Westward Expansion

A History of the American Frontier

5Th

EDITION

Ray Allen Billington

Late of the Henry E. Huntington Library and Art Gallery

Martin Ridge

Senior Research Associate, Henry E. Huntington Library and Art Gallery

MACMILLAN PUBLISHING CO., INC.
New York

COLLIER MACMILLAN PUBLISHERS
London

Macmillan Publishing Co., Inc.
866 Third Avenue, New York, New York 10022

Collier Macmillan Canada, Inc.

Library of Congress Cataloging in Publication Data

Billington, Ray Allen
  Westward expansion.

  Bibliography: p.
  Includes index.
  1. United States—Territorial expansion.
2. United States—History. 3. Mississippi Valley—
History—1803–1865. 4. West (U.S.)—History.
I. Ridge, Martin. II Title.
E179.5.B63 1982   973   81-8450
ISBN 0-02-309860-0   AACR2

Printing: 4 5 6 7 8   Year: 8 9 0

Preface

When the first edition of this book was conceived almost forty years ago, it was seen as a joint project with its senior author, Professor James Blaine Hedges of Brown University, generously allowing me to share equally in its composition—and such benefits as it generated. His was to be the responsibility for the chapters on the trans-Mississippi West; I was to trace the frontier's progress westward from the first Atlantic settlements to the crossing of the Mississippi River.

From the first these plans went astray. Professor Hedges, deeply involved in a significant research program and ill at ease when preparing a warmed-over narrative, was able to write only three of the book's chapters, forcing me to add a few years and a major amount of reading to the preparation. It finally appeared in 1949 with my name as author, but "with the collaboration of James Blaine Hedges" properly displayed on the title page. In subsequent editions I assumed sole responsibility for the extensive changes made until virtually no mark of Professor Hedges' contribution remained.

With this edition, however, the title page is again resplendent with the name of a collaborator, and one who has played a far larger role in preparing the text than did Professor Hedges in the first edition. The addition is much to my liking. Having been forced to delay my own researches by keeping abreast of all phases of frontier scholarship for the thirty years that revisions of this book have been required, I have been eager to find a younger colleague willing to assume the burden of the periodic revisions.

Fortunately an ideal choice could be found no farther away than across the hallway from my office on the Huntington Library's second floor. Martin Ridge had been a student of mine at Northwestern University during the post-World War II years (and a very good student he was), and had prepared his doctoral dissertation under my direction. That dissertation blossomed into the first of his several books, *Ignatius Donnelly: The Portrait of a Politician*, published in 1962. Its author climbed rapidly up the academic ladder, teaching first at Westminister College in Pennsylvania and San Diego State University, then at Indiana University where he was editor of the prestigious *Journal of American History*. In 1977 he joined the staff of the Huntington Library as Senior Research Associate and Coordinator of Research and Publication, a post that he has occupied with distinction since that time. He also serves as part-time Professor of History at the California Institute of Technology.

Martin Ridge is responsible for the extensive revisions in the text for this fifth edition; he has brought to the task an unparalleled knowledge of current approaches to historical studies, as well as the vast experience with frontier history and historians gained during his years as editor. I have happily surrendered this task to his capable hands, and have confined my own contribution to the preparation of the revised bibliography. This in itself was a major task, for publication in the field continues to accelerate rapidly. The resulting listing of books and articles published since 1972 has been kept manageable only by eliminating hundreds of items listed in earlier editions. Indeed, the current bibliography contains almost none of the studies in circulation in 1949 when the bibliography to the first edition was prepared.

In subsequent editions, the entire responsibility for both text and bibliography will be borne by Martin Ridge. In retiring from association with a book that has occupied my interest for almost forty years I can only wish him well, confident that his knowledge of frontier history, and his abilities as an outstanding historian, assure the volume the respect that it has enjoyed in the past.

R.A.B.

Introduction

The first edition of *Westward Expansion*, which appeared in 1949, set a high water mark for scholarship in western American history. As the first full-scale attempt to present American frontier history in the context of Frederick Jackson Turner's thought and to compress the voluminous literature of the field, it startled reviewers; one of whom insisted that no one but Turner could string the master's bow. The success of that edition and the three others that followed disproved that observation. For a generation of students and scholars, "Billington's *Westward Expansion*"—almost as a title—has been the benchmark against which other studies in the field have been measured. The author's robust masculine style, engaging personality, and point of view gave the book a special flavor that has remained unchanged even as the content of the book was updated. His basic faith in political and social democracy was drawn more sharply into focus as the nation's scholarship reflected an increasing sensitivity to the human issues of our time. Over the years the superb and updated bibliography reflected his remarkable knowledge not only of the staggering quantity and enhanced quality of research in western history but also its remarkable dynamism.

This new edition seeks to preserve Ray Allen Billington's unashamedly graceful narrative style. It is written within the context of José Ortega y Gasset's reminder that there can be analysis as well as explanation through narrative. In that sense the structure and presentation in this edition remains unchanged from the previous edition. The focus too centers on the primary period of settlement and the immediate social and political implications of that initial westering experience of the American people. The heroes and heroines of this book are plain people—farmers, ranchers, merchants, traders, soldiers, laborers, teamsters, drovers—who subdued the heart of the

vii

continent and set the nation on a remarkable course. It is too often forgotten that western history was the first social history written by American scholars, when they analyzed the experiences of the working people in the settlement of the country. The names of the great and near great are few and far between in the history of the West, for pioneering in the wilderness or the desert rarely earns one that kind of distinction; yet the record of achievement of the men and women who built a town, settled at the fork or ford on a river, traveled the overland trail, survived an Indian attack, or pastured cattle on a thousand hills should be kept. The history of this nation is incomplete without a knowledge of its internal development because the frontier environment had an impact on the angle of vision of statesmen as well as common folk. It is a far from simple story, and to synthesize it adequately means that the focus often shifts from looking at history in terms of change over time to dealing with specific episodes.

This only becomes clear to the reader of *Westward Expansion* if the book is used properly. The extensive bibliography is an integral part of the study; not only does it set out the standard works on which the narrative is based, indicate where new work has been done, and identify the conflicting interpretations that are reconciled in the text, but also it goes beyond the text in many cases to discuss areas that could not be included for reasons of space as well as subjects where additional or new work should be done. The serious student only at peril can ignore the bibliography and hope to understand the field.

The history of the American West is, almost by definition, a triumphal narrative for it traces a virtually unbroken chain of successes in national expansion. Although the text sets forth this story and the authors accept in large part a theory of American exceptionalism, which places great stress on the frontiering experiences of the American people, they have tried to mark out quite clearly the shortcomings, contradictions, and anomalies in this intepretation. Americans are justified in taking pride in the frontier heritage and myth, but they should view it quite critically lest they succumb, as did an earlier generation of writers on the West—Theodore Roosevelt, for example—to the poisonous venom of excessive nationalism. The American westering experience offers a mixed model of human behavior; a fact that a careful reading of this book makes clear. If we are to lay claim today to being a democratic, innovative, and progressive people, it will be because of what we make of our frontier past, for certainly it alone offers no guarantees for the future.

This edition benefited from the help of many friends. Some—Robert Athearn, Paul Hutton, Calvin Martin, and Glenda Riley—were kind enough to read parts of the text and comment on it. Others—Rodman W. Paul, Andrew Rolle, John Reid, Paul Prucha, Sandra Myres, and Wilbur Jacobs— were unwitting contributors. As sometime members of the seminar that is the daily luncheon conversation at the history table at the Huntington Library, they generously answered questions in areas of their expertise. They are, of course, not responsible for the use I made of their insights.

In the largest sense this book remains Ray Allen Billington's *Westward Expansion*. Anyone who seeks a different interpretation of the American frontiering experience need look elsewhere.

In a very special sense this edition was prepared with my youngest son, Wallace, in mind for when he learned that the family was leaving Indiana for the West because I had accepted a position in the Huntington Library he brightened and said, "Let's go see California."

San Marino, California   M.R.

Contents

SECTION III

THE TRANS-MISSISSIPPI FRONTIER

Maps

1

---------❖---------

The Frontier Hypothesis

Suggest the term *frontier* to the average movie-addicted, TV-Western-oriented American of today and you will conjure up in his mind happy visions of painted Indians, gaudily-dressed hurdy-gurdy girls, straight-shooting cowboys, and villainous badmen, all besporting themselves beneath sun-bathed western skies. The frontier was truly a land of romance, but it also helped shape the distinctive civilization of the United States. America's unique characteristics stemmed from no single source; the European heritage, the continuing impact of ideas from abroad, the mingling of peoples, the spread of the industrial revolution, and the growth of class consciousness all contributed. Yet no one force did more to Americanize the nation's people and institutions than the repeated rebirth of civilization along the western edge of settlement during the three centuries required to occupy the continent.

This was first realized during the 1890s by Frederick Jackson Turner, a young history instructor at the University of Wisconsin. Trained in the seminars of Johns Hopkins University, where he was taught that institutions evolved from earlier "germ cells" without reference to environmental factors, Turner rebelled against a concept which was at variance with observable phenomena in his own Middle West. His historical declaration of independence was a paper, "The Significance of the Frontier in American History," which he read at the Chicago meeting of the American Historical Association in 1893. The European heritage he insisted, accounted only for the similarities between European and American society; to explain the hitherto neglected differences historians must look to the distinctive environment of the United States.

The most unique characteristic of that environment, Turner felt, was the presence of an area of free land on the western edge of the advancing

1

settlements. Into that unoccupied region poured a stream of settlers from Europe or the East, attracted by the hope of economic betterment or the chance for adventure. They came as easterners, bringing with them the complex political, economic, and social customs required in the stratified societies they left behind. In their new homes on the "hither edge" of the wilderness these imported institutions were out of place; hence the "cake of custom" was broken as new customs better adapted to a primitive society were substituted. Highly developed political forms gave way to simple associations of settlers or rudimentary representative bodies. Specialized trades were forgotten in a land where tasks could best be accomplished by individuals or groups without a division of labor. Complex social activities were abandoned in favor of simpler pastoral pursuits: husking bees, cabin raisings, log rollings, and play parties. Cultural developments lagged as emphasis shifted to the primal tasks of providing food, clothing, and shelter. In thought and habit easterners shed the trappings of sophisticated society; they altered their ways of life, sought new means for using natural resources, or adapted older practices to the new environment. Innovation, adaptation, and invention—in economics, social organization, and government—were characteristics of frontier life.

As newcomers drifted into each pioneer settlement, increasing the ratio between man and nature, the social organization steadily climbed back toward complexity. Governmental forms grew more rigid. Economic specialization set in as eastern capital was imported to begin roads, mills, and primitive industries. Social activities expanded and grew more complex. As men and women conquered the wilderness, a fully developed society evolved, complete with manufacturing establishments, accumulated capital, cities, cooperative institutions, mature governmental practices, and cultural outpourings. The resulting civilization, however, differed from that of the East, modified by the accident of separate evolution and by the unique social environment. As the matured area assimilated itself with the region just to the east, the frontier passed on westward to begin the transformation of a more advanced area.

This was the process that was repeated for three centuries as Americans colonized the continent. The story of westward expansion was one of the continuous rebirth of society, a repeated "beginning over again" in the West, with the results the same on every frontier, although with differences due to time, place, and the manner of men and women who peopled each area. This continuous throwing of people into contact with the simplicity of primitive society left traditions, memories, and characteristics which persisted long after the frontier passed. Those pioneer traits were strongest in the newer regions, but they greatly influenced the adjacent transitional zone and to a lesser degree the matured social order still farther east. The result was the Americanization of people and institutions. The unique character of American civilization, Turner believed, could be ascribed to the continuous "evolution and adaptation of organs in response to changed environment."

"The existence of an area of free land," he wrote, "its continuous recession, and the advance of American settlement westward, explain American development."

Since Turner first advanced the "frontier hypothesis," scholars have subjected his concept to a minute examination. Their careful study modified, but did not refute, his basic doctrine. Few would agree today that the westward-moving "area of free land" alone explains "American development;" indeed Turner himself was less guilty of such overstatement than some of his too-enthusiastic disciples. The persistence of inherited European traits, the continuous impact of changing world conditions, and the influence of various racial groups were equally important forces in shaping the nation's distinctive civilization. Yet the continuous rebirth of society in the western wilderness helped endow the American people and their institutions with characteristics not shared by the rest of the world.

The moulding effect of this unique environment can best be understood by picturing the Anglo-American frontier as a migrating geographic area which moved westward from Atlantic to Pacific over the course of three centuries. Here was the outer edge of advancing settlement, the meeting point of savagery and civilization, the zone where civilization entered the wilderness, the "region whose social conditions resulted from the application of older institutions and ideas to the transforming influences of free land." In this geographic sense, the frontier has been usually defined as an area containing not less than two nor more than six inhabitants to the square mile. Census bureau statisticians have adopted this definition in tracing the frontier's advance from the records of each population poll since the first tabulation of 1790. Decade by decade they have drawn narrow bands across the map of the United States, each farther west than the last, as virgin territory was engulfed by migrating pioneers.

This exact definition, although satisfactory to statisticians, fails to reflect the evolutionary nature of the frontier process. The frontier can be pictured more meaningfully as a vast westward-moving zone, contiguous to the settled portions of the continent, and peopled by a variety of individuals bent on applying individual skills to the exploitation of unusually abundant natural resources. As the westward movement gained momentum, a number of frontier "types" emerged, each playing a distinctive role in the advance of civilization. Although varying with time and place, each is identifiable on the successive frontiers until the conquest of the continent was completed.

Normally, the assault on nature was begun by the fur traders. These restless nomads led the way westward virtually from the time Europeans first set foot on American soil. They blazed the trails across the Piedmont and through the Appalachian Mountain barrier, pioneered on the "Dark and Bloody Ground" of Kentucky, crossed the Mississippi far in advance of the first farmers, traced the eastward-flowing streams to their sources in the Rockies, scaled the Sierras, and descended the Pacific slope to run their trap lines through California's interior valleys or along the beaver streams of the far Northwest. Always far in advance of civilization, the fur traders crossed the continent with such speed that they made little permanent impression on the wilderness. Usually they were psychological types who found forest solitudes more acceptable than the company of other people. So they adapted themselves to the ways of warriors, borrowing their clothes, their living habits, their forest lore, and often their wives. Yet traders did much to prepare the way for later comers. They broke down Indian self-sufficiency, accustoming the native to the guns, knives, and firewater of the white men's material civilization. They weakened the natives by spreading diseases and vices among them, or by providing some tribes with the guns that led to the slaughter of their wilderness enemies. They explored every nook and cranny of the West, seeking out passes through mountain barriers, investigating river routes to the interior, and discovering favored agricultural sites. Traders' posts served as nucleuses for hamlets and cities; traders' "traces" were widened into roads over which came later pioneers. Theirs was the role of advertising the West and introducing the disintegrating forces of civilization into the Indian society of the forest and plain.

As ever-present on successive frontiers as the fur trappers were the cattlemen. Early Boston had its cattle frontier in the Charles River Valley; early Virginia boasted cowpens among the canebrakes and peavine marshes that fringed the farming regions a few miles from the coast. As farms advanced westward the cattle frontier steadily retreated, into the Piedmont and Great Valley of the Appalachians, across the mountains to the rich valleys of Ohio or the grass-blanketed prairies of Illinois, southward to the piney woods of Mississippi where, mounted on "low built, shaggy, but muscular and hardy horses of that region, and armed with rawhide whips . . . and sometimes with a catching rope or lasso . . . they scour the woods . . . sometimes driving a herd of a thousand heads to the pen." Ranchers led farmers into the trans-Mississippi West, there to build their cattle kingdom on the gargantuan grassland of the Great Plains before succumbing once more to pressure from farmers and retiring to the fenced pastures of today.

Whenever conditions were favorable, trappers and herders were joined by miners. The mining frontier, which depended on the exploitation of rare pockets of mineral wealth, advanced in less orderly fashion than that of the traders or ranchers; at times it leaped far in advance of settlement, at others it lagged behind while previously discovered riches were developed. Yet miners played a persistent role in the frontier advance. They were present in colonial Virginia and Masssachusetts, seeking deposits of "bog iron" in the forest beyond the settlements. During the early nineteenth century they led the way into western Georgia and Alabama where gold discoveries were responsible for Wild West boom towns, grizzled prospectors, and a moral level considered by easterners to be "deplorably bad." At the same time, the discovery of lead outcroppings in northwestern Illinois transformed the hamlet of Galena into the leading Gomorrah of the West as well as the territory's most populous city. During the next generation the mining frontier engulfed the trans-Mississippi country in the wake of exciting "strikes" in California, Nevada, Colorado, and the northern Rockies. Many who participated in these "rushes" were from older mining areas; Georgia's mines contributed heavily to the Colorado gold fields, lead miners from Illinois were prominent among the San Francisco '49ers, and "yonder siders" from California pioneered in the Rocky Mountain country. The miner was a distinct frontier type, ready to rush wherever opportunity beckoned. Miners, like the traders and ranchers, were content with surface exploitation; after skimming off the visible wealth they moved on, leaving the still rich land to actual settlers.

They were the pioneer farmers. Unlike those who preceded them, the farmers made no compromise with nature; their task was not to adapt but to conquer. They viewed the forests or grasslands of the continent as obstacles to overcome; millions of acres of virgin timber were stripped away by their axes, millions of acres of prairie sod were turned under by their plows. They hated the Indians with a fervor born of experience in massacres, cursed traders for supplying them with firewater or firearms, and wanted only to see the natives exterminated. They professed, some of them, to prefer wilderness solitudes to the fellowship of other humans, but all were anxious for new settlers to join them, knowing that numbers meant safety and an increase in land values. Although many pioneer farmers were perennial movers who shifted with the frontier until they became shiftless themselves, their objective was to transform the western wilds into replicas of eastern communities, with no trace of the natural environment remaining.

Theirs was a romantic, if arduous, existence. They were first into each new area, alone or with a handful of kindred spirits. They made the first rude clearings, built the first rough dwellings, laid out the first passable trails through the underbrush or across the plains. Often they made no attempt to buy land, simply squatting on the public domain. As year after year of backbreaking labor passed, more and more land was cleared. In time enough was under cultivation to support the pioneer family; then still more timber was cut away to produce agricultural surpluses for export. As this went on other settlers moved in, roads reaching back to the eastern settlements were improved, and cultivated land vied with forested regions for supremacy. When this occurred the pioneer family was often infected with the wanderlust. Sometimes they were driven onward by dislike of civilization and its ways, sometimes by the prospect of better lands ahead, but more often by the hope of gain. Cleared fields mounted steadily in value as population increased; a squatter could sell "improvements" at a profit; a farmer could dispose of excess holdings, then the farm itself, for a handsome sum, while moving on westward to begin the process anew. Many pioneer farm families shifted their homes six times or more in their lifetimes.

When they sold it was usually to "equipped farmers." These were men and women with capital who were drawn from adjacent farming regions, the East, or Europe. They came intending to stay and develop their newly acquired acres; hence they continued the clearing process with greater thoroughness, grubbed out the stumps, built frame houses, fenced their lands, and improved the roads. Each year, as the cleared areas increased, the amount of exportable surplus mounted, and each year, in return, more wealth flowed into the community. As this mounted the prospering farmers were able to pay for services they formerly performed for themselves. Their demands not only led to a division of labor, which marked the maturing of civilization, but also laid the basis for the towns and villages that climaxed the farmers' frontier.

An urban frontier was truly a part of advancing settlement. Towns sprang up as if by magic, some founded by speculators who hoped to turn a tidy profit, others by merchants seeking a favorable spot for their enterprises, others by politicians determined to fix territorial or state capitals, sites for prisons and universities, and seats of county government. Usually a strategic location was chosen—at a crossroads, an advantageous spot on a canal or railroad, at the head of navigation on a stream. Whenever possible, the town site was surveyed, and streets, lots, and open spaces were set aside. Prudent investors placed their businesses in predetermined locations. To the casual observer these pioneer villages varied little from the towns in the East, but actually they differed markedly in the sophistication of their economic activity, institutions, and attitudes. Their unique characteristics stemmed largely from the manner in which urban pioneers made their living. Towns in farming regions erected sawmills to produce lumber, grist mills or distilleries to transform bulky grain into exportable commodities. They also supplied farmers with machinery, furniture, food, and other goods that were no longer produced on the farm. The towns provided legal services, newspapers, and whatever culture otherwise isolated farm families sought. Many of the frontier's important cities owed their origins to the discovery of precious metals, and they functioned primarily to extract, process, and ship ore, while they distributed the goods and services that well-paid workers wanted. The chief supply centers of the mining and farming frontier grew with the diversification of their economic base.

The attitudes of urban pioneers differed from those of eastern city dwellers. Most were restless seekers after wealth who, driven onward by failure at home or the hope of greater profits in a new country, deliberately selected a promising frontier community as the site of their next experiment in fortune making. There they built a mill, opened a general store, set up a portable printing press, or hung out a shingle as lawyer or dancing teacher, confident that the town's rapid growth would bring them affluence and social prominence. They would "grow up with the country." When they guessed right and the village did evolve into a city they usually stayed on as prosperous businessmen or community leaders. When, more often, they were unsuccessful, they moved on again to a still newer town. Urban pioneers advanced westward just as did pioneer farmers; one might live in Rochester, Buffalo, Cleveland, Detroit, Chicago, and Milwaukee before fortune nodded. Their mobility and restlessness distinguished them from the more stable souls who filled the eastern cities.

Institutions also marked the frontier towns as distinct from their counterparts in the East. Most rooted their political systems in eighteenth-century liberalism, with emphasis on legislative power, frequent public meetings for charter changes, and provisions for constant civic improvement. Yearly elections to the town councils were the rule; in one an ordinance allowing councilmen to hold office three years was defeated as "placing them beyond the reach of public opinion for a time almost equal to an age in older communities." Yet, with typical frontier inconsistency, all regulated services touching upon the public welfare with a stern hand. Ordinances in pioneer towns provided for a strict control of markets, fuel distributors, and food handlers, and for careful provisions respecting health and cleanliness. The most striking characteristic of the frontier cities was the similarity of their institutions. Cleveland copied its charter from Buffalo, Chicago from Cleveland. Practices found suitable to the western environment were first tested, then generally applied along the advancing urban frontier.

One would like to believe, with Frederick Jackson Turner, that the West was subdued by a procession of frontier types, each following the other in an orderly pattern of conquest. Unfortunately, human motives and behavioral patterns are too complex to fit such a neat formula. Instead the frontier process can be roughly visualized in terms of two loosely defined groups. One—made up of fur trappers, missionaries, herdsmen, and others whose enterprise depended on preserving the wilderness—was interested in *using* nature. The other—comprised of farmers, speculators, town-planters, merchants, millers, and a host more whose profits depended on an expanding economy—was bent on *subduing* nature. Usually the Users preceded the Subduers, but even this broad division broke down amidst wilderness conditions. Sometimes town-planters led the way to monopolize favored sites; at others miners advanced more rapidly than fur traders; at still others farmers were in the van. Every frontier was a beehive of activity as the many specialties needed to plant civilization were applied in every sort of sequence.

Whatever the pattern—or lack of pattern—the movement went on at a rate of advance that varied greatly with time and place. Three factors contributed to everyone's decision to move to the frontier: conditions at home, the ease with which the West could be reached, and the attractiveness of the region ahead. If lands in the East were worn out by repeated cultivation, if overcrowding had reached the point where men and women were unable to adapt themselves to the diminished area, if overcompetition lessened economic opportunity, the dissatisfied were inclined to look to the frontier for rehabilitation. "Our lands being thus worn out," wrote a Connecticut farmer in the eighteenth century, "I suppose to be one Reason why so many are inclined to Remove to new Places that they may raise Wheat: As also that they may have more Room, thinking that we live too thick." Yet no amount of dissatisfaction could set the westward-moving tide flowing unless the road to the frontier was open. Whenever natural obstacles stood in the way—whether an Appalachian Mountain barrier, a phalanx of hostile Indians, or an unfamiliar environment such as the Great Plains—the frontier advance slowed or even halted momentarily. Then the dammed-up population increased to the point where the sheer force of numbers pushed the barrier aside. Always progress was most rapid when adequate transportation routes led westward; highways—whether forest trails, roads, or railroads—were the arteries that fed each new frontier. Equally essential in accounting for the ebb and flow of the westward movement was the desirability of the area just ahead. Whenever a particularly attractive spot beckoned, the advance was rapid; the rush into the bluegrass country of Kentucky, the cotton lands of the Gulf Plains, and the fertile prairies just west of the Mississippi illustrated the effect of unusual soils on migration. Economic opportunity, however, was not the West's only lure. The challenge of a new country, the call of the primitive, were important psychological attractions to men (and some women) "with the West in their eyes." Many a pioneer left the East in search of the adventure and romance that waited on the hither edge of the wilderness.

Modern statisticians tell us that five variables normally determined the pace of mobility: the relative per capita income in the expelling and attracting areas, the job opportunity in each, the distance separating them, population density, and regional affinity; a person adjusted to a distinctive social climate usually sought a similar social climate when he moved. An analysis of census statistics for 1850 (the first with sufficient data) shows that the better the job opportunity, the smaller the distance, the lower the population density (and hence the greater chance to secure land), and the more alike the cultural and physical climate of a region, the larger the migration into it. Statistical evidence, in other words, simply supports the generalizations of Frederick Jackson Turner and his disciples; people moved to the frontier to secure more land and greater opportunity; they tended to shift into nearby areas least isolated by geographic barriers; they moved along isothermic lines rather than northward or southward into differing cultural areas. The data also reveal that those born west of the Appalachians were more sensitive in income differentials (and hence more inclined to migrate) than those from east of the mountains, and less provincial than easterners in their willingness to settle in regions unlike those in which they had been born. The westerner, these figures suggest, was slightly more adaptable and somewhat more flexible than the easterner in migration patterns. A westerner's inherent traditionalism had been shaken by the frontier experience.

An eighteenth-century traveler summed up all that statisticians have told us when he described the migrations from his native New England: "Those, who are first inclined to emigrate, are usually such, as have met with difficulties at home. These are commonly joined by persons, who, having large families and small farms, are induced, for the sake of settling their children comfortably, to seek for new and cheaper lands. To both are always added the discontented, the enterprising, the ambitious, and the covetous. . . . Others, still, are allured by the prospect of gain, presented in every new country to the sagacious, from the purchase and sale of new lands: while not a small number are influenced by the brilliant stories, which everywhere are told concerning most tracts during the early progress of their settlement."

The lure of the West did not affect all easterners in the same way. Perhaps many desired to take advantage of frontier opportunity, but few were able to do so; every individual's migration depended on three ingredients: proximity, skill in pioneering techniques, and capital. Certainly the history of westward expansion demonstrated that proximity was of primary importance; unless nature's obstacles intervened each new region was settled from neighboring areas rather than distant points. New Englanders peopled western New York, their children moved on to the Old Northwest, their grandchildren to the upper Mississippi Valley. This was a universal rule; even in the 1850s when abolitionists and southern fire-eaters urged partisans in the slavery controversy to occupy disputed Kansas, few responded; instead that territory was settled by hard-headed realists from Missouri, Illinois, Indiana, Kentucky, and Tennessee. "In thirty States out of thirty-four," wrote the Superintendent of the Census in 1860, "it will be perceived that the native emigrants have chiefly preferred to locate in a State immediately adjacent to that of their birth."

Distance and inadequate training in agricultural pursuits closed the frontier to eastern workingmen; instead America was settled by successive waves of farmers who were already skilled in wresting a living from the soil. Farming, even before the day of mechanization, was a highly technical profession; frontiering required a knowledge of even more specialized techniques. Clearing the land, building a home, fencing fields, solving the problem of defense, and planting crops on virgin soil all demanded experience few workingmen could boast. During the colonial period, when the distance between East and West was small, numerous workers made the transition to farming, not because the prospect pleased them, but because industrial opportunities were so few that mechanics were forced to turn to agriculture. After the industrial revolution of the early nineteenth century, however, the frontier seldom served as a "safety valve" for workingmen, although a few skilled workers from the East and a larger number from Europe did succeed in making the change.

The cost of moving west was a barrier that few easterners could overcome. If a prospective pioneer wanted to begin life anew, he must move to the extreme edge of the frontier, appropriate government land, clear his fields, and personally conquer the wilderness; this required technical knowledge acquired by prior experience. When such skills were lacking, his only choice was to settle in a community already undergoing development. This was expensive. In the middle-nineteenth century he would be forced to pay between $1.25 and $10 an acre for land, $5 to $20 an acre to have it cleared, $112 for a split-rail fence, from $100 to $375 for tools, $150 for draft animals, $50 for a log cabin, $25 for transportation, and $100 for food to support his family until his own farm came into production. Few eighty-acre farms were established that did not cost their owners at least $1,500—a sum far beyond the reach of the average eastern workingman whose wages seldom rose above $1 a day. Morever when the pressure to escape to the frontier was greatest—in periods of depression—laborers were particularly unable to make the transition, for each panic was preceded by a boom period of high prices which swept away their savings. Even those who sought to become independent farmers by working first as hired hands in the West found the path difficult; they learned the needed skills but often found it impossible to save the money to buy a farm from their wages of $150 a year and keep.

What was true for workingmen was also true for working women. Little wonder that most new areas were occupied by farmers from nearby regions who had either the frontier skills to begin life anew cheaply or the capital necessary to put land into production. Yet the drain of farm workers from eastern to western lands was not without its effect on the East. Many who drifted westward might otherwise have gone into the cities in quest of factory jobs. The frontier served as a safety valve during the first half of the nineteenth century by draining off potential laborers; in the post-Civil War years even that influence declined as the gap between the pioneer zone and industrial areas widened. The trans-Mississippi frontier recruited its settlers from adjacent agricultural regions rather than from the industrialized East. Through the history of America's westward expansion the farmer, blessed with wealth, skills, and proximity, was the average pioneer.

The frontier communities that were the end product of this migration process differed only in degree from their eastern counterparts; the popular picture of a predominantly male social order, where youth reigned and equality was the order of the day, bears little resemblance to actuality. On virtually all frontiers that had reached the agricultural stage men outnumbered women only in slight degree, the average male age at marriage was in the late twenties rather than the late teens, families were of normal size, wealth was so unevenly distributed that the upper tenth of the population controlled 40 per cent of the wealth, and aliens were denied social equality or equal economic opportunity. Variations in this pattern were numerous; thus Scandinavians and Germans in Wisconsin found no barriers before them, but Mexicans in the southwestern borderland were denied the right to own slaves, hold equal jobs, or attend school. Frontiering did not automatically wipe out the class distinctions or prejudices carried westward by the pioneers; it did allow a greater number (including many aliens) to step aboard the escalator, and it did offer a hand up to easterners who had been handicapped by improper lineage or social position.

The variations wrought by the changed social environment were accentuated by the variety of physical environments that waited the pioneers as they pushed westward. The North American continent was not uniform; instead a series of differing physiographic provinces lay before the migrating peoples, each with a distinct soil structure, topography, and climate. In this checkerboard of unique environments occurred an interplay of migrating stocks and geographic forces, to produce in each a distinctive type of economic enterprise best suited to the natural conditions and imported habits of the settlers. In many ways these sections resembled the countries of Europe; each had its own history of occupation and development, and each was so conscious of its differences that it possessed a sense of distinction from other parts of the country. This stemmed largely from the economic habits of the people; in one, staple agriculture might be best suited to natural conditions, in another diversified farming, in another cattle raising, in another industry. As specialization developed, each section demanded from the national government laws beneficial to its own interests; hence the sectional concept implied a degree of rivalry comparable to the ill-feeling that has marked Europe's national history.

This was the heritage of the frontier's advance. As the successive Wests became Easts a mosaic of sections was left behind, each bent on shaping national legislation to its own ends. At times sectional antagonism led to civil war; more often the federal government reconciled antagonisms by compromise or allowed the sections themselves to effect workable combinations for legislative purposes. These conflicts were not solely responsible for the pattern of American history. Sectional lines were often blurred by the influence of national parties, the growth of class divisions, the intellectual traits and ideals of the people, and the presence within each section of smaller regions differing from the majority point of view. Yet no understanding of American development in the eighteenth and nineteenth centuries is possible without a proper recognition of sectional influences.

The following pages tell the story of the successive occupation of America's physiographic provinces by advancing waves of pioneers. Romantic characters took part: coon-skinned trappers and leatherclad "Mountain Men," starry-eyed prospectors and hard-riding cowboys, badmen and vigilantes. But the true heroes of the tale were the hard-working farmer and his wife who marched ever westward until the boundaries of their nation touched the Pacific. They were acutely aware that small-scale capitalism flourishes and is most effective in areas of great uncertainty and high returns. Out of such circumstances develop not a simple farming society but an increasingly sophisticated and competitive corporate community. They and their urban counterparts planted the seeds for modern America. The history of the American frontier is not only one of the conquest of a continent and of expanding opportunity for the downtrodden; it is the history of the birth of a nation, endowed with characteristics that persisted through its adolescence and influenced its people long after the West itself was gone.

THE COLONIAL
FRONTIER

The Land and Its People

Had the first Europeans to reach the New World realized the harshness of the land that lay before them or the strength of the native population that must be conquered they might well have scurried back across the Atlantic. Fortunately for them they were pleasantly misled by what they saw on their first landfalls. In their eyes the North American continent was a reasonable facsimile of their homelands; they were delighted with the equitable climate, the plentiful rivers, the dense forest growth, the abundance of bushes and plants that seemed familiar despite variations. Here, they reasoned, was an environment so familiar that adaptation would pose no problems. When they called one region New England and another Virginia (after the virgin Queen Elizabeth) they simply symbolized that belief. Too, they found the native peoples so few in some places that they could be easily brushed aside and so docile that they seemed incapable of resistance, eager to receive the newcomers from beyond the sea, and happy to exchange furs and bits of gold and fresh-water pearls for knives and pots and blankets. So friendly was the land and so welcoming its people that its occupation offered scarcely a problem.

So they thought, those pioneers on Europe's first New World frontier, but they were tragically wrong. They could not know that the coastal lowlands where they made their first clearings were far from typical, and that the unknown interior concealed a checkerboard of different environments, some of them easily subdued, but others so brutally hostile that they would test the stamina of any invaders. Nor did they realize that the handful of friendly Indians who greeted them with rejoicing were far from typical of the multitudes that firmly held the continent and could be subdued only at the cost of thousands of lives and an abundance of suffering. Not until much later did the invaders learn that the heaviest Indian populations were quite naturally situated on the very best lands most coveted by the whites. Europeans were to discover at frightful cost that North America could be won only by the overrunning of a succession of environments, some of them forbidding, and by the tragic displacement of native peoples who were determined to hold their homelands at all cost.

Their error is understandable, for they made their landfalls in a coastal lowland highly suitable to their needs. There they found the familiar climate of the North Temperate zone, varying from north to south to a greater degree than in Europe, but still suitable for comfortable living. There they found the heavy forest growth that they knew at home, interspersed with cleared fields left by the Indians, where grain could be grown and cattle pastured. Rivers were plentiful, most of them flowing into the sea from the distant interior, and many of them large enough to allow the small ocean-going vessels of that day to penetrate far inland. The soils, they soon found, varied greatly, from the rocky gravels of New England strewn with glacial debris to the rich humus of the southern Tidewater, but all were easily cultivated by techniques and implements familiar to the colonists. The Anglo-American settlers readily adapted to the differences that did exist, developing a plantation system in the South where the long summers, the warm climate, and the availability of river transportation allowed the cultivation of such bulky staples as tobacco and cotton, and in New England with its short growing season and rock-strewn soils building a civilization based on village-oriented small-farm agriculture. These were minor adjustments for an agricultural people and were made without undue hardship.

Most of the seventeenth century was needed to occupy this coastal lowland, but by the 1680s pioneers were beginning to make their clearings in the uplands that lay just beyond. This again proved an easy transition. The so-called fall line—easily mapped by connecting the first waterfalls encountered when ascending the rivers that flowed into the sea—might appear a formidable barrier but it proved scarcely a deterrent. The goods carried along the river highways were easily transshipped around the obstruction (cities emerged at each point to provide labor), so that staples could be grown in the southern upland (the Piedmont, it was called) as they could nearer the coast. There in that hilly province New Englanders practiced their small-farm agriculture and southerners their plantation farming just as they did farther eastward. Yet a maturing society along the seaboard found little in common with the more primitive frontier society of the interior, giving rise to social conflicts that hurried the westward movement during the eighteenth century.

Beyond the uplands stretched the Appalachian Mountain system, a complex of ridges and valleys running for thirteen hundred miles along the colonial backcountry from the White Mountains of New Hampshire to the highlands of Georgia. This, too, proved no serious deterrent to the westward-moving frontiersmen. Two passes led directly to the interior—the Mohawk

River valley in the North and the Cumberland Pass into Kentucky in the South—and both were to be used by the end of the eighteenth century. Until that time, however, the Appalachians did hold back migration, not because they were difficult to cross, but because they offered a base for powerful Indian tribes who operated with French allies from Canada and Louisiana to guard the interior. Until those defenders could be conquered, as they were in the French and Indian wars of the eighteenth century, the Anglo-American frontier would be forced to hug the seaboard.

Once that barrier was breached, as it was in 1763, the gates were open and a hoard of settlers invaded the interior. The first-comers found a region strangely familiar: the Appalachian Plateau province differed little from the rugged hill country of the Piedmont east of the Appalachians. The rough countryside and the problems of transportation discouraged the occupation of much of the plateau, but within it were a number of garden spots destined to play a spectacular role in frontier history: the rolling uplands of western New York state, the Bluegrass region of Kentucky, the Nashville Basin of Tennessee, and the network of small valleys formed by the upper tributaries of the Tennessee River. All were eagerly sought by pioneers just before and after the American Revolution, and all were eventually occupied at a heavy cost in lives and national honor.

Once the Appalachian Plateau country had been skimmed of its best lands, the pioneers swept onward into the Mississippi Valley which was occupied during the first half of the nineteenth century. Here was a settler's dream come true: millions of acres of level prairie, crisscrossed by the tributaries of the Ohio, interspersed with hills, and rich in deep humus soils that promised unheard-of bounties to the farmer. Forests blanketed the area, but the clearings made by Indians were now supplemented by natural prairies where grass and wild flowers grew rank to signal the richness of the land. Easterners accustomed to the back-breaking labor of clearing their fields of stones or felling the forest giants to bring sunlight to their crops found in the Mississippi Valley an agricultural Valhalla where clearing was easy, the yields excellent, and the markets readily available over the water routes provided by the Mississippi and its tributaries. So great was the lure of this last woodland frontier that by 1825 the whole area east of the Father of Waters had been carved into states save Wisconsin and Michigan which were territories. Nature's abundance had proven to be an irresistible magnet.

Irresistible it might be, but the settlement of the eastern United States was accomplished only after two centuries of warfare and bloodshed on a scale that would have been incomprehensible to the first English explorers. Their impression of the native peoples was misleading; the Indians who greeted them on the Atlantic's shore were less warlike if not less numerous than those who occupied the continent's interior. America, the Europeans were to discover to their sorrow, was peopled by a native population with cultures unique to Europeans, all stubbornly determined to protect their lands from the alien invaders, and nearly all endowed with the weapons and skill to do so. They were ultimately subdued, but only after a series of wars far more brutal than those among the European nations of that day. The true story of the occupation of North America is the story of a conquest, not of an uncontested march westward of Anglo-American frontiersmen.

This, true, is not the traditional picture painted by historians. If they have mentioned Indians at all they have seen them only as stone-age barbarians who stood in the path of an advancing civilization and whose stubborn refusal to recognize this fact justified the sad fate awaiting them. Frederick Jackson Turner in his many essays on the frontier scarcely mentioned the red man or his contributions to the social order that emerged from the pioneering experience; he saw the Indian as an annoying obstacle to progress significant only because his resistance forced the colonists to unified action, thus hurrying the trend that was climaxed in the united front against Britain in 1776. Other writers were even less charitable; Theodore Roosevelt in his monumental study of the southern frontier judged the Indian's defense of their homes against white aggression unjustified because "this great continent could not have been kept as nothing but a game reserve for squalid savages."

This hostile evaluation stemmed partly from a basic misconception, partly from the sources on which historians based their judgments. That they subconsciously aligned themselves with the pioneers whose march they recorded is easily understandable. Their heroes were the whites who won America, the vanguard of the nation's civilization; these were the venturesome conquerors who deserved the plaudits of subsequent generations that benefit so vastly from their sacrifices. That a few "savages" died along the way was regrettable, but all who stood in the way of "progress" must go, whatever the cost in human decency. Americans have generally parroted frontiersmen in their belief in a *conquistador* psychology that branded the conquered deserving of conquest. The Indian, pioneers insisted, no less than the forests, must be displaced as an enemy of cultural advance.

This viewpoint has been accentuated by the documentary sources available to historical writers. The Indian left almost no written records to tell his side of the story; the conquerors left records aplenty. To them there was no compromise with self-evident truth. They viewed themselves as heralds of civilization, destined to win the new world for their emperors and their church. At no time in history have people been driven by such zealous ambition; the age of discovery was the age of a rising merchant class, of competitive search for new trade routes, of the blood-bath of war as the forces of the Reformation and Counter-Reformation met on Europe's battle fields. The American Indians' misfortune was to fall victim to European contact at the precise moment when an aggressive nationalism, an inordinate lust for profits, and a fanatical crusading zeal motivated their conquerors. The whites were self-confident in their righteousness, unrestrained as yet by the tempering humanitarianism of the Enlightenment, and virtually unhampered by the slightest compassion toward any who stood in their path.

These were the views of the European invaders who saw the Indian as the supreme enemy of civilization, Indians were a personification of the savagery and heathenism from which the Old World had emerged; they were a relic of an earlier age who must be elevated or eliminated lest they drag Europeans back into the barbarism they had so recently escaped, for his very nakedness represented a threat to an orderly Christian society. To abide the Indian was to risk fatal contamination. Here was the basis of a racism that the frontier experience reinforced.

That racist image shaped Indian-white relations for centuries and still clouds the American vision today. Because the Indians did hunt and kill, because they did sometimes torture prisoners, because they were not driven by a Puritan work ethic to labor beyond their needs, because they indulged in unfamiliar religious practices, because they viewed nature as an ally rather than as an enemy, they were transformed in the eyes of Europeans into brutal savages, cruel, treacherous, not to be trusted. They saw the Indian male as indolent and lazy, lolling in sloth while his wife-slave did such work as was necessary. They pictured him a rootless wanderer, roaming the face of the earth after game as had their own primitive ancestors centuries before. The Indians were, in Europe's judgment, souls hopelessly lost to heathenism; learned scholars in the sixteenth century debated whether the Indians had souls, whether they were descended from Adam and Eve, whether they antedated the Garden of Eden and hence were a subhuman species more animal than man. Why show compassion to such creatures? To whites of this bias, "the only good Indian was a dead Indian."

Those suffered to live underwent a threefold transformation in the eyes of European chroniclers. To the earliest explorers and conquerors, and to their contemporaries who interpreted their discoveries for the information of the learned men of the day, the Indian was a simple child of the forest, enjoying the plenties of nature without the curse of labor, and much to be envied and imitated. "They have on several accounts," wrote an Englishman who knew them well, "reason to Lament the arrival of *Europeans,* by whose means they seem to have lost their Felicity, as well as their Innocence." This idyllic image changed abruptly when the native wars began; overnight the Indian became a bloodthirsty savage, bent on murder and rape and pillage, a pitiless foe to be killed before he killed you. With defeat in warfare the European's picture of the Indian changed once more; their numbers depleted by slaughter and disease, their warriors weakened by liquor, their lands seized by avaricious speculators, their life patterns altered by the white society's tools and guns, their cultures fragmented with devastating psychological effect, their racial self-confidence shattered, the Indian became in the eyes of whites a degraded race, impoverished and indolent, seeking escape in whisky, incapable of caring for themselves and unworthy of the care of others.

All of these images resulted from the European's pride in his own identity and culture. To Europeans their own civilization was the world's only civilization; any culture that differed was, by definition, corrupt and doomed to extinction. They brought with them from Europe a firm Judeo-Christian religious tradition, the heritage of a culture that had emerged over the centuries in the Near East, Greece, and Rome. They brought economic and social practices that had, in their eyes, achieved near-perfection. Wedded as they were to their own cultural patterns, they were incapable of admitting that the American Indian had valuable skills and traits at the same time that the whites were appropriating them. Because the Indians' behavior and philosophical concepts differed from those of the white, they had no culture at all. European misconceptions concerning native customs, religion, literacy, social controls, sexual habits, and technological skills contributed to the conflict between the races.

Only recently have anthropologists delved deeply enough into the Indian past to allow us to appreciate the complexities of the cultures that had matured in the Americas before they were disrupted by the coming of the whites. These differed greatly, one from the other, due both to ethnic and environmental differences. Archaeologists can set no precise date, but in all probability the ancestors of the native Americans began crossing from Asia into Alaska about thirty or forty thousand years ago, using the thousand-mile wide land bridge that emerged when the oceans fell some 300 feet during the Ice Age. They came in a series of migrations, interrupted now and then when the Bering Sea rose to cover the land mass, resumed when the oceans sank and the food-quest may have led them to follow herds eastward once more. The last great influx probably reached America only about eight thousand years ago. In the meantime the prior comers were spreading to the east and south from Alaska, following the river valleys as the glacial ice melted, until some 25,000 years after their invasion began they occupied all of North and South America.

As each migrating band of hunters and gatherers staked out its own territory some, responding to environmental forces, turned to farming. Each adopted the customs and technology suitable to survival in its own habitat, whether desert or mountain valley or prairie or woodland. Some lived primarily by farming, others by hunting, fishing, and gathering foods from native wild plants. Each specialized occupation required new weapons, new tools, new living arrangements. As these developed over the centuries, social customs, subsistence strategies, and religious beliefs emerged that were adjusted to the peculiar living habits of the region. As communication between the groups increased, borrowing began, with customs or ideas from one culture engrafted onto another. Thus there emerged in the Americas a complex of cultural areas, each differing from its neighbors very much as European nations differed one from another. Even the languages varied so widely that intertribal understanding was sometimes difficult; no less than 2,200 languages were spoken when the European conquest began, 200 of them north of Mexico.

The richness of the Indian cultures underlines the fact that the early Europeans who characterized all as "Indians" showed little understanding of the natives' manner of life and thought. Had they been less ethnocentric and more observing they would have recognized that "Indianness" was impossible to define. Indians varied in size, shape, coloration, language, and beliefs as widely as did whites. Some were tall, some short; some were dark-skinned, some light; some were round-headed, some long-headed; some were coarse featured, some delicate. They farmed, they fished, they hunted, they subsisted on native wild plants. Some gloried in warfare, but homicide within a group was abhorrent. The Iroquois hunted with bows and arrows, the Seminole with blow guns; the Chippewa rode in birch canoes, the Chickasaw in dugouts. Nor were these differences a product of distance; the Choctaw and Chickasaw were neighbors, yet one tribe was known for its agricultural skills and peaceful practices, the other for its hunting and belligerency. So deep was the gulf between groups that the Indians never thought of themselves as a distinct race; to the Iroquois, a Creek or a Sioux was just as much an outsider as an Englishman, and to be viewed with equal suspicion. In fact, during the early stages of colonization, tribes often welcomed whites as allies in wars against their traditional enemies. Not until the eighteenth century did the Indians begin to realize that they had something in common as opposed to the whites.

If early Europeans—and later historians—failed to realize the nature of Indian cultures, they had even less realization of the numbers of native Americans in possession of the continent when the invasion began. Their estimate of a handful of scattered tribes so thinly spread that they had no claim to the land was a wish-fulfilling dream that justified driving the Indians from their holdings. Today many anthropologists believe that somewhere between 4,500,000 and 9,800,000 Indians lived north of Mexico at the time of the first white contact. If these figures are accurate, not until 1815, two centuries after the conquest began, did the United States number as many inhabitants as the territory had in 1450. Nor were the native occupants uncivilized nomads, roaming the wilderness in search of game. Most Indians in eastern North America lived in towns or villages, many of them sizeable, with streets, houses, palisaded fortifications, and well-constructed centers for religious or civic ceremonies, usually surrounded by garden plots, fields of hybridized corn, and cultivated orchards. Most, too, had perfected sophisticated social controls, religious practices, and a stratified social structure.

Given these numbers and this cultural level, why did Europeans fail to realize either the strength or the cultural maturity of the native Americans? Even with their vision blinded by ethnocentric bias they could not fail to be impressed with the wooden buildings fifty feet long, the elaborate villages, the mature societies that had been reared in the continent's interior. The tragic answer is that the greatest of North America's Indian civilizations were decaying before the two races came in actual contact, the victim of diseases the white man unintentionally carried to the New World. The first explorers, the first fishermen and *conquistadores,* came laden with a variety of diseases that were relatively harmless in the Old World but lethal to peoples who had built up no immunities. These spread from the coast like wildfire, devastating tribe after tribe, and killing hundreds of thousands of Indians long before the first whites reached their villages. Measles, malaria, typhus, and influenza all were ruthless killers, but smallpox was the most virulent of all, decimating whole populations, then returning for a second or third time to strike down the survivors. Few conquering peoples have been aided by such potent allies as the diseases that paved the way for Europe's conquest of America.

Despite their devastation, sizeable native populations guarded their homelands against the Anglo-American invaders who swept the frontier westward. They were no handful of incompetents who could be brushed aside, but well-established tribesmen determined to defend their possessions against alien hordes. They lacked, however, viable political structures that allowed them to cooperate; instead they often found it desirable and convenient to side with whites against neighboring tribes. Eventually the contest between the two races became a full-scale war—a war far more devastating than Indians could ever have imagined—with the lands of a continent the prize for the winner.

For the Indians boasted a mature society, even by the standards of today. Generalizations can only be misleading when applied to such diverse cultures, but most woodland Indians in the eastern United States shared traits and beliefs that can be roughly defined. Common to nearly all was a social organization built upon the family and the clan. The latter was a kinship group formed of families descended from a common ancestor; most were given the names of animals—called "totems" or "brothers"—who were believed to be the supernatural or spiritual creators of the members. The clans played a significant role in both social, political, and family life; in some tribes they assumed part of the responsibility for raising children and conducting them into adulthood with appropriate rites.

The spiritual beliefs of the woodland Indians also had much in common. None accepted a set orthodoxy; an essence of tribalism was freedom of conscience for each individual which outlawed proselytizing in the manner of Christian missionaries. Yet most shared a common faith in a vast superior force that linked each man's spirit with every tree, every plant, every animal in the world of nature. The sum total of the spiritual powers in the universe was a force called the *orenda* by the Iroquois and the *manitou* by the Algonquians. Indians accepted a single creative force that the whites taught them to call the Great Spirit or Supreme Being. They all believed in an invisible world of spirits. Shamans, or medicine men as they were called later, served as spiritual leaders in some tribes, as well as doctors with a surprising record of cures. Venerated as possessing supernatural powers that allowed them direct contact with the spiritual world, they were called upon to tell the whereabouts of game or provide safety in battle, usually in rituals accompanied by music and dancing. Nearly all Indians anticipated life after death. Few pictured a hunter's paradise; the term ''Happy Hunting Ground'' was the white man's creation.

The woodland Indian's spiritual concepts governed his attitude to the material world about him. His acceptance of totemism, which symbolized the unity of all living things by linking humans with plants and animals, gave him a view of nature completely alien to European thought. The Indian revered the earth, the great mother of all things. He must use its bounties, for their purpose was to sustain him as his was to sustain them, but he strove always to maintain an equitable balance between himself and nature's resources. The overkill was contrary to his basic beliefs; he took only the animals and plants needed for existence. ''Their Manitou or good spirit,'' wrote one who knew them well, ''gave them the beasts of the woods for their support, to feed and Cloth themselves withal; that it was therefore lawful to kill them for these purposes—but that it was highly criminal to kill them for any other.'' The Indians' spiritual ties with nature were mirrored in their religious rites, their songs, their mythology, for all were geared to the rhythm of the seasons and all showed a mystic veneration for the natural objects about them. To covet an unjust share of these was to court pain, illness, and even death. These spiritual ties were broken or severely strained with Indian-white contact.

His religious concepts shaped his understanding of the function of land in the lives of men. Like the skies above and the bounties of nature, the earth was a common benefaction for all men, and could not be owned or traded. The concept of private ownership of the soil was alien to the Indians' thinking. They recognized the need to divide the *use* of the land; each tribe occupied a loosely defined area that was respected by its neighbors, and some allotted garden plots or partitioned hunting preserves among families to preserve fur-bearing animals. They also on occasion favored friends (including Europeans) by ''giving'' them plots they wanted in return for presents, but again they thought only in terms of mutual gift-giving, not of sale. This was a basic concept, built on the belief that the planet was a gift from nature, to be used collectively as nature intended. No man and no tribe owned land, and hence none could sell. The basic contradiction between the way Indians and whites viewed land made conflict between them inevitable.

As the Indians sought an accommodation with nature, so many of them wanted to achieve an accommodation with their neighbors. This was not true of all; warfare was common among all woodland Indians, and with some was an avocation. A few, too, elevated cruelty to a fine art, taking sadistic delight in torturing prisoners, burning captives at the stake, or forcing their victims to run the gauntlet while being beaten or slashed. Yet for every warlike tribe there was another that saw conflict as a necessary evil, to be used only to avenge a murder, protect crops and hunting grounds, or augment a dwindling supply of horses or slaves. None kept standing armies as did European nations, and most confined fighting to sporadic raids. The bloody battles and prolonged sieges common in the Europe of that day had little appeal to the Indian; no victory, he reasoned, was worth excessive effort or casualties.

In sum, the Indians who peopled the North American woodlands were culturally mature, reasonably healthy, responsibly governed, spiritually well-assured, and far better adjusted to their environment and its preservation than the Europeans who displaced them. "I can assure you," wrote a Britisher who had lived among them, "that they are a much better sort of people than commonly represented; they are hospitable, friendly and civil to an immense degree; in good breeding I think they infinitely surpass the French or any other people that I ever saw, if you will allow good breeding to consist in the desire to do everything that will please you, and in strict carefulness not to do anything that may offend you." Few at that time or since were sufficiently unbiased to agree with that judgment, but it was far more accurate than the distorted portrait handed down to later generations.

To refine these generalizations by surveying eastern North America's native inhabitants when the European conquest began is to underline the fact that cultural differences could transcend cultural similarities. Living as they did in a forest environment that varied little from north to south or east to west, they might be expected to show many common traits and beliefs, and such was not the case. They hunted, fished, and gardened. Some glorified war; others shunned combat. They spoke in a babble of tongues although all fell within one or the other of four linguistic groups: Algonquian, Iroquoian, Muskhogean, or Siouan. Each occupied a roughly defined territory, but its boundaries were largely fictitious and shifted constantly. The Indians, in other words, were diversified as individuals and groups.

First to be encountered by the invading Europeans were the coastal tribes. These were small and culturally variegated, sharing in common a marine and land economy. Far to the north, in present-day Maine and beyond the Canadian border, lived the Micmac, Abnaki, Penobscots, and other tribes who subsisted on fish and game, although along their southern fringes some farming and maple-sugar-gathering supplemented their diets. South of them, in New England and the Hudson River valley, were the villages of the Algonquian-speaking Pennacook, Nipmuc, Massachusetts, Wampanoag, Nausets, Pequot, Mohegan, Mohican, and other small groups; still further south in the Jerseys and Virginia lay the preserves of the Delawares, Powhatans, and Shawnee, as well as the Siouan-speaking Catawba and Monacan and the Iroquoian Tuscarora and Nottaway. In modern-day Georgia lived the Muskhogean Creeks, Hitchiti, and Yamasees, while Florida was the homeland of the Apalachees, Timucua, and other tribes. All were fishers and hunters, but agriculture was the foundation stone on which they built their economies. Most were skilled farmers, adept at clearing the forest by girdling the trunks of trees and burning the brush. Their clearings, left vacant by the diseases that ravaged their ranks, were the first fields used by Europeans to grow grain.

Beyond the coastal tribes lay the villages of far more numerous and powerful confederations. Far to the north, in present-day Ontario, stood the villages of the Huron, surrounded by stockades, and boasting populations of more than a thousand people in each. South of Lake Erie, in upper New York state, lay the land of the Iroquois, whose confederacy of Five Nations (later expanded to the Six Nations by the addition of the Tuscarora) was one native culture at a time when first contact was made with the whites.

The Iroquoian social structure was based on the "fireside" of mother and children; each in turn was part of a *ohwachira* of families tracing their relationship through the mothers. Two or more *ohwachiras* formed a clan, and a combination of clans constituted the tribe or nation. Over all, the women who headed the *ohwachiras* exercised supreme authority; they named delegates to the clan and tribal councils, selected the fifty Peace Chiefs who made up the ruling council of the Five Nations, and chose a group of sachems known as the Pine Tree Chiefs who were authorized to speak at the all-important meetings of the Iroquoian League. This met each summer at a principal town, with the fifty members voting by tribe rather than as individuals and a unanimous vote required on all major decisions. Within this sophisticated structure the individual tribes governed their internal affairs, with the League keeping peace among them and intensifying their strength by its sense of unity.

The life pattern of the Iroquois was equally indicative of their cultural level. They lived in villages of six or seven hundred people, surrounded by palisades of up-ended logs, so imposing that they were called castles by the first Europeans who saw them. Within these enclosures were the longhouses for which the confederation was famous: a structure some three hundred feet long so skillfully covered with elm bark that rain and cold were kept out. Within were spacious rooms for religious ceremonies and civic meetings, as well as apartments for from ten to twenty families, each with its own fire. Beyond the village walls was a ditch not unlike a castle moat, and beyond this the fields where corn and beans and squash were grown. Iroquois women were superb farmers, cultivating fifteen varieties of hybridized corn, eight varieties of squash, and sixty of beans; they also gathered from the forest fifty forms of edible roots and thirty-four types of fruit. Each year their fields were burned, returning minerals to the soil so successfully that crops could be planted a dozen years in a row. They had also learned by experimentation that beans, when grown with corn, gathered bacteria on their roots which fixed nitrogen in the soil, vastly increasing fertility. The Iroquois male was a diplomat, warrior, hunter, and fisherman.

South and west of the Iroquois was a land occupied by less powerful tribes: the Susquehannocks and Eries in Pennsylvania and eastern Ohio; the Algonquian-speaking Sauk, Foxes, Potawatomi, Ottawa, Menominee, Kickapoo, and Chippewa about the Great Lakes, and the Siouan-speaking Win-

nebago in Wisconsin. South of the Great Lakes lived others of the Algonquian linguistic family—the Kaskaskia and Miami among them—and along
the Kentucky-Tennessee border the Shawnee. All were village farmers who
planted corn and beans and squash and supplemented their diet by hunting,
fishing, and gathering. Their dwellings varied, some occupying rectangular
longhouses, others dome-shaped lodges fashioned of saplings covered with
birch bark strips. Both economically and politically they were self-sufficient
and independent; the Chippewa and Ottawa particularly became traders
traveling hundreds of miles to barter copper and furs and wampum belts
among the tribes. Each tribe governed itself efficiently, while at times as
many as thirty banded together in loose confederations designed to keep
peace among the members and protect themselves from others.

The first European invaders in the lower Mississippi Valley encountered
the decaying relics of still another variety of the Woodland Culture more
sophisticated than any other in eastern North America. The roots of the
Mississippian Tradition that thrived between southern Illinois and Natchez
between 700 and 1600 A.D. lay in an agricultural revolution that occurred
among the tribes that had occupied the region for thousands of years. With
new implements, new techniques, and successful hybridization of corn, adequate foodstuffs allowed a population and cultural explosion during the
seventh and eighth centuries that climaxed in a truly remarkable civilization.

This clustered about major ceremonial centers, many of them huge, with
a wooden temple built atop a large earthen mound usually flanked by an
imposing council house on an adjacent mound. Within the temple a perpetual
fire burned, renewed yearly with appropriate ceremonies. About the mounds
were sizeable metropolitan centers holding several thousand people, most
of them farmers, and all of them united in a southern ceremonial complex
that may have been a universal religion. The remarkable civilization of the
Mississippian Tradition began to decline in the sixteenth century when its
cities were swept by diseases introduced into the eastern forests by Europeans, diseases that wrought particular havoc among Indians living in close
proximity to each other. During the next half-century thousands died and
survivors scattered, leaving behind only the giant mounds at Cahokia, Illinois; Moundville, Alabama; Etowah, Georgia; and other sites as relics of
a golden age.

One, however, did survive long enough to be visited by French explorers
in the late sixteenth century. They found near Natchez a group of 4000
Indians living in nine towns that surrounded an imposing temple where an
eternal fire burned and the bones of former rulers were preserved. Ruling
over all was a despot known as the Great Sun who was believed to be a
lineal descendant of the Sun God; he was carried about on a litter and
venerated as a deity. With his relatives, the Little Suns, the Great Sun
constituted the ruling "Sun Clan" from which the high priests and warriors
were recruited. Below them in the highly structured social order were Nobles, Honored Men, and ordinary people that the earliest French explorers

called "stinkards." The society was not so aristocratic as it first appeared, for Great Sun women were required to mate with stinkard males.

By the time major contact with the whites began, the remnants of the Mississippian Tradition had regrouped into a number of tribal organizations. In Georgia and Alabama were the Muskogis, or Creeks as the English labeled them, bound together in a loose confederation, and occupying some fifty towns, half of them Red Towns that supplied military leaders and fought wars, half White Towns that controlled civil functions and trained future chiefs for the confederacy. Their near-neighbors were the Chickasaw, Choctaw, and Cherokee who lived in sixty villages in the hill and mountain country of North Carolina and Tennessee. In Florida the earlier tribes—Calusas, Timucuas, and Apalachees—had been virtually exterminated by the Spaniards by the early eighteenth century; that vacuum was filled when the few survivors intermarried with refugee Creeks from Georgia and runaway Negro slaves to form a new tribe known contemptuously to the Creeks as the "Isty-Semole," or "wild men." Later, as these "wild men" settled into villages and became farmers, their name was corrupted into Seminole. They, with the Choctaw, Chickasaw, Cherokee, and Creeks, came to be known as the Five Civilized Tribes.

The southern Indians during their historic period usually occupied stockaded towns, some of them with a hundred dwellings or more clustered about a central square that was used for religious ceremonies and festive occasions. Their houses, built of grass or plaster or thatch fastened to a pole framework, showed genuine architectural ingenuity; so did the large community house or temple that usually dominated their towns. Farming was their principal occupation, with corn, beans, squash, and tobacco the basic crops, supplemented with nuts and berries and with the meat of deer, bear, wildfowl, and fish. The southern Indians displayed surprising sophistication in the culinary arts, producing jelly made from wild roots, cakes of corn flour, a sweet syrup extracted from corn, and hominy. Yearly they blessed nature for the bounties bestowed on them in a *puskita,* or Creek Corn Ceremony, held just after the harvest to symbolize the renewal of life. Then fires were extinguished and relighted, broken pottery discarded, the village cleaned, and feuds settled. For a time, at least, they lived at peace with the world.

Whether they lived in the palisaded villages of the Creeks or Cherokee, or in the long houses of the Iroquois, the woodland Indians of eastern North America were unworthy of the treatment that they inspired in racially-biased Europeans. They were a viable cultural group accustomed to social controls and racial stratification often as structured and demanding as those of English villages. They held profound spiritual beliefs, including the idea of an afterlife. They were usually excellent farmers, living a sedentary life in a village community, and moving only when their routine was disrupted by war or famine. They ate well, cultivating a variety of vegetables with skill, and supplementing them with meat and fish from nature's larder. Unlike the Europeans who displaced them, they struggled to keep this always well filled by preserving a natural balance. Spiritually the eastern Indian lived as well, and almost as peacefully, as the Anglo-American settler.

Nor were their material standards noticeably inferior to those of their conquerors. They garbed themselves in raiment that was both functional and colorful, dressing in breechcloth, leggings, and shirt of leather softened by skillful tanning, and often ornamented with floral designs fashioned of shells or dyed porcupine quills. They decked themselves with jewelry, for the Indians were excellent artisans, adept at creating rings and ornaments from fresh-water pearls and the copper mined near Lake Superior and distributed over much of North America by barter. He knew how to use exactly the right wood for his bows and arrows, while his animal snares and canoes were marvels of expert construction. The North American Indians lagged behind their European rival principally in their failure to perfect a written language, develop a metal culture, or adapt the wheel to his use.

The American inheritance from the Indian is by no means insignificant; he taught us to use many of the foods that we eat (corn, potatoes, squash, pumpkins, and many others), many of the phrases that we use (including wigwam, wampum, caucus, papoose, sachem, mugwump, and succotash), many of the objects that we employ (hammocks, smoking pipes, snow shoes, and rubber balls, to name a few), many of the drugs that minister to our ills (at least fifty-nine in common usage derive from Indian medicine men), many of the names of our cities and towns (more than five thousand have been counted). From the American natives we learned how to smoke tobacco and an art of guerrilla warfare. Most important of all, they had learned to live within nature's bounds. One of the facts of history is that our European ancestors failed to recognize the virtues of Indian culture, and that they virtually rejected a civilization which had so much to offer their own.

Europe's First Frontier
1492-1615

The occupation of the western hemisphere was one stage in the mighty movement of peoples that began in the twelfth century when feudal Europe began pushing back the barbarian hordes that had pressed in from east, north, and south to threaten the Holy City of Rome itself. The first step in this expansion was taken by zealous crusaders who in the twelfth and thirteenth centuries battered back the Moslems upon their eastern borders in a vain effort to wrest Jerusalem from infidel hands. They failed, but the plundered wealth with which they returned sent new life coursing through Europe's stagnant economic system, and their tales of the riches of the Near East conjured up dreams of splendors all but forgotten by peoples accustomed to frugal feudalism. Venetian traders followed close on their heels to establish trade routes with Constantinople and other Levantine cities which sent unaccustomed luxuries of the Levant flooding over Europe: spices to relieve the monotony of coarse food, "notemuge to putte in ale," rich tapestries, gems, and precious stones.

Quickening economic life stimulated the monarchs of the shadowy realms that survived the Middle Ages to reassert themselves; from the thirteenth to the sixteenth centuries they waged bitter war on their feudal lords to build on the ruins of the seignorial system the nations of modern Europe: Portugal, Spain, France, England, and the Netherlands. In each country this conquest was aided by the rising merchant class, thus placing the monarchs in the debt of the monied interests. Royal efforts to repay these obligations hurried the commercial exploitation of the New World. Business leaders knew that the exotic goods of the Levant were brought by caravan from distant eastern lands. Travelers—such as Marco Polo—told them that in those mysterious realms of Cathay (China) and Cipango (Japan) the cities had "walles of silver and bulwarkes or towers of golde" and were filled with palaces "entirely roofed with fine gold," and with lakes of pearls. "Whoever won-teth golde," Europeans read, "diggeth till he hath found some quan-titie." Their own wealth was steadily draining eastward to purchase the exotic goods that Europe now demanded, while the end of crusading had stopped the flow of plundered Near Eastern gold into their coffers. What magnificent profits would be theirs if they could establish direct trade with the Orient!

This was the incentive that sent the nations of western Europe along the path to new frontiers. Portugal, a compact, well-governed little country, took the lead by sending her explorers southward during the fifteenth century in search of a route around Africa. When Bartholomew Diaz rounded the Cape of Good Hope in 1486 the goal was in sight, and a suddenly alarmed Europe awakened to the possibility that the Portuguese might monopolize the rich Oriental trade. Spain was especially fearful, but Ferdinand and Isabella, the joint rulers, were busy driving Moorish invaders back to Africa and could do nothing until the last enemy stronghold at Granada fell in 1492. Six months later they sent a Genoese navigator named Christopher Columbus on his memorable voyage across the Atlantic, realizing, as did all intelligent people of the day, that the world was round and that ships could reach the East by sailing west. Seventy days after his three tiny vessels left the Azores, Columbus made his landfall in the West Indian islands. He found no crowded city of Quinsay, no rich realms of Cipango or Cathay, no empire of the Grand Khan. But he returned to Europe convinced that he had hit on some outlying portion of Asia and that further exploration would reveal the fabled riches of that fabulous land.

Within ten years after Columbus' first voyage the Spanish explorers who followed in his wake showed that he had discovered not the Orient but a great interocean barrier between Europe and the Far East. The disap-pointment caused by this revelation was only momentary; might not this mysterious new world hold wealth to rival that of Asia? Columbus had found a few gold trinkets among the natives on his first voyage, and on his second in 1493 carried 1,500 colonists who built the first permanent European set-tlement in America on the island of Hispaniola (Haiti) and turned at once to the search for the precious metal. They soon found that enslaved Indians could be forced to work the primitive gold mines which existed on many of the islands. Here at last was the wealth Spain sought; excitement swept the nation as eager colonists fought for the privilege of going to America. These adventurers, wrote one chronicler of that day, "dreamed of nothing but gold, . . . it was gold that they there sought for, gold that they extracted from the Indians, gold that was given to satisfy them, gold that clinked in their letters to give them standing at Court, and gold that the Court demanded and coveted."

Under this stimulus, plus royal zeal for conversion of a vast new heathendom, the settlement on Hispaniola expanded rapidly until by 1513, when Spain made her first assault on the North American coast, seventeen towns dotted the island, and colonies were established on Puerto Rico, Jamaica, and Cuba. Life in these villages followed a pattern that was to be often duplicated as America's mining frontier moved westward across the continent. Lavish spending and utter profligacy were the rule. Officials strutted about in rich silks, brocades, and embroideries, lived with Indian mistresses, and gambled for preposterous stakes; they taught their horses to dance and curvet, and their principal sport was hunting Indians with hounds. Banquets were given where gold dust was served instead of salt and musicians were imported "to make the people merry." Only lynch law was needed to transform these boisterous towns into the typical American mining camps of a later period.

For a few years the island settlements provided Spain with sufficient wealth, but the mother country's insatiable appetite for gold and souls soon turned attention to the mainland. With this move there rose to prominence a new type of Spanish frontiersman, the *conquistadors*. These hardy adventurers were minor noblemen who, having lived by their swords during the long Moorish wars, were left at loose ends when peace settled on Spain in 1492. Their adventurous past made industry or commerce seem prosaic, and their independent spirits rebelled against servile adherence to royal absolutism. Many drifted to America, lured by the promise of excitement and wealth. Cruel, devout, hard-fighting men, they blazed a trail of conquest and salvation westward as they planted the flag of their king and the cross of their church across the face of the continent. Pity and fear were unknown to these robust swashbucklers who led Spain's assault on North America; they slew their enemies as boldly as they faced death themselves.

Juan Ponce de León was the first. Unable to settle down to court intrigues after the Moorish wars, he turned to the New World, going with Columbus on his second voyage and later "pacifying" Puerto Rico by the usual process of killing or enslaving the natives. There he heard of the island of Bimini lying to the north, where gold was plentiful and a magic spring spouted waters that brought perpetual youth to all who drank. Armed with a patent to discover and people this island, Ponce de León sailed from Puerto Rico in March, 1513. Sighting a strip of coast which he named Florida, he landed near the mouth of the St. John's River, then journeyed around the peninsula as far as Pensacola Bay. Hostile Indians thwarted him at every stop, and he returned to the islands without gold and without having drunk of the fabulous fountain. Two other explorers took up the task of determining whether Florida was really the magic isle of Bimini. In 1519 an expedition under Alonso Álvarez de Pineda skirted the northern coast of the Gulf of Mexico, stopping to trade with the natives, investigate bays, and take possession of the land. Álvarez returned to Jamaica with lying tales of plentiful gold and giant natives, but he did establish the fact that Florida was part of a larger mainland. A year later a second party equipped by Lucas Vásquez de Ayllón added proof by exploring the eastern shore as far north as Cape

Fear, where 150 natives were captured and taken back to the West Indies as slaves.

Ponce de León was sufficiently alarmed by these encroachments on a domain that he considered his own to obtain a new patent authorizing him to settle "the Island of Bimini and the Island of Florida," and in 1521 he landed two ship loads of men near Charlotte Bay. Again hostile Indians drove off the colonists, wounding Ponce de León so severely that he died a short time after returning to Cuba. Vásquez de Ayllón immediately set out for Spain to secure the patent vacated by Ponce's death, taking with him an Indian named Francisco Chicora who delighted Charles V and his Spanish court with marvelous tales of his homeland. The people there, he told his credulous listeners, were white with long tails which were "not movable like those of quadrupeds, but formed one mass, as in the case with fish and crocodiles, and was as hard as bone. When these men wanted to sit down they had consequently to have a seat with an open bottom; and if there were none, they had to dig a hole more than a cubit deep to hold their tails and allow them to rest." Gold and precious stones, of course, abounded among these natives. The king was charmed by this gifted liar into granting Ayllón the charter needed to settle that fantastic country.

After preliminary explorations, Ayllón set out from Spain in 1526 with six vessels and five hundred settlers. Failing to find the country described by Chicora in the Cape Fear region, he moved his elaborate force southward, to the banks of a river—probably the Pee Dee—where he built a few flimsy huts that were glorified as the settlement of San Miguel de Guadalupe. Cold, starvation, and disease took a frightful toll during the winter of 1526-27, and in the spring the 150 survivors struggled back to Hispaniola, leaving behind them the body of their leader who had fallen prey to the wilderness he tried to conquer. Thus ended Spain's first serious effort to found a colony in what is now the eastern United States. Insufficient knowledge of frontier technique proved so disastrous that for twenty years the Spaniards made no further attempt to settle that forbidding coast.

Instead new prospects lured them into the interior of the continent. Their interest was turned in this direction by the conquests of Hernán Cortés in Mexico (1519-21) and Francisco Pizarro in Peru (1528), for these two *conquistadors* found in the central cities of the Aztecs and Incas the fabulous wealth that Spaniards had long been seeking. If Central and South America concealed such riches, the unknown interior of North America might hide even greater fortunes. New Spain was rich enough to make the assault now, for its island possessions were thriving; Negro slaves, first introduced in 1501, numbered no less than ten thousand by 1527 and were ready to provide sinew for any conquest. Three hundred black men had dragged the cannons used by Cortés to subdue the Aztecs and others had been at the side of Pizarro and Ponce de León. Now they were ready to aid the search for loot, lands, and souls that became the objective of Spanish adventurers.

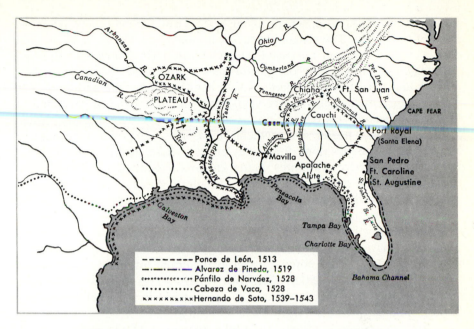

The Spanish in Eastern North America, 1513–1590

First to take up the quest was Pánfilo de Narváez, who landed at Tampa Bay with four hundred followers in April, 1528. His ambitious plans called for the founding of several cities along the Gulf coast to serve as bases for raids on the interior Indian tribes, but these were forgotten when natives showed him a few gold trinkets which, they said, came from the village of Apalache where the white men would find all the yellow metal they could carry. Why wait to establish towns when a second Mexico City lay just ahead? For two months Narváez led his men northward through swamps and thickets and hostile natives, until finally they burst upon Apalache. Instead of a great city they found forty thatched huts, instead of gold and silver a few half-starved natives, instead of rich mines a countryside of "great lakes, dense mountains, immense deserts and solitudes." The disappointed Spaniards did not stay long, for the Indians were anxious to be rid of the ravenous invaders and sent them on by telling them that a town to the southward held the yellow metal they sought. Again the tiresome march was resumed, and again the hoped-for city proved to be a miserable Indian village. Thoroughly discouraged, the Spaniards pressed on to the sea at Apalache Bay.

The hope of the 242 survivors was to reach Mexico. Five crude boats were built of boards hacked out with swords and held together by nails melted down from armor. In these overloaded craft they set out to sea in September, 1528, sailing westward along the coast until they reached the mouth of the Mississippi where raging waters and strong winds swamped three of the boats. The remaining two, with eighty survivors, kept on until they were wrecked on an island near Galveston Bay. Friendly Indians, "howling like brutes over our misfortunes," took the Spaniards to their villages and tried to nurse them back to health, but by the spring of 1529 only fifteen remained alive. Six years later this number had dwindled to two, one of whom was Álvar Núñez Cabeza de Vaca, who had established a reputation as a healer and medicine man. Resolving at last to escape, Núñez set out alone along the Texas coast, where he found three other Spaniards and Andres Dorantes, better known as Estevan the Black, a Morocco-born Negro slave who had been brought to America by his master in 1527 to join the Narváez expedition. With them he started the overland journey to Mexico. In each village he used his healing arts with such success that marvelous cures followed his prayers and mystical rites. Estevan the Black also charmed the natives who never ceased to wonder at the color of his skin. He was, Núñez noted, "our go-between; he informed himself about the ways we wished to take, what towns there were, and the matters we desired to know." Their journey became a triumphant procession—four tattered Spaniards and a Negro slave marching at the head of as many as four thousand painted natives—until they arrived in Mexico City in April, 1536.

Cabeza de Vaca's straightforward account of what he had seen should have ended Spanish interest in North America, for he had found no permanent cities, no gold or silver, and only impoverished Indians who lived on roots, spiders, and an occasional deer that was exhausted by an all-day chase. Instead Spaniards preferred to listen to the fanciful imaginings of Indians who were always ready to conjure up tales that would please the white men—of wealthy interior tribes and especially of "seven very large towns which had streets of silver workers" and gold in plenty. Could these be the cities of the seven bishops who, according to hoary Spanish legend, had fled west in the eighth century to set up seven episcopates on fabulously rich lands across the Atlantic? Even Cabeza de Vaca, succumbing to popular pressure, decided to tell his countrymen what they wanted to hear rather than the truth. When he visited Spain a year after his return he found such eager listeners among the nobles that he let his imagination run wild and in great secrecy "gave them to understand that it was the richest country in the world."

One man listened with particular interest. Hernando de Soto, a wealthy noble with considerable colonial experience who had just secured Narváez's grant to eastern North America, realized that Cabeza de Vaca's ramblings promised him not only great wealth but plentiful recruits for the expedition he was organizing. All Spain caught the excitement; noblemen sold their estates to buy places on de Soto's ships or fought for the privilege of going, and when he sailed in 1538 so great a company assembled on the docks that many "who had sold their goods, remained behind for want of shipping."

After wintering in Cuba, the elaborate force of six hundred soldiers, great herds of horses and swine, packs of hounds, and mountains of equipment, landed on the east shore of Tampa Bay in May, 1539. There began four years of fruitless wandering over 350,000 square miles of wilderness, guided only by Indians who discovered that they could best rid themselves of the plundering Spaniards by telling them that the next village was richer than their own.

De Soto spent the first winter at Apalache, where he learned of a northern province governed by a woman, "the town she lived in being of an astonishing size, and many neighboring lords her tributaries, some of whom gave her clothing, others gold in quantity." They found this woman on the Savannah River, but her "astonishing" village held only a few flimsy huts, and her wealth consisted of a handful of spoiled fresh-water pearls. The country about the upper Savannah proved so uninviting that the Spaniards headed south again as far as Mavilla where a disastrous fire destroyed even the meagre plunder they had gathered, then turned to the northwest and spent the winter of 1540-41 near the Yazoo River. With spring they wended their weary way onward until they came upon the Mississippi a few miles south of present Memphis. De Soto was annoyed rather than pleased at his discovery, for the expedition had to pause while barges were built before the men could cross. Again the northern country proved unattractive, but the Indians told of large towns to the south, and the summer was spent searching the Ozark region for the fabled seven cities. After wintering on the Arkansas River near its junction with the Canadian, de Soto started his tattered followers back toward the Gulf to renew their equipment. To his great disappointment the Arkansas River led them again to the broad Mississippi rather than to the sea. There, while his men were building boats and fighting off hostile natives, de Soto "took to his pallet" and died.

The remnants of the expedition first tried to march west to Mexico, but after a year of wandering turned back to the Mississippi, built seven boats, and floated down to the Gulf on the spring floods of 1543. Alternately praying and rowing, they made their way along the coast until September 10, 1543, when they turned into the Río De Pánuco. There they learned that a Spanish town was only fifteen leagues away. "Many, leaping on shore, kissed the ground"; wrote their chronicler, "and all, on bended knees, with hands raised above them, and their eyes to heaven, remained untiring in giving thanks to God." Of the six hundred men who started with de Soto four years before, 311 survived the incredible hardships with sufficient spirit to criticize the poverty of the Spanish town where fate had cast them! Here was proof of the prowess of the *conquistadors*.

De Soto's disastrous failure, by ending hope of rich finds in the interior of eastern North America, ushered in a phase of the Spanish conquest in which colonization rather than exploitation became the ambition of the nation's rulers. This decision was forced upon them by the need of occupying the Florida coast, a step deemed necessary to protect Spain's thriving possessions in Central and South America. By this time Mexico City was the principal city of New Spain, its treasure houses bulging with wealth from native mines. This gold and silver was carried to Spain in great galleons which sailed across the Gulf, through the Bahama Channel, and northward along the coast of Florida before spreading their sails to the easterly blowing Atlantic trade winds. If enemy vessels were allowed to lurk in the many inlets along the Florida coast they could pounce on Spanish shipping almost at will. As France, England, and Holland, the other maritime powers of the Atlantic seaboard, were casting covetous eyes at Spain's New World wealth, the Spanish authorities realized that they must act. Only by winning over the coastal natives and making eastern Florida so thoroughly loyal that no enemy vessel dared touch there could they protect their treasure route.

Philip II, ruler of Spain, planned two settlements, one at Santa Elena and the other on the Gulf of Mexico. In June, 1559, an expedition sailed, with 1,500 colonists under the command of Don Tristán De Luna y Arellano. They landed at the port of Ochuse, on Pensacola Bay, where De Luna ordered the first settlement built. De Luna, who had been with de Soto, planned to send a part to Coca, the only rich Indian settlement de Soto had found. When 300 badly needed soldiers returned from a futile search that ended at a miserable little village of thirty huts on the Coosa River, they found the colony torn by dissension, with its leaders bickering among themselves and most of the settlers anxious to return home. News of this sorry state of affairs finally reached Mexico. De Luna was sent packing, and a new leader, Ángel de Villafañe, took over the ill-fated expedition. He fared no better, for when he tried to move the colonists to Santa Elena in the spring of 1561 his ships were buffeted by storms that finally drove him back to Hispaniola. Discouraged, Philip II was no longer willing to expend treasure and life to settle Florida.

But Philip had no choice for an interloper forced a reversal of Spanish policy. The ambitions of Gaspard de Coligny, Admiral of the Realm, were responsible. Staunch patriot and zealous Huguenot, he had long dreamed of establishing the colonial prestige of his beloved France by founding a Protestant settlement on the northern Florida coast. An opportunity arose in the spring of 1562. His three shiploads of volunteers under Jean Ribaut selected a site for their colony at Santa Elena, which they renamed Port Royal, and there began constructing crude mud huts surrounded by log fortifications. While work was going on, Ribaut sailed back to France for more supplies, but mutiny broke out among the settlers and, when fire destroyed the food supply, his colonists were reduced to near-starvation. In desperation they finally set out for France in a tiny vessel built with their own hands, only to lie becalmed in mid-Atlantic until their food gave out and they were almost reduced to cannibalism before being rescued by a passing British ship. A Spanish expedition that sailed from Cuba to drive out the hated French found only the abandoned fort and a French youth who preferred life among the Indians to fleeing by boat.

Coligny was not ready to give up. Even as the Spaniards were returning triumphantly to Cuba a second French expedition under René de Laudonnière was on its way to Florida. This time the French built their settlement, which they called Ft. Caroline, on the St. John's River. The hardships of the first winter almost forced them to give up the attempt, but when Jean Ribaut arrived to take command in the spring of 1565 with seven shiploads of supplies, new colonists, and abundant food, the outpost's future seemed secure. Not so that of the Spaniards. Ribaut planned to build a fort on the Florida Keys as a headquarters for six galleys that could sally forth against Spain's treasure ships as they sailed northward through the nearby Bahama Channel—the lifeline of empire. The Spanish were horrified. "They put the Indies in a crucible," one wrote frantically from Mexico, "for we are compelled to pass in front of their port, and with the greatest ease they can sally out with their armadas to seek us, and easily return home when it suits them." Philip II acted quickly, selecting a noted soldier, Don Pedro Menéndez de Avilés, as Spain's avenger with orders to drive out the French "by what means you see fit" and found a colony in Florida that would forestall future intrusions.

The first task proved easier than the second. Menéndez, with a strong fleet and 800 followers, dropped anchor on August 28, 1565, at the mouth of a small river which he called the St. Augustine. After seven days preparation he sailed north, only to have the French cut their cables and sail before he could attack. When an all-night pursuit of the fleeing enemy proved fruitless he returned to Ft. Caroline, which was now well guarded by three warships that had been lurking in the river. Menéndez, afraid to risk an open attack, retraced his steps to the St. Augustine where his men began constructing the first enduring white settlement in what was to become the United States. While this went on both commanders decided to take the offensive, Ribaut by sea and Menéndez by land. Fate played against the French. Violent storms scattered their fleet on its way to St. Augustine and left Ft. Caroline's 240 defenders at the mercy of the Spaniards when they struck on September 30 after a quick overland march. Within an hour 138 had been put to the sword, even the sick being dragged from their beds and murdered. Only sixty Frenchmen escaped. During the next weeks nearly 400 more Frenchmen who survived the wreck of their fleet, including Ribaut himself, were slaughtered along the Florida coast. "I put Jean Ribaut and all the rest of them to the knife," Menéndez wrote Philip, "judging it to be necessary to the service of the Lord Our God, and of Your Majesty."

The founding of outposts to hold Florida against future intruders proved more difficult. Menéndez set out from St. Augustine in 1566 with three ships and 150 men, going first to Santa Elena where, on the swampy shores of Parris Island, the willing ship's crew fell to building a fort or presidio which they called San Felipe. After leaving 110 men to guard that strategic spot he turned south to Cumberland Island where the presidio of San Pedro was built and garrisoned by eighty soldiers. The spot on the St. John's where the French had reared Ft. Caroline was selected for the final northern fort, which was called San Mateo. South of St. Augustine a presidio was located on the St. Lucie River and two more on the west coast at Tampa and Charlotte bays. With the coast secure Menéndez turned to the more difficult task of fortifying the back country. Captain Juan Pardo was sent west from Santa Elena with a small force, first to the upper reaches of the Broad River where he built Ft. San Juan, then on to the Indian villages of Chiaha and Cauchi near the headwaters of the Chattahoochee River where small presidios were constructed. A handful of men was left at each of these tiny outposts with instructions to convert the natives to Christianity and search for the fabled mines supposedly in that region.

From the first these frontier posts fared badly. Most of them were located on swampy ground where mosquitoes made life intolerable, diseases took a heavy toll, and the few farmers assigned to each presidio were unable to raise sufficient grain for the garrisons. Hostile Indians and delays in importing food from Spain increased the hazards of presidio life. Dissension soon developed among the idle troops, who had little to do but complain, and Menéndez spent his declining years in a losing struggle to hold his feeble domain together. His death in 1573 was the signal for an outbreak of Indian hostility that his nephew, Pedro Menéndez de Márquez, who succeeded him as governor of Florida, was unable to check. The garrison at Tampa Bay was killed, the post at Charlotte Bay was abandoned in the face of hostile demonstrations, and lurking Indians surrounded each of the other presidios, ready to pounce on stragglers. This smouldering enmity burst into open rebellion in 1576 when the starving soldiers at San Felipe attempted to force corn from a neighboring tribe. Two thousand war-crazed Indians swept down on the feeble outpost, forced the tiny garrison to flee toward St. Augustine, and burned the fort. The interior posts suffered a similar fate, and even the presidio of San Mateo was dismantled under the pressure of native hostility.

Menéndez de Márquez tried to salvage what he could from the wreckage of his defenses. A new fort of logs and oyster shells, surrounded by sixty sturdy houses, was built at Santa Elena during the summer of 1577, but the task was hopeless. Even while he was at work on this outpost word reached Menéndez that Frenchmen had landed a few leagues to the north where they were erecting a fort. He had too few men to drive out the intruders, but the following spring he led the largest force he could muster along the coast, capturing nearly a hundred French interlopers and killing their leader, a piratical corsair named Nicolas Estrozi. This step only made the situation worse, for the Caribbean swarmed with English and French pirates and freebooters, many of whom now vowed to avenge their comrade's death. For the next two years these adventuresome outcasts kept the Florida coast in a constant state of turmoil, fomenting Indian rebellions and raiding Spanish supply ships on their way to aid the harassed garrisons. Not until the autumn of 1580, when additional troops arrived from Spain, was Menéndez able to punish the offending natives by a northward march that ended for the time being the danger of a joint French-Indian attack on St. Augustine.

This warfare along the borderlands showed that Spain's frontier technique, which depended on native labor to exploit a region's tangible wealth, was entirely unadapted to eastern North America. In Central and South America the labor of large numbers of relatively advanced and frequently docile Indians could be utilized for work in mines and fields, so that comparatively few Spaniards could control large areas. North of the Gulf of Mexico, however, the country was poor and the native population too proud to be enslaved. The disastrous experiences of the two Menéndez demonstrated that these independent Indians could not be forced to work, while the colonists, accustomed to living on the labor of submissive natives, were usually unwilling to perform the back-breaking tasks themselves. Nor could the mother country send out enough white settlers to hold the northern coast; all but the most loyal Catholics were forbidden to emigrate, and most of these preferred the safety of their native land or the greater opportunities elsewhere.

Under these circumstances Spain was forced to devise a new frontier technique suitable to the peculiar conditions of North America. Her answer was the mission station. Earnest friars, clad in fibre sandals and sackcloth gowns worn scant and thin, painfully learning the native tongues when they found to their mild amazement that "the Indians did not understand Latin," succeeded where the armed might of Spain failed. They established their tiny chapels in the forbidding wilderness, gathered about them groups of Indians who were taught crafts and agriculture as well as Christianity, and gradually extended their influence through conversions until all northern Florida was pacified. Thus the holy fathers built up a loyal population, ready to defend for crown and church a great domain that might otherwise have fallen sooner into alien hands.

Jesuit and Franciscan missionaries visited North America with the early explorers, but not until 1593, when a band of twelve Franciscans under Fray Juan de Silva reached Florida, did they play a major role in the Spanish conquest. A number of mission provinces were established at once. Apalache on the northern Gulf coast, Timucua in the Florida peninsula, Guale in present Georgia, Orista extending northward through modern South Carolina, and Tama embracing the interior. The first arrivals were dispersed over Guale, where the Indians were so hostile that the presidio garrisons did not dare hunt or fish beyond the protection of their forts. Within three years the whole region was at peace, 1,500 natives had been baptized, and others were flocking from the interior to seek religious instruction. The friars used these willing neophytes to erect chapels at the principal Indian villages along the coast: San Pedro on Cumberland Island, Santiago De Ocone on Jekyl Island, Asao on St. Simon Island, Tolomato and Tupique on the mainland. Garrisons were still maintained near these mission stations at presidios on Amelia, Cumberland, Sapelo, and St. Catherine islands, but the soldiers had little to do. By 1596 the whole northern frontier was peaceful and loyal to Spain, and plans were being laid to extend the missionaries' activities into Tama.

This tranquil progress was rudely checked in 1597 by the Juanillo Revolt. Trouble began when Juanillo, a warlike Guale brave who was angered by the friars' refusal to let him become chief of his tribe, gathered other discontented spirits and murdered the missionary at Tolomato in the midst of morning devotions. This act, he told neighboring tribes, would result in general punishment unless they drove the white men from the land. The simple Indians were so much impressed by this warning that they slaughtered the Franciscan friars on St. Catherine, St. Simon, and Jekyl islands in a series of sudden raids. Word of the revolt was hurried to St. Augustine, but a relief expedition that marched from that stronghold in October failed to capture more than a handful of the rebels, although several Indian villages were burned and crops destroyed. The mission station on Cumberland Island, which had survived one attack with the aid of friendly natives, was judged unsafe and abandoned before winter. In a few months the natives destroyed the patient labor of years, leaving the northern Florida frontier a wilderness, broken only by the isolated presidio at Santa Elena.

Starvation which swept through the native ranks following a punitive expedition in 1598 broke their rebellious spirit, and by the spring of 1600 humiliated chiefs were flocking to St. Augustine to ask forgiveness. The task of restoring the missions was begun in 1603 and went on rapidly; within three years new stations were erected at San Juan, Santa María, San Pedro, Macoma, Talaxe, and Santa Catalina de Guale, all occupied by newly arrived Franciscans who administered to a growing group of docile Indians. This triumph was celebrated in 1606 when the Bishop of Cuba, with an elaborate retinue of civil and ecclesiastical followers, visited each station in turn to baptize 2,453 natives in impressive ceremonies.

This episcopal visitation launched the Spanish missions on a period of prosperity that lasted for half a century. During these years steady streams of Franciscan friars reached St. Augustine and plunged into the wilderness to found new stations on the fringe of advancing civilization. One group turned to the north where they strung their missions along the sea islands of Guale and Orista as far as San Felipe and Chatuache; another scattered over the province of Timucua where eighteen stations stretching westward from St. Augustine ministered to a loyal band of Christian Indians. Still farther to the west the Franciscans in 1633 began establishing their outposts in Apalache, clustering most of them about the principal station and presidio at San Luis. By 1650 these holy fathers, with a handful of soldiers in a few strategically located forts, controlled almost 26,000 Indians.

The mission stations won southeastern North America for Spain. Zealous friars, willing to live with their wards, follow them through the forests in search of acorns during the starving times, and tremble before their treachery in periodic revolts, secured the empire that the *conquistadors* had failed

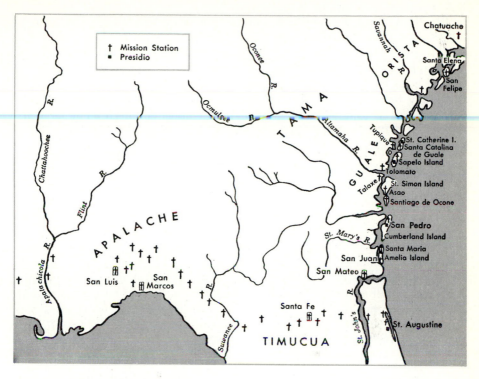

The Spanish Mission Station Frontier in the Southeast, 1590–1630

to win. Their loyal native converts were ready to drive out any intruders, be they hostile tribesmen from the north or heretic Europeans from overseas. The Franciscans gave their church and king a monopoly in the Florida country which latecomers would have to break.

While Spaniards struggled to win yellow gold and red souls in the South, other Europeans were carving an empire from the northern lands tributary to the St. Lawrence River, lured by the less romantic flesh of the cod and skin of the beaver. The French who sought their share of the New World's wealth amidst the sparkling streams and deep forests of this north country entered the race for America late; until 1529 when the Peace of Cambrai ended a long period of war at home they had neither time nor energy for overseas conquest. With peace their monarch, Francis I, displayed an immediate interest, for he lived in extravagant splendor and coveted "diamonts" and "golde ore" as did few other men. To find them, and to seek the fabled Straits of Anian that would allow ships to sail through the North American continent to the riches of the Orient, he sent out Jacques Cartier in 1534 on the voyage that laid the basis of France's American empire.

Cartier, with two tiny vessels, touched first on Newfoundland, then sailed north and through the Straits of Belle Isle into the Great Bay, as he called the Gulf of St. Lawrence, which he explored thoroughly. He found no gold or precious stones, but the broad river that entered into the Great Bay might lead to the Pacific Ocean, and he returned a year later to venture as far inland as the present site of Montreal. That winter of 1535-36 he spent on the St. Charles River, near present Quebec, among Indians so friendly that they bribed the Frenchmen not to leave and even dressed as devils "with horns as long as one's arms and their faces coloured black as coal" to overawe the explorers into staying. Cartier returned to France in the spring, still without gold or silver, but with tales of a fertile and beautiful country that deserved further exploitation.

By this time France was at war again, and not until 1541 could Cartier start on his third voyage. His backer now was Sieur de Roberval, a Norman knight and freebooter, who had glimpsed a vision of empire and wanted to plant a colony of his own. Cartier sailed first with five ships and wintered near present Quebec; his patron followed a year later with three more vessels laden with colonists recruited from Paris slums and jails. In a Newfoundland harbor he met Cartier heading back for France, wild with excitement over a few barrels of iron pyrites—mica and quartz that he had mistaken for gold. Roberval continued on, but one winter with his unruly convict crew was enough, and in 1543 he returned to France. This ended the first French attempt to found an outpost in the New World, for the mother country was so weakened by renewed religious dissension and civil war that her rulers lost interest in a barren wilderness promising no immediate returns.

For the next half-century France was too absorbed in her internal difficulties to concern herself with nebulous wealth beyond the seas. Yet during this interim her claim to northern North America was firmly established, not by haughty nobles in tall ships, but by humble fishermen. The first explorers to cross the Atlantic brought back tales of seas off Newfoundland "full of fish, which are not only taken by a net, but also with a basket, a stone being fastened to it in order to keep it in the water." This was important news to Catholic Europe, and as word of these Newfoundland Banks spread through the docks of Bristol, Lisbon, Rouen, St. Malo, Dieppe, and other ports, hardy fishermen set out to exploit these fishing grounds. As early as 1527 an explorer who put into the harbor of St. Johns found "eleven sail of Normans and one Britaine and two Portugal Barques, and all a-fishing." Frenchmen were especially active on the Banks, particularly after 1539 when the discovery of the principle of tacking reduced the time required by the Atlantic crossing from months to weeks. By 1578, one hundred fifty French vessels were busily engaged in the trade, against fifty from England, Holland, Spain, and Portugal.

An unrecorded event that took place somewhere, sometime, on the bleak Newfoundland coast turned the attention of France from the sea to the land. Each year the fishing fleets, after casting their nets at the Banks, put in to the nearest harbor to split, salt, and dry the codfish before journeying back across the Atlantic. The Indians who gathered to watch these strange rites were fascinated by the knives of the Frenchmen, for their own bone and stone implements seemed crude by comparison. One of them, watching with covetous eyes a gleaming knife of a fisherman as he split open a fat cod, managed to signal that he would give anything he possessed for that glittering blade. The sailor, noticing the fine cloak of beaver skins worn by the Indian, indicated that he was willing to trade. Thus was born the fur trade on which the French occupation of North America rested.

What a profitable trade it was. Furs were light in weight, easy to pack and carry, and possessed the basic requisite of any staple: they could not be produced in the mother country. No special skills were required; a ship sturdy enough to cross the Atlantic and a crew hardy enough to stand the voyage were the only requisites. The market was limitless. During the late sixteenth century Europe's world of fashion decreed that every gentleman must wear a felt hat, and in those days the principal source of good felt was the beaver. Each strand of the soft underfur had tiny barbs at the tip; these meshed to form a permanent matting that wore better and held its shape longer than any other material. Canadian beaver pelts were best of all, for the cold winters assured a thick coat and hence ample felt. With the "beaver" hat a necessity for every well-to-do European, and price no object, rich returns were assured traders. A knife or an ax or a few cheap trinkets worth about a *livre* could be bartered for a beaver robe that would fetch two hundred *livres* in Paris. One good season would assure a man a small fortune. Here was the economic basis for France's American empire.

At first the trade was haphazard, carried on by ships' crews and captains who stuffed their sea chests with knives, beads, metal mirrors, pots and pans, and other items that the natives seemed to want. But by the 1580s French merchants who entered the field were sending their vessels farther and farther up the St. Lawrence to intercept the interior furs on their way down to the coast. Through the next two decades a number of small companies plied the trade vigorously, making yearly trips to Tadoussac to meet the Indians who slipped down the Saguenay River with canoes brimful of shining peltry. Just why the Indians willingly repudiated a culture that set a balance in nature remains a mystery, but repudiate they did, launching a devastating campaign against the beaver. Moreover, the natives learned to wait until several ships arrived, then play one against the other to drive the price of pelts upward. Monopoly alone would assure the French continued spectacular profits. King Henry of Navarre had already decided that France must secure Canada as a royal province, for his national coffers were so depleted by religious wars that the fees paid by merchants for monopolistic privileges would help stave off financial disaster. These were the circumstances that in 1603 brought together a little band of King Henry's former military associates —Sieur de Chastes, Sieur du Pontgravé, Sieur de Monts, and Samuel de Champlain—with the promise of a fur monopoly in return for establishing a colony in Canada.

The company's first expedition linked the men who contributed most to Canada's early history, Champlain and Pontgravé. Pontgravé was the sailor, making dangerous journeys across the North Atlantic as regularly as clock work and minimizing by his skill the difficulties of navigation in that primitive day. Thirty-six-year-old Champlain was the explorer, driven always by a burning desire to see what lay beyond the next bend in the stream or over the next hill. Colonization and the fur trade interested him far less than the sight of a new mountain range or the discovery of a new lake or river. His wanderings, as he sought to satisfy that insatiable curiosity, gave France an empire in the New World.

Champlain began to pry into Canada's secrets in 1603 when Pontgravé's ship carried him to Tadoussac. There he had his first chance to talk with the Indians. He learned from them of a river and portage route along the Saguenay-Mistassini traverse to a great body of salt water lying to the north (Hudson Bay), of a passage through lakes and rivers south of the Richelieu River "which leads down to the coast of Florida" (Lake Champlain and the Hudson River), of a portage route to large inland lakes (the Great Lakes) along the Ottawa River, across Lake Nipissing, and down the French River. The St. Lawrence intrigued him most, for the natives told him of Lake Superior and Lake Erie, and gave him a sketchy picture of Lake Huron. Here, he thought, might be the long-sought route to the Pacific. While Champlain was making these surprisingly correct deductions on American geography, Pontgravé loaded his ship with enough furs to show a handsome profit when they returned to France in the autumn of 1603.

This tidy sum allowed the company, now enlarged and headed by de Monts, who succeeded to the presidency on de Chastes' death, to attempt its first colony planting a year later. Two ships were sent out, one to trade at Tadoussac, the other to found a settlement on the Bay of Fundy. De Monts, who accompanied the latter vessel, finally chose a site on St. Croix Island where, in June, 1604, Frenchmen began building their first homes in the New World. His selection was unfortunate; the tiny island offered neither shelter from the cold winds of the North Atlantic nor game to vary the monotonous diet of salt meat, and the little group under Champlain who wintered there suffered severely. In the spring of 1605 they showed that they had learned their first lesson in frontier technique by moving their colony to Port Royal, on the mainland of Nova Scotia, where they planted grain and erected a sturdy log fort containing comfortable living quarters, warehouses, magazines, and a forge, all surrounding a spacious central court. Here the colonists lived regally during the next winter. The fifteen officers, organized informally as "L'Ordre de Bon-Temps," each day elected one of their members a Grand Master whose duty it was to provide the company with food obtained by hunting or barter. Every dish was served with elaborate ceremony; the table frequently groaned under the flesh of moose, caribou, deer, beaver, otter, hare, bear, ducks, geese, sturgeon, and trout.

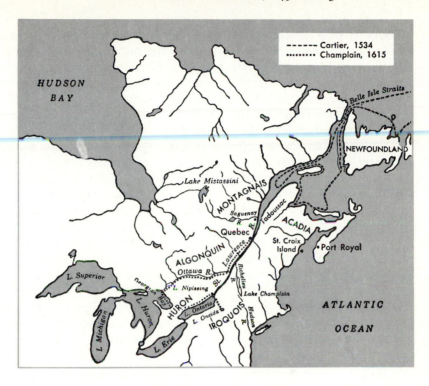

- - - - - Cartier, 1534
· · · · · · · Champlain, 1615

New France, 1534–1615

These merry times, which contrasted markedly with the suffering of the year before, attested to the ease with which the French adapted themselves to a forest environment.

For three years the tiny settlement prospered while Indian friendship was won and Champlain spent happy days exploring the Acadian coast. But while de Monts' company triumphed over the wilderness, de Monts proved less successful with the intrigue of the French court. Jealous merchants finally persuaded the king to break the company's monopoly in 1607, leaving Champlain and his followers no choice but to return to France that fall. Neither he nor Pontgravé were willing to abandon their wilderness life, however, and their arguments finally convinced de Monts that a permanent post on the St. Lawrence would allow the company to prosper even without the advantages of a monopoly. By the summer of 1608 both were back in Canada, where Pontgravé fought off Basque intruders while Champlain searched for a favorable site for their colony. He finally chose a spot beneath a high promontory overlooking the St. Lawrence, and there in July, 1608, were built the first crude huts of the town of Quebec. A year later de Monts' company failed, but this tiny outpost continued to cling to existence amidst the Canadian wilderness.

Champlain was its guiding spirit. Neglected by king and countrymen and ignored by the royal favorites who held the fur monopoly during the next quarter-century, he clung tenaciously to his forest post, contented to rule over his handful of turbulent followers, seek the friendship of the neighboring tribes, and press the explorations that were his real love. Quebec was a colorful place under his rule. Here each summer the trading ships from France dropped anchor and sent their men ashore to erect booths where they could display their knives and mirrors and bright colored cloths. Indians gathered from miles around, bearing the furs accumulated during the past winter. Never had the rich green forests of Quebec witnessed such sights as these—the painted Indians decked in their primitive finery, the Bretons gorgeous in blue and red and purple coats, the Basque and Norman fishermen in their colorful garb, all shrieking in a medley of a dozen tongues as they haggled over the price of a shining beaver skin. Over these wild scenes presided Champlain, ready always to settle disputes or soothe feelings ruffled by too enthusiastic bartering, and far more at home among the natives of America than his own people.

His principal task was to maintain the Indian alliances which kept a steady stream of peltry flowing toward Quebec. This was difficult, for when the French settled in Canada they became unwilling participants in an ancient wilderness war being fought for the control of the St. Lawrence Valley. On one side in this struggle were three tribes living north of the waterway: the Montagnais who roamed the country about the headwaters of the Saguenay, the Algonquin of the Ottawa River valley, and the Huron who lived between the Ottawa River and Lake Huron—all determined to use the French as allies—on the other the loose confederation of five Iroquois tribes whose longhouses dotted the region south of Lake Ontario. When Europeans first entered the valley the triumphant Iroquois, who controlled Lake Ontario and the upper St. Lawrence as far as Quebec, were steadily extending their conquests eastward. The French, unwitting recruits, took sides in this forest war when they opened trade with the Montagnais at the mouth of the Saguenay River. Within a few years the Algonquin and Huron were also making regular trading trips to Tadoussac over a difficult route that crossed the headwaters of streams tributary to the St. Lawrence.

This trade gave the Montagnais-Algonquin-Huron confederation both an immediate advantage over the Iroquois, and a new incentive to press the war against their ancient enemies. Their objective now was to drive their rivals from the St. Lawrence Valley. This would assure their continued monopoly over the French trade; an important consideration to peoples who viewed knives and utensils with such awe that they sincerely believed the king of France made all the pots and pans himself—surely a man capable of such wonders deserved to rule his people. The expulsion of the Iroquois would moreover allow the Algonquin and Huron to reach Tadoussac over the Ottawa River or St. Lawrence routes, rather than along the difficult path to the Saguenay. Inspired by these prospects, the northern tribes waged a bitter war through the sixteenth century, so intense that peaceful bands of Indians seen by Cartier were gone when Champlain reached Canada, crushed between the two powerful foes. By 1608 they had driven their enemies south of the St. Lawrence and controlled the prized valley.

The Iroquois menace still remained; warriors of that powerful confederation might push northward at any time, cut the trade routes between the Huron or Algonquin country and Quebec, and stop the eastward flow of furs. Champlain, who saw that this vital highway could be kept open only by crippling the Iroquois, was so concerned that he consented to join the northern Indians in their continuous warfare against the southern tribes, particularly because he saw that these raiding parties offered an excellent chance for exploration. His first journey was in 1609 when he and two other Frenchmen joined a band of Algonquin in a march up the Richelieu River, across Lake Champlain, and to the present site of Ticonderoga, where a group of Iroquois, terrified by their first sight of guns, were decisively defeated. In 1615 he set out again, this time to aid the Huron in their perpetual war against the Onondaga, one of the Iroquois tribes. With a few Norman musketeers he journeyed up the Ottawa River, across Lake Nipissing, and to Georgian Bay, blazing a trail that was to be the principal French route to the interior for many years. There he joined five hundred Huron in a march to the eastern narrows of Lake Ontario, which they crossed in canoes, to fall on an enemy village near Lake Oneida. Stout Iroquois defenses turned back the badly organized Huron assault. Severe casualties were inflicted on the attackers, and Champlain himself suffered two wounds before he and his allies beat a retreat to Huronia. That minor skirmish cost New France heavily. Until this time the Iroquois had been on the defensive, beleaguered by foes who surrounded their hunting grounds and kept them from the prime beaver country. Now all changed. The French, in spite of their firearms, had been beaten back so decisively that they would not return. After 1615 the Iroquois took the offensive, pressing relentlessly on the French borderlands. Champlain, all too innocently, had created a Frankenstein monster that would eventually doom France's hopes for a New World empire.

Fortunately he could not peer into the future as he returned to Quebec to spend the last nineteen years of his life, leaving to younger men the hardships of exploration. His tiny outpost nestled against the banks of the St. Lawrence was the one tangible monument to the men and treasure that France poured into the New World. Far to the south the other minute settlement of St. Augustine with its surrounding ring of presidios and mission stations stood guard over a forest empire that bore but faint resemblance to the dream worlds of the *conquistadors*. Between the two lay a great unoccupied wilderness that seemingly contained none of the gold or furs so eagerly sought by the Spaniards and French. Into this area came a little group of English laborers and gentlemen, to begin that slow process of expansion which ended only when France and Spain and the wilderness were pushed aside and the continent settled.

The Southern Frontier
1600-1700

During the first half of the sixteenth century—while Frenchmen and Spaniards greedily staked their claims to the New World—England's Tudor monarchs were too interested in separating their newly united realm from continental intrigue and papal power to concern themselves with colonies beyond the seas. Bold navigators occasionally searched the icy waters about Labrador and Hudson Bay for the fabled Northwest Passage to Cathay, and hardy fishermen regularly cast their nets off Newfoundland for the cod and mackerel that economics, if not religion, demanded in England, but these voyages served only to give the English a thorough knowledge of the North American coast. Not until the 1570s were they ready to make their first assault on that wilderness.

At that time Queen Elizabeth, sensing that her nation was strong enough to enter the race for colonial possessions, abruptly reversed her traditionally friendly policy toward Catholic Spain. Swashbuckling adventurers, led by Francis Drake, sallied out to plunder Spanish treasure ships or raid the rich towns of Central and South America. The success of these piratical ventures convinced Sir Walter Raleigh, a wealthy court favorite of great influence, that the time was ripe to plant a colony in America; such an outpost, he saw, would not only limit Spain's expansion but would serve as a base for further raids on that nation's possessions. With the queen's tacit consent, he sent three expeditions to Roanoke Island in 1584, 1585, and 1587, but the first two returned to England and the last—the famous Lost Colony—disappeared before a relief ship arrived. These futile efforts irked Spain as much as the plundering Sea Hawks and contributed to the outbreak of the open warfare which began in 1588 when the mammoth Spanish Armada sailed north to suffer the defeat that established England as mistress of the seas.

The English learned two valuable lessons from Raleigh's disastrous experiments. One was that the type of colony traditionally used by Europeans—a trading post to collect goods already gathered by the native population—was not suited to the North American wilderness. Indian society was essentially self-contained; no colony could prosper if it had to rely alone on wealth derived from Indians. To succeed in the New World, settlers required a permanent establishment that could produce adequate foodstuffs for its population and a civil government that could control colonists who were suddenly removed from legal restraints. Raleigh's ill-fated efforts also taught England that the wealth of any one man, no matter how great, was insufficient for colony planting; the resources of many individuals must be combined to support an overseas plantation until it attained self-sufficiency. This realization discouraged the efforts of the old individualistic feudal class to tap the New World's wealth, but the rising merchant class was unwilling to forsake any field that promised profits. Their solution was to apply joint stock company methods to colony planting. These companies, which had been used since the sixteenth century to finance trading ventures, were even better suited to establishing settlements; depending as they did for support on many investors they could collect the large sums needed to nurture a plantation to maturity.

These lessons could not be applied so long as the war with Spain gave Elizabethan Sea Dogs the chance to chase enemy treasure ships, but the peace arranged by James I shortly after he ascended the throne in 1603 closed this exciting source of profits and turned Englishmen to the more prosaic task of founding settlements. The time seemed ripe for overseas expansion. Times were bad in England, for the long war had closed old continental trading routes and the enclosure of fields for sheep growing had loosed "monstrous swarms of beggars" upon the countryside. Colonies, the people were told by Richard Hakluyt and a host of other propagandists, would restore prosperity by reviving commerce and draining away surplus population. Moreover religious fervor was high after the wars with Catholic Spain, and Englishmen were anxious to preach their version of the Gospel to the heathen. These forces—economic, social, and spiritual—which were to send men to new frontiers across the face of the American continent, were all operating in the England of James I.

Two groups of merchants and governmental officials in London and Plymouth responded first when, in 1605, they separately petitioned the crown for the right to establish colonies. James I brought both together as the Virginia Company. The Royal Charter of 1606 provided for a central governing board, meeting in England and appointed by the king, which would supervise the two plantations planned. The London group was authorized to plant its settlement between the 34th and 41st parallels, the Plymouth group was given the region between the 45th and 38th parallels, and the overlapping strip between 41° and 38° was opened to both. Each group was empowered to "make habitation, plantation, and to deduce a colony of sundry of our people into that part of America commonly called Virginia." The colonists were guaranteed the "liberties, franchises, and immunities" that they enjoyed as Englishmen, but they were expected to work for the companies, which would give them their support and a share of the profits. Each colony was to be governed by a council of thirteen, appointed by the central board, and authorized to name one of its members as president. Thus general administrative control was retained by the king but the actual business of settlement was left to the companies.

The London group, which succeeded in planting the first permanent English settlement in North America, was granted the physiographic region known as the Southern Tidewater. This low-lying area, laced by rivers and cut by swampy inlets, stretched along the coast from New Jersey to Georgia and extended inland from 50 to 150 miles. The northern portion was dotted with great bays and river estuaries that allowed the small ships of that day to sail far inland; farther south lay the Cape Fear region with its multitude of sea islands and its vast swamps where rice culture was to center. The many rivers that twisted their slow way through this flat countryside formed numerous peninsulas and promontories where the silt-laden soil was ideal for agriculture, even south of the Savannah River where the streams ran almost level with the land and inundated great areas during the spring floods. Near the western edge of this coastal plain a fifty-mile belt of sandy soil covered by twisted pine forests ran across the Carolinas and Georgia, serving as a barrier to the westward movement of the agricultural frontier.

The soil of the Southern Tidewater was rich but thin, particularly on the ridges between river valleys where erosion left only four or five inches of fertile land over a sterile subsoil. The river bottoms, where the land was deep and enduring, were the prized farming areas. The heavy rainfall, averaging between forty and seventy inches a year, and the warm climate which assured a long growing season, made the Tidewater ideal for the production of staple crops suited to semitropical conditions. Nor was the task of clearing the land so difficult here as on later frontiers, for while the coastal plain was covered with a dense growth of hardwoods, pine, palmettoes, and cypress, the underbrush which plagued most pioneers was lacking. For this blessing the settlers could thank the Indians, who regularly burned over the region to drive game into traps. The forests were teeming with wild life: deer, buffalo, bears, and other animals in profusion, turkeys that weighed seventy pounds or more, and ducks so numerous that flocks seven miles long shut out the sunlight as they passed overhead. Streams swarmed with fish so large that ordinary nets would not hold them and so plentiful that a horse could not wade across a river where they were running. Sturgeon twelve feet long were killed with axes, and oysters thirteen inches across were seen along the coast. Once the Englishmen learned to use these resources they were assured a bountiful living.

Yet the first settlers starved to death amidst this plenty. They came in the spring of 1607—three shiploads of laborers and gentlemen sent out by the London Company to transfer England's civilization to the New World. The James River was selected for their settlement because its broad estuary seemed to promise a giant river system that might lead to the fabled Northwest Passage. After exploring the stream's lower reaches for about thirty miles the colonists came upon a peninsula two or three miles long and a mile and a half wide, covered with marsh and woodland, where the water was so deep that ships could be tied to trees on shore. Here, on May 24, 1607, the 105 settlers began building the fort and clustered houses which they called James Fort, and later Jamestown. From the first the settlement suffered. Cutting trees and erecting defenses was cruelly hard work for the gentlemen in the party who had hoped to stuff their pockets with gold. Those of lesser status were no better equipped to labor at needed tasks; instead they spent their time in play or bowling on the green. This did not mean that they were unusually lazy; they were simply conforming to the English work habits with which they were familiar. Too, they knew that soldiers or foresters then subduing northern Ireland were customarily fed and clothed from home; why then should they provide their own subsistence? Moreover, most of them soon suffered from malnutrition, with energy so sapped that they were neither psychologically nor physically capable of more than a few hours of work at a time. Such work as they did brought disheartening results. As land was cleared for lumber, wheat was planted, only to shoot into stalks seven feet tall with no grain. Not until two years later did they learn from the Indians that the excessive fertility of the soil must be drained by several plantings of corn before wheat could be grown. This disappointing crop, inadequate supplies from England, and the mosquitoes and diseases natural in that swampy country took a heavy toll that first winter; by spring only thirty-eight men remained alive.

The "Starving Time" had two beneficial results. It elevated to the presidency of the local council a robust braggart named Captain John Smith who stopped treasure hunting, forced all to work at useful tasks, and secured enough grain from the Indians to support the feeble colony. And it led the king to grant a new charter to the London Company in 1609 which substituted an autocratic governor for the bickering council, changed the boundaries by granting the company a strip of land running two hundred miles north and south of Point Comfort then "up into the land, throughout from sea to sea, west and northwest," and provided that the governing council in England be elected by the stockholders rather than appointed by the king.

The results of these changes began to show in 1611 when Sir Thomas Dale began an eventful seven-year period as deputy governor. Settlers were sent out, fields planted, the forts and houses put in good condition, and a new settlement begun at Henrico, near the "Falls of the Farre West." The high ground of this site proved so much healthier than the swampy Jamestown peninsula that by 1616 Henrico was the colony's leading town, with substantial brick or frame houses, and a thriving agricultural population protected from Indian attack by a two-mile palisade between the James and Appomattox rivers. By this time the Virginia settlement was beginning to assume an aspect of permanence. The Englishmen were becoming "seasoned"—which meant they had acquired an immunity against American diseases and a rudimentary knowledge of frontier technique. Friendly Indians taught them how to plant corn, capture wild turkeys, catch fish, and clothe themselves in the warm skins of animals; from less hospitable natives they learned to venture into the forest only in groups. These lessons were to be applied during the whole history of American expansion.

Yet two things were needed before Virginia could prosper. One was a staple crop which could be sold in England, the other a more satisfactory land and labor system than that imposed by the London Company. The first was provided in 1612 when one of the colonists, John Rolfe, began experimenting with native tobacco. He soon produced a type that was "strong, sweet and pleasant as any under the sun." An acre of Virginia bottom land would produce five hundred pounds of the weed, which sold in England for five shillings a pound. Here was wealth undreamed of by the peasants who had come to America. The second proved more difficult. The company pictured the settlers as its servants, employed to labor on company lands and deposit their produce in company storehouses, in return for their keep and one share of stock which sold on the London market for £12 10s. In addition the governing council decided in 1612 to grant each planter one hundred acres of land after seven years, with additional grants if the first was used properly.

This system proved unworkable, largely because colonists refused to labor for absentee English stockholders even when driven by such a tyrannical governor as Dale. The only solution was a transition to private ownership. In 1616 Dale began granting one hundred acres to each settler with the incentive of an additional hundred acres if the first was well cultivated, the company retaining several large reserves which it hoped to develop with tenant farmers. By 1619 this transition was completed. The second means used was inaugurated in 1617 when the company granted large tracts of land, called "Hundreds" or "Particular Plantations," to groups willing to buy a sizeable block of stock in return for the privilege of sending out their own settlers. The first, a grant of 80,000 acres to the Society of Smith's Hundred, was followed by forty-three others between 1617 and 1623, although only a few of these were actually settled. Eventually most of this land was assigned to private individuals.

Tobacco planting and private ownership brought Virginia its first real prosperity. In vain did company and king rail against "this deceavable weede Tobacco, which served neither for necessity nor for ornament to the life of man." A man could earn £25 a year growing tobacco—five times as much as he could with grain—and by 1619 even the company bowed to the inevitable by sending out farmers to plant the "weed." At the same time, to

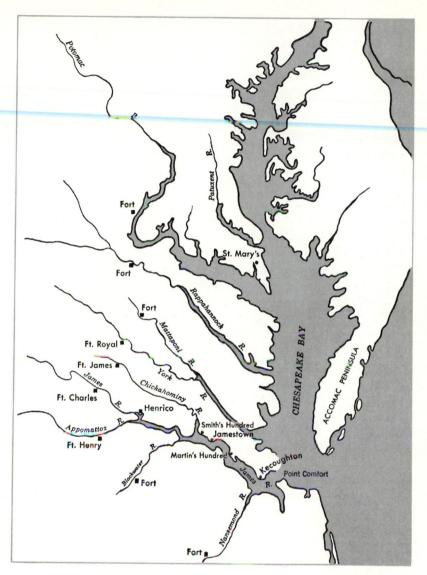

The Tidewater Frontier, 1607–1675

make the colony more attractive and lure other settlers, it granted Virginia a legislative assembly to execute "those things as might best tend to their good." During the next three years the population increased from six hundred to more than three thousand, all eager seekers after good tobacco lands. At first the palisaded peninsulas held them in, but they soon burst these bonds and spread along the lower James from Kecoughton to Henrico. They felt secure against Indian attack even though far from the forts, for

John Rolfe had married Pocahontas, daughter of the Indian chieftain Powhatan, and the two races seemed destined to perpetual peace.

Lulled by this false sense of security, the colonists were unprepared when the death of Powhatan elevated a hostile chief named Opechancanough to the leadership of his tribe. Thoroughly alarmed by the rapid extension of white settlements, he decided to make one great effort to drive the intruders into the sea. The blow that fell on March 22, 1622, took the Englishmen so completely by surprise that 357 were killed and every isolated plantation destroyed overnight. Those still alive scampered for the safety of Henrico, Shirley Hundred, Jamestown, or Kecoughton, formed armies, and marched against the foe. For two years this warfare went on, with regular fall marches into the tribal villages to destroy crops, until the Indian power was broken. The two races lived in peace for the next twenty years.

The uprising of 1622 did much to destroy the waning fortunes of the London Company, already torn by factional disputes and engaged in a bitter controversy with the king over customs duties on tobacco. James I seized on the opportunity to appoint an investigating commission which reported that the company was ready for receivership. When its officers refused the offer of a new charter the king began legal proceedings that only ended in 1624 with the company overthrown and Virginia a royal colony, its governor and council appointed by the crown rather than by the stockholders. Charles I, who now ruled England, was an absolutist with no intention of re-establishing representative government in America, but in this he reckoned without the wishes of the Virginians. Like all Englishmen they treasured their liberties; like all frontiersmen they believed that no outsider understood their peculiar problems. Thus motivated by tradition and environment, they demanded authority to discuss specific subjects in 1628 and 1629, and after 1630 held regular assemblies that gradually assumed the law-making power. The king, busy with his affairs at home, finally accepted the authority of this House of Burgesses, thus giving America the precedent on which its representative rule was to be based.

The new government was successful from the first. Its immediate task was an efficient defense system, for the Massacre of 1622 indicated that continued friendly relations were impossible. "Either," wrote a governor, "we must cleere them or they us out oft the country." Two methods were devised: marches and palisades. The former were regular expeditions into the Indian country, staged by militiamen whose heavy armor made them walking fortresses safe from the arrows of the enemy. They seldom caught an Indian, but their systematic destruction of crops after the harvest season drove them westward to safer regions. The use of a palisade was suggested shortly after the massacre when the assembly proposed erecting a six-mile-long wall, interspersed with blockhouses that could house garrisons, between Martin's Hundred and the York River. This, when completed in 1630, provided protection for 300,000 acres containing many of the settlements. Yet even by this time the palisade had outgrown its usefulness; it could not shift with the advancing frontier and was soon left behind by westward moving settlers. This was recognized when the legislature in 1630 tried to form a living wall against attack by offering large land grants to groups who would settle at dangerous spots. Although only one adventurous band took advantage of this offer, precedent was provided that was to be imitated often in the westward march of civilization. Thus did Englishmen, confronted with problems rising from a totally new environment, experiment until they found a solution.

The colonists might grope toward a satisfactory system of defense, but they were less successful in placing their economy on an even keel. Some, true, thought of the years between 1618 and 1630 as a boom period in contrast with the hard times before, with prosperity sustained by a private-enterprise system that provided a needed work incentive. Yet cold statistics show that in the half-dozen years after 1618 no less than 3,000 Englishmen died in Virginia; total migration to the colony numbered 3,500 persons during these years but population increased from only 1,000 persons in 1618 to 1,500 in 1624. Death was tolling for a disproportionate number of the newcomers. Some lost their lives in the Indian attack of 1622; others were victims of the company's eagerness to build the colony so rapidly that more immigrants were sent than Virginia could absorb. Ship captains during those years crowded their vessels with laborers who were dumped in America more dead than alive, without means to survive.

This was the fate of hundreds, despite the fact that grain supplies were consistently sufficient to feed all newcomers save for a brief period following the 1622 war. To blame for this sad situation were private entrepreneurs and officials of the Virginia Company who knew how to turn public distress into private profits. These small planters lived high; tobacco prices were constantly soaring, profits unbelievable, and money plentiful. They reacted as did all frontiersmen showered with unaccustomed wealth, embarking on a spending spree that supplied them with handsome clothes, luxurious living, and especially the abundant quantities of alcoholic beverages needed to offset the drabness of life. The planters could maintain this level of expenditure only by constantly increasing their labor supply, for profits from tobacco increased proportionately to the number of workers engaged in its cultivation. Hence they bid high for the servants and apprentices arriving in such numbers; such was the demand for servants that some planters even ransomed captives from the Indians in return for their services.

The sufferers from this speculative orgy were the laborers themselves and the Virginia Company. The company sent out far more "tenants" than needed to produce adequate food supplies if they had been assigned to farming as intended; instead they were diverted by selfish company officials to labor for tobacco planters. Even food sent from England to feed the tenants until they became self sufficient found its way into the warehouses of the managerial class rather than into the mouths of the poor. Maladjustment of the system of distribution, brought about by selfish planters whose

consciences had been deadened by the unusual profits obtainable from tobacco cultivation, spelled disaster. Not until the price of the weed tumbled
from the two or three shillings a pound paid between 1618 and 1629 to the
penny a pound that it fetched in 1630 could Virginia develop the diversified
economy needed for its proper growth.

The lessons learned by Virginia's pioneers made the establishment of
the second Tidewater colony far easier. The region north of the Potomac
was granted in 1632 to George Calvert, Lord Baltimore, a prominent English
Catholic who wanted to found a New World haven for the persecuted members of his church. His first colonists reached Maryland in February, 1634,
and after selecting a site for their town of St. Mary's on the St. George
River, fell at once to building a fort, a storehouse, a chapel, and substantial
houses. The high, fertile spot, and the generous price paid the Indians for
the land, assured them freedom from the disease and warfare that had harried
the Virginians. From their neighbors they learned to fell the timber, plant
corn and tobacco, and live bountifully from the wilderness. From them, too,
they caught the frontier spirit of independence; when Lord Baltimore tried
to establish an archaic governmental system which restricted the legislature
to advisory functions they resisted so lustily that within fifteen years the
Maryland assembly virtually ruled the colony.

For the next half-century the two tobacco colonies expanded rapidly.
The Virginia settlements, which had been confined to the James Valley and
the Accomac peninsula during the 1620s, pushed northward during the next
decade to the banks of the York River. The bottom lands of that stream
proved just as fertile as those of the James, and the deep-flowing river
provided equally good transportation facilities for the shipment of tobacco.
Encouraged by this, planters moved on to fill the valleys of the Rappahannock and Potomac rivers, advanced slowly westward until they reached the
first waterfalls that stopped navigation, then spread out between the streams
into the less-fertile uplands. Another group carved their homes from the
country south of the James, occupying the valleys of the Nansemond and
Blackwater rivers first, then the higher land between. The expanding tobacco
frontier in Maryland also followed the waterways, moving first around Chesapeake Bay where ocean-going ships could come directly to the plantations
for the heavy hogsheads of tobacco, then up the northern bank of the Potomac. By the 1670s the Tidewater in both colonies was comfortably settled
by hard-working farmers.

The causes of this rapid expansion were those that led to the peopling
of the entire American continent: expelling forces which drove people from
their homes and attracting forces which lured them westward. Most important was a large reserve population sufficiently dissatisfied with existing
conditions to brave the wilderness. The troubled England of the late seventeenth century provided this; for a time the autocratic rule of Charles I
drove a stream of Protestant dissenters beyond the seas, then the period of
Puritan control between 1649 and 1660 sent thousands of Anglican yeoman

farmers to Virginia and Maryland. With the restoration of Charles II in 1660 it was the turn of Roundheads and Puritans to flee once more. All of these swelled the population of the tobacco colonies. In America the newcomers were driven to the frontier by the agricultural methods employed, the ease with which they could secure land, and the distinctive labor system.

The primitive farming methods of the seventeenth century sent many pioneers westward. Tobacco was planted year after year, without any attempt to restore the soil's fertility by crop rotation or fertilization, until the mineral salts were exhausted. Usually three successive plantings were enough to cause the yield to decline, as tobacco was a heavy consumer of nitrogen and potash. Then the planter grew several crops of corn or wheat before abandoning the worn-out land and pushing farther into the wilderness, leaving behind a wake of "old fields" that rapidly reverted to forest. This process went on with increasing rapidity as the century advanced. By this time the river bottoms, with their deep silt deposits, were settled, turning pioneers to the thin surface soils of the uplands which disintegrated rapidly under intensive cultivation. In this hilly country, too, the primitive, surface-scratching plows encouraged rapid erosion during the heavy summer rains. Moreover the attempts of the colonial legislatures to prevent a glutting of the market by limiting the number of plants that each farmer could grow encouraged a rapid movement to virgin soils where the plants would be large and the crop, sold by weight, proportionately more valuable. Parliament also speeded the westward movement by the Navigation Act of 1669 which forbade the direct export of tobacco to Europe, for this discouraged the production of cheaper types that could be grown on poor land. All these factors accounted for the rapidity with which the soil's fertility was exhausted, driving frontiersmen steadily onward in their search for wealth.

The evolution of a land system that allowed planters to secure their farms cheaply and easily also contributed to the rapid westward movement of the frontier. In neither Virginia nor Maryland could lands be purchased during the seventeenth century, for the rulers believed that the colonies would develop most rapidly if plots were given to individuals only in return for meritorious service. Both, however, awarded a "headright" of fifty acres to every person transporting a servant to America. As the demand for land increased with the rising population, these headrights were converted into convenient means for its sale. They were easily obtainable; accommodating officials granted them so freely that two hundred acres passed into private hands for each person crossing the Atlantic; the merchant sending him, the ship captain carrying him, the planter purchasing his services, and the servant himself all secured headrights at no expense. By the last of the century prudent planters began to accumulate headrights and use them during periods of speculative buying, periods when the slave plantation system was most profitable. When government clerks began selling these warrants openly the authorities finally succumbed to popular pressure, and Maryland in 1683 and

Virginia in 1705 legalized their sale. After this they were peddled legally at the rate of five shillings for fifty acres.

Some of the headrights issued to ships' crews, servants, and travelers were sold directly to farmers who used them to secure certificates from county authorities entitling them to fifty acres of unoccupied land. More found their way into the hands of investors. Ship captains and contractors who received large grants were always ready to sell their rights for a low cash price, and even those granted sailors were secured by jobbers who herded whole crews into the county offices, helped them to secure their headrights, and then purchased all the warrants immediately. In this way absentee owners engrossed much of the best land in advance of settlement, forcing newcomers to extend the settled areas by seeking less valuable spots in the interior. The activity of speculators was partially responsible for the 135 per cent increase in Maryland land prices between 1660 and the end of the century.

Almost as important as soil exhaustion and the land system in explaining the rapid settlement of the Tidewater was the type of labor employed. Much of the work was done by indentured servants who bound themselves to labor seven years for a planter in return for their passage across the Atlantic, their keep, and equipment to start a farm of their own when they earned their freedom. Although most of these servants were honest English cottagers who came to America because their only saleable asset, their labor, brought a higher price than in crowded England, their coming hurried the westward movement. Like all bond labor they encouraged soil exhaustion, having neither the knowledge nor the inclination to preserve the fertility of the fields they tilled. Moreover, when they completed their period of indenture, they usually sold the hundred acres granted them by the colony, then sought a cheaper home on the fringe of settlement. Through the seventeenth century a steady migration of these freed servants pushed the frontier westward.

The results of this expansion were as important as the forces that called it into being. From it stemmed two problems that plagued frontiersmen across the face of the continent: how could they protect themselves from the Indians who pressed upon them from the west? How could they guard themselves against easterners who tried to make them accept institutions ill suited to the wilderness environment?

The need for defense rose during the 1640s when the natives, alarmed by the steady encroachment of whites upon their lands, rose in revolt. Isolated raids by the Susquehannocks of the Susquehanna Valley on the Maryland back country began in the first years of the decade, but warfare was not serious until 1644 when the old Powhatan chief, Opechancanough, determined to strike while the English were torn by the Puritan Revolution. So helpless that he could not rise from a litter and so weak that attendants lifted his eyelids when he wished to see, his cunning mind could still plan an attack that took the colonists completely by surprise. This fell in the spring of 1644, so suddenly that before the whites could rally their forces nearly 500 men, women, and children were killed. The English struck back with fierce marches that destroyed the Indians' crops, but not until Opechancanough was captured and treacherously put to death did the disheartened natives retreat into the wilderness. With the war over, the victors turned belatedly to the problem of defense.

Their solution was twofold. Recognizing that friction between whites and red men was one cause of difficulty, they made separation a definite policy. A treaty in 1646 forced the Indians in the James-York peninsula to move into the country west of the Tidewater. Three years later Maryland attempted to remove another source of irritation by forbidding settlers to purchase land directly from the natives; Virginia imitated this excellent example in 1658, and in 1662 went so far as to declare all such transactions void. Maryland also in 1650 forbade Indians to enter certain settled areas under any pretext. In 1653 a more significant step was taken when the English began assigning some of the tribesmen to reservations, giving each warrior fifty acres of land and the privilege of hunting over other unoccupied territory. In groping after answers to an important frontier problem, the colonists established practices that were to be employed repeatedly in the next two centuries.

Yet separation might not keep peace, and even while working out this policy the authorities turned their attention to other means of protection. Palisades were unsatisfactory and marches more valuable in punishing Indian attacks than defending the settlements. Hence Virginia in 1645 decided to erect a chain of forts along the western edge of the Tidewater, manned by small garrisons which could beat back minor attacks or warn the colonists of threatening danger. Before these were built the legislature in 1646 hit on the happier scheme of offering land bounties to prominent citizens who would assume the burden of defense. Grants of 600-acre plots were sufficient to secure four forts: Ft. Royal on the York, Ft. Charles on the James, Ft. James on the high ridge overlooking the Chickahominy, and Ft. Henry on the Appomatox, each defended by a small garrison and governed by a frontier leader. As the threat of danger passed, most of these fell into decay, but they were re-established at public expense in the 1670s when a new Indian attack was rumored. By this time the more extended settlement required more forts, and the legislature in 1675 and 1676 provided for additional outposts on the Potomac, Rappahannock, and Mattaponi rivers in the north, and at the headwaters of the Blackwater and Nansemond rivers south of the James. Together they formed a ring of forts about forty miles apart around the colony.

Forts were expensive to maintain and as the threat of danger again passed the settlers cast about for other means of protection. In 1682 both Virginia and Maryland began employing patrols of mounted border rangers to ride constantly along the frontier, ready to fend off minor raids or give warning of major attacks. Clad in buckskin, carrying guns and long knives, mounted on spirited ponies, and steeped in the lore of the Indian and forest, these rangers were true frontiersmen whose wilderness skill testified to the amount learned by the English since the first colonists starved to death amidst plenty at Jamestown. Yet the border patrols were so costly that Virginia cast about for a better system of defense. Her Burgesses made a final attempt to solve the problem in 1701 when they agreed on grants of from ten to thirty thousand acres to groups of individuals who would settle at exposed spots. The statute decreed that each settler must be a "warlike christian man between sixteen and sixty years of age perfect of limb, able and fit for service"; they were to erect a palisade to be used in case of attack, and each was to be assigned a half-acre house lot and a two-hundred-acre farm near the fort. The "warlike christian men" desired by the House of Burgesses never assembled—the Virginians were too individualistic to be confined within a narrow fort—but the measure provided a precedent for the Kentucky "Stations" of a later generation.

Dominating easterners always bothered frontier settlers as much as menacing Indians. Virginians discovered this as early as the 1620s when they demanded their own legislature to solve problems that a distant monarch could not understand, but not until half a century later did a serious East-West conflict develop within the colonies. The rapid advance of settlement made this struggle inevitable, for by the 1670s the westward movement of the frontier had created a series of distinct zones, each representing a transitional stage in the development of civilization, and each with peculiar problems that demanded home treatment. The attempt of the more thickly settled East, which controlled the colonial legislatures, to force its institutions on the western zones, bred the first of a series of bitter conflicts that marred the history of the American frontier.

The extreme westerly areas of settlement were most affected by the wilderness environment. Along the edge of the Tidewater and spilling over into the hilly country beyond was the fur-trading frontier. Here, in the log forts erected at the falls of the rivers, lived leather-clad pioneers who felt more at home leading their pack trains along silent forest trails than in the cramped streets of Jamestown. Over them ruled a number of border barons who owned the forts—Colonel William Byrd, Captain Abraham Wood, Major Lawrence Smith, Henry Fleete—busily engaged in harvesting a fortune from their peltry traffic while they spied out the riches of the western country. Also near the western edge of the Tidewater and extending slightly beyond was the cattle frontier where cows and horses roamed wild, watched over by nomadic herdsmen who built crude huts near the peavine marshes where the animals grazed. Each fall the cattlemen staged a roundup to single out beeves for market and burn their identifying brand on the new-born calves. "They go in ganges," a traveler wrote, ". . . which move (like unto the ancient patriarchs or the modern Bodewins in Arabia) from forest to forest in a measure as the grass wears out or the planters approach them." In the wild lives of these cattlemen and fur traders there was little of the civilization they had left behind.

East of the cattle and trading frontiers was the zone where pioneer farmers were busily transforming the wilderness into fertile tobacco fields. To this outpost came indentured servants who had worked out their terms of servitude, new immigrants from England, younger sons of established easterners, and planters from the East whose lands were exhausted by successive plantings of tobacco. Most were so poor that they could not pay the high prices demanded by speculators for good land near civilization; many were squatters. All were willing to pit their strength against nature in quest of the wealth that society denied them.

The manner in which the pioneer farmers lived showed how quickly Englishmen learned the frontier technique. They usually moved west in the autumn until they found a heavily timbered spot that pleased them, for large trees meant good soil. The first task was to girdle the trees by cutting a notch around the trunk a few feet from the ground; this allowed sunlight to penetrate their skeleton-like dead branches. Crude axes and mattocks were then used to fell enough timber to build a house, the great trees being trimmed on two sides and fitted together into solid walls. A heavy oak door facing a hand-dug well, windows with sliding wooden panels, holes bored at intervals to hold guns, and a plank roof completed the crude home. Nails were used as sparingly as possible for they were expensive; when a settler moved he frequently burned his house to retrieve the precious metal. With a shelter erected the pioneer farmer spent the winter cutting the giant trees and piling them for burning. In April he planted his first crop of corn among the standing dead timber and by August the ripe ears were ready for drying on tall wooden frames. This dried corn, with turnips and beets grown in a small garden and pork from acorn-fattened hogs, assured his family a plentiful diet of those foods already becoming staple in the southern diet: hog and hominy, bacon and greens, corn bread, hoe cake, and corn pone.

Sometimes during the first year, always in the second, the best portion of the cleared land was set aside for tobacco. A sheltered, sunny spot near the forest edge was planted to seed in March; two months later the fragrant green plants were moved to other fields where they were hoed regularly until September when the yellowing leaves warned that harvest time was near. Then they were cut, tied on strings to cure, and finally fastened in bundles which could be laid in huge hogsheads for shipment to England. The hogshead or two of tobacco sold each year paid for the gunpowder, sugar, tea, and iron implements that the farmer could not fashion with his own hands. Beyond this the farm family was self-sufficient; they raised their own food, built their own crude furniture and primitive agricultural implements, and dressed in clothes sewn from the skins of animals or from wool produced in the neighborhood. The farm family wanted little from society and expected to give little in return.

East of the pioneer-farmer zone was the fully matured social order of the seaboard. The planters who lived there dwelt on farms no larger than those of the frontier, for the great plantations of the South did not develop until the eighteenth century when slave labor was introduced in large quantities. Seventy-five per cent of the Maryland farms contained less than 250 acres at the close of the century and in Virginia the proportion of large estates was even smaller except on the Accomac peninsula where some tendency toward combining holdings was noticeable. Despite this, the eastern planter differed from the western farmer in his social attitudes, largely because he was less self-sufficient. Tobacco was the region's staple crop— even food was imported from the up-river settlements—and the whole area was bound to England by close commercial ties. Looking always to the mother country, the average planter of the lower Tidewater consciously patterned his life on the model of the English aristocracy. He dressed in a peculiar assortment of homespun and imported fineries, lived in a small frame dwelling with a chimney at either end which he casually referred to as the "Manor House" or the "Great House," sat in the best pew of the parish church, sent his children to England for a polite education, and considered himself on a higher social plane than the farmers of the back country.

The development of these two antagonistic societies in the upper and lower Tidewater predestined trouble. One was aristocratic, conservative, and bound by close cultural ties to England; the other democratic, liberal, and dominated by free and easy frontier concepts. Both were bound together by artificial colonial boundary lines. Only a specific grievance was needed to precipitate a serious conflict.

This was provided by the economic depression that plagued the tobacco colonies during the 1670s. Wars with Holland in 1664 and 1673 that disrupted trade, bad storms, a "Dreadful Hurry Cane," and a glutting of the world's tobacco markets all contributed to a downward price spiral that gave every evidence of permanence. Planters pleaded in vain with the legislatures to limit production by law, but neither colony dared act without the cooperation of the other, and this was not forthcoming. By the mid-1670s tobacco went begging at a penny a pound while mobs roamed the countryside burning crops in a vain attempt to force prices up. Conditions were particularly bad in the back country, where small farmers lacked the reserves that allowed eastern planters to weather the worst years. To compound injury, taxes must be paid in tobacco, and as tobacco prices declined the quantities needed to satisfy the tax officials increased. Farmers in the interior complained that too much of their time was spent laboring for a government that benefited them little if at all. Particularly resented by small planters were the poll taxes that fell equally on rich and poor alike. These were levied at secret sessions of the justices of the peace in each county, "by which the poor people not knowing for what they paid their levy did allways admire how their taxes could be so high."

Economic distress bred political discontent. Both small planters and the newly arrived larger holders resented the dictatorial practices of the governors, Sir William Berkeley in Virginia and Charles Calvert in Maryland. Berkeley especially mirrored the conservative atmosphere of the Restoration period by ruling with an iron hand, refusing to allow the election of an assembly to replace the docile body chosen in 1661 that faithfully did his bidding. He might have survived the mounting discontent if a simple division between Berkeleyites and anti-Berkeleyites continued, but during the 1660s the Virginia scene was complicated by the rise of a complex of factions. Most of these were groups of planters that clustered about the local justice of peace in each county. For a time Berkeley allowed them a large degree of self control in their own counties in return for his right to rule the colony, but as they grew steadily more powerful with the expansion of the county courts' authority, a volcanic situation developed. Each faction, although differing in composition and purpose from county to county, was thirsty for power that could be obtained only by stripping authority from the governor. Matters were brought to a head when the aging Berkeley showed an increasing tendency to ignore crises instead of meeting them squarely. He was slipping, the planters whispered among themselves, and could no longer be trusted to rule the colony. A power vacuum had developed that spelled doom to orderly protest.

The spark that touched off this tinderbox was set in the Potomac Valley frontier in July, 1675, when Indians killed the servant of a planter who had refused to pay them for goods that he had purchased. Retaliation was swift; a hastily formed army of backwoodsmen marched against the offending tribesmen but made the mistake of falling instead on the village of friendly Susquehannock Indians which was ruthlessly destroyed. A few weeks later another army of unauthorized militiamen added injury to insult by putting to death five Susquehannock chiefs who had approached to parley under a flag of truce. This was too much for even the friendly Virginia Indians to accept. Although hopelessly outnumbered—the nineteen tribes that lived peacefully on the borders of the colony could command no more than 725 bowmen between them—they fell on the outlying plantations with such fury that thirty-six settlers were killed in January, 1676. Governor Berkeley, although sternly disapproving the unauthorized acts of the Virginians that had provoked the attacks, immediately called a special meeting of the Assembly to adopt defensive measures. Money was appropriated to build a ring of forts, to arm five hundred rangers who would ride between these bastions, and to restrict the fur trade to a few trusted men who could be counted on not to supply the natives with arms or ammunition.

When this Assembly was prorogued in March, 1676, rebellion seemed far away, for while backwoodsmen grumbled at the new taxes necessary to support these defensive measures and complained that forts were less effective than marches against the Indians, they seemed inclined to follow a policy of watchful waiting. This atmosphere of uneasy calm was shattered by the ambitions of the elite groups that had long been vying for power within the counties, particularly in the interior. Their tools were the pioneers who, driven from their homes by marauding tribesmen, gathered in ever-increasing numbers at the Falls of the James to await the return of peace.

As these sufferers exchanged tales of the indignities they had endured, their wrath not only mounted but focused on the friendly Indians whose villages lay nearby. That these subject red men had not joined in the border forays made no difference to the hot-headed westerners; their extermination would open new lands to settlement, and new lands would ease the economic blight that beset the interior. Only a high priest was needed for a blood sacrifice of innocent victims.

One was soon provided by Colonel William Byrd and other border barons who were itching to punish Governor Berkeley for ending their lucrative fur-trading operations. Seizing upon a young hot-head recently arrived from England, Nathaniel Bacon, they persuaded him to journey to Jordan's Point where the malcontents were gathered, bolster their spirits with liberal portions of rum, and lead them against the nearest Indian villages. News of this mutinous action brought Governor Berkeley to the scene with three hundred followers and a firm determination to "call Mr. Bacon to accompt," but when he arrived, the rebel had vanished into the forest at the head of two hundred frontiersmen in search of "a more agreeable destiny than you are pleased to designe mee." The governor, realizing for the first time the depth of frontier discontent, promised amnesty to all who had defied his orders and agreed to call a general election to choose a new assembly that would more accurately reflect western sentiment. While he was thus occupied, Bacon and his Indian-hunting frontiersmen reached the Roanoke River where they enlisted the aid of friendly Occaneechee Indians to wipe out a village of Susquehannocks, then turned on their Occaneechee allies and slaughtered many of them as well. They returned to a hero's welcome; Bacon was elected a back country delegate to the new Assembly and started for Jamestown with fifty armed followers sworn to protect him with their lives should Berkeley persist in treating him as a rebel.

"Bacon's Assembly" was no band of radicals; of the twenty-one members identifiable all but four were justices of the peace and at least five were hold-overs from the Long Assembly. The laws that were passed—liberalizing the franchise, opening offices to small property holders, recasting the tax structure along more democratic lines, caring for Indian defense—had long been sought by the elitist county groups, particularly in the interior where rising young aristocrats wanted a chance to rise politically as well as economically. In them Bacon took no part. Instead he soon left Jamestown for the back country, only to return on June 23 with six hundred rough followers and the demand that he be named commander of all Virginia's armed forces. The stout old governor staunchly resisted, but the assemblymen were of less stern stuff and on June 25 voted Bacon the authority that he sought. Armed with this he departed for the interior once more, bent on wiping out more friendly Indians.

His army never reached the frontier, for Bacon heard that Berkeley was raising troops of his own and hurriedly retraced his steps as the governor fled to the safety of the Accomac Peninsula. After issuing a "Declaration of the People'' commanding his enemies to surrender as traitors, the rebel leader vanished into the Great Dragon swamp to kill a few harmless red men. His absence allowed Berkeley to recapture Jamestown early in September, a maneuver that brought Bacon hurrying back to lay siege to the capital. When the government forces finally withdrew to the eastern shore once more, Jamestown was burned to the ground on September 19. In his hour of triumph, Bacon suddenly died of a ''Bloody Flux,'' bringing the rebellion to an abrupt end. Thirty-seven of his rebels paid with their lives for their part in the uprising. He had led no democratic revolution—the ''Bacon's Laws'' passed by the June Assembly were the work of others— but he did typify the frontier belief that Indian lands should be taken whatever the cost in human decency or national loyalty.

Maryland's outburst was less violent than Virginia's. In September, 1676, a band of discontented backwoodsmen gathered at the plantation of Thomas Barbary on the Patuxent River to demand reform, but popular sympathy was lacking and the authorities easily captured and hanged the leaders. Hatred of the colony's aristocratic rulers continued strong along the frontier where several minor outbursts occurred during the early 1680s. This reached a climax in 1689 when the Maryland officials refused to support the Glorious Revolution or to recognize William III as their new monarch. ''Two rank Baconists,'' Josias Fendall and John Coode, seized the excuse to gather an army of frontiersmen, march on St. Mary's, and seize control of the government. The popular assembly that they called asked the king to abolish proprietary control by making Maryland into a royal colony—a step taken in 1691. Frontier dissatisfaction temporarily cost the Calvert family a province.

One unforeseen result of these frontier uprisings was a steady exodus of dissatisfied backwoodsmen southward to bolster a new colony taking shape there. This was Carolina, stretching between Virginia's southern boundary and the 31st parallel. Virginians had been probing that unpeopled land for a generation, led by such fur traders as Nathaniel Batts who began his explorations there in 1655. Others followed, but they were few until the crown in 1663 granted the whole region to a group of eight commercially minded proprietors, all of whom were already engaged in flinging back the borders of Britain's expanding empire in other parts of the world. By the 1670s two centers of settlement were developing. One was nestled in the forests and swamps about Albemarle Sound, where Virginia had planted a band of pioneers in 1653 to guard her southern border. Others filtered in during the next years, attracted by the prospect of living in an isolated region where they would be safe from tax collectors or reforming ministers, until by 1677 some 2,500 people lived there. The other center of population was established when the proprietors in 1670 sent colonists to lay out Charles Town on the Ashley River some twenty-five miles from its mouth. This site proved so unsatisfactory that ten years later the whole colony was moved to the junction of the Ashley and Cooper rivers. There a stout palisade

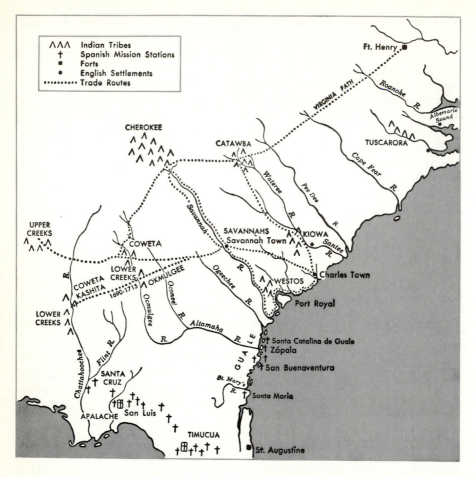

The Carolina Frontier, 1670–1700

enclosed government buildings and thirty houses, surrounded by settlers' fields.

The settlements about Charles Town grew slowly. Thirty years after the colony was founded the frontier line was nowhere more than fifty or seventy-five miles from the coast and extended from Port Royal to the valley of the Santee River. Two things prevented the rapid dispersal of population that had marked the westward advance in Virginia and Maryland. One was the failure of the colonists to find a suitable staple; tobacco did poorly in this swampy country and England's own crops were ill suited to the semi-tropical climate. Not until the 1690s did Carolinians begin the experiments with rice culture that brought them fortunes in the next century. The other was the need for defense. Southern Carolina was flung into the very teeth of the Spaniards and their Indian allies; Charles Town was only 250 miles from St. Augustine while to the north some 400 miles of lonely forests and dreary swamps separated it from the James River settlements. Almost at its doorstep were the outposts of the Florida mission frontier, which had been driven back beyond the Savannah River by Indian attacks in 1661 but still stretched northward as far as St. Catherine's Island where the Franciscan station of Santa Catalina de Guale and its protecting presidio guarded a band of loyal Indians. Normal agricultural expansion was impossible where isolated settlements might fall prey to marauding Indians or Spanish troops.

Instead the Carolinians turned to the fur trade in their search for wealth. This promised them not only an export staple but a chance to build up Indian alliances against the inevitable day of reckoning with Spain. The situation was ideal for their purposes. In Guale, Apalache, and Timucua lived some 26,000 natives whose loyalty to the Spanish mission fathers was beginning to crumble. Poverty, resentment against discipline, and woefully inadequate support had by this time eroded the influence of the stations; by 1676 only forty men were available for seventy mission posts and by 1681 only thirty-four. The missions were dying, and with their death came opportunity for Englishmen. Too, the gateway to that Spanish domain was swinging open. Just to the north was a borderland occupied by three small tribes only nominally under Spanish influence: the Westos about Port Royal, the Savannahs along the middle Savannah River, and the Kiowa in the country west of Charles Town. Beyond these was a circling ring of powerful tribes over which the Spaniards had no control: the Tuscarora whose hunting parties ranged between the Roanoke and Cape Fear rivers, the Catawba along the upper waters of the Wateree River, the Cherokee about the headwaters of the Savannah River, and the Lower Creeks whose villages dotted the valley of the middle Chattahoochee River. Across the mountains, but accessible by the ancient trails that ran around the southern tip of the Appalachians, were three other powerful tribes: the Upper Creeks, the Chickasaw, and the Choctaw. All of these interior Indians were so eager for the guns and knives and firewater of the white man that they might welcome English traders where they had rebuffed Spanish friars.

The English saw their problem clearly. They must establish trade with the Catawba, Cherokee, and Lower Creek tribes that had resisted Spain's pressure. To do this they must first, however, either exterminate the Westos, Savannahs, and Kiowa, or win their friendship lest they menace the trading routes to the interior. The latter course was preferable; these tribes as allies would form a buffer between Charles Town and the Guale Indians. Fortunately the colony contained a man capable of cementing this alliance: Dr. Thomas Woodward, an adventurer who had lived among the coastal Indians for some years before Charles Town was founded and was thoroughly familiar with their languages and customs. In 1674 he visited the Westos villages on the lower Savannah and opened a trade in "deare skins, furrs and younge Indian slaves" that thrived for the next six years. This ended in 1680 when a dispute between the tribal leaders and the Carolinians burst into open warfare. The Westos War that followed wiped out the tribe, leaving the Savannahs as friends of the English and protectors of their trade routes.

The Westos War convinced the Englishmen that they would never be safe so long as Spaniards threatened their southern borderland. Hence, with 300 friendly tribesmen, the Carolina militia fell on the mission stations at Santa Catalina and San Buenaventura early in the 1680s, driving the friars to the protection of the presidio of Zápala on Sapelo Island. Even this strong post was menaced by English raiding parties and marauding pirates, until the Spanish in 1684 gave up the struggle for Guale and retreated to Amelia Island where the Santa María station became their new northern outpost. Even more alarming to the Spaniards was the way in which their Indian allies deserted to the side of the victorious English rather than following the missions southward; the powerful Yamassee in particular went so far as to move their villages to the lands formerly occupied by the Westos on the lower Savannah. An attempt to regain prestige failed when an expedition sent to demolish Charles Town in 1686 was scattered by "a Hurricane wonderfully horrid and destructive," after wiping out a small settlement of Scotch covenanters at Stuart's Town on Port Royal.

The English traders, no longer fearing a flank attack from northern Guale, immediately extended their operations toward the interior. This was a move long dreaded by the Spaniards, for if the Carolinians won over the Lower Creeks they would be within striking distance of the important Apalache mission station and presidio of San Luis. Even while the war in Guale was going on, officials of New Spain vainly sought permission to found a mission in the Creek country, and when this was not forthcoming, set up the station of Santa Cruz de Sábacola at the junction of the Flint and Chattahoochee rivers in 1681 as a center for a few friendly Indians. These preparations were not wasted. Four years later Dr. Woodward with a handful of followers reached the Creek villages of Coweta and Kashita with a small pack train of trading goods. The horrified commander at San Luis marched north to drive him out, but Woodward only disappeared into the forest while the Spanish were near and continued trading until the fall of 1685 when he left for Charles Town with 150 natives laden with furs. Other traders who followed on his heels finally forced Spanish officials to agree to a fort in the Creek country, although the construction of this post—in 1689—had hardly the effect intended. Instead of welcoming the Spaniards the Indians were so angered by the attempt to end their trade that a year later the entire tribe moved east to the valleys of the Oconee and Ocmulgee rivers where they could be nearer the English.

From this time on the Carolina traders did a prosperous business. Every spring they gathered, almost 400 strong, at Savannah Town, a frontier village established on the Savannah River about 1690, where each fitted out his twenty-horse pack train with blankets, ironware, guns, knives, rum, and trinkets. Forming into caravans of a hundred horses or more they set out along the well-marked trails into the Indian country. Some followed the

Savannah River to the Cherokee villages, then on to the Catawba country where they usually met rivals from Virginia. Others continued along the trail to the ford over the Ogeechee River where they divided to take either the Upper Path that led to the Lower Creek village of Coweta or the Lower Path to Okmulgee. All during the fall and winter they wandered from tribe to tribe carrying on their trade. If they were honest they drove as hard a bargain as they could; if they were unscrupulous, which was far more likely, they treated the Indians to liberal portions of rum before beginning negotiations. In the spring they turned their pack horses, laden now with bundles of deer skins and peltries, back to Charles Town for a few weeks of riotous living while they sold their catch and bought fresh goods. This tiny town was a colorful spot during their visits. Their caravans clattered through its quiet streets, their picturesque costumes lent variety to the dull garb of its citizens, and their inordinate thirst cheered the heart of many a tavern keeper. "Those sparkes," wrote one observer, "make little of drinking 15 or 16 £ in one Bout in Towne." Most important of all, they brought prosperity to southern Carolina, for during the 1690s Charles Town annually shipped some 54,000 deer skins to London markets.

By the end of the seventeenth century England's hold on the southern coast of North America was secure. Its colonies were firmly planted, with a strong economic base, but even more heartening for their future growth was a subtle change taking place in the attitude of the ruling gentry. Bacon's Rebellion and the exodus of the Carolinians brought home the fact that the social and political system must be altered to conform to the more democratic atmosphere of frontier America. During the half-century after Governor Berkeley's departure for London in 1676 the ruling elites in the southern colonies, although never relinquishing their control of political or economic institutions, slowly shifted their philosophy. Instead of ruling solely in their own interest they made an honest attempt to determine the wishes of the lower orders, and in some instances at least to do the will of the small planter class. This was an important transition in practice if not in law; it found no better expression than the virtual abandonment of the aristocratic inheritance laws of primogeniture and entail in Virginia during the early eighteenth century—their repeal after the Revolution was only a gesture. The yeoman farmers and adventurous fur traders who were driving back the Spaniards on the southern frontier still had no direct voice in government, but neither were they completely ignored. A broad base was being laid for the conquest of still more territories by England—and for the eventual conquest of the continent.

5

The Northern Frontier
1600-1700

While some Englishmen moved slowly across the southern Tidewater seeking fertile soil for their tobacco plants or friendly Indians along the Spanish borderlands, others carved out a new frontier in the region that became the northeastern United States. During the seventeenth century the coastal lowlands and river bottoms of this domain were filled by homeseekers who transformed the wilderness into a new civilization vastly different from that of the South.

The first assault on this northern frontier ended disastrously when colonists sent out by the Plymouth Company in May, 1607, returned to England a year later after an "extreme unseasonable and frosty" winter on the Kennebec, then called the Sagadahoc River. With this half-hearted effort the company lapsed into inactivity that only ended in 1620 when its more ambitious members effected a reorganization into the Council for New England. Although blessed with a royal grant to all lands between the 40th and 48th parallels the Council failed to secure enough financial support to plant its own colony and contented itself with granting lands to small groups of settlers. These hardy pioneers founded the New England colonies.

The first grant was to a little band of religious dissenters called Separatists whose dissatisfaction with the established English church drove them first to Holland early in the century, and then to America. Their objective, when they sailed on the *Mayflower* in 1620, was a "Particular Plantation" in Virginia which had been purchased from the London Company, but storms which blew them from their course cast them on the Massachusetts coast. Realizing that they were beyond the pale of the law and intruders on lands to which they had no title, the Pilgrims signed a brief agreement before they landed, binding themselves into a "civill body politick" to enact laws "unto

70

which we promise all due submission and obedience." The famous May-flower Compact, applying as it did the principles of church covenants to this unique civil problem, was the first of a series of squatters' agreements to which pioneers resorted as a basis for temporary self-government whenever their westward march carried them beyond the bounds of orderly society. With their immediate governmental needs provided for, the 102 colonists landed, and in December, 1620, began building their homes at Plymouth.

The land system insisted upon by the London capitalists who financed the voyage—they were to labor for seven years on a company plantation—worked so badly that in 1623 the division of lands among private owners began. This proved successful; within ten years the colony was completely self-sustaining, with its English backers paid in full and the people prosperous. The Pilgrims' ability to maintain themselves without aid from the mother country impressed contemporaries far more than the religious experiment they were conducting, and encouraged other groups to migrate to the New World. While realizing this state of happy self-sufficiency the Plymouth settlers constantly cast about for some exportable staple comparable to Virginia's tobacco. When experiment showed that the diversified agriculture suitable to the climate and soil of Massachusetts could produce no crop sufficiently prized in England to be profitable, they turned, like the Carolinians, to the fur trade. Here they were more fortunate. The neighboring Indians were skilled in producing wampum—the native currency made by stringing together tiny beads carved from the inner whorls of coast shells and bored with a flint drill—which was highly valued by the more primitive tribesmen of Maine. By 1628 the Pilgrims were buying up wampum in Massachusetts, carrying it northward in their shallops, and bartering there for beaver, marten, and otter skins. Within a year they were able to erect a trading post, or "trucking house," at Cushenoc on the Kennebec River to serve as a center for their traffic, and until 1640, when the near-extermination of the beaver ended trade, this was their principal source of wealth.

By that time the Plymouth colony was well established. New settlers who arrived during the 1620s moved first north along the low-lying coast to found Duxbury, Marshfield, and Scituate, then turned southward to lay out Taunton and build their homes about Buzzard's Bay and the lower reaches of Cape Cod. There they discovered coastal marshes where they could pasture their cattle and fertile fields to grow corn and other foodstuffs. This expansion gradually transformed Plymouth into a prosperous agricultural colony, with cattle raising as its principal industry. The whole process was carried on without serious Indian opposition, for Chief Massasoit of the Wampanoags, whose country the Pilgrims occupied, kept a pledge of peace made with the first settlers until his death in 1662.

While the Plymouth colony was taking root in Massachusetts soil other English outposts were planted to the northward. Fishermen and traders found that stern and rockbound coast such an attractive field for their operations that by the end of the 1620s their tiny settlements dotted the New

England shoreline from Casco Bay to Boston Harbor. The most important of these trading posts was one at Salem operated by a small English corporation. The struggles of this company to maintain its precarious foothold attracted the attention of a group of wealthy Puritan clergy and business men who conceived the idea of taking over the colony as a joint commercial and missionary enterprise. With this in mind they formed the Massachusetts Bay Company and in 1628 secured a grant from the Council for New England to a strip of territory lying between a point three miles north of the Merrimac and another three miles south of the Charles, extending from sea to sea. A year later a royal charter confirmed this allotment and officially incorporated the company.

Among the stockholders of the Massachusetts Bay Company was a locally influential Puritan, John Winthrop, who was interested in founding a New World colony where members of his sect could follow the dictates of their consciences on religious matters. Noticing that the charter, probably through oversight, failed to state that meetings of the corporation must be held in England, Winthrop conceived a bold plan. Why not transfer the entire government to America, setting up there a Puritan commonwealth that would be virtually self-governing within its corporate rights? The rest of the stockholders readily agreed to his proposal and in 1630 Winthrop, newly elected governor, sailed away with a thousand colonists to plant his wilderness Zion. Destitute Salem proved little to the Puritans' liking so they continued south until they found a magnificent harbor into which jutted a broad peninsula. On this safe and healthy site they built the town of Boston. Englishmen were now so skilled in frontier techniques—planting corn, establishing friendly relations with the Indians, importing cattle to graze on the marshes—that the colony was firmly established within two years. By this time half a dozen small towns were clustered about the shores of Boston Harbor: Roxbury, Dorchester, Watertown, Medford, and Newtown or Cambridge.

During the next decade the Massachusetts Bay Colony expanded rapidly. Some 24,500 newcomers arrived at Boston during those ten years of the "Great Migration," driven overseas by bad conditions in the homeland. They came in family groups from southeastern England where poor harvests and a declining textile trade brought hard times. Others fled to the colonies from the absolutism of Charles I, who dissolved parliament in 1629 and entered upon a period of personal rule which only ended with revolution. Puritans suffered greatly during his reign, for he was an uncompromising believer in high-church Anglicanism and staunchly supported the campaign begun in 1633 by William Laud, Archbishop of Canterbury, to stamp out England's dissenters. Non-conformists' services were broken up, their churches dissolved, and their ministers deported. Thousands of believers, convinced that salvation was impossible in an England unaccountably delivered into the devil's hands, departed for homes beyond the seas between 1630 and 1640.

Few stayed in Boston where the system of government was nearly as autocratic as that from which they fled. John Winthrop and the Puritan clerics who guided his hand were no believers in democracy. They knew that they, as divinely appointed interpreters of the Holy Writ, alone understood God's will; popular rule would defeat His whole purpose in establishing this wilderness Zion. At first they tried to rule without the General Court, or legislature, authorized by the charter, but popular resentment forced them in 1634 to call an assembly made up of delegates from the various towns. Before doing so they carefully protected themselves by decreeing that only freemen could vote or hold office. As only church members could become freemen, and only men approved by the clergy become church members, the leaders were able to continue their autocratic rule behind this democratic facade, ruthlessly stamping out all dissent against the established order. Their harsh rule bred a whole stream of rebels, some famous but more unsung, who went forth into the wilderness to found villages where they could practice their own beliefs—and be intolerant of others.

The dispersal of population went on so rapidly in New England that the usual sequence of frontier types was less apparent than later when fur trader, cattle raiser, pioneer farmer, and equipped farmer were more or less recognizable. All were present, but they succeeded each other so rapidly that only the fur trader was distinguishable. He was in the van as usual, spying out the best lands, reducing the self-sufficiency of the Indians by giving them the tools and vices of the white man, and paving the way for later settlers.

Interest in an interior trading frontier was awakened in 1631 when the chief sachem of the Mohegan Indians—a Connecticut Valley tribe—visited the settlements. He brought tales not only of plentiful furs and natives eager for trade, but of a hated rival already in the field. The Dutch, he told the horrified Englishmen, had founded a settlement called New Amsterdam on Manhattan Island, and were sending their expeditions northward along the coast to barter for peltries. The Plymouth authorities were sufficiently aroused to send out an exploring party under Edward Winslow in 1632. His glowing reports, and news that the Dutch were establishing a post at the House of Good Hope on the lower Connecticut, sent both colonies into action in 1633. A Plymouth expedition under Captain William Holmes reached the valley first and sailing boldly past the Dutch, built a trucking house at the mouth of the Farmington River. This was followed a few months later by a small party from Massachusetts Bay led by John Oldham which investigated the Connecticut Valley during the autumn months. Oldham was back in the spring of 1634 to build a trading post at the present site of Wethersfield. A second Massachusetts trader, William Pynchon, explored the country in quest of a good spot for a trucking house during 1635. All of these men brought back enthusiastic accounts of rich soil, level fields, and friendly Indians.

These reports fell on the ears of men willing to listen, for by 1635 the people in the towns clustered about Boston felt the effects of overcrowding.

Many, finding the sandy soil of their new homes unsuitable to agriculture, were anxious to turn to cattle raising, but the limited lands of Newtown, Dorchester, Roxbury, and Watertown gave them no room for pasturage. Others chafed under the autocratic rule of the Boston governors, especially as the clergymen in each of these towns quarreled with the ruling hierarchy and infected their congregations with dissatisfaction. Still others were moved, as they put it, by "a strong bent of their spirits for change," as they felt that restlessness which was becoming an American trait. They began drifting into the Connecticut Valley in small groups during the summer of 1635 when the General Court, after vainly trying to divert migration to the Merrimac River, finally authorized their departure. Crude huts were thrown up about the trucking houses at Windsor and Wethersfield and a settlement was begun on the site of present Hartford before an extreme winter drove most of the pioneers back to the comparative comfort of Boston. Only one settlement survived: a small outpost called Saybrook established during 1635 by a group of wealthy Puritans under the leadership of John Winthrop, Jr. The relatively milder climate of the Long Island Sound spared its settlers the rigors of that cold winter.

With the spring of 1636 the movement began again. In the lead were the inhabitants of Newtown who sold their homes to a newly arrived congregation from England and, led by their minister, the Reverend Thomas Hooker, started westward along the old Bay Path, driving their 160 cattle before them. This first mass migration in the history of the American frontier lasted two weeks before they began building their houses at Hartford. Other eastern groups were also on the move. From Dorchester went the settlers who had been driven back during the winter, taking their friends with them in another overland expedition to found Windsor. Most of the Watertown citizens joined in chartering a ship to carry them to Wethersfield where they gave that infant settlement its first permanent character. Another band from Roxbury followed William Pynchon, whose fur trading activities made him familiar with the entire valley, to Springfield where they signed a compact governing their civil and religious affairs and laid out their town. Through the remainder of 1636 and the summer of 1637 newcomers continued to arrive, until the Boston authorities grew alarmed lest their own population be seriously depleted.

For a time these river towns were claimed by both Massachusetts and the Saybrook colony until the settlers, distrustful as were all frontiersmen of outside authority, took matters into their own hands. Inspired by a sermon of Thomas Hooker's which defended the right of people to name their own rulers, they sent delegates to a Hartford convention in January, 1639, to draw up the famous Fundamental Orders of Connecticut. This compact vested the principal power to rule in a legislature made up of four delegates from each town; its members could call meetings or adjourn when they chose and its laws were not subject to veto by the governor. Although the provision that only religiously orthodox freemen could vote for delegates to the General

Court excluded some two-thirds of the people from the franchise, the system was far more democratic than that of Massachusetts Bay where an autocratic governor and a small oligarchy of assistants and ministers reigned supreme.

While these Puritans carved their homes from the Connecticut wilderness another group of rebels against Massachusetts authority founded the first towns of Rhode Island. Roger Williams, a kindly humanitarian whose belief in religious toleration and Indian rights made him unpopular in both Salem and Boston, led the way when he was banished from the Bay Colony in 1635. After spending the winter with Massasoit he moved south with a few friends from Salem to found Providence. At his heels came others who had aroused the ire of Massachusetts' authorities by listening to the unorthodox teachings of Anne Hutchinson; they established Portsmouth in 1638. A year later this tiny settlement split in two, with one faction under the eccentric Samuel Gorton breaking away to found Newport and Warwick. Roger Williams erected such a liberal governmental structure for the Narragansett Bay communities that they served during the next years as a constant haven for discontented elements from Massachusetts.

Rebellion against harsh Bay Colony rule drove another stream of dissenters north to lay out the first New Hampshire towns. First to arrive was the Reverend John Wheelright, a victim of the Anne Hutchinson controversy, who established Exeter in 1638. In the same year a group that had seceded from the Lynn church laid out pastures for cattle raising at Hampton. Nearer the coast Rye, Portsmouth, and Dover were settled at about the same time by English Anglicans. When these towns found themselves the subject of a jurisdictional dispute between Massachusetts and the Council for New England they followed the usual frontier practice of drawing up a compact "to make and set up such government as shall be to our best discerning." This instrument, more democratic than the Mayflower Compact or the Fundamental Orders, provided the colony with an orderly government until it was absorbed by Massachusetts in 1641.

The first extension of the northern frontier into Connecticut, Rhode Island, and New Hampshire, dictated as it was by a desire for fertile land, left great stretches of hilly wilderness still occupied by Indians. These natives, and particularly those between the Connecticut River and Narragansett Bay, viewed the advance with alarm, realizing that they were caught between two arms of settlement which threatened to squeeze them from their hunting grounds. Most fearful were the Pequots, newcomers to the area between the Thames and Pawcatuck rivers, who could not count on the friendship of surrounding tribes: the Podunks and Mohegans of the Connecticut Valley, a dissident faction of the Pequot, and the Narragansetts who lived east of the Pawcatuck River. Warlike and quarrelsome, they were feared and hated by the Dutch, the English, and their neighbors.

The spark that ignited this tinderbox was the murder of a Boston renegade, John Oldham, during the summer of 1636. Massachusetts authorities insisted his death was an insult; with their colony solidly planted they seemed

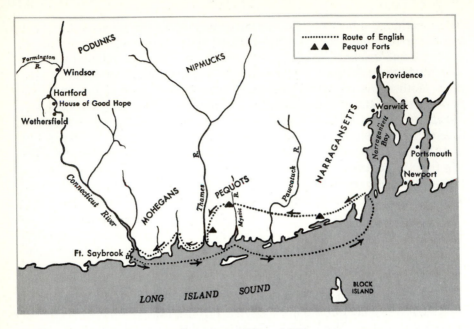

The Pequot War, 1637

eager to test their strength. Too, the Pequot shamans were boasting that they could defeat any enemy by witchcraft, and this was a challenge to the devout Puritans. Hence they sent ninety men under John Endicott to demand the surrender of the murderers. When the Indians delayed, fighting broke out and continued as the soldiers swept through the country, destroying villages and crops. When the Pequots retaliated by torturing and slaying every Englishman they could find, the General Court declared war on May 1, 1637.

The outcome was never in doubt. The Mohegans, eager to settle old scores, saw the Puritans as "handy tools," while the Narragansetts pledged their allegiance to Roger Williams when he visited their villages. Thus isolated, the Pequots were at the mercy of 180 colonials and Mohegans under Captain John Mason sent against them. Instead of risking a frontal attack, Mason capitalized on the Narragansetts' friendship by sailing out of the Connecticut River, past the Pequot villages, and into Narragansett Bay. Landing there, the English marched overland so swiftly that they completely surprised the Indian fort on the Mystic River. Caught unawares, the Pequots offered such scant resistance that nearly 500 men, women, and children were put to the sword. The survivors fled westward, with Mason in pursuit, until all were slain or captured in a swamp near present-day Southport. In one heartless campaign the entire tribe was practically exterminated.

This decisive conquest, which brought peace to the northern frontier for forty years, opened a new period of expansion. At the close of the Pequot

War the settled areas extended in a straggling line down the Maine coast, broadened to include the towns about Boston Harbor, hugged the coast again at Plymouth, and then swept inland to encompass the settlements along the Taunton River and about Narragansett Bay. West of the Connecticut River in the lands explored during the Pequot War lay another region that was developing rapidly; New Haven was founded there by a group of English Puritans in 1638 and Guilford, Branford, Milford, Fairfield, Stamford, and Greenwich followed within five years. All of these settlements bordered the coast; only the Connecticut Valley frontier—which stretched northward to Springfield—penetrated the interior. The task of the colonists in the forty years of peace between the Pequot War and King Philip's War was to fill the gaps between their coastal settlements and begin the conquest of the upcountry. The speed with which this was accomplished showed how well Puritans had mastered frontiering techniques.

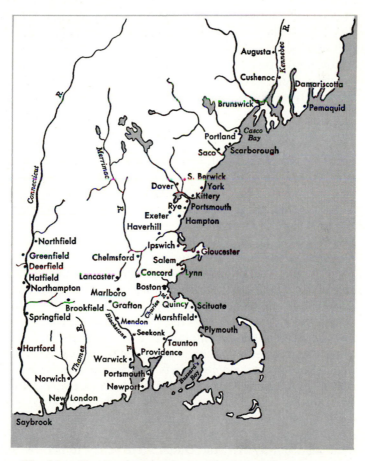

The New England Frontier in the Seventeenth Century

As usual the fur traders were in the van. The trail to a new northern frontier for Massachusetts was blazed by Simon Willard, who as early as 1635 established a post at Concord where he could intercept the furs coming down the Merrimac and Concord rivers on their way to trucking houses at Cambridge. His success not only inspired a rival outpost at Lancaster on the Nashua River, but finally led Willard to move nearer the Merrimac and found Chelmsford in 1655. There he did a profitable business for the next twelve years, buying out the Lancaster post, exploring much of lower New Hampshire, and amassing a fortune in the process. This same role in the Connecticut Valley was played by William Pynchon and his son, John, who dominated trade there after his father's retirement in 1652. Their agents established trucking houses at Northampton in 1654 and Hadley in 1665 as well as exploring the northern country where Deerfield and Northfield were soon to be founded.

The rapid expansion of the fur trading frontier brought New England traders into conflict with two other colonizing powers, Holland and Sweden. The commercial war that followed was fought on two fronts—the Hudson and Delaware river valleys—and ended only with the expulsion of those troublesome rivals from the American continent.

A three-cornered struggle for the Delaware Valley trade touched off the rivalry. First in the field was the Dutch West India Company which in 1623 sent a small force from New Amsterdam to build Ft. Nassau at the mouth of the river where furs from the interior could be intercepted. The Dutch monopolized this rich area until 1638 when Sweden, tempted by tales of the region's wealth, chartered a trading organization known as the South Company to build a palisaded post—Ft. Christina—on the lower Delaware. For a time this settlement languished but in 1643 Johan Printz became its governor and threw himself into his task with an energy that belied his 400 pounds. Farmers were brought out, the fort strengthened, and a new post— Ft. Gothenburg—founded on the Delaware just above Ft. Nassau to command the trade of the upper river. To make matters even worse for the Dutch, the English chose this same time to invade their country. A group of New Haven merchants, organized as the Delaware Company and led by George Lamberton, sailed boldly into the river and built their post at the site of Philadelphia, above those of both rivals. This was too much. A hastily organized Dutch force swept down on the English fort in 1643, trounced its defenders, and carried them in triumph to New Amsterdam. Nor did a second New England attempt to invade the region a year later succeed. When a ship financed by Boston capitalists entered the river it was fired on from Ft. Christina and turned back at Ft. Nassau—only escaping after agreeing to compensate the thrifty Governor Printz for the cost of the shot.

The Swedes remained to be reckoned with. For a time the two nations sparred by building new posts, each higher up the Delaware or Schuylkill rivers than the last, but by 1651 the Dutch were ready to act. With a fleet of eleven ships and an army of 120 men they appeared suddenly before Ft.

Christina to demand its surrender. Governor Printz grumblingly turned over his command to the Dutch who insured their conquest by building Ft. Casimir at the entrance to the Delaware. Three years later a Swedish fleet that surprised Ft. Casimir when its defenders were inopportunely out of powder recaptured the region, but the intruders were driven out by a superior Dutch force in 1655 to end the days of New Sweden in America. In this Delaware River battleground Holland was completely victorious.

The commercial warfare between Dutch and New Englanders for the trade of the Hudson River valley was more serious. This was the heart of New Netherland. The Dutch West India Company, failing to lure many farmers to its New World possessions, depended for its prosperity on trade with the powerful Iroquois Confederation of the Mohawk Valley. They found the Indians especially eager for guns that would allow them to regain superiority over their traditional Algonquin-Huron enemies who had been armed by the French, and a thriving trade that brought wealth to the Hollanders and power to the natives was soon in progress at the Dutch post of Ft. Orange. Boston and New Haven merchants, covetously watching this business grow, were soon plotting to establish posts in the Hudson Valley.

They tried first in 1646 when a group of New Haven business men established a small trucking house on the Naugatuck River near its junction with the Housatonic and only about sixty miles from Ft. Orange. This threat sent the Dutch governor, bluff old Peter Stuyvesant, storming into Hartford to protest. He won his point; by playing on divisions between the New England colonies that still wanted to expand (New Hampshire and Connecticut) and those that did not (Massachusetts and Plymouth), he won a firm commitment on a Hudson River boundary between the two nations. The Treaty of Hartford ended New Haven's attempt to challenge Holland for the interior trade, but the spirit of expansion was too dynamic in New England to be long restrained. A Boston firm made another attempt to tap the Iroquois trade in 1659 when it sent William Hawthorne and John Pynchon to spy out the ground and secure permission to found a town near Ft. Orange, ostensibly to raise cattle for the Dutch traders. Wily Peter Stuyvesant was not deceived by this stratagem; his refusal forced the new company to cast off all pretence and obtain a Massachusetts charter authorizing a trading post near present Poughkeepsie. Colonial authorities supported the traders' claims so vigorously that war threatened for a time, before excitement attending the restoration of monarchy in England ended this second venture.

These squabbles over trade led directly to the annexation of New Netherland. Charles II, anxious to reward the commercial classes which had aided his restoration, in 1664 ordered the seizure of the Dutch possessions in America. New Netherland became New York, a proprietary province under the control of the Duke of York, who granted its southern portion to other court favorites as the colony of New Jersey. Clashing trading frontiers had helped to add another possession to the growing British empire.

The westward march of the traders paved the way for a rapid expansion of the agricultural frontier between the Pequot War and King Philip's War. As this movement went on, certain differences distinguishing the New England advance from that of the southern colonies became clear. In the South the wilderness was pushed back by individuals who sought out the best lands, purchased them with headrights or from speculators, cleared their own fields, and turned as rapidly as possible to the production of staples. In the Puritan colonies the people moved west in groups, judged their land by its adjacence to settled areas rather than fertility, secured their titles from the General Court without cost, subdued the forest by cooperative effort, and devoted themselves to diversified agriculture. The explanation for these radically different frontier techniques—developing simultaneously among settlers with approximately the same English background—can be found in the New England land system. This, in turn, was based on the section's peculiar geographic features and the religious concepts of the settlers.

To the Puritan fathers who shaped the method of land disposal, profits were less important than achieving stability in a growing commonwealth of people with unquestioned faith who would rigorously obey God's ordinances. This belief led them to abandon the system of headrights and individual grants authorized in the colonial charters and vest in the legislature of each colony sole control over the "sitting down of men," with the understanding that the public domain be divided among the orthodox in any way that would advance the true religion. This could best be done by gifts of plantations or town sites to believers. Hence the New England legislatures made two types of grants: to individuals and to groups. The former were relatively unimportant, although magistrates and governors who controlled land disposal showed some tendency to allot themselves sizeable plots. Thus of 130,000 acres given individuals by the Massachusetts General Court between 1630 and 1675 about half went to favored officials and the remainder to ministers, military veterans, and schoolmasters. Far more important were grants to groups of men willing to plant a new town on the frontier.

The procedure for allotting town sites was simple. Several families wishing to move west would together petition the General Court for a "Plantation Right" authorizing settlement. The legislature, after deciding that the petitioners were of proper economic and religious orthodoxy, and that the proposed site was fertile, easily defended, and sufficiently near other habitations, named a committee to locate the town and extinguish the Indian title. Usually a plot about six miles square contiguous to other settlements was chosen, but all efforts to run boundaries "in a comely form" through the hilly countryside failed, and the towns were often irregularly shaped with ungranted lands lying between. This having been done, the original petitioners became the proprietors of the new town with sole authority to sell the land, give it away, or will it to their heirs. In return they were expected to divide the plot, build roads and a church, locate a minister, and bring in acceptable newcomers within a two- or three-year period.

The proprietors' first step was to select a committee to lay out the town. Near the center they set aside a plot for the village green, with a church, parish house, and usually a school nearby. Often they offered other lots to grist mill operators, blacksmiths, and even, in at least one case, a midwife "to answer the town's necessity, which at present is great." About the green they laid out house lots to be divided among the proprietors, varying in size from half an acre to ten acres but always large enough for a home, barns, a garden, and an orchard. These were assigned the settlers by lot, which was believed a just way of determining "the judgement of God." The marshy lands along the river or sea were then apportioned in the same way for use as pasturage or as a source for hay. Finally a large upland field of several hundred acres was divided into rectangular strips which were again distributed among the proprietors according to the laws of chance, although those drawing particularly undesirable plots could "pitch" their land elsewhere. As soon as this field was cleared and under cultivation a second was laid out and similarly apportioned. After several of these divisions an inhabitant would own a number of strips scattered through the town fields as well as a home and meadow lot. The "undivided land" remaining belonged solely to the proprietors, who also controlled a "common field" that was usually used for pasture.

In all divisions of land the settlers were given not equal amounts but a share proportionate to their wealth. In Windsor, Connecticut, for example, the wealthiest 10 per cent of the population received 41 per cent of the land; the poorest 20 per cent a mere 3.5 per cent. But this was far more equitable a distribution than existed in England in the seventeenth century where in a comparable village half of the population would have owned no land at all. This inequality was defended by the Puritans on two grounds; the wealthy,

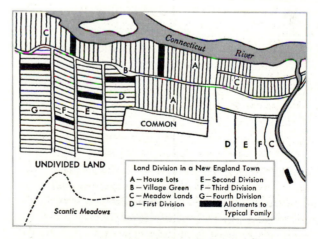

A Typical New England Town: Enfield, Connecticut

they said, contributed more to the cost of planting the town, and they had demonstrated their ability to use the land wisely by the mere fact of becoming rich. Actually these excuses only rationalized the aristocratic prejudices of the New England leaders who instinctively distrusted the leveling effects of an equal land division. Some feared, too, that liberal grants to the poor would lead, as John Winthrop put it, to "the neglect of trades" as mechanics and workers were drawn west by the magnet of free lands. Through the history of the frontier eastern employers opposed a liberal land policy on this ground.

The New England land system, through both its merits and defects, led to a rapid dispersal of the population. Its advantages were obvious: it induced a planned migration that spared the settlers most of the discomforts of pioneer life and assured them spiritual and economic security. Less apparent, but more important, were the system's deficiencies, for these sent a steady stream of disgruntled farmers westward.

Their dissatisfaction rested on the fact that a small group of proprietors or their heirs in each town not only owned all the land but exercised sole authority over its disposal until the last division was made. At first this caused no difficulty; so long as settlers were few and lands plentiful the proprietors lived up to their implied trust by granting lots freely to all families of adequate means and orthodox beliefs. As newcomers increased, however, three distinct classes developed in each town: the small group of original proprietors who controlled all the undivided land, the later arrivals, or "freemen," who owned the fields that had been granted them and enjoyed full political rights but had no voice in the disposal of the lands not yet divided, and the laborers, or "cottagers," who built their huts on unwanted land "onely at the towne's courtesie" and had no vote in the town meeting. Trouble began as soon as the freemen and cottagers outnumbered the proprietors and demanded a further division of the town's lands in which they would share.

The proprietors could meet these protests either by admitting the freemen to their closed corporation or by dividing the land more equitably among them. This they were reluctant to do, for as lands grew scarce in the older towns they felt a normal desire to retain their excessive holdings against the day when sale at high prices would be possible. This speculative spirit existed only in embryo form in seventeenth-century New England, but it was sufficiently strong to array the proprietors against the freemen as soon as the latter demanded a share of the undivided lands. Wherever this occurred a bitter conflict developed. Sometimes this was settled by a compromise that gave the freemen small concessions; sometimes by arbiters called in from neighboring towns to decide how much territory the proprietors should relinquish. More often the struggle ended before the law courts which inevitably ruled against the freemen. The proprietors then usually formed separate corporations to control the undivided lands without interference from the town meetings, a step that was legalized by the colonial legislatures in the late seventeenth century.

These controversies, culminating in proprietory victory in each case, were an important factor in propelling freemen and cottagers toward the frontier. Probably few of the disgruntled individuals whose dreams of expanding acres and greater prosperity were shattered by adverse court decisions became proprietors themselves; the aristocratic General Court hesitated to assign the task of laying out new towns to men of such small property. Instead most of them moved as individuals to frontier communities where proprietors had not yet caught the speculative fever and would be more generous in their allotments.

Conflicts over land holdings also helped shape the political character of the New England colonies, with important implications for the future history of the United States. Vesting control of land in the hands of proprietors tended to create an elitist faction politically as well as economically; they turned their faces toward the past, were distrustful of innovation, and sought to uphold the "old ways" both in politics and religion. Voting lists and tax records in Dedham, for example, show the extent and persistence of their control; there the medieval heritage was so prevailing and the weight of Puritanism so enervating that for half a century the proprietors ruled with an iron hand, using the town meeting only as a tool for their own ends. During this time they allotted only half the lands granted them, clung to a subsistance agriculture, and sought to live as their fathers had lived. What was true of Dedham was apparently true of other communities; until 1664 at least a segment of well-to-do church members barred access to the franchise and exercised almost complete control. Not until the late seventeenth and early eighteenth century did the situation change, and then not from rebellion from within but from pressures from without—pressures generated by the advance of the frontier. As the older generation passed from the scene, as towns multiplied each competing with the other for men and resources, the whole aristocratic structure began to disintegrate economically and politically. Democracy did not come overnight to eighteenth century Massachusetts, but frontier-bred forces were tending toward greater popular participation in the governmental processes well before the Revolution, marked by increasingly aggressive town meetings, the parcelling of authority more widely by the selectmen, and the emergence of a new politics more broadly based than the old.

Whatever its impact on the future, the New England land system fathered a distinct form of settlement—one of advancing tiers of adjacent towns—ideally suited to both the religious ideas of the Puritans and the geographic conditions of New England. Isolated settlements by individuals were frowned upon by all-powerful ministers whose sole concern was to assure each pioneer proper church facilities "for safety, Christian communion, schools, civility and other good ends." Moreover many of the new towns were laid out by groups from older towns who, having differed with their neighbors on matters of religious opinion, moved west in a body to found a settlement where they could enforce their own doctrines. Even these strong religious forces working toward compact settlements might have broken down if New Englanders were able to produce a staple, for then the temptation to leap ahead to rich soil areas would have been irresistible. Instead the short growing season, the hilly countryside, the sandy soil strewn with rocky glacial debris, and the absence of navigable rivers condemned them to a self-sustaining type of agriculture that emphasized cereal production and grazing. With neither a staple nor a market, 85 per cent of the farmers were content to care for themselves and grow the small surplus needed by the 15 per cent engaged in nonagricultural pursuits.

The New Englanders, moving westward in groups, were forced to develop different frontier techniques than those employed by the Virginians. They soon learned to girdle trees and plant their first corn crop among standing dead timber as did the southerners, but here the similarity ended. The land was always cleared by joint enterprise with the town authorities deciding which trees should be removed and which preserved, for community spirit overbalanced the natural frontier tendency to squander natural resources. As soon as the fields were laid out each farmer planted his strips to the crops best suited to the soil—usually corn, barley, or rye, although wheat was widely grown in such favored areas as the Connecticut Valley. New Englanders soon found that much time was wasted in going between their scattered plots and began to concentrate their holding by exchanging lots, despite official warnings against this "buying and purchasing Home Lotts and laying them together;" by the end of the seventeenth century most of them owned large fenced fields. They supplemented their income with cattle, which were as important as corn in the primitive life of the section. In every town large herds of tough, big-boned beasts pastured on the undivided land or the common, each marked with a brand that his owner registered with the authorities.

Few New England farmers grew wealthy, but they lived well. Their homes, clustered about the village green, were sturdy frame dwellings, with outbuildings and barns attached to make chores easier during the long winters. Each morning they left their houses to labor in their fields, using crude wooden hoes and mattocks fashioned by their own hands, or a clumsy plow pulled by four oxen. Each night they returned, to sit before the broad stone fireplace on fall or winter evenings and build the many necessities that their slender resources did not allow them to buy from England. Everything from plows to furniture was constructed at home; a task in which the wives joined with their spinning wheels, candle moulds, and churns. Yet this marginal existence had its compensations. Near at hand were neighbors for pleasant companionship, the church to assure salvation, and a school to dose the young with liberal potions of piety and knowledge. Such conservative easterners as Cotton Mather might bemoan the tendency of people to *"Go Out from the Institutions of God, Swarming into New Settlements, where they* and their Untaught Families are like to *Perish for Lack of Vision*," but the New England frontier family enjoyed far more comfort than the isolated pioneer in the southern colonies.

The attractiveness of frontier life, the dispersing effects of the land system, the restlessness of new immigrants, the opportunity to own land, and religious disputes sent the New Englanders westward between 1640 and 1675. In Maine and New Hampshire settlements still clung to the coast where the many trading posts were converted into farming communities, but in Massachusetts, Rhode Island, and Connecticut the conquest of the interior proceeded rapidly. From Boston and Plymouth settlers pushed outward along the river bottoms to found Lancaster, Marlboro, Grafton, Mendon, and a host of other towns during the 1650s, while another advancing stream from Rhode Island moved up the Blackstone Valley to Woonsocket and Seekonk. West of this line the forest stretched unbroken—except for the tiny outpost at Brookfield where six or seven adventurous families built their homes in 1667—as far as the former Pequot country about the Thames River. Here New London, founded in 1646 by John Winthrop, Jr., served as a center for a steady expansion that scattered several towns along the upper Thames. Another arm of settlement extended northward along the Connecticut, filling in the lower reaches of that rich valley, pushing west along the Farmington River as far as Simsbury, and moving steadily north to plant Hatfield, Deerfield, Greenfield, and Northfield. In the New Haven country pioneers not only laid out new coastal towns between Guilford and Greenwich but during the 1660s advanced up the river valleys to establish Killingworth, Wallingford, Waterbury, and Woodbury. Some 50,000 men, women, and children lived in the settled regions guarded by this northern frontier in 1675, while other New Englanders had left their native soil to establish towns on the eastern tip of Long Island and in New Jersey.

The fruits of this rapid expansion were harvested between 1675 and 1677 when King Philip's War, one of the most devastating conflicts in the history of the frontier, ravaged the New England back country. To the Indians, hostilities appeared not only justified but necessary. Advancing tiers of towns were pressing upon their tribal lands, catching in a crushing vise the Wampanoags who occupied the territory east of Narragansett Bay, the Narragansetts and Nipmucks who were caught between the coastal and valley settlements, and the Mohegans, Podunks, and River Tribes of the Connecticut Valley. They must either fight to retain the large areas needed for their economy or become vassals of the white men. The fate of Indians who had already submitted to English rule made this choice easy. Some had been pushed onto six Massachusetts reservations where they were compelled to obey Puritan laws that forbade them to hunt on the Sabbath, denied them firearms and firewater, ended their accustomed freedom, and condemned them to servile dependency. Others who lived near the settlements were mercilessly abused. Thus one Connecticut law forced any drunken Indian to work six days for the colony and six for the informer; any unscrupulous colonist could secure free labor by giving a brave a few drinks of rum. Still others who succumbed to the lures of well-meaning missionaries were gathered in villages of "Praying Indians." The restricted lives of these Christian warriors did not appeal to free-living red men who treasured their independence and ancient customs above all else. Even war against the whites was preferable to such a fate.

Their smouldering discontent was fanned to open rebellion in 1671 when the English attempted to disarm the Wampanoags. King Philip, the sachem of the tribe, knowing that his people would starve without their hunting guns, resisted strenuously, but the Plymouth and Boston authorities remained firm. A humiliating treaty which warned Philip that "if he went on in his refractory way he must expect to smart for it," left him so angry that he spent the next three years trying to arrange alliances with the Narragansetts and Nipmucks against the colonists. In this he failed, but the young warriors of his tribe sensed their chief's resentment and decided to act. Raiding parties fell on the Plymouth frontier in the spring of 1675; by July the whole back country was aflame. Five hundred soldiers from Plymouth and Boston were hurriedly gathered, and after a march through the Mount Hope country, they drove Philip and his followers into Pocassett Swamp.

English strategy at this point was obvious. They should have penned in the few rebellious Indians by surrounding the swamp, while agents convinced the other New England tribes to remain neutral. These steps would have nipped a minor insurrection in the bud. Instead the colonists committed two grievous errors. One was to leave the rear of the swamp unguarded; the other was to send the entire Massachusetts army into the Narragansett country to overawe that powerful tribe. If the authorities had consciously tried to prolong the war they could have taken no more effective steps than these, for Philip's forces promptly swam the Taunton River and slipped northward to join the Nipmucks, while the Narragansetts took to the warpath to protest the invasion of their tribal lands.

The Massachusetts officials responsible for this blunder probably wanted to carry the war into the Narragansett country. Hatred of Rhode Island and the ambitions of land speculators were responsible. Roger Williams' colony had long been a sore spot in Puritan New England; the freedom of conscience allowed dissenters, the tolerance extended to all creeds, and the humanitarianism shown in dealings with the Indians constantly rankled the stern Bostonians. They knew that war on the Narragansetts would hurt the many Rhode Islanders who traded with that tribe. Extermination of the Narragansetts would also benefit Massachusetts land speculators who found Rhode Island a profitable field for exploitation. Their activities in the Narragansett country had long annoyed colonial officials; now they seized on the outbreak of warfare as a golden opportunity to settle their claims for all time.

Massachusetts land jobbers began to operate in Rhode Island during the late 1650s when two groups of merchants organized as the Pettiquamscutt

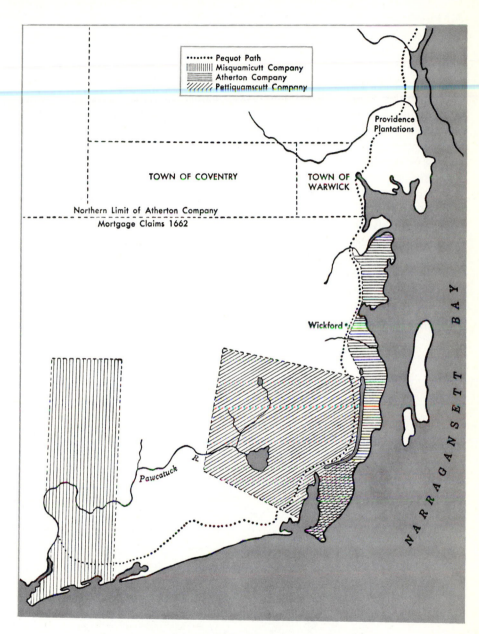

Land Speculation in the Narragansett Country

Company and the Misquamicutt Company illegally purchased blocks of land from the Indians, but not until 1659 when the Atherton Company was formed did their speculations arouse Williams' followers. This corporation, which included in its ranks most of the leading capitalists of Boston, Taunton, and Portsmouth as well as Governor John Winthrop, Jr., of Connecticut, began operating modestly by buying two tracts of Indian territory lying south of Warwick. A year later it extended its claims over the entire Narragansett country by assuming a heavy fine levied against the tribe, securing in return a mortgage on all their lands. When the natives failed to meet the impossible payments within the required six months, the Atherton Company laid claim to their hunting grounds and prepared to battle the horrified Rhode Islanders for possession. This conflict raged for the next fifteen years, with the company directing most of its efforts toward securing a new colonial boundary that would include the disputed area in Connecticut, and was still going on when King Philip's War broke out. Its leaders, knowing that the lands could be opened only by exterminating the Narragansetts, probably had a hand in arranging the Massachusetts expedition into the Indian territory. This was sufficient motive to endanger the peace of the frontier and plunge New England into its bloodiest war.

The invasion sent the tribes of all New England on the warpath, for the Narragansetts had no alternative but to defend their hunting grounds and the Nipmucks and Valley Tribes only needed the incentive of Philip's arrival

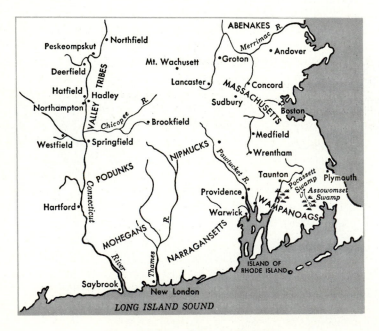

King Philip's War, 1675–1676

to take up the tomahawk. The first blow fell on isolated Brookfield whose few families watched the destruction of their homes from a strong garrison house, then scurried to the safety of fortified Hadley. There too the Indians threatened until an English force from the valley towns fell on them at Hopewell Swamp in August, 1675, administering a sound defeat. These early successes lulled the overconfident English into a sense of false security that was shattered only when another raiding party burned Deerfield and swept northward to lay siege to the stockaded outpost of Northfield. A relief expedition from Hadley drove off the attackers, but the Massachusetts authorities, deciding the town was too dangerous to defend, sent sixty men with wagons to bring in the crops from all the northern Connecticut Valley. On their return they were ambushed a few miles south of Deerfield while fording a small stream since known as Bloody Brook. Only two white men escaped, and crops needed to feed the troops in the lower valley were destroyed. Flushed with success, the Indians fell on Northampton, Hadley, Hatfield, and even Springfield so long as the fall foliage clung to the trees to give them ambush.

With the coming of winter the center of fighting shifted to the Narragansett country where that tribe, after a few forays against isolated settlements, had retreated to several islands in the great coastal swamps. There they were found by an army of 1000 men sent south from Massachusetts. Marching over the frozen ground, the troops surprised the principal Indian village on December 19, 1675, slaughtering some 300 women and children with merciless thoroughness. Most of the braves escaped but for the next month the English tramped through the tribe's lands on a famous "hungry march," burning towns, destroying crops, and putting captives to death with such heartless cruelty that their purpose seemed one of extermination. By the end of January most of the women, children, and old men of the Narragansetts were killed, some escaped to live with the neutral Niantics, while the warriors had fled northward to join the Nipmucks. The Atherton Company lands were freed of Indians.

The maneuver, however, created new difficulties on the northern frontier. The Nipmucks' slender food supplies were soon exhausted by the new arrivals, forcing the Indians to plunder towns or face starvation. All through the winter of 1675-76 these raids went on, as the natives fell upon Lancaster, Concord, Groton, and Medfield in turn. Their victory at Lancaster was most complete; they not only destroyed the town but captured one of the garrisoned houses, killing the men and carrying the women into captivity.

With the coming of spring Philip and his followers continued to attack the eastern settlements, hoping to lure troops from the upper Connecticut Valley so that they could grow food there. Using Mt. Wachusett as their headquarters, they struck along the entire frontier with such devastating thoroughness that the skies from Warwick to Groton were lighted with the flames of burning dwellings. Town after town was deserted before this steady onslaught, until the line of settlement was driven back to Sudbury, Wrentham, and Providence. Even the seaboard cities trembled before the marauders as citizens fled Providence for the safety of the island of Rhode Island, and Cambridge and Boston hurriedly threw up fortifications against the impending attack. For a time in that dread spring of 1676 victory seemed within the grasp of the red men, but the turning point was near. In April reluctant Massachusetts authorities finally consented to employ "Praying Indians" as scouts to protect their troops from the ambushes that had taken such a heavy toll in the past. For the first time the English armies were able to win some engagements. The most important success was enjoyed by a small force that marched north from Hadley in May, 1676, to take the Indian village of Peskeompskut by surprise, slaughter a large number of men, women, and children, and destroy vast quantities of crops.

Indian resistance suddenly collapsed after the Battle of Peskeompskut, much to the surprise of the English who did not know that they had accidentally hit on the one vulnerable spot in the red men's armor when they ravaged the grain fields of the upper valley. Realizing that starvation almost certainly faced them in the coming winter, the natives abruptly lost heart. A combined force of Connecticut troops and friendly Mohegan Indians that swept northward in June found resistance at an end and drove the weary enemy into the wilds of New Hampshire. Philip knew the day of reckoning was at hand. With a few faithful followers he fled back to his old hunting ground east of the Taunton River. There the English forces began the task of "exterminating the rabid animals, which, by a most unaccountable condition from heaven, had now neither strength or sense left them to do anything for their own defense." Philip managed to escape into Assowomset Swamp, but one of his followers betrayed him to the colonial troops, and on the night of August 12, 1676, he was captured and shot. Neither a great fighter nor a particularly gifted leader, Philip had little to do with the war to which he gave his name and his life. Yet to the thousands of New Englanders who had trembled before the tomahawk he was a symbol of all the cruelty of Indian warfare; for the next quarter century the sight of his mummified head perched on a pole in Plymouth gave them cheerful assurance that Indian resistance was crushed.

There was good reason for their relief. King Philip's War was one of the bloodiest in the history of the frontier. More than six hundred men—one-sixth of the male population of New England—were killed, £90,000 expended, and twenty-five towns destroyed. In Maine where fighting went on until 1678, only six villages managed to withstand attack. Little wonder that the colonial authorities treated the remaining Indians with a cold brutality that belied their Christian principles. Those suspected of taking part in the war were slaughtered or sold into slavery, while the remainder were herded onto reservations or bound out to work for white men. In every colony their lands were awarded the soldiers as bounties. Indian power, however, was far from broken and sporadic fighting continued along the northeast seaboard. The English were convinced that French intrigue was at the root of their problem in New England.

For the remaining years of the seventeenth century the expansion of New England went on only at great cost, until by 1700 the lowland areas were filled. Ringing the settlements now to ward off enemy blows was a chain of frontier towns, protected by palisades or garrisoned houses, each inhabited by thirty or forty families who were willing to risk their lives for the generous land grants offered settlers at these outposts. Massachusetts initiated this system in 1695 when the legislature designated eleven towns— York, Wells, Kittery, Amesbury, Haverhill, Dunstable, Chelmsford, Groton, Lancaster, Marlboro, and Deerfield—as frontier posts, and Connecticut completed the protective circle in 1704 when Symsbury, Waterbury, Danbury, Colchester, Windham, Mansfield, and Plainfield were added. Behind this living screen the older settlements grew rapidly. The New Englanders, like the Tidewater planters, were thoroughly adjusted to the strange environment of the New World and ready to begin that march upward into the western hills that only ended when they spread over the interior of the continent.

The Old West
1700-1763

By the closing years of the seventeenth century the choicest lands of the coastal plains and tidal valleys were cleared and pioneers were ready to swarm over the physiographic province known as the Old West. Here, in the New England highlands, the broad river bottoms of New York and Pennsylvania, and the rugged uplands of the southern Piedmont, they created during the first half of the eighteenth century a new society with distinctive frontier institutions and social attitudes that retained few remnants of the Old World heritage.

Peculiar geographic features gave the Old West a unity which transcended artificial colonial boundary lines. In the south the province was separated from the Tidewater by the "Fall Line," where tumbling cataracts two hundred feet high ended navigation on the coastal rivers, and, south of the Roanoke, by a thirty-mile strip of forbidding pine barrens that towered six or seven hundred feet above the level countryside. Beyond these barriers the Piedmont sloped gradually upward toward the Appalachian Mountains. A land of rolling hills and swift-flowing streams, of abundant rainfall and temperate climate, of rich, red, residual soils, its forest-covered slopes offered tempting farm sites for land-hungry easterners. Along its western edge stretched the steep walls of the Blue Ridge Mountains, cut at intervals by flaring water gaps where the Delaware, Susquehanna, Potomac, and James rivers tumbled downward toward the sea. Pioneers passing through these emerged on the Great Valley of the Appalachians, a broad floor dotted with hills and interlaced with level plains where the limestone soil was deep and good. Seventy-five miles beyond rose the jagged peaks of the Allegheny Front, a jumbled mass of mountains three or four thousand feet high where passes were few and crossing difficult.

The Great Valley of the Appalachians linked the southern and northern portions of the Old West, for it extended across Pennsylvania and New York as far as Lake Champlain. The river bottoms of this region attracted settlers early in the eighteenth century—a restless stream that filled the valleys of the Delaware, Susquehanna, Hudson, Mohawk, and upper Connecticut and Merrimac before spilling over into the highlands and plateaus on either side. Here, as in the South, their westward march was checked by forbidding mountain ranges that stretched along the back country from the White Mountains of New Hampshire to the point where the Appalachian Ridges of Pennsylvania blended into the Allegheny Front. This barrier, the unifying influence of the Great Valley, and the impossibility of direct communication between the interior uplands and the seaboard bound the pioneers who settled the Old West together, whether they built their cabins along the sparkling Juniata or staked their "tomahawk claims" on the upper reaches of the Yadkin.

The southern Piedmont was settled first. The exploration of this hilly region was begun in mid-seventeenth century by the commanders of Virginia's Fall Line forts who were naturally interested in the trading or mineral wealth concealed in the unknown West. Captain Abraham Wood, who ruled over Ft. Henry at the falls of the Appomattox, led the way in 1650 when he and a companion, Edward Bland, made a five-day journey to the forks of the Roanoke in search of choice spots for a land-jobbing scheme they had

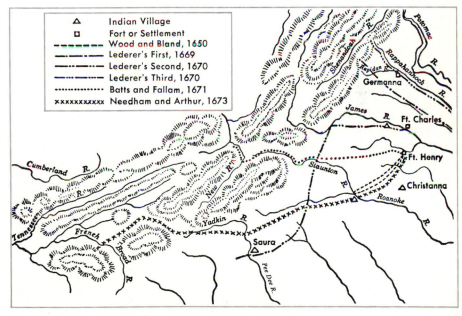

The Exploration of the Piedmont

in mind. They were highly pleased with the rolling countryside, but settlement was not ready to follow, and not until the late 1660s was exploration
resumed by both Captain Wood and Governor Berkeley. Passes through the
Blue Ridge to allow trade with the western Indians were now the objective.
Berkeley sent out three expeditions under a German physician, John Lederer, in 1669 and 1670, one across the Rapidan River to the mountains,
another southward as far as the Indian village of Saura on the Pee Dee River,
and a third up the Rappahannock, but each was blocked by the mountains
and returned without success. Captain Wood's attempt the next year was
crowned with better fortune; the little band of pioneers under Thomas Batts
and Robert Fallam that he sent westward followed the Staunton River
through the Blue Ridge to emerge on the westerly flowing New River. They
took possession of all the lands drained by this stream for their sovereign,
and after convincing themselves that some slight movement of the water
was caused by the ebb and flow of tide, returned with news that they had
found the route to the Pacific.

Wood's explorers turned next to the southern Piedmont in an attempt
to tap the trade of the Carolina back country. James Needham and an
illiterate lad named Gabriel Arthur were sent out with eight Indian guides
in 1673, and after traveling southwesterly for nine days, reached the Yadkin
River which led them westward through a pass in the Carolina Blue Ridge.
Fifteen more days brought them to a village of the Tamahita Indians on the
French Broad River, where Needham turned back, leaving Arthur to live
with the red men and roam with their war parties from the Ohio to the
Floridas before returning safely to Ft. Henry in June, 1674.

Bacon's Rebellion ended further official exploration, but by this time
the fur traders were ready to take over the task. From each of the Fall Line
forts their hundred-horse pack trains, with harness bells tinkling a merry
song, moved farther and farther into the wilderness. Some followed the trail
blazed by Batts and Fallam along the New and Kanawha rivers until by the
1690s they were trading on the banks of the Ohio. Others who made the
fort on the Rappahannock their headquarters crossed the Blue Ridge in the
1680s to drain peltry from the Shenandoah Valley. Still others made their
way along Needham's route—known to woodsmen as the Occaneechi Path—
to the Carolina Piedmont or the interlacing waters of the Savannah and
Tennessee river systems where the Cherokee eagerly awaited them. The
more adventurous pressed even farther south to round the tip of the mountain
system and compete with the Carolina traders for the business of the Creek
and Chickasaw Indians. Wherever they went they spied out the choice lands
and broke down the self-sufficiency of the natives. The way was prepared
for the first settlers.

The westward push of Virginia farmers began soon after Bacon's Rebellion and was in full swing by 1710. In the van as usual were the cattle
ranchers who grazed their herds on the open meadows and canebrakes or
built enclosed cowpens surrounded by rude cabins and half-cleared fields

where they grew corn for themselves and their animals. Each of these rude clearings became the nucleus for a small settlement as homeseekers from the Tidewater moved west. Some of these newcomers came directly from England, but more were from the East where large importations of Negro slaves at the turn of the century stimulated the rapid development of plantation agriculture. The expansion of these great estates crowded out thousands of small farmers who turned west to begin life anew. This whole process was stimulated between 1710 and 1722 by Governor Alexander Spotswood, who herded the Piedmont Indians onto a reservation at Christanna, founded a settlement of indentured German servants at Germanna on the Rapidan to protect the northern frontier from attack, and in 1716 led an elaborate exploring party through the James River watergap into the Shenandoah Valley where these Knights of the Golden Horseshoe, as they styled themselves, toasted each new discovery with the rum and wines provided for the occasion.

Governor Spotswood's solicitous interest in the West was not unselfish for he, with other governmental officials and influential easterners, had succumbed to the speculative fever which raged through the colonies during the eighteenth century. This was a day of bold enterprise on both sides of the Atlantic—of reckless commercial ventures, of sudden wealth, of the fantastic South Sea Bubble—when business leaders scrambled to pyramid fortunes amidst the limitless possibilities of an expanding empire. In America this spirit was expressed by a mad rush to engross the best lands against the day when they could be resold to settlers at fabulous profits. The speculator was suddenly catapulted into a position of importance; from New England to the Carolinas his agents were at work, hunting out choice spots, bribing legislatures and officials into favorable terms of sale, and reshaping the whole course of the westward movement by their shady dealings.

Governor Spotswood could no more remain aloof than any other wealthy man. He first tried to check speculative buying as his royal instructions ordered, then gave up the struggle and not only built up large estates for himself and his Tidewater friends but shaped Virginia's laws to increase the value of his holdings. Typical of his efforts was an act of 1720 which divided the Piedmont into the two counties of Brunswick and Spotsylvania, bound the colony to care for all their religious and educational needs, and exempted landholders there from taxes or quitrents for ten years. When the crown refused to approve this outrageous measure until land grants in the new counties were limited to a thousand acres, Spotswood and his fellow planters were not discouraged. They used dummy grantees for a time, then the law was simply ignored by speculators who secured grants of from ten to forty thousand acres from the governor by the simple expedient of winning his friendship and promising future payment.

In the Carolinas, where royal officials vainly tried to stop the assembly from making large speculative grants to Tidewater planters, the situation was even worse. The legislators were so determined to award themselves and their friends western estates that they sliced away most of the governor's salary to show their displeasure, then defied a royal agent who appeared in 1739 with orders to limit the size of holdings. This official not only recognized the force of public opinion by giving up the struggle, but stayed on to build up grants of a million acres for himself.

By the middle of the eighteenth century the entire Virginia and Carolina Piedmont was in private hands, and speculators were beginning to accumulate estates in the Great Valley. Most of the grants, which ranged from ten to forty thousand acres, were held by Tidewater planters, but two were awarded court favorites by the Restoration monarchs. One, controlled by Lord Fairfax, comprised the whole Northern Neck of Virginia between the Rappahannock and Potomac rivers including much of the Shenandoah Valley; the other was owned by the Earl of Granville and covered most of northern North Carolina. On both of these giant estates minor agents assigned lands, collected rents, and engaged in fraudulent practices that kept the tenant farmers in a turmoil of discontent.

The engrossment of western lands by speculators both encouraged and discouraged the movement to the frontier. Some owners tried to lure settlers to their holdings by making elementary improvements, bringing out immigrants from Europe, maintaining agents in eastern ports to steer new arrivals toward the Piedmont, and circulating promotional literature which described the West as "the best, richest, and most healthy part of our Country." More, however, simply held their lands while they waited for the price rise that would make them rich. Some refused to sell at all but insisted on renting, others encouraged settlement and then demanded an exorbitant fee for the improved land. Worst of all was the fact that hastily drawn boundaries between the grants were usually so inaccurate that a farmer who purchased from one speculator was often forced to repurchase at a higher price from another after ownership was finally settled. The total effect of speculation was to hinder, rather than hurry, the westward advance.

Yet settlements spread westward, moving up the river valleys of the Virginia and North Carolina Piedmont, then out over the highlands to form a compact agricultural frontier. In South Carolina, the advance was less rapid, for Indian troubles, the forbidding barrier of pine barrens, and the slow development of that colony combined to keep the frontier east of the Piedmont until after 1730. Not until another column of pioneers moved down the Great Valley from the Middle Colonies, pushed through the mountain gaps, and overflowed the Carolina back country from the west did the southern Piedmont receive its first sizeable migration.

This stream of homeseekers was deflected southward from New York and Pennsylvania by conditions within those colonies that discouraged frontier settlements there. In New York the activities of fur traders and land speculators were responsible. Powerful trading interests, centered at Albany where they bartered with the Iroquois for peltry, blocked the only path that settlers could follow toward the interior: up the Hudson between the towering peaks of the Catskills and Berkshires and westward along the level Mohawk Valley. This gateway the traders guarded jealously, knowing that any advance of the farming frontier would drive away the Indian middlemen who supplied them with furs. Schenectady was settled in 1661 with their reluctant permission only after the fourteen families who founded that town agreed not to engage in trade. From that time on they resisted every invasion of their domain.

The expanding population east of Albany which might have brushed the traders aside failed to develop until late in the eighteenth century because of deficiencies in New York's land system. The colony's laws provided that to obtain a grant a colonial favorite had only to obtain authorization from the governor, purchase the plot he desired from the Indians, finance a survey, and then secure the final patent from the governor and his council. Every step in this process invited fraud. Influential colonists found that they could trade their political support for vast estates, or that greedy officials were willing to make large grants in return for a share of the proceeds. Moreover the taxes and quitrents were low; the legislature hesitated to relinquish its control over the purse strings by allowing royal governors to supplement their incomes by revenues from land, and ordinarily demanded only a raccoon skin, a bushel of wheat, or a few shillings a year from the largest holders.

The first large grant was made in 1684 to strengthen royal authority by establishing a manorial class, and others followed, particularly between 1702 and 1708 when an avaricious governor, Lord Cornbury, rewarded his favorites with a free hand. By 1710 the entire Hudson River valley was in the hands of landlords, whose holdings varied from the millions of acres of the giant Kayaderosseras and Hardenbergh patents to the smaller but still sizeable estates of the Cortlandt and Philipsborough manors. In the long run these giant land holders played a positive role in peopling New York; their promotional activities and their willingness to lease rather than sell attracted a great many small farmers who could not otherwise have afforded to move to the frontier. Eventually many obtained freeholds and became permanent settlers, often at the expense of the speculators whose returns were always modest. For the time being, however, many would-be pioneers were unwilling to live in New York under these conditions when neighboring colonies offered full ownership at fairly low prices. Little wonder that most of the estates had only a few families scattered over their thousands of acres, or that virgin forest blanketed nearly all of this fertile valley at a time when other coastal river beds were under cultivation.

This state of affairs alarmed royal officials, and their concern started a new immigrant stream toward the Old West—the Palatine Germans. These sturdy aliens came from the Rhinish Palatinate, a fruitful area which was laid bare by marching armies during the Thirty Years' War, by plundering petty princes who wrung from starving serfs the money needed to transform their tiny courts into replicas of fashionable Versailles, and by French invaders who swept over the countryside with the outbreak of the War of the Spanish Succession in 1702. On the ears of suffering Palatines fell tales of America's riches; they read glowing letters sent by fortunate relatives who had reached the land of promise, or listened eagerly to *Neuländers*—men hired by immigration and shipping companies to loaf about villages in gaudy clothes boasting that their fortunes were made in the colonies. The rumor spread, too, that England would transport all Protestants who reached her shores to America.

This agitation bore its first fruit in 1708 when a little group of Palatines led by the Reverend Joshua Kocherthal loaded their scanty possessions on boats and drifted down the Rhine to Holland, where English ships carried them to London. That fall fifty-five of them were sent to New York where land along the Hudson was given them to lay out the town of Newburgh. News of their success drifted back to a Germany caught in a new disaster, for the winter of 1708—09 was one of such unseasonable cold that vines and fruit trees of countless peasants were killed. With spring the mass migration began, gathering momentum steadily until June when Palatines arrived in the Low Countries at the rate of a thousand a week. British agents welcomed them there and sent all Protestants to England; that nation was delighted to build up its colonies without depleting its home population. By the fall of 1709, some 13,500 Germans overflowed London, filling the taverns and public squares where the army erected tents to house them. Their dispersal through the empire began in the spring; some stayed in England, others were sent to Ireland or the Carolinas, but the largest group of 3,000 was dispatched to New York.

Here, officials planned, they would earn their keep by producing naval stores—tar, pitch, and tall masts—needed by the royal navy. Governor Robert Hunter selected a site for the experiment near the estate of a great landholder, Robert Livingston, who was authorized to feed the Germans at government expense. There, in October, 1709, two villages of East Camp and West Camp were laid out, the Palatines established, and the work of producing naval stores begun. The project fared badly from the first, largely because the local farmer hired to supervise production knew nothing about extracting pitch from virgin pine. After two years of blundering, Parliament ended the whole disastrous enterprise in 1712, leaving the Germans free to go where they wished.

Some scattered along the Hudson or over the neighboring colonies, but the largest group turned toward the Schoharie River valley where, rumor had it, Governor Hunter had intended to plant them in the first place. Sending a few deputies ahead to buy land from the Indians, the Palatines wintered in Albany before pushing on to their new homes in the spring of 1713, dragging their humble belongings on sleds through waist-deep snow. Seven villages were laid out to hold the 500 settlers who reached there that year. Their poverty was appalling; they borrowed one horse and one cow which were teamed to a crude plow, fashioned essential farm tools from wood and

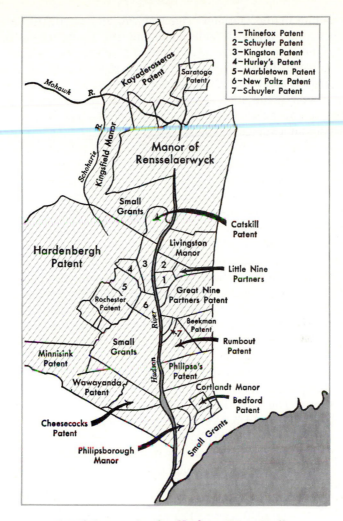

Land Grants in the Hudson River Valley

stone, carried their grain on their backs to Albany or Schenectady mills fifty miles away, and subsisted until the first harvest on roots and berries. Yet perseverance triumphed, and by 1714 the little community was firmly established. Their difficulties were not over, however. For the next seven years they fought a losing battle with Albany speculators who owned the land on which they had located, a struggle that only ended in 1721 when the governor offered all Palatines who would move free lands farther along the Mohawk. Some took advantage of this opportunity to establish the towns of Palatine and Stone Arabia, others went on to found Herkimer in 1723, while the remainder either moved to the Tulpehocken district of Pennsylvania or came to terms with the speculators.

The coming of the Germans signaled the end of the Albany traders' monopoly over the Mohawk Valley and opened a new period of feverish activity for land jobbers. Between 1713 and 1738 they scrambled for grants there, then turned their attention to the unexploited country south of the Mohawk. This region, cut off from the older New York settlements by mountains, seemed uninviting so long as land was available along the Hudson, Mohawk, and Schoharie rivers, but in 1740 a pioneering Scot, John Lindesay, laid out a village on Cherry Valley Creek and the land rush began. Not of settlers—Cherry Valley grew slowly and no other towns were started for many years—but of speculators. Again they besieged the governors; again great estates were erected in this remote wilderness, until most of the best land was absorbed by individuals or small companies. New York, as a result of this overabundance of speculative activity, presented a sorry picture in the 1750s. Its prized river valleys and rolling hills were blanketed with land patents, but of settlers there were few. A scattering of tenant farmers on the great estates along the Hudson, a few pioneers grouped around Albany and Schenectady, a cluster of settlements built around Ft. Hunter after that blockhouse was erected in 1712, the isolated outposts at Cherry Valley, a row of tidy German towns along the Schoharie and upper Mohawk—those were the only monuments to a generation of frontier activity. Those and the land warrants locked in the trunks of a legion of speculators.

Conditions in New York deflected the immigrant tide that flowed from Europe during the eighteenth century southward to the beckoning harbors of Pennsylvania. There the tolerant Quakers who had built their homes in Philadelphia and along the banks of the Delaware and Schuylkill rivers made them welcome, knowing that William Penn viewed his colony as a sanctuary for Europe's oppressed. News of this haven was carried to the continent by Penn himself, who not only visited Germany to tell persecuted minorities that land and understanding waited them in America but used printer's ink liberally to make Pennsylvania the best known of all the colonies. While this invitation was spread among European peoples, Penn and his cohorts were preparing lands for their occupation. The Delaware and Schuylkill valleys would accommodate some but the rich Susquehanna Valley in the interior was also needed. William Penn began purchasing land from the Indians there as early as 1683, only to find himself involved in a conflict with the Albany traders who feared the intrusion of settlers into lands hunted by their Iroquois suppliers. He eventually won his battle, and with it a royal grant to the Susquehanna Valley in 1697. From that time on Penn's lieutenant, James Logan, built a lucrative Indian trade there, at the same time using trading posts on Conestoga and Pequea creeks as centers for expeditions sent to spy out the best farming regions. As more and more of these were purchased from the natives, the Indians were forced to shift westward to the area about Shamokin where the fur trade centered after 1708. At the same time settlers were sent in, a few at first, then in increasing numbers

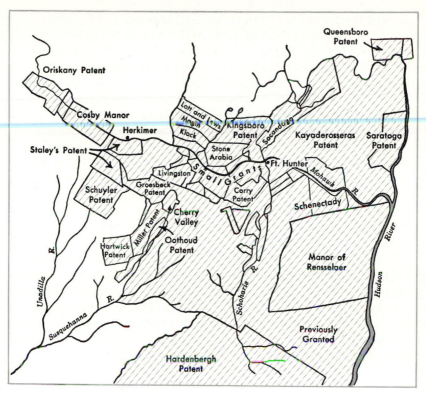

Speculation on the Mohawk Frontier, 1700–1763

to occupy the lower Susquehanna Valley. By 1710 that fertile farmland was ready to receive a mass migration.

The tide began to flow that year when some of the Palatines shipped from London found their way to Pennsylvania. Their letters home encouraged others to follow. "The farmers or husbandmen live better than lords," they wrote. "If a workman will only work four or five days a week, he can live grandly. The farmers here pay no tithes or contributions." Each year more came, many paying their way by working as indentured servants, or redemptioners. By 1717 a mass migration was under way. For the next decades every ship that docked at Philadelphia left a cargo of German-speaking peasants to work out their indenture terms with the farmers who financed their passage, then push into the interior after lands of their own. Most of them could not afford the £10 per hundred acres charged by the colony, let alone the exorbitant fees demanded by speculators who had engrossed the best land, and simply squatted on a spot that pleased them. In 1726 more than 100,000 of them lived on farms to which they had no title; by mid-century the proprietors were forced to recognize the right of squatters to pre-empt sites and pay for them later.

At first the Palatines swarmed up the Delaware and Schuylkill valleys as far as Bethlehem and Tulpehocken Creek or spread out around their early settlement at German Valley in New Jersey, but the Susquehanna Valley was the mecca that attracted most of them. In the rolling countryside, reminiscent of their native Palatinate, the "Pennsylvania Dutch" found the haven of their dreams. Building farms, they advanced northward until they reached the less fertile lands about the Juniata, then the stream turned southward. This transition was natural. Before them lay the broad floor of the Great Valley of the Appalachians, easily accessible in eastern Pennsylvania through gaps in the low South Mountains, where streams were plentiful and the limestone soil fertile. As they moved along this natural highway they found that land prices steadily declined; Pennsylvania charged £15 for each 100 acres after 1738, Maryland only £5, and Virginia speculators in the Shenandoah Valley even less. This was the magnet that drew the Palatines steadily southward.

The movement began in 1726 when German families crossed the South Mountains through Crampton's Gap and followed Monocacy Creek into the Potomac Valley where they built such towns as Monocacy and Frederick. Others went on across the Potomac at Old Packhorse Ford to lay out New Mecklenburg that same year. The first Palatine to make his way into the Great Valley of Virginia was Adam Müller who settled on Hawkswill Creek in 1727; within three years he had the satisfaction of luring half a dozen more

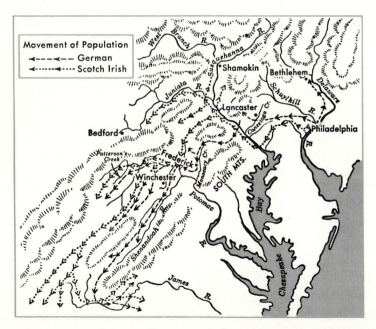

The Settlement of Pennsylvania and the Great Valley of Virginia

German families to his clearing. More prominent was the town of Winchester, laid out in 1731 by a band of eleven families under Justus Hite. This became a center for the German migration that filled the Virginia back country during the next decade; by 1740 their settlements extended as far west as Patterson's Creek and south to the James River, while an overflow was already spilling eastward through the mountain gaps into the Piedmont. When a colony of German Moravians purchased 100,000 acres near the Yadkin River in 1751 the march southward began once more, ending a decade later when the North Carolina Great Valley and Piedmont were comfortably settled. A zone of German farmers fringed the colonies from the Mohawk Valley to the Carolinas.

The Palatines did not have the West long to themselves. Close on their heels came another European migratory stream, this one from northern Ireland. The bulk of these Scotch-Irish were lowland Scots and Englishmen who had been planted there early in the seventeenth century in a vain British effort to tame and convert the wild Irish tribesmen, but they included a liberal sprinkling of Scotch Highlanders and southern Irishmen. Most had learned the rudiments of frontier technique when they cleared their Ulster fields or battled the fierce Irish tribes; all hated England for the harsh laws that drove them to the New World. Parliament passed a series of these acts between 1665 and 1680 forbidding the importation into England of Irish livestock, meat, and grain; then, when Ulsterites built a new economic life based on wool growing, ended that in 1699 by prohibiting the export of woolen goods. While they still staggered under this blow a Penal Act of 1704 excluded Presbyterians from all civil and military offices and forbade their ministers to perform the marriage service. This was too much. When their leases fell due in 1717 and 1718 thousands took passage for America. From that date until the Revolution the tide flowed steadily, increasing in depression years such as 1740 and 1741 when more than 12,000 crossed the Atlantic, until 300,000 lived in the colonies.

Some went to New England, others to the Mohawk and Cherry Valley frontiers, but most made Pennsylvania their New World mecca. Like the Germans they were too poor to buy lands and sought isolated spots in the interior where they squatted unmolested or defied the few rent collectors who invaded their domains with the bold assertion that "it was against the laws of God and nature, that so much land should be idle while so many Christians wanted it to labor on to raise their bread." By the 1730s they were moving west in large numbers, following a trail that paralleled the banks of Octorara Creek, then turned northward along the Susquehanna and its tributaries. Much of the land was occupied by Germans, forcing the Scotch-Irish into the hillier country beside the Juniata River and west of the Cumberland Valley. This whole mountainous region as far as the frontier post of Bedford was filled with these turbulent immigrants by mid-century, while others were only restrained from moving on to the lands about the Forks of the Ohio by the Pennsylvania proprietors.

As the lands of interior Pennsylvania filled, the stream turned south-ward, particularly after 1738 when Virginia and North Carolina promised freedom of worship to Presbyterians. By this time the northern-sloping half of the Great Valley of Virginia was occupied by Germans, forcing the Scotch-Irish to push on southwest of the James River. North Carolina doubled its population between 1732 and 1754, largely by their influx. Some overflowed into the Carolina Piedmont, but most of the migrating families sought homes in the limestone valleys that fringed the western edges of the Appalachian Mountains. There they were led onward by the western-flowing rivers of the upper Tennessee system, until their settlements dotted the banks of the Greenbrier, the Holston, the Watauga, and the Nolichucky. These were plain folk, not a planter class. They built their crude cabins, raised their large crops of children and their small crops of corn, and succumbed rapidly to the forest environment. "The clothes of the people," wrote a visitor to one of their villages, "consist of deer skins, their food of Johnycakes, deer and bear meat. A kind of white people are found here, who live like savages. Hunting is their chief occupation." Bold, devout, shrewd men, hating In-dians and easterners with impartial vigor, and determined to "keep the sabbath and everything else they could lay their hands on," the Scotch-Irish made ideal pioneers in the westward march of empire.

While they and their German cohorts subdued the southern back coun-try, other frontiersmen advanced into the upland plateaus and mountain valleys of New England. The settlers who made their homes in this rugged hill country came not from Germany or Ireland but from the coastal lowlands where Puritan mothers proved more productive than their rock-strewn fields. The large families which overcrowded the bottom lands, eager to be on the move at the close of the seventeenth century, proved a greater temptation for speculative enterprise than officials and businessmen could resist. Money overflowed the coin chests of eastern merchants, for fortunes were being made in commerce, and crown restrictions on manufacturing closed that form of investment to their capital. If they could buy up land in anticipation of the impeding rush, the riches of Midas would be theirs! Under this pres-sure the New England land system was completely transformed as legisla-tures, succumbing to the speculative fever, saw profits rather than an orderly and stable society as their goal. This transition reshaped the whole course of settlement.

The spirit of speculation was first shown early in the eighteenth century when Boston and Salem businessmen began buying plots from proprietors of new towns or from old towns where undivided fields were still available. For a time the Massachusetts General Court resisted their demand and made grants as it had in the seventeenth century—to non-profit-seeking groups of religiously orthodox individuals—but by 1727 the pressure was too strong. In that year nine new towns were laid out along the northern border to satisfy land bounties issued during King Philip's War; in the next five years thirty-five more were created in Maine, Massachusetts, and New Hampshire, all for the benefit of investors. From this time on all pretext of creating contiguous, church-dominated towns was abandoned as the legislature granted lands freely to any speculative group able to bring enough pressure. The next logical step, the sale of town sites by the colony, followed by the late 1740s and continued until 1762, when the last remaining land in Massachusetts was auctioned off.

The other New England colonies followed a similar course. Connecticut sold a large block at auction first in 1715, and by 1720 was committed to this policy of land disposal. These sales reached their height in the late 1720s when the vast area west of the Connecticut River was divided between the colony and the towns of Hartford and Windsor, carved into towns, and disposed of at a series of spectacular sales that attracted speculators from the entire seaboard. In Maine, which was an undisputed part of Massachusetts after 1677, land jobbers revived twenty-four "ancient patents" issued by the Council for New England a century before, formed themselves into such companies as the Masonian Proprietors, Lincolnshire Company Proprietors, and Pemaquid Proprietors, and set out to lure European immigrants to their shadowy domains. In their eagerness to sell they not only built forts, sawmills, and other necessities, but introduced into America the device of free grants to enhance the value of sections retained. Even Vermont, which was claimed by both New York and New Hampshire, felt the impact of this speculative fever. Between 1749 and 1764 Governor Benning Wentworth of New Hampshire granted 129 townsites there to speculators, carefully reserving 500 acres in each for himself. Most of the recipients of these infamous "New Hampshire Grants" had no intention of settling in their towns; instead many owned shares in several villages and one notorious speculator was a proprietor in at least eighteen towns at the same time. Wentworth knew full well that speculators would profit, but he also knew that this was a small price for the rich New Hampshire countryside that he had been ordered by the crown to secure. Nor was he wrong. The great holders skimmed off their profits—modest ones, as time was to show—but their promotional activity attracted settlers who developed western New Hampshire and Vermont far more rapidly than would otherwise have been the case.

This burst of activity changed the whole course of New England's westward movement. No longer was each town controlled by an interested group of resident proprietors who cared for its needs and divided its fields among acceptable newcomers. Now absentee proprietors, concerned only with allotting the lands among themselves and selling their portions profitably, governed each new settlement. Some made a conscious effort to lure immigrants by sending agents through the colonies or to England to sell lots, but far more were content to do nothing while waiting for prices to rise. Pioneers accustomed to the benevolent paternalism of the older system, which had provided them with mills, schools, churches, and defense, were quick to object. They complained that the Boston capitalists who owned the land not only did nothing to make pioneer life easier, but charged exorbitant prices, withheld the best land from sale in anticipation of price rises, and reaped an unearned profit without sharing the dangers and poverty of the frontier. Worse still, settlers insisted, was the tendency to create towns so rapidly under speculative pressure that settlers were not available to fill them, leaving a weak frontier line at the mercy of attacking Indians. Dissatisfaction bred of this eastern proprietary monopoly did much to foster the spirit of radicalism which flourished in western New England through the Revolutionary Era.

The rapid settlement of the back country in the face of these handicaps testified to the section's expansive power. All through the early eighteenth century advancing waves of settlers moved upward from the coastal lowland into the New England hill country, augmented now and then by a trickle of immigrants from Europe. One group, led by bands of Scotch-Irish, began the assault on the hilly plateau of central Massachusetts about 1718. Worcester, the principal town, became the center for westward-moving pioneers who founded villages as far west as Ware and Amherst, many of them Scotch-Irish driven from older settlements by the hostility of Puritan clergy who feared the corrupting effect of Presbyterianism on their charges. Other pioneers moved west from the Connecticut Valley into the Berkshires, where they met another stream advancing up the Housatonic River from Connecticut and joined with them in founding a string of picturesque hill towns between Sheffield and Williamstown. By mid-century the Berkshire regions of both Massachusetts and Connecticut were filling so rapidly that settlers spilled over into lands claimed by New York. Their coming aroused such dissatisfaction among the tenant farmers on the manorial Hudson Valley estates—who hoped that Massachusetts would allow them to trade their serflike status for actual ownership of their farms by annexing the area— that they waged war on their landlords during the 1750s. Only a crown decree fixing the New York-Massachusetts boundary at a point twenty miles east of the Hudson ended this border fighting.

The establishment of this boundary turned the westward-marching New Englanders northward toward Vermont, New Hampshire, and Maine. These border regions had grown slowly to that time, despite a flurry of activity in New Hampshire when Londonderry, Concord, Amherst, Atkinson, Rochester, and a few other isolated towns were planted by Scotch-Irish and lowlanders in the 1720s. Now the boom began. Between 1760 and 1776 seventy-four new towns were settled in Vermont, one hundred in New Hampshire and ninety-four in Maine, many of them peopled by restless migrants making their second or third move toward the frontier. By the time of the Revolution this great northern country was being converted into a peaceful farming area. Yet so strong was the expansive spirit that even these provinces failed to satisfy the New Englanders. In 1754 a group of Connecticut speculators, organized as the Susquehanna Company, purchased from the Indians a two-hundred-mile tract in the beautiful Wyoming Valley of Pennsylvania, and with the blessing of their colony (which claimed that region under an ancient charter), began sending out settlers in 1762. Despite Indian troubles and indignant protests from Pennsylvania, the towns of Wilkes-Barre and Plymouth were laid out by 1768. Another Connecticut enterprise, the Delaware Company, enjoyed less success but did plant a handful of pioneers along the upper Delaware River in Pennsylvania.

The pioneers who hewed out their clearings beneath the long shadows of Vermont's Green Mountains or beside the rippling waters of the Susquehanna typified the changes wrought on New England's institutions by contact with the American wilderness. No longer were the Puritan leaders content to move slowly westward, taking their neighbors and ministers with them, in an orderly march of contiguous settlements. Instead the speculative fever was on them; they were more interested in saving dollars than souls, more concerned with good land than compact villages, more excited about individual wealth than group welfare. They still settled in communities, but good soil rather than adjacence to other towns and churches dictated their choice of sites. Some, indeed, were ready to leave the settled frontier far behind in their search for favored agricultural regions. "The newcomers do not fix near their neighbors and go on regularly," complained one observer in Vermont, "but take spots that please them best, though twenty or thirty miles beyond any others." Limitless opportunity, in the form of cheap land that could be farmed or resold, was the dynamic reshaping New England's social structure.

This transformation typified the changes taking place along the entire back country. In the Old West a new society was born in the eighteenth century, enriched by borrowings from European peoples and shaped by the frontier environment. Each of the migratory groups that sought homes there—the Yankees, Southerners, Scotch-Irish, Germans, Welshmen—contributed something to the social order as they adapted themselves, for the first time in the history of the frontier, to a life completely isolated from European influences. From this blending emerged distinctive characteristics that stamped these pioneers as typical Americans: emphasis on the practical, intense optimism, impatience with the slow workings of the law, a compelling restlessness, love for oversimplification, mechanical ingenuity, versatility, respect for the individual, tolerance of different religious ideas. Neither the forest nor the European heritage alone shaped these points of view; both contributed.

Every pioneer who moved to the Old West, carrying his ax and gun and driving his livestock before him, felt the impact of the wilderness environment. He knew that he would be able to till only a few acres of land yet he always took out more than he needed, realizing that any excess could be sold at a profit to later comers. With this purchased, or acquired by the simpler expedient of squatting, he felled trees to build a log cabin, notching the ends to fit snugly together, and leaving a hole in the split-board roof to let some of the smoke out—a technique acquired from the Swedes who contributed this distinct architectural form to America. Neighbors usually assisted in this task, for settlements were always near enough together to encourage community cooperation. "They make it a point of hospitality to aid the new farmer," a traveler wrote. "A cask of cider drank in common, and with gaiety, or a gallon of rum, are the only recompense for these services." Only the methodical Germans scorned these methods. Their homes were built of square-hewn logs, with thatched roofs and a center chimney to conserve fuel, dominated by a great barn with stone basement, broad threshing floor, and ample lofts. The "Palatine barns" proved so useful that they were generally adopted through the West.

With shelter assured, the frontiersmen began clearing his land. If he lived in New England or was a German he followed the "Yankee method" of cutting down the trees and calling in neighbors to roll the logs together for burning; if he was southern or Scotch-Irish he girdled the trunks and let them rot away. Four or five years of back-breaking labor was needed to clear the ten or fifteen acres necessary to support a family. During this period the pioneer family lived on grain purchased from nearby farmers, but two good crops would pay for the farm and all improvements. Corn was the great staple of the Old West, although rye was often grown as a first crop in northern New England, and wheat in the Mohawk and Shenandoah valleys. The Germans especially found the latter profitable; they shunned the usual exploitive methods of frontier agriculture, guarding their soil so carefully that they made fourteen successive plantings before allowing a field to renew its fertility by lying fallow. The grain was consumed at home, sold to newcomers, or transported to the nearest markets either on the backs of settlers or in the Conestoga wagons that the Palatines introduced into Pennsylvania and the Great Valley. These sturdy vehicles, painted blue and covered with tightly stretched cloth, were soon adopted generally along the frontier and, as covered wagons, carried thousands of migrating families westward.

Most of the frontier settlers, even in the primitive settlements that fringed the western edge of civilization, lived well. Self-sufficiency was a necessity here. Only two things the pioneer must have: an ax and a gun. The long-handled ax was a universal tool; with it the farmer built his cabin, cleared his land, fashioned crude furniture and wooden dishes, hacked out his cumbersome farm instruments and even "edged her up a bit and shaved with her" on rare state occasions. Often his skilled hands fashioned a spinning wheel and loom so that his overworked wife could make her own poke bonnet, jacket, and linsey petticoat. She patterned his clothes after the Indians': a fur cap, leggings of buckskin or elk hide, and a fringed hunting shirt that hung loose from the shoulders to the knees and was drawn in at the waist by a broad belt. All these were made at home; only iron, powder, and a few luxuries were imported.

The rifle was just as essential. On it the frontiersmen depended for game to feed his family, protection against outlaws, and defense against Indians. Every male over twelve expected to share these burdens; those who refused were "hated out" of the community. Because a straight-shooting gun spelled food and security to the pioneer, his pointed criticism of European weapons—directed at German gunsmiths in western towns—brought important changes. These craftsmen gradually modified the cumbersome imported weapons to meet American conditions. They lengthened the stubby barrels to some five feet for accuracy, reduced the bore to less than half an inch to conserve heavy lead bullets, enlarged and strengthened the trigger guards to withstand hard treatment, increased the size of the sights for better aim amidst the forest gloom, and more important of all adopted the "grease patch" which had been used only occasionally in Europe. This was a small circle of tallow-soaked cloth that was placed under the bullet for loading. Instead of driving the ball down the barrel with an iron ram, as in older guns, the frontiersman could load quietly and quickly with a light hickory ramrod. The result was the deadly Kentucky Rifle, a weapon that had much to do with the speedy conquest of the frontier. So accurately did they shoot that a skilled frontiersman could snuff out a candle at fifty yards, slice off a turkey's head at eighty yards, and split a sapling at two hundred and fifty yards.

One of these rifles, a well-poised ax, possibly a horse or cow—these were the only tools needed to start life anew in the wilderness. The men who used them, justly proud of their skill, pitied greenhorn easterners, all unaware that they themselves were scorned by coastal settlers for their crude manners, lack of education, emotional religions, and unorthodox legal devices. Frontier arrogance bound the people of the Old West together, for whether they lived amidst the Berkshires or in the Carolina Piedmont they were proudly aware that they were westerners, and hence superior to the rest of mankind. They were united, too, by their tendency to look to Pennsylvania for leadership. From this colony Lutheran and Moravian ministers went forth to preach at the tiny log chapels built by the Palatines or to plod along a thousand-mile circuit through the back country. Presbyterian ministers who carried the word of God to Scotch-Irish settlements in the Great Valley were trained there, many of them at the famed Log Cabin College established in 1728 by the Reverend William Tennent or, after his death in 1746, at Princeton. Pennsylvania also was the terminus of most of the trade routes of the Old West, for farmers living in the Great Valley of Virginia or the Carolinas found that their best markets lay not across the mountains but in Philadelphia, or, after 1730, Baltimore. The volume of this trade controlled the growth of these cities; when commerce was heavy, as it was between 1681 and 1700 or again after 1730, they grew with amazing speed, then remained almost stable during eras of commercial stagnation such as that between 1700 and 1730. Common problems, common interests, and common grievances bound the people of the uplands together.

This unity was not without its dangers. By mid-eighteenth century the Old West stood apart as a distinct section, differing in ethnic composition, agricultural methods, and social attitudes from the Tidewater and coastal lowlands. Its democratic, poverty-stricken small farmers had little in common with the aristocratic plantation owners or merchant capitalists of the seaboard, yet the two were bound together by artificial boundary lines in each of the colonies. Neither could understand the other. Westerners looked on easterners as money-mad tyrants selfishly engaged in accumulating fortunes or aping English society while others performed the arduous task of subduing the wilderness. Easterners looked on westerners as illiterate, ungodly savages who were poorly equipped by their over simplified life to handle complex problems of government. Unfortunately for the frontiersmen, the planters and merchants were in a position to carry their prejudices into practice. They dominated the colonial legislatures at the beginning of the eighteenth century, and as the West was settled perpetuated their control, either by erecting large western counties with the same number of representatives as the smaller eastern units, or by assigning interior counties fewer delegates than those along the coast. This thoroughly enraged the westerners. Not only were they deprived of an equal voice in government but their counties were so large that local govenment broke down, inadequate defense was provided, and county courts were so distant that few could seek the protection of the law. Their discontent, and eastern misunderstanding, gave birth to the first sectional conflicts in the history of the frontier.

In most of the northern colonies and Virginia frontier dissatisfaction seethed below the surface until after the Revolution, although in New York some tenant farmers rebelled against their landlords during the 1750s and in New Jersey a proprietary attempt to eject squatters aroused rioters who raged through the back country between 1745 and 1754. The outburst in Pennsylvania was more serious. There the westerners, already rankled by the fact that their five interior counties were allowed only ten representatives in the legislature to twenty-six from the three eastern districts, were goaded to rebellion by Indian attacks between 1754 and 1763. For nine years the natives ravaged the back country while pioneers pleaded for aid from the Quaker assembly, only to be turned away with pacific platitudes or the galling assurance that their own quarrelsome actions caused all the trouble. Rumors, natural in such a tense atmosphere, flew through the West: the easterners refused to fight because war would interfere with their fur trade; a group of peaceful Moravian Indians in Northampton County was harboring raiding parties; another village of Christianized Conestoga Indians in Lancaster County was supplying the enemy with guns. The governor finally consented to move the Moravian Indians to Philadelphia, but before he could protect the Conestoga village the frontiersmen acted. A mob from Paxton and Donegal descended on the harmless Indians on December 13, 1763, killing six and wounding several more, then attacked again on December 27 after the tribe had been hurriedly removed to Lancaster by the government.

The horrified assembly immediately issued warrants for the arrest of the "Paxton Boys," ordering them brought east to Philadelphia to stand trial for the cold-blooded murder of friendly Indians. This was the signal for a new outbreak. The frontiersmen, knowing they could never expect justice from an eastern court, formed a ragged army which marched toward Philadelphia. A government force was sent against them, but fortunately the persuasive Benjamin Franklin, who met the rebels first at Germantown, convinced them to substitute a moving "Declaration and Remonstrance" for battle. This heartrending protest won them only a few minor concessions in the form of greater representation, and western antagonism continued into the Revolutionary Era.

Conditions in the back country were particularly bad. In North Carolina the sectional struggle took its most violent form. Tidewater planters not only controlled the legislature but dominated western local government through the governor who appointed both the law-making justices of county courts and the law-enforcing sheriffs. These ruling bodies levied a whole portfolio of taxes that discriminated against those in the lower income brackets; the crown, Parliament, the North Carolina legislature, county courts, and parish vestries all tried, at least, to take their share of whatever profits the backwoods family could earn. Most burdensome of all were the poll taxes which fell equally on rich and poor. This was bad enough, but corrupt tax collectors made life intolerable. Usually they called when least expected, demanded payment in specie, and when this was not forthcoming hurried off to sell the farm for tax arrears to one of their speculating friends. Sometimes the farmer was able to borrow money from neighbors to beat the collector in a race to the county seat; more often he could only recover his property in the law courts where fees from lawyers, clerks, and judges left him penniless. It was no secret in North Carolina that wealth in the backcountry was unevenly distributed, for 10 per cent of the settlers owned 40 per cent of the property.

Pioneers who lived on the Granville estates in the northern half of the colony were especially restive; they had to pay high quitrents to the proprietor's agents. Resistance started there in 1759 when rioters who captured one of Lord Granville's collectors were jailed, then released by a mob that swept through the West until subdued by hastily summoned sheriffs from the East. Ten years of peace followed, but in 1768 the frontiersmen began forming an extralegal body which they called "The Regulation," binding themselves by compact to pay no taxes until they were satisfied that the money was legally used and collected. At first the Regulators asked only to meet with proper officials to air their grievances. They were less interested in who ruled than in securing a responsive government that was free of corruption. Only when Governor William Tryon unjustly branded them as insurrectionists and called out the militia to capture their leaders did they turn from protest to rebellion. Rioting about Hillsboro grew increasingly violent until 1770 when the governor issued warrants for the arrest of the Regulators and ordered out troops to enforce them.

An attempt to serve these warrants in the spring of 1771 brought matters to a climax. Tryon, at the head of one provincial army, marched into Hillsboro without resistance, but another body of troops under General Hugh Waddell was turned back at Salisbury by a band of Regulators. When Tryon attempted to join his confederate he was met by a tattered mob of some 2000 Regulators drawn up on the banks of the Alamance River. Thinking that they could overawe the governor by this show of force, they were taken completely by surprise when the militia fired on them. This Battle of the Alamance, fought on May 16, 1771, cost each side nine men killed and a number wounded, and broke the strength of the Regulator movement, for the rioters were not rebels and dispersed rapidly before this show of force. By midsummer most of the leaders who had not been caught and executed had fled the colony; resistance was at an end.

South Carolina had a Regulator movement of its own with results almost as serious. The grievances were the same—high taxes, corrupt officials, underrepresentation in the legislature, oversized counties—plus two others: a complete lack of courts in the interior which necessitated a two-hundred-mile journey to Charleston for every legal action, and the assembly's refusal to erect any new western counties until their inhabitants agreed to support the Anglican Church. Resistance first developed in 1767 when settlers on the upper Pee Dee and Congaree rivers organized groups of vigilantes to defend their property and punish criminals, calling themselves Regulators. Their motives were as thoroughly misunderstood as in North Carolina. They were denounced as traitors, the militia was called out against them, and scattered fighting went on between the summer of 1768 and March, 1769, when the two forces met in a pitched battle on the Saluda River. Civil war was only averted when the troops were withdrawn and the legislature hastily summoned to pass a circuit court bill which provided adequate protection for the interior. With this victory the Regulators dissolved, although lack of representation rankled for many years.

The back country gained little in a sectional struggle which only intensified eastern fear of western ''radicalism,'' but the results were far reaching. So bitter was the hatred engendered that for many years the two sections remained at swords' points. This was shown during the Revolution when internal antagonism led them often to take opposite sides whatever their personal convictions; thus in Pennsylvania the West more actively supported independence when the seaboard remained cautious if not loyal to England, while in the South the back country had strong centers of loyalism because the Tidewater in general favored the patriot cause. A more important immediate result was to send a new stream of population westward as disgruntled pioneers, their hopes for reform dashed by eastern victories, turned to isolated lands beyond the mountains where they could rule themselves as they pleased. Before they could people the broad plains of the Ohio Valley, however, that region must be won by England. There the French were firmly established; only a series of imperial wars lasting over the course of a century expelled the rivals and opened the heart of the continent to Anglo-American settlers.

7

The French Barrier
1615-1763

While farmers in the English colonies toiled over the hills of the Old West, the pioneers of New France swept their frontier westward with breathtaking speed. For a century and a half their spectacular conquest of the continent went on, until the whole interior, from the Great Lakes to the Gulf of Mexico, was in their hands. Before the British could crowd through the mountain gaps to overrun the Mississippi Valley the French barrier must be pushed aside—by intrigue, Indian diplomacy, commercial conflicts, and four great wars.

France built her New World empire on the fur trade, and Samuel de Champlain was its architect. At Quebec, where he presided over a nondescript crew of traders until his death in 1635, Champlain laid down the broad principles on which French expansion rested: trade with the Huron Indians of the Georgian Bay region who could first serve as middlemen, then open the road to the tribes of the Great Lakes country. Too old to do more than plan wisely, Champlain sent out a number of reckless youths to cement the necessary forest alliances: Etienne Brulé who explored the northern shore of Lake Huron and probably ventured into Lake Superior; Jean Nicolet who followed the Ottawa River route to Georgian Bay, passed through the Straits of Mackinac to Lake Michigan and Green Bay, and ascended the Fox River to a point where the Mississippi was only three days travel away. There he found the Winnebago Indians so friendly that he was fired with ambition to extend the trade of New France to the Wisconsin country. "Champlain's Young Men" were aided in their explorations by Jesuit missionaries who first reached Quebec in 1632. During the next years hundreds of black-robed friars arrived, to master the Indians' tongues, eat their food, live in their hovels, minister to their ungrateful souls, and frequently earn the highest

113

tribute they could pay a foe: death by slow torture. By 1641 a dozen devout Jesuit fathers were laboring in as many Huron villages, while two were at Sault Ste. Marie where they said mass before a group of awestruck Algonquin. Gradually French influence reached out toward the Great Lakes country.

Expansion was brought to a rude halt in the 1640s by the sudden rise to power of the Iroquois. Supplied with guns by Dutch traders and united in a loose confederation, the five tribes that had earlier lived peacefully between Lake Champlain and the eastern tip of Lake Erie—the Mohawk, Oneida, Onondaga, Cayuga, and Seneca—overnight blossomed into one of the continent's most powerful Indian nations, ready to spread devastation among weaker neighbors who still depended on primitive bows and arrows. Iroquois wrath would naturally have been directed against their traditional enemies, the Algonquin-Huron group, but warfare was made even more serious by the realization that this was no wilderness skirmish. The Five Nations were middlemen for the Albany Dutch, the Hurons for the Quebec French. Each wanted the trade of the Great Lakes Indians. Only the actual extermination of the Hurons and their French backers would open the continent to Iroquois traders.

The Iroquois Wars began in 1642 when raiding parties sliced northward through the Huron lands to close the Ottawa River route to the interior. This accomplished, the raiders turned against their forest enemies, slaughtering Huron and Jesuit missionaries indiscriminately, until all the country east of Lake Huron was in their hands. News of their victories spread panic among the Lakes Indians. Through Michigan and the Ohio country small tribes folded their lodges and retreated westward, pursued by roving bands of Iroquois, who reached the shores of Lake Michigan in 1652. "They came like foxes," wrote a weary French chronicler, "attacked like lions, and fled like birds." Algonquin from northern Michigan, Sauk from the Saginaw Valley, Potawatomi, Ottawa, and Miami from southern Michigan and Ohio, all crowded into Wisconsin on the heels of the Huron in a headlong flight that only ended when they reached the upper Mississippi Valley lands of the powerful Sioux. Not until 1653 did the Iroquois win their objective: a trading treaty with France and with it control of the fur traffic of the entire interior. Under its terms Jesuit missionaries were allowed to establish themselves in the Five Nations in return for the Iroquois' right to trade directly with Canada. Now they could play off Montreal dealers against those of Albany to secure the best prices. Yet this victory was more apparent than real, for while the Huron were displaced as middlemen between the French and the upper Mississippi tribes, the Ottawa Indians took their place, garnering peltry from all tribes save the Sioux (their ancient enemies) in the region west of the Great Lakes.

The French traders had a new objective now: to penetrate this shield of middlemen and reestablish relations with their former customers who were dispersed beyond Lake Michigan. Fortunately, the Indians were as

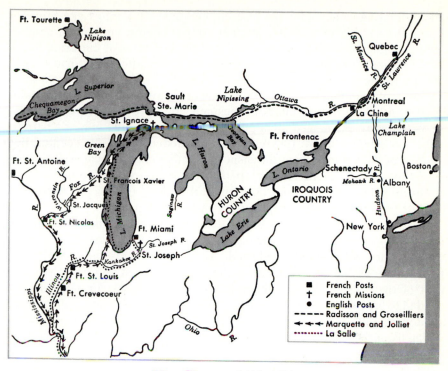

New France, 1615–1689

anxious to resume direct trade as the white men. In 1654 a party of Algonquin from Green Bay reached Three Rivers over the difficult St. Maurice River route with a few furs and such an insatiable appetite for trading goods that an adventurous *voyageur*, Médard Chouart, Sieur des Groseilliers, was dispatched to accompany them on their return journey. His report, when he reached Quebec again in 1656, was enthusiastic: Wisconsin teemed with natives who were starved for French goods and rich in furs. During the next few summers some thirty traders rushed west to tap this market, either traveling by canoe over the Ottawa River route or portaging across southern Michigan. Again New France prospered, and again expansion into new trading areas began.

The leaders in this period of activity were Groseilliers and his brother-in-law, Pierre Esprit Radisson. They made an ideal pair. Radisson was the impetuous adventurer, Groseilliers the shrewd businessman; both were experienced Indian traders and both loved the lonely life of forest and stream. "We weare Cesars," wrote Radisson on one voyage, "being nobody to contradict us." They set out in August, 1659, with seven canoe loads of friendly natives, slipping quietly away without the official observer appointed by the governor to accompany them. Quickly traversing the Ottawa River-

Lake Nipissing route, they passed from Georgian Bay into Lake Superior, skirted the southern shore of that great body of water, and on the banks of Chequamegon Bay built a sturdy trading hut. A winter of bartering for the thick northern furs of that cold country convinced them they had found a solution to the trading problem of New France. Traders could profit most, they saw, by avoiding sophisticated Huron or Ottawa middlemen and dealing directly with the primitive interior tribesmen who were so eager for European goods that they exchanged great piles of peltry for an old knife or a battered sauce pan. Hence the St. Lawrence was outmoded as a trading center, both because of its distance from the dispersed Indians, and because the Huron and Ottawa straddled the traders' paths. Better to establish a new outpost on Hudson Bay, the great northern outlet described by natives, in the very heart of the richest fur-bearing country in North America.

Radisson and Groseilliers were filled with these dreams when they returned to Quebec in the summer of 1660, leading a flotilla of sixty fur-laden canoes. They were rudely awakened. The governor, instead of welcoming them as heroes, penalized them for their unauthorized trip by confiscating most of their peltry, leaving them so embittered against France that they decided to lay their plan before English capitalists. When they finally reached London in 1665 they found both Charles II and his merchant supporters willing listeners. A vessel was sent out in 1668 with Groseilliers aboard, the winter was spent trading in Hudson Bay, and in 1669 the expedition returned triumphantly with £19,000 worth of furs which had been obtained for £650 in goods. With success assured, the king in 1670 signed a charter creating the Hudson's Bay Company under the patronage of Prince Rupert. From the visions of Radisson and Groseilliers a new commercial rival had risen to plague the northern borders of New France.

In the meantime the settlements along the St. Lawrence were being strengthened. When Louis XIV assumed the reins of French government in 1661 a new day dawned for French colonial possessions. Prodded by his principal minister, Jean Baptiste Colbert, he decided in 1663 to convert New France into a royal province, governed by a royally appointed council of seven, a governor to carry out the council's orders, and an intendant to enforce the royal will. The intendant, as personal representative of the king, was the most important of these officials. To this vital post Colbert in 1665 named an experienced administrator, Jean Talon, the "Great Intendant," whose able rule elevated New France from a struggling outpost to a thriving colony. The next ten years witnessed the most remarkable expansion in the history of the New World.

When Talon took over his post he found trade disrupted by a renewal of the Iroquois Wars. Disdaining halfhearted measures, he marched an army of a thousand men into the country of the Five Nations, crushing resistance so thoroughly that the Indians sued for peace in 1666. With the Ottawa River-Lake Nipissing route again open, a trader, Nicolas Perrot, was hurried westward to recement trading alliances; through 1668 and 1669 Perrot traveled through the Wisconsin country making treaties with the principal tribes before returning to Quebec with almost 900 Indians and so many furs that the bottom dropped out of the market. The dispersed tribes, he reported, were drifting back to their old homes—the Huron, Algonquin, and Ottawa to the upper peninsula of Michigan where they could catch whitefish, the Sauk, Potawatomi, Fox, and Winnebago about Green Bay where they could feast on wild rice, the Ouiatanon around the lower tip of Lake Michigan. All were eager to trade.

Here, Talon saw, was a golden opportunity to win the whole interior for his king. His first step was to send an expedition to take formal possession, guided by Nicolas Perrot and headed by a young nobleman newly arrived from France, Francois Daumont, Sieur de St. Lusson. Their elaborate following reached Sault Ste. Marie in June, 1671. Before chiefs and delegates from fourteen tribes, St. Lusson broke off a piece of turf, raised it aloft, and officially proclaimed his monarch the ruler of this vast domain. The elaborate pageantry, the booming muskets, the shouts of "Vive le Roi" echoing through the wilderness silence, sent the Indians back to their villages deeply impressed with the power of this master who proclaimed himself their ruler.

But Talon knew that permanent conquest must rest on trade rather than ceremony. Each year, he decreed, twenty-five licensed traders would make the journey westward to supply the Great Lakes Indians with needed goods. Jesuit missionaries, too, were urged to extend their operations into Wisconsin; between 1670 and 1672 two stations were built—St. Francois Xavier on Green Bay and St. Jacques on the Fox River—where ten earnest friars labored to win souls for their God and subjects for their sovereign. Even then Talon was not satisfied. Beyond the Wisconsin tribes, he knew, were other natives who might welcome French brandy and firearms. To open trade with them, and to explore a great interior river that the Indians described to traders, he sent out an important exploring expedition, ably commanded by two seasoned woodsmen, Father Jacques Marquette and Louis Jolliet. Starting from St. Ignace where Father Marquette had conducted a mission station since 1670, they traversed Green Bay and the Fox River, portaged to the Wisconsin River, and entered the Mississippi on June 17, 1673. Their journey down the Father of Waters was disappointing, for when they reached the mouth of the Arkansas River they learned that the Mississippi emptied into the Gulf of Mexico rather than the Pacific Ocean, and turned back. Returning by the Illinois portage to Lake Michigan, they reached Quebec early in 1674, excited by the prospect of an all-water route between the Great Lakes and the Gulf of Mexico.

Two men listened to the explorers' tales. One was Louis Count de Frontenac, who became governor of New France on Talon's recall in 1672. The other was Robert Cavelier, Sieur de La Salle, an energetic visionary whose trading expeditions had carried him into the Ohio Valley and given him a thorough knowledge of Indian ways. Why not, they reasoned, establish a chain of posts across the Lake country and down the Mississippi River, each controlled by a trader who would gather furs from neighboring tribes, and visited yearly by large vessels that would ply the Great Lakes and the interior river systems. The furs, exported through either Quebec or the town they hoped to establish at the mouth of the Mississippi, would spell prosperity to New France, while the chain of posts hemming in the English colonies would secure the heart of the continent for their sovereign. Moreover they would reap fortunes for themselves through the trading monopoly they hoped to obtain in return for this service to the crown.

The scheme was launched auspiciously in 1675 when La Salle returned from Paris with official blessings and a five year monopoly over the fur trade. Four more years were needed for preparations, including the building of a stout stone fort, Ft. Frontenac, as a basis for operations on Lake Ontario, but in August, 1679, La Salle started west in a large sailing vessel, the *Griffon,* while his lieutenant, Henry de Tonti, pushed ahead with a small party to collect furs. At Green Bay the *Griffon* turned back with a full load of peltry while La Salle and fourteen men pressed on by canoe along the shore of Lake Michigan. At the mouth of the St. Joseph River, where they paused to build a palisaded post, Ft. Miami, they were joined by Tonti and seventeen more *voyageurs.* The enlarged party used the Kankakee portage to reach the Illinois River where a second post, Ft. Crevecoeur, was constructed. There they separated. Tonti was left in charge of the fort while a missionary member of the party, Father Louis Hennepin, started north to explore the upper Mississippi and La Salle returned to Ft. Frontenac. There disquieting news awaited him: the *Griffon* had been lost with its cargo of furs, and the garrison at Ft. Crevecoeur was in revolt against Tonti. Hurrying west once more, he found the whole country ravaged by a new Iroquois invasion, which precluded further activity that year.

Not until the autumn of 1681 was the frontier sufficiently peaceful to begin the task of post-planting anew. Starting from Ft. Miami, La Salle and a little party of twenty-three Frenchmen followed the Kankakee portage to the Illinois River, then descended that stream and the Mississippi in an uneventful journey that brought them to the Gulf of Mexico on April 9, 1682. On the return journey a new fort, Ft. St. Louis, was built on an easily defended natural fortress called Starved Rock which overlooked the Illinois River. Around this La Salle gathered several thousand friendly Indians, all eager to trade. Apparently his dream of an interior empire was near realization; he had won over the Illinois Indians, built a strong post as headquarters, and developed a year-around route for the export of furs. Only a post at the mouth of the Mississippi was needed to crown his enterprise, but this proved La Salle's undoing. Realizing that such a fort could best be established from the mother country, he returned to France, then set out in February, 1684 with four ships and about 400 men. After a stormy voyage, they missed the mouth of the Mississippi, landing instead at Matagorda Bay, where La Salle was murdered by his rebellious followers. Thus ended his dream, and Frontenac's, of a trading monopoly that would enrich them, whatever its advantages to New France.

Fortunately for the course of empire, neither they nor their monarch could hold back the small merchants whose trade was the lifeblood of the colony. By 1680 at least 800 of these *coureurs de bois* roamed the wilderness, most of them operating out of a base at Michillimackinac and bartering with the Sioux on the upper Mississippi, the Assiniboin beyond Lake Superior, and the tribes above Lake Nipigon. "I have," reported the Intendant, "been unable to ascertain the exact number because everyone associated with them covers up for them." Theirs was a life of wearisome toil that eliminated all but the most hardy. For mile after mile their paddles bit the water as they squatted on a narrow canoe thwart, their legs cramped by bales of trading goods, pausing only for an occasional pipe or to gulp a meal of corn meal mush flavored with salt pork, every now and then portaging their heavy burdens over rocky trails. Life was hard, but profits were so spectacular that every effort of Colbert to stop their illegal operations failed. This was fortunate for France, for these were the unsung heroes who fastened its precarious hold on the continent's interior. By 1681 Colbert was forced to admit that too many were spread through the wilderness to be counted—or punished—and issued a royal edict promising them amnesty if they returned to Quebec where licenses would be issued to twenty-five traders. This feeble attempt at regulation was completely ignored. Such was the expansive dynamism of the *coureurs de bois* that nothing could restrain them.

One by-product of their far-ranging activity was an increased concern with the hitherto neglected Lake Superior country. There in 1684 Daniel Greysolon, Sieur Duluth, a Frenchman of good family who had come to America to recoup his fortunes, built a trading post, Ft. Tourette. His dreams of a profitable trade in that rich northern country were soon dashed, however, for in that same year the outbreak of a new Indian war forced him to retire from the West. The French-Iroquois War that began in 1684 was apparently only another of the wilderness conflicts that had occurred intermittently since the days of Champlain. Actually it was far different. Ranged behind the warriors of the Five Nations now were a group of newly awakened British officials who, unlike the Dutch merchants of old, were well aware of the connection between trade and empire. The flag, they saw, would inevitably follow the paths blazed by traders. The nation that controlled the commerce of the Mississippi Valley would eventually win the continent's interior. This realization transformed the Iroquois Wars from forest skirmishes into a century-long conflict between England, France, and Spain, with North America as the prize for the victor.

The struggle began in 1684 when an imperial-minded governor of England's New York, Thomas Dongan, goaded the Iroquois into striking westward and northward against the French and their Indian allies. Once more tribesmen in the Great Lakes country trembled before the wrath of the dread raiders; once more *voyageurs* and missionaries fled eastward for their lives.

Within two years the West was deserted, while bands of Iroquois carried the war to the gates of Montreal itself. An energetic governor, the Marquis de Denonville, who assumed control of New France in 1686, tried to rescue something from the debacle. Nicolas Perrot, the skilled forest diplomat, was hurried to Wisconsin to supervise the building of two forts—Ft. St. Antoine on Lake Pepin and Ft. St. Nicolas on the Wisconsin River—to impress the Indians with French power; the Jesuits were goaded into founding a new mission at St. Joseph; and Denonville himself led 1,500 troops in a destructive march through the Iroquois country during 1687. He killed so few Indians, however, that the infuriated warriors only struck back with new fury during the next two years. Their raids reached a climax on a stormy night in August, 1689, when 1,500 painted Indians surprised the little village of La Chine, killed almost 200 of its settlers, and carried away ninety more as captives. Before this assault even Ft. Frontenac was abandoned while Denonville concentrated his defenses in the lower St. Lawrence Valley.

Yet worse was to come. In 1689 Louis XIV's refusal to recognize the ascension of William of Orange to the English throne plunged the two nations into the first of four wars for control of North America: the War of the Palatinate, or King William's War as it was known in the colonies. Fortunately for New France, royal officials recognized the gravity of the situation and returned Frontenac as governor. That grizzled old warrior threw himself into his task with an energy that belied his seventy years, perfecting defenses, whipping an army into shape, rebuilding decayed Indian alliances, and planning an invasion of the English colonies. Throughout Quebec hope displaced despair as the "Iron Governor" won over tribe after tribe in the Northwest; on one occasion Frontenac convinced a visiting party of chiefs to cast their lot with New France by interrupting a conference with a war whoop, seizing a tomahawk, and leading the excited Indians in a furious war dance. Here were allies to carry the scalping knife against English settlements on the three fronts where the war was fought: the New England-New York borderland, the Great Lakes country, and about Hudson Bay.

Frontenac might rally Quebec's sagging spirits, but no amount of enthusiasm could compensate for his own inept leadership. Instead of sending a force to wipe out Albany where the Iroquois raiding parties that harassed Canada were armed and inspired, he decided to send three small expeditions against backwoods settlements in New England and New York. One fell on the hamlet of Schenectady on the bitterly cold night of February 9, 1690 when a force of about 200 French and Indians struck just after its guards had retired to warm beds, leaving two dummy snowmen to watch the gates. Sixty were killed and twenty-seven more carried into captivity on that raid. Other French-Indian parties devastated Salmon Falls and Fort Loyal in New England where another 100 British settlers died. From that time on attacks followed attacks with terrifying regularity along the whole back country. Their savagery was shown by an incident that occurred after an assault on Haverhill, Massachusetts. One of the captives carried away was a housewife, Hannah Dustin, who was captured by a band of two braves, three Indian women, and seven children. During the march to Quebec she managed to escape. Instead of slipping quietly away, she recalled the sizeable bounty paid by Massachusetts for scalps and, seizing a tomahawk, killed ten of her sleeping captors, sparing only a young child and a wounded woman. These border forays bred frontier legends, but they did New France little good. Instead they served only to unite the divided English colonies in a common war effort. Many a Canadian defeat over the next years stemmed from the common purpose that Frontenac's ill-advised warfare inspired.

The French were slightly more successful in the Great Lakes country where the conflict was not of arms but of Indian diplomacy. Frontenac, fearful that British competition and the cordon thrown around the Ohio Valley by Iroquois warriors would end French trade there altogether, determined to reap such profits there as he could. Every year he sent expeditions westward, ostensibly to supply posts and traders, but actually laden with trading goods including plentiful supplies of brandy. His example encouraged a burst of activity there; within two years more Canadian traders roamed the West than at any time in history. Their harvest of furs was embarrassingly rich, for just at this time the home market was shrinking; an inexplicable shift in styles now decreed a smaller brim on the ever-popular felt hat, and a texture that could be obtained only by mixing rabbit or Peruvian llama wool with the under-fur of the beaver. By 1695 no less than 3,500,000 *livres* worth of pelts clogged the warehouses of New France. The tottering trade economy could be bolstered only by checking the supply, whatever the diplomatic consequences. In 1696 a royal decree ordered that all western posts save that at Ft. St. Louis in Illinois be abandoned and that no further permits be issued for western expeditions. Vigorous protests softened this decree slightly—posts at Michillimackinac, St. Joseph, and Ft. Frontenac were retained as well as that at Ft. St. Louis—but Frenchmen were still forbidden to leave the St. Lawrence Valley. *Coureurs de bois* continued to traffic for furs as they had before, but Frontenac's greed and Louis XIV's vacillating policy had done the colony no good.

Only on a third front, about the icy shores of Hudson Bay, were French gains more enduring. There the Hudson's Bay Company operated a number of posts commanding the interior rivers: York Factory on the Hayes River, Albany on the Albany River, Moose Factory on the Moose River, and Rupert's House on the Rupert River, all established during the 1670s. Skirmishing for these posts began even before war broke out in Europe, for in 1686 a French commander, Pierre Le Moyne d'Iberville, led a large party overland from Quebec to capture Moose Factory, Rupert's House, and Albany after a brisk fight. This started a seesaw battle, which lasted more than ten years, with forts changing hands almost yearly. The climax came in 1697 when Iberville, in a single ship, routed four English vessels protecting York Factory, then captured the post. The war ended with York Factory in French hands, but with England in control of the three forts about James Bay.

King William's War came to a close in 1697 with neither side completely victorious. The indecisive results were reflected in the Treaty of Ryswick which provided that each nation must return its conquests, with the exception of York Factory which remained a French possession. Clearly this was only a truce designed to give the warring factions a breathing spell. Both nations, certain that war would soon be renewed, spent the next five years jockeying for position in America's interior. England's moves were made by traders and a few farseeing colonial governors; those of France were part of a well-conceived scheme to secure control of the heart of the continent. The effect of both was to shift the scene of conflict from the Great Lakes to the lower Mississippi Valley.

Attention was focused on that region by the action of Charleston traders. Those adventurous wanderers, extending their trails around the southern Appalachians farther westward each year, reached the Mississippi as early as 1698, to ply their trade with the Chickasaw and the smaller tribes about the mouth of the Arkansas River. That was bad enough in the eyes of New France, but even more alarming was the conduct of her own *voyageurs*. Many of these woodsmen, when deprived of a market for their peltry at Quebec by the royal order of 1696, turned instead to the English colonies. Here was a real danger! If those renegades, or *coureurs de bois* as they were derisively labeled, should lead the English back through the passes in the mountains, all the interior might fall into England's hands. The danger was brought home to New France when a *coureur de bois,* Jean Couture, a deserter who had served with La Salle and Tonti, reached the Carolinas after an eastward journey along the Tennessee River, then returned at the head of a trading party which descended the Tennessee, Ohio, and Mississippi rivers to the Arkansas River. Unless the French acted quickly British traders would overrun the whole western country! Frantic pleas from Quebec officials finally bore fruit when Louis XIV, at the close of the century, rescinded his order of 1696 and threw the interior open to French trade once more.

Voyageurs swarmed into the Great Lakes country during the summer of 1700, but wise Quebec leaders realized that trade might not be enough to hold the wavering Indians in the face of cheaper English manufactured goods. Occupation was the only answer. That year a stout warehouse, with a garrison attached, was built on strategic Mackinac Island; a year later the important post of Detroit was constructed on the narrow waterway connecting Lake Erie and Lake Huron. Friendly Indians were encouraged to settle nearby, partly to satisfy traders, partly to strengthen the feeble garrisons left in control. The occupation of the Illinois country was entrusted to missionaries. First to arrive were a band of priests from the Seminary of Foreign Missions; they reached the West under Tonti's guidance in 1699 and selected a site for their chapel at the Indian village of Cahokia. The Jesuits, resenting this intrusion of a rival order, promptly retaliated by founding their own mission station among the Kaskaskia Indians on the fertile bottom lands just south of the Kaskaskia River. Traders and farmers who drifted in during the next few years transformed Kaskaskia and Cahokia into thriving wilderness towns.

The French founded outposts in the Northwest without opposition, but when they tried to occupy the lower Mississippi Valley they became involved in a three-cornered conflict with England and Spain. Spain was naturally interested, for she considered the northern shore of the Gulf of Mexico her exclusive domain. England's ambitions were centered in an adventurer, Dr. Daniel Coxe, who had inherited an ancient royal patent to the province of Carolina which entitled him to all territory between the 31st and 36th parallels. His ambition was to found a colony at the mouth of the Mississippi, peopled by French Huguenots driven from their homeland by the revocation of the Edict of Nantes.

All three contestants moved into action in October, 1698; when a Spanish force sailed from Vera Cruz to secure both Pensacola Bay and the Mississippi outlet, Dr. Coxe left England with two shiploads of colonists, and Pierre Le Moyne d'Iberville set out from France in command of some 200 soldiers. The race was won by Iberville, who in March, 1699, built a small post on the lower Mississippi while the Spaniards were still at Pensacola Bay and Dr. Coxe's party lingered at Charles Town. Quickly he cemented his hold by building other posts: Ft. Maurepas at Biloxi Bay, Ft. Mobile at the mouth of the Tombigbee River, and a small outpost at the mouth of the Ohio River. His new colony of Louisiana doomed all hope of regulating the Great Lakes fur trade, even though selfish Montreal merchants secured a royal decree ordering the export of all upper Mississippi Valley furs over the St. Lawrence route. The hundreds of *coureurs de bois* were regulated by market conditions, not orders from their monarch, and so long as beaver pelts could be sold more profitably in New Orleans than in Montreal, to New Orleans they would be taken. This trade allowed Iberville's colony to grow slowly. It had unquestionably strengthened the imperial position of New France. When the next colonial war began, a string of French outposts hemmed in the English colonists.

The War of the Spanish Succession, or Queen Anne's War, broke out in 1702 when a vastly strengthened France challenged England's might by denying Anne's right to the throne. The American phase, which lasted until 1713, was fought on two fronts: the borderland between the Carolinas, Florida, and Louisiana; and the wilderness frontier separating New England from Canada.

England's campaigns in the southern theater were mapped by Governor James Moore of the Carolinas. Realizing that the road to Louisiana could only be opened by first defeating France's Spanish allies along the Gulf of Mexico, he sent his troops storming into Guale and Florida with such success that by the end of 1702 all that land was at his mercy except for a band of

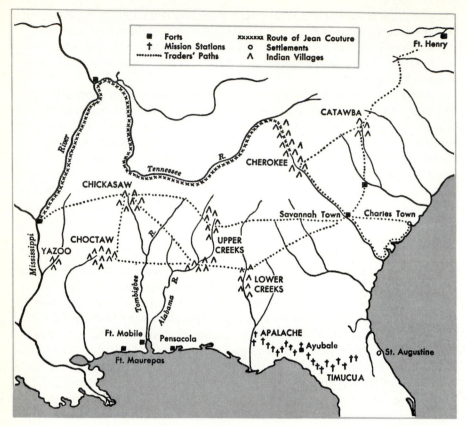

The Southern Theater of Conflict, 1697–1713

defenders besieged in the strong stone fortress outside the city of St. Augustine. A year later English troops overran Apalache, destroying the fort at Ayubale and thirteen mission stations, and assuring England's forces an unguarded path for the planned attack on Louisiana. To prepare for this decisive expedition, traders were sent westward between 1703 and 1707 with orders to win over the Indians by offering them fantastic bargains. One by one the tribes succumbed: the Alabama in 1703, the Chickasaw in 1704, the Creeks in 1705, and the Tallapoosa and Yazoo in 1706, until only the Choctaw remained loyal to France. Yet the English attack never materialized; inefficiency and the constant threat of a naval attack on Charles Town kept the Carolinians at home and deprived England of a golden opportunity to win the lower Mississippi borderland.

On the northern front fighting was confined to the New England borderland where the Iroquois, with bitter memories of their sacrifices in King William's War, declared their neutrality. The conflict began in August, 1703, when a band of Frenchmen and Indians destroyed the town of Wells, Maine, and grew in intensity during the next five years. By 1709 conditions along the frontier were so bad that the New Englanders decided to take matters into their own hands. Forming an army of 1,900 men, they sailed away for Port Royal, the powerful Acadian outpost of New France, whose several hundred defenders had no choice but surrender. This important fort, which had long served as a nest for attacks on English shipping, passed forever into the hands of Englishmen, who renamed it Annapolis. A year later a giant naval expedition against Quebec ended in failure when its inefficient leader, insisting on using his own meagre skill as a navigator in the treacherous Gulf of St. Lawrence, sacrificed ten of his ships and more than 900 of his men on the fog-hidden shoals of the lower bay.

This was the last expedition of the war, for preliminary peace terms were accepted in 1711 and the Treaty of Utrecht signed two years later. Both France and Spain were made to pay heavily for the success enjoyed by British arms throughout the world. Spain gave up Gibraltar; France surrendered Newfoundland, Acadia, and all the territory draining into Hudson Bay, and recognized the British overlordship of the Iroquois. Yet the Treaty of Utrecht, favorable as it was to the English cause, left many problems unsettled. The ownership of the interior of the continent, the division of the disputed territory about the Gulf of Mexico, and the exact limits of Acadia, or Nova Scotia as it was now called, were still to be determined. These differences made another war inevitable. That the two nations remained at peace between 1713 and 1744 was due to the cautious policy of Sir Robert Walpole, Britain's prime minister; both used the period of truce to strengthen their positions for the final struggle. On five frontiers—the

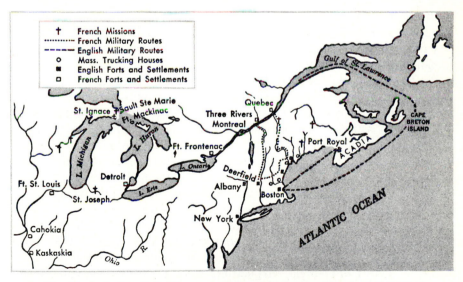

The French-English Theater of Conflict in the North, 1697–1713

lower Mississippi Valley, the Hudson Bay region, about Lake Ontario, in the Lake Champlain country, and on the borderland between Nova Scotia and New England—this jockeying for position went on, with the English gradually gaining strength .

In the southern debatable land, where Carolina trappers, Spanish missionaries, and French *voyageurs* battled for control of the interior valley between 1713 and 1744, France gained the initial advantage. Between 1717 and 1731 Louisiana prospered, nurtured by the profits of John Law's fabulous Company of the Indies which was given royal permission to develop the entire Mississippi Valley. New towns were founded—New Orleans in 1718, Fort de Chartres in 1720, St. Philippe in 1726—settlers were sent out by the thousands, and trade was fostered by building a new post, Ft. Toulouse, on the Alabama River among the Creek Indians. Impressed by this show of strength, the tribes of the southern debatable land drifted rapidly into the French sphere of influence; the Lower Creeks moved their villages from the Ocmulgee to the Chattahoochee River, the Upper Creeks, Apalache, Alabama, and Choctaw closed their towns to English traders, and the Yamassee showed their changing allegiance by attacking the Carolina back country. The British, placed upon the defensive by this gradual shift, were forced to protect themselves by throwing up a ring of fortifications around their borders: Ft. King George on the Altamaha, Fts. Palachacola and Moore on the Savannah, and Ft. Congaree on the Santee.

If English prestige was to be restored, however, something more was needed. By the middle 1720s the South Carolina officials were busily at work among the wavering tribes, showering chiefs with presents, offering trading goods at low prices, and promising generous rewards for support. Their tactics succeeded. The Lower Creeks shifted allegiance first, followed by the Upper Creeks and portions of the Chickasaw. Only the Alabama, who lived under the shadow of Ft. Toulouse, and the Yamassee, who still smarted under their defeat at the hands of the Carolinians a few years before, remained friendly to France, and the latter were virtually exterminated in a new English-Yamassee War that flamed in 1728. To make matters even worse for Louisiana, the Yazoo and Natchez Indians of the Mississippi Valley, jealous of the superior goods that British traders offered eastern tribes, joined with the Chickasaw to fall suddenly on the French settlements in 1729. This blow launched the decade-long Natchez War, with the Louisianians and their Choctaw allies ranged against the rest of the lower Mississippi Valley tribes. By the closing years of the 1730s the hard-pressed French were reduced to protecting their homes within Louisiana, with all hope of dominating the surrounding areas temporarily gone.

The Natchez War served as a protective screen behind which the English could continue their expansion in the southern debatable land. In 1732 James Edward Oglethorpe, a wealthy humanitarian, secured royal permission to found the colony of Georgia. His settlers were a sturdy crew, half enlisted from the Continent, nearly half from the worthy poor of England, and a

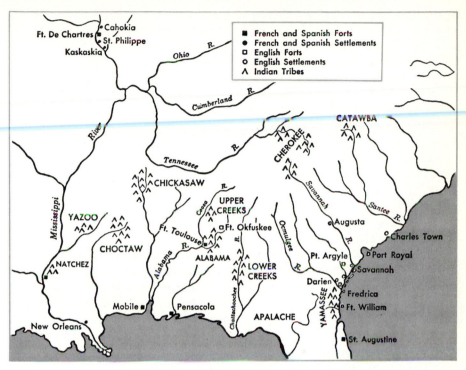

The Southern Borderland, 1713–1744

handful of refugees from British debtor prisons, all of them able to work and willing to do so. This was well, for from the day they began building their homes at Savannah, Oglethorpe devoted himself wholeheartedly to the problem of defense, realizing that Spanish or French retaliation was certain. He limited holdings to fifty acres to insure a compact village, banned Negro slaves, built a ring of forts to keep off raiding parties—Ft. Argyle on the Ogeechee, Ft. St. Andrews on Jekyl Island, and Ft. William on Cumberland Island—encouraged bands of immigrants to settle at such danger points as Darien and Fredrica, and regulated the Indian trade with an iron hand lest cheated tribesmen take to the war path. Even liquor was outlawed in the colony rather than risk its falling into Indian hands, despite the settlers' complaint that they were ravaged with disease because "Water without any Qualification was the chief Drink." By 1735 England's latest frontier outpost was firmly established, with its traders roaming the forest as far west as the Chickasaw villages from two posts established by the colony: Augusta on the middle Savannah River and Ft. Okfuskee on the Tallapoosa River.

These preparations were not in vain. When the English government, aroused by tales of Spanish cruelty to her merchant seamen, declared war on Spain in October, 1739, only the Yamassee were ready to take up arms against the Georgians; the Creeks, Cherokee, and Chickasaw were safely in the British camp, while the Choctaw were too busy defending Louisiana to take any part. With peace assured in western Georgia, Oglethorpe was free to march an army against Florida. One by one the towns of that Spanish domain capitulated during the spring of 1740, until only the stout fort at St. Augustine held out. A Spanish counterattack two years later was beaten off when the English successfully defended themselves at the gory Battle of Bloody Swamp on St. Simon Island. Georgia's victories in the War of Jenkins' Ear, as this Anglo-Spanish struggle was called, typified England's new strength on the southern borderland. With a new colony founded, Indian allegiance won, and Spanish rivals cowed, England was in a far better position to challenge French might in the 1740s than she had been a generation earlier.

The French hoped to buttress their position in the Lakes country during those years. The region was not officially in dispute—English traders were not yet ready to invade that distant country—but the officials of New France determined to use the period of peace after Queen Anne's War to prepare for a struggle that seemed inevitable. French policy was two-pronged: to offset the superiority of English trading goods by carrying their own knives, blankets, and brandy into the Indian country and to establish military posts at any point where there seemed a possibility that Anglo-American traders would break through. Both operated successfully. Each spring some hundred canoes, each manned by from five to ten men, left Montreal for the West, laden with goods that would discourage the Indians from making the long voyage to Albany. At the same time between 1715 and 1718 half a dozen new forts were scattered through the area on strategic waterways and portages, ranging from Ft. Miami on the Maumee-Wabash portage to Ft. Kaministiquia at the entrance to the Grand Portage into the Rainy Lake country.

These gains were offset when the French determined to crush the Fox Indians of the Wisconsin River valley who had long served as middlemen for the Sioux, thus opening the way to direct trade with that nation. Such a move was imperative as overtrapping lessened the beaver take in the Great Lakes region just at a time when a recovering European market drove the price of pelts to highly profitable levels. This decision made, a full-scale attack was launched in 1730 when some 400 Canadians and 1,200 friendly Indians marched through the Fox country, destroying crops and villages. Again in 1731 and 1734 French expeditions ravaged the countryside until the power of the tribe was broken. The Fox War cost Canada heavily in supplies, but its side effects were still more devastating. Tribe after tribe in the interior, alarmed at French ruthlessness, took to the warpath to avenge their brethren. Greed for profits had dealt French prestige a serious blow during those years.

On two other friction points, New France gained steadily at English expense between 1715 and 1740. One was in the vast wilderness south of Hudson Bay where Quebec traders, led by the Sieur de la Vérendrye, made a valiant effort to divert the flow of peltry southward from the Hudson's Bay Company posts to the St. Lawrence Valley. By 1740 Vérendrye's strategically located trading factories dotted the country between the Grand Portage and the Assiniboine River, and the English company was expressing alarm at the diversion of peltry eastward. Even more concerned were royal officials who saw in the T-shaped string of forts thrown across the continent by France—from the St. Lawrence to the Rocky Mountains and extending southward along the Mississippi—a device to cut Britain's possessions in two.

The situation in the region of Lake Ontario and the New England back country was even more threatening to England. Here, the bold and forceful administrator who now served as Governor General of Canada, Philippe de Rigaud Vaudreuil, skillfully dangling for alliances, set out to build a living barrier of Indians who would check British expansion. His major triumph came in 1720 when a *voyageur*, Chabert de Joncaire, secured Seneca consent for a post on the Niagara River. The alarmed English officials, realizing that Iroquois furs—and allegiance—might swing to the French, retaliated by beating down opposition from the Albany traders and establishing Ft. Oswego on the Oswego River in 1725. From that time on agents from Ft. Niagara

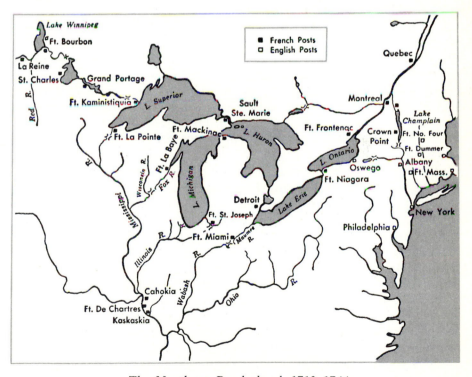

The Northern Borderland, 1713–1744

and Ft. Oswego roamed the Iroquois country, competing for peltry in every village. At this friction point the two nations were in direct commercial conflict by 1740.

Equally irritating to both was the contest for control of the Lake Champlain waterway and the New England-Nova Scotia borderland. The French, having learned the military value of Lake Champlain during the first two colonial wars, attempted to secure control of the lake in 1731 by building Ft. Crown Point at its lower end. Lethargic New York officials allowed this invasion of their territory to go on with only feeble protests, but Massachusetts, with vivid memories of Queen Anne's War fresh in mind, showed more initiative in protecting the Connecticut Valley route between the nations. Ft. Dummer and Ft. Number Four on the upper Connecticut, and Ft. Massachusetts on the Housatonic, were built to guard that approach from Canada. The struggle for domination of strategic spots was just as bitter in the country north of New England. There, too, France gained the initial advantage, building a powerful new fortress at Louisbourg on Cape Breton Island in the 1720s, then sending priests into Nova Scotia to urge the French farmers of that newly lost territory to rebel against their English overlords, and dispatching missionaries among the border Indians to win allies. This policy was particularly successful with the Abenaki tribe in the wilderness east of the Kennebec; they welcomed the Quebec Jesuits, fortified their villages to form a ring of palisaded posts around the Maine settlements, and sent out raiding parties that carried torch and scalping knife deep into Massachusetts. In vain did the English establish colony-owned trucking houses that would win back the natives through cheap goods; the Abenaki were too loyal to France to go near the trading posts. Vaudreuil's well-planned policy had built the barrier he desired, with the English advance halted at the St. George River near Kennebec and the buffer zone beyond well guarded by loyal Indian allies. New England conceded his success when it began building forts in the back country during the 1730s, thus acknowledging that it was on the defensive in that borderland.

On each of the French-English friction points tension was high by 1744; in Georgia and Maine haphazard skirmishing had begun, in the regions about Lake Superior and Lake Ontario the two nations were locked in a bitter commercial war, and in the Lake Champlain country both were occupying military routes through which attacks must come. Yet friction had not reached the point that either welcomed the war that broke out in 1744. King George's War, or the War of the Austrian Succession as it was called in Europe, began when Frederick II of Prussia upset the balance of power by seizing Silesia, then found allies in France and Spain against England and Austria. Fighting was largely confined to the European theater; only on the New England-Nova Scotia frontier was any major engagement fought in America.

There the French struck first, sending an expedition to lay siege to Annapolis during the summer of 1744. Although the attack was beaten off, the English realized that their Nova Scotian fortress would never be safe as long as the enemy controlled near-by Louisbourg. This was the objective of a force of 4,000 provincials who sailed from Massachusetts on a fleet of merchant vessels in the spring of 1745. Frenchmen watched the approach of the expedition with incredulous amazement; what could these untrained colonials hope to accomplish against a fort so impregnable that it was referred to as the Gibraltar of America? They soon found that Yankee ingenuity could offset a lack of military training. The Americans landed under the stone walls of Louisbourg on April 30, 1745, captured a French battery, and turned the defenders' own guns against them with such devastating effect that after forty-nine days the fortress surrendered.

The wartime years were also notable for a shift in Indian diplomacy on the New York frontier. In the past England's relations with the Iroquois had been shaped by the Albany Commissioners, a small group of locally elected magistrates who reflected the traders' viewpoint in their concern for profits rather than expansion. Their insistence on keeping the Five Nations neutral at the start of King George's War so irked imperial authorities that their powers were stripped away and an Indian commissioner was named to formulate the colony's policy. William Johnson, who was to dominate frontier diplomacy for the next generation, was ideally suited for that post. As a trader on the New York borderland since 1738 he had won the respect of the Iroquois through his scrupulous honesty, lavish entertainment at his Mohawk Valley home, Ft. Johnson, and his sympathetic understanding of the native point of view. Under his prodding the tribe took to the warpath during the last years of the war, although their raids did little more than inspire retaliatory French attacks on Albany and Schenectady. Johnson's influence, however, insured Iroquois support in future struggles.

The halfhearted efforts of both French and English in King George's War indicated that neither expected the results to be decisive. The Treaty of Aix-la-Chapelle which ended the conflict in 1748 proved them right; it provided simply that each nation must restore its conquests in Asia, Europe, and America. Although New Englanders grumbled when hard-won Louisbourg was returned to France, they consoled themselves with the thought that peace was only temporary and an opportunity for revenge near.

During the next six years both nations girded themselves for the last of the eighteenth-century wars, fully aware that ownership of North America and of imperial possessions scattered over half the globe would be the prize of the victor. The French gained most during this breathing period, despite the neglect of the dissolute Louis XV who preferred to lavish wealth on mistresses rather than colonies, and despite the indifference of a succession of weak Quebec governors who showed more skill in plundering the royal treasury than the lands of their enemies. Minor officials—realizing as the English did not that any Indian tribe committing itself to either antagonist expected to be protected from the other—used the period of truce to construct a chain of forts that not only won New France invaluable allies but seriously threatened England's position in America.

This building program went on at each of the friction points where frontiers clashed. On the Lake Ontario borderland Ft. Toronto, at the foot of the Toronto portage, and Ft. Présentation on the upper St. Lawrence, served as headquarters for Joncaire and other French agents who worked effectively among the Iroquois. They found the tribesmen, disgusted by English inaction, ready to listen, especially after Johnson resigned his superintendency when the colony refused to reimburse him for presents given the Indians. On the New England-Nova Scotia frontier England took the initiative by constructing a strong naval base at Halifax in 1749, and a new outpost, Ft. Lawrence, on the south side of the Missaguash River to guard the entrance to the peninsula. France responded by throwing up a strong fort, Ft. Beauséjour, on the opposite bank of that stream, and by urging the Acadians to rise against the English. In the southern debatable land English prestige also waned when the transfer of Georgia from proprietary to royal control in 1752 so absorbed colonial officials that they neglected their Indian allies. Alert Louisiana leaders seized the opportunity to make peace with the Chickasaw and to send such persuasive agents among the Cherokee and Creeks that by 1753 most of the latter were won over and the Cherokee so tempted that South Carolina built Ft. Prince George among them to prevent their defection.

Yet France, strong as it was on all these borderlands, would never have risked another conflict if war had not been necessary to keep the English from overrunning the Ohio Valley. Canadians first recognized the strategic importance of that waterway in the 1720s when the Fox Wars forced them to shift their trade routes from the Wisconsin and Illinois portages to the Maumee and Wabash rivers. The advantages of this path were obvious; not only did it shorten the distance between Montreal and the Illinois-Louisiana settlements, but won for France all territory west of the Wabash. Hence three garrisoned posts were erected to guard the portage route: Ft. Miami on the upper Maumee, and Fts. Ouiatanon and Vincennes on the Wabash, all completed before 1731. Frenchmen controlled the lower Ohio River valley from that time on.

In the meantime English traders began entering the upper Ohio Valley. They came from Pennsylvania, lured west by migrating Shawnee and Delaware Indians who in the late 1720s were pushed from their Pennsylvania hunting lands to new homes at Kittanning and Logstown about the Forks of the Ohio. Traditionally friendly to the English, these tribes welcomed merchants from Lancaster who struggled westward over the West Branch and Juniata rivers, their packs bulging with rum, guns, and ironware. By the close of the 1730s, Englishmen dominated the trade of the upper Ohio Valley, just as the French controlled the lower reaches of that stream. Between the two was a wilderness occupied by tribes nominally friendly to France: the Wyandot, Miami, and Huron. Any expansion of either trading frontier would mean a clash, particularly if the English pushed far enough westward to threaten the Maumee-Wabash portage.

King George's War gave them a chance to do so, for Britain's mighty navy so disrupted French trade that Canadian merchants were unable to secure goods needed for the Ohio Valley tribes. Here was a golden opportunity for the Pennsylvania frontiersmen. That they rose to the occasion was largely due to the skill of a robust Irish trader, George Croghan, who owned a post on the Susquehanna frontier. By the close of 1744 he was operating trading centers at Pine Creek, Logstown, and Beaver Creek on the upper Ohio; from those bases trading expeditions were sent to the Miami and Huron villages and even to the Illinois Indians of the Mississippi Valley. Other traders who followed on the heels of this bold pioneer sent their pack trains along the Great Trail into the depths of the Ohio country, or threw up rough posts at Sandusky, on the Muskingum River, and at the mouth of the Scioto. Croghan climaxed this rapid expansion of the trading frontier in 1748 when he ordered the construction of a palisaded fort at the Miami village of Pickawillany in the very heart of French territory. By the close of King George's War Pennsylvania traders reigned supreme over the wilderness from the Alleghenies to the Wabash River.

Croghan, whose vision was broad enough to see the connection between trade and empire, realized that the time was ripe to perpetuate the new wilderness alliance through formal treaties. With the able assistance of Conrad Weiser, a soft-spoken Palatine Pietist well skilled in Indian ways and languages, Croghan finally persuaded Pennsylvania's Quaker assembly that this was necessary, then lured chiefs of the Miami tribe to Lancaster where

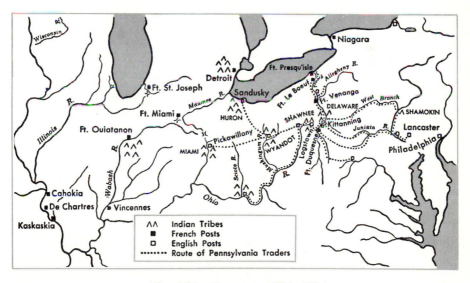

The Ohio Country, 1730–1754

in 1748 they signed a formal treaty of friendship. A few months later, in August, 1748, leaders of the Delaware, Shawnee, Iroquois, and Wyandot tribes gathered at Logstown, accepted gifts from Croghan and Weiser, and pledged perpetual allegiance to England in the Treaty of Logstown. English trade and diplomacy had driven the French from the Ohio debatable land.

With the close of King George's War Canadian officials swung into action in an attempt to regain lost ground. During the summer of 1749 a few hundred soldiers under Céloron de Blainville were sent through the Ohio country, but the inept commander did not dare attack Pickawillany with his small force and retired in disgrace after burying a number of lead plates proclaiming French ownership of the land. This initial failure was more than overcome two years later when the able Marquis Duquesne became governor of New France. By this time the Ohio Indians were growing restless under English rule, some aroused by the corrupt practices of the Pennsylvania traders, others by the failure of the colony's Quaker legislature to build a fort that would protect their villages from French attacks. Sensing this dissatisfaction, Duquesne ordered a sudden attack on Pickawillany during the summer of 1752. The invaders—a band of French traders and Ottawa Indians under Charles le Langlade—struck so suddenly that Croghan's post was taken by surprise, its defenders killed, their cabins burned, a Miami chief who had aided them killed, boiled, and eaten, and £3,000 in trading goods carried triumphantly to Detroit. Awed by this show of strength, the Miami, Huron, and most of the Shawnee deserted the English. The nation's prestige was as low at the end of 1752 as it had been high a year before.

Duquesne saw his opportunity. Why not secure the Ohio country for all time by building a chain of posts from Lake Erie to the Forks of the Ohio? This would close the West to the hated Pennsylvania traders, guard interior tribes from Iroquois attacks, and give France control of the short French Creek-Allegheny River portage route between Montreal and the Mississippi River. Duquesne acted before the snow melted in the spring of 1753. A construction party that set out from Ft. Niagara in April stopped first at the Lake Erie entrance to the portage to throw up a strong post called Ft. Presqu'Isle, then moved inland to the head of navigation on French Creek where Ft. Le Boeuf was built. Leaving several hundred men to garrison those posts, the party moved on to the junction of French Creek and the Allegheny River where Ft. Venango was begun. By this time over 400 of the original 2000 men in the work party had died from overexertion, while only 800 of the remainder were strong enough to walk. Plans to build a final fort at the Forks of the Ohio had to be postponed.

Alarm flared through the middle colonies. Particularly concerned was Virginia's vigorous Scotch governor, Robert Dinwiddie, who saw that the French move not only threatened his own trading and speculating activities but promised to deprive his colony of a vast territory claimed under its 1609 charter. In this emergency, he shouldered the burdens of empire by sending a small party under twenty-one-year-old George Washington to warn the

Frenchmen that they were on Virginia soil. Washington reached Ft. Venango late in December, 1753, and was well received by Joncaire. "The Wine, as they dosed themselves pretty plentifully with it, soon banished the Restraint," but the English accomplished nothing, for the French declared "that it was their absolute Design to take Possession of the *Ohio,* and by G— they would do it." After a similar reception at Ft. Le Boeuf Washington returned home to report that force alone would drive out the intruders.

Dinwiddie acted at once. In January, 1754, he ordered a construction crew westward to forestall the French by building an English fort at the Forks of the Ohio. The army of 150 men under Washington designated to occupy the fort did not start inland until April. At Wills Creek they met the work party, returning with the disquieting news that a large enemy force was already erecting a powerful fort, Ft. Duquesne, at the Forks. Washington, with more courage than good sense, decided to march against the French although his army was outnumbered ten to one. At Great Meadows, a treeless valley where traders pastured their pack animals, he stumbled on a small French scouting party which was decisively defeated. This foolish act placed Washington in difficulty, for if he advanced or retreated he would surely be surprised by an army from Ft. Duquesne bent on revenge. Hence he ordered his men to throw up earthworks, which they called Ft. Necessity, to wait the attack that was sure to come. There they were found by a French force on July 3, 1754, and after defending themselves valiantly in an all-day battle, accepted honorable terms of surrender. The English were driven from the Ohio country and the Seven Years' War had begun.

The next few years were dreary ones for England. General Edward Braddock, who arrived to take command with two regiments of regulars and a portfolio of very bad advice from the home government, devised a plan of campaign that courted disaster. Instead of concentrating his inadequate force in a drive northward that would cut New France in two, he split his meagre army into four parts, one to attack Ft. Duquesne, another to march on Ft. Niagara, a third to move against Ft. Crown Point, and the last to assault Ft. Beauséjour. This inept strategy brought disaster to three of the four expeditions.

He suffered the worst defeat himself. With a party of 300 axmen cutting the way, Braddock started for Ft. Duquesne in June, leading 1,400 redcoats, 450 Virginia militiamen under Washington, and fifty Indian scouts. The large force moved slowly as streams were bridged and small hills leveled for the supply wagons. Sixteen days later, when word reached the English that French reinforcements were on the way, Braddock decided to press on more rapidly with 1,200 men, leaving the artillery and supply trains to advance more slowly. On July 8, 1755, this well-equipped army with flags flying and bagpipes shrilling emerged on an open plain seven miles from its objective. There 250 Frenchmen and 600 Indians, sent from Ft. Duquesne to delay rather than stop the English awaited them. The two forces clashed at once, fighting in the open in the best European tradition of eighteenth-century

warfare. With the first burst of fire Braddock's advance column fell back
as it should, but the main body of troops failed to halt and the two surged
together in a scene of incredible confusion. The French seized the chance
to occupy a hill and ravine on either side of the British, and from this natural
cover poured a deadly fire into the struggling mass of redcoats. The British
panicked; the retreat finally ordered by the mortally wounded Braddock
turned into a rout; of the 1,900 men who started west with Braddock, only
590 returned unharmed to Ft. Cumberland.

The other English campaigns of 1755 fared little better, partly because
documents abandoned by Braddock's force described them in detail, allowing the French to know when and where each blow was to fall. The British
force sent against Ft. Niagara delayed so long that winter overtook the army
while it was still at Oswego, while delays were also responsible for the failure
of the attack on Ft. Crown Point, although the British did succeed in protecting the entrance to Lake Champlain by building two forts—Ft. Edward
and Ft. William Henry—there. Only the third expedition enjoyed any success; Ft. Beauséjour surrendered to 2,000 New England militiamen in June.
These inglorious defeats had their inevitable consequences; all along the
back country Indians, impressed by French power, flocked to the aid of
New France. Their war parties, armed at Ft. Duquesne, harried the frontiers
of Pennsylvania, Maryland, and Virginia during the winter and spring of
1756, until heartrending petitions and grisly relics sent east by the suffering
pioneers finally forced the legislatures of those colonies into action. Maryland and Virginia built almost 200 posts and blockhouses to guard their
western mountain passes during the next two years; Pennsylvania followed
the same policy after outraged public opinion forced the resignation of its
pacifistic Quaker assembly at the end of 1756. When the building program
was completed a line of forts stretched from Ft. Augusta on the northern
Susquehanna to Ft. Mayo on the Carolina frontier, with two—Fts. Bedford
and Ligonier—guarding the route to the Ohio. They brought peace to the
back country, but their construction signaled the end of British westward
expansion. The British were content to hold what they had rather than
dream of conquering the interior.

Until 1756 both nations remained officially at peace, but in May of that
year a formal declaration of war brought all Europe into the struggle, with
Frederick the Great of Prussia on the side of England, and Russia, Austria,
and Poland aligned with France. France now must use most of her military
force to combat the efficient Prussian armies; England could entrust its
continental war to Frederick the Great while concentrating its own attack
on French colonial possessions. Most of these efforts were directed toward
North America, but with remarkably little success during the next two years.

England's tribulations during this trying time were caused partly by
colonial provincialism, partly by the refusal of the thirteen colonies to forget
their internal differences in the face of a common enemy, and partly by the
complete inefficiency of the military leadership. For the latter the com-

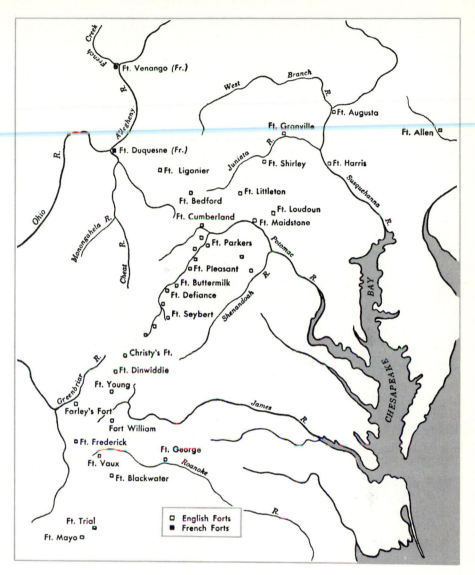

Defense of the Middle Colony Frontier, 1755–1757

mander in chief of the British forces, the Earl of Loudoun, was primarily responsible. That pompous windbag did nothing for the next two years save launch an expedition against Louisbourg that never got beyond Halifax. The general who commanded Canada's armies, the Marquis de Montcalm, capitalized on this period of English lethargy as fully as his resources allowed. Ft. Oswego fell to one of his armies in 1756; a year later he led a strong force southward along Lake Champlain, captured an English army of 2,000 men sent to meet him, and overran Ft. William Henry. Although Ft. Edward withstood his assault, French control of the lower Lake Champlain country opened the New York settlements to Indian raids from Canada. These went on through the winter of 1757-58, spreading such desolation along the Mohawk Valley that settlers scurried to the safety of Albany or Schenectady. There, as in the West, the victorious French and Indians pressed deep into the English colonies.

That New France should win these victories was not surprising. The manpower differential between the antagonists was far from favorable—1,500,000 in the English colonies to 70,000 in the French—yet all but a handful of the Americans were farmers or tradesmen, untrained in war, provincial in interest, and resentful of all authority that sought to curb private interests for the public good. The Canadian frontiersmen, on the other hand, had been trained in wilderness ways and warfare by their long experience in the fur trade, were expert guerilla fighters, and could count on the aid of Indians capable of paralyzing any section of the back country where they chose to strike. Too, they had no grandiose plans of conquest, wanting only to hold their own until peace was made in Europe, a strategy that allowed them to fight along interior lines. New France could survive so long as its heartland—the St. Lawrence Valley—resisted attack. This core area could be approached by only three routes: up the St. Lawrence from the sea, northward along the Lake Champlain-Richelieu River portageway, or from Lake Ontario and the west. All were well guarded by natural obstacles as well as French forts. British armies converging over these three avenues would be out of touch with each other, handicapped by over-thin supply lines, and subject to harassment by French-Indian armies that could shift from front to front along the interior water routes that they controlled.

Given these circumstances, the failure of New France must be traced not to inferior numbers but to inferior leadership. Its most fatal weakness was a divided command. Montcalm was a hot-tempered, supercilious, fussbudget whose concern for petty detail obscured the broad vision needed by a successful commander. As leader of the French regulars he believed that he should plot strategy. This was disputed by the Governor General of New France, Pierre-Francois de Rigaud, Marquis de Vaudreuil-Cavagnal, a resentful man, unsure of himself, vain, and insistent that his office gave him the right to plan the overall campaigns. Not only did the bickering between these two would-be dictators occupy more of their time than the direction of hostilities, but soon spread to their subordinate officers, splintering the army into hopelessly divided factions. Vaudreuil wanted to wage an offensive war stressing guerilla tactics and Indian raids; Montcalm, trained on the battlefields of Europe, had only contempt for these backwoods tactics and longed to fight traditional battles where superior strategy would win victory. When the royal court in 1758 ended their quarreling by ordering Vaudreuil to defer to Montcalm on all military matters the French fate was sealed.

It was already on the wane, for in the fall of 1757 a new British ministry, dominated by the forty-eight-year-old William Pitt, was called upon to save the tottering empire. Pitt's imaginative enthusiasm, his reckless theatricalism, his bold energy, turned defeat into victory. Prussia, he saw, could handle the war on the Continent; England must furnish money, ships, and men to carry the attack against the enemy's far-flung world possessions. Parliament, catching his enthusiasm, voted unprecedented sums; "you would as soon hear 'No' from an old maid as from the House of Commons," wrote Walpole. Volunteers flocked to the colors, ships slid from the ways, and all England bustled with preparation, confident that victory was near. Most important of all was Pitt's selection of officers for the new offensive. Brushing aside the antiquated relics elevated to important positions in army and navy by age or social position, he raised brilliant young unknowns from the ranks to positions of power. Two of these dashing young commanders, Colonel Jeffrey Amherst and General James Wolfe, won North America for England.

Yet the first campaign of the spring offensive in 1758 was a failure, largely because its leader was General James Abercromby, an older general who had supplanted Loudoun as American commander the preceding autumn. Hoping to secure the water route that must some day be used for the assault on French Canada, Abercromby headed northward from Albany at the head of 15,000 troops, with a newly built French fort on Lake Champlain, Ft. Ticonderoga, as his objective. There Montcalm, with 3,600 men prepared his defenses carefully. Electing to defend a low ridge just outside the fort, he threw up zigzag breastworks of earth and logs, reinforced with trees that had been felled to make their branches, trimmed and sharpened, comparable to a modern barbed wire entanglement. Instead of blasting this formidable barrier to pieces with his artillery, Abercromby led his closely packed redcoats in a direct frontal attack that began on the morning of July 8, 1758. Again and again brave troops hurled themselves onto the jagged timber barricade, only to melt away before the deadly fire of concealed Frenchmen. When Abercromby finally ordered a retreat he left 2,000 of England's best fighting men dead on the battlefield.

Montcalm's victory was in vain, for while he held the middle approach to Quebec the eastern and western gateways fell before the English assault. A formidable army of 12,000 men under Amherst and Wolfe captured the stronghold at Louisbourg on July 26, 1758, after battering breaches in its stout stone walls. At the same time another English force under Colonel John Bradstreet swept westward across the Mohawk Valley, built Ft. Stanwix to guard the Oneida Lake portage, and slipped northward to surprise Ft. Frontenac. When that outpost surrendered after a day's bombardment Canada was cut in two and the way opened for the conquest of the interior. This began in the fall of 1758 when 6,000 men, led by General John Forbes, cut their way slowly across Pennsylvania on the road to Ft. Duquesne. By the time they arrived the Indian allies of New France had deserted, and the handful of defenders, realizing the futility of resistance, blew up their once proud stronghold on November 24. The fall of Ft. Duquesne and its reconstruction as Ft. Pitt so influenced the interior Indians that they took over the task of driving the French from the Great Lakes country. Through the winter of 1758-59 they carried the torch and tomahawk against their former allies so effectively that within a year only Ft. La Baye, Detroit, Mackinac, and the Illinois villages remained in the hands of New France.

Little wonder, with the West won and the approaches to New France secure that England heralded the dawn of 1759 with elation. This was the year of the kill. Two expeditions were to close in on the St. Lawrence Valley, one under Wolfe striking from the sea, the other under Amherst by land over the Lake Champlain portage; while a minor force subdued Ft. Niagara. These well-laid plans were carried out with only one hitch. Niagara fell to a British army on July 25, but Amherst, moving with glacial speed, advanced no farther than Crown Point, then paused to build a massive fort, so imposing that he had apparently abandoned all hope of conquering Canada and believed the Lake Champlain route must be guarded against attack.

These less-than-exciting maneuvers were eclipsed by Wolfe's campaign against Quebec. The thirty-two-year-old commander, with a fleet carrying 18,000 men, dropped anchor on June 26, 1759, below the towering cliffs that guarded the formidable French fortress. Montcalm, with 15,000 regulars and provincials in his command, stayed safely within his stronghold while British batteries were mounted on the opposite shore of the St. Lawrence. During

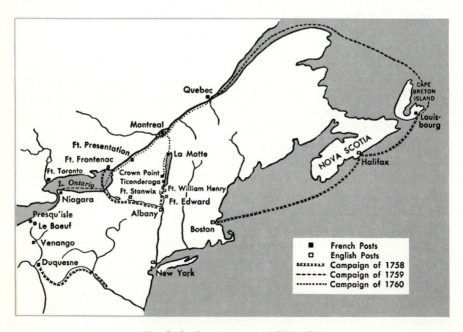

English Campaigns, 1758–1760

the summer cannon pounded the city to rubble, while American rangers roamed the countryside ravaging and pillaging in the hope of forcing Montcalm into the open to defend his people. In all 1,400 homes and manor houses went up in flames that year. Wolfe, failing to capitalize on his naval control of the St. Lawrence by moving up the river for an attack, spent the entire summer probing Quebec's defenses, with no success.

By the end of August, with winter at hand, he decided on a bold stratagem. On the night of September 12, he ordered his ships below the town to begin a heavy bombardment, then, with thirty boat loads of picked troops, started quietly up the river. Slipping past the sleepy French sentries, they landed at a small bay, Anse au Foulon, two miles above Quebec, where a path led upward through a rocky ravine. The twenty-four volunteers who ascended surprised the sentries at the top into surrendering without a shot. Sunrise found 4,500 British redcoats drawn up on the Plains of Abraham. Montcalm, so caught in panic that he did not wait the arrival of 3,000 regulars on their way from a nearby town, rushed into battle with 4,500 men, only half the force he had available. His provincials were ill-equipped for this type of open fighting; undisciplined and untrained in European military tactics, they fired too soon, broke ranks to reload, and lost the shock effect of volleys fired at lethal range. The British regulars, in contrast, held their fire until the enemy was within sixty yards, then fired by platoons. The French lines crumbled before this withering rain of death. Those still standing broke and ran, the British in pursuit. Both Wolfe and Montcalm laid down their lives in that epic battle, but Wolfe's sacrifice was not in vain. Four days later the Union Jack floated over the supposedly impregnable French citadel. A year later Montreal surrendered to three giant armies that moved in from the south, east, and west. The articles of capitulation signed on September 8, 1760, gave England Canada and all its dependencies.

Although the Seven Years' War was over in America, fighting continued in the rest of the world, with British armies sweeping all before them. Spain, in a futile effort to check the English juggernaut, entered the struggle in 1761, but this only gave England more territory to conquer. One by one the West Indian islands of that proud colonial power fell before the triumphant victors, until finally Cuba passed from Spanish hands in August, 1762. Two months later the Philippines surrendered, just as England's continental ally, Frederick the Great, trounced the last of his foes in Europe.

The Treaty of Paris, signed in 1763, reflected these triumphs. France ceded all territory east of the Mississippi excepting two tiny islands in the St. Lawrence Bay and the city of New Orleans, which was retained when gullible English ministers accepted a boundary drawn down the Iberville River rather than the main channel of the Mississippi. Spain gave up the Floridas in exchange for conquered Cuba and received from France, as an award for an immediate peace, the vast Louisiana Territory lying west of the Mississippi. The Seven Years' War drove the French from North America and opened the great valley of the Mississippi to eager Anglo-American frontiersmen.

British Western Policy
1763-1776

England's triumphs in the Seven Years' War brought that nation face to face with a problem of unprecedented difficulty. What should be done with the western territories taken from France and Spain? Should they be opened to settlers or held for traders? Should they be governed by the crown or by the colonies? Should they be reserved for Indians or carved into new provinces? The blundering attempts of successive British ministries to answer these questions kept the West in a turmoil between the Treaty of Paris and the outbreak of the American Revolution.

The occupation of the western country began four days after Montreal fell when Major Robert Rogers was dispatched with some 200 Royal Rangers to force the interior French forts to surrender. As the English moved west along the shore of Lake Erie Indians hailed them as saviors, knowing that their coming foretold a day when trading goods would replenish stores exhausted by seven years of war. Rogers wisely encouraged this belief, promising that "all the Rivers would flow with Rum—that Presents from the Great King were to be unlimited—that all sorts of Goods were to be in the Utmost Plenty and so cheap." As overjoyed Indians hastened to make peace with the advancing Englishmen, the French saw that resistance was useless, for without tribal aid their cause was lost. Many slipped down the Mississippi to New Orleans, leaving only a skeleton force to surrender Detroit to Rogers' Rangers in November, 1760. During the following summer the forts at Mackinac, St. Joseph, and La Baye were occupied and rebuilt, the latter as Ft. Edward Augustus. By the end of 1761 British arms were planted through the West, except in the Illinois country which was not molested until after the Treaty of Paris.

Traders and landseekers followed close on the heels of the army. From Montreal and Albany and Lancaster they came, their pack trains and canoes heavily laden with trading goods, to swarm over the Michigan and Wisconsin country during the summers of 1760 and 1761. Some of them represented established Albany or Montreal firms, but more were dissolute wretches who took advantage of the ease with which licenses could be obtained— anyone could become a trader by paying a small fee to a colonial governor— to cheat and debauch the Indians. "The most worthless and abandoned fellows in the Provinces," they were called, "being proficients in all sorts of vice and debauchery." They left in their wake a trail of Indian dissatisfaction, which grew so intense by the fall of 1761, that Sir William Johnson was hurried to Detroit to quiet thirteen northwestern tribes threatening warfare. Homeseekers caused just as much trouble as they streamed west along the road cut by Forbes' army to the region about Ft. Pitt. By October, 1761, the neighboring tribes were so resentful of their encroachment that the commander, Colonel Henry Bouquet, issued a proclamation forbidding all settlement west of the mountains. Yet this was clearly a temporary expedient. On the shoulders of the home government fell the formidable task of developing a permanent policy for the trans-Appalachian regions.

Clashing interests, in England and America, made this difficult. Ministers, with no precedents to build upon, must devise a system that would satisfy zealous provincials, greedy traders, land-hungry speculators, English merchants, rabid imperialists, sentimental humanitarians, and individualistic pioneers. They had to weigh the claims of colonies whose boundaries extended to the Mississippi against the crown's own rights in the interior. They had to reconcile powerful interests that believed the West should be administered from England with equally outspoken provincials who wanted the colonies to control the trans-Appalachian country. Most discouraging of all was the fact that any western policy would certainly be opposed by one or the other of the two most powerful pressure groups in the eighteenth century—the fur traders and land speculators—for any system that would satisfy one was bound to arouse the ire of the other.

The traders wanted the West to become a permanent Indian reservation. They were supported by mercantile thinkers who insisted that colonies were valuable only for the agricultural raw materials that they supplied the mother country, and by humanitarians with the natives' interests at heart. These groups, and particularly the traders, were in a position to bring strong pressure on the government. Many of the woodsmen who roamed the American forest acted as agents for frontier firms which secured their goods from large merchant houses in Montreal or Philadelphia. These, in turn, purchased supplies from English companies—Robert Hunter Company, Watson and Rashleigh Company, Dyer, Allen and Company—which were influential in both Parliament and the court. Moreover the large number of Scotch traders who settled in Montreal immediately after the English conquest enlisted the solid support of the Scottish parliamentary delegation so completely that any ministry attacking trade risked its opposition.

Even more influential were the land speculators who demanded that the West should be opened to settlers. They argued that the principal value of colonies lay in their ability to consume manufactured goods produced by the mother country. Expansion would encourage this, both by building up a large interior population and by checking local manufacturing which might develop if the Americans were confined to the seaboard provinces. These plausible rationalizations, however, concealed the speculators' real ambition: to expand their own fortunes rather than the empire. They realized that westward expansion, checked for almost a decade by war, would be resumed with peace; fabulous fortunes waited those fortunate enough to engross the interior lands before settlers reached there. These beliefs sent speculative fever surging to new heights during the years between the Seven Years' War and the Revolution. Land was the magic lodestone to wealth, the panacea for all misfortune, the one word inevitably capitalized in all correspondence of the day. In England and in America humble commoners, merchant princes, and cabinet ministers scrambled to share the riches sure to be made; the people of all the empire, wrote George Croghan after a visit to London, were "land crazy."

Excitement was greatest in Pennsylvania and Virginia. In the former colony speculation was encouraged by the capital surpluses accumulating in the chests of thrifty Quaker and Jewish merchants and by the westward flow of migrating Scotch-Irish and Germans; prospective land jobbers received an exaggerated impression of the demand for interior lands. In the latter, poverty rather than wealth was responsible. When war and declining tobacco prices fastened a prolonged depression on the Tidewater during the 1760s, planters turned their eyes westward, hoping to restore their dwindling fortunes by speculation. In both colonies speculators were encouraged by the colonial governments; Virginia claimed much of the West under its 1609 charter, and Pennsylvania, with no such claims, was anxious to see the interior divided into new colonies by the crown. Yet jobbers realized that royal approval, as well as provincial support, was needed for any extensive grant. This could be obtained only by direct pressure on England's governing officials. For a dozen years speculators' agents swarmed over London, writing pamphlets, buttonholing ministers, and offering generous blocks of stock to governmental leaders in return for support. Bold indeed was the minister who dared defy them.

Several land-jobbing concerns were in existence by 1762 when the government began formulating its western policy, some of them dating back to the years before the Seven Years' War. First on the scene was the Ohio Company, formed by several prominent Virginians in 1747 as a trading and speculating enterprise. Its petition for a grant in the West reached the Board of Trade just as that royal bureau was seeking a means of strengthening England's position in trans-Appalachia. Hence in May, 1748, the company was given 200,000 acres in the area bounded by the Ohio and Great Kanawha rivers and the Allegheny Mountains, with the provision that 300,000 more would be granted if one hundred families were settled within seven years. Although all efforts to secure immigrants failed, the Ohio Company engaged in extensive trading activities under the direction of a skilled woodsman, Christopher Gist, who established a storehouse at Wills Creek, laid out a crude trail to Redstone Creek, and explored much of the region. In 1752 the company petitioned for a revision of its charter, asking that it be given seven more years to plant 300 settlers in the West, but an expected German migration failed to materialize and others hesitated to move to the frontier while war threatened between France and England.

The failure of the Ohio Company was due partly to Virginia's opposition; the Old Dominion never ceased insisting that the Board of Trade had no right to grant lands given the colony by the charter of 1609. Further crown raids on this territory, colonial officials believed, could be forestalled only if Virginia granted away its own lands. One man who felt this way, John Robinson, speaker of the House of Burgesses, gathered Colonel John Lewis, Dr. Thomas Walker, and other influential citizens together as the Loyal Land Company and obtained 800,000 acres of western territory from Virginia in July, 1748. Walker was sent to locate the lands, but although he discovered Cumberland Gap through the mountains he failed to locate the fertile Kentucky bluegrass region, and the company decided to lay out its grant in the Clinch and Holston valleys. By 1754 almost 200 families were settled there. Robinson also helped organize a second Virginia concern, the Greenbrier

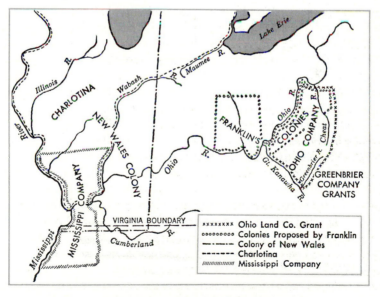

Land Speculation, 1748–1763

Company, which obtained a tract along the Greenbrier River from the colony in 1751.

Pennsylvania speculators were equally interested in the West during the 1750s. Benjamin Franklin was most active; in 1756 he petitioned the crown to create two new colonies along the upper Ohio in an area claimed by Virginia. More visionary was the plan of a Philadelphia merchant, Samuel Hazard, who sought permission to plant several thousand settlers in a giant province lying north of the Tennessee River. Before the crown could act on either of these requests the Seven Years' War pushed all plans to settle the West into the background.

With peace the speculative fever swept over America once more. Both the Loyal Land Company and the Ohio Company petitioned for renewals of their grants, the latter sending an agent to London to press its claims. More important were the dozens of new companies that sprang up in England and the colonies. Many were abortive enterprises without capital or influence, but others enlisted the support of important financial and political leaders. Among the visionary schemes were the plans of a group of Scotch merchants to establish the colony of Charlotina west of the Wabash River, the ambitions of New York speculators to plant the province of New Wales on the lower Mississippi, and the efforts of a New Jersey company to convert the lands about the Forks of the Ohio into the colony of Pittsylvania. More practical was the effort of leading Virginians to capitalize on the land bounties granted soldiers in that colony's militia. Forming themselves into the Mississippi Company, with George Washington as its principal promoter, they purchased most of these small grants at a fraction of their value, then, in June, 1763, petitioned the crown for enough land at the junction of the Ohio and Mississippi rivers to satisfy the warrants. This company, in common with most of the others, kept an agent in London after 1763 to urge favorable action on its request.

It was amidst this atmosphere of conflicting demands from speculators and traders that the British government turned to the task of formulating a western policy. The principal burden fell on the shoulders of the Earl of Egremont, whose post as Secretary of State for the Southern Department gave him control of the colonies. He searched during 1762 for a satisfactory solution but before he could act a ministerial shift removed American affairs from his department and vested them in the president of the Board of Trade. The young man who held this post, the Earl of Shelburne, although inexperienced, had enough common sense to follow the advice of his more learned colleagues. Using the detailed outline already prepared by Egremont, and relying heavily on the help of Americans in London and sage advice from John Pownall, permanent secretary of the Board of Trade, Shelburne worked out a comprehensive plan which he submitted to the king on June 8, 1763.

This made no attempt to solve all American problems; such ticklish questions as the disposal of 10,000 troops then in the colonies, and the management of Indian affairs, were left for later study. Instead it sought to provide temporary protection for Indians by forbidding settlement west of a line drawn down the crest of the Appalachians—a line that veered to the east in New York and Georgia where Indians still lived and to the west in Virginia to embrace white settlers there. Although the temporary nature of this boundary was stressed, Egremont and Shelburne realized that any restriction would be resented unless excess population was drained away to the north and south. This they hoped to accomplish by erecting three new colonies: Quebec, East Florida, and West Florida. Each was to be ruled by a royally appointed governor and council until the population was large enough, or well enough versed in English ways, to warrant a representative legislature.

This report was as intelligent as could be expected from ministers who knew little of American conditions. If adopted it would probably have satisfied both traders and speculators for the time being, or at least until a better plan could be evolved. Before the cabinet acted, however, disquieting news from America ended all hope of settling the western problem. The Indians were on the warpath once more, and England must push questions of administration aside until the Mississippi Valley was reconquered.

The causes that led to Pontiac's Rebellion were many. Most of the native leaders realized that the expulsion of the French from North America placed them at England's mercy, unable longer to play one nation off against the other. Fur traders and land speculators gave them a taste of their inevitable fate. Traders, left free by indifferent authorities to operate as they pleased, cheated and plundered Indians unmercifully; speculators, disguised as hunters to evade Bouquet's proclamation, spied out their lands and told them of the thousands of white men who would soon cross the mountains. Matters were made far worse by the attitude of Lord Jeffrey Amherst who, as commander of the military establishment, controlled Indian affairs. He despised Indians as he did the beasts of the forest; "could it not be contrived," he wrote to Bouquet, "to send the Small Pox among those dissatisfied tribes?" And Bouquet replied that he would try to distribute germ-laden blankets among them, adding, "as it is a pity to expose good men against them, I wish we could make use of the Spanish method, to hunt them with English dogs . . . who would, I think, effectually extirpate or remove that vermin." Officials with these views were hardly inclined to adopt the conciliatory attitude necessary to quiet native fears. In 1762 Amherst suddenly reduced the appropriation for the Indian department 40 per cent, at the same time writing Sir William Johnson: "Nor do I think it necessary to give them any presents by way of *Bribes,* for if they do not behave properly they are to be punished." The abrupt announcement that accustomed gifts would not be distributed during the winter of 1762-63 seemed to symbolize the fate awaiting Indians in English hands.

In this mood they listened eagerly to French travelers who told them that their Great Father in France had been sleeping but now was ready to help them drive the "red-coated dogs" into the sea, and to a religious leader dubbed "The Prophet" who assured them that they had only to abandon the ways of the white men to regain the strength that would restore their lost hunting grounds. One who heard these messages was an Ottawa chief named Pontiac whose village lay only a few miles from Detroit. Whipping his followers into a warlike mood, he led them in an attack on this stoutly palisaded fort on May 7, 1763. Its defenders beat off the onslaught, but the Indians killed a number of farmers living nearby before settling down to a prolonged siege. News of the attack on Detroit spread rapidly through the forests, inspiring a massive uprising as the Indians made a last desperate bid to regain their over-mountain lands. Ft. Pitt, assaulted by Shawnee and Delawares late in May, managed to resist, but other posts were less fortunate. Mackinac succumbed on June 2 when a band of Chippewa who were playing lacrosse beneath the walls of the fort rushed into the enclosure after a ball, then turned suddenly on the defending troops. One by one the other western forts followed, until by the end of July only Detroit, Ft. Pitt, and Ft. Niagara still held out against the triumphant Indians. In two months England had lost all of the hard-won West.

Amherst struck back promptly. On June 12, 1763, he ordered two expeditions to the relief of besieged western posts. One, under Captain James Dalyell, reached Detroit with goods which allowed the defenders to hold their position; the other, led by Colonel Bouquet, defeated the Indians at the bloody Battle of Bushy Run on August 5 to lift the siege of Ft. Pitt. In October Pontiac, discouraged by these setbacks and heartbroken at the failure of the French to come to his aid, arranged a truce which allowed him to slip away to the Illinois country where he hoped to organize a new offensive. By that time, however, most of his followers had deserted him. Nearly all the western tribes accepted Sir William Johnson's invitation to a peace conference at Niagara in the early summer of 1764; and those that did not—notably the Shawnee and Delaware—were crushed by two expeditions that marched through the Ohio country in the next months, one under Bouquet which shattered Delaware resistance along the Muskingum River, the other under Colonel John Bradstreet which subdued the area below Lake Erie. Mackinac was rebuilt in September, 1764, as a powerful fortress on the south side of the straits, and the West was once more at peace.

Pontiac, however, still lurked in the Illinois country, and to General Thomas Gage, who succeeded Amherst as military commander, the time seemed ripe for an expedition to subdue that sullen chieftain and extend English authority over the neglected French villages. An earlier expedition in January, 1764, commanded by Major John Loftus went up the Mississippi River but was routed by Indians. Now the task was entrusted to the Pennsylvania trader, George Croghan, who started from Ft. Pitt in May, 1765, with a few companions and two boatloads of presents. Near the mouth of the Wabash the party was captured by Kickapoo and Moscoutin Indians and carried to the vicinity of Ft. Ouiatanon, but soon released when protests from the neighboring tribes convinced the captors of their mistake. A short distance beyond they met Pontiac, on his way to confer with Croghan; arm in arm the two returned to the fort where they smoked the calumet and arranged the final peace. "Pontiac and I are on extreme good terms," Croghan wrote, "and I am mistaken if I don't ruin his influence with his own people before I part with him." News of the treaty was hurried to Ft. Pitt, where a hundred troops set out to join Croghan for the final march to the Illinois villages. They reached Ft. de Chartres on October 9, 1765, and set up a military government to control the colorful crew of *habitants* and traders who lived in the wilderness outpost. Pontiac's Rebellion was ended.

The uprising, however, upset the plans of British ministers who were struggling to develop a satisfactory western policy. News of the Indian war reached them in August, 1763, just as a ministerial crisis drove Shelburne from the presidency of the Board of Trade. On September 28 his place was taken by the Earl of Hillsborough, a man of poor judgment and inadequate experience, who was nevertheless wise enough to see that the plan worked out by Egremont and Shelburne must be changed in one essential detail. No careful demarcation line could be run in the midst of an Indian rebellion; therefore he recommended that the western boundary for white settlers follow the Appalachian highlands, that Quebec, East Florida, and West Florida be thrown open to settlement at once, that the trade of the Indian reservation be opened to all who obtained licenses from colonial governors or the military commander, and that all private land purchases from Indians be forbidden. In this form the proclamation was issued by the king on October 7, 1763.

Ignorance and indifference, combined with grim necessity, were responsible for several grievous errors in the Proclamation of 1763. Most glaring was the poorly run boundary which left several hundred whites in Indian territory. Pious phrases ordering pioneers who had "willfully or inadvertently seated themselves" on these lands "forthwith to remove themselves from such settlements" could not ease the suffering of those unfortunates. Almost as bad was the failure to provide any civil government for French settlers about Detroit and in the Illinois country; instead they were placed under military rule without access to courts or other bulwarks against tyranny. Even more tragic was the fate of the 80,000 inhabitants of Quebec, where, the Proclamation decreed, the laws of England were to be enforced. This thoughtless edict, which extended harsh antipapal statutes to a Catholic province, deprived the people of nearly all civil and political rights and left them at the mercy of unscrupulous Englishmen who during the next decade systematically stripped them of their property.

At least three men in America saw another fundamental defect in the Proclamation of 1763. Sir William Johnson, his deputy George Croghan, and Colonel John Stuart who became Indian Superintendent for the Southern Department in 1763, realized that trade with the Indians must be carefully regulated to ward off another uprising. General Gage was impressed with their arguments, and during the winter of 1763-64 they planned with him a workable method of control. They retained the northern and southern districts, with the boundary line at the Ohio River and a superintendent over each. These were to be divided into two or three subdistricts under deputy superintendents, and into twenty-six smaller areas each embracing one tribe. A commissary, interpreter, and blacksmith were to be maintained at small posts in each tribal division. All trade was to be confined to these posts, where the commissary would set prices, supervise bartering, and protect the Indians from unscrupulous traders. This was the plan that Croghan carried to England in February, 1764, seeking royal approval. For some time he cooled his heels in statesmen's offices; "Nothing has been Don Respecting North America," he wrote in March. "The people hear Spend thire time in Nothing butt abuseing one Another and Striveing who Shall be in power with a view to Serve themselves and Thire frends, and Neglect the Publick." Finally, on July 10, 1764, the Board of Trade tentatively adopted his proposals.

The measure, which called for a tax on trading goods to support the elaborate structure, required parliamentary approval, but the Board of Trade was so confident of favorable action that it ordered the two superintendents to put the system in force at once. Stuart was anxious to act, for his southern territory was so overrun with traders that competitive bidding forced fur prices down to a point where profits could only be made by cheating the Indians. This could be remedied, he knew, only by limiting the number of merchants entering the Indian country. Hence when he called natives and colonial officials together at a Pensacola conference to explain the new ruling he not only suggested that commissaries regulate trade in each village but asked that governors grant licenses only to a few selected traders. Although the Indians hailed the plan with rejoicing, colonial authorities remained unmoved, knowing that traders' bribes and profits from license fees were two of their principal sources of income. The governors of Georgia and South Carolina flatly refused to limit the number of permits, while the governor of Virginia insisted that he had never heard of the Proclamation of 1763! All closed their courts to Stuart when he tried to punish offenders. With this the whole system broke down, leaving southern trade as chaotic as before.

Conditions in the Northwest were no better. Sir William Johnson ruled that all trade must be conducted at Detroit or Mackinac—Ft. Edward Augustus was never rebuilt after Pontiac's Rebellion—and forced all traders to post bonds that would be forfeited if they operated elsewhere. The results were disastrous. The Indians, long accustomed to regular visits from French traders, refused to make the trek from Wisconsin or Ohio to Detroit and Mackinac; honest traders who posted bonds and took out licenses waited in vain for natives who never came. Instead trade passed into the hands of two other groups: unlicensed traders from Montreal and Albany who slipped quietly into the wilderness to barter with the Indians, and illegal French *voyageurs* who swarmed over the northwest from the Spanish posts of St. Genevieve and, after 1765, St. Louis. Both sent their furs south to New Orleans and obtained trading goods from that port. By the close of 1766 the commandants at Detroit and Mackinac were complaining that the Plan of 1764 had diverted the trade of all the Northwest from England to Spain and demanding the right to send traders to the Indians once more. This was done during 1767 by the Mackinac commander, who paid for his folly with a court martial, but Johnson was finally convinced. That fall the region north of Lake Superior and the Ottawa River was opened to all licensed merchants; through the rest of the Northwest illegal traders gradually usurped most of the peltry traffic.

Only in the Illinois country did the Plan of 1764 operate with any success. The riches concealed in that neglected region were first realized by George Croghan, who returned from his western journey in 1765 fully convinced that a fortune waited the firm that secured the right to supply the Illinois Indians, *habitants*, and garrisons with supplies. With this in mind he sought out friends in the prominent Philadelphia company of Baynton, Wharton & Morgan, and, with a quarter of the profits as his own reward, helped secure them a monopoly over the trade. Thus was launched the "Grand Illinois Venture," the most elaborate trading scheme in colonial America's history. All through the summer of 1766 pack trains plodded between Philadelphia and the Ohio, fighting off hostile settlers who objected to the sale of guns and scalping knives to the Indians, while at Ft. Pitt a crew of carpenters built boat after boat to carry goods westward. In the autumn a fleet of sixty-five barges manned by 350 boatmen set out, bound for stores that one of the partners, George Morgan, had built at Vincennes, Kaskaskia, Cahokia, and Ft. de Chartres. When the vessels reached their destination without mishap the Illinois venture seemed launched on the road to success.

Almost from the first, however, the scheme was destined to failure. Its magnitude was a drawback; not even the wealthy firm of Baynton, Wharton & Morgan could stand the financial drain necessary before such a giant enterprise paid profits. To make matters worse, the expected trade did not develop. A rival concern secured the contract to supply the garrison when Morgan refused to match its bribe, the French *habitants* preferred to buy from their own countrymen across the Mississippi, and hoped-for orders from the Indian commissary failed to materialize when General Gage in 1768 forbade further presents to the tribes. Most serious of all was the failure of the fur trade to show any profit. This was due partly to the extermination of fur-bearing animals in that hunted-over region, but more to the Indians' refusal to come to Morgan's stores when they were offered equally good prices by French traders from St. Louis and St. Genevieve. By the end of 1768 the Grand Illinois Venture was an admitted failure, and the firm of Baynton, Wharton & Morgan trembled on the verge of bankruptcy.

The collapse of this trading structure demonstrated the failure of the Plan of 1764. The need of reform was brought home to the British government by cold figures: peltry exports declined from £28,067 in 1764 to £18,923 in 1768. Officials at home and abroad conjured up schemes to frustrate the French *voyageurs* who robbed England of her wealth: to build forts at the mouth of the Ohio and Illinois rivers to turn back their canoes and a canal along the Iberville River to give English traders a direct outlet to the Gulf. Johnson, on the other hand, insisted that his plan could never be properly tested until new posts were established at La Baye, Sault Ste. Marie, Sandusky, St. Joseph, Ouiatanon, and the Maumee River. He was answered by government agents who held that the cost of the system would then exceed its profits. These arguments gained strength after February, 1767, when a 25 per cent reduction in the English land tax made colonial economy imperative. Why, members of Parliament demanded, should they be taxed for the benefit of distant Indians who paid back kindnesses with tomahawk and scalping knife? A less expensive establishment was needed.

Dissatisfaction with the Plan of 1764 was only one factor underlying the demand for a revision of England's western policy. Even more insistent on reform were the land speculators. These avaricious individuals were not discouraged by the Proclamation of 1763. George Washington summed up their views when he wrote: "I can never look upon that proclamation in any other light . . . than as a temporary expedient to quiet the minds of Indians. . . . Any person, therefore, who neglects the present opportunity of hunting out good lands, and in some measure marking and distinguishing them for his own (in order to keep others from settling them), will never regain it." In this mood, wealthy easterners listened eagerly to traders and hunters who returned from the West with tales of fertile lowlands in Kentucky and Ohio, of grassy plains in Illinois, of level timber lands about the Great Lakes—all waiting the magic touch of man to become prosperous farming communities. Fortune would surely smile on the landowner who was there when the teeming coastal settlers burst through the mountains! All along the seaboard influential colonists plotted means of engrossing western lands: George Washington kept a regular agent in the upper Ohio country staking out claims, George Croghan accumulated several hundred thousand acres about Ft. Pitt, Richard Henderson of North Carolina employed Daniel Boone to hunt out the choice Kentucky regions on his hunting trips, and hundreds of others scrambled to absorb the best regions before the Proclamation Line was moved west.

More important were the speculating companies that blossomed by the score between 1763 and 1767. Most of them were too small to influence the British government, but three made their weight felt. One was formed by General Phineas Lyman of Connecticut who in 1766 gathered some of the officers who had served together during the Seven Years' War into an organization known as the Military Associates. They petitioned the crown for a grant at the mouth of the Ohio. Another was originated by George Croghan, who saw that losses suffered by traders at the outbreak of Pontiac's Rebellion might be put to profitable use. During 1764 and 1765 he brought these

"Suffering Traders"—who included the wealthy Philadelphia firms of Baynton, Wharton & Morgan, and Simon, Trent, Levy & Franks—together into a compact organization, secured the blessing of Sir William Johnson and General Gage, and in March, 1766, launched the Illinois Company with the avowed purpose of securing 1,200,000 acres of land along the Mississippi as compensation for their losses. Benjamin Franklin was soon added to press its claims in England.

The third company formed between 1763 and 1767, the Indiana Company, illustrated the careful planning of the speculators. Its members were the same "Suffering Traders" who made up the Illinois Company: George Croghan, Joseph Galloway of Pennsylvania, Governor William Franklin of New Jersey, Benjamin Franklin, and the Philadelphia firms of Baynton, Wharton & Morgan, and Simon, Trent, Levy & Franks. Its objectives, however, were different. Instead of seeking a grant in the distant Mississippi Valley, the Indiana Company petitioned for a tract lying just west of the Proclamation Line between the Monongahela, Little Kanawha, and Ohio rivers. The astute jobbers who worked with Croghan were thus assured lands whatever the government's decision; if officials agreed to shift the Proclamation Line westward the Indiana Company was on hand with its claims, if interior colonies were deemed wiser the Illinois Company could press for recognition. Both clamored constantly for a revision in western policy that would open the trans-Appalachian country to settlers.

Pressure from greedy speculators, dissatisfied traders, economy-minded parliamentarians, and idealistic Indian agents was so great by 1767 that the British government turned at last to revising its frontier policy. Underlying this decision were forces that were to culminate in the clash between colonies and mother country a few years hence: colonial unrest requiring the transfer of troops from the interior to the east, political instability in England, and the necessity of financial retrenchment in a weakening economy. Once more the task of formulating a satisfactory system fell to the Earl of Shelburne who became Secretary of State for the Southern Department in a new ministry formed by William Pitt in July, 1766. His solution, embodied in a report that he laid before the cabinet on September 11, 1767, showed how completely he had succumbed to the wiles of the land speculators. He proposed to abolish the whole Indian department, return control over trade to the colonies, withdraw all troops from the West except for small garrisons at Niagara, Ft. Pitt, Ft. de Chartres, and Natchez, build a new post on the Iberville River, and throw the whole Mississippi Valley open to settlement. Shelburne suggested three interior colonies: at Detroit, in Illinois, and on the upper Ohio,—two of them, strangely enough, on lands claimed by the Illinois and Indiana companies! Fortunately this scheme was never adopted, for it would have bred a new Indian war more serious than Pontiac's Rebellion. Before it could be acted upon a ministerial shake-up deprived Shelburne of his control over American affairs. These were centered in a new office, Secretary of State for the Colonies, which was assumed by Lord

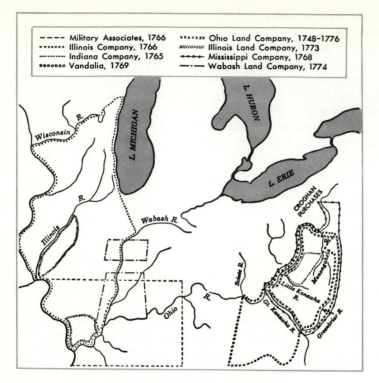

– – – – Military Associates, 1766	✗✗✗✗✗✗ Ohio Land Company, 1748–1776
• • • • • • Illinois Company, 1766	∽∽∽∽∽ Illinois Land Company, 1773
········· Indiana Company, 1765	+++++ Mississippi Company, 1768
●●●●●● Vandalia, 1769	—·—·— Wabash Land Company, 1774

Land Speculation, 1763–1776

Hillsborough in January, 1768. Once more, as in 1763, policies developed by Shelburne were left to Hillsborough for application.

The new minister immediately recognized the glaring weakness of the proposals. His own recommendations, adopted by the cabinet in March, 1768, contained the first workable plan for the West yet devised. The Indian superintendents were retained, but with powers restricted to imperial functions: land purchases from the Indians, readjustments of the boundary line, and settling diplomatic questions. Local matters, such as the fur trade, were left in the hands of the colonies. This made western posts unnecessary and all were ordered abandoned except those at Detroit, Mackinac, and Niagara which were needed for protection or to offset French intrigue. Instead of setting up three western colonies, Hillsborough attempted to satisfy expansionists by ordering the Proclamation Line shifted westward. This pleased the fur traders, as well as assuring English merchants the interior trade which might have flowed south to New Orleans.

General Gage accepted the new regulations without comment and immediately began withdrawing the western garrisons; within a year only Niagara, Detroit, Mackinac, and Fort de Chartres remained, and in 1772 the latter was evacuated as a costly luxury that had outlived its usefulness. With

Ft. de Chartres abandoned, Ft. Pitt was no longer necessary; its principal function had been to guard the supply lines between the coast and the Illinois country. In November, 1772, troops were withdrawn and the fort allowed to fall into ruins. At the same time the Indian superintendents dismantled their elaborate structure of commissaries, blacksmiths, and interpreters. The traders were delighted. Once more they swept into the West to establish their posts through the northern country as far as Lake Winnepeg and the Sioux lands beyond the Mississippi; in 1769 seventy-seven licenses were granted to small companies and the number steadily increased during the next years. Peltry again moved toward Montreal rather than New Orleans, but the change was not without its disadvantages, for Indians were soon grumbling their dissatisfaction at the conduct of the unregulated traders.

In the meantime orders to shift the Proclamation Line westward reached America. Both Stuart and Johnson welcomed the assignment. Stuart especially recognized the injustice of the older line; since 1765 he had sounded out the Creeks, Cherokee, and Chickasaw on a more acceptable boundary. By the close of 1767 he and the Indians agreed on a line running from Tryon Mountain in northern South Carolina across Georgia and around the coast of the Floridas to the Iberville River. The Creeks, who gained the portion of Georgia between the Ogeechee River and the original Proclamation Line, readily confirmed these earlier treaties at a conference in Pensacola in November, 1768. Although Stuart was unable to negotiate with the Choctaw and Chickasaw because of a Creek-Choctaw war then in progress, these tribes had agreed to a preliminary treaty in 1765, and for all practical purposes the boundary extended from North Carolina to the western limits of English territory.

These arrangements were made without difficulty because speculators had no interest in the Georgia and Carolina back country, but when Stuart attempted to extend the line northward across Virginia his troubles began. Dr. Thomas Walker and Colonel Andrew Lewis, who dominated the Loyal Land Company and the Greenbrier Company, were the principal architects of the colony's obstructionist tactics, for they knew that any properly negotiated treaty between Stuart and the Cherokee would place their lands beyond the white settlements. Under this prodding Virginia refused to recognize Stuart's authority to negotiate until royal orders arrived during the spring of 1768, then named Walker and Lewis to serve as the colony's representatives at the conferences. The superintendent recognized the folly of drawing up a treaty with these worthies present, especially as both openly declared their intention of pushing the demarcation line westward to the Tennessee River. Hence instead of struggling with two such uncompromising delegates he neglected Virginia entirely when he assembled the Cherokee at the Indian village of Hard Labor on October 14 to draft the Treaty of Hard Labor. This extended the boundary northward from Tryon Mountain to Chiswell's Mine, then straight to the mouth of the Great Kanawha. Probably Stuart hoped that this line, which gave Virginia more territory than one originally plotted along the Great Kanawha, would so please the colony's officials that they would overlook his breach of diplomatic etiquette.

Sir William Johnson's task was to extend the boundary northward from the mouth of the Great Kanawha River across Pennsylvania to the Indian village of Owege in southern New York, leaving for subsequent negotiations the troublesome question of demarcation in the Iroquois country. To arrange this, he called a conference of most of the northern tribes at Ft. Stanwix in the autumn of 1768. This was the signal for speculators all along the colonial front to spring into action. In Virginia their pressure forced the appointment of Dr. Thomas Walker as the colony's official delegate to the meeting; he set out for Ft. Stanwix pledged to open as much of Kentucky as possible. In Pennsylvania officials impressed their commissioners with the importance of securing the country between the Susquehanna and West Branch rivers. In New York the Indiana Company set to work with a will. Two of its most influential members, Samuel Wharton and William Trent, spent the summer securing Johnson's promise to press their company's claims for the grant on the upper Ohio, then traveled through the Iroquois country distributing gifts lavishly to win native good will. The stage was set for a battle between rival speculating groups, with Indians the innocent sufferers.

This began as soon as the 3,400 natives and the small army of colonial agents and speculators assembled beneath the palisaded walls of Ft. Stanwix. The lines were clearly drawn. On one side were the Virginia interests, who hoped to upset Stuart's work and open the Kentucky country to settlement, at the same time keeping any other company from a share of their back country. On the other side were the members of the Indiana Company, eager to obtain their upper Ohio grant, and conscious that the territory lay within Virginia's boundaries. They held the upper hand from the first, for Johnson was apparently a secret member of their group. With his aid, they persuaded the Iroquois to sell them their coveted 1,800,000 acre tract on November 3, 1768, but Walker's consent was still needed. It was clear this Virginia delegate would hesitate to sign a treaty ceding away part of his own colony. In this crisis the speculators probably arranged a bargain. They seemingly suggested to Walker that if he would accept the Indiana Company grant, Johnson in turn would extend the new boundary line past the mouth of the Great Kanawha to the Tennessee River. This would either force Stuart to redraw the southern demarcation line in such a way that lands of the Loyal and Greenbrier companies would be opened to settlers, or so confuse the whole boundary system that all Kentucky would be legitimate prey for speculators. The jobbers were realistic enough to know that Johnson would accept such a surrender; they were well aware that his consistent policy had been directed to two ends: to guard his Iroquois wards and to satisfy his land-jobbing friends.

These were the provisions embodied in the Treaty of Ft. Stanwix which was signed on November 5, 1768. The line began, not at Owege, but near Ft. Stanwix—thus securing much of southwestern New York for the Eng-

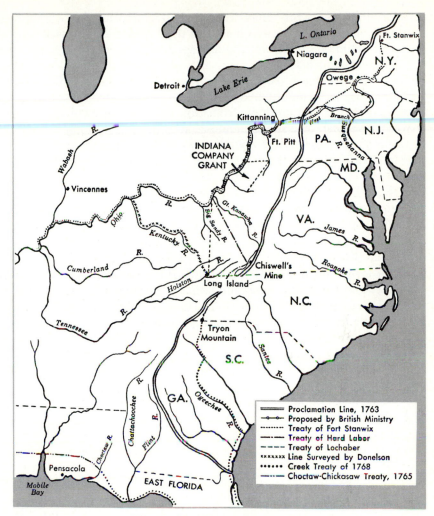

The Indian Demarcation Line

lish—cut west across Pennsylvania to open the Susquehanna Forks region to pioneers, and extended along the Allegheny and Ohio to the mouth of the Tennessee. In return the Indians were given gifts worth £10,460. Johnson explained the violation of his orders—which bound him to end the line at the Great Kanawha—by saying that the Iroquois insisted on ceding Kentucky to the English as proof of their ownership. There is no doubt that they were willing to sell their shadowy claims as a gesture of good will but also Johnson should certainly never have accepted. He was wise enough in frontier ways to know that his action not only upset the whole demarcation system, but angered the Cherokee, Shawnee, and Delaware tribes by depriving them of

hunting ground they rightly considered their own and left the whole West
in a turmoil. Worst of all, his acceptance of the Tennessee boundary showed
that the line could be shifted west by any speculators with enough influence
over the superintendents.

The results of this ill-advised policy were foreordained. Dr. Walker
returned to Virginia so determined to force a new treaty from Stuart that his
pressure, combined with prodding from Colonel Lewis and colonial authorities, was irresistible. The superintendent, after delaying as long as possible,
finally consented to extend the boundary west along the northern border of
Tennessee to a point near the Long Island of the Holston River, then north
to the mouth of the Great Kanawha. This was done at the Treaty of Lochaber, signed in October, 1770, with the Cherokee receiving compensation
in the form of £2,500 worth of gifts provided by Virginia. Even now, with
most of the lands claimed by the Loyal and Greenbrier companies opened
at last, the process of grabbing Indian territory did not end. The party sent
to survey the Lochaber treaty line in the spring of 1771, instead of turning
north from Long Island toward the mouth of the Great Kanawha, started
in a northwesterly direction—the fault either of poor instruments or of pressure from speculators on its leader, John Donelson. Reaching a river which
they took to be the West Branch of the Big Sandy, Donelson persuaded the
Cherokee accompanying him that it would be easier to run the line along the
stream than directly through the wilderness. They agreed, for an additional
£400, but unfortunately the river was the Kentucky rather than the Big
Sandy, and their acceptance opened another large territory to the whites.
Stuart accepted the Donelson line reluctantly, partly because the inaccurate
maps of that day minimized the error, and partly because he recognized the
futility of opposing the speculators.

The rapid westward shift of the boundary between 1768 and 1771 plunged
the English and Americans into a new period of speculation—with lands
opened by the treaties of Hard Labor, Lochaber, and Ft. Stanwix as the
prize. The older companies, many of them dormant for several years, led
the scramble; the Ohio Company sent petitions and agents to London to
urge a renewal of its grant, the Military Adventurers ambitiously requested
the whole area between the Ohio and the Alleghenies, the Mississippi Company begged rights to the same vast region, and individual operators such
as George Washington started west to stake out lands in the Great Kanawha
country. More important were efforts of the Indiana Company to secure
royal confirmation for its grant, for they launched the greatest speculative
enterprise of America's colonial period .

These started modestly enough in December, 1768, when Samuel Wharton reached London with instructions to seek support from the Privy Council,
rather than Lord Hillsborough, the Colonial Secretary, who was known to
be unalterably opposed. Wharton saw at once that two steps were necessary:
the Indiana Company must absorb rivals whose claims interfered with its
own, and it must win enough political support by judicious stock distributions

to override Hillsborough in the ministry. If all these groups were to be rewarded with land a larger territory was needed. Wharton worked through the summer of 1769, buttonholding politicians and bargaining with agents of other companies, to shape a new organization that would make this possible. The Ohio Company and George Washington were persuaded to join in return for promises of sizeable grants. Thomas Walpole, a prominent banker and politician, was won over and helped to enlist a roster of distinguished men— George Grenville, Lord Hertford, Lord Camden, Thomas Pownall, and others from the Privy Council—all chosen carefully to give the company representation in the various political factions governing England. By December 1769, Wharton felt strong enough to lay his proposition before Lord Hillsborough. The Indiana Company, he announced, wished to buy the entire Ft. Stanwix cession, paying the crown £10,460, the exact amount spent at the conference.

Wharton, who expected immediate disapproval from Hillsborough, could scarcely contain his surprise when the Colonial Secretary not only seemed friendly but even suggested that the company's request was too modest. Why not, he proposed, petition for a grant large enough to form a new colony? The delighted speculators acted at once. On December 27, 1769, they met in London, drew up articles of agreement as the Grand Ohio Company and petitioned the crown for a tract extending from the Forks of the Ohio south to the Greenbrier River and west to the mouth of the Scioto— some 20,000,000 acres in all. They would, they agreed, establish a proprietary colony known as Vandalia (in honor of the royal consort who was supposedly descended from the Vandals), bear all expenses of colonization, and pay the king a quitrent after twenty years.

When Hillsborough suggested the larger grant he did so only because he believed that the request would be too unreasonable to be considered by the government. He failed, however, to count on the enormous political power of the company. The petition was approved by the Lords of the Treasury in April, 1770, sent to the Privy Council in May, and referred favorably to the Board of Trade. Hillsborough's influence was strong enough in that body to delay action until April, 1772, when the board finally reported against the grant. This was the signal for the Colonial Secretary's political opponents, who were strongly represented in the company, to leap to the attack. They were so successful that Hillsborough was forced to resign from the ministry on August 1, 1772. The new Colonial Secretary was the Earl of Dartmouth, an enthusiastic supporter of the Vandalia claims, who ten days later issued a report endorsing the colony. This was accepted by the king and Privy Council on August 14, 1772. All seemed clear sailing for the jubilant Wharton who had apparently engineered the greatest speculative *coup* of the eighteenth century.

Only one thing more was needed: a charter authorizing the proprietors to set up a governmental system for Vandalia. This step, which seemed a simple formality, actually proved a fatal stumbling block, largely because interest in the colony declined steadily after August, 1772. This was partly due to the fact that many ministers who voted for the grant only to embarrass Hillsborough were no longer interested, and partly to the growing revolutionary agitation in America; the home government hesitated to establish a new province until excitement died down. Wharton stormed and pleaded in vain. Ministers turned a deaf ear to his entreaties until the Revolutionary War ended all hope for Vandalia's promoters.

The collapse of the Walpole Company, as it was known after its principal patron, opened the way for several minor speculating schemes that flourished briefly just before the colonies declared their independence. One was hatched by General Phineas Lyman who obtained several thousand acres of West Florida land in 1773 and vainly petitioned the crown to recognize his holdings as the colony of Georgiana. More important was a surge of activity by small companies and individuals who began buying large tracts directly from the Indians. Samuel Wharton engineered this enterprise when on July 21, 1771, he sent sealed instructions to George Croghan to begin major purchases west of the Forks of the Ohio. Croghan carried out his instructions faithfully over the next five years, acquiring some 6,000,000 acres, many purchased with goods originally intended for the Vandalia purchase.

Others, in both England and America, caught the infection. William Murray, a prominent speculator active in the Grand Ohio Company, returned from London and in the spring of 1774 helped form the Illinois Land Company and the Wabash Land Company, with Lord Dunmore, governor of Virginia, a member to assure that colony's support. Four giant tracts in the Illinois country and along the Wabash River were acquired from the Indians during the next year. Croghan and William Trent attempted to revive the Indiana Company, even to selling land at a Pittsburgh office opened in January, 1776.

This flurry of speculative activity was a product of the troubled times. Sharp-witted speculators recognized that land purchases directly from the Indians were illegal and would never be sustained by a British court; they also saw, however, that relations between the colonies and mother country were straining toward the breaking point. In the impending controversy, the individual who had even the flimsiest title to western lands might make good his claim. In the meantime they could pretend legality by hiding behind the so-called Camden-Yorke decision. This was a valid legal opinion issued in 1757 by the Earl of Camden, the Attorney General, and Charles Yorke, the Solicitor General, concerning land ownership in India. "In respect to such places, as have been or shall be acquired by treaty of grant from the Grand Mogul or any of the Indian princes or governments," it read, "your Majesties' letters patent are not necessary, the property of the soil vesting in the grantees of the Indian-grants." Somewhere, sometime, in the early 1770s a sharp-eyed speculator recognized the possibilities of this decision. It was copied with the words "Grand Mogul" omitted to make it appear to apply to America, and was passed from hand to hand among the land-jobbers.

Thus armed, they could pretend that they had a legal right to purchase directly from Indians, even though every precedent opposed such a practice.

If the Camden-Yorke decision gave speculators a pretended authority to engross Ohio Valley lands, the Quebec Act of 1774 provided them with an incentive to do so. This tolerant measure was intended to right the wrongs inflicted on French-Canadians under the Proclamation of 1763. It established civil governments for the inhabitants of Detroit, Mackinac, and the Illinois villages; granted religious toleration to Quebec's Catholics and offered them a measure of self-government as well as the benefits of French civil law; and extended the boundaries of the province of Quebec west to the Ohio and Mississippi rivers. The Quebec Act stirred a storm of protest; Virginia vehemently denied the crown's right to award her western territories to another colony; traders protested against a measure that would subject them to closer regulation by Montreal officials; and Yankees raised a hue-and-cry against the recognition given "Popery" by its tolerant religious provisions. Speculators were also concerned, for they realized that a strong new government in the West would end their illicit land purchases there. Hence they hurried into renewed action, conscious that they must accumulate all possible before the gates were closed.

The persistence of these activities, all patently illegal and known to be such by land buyers and crown officials alike, demonstrated the failure of Britain's western policy. Instead of curbing land jobbers, the revised Proclamation Line of 1768 only inspired them to new efforts; instead of bringing order to the frontiers the Quebec Act of 1774 stimulated a wave of illegal purchasing there. Defiance of authority was the way of life for speculators on both sides of the Atlantic and would continue to be, so long as they believed that the West would eventually be opened to settlement. So long as this belief persisted they would defy officials, retard the advance of small farmers who could not afford to risk purchasing claims that might later be held void, and defraud the Indians of their hunting grounds. American greed and British blundering combined to sire an ill-conceived and poorly executed western policy that bred colonial discontent without solving any of the major problems of the frontier.

Settlement
Crosses the Mountains
1763-1776

The investors who argued for a western policy that would foster colonies in the Mississippi Valley realized that nothing could restrain the pioneers who in 1763 were poised on the crest of the Appalachians, ready to move into the interior of the continent. For a century and a half they had been hemmed in by towering mountains, hostile Indians, and warlike Frenchmen, while immigrants and natives vied for overcrowded coastal lands. Now the barriers were down—the French expelled, the Indians cowed, the mountain barriers pierced by military roads—and even before the Seven Years' War ended pioneers cast covetous glances toward the rolling hill country that fringed the western edge of the Great Valley. During the next dozen years pioneers invaded that wilderness so successfully that by the time of the Revolution their lonely cabins dotted the lowlands about the Forks of the Ohio, the bluegrass region of Kentucky, and the winding valleys of the upper Tennessee River.

That Pennsylvania, New Jersey, Virginia, and North Carolina contributed most heavily to this migration was due partly to the pressure of surplus population in these Middle Colonies, partly to the presence there of routes to the interior. The Scotch-Irish and German immigrants who made their homes in the western valleys of those provinces filled them to the saturation point. Before the cramped pioneers lay tempting trails westward. From Pennsylvania, Maryland, and Virginia they could follow the crude traces—Braddock's Road or Forbes' Road—cut by Britain's armies to the Forks of the Ohio. From western Virginia and Maryland they could make their way through the valleys of the Cheat or Youghiogheny rivers to that same spot. Farther south lay one of nature's grandest passageways, Cumberland Gap, which offered easy passage from back-country Virginia and North Carolina

162

into the hilly uplands of Kentucky. Other travelers could follow the Watauga, Holston, and Clinch rivers into eastern Tennessee. This combination of land-starved farmers and easy transportation routes explains why the Appalachian frontier bulged first in the center.

The movement began long before the Seven Years' War. Thomas Cresap, a restless woodsman, spied out the country about the Forks of the Ohio as early as 1750. Three years later Christopher Gist blazed a trail from the Potomac River to Redstone Creek, a tributary of the Monongahela, where he built a cabin and persuaded eleven other families to settle nearby. Not far away William Stewart founded a small settlement at Stewart's Crossing during the same year; others followed until by the end of 1754 a sizeable group peopled the middle Monongahela. The outbreak of the Seven Years' War drove them back, but Forbes' successful expedition against Ft. Pitt in 1758 set the tide flowing again. They came by the score now, some along Braddock's Road and an extension built by Colonel James Burd to Redstone Creek in 1759, others along the Ft. Pitt highway cut through the wilderness by Forbes. By 1760 a dozen cabins clustered about the mouth of Redstone Creek, while Ft. Pitt was surrounded by 146 hastily built houses.

This rush of settlers into a region reserved for the Indians by treaty— the Treaty of Easton (1758)—alarmed British officials who realized that tribesmen would not sit idly by while pioneers turned hunting grounds into corn fields. Colonel Henry Bouquet, the commandant at Ft. Pitt, sought to check the movement in 1761 by forbidding all settlement west of the mountains, but still they came, disguised now as hunters to escape royal wrath. In vain the indignant colonel stormed through the countryside, burning cabins and herding inhabitants eastward; the wilderness was too large to patrol, the craving for cheap lands was too strong to check. The people, wrote one official at the time, "will remove as their avidity and restlessness incite them. They acquire no attachment to Place: but wandering about

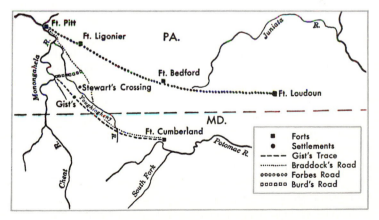

Western Pennsylvania, 1760–1776

Seems engrafted in their Nature; and it is a weakness incident to it that they Should forever imagine the Lands further off, are Still better than those upon which they are already Settled." The movement went on until 1763 when Ft. Pitt was surrounded by several hundred houses and a thin band of settlements bordered the upper Monongahela River.

Chief Pontiac succeeded where Colonel Bouquet failed. His Delaware and Shawnee warriors wiped out hundreds of settlers and sent the rest scurrying for the safety of Ft. Pitt, Ft. Ligonier, or Ft. Bedford. For two years western Pennsylvania was deserted except for garrisons and triumphant Indians, until Colonel Bouquet's 1764 Ohio expedition allowed a new westward surge of the frontier. Then the Monongahela Valley filled rapidly with persistent pioneers who recrossed the mountains to bury their dead and build new cabins on the blackened ashes of the old. By 1768 2,000 Americans lived along the Youghiogheny, Monongahela, Redstone, and Cheat valleys and this time they were there to stay. Not even the frantic efforts of General Gage and George Croghan, who issued repeated proclamations against encroachment on lands guaranteed Indians, could dislodge them; nor were they frightened when the Pennsylvania legislature in 1768 decreed the death penalty for those who did not return to the white territory east of the Proclamation Line. A few timid souls obeyed, but more defied Pennsylvania and the crown until the Treaty of Ft. Stanwix opened the whole region south and east of the Ohio River in 1768.

This treaty, which removed the last obstacle to expansion, sent a stream of settlers westward toward the Forks of the Ohio. Land was easily obtainable; both Virginia and Pennsylvania claimed the region and sold territory freely to homeseekers and small speculators. Most of the farmers bought directly from a Pennsylvania land office established at Pittsburgh (as the settlement at the Forks was now called) in April, 1769; on its first day of business, 2,790 purchasers stormed the office doors and within four months a million acres were sold. By this time nearly 5,000 families lived on the Pennsylvania frontier. "All this spring and summer," wrote Croghan in 1770, "The roads have been lined with waggons moving to the Ohio." In 1771 the population reached 10,000 families; two years later a traveler reported the country thickly settled for 150 miles south of the Forks. So rapid was the expansion that by 1774 General Gage was again warning pioneers not to cross the Ft. Stanwix boundary into the Indian reservation.

While the Pennsylvania frontier was filling, other immigrants moved down the Greenbrier and New rivers to the fertile valley of the Great Kanawha. Lewisburg and Peterstown were laid out in 1769 and 1770 by pioneers from Virginia, and three years later Thomas Bullitt, another adventurer from the South Fork frontier, built his cabin on the Great Kanawha. The few dozen families who followed him were joined by others who advanced along the south bank of the Ohio from Pittsburgh, until by 1776 the whole triangle between that river, the Great Kanawha, and the mountains was being settled. As the newcomers were well in advance of Virginia's surveyors, most of them simply blazed a few trees and constructed a cabin to establish a "to-mahawk claim" to their lands. All were seasoned frontier families, who, having learned the ways of the wilderness in the mountainous valleys they left behind, were equipped to live well in their forest surroundings.

A third trans-Appalachian area settled during those years was in eastern Tennessee where the twisting tributaries of the Tennessee River promised home seekers rich valley farms. The prospects of that region were made known by a few pioneers who settled there before the Seven Years' War—a hunter, Stephen Holston, built a cabin on the banks of the stream that bears his name as early as 1746 and a few others followed—but Indian raids drove them back and not until 1768 did immigration set in. In the van was William Bean, a trader and farmer from western Virginia, who selected the Watauga River valley as a site for his cabin, hiding it well as protection against Cherokee attacks. His tales of the fertile soil and natural beauty of his new home attracted others during 1769 and 1770; by the autumn of 1770 their clearings dotted the banks of the Watauga for several miles. This tiny outpost was visited that fall by the man destined to become its leader: James Robertson, a young Scotch frontiersman from the Yadkin River settlements of North Carolina. He was so pleased with the country that he returned in the spring of 1771, accompanied by his family and sixteen friends. The cluster of cabins that they built near the mouth of the Doe River became the center of the Watauga settlements.

Other pioneers moved in around them. John Carter, a trader who established a post just west of the Holston in 1769, was followed to that outpost by a handful of settlers. More of them drifted toward the valley country north of the South Fork of the Holston. Maryland contributed heavily to that migration, as one of its prominent frontiersmen, Captain Evan Shelby, induced many of his fellow colonists to settle near his store at Shelby's

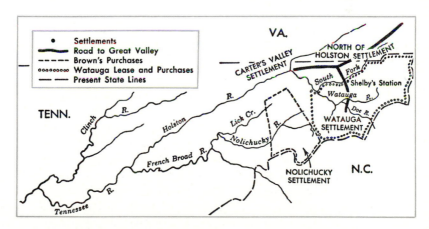

The Eastern Tennessee Frontier, 1760–1776

Station. In the same year Jacob Brown of North Carolina established a few families on the Nolichucky River, while to the west Jacob Castle and a handful of followers built their fort and cabins at Castle's Woods on the Clinch River. These migrations planted a cluster of settlements in eastern Tennessee by the close of 1771: Watauga, Carter's Valley, North-of-Holston, Castle's Woods, and Nolichucky.

During the next two years those isolated communities grew rapidly, as settlers were drawn west by glowing reports from the pioneers or driven to the frontier by intolerable conditions in their native Virginia and North Carolina. Many came from North Carolina, where the defeat of the Regulators at Alamance in May, 1771, apparently doomed the frontier to continued high taxes, unjust fees, and corrupt administration. So rapid was the emigration that the membership of one Baptist church in the Carolina upcountry declined from 606 to 14 during 1771. The movement continued during 1772 as discontented Regulators who delayed to sell their lands before migrating swelled the stream. Others moved west from Virginia and Maryland, lured by the promise of fertile farms and the speculative profits that awaited pioneers on any new frontier. By the close of 1772 several hundred families lived in eastern Tennessee.

Then, suddenly, the very existence of the Watauga settlements was threatened. The surveys of the Lochaber Treaty line, completed in 1772 along the southern boundary of Virginia, disclosed that while the North-of-Holston settlements lay within the area granted England by the Cherokee, the Watauga, Nolichucky, and Carter's Valley communities were in Indian territory. News of this disturbing decision, carried to the frontier settlers by Colonel Stuart's agents, threw them into a turmoil. Some who lived deep in the Indian country saw that resistance was useless—John Carter abandoned his outpost in Carter's Valley and Jacob Brown led his Nolichucky followers northward—but instead of retreating into the region opened by the Treaty of Lochaber, both groups settled in the Watauga settlement where they prepared to defy Stuart and all other royal officials who might try to drive them from their homes.

Their first need was an agreement with the Indians. Two commissioners, James Robertson and Robert Bean, were delegated to obtain a long-term lease from the Cherokee, for all purchases from natives were illegal under the Proclamation of 1763. Fortunately the Indians were in such a friendly mood that two large tracts were secured without difficulty, one embracing the region south and east of the South Fork of the Holston, the other the country where the Nolichucky settlers made their homes. Probably the money for this transaction was supplied by some eastern speculator, such as Judge Richard Henderson of North Carolina, who hoped eventually to transform the lease into a sale.

With land secured, the Wataugans turned to the related tasks of providing law and stability for their isolated community and forming a united front against royal officials wishing to oust them from their illegally held homes. In this situation they resorted to a practice usual to frontier people whose westward advance temporarily carried them beyond the protection of the law: they called a convention of all arms-bearing men to draw up a compact. All signers of the Articles of Association agreed to obey five commissioners who were given both legislative and judicial powers; they were to keep order, enlist a militia, record deeds for land sales, issue marriage licenses, and try offenders. This Association was not, as some historians have stated, a landmark in the development of American democracy. Instead it was an ordinary squatters' agreement, stemming from necessity and rooted in Presbyterian religious beliefs which emphasized the original compact between God and man. The Wataugans viewed their Association just as the Pilgrims viewed their Mayflower Compact: as a temporary expedient to endure only until a regular government was established and as a means of protecting illegal land holdings.

Certainly the Watauga Association did not attract other liberty-seeking pioneers to that isolated valley, for while the westward movement continued unabated during 1773 it was directed now to the North-of-Holston settlements that were clearly within Virginia. These grew rapidly, fed by a steady stream of homeseekers from western Virginia and North Carolina. As early as 1773 they had reached such an advanced stage that two roads were begun to connect them with the Great Valley of Virginia, the "Island Road" to the Long Island of the Holston River, and the "Watauga Road" to the Doe River. Along these crude highways trundled the heavy wagons of the early settlers, carrying grain and tobacco to Baltimore or Philadelphia markets, and returning with the few manufactured goods that the pioneers could not produce themselves. By the time of the Revolution the eastern Tennessee communities were beginning to pass beyond the primitive stage.

Beyond them a new frontier took shape in 1774 and 1775 as pioneers pushed deep into the wilderness to plant England's most westerly outpost on the banks of the Kentucky River. There, in a land of forest clad hills and fertile lowlands where lush bluegrass grew tall and thick, they reared the "Kentucky Stations" that held back the Indian tide during the war for independence and helped win the continent's interior for the newborn American republic.

The usual shock troops of civilization swept across the Kentucky country for some years before white families made their first permanent intrusion on that "Dark and Bloody Ground." First came the explorers, led by Dr. Thomas Walker, who started west in March, 1750, hunting a site for the 800,000 acres that Virginia had granted his Loyal Land Company. Leading his tiny party through the Blue Ridge, across the Holston Valley, and over Powell's Mountain, he emerged in April in Powell's Valley, where the flaring portals of Cumberland Gap led to the interior lands he sought. Whether Walker stumbled on this gateway or learned of its existence from Indians was less important than the fact that he had discovered the outlet which governed the course of western settlement until after the Revolution. Passing through the gap, the explorers followed a well-worn Indian trail, the War-riors' Path, northward, pausing only to build a cabin that would bolster their claims to the region. The hilly country discouraged Walker before he found the level fields along the Kentucky River, and he turned his followers east-ward to explore the forks of the Big Sandy River. There too the rough, mountainous terrain was so uninviting that the disgusted explorers continued east across the Cumberland Mountains to Staunton, Virginia, having failed to find the garden spot that was to become the mecca of pioneers a generation later: the bluegrass country.

To a Pennsylvania trader fell credit for first confirming Indian stories of the richness of that prized spot. John Finley, on his way down the Ohio with several canoes of trading goods, was captured by a party of Shawnee near the Falls of the Ohio late in 1752 and carried to the Indians' village in the Kentucky lowlands. There he learned from visiting traders that the fertile country where he found himself was readily accessible from Cumberland Gap. Finley returned to Pennsylvania filled with the importance of his dis-covery, but before his news could do more than spread among his frontier acquaintances, the Seven Years' War ended further exploration. Not until the war was won and Pontiac's Rebellion crushed did interest in Kentucky revive along the back country.

First to reawaken to the possibilities of that new frontier were hunters, their appetites whetted by traders' tales of wild turkeys so thick they broke branches from trees where they settled, deer that crowded unafraid around salt licks, and buffalo so numerous that herds might trample an unwary wanderer to death. Small parties of riflemen invaded Kentucky during the summer of 1766. Captain James Smith of Pennsylvania was probably the first; with four companions he passed through Cumberland Gap and hunted along the Cumberland and Tennessee rivers. Another party of five hunters under Isaac Lindsey followed the same course but continued down the Cumberland as far as Stone River where two other woodsmen, James Harrod and Michael Stoner, who had made their way along the Ohio and Cumberland rivers from Ft. Pitt, were encountered. Even more spectacular were the exploits of another expedition led by Benjamin Cutbird of North Carolina. Crossing the Appalachians by a little-known Indian trail, Cutbird hunted across southern Kentucky and northern Tennessee to the Mississippi, then descended that river to New Orleans where he sold his furs.

The principal importance of this bold journey was to interest Daniel Boone in Kentucky, for his brother-in-law, John Stewart, was a member of Cutbird's party. This remarkable woodsman, whose name is forever asso-ciated with the early history of the Southwest, had been reared in the pri-mitive Yadkin Valley settlements where he learned to farm and hunt and to love the haunting solitude of the deep forest. He fought for a time during the Seven Years' War, serving as a wagoner in Braddock's expedition where he met John Finley, then returned to his beloved Yadkin Valley where he slipped back into the seminomadic life of the advanced frontier. His was a

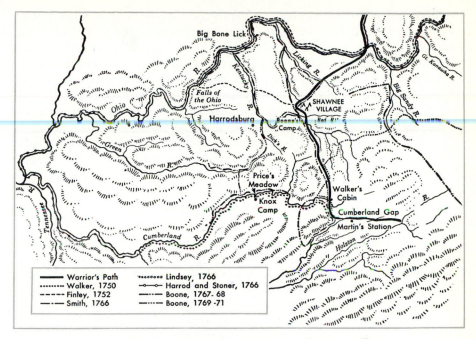

The Exploration of Kentucky, 1750–1774

pleasant existence for one who enjoyed silent woodlands more than his fellow men. Each spring Boone planted a crop on his half-cleared fields; each fall when the harvest was in he shouldered his long rifle and stalked alone into the forest, leading a pack horse to carry out the deer skins and beaver peltry he would capture during the winter. In the spring he emerged to rejoin his family, sell his furs, and dream through the summer of his next hunting trip. After 1764 he extended his lone expeditions farther and farther afield under the prodding of a North Carolina speculator, Judge Richard Henderson; Henderson provided the hunting equipment, receiving in return information on choice interior sites. The combination was ideal for both parties.

That was the situation in 1766 when Daniel Boone first heard hunters tell of the fine lands they had found in Kentucky. Boone listened eagerly to these tales, particularly to those of John Stewart who had been with Cutbird's party. The information, he realized, fitted well with things learned from John Finley while on Braddock's expedition. Hunters had discovered Cumberland Gap; traders, the bluegrass country. The explorer who could piece those two bits of knowledge together and discover a route from the southern back country to that paradise would reap a fortune from speculators who would squander their resources for news of such a find. This became Boone's consuming ambition.

His first try, made during the winter of 1767–68, failed when Boone crossed the Blue Ridge to emerge in the jagged hillcountry south of the Big Sandy River. This was not the Kentucky of Finley's descriptions, and he returned in the spring of 1768 with a harvest of furs but with his appetite for knowledge of the bluegrass region still unsatisfied. Before he could set out on his wanderings again his plans were upset by the unexpected arrival in the Yadkin Valley of John Finley, who had abandoned the adventurous life of the fur trader for a less hazardous career as peddler of pins, needles, linen, and other wares designed to catch the eye of frontier housewives. Finley was easily persuaded to spend the winter as a guest in the Boone cabin; all through the cold months the two men talked of Kentucky, and planned an elaborate assault on its mysteries. Finley, who was sure that he could find Cumberland Gap from descriptions given him by traders, was to serve as guide. Boone and four backwoods companions were to hunt, and Judge Henderson was to provide supplies. In May, 1769, the little party set out, each riding a wiry mount and leading a pack horse.

Finley located Cumberland Gap easily enough and the group followed the Warriors' Path across Kentucky as far as Station Camp Creek where they built a shelter to house the furs they captured. There the men separated into pairs to explore the countryside. All went well until December, 1769, when Boone and Finley were captured by a band of Shawnee who raided the main camp and carried away most of the stores and ammunition. The two seasoned woodsmen managed to escape by diving into a giant canebrake where thirty-foot-tall weeds hid them, but most of the party were so disheartened by the loss of their supplies that they wanted to return home. Only Boone and his brother-in-law, John Stewart, stayed on, moving their camp to the mouth of the Red River where they would be safe from war parties using the Warriors' Path. There they were joined by Daniel's brother, Squire Boone, who came out to meet them with fresh supplies and a lone companion.

Things went badly during that winter of 1769–70; Stewart failed to return from one of his solitary hunting trips, and Squire Boone's comrade lost heart and returned east, leaving the two brothers alone in the wilderness. In the spring Squire Boone set out for North Carolina to replenish their dwindling supply of ammunition. Daniel, completely alone, spent the next few months roaming the forest, dodging Indian war parties, sleeping in canebrakes, and living from the country. His solitary wanderings took him as far north as the Ohio, along the Kentucky and Licking river valleys, and over most of the bluegrass region. By July 27, 1770, when he rejoined Squire Boone at their old camp on the Red River, he knew more of Kentucky than any other white man. That summer the brothers hunted along the banks of the Kentucky River, then in the fall shifted their operations to the Green and Cumberland valleys where they spent the winter of 1770–71. Finally, in March, they started east, their pack horses loaded with a modest fortune in furs. Fate, however, was unkind. Near Cumberland Gap they encountered a band of Indians who took their peltry, their horses, and their supplies, leaving the discouraged men to tramp homeward with nothing to show for two years of hunting.

Boone's disastrous experience typified the fate awaiting any individual who ventured alone into Kentucky, for there, as on all frontiers, the group was needed for protection. This was realized by Uriah Stone, a skilled hunter who had accompanied Captain James Smith's exploring party, even before Daniel Boone and his brother had returned empty handed from their journey. Stone saw that safety could be assured only if hunters ventured into Kentucky in large bands capable of beating off Indian war parties. With this in mind he sent word along the back country for all hunters interested in Kentucky to meet on the New River in June, 1769. The several dozen who responded followed the well-marked trail through Cumberland Gap, then separated to found camps at Price's Meadow on the Cumberland and Station Camp Creek. From these bases they roamed the country, shooting and trapping. Game was plentiful and easily captured; riflemen had only to wait along trails converging on the numerous salt licks to slaughter deer and buffalo crowding down to lap the briny fluid. They returned east in the fall with pack horses staggering beneath a wealth of furs.

The success of that expedition encouraged another the next year, this time under the leadership of James Knox and made up of forty hunters from upcountry Virginia. From a base near Price's Meadow they roamed over most of western Kentucky, operating especially in the hitherto neglected Green River valley. There in the fall of 1770 they happened upon Daniel Boone, lying on his back and singing so loudly for the sheer joy of his wilderness life that they believed when they first heard him they had discovered some strange new animal. Boone spent the winter of 1770–71 with them, then left for the East in the early spring while the Knox party stayed on to hunt southward toward the Cumberland. When they returned to the Green Valley in the fall they found that Indians had carried away their carefully cached furs. After carving a lusty protest on a tree—"2300 deer-skins lost. Ruination, by God"—they set out for home, still carrying a comfortable catch to pay for their two years of wandering.

These "Long Hunters," as they were dubbed because of their extended journeys, were living examples of the Americans' mastery of frontier techniques. Half civilized and half savage, they were as much at home in the towering Kentucky forests as in the cabins that dotted the agricultural settlements. To them the woods held no mysteries; they could read the message told by a broken twig or the cry of a distant animal as easily as their red-skinned foes. They saw the wilderness not as a forbidding obstacle but as a source of adventure and wealth. From it they took the necessities of life: game and wild vegetables and salt for food, hides to fashion their coonskin caps and leather hunting shirts and buckskin leggings, furs to trade for the few things the wilderness did not provide: a hatchet and hunting knife to thrust into their belt, a long rifle to carry in the crook of their arm, "traps, a large supply of powder and lead, a small hand-vice and bellows, files and screw-plates for fixing the guns if any of them should get out of fix." That was all, for so long as their long rifles could shoot, the woods offered them safety and comfort. They loved their nomadic life, and their tales of the level fields, gently flowing streams, and majestic forests of "Kaintuck" did much to interest less adventurous frontiersmen in moving there as settlers.

After the explorers and hunters, in the succession of pioneers who subdued Kentucky, came the land speculators. These astute individuals, whose fingers were always on the pulse of the frontier, realized that Americans were ready to storm across the mountains, regardless of royal proclamations or Indian treaties. Fortunes awaited the lucky land jobbers who could engross the best lands before they arrived. Speculators knew, moreover, that the land bounties issued to Virginia's soldiers during the Seven Years' War offered a means of securing title. Because these warrants antedated the Proclamation of 1763, Virginia maintained that none of the subsequent treaties affected them; their holders could locate claims anywhere in the Indian country. Although most of the bounties had been purchased by a group under George Washington there was scarcely a speculator in the Old Dominion who did not have at least one. Any land jobber could go west, ostensibly to locate his bounty claim, and while there survey a larger grant in anticipation of the rush of settlers to come.

The first surveying party was organized by a speculator, Captain Thomas Bullitt, who in October, 1772, advertised in Virginia and Pennsylvania newspapers that all interested in marking out bounty lands should gather at the mouth of the Great Kanawha the following spring. The large expedition that formed moved slowly down the Ohio, pausing to survey choice spots: the mouth of Limestone Creek, Big Bone Lick where the bones of thousands of animals whitened the ground about a salt spring, the Kentucky Valley, and the Falls of the Ohio. In the spring of 1774 the jobbers were back again, in three groups this time, headed by Colonel William Preston who was official surveyor for western Virginia, William Crawford who had long served as Washington's land agent, and a minor speculator named James Harrod. Once more they worked through the early summer staking out extensive claims for themselves and their backers along the Ohio, Kentucky, and Licking rivers. "What a buzzel is this amongst People about *Kentuck*," wrote a Virginia clergyman as he observed this speculative mania. "To hear people speak of it one would think it was a new found paradise." The Virginians under James Harrod were so impressed with the rich country near Dick's River that they built cabins and laid out the town of Harrodsburg.

That the conquest of Kentucky could go on without Indian retaliation was too much to expect. Although no tribe actually occupied the "Dark and Bloody Ground," both the Cherokee of Tennessee and the Shawnee of Ohio fought and hunted there. The Shawnee especially looked on the region as their own, remembering that before moving to the Scioto Valley as vassals of the Iroquois they had lived along the Cumberland River. For some years they watched the gradual encroachment of white men: hunters who ruthlessly slaughtered game, traders who carried compasses—"land-stealers," the natives called them—to mark out choice sites, surveyors who told of settlers soon to come. Little wonder that by 1771 the Shawnee were seeking alliances with the Cherokee, Seneca, and other tribes to drive the intruders from Kentucky.

That they failed to recruit allies was due to the patient efforts of the Indian superintendents, Sir William Johnson in the north and John Stuart in the south. Sir William, intimate as always with the Iroquois, used his personal influence to keep that tribe at peace. Stuart played an even more heroic role. Alert to happenings among his charges, he heard rumors during the winter of 1773–74 of a confederation forming among the Choctaw, Chickasaw, Cherokee and Creeks—a confederation that would menace the whole southern frontier should the Shawnee elect to join and direct its war effort. Stuart's able maneuvers nipped this alliance in the bud; by playing off long-time rivalries (such as those between the Choctaw and Creeks), and by withholding ammunition from all the tribes, he divided them so completely that the threat soon passed. In the end the southern Indians vowed to maintain peace when they met with Stuart at a conference at Savannah in 1774. The Shawnee were left isolated to brave the assault of land-starved frontiersmen—and thus doomed to certain defeat.

The conflict that broke out then—Lord Dunmore's War—was a struggle for land between peoples of two antagonistic cultures. The Indians wanted Kentucky for a hunting ground; the Americans wanted Kentucky for farms. There was no reconciling these views; war was inevitable. Lawless frontiersmen who realized this began the conflict in 1773 with vicious attacks on the natives: one trapper killed an Indian and a squaw suspected of stealing his dog, another murdered a dozen friendly warriors after plying them with liquor until they were helplessly drunk. Until the spring of 1774 the Shawnee showed greater restraint than these outrages warranted, hoping that the Pennsylvania Quakers who controlled the Forks of the Ohio would find some peaceful solution. This last hope went glimmering early in 1774 when Virginia, which claimed all western Pennsylvania under its 1609 charter, forcibly seized the disputed area. Governor Dunmore's appointment of a wild Irishman, Dr. John Connolly, as commander at Pittsburgh was the last straw. Now the whole frontier was controlled by land-hungry Virginians.

Dr. Connolly, who claimed extensive tracts of Kentucky land himself, evidently decided to hurry the coming of the inevitable conflict. In April, 1774, he used a minor Shawnee attack on a surveying party as an excuse for a fiery proclamation which urged the frontiersmen to defend themselves. Such an order as this was as good as a declaration of war to Indian-hating pioneers; all along the back country they waylaid Shawnee hunting parties and raided native villages. Even this was not enough to goad the Indians into war. Only when messengers sent to Pittsburgh to plead for peace were first rebuffed, then attacked by Dr. Connolly's troops did Shawnee patience finally reach a breaking point. Then hot-headed young warriors fell on several outlying settlements, killing thirteen men to avenge the thirteen Indians who had died in the skirmishing. There was no turning back now; on June 10 Governor Dunmore sent word to the frontier settlements that war had begun.

A terrifying alarm swept through the West, for with the Shawnee on the warpath farmers and hunters from the upper Holston to the Ohio faced death. Dunmore's first thought was for the surveyors scattered over Kentucky. Daniel Boone and another woodsman, Michael Stoner, were hurried west to warn them of their danger. Traveling through the virgin forests on foot, those two skilled frontiersmen journeyed 800 miles in sixty days, stopping only at Harrodsburg where Boone's land hunger so overbalanced his caution that he paused to stake out a claim and build a cabin before issuing his warning. The Watauga settlers, living beyond the pale of civilization, could expect no such attention. Their only hope was to keep the Cherokee neutral. James Robertson was called on to use his considerable diplomatic skill in this emergency, and after a prolonged conference his persuasive eloquence won the day. This not only saved the Watauga settlements but cost the Shawnee their principal southern allies. At the same time Sir William Johnson and George Croghan worked feverishly to win the Iroquois and Delawares to the English side. In the end the Shawnee were left with only the Ottawa and Mingo to aid them.

With the safety of isolated settlers secured and the diplomatic battle won, Governor Dunmore turned to the conquest of his enemies. On July 24, 1774, he dispatched nearly 400 men under Major Angus McDonald to the newly built Ft. Fincastle with orders to march up the Muskingum Valley and destroy any Indians they found, thus throwing a screen between the Ohio tribes and the upper Ohio settlements. This done, Dunmore planned two expeditions into the Shawnee country, one from Pittsburgh, the other from upcountry Virginia, which would unite at the mouth of the Great Kanawha to march northward. Dunmore, who commanded the Pittsburgh army, changed his plans as his 1,100 militiamen drifted down the Ohio, and decided to strike directly at the Shawnee villages by way of the Hocking River. Pausing only to build an outpost, Ft. Gower, to guard his supply lines, he sent word to the thousand Virginians under Colonel Andrew Lewis who were moving down the Great Kanawha to cross the Ohio and ascend the Scioto, then headed northward into the wilderness.

The Shawnee commander, Chief Cornstalk, was overjoyed when scouts told him of this change. The Virginians were divided; he could fall first on one army and then the other! Gathering a thousand warriors, he slipped quietly southward, crossed the Ohio in the very teeth of Colonel Andrew Lewis' advancing troops, and prepared to fall on the upcountry militiamen who had descended the Great Kanawha to Point Pleasant, near the river's mouth. The attack came at daybreak on the morning of October 9, 1774. What might have been a complete surprise was averted when hunters who saw the Indians gave the alarm; the militiamen sprang to their guns and deployed through the woods for a typical frontier battle. All day long the fight raged, with neither side able to gain any advantage, until dusk when Chief Cornstalk mistook a Virginia flank attack for the arrival of reinforcements. Disheartened, he ordered a retreat. That night the Shawnee slipped across the Ohio as quietly as they had come. Colonel Lewis, who had expected fighting to continue, thankfully gathered his battle-scarred forces for the march northward along the Scioto War Trail to the Shawnee villages.

News of the Battle of Point Pleasant reached Dunmore while he was still moving slowly up the Hocking Valley. He was wise enough to realize that a sudden attack on the Indians now, while they were cowed by defeat, would probably end the war. Hence instead of waiting for Lewis he marched boldly into the Shawnee country. The warriors, fearful lest their women and children suffer, sued for peace at once. Dunmore forced the leading chieftains to sign the Treaty of Camp Charlotte; they would, they agreed, consent to the occupation of Kentucky, cease hunting there, and stop molesting boats plying the Ohio River. Lord Dunmore's War was over, the last obstacle to the settlement of Kentucky removed.

The one man who above all others realized the importance of the Shawnee defeat was Judge Richard Henderson. That wealthy speculator, who had dabbled in western lands for a decade as Daniel Boone's employer, had just retired from the North Carolina bench to concentrate on land sales. He saw that two factors favored a bold bid for the interior. One was the presence of a vast population poised to push across the mountains, including many men who had learned something of Kentucky while serving with Colonel Lewis' army. The other was the undisputed ownership of that region by the Cherokee, for the Iroquois gave up their claims at the Treaty of Ft. Stanwix, and the Shawnee at the Treaty of Camp Charlotte. Direct purchase was impossible, but an alert speculator might obtain a long-term lease to Kentucky that would be just as profitable. Such a land jobber, moreover, would probably be able to turn possession into ownership should the crown ever open the region to settlement.

With this in mind, Henderson called some of his well-to-do North Carolina friends together in August, 1774, to form the Louisa Company. They planned to lease a large tract south of the Ohio and west of the Great Kanawha, together with a right-of-way through Cumberland Gap. Henderson and one of his partners set out at once to open negotiations with the Cherokee, who assured the speculators they were willing to negotiate if a price could be agreed upon. So confident were the members of the Louisa Company that Kentucky was theirs that in December, 1774, they advertised for settlers in Virginia and North Carolina newspapers, offering 500 acre plots at a price of twenty shillings for each 100 acres with an annual quitrent of two shillings.

During the next few weeks Henderson, suddenly changing his plans, decided to buy rather than lease Kentucky from the Indians. This reversal may have been due to word of the Camden-Yorke decision but was more probably a product of turbulent conditions in the colonies. The drift toward revolution during the winter of 1774–75 undoubtedly convinced Henderson that he could make good a purchase from the Indians in the troubled times ahead. Whatever the reason, in January, 1775, he reorganized the Louisa Company as the Transylvania Company and sent runners to summon the Cherokee chiefs to a conference at Sycamore Shoals on the Watauga River in March. Negotiations lasted from March 14 to March 17 when the Treaty of Sycamore Shoals was signed. In return for £10,000 worth of trading goods the Indians ceded all lands between the Kentucky River and the highlands south of the Cumberland, together with a strip between the Holston and the Cumberland Mountains. In addition the Watauga settlers took advantage of the natives' generous mood to turn their lease into a purchase, and Jacob Brown bought two large tracts along the Nolichucky River where his followers were established. Only when the last transaction was completed did Henderson wheel out the casks of rum which launched a wilderness celebration wild even for those frontier peoples.

The Treaty of Sycamore Shoals had no more validity than any other purchase made under the Camden-Yorke decision. Every English precedent vested title to colonial lands in the crown, not in the native population; Indian treaties were only devices to remove troublesome occupants from lands already owned by the king. Individuals who made such treaties actually usurped territory which legally belonged to their sovereign. Henderson, like most of the other speculators who used the Camden-Yorke decision, probably realized this. His object was to obtain possession of Kentucky, then hold the region during the confusion of the coming revolution.

Certainly he moved with unseemly rapidity to establish his company's claim. On March 10, 1775, when negotiations were just getting under way, he sent Daniel Boone with thirty axmen to cut a road to the Kentucky River where Henderson planned to plant his first settlement. That was the origin of the famous Wilderness Road, which began at the Long Island of the Holston, passed through Powell's Valley and Cumberland Gap, and emerged on the Kentucky River where Boone and his followers built their cabins. Henderson set out over this trail on March 20, with forty riflemen, a number of Negro slaves, and a train of wagons and pack horses loaded with provisions and ammunition. In Powell's Valley he found the first intruder on his domain, a trader, Joseph Martin, who was operating a newly built trading post. Henderson, recognizing the value of a station at that strategic point, gladly guaranteed Martin his land in return for aid given settlers on their way west. While still there he was joined by a small group of immigrants under Benjamin Logan who were bound for Kentucky, and on April 8 the combined party started westward over the Wilderness Road.

At Cumberland Gap they met forty pioneers fleeing toward the East with tales of a new Indian uprising, but Henderson only sent a runner ahead to warn Boone to hold his ground and pressed on more rapidly than before.

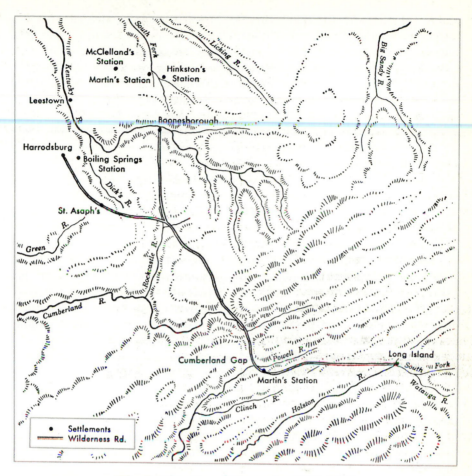

The Settlement of Kentucky, 1775–1776

A second setback occurred just beyond Rockcastle River when Logan, who refused to recognize the Transylvania Company's authority, broke away from the main party and led his followers off toward Harrodsburg to found their own settlement, St. Asaph's Station. The remainder pushed on to the Kentucky River where they were welcomed by a twenty-five gun salute from Boone's men. All were enchanted by the beauty and richness of the level country that lay before them. "Perhaps no Adventureor Since the days of donquicksotte or before," wrote one awe-struck pioneer, "ever felt So Cheerful & Ilated in prospect, every heart abounded with Joy & excitement." That sight of tossing white clover, level bluegrass, and the gently flowing river was to cheer many a weary traveler at the end of the Wilderness Road.

Boone's axmen had thrown up a few cabins but no stockade, for the men had suffered so severely from land fever that they had spent their time

staking out sites for themselves rather than preparing for Henderson's settlers. Nor could Henderson dissuade them from this exciting task. He
planned to erect a fort called Boonesborough on the model of Martin's
Station, with a series of cabins connected by log stockades to house the
pioneers. Instead his settlers spent the first week marking out lots, surveying
fields, and prospecting for land despite all the pleas of their proprietor. Even
after the first excitement passed they showed so little inclination to work
that the fort was not completed until after the start of the Revolution. Only
the friendliness of the natives saved Boonesborough from extinction during
those months.

More annoying than this to Henderson was the steady intrusion of
newcomers who had no respect for his authority. Benjamin Logan's followers at St. Asaph's Station had already defied him. James Harrod also returned in May, 1775, to rebuild Harrodsburg, while some of his fellow immigrants split away to found Boiling Springs Station in the Dick's River
valley. All of these settlers denied the Transylvania Company's right to
Kentucky and stoutly maintained that Virginia was in control—largely because that distant colony would not bother them. Henderson was wise
enough to see that he could establish his authority over these unruly settlers
only by giving them such an orderly government that they would be willing
to pay for their land in return. His opportunity came when thirty new arrivals
from North Carolina established themselves near Harrodsburg over the protests of that town's inhabitants. This, he insisted, showed the need of some
agency to settle disputes, and he invited the four stations to send delegates
to Boonesborough on May 23, 1775, to enact laws for the colony of Transylvania.

On the appointed day eighteen frontiersmen selected by the towns met
under a great elm tree at Boonesborough and listened to a resounding address
in Henderson's worst eighteenth-century style. "You are," he told those
roughhewn woodsmen, "fixing the palladium, or placing the first cornerstone of an edifice, the height and magnificence of whose superstructure is
now in the womb of futurity, and can only become great and glorious in
proportion to the excellence of its foundation." Lulled by this oratory, the
delegates passed laws setting up a court and militia system, and providing
for the punishment of criminals, the preservation of game, and the proper
breeding of horses. They also adopted something like a constitution which
was carefully drawn by Henderson to vest governmental power in the Transylvania Company, despite a number of deft phrases seemingly promising
democracy. He was, he sincerely believed, erecting a new proprietary colony in the heart of America, with himself at its head.

This constitution, and the land system that Henderson tried to introduce,
were both monuments to his dreamy impracticability. Any sensible man
would have known that the woodsmen of Kentucky, suddenly freed from
taxation and quitrents, would never accept a proprietary government just
as they were on the verge of rebelling against a distant king who had denied
them the right to rule themselves. Common sense should also have told

Henderson that his land system would never be accepted. His price was low enough—twenty shillings for each 100 acres—but each purchaser was to pay an annual quitrent of two shillings for every 100 acres he held. Although this archaic system had long since failed in the East, Henderson had the audacity to believe that he could force unruly, individualistic frontiersmen to promise him regular payments through their lifetimes. He was completely out of touch with his times, a renegade from an earlier century.

Henderson's outmoded idealism doomed the Transylvania Company to many dreary months of conflict. New settlers crowded onto its lands during the summer of 1775, to fill the older towns and to lay out new stations: Leestown, McClellands's Station, Hinkston's Station, and Martin's Station. No one paid the slightest attention to the company; the immigrants reasoned that it had obtained possession illegally and they would do the same. The Transylvania proprietors were too busy to protest, for the Continental Congress was meeting and they were in the East vainly petitioning for recognition as the fourteenth colony. Realizing that this would never be forthcoming over the protests of Virginia and North Carolina, they finally determined to snatch what profits they could. Land prices were raised sharply on December 1, 1775—from twenty shillings to two pounds ten shillings per 100 acres. This unwise step only increased dissatisfaction, nor did Indian raids during the winter strengthen the company's position. By the spring of 1776 discontent was boiling through Kentucky.

This came to a head in June, 1776, when a leader arrived to shape the popular revolt. George Rogers Clark, a fiery twenty-four-year-old Virginian, well trained in wilderness ways, sensed the discontent of the people at once and issued a call for a convention to meet at Harrodsburg on June 6, 1776. The assembled delegates from all stations divided their time between denouncing the Transylvania Company and drawing up a petition to Virginia asking that Kentucky be made a county of that colony. On adjournment they named a revolutionary Committee of Twenty-One to govern the region until Virginia's authority was extended over them. Henderson hurried away to the colonial capital to protest this rebellion, but his efforts were in vain. Early in 1777 the House of Burgesses formally annexed the Transylvania Company domain as Kentucky County. Henderson was given 200,000 acres between the Ohio and Green rivers as compensation for his efforts, and in 1783 North Carolina awarded him the same amount in the Powell and Clinch river valleys. Thus ended the grandiose scheme of one of America's most visionary speculators.

But neither Henderson nor other pioneers who dreamed of trans-Appalachian colonies labored in vain. They had built a new frontier—one that stretched from the Monongahela Valley across western Virginia to Kentucky and eastern Tennessee by 1776. There lived thousands of men and women, all engaged in clearing away the age-old forests and planting civilization in a conquered wilderness. These were the pioneers who bore the full brunt of Indian raids during the Revolutionary War, and helped win the West for the new nation born of that struggle.

10

The West in the American Revolution

1776-1783

The West played only a minor role in the epic events leading to the Revolution. The provincialism, individualism, and distrust of external interference underlying that rebellion were all frontier characteristics, bred into the colonists by the New World environment, but the isolated westerners showed little concern with the issues that started Americans along the road to independence. Duties on molasses and tea aroused scant interest among people who had never seen those luxuries, nor could they grow wrathful about "taxation without representation" when they were often underrepresented in colonial legislatures. They resented British attempts to limit expansion, but even on this sore point they knew better than easterners that mythical boundary lines could be crossed at will. Yet the indifferent westerners were destined to play a major role in the war. For seven years they trembled in their cabins with fear of the tomahawk and scalping knife heavy in their hearts or ventured forth to hurl back fierce attacks by redcoated or redskinned warriors. They fought savagely; war is rarely so inhumane as when it is waged by amateurs. Thousands paid with their lives for the right to freedom and expansion.

From the beginning of the war it was clear that Indians would play a leading role in the West, and both English and Americans set out to win their support. The British enjoyed a marked advantage in this wilderness contest. They could offer the natives proven friends in the Indian Superintendents—John Stuart in the South and Sir John Johnson, who ascended to the northern superintendency on the death of his father in 1774, in the North—protection at Detroit, Mackinac, Oswego, Niagara, and other English-controlled posts, a well-established fur trade, and superior trading goods. The Americans, on the other hand, having no manufactured goods of their own, could give the Indians only high-flown speeches on liberty which sounded ironical to natives who knew the land-hungry colonists wanted their lands. Most Indians believed they could win back their lost hunting grounds only by casting their lot with England.

Hence British commanders had only to give the word to send most tribes storming against the settlements. They hesitated to do so for they shrank from the barbarism of frontier warfare. Their problem was to solicit enough native aid to protect their interior posts, while restraining the Indian from shedding the blood of innocent victims. Yet the Americans, who would have welcomed active aid against their enemy's forts, were wise enough to see that this was unobtainable. Instead the three Indian Commissioners appointed by the Continental Congress in July, 1775, concentrated on keeping the tribes neutral. In a series of conferences held with the Iroquois at German Flats from August, 1775, onward, the commissioner for the Northern Department promised gifts and waved tempting treaties before the Indians, but they knew that his promises meant nothing. Trading goods were in short supply and an effective gift policy impossible for a tiny warring nation without manufactures of its own. Two years of negotiations did no more than win halfhearted promises of neutrality from the two weakest of the Six Nations.

Nor did the commissioners for the Central and Southern Departments fare better. Congresses with the middle-colony Indians at Pittsburgh during the summers of 1775 and 1776 showed the magnitude of their task; only two, the Shawnee and Delawares, responded favorably, and their action was due more to smarting memories of Lord Dunmore's War and fear of the fierce Virginia "Long-Knives" than to any sympathy with the American cause. The southern commissioner enjoyed even less success. Although the Creeks grudgingly agreed to refrain from attacks for a time, the Cherokee broke up a conference at Ft. Charlotte in April, 1776, by proclaiming their allegiance to George III. The colonists began their Revolutionary War hemmed in by a ring of hostile Indians, all poised to pounce on back-country settlements whenever British commanders gave the word.

The threat to the southern back country was compounded by the large number of Loyalists there, most of them ready to join the Indians in attacking the overmountain settlements. The British government, well aware of their strategic value, planned to launch the war against the southern colonies with a naval expedition that would seize their ports timed to coincide with a Tory uprising in the interior. This plan went askew when the North Carolina governor, Josiah Martin, was so overeager that he called on the Loyalists to rise prematurely. Without the diversionary naval action, they were no match for a hurriedly recruited force of patriot militiamen who defeated them at the Battle of Moore's Creek Bridge in February, 1776. The naval squadron, recognizing the futility of an attack without land support, was diverted to an assault on Charleston.

The defeat of the Loyalists ended one threat in the North Carolina interior, only to give way to another that was far more serious. The Cherokee, chafing under the presence of the Watauga and Nolichucky settlers, wanted to attack at once, despite Colonel John Stuart's determination to restrain them. He did his best. His brother, Henry Stuart, was sent to visit the Cherokee villages in April, 1776, only to find the tribe so inflamed that there was no stopping them. Convinced that he could not hold back the onslaught, Stuart hurried to warn the Wataugans that they must either defend themselves or move to safer quarters. Hence the Americans were ready when the blow fell, safe within two strong fortifications: Eaton's Station at the Long Island of the Holston and Ft. Watauga at Sycamore Shoals. There, on the morning of July 20, 1776, word reached them that 700 Cherokee under Chief Dragging Canoe were approaching. Instead of waiting, the 170 defenders of Eaton's Station sallied forth to meet the Indians, who were defeated after a fierce battle beneath the walls of the fort. A similar attack on Ft. Watauga the next day also failed, and the Cherokee retreated in disgrace to their villages. This raid ignited the torch of war along the southern frontier; overnight the inflamed Cherokee, Creeks, and Choctaw swept down on outlying settlements.

The southern states struck back relentlessly in September and October, 1776. Twenty-five hundred regulars and militia from North Carolina fell first on the Middle Cherokee towns, then joined with a smaller force from South Carolina to lay waste the Lower Towns while a Virginia expedition spread devastation among the Overhill tribe. By the end of October, when the victorious southerners returned to their homes, Cherokee power was broken, tribal villages smoking ruins, crops destroyed, and warriors scattered. A few months later the remnants of the once-powerful tribe were forced to sign two humiliating treaties: the Treaty of DeWitt's Corner (May 20, 1777) in which the Lower Cherokee surrendered their remaining territory in South Carolina, and the Treaty of Long Island (July 20, 1777) where the Overhill Cherokee gave up their lands east of the Blue Ridge together with the region occupied by the Watauga and Nolichucky settlements. This decisive victory assured two years of peace for the southern frontier.

This was fortunate, not only for the pioneers of the Carolina back country but also for Kentuckians, as those harassed pioneers were left free to repel Indian and British raiders from across the Ohio. To the Indians of that country—the Delawares, Shawnee, Ottawa, and Miami—the Revolution was a golden opportunity to drive American intruders from their hunting ground, for on no other frontier were the British so willing to aid the Indian. Captain Henry Hamilton, lieutenant-governor of England's northwestern territories, had only 120 men to protect his own post at Detroit and smaller garrisons at Mackinac, St. Joseph, Ouiatanon, Vincennes, and Kaskaskia. This skeleton force must guard thousands of miles of wilderness, a dozen Indian tribes, and a population of Frenchmen whose sympathy lay more with the Americans than with George III. Hamilton, who had no more liking for

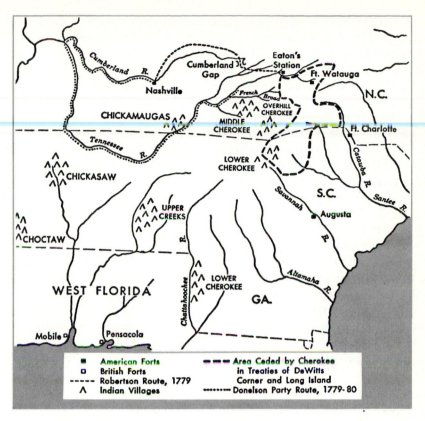

The Southern Frontier in the Revolution, 1776–1780

frontier warfare than Colonel Stuart, did his best to keep his Indian allies in check, but circumstances compelled him to use them almost from the beginning of the war.

Raids began in the summer of 1776, when bands of Shawnee and Delaware warriors slipped across the Ohio to lurk about the Kentucky stations. As the attacks grew in intensity, station after station was abandoned, the inhabitants either trudging back east or moving into one of the stronger settlements, until by the beginning of 1777 the whole Kentucky population was concentrated in the three largest posts: Boonesborough, Harrodsburg, and St. Asaph's. These were feverishly transformed into strong forts. Each was a large rectangle—that at Boonesborough was 260 by 180 feet—formed by the backs of cabins and a ten-foot-high stockade of pointed oak logs set upright. At each corner a block house with a projecting second story allowed defenders to fire along the walls, while the stockades were also equipped with loopholes. Even the roofs of the cabins sloped inward so that protectors could extinguish flame arrows without showing themselves to the enemy.

Within these hollow squares a large population could live safely, if not comfortably, through any siege that impatient Indians could conduct. The Kentucky Stations were to prove themselves, in the dark days of the Revolution, the most efficient means of defense devised on the frontier.

Their completion in the spring of 1777 came none too soon, for that "year of the three sevens" was long known as the "Bloody Year" in Kentucky's history. Raids began on March 7 when Chief Blackfish and several hundred Shawnee warriors fell on Boonesborough. The inhabitants managed to "fort up" safely, but throughout that summer Blackfish slipped from station to station, keeping all in what amounted to a state of siege. Outside aid was needed if Kentuckians were to be saved and crops planted. A plea to Virginia finally bore fruit in August when Colonel John Bowman with about 100 troops reached Harrodsburg from the East, to be followed in September by fifty more from the Yadkin district. Chief Blackfish retreated across the Ohio rather than face this new army, leaving a badly battered Kentucky behind him; no crops were planted, every larder was empty; in all the land, one soldier complained, there was "no bread, no salt, no vegetables, no fruit of any kind, no ardent spirits, nothing but meat."

The Kentuckians could endure this meagre fare but complaints from eastern soldiers were so insistent during the winter that in January, 1778, Daniel Boone determined to silence them. With thirty men he set out for a salt spring at Blue Licks on the Licking River, where the whole party

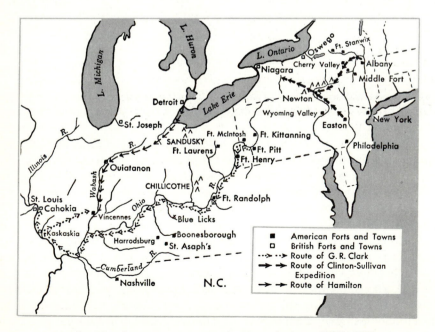

The Northern Frontier in the Revolution, 1776–1780

settled down to the tedious task of boiling down the briny water that gushed from the ground. While the men were still there, Boone, on a lone hunting trip, was captured by a large Indian war party bound for Boonesborough. Realizing that an attack on the unprepared settlement would mean the killing of women and children, he led the raiders to Blue Licks where he persuaded the salt-makers to surrender, knowing that such a prize would satisfy the warriors. They were carried triumphantly to the Indian village of Chillicothe where their bravery so impressed the Indians that sixteen were adopted into the Shawnee tribe, Boone becoming the foster-son of Chief Blackfish. That winter and spring the Kentuckians lived with the tribe until early June when Boone learned that another attack on Boonesborough was planned. He must, he knew, warn the Kentuckians. Opportunity came while returning from a salt-boiling expedition; he fell behind his captors under pretext of adjusting his salt kettles, then dashed into the wilderness. Four days later, on June 20, 1778, Boone reached Boonesborough, having covered 160 miles of trackless forest.

His warning that 400 raiders were on their way came none too soon, for the station's defenses had been allowed to rot away. The sixty men in the fort worked so furiously that by September 7, 1778, when Chief Blackfish and his party appeared, Boonesborough was again able to resist. For a time the two forces parleyed, as Blackfish reprimanded Boone for leaving the Shawnee and tried to persuade the settlers to surrender peacefully, but after two days the attack began. The Indians followed their usual tactics: they rushed the fort, were beaten back, noisily prepared to depart, and filed away into the forest. When this traditional ruse failed to deceive the Boonesborough settlers the Shawnee returned and settled down to a siege. This lasted for nine days, until a heavy rain renewed the fort's water supply and caved in a tunnel the Indians were digging beneath its walls. This time, when the attackers slipped away into the wilderness, they were gone for good. The cheering settlers, warmed by the thought they had withstood the longest siege in the history of Indian warfare, led their half-starved cattle out to pasture once more. Yet bands of Indians roamed Kentucky through the autumn of 1778, pouncing on unwary wanderers, seizing livestock, and for the second year preventing the harvesting of badly needed crops. The settler's defensive policy was an obvious failure.

This lack of aggressive tactics also spelled disaster on the rest of the northern frontier between 1776 and 1778. Along the upper Ohio River Virginia contented itself with throwing up four forts to guard its long border: Ft. Kittanning, Ft. Pitt, Ft. Henry at the site of Wheeling, and Ft. Randolph at the mouth of the Great Kanawha. These did little good; Ft. Henry was raided twice by Delaware and Shawnee war parties during 1777 and the whole back country between Pittsburgh and Kentucky ravaged by such savage attacks that no crops were planted. The Continental Congress made only one attempt to improve the situation. In February, 1778, it ordered Brigadier General Edward Hand, who commanded the few federal troops at Ft. Pitt, to invade the Indian country as far as Sandusky, destroying villages and crops as he went. Heavy rains, poor leadership, and inadequate supplies doomed the expedition from the start, and Hand returned in disgrace after killing a few friendly Delawares. On the Upper Ohio, as in Kentucky, the Americans were hard pressed by 1778.

The New York frontier looked even worse during the first two years of the Revolution. There the British could rely not only on several of the powerful Iroquois tribes under their able Mohawk chieftain, Joseph Brant, but also on a number of Loyalists whose bloody deeds made even their Indian allies shudder: Sir John Johnson and Guy Johnson, son and nephew of Sir William Johnson, Colonel John Butler and his band of renegades who called themselves the Tory Rangers, and Colonel Guy Carleton, all well equipped and strategically based at Niagara or Oswego. They swung into action during the summer of 1777 when the English high command sent General Barry St. Leger to Oswego with orders to march his army of Indians and Tories east along the Mohawk to join General John Burgoyne—who was descending Lake Champlain from Canada—on the Hudson River. St. Leger, with 1,700 followers, met his first obstacle at Ft. Stanwix where 750 well-armed Americans awaited him. Unwilling to accept information about rebel strength, he began a siege that ended seventeen days later when the British gave up hope of routing the stubborn patriots and retreated to Oswego. Yet the American triumph was not complete; a relief expedition of 800 men and boys under General Nicholas Herkimer, bound for Ft. Stanwix from the East, marched into an ambush only eight miles from the fort on August 5. The Battle of Oriskany, which cost 200 lives, was one of the most disastrous in the history of the frontier.

With the spring of 1778 the attacks began again. Joseph Brant led the assault on May 30 when his 300 Iroquois stormed the little town of Cobleskill, then swept westward along the Mohawk, destroying farms as they went. While this force ravaged outlying New York settlements, another under Colonel John Butler moved quietly southward toward the Wyoming Valley of Pennsylvania. The 5,000 inhabitants of that fertile region, left virtually without protection by the exodus of men to serve in Washington's army, were crowded into the one defensible spot in the valley, a large palisade known as Forty Fort, when Butler's 1,000 Indians and Tories arrived on June 3. Instead of defending themselves 300 American men and boys fool-ishly sallied out to meet the attackers. The result was the Wyoming Massacre; 360 were killed outright and countless others who escaped into the forest died of exposure or starvation. His bloody work done, Butler rejoined Brant to raid along the Mohawk and Schoharie valleys. By the end of June, 1778, no frontier settlement was safe; even the people of Albany and Schenectady trembled lest they feel the Indians' wrath.

Clearly the defensive policy followed in the West had failed; aggression alone would drive back the enemy hordes. Only a practical demonstration of the success of offensive action was needed to convince Congress. This was provided by George Rogers Clark, a fiery young Kentuckian, who, suffering with his fellow frontiersmen in their wilderness stations, decided that Indian attacks could best be ended by striking against the British posts north of the Ohio. During the winter of 1777-78 he persuaded the Virginia authorities to authorize an expedition against the Illinois villages, knowing that the French inhabitants would aid the invaders. Moreover the capture of that region would allow Americans to import supplies from New Orleans over the Mississippi route, as well as bolster Virginia's claim to the Northwest. Clark was made a lieutenant colonel with authority to raise a force of militiamen for his task.

Near the ruins of Ft. Massac, a few miles below the mouth of the Tennessee River, on June 26, 1778, Clark's force of 175 well-trained Indian fighters left their boats and started overland rather than risk discovery along the river. The little army reached Kaskaskia on July 4, approaching so stealthily that the English commander did not know of their presence until the Americans pushed open the gates of the palisade. The British had no choice but surrender, particularly when Clark won over the French inhabitants by telling them of the newly concluded alliance between the United States and France. Cahokia also capitulated without resistance; a little later Vincennes surrendered to a Kaskaskia priest who journeyed to that village with news of the Kentuckian's arrival. By mid-August Clark controlled the Illinois country. He capitalized on his success by summoning neighboring Indians to a conference at Cahokia, where his arrogant speeches, blustering manner, and judicious distribution of presents completely captivated his audience. Before the session adjourned most of the Wisconsin and upper Mississippi tribes, as well as a few from Ohio, swore allegiance to the United States.

Clark's convincing proof that an offense was the best defense forced Congress to imitate his example elsewhere on the frontier—with less satisfactory results. An expedition into the Ohio country, with Detroit as its final objective, was clearly called for. After the Delawares had been cajoled into permitting an army to cross their tribal lands, the force set out from Ft. Pitt in October—1,000 men under General Lachlan McIntosh. They paused to build Ft. McIntosh at Big Beaver Creek—the first American foothold on the right bank of the Ohio—then turned westward, driving fleeing natives before them, until cold weather turned them back. The expedition did little good; few Indians were killed and fewer villages destroyed, while garrisons left at Ft. McIntosh and Ft. Laurens, a more advanced outpost on the Tuscarawas River, irritated rather than overawed the Indians. Nor did the aggressive program attempted in western New York during the autumn of 1778 fare better. A small army from the East which wiped out the two Indian villages of Unadilla and Oghwaga so infuriated Joseph Brant that he turned his raiders against the substantial town of Cherry Valley, one of the few remaining strongholds south of the Mohawk. Striking suddenly on November 11, 1778, his well-trained fighters cut down thirty of the defenders and wounded seventy-one more before they withdrew.

These disastrous autumn campaigns in New York and Ohio did much to offset the influence of Clark's success; Indians who manifested friendship toward Americans during the summer swung abruptly back into the British camp. To make matters worse, Captain Hamilton at Detroit threatened to undo all Clark accomplished. As soon as Hamilton heard that the Illinois villages were captured, he set out with an army of 500 Indians and British to retake them. Vincennes fell in December, when the French garrison deserted, but constant rains forced Hamilton to stay there all winter.

Clark first heard this discouraging news from a trader who reached Kaskaskia on January 29, 1779. Realizing that his only hope was a surprise attack, he set out for Vincennes, 180 miles away, on February 6, leading a little force of 172 men. The journey was one of unprecedented difficulties. Trails were ankle-deep in mud, game was scarce, and cold rain fell steadily. For the last twenty miles the men waded through water, sometimes up to their shoulders, breaking ice as they went. Yet on the afternoon of February 23 they reached their goal. Captain Hamilton, not anticipating Clark's bold move, was caught napping when the Americans marched quietly into Vincennes under cover of an early winter dusk. His supplies were woefully low, while desertions and illness had cost him so many men that he had only thirty-three soldiers capable of bearing arms. Although recognizing the futility of pitting this tiny force against Clark's 170 seasoned fighters, Captain Hamilton ordered his men to defend the fort that stood in the heart of the village. All that night the battle raged, as weary Americans displayed their wilderness skills by picking off the English gunners through the port holes of the fort. With the morning of February 24 Hamilton realized that further resistance was suicidal and offered to surrender. He and his fellow officers were packed triumphantly off to Virginia, and again American prestige was high throughout the Northwest.

Clark, knowing that nothing impressed the Indians like success, laid plans to march on Detroit at once. Fresh troops were needed to replace the exhausted veterans of the Vincennes campaign. A hurried call to Virginia brought only 150 raw recruits rather than the 500 requested, while the expected contingent from Kentucky never arrived. Its commander, Colonel John Bowman, succumbing to the blandishments of his frontier followers, turned aside to burn the Shawnee village of Chillicothe. By that time the two-month enlistment term of his troops was up and they returned home, leaving Bowman only thirty men when he finally reached Vincennes. Clark did not dare proceed with that small force; "Detroit lost for want of a few men," he ruefully wrote.

He could find consolation in the fact that his brilliant triumphs inspired victories on other frontiers during 1779 when American military success in the West reached its high water mark. The decision to mount a major campaign in western New York was wise. Something must be done to end the

Iroquois-Tory raids that had ravaged the back country since 1778, raids that grew in numbers and brutality as the Tory rangers recruited new members and learned the art of guerilla war. These cost heavily in scalps and homes, but by the end of 1778 they were also influencing the grand strategy of the war, partly by destroying the Mohawk Valley grain crops needed to feed General Washington's soldiers, partly by keeping in the West militiamen badly needed in the East. Moreover a sweep through the Iroquois country would avenge the Americans who had been killed, wipe out crops needed by the Indians during the winter, and demonstrate the failure of Britain's ability to protect its Indian allies, thus weakening that unholy alliance. Washington planned well; given the resources available at the time he could have devised no better scheme to chastise the enemy.

The decision made, General Washington started his main army toward Connecticut, feigning an attack on Canada designed to check the British from moving troops southward. This stratagem succeeded admirably; a regiment under Sir John Johnson scheduled to move into the Iroquois country was kept at home instead. With this threat removed, two strong armies under General James Clinton and General John Sullivan were ordered to start westward, moving so rapidly that England's defenses would be kept off balance. Sullivan, with the main force of 2,500 men, started from Easton, Pennsylvania, June 18, 1779, and at Tioga joined with Clinton's 1,500 troops who had marched from Canajoharie. From there the combined force started west along the Chemung River into the heart of the Indian country. British and Indians, securely entrenched behind earthen embankments, awaited them at the native village of Newtown. The Battle of Newtown (August 29, 1779) was disastrous for the British. Sullivan's seasoned fighters battered down their defenses with cannon fire, then dashed upon the terrified Indians. Only thirty-three of the enemy were killed, but the rest fled in disgrace with Sullivan at their heels, cutting a swath of destruction through the Iroquois country. For a time at least the Six Nations were so cowed that the New York frontier was safe from attack.

This happy state of affairs did not last long. Most of the 380 Indians who died in battle or from starvation were women, children, or old men, leaving the warriors at near-full strength and thirsting for revenge. Even worse, Sullivan's raid drove the neutral Indians to join the pro-British faction. By 1780 the Iroquois were ravaging the New York back country with as much fury as before; more raiding parties swept through the frontier settlements that year than in 1778. Yet the Sullivan-Clinton campaign was still a success; it heightened American morale, diverted British troops and supplies from the East, and kept the peace long enough in 1779 for the Mohawk Valley to produce the bountiful grain crop so desperately needed by Washington's troops.

The Americans were just as successful in subduing a new flare-up in the South during the summer of 1779. This centered in the Chickamauga villages along the Tennessee River where 1,000 disgruntled Cherokee warriors had lived since they fled west in 1776. Aroused by American victories, they took to the warpath in the spring of 1779. A Virginia-North Carolina expedition under Colonel Evan Shelby moved through the Chickamauga country in April, destroying eleven villages and 20,000 bushels of grain. Again in the fall when the Indians showed warlike tendencies a South Carolina force wiped out six more towns. This was enough; for the rest of the war the southern Indians remained neutral. There, as in New York and Ohio, the war seemed over by the autumn of 1779.

This was cheering news to harassed frontier settlers. Since the start of the war they had fled eastward before threatened Indian attacks, now, even though the frontiers were far from safe, population moved west once more. Land in Tennessee and Kentucky was easily obtainable under liberal laws enacted by North Carolina and Virginia; the North Carolina statute, passed in 1777, allowed purchasers as much as 640 acres at fifty shillings for each 100 acres, while a Virginia law of October, 1779, set a price of £40 for a hundred-acre plot. Actually settlers paid far less than this, as both states accepted payment in their own depreciated paper currency. Pioneers bought Kentucky land for about ten shillings for 100 acres, while those living in the West before 1778 were given 400 acres free of charge.

The settlers who took advantage of those bargains moved westward in a steady stream all through the summer and fall of 1779. By the end of the year their cabins dotted the Tennessee countryside along the Holston as far south as the French Broad River. Migration to Kentucky was spurred by an "Ancient Cultivation" law adopted by the Virginia legislature in 1777 promising free land to all who had lived in the county before June 1, 1776. Word quickly spread that latecomers would be granted the same bounty, and the rush was on, largely of perennial wanderers from the back country of the eastern colonies. By the spring of 1780 it was running flood tide, with the Wilderness Road crowded with new arrivals. So many came down the Ohio by barge and flatboat that by midsummer Louisville, founded at the Falls of that stream, boasted a thriving population, rectangular streets, and even a city park. Before snow fell Kentucky teemed with 20,000 inhabitants who filled the old stations, spilled over into new towns, and turned the war-scarred wilderness into a busy frontier of civilization.

Many who came in this first wave were destined to disappointment; the early comers felt the full brunt of Indian warfare while the free lands that they expected never materialized. By the end of 1780 disgruntled Kentuckians were petitioning Congress to annex the region and distribute land there; others were so angered that they joined the Loyalist cause; still others made no pretense of obtaining legal title but defied authority by squatting on the lands they wanted. The divisions that eventually led Kentucky to separate from Virginia were already taking shape.

Despite the tribulations of the Kentuckians, the spirit of expansion was so strong that an entirely new settlement sprang up during the winter of 1779-80. This outpost, at Nashville on the Cumberland River, originated in the speculative ambitions of Judge Richard Henderson who turned his attention to the southern portions of his Cherokee purchase after Virginia in 1777 decided against the Transylvania Company's claim to Kentucky. As leader for his enterprise he selected James Robertson, already trained in frontier life by his long career at Watauga. Robertson started westward with a small advance party in February, 1779, to lay out a town and plant corn against the coming winter. Henderson sent the rest of his prospective settlers to Nashville in two parties, one overland through Cumberland Gap during the cold winter of 1779-80, the other by boat along the circuitous Tennessee-Cumberland River route. The latter arrived in April, 1780, just as Henderson returned from a corn-buying trip into Kentucky, and the work of planting the new settlement began. Eight small stations, centered about Bluff Fort at French Lick, were erected along the river bank to hold the 300 inhabitants. Having launched his enterprise successfully, Henderson headed east to protest in vain while North Carolina followed Virginia's example by holding his claim invalid. Nashville, as a part of North Carolina, expanded slowly under Robertson's leadership during the next years.

The rapid advance of the frontier during 1779 and 1780 was based on the belief that war in the West was over. Unfortunately this was not the case, for the successes of 1779 were more apparent than real. Clark's victories were based on audacity rather than military power, Bowman's campaign antagonized rather than crushed the Shawnee, and Sullivan's devastating march through New York left the British in control of Niagara and Oswego. English goods still reached the Great Lakes Indians over Lake Ontario and Lake Erie, and the poverty-stricken Continental Congress could not afford the gifts needed to cement its newly won Indian alliances. By the end of 1780 most of the interior tribes were back in England's camp, and for the next three years Americans fought a losing battle to retain control of the West.

In New York the counterattack began in the early spring when a raiding party from Oswego swooped down on the little town of German Flats. Again in May, Sir John Johnson led his charges in a sweep westward along the Mohawk from Lake Champlain to the site of his father's old home, while Brant cut a swath of destruction between Ft. Stanwix and Canajoharie. In August the two armies, after joining at Unadilla, marched eastward along the Charlotte River, laid waste the Schoharie Valley, burned Middle Fort, and killed more than 100 people. A hastily summoned militia force from Albany chased the raiders to Stone Arabia, where they were defeated, but when the cautious American commander refused to pursue farther, the British returned to the attack. Even Albany and Schenectady feared an Indian raid during the dismal fall of 1780.

The plight of settlers along the upper Ohio and in Kentucky was almost as desperate, due largely to the failure of two American expeditions aimed at Detroit. General Washington planned one of these, with Colonel Daniel Brodhead of Ft. Pitt in charge, but the militia needed to guard the Ohio

River forts while regulars marched against the enemy refused to leave their homes, and the Continental Congress was unable to provide supplies. Instead of leading a triumphant army into Detroit, Brodhead spent the summer of 1780 fighting off Seneca raiding parties that operated as far south as the Monongahela River. The second expedition was authorized by Virginia, which instructed George Rogers Clark to raise 1,000 men and subdue the enemy outpost. Clark began his enlistment campaign with high hopes of success, but the Kentuckians simply refused to serve. They were willing to fight the Shawnee whose troublesome raids began again in 1780, but could see no reason to attack a distant enemy post. Clark railed and ranted in vain, even closing the land office to turn the people from speculation to fighting. In the end he bowed to frontier provincialism, sullenly retiring to build a new fort, Ft. Jefferson, near the mouth of the Ohio.

These failures vastly strengthened England's hand as vacillating Indians, sensing the declining American power, hurriedly aligned themselves with the British. Two English expeditions were planned to capitalize on this shift in the wilderness balance of power. A major force under Emanuel Hesse was to move south from Mackinac, overwhelm the Illinois villages, descend the Mississippi River, and help recapture West Florida from its Spanish conquerors. At the same time a smaller army, led by Captain Henry Bird, was to draw Clark's troops east by harrying Kentucky, thus opening the Mississippi to Hesse's force.

Fortunately for the Americans, these well-laid plans went astray. Hesse reached Cahokia in May, 1780, with almost 1,000 British and Indian followers, but Clark had anticipated his coming and was waiting in that garrisoned post. His mere presence was enough to overawe Hesse's warriors who, after a few halfhearted sallies, forced their commander to move on to St. Louis. There too they were expected. Instead of surprising a handful of demoralized Spaniards, the English were met with cannon fire which sent them scurrying to safety. The expedition retired to Mackinac in disgrace after burning a few farmhouses. Hesse, fearful that Clark was at his heels, hastily moved his fort to an island in the Straits of Mackinac. The American commander, with too few troops to pursue the fleeing enemy, contented himself with sending a small force under Colonel John Montgomery to punish the Wisconsin Sauk for participating in the British raid.

Captain Bird enjoyed more success than Hesse. He left Detroit in April with 150 whites and 1,000 Indians, crossed the Ohio, and ascended the Licking Valley which was dotted with small settlements. The pioneers in the first of these, Riddle's Station, prepared to resist, knowing that their palisaded fort could withstand a long siege, but when Bird's men produced two cannon they saw their cause was lost. On June 20, for the first time in history, a Kentucky Station surrendered. A week later Martin's Station fell before the battering of British artillery, and terror swept over the countryside. Bird, it appeared, could sweep all before him. But by this time the

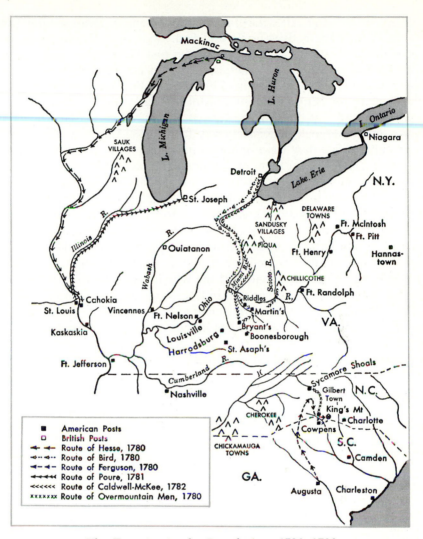

The Frontier in the Revolution, 1780–1783

English commander, who deplored Indian warfare and feared his followers would get out of hand, had enough. With 100 prisoners he started for Detroit.

When news of the "Bird Raid" reached George Rogers Clark at Kaskaskia on June 5, 1780, he immediately started east, disguised as an Indian to escape enemy raiders. This time recruits for the retaliatory expedition which he organized at Harrodsburg were plentiful. With 1,000 men, Clark marched to Old Chillicothe, burned the town, then moved on to the Indian village of Piqua on the Big Miami River where several hundred natives under a Tory, Simon Girty, awaited him. This time it was the Americans' turn to produce a cannon and batter down the enemy defenses. After several hours of fierce fighting the natives broke and fled. Again Clark's vigorous campaigning freed Kentucky from attack for the rest of the year.

Despite this victory the American position in the Northwest was far weaker at the close of 1780 than in 1779. Most of the Indians were still loyal to the British, for Bird was as successful as Clark, and England's trading goods far superior to those of the United States. More serious, however, was the drift of French Illinoisans away from their American alliance. By the autumn of 1780 they were on the point of revolt, angered by the strict military rule imposed on them by Virginia, the lack of trading goods, the corrupt speculators who appropriated their lands, and the flood of depreciated Continental currency which disrupted their business. Their discontent was fostered by a fiery French agitator, Colonel Mottin de la Balme, who began plotting against Virginia soon after he reached Kaskaskia in July, 1780. De la Balme was massacred that fall while leading a French force against Detroit, but dissatisfaction remained. Apparently the United States was on the verge of losing control of the whole region that Clark had won.

Only in the South did Americans in 1780 retain prestige won the previous year, and there the victories were gained at the expense of British regulars rather than Indians. By that time the center of the eastern war was in the southern states; Charleston fell to England in May, 1780, and a strong British army under Lord Cornwallis started north to crush the rebellious colonists between that city and New York. Cornwallis, to guard his left flank, dispatched a dashing young Scotch Highlander, Major Patrick Ferguson, to enlist Tories in the Carolina back country. Ferguson's appeal was so great that he soon commanded 1,000 Loyalists who roamed the interior, destroying Whig property and lives. For a time a group of mountain men under Colonel Charles McDowell and Isaac Shelby offered some resistance, but when the American defeat at Camden in mid-August 1780, left them at the mercy of the British they fled westward with Ferguson's horsemen in hot pursuit.

There they might have stayed had not the arrogant Tory commander sent word that he planned to invade their hilly lair. Frontiersmen trained in the Indian tradition of aggressive fighting had only one answer to such a challenge; a call went through the back country for volunteers to assemble at Sycamore Shoals on September 25, 1780. As the leather-clad woodsmen who responded moved east from their rendezvous they were joined by others, until the force that crossed the Blue Ridge numbered 1,500 trained forest fighters. Ferguson, rather than risk open combat, started east from Gilbert Town to join Cornwallis' main British force at Charlotte.

News of this move reached the Americans while they were camped at Cowpens, feasting on cattle seized from a Tory owner. Nine hundred horsemen set out in pursuit, and after an all-night ride through a steady drizzle, caught their quarry at three o'clock in the afternoon of October 7, 1780. They found the British camped on a rocky spur that jutted from King's Mountain—a flat table of rock rising sixty feet above the level countryside—

a spot chosen by Ferguson because he believed frontiersmen could not stand against bayonet charges. The Americans attacked at once, creeping upward through the trees and debris in Indian fashion. The advantage was theirs from the outset. When Tory troops charged down one side of the mountain, driving patriots before them, they exposed their backs to the withering fire of others. At last the Americans, reaching the summit, closed in among the trees, dropping Ferguson's men with their deadly long rifles. When the valiant commander fell the British gave up; 225 Loyalists were killed, 163 wounded, and 715 taken prisoner in the Battle of King's Mountain, while the Americans lost only twenty-eight killed and sixty-two wounded.

This famous engagement ended Tory raids on the back country and allowed the overmountain men to return home in peace. There, however, disturbing news awaited them: the Cherokee had seized on their absence to begin raiding again. They acted at once. A force was raised, commanded by Colonel Arthur Campbell of Virginia and Colonel John Sevier who became leader of the Watauga settlements on Robertson's departure. Through the autumn of 1780 they marched through the country of the Overhill Cherokee, destroying crops and towns, and leaving the Indians to face a winter of starvation. Again in the spring of 1781 Sevier took to the warpath, this time against the Middle Towns along the upper French Broad, striking swiftly and cruelly. When he led his raiders back to their Watauga homes the natives' power was broken. Sevier forced the subdued Cherokee chiefs to sign the second Treaty of Long Island (July 26, 1781) in which they surrendered another slice of territory to the land-hungry Americans. For the next two years the southern back country enjoyed a well-earned peace.

Vigorous action also ended the Revolution on the New York frontier during 1781. This only came after British and Indian raiding parties had reduced the Mohawk Valley to a virtual desert and carried their attacks to the doors of Schenectady and Kingston; by midsummer only some 800 arms-bearing men remained in the whole valley and even they dared not venture beyond the blockhouses that offered the sole means of defense. The plight of these unfortunates finally forced New York to act. A strong army of seasoned soldiers, led by Colonel Marinus Willett, marched west in August, driving the intruders before them. In October the campaign reached its culmination when Willett caught the retreating British as they forded West Canada Creek, fell upon them, and slaughtered large numbers. Only a few isolated raids by Brant's declining forces broke the calm in western New York after that.

In the Northwest, however, Americans during 1781 and 1782 lost much they had won during the first years of the Revolution. Their cause appeared bright enough in the spring of 1781, particularly after a band of Spaniards and Indians from St. Louis, led by Captain Eugene Pourée, demonstrated British weakness by destroying the post at St. Joseph. But from that time on the list of disasters mounted. Clark spent the summer urging Kentuckians and Virginians to enlist for the often-planned attack on Detroit, but frontier provincialism, military jealousy, and the poverty of Congress proved obstacles that even this forceful leader could not overcome. By fall he had given up hope and fell to constructing a new fort, Ft. Nelson, at Louisville, while Indian raiders stormed about his ears. All through that dark winter attacks continued while Virginia, its economy strained to the breaking point by a depreciating currency, allowed the chain of forts along the Upper Ohio to moulder into decay. Yet worse was to come. In the spring of 1782 about 300 hot-headed Pennsylvanians, ousted from their homes by the settlement of the Virginia-Pennsylvania boundary dispute, crossed the Ohio to seize lands. They were entertained for three days at the Indian village of Gnadenhutten, where ninety friendly Delawares lived under the guidance of Moravian missionaries; on the fourth day the white men fell on their hymn-singing hosts in the Moravian church, slaughtering all of them—men, women, and children—"in a most cool and deliberate manner." This wanton brutality gave the Ohio Indians a new motive; the Delawares threw off all pretext of neutrality to join the Shawnee and Wyandot in a savage assault upon the northwestern borderland. By May the raids were so intense that the whole frontier was threatened. Again an expedition from Ft. Pitt marched into the Ohio country, this one under Colonel William Crawford, with the Sandusky villages as its objective. On the upper reaches of that river the Americans met a band of Shawnee and Delawares, fought a bitter one-day battle on June 4, and began a retreat that soon turned into a panic-stricken rout. Fifty were killed and nine carried away to the Delaware villages to be tortured to death. Crawford himself died by slow roasting—the sign of supreme Indian contempt.

The British were quick to take advantage of the aggressive spirit in their allies. During the summer of 1782 two expeditions left Detroit. One, led by Joseph Brant, attacked Ft. Henry and carried faggot and tomahawk as far as Hannastown, Pennsylvania. The other, under Captain William Caldwell and Alexander McKee, followed the usual path into Kentucky where Bryant's Station was stormed unsuccessfully, then headed east with a hastily formed army of Kentuckians at its heels. Canny old Daniel Boone warned his comrades that something was wrong; there was so much Indian "sign" left by the fleeing British that an ambush seemed likely. The reckless young men refused to heed his sound advice, even when Boone pointed out a likely spot for a surprise attack in a ravine just across the Licking River. Instead they rushed into the very trap the wise old frontiersman feared; sixty Americans died in that Battle of Blue Licks, the British escaping to Ohio. Not even a successful march against Chillicothe and Piqua in November, led by George Rogers Clark, wiped out the sting of that defeat.

That was the last campaign of the Revolution; when Clark returned to the Ohio he learned that a preliminary peace treaty had been signed. Not since 1779 had American fortunes in the West been at lower ebb. Kentucky was still theirs, but the Indians were all in the enemy's ranks, Detroit and Mackinac were British-held, and even the Illinois country was lost when

Virginia withdrew its troops from Kaskaskia in 1781. What Clark had won in his brilliant campaigns was lost through vacillating American policies, the poverty of Congress and Virginia, and the provincialism of frontiersmen who would defend their homes but refused to march against vital distant objectives. England had a far better claim to the Northwest at war's end than in 1780, but what the Americans lost on the battlefield they gained at the peace table. The diplomats who met at Paris in 1782 to write the treaty giving the United States independence accomplished more for the West than all the bloody campaigns of the war.

Each negotiator had his own ambitions. Benjamin Franklin and John Jay, who represented the United States, wanted England to recognize their country's independence as a preliminary to further negotiations, then hoped to secure as favorable boundaries and concessions as possible. The Earl of Shelburne, who became British prime minister in July, 1782, and his agent, Richard Oswald, wished to separate the Americans from their French and Spanish allies. The Comte de Vergennes, French foreign minister, faced a more difficult problem. He had carried his country into war in 1778 by signing a treaty which bound France to continue fighting until American independence was won. He had lured Spain into the struggle a year later by promising continuous war until Gibraltar was restored to that nation. Now France was ready for peace, but the Mediterranean fortress was still in English hands. Vergennes' task was to secure independence for the Americans, then end the war by satisfying Spain with territorial concessions less difficult to obtain than Gibraltar. The fourth nation, Spain, was dominated by an able and aggressive foreign minister, the Count de Floridablanca. That hard-headed realist was determined to secure Gibraltar and to transform the Gulf of Mexico into a Spanish lake by acquiring the Floridas, exclusive navigation of the Mississippi River, and possibly a strip of territory east of that stream.

Vergennes saw his problem clearly. He knew that both France and the United States, although anxious for peace, were bound by treaty obligations to continue fighting until Spain was ready to lay down its arms—or until Gibraltar was restored. War might go on for years unless he could bribe Floridablanca into accepting peace. Why not, Vergennes reasoned, offer the Spaniards enough territory in the American West to compensate them for their failure to recapture that rocky fort. This seemed reasonable to the French foreign minister; he had made no boundary commitments to the United States and could with a clear conscience look on the trans-Appalachian country as conquered territory which could be assigned to any one of the allies. Hence he asked his secretary, Gerard de Rayneval, to work out a division of the West satisfactory to the Spanish ambassador to Versailles, the Count of Aranda. After several conferences Aranda agreed that the region north of the Ohio should be retained by England, Kentucky and eastern Tennessee should go to the United States, and the area south of the Cumberland and west of a line zigzagging to the Gulf at Apalachicola Bay

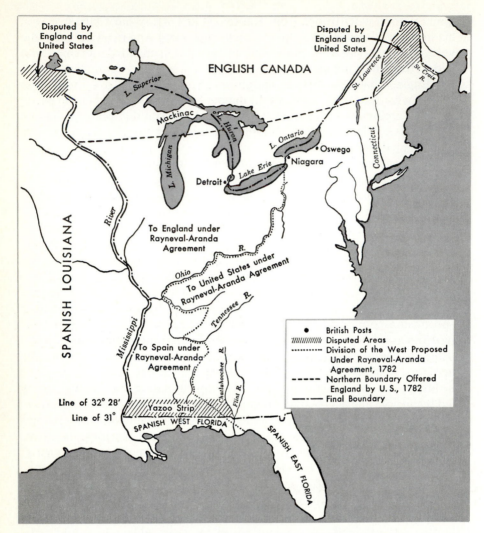

The West in the Peace Negotiations

should be assigned to Spain. This would give the Spaniards control of both banks of the Mississippi south of the Ohio and bar Americans from the river entirely. On September 6, 1782, Vergennes delivered this proposal to the American commissioners as his "personal ideal," keeping Spain's part in its formulation secret.

John Jay, who was acting alone due to Franklin's illness, was horrified. Vergennes, it seemed, was willing to carve up the new-born Republic for the benefit of greedy European neighbors even before independence was won. While Jay still pondered this unpleasant fact he received two other bits of information that apparently confirmed his worst fears. On September 10, 1782, Oswald handed him captured dispatches that proved the Chevalier de La Luzerne, French minister to the United States, guilty of trying to influence Congress to accept an Appalachian boundary. On the same day he learned that Rayneval had departed secretly for London to confer with Shelburne. Jay leaped to the conclusion that he had gone to persuade England to accept the Appalachian boundary or even offer that nation a separate peace. In the face of this seeming betrayal by an ally, why should the United States adhere to its outworn pledge of 1778? Better to protect the national interest by concluding an immediate treaty with Britain.

Jay acted at once. Oswald was told that the Americans were ready to negotiate, even without preliminary recognition of their independence, if his commission was altered to authorize dealings with agents of the United States—this being considered tacit recognition. At the same time Jay sent one of his own employees, Benjamin Vaughan, to assure Shelburne that the United States was ready to make an immediate peace if England would grant the Mississippi boundary and other concessions. The canny prime minister saw at once that this was a golden opportunity to split the allies. Oswald's new instructions were hurried to Paris by courier, reaching there on September 27, 1782. Negotiations began at once, and by October 5 Jay and Oswald agreed on a preliminary treaty which included the Mississippi line and a provision that both nations share navigation of that river. This draft proved unacceptable to England, for by the time it reached London on October 11 the government knew that a last allied assault on Gibraltar had failed. Hence Shelburne insisted on further concessions from the United States, particularly compensation for British merchants with outstanding loans in America and Loyalists who had abandoned property there.

John Adams, a third American delegate who arrived in Paris at that time, readily agreed to follow Jay's leadership. Together they persuaded Franklin to proceed without consulting Vergennes. Negotiations went forward rapidly until November 3, 1782, when preliminary articles were signed. These gave the British their choice of two northern boundaries. Both began at the St. Croix River and followed the "highlands" between the Atlantic and St. Lawrence to the Connecticut—a provision that led to a prolonged controversy, as the location of both the St. Croix and the "highlands" was disputed. One possible boundary ran due west from the Connecticut along the 45th parallel to the Mississippi; the other followed that parallel to the St. Lawrence, then through the Great Lakes and across the Grand Portage to the northwest corner of the Lake of the Woods. From that point the line extended "due west to the Mississippi"—another source of dispute as that river terminated south of the Lake of the Woods—down the Mississippi to the 31st parallel, east to the Chattahoochee, south along that stream to its junction with the Flint, east once more to the St. Mary's, and down the center of that twisting river to the sea. Because the fate of the Floridas was unknown at that time, a secret provision in the preliminary treaty provided that should England secure those provinces the southern boundary of the United States was to begin at the mouth of the Yazoo River and run east to the Chattahoochee along the line of 32° 28' rather than along the 31st parallel. This too caused controversy, as Spain ultimately secured the Floridas and laid claim to the whole "Yazoo Strip" that Jay and Adams were willing to grant their enemy but not their ally.

These boundaries were as advantageous as could have been expected. By deserting France and playing on England's desire for an immediate peace, the American commissioners gave their country a vast western territory that might otherwise have gone to Spain. In its other provisions the preliminary treaty was almost as favorable. The United States and England shared the right to navigate the Mississippi, Americans were granted fishing rights off Canada, and agreed to put no obstacles in the way of merchants or Loyalists trying to recover their property. British garrisons in the Northwest Posts that lay south of the border were to be evacuated "with all convenient speed." Shelburne accepted those provisions at once, after choosing the Great Lakes boundary, and on November 30, 1782, the preliminary treaty was signed by both sets of commissioners. Vergennes, who was shown a copy the next day, was probably secretly pleased that the Americans had violated their pledge and made a separate peace, for the desertion of an ally helped him persuade Spain to give up the fight. Five days later the Spanish government agreed to accept the Floridas and Minorca instead of Gibraltar. Anglo-French and Anglo-Spanish treaties were concluded by January 20, 1783, automatically putting the Anglo-American agreement into effect. By September 3, 1783, both England and the United States had ratified and signed the final treaty.

American diplomats won a significant victory for their fellow countrymen when they secured the West—even at the risk of angering their French allies and saviors—after military conquest failed. Yet even their repudiation of the Franco-American treaty would not have brought this triumph but for the generosity of Lord Shelburne. He, above all other statesmen, realized that frontier expansion was inevitable and that the American people would never be satisfied if their westward path was blocked. "The deed is done," he wrote later, "and a strong foundation laid for eternal amity between England and America." The vision of an enemy minister and the willingness of American negotiators to place national interest above international ethics secured the trans-Appalachian wilderness for the new republic.

THE TRANS-APPALACHIAN FRONTIER

The Western Problem
1783-1790

The Treaty of 1783 brought the infant American government face to face with the same staggering problems that plagued England's ministers after the Seven Years' War: how could Indians be removed from the trans-Appalachian wilderness, lands disposed of, and settlers governed? Britain's best statesmen failed to find an answer; now an untried congress, torn by dissension and weakened by sectional jealousies, must succeed or witness the collapse of the entire democratic experiment. To make matters even worse, the solution was complicated by the presence of a welter of conflicting interests involving land companies, traders, foreign intrigue, and state claims. Little wonder that some observers who remembered England's groping efforts viewed the task as insurmountable.

Congress' first step was to secure undisputed control of the West, for at the start of the Revolution the overmountain region was claimed by seven of the thirteen states on the basis of the crown-granted sea-to-sea charters to which they owed their origin. Massachusetts, Connecticut, North Carolina, and Georgia contended that their original grants, which provided each with a strip of coast and northern and southern boundaries running to the Pacific, extended their territories to the Mississippi. South Carolina, whose sea-to-sea charter was disputed by Georgia, laid claim to a fifty-mile strip between the 35th parallel and a line drawn west from the junction of the Tugaloo and Keowee rivers. Virginia insisted that her 1609 charter, extending the Old Dominion's boundaries "up into the land, throughout from sea to sea, west and northwest," gave her control of Kentucky and virtually all lands north and west of the Ohio River. New York claimed the same region, not on the basis of a colonial grant, but because her jurisdiction over the Iroquois applied to all lands conquered by that tribe.

From the beginning of the Revolution both national statesmen and representatives of the six landless states urged the cession of the western lands to the United States. The former argued that the trans-Appalachian domains were common property because they were "wrested from the common enemy by the blood and treasure of the thirteen states," that a nationally owned West would serve as a bond of unity during trying days when interstate rivalries threatened the Republic, that central control would satisfy frontiersmen who clamored through the war for a better form of government than individual states could provide, and that the lands were needed both for revenue and for satisfying bounties promised men who had enlisted in the Revolutionary armies. Spokesmen for the six states that did not claim western territories not only echoed these arguments but pointed out that cession was necessary to protect their own commonwealths. States with territories in the West, they argued, could care for most of their expenses by selling land. Those without would be forced to resort to higher taxes, driving their inhabitants to the landed states. The depopulation of stretches of the seaboard loomed as an unpleasant possibility.

Most of those who argued in this way were sincere, but the more vociferous were representatives of land companies who saw a chance to turn the conflict to their own advantage. Firmly against cession in each commonwealth were speculators who hoped to use their local influence to secure state-granted lands in the West. Arguing for cession were two organizations that antedated the Revolution, the Indiana Company and the Illinois-Wabash Land Company, both of which claimed lands in western Virginia on the basis of purchases made under the Camden-Yorke decision. Their leaders knew that Virginia would never recognize their claims, especially after 1776 when the legislature specifically voided all titles acquired directly from Indians. Congress, however, might be more lenient. With this in mind both companies were reorganized soon after independence to include leading politicians in the landless Middle States. These men, working together under the able leadership of Robert Morris of Pennsylvania, formed a solid congressional bloc in favor of immediate cession. They were a power to be reckoned with, for they could always count on the support of Maryland, Pennsylvania, New Jersey, and Delaware, and could usually capture additional votes from Rhode Island and New Hampshire.

The Middle States speculators showed their hand first by attempting to write a clause into an early draft of the Articles of Confederation authorizing Congress to define state boundaries and erect new western states, but the seven land-owning states defeated that proposal, substituting in the final draft a guarantee that "no state shall be deprived of territory for the benefit of the United States." When the Articles were submitted to the states for ratification, the speculators and nationalists had their revenge. On December 15, 1778, Maryland announced it would never ratify until the landed states surrendered their holdings to the central government. This resolution was couched in patriotic language and stressed Congress' need for territories to satisfy soldiers' bonuses, but the influence of jobbers became apparent two days later when Virginia offered to provide all lands required for this purpose free of charge. Now the Maryland speculators had no choice but to state their position openly. The formal declaration of the state's intentions, submitted to Congress on January 6, 1779, stressed only the common right of all the people to all parts of trans-Appalachia not granted to individuals before the war. The issue, as Virginia saw it, was clear: should she surrender her western lands to the Indiana and Illinois-Wabash Land companies, or keep them to be exploited by her own speculators?

Others, however, did not realize this, and Virginia's position grew steadily weaker during the next two years. Her attempt to expose the companies by opening the West to settlement backfired when a congressional committee, dominated by representatives of the landless states, adopted a resolution in November, 1779, urging that no western territory be sold until after the war. To make matters worse, New York ceded its shadowy claims in February, 1780, setting a precedent dangerous to Virginia's interests. Many prominent men, even within the Old Dominion, were won to cession by the military reverses of that year. Better to strengthen the American cause by ceding the West and allowing the Articles of Confederation to go into effect, they argued, than risk defeat by England. This mounting pressure was too much to resist, but Virginia was not ready to surrender completely. In September, 1780, it agreed to turn over its western lands only if Congress guaranteed that no private purchases previously made there would be recognized.

This unlooked-for development sent the speculators into action. Petitions were signed, pamphlets circulated, and stock judiciously distributed among doubting congressmen. These efforts bore fruit in October when Congress accepted the Virginia cession only after striking out the provision respecting private purchases. Undaunted, the House of Burgesses on January 2, 1781, ceded the United States all lands north of the Ohio, but with restrictions on land companies intact. This maneuver placed the decision squarely up to Maryland; refusal to ratify now would prove it was acting in the interest of speculators rather than with the nation's welfare at heart. On February 2, 1781, the state's legislature formally accepted the new frame of government.

The land companies were still not ready to surrender. Virginia had ceded, but Congress might be persuaded not to accept the cession until the obnoxious provision on private purchases was stricken out. For the next three years they worked frantically, but to no avail. Twice speculator-dominated committees insisted that the national government already owned the trans-Appalachian country and could grant it without respect to Virginia's wishes, one maintaining that Congress inherited the West from England, the other that the New York cession included all territory claimed by the Old Dominion. Fortunately neither report was adopted, for sentiment was swinging against the speculators as their role in the sordid controversy became clear. A few greedy individuals, Americans saw, were denying Congress a domain badly needed to ease the nation's financial burdens and satisfy bounty-holding Revolutionary heroes. The shift in popular opinion was shown in June, 1783, when a new committee, made up largely of representatives of landholding states, urged Congress to accept the Virginia cession with all restrictions attached. This report was adopted in September, and on March 1, 1784, jubilant Virginia officials, happy in their victory over the speculators, transferred their state's western holding to the United States.

In her cession Virginia set a pattern that other states later followed. All had issued land bounties to their Revolutionary militia and were now faced with the necessity of retaining enough western territory to satisfy those claims. Hence the Virginia assembly retained a "military reserve" between the Scioto and Little Miami rivers as well as a 150,000 acre plot opposite Louisville which was awarded George Rogers Clark and his men. Only the lands north of the Ohio River were included in the cession, as most of Kentucky was already sold and that region was kept as a county until ready for statehood.

The other northern states quickly followed the example of New York and Virginia. Massachusetts ceded all its lands west of New York in November, 1784, reserving a claim to the western portion of that state. Connecticut, after vainly trying to retain title to the Wyoming Valley of Pennsylvania, succumbed to popular pressure in May, 1786, when it surrendered all of its interior territory save a "Western Reserve" of nearly 4,000,000 acres in northwestern Ohio. This it managed to hold by bargaining so skillfully with other states that they finally agreed to a land grab that had few precedents and less justification. By the end of 1786 the United States controlled all of the Northwest, except the Virginia and Connecticut reserves.

The states south of Virginia proved less responsive to public opinion, for most of them had suffered heavily during the war and were anxious to profit from their western lands. The eagerness of the legislatures of North Carolina, South Carolina, and Georgia to reap large returns from their interior territories proved an irresistible lure to speculators and plunged those southern governments into a labyrinth of intrigue that lasted for a quarter-century.

The situation was particularly bad in North Carolina. As soon as popular interest in cession began to develop, the assembly, in 1783, hurriedly threw open the Tennessee country to settlers, setting aside only a military reserve for bounty holders in the Cumberland Valley. The low price asked—about $5 for 100 acres—sent Carolina land jobbers upon a speculative rampage; within seven months 4,000,000 acres were sold at the Hillsboro office. By that time sentiment for cession was developing rapidly, fomented by eastern planters who disliked paying taxes to protect distant frontiersmen and by western speculators who looked to the national government for improvements that would increase the value of their holdings. Their influence resulted in an act in June, 1784, ceding the Tennessee country to the United

States and specifically stating that all previous grants there must be respected. The measure was passed over the protests of frontiersmen who hesitated to trade the assured protection of North Carolina for the nebulous advantages of national control.

The westerners determined not to accept the decision without protest. When news of the cession reached their overhill homes a spontaneous call went forth for a convention to meet at Jonesboro in August, 1784. The rough woodsmen who assembled in that wilderness town decided on their future course at once: they would set up a government and enter the Union as an independent state. This seemed legal and proper; Congress had just resolved to admit new states into the Republic, and only separate existence would assure protection for their homes and lives. Hence they drew up a petition to Congress, laid out boundaries that included much of southwestern Virginia

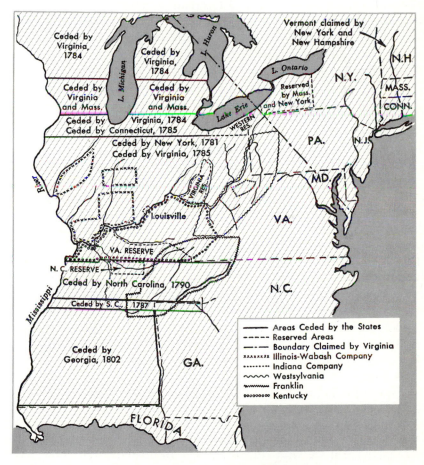

Western Land Cessions, 1780–1802

as well as eastern Tennessee in their new commonwealth, and provided for a second convention to frame a constitution.

Before this convention met the situation had changed. In November, 1784, the North Carolina legislature, alarmed by the separate-statehood movement and swayed by a humanitarian desire to deal more fairly with the westerners, repealed the act of cession. At the same time it tried to win back the rebellious settlers by giving them their own court system and an efficient militia force. The effect of this appeasement policy was shown when the frontiersmen assembled in December to draw up a constitution for their new state. Where the August meeting had been harmonious, the new gathering was divided into two groups. One, headed by John Sevier of the Holston settlements who had been a leader of the statehood movement from the first, insisted on separation despite North Carolina's action. The other, led by Colonel John Tipton, long a rival of Sevier, favored immediate capitulation. The separate-state men were in a majority and after riding rough-shod over their opponents, agreed to create a new state of Frankland—or Franklin as it was soon called. After the laws of North Carolina were adopted as a temporary constitution, Sevier was chosen governor by acclamation. Frontier pride and provincialism had launched a wilderness experiment in self-government.

The State of Franklin fared badly from the first. Its survival depended on congressional recognition, yet Congress not only refused to consider admitting the new state but adopted a decidedly hostile attitude which was shown especially in dealing with the Indians. The Franklinites, with the usual frontier disregard for native rights, attempted to secure lands for expansion by forcing a handful of minor Cherokee chiefs to sign the so-called Treaty of Dumplin Creek in May, 1785. This illegal agreement, which extended the whites' territory as far as the watershed of the Little River, was protested so vigorously by the rest of the tribe that national authorities felt called upon to intercede. The United States commissioners sent to meet the Indians in November, 1785, not only disavowed the Treaty of Dumplin Creek but drew up their own Treaty of Hopewell in open defiance of the Franklin government. The lines established by the Treaties of DeWitt's Corner and Long Island were recognized, a narrow strip in North Carolina purchased from the Cherokee, a boundary run westward from Long Island through Cumberland Gap and along the Cumberland River to place the Nashville settlements in American territory. The disgruntled pioneers were forced to watch their lands turned over to Indians by a government whose support they had anticipated.

Neither congressional hostility nor internal dissension could discourage the optimistic westerners; instead they believed that the constant disputes between Franklinites, anti-Franklinites, and government men would "be found useful in forming the manner of the people; . . . the next generation in Frankland will vie with Athens itself." In this cheerful mood they met together in November, 1785, to draw up a constitution for their state. The document that emerged was surprisingly democratic; it swept away nearly all property qualifications for office holding, introduced manhood suffrage, a popularly elected one-house legislature, the registration of voters, election by ballot, and a crude form of referendum. These liberal features were little to the liking of Governor Sevier or his little clique of friends who had no more sympathy with true democracy than any other representatives of the planter class of frontier society. Their influence was sufficient to defeat the constitution and substitute a modified version of the North Carolina frame of government.

More than this was needed to save Sevier's tottering government. During the summer of 1786 the North Carolina legislature, determined to stamp out the rebellion, adopted a series of laws designed to bring the outlaws back into the fold—one forgave all taxes for any man accepting the state's authority—and named officials to take over "Franklin County." These two steps swung most of the Franklinites into line, but Sevier with a few friends doggedly maintained his right to the governorship. Conflicts between the outlawed Franklinites and loyal North Carolinians grew increasingly serious

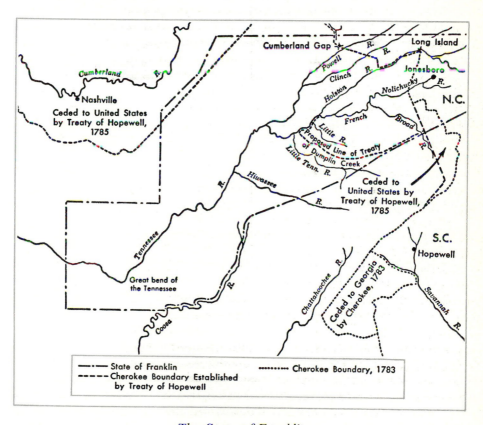

The State of Franklin

until they reached a climax in February, 1788. At that time several state officers, led by John Tipton, seized some of Sevier's slaves for nonpayment of North Carolina taxes. The outraged governor retaliated by storming the homes of his enemies. A pitched battle followed, in which Sevier's outnumbered party was soundly defeated, although the discredited leader escaped capture until October, 1788, when he ventured into the Nolichucky settlements. The state authorities were wise enough to pardon him rather than allow him to develop a martyr's following, and Sevier returned to his old position as a western leader. The State of Franklin was dead for all time.

With the West at peace, North Carolina again ceded its Tennessee lands. By that time so much of the region was sold that the act of cession, passed in December, 1789, and accepted by Congress two months later, conveyed little more than jurisdiction. In the meantime South Carolina turned over its narrow strip in August, 1787, leaving Georgia the last state to surrender its western territories. There too the hope of financial returns delayed the final surrender; the legislature in 1789 and again in 1795 sold the whole tract to speculating companies, then rescinded the sales. Not until 1802 was the last cession completed and the United States assured possession of the vast wilderness between the Appalachians and the Mississippi.

Congress had begun to shape the United States' western policy long before this, for when Virginia ceded its holdings in 1784 the others were bound to follow. During the next few years, and with a systematic progression that resulted from chance rather than plan, the three most important problems were solved: how to sell the public domain, how to clear away the Indian inhabitants, and how to govern the federal territories. The monumental laws embodying these decisions set a pattern that was followed through the history of the frontier in determining relations between the government and the West.

The nation's first concern was a means of selling the newly acquired lands, for money was needed to reduce the Revolutionary debt and meet part of the government's expenses. The complexities of the problem immediately became clear. Congress must choose between two established systems: the New England practice of surveying lands before settlement and selling them in orderly blocks, or the southern custom of "indiscriminate location and subsequent survey" which allowed a settler to purchase a warrant, lay out his plot where he wished, and then have it surveyed. Both methods had elements of strength and weakness. The northern system did away with conflicting titles and assured pioneers protection as they advanced westward in compact tiers, but discouraged migration by overemphasizing the social group and by forcing the purchase of bad land along with good. The southern system, although favored by westerners, bred a welter of conflicting titles, for each homeseeker avoided poor soil by laying out irregularly shaped plots which could not be surveyed accurately. Somewhere between those two extremes—one sacrificing settlement for order and the

other impossible to administer—Congress must find the answer to its problem.

Suggestions began pouring in as early as 1781 when a pamphleteer,
Pelatiah Webster, urged the government to divide the West into square
townships to be auctioned off at a minimum price of a $1 an acre. For the
next three years the question was debated occasionally, but not until March,
1785, when a committee was set up to recommend a definite program, did
Congress act. The report proposed that the public domain be divided into
townships seven miles square, that these be sold at auction with a minimum
price of $1 an acre, and that only whole townships be disposed of to united
groups of settlers. This proposal, which virtually adopted the New England
system, aroused southern congressmen. They pointed out that individualistic
pioneers from their states were unwilling to band together for township
purchases, thus giving socially minded northerners an undue advantage.
These valid criticisms led to a general modification of the proposal in the
month of debate that followed. The result was the Ordinance of 1785,
adopted on May 20 of that year—one of the most important legislative measures in American history.

All government-owned lands, it stated, would be divided into townships
six miles square. These, in turn, would be subdivided into thirty-six numbered "sections," each containing one square mile or 640 acres. Alternate
townships would be sold as a whole and in sections, thus satisfying both

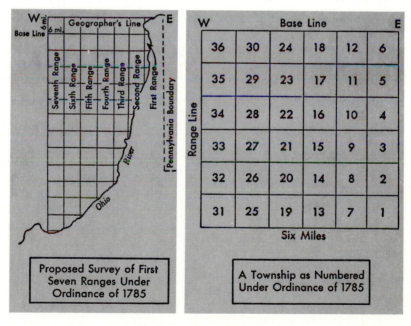

Proposed Survey of First
Seven Ranges Under
Ordinance of 1785

A Township as Numbered
Under Ordinance of 1785

The Ordinance of 1785

New Englanders who wanted large units and southerners who wished smaller plots. The auction method was adopted, with regular sales in each state, and a minimum price of $1 an acre. Congress reserved four sections in each township for subsequent disposal and set aside one—section sixteen—to maintain schools. The Ordinance stated that the first "base line," as the east-west surveys were called, should run due west from the point where the Pennsylvania boundary crossed the Ohio River, and that north-south "range lines" should extend southward from this to the Ohio. As soon as the first "Seven Ranges" were surveyed the whole tract, in the southeast corner of present Ohio, would be opened to settlers.

When Congress adopted the Ordinance of 1785 it traded the immediate benefit of land sales for a well-ordered future. The measure did end the confusion prevalent under the southern warrant system; now a prospective settler purchased a definite, previously surveyed tract—section twenty in township number three, for example—rather than title to a plot that he could lay out himself. Yet months, or even years, would be needed to complete the laborious surveys necessary before sales could begin. More years might be required to persuade independent men and women to buy well-marked government tracts rather than to select choice lands that pleased them. The warrant system not only promised Congress better financial returns, but was better suited to the needs of the frontier. By limiting sales to auctions in eastern states, barring purchases of less than 640 acres, and decreeing that the minimum price for a plot should be $640, the Ordinance prevented pioneer farmers from buying government land, for few settlers needed such

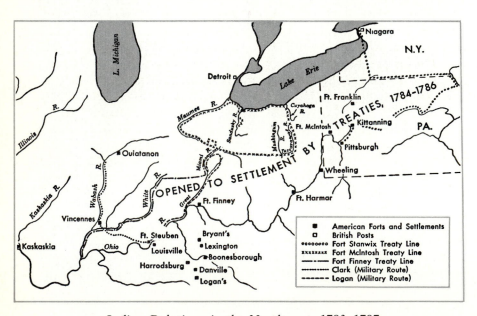

Indian Relations in the Northwest, 1783–1787

a large tract nor could they afford to buy on those terms. Instead the door was opened to speculators who could purchase sections or townships at eastern auctions, then parcel them out to users in smaller tracts and on credit. This probably was in the minds of congressmen, many of whom were land jobbers themselves. While surveys were getting under way, Congress turned to the second step needed to open the West: removal of the Indians. The five commissioners already named to treat with the northwestern tribes were instructed to visit the Ohio country, meet the natives, and establish a boundary extending the area open to settlement west to the Falls of the Ohio. Three of them went at once to Ft. Stanwix where they badgered the Iroquois into surrendering all claims to the Northwest for a few paltry presents. A little later, on January 21, 1785, the Chippewa, Ottawa, Delaware, and Wyandot tribes were summoned to Ft. McIntosh and intimidated into giving up all their Ohio lands except a reservation between the Cuyahoga-Tuscarawas portage and the Maumee River. Even this region was not completely theirs; the United States retained several strategic spots on the Maumee, Sandusky, and Great Miami rivers for trading posts.

The Treaties of Ft. Stanwix and Ft. McIntosh complicated, rather than solved, the northwestern Indian problem. Neither satisfied the natives; the Iroquois cession only angered Ohio tribesmen who claimed the Six Nations had no right to cede their hunting grounds, and the Ft. McIntosh agreement was useless because the Shawnee refused to sign. To make matters worse they gave lawless squatters an excuse to swarm across the Ohio River onto lands still claimed by the Indians. From Kentucky, Virginia, and Pennsylvania these adventurers came, to elbow into the peaceful Illinois villages, crowd into Vincennes, and stake out their tomahawk claims along the north bank of the Ohio from Pittsburgh to the Muskingum. The commissioners, alarmed lest this invasion arouse native resentment, instructed Colonel Josiah Harmar, who commanded the federal troops on the northwest frontier, to drive them out by any means necessary. This was done in the spring of 1785 but the commander of the force brought back discouraging news. He found several thousand "banditti whose actions are a disgrace to human nature" squatting on the federal domain well organized with their own elected governor, and firm in the belief that every American had "an undoubted right to pass into every vacant country and there to form their constitution." Strong measures would be needed, he reported, to drive back those defiant wilderness spirits.

Harmar, realizing that merely policing the frontier would not suffice, secured congressional consent for a new fort, Ft. Harmar at the mouth of the Muskingum, but even this failed to halt the oncoming tide during the summer of 1785. Most embarrassed of all by the illegal migration were the Indian commissioners who were laboring to secure Shawnee consent for the northwestern land cessions. In an effort to placate their native charges they sent out runners summoning the Ohio tribes to a new conference at the mouth of the Great Miami in October, 1785. After a month of waiting a few

Wyandot and Delaware chiefs straggled in, although the Shawnee remained aloof until a threat of war brought 150 sullen warriors to the meeting ground early in January 1786. Three weeks of negotiations, marked by threats from the officials and grudging concessions from the Indians, were climaxed by the signing of the Treaty of Ft. Finney—named after a blockhouse thrown up by the American troops while they were waiting—on January 31, 1786. The Shawnee reluctantly agreed to the Ft. McIntosh cession and to an extension of the boundary westward along the White River to the mouth of the Wabash, but they repudiated the agreement as soon as they returned to the safety of their villages.

That tribe's defiance of the United States brought Indian dissatisfaction to the boiling point in the spring of 1786. Through the Ohio country irate warriors attacked traders and raided settlements, while the Iroquois renounced the Ft. Stanwix treaty and threatened war if their lands were occupied. These attacks were climaxed on July 15 when 500 Miami warriors surrounded Vincennes and demanded the right to slaughter all Americans there. When their cold-blooded request was refused they retreated grumblingly, letting it be known they would soon return. If the frontier was to be saved from war something more was needed than the feeble efforts of an impoverished Congress and the inadequate protection of the few soldiers at Ft. Harmar and Ft. Finney. As usual in such a situation westerners took matters into their own hands. Throughout Kentucky the demand rose for George Rogers Clark to save the Northwest.

Clark, despite advancing years and a growing tendency toward alcoholic overindulgence, rose to the emergency in his usual capable fashion. Two expeditions were planned; one under Clark to march north from Ft. Steuben, a new federal outpost across the river from Louisville, to destroy the Miami villages on the upper Wabash and Miami, the other to advance along the Great Miami River into the Shawnee country. The latter, led by Colonel Benjamin Logan, destroyed ten towns and 15,000 bushels of corn, but Clark's 1,200 militiamen mutinied at the mouth of Vermillion Creek and returned in disorder without sighting a single foe. The Indians, encouraged by this failure, held two conferences during the winter of 1786-87 to repudiate the treaties of Ft. Stanwix, Ft. McIntosh, and Ft. Finney and declare that "the line now cutting Pennsylvania shall bound them on the sun-rising, and the Ohio shall be the boundary between them and the Big Knives."

Congress was helpless in face of this native demand for the whole Ohio country. It attempted to better relations by passing the Ordinance of 1786 which set up an Indian Department patterned after the earlier English model, with superintendents for the regions north and south of the Ohio River authorized to bar unlicensed traders and guarantee the Indians fair prices for furs. This halfhearted palliative meant nothing, as the United States had no manufacturing establishments to provide trading goods, even if the day for peaceful negotiation had not passed. When raids mounted in intensity during the spring of 1787 Congress, recognizing the need for force, strengthened the garrisons at Ft. Pitt, Ft. McIntosh, Ft. Harmar, Ft. Finney, Ft. Steuben, and Vincennes. A war was needed before the Northwest was safe for settlers.

Yet the government's financial needs required an immediate sale of western territory. Hence as soon as the treaties of Ft. Stanwix and Ft. McIntosh were signed, work began on the first base line, or "Geographer's Line" as it was called, of the "Seven Ranges." The task proved formidable—surveyors worked over rough, forested country under constant threat of Indian attack—but the little band of men stuck doggedly to their task between September 1785 and April 1787. By that time only four ranges were laid out and Congress, impatient under its financial burdens, decided to throw these open to settlement at once. The first sales, held at New York in September and October, 1787, were disappointing; buyers were few, bidding so listless that the price seldom rose above the minimum, purchases small, and the total profit only $176,090 in depreciated currency. This was not the fortune needed to retire the national debt. The land system must be revised to bring in larger returns.

Congress was moved to make this change by pressure from one of the most important land companies in history, the Ohio Company. This influential organization was the brain child of Brigadier General Rufus Putnam, a Revolutionary veteran from New England. Putnam knew that Washington's soldiers were mustered out with their pockets stuffed with "certificates of indebtedness"—depreciated government securities issued in lieu of back pay—which Congress would accept at par value in any land sales. Why not form a company, sell stock to veterans in return for those worthless certificates, and purchase a large tract in the Ohio country? With this in mind Putnam persuaded his close friend, Brigadier General Benjamin Tupper, to join the party surveying the Seven Ranges with an eye to spying out a suitable spot for a colony. Tupper's few months in the West had convinced him that the garden spot of the Ohio region was the Muskingum Valley, a fertile area guarded by Ft. Harmar and adjacent to the Seven Ranges.

His glowing report so fired Putnam's enthusiasm that the two men lost no time in inserting "A Piece called Information" in the Massachusetts papers, asking all former soldiers interested to meet at the Bunch of Grapes Tavern in Boston on March 1, 1786. The eleven delegates who gathered that day were easily persuaded to endorse the scheme. Then and there they formed the Ohio Company, pledged themselves to sell $1,000,000 worth of stock for Continental certificates, and agreed to migrate to the Ohio lands that would be purchased with this sum. When they met again a year later only 250 thousand-dollar shares had been sold, but they decided to buy as much as possible with the money on hand, hoping to expand their holdings when their successful colony brought a rush of new subscribers. The task of negotiating with Congress was entrusted to a shrewd Ipswich clergyman, the Reverend Manasseh Cutler, who reached New York, where the government was meeting, on July 5, 1787.

His proposal—that Congress overthrow the entire principle of small sales underlying the Ordinance of 1785 by selling his company a plot at less than a depreciated dollar an acre—aroused so little congressional enthusiasm that by July 20 Cutler was on the point of admitting defeat and returning to New England. At that point, he received a call from Colonel William Duer, secretary of the Board of Treasury which handled all land sales. A "number of the principal characters in the city," his visitor explained, were interested in the success of the Ohio Company sale, but only if they could share secretly in the proceeds. This was sufficient to interest Cutler, who was enough of a Yankee to know an opportunity when he saw one, and the two men set out for Brooklyn where, over an excellent oyster supper, they hatched one of the nation's important speculations.

Duer's scheme was as simple as it was dishonest. He represented a number of congressmen, government leaders, and businessmen who were eager to buy Ohio land but could not because of their official positions. They wished the Ohio Company to apply for 1,500,000 acres for itself, to be paid for in two $500,000 installments, one when the sale was made and the other on completion of the surveys. At the same time it was to purchase an additional 5,000,000 acres for Colonel Duer's associates, who were to organize as the Scioto Company and pay for their tract in six installments. In return for this service Colonel Duer agreed to loan the Ohio Company the money needed to complete its down payment and to take Cutler and one of his associates, Winthrop Sargent, into the Scioto Company. They would, Duer explained, be given thirteen shares between them, Duer and his friends would keep thirteen more, and six would be sold in Europe. The profits from those six would allow the company to meet the few payments necessary until its option was sold to some other speculating concern at a handsome profit. All parties would benefit: the Ohio Company would get 1,000,000 acres of choice land for about eight cents an acre, Duer and his associates would have an option on 2,000,000 more acres, and Cutler and Sargent would control an equal amount—all for the cost of one oyster supper and a loan of $200,000 in depreciated currency. Little wonder that the speculation promised to be one of the most profitable in history.

Colonel Duer, who agreed to push the sale through Congress, lived up to his bargain well. He and Cutler reached an agreement on July 21, 1787. Two days later Congress authorized Duer's Board of Treasury to sell large blocks of land to companies, and on July 24 Cutler laid down his terms, announcing with a great show of bluster that he would leave the city unless they were accepted. After three more days—to create an impression of proper deliberation—the board agreed to the sale. Two plots were turned over to the Ohio Company. One lay along the Ohio River between the seventh and seventeenth range lines and extended inward far enough to include 1,500,000 acres—although when the surveys were completed the company actually received 1,781,760 acres. The second embraced 5,000,000 acres between the first tract and the Scioto River. Cutler received only an

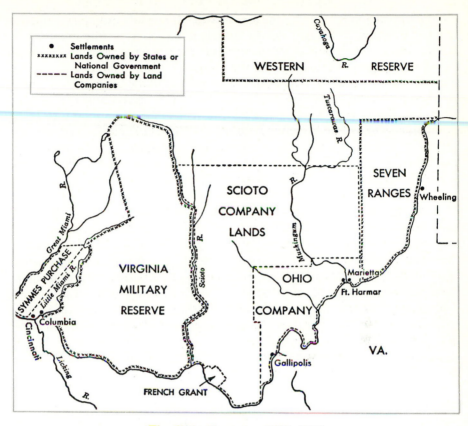

The Ohio Country, 1787–1790

option on those lands requiring payment at the rate of 66⅔ cents an acre in four semiannual installments beginning six months after the external surveys were completed. This he turned over to the Scioto Company. Cutler was still not satisfied, even with a bargain that gave his company 1,500,000 acres at eight cents an acre and himself a sizeable interest in a giant speculation. He pointed out to Congress that orderly government for the Ohio country must be provided before the Ohio and Scioto companies could hope for profitable sales. His prodding spurred adoption of the Ordinance of 1787, a measure that ranked with the Ordinance of 1785 in shaping the future of the West.

Cutler and his fellow landjobbers had nothing to do with shaping the Ordinance; congressmen had long wrangled over a governmental system for the western territories before he whipped them into action. On one point they agreed unanimously: they must not repeat the mistakes that had been responsible for the Revolution. Their problem, they knew, was the same that faced Parliament before 1776, for the public domain was really a vast colony owned jointly by the thirteen states. England's American empire collapsed because it failed to grant sufficient autonomy to the component parts; American Revolutionists had insisted on a system of coordinacy which would have placed colonies and mother country on an equal footing, bound together only through the allegiance both paid the king. When Parliament failed to recognize this and tried to rule the king's American subjects, war followed. Hence congressmen realized they must grant autonomy to their own colonies to escape a second revolution. The Union could exist only so long as no one of its parts was subservient to any other.

This was made clear by the rebellious attitude of westerners during and just after the Revolution. The pioneers who lived beyond the mountains were men and women of a different world—the "Western World" they called it—who demanded the right to shape their own destiny. What did self-satisfied easterners know of life on the frontier, of the need for protection, easy land laws, and less burdensome taxes? Petitions sent over the mountains to protest rulings of a distant legislature were strangely reminiscent of protests that colonists of an earlier generation showered on Parliament. Moreover, when demands were ignored, these colonists of the West showed a dangerous tendency to take matters into their own hands. Separate state-hood movements flourished and died in the West all through the Revolutionary Era. Pennsylvania was so plagued by demands of its overmountain citizens for independence that in 1783 it threatened all agitators with the death penalty. North Carolina lost control of its frontier settlers entirely for a time when they formed their own state of Franklin. Kentucky nourished a similar separatist movement for some years after 1780. North of the Ohio squatters fought eviction by petitioning for admission as a new state. Even the handful of settlers on Clark's grant opposite Louisville in 1785 proclaimed the right to make their own laws in the absence of adequate government. Surveying this turbulent scene, congressmen realized that the West would be satisfied only with the same rights and privileges under the central government that the East enjoyed. Those could be granted only by erecting the trans-Appalachian territories into states, to be admitted into the Union on terms of full equality with the original states.

This principle was clearly stated in October, 1780, when Congress tried to persuade the landed states to cede their western holdings by promising that all cessions would be "formed into separate republican states which shall become members of the federal union, and have the same rights and sovereignty, freedom and independence as the other states." From that time debate hinged only about the size and method of admission of new states. Numerous plans were suggested. An "Army Plan" submitted by a group of officers in 1783 proposed statehood for present Ohio as a means of caring for soldiers' land bounties; a "Financiers' Plan" offered by several business leaders two months later would have divided the West into territories embracing two degrees of latitude and three of longitude which would become states as soon as their population reached 20,000. More important was a plan submitted to Congress in March, 1784, by one of its own committees. Thomas Jefferson, who as chairman was largely responsible for the report, suggested that the Mississippi Valley be divided into fourteen dis- tricts, each with an impressive classical name. The first settlers would set up a temporary government with a legislature, elective officials, and delegate to Congress, which would control the district until its population reached 20,000 when it would be admitted "into the Congress of the United States, on an equal footing with the said original states."

Jefferson's Ordinance of 1784 never went into effect, for Congress ruled that it should operate only after all landed states ceded their western terri- tories and long before that time several of its features were attacked. West- erners disliked its emphasis on rectangular state boundaries rather than divisions provided by nature. Easterners had two more important com- plaints. One was levelled against the large number of states planned for the Mississippi Valley. These would, alarmed congressmen pointed out, even- tually outnumber the older dominions, wrest control of the government from the East, and rule the nation in the interests of frontier agriculture. Fewer and larger western states would alone protect the seaboard's economy. Equally alarming to conservative eastern representatives was the complete democracy provided by Jefferson's ordinance. They insisted that frontier settlers were incapable of ruling themselves and that external control, at least in the early stages of each new territorial government, was needed to assure an orderly administration.

Congress was still debating these controversial points in July, 1787, when the Reverend Manasseh Cutler appeared with his petition. His prod- ding forced the appointment of a new committee on July 9; two days later its report, modified by many congressmen's suggestions, was presented and on July 13 the Ordinance of 1787 was adopted by the unanimous vote of the eight states present. The first of its three sections erected the "Territory North West of the Ohio" into one temporary district with the provision that it eventually be carved into not less than three or more than five territories. If Congress decided on three, one north-south boundary was to run through the mouth of the Great Miami River, the other through Vincennes to the Wabash and down that stream to the Ohio. If five territories were agreed upon an east-west line touching the southern tip of Lake Michigan was to be added.

The second section of the Ordinance established three stages in the evolutionary process by which each territory was to become a state. In the first the people were to be controlled by a governor, secretary, and three judges named by Congress, authorized to enforce laws and control the militia. When the adult male population reached 5,000 the territory would enter the second stage, with an elected legislature to share its power with a council of five selected by the governor and Congress. The assembly was to name a delegate to Congress who could speak but not vote. The final stage would be attained when the territory's inhabitants numbered 60,000. It then could frame a constitution and apply for admission into the Union on equal terms with the older states. The third section of the Ordinance contained a noteworthy bill of rights which guaranteed the people of the Northwest Territory freedom of worship, proportional representation, jury trial, privileges of the common law, the writ of habeas corpus, and security for private contracts. Slavery was prohibited and aristocratic inheritance laws designed to perpetuate great estates were forbidden.

The Ordinance of 1787, a conservative document written by jealous easterners who wanted to guard their own political and economic supremacy, failed to satisfy the West. Frontier settlers objected to the oversized states, the complete lack of self-rule during the early territorial stage, and the absolute veto power of the governor during the second. They resented property qualifications which required all voters to own fifty acres of land and all legislators 200, not because these restricted the franchise, but because such checks were out of keeping with the democratic spirit of the frontier. Despite these faults the Ordinance of 1787 did more to perpetuate the Union than any document save the Constitution. Men could now leave the older states assured they were not surrendering their political privileges. Congress had not only saved the Republic, but had removed one great obstacle to the westward movement.

This was shown by the immediate burst of activity in lands opened by the Ordinance. The Ohio Company moved first. Its advance parties, setting out from Massachusetts and Connecticut during the winter of 1787-88, beached their boats on the sloping shores below Ft. Harmar on April 7 and fell at once to building a town they called Marietta. The whole process was carefully supervised by the company which donated land for the village, paid for the first buildings, laid out lots and farms, awarded free "Donation Lands" to "Warlike Christian Men" who would settle at dangerous spots in the interior, offered waterpower sites to gristmill and sawmill operators, and divided the lands among the settlers: a town lot, an eight-acre field near the village, and a 116 acre pasture along the Ohio going to each. Here, in other words, was a New England village transplanted bodily to the Ohio wilderness, with a paternalistic colonizing company playing the same valuable role that town proprietors played in seventeenth-century Massachusetts. Their concern was the welfare of their people, not profits, and they looked after their charges with solicitous attention, even planting shade trees along the Marietta streets and issuing each settler half a pint of whiskey to assure a proper celebration of the first Fourth of July spent in their new homes. Seldom have a people migrated with less hardship than the New Englanders who moved west with the Ohio Company.

This was in marked contrast to the suffering of immigrants lured to Ohio by less scrupulous speculators between 1787 and 1789. First to arrive were a group under John Cleves Symmes, a New Jersey politician who in October, 1787, petitioned Congress for 1,000,000 acres of the rich, rolling country between the Great Miami and Little Miami rivers. Without waiting for final action on his request he started west in the spring of 1788 with a few followers who purchased sites along the Ohio. Scarcely had Symmes reached his projected colony when he learned that Congress had sold him only a twenty-mile-wide strip on the east bank of the Great Miami rather than the lands requested. Many of the plots already sold lay beyond his purchase and Symmes, hoping to persuade the government to give him the tract he first requested, continued to make grants in that region. One was to a group of pioneers who laid out the town of Columbia a short distance below the mouth of the Little Miami in November, 1788. More important was the sale of a plot opposite the mouth of the Licking to a small company of Kentucky speculators. These frontiersmen—who demonstrated their classical knowledge by naming their settlement Losantiville (L for Licking, os for mouth, anti for opposite, ville for city)—hit upon one of the garden spots of the Ohio Valley. Their village was destined to expand into the West's principal metropolis under the slightly less burdensome name of Cincinnati. Yet neither of these outposts prospered as did Marietta, for Symmes contributed nothing but oppressive prices and conflicting titles which discouraged settlement. He, like most speculators, hindered rather than aided the frontier advance.

This was even more true of the Scioto Company. Colonel Duer and his associates, all of whom were involved in a score of bold speculations, had no intention of developing their 5,000,000 acres. Instead they hoped to sell six of the company's thirty-two shares in Europe, use the returns from these to make payments needed to keep their option, and finally unload the whole tract on other speculators to parcel out among individuals. This scheme depended on selling the six shares in Europe at a price high enough to meet at least the first installment due the government. That task was intrusted, strangely enough, to Joel Barlow, a dreamy young lawyer who was famed for his authorship of a bombastic poem called *The Vision of Columbus* rather than for his business acumen. His success in selling Ohio Company shares endeared him to Cutler, however, and Colonel Duer reluctantly consented to his appointment, perhaps thinking that a poet was well-suited to sell lands that the company did not own.

Barlow never understood the scheme in which he was involved. Instead of disposing of the option or shares in the Scioto Company he tramped the streets of Paris for ten months trying unsuccessfully to peddle small tracts of territory. At this point, in the summer of 1789, he had the bad fortune to fall into the hands of a corrupt Englishman, William Playfair, who made a most sensible suggestion. The French, he said, would never purchase land from an unknown foreigner, but would buy anything from a seemingly respectable company. Barlow was so impressed that he agreed to help form a new corporation, the Compagnie de Scioto, and to sell it 3,000,000 acres of Scioto land, to be paid for in regular installments as the territory was sold. Playfair, as the concern's agent, launched an intensive selling campaign at once. Maps and pamphlets were strewn over Paris, showing the Seven Ranges and Ohio Company tracts as settled, describing a gleaming white city of Gallipolis (City of the French) at the mouth of the Great Kanawha, hinting that the capital of the United States would soon be moved there, and urging Frenchmen to seize the opportunity to live in comfort supported by a bountiful nature. Hundreds rose to the bait; by the end of 1789 150,000 acres were "sold," to innocent victims who never suspected that the Compagnie de Scioto owned no land and that the elaborate certificates they purchased conveyed no title whatsoever. Proudly Joel Barlow gathered those unfortunates together, sending word to Duer in January, 1790, that he was sailing with 600 immigrants who had been promised transportation and homes in Gallipolis.

Duer was thunderstruck. Settlers would mean expense—for the journey to Ohio, homes, and surveys—but worse was the fact that the Scioto Company owned no land on which to plant them. The first payment to Congress had not been made, and even the site of Gallipolis was shown by surveys to be on the Ohio Company grant. Something must be done. Frantically Duer arranged to purchase the tract opposite the Great Kanawha for his unwanted colonists, then send a crew of axmen west to build huts for the newcomers. In the meantime the 600 Frenchmen arrived at Alexandria, Virginia, where agents met them with the sad news that they had been duped. Some drifted to New York or Philadelphia, others returned to Paris, but most insisted on being moved to the promised lands. Finally, in June, 1790, they were started west, and by mid-October all reached Gallipolis. What disappointments waited the weary travelers! No gleaming white city, no fertile countryside, no luxurious homes, no golden fields ripe for the harvest—only an unbroken forest, a half-cleared village, a few rows of ugly log cabins met their eyes. If they had only known they could have found consolation in the fact that William Playfair vanished with all funds collected by the Compagnie de Scioto, leaving Colonel Duer the unpleasant task of meeting all their expenses himself. But even this cheering news did not reach them as they settled down to the backbreaking task of clearing a frontier and planting vineyards. Some eventually moved to a 24,000 acre "French Grant" given them by a pitying Congress in 1795, but most stayed at Gallipolis to live out their lives in squalor and poverty—a fitting monument to the Scioto Company's unethical manipulations.

Yet darker years lay ahead for those suffering Frenchmen and for the sturdy Kentuckians and New Englanders who were hewing out the first clearings on the north bank of the Ohio. Congress had solved two western problems; it had set up a land system and installed a form of government which promised better times for the future. But all attempts to cope with the third task—removal of the Indians—failed. Once more, during the 1790s, the frontier was destined to ring with the war whoops of warriors and the agonized shrieks of their victims. Diplomatic skill and military valor had to be called into play before the pioneers at Marietta and Gallipolis and Losantiville could rest peacefully in their wilderness homes.

The West in American Diplomacy

1783-1803

Of the three western problems facing Congress during the Critical Period —erecting a satisfactory land system, devising a form of government, and pacifying the Indians—the last proved hardest to solve. For the tribes that harassed the borderland were only pawns in the hands of intriguing European nations that hoped to fatten their empires at the expense of the dissension-torn American Republic. Both its former allies, France and Spain, and its erstwhile enemy, England, were only too glad to use the loosely worded Treaty of 1783 as an excuse to devise plots that were to keep the West in a turmoil for twenty years and at times to threaten the nation's existence.

The conflict with England involved the string of Northwest Posts that controlled waterways along the Canadian-American border: Dutchman's Point and Point-au-Fer on Lake Champlain, Oswegatchie and Oswego near the eastern tip of Lake Ontario, and Niagara, Detroit, and Mackinac at the Great Lakes passageways. All were south of the border and were, according to the treaty of peace, to be "evacuated with all convenient speed," but Canada's officials found at least two good reasons to retain them when the war was over. One was the desire to keep control of the fur trade in the Great Lakes country, the other the fear that removal of British troops would incite the Indians to rebellion, for the interior tribes were already on the verge of revolt against their new overlords. Economic good sense and humanitarian idealism both determined General Haldimand, the Governor General of Canada, to stand firm. Having made up his mind, he three times refused to surrender the posts to congressional emissaries from the United States, at the same time besieging his home government for authorization for his stand.

223

This was not long in arriving. British ministers at London were just as anxious to hold the Northwest Posts as Canada's officialdom, partly because they, too, were subjected to pressure from fur traders, partly because England's control of the back country would be advantageous should the quarreling American states give up their attempt to live peacefully together, as appeared likely at the time. But some justification must be found to occupy another nation's territory! The ministers wrote their answer into instructions sent to Haldimand on April 8, 1784. The United States, they said, had failed to live up to the sections of the Treaty of 1783 which forbade the states to put obstacles in the way of merchants or Loyalists seeking to recover lawful debts. Hence England would keep the Northwest Posts "at least until" her traders could remove their goods. This stand placed Congress in a hopeless situation. It had no power to coerce the states under the Articles of Confederation, and although it urged them to open their courts to British creditors, state judges turned a deaf ear.

With this official backing, Haldimand moved into action in the Ohio country, for he realized that more than the Northwest Posts were at stake. If he could unite the tribes there in a strong confederation, they could not only keep out American settlers but perhaps bludgeon the United States into relinquishing the whole region to the Indians as a buffer state under English protection. With this as their objective, Haldimand's aides—Sir John Johnson, Joseph Butler, and especially Joseph Brant—worked steadily among the tribes between 1785 and 1787, gradually shaping the needed confederation. By the beginning of 1788 the Iroquois, Wyandot, Shawnee, Delaware, Miami, Ottawa, Chippewa, and Potawatomi had joined; all had pledged themselves to cede no more land to the United States without the consent of the confederacy, to repudiate the treaties of Ft. Stanwix, Ft. McIntosh, and Ft. Finney, and to insist on the creation of an Indian buffer state with its borders at the Ohio River. Yet Haldimand's efforts were to no avail, for two insurmountable obstacles precluded the peaceful establishment of the Indian nation that he envisioned.

One was the refusal of individualistic Indians to cooperate. This became apparent in 1788 when some of the more aggressive chiefs, spurred on by British agents, decided to press for a treaty with the United States recognizing their right to the entire Ohio country. Preliminary conversations showed the natives hopelessly divided; the Shawnee, Kickapoo, and Miami insisted on the Ohio River boundary at all costs, the Wyandot, Delaware, and Seneca refused to endorse a plan that would surely lead to war. In vain did Joseph Brant suggest a compromise line giving Americans the region east of the Muskingum. When the sought-for conference with agents of the United States was finally held at Ft. Harmar in January, 1789, the Indians were so torn by dissension that Arthur St. Clair, who represented the United States as governor of the newly created Northwest Territory, was able to dictate a treaty almost as obnoxious as the old. By the Treaty of Ft. Harmar the Indians accepted the lines drawn at Ft. McIntosh and Ft. Finney, receiving

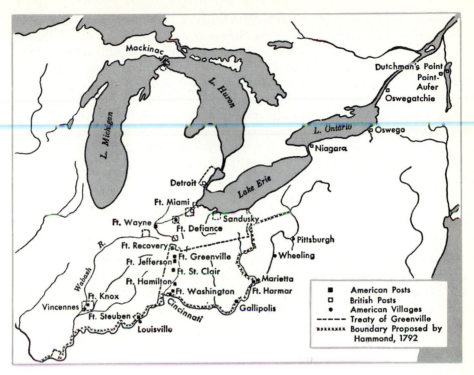

The Northwestern Indian Problem, 1789–1795

in compensation trading goods worth $9,000. This token sum signaled a basic shift in Indian policy; from this time on the government was to pay for appropriated lands rather than seize them by conquest. The Indians cared little; they drifted back into the wilderness, sick at heart that their union had failed them. Equally destructive of any peaceful solution was the attitude of the Kentucky settlers. Fearful lest the proposed confederation engender a new war, these bold spirits began sending small raiding parties against the Indians as early as the summer of 1788. When the natives struck back the United States found itself involved in a new Indian war by the autumn of 1789.

The first two expeditions formed to crush the rebellious Indians fared badly. General Josiah Harmar, commander of the western army, led the first northward from Ft. Washington in the autumn of 1790, but he moved so slowly that the Indians were amply warned and disappeared into the forest about the Maumee River. After searching vainly for the foe, Harmar started south again in late October, then paused while a detachment of several hundred militiamen slipped back toward the Maumee in the hope of surprising the returning Indians. Instead the tables were turned; the poorly trained militia walked straight into an ambush that cost 183 lives. The second expedition was made up of an elaborate force of 3,000 men under Arthur St. Clair. That inept commander fussed the summer of 1791 away at Ft. Washington, then led his men toward the Maumee country, pausing to build three log forts—Ft. Hamilton, Ft. St. Clair, and Ft. Jefferson—on the way. When the troops camped south of the Maumee on November 3, St. Clair allowed them to pitch their tents in haphazard fashion and sleep virtually without guards. All through the night Indians slipped past the drowsing scouts until the camp was surrounded; at sunrise the yelling Indians rushed upon the surprised Americans. Within a few moments the whole force was huddled in the center of the camp while the attackers raced about, shooting at will. When St. Clair and a few others broke through the encircling foes they left 630 dead and 283 wounded behind; those who escaped were so anxious for safety that they reached Ft. Jefferson in twenty-four hours—a distance that took ten days to cover on the outward march.

The effect of St. Clair's defeat was great on both the Indians and their British supporters. The warriors, confident that nothing could stop them, carried the war against every settlement north of the Ohio during the winter of 1791-92, while settlers abandoned their homes to huddle together at Marietta or Cincinnati. The English, in both Canada and the mother country, reacted scarcely less violently. The time was ripe, they believed, to bring their plan for an Indian buffer state into the open; surely the beaten United States could not refuse now! With this in view, Sir Guy Carleton, Lord Dorchester, who governed Quebec, and Colonel John G. Simcoe, who controlled Upper Canada, sent their agents to convince the tribes to unite behind this demand. By the autumn of 1792 the Canadian governors could call their wilderness charges into a conference at the Maumee River rapids, assured that all were represented. There the Indians agreed to demand the Ohio River boundary when they met with American commissioners in a scheduled conference at Sandusky the next spring. If the United States refused, they decided, the war would go on until the Ohio country was won.

While Simcoe and Dorchester carried on their forest intrigue, British statesmen worked steadily to secure the barrier state through diplomatic channels. Negotiations began when the new American government under President Washington, with power now to force the states to deal fairly with British merchants and Loyalists, began hinting commercial retaliation unless England consented to discuss the differences between the two nations. The young minister named to carry on these conversations, George Hammond, bore rigid instructions concerning the Northwest: he was to press for a neutral state bounded by the Ohio or, if that was impossible, a line following the Cuyahoga-Tuscarawas portage and the Muskingum River; offering in return British mediation with the Indians and surrender of the Northwest Posts. These demands made little impression on Thomas Jefferson, the American secretary of state. When conversations opened in March, 1792, Hammond's earnest argument for retention of the posts was speedily demolished by the skillful American secretary, his offer of mediation was summarily dismissed on the ground that there was no call for external interference between a government and its subjects, and his request for a new boundary was answered by the indisputable phrases of the Treaty of 1783. By December both he and his home government recognized that negotiations were futile; only further victories by their Indian allies would force the United States to back down on a buffer state.

This realization focused the attention of both nations on the American-Indian conference scheduled to meet at Sandusky in the spring of 1793; perhaps the natives could use the threat of renewed war to secure the settlement desired by England. The three commissioners named by Washington to attend this meeting expected to make radical concessions, even to surrendering all Ohio lands not actually occupied by the Ohio Company and Symmes Associates, but fortunately for them the conference never assembled. The American agents, learning on their way west that the Indians would insist on the Ohio River boundary, retraced their steps to warn President Washington that continued war was inevitable. The President, having anticipated such a report, sent word at once to his new military commander in the West, General Anthony Wayne, to begin the attack. Wayne, too wise to risk a fall campaign, advanced instead to a point six miles beyond Ft. Jefferson where he built a new outpost, Ft. Greenville. There he spent the winter of 1793-94, drilling his 1,000 seasoned troops, subjecting them to rigid discipline, and preparing for a spring offensive that would forever settle the troublesome northwestern problem.

His preparations were necessary, for during the winter the situation changed radically. England, plunging into war against the French Revolutionists, was again interfering with American shipping so drastically that the United States threatened to enter the conflict on the side of France. The tense atmosphere created by this possibility led Lord Dorchester to commit two colossal errors. In February, 1794, he told a visiting delegation of western chiefs that war was inevitable; when it came, he said, British and Indians would fight side by side to restore the natives' hunting grounds. A week later he ordered Simcoe to build a new post, Ft. Miami, on the Maumee River to protect Detroit from an attack by Wayne's army. These two moves convinced the overjoyed Indians that they could count on British aid against the Americans; war belts were hurried through the forest to summon warriors, until by mid-June some 2,000 warriors waited under the walls of Ft. Miami, all confident of ultimate victory.

Meanwhile Wayne moved his army slowly northward, stopping at the site of St. Clair's defeat to build Ft. Recovery where, in late June he beat off a sizeable Indian attack. With the natives weakened by that defeat, he pushed on along the Au Glaize River until the Maumee was reached on August 8, 1794. From a rough fortification thrown up there by his seasoned campaigners Wayne sent word through the forest that on August 17 he would march against the position selected by the Indians for their defense—a spot near Ft. Miami where a tangle of fallen trees afforded excellent protection.

This misinformation was broadcast intentionally, because the American commander knew the Indian habit of fasting before a battle. On the appointed day he started forward, but instead of attacking, camped ten miles away. For three days he stayed there, while his starving enemies waited impatiently. Finally, on August 20, several hundred warriors wandered away to gorge on food provided by the garrison at Ft. Miami. This was the moment chosen for the American attack. The well-trained troops moved forward in two columns, one for a frontal attack, the other to pour a withering fire into the left flank of the almost 800 warriors who crouched behind their jagged barrier. For a few minutes the Indians stood their ground, then broke and fled. The Battle of Fallen Timbers, which had required months of preparation, was over in less than two hours.

Wayne's victory was decisive not because he killed his enemies—only fifty Indians were killed—but because their spirit was broken when the British refused to aid them. For in the supreme test the commander at Ft. Miami dared not risk war with a neutral nation by sending his men to fight at Fallen Timbers. Disheartened by the realization that they must fight alone, the natives crept back to their villages with word that they must move west once more, to lands not wanted by the white men. Wayne took advantage of their broken spirit. After destroying a few villages and building a new fort to guard his conquest—Ft. Wayne at the head of the Maumee—he gathered the scattered chiefs together at Ft. Greenville early in 1795 to dictate the terms of the Treaty of Greenville. The Indians surrendered all Ohio except a strip along Lake Erie, a triangle of land in Indiana, and sixteen small spots for trading posts on strategic waterways. Wayne had broken the power of the northwestern Indians, temporarily severed their alliance with the British, and cleared a new stretch of territory for American expansion.

There remained only the task of driving the English from the Northwest Posts. Negotiations to settle that thorny issue began during the summer of 1794 when President Washington, in a last effort to dissolve the difficulties between the two nations by any means short of war, sent John Jay to London with full authority to make any concessions necessary. The times were auspicious for such a move. Britain's European position was weakening rapidly; the First Coalition built up to fight the French Revolutionists was crumbling as Spain talked of a separate peace and Prussia showed a declining interest; the countries of northern Europe were uniting in a League of Armed Neutrality to protest England's high-handed interference with their shipping. Rumors were rife that the United States would join the League, and this the British could not allow, depending as they did on American trade to finance the war. Better to back down on the Northwest Posts than lose everything, especially as those forts were no longer deemed as important as in the past. Reports from Montreal showed the fur trade south of the Great Lakes declining. In this case, why waste the £5,000 needed to repair the posts and the 4,000 men necessary to garrison them? Better to give them up in a munificent gesture that might keep the United States out of the League of Armed Neutrality.

England's decision to surrender the Northwest Posts was reflected in the first conversations between Jay and Baron Grenville, Secretary of State for Foreign Affairs, but in September, 1794, Grenville's attitude suddenly stiffened. Dispatches from George Hammond, his minister to the United States, were responsible. Alexander Hamilton, Hammond reported, had assured him that the United States would not enter the League and that all talk of war against England was mere bluff. Supported by this guarantee, Grenville made no more concessions; from that time on he dictated terms while Jay humbly acquiesced. Jay's Treaty, signed on November 14, 1794, was a monument to Hamilton's colossal blunder. England agreed to surrender the Northwest Posts by June 1, 1796, but in return the United States guaranteed Canadian traders perpetual passage over portages along the border, allowed them to operate south of the boundary, promised not to tax the furs they carried back to Montreal, and agreed to levy the same tax on their trading goods as on those of its own nationals. Yet Jay's Treaty, and the Treaty of Greenville that followed a few months later, freed one important borderland from intrigue and brought peace to the Northwest for a generation.

On the southwestern frontier the post-Revolutionary diplomatic conflicts were settled less easily. The antagonists there—Spain and the United States—were both well equipped for the struggle. Spain's North American colonies were governed efficiently under the able Charles III (1759-88); an army officer in each town, directly responsible to the governor of Louisiana, rigidly controlled the 25,000 French, Spanish, British, and Greek inhabitants who occupied East Florida, West Florida, and Louisiana. In addition Spain could count on the aid of some 14,000 warriors from the four principal tribes of the southern borderland: the Creeks, Cherokee, Chickasaw, and Choctaw. This was sure to be needed, for pressing upon the Spanish lands were the 120,000 Americans whose homes fringed the southwestern frontier in 1783— in Kentucky, the Nashville and Holston settlements, and the Georgia back country. All were aggressive expansionists, eager to overrun international boundaries in their search for wealth. Little wonder that Spain feared she had created a Frankenstein monster by helping them win independence, for now England's restraining hand no longer checked their westward march. Instead they were poised to sweep over the debatable land between Louisiana and Georgia like the "Goths and Vandals, with the Treaty of 1783 in one hand and a carbine in the other." Spain's principal task was to hold back that surging horde.

Her most effective weapon was control of the mouth of the Mississippi; by closing the river to American trade she could strangle the West economically, as settlers could market their bulky agricultural products only by sending them to New Orleans on flatboats. Spain realized she must use the weapon carefully, lest western dissatisfaction lead to retaliation in the form of filibustering expeditions against Louisiana, yet even that danger was not serious. The distance from Kentucky or Tennessee was too great for a sustained attack unless the settlers were aided by some strong naval power. Through the whole controversy Spain's principal fear was an Anglo-American alliance which would give the westerners sea power; whenever such a union seemed possible she adopted a conciliatory attitude.

The immediate cause of conflict was the disputed Yazoo Strip. That territory was granted the United States in the Anglo-American Treaty of 1783, which established the 31st parallel as the southern boundary of the new Republic, but was also claimed by Spain on the basis of the Anglo-Spanish Treaty provision that she "retain" West Florida. Her ministers rightly argued that this meant control of the region north to the line of 32° 28', as that was the boundary of the province under English rule. Neither nation was eager to take the first move toward settling the conflict. Spain, in actual possession of the Yazoo Strip, saw no reason to upset the *status quo*; the United States was content to wait until time worked in its favor, knowing that its population was increasing while Louisiana's remained static. Yet each was ready to take advantage of any shift in the international situation to press for a settlement.

Until the right moment arrived the struggle for the Southwest was carried on by those perennial shock troops of empire—speculators and traders. They clashed first when land jobbers, eager to exploit Georgia's western lands before the state ceded its holdings to the United States, persuaded authorities to negotiate the Treaty of Augusta (November 1, 1783) with two weak Creek chiefs. The principal effect of this land-grabbing treaty, which transferred a tract between the Oconee and Tugaloo rivers to the state, was to elevate a young chief, Alexander McGillivray, to leadership of the Creek tribe. A gifted halfbreed, McGillivray had a frail body, a cowardly temperament, an undying hatred of Americans, and an uncanny skill as a diplomat. Having fled westward to join his mother's people when his Loyalist father was driven from Georgia during the Revolution, he was one of several minor chiefs when the Treaty of Augusta gave him a chance to show his ability. Quickly calling representatives of the thirty-four Creek towns together, he persuaded them to repudiate the cession and agree to sell no more land without the entire tribe's consent. From that time the Creeks looked to McGillivray for leadership.

The chief, realizing that his followers could resist Americans only if they were backed by some European power and adequately supplied with arms, on January 1, 1784, addressed a letter to the New Orleans officials, suggesting a Creek-Spanish alliance against American aggression, and asking the right to buy unrestrictedly from Panton, Leslie and Co., an East Florida Loyalist firm which could sell the Indians superior English guns. Governor Esteban Miró of Louisiana, eager to welcome any ally against the United States, lost no time in arranging conferences with both McGillivray and representatives of the Choctaw and Chickasaw tribes. All agreed to keep

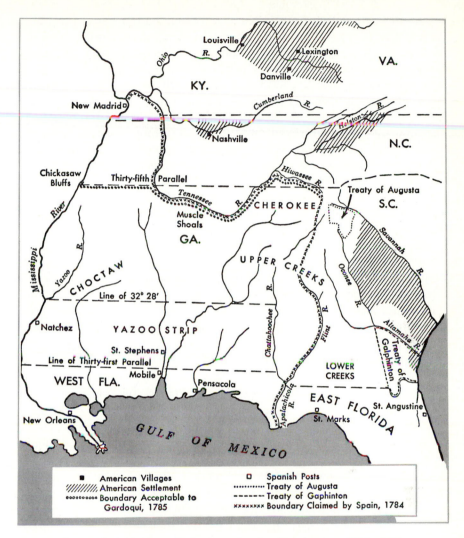

Spanish-American Relations in the Southwest, 1783–1788

peace among themselves, exclude American traders, and accept Spain's protection, in return for trading privileges with Panton, Leslie and Co.

These threatening gestures failed to still the economic ardor of the southwestern speculators. During 1784, one group, led by a prominent North Carolinian named William Blount, formed the Muscle Shoals Company to plant a colony at the Great Bend of the Tennessee River; another, dominated by James Robertson of Nashville, projected an outpost at Chickasaw Bluffs in the heart of the Chickasaw hunting grounds. Worst of all was the step taken by the Georgia legislature in February, 1785, when, bowing to the demands of the few Americans in Natchez, it erected the western end of the Yazoo Strip into the County of Bourbon which was thrown open to settlers. This was too much for McGillivray and his confederates. By midsummer the whole back country was aflame with a Creek-Georgia war. Nor was the federal government able to end this conflict which threatened to involve the United States with Spain. A peace delegation sent south in the fall of 1785 returned in disgust when only eighty Indians appeared at the treaty grounds. In the end this futile effort did more harm than good, for a delegation of Georgians who had accompanied the American agents stayed on to negotiate the Treaty of Galphinton (November 12, 1785), which ceded additional Creek lands south of the Altamaha River. This was immediately repudiated by the rest of the Creeks, who now redoubled their attacks.

Nor did Congress fare any better in diplomatic negotiations going on at the same time. These were initiated by the Count of Floridablanca, Spain's able foreign minister, who on June 26, 1784, closed the Mississippi River to American navigation, then dispatched an agent to the United States in hopes of capitalizing on western discontent by wringing a favorable treaty from that dissension-torn nation. The diplomat selected for this post, Don Diego de Gardoqui, was ordered to press not only for the Yazoo Strip and American recognition of Spain's exclusive control of the Mississippi, but for all the western country south of the Tennessee and west of the Hiwassee and Flint rivers. This region, Floridablanca contended, was Spain's by right of conquest and occupation. In return Gardoqui was allowed to offer the United States trading concessions and a defensive alliance containing mutual territorial guarantees.

The first conversations between this shrewd bargainer and John Jay, secretary of foreign affairs, showed that they stood so far apart on boundaries that there could be no compromise; Gardoqui would offer nothing more than a line along the 35th parallel and the Hiwassee-Flint rivers, while Jay clung to the 31st parallel. On other questions the commercially minded American diplomat adopted a more conciliatory tone, for he was dazzled by the promise of Spanish trading privileges. By August, 1786, they had reached a tentative agreement, which Jay laid before Congress. American ships, the negotiators proposed, would be admitted to Spanish ports, each nation would guarantee the other's possessions against external attack, the United States would give up the right to navigate the Mississippi for twenty-five years, and the boundary dispute would be settled later. Was Congress willing, Jay asked, to grant him the right to close the Mississippi for that period? The seven northern states, tempted by the prospect of trade, voted "Yes," the five southern states "No," while Delaware's delegates refused to commit themselves. This victory for the commercial elements meant nothing, as the votes of nine states were required to ratify a treaty and the southern representatives announced they would never yield. Jay and Gardoqui, realizing that further conversations were useless, abandoned their meetings.

But the harm was done. News of the vote, reaching the West in December, 1786, spread like wildfire among the frontier settlements. Seven states were willing to inflict economic strangulation on the Mississippi Valley to further their selfish commercial ambitions! Why remain loyal to such a government—a government that gave them no right to rule themselves, no protection from Indians, no cheap lands, no manufactured goods? Why not set up a trans-Appalachian republic under Spanish protection? Spain might be willing, in return, to open the Mississippi to their goods. All during the summer of 1787 revolutionary documents were exchanged by committees of correspondence in Nashville, Holston, Franklin, Kentucky, and even western Pennsylvania. Never had separatist sentiment in the West been higher.

Two alternatives lay before the malcontents: they could move into Louisiana as permanent Spanish settlers, or they could form their own republic by seceding from the United States. The first alternative became a possibility when Governor Miró set out to convince his Madrid superiors that American settlers would make ideal colonists if they accepted the Catholic religion. His emissary was a French adventurer, Pierre d'Arges, who visited New Orleans in 1786 and listened to Miró expound his ideas. To d'Arges this was a chance to turn a quick profit as land agent. Hence he readily acceded when Miró proposed that they draft a resolution to the Spanish crown which would be forwarded by the French minister to Spain. This they did, arguing that an enlarged population was essential to the economy and defense of Louisiana, and insisting that religious faith was less important than the protection of the colony. It would, they insisted, be overrun by Americans if its own loyal population remained small. Spanish officials were sufficiently interested in the proposal to invite d'Arges to visit Madrid in July, 1787; there he received authorization to import 1,500 Kentuckians with the understanding that they accept conversion at the hands of Irish priests recruited for the purpose.

Before d'Arges could reach New Orleans with news of his colonization project, a group of Kentuckians had launched a scheme designed to solve their problems by the second method: independence from the United States, and the creation of a separate republic. At their head was James Wilkinson, a colorful scoundrel fast rising to an influential position in Kentucky. Why not, Wilkinson reasoned, turn the dissatisfaction bred of congressional neglect and the anger engendered by the Jay-Gardoqui negotiations to his own benefit? If he could foment a revolution with Spain's aid a glittering future lay ahead: unrestricted trading privileges and land grants, leadership in a Mississippi Valley republic, the plaudits of a grateful people who would hail him as the Washington of the West. With this mirage leading him on, Wilkinson during the summer of 1787 enlisted the support of other Kentuckians who were dissatisfied with American rule: John Brown, Harry Innes, Benjamin Sebastian, and others. As soon as these separatists began to stir up discontent, Wilkinson set out for New Orleans, taking with him a fleet of flatboats laden with tobacco and flour. There he was well received by Governor Miró, who listened gullibly to Wilkinson's tales of a western republic and pressed the American for advice on how to proceed. He was then told that the desired objective could be secured if several prominent men in each settlement were allowed to ship goods down the Mississippi; they in return would forestall any attack on New Orleans and win converts for the proposed revolution. Wilkinson, of course, suggested himself as agent for Kentucky, and asked the privilege of sending $60,000 worth of goods south yearly.

Governor Miró was delighted. He promised to lay Wilkinson's plans before the king, authorized the Kentuckian to ship $30,000 worth of supplies to New Orleans annually, and had him swear allegiance to Spain—a ceremony that meant nothing to that gifted fabricator who would swear to anything if he could turn a dishonest dollar. Having completed arrangements, Wilkinson departed for Kentucky where he arrived early in 1788. His first opportunity to serve his Spanish masters came in July when a convention of Kentuckians assembled to protest Virginia's refusal to grant them separate statehood. Wilkinson, Sebastian, Brown, Innes, and other conspirators were much in evidence, but all their pleas for revolution fell on deaf ears. Much as westerners hated Congress, they realized that they lacked the wealth and numbers to erect an enduring new government; many, too, shrank from aligning themselves with autocratic Spain. In the end the convention, after defeating a proposal to draft a new constitution, adjourned to wait the outcome of the constitutional convention then meeting in the East, hoping the new Congress might give them statehood where the old one failed.

This was a sad blow to Wilkinson, but more were to come, for the immigration scheme hatched by d'Arges and Miró was bearing fruit. D'Arges had returned to New Orleans in the spring of 1788 with news that Spain was ready to welcome into Louisiana not only individuals but whole colonies of settlers. That sad fact came to Wilkinson's attention that fall when he heard that Spain's officials had granted George Morgan, of Indiana Company fame, authority to plant a colony on the west bank of the Mississippi not far below its junction with the Ohio. If this plan were carried out, Wilkinson knew, Kentuckians would be able to sell their produce at the proposed town, New Madrid, rather than through his own profitable monopoly in New Orleans. Hastening southward in the spring of 1789 to protest, he was met at New Orleans with still more disquieting news. The king, Miró informed Wilkinson, had not only refused to enter into any conspiracy with the Kentuckians, but had ordered a complete reversal of Spanish policy. From that time on all Americans willing to pay a 15 per cent duty were to be allowed to ship their goods through New Orleans. Those who wished to escape this fee were encouraged to move into Louisiana; to stimulate migration Americans were to be granted easy conditions of entry, religious toleration, equal commercial privileges, free land, and the right of selling tobacco at high prices to the king's warehouses. Spain, wisely placing no hope in conspiracy, had determined to strengthen her feeble colonies by supplying them with the settlers needed to build up a strong population. Wilkinson's intrigue was nipped in the bud, for the time being at least. When he returned to Kentucky late in 1789 he found his countrymen busily engaged in drawing up the constitution under which the state entered the Union three years later.

In other parts of the West the Spanish Conspiracy never reached serious proportions, largely because the conspirators were more concerned with winning concessions for themselves than independence for their neighbors. The plot in eastern Tennessee was originated by James White, a former congressman, and John Sevier, the discredited leader of the defunct State of Franklin. Sensing frontier dissatisfaction with the Creek-Georgia War and the failure of Congress to agree to separate statehood for the region, they drew up several memorials to Gardoqui, promising to forge a western state under Spanish protection in return for commercial concessions and the right to plant a colony at Muscle Shoals—a speculation in which both men were interested. When the Spaniard refused to grant them any financial aid and suggested that they lay the subject of the Muscle Shoals settlement before Governor Miró the conspirators lost interest. The intrigue in the Nashville settlements was equally halfhearted. There James Robertson, eager to end the Creek attacks that cost his followers so heavily, suggested to Miró that he might be willing to lead his people out of the United States and into the Spanish empire if the Indians were restrained. In all probability he, like Sevier, was simply pulling Spain by the nose; Robertson was willing to talk disunion if his words paid dividends, but his loyalty was unquestioned. When the Spanish governor showed no interest, plotting came to an end.

Athough the collapse of the Spanish Conspiracy in 1789 temporarily ended the threat of secession in the West, the new government under George Washington which assumed office at the same time realized that the problem was not settled. The bitter dregs remained: disgruntled leaders, dissatisfied frontiersmen, and above all the rankling causes of western discontent. Washington saw that the West could never know peace until the former plotters were pacified and the conditions that bred rebellion removed. The first task was easily accomplished, for most of the conspirators had embarked on their intrigue with Miró not because they were disloyal to the United States but because they thirsted for power or wealth. The President, wisely reasoning that they could be won back by suitable rewards from their own government, made William Blount governor of the Southwestern Territory that was created in 1790, appointed John Sevier and James Robertson brigadier-generals in the western army, and named James Wilkinson a lieutenant-colonel in the federal forces. Washington was so eager to convince westerners that his administration was friendly to them that he chose Thomas Jefferson rather than the hated John Jay secretary of state in his first cabinet.

Removing the causes of western discontent proved more difficult. The frontier settlers wanted two things: a diplomatic settlement with Spain that would open the Mississippi to free navigation, and peace with the Indians. The first would have to wait until the shifting sands of European diplomacy forced Spain into a position where she would have to back down, and even the second seemed impossible to achieve. The greed of the Georgia legislature was responsible. Knowing that all other states had ceded their western lands to the United States and that popular pressure would soon force them to follow, the members of that body determined to reap all possible profits first. On December 21, 1789, the assembly sold 25,400,000 acres in the Mississippi, Tombigbee, and Tennessee valleys to three speculating companies formed for the purpose: the South Carolina Yazoo Company, the Virginia Yazoo Company, and the Tennessee Yazoo Company. The presence in the concerns of such seasoned speculators as John Sevier, George Morgan, George Rogers Clark, James White, and Patrick Henry accounted for the fact that they purchased the vast tract for $207,580. With the sale

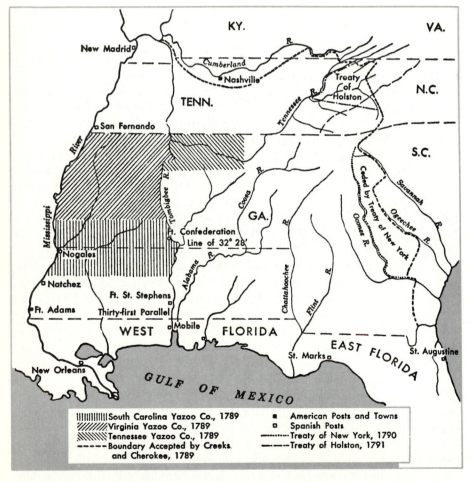

Spanish-American Relations in the Southwest, 1789–1803

completed, all three began selling lands and organizing colonists, with the lead taken by the South Carolina Yazoo Company under the colorful Irish rogue that acted as its general agent, Dr. James O'Fallon.

President Washington was horrified, knowing that continued invasion of the southern Mississippi Valley would not only antagonize Spain but prolong the Creek War. While he was still casting about for some means of stopping the companies, a fortunate incident, the Nootka Sound Controversy, provided him with the answer. This conflict centered in Nootka Sound, a relatively unimportant harbor in the Pacific Northwest where British ships stopped on furseeking expeditions. During the summer of 1789 the Spaniards, long resentful of England's invasion of their Pacific domain, confiscated several vessels that were anchored there. Britain, seizing the opportunity to challenge Spain's monopoly in the Pacific while that country's ally, France, was in the throes of revolution, first demanded immediate satisfaction, then began preparations for war. For several months a conflict seemed certain before Spain backed down. In October, 1790, her ministers signed the Nootka Sound Convention which yielded every disputed point to England.

The threat of an Anglo-Spanish war during the summer of 1790 played directly into Washington's hands in his dealings with both the Creeks and the Yazoo companies. Alexander McGillivray, realizing that war would leave him at the mercy of the Georgians by cutting off his supply of arms, was ready to receeive the peace emissary sent south by the President in the spring of 1790. Together they journeyed northward in an elaborate procession—a few favored chiefs on horseback at its head, twenty-six others in three wagons next, and the American agent bringing up the rear in a sulky. At New York they were escorted to Federal Hall by the largest crowd to assemble since the inauguration of Washington, led by the Sons of St. Tammany in full regalia. McGillivray was too canny to be swept away by this display, and the Treaty of New York that was signed on August 7, 1790, was by no means a complete surrender. McGillivray secured what he wanted most: a secret clause allowing him to import trading goods through a free port in Georgia, thus relieving the Creeks of dependence on British traders in Florida and at the same time assuring McGillivray a virtual monopoly of a very lucrative business. In return the Creeks ceded a large strip between the Ogeechee and Oconee rivers, receiving in return a perpetual guarantee to their remaining territories, including those claimed by the Yazoo Companies. At the same time McGillivray was made a brigadier-general in the American army at a salary of $1,200 a year. This shameless bribery did little good; Spain and the anti-McGillivray faction among the Creeks were so opposed to any land cession that they forced him to refuse to obey the treaty and to retreat back into his close relations with the Spanish. For the time being, however, the southern frontier knew peace.

The Nootka Sound crisis also doomed the Yazoo companies. Dr. O'Fallon first heard of the threatened war between Spain and England while he was gathering colonists for the South Carolina Yazoo Company in Kentucky. To him, and to thousands of other westerners, this seemed the long-awaited chance to wrest New Orleans from the Spanish with England's aid. Hence in July, 1790, he addressed a bellicose letter to Governor Miró, threatening to lead an army against Louisiana unless his company was granted the right to plant its settlers peacefully. At the same time he recruited a warlike force, secured George Rogers Clark as its leader, and made plans for a joint military-colonizing expedition against New Orleans. Having displayed his hand, O'Fallon could not back down when the hope of war went glimmering in the fall of 1790. By winter not only his grandiose plan, but the Yazoo companies', as well, had collapsed. An international crisis over which he had no control had helped Washington remove a serious threat to the peace of the southwestern frontier.

More important than the effect of the Nootka Sound crisis on either the Creeks or the Yazoo companies was its impact on Spain. That country's officials emerged from the controversy with the firm conviction that their frontier policy was a failure. They had relied on three devices to defend Louisiana against the United States: Indian alliance, intrigue, and immigration. The Treaty of New York indicated that Indian allies could not be depended upon, intrigue was dead with the collapse of the Spanish Conspiracy, and every dispatch from Louisiana testified to the failure of the immigration policy. American settlers simply were not responding to the bait of free lands, religious liberty, and commercial privileges promised them. The reasons for their reluctance were not hard to find. New Spain could not offer them the democratic institutions of their homeland, the promised religious freedom included only the right to practice Protestantism in private, and the hoped-for relief from Indian attacks failed to materialize. More important was the discovery that Spanish law made land grants nontransferable, thus removing the opportunity for speculation that every westerner sought, and a royal order of December, 1790, drastically reducing the price paid for tobacco at government warehouses, an act that demonstrated the insecurity of property under an absolute monarchy. Deterred by these handicaps, only a handful of Americans crossed the Mississippi. Spain's immigration system was an admitted failure by the close of 1791.

This realization resulted in a complete revision of Spanish policy which led first to a momentary flurry of expansion, then to a period of retreat as American settlers pressed in from east and north, and finally to the diplomatic settlement that ended intrigue in the Southwest. The era of expansion was inaugurated by the Louisiana governor who replaced the disgraced Miró late in 1791, Hector, Baron de Carondelet. A man of poor judgment and furious action who lacked knowledge to move wisely and humility to accept the advice of others, Carondelet needed only three months to perfect his plans. He would build up a giant Indian confederation, shower arms upon the natives, and send them forth to drive Americans back across the mountains! Anyone familiar with the frontier could have told him that the Indians were so torn by dissension and such poor fighters that the scheme was predestined to failure. But Carondelet refused to listen. Instead, he sent his emissaries through the forest during the summer of 1792, promising Creeks, Cherokee, Chickasaw, Choctaw, and Chickamauga guns, ammunition, land guarantees and unrestricted trading rights with Panton, Leslie and Co. if they joined his confederation. The Indians were ready to listen—McGillivray even accepted a pension $800 larger than that being paid him by the United States—but when Carondelet tried to bring them together in the spring of 1793 to establish the confederacy, he realized the futility of his efforts. By that time the Creeks and Choctaw were engaged in a minor war, and the remainder wanted only protection from the Americans, not aggression. The discouraged governor agreed to build a new post, Ft. Confederation, in the Choctaw country, then skulked away to New Orleans, knowing his plan a failure.

The collapse of the Spanish offensive opened the way for new attacks on Louisiana from both the north and the east. The attack from the north materialized when the Kentuckians, wildly supporting the newly formed revolutionary government in France, suddenly realized that the international situation played into their own hands. Spain and France were at war; Louisiana was filled with liberty-loving Frenchmen who sympathized with the revolutionists across the Atlantic. Surely an expedition against New Orleans would succeed now. So reasoned excited frontiersmen as they gathered to talk of these prospects during the summer of 1793, or formed themselves into Democratic societies modeled on the Jacobin clubs of France. Only a leader was needed to send the westerners storming against the ramparts of Spain's Mississippi Valley colony.

That individual reached America during the summer of 1793 in the person of Citizen Edmond Genet, the fiery French minister to the United States. Inspired by his faith in the revolutionary cause and backed by the plentiful resources of his home government, Genet immediately laid plans for a large expedition against Louisiana. George Rogers Clark, who volunteered his services, was made major general of the "Independent and Revolutionary Legion of the Mississippi," agents with well-stuffed pockets were sent west to enlist recruits, and the secret approval of Secretary of State Jefferson was secured. During the summer and fall of 1793 Kentucky hummed with activity as Democratic societies carried on a furious correspondence, Clark supervised boat building, recruits drilled, and prominent citizens such as Governor Isaac Shelby issued proclamations urging support for the expedition. The doom of New Orleans seemed at hand. President Washington watched these preparations with dismay. Success for Clark's legion meant either the loss of Kentucky by the United States or war with Spain. His only hope was to delay the expedition until the European situation was more favorable. Governor Shelby refused to cooperate in that worthy cause, but a well-known Kentuckian, James Innes, was enlisted to spread the word that Kentucky's best interests could be served by following Washington's leadership. Little but delay was won, but that proved sufficient.

Before Clark could move, Genet was recalled by his home government, charged with violating American neutrality. With his departure in November, 1793, the whole movement collapsed.

Scarcely was that menace removed when another rose to plague New Spain. This time the "Goths and Vandals" threatened from the east, where Georgia speculators were again on the march. In January, 1795, the state legislature, still hoping for some profit before ceding its western holdings, sold most of Alabama and Mississippi to four large concerns: the Upper Mississippi Company, the Tennessee Company, the Georgia Company, and the Georgia Mississippi Company. The second Yazoo Sale was even more fraudulent than the first; the speculators secured the vast region for about one cent an acre, tax free until it was settled. Their dreams of vast profits were short-lived, for when Georgians learned that every legislator but one who voted for the grant was a member of the companies, an "Anti-Yazoo Ticket" swept the next election, rescinded the sale, and publicly burned the deed by fire drawn from heaven—with the aid of a magnifying glass.

Yet the Yazoo sale, coming on the heels of the threatened attack by Genet's Legion of the Mississippi, convinced the terrified Carondelet that Louisiana could be saved only by falling back on two oft-used devices: forts and intrigue. During the spring of 1795 he strengthened the posts at St. Louis, Nogales, Natchez, and St. Stephens, improved newly built Ft. Confederation, and erected a new fort, Ft. San Fernando, at Chickasaw Bluffs. At the same time he welcomed the intrigue that was suggested to him by that irrepressible scoundrel, James Wilkinson. The fact that he was now an officer in the American army did not deter that polished liar from conniving with foreign officials; in January, 1794, he wrote Carondelet a full account of the Genet expedition, hinted that he had been responsible for saving Louisiana from attack, and warned that other assaults might come unless Spain hired trusted agents to keep the frontiersmen peaceful and foment a separatist movement. Wilkinson, of course, suggested his willingness to serve and volunteered to find others. Carondelet, who knew little of Miró's fruitless plotting, was delighted. He dispatched urgent letters to Madrid asking for money and then, afraid aid might come too late, took matters into his own hands. Wilkinson was granted $16,000 in addition to his $2,000 pension and told to enlist leaders for the cause.

That proved easy. The time was ripe for a western uprising against Washington's government. In the five years the President had held office, he had failed to open the Mississippi River, refused to aid France's struggle for liberty, enacted a whiskey tax that fell heavily on the frontier's principal export crop, and generally had governed the nation to please commercially minded Federalists rather than interior Jeffersonians—especially after December, 1793, when Thomas Jefferson, their last friend in the cabinet, resigned. Yet most of the prominent Kentuckians who joined with Wilkinson were probably loyal to the United States; the threat of rebellion was, in their eyes, only a device to force more equitable treatment from their own government. This was shown when Carondelet sent an agent to New Madrid in July, 1795, to arrange the delivery of twenty cannon and 10,000 rifles that Spain set aside for the conspirators' use; not even Wilkinson dared meet him to launch the revolution. By the end of 1795 Carondelet reluctantly concluded that he was only serving as a pawn for the Kentuckians, and the second Spanish Conspiracy came to an end.

All the events that had kept the southwestern borderland in a turmoil between 1789 and 1795—plots and counterplots, Indian wars and tribal confederations, infamous speculations and abortive military expeditions—apparently were of little significance, for the relative positions of the two quarreling powers remained unchanged over those years. Spain still held the mouth of the Mississippi, still exacted duties from American shippers, still clung to the Yazoo Strip, and still dominated most Indian tribes. Actually, however, the backwoods conflicts formed the backdrop against which the United States and Spain eventually settled their differences over the conference table. Had American frontiersmen not conspired and fought and speculated as they did, the treaty that ended the contest for the southern debatable land would not have been so favorable to their nation.

The chain of events leading to the diplomatic settlement began when Spanish alarm over the Nootka Sound Crisis forced that haughty nation to suggest it was willing to negotiate its differences with the United States. When this news reached the United States in December, 1791, Secretary of State Jefferson saw the occasion was not auspicious; by this time the Anglo-Spanish war threat had passed and Spain would never back down unless her position in Europe was so perilous that she was forced to court American friendship by making unusual concessions. Hence instead of accepting the invitation, he ordered two minor employees of the State Department, William Short and William Carmichael—neither sufficiently influential to inspire Spain's confidence—to proceed to Madrid as slowly as possible. When they arrived in February, 1793, they realized that the new Spanish chief of state, Manuel de Godoy—an impetuous young incompetent who had risen to power through the queen's influence—was no more anxious to reach a settlement than they. Half-hearted negotiations dragged on until the spring of 1794 with nothing accomplished. Both parties were waiting a more favorable European situation to press for a solution.

At that time the turn of fortune's wheel favored the United States. Things were going badly for Spain in the European war, her treasury was bankrupt, and her alliance with England crumbling. From America, too, came disquieting news: an army forming in Kentucky to attack Louisiana, an envoy named John Jay on his way to London to draft a treaty that might ally England with the United States against Spain. Better to secure American friendship than risk an Anglo-American attack on New Spain when conditions in Europe were so bad that colonies could not be defended. In May, 1794, Godoy told Short and Carmichael his nation might be willing to trade the Yazoo strip and navigation rights on the Mississippi for a defensive alliance if a properly authorized plenipotentiary could come to Madrid.

Thomas Pinckney, American minister to Great Britain, was selected for this important task. He had so little faith in his mission that he delayed until June 29, 1795, before reaching Spain, thus losing a chance to capitalize on Spanish fear of an Anglo-American alliance. By the time he arrived Godoy had seen a copy of Jay's Treaty and had assured himself that there was no danger of an accord which would send the navies of England and the armies of the United States against Louisiana. Yet conditions were far more favorable than Pinckney knew. As early as March, 1795, Godoy had decided to withdraw Spain from a war that meant only military defeats, popular resentment at home, and court intrigue aimed at his regime. This meant withdrawal from the alliance with England, and almost certain retaliation from that nation, probably in the form of a naval attack on Spanish colonies in the Gulf of Mexico. Should that come, American friendship was essential to save Louisiana. Surrender on the minor points in dispute was a cheap price to pay for aid against the English dogs of war.

Having reached his decision, Godoy first made separate peace with France through the Treaty of Basle (July 22, 1795), then called his Council of State together to disclose his intention of backing down before the American demands. Retreat was justified, he told the ministers, by the failure of Spain's frontier policy. Indian alliances built up by Miró and Carondelet were useless, the immigration policy a failure, and the intrigue between the Louisiana governor and Wilkinson futile. Spanish resources were too depleted by the European war to defend New Spain against a combination of wrathful frontiersmen and vengeful English men of war. Spain must surrender the Yazoo Strip and navigation of the Mississippi or lose all. His gloomy advice carried the day; the Council of State voted to seek a treaty that would cement ties of Spanish-American friendship.

With this decision made, negotiations between Pinckney and the Spanish spokesmen moved rapidly forward until October 27, 1795, when the Treaty of San Lorenzo was signed. Spain gave up the Yazoo Strip and agreed to move all garrisons from the territory north of the 31st parallel within six months. Americans were granted the right to navigate the Mississippi from its source to its mouth, and were extended the "privilege" of deposit at New Orleans for three years, with the understanding of probable renewal. This was an important concession, for now westerners could land their goods at designated warehouses and transship them to ocean-going vessels without paying custom duties. The agreement also gave the United States commercial privileges in Spain, but not in the Spanish colonies.

The Treaty of San Lorenzo—or Pinckney's Treaty—ended the troublesome conflicts that had kept the frontier in a turmoil for a dozen years. Carondelet, heartsick though he was at the surrender, undertook to carry out its provisions to the letter. The Mississippi was opened to American ships in December, 1796, and two months later the task of dismantling the forts at Natchez, Nogales, Confederation, San Fernando, and St. Stephens was begun. Scarcely had work started when new dispatches from Madrid caused an interruption. These orders, dated October 29, 1796, told of the outbreak of war between Spain and England, of the necessity of warding off an English attack on Louisiana from Canada, and of the dangerous manner in which the Federalist Presidents, George Washington and John Adams, were openly aligning themselves with Britain. Carondelet was ordered to delay executing the treaty until the situation changed. Joyfully the Louisiana governor hurried word to his followers, telling them to regarrison the forts once more. The American commissioner at Natchez, watching with grim satisfaction as Spanish soldiers carried guns and supplies from that fortification, was amazed on March 22 to see them suddenly retrace their steps, remount their cannon, and prepare to defend their outpost once more.

The result of this shift in policy was nothing Godoy could foresee: his hasty action set in motion a chain of events that led finally to Spain's loss of Louisiana. Had he been better versed in frontier affairs he would have known that the settlers in the southern borderland would never accept renewed Spanish rule, for most of them were British Loyalists or Americans, now united by the Anglo-Spanish war. They made their feelings known as soon as they learned of Spain's decision to retain the Yazoo Strip. In Natchez mobs that raged through the town held the Spanish deputy governor a prisoner until he resigned. In the border towns of West Florida dozens of conspirators—British, American, and Spanish—hatched revolutionary plots to free the Floridas and Louisiana from Spanish rule. In the southern United States William Blount, now senator from Tennessee but still an enthusiastic plotter, planned four military expeditions to wrest away Spain's North American colonies. Faced by this solid phalanx of opposition, Godoy was forced to reverse his policy once more and in March, 1798, directed Carondelet to surrender the disputed territory. But the harm was done. Having tasted action, the Americans were unwilling to accept a peaceful settlement.

Their objective now was nothing less than ownership of both West Florida and Louisiana. A successful attack on those Spanish colonies would not only insure the West against any future closing of the Mississippi but open new trading routes along the Alabama and Tombigbee rivers and allow the filibusterers to grab off speculative land claims in the conquered territory. The United States, drifting toward war with both France and Spain during 1797 and 1798, would probably welcome such a blow. Through those two years westerners talked constantly of expeditions or laid elaborate plans. Alexander Hamilton suggested one scheme—a march to liberate not only Louisiana but Mexico and Latin America from Spanish rule—but settlers refused to follow this arch-Federalist who was more interested in aiding England than helping them. More to their liking was a filibustering expedition launched in 1799 by a Loyalist, William Augustus Bowles. With 300 Indians and renegade whites, that adventurer captured the fort at St. Marks in May,

1800, and seemed on the point of overrunning the Floridas when a larger Spanish force dispersed his followers and sent Bowles off to death in Spain.

These attacks were of more than local importance, for they strengthened a belief growing in the minds of Spanish rulers since the Treaty of San Lorenzo: Louisiana was an expensive luxury that must be sold before England or the United States took it by force. The colony cost Spain dearly—customs duties never paid more than one-fifth the sums needed for its administration—and gave the Spanish little in return, for Louisiana purchased its industrial goods from France and shipped its agriculture produce there in payment. Little wonder that Spain was willing to dispose of its American white elephant at almost any price after Pinckney's Treaty removed its value as a bargaining instrument in dealings with the United States.

France was anxious to buy, partly because its rulers envisaged future profits from the growing sugar and cotton production in Louisiana, partly because Napoleon's victories reawakened dreams of a vast new empire. Negotiations between the two powers, carried on since 1795, reached a climax in 1800 when Napoleon's European conquests gave France the territories needed to bargain with the Spanish monarch, Charles IV. In the Treaty of San Ildefonso, signed on October 1, 1800, Spain agreed to transfer Louisiana to France, in return for Napoleon's promise to carve out a Tuscan kingdom for Charles' indigent relatives of the House of Parma. The First Consul never lived up to his part of the agreement. Instead of continuing the continental war until he secured the promised Italian lands, he abruptly brought his war with England to a close through the Treaty of Amiens (1801), then demanded that Spain turn over Louisiana at once without compensation. The powerless Spaniards, unwilling to risk the enmity of both France and England, reluctantly complied. On October 15, 1802, orders reached New Orleans to surrender the colony to its new masters.

News of the cession sent a wave of terror through the West. Spain could be bullied into keeping the Mississippi open, but powerful France would be impossible to control. As westerners discussed their fate, an event occurred that seemed to confirm their worst fears. On October 18, 1802, New Orleans officials quietly posted a proclamation ending the right of deposit. Actually France had nothing to do with the order, which was a belated Spanish attempt to stop American abuses of the deposit privilege: contraband trade, evasion of duties, and smuggling of gold and silver. But westerners did not know these circumstances. In their eyes this was an example of the treatment they could expect from the new masters of the lower Mississippi. As the news spread northward newspaper extras were published, people gathered in excited knots to discuss and condemn, and legislatures passed fiery resolutions urging France to retract. Nor did the half million people in the West stand alone. New York and Philadelphia merchants who supplied the interior with manufactured items, eastern ship owners who imported goods for the frontier, and New England wholesalers who shipped their produce across the mountains, all faced ruin if western buying power declined. A united nation demanded that the government meet this crisis, even if it were necessary to take New Orleans from France by force.

President Thomas Jefferson, the anti-Federalist now controlling national affairs, was particularly alarmed, not only because of his inherent sympathy for the West but because the growing anti-French sentiment would react against his party in the elections of 1804. As usual he hit upon the correct strategy. The United States, he realized, must purchase New Orleans and enough of West Florida to give it control of the mouth of the Mississippi. This could be arranged only if a new Anglo-French war broke out, for then France might be willing to cede rather than risk a British naval attack on Louisiana. A waiting game was clearly called for, but in the meantime Jefferson subjected France to a barrage of propaganda designed to show that the United States was so hostile to the French and so friendly to the English that an attack on New Orleans was imminent. Letters proclaiming America's intention to "marry ourselves to the British fleet and nation" were allowed to fall into the hands of the First Consul's agents; hours were spent convincing French and Spanish ministers that the whole nation wanted war so ardently that only the President's desire for peace prevented an immediate invasion of Louisiana. Jefferson also persuaded Congress to authorize an army of 80,000 troops and a navy of fifteen Mississippi gunboats. Then, amidst this carefully created hostile atmosphere, he sent James Monroe to Paris to buy New Orleans. Jefferson also secretly kept the Kentuckians informed of his negotiations to prevent any western attack on New Orleans.

The results of Jefferson's blustering policy were gratifying. Spain backed down first, hurrying word to New Orleans to reopen deposit at that port before the frontiersmen could attack. At the same time Napoleon decided that he would sell not only New Orleans but all Louisiana. The war with England, he knew, would soon be resumed, and he could no more risk an Anglo-American attack on his new colony than could Spain. Moreover the failure of his best troops to subdue a slave insurrection in Santo Domingo had lessened his enthusiasm for empire building. Having reached his decision in March, 1803, Napoleon instructed Talleyrand, his foreign minister, to broach the subject to the resident American minister, Robert Livingston. Talleyrand waited until April 11, then in the midst of an ordinary conversation suddenly asked, "What would you give for the whole of Louisiana?" Livingston, who was slightly deaf, could scarcely believe his ears but he had the presence of mind to indicate that he was interested. Negotiations went forward rapidly until April 30, 1803, when a treaty was signed transferring Louisiana to the United States for 80,000,000 francs—about $15,000,000.

There remained only the task of taking over control of New Orleans and its far-flung hinterland. Spain was still in possession when news of the purchase reached the city in August, 1803, but the French agent waiting to take over Louisiana insisted that he have the glory of surrendering the territory to the United States. Hence on November 30, 1803, the colony passed into French hands, just as James Wilkinson with 150 men set out from newly built Ft. Adams to receive jurisdiction. The second ceremony was held in the public square of New Orleans on December 20. Beneath a clear warm sun the French agent delivered the city's keys to Wilkinson and William C. Claiborne, the second American commissioner. Claiborne then addressed the small crowd, assuring the people protection for their property and religion, before the three-colored flag of France was hauled down and the Stars and Stripes hoisted in its place. Wilkinson, who had carried out the transaction in an efficient manner, characteristically wrung $12,000 from the retiring Spanish governor for his ''Reflections'' on Spain's policy—a hodge-podge of outworn revelations and obvious advice—then used the same information as the basis for a long report to President Jefferson. The man's duplicity was unequalled.

The Louisiana Purchase fittingly climaxed the diplomacy of the Revolutionary period. Gone from the Mississippi Valley were foreign agents who incited Indians to attack American settlers, commercial restrictions that throttled the economic life of the West, unpatriotic westerners willing to preach rebellion for a price. With the extension of American rule over the interior of the continent peace settled upon the frontier. Once more the westward march could be resumed, as homeseekers pushed inland to exploit the domain won by the blood and sweat of their nation's statesmen and soldiers.

13

Settling the Appalachian Plateau

1795-1812

For a generation before 1795 the westward march of the American people was halted while independence was won, a workable government system established, Indians subdued, and foreign intrigue swept from the borderlands. Now Americans were ready to move again, as Jay's Treaty, Wayne's victory, the Treaty of Greenville, and Pinckney's Treaty cleared the way. From New England, the Middle States, and the South they came— eager homeseekers with their families, young axmen hunting a homesite for the expectant bride waiting patiently behind, starry-eyed speculators in search of choice lands, shiftless ne'er-do-wells cast out by the older societies of the East, zealous ministers in quest of souls, impatient young lawyers seeking a more liberal atmosphere to nurture political ambitions, journeymen printers carrying type for a frontier newspaper, merchants, millers, black-smiths, artisans, rogues, and saints—all rubbing elbows on the trails that led to the mecca beyond the mountains. For seventeen years the tide of pop-ulation flowed west—the greatest movement of peoples America had known—until 1812 when a new war closed the gates of the frontier once more.

Unusually choice lands were not the magnets that drew these pioneers toward the frontier, for the best spots had already been appropriated by the bolder spirits who had ventured across the Appalachians just after the Rev-olution: the valleys of eastern Tennessee, the Nashville Basin, the limestone areas of Kentucky, and the Ohio River lowlands. For the newcomers there remained the hilly areas of the physiographic region known as the Appala-chian Plateau. There rolling foothills, sloping gradually downward to merge

247

with the level Lake Plains Province, and broad valleys that marked the former course of glacial rivers, offered tempting prospects to farmers grown weary of wresting a living from New England's stubborn soil or crowded from their southern homes by advancing plantations. The whole region, between New York and northern Alabama, was interlaced with swift-flowing streams and covered with a heavy growth of hardwood that testified to the soil's fertility. Yet settlers who went west during those years were less concerned with finding ideal conditions in their new homes than escaping bad conditions in the old. In each of the three sections contributing to the migration—New England, the Middle States, and the South—people were discontented and anxious to be on the move.

Overcrowding was the principal expelling force in New England. For more than a century the Yankees had been held back, their path westward across New York State blocked by the powerful Iroquois Confederation. A few bold spirits made the lengthy trek to the Wyoming Valley or the Ohio country, a few others moved northward to hilly Vermont, but the majority remained at home to compete for the few lands available. This sent prices soaring, until by the 1790s even moderately good farms sold for from $14 to $50 an acre. Younger sons—and they were plentiful in prolific New England families—refused to pay such prices for rock-strewn hillsides when they could buy fertile lands in the West for $2 or $3 an acre. That price discrepancy underlay the migration, but other New Englanders went west to escape the established Congregational church of Massachusetts and Connecticut, or to seek a more liberal social order than that rock-ribbed Federalist stronghold. High taxes, normal in well-established communities, drove others toward the frontier.

Those same conditions—overcrowding, high prices, exorbitant taxes, and conservatism—also existed in the Middle States and South, but other factors in both those sections helped speed the exodus. Many who left New York and Pennsylvania were pioneers who, living on the western fringe of civilization, drifted naturally with the moving tide. In Virginia, Maryland, and North Carolina soil exhaustion forced thousands to abandon their farms, particularly in the hilly Piedmont region where heavy rains had washed essential minerals from cultivated soil. More were driven from their homes by the expansion of plantation agriculture into the Piedmont and Great Valley during the post-Revolutionary years. Some of the democratic small farmers occupying the region went west to escape contact with slavery, others disliked blacks, some fled the new class stratification which placed them on a lower level than the great planters, while still others were displaced when their lands were absorbed by plantations. Between 1790 and 1800 thirteen counties in Maryland and twenty-six in Virginia lost population, so rapid was the migration.

Important as these expelling factors were, the mass exodus of the post-Revolutionary years owed its magnitude also to improved roads connecting East and West. These had been built during an internal improvement craze

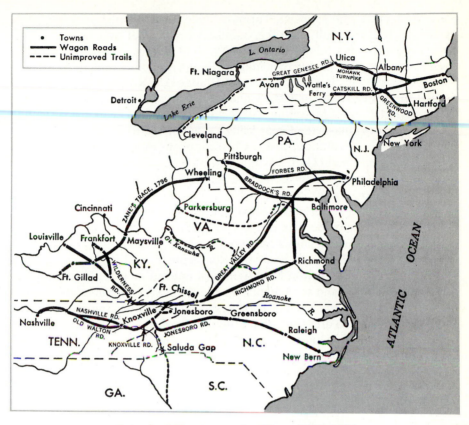

Principal Routes to the West, 1795–1812

that swept over the new nation in th 1790s. Most of the highways scarcely deserved the name; they were made by chopping out underbrush and small trees in a swath ten to thirty feet wide, cutting off the larger timber eighteen inches from the ground, and leaving the largest trees standing even in the middle of the thoroughfare. Small streams were bridged with logs, but only fords or ferries on the main-traveled routes allowed passage over rivers. Although these roads were impassable quagmires in wet weather and unsatisfactory under the best conditions, they were still better than the trails used in the past. In winter especially, when deep-packed snow smoothed the rough surfaces, pioneers could quite easily move household goods westward by sled. Most settlers migrated just before the spring thaw for that reason.

The three road systems built westward from New England, the Middle States, and the South had much to do with the course of the westward movement, for all converged in the Ohio Valley. One led from Boston and Hartford to the Hudson River where it connected with two highways across

New York State, the Mohawk Turnpike which was opened as far at Utica by 1793, and the Catskill Turnpike, built between Catskill and Wattle's Ferry on the Susquehanna in 1792. The Middle States were connected with the West during the 1780s by two military highways constructed during the Seven Years' War, Forbes' Road and Braddock's Road, which were improved by Pennsylvania and Maryland until they were passable for wagons as far as Pittsburgh. Migrating Virginians could travel over those Middle States routes, or follow the Great Valley Road or the Richmond Road, both built before the Revolution, to Ft. Chissel. From that post a single wagon road led to Cumberland Gap, 200 miles away, where it joined the Wilderness Road across Kentucky to Louisville and Frankfort. That highway was opened to wagon traffic in 1795, while a branch built a few years before allowed settlers to reach either Maysville on the Ohio or Ft. Gillad on the Green River. Tennessee was equally accessible over the Knoxville Road, built between the Wilderness Road and the mouth of the French Broad River between 1791 and 1795, the Nashville Road constructed by North Carolina in 1788, and the Old Walton Road that was opened in 1795 as an alternate route to the Cumberland settlements. In addition to the wagon roads, several unimproved trails were widely used, especially the twisting paths across western Virginia to Parkersburg and the mouth of the Great Kanawha, and the trace that used Saluda Gap, in the eastern mountain wall, to connect Georgia with the Holston frontier.

Over those roads went the pioneers. Between 1790, when the Southwest Territory was erected with William Blount as governor, and 1795, the migratory stream moved toward eastern Tennessee. The Holston settlements could not hold the thousands who sought homes there; instead the frontier surged westward so rapidly that when Blount chose a central site for the territorial capital in 1792 he laid out the new town of Knoxville at the mouth of the French Broad. As soon as Pinckney's Treaty ended the threat of Indian attacks and Spanish intrigue the tide set in toward Nashville. Immigrants were so thick on the Old Walton Road during the summer of 1795 that they crowded each other from the highway; 26,000 crossed the Cumberland in two months. Through the cold winter that followed the exodus continued—thousands of ragged men and women tramping barefooted through the snow because "every body says it's good land." By 1796, when 77,000 people lived in Tennessee, the territory was ready to enter the Union as a state. Others sought homes in Kentucky after Wayne's victory ended fear of Indian raids, filling the Blue Grass country, pushing into the hills about the Big Sandy, and spreading westward along the valley of the Green River. More than 220,000 people occupied Kentucky by 1800.

Both Tennessee and Kentucky filled so rapidly that the transition from frontier to civilized community was accomplished almost overnight. Pioneers in each new settlement bore the typical backcountry stamp; they built crude log cabins, cleared thirty or forty acres from their larger speculative holdings, lived on corn meal, pork, and game, and dressed in the fringed hunting shirt, leggings, and moccasins that were standard garb in the West. As their fields extended year after year their wealth steadily increased, for the rich bottom lands produced almost 100 bushels of corn an acre and the price was steady at twenty-five cents a bushel. Four years of such harvests allowed a farmer to build a frame house, buy a suit of clothes, subscribe to the weekly newspaper just started by a journeyman printer in the nearby town, send his children to the classical academy opened there by an itinerant schoolmaster, and perhaps buy a carriage to carry his proud family to church on Sundays. Most made this transition; the unlucky or unskilled who could not moved farther west after selling their improvements to newer settlers.

Despite the rapid evolution, society remained predominately rural. Lexington, the largest city in the West, had only 1,795 inhabitants in 1800, while the population of Louisville, Frankfort, Nashville, Knoxville, and the other towns was less than five hundred. Farming was the principal occupation, corn the leading crop. Transportation difficulties discouraged the production of tobacco, cotton, and wheat except in the Cumberland and bluegrass settlements where flatboats were used to carry those bulky goods to the New Orleans market. Corn, on the other hand, was ground into meal for local consumption, concentrated into whiskey for export, or fed to cattle and hogs who could carry themselves to market. By 1800 whiskey from the many small distilleries that dotted Kentucky and Tennessee was displacing rum as America's national drink, while large herds of cattle and hogs, driven north along the Great Valley Road or south through Saluda Gap, were bringing prosperity to the frontier. Yet money remained scarce, for profits went to buy manufactured goods in Baltimore and Philadelphia, or to pay the $6 or $7 per 100 pounds demanded by wagoners who carried freight between the seaboard and the West. Only the Nashville settlements and the bluegrass country, where cotton and tobacco were grown, rose above the primitive economy usual in frontier communities. There, in the first years of the nineteenth century, thrifty farmers expanded their holdings at the expense of less fortunate neighbors, elaborate frame houses testified to a new affluence, and young lawyers such as Andrew Jackson dominated political affairs rather than the Indian fighters who had captured the imagination of an earlier generation.

The transition from frontier to civilized community was particularly rapid in Tennessee and Kentucky because land could be purchased cheaply from either the states or the army of small speculators operating there. In the northern portions of the Appalachian Plateau—New York, western Pennsylvania, and the Northwest Territory—the course of settlement was different, largely because neither the states concerned nor the national government had developed a satisfactory method of selling the public domain to pioneer farmers. Failure to do so plunged the United States into a period of speculative activity unrivaled in its history. Everywhere land-jobbing companies sprang up, financed by European or American capitalists who saw in the combination of a westward-moving population, a stable new government, and greedy states eager to sell their western holdings, a formula almost certain to spell handsome returns. Land companies played a larger role in the westward movement during those years than at any time before or since.

Western New York felt their influence first. Settlers from the eastern part of the state and New England drifted into that war-torn region after 1783, to lay out a few scattered towns along the upper Mohawk and Unadilla rivers, but no mass migration could begin until Indians were removed and ownership of the area—which was claimed by both Massachusetts and New York—finally established. The first proved easy, for the ravages of the Revolution and an exodus to Canada left only about 6,000 of the once-proud tribesmen in the coveted territory. A commission named by the state legislature set to work in the spring of 1785; by 1789 the Oneida, Tuscarora, and Cayuga tribes had surrendered their former hunting grounds in return for cash settlements, annuities, and small reservations. New York then possessed all lands west to Lake Seneca except those north of the Mohawk River claimed by the departed Mohawk Indians, and these were secured in 1797 for a payment of $1,600. Thus were the mighty warriors who had held the English at bay for a century reduced to a servile life on the scattered reservations allotted them.

While that was going on, the New York legislature opened negotiations with Massachusetts to determine which state really owned the ceded lands, for Massachusetts had specifically retained its colonial claims to a strip across New York when turning its western territory over to Congress. Commissioners from the two states met at Hartford during the summer of 1786 and after the usual amount of wrangling settled the problem by drawing a Pre-emption Line south from Sodus Bay to the Pennslyvania border. New York retained all territory east of the line, together with a mile-wide strip along the Niagara River and sovereignty over the whole region on both sides of the boundary. Massachusetts was given the lands west of the Pre-emption Line, and 230,400 acres on the Susquehanna River.

Both states were ready to dispose of their holdings immediately; moreover their empty coffers suggested rapid sales in wholesale quantities rather than the slower process of parceling out the land to individual farmers. Massachusetts, in 1787, sold its entire Susquehanna Tract, known as the Boston Ten Towns, to a group of speculators for 12½ cents an acre. New York, which began selling its lands in 1789, auctioned off the whole region between the Unadilla River and the Pre-emption Line during the next few years. Nearly all went to speculators, some organized into companies to purchase such large tracts as Chemung Township, the Watkins and Flint Purchase, or the Chenango Triangle. Other areas, such as the Chenango Twenty Townships, went to a number of small buyers. This was also the fate of the Military Tract that New York set aside to satisfy bounties issued Revolutionary soldiers. Distribution of those lands began in 1791 and as the

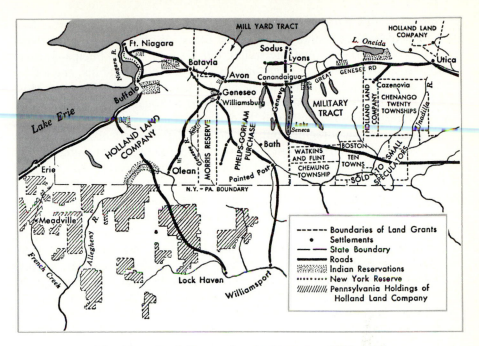

The New York-Pennsylvania Frontier, 1790–1812

military warrants were transferable, most were absorbed by land jobbers. Speculators sold their purchases to settlers so readily that by 1795 the region east of the Pre-emption Line was thinly settled.

In the meantime Massachusetts turned to the disposal of its 6,000,000 acres west of the line. For a time individual sales to farmers were considered, but the need for quick profits and pressure from speculators who hoped to divide the land among themselves finally proved decisive. On April 1, 1788, the whole tract was sold to Oliver Phelps and Nathaniel Gorham, two wealthy land jobbers with excellent political influence. They agreed to pay the state £300,000 within three years—in Massachusetts currency which was so depreciated the actual purchase price was only $175,000 in gold, or about three cents an acre. Even that sum was more than Phelps and Gorham could raise and for the next year they struggled frantically to secure help from other capitalists of New England, New York, and Pennsylvania.

While Gorham sought out fellow speculators in the quest for additional capital, Phelps went west to supervise surveys and sales. His first task was to extinguish Indian title to the tract, as the New York treaties secured only the region east of the Pre-emption Line. Hence he went immediately to Buffalo Creek where, in July, 1789, he persuaded the Seneca to give up 2,500,000 acres east of the Genesee River, plus the Mill Yard Tract on the west bank of that stream, for $5,000 and an annuity of $500. That done,

Phelps set surveyors to work, built a storehouse and land office at the foot of Canandaigua Lake, and began public sales. Within a year a thousand settlers were scattered over the rolling hill country of the Phelps-Gorham Purchase, Canandaigua was a bustling little town of thirty cabins, and a rival village called Geneva was taking shape at the foot of Lake Seneca. Most of the newcomers were from New England, although New Yorkers and Pennsylvanians who had followed the Susquehanna north were in evidence.

Sales were encouraging, but the credit system used brought in little actual cash and left Phelps and Gorham with the task of raising money needed for their three annual payments to Massachusetts. That proved difficult. Many New York and Pennsylvania speculators who had promised aid backed out, while the hope of selling Pennsylvania the so-called "Erie Triangle" vanished when the federal government decided that area was not a part of New York. Worse still was the rapid rise in the price of Massachusetts securities. Phelps and Gorham planned to buy depreciated state notes at a low figure, then turn them over to Massachusetts at par. During 1789 those seemingly worthless notes skyrocketed in value as rumors spread that the national government planned to assume the state debts. Dozens of speculators, including Phelps and Gorham, who counted on making payments in a depreciated medium were faced with the dismal prospect of cash prices, particularly after 1790 when Secretary of the Treasury Alexander Hamilton carried his funding plan through Congress. To make matters even worse an opposition party within the Massachusetts legislature, led by the ever-popular Samuel Adams, threatened to revoke the contract on the slightest excuse.

Phelps and Gorham managed to pay their first installment, but hopes of meeting the next two were slim. Rather than risk losing all, they agreed in March, 1790, to turn back the western two-thirds in return for full title to the eastern third. The exploitation of even that smaller plot so strained their resources that they leaped at the first opportunity to sell. On November 18, 1790, Robert Morris of New York bought the Phelps-Gorham Purchase for £30,000—about eight cents an acre. A few months later Morris purchased from Massachusetts the whole western portion of New York for an additional £45,000. This wealthy speculator, whose two spectacular bargains made him the largest landholder in America, was already well known in the money markets of the United States and Europe. He was wise enough to know that even his vast resources were insufficient to develop the tract he had contracted to buy; instead he made the purchase to test a shrewd theory of his own. The speculative spirit, he knew, was running high among European bankers who commanded far more capital than any jobber in poverty-stricken America. He realized, too, that his own name was known and trusted abroad, for he had served successfully as secretary of finance during the latter years of the Revolution. Therefore he would market his New York lands in Amsterdam, London, and Paris, hoping to find there the profitable resale that was every speculator's dream.

For that purpose Morris divided his holdings into three tracts. The middle section along the Genesee River was the best; this he kept himself. The eastern portion, consisting of the Phelps-Gorham Purchase, he sold for £75,000 early in 1791 to a syndicate of English capitalists headed by Sir William Pulteney—a sum that gave him a tidy profit of £45,000. In casting about for a purchaser for the western half of his property, Morris hit on four prominent Amsterdam business concerns then speculating in American securities. Their agent in the United States, Theophile Cazenove, proved interested, partly because Hamilton's funding program was reducing profits from financial ventures, and partly because he had already made two minor purchases from New York—one just east of the Military Tract and the other north of the Mohawk—and was sufficiently infected with land fever to want more. Cazenove's enthusiasm proved so contagious that his Dutch backers decided to enter the speculative field on a wholesale scale. They added two more banking houses to their number, organized themselves as the Holland Land Company, and instructed Cazenove to buy widely for them. By December, 1792, the ambitious agent completed arrangements with Morris to take over 2,500,000 acres in western New York, and in the next few months he secured another 1,500,000 acres in Pennsylvania.

The series of purchases which delivered most of western New York and Pennsylvania into the hands of European speculators greatly affected the development of that region. The English and Dutch business men now in control had capital to develop their holdings—something completely lacking among American jobbers who usually operated on a shoestring and counted on a quick turnover for profits. This advantage was first realized by Charles Williamson, the agent sent to the United States by the Pulteney Estates. He reached western New York in the spring of 1792 filled with ambitious plans; he would build roads, improve rivers, erect stores, taverns, gristmills, and sawmills, provide centers for amusement, and turn his wilderness estate into the garden spot of the West. His backers, he knew, were wealthy enough to afford the expense, and he reasoned that grateful Americans would repay them by purchasing lands at unusually high prices. Thus originated the "hothouse" method of developing the frontier.

A rapid survey of the Pulteney Estates convinced Williamson that export centers should be established on Lake Ontario, the Genesee River, the Seneca River, and the Cohocton River. Hence he set crews to work on carefully planned cities controlling those routes. At Bath, at the head of navigation on the Cohocton, he built houses, farm buildings, a gristmill, two sawmills, a tavern, a theater, and a race track. Williamsburg on the Genesee and Lyons on the Seneca were also provided with homes, storehouses, distilleries, and mills. The Sodus development on Lake Ontario was even more ambitious; in addition to constructing dwellings, stores, and mills, Williamson improved the harbor and erected a large wharf. Settlements already begun at Canandaigua and Geneva were similarly improved. Over the whole area he scattered gristmills, distilleries, farmhouses, and cleared fields to lure homeseekers. Equal care was spent on a road system connecting the cities with rural regions. One long highway was built from Williamsport, on the Susquehanna River in Pennsylvania, to Williamsburg, another from Sodus to Geneva. At the same time Williamson in 1794 persuaded New York to extend the Mohawk Turnpike through Geneva and Canandaigua to the future site of Avon on the Genesee. The Great Genesee Road, as it was called, gave the Pulteney Estates direct access to Albany and New York markets, while the southern road to Williamsport allowed shipments to Philadelphia and Baltimore.

In the ten years that Williamson pushed this building program he spent $1,000,000 and took in just $146,000 from land sales, although more was due under the six-year credit system allowed. By that time his wealthy supporters were so alarmed that he was displaced in 1801 by an agent who emphasized returns rather than expenditures. Although the Pulteney interests did little more than break even on their investment, they took solace in the fact that Williamson's efforts hurried the advance of settlement. By 1800 population was well established over the whole region, with most of the settlers scattered along the Great Genesee Road and about Bath. The frontier was ready to pass beyond the Genesee River, where the lands of the Morris Reserve were filling rapidly, into the domain of the Holland Land Company.

During the 1790s that wealthy European concern was experimenting with the "hothouse" method of settlement on its two tracts in eastern New York. Within five years $128,000 was squandered on the plot south of Lake Oneida, much of it on the city of Cazenovia where a brewery, a distillery, sawmills and gristmills, a potash works, two stores, and a tavern were built. Even more was spent on the region north of the Mohawk River, where a disastrous experiment in maple sugar production cost the company $15,000 even before the usual developments began. These included model farms, two well-equipped towns, and purchase of a tract along the Mohawk for a new village, Utica, to provide a market and export center. Between 1794 and 1798 $15,000 a year was poured into the small area. By that time the directors of the Holland Land Company, disturbed by the large expenditures, ordered an end to developments in both tracts. Theophile Cazenove was replaced by a more conservative agent, and the company prepared to reap some return on its investments.

Those expensive experiments convinced the thrifty Dutch bankers there should be no "hastening of civilization" west of the Genesee. Settlers were paying the high prices asked for improved lands, but just as many were going to nearby regions on which the owners spent nothing. The American pioneer, they saw, did not want cleared fields and trim frame houses; he was enough of a speculator to want cheap land that he could improve with his own labor. The "hothouse" method transferred the profits gained from the initial risk to the company. Nor were gristmills, sawmills, and distilleries necessary; they sprang up in each frontier community as soon as the demand was great enough. The company's decision to leave all but necessary improvements to private initiative was a wise one.

The first step in opening the Holland Land Company's territory was to extinguish Indian title. That was accomplished in the Big Tree Treaty, signed by the Seneca on September 15, 1797, after chiefs, interpreters, and watching government officials were bribed into accepting terms distasteful to the majority of the tribe. With the way cleared for settlement, Joseph Ellicott, an experienced American woodsman who had no sympathy with "hothouse" methods, was appointed agent. By the spring of 1800 the region was divided into townships six miles square, while those marked for immediate sale were subdivided into three-hundred-and-sixty-acre plots. Sales started in 1802, at a land office in the new town of Batavia. When the paucity of purchasers convinced Ellicott that the $2.75 an acre asked by the company was too high, he lowered the price to between $1.50 and $2, eliminated down payments, and allowed ten years credit. Such a rush of customers followed that he was obliged to open the whole Genesee country to settlers. The price was gradually increased over the next years, until by 1811 the average sum received for an acre was $2.30 and in 1817 $5. Although collections were slow and payment often in goods rather than cash the Holland Land Company eventually retired from its venture with a comfortable profit.

This was partly due to the manner in which the economy-minded Ellicott confined himself to the most essential improvements. Some roads were built to supplement the Great Genesee Road after the state extended that highway to Buffalo between 1798 and 1803: one from Niagara through Batavia to Geneseo where it connected with the transportation system of the Pulteney Estates, another from Geneseo to Olean at the head of navigation on the Allegheny River, and a third from Buffalo along the shore of Lake Erie to Erie, with a branch running southest to the Pennsylvania border. Although these highways were well built—underbrush and small trees were cleared away in a forty-foot path and a sixteen foot swath level with the ground cut down the middle—they cost little as Ellicott allowed farmers to pay for land by road work. Those were virtually the only improvements, aside from two unsuccessful mills at Batavia and a grant of 200 acres in each township for schools and churches. Individual artisans soon appeared to supply the sawmills, gristmills, and distilleries needed.

The Holland Land Company and other European speculative concerns vastly stimulated the peopling of western New York. Their improvements, whether confined to road building or on a needlessly grandiose scale, made settlement easier; their advertising in eastern states lured thousands of home-seekers westward. Much of this was concentrated in New England, where, speculators realized, the people were ready to move. As hard-working farmers in that section read gaudy circulars distributed by the companies or listened to enthusiastic letters from the first arrivals in western New York, their dissatisfaction with their rock-strewn soil increased. Why dedicate yourself to a lifetime of backbreaking toil when the western country beckoned? As more and more reasoned in that way a "Genesee Fever" swept through the eastern states. Everywhere, from Massachusetts to New Jersey, men sold their farms and began the long trek to the frontier.

All through the 1790s the numbers moving west increased year by year until by 1800 a mass exodus was under way. A traveler in 1797 counted almost 500 wagons a day on the roads through Albany, and a few years later the Catskill Road, now extended to Canandaigua, was just as crowded. By 1800 immigrants overran the Military Tract and Pulteney Estates; five years later they were moving across the Genesee lands of the Holland Company where Batavia, Buffalo, Stafford, and other towns blossomed into tiny cities overnight. "The woods are full of new settlers," wrote an observer near Batavia in 1805. "Axes are resounding, and the trees literally falling about us as we passed. In one instance we were obliged to pass in a field through the smoke and flame of the trees which had lately been felled and were just fired." In 1812, almost 200,000 people lived in western New York, 25,000 of them in the Holland Land Company purchase, and the region was passing beyond the frontier stage.

More than two thirds of the pioneers were New Englanders, most of whom came from Massachusetts, Connecticut, or Rhode Island. The wholesale departure of these thousands spread alarm through the ranks of those who stayed behind. Their own states, they noted, were lagging significantly behind the rest of the nation in population increase, their best and youngest citizens were moving away, and both land values and the social structure were suffering. These good fathers could not know they were witnessing the first stages of that century-long process known as the rural decay of New England. Instead they sought vainly to offset the advertising of the land companies by propaganda of their own. Newspapers in the early 1800s bristled with lurid descriptions of dangers of frontier life or with such verses as:

> Let the idle complain
> And ramble in vain,
> And Eden to find in the West,
> They're grossly deceiv'd,
> Their hearts sorely griev'd,
> They'll sigh to return to the East.

"Actual calculation has evinced," wrote the Reverend Jedidiah Morse in the 1796 edition of his famous *Geography*, "that any quantity of the best mowing land in Connecticut produces about twice as much clear profit as the same quantity of the best wheat land in the State of New York." These calamitous voices cried in a wilderness of indifference. More than words were needed to keep an American at home when good soil lay ahead.

Or even, in that restless day, poor soil. For while the main stream of westward-moving population inundated the Genesee country, two subsidiary rivulets branched off to engulf the mountainous wastes of Pennsylvania and northern New York. Pennsylvania threw open its last unsettled portions, the northwestern region obtained from the Iroquois in the second Treaty of Ft. Stanwix, in 1792. The land law passed at the time was so loosely worded that untold confusion had resulted; farms could be obtained for twenty cents an acre either by squatting or buying a warrant, all plots were to be settled within two years unless Indian disturbances intervened, and surveys were to follow rather than precede purchase. Those vague phrases, intentionally inserted by speculators, made Pennsylvania a happy hunting ground for land jobbers. Within a few years the whole area was engrossed by their agents, most of it by two large companies: the Holland Land Company, and the Pennsylvania Population Company. Neither had any hope of settling its domains within the prescribed two-year period. When the state finally tried to force them to do so in 1797 they began a long legal battle that only ended in 1805 when the United States Supreme Court ruled that the 1792 law was too poorly worded to be binding. This litigation discouraged settlement, although a large number of squatters—some hired by companies organized for the purpose—planted themselves on speculators' lands in hopes of securing title through possession. After 1805, with ownership clear and a state road opened from Lock Haven to the border, sales began at the Holland Land Company's offices in Meadville and Kittanning. By 1812 the region was sparsely settled with Erie and Meadville its principal towns, but the mountainous terrain failed to attract a large population. Certainly speculators discouraged rather than aided the westward movement there.

They played a more valuable role in peopling the two habitable portions of northern New York: the hill country between the Black River and Lake Ontario, and the woodlands bordering the St. Lawrence River. A commission created by the legislature began selling plots in the first area during the late 1780s; by 1795 nearly all was in the hands of small speculators who spent the next years developing their tracts. The most ambitious of those jobbers was a New York merchant, George Scriba, who secured the region north of Lake Oneida, laid out two towns, built a connecting road, and made the usual improvements designed to lure settlers. It was in this territory, and just south of a grant made to Baron Steuben for his part in the Revolution, that Cazenove bought the tract the Holland Land Company placed on the market in 1794.

Speculation in the St. Lawrence country was on a more spectacular scale. The first region to be surveyed, a fertile area known as the St. Lawrence Ten Towns, was auctioned off in 1787 to a syndicate of jobbers led by Alexander Macomb, a bold plunger with large resources. Macomb's appetite for land was only whetted; he began negotiating at once to secure the millions of acres surrounding his tract. Arrangements were completed in 1791 when he bought all of the unpatented lands remaining in northern New York—4,000,000 acres in all—for eight cents an acre. Macomb, who realized he could meet the first of five annual payments only by immediate resale, divided his purchase into six tracts which were assigned to lesser

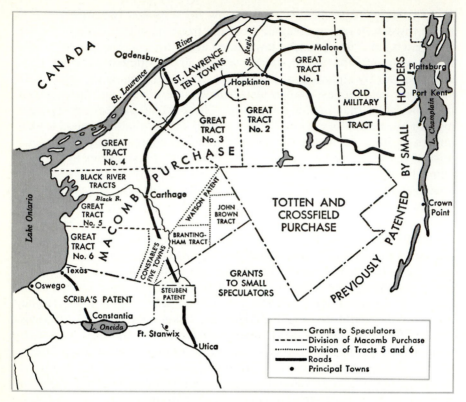

Northern New York, 1790–1812

speculators for development and sale. Most prominent among these was William Constable, who received Tracts Four, Five, and Six. Those were disposed of during the next few years, Tract Four to a group of Belgian capitalists organized as the Antwerp Company, part of Tract Five to a group of refugees from Revolutionary France, and the remainder to smaller American operators such as William Inman and John Brown, the wealthy Providence merchant. The land Constable was unable to sell he developed himself as Constable's Five Towns. In this way most of the Black River region was parceled out between 1793 and 1812, but the distance from markets and the rough country kept the population small.

The northern portions of the Macomb purchase went through a similar evolution, for these too were assigned to smaller speculators for improvement and sale. One, Samuel Ogden, laid out the town of Ogdensburg in 1801, built the usual mills, and constructed a passable road to the Black River where it connected with a highway just completed to Utica. Some settlers drifted in over this, but more came from Vermont, attracted by Ogden's advertising and the cheap lands of the wild St. Lawrence country.

Some were pioneers from southern New England who drifted on now with the advancing frontier; others were established farmers weaned from rugged Vermont by promises of "lands not lying edgewise." The crude "winter road" from Lake Champlain to the mouth of the St. Regis River was crowded each year with hundreds of moving families, dragging their household goods on sleds over the hard-packed snow. The region around Ogdensburg and the valley of the Oswegatchie River filled up first, but three toll roads built by turnpike companies between 1810 and 1812—the St. Lawrence Turnpike between Carthage and Malone, and two highways connecting Hopkinton with Lake Champlain—turned the tide of settlement toward the interior. Although northern New York did not pass beyond the primitive stage of frontier development before the War of 1812, great timber rafts drifting down the St. Lawrence to Montreal and barges deep laden with flour and potash bound for that Canadian port testified to an advancing civilization.

Northern New York and western Pennsylvania developed slowly because they were only eddies in the main frontier stream sweeping westward from New England and the Middle States. Settlement was more rapid at the terminus of that swift-flowing current in the Northwest Territory. The peopling of that region began in 1795 when Wayne's Treaty of Greenville removed Indians from much of the Ohio country. In the van were the pioneers who had crowded together in the river towns during the wars; all through the summer of 1795 they poured out of Marietta, Massie's Station, Columbia, Cincinnati, and North Bend on their way to the back country. Before autumn set in they were joined by a horde of land-seekers from Pennsylvania, Virginia, and Kentucky, who started west as soon as news reached them that the frontier was safe. Some followed the Wilderness Road to Maysville; more reached Redstone or Pittsburgh over Forbes' or Braddock's Roads, bought flatboats, and drifted down the Ohio to a site that pleased them. For the next dozen years a regular procession of those ungainly craft floated westward with a perspiring farmer at the sweeps, a horse and a few cows munching at the haystack in the prow, a handful of ragged children playing on the roofed portion of the stern, and a busy housewife hanging out her washing or churning her butter as she would on shore. Seldom had the frontier developed a more convenient form of transportation than flatboats. They cost only $30 or $40, allowed normal life to continue during the journey, and were broken up for lumber to build the settler's home.

Some pioneers purchased land from the small speculators operating in the Seven Ranges or about Steubenville. Others bought from the Ohio Company in such quantities that the villages there—Marietta and newly established Athens—began to lose their New England character. Still more made their homes on the lands east of the Scioto which the government took back from the defunct Scioto Company, or in the federal Military Reserve that was laid out in 1796 to satisfy the bounties promised Revolutionary veterans. There, as in the Virginia Military Reserve, nearly all purchases were made

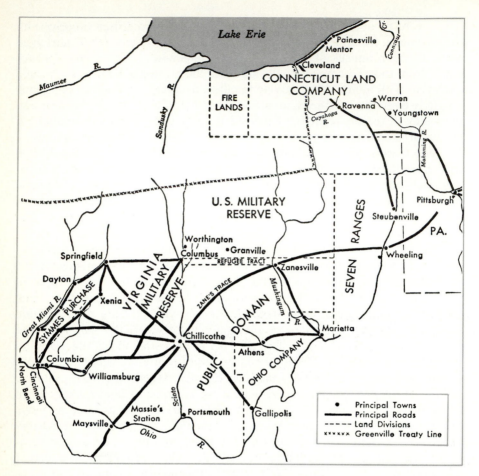

The Ohio Country, 1790–1812

through speculators, for the transferable warrants issued soldiers usually found their way into their hands. Symmes Purchase also filled rapidly during the late 1790s. By the end of the century squatters in the unsurveyed region west of the Great Miami River had extended the frontier as far as the boundary established at Greenville only five years before.

Speculators in the Ohio country not only provided pioneers with needed credit but helped establish interior towns. Speculation in village sites, which absorbed more and more of the energy of land jobbers, promised even greater profits than farm lands. Most "paper towns" never passed beyond the planning stage, but some expanded into Ohio's leading cities. Hamilton was founded by a prominent speculator, Israel Ludlow, in 1795; in the same year a syndicate that he headed laid out the streets of Dayton. Nathaniel Massie played a similar role. The station he established on the north bank of the

Ohio in 1790 grew into the city of Manchester, and the site he selected for another town, Chillicothe, proved so advantageous that the village soon rivaled Cincinnati. Most of the other towns founded between 1796 and 1803—Portsmouth, Columbus, Williamsburg, Deerfield, Caesarville, Xenia, and a dozen more—owed their existence to the vision and luck of some land jobber. Pressure from speculators was also partially responsible for the congressional grant that made possible the first road across Ohio, Zane's Trace, in 1796.

They were even more influential in peopling the Western Reserve, that northeast corner of Ohio retained when Connecticut ceded its lands to Congress. The first step toward disposing of the area was taken in 1792 when the legislature granted 500,000 acres on the western edge of the Reserve to 1,870 inhabitants of coastal towns whose property was destroyed by British raids during the Revolution. When it became clear that these "Fire Lands" could never be disposed of until the region east of them was thrown on the market, the whole tract was sold in 1795 to a group of thirty-five speculators under Oliver Phelps, organized as the Connecticut Land Company, for $1,200,000. Moses Cleaveland, an able young Yale graduate who was named general agent, started west in the spring of 1796 with a party of surveyors and instructions to begin sales at once. Stopping first at Buffalo, where he purchased the region east of the Cuyahoga from Indians for £500, two beef cattle, and almost 100 gallons of whiskey, Cleaveland reached the mouth of Conneaut Creek on July 4, 1796, and there established his headquarters. Surveys went on rapidly, a village bearing the agent's name—later shortened to Cleveland—was laid out at the mouth of the Cuyahoga River, and settlers began flocking in. Nearly all came from New England, over the Great Genesee Road and an extension built by the company from Erie to Cleveland, attracted by good land which sold for only $1 an acre with five years credit. By 1800, more than 1,200 people lived in the Western Reserve, most of them clustered about villages that sprang up in the Mahoning and Cuyahoga valleys or along the lake shore.

The influx of settlers, in the Western Reserve and the river bottoms north of the Ohio, fostered a growing demand for a greater degree of self-government. The frontiersmen were not only familiar with the provisions of the Ordinance of 1787 but thoroughly dissatisfied with the administration of Governor Arthur St. Clair. That crotchety general, who was disliked for his military failures, his autocratic leanings, and his staunch Federalism, was finally goaded into ordering a census in 1798. When this showed that many more than the needed 5,000 adult males lived in the territory he was forced to call a general election to select a legislature. The twenty-two men named to that body in December, 1798, were not completely representative, for property qualifications kept many people from voting, yet nearly all were anti-Federalists and a contest between them and the governor was inevitable. The clash came over the election of a delegate to represent the Northwest Territory in Congress. St. Clair and his small following of aristocratic Federalists backed the governor's son, Arthur St. Clair, Jr., while the opposition chose as their candidate a twenty-six-year-old stripling already distinguished as a military leader in the Indian wars, William Henry Harrison. After a spirited campaign the legislature selected Harrison by a vote of eleven to ten. Despite all of St. Clair's ranting that able young Jeffersonian set out for the nation's capital during the winter of 1799–1800.

The Jeffersonian revolt against Federalist control of the frontier forced Congress to recognize the growing influence of the West in its legislative program, and it led to the first division of the Northwest Territory and statehood for Ohio. William Henry Harrison was responsible for the first. He reached Washington aflame with zeal for one great cause: he would remake the land laws to allow direct individual purchases of small plots on extended credit at offices conveniently located along the frontier. Fortunately the time was ripe for such a change, for when he laid his proposals before Congress in February, 1800, the political revolution that led to the overthrow of the Federalists a few months later was already taking shape. Most western congressmen were sympathetic, and some—notably those from Kentucky, Tennessee, western Pennsylvania, Virginia, and the Carolinas—were as enthusiastic as their frontier constituents. Harrison's ready tongue made him an admirable spokesman for this western pressure group. The result was the first workable land law in American history.

The East did not bow completely before frontier demands when it accepted the measure that passed Congress on May 10, 1800; while the law was more liberal than the Ordinance of 1785 or the modifying act of 1796 which raised the price to $2 an acre but allowed a year's credit on half the amount, it still reflected eastern conservatism. The minimum price of $2 an acre was retained, with the additional provision that lands not sold after three weeks on the auction block could be purchased for that sum at land offices in Cincinnati, Chillicothe, Marietta, and Steubenville. The smallest amount purchasable was lowered from 640 acres to 320 acres. More important was a provision in the Act of 1800 that allowed a buyer to pay only one quarter of the purchase price down and the remainder within four years. This credit feature, which made it possible to buy 320 acres for only $160 in cash, did much to satisfy western demands. Speculators, other than those dealing in town sites, were virtually eliminated as settlers flocked to buy directly from the government in such large numbers that the phrase, "doing a land-office business," was added to the American vocabulary. Congress was so impressed by the financial returns that in 1804 it further liberalized the land system by lowering the minimum amount purchasable to 160 acres.

Just as influential in speeding the advance of settlement were the governmental changes that followed Harrison's election to Congress, for that manifestation of public discontent with Federalist rule set in motion the chain of events leading to statehood for Ohio. St. Clair, seeing the way the wind blew, acted first, hoping to ward off the admission of a new state that would almost certainly support Jefferson. In February, 1800, he asked Harrison to introduce a bill dividing the Northwest into three territories, with boundaries running north from the mouths of the Scioto and Kentucky rivers. This, St. Clair reasoned, would not only split the Republican strength, which was concentrated in the Scioto Valley, but allow the strong Federalist organization in Marietta to dominate the region east of the river and his own Cincinnati machine to control the West. Moreover no one of the three territories would have the 60,000 inhabitants needed for statehood. No sooner had St. Clair shown his hand, however, than the Jeffersonians leaped into action. The scheme they laid before Harrison called for two territories, divided by a line running north from the mouth of the Great Miami River. This plan was as clever as that of the Federalists; it would keep the Scioto Valley Jeffersonians united, assure immediate statehood for the eastern territory they dominated, and probably shift the capital from Cincinnati to the centrally located city of Chillicothe.

Harrison, when confronted with the two proposals, decided to support the second, although he realized the difficulty of pushing a Jeffersonian-sponsored bill through a Federalist Congress. His strenuous efforts were rewarded on May 7, 1800, when an act setting up two territories, separated by a line running from the mouth of the Kentucky to Ft. Recovery and then north to the Canadian boundary, finally passed. Harrison was rewarded by the governorship of the new Indiana Territory created in the West.

From that time on the movement for Ohio statehood was rapid, for St. Clair's obstructionist efforts made more enemies than friends. A relentless Jeffersonian campaign, inspired partly by a desire to oust the ill-tempered St. Clair, reached a climax on April 30, 1802, when Congress passed an enabling act authorizing a convention to decide whether statehood was desirable. This met at Chillicothe in November, and after listening to an anti-Jeffersonian tirade from St. Clair, the delegates voted with only one dissenting voice for immediate admission into the Union. The constitution as adopted reflected both the southern background of most of the delegates and the liberal influence of the frontier. It was modeled after Tennessee's frame of government, but swept away all property qualifications for voting, vested more power in the legislature, and made the governor a figurehead who could hold office only two years and had no veto power. Even the state judges were to be elected by the legislature. The convention also agreed the new state would not tax public lands until five years after they were sold, if the United States in return would set aside one section in each township to support schools and donate 3 per cent of all land sales for road building. Congress accepted both the constitution and these provisions, and Ohio, the first state to be formed from the public domain, entered the Union.

Both the governmental changes and the liberal Land Act of 1800 stimulated the settlement of the Northwest. From New England, the Middle States and the South the immigrants came in ever-increasing numbers: southern Quakers fleeing before the advancing slave frontier; upcountry farmers from the Virginia or Carolina Piedmont driven westward by worn-out soils;

pioneers from Kentucky and Pennsylvania drifting onward with the advancing settlements; New Englanders who moved as individuals or in whole villages, intact with pastors and school masters and deacons, to found at Granville and Worthington and other Ohio towns exact replicas of the quiet villages they left behind. Some bought from intermediaries who offered land in the United States and Virginia military reserves, or in the Refugee Tract set aside by Congress for Canadians who aided the American Revolution. More patronized the government land offices; 3,374,843 acres were sold in the Northwest in the first eleven years after the passage of the Act of 1800. Still others purchased from the Connecticut Land Company or from the Firelands Company which was formed by the shareholders in the Fire Lands of the Western Reserve. By 1812 more than 250,000 people lived in Ohio, and the whole region north and west to the Greenville Treaty line was beginning to resemble an eastern state with passable roads, bustling cities, and a spreading blanket of cultivated fields.

So rapid was the influx into Ohio that some newcomers moved over into Indiana Territory, which increased its population under Harrison's able leadership until a legislature could be called in 1805. At the same time the northern portion was set aside as Michigan Territory, although that isolated region did not feel the impact of any considerable migration until after the War of 1812. More new settlers sought homes in the country west of the Wabash, where they clustered about the French villages of Kaskaskia and Cahokia, laid out primitive new outposts at Ft. Massac and Shawneetown, or cleared the fertile lands of the American Bottom opposite St. Louis. The difficulty of administering those distant settlements from the Indiana territorial seat at Vincennes led Congress in 1809 to set up the separate Territory of Illinois, governed by Ninian Edwards of Kentucky. By 1812, when Illinois entered its second territorial stage with the election of a legislature, 13,000 persons were scattered through the region, while Indiana's population was 25,000. Both were in a primitive frontier stage when the outbreak of a new wilderness war brought the westward movement to a temporary close.

14

The West in the War of 1812

1812-1815

The issues that plunged the United States into its second war with England seemingly were of little interest to westerners. Why should they grow wrathful over a distant death struggle between Britain and the newly risen colossus of the Continent, Napoleon? What matter to them that both warring powers confiscated American cargoes or that England's navy impressed British deserters (and a few United States citizens) from American ships? As loyal Jeffersonians, westerners could be expected to applaud their President's efforts to keep peace and to support his application of economic sanctions to both belligerents. As ardent nationalists they would certainly boil with indignation at each new attack on their country's shipping or each added insult to its honor. But neither partisanship nor patriotism seemed sufficient to send them along the road to war.

Yet frontier demands, coupled with those of the South, forced the War of 1812 on a reluctant East, frontier arms accounted for the few American victories, and frontier ambitions dictated the peace. The answer to this apparent paradox can be found in both the practical problems facing the West in 1812 and the psychological attitudes persistent there. A serious depression engulfed the back country, fur traders were engaged in a losing battle with intruders, an Indian war ravaged outlying settlements, and a younger generation of revolutionists bristled with each new sullying of the national honor. The average westerner believed that England was responsible for all troubles and that only a war with that power would allow the conquest of Canada, which was the sole means of their solution. Such a conquest would automatically solve the fur-trading problem and end Indian attacks; then at war's end the plundered colony could be offered to England as the price for respecting America's neutral shipping rights. With freedom of the seas guaranteed, the West could shake off the depression by again exporting its surpluses to a hungry Europe.

This depression that shackled the Ohio Valley between 1808 and 1812 underlay all other grievances. Its cause was the unsound economy forced on the Ohio Valley by its inadequate transportation system. The bulky farm goods produced there could be marketed only in New Orleans. Western farmers had to select their cargoes for export in the light of price information a month old, spend another month and a large sum of money reaching the market, and compete with dozens of other sellers who arrived at the same time. Often backwoodsmen who had braved snags and pirates in the tortuous journey down the Mississippi were so overawed by the bustling strangeness of teeming New Orleans or so afraid of contracting tropical fevers that they sold their cargoes hurriedly at ridiculously low prices. Only the fortunate few were able to sell at a profit under those conditions.

The West did not feel the full impact of its economic maladjustment until 1808, for until that time the influx of new immigrants not only absorbed agricultural surpluses but kept the frontier supplied with ready cash. Thus the depression coincided with England's blockade, and to frontiersmen the two events were intimately connected. So long as American ships reached Europe the Ohio Valley enjoyed prosperity; when Britain closed that market hard times followed. Prosperity would only return when the English fleet allowed the United States to trade with the Continent once more. Westerners, reasoning in that fashion, solidly supported the Embargo of 1807, objected strenuously when eastern pressure forced Congress to adopt the less stringent Non-Intercourse Act in 1809, and adopted a belligerent I-told-you-so attitude when hard times grew more acute in the next three years. By 1812 westerners agreed that war was necessary to restore prosperity. "The true question," said one of their congressional representatives, ". . . is the right of exporting the productions of our soil and industry to foreign markets."

This goal could be achieved, westerners agreed, only by using a conquered Canada as a hostage to force England to her knees. This was Britain's only vulnerable spot; not even the most optimistic patriot could hope that the few American vessels could challenge the might of the world's dominant naval power on the high seas. But poorly protected Canada could be easily taken, then dangled before England in return for the promise to allow American ships freedom to trade wherever they pleased. To the westerners, this was all-important. Wealthy Boston or New York shipowners could afford to lose two vessels in every three to Britain's raiders and still count a respectable profit; even greater losses could be sustained so long as their cash reserves and ready credit held out. To these easterners war spelled disaster, for they well knew that all their trade would end at once. The pioneers of the Ohio Valley, however, had no such fears. With their near-marginal economy, they were convinced that the export of only a fraction—5 or 10 per cent—of their corn and wheat surpluses to starving Europe would

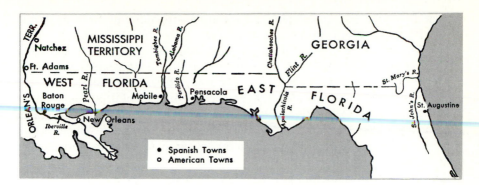

Expansion in Florida, 1803–1812

lift them from their depression and assure them perpetual prosperity. Maritime rights and neutral trade were more important to them than to New England's merchants, despite their relatively small stake in European commerce.

To western expansionists, then, the overrunning of Canada was not an end—they were aware that the nation's supply of unoccupied lands would suffice for generations to come—but a means through which they would restore prosperity and avenge the sullied national honor. That this was the case was amply demonstrated by the correlation between belligerency and inadequate trade outlets. On the one hand the farmers of northern New York and Vermont, long accustomed to exporting their grain and potash to Montreal via the St. Lawrence River, not only opposed war but persisted in their trade after the 1807 Embargo made such trade illegal. On the other hand the planters of South Carolina and Georgia, where glutted cotton markets sent prices tumbling, and the farmers of the Ohio Valley, where a faulty marketing system doomed prosperity, were the most violent spokesmen for conflict.

Southerners had another reason for war, for a conflict with England and that nation's ally, Spain, would allow the conquest of Spanish Florida. This would open new trade routes to the Gulf along the Alabama, Pearl, and Apalachicola rivers and end chaotic conditions along the southern borderland where renegades, runaway slaves, and lawless Indians took advantage of Spain's preoccupation at home to roam about unmolested. The South's appetite for this tempting prize had been whetted by a series of events that had taken place in the decade preceding 1812. Chief among these were the gradual infiltration of Americans into West Florida and growing official interest in the region. Settlers, lured southward by Spain's liberal land policy, drifted into the region west of the Pearl River in such large numbers that by 1809 nine tenths of the district's inhabitants were loyal to the United States. Their presence encouraged President James Madison to make a bold bid for the whole region. Taking advantage of Spain's absorption in the Napoleonic Wars, President Madison advanced the theory that West Florida was part of the Louisiana Purchase. The Treaty of 1803, he pointed out, gave the United States Louisiana "with the same extent that it now has in the hands of Spain, and that it had when France possessed it." Actually those two provisions were irreconcilable; the eastern boundary of Louisiana under Spain was the Iberville River, while under France in 1763 the province extended on to the Perdido. Madison's determination to secure West Florida by claiming the latter boundary was an invitation to Americans there to take matters into their own hands.

They acted in September, 1810, when a group of revolutionists formed an army, seized the Spanish fort at Baton Rouge, and captured the governor. Three days later a convention of insurrectionists formally requested annexation by the United States. President Madison responded on October 27, 1810, when he issued a proclamation annexing the region between the Iberville and Perdido rivers. This order was carried into West Florida by Governor David Holmes of Mississippi Territory with a detachment of regular troops; no resistance was encountered and on December 10 the American flag was raised over Baton Rouge. Mobile, however, remained in Spanish hands, nor did the President dare use force to oust its strong garrison so long as the United States remained at peace. The promise of that rich prize, which controlled the trade of the Alabama Valley, helped to create a western demand for war with Spain and her English ally.

The war spirit was fanned in the southeast by demands for East Florida, although there the situation was slightly different. The many Americans living in that province were not only well satisfied with Spanish rule but realized that annexation would stop the importation of slaves and end the smuggling of foreign imports across St. Mary's River—a trade that brought prosperity to northern Florida after passage of the Embargo Act. North of the border, however, desire for East Florida was strong, inspired partly by land hunger, partly by a desire to end turbulent border conditions, partly by the success of the West Florida revolution, and partly by the enthusiasm of an ardent expansionist, George Mathews, a former governor of Georgia who began building up a revolutionary party in the autumn of 1810. That winter Mathews laid his plans before President Madison with such success that when he returned to Georgia in the spring of 1811 he carried an official proclamation authorizing him to secure East Florida for the United States either by negotiation or, if any foreign power threatened to take possession, by force. With him too, in all probability, went the President's assurance of aid should Mathews succeed in stirring up a rebellion. Certainly the troops and warships that Madison dispatched to the Georgia border indicated a plan for armed intervention on the slightest excuse.

Mathews spent the rest of 1811 building up a revolutionary party among Americans in East Florida. By March, 1812, he was ready to act. With a following of 200 volunteers he attacked first the Spanish town of Fernandina on Amelia Island, then started a march on St. Augustine, followed closely by American troops who refused to take part in actual fighting but occupied each conquered town. By mid-April the Florida capital was under siege and Mathews was dispatching urgent messages to Madison asking authority to use the regular army for its reduction. The President dared not go that far in face of Spain's vigorous protests and the criticism from the antiwar faction in Washington. Instead he dismissed Mathews, ordered the army back to the St. Mary's River, and placed control of border relations in the hands of the Georgia governor. News of this step aroused resentment throughout the southern borderland from Savannah to Nashville. Expansionists, with East Florida snatched from their grasp, believed war with England and Spain necessary before they could complete a conquest they considered rightfully theirs.

In the Northwest expansionist sentiment was stimulated by a desire for Canada. Neither land hunger nor hope for new trade routes was responsible; plentiful lands still awaited the westward marching pioneers while the St. Lawrence route to the sea, although closed to Americans, was too round-about to be coveted. Instead conquered Canada promised two important benefits: it would end an irritating dispute over the fur trade, and check a serious Indian outbreak then well underway.

The trading dispute was more imagined than real. Since the drafting of Jay's Treaty Canadians roamed the country south of the border, operating from posts at Green Bay, Prairie du Chien, and other strategic spots. Zebulon M. Pike, an army officer sent to explore the Mississippi headwaters in 1805, found them everywhere in the northern woods, entirely unaware that they were on American soil. Their presence alarmed westerners who not only resented the drain of peltry northward, but believed Canadian trappers armed and incited the Indians. Those fears were not shared by the men most affected—the American traders. United States trade was dominated by John Jacob Astor's American Fur Company which, after a period of cutthroat competition with the Canadian North West Company, agreed in 1811 to divide the trade of the West with its rival. The American Fur Company, operating through a subsidiary corporation known as the South West Company, was given exclusive trading rights east of the Rockies, while the Canadian concern was awarded the far-western area. Astor was well satisfied with that arrangement and shied from a war that would upset his carefully worked out plans. Westerners, however, knowing nothing of those international agreements, believed a conflict with England desirable if only to wipe out the clauses of Jay's Treaty that allowed Canadian traders to operate south of the border.

Far more important in sending the westerners along the road to war was the Indian unrest that boiled through the back country by 1812. Responsible for this were land-grabbing treaties, forced upon the natives by avaricious frontier officials. Thomas Jefferson, whose frontier background transcended his well-known humanitarianism, was to blame for these. Under his administration Indian agents were instructed either to convert western Indians to agriculture or move them to unwanted lands beyond the Mississippi. Those harsh orders invited trouble in both South and North. The principal southern agent, a sincere friend of the Indians named Benjamin Hawkins, made an honest attempt to transform his charges into farmers, but when this failed he had no choice but to begin absorbing their lands. Between 1802, when the Creeks ceded territories east of the Oconee and north of the St. Mary's rivers, and 1806, millions of acres in central Georgia, southern Tennessee, and Mississippi Territory were taken from the Cherokee, Choctaw, and Chickasaw, leaving the Indians dissatisfied within their restricted hunting grounds.

Conditions in the Northwest were even worse. Jefferson's agent there was Governor William Henry Harrison of Indiana Territory whose insatiable desire for Indian lands was tempered by neither sympathy nor humanitarianism. He showed his colors first in 1802 when he called representatives of the Kickapoo, Wea, and Delaware tribes together at Vincennes to adjust disputes growing out of the Greenville Treaty line surveys across Indiana. To their amazement Harrison not only proposed to define that boundary, but demanded they cede the territory supposedly purchased by the Wabash Land Company a quarter of a century before. When the chiefs indignantly refused, the governor assured them the lands already belonged to the United States and would be occupied by force unless they backed down. This threat, together with bribes and cajolery, proved effective, although the cession was smaller than Harrison wished.

The Treaty of Vincennes set a pattern that was duplicated time and time again over the next seven years. Conferences were called almost yearly, some at the insistence of the natives to protest illegal cessions, others by Harrison to correct an alleged wrong done the Indians. In each the result was the same, for the natives were powerless before the governor's bribes and threats of force. In 1803 he persuaded the weakened Kaskaskia to surrender their flimsy title to the Illinois country by promising them aid in a threatened war with the Potawatomi. A year later the Sauk and Foxes gave up 15,000,000 acres south of the Wisconsin River in return for annuities and the surrender of an Indian accused of murdering a white man. When native objections to these tactics reached Harrison's ears he called a conference at Grouseland, his newly completed mansion at Vincennes, then pitted the assembled tribes against each other to extract another 2,000,000 acres from them. Those treaties, together with smaller cessions from the Delawares and Piankashaw and a giant grant arranged by Governor William Hull of Michigan territory, gave the United States control of eastern Michigan, southern Indiana, and most of Illinois by the close of 1807.

Indian resentment at Harrison's land-grabbing activities would probably have subsided eventually had not two unforeseen events altered the situation. One was the advance of the powerful upper-Mississippi tribes—the Sioux and Chippewa—into the Wisconsin country in search of peltry. There they

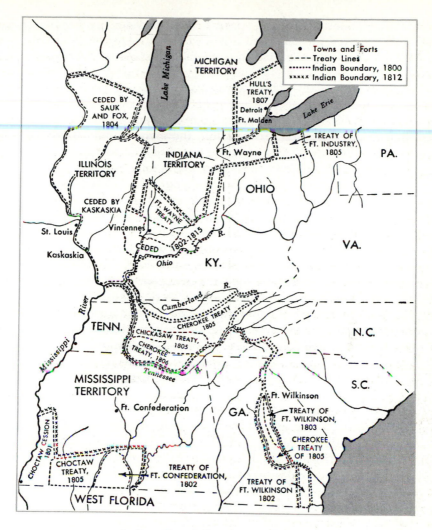

Indian Land Cessions, 1800–1812

formed an impenetrable barrier; Great Lakes Indians, no longer able to move westward to new hunting grounds, must fight to maintain their homes. The other was the rise of two Indian leaders: a Shawnee chieftain, Tecumseh, and his brother, The Prophet. Tecumseh saw that his people suffered because small tribes bowed to Harrison's pressure. If all natives were united in a confederation, with members pledged to make no land cessions without the consent of all, they could resist American demands. That was the message Tecumseh began spreading through the Northwest in 1805, aided by The Prophet, a one-eyed, epileptic medicine man believed by the natives to possess supernatural powers. Together they traveled among the tribes, preaching the need for unity and urging Indians to give up the foibles and firewater of the white man that they might gain strength to win back their lands.

Harrison first heard of their spreading influence in 1806, and although not greatly alarmed, decided to warn the natives against their newly risen prophet. "If he is really a prophet," the governor wrote the Delawares, "ask him to cause the sun to stand still, the moon to alter its course, the rivers to cease to flow." Unfortunately word of this message reached The Prophet, who had heard from the whites that a total eclipse of the sun was to take place on June 16, 1806. By forecasting this, he realized, his reputation would be forever made. From that time on the word of both Tecumseh and his brother was accepted as law by the Indians; had they not accepted Harrison's challenge to blot out the sun? As tribe after tribe aligned itself with their confederation, the two conspirators were encouraged to take two significant steps during 1808. One was to found the village of Prophetstown at the junction of the Wabash River and Tippecanoe Creek where they could extend their influence over Illinois and Wisconsin tribes. The other was to visit the British post, Ft. Malden, established on the Canadian shore of the Detroit River after Jay's Treaty had forced the evacuation of Detroit. Tecumseh was warmly received by the skilled agent in charge, Captain Mathew Elliott, for the English expected war to follow the controversy over impressment and welcomed a chance to build Indian alliances. At a great council Elliott urged the Indians to unite and expressed concern over their loss of lands, but cautioned them not to strike the first blow. Tecumseh, however, was convinced that he could count on British aid.

In the meantime, Harrison, blissfully unaware of this forest intrigue, went ahead with plans for another land-grabbing treaty. The occasion was the creation of Illinois Territory in 1809; many of the earlier cessions were in what was now Illinois and the inhabitants of Vincennes professed alarm at a demarcation line only twenty miles from their doors. Runners spread word of the conference so widely that 1,100 natives were assembled at Fort Wayne when the governor lighted the council fire in September, 1809. Again one tribe was played off against another, particularly after Harrison found the Delawares and Potawatomi anxious to increase their annuities by selling some of their territories; again bribes and presents were dangled before wavering chiefs. In the end the Treaty of Fort Wayne transferred 3,000,000 acres of Indiana land to the United States, in return for $7,000 in cash and an annuity of $1,750.

That was the final blow. Since the turn of the century nearly 110,000,000 acres of choice hunting land had been wrung from the natives by bribery, threats, and treaties with tribal fragments. Tecumseh, hurrying to Vincennes with a small group of followers, recited his people's grievances in a great open-air council. The land, he told Harrison, was the common property of all the Indians; no one tribe had a right to sell. Hence the Treaty of Fort

Wayne was invalid, and any attempt to occupy the territory would be resisted. Harrison replied that the lands were acquired legally and would be settled by force if need be. The issue was now clear and war certain.

Attacks on outlying settlements began in the spring of 1810. By autumn, when 6,000 Indians visited Ft. Malden to plead for arms, a border war was in full swing. Major General Isaac Brock, governor general of Upper Canada, was thoroughly alarmed by these developments, fearing England would be blamed for inciting the natives, but his pleas for peace came too late. Young warriors, their fear of the dreaded "Long Knives" forgotten, passed war belts through the forests during the winter of 1810–11 or boasted about council fires that their new unity would drive the whites back to the sea. Tecumseh, however, worked frantically to restrain his overeager braves so long as Harrison made no attempt to occupy the Fort Wayne Treaty lands. In July, 1811, he visited Vincennes with news that he was on his way to enlist southern tribes in his confederacy, and to assure the governor that war could still be avoided if the disputed territory were left alone. When Harrison reiterated his determination to carry on surveys, the two men parted in an atmosphere of mutual distrust.

Tecumseh, whose mother was a Creek, continued south to meet with the Creeks, Cherokee, and Choctaw. In a conference on the banks of the Tallapoosa River, with his face painted the black war color, he urged 5,000 Creek listeners to join in a to-the-death attack on their oppressors. "Burn their dwellings," he shouted. "Destroy their stock. The red people own the country. . . . War now. War forever. War upon the living. War upon the dead; dig up their corpses from the grave; our country must give no rest to a white man's bones." His fiery pleas inflamed the anti-American element among the Creek—later called the "Red Sticks"—but the Choctaw and the Cherokee, fearful of their more numerous Creek neighbors, preferred to remain neutral rather than risk annihilation at the hands of the Americans.

In the meantime hostilities began in the North. When Tecumseh left Vincennes on August 5, 1811, Harrison recognized a golden opportunity. A march on Prophetstown would goad young warriors, freed from their chief's restraining influence, into an attack that would allow him to administer a crushing defeat. With a thousand troops from Washington and Kentucky he started northward along the Wabash on September 26, 1811. Pausing on the way to erect two strong fortifications, Ft. Harrison at the site of Terre Haute, and a log blockhouse at the mouth of the Vermillion River, the army reached Prophetstown on November 6 and camped three quarters of a mile from the town, choosing a ten-acre triangle of level land bounded by a thick marsh, a creek, and heavy woods. That night the men slept on their arms, while in the neighboring village The Prophet performed magic rites to render the enemy impotent and his own warriors invincible.

Just before daylight on the morning of November 7 the Indians moved forward through a cold, slow-falling rain to surround the sleeping Americans. Before they attacked, however, one of Harrison's guards detected a move-

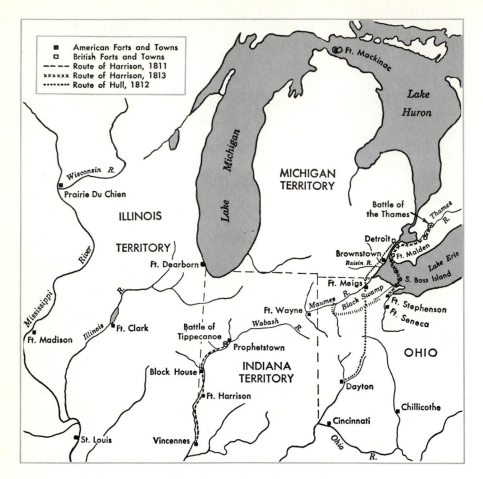

The Northwest in the War of 1812

ment in the bushes and fired. With this the Indians rushed pell-mell into the camp, sweeping past the outposts and into tents where soldiers were still asleep. No surprise could overawe the seasoned fighters Harrison had assembled. Within a few minutes they beat off the first attack, formed solid lines, and began pouring a murderous fire into the attackers. The Indians, disheartened by resistance from soldiers supposedly made helpless by The Prophet's magic, first fell back, then broke completely when Harrison's cavalry charged upon them from two directions. The commander, unable to believe victory was his, kept his men erecting breastworks until November 8 when scouts brought back word that Prophetstown was deserted. The village was destroyed before the American army started back to Vincennes.

The Battle of Tippecanoe was no decisive victory. Harrison's men, who outnumbered The Prophet's warriors by almost 300, held their ground, but their losses were as large as those of the Indians, each side counting thirty-eight killed and 150 wounded. Nor did the victory end the Indian menace in the West. Instead Tecumseh, on his return, sent his followers storming against American outposts with fire and tomahawk. Tippecanoe only scattered Prophetstown fanatics along the frontier to launch the Northwest on a serious Indian war. By the spring of 1812 settlers were fleeing from outlying cabins, and fear was sweeping even the thickly settled regions of Ohio and Kentucky.

Hostilities, every westerner believed, could be laid directly at England's door. British agents lured the Indians to Ft. Malden, supplied them with guns and ammunition, and drove them forth to murder American backwoodsmen! Harrison reflected the popular view when he wrote: "The whole of the Indians on this frontier have been completely armed and equipped from the British King's stores at Malden." The solution seemed equally simple. The United States must conquer Canada, wipe out Ft. Malden, and end forever the unholy alliance between redcoats and Indians. The conquest would not only end Indian attacks but also would lift the depression by forcing Britain to respect American shipping as the price for the return of her colony. Little wonder that westerners drank toasts to "the starry flag of 1812" which would soon "float triumphant over the ramparts of Quebec," or that western representatives assured Congress that "the militia of Kentucky are alone competent to place Montreal and upper Canada at your feet." "We have heard but one word," wrote a disgusted easterner, "—like the whip-poor-will, but an eternal monotonous tone—Canada! Canada! Canada!"

The West wanted war, but that thinly peopled region was too underrepresented in Congress to inflict its will on the nation. This became clear when the elections of 1810 sent to Washington a noisy band of "War Hawks," as they were derisively labeled by their enemies. These fire-eaters took control in the House, naming Henry Clay of Kentucky their speaker, packing committees with their numbers, and flooding Congress with petitions and reports demanding heavier military expenditures. Westerners were prominent among the War Hawks, but they were more noticeable for the shrillness of their demands than the weight of their numbers. Of the sixty-one delegates in the House of Representatives who consistently favored war measures, only seven were from the West, while ten were from New England, fifteen from the Middle States, and twenty-nine from the South. Clearly hard times in the Ohio Valley or Indian raids along the frontiers were of only remote concern to the majority of the War Hawks. Pennsylvania's delegates, thus, favored war measures even though the region was experiencing unaccustomed prosperity, had no interest in acquiring Canada, and heartily opposed an Indian conflict. Michigan citizens generally supported a declaration but hesitated lest an Indian war mean the invasion and devastation of their territory. Throughout the West, war was seen as the only alternative to humiliating submission to the British commercial system and a surrender of the national honor.

Viewing the record of Congress as a whole as it voted on a succession of warlike measures, the division was along party rather than sectional lines, with westerners supporting or opposing Madison as their loyalties dictated, and with little concern for Indian war or Canada. In the Senate factionalism within the Republican Party complicated the situation but did not alter it. There the six Federalists normally voted as one, but the twenty-eight Republicans were hopelessly divided: twelve under William H. Crawford consistently supported war measures, four "Invisibles" so disliked Madison that they favored an aggressive policy only to embarrass the federal treasury, three "Clintonians" from the northern states unalterably opposed war, and the remainder wavered with the times. For a time they squabbled among themselves as the Senate tested administration strength with a series of votes on military expenditures, then most of the "Invisibles" and some of the "Waverers" swung into line largely because they feared a Republican defeat in the election of 1812 if they voted against the President. The narrowness of the vote—a switch of only three members would have caused a deadlock—and the prevalence of party rather than sectional loyalties demonstrated that local factors such as an Indian war or depression were less determinative than resentment against Britain's sullying of the national honor. President Madison had sought a decision for war, and on June 18, 1812, the United States officially entered the conflict.

Seldom had a nation been so poorly prepared for a major conflict. Half a dozen war ships, an ill-trained army of 6,700 men led by two inept major generals, Henry Dearborn and Thomas Pinckney, a rather timid President, a people generally indifferent to or, in the case of most New Englanders, openly hostile to war—these were the assets on which the United States relied to win victory from the world's mightiest military power. Nor did public apathy dissolve when fighting began; an appeal for an $11,000,000 loan brought in only $6,000,000, while a call for volunteers was so disappointing that for the rest of the war reliance was placed on state militia. Yet westerners were not discouraged. Canada was defended by only 4,500 troops, and Florida poorly guarded; both would surely fall to American arms before the year was out.

Those dreams were rudely shattered. Within a few months after fighting began even the cocksure Ohio frontiersmen found themselves on the defensive rather than engaged in a spectacular conquest of Canada. The first blow fell when one of their own outposts, Ft. Mackinac, was surprised by a superior British force from nearby St. Joseph Island on July 17, 1812, and forced to surrender without a shot being fired. This disappointment was forgotten amidst plans for an invasion of Canada which would not only recapture Ft. Mackinac but reduce Ft. Malden as well. Westerners could not know that their very enthusiasm for the war ruined their nation's chance for victory. Proper American strategy called for a drive against Montreal through the Champlain Valley, cutting Canada in two, stopping the flow of British supplies to western Indians, and forcing Upper Canada to surrender. Such a campaign was impossible. Only the West would provide men and materials needed for a Canadian invasion, and the West demanded the immediate capture of Ft. Malden. Hence American strategists decided to direct their principal attack against that distant fortification.

General William Hull, the sixty-year-old governor of Michigan Territory named commander of the western army, realized the hopelessness of his task. His force, he pointed out, must be supplied from Ohio. Food, ammunition, and other essentials could be shipped to Detroit either across Lake Erie or along the banks of the Detroit River. Neither route could be used; English gunboats controlling the lake menaced shore roads, while land transportation was made additionally difficult by the Black Swamp, a tangled morass along the Maumee River lying squarely across the American path. Ft. Malden could never be taken, Hull insisted, until the United States controlled Lake Erie, but like every good soldier he obeyed his orders. Raising 2,000 men, he marched rapidly to Detroit which was reached on July 7, 1812. After a brief pause, the army crossed the Detroit River to Canadian soil where the overly cautious Hull hesitated before launching his attack. General Isaac Brock, British commander in Upper Canada, seized on this opportunity. A small British force was dispatched by water to capture the little village of Brownstown which lay squarely athwart American supply lines on the lower Detroit River. Hull was terrified. When an attempt to dislodge the Brownstown captors failed, he fell back to Detroit, then, as his supplies dwindled, sent one quarter of his men southward to bypass his troublesome enemies and reopen communication lines.

That was the moment chosen by General Brock for his attack. On August 16 the entire English army crossed the Detroit River to storm the town's defenses. Hull, his supplies dwindling and his force weakened, had no choice but surrender. The first Canadian invasion resulted not only in defeat but the loss of Detroit to the enemy! Nor did disasters end there, for just as Hull surrendered, another western outpost, Ft. Dearborn, fell. The garrison of that fort, marching to join the defenders of Detroit, was ambushed by Indians amidst the sand dunes of lower Lake Michigan; twenty-six men were killed outright and nine others tortured to death in the "Dearborn Massacre."

Even now the West was not discouraged. The energetic William Henry Harrison, who succeeded Hull in command, had no difficulty raising troops for a fall attack on Canada. Before the Americans could march, they found themselves, to their surprise, on the defensive as British and Indian raiding parties swept down from Detroit against the Ohio forts. Harrison was forced to spend the summer beating off attacks on Ft. Wayne and Ft. Harrison rather than leading a triumphant army northward. When he was finally ready to march in October, 1812, the Black Swamp was impassable and he set his men building military roads across its treacherous surface. Thus ended the glorious dreams of the expansionists in that winter of 1812–13, with their army grubbing its way through the mud of an Ohio swamp and both Canada and three of their own forts in British hands.

Nor did the 1812 campaigns on the New York frontier succeed any better. Two invasions of Canada were planned for that autumn, one across the Niagara River, the other along Lake Champlain. The former was launched on October 18, 1812, when the commander of the state militia at Ft. Niagara threw 6,000 men across the river to capture the heights surrounding the strong British fort of Queenston. Reinforcements needed to turn this initial triumph into a victory never arrived, for Brigadier General Alexander Smyth, commander of the regular army at Niagara, refused to let his men cross the river, insisting that a militia action was no concern of his. As more British troops were rushed into action the outnumbered militiamen fell back slowly until they reached the rushing waters of the Niagara where they surrendered. Petty jealousies and weak discipline cost the United States an army. Equally disheartening was the American failure at Lake Champlain. There General Henry Dearborn drilled 5,000 troops until mid-November, then marched northward. At the Canadian boundary the militia refused to go on, insisting they were to fight only in their own state. Dearborn, who was old and weak, bowed to the mutineers and led his men back to winter quarters at Plattsburg. He alone among the American commanders saved his army, but only by keeping it well away from the enemy.

Events in the southern theater during the first year of war were slightly more favorable. When hostilities began only Mobile and Pensacola remained in Spanish hands in West Florida, while in East Florida the American army of occupation, commanded by Governor D. B. Mitchell of Georgia, controlled the country west of the St. John's River and held St. Augustine in a state of siege. Every expansionist was certain that a formal declaration of war would be followed by a rapid conquest of the whole region by the regular army. Spain, however, refused to play into their hands, for her officials, recognizing their country's weakness, steadfastly refused to abandon their neutrality. President Madison, sorely disappointed, was forced to leave the situation to Governor Mitchell and his small army of "patriots." Even they fared badly after St. Augustine officials encouraged the Florida Indians to take to the war path. So many American soldiers scurried off to protect their homes that the remainder, fearing an attack on their thin supply lines, gave up the siege of St. Augustine and fell back to Georgia soil. In November, 1813, disappointed expansionists in that state's legislature grumblingly informed Congress that unless troops were sent against East Florida they would take matters into their own hands.

President Madison, certain that this show of feeling would persuade Congress to authorize an attack on Spanish possessions, hurried word to Andrew Jackson, commander of the Tennessee militia, to raise 1,500 men for a march on Mobile, Pensacola, and St. Augustine as soon as congressional approval was secured. With preparations made, the President in January,

1813, asked Congress for authority to annex both Floridas, charging that negotiations with Spain had broken down and that England or France would occupy the strategic territories if the United States did not. His proposal was decisively defeated on February 2, 1813, by a combination of northern and Federalist votes, leaving Madison no choice but to dismiss Jackson's army. Southern expansionists were only partly placated when Congress did authorize the occupation of Mobile and West Florida, a move carried out by General James Wilkinson during the next months.

Disheartening as were these events, the Americans were destined to still more trying days before they tasted the sweets of victory. The winter of 1812-13 in the Northwest was spent preparing for a march across the ice to Ft. Malden. That expedition was abandoned when a thousand of Harrison's men, disregarding his orders, struck out on their own to capture Frenchtown, a little settlement on the Raisin River. There they were surprised by a war party of British and Indians on the morning of January 22, 1813. The Raisin River Massacre not only cost the Americans 250 dead and 500 prisoners, but ended all hope of a Canadian invasion. Instead Harrison devoted himself to strengthening Ohio's defenses, knowing the jubilant British could now count on aid from most of the western Indians. Nor was he mistaken. While his men labored on the stout walls and blockhouses of a well-located new fort, Ft. Meigs, skilled English agents scoured the forests between Georgian Bay and the Mississippi for native recruits. By spring 1,000 warriors were camped about Ft. Malden, waiting the signal to attack from Colonel Henry Proctor, who succeeded to the western command when General Isaac Brock was killed at the Battle of Queenston.

This came in mid-April, 1813, when Proctor led his 1,000 regulars and an equal number of Indians southward to lay siege to Ft. Meigs. From April 28 to May 7 British batteries hammered at the American works, but Harrison's defenses were so well planned that the cannon balls buried themselves harmlessly in earthen barricades protecting the fort's wooden walls. When 350 frontiersmen braved enemy fire on May 6 to spike the English guns, the attackers lost heart; the next day they silently dismantled their cannon and vanished into the forest. Three months later they were back again, this time with 1,400 Indians recently arrived from the Wisconsin country. Harrison, sure that Ft. Meigs could care for itself, left its defense to subordinates while he moved his main force to the Sandusky River country. Two forts commanded that valley: Ft. Stephenson on the lower river and Ft. Seneca several miles to the south. Deciding the former was too weak to withstand a serious attack, Harrison concentrated his men at Ft. Seneca, leaving only 150 militia under a twenty-one-year-old stripling, Major George Croghan, at Ft. Stephenson. The American commander diagnosed the situation correctly; on July 29, 1813, the British abandoned their siege of Ft. Meigs to descend on the Sandusky Valley, marching first against the poorly defended lower fort. Major Croghan, instead of burning the palisade and retreating, decided to make a stand. Loading his one cannon with grapeshot and arranging his handful of followers carefully about it, he waited until the enemy rushed through a breach in the walls, then raked them with a deadly fire from pointblank range. Those not killed broke for the woods where they encountered a strong force under Harrison that had started north at the sound of gunfire. Within a few hours the thoroughly beaten attackers were slinking back toward Ft. Malden, their spirits broken by two failures to penetrate American defenses.

The victory gave Harrison a chance to turn to a task more to his liking: a new attack on Detroit and Ft. Malden. Preparations were already under way. Washington officials, finally realizing that control of Lake Erie was essential to a successful western campaign, had entrusted twenty-seven-year-old Oliver Hazard Perry with the task of building a fleet strong enough to defeat the British gunboats. Perry's sturdy vessels, painstakingly built at Erie of materials transported from the East by wagon train, sailed westward on August 12, 1813, in search of the British force, which was anchored under the guns of Ft. Malden. Not daring to engage the enemy amidst the treacherous currents of the lower Detroit River, the Americans waited at Put-in-Bay Harbor on South Bass Island, knowing the enemy would have to attack or lose control of Lake Erie by default. On September 10, 1813, the two fleets met in a furious three-hour engagement that ended in complete victory for the superior American force. Harrison heard the good news a day later when a small boat rowed furiously up the Sandusky River bearing an officer who delivered Perry's famous message scribbled on the back of an old envelope: "We have met the enemy and they are ours."

The imposing task of ferrying the whole United States army—recently augmented by the arrival of 3,500 Kentucky militia—to the Canadian shore began at once, and on the afternoon of September 27 a landing was made three miles below Ft. Malden. There word reached Harrison that the British, acting on the sound assumption that it was better to lose a province than an army, had started east along the Thames River. The pursuit began at once, with 3,000 picked men leading the way and supplies following on river boats—an advantage that allowed the Americans to gain rapidly on the slow-moving enemy. On October 5, when only a few miles separated the two armies, General Proctor decided to make a stand. The battle ground selected was a level plain between the Thames River and a dense swamp. There Proctor posted his scanty force: some 400 regulars spread between the swamp and river in two thin lines, about 600 Indians under Tecumseh scattered through the swamp to pour fire upon the attackers.

These elaborate preparations were in vain. At 2:30 on that quiet afternoon Harrison ordered a charge. His Kentucky cavalrymen, yelling like demons, swept through the flimsy British lines, slaughtering as they went, while the infantry plunged into the swamp after the outnumbered Indians. A few minutes of furious fighting and all was over; the entire English force was either killed or captured, Tecumseh dead, and Proctor fleeing toward the neighboring village of Moravian Town. The Battle of the Thames was one of the decisive victories of the War of 1812, for it broke Indian power in the Ohio and Wabash country, scattered Tecumseh's confederation, and convinced the Indians they could not depend on their English allies. To make matters even worse from the Indian point of view a second American army, made up of 1,400 Illinois and Missouri militia and commanded by General Benjamin Howard, at the same time spread a path of destruction through Illinois. By the winter of 1813 all the Northwest was in American hands, with the exception of a few British-held posts.

On other fronts the United States enjoyed less success during 1813. Minor skirmishing along the New York frontier accomplished nothing. In the Southwest a new British ally, the Creek tribe, took to the warpath during the spring, and by midsummer settlers in the whole southern borderland were scurrying into hastily built blockhouses for protection. One sizeable fortification, built by Samuel Mims on the lower Alabama River, was to suffer the most devastating attack. Adequate troops were assigned for its protection, but the local commander, Major Daniel Beasley, was a master of inefficiency who took no notice when Indians piled so much sand about the fort's gates that they could not be closed. The settlers who had "forted up" there were helpless when the Red Sticks, the hostile faction of the Creek nation, struck on August 30, 1813. Between 247 and 260 died at Ft. Mims, while nearly 100 women, children, and Negro slaves were carried away as prisoners. The Creeks were committed to war now, and the southern states belatedly aware that they must defend themselves or suffer.

Although the two small armies that marched west from Georgia accomplished little, a third column from Tennessee was more successful. This was commanded by Andrew Jackson and composed of 5,000 militiamen who assembled at Fayetteville on October 4, 1813. Marching rapidly south to save Huntsville from a rumored attack, the Tennesseans moved into the heart of the Creek country, pausing only to construct a supply road between the Tennessee and Coosa rivers. Conditions were ripe for their success, for the Creeks were hopelessly divided over participation in the war, with the majority favoring peace and only the fanatical Red Stick faction bent on hostilities. The Red Sticks were to be feared, however; they believed themselves endowed with mystical powers gained from the visit of Tecumseh and The Prophet, and were ready to die in a holy cause. Jackson knew nothing of this as he sent a series of raiding parties against their villages; Tallushatchee was wiped out with its nearly 200 defenders and Talladega subdued with almost 300 more. By that time winter ended operations except for one unsuccessful January raid on the Creek town of Tohopeka at Horse Shoe Bend on the Tallapoosa River. Even that defeat reacted in Jackson's favor, as the Indians, convinced this village was impregnable, flocked there in large numbers during the next months. The Americans had only to wait until spring to strike a decisive blow at the whole Creek tribe.

By March 27, 1814, 3,000 troops were camped before Tohopeka where 1,000 braves awaited them behind a zigzag log barricade that protected a

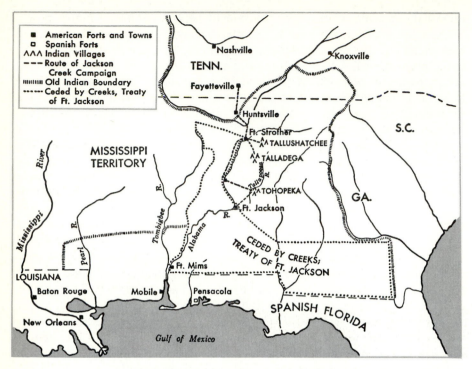

The Southwest in the War of 1812

hundred-acre peninsula. Jackson turned his cannon against the fortification at once, but before his six-pounders opened a breach, a number of friendly Indians swam the Tallapoosa River to attack the defenders from the rear. Instantly all was confusion within the village. Jackson seized the opportunity to order a charge which sent his shouting infantry swarming over the barricade and into the midst of the outnumbered Indians. None attempted to escape; none asked quarter. For hours the slaughter went on; when the Battle of Horseshoe Bend was over 800 warriors lay dead on the battlefield. Jackson ordered the few survivors to appear at newly built Ft. Jackson to draw up a treaty of peace. There, on August 1, 1814, the Tennessee commander dictated the terms: the Creeks must surrender sites for military roads and posts, stop all trade with the Spaniards of Florida, and give up about half their lands—an L-shaped plot lying between their hunting grounds and those of the Choctaw and Chickasaw. The bewildered natives protested in vain; Jackson was adamant and on August 9, 1814, the Treaty of Ft. Jackson was signed. Indian power in the Southwest was broken.

Along the northern borderland the Americans enjoyed less success during 1814, the last year of fighting. A small force of frontiersmen, mindful that the peace treaty might award each nation the lands in its possession when the war ended and aware of the importance of the Wisconsin-Fox River portage route to the fur trade, succeeded in capturing the British-held post of Prairie du Chien in June, 1814, but a larger English party from Mackinac recaptured the fort a month later. Nor did an effort to subdue Mackinac fare any better, for an attempt to land there in August, 1814, was beaten off. Fighting ended with both those strategic outposts in British hands.

On the Niagara frontier the record of dismal defeats also continued. Ft. George, a Canadian outpost captured by a United States naval force early in 1813, was recaptured by the English in December of that year. From that time on they harried Americans constantly; expeditions that crossed the Niagara River during the winter of 1813–14, destroyed Ft. Niagara, burned Buffalo, and ravaged the countryside. Not until March, 1814, when two able generals, George Izard and Jacob Brown, replaced inefficient commanders did the tide turn. After whipping an army into shape, Brown led his men across the river in July to best British defenders at the Battles of Chippewa and Lundy's Lane before returning to American soil. The summer of skirmishing accomplished little but did prevent an invasion of New York at that point.

Fighting on the Lake Champlain frontier was more serious, as that was the route chosen by British authorities for the final attack on the United States that would end the war. There they concentrated the seasoned veterans released for American service by Napoleon's defeat; by September 18,000 trained troops stood poised at the northern end of Lake Champlain, waiting the signal to advance. Opposing them at Plattsburg were 3,300 American regulars and militiamen commanded by General George Izard. In this apparently hopeless situation only one factor favored the United States. The British must gain naval control of Lake Champlain before they could attack, and a sufficiently powerful American fleet might turn the scales toward victory. All that summer of 1814 skilled shipbuilders labored at the southern lake ports, while in the north English workers fashioned vessels for their commanders. By September 3 the Canadian general, Sir George Prevost, was ready. His fleet of sixteen vessels and his army, reduced to 11,000 men when no more appeared necessary, started south.

At Plattsburg fourteen American gunboats waited them. Their brilliant young commander, Captain Thomas Macdonough, knowing he was outnumbered and must make every shot tell, prepared for the onslaught by providing his anchored vessels with devices that allowed them to swing about quickly. This proved the deciding factor. When the English fleet sailed into Plattsburg Harbor Macdonough's gunboats were able to exchange broadside for broadside, then as British fire weakened, warp about to bring freshly loaded cannon to bear. A few hours of this crippled the strongest enemy ships and forced the remainder to surrender. The Battle of Lake Champlain was decisive, for when Prevost heard of the defeat he turned his army back toward Canada.

New York, and perhaps the whole nation, was saved by a young commander's strategy.

Only one more battle remained to be fought, and that in the Southwest. There the English, hoping to secure control of strategic ports against a possible peace treaty that would award spoils to the victors, began an offensive in August, 1814, by landing at Pensacola as a prelude to attacking Mobile. Their plan posed a serious threat to the United States; there was every possibility that the Indians would rally to their side and that they would be joined by hundreds of liberated Negro slaves. Thus strengthened they could ravage the southern back country just at a time when another invading force was moving down the Lake Champlain route to subdue the Northeast. Admiral Sir John Warren, who hatched this strategy, made his first move in August, 1814, when 2,000 men under Major Edward Nicolls landed at Pensacola. The results were discouraging, for not only did the Indians show little stomach for fighting but Nicolls alienated his Spanish allies by absconding with some of their slaves. Yet Britain still threatened; should Pensacola and Mobile be won they would be able to move against New Orleans almost at will.

This was the situation that confronted Andrew Jackson, whose triumph at Horse Shoe Bend had been rewarded with a generalship in the regular army and responsibility for defense of the Gulf Coast. A less experienced commander would have hurried at once to protect New Orleans but Jackson realized that city would never be safe so long as Pensacola and Mobile were in British hands. Hence he postponed his main task as he moved directly against those outposts in November, 1814, taking first Pensacola and then Mobile. So impressive was his show of strength that the Spanish officials there were won to his side; he could leave them in charge knowing that this strategic flank was secured. By this time New Orleans needed his aid; Jackson's intelligence informed him that fifty ships bearing 10,000 men had just sailed from Jamaica bound for that city. Hurrying there with 12,000 Tennessee volunteers, he began preparing for the attack on December 1, 1814, building forts along the lower river and at the entrance to Lake Ponchartrain, throwing up earthworks along the Chef Menteur Road that offered the one land approach, and clogging the bayous along Lake Borgne with fallen trees.

Unfortunately the English hit upon the one flaw in those defenses. On December 22 a landing party found the Bayou Bienvenue was not yet blocked; by noon of the next day several thousand redcoats were drawn up below the city. Jackson, although caught napping, threw the enemy into confusion by an immediate attack, then used the time gained to build earthworks between the British and New Orleans. That delay cost the English leader, Sir Edward Pakenham, the battle, for by the time he turned to the assault the Americans were too well entrenched to be dislodged. A frontal attack failed first, then a heavy bombardment that scarcely marred Jackson's stout defenses. Finally on January 7, 1815, Pakenham adopted the one device that might have succeeded: he sent part of his army across the Mississippi to turn captured American batteries against Jackson's earthworks while his own infantry stormed forward. A sudden fall in the river that night delayed the troops assigned the task of crossing the Mississippi; at the time agreed on for attack on the morning of January 8 they were still far below the American batteries. Pakenham, unaware of this, ordered his men to charge. Wave after wave swept forward, to be met with the steady fire of the frontiersmen. By nightfall Pakenham and 2,000 of his men lay dead on the battlefield, while Jackson had lost only six men. A few days later the British force straggled back to its ships. The War of 1812 was over, Jackson the new hero of the West.

The Battle of New Orleans did not affect the outcome, for two weeks before Jackson's victory the peace treaty had been signed. Negotiations were begun at Ghent in August, 1814, just as American fortunes were at their lowest ebb; Mackinac, Niagara, and eastern Maine were in British hands, the capitol and White House recently burned, and two powerful English armies preparing to invade the United States through Lake Champlain and New Orleans. From this debacle of wrecked hopes the able American commissioners—John Quincy Adams, Albert Gallatin, Henry Clay, James A. Bayard and Jonathan Russell—must gain what concessions they could. Little wonder that few informed men on either side of the Atlantic expected them to emerge with one, let alone both, of their avowed objectives: a specific English agreement to respect American maritime rights in the future, and the abrogation of the sections of Jay's Treaty that gave Canadian traders the right to operate south of the border. The victorious British would scarcely back down on those two points.

Preliminary negotiations convinced the American agents they had no hope of securing both their demands and that peace could only be secured if they gave ground on one. This one, they saw, must concern neutral rights, partly because the English would never compromise on that issue, partly because westerners would rebel against a treaty unfavorable to their section. Hence they informed the British negotiators that the United States would accept a treaty that did not mention neutral rights—a tacit admission that England's stand was accepted—if the British would agree to their contentions on the West. For a time negotiations hung in the balance as commissioners deliberated this offer, but time was on the side of the Americans. Word that Prevost's Lake Champlain expedition had failed helped convince the English; so did mounting pressure for peace from taxpayers tired of twenty years of war, and the realization that the United States could never be conquered until Lake Erie and Lake Champlain were controlled. England did not dare begin that slow and expensive task when her crumbling European alliances made a new continental war seem possible. Hence her agents agreed to back down in their western demands for a barrier state, a renewal of Jay's Treaty, and a boundary revision giving Mackinac, Prairie du Chien, and the head of the Mississippi River to Canada. With those mutual concessions, the Treaty of Ghent was signed on December 24, 1814.

Its provisions were far from happy for the United States: a restoration of all territorial conquests by both nations, and a tacit recognition, by omission, that the United States accepted England's provisions concerning neutral rights, while Britain gave up all claims to trade south of the Canadian border. Only one section referred to the Indians and this, although promising them all rights enjoyed in 1811, was so vaguely worded that it meant little. Technically the United States lost the war, as none of the objectives for which it fought was attained. Actually the peace spelled victory, particularly for the West. By signing a treaty of *status quo ante bellum* the British signified their intention of abandoning the Indians to land-hungry Americans. No longer could the Indians count on aid from Canadian trappers or rally behind a prophet who promised them English aid. The way was cleared for a new era of westward expansion that would carry the frontier to the Mississippi.

15

Settling the Lake Plains
1815-1850

When the Treaty of Ghent rang down the curtain on the War of 1812 the settled portions of the United States comprised a giant triangle, its base the Atlantic seaboard and its apex the junction of the Ohio and Mississippi rivers. To the north and south lay two physiographic provinces, the Lake Plains and Gulf Plains, whose towering forests and rolling prairies were virtually unsullied by the cabin homes of pioneers. In the next quarter century those two areas were inundated by a surging tide of westward-moving, land-hungry farmers who swept forward in the greatest population movement the nation had known. By 1850 the peopling of the eastern half of the continent was completed.

Scarcely was the last shot fired when western pressure forced the federal government to open the Lake Plains to pioneers. The first step was to pacify the Indians who, sullen and restless after a war that cost them dearly, seemed ready to take to the warpath at any moment. Three peace commissioners named by President Madison met 2,000 tribesmen at the little village of Portage des Sioux in July, 1815. One by one the grievances of various tribes were settled until by September, when the last partially placated warrior departed, the frontier was technically at peace once more. Yet the Treaties of Portage des Sioux did not completely end the threat of war, for delegates from the Fox and Sauk tribes had stalked angrily from the conference grounds after refusing the terms offered them, and the Kickapoo and Winnebago were left discontented. Clearly something more than presents and promises were needed to control the Indians and protect the line of settlements and farms that shifted ever westward.

This realization led the national government to launch a fort-building program designed to throw a protecting screen between Indians and pioneers.

Work went on rapidly through 1816 and 1817; older outposts at Ft. Wayne and Ft. Harrison in Indiana were rebuilt, Ft. Shelby in Detroit and Fts. Gratiot and Mackinac along the eastern edge of Michigan were garrisoned, and Fts. Dearborn and Clark were re-established to protect the Illinois settlements. More important were new fortifications in the Mississippi and Wisconsin country. Ft. Edward in western Illinois, Ft. Armstrong on Rock Island, Ft. Crawford at Prairie du Chien, and Ft. Howard near the mouth of the Fox River, all built in 1816, together guarded a 400-mile strip of virgin back country between Lake Michigan and the warlike northwestern tribes. Each fort consisted of a stoutly built stone or timber palisade, with blockhouses at each corner and barracks within to house a hundred or more troops. For the next years these outposts stood guard over the Indians, ready to quell rebellious warriors or nip incipient uprisings in the bud. As their garrisons restored order to the hinterland the federal government extended its control over more and more tribes; Ft. Snelling on the upper Mississippi, Ft. Saginaw in Michigan, and Ft. Brady at Sault Ste. Marie, all erected between 1819 and 1822, testified to the expanding sphere of American influence.

While establishing those garrisoned outposts, the United States sought to break the traditional British-Indian alliance by expelling Canadian traders from native villages. The need for action was demonstrated in 1817 when a military expedition under Major Stephen Long reported the upper Mississippi country swarming with Montreal *voyageurs* and the tribes completely loyal to England. Authorities at Washington were wise enough to see that the intruders could never be driven out, despite the provisions of the Treaty of Ghent, and that their influence could best be nullified by persuading the natives to trade with American agents. With this in mind government trading factories, which had offered goods at cost at a few strategic sites since 1795-1796, were multiplied throughout the Northwest in the years after the war. They proved effective for a time, buying Indian friendship with their low prices and quality goods. But not for long.

The doom of the trading-factory system was spelled when the giant American Fur Company began invading the lower Great Lakes country in 1817. Operating from their headquarters at Mackinac, company agents established posts along all the principal rivers of the region, situated only forty or fifty miles apart, all supplied from Ft. Mackinac, and all manned by experienced British and Canadian traders attracted by high wages. The company's guiding genius, John Jacob Astor, would be content with nothing less than a trade monopoly for the entire Northwest. This meant that he must drive out the government factories. Astor declared war in 1818, cutting prices, sending traders to the Indian villages, selling the whiskey that the government agents could not. In this unequal struggle there could be only one victor; a factory system supported by a niggardly congressional appropriation was no match for the energetic American Fur Company with its vast resources. One by one the factories began closing their doors in 1821, and a year later Congress ordered the end of the whole system. With one foe vanquished, the company focused on the smaller private traders still operating, driving them from business one by one until by 1825 it monopolized the trade of the Great Lakes country. It had by this time achieved such dominance that the Indians were completely at its mercy.

This played into the hands of the federal government, for national Indian policy had only one objective: to bring the tribes so completely under American control that they could be pushed from their ancestral lands. This ambition was as old as English settlement in the New World, but the methods were new. Instead of bribing a few weak chiefs into signing a land-grabbing treaty, the commissioners named to deal with the northwestern Indians acted with brutal directness. The pattern was set in September, 1817, when representatives of the half-dozen tribes still owning lands in Ohio were called together, informed they must cede their claims in return for annuities and presents, and forced to sign a treaty of cession. For the next four years that ruthless process went on, with tribe after tribe surrendering its territories and agreeing to live within the confines of a reservation or move to the unwanted wilderness beyond the Mississippi. Powerless without the help of their British allies, the natives had no choice but to give way. By the end of 1821 nearly all of Indiana, Illinois, and Michigan was in American hands, ready to receive westward-moving pioneers.

Nor were the settlers long in coming. Both the attractiveness of the Lake Plains country and disturbed conditions in the East combined to drive the frontier rapidly westward. Certainly the Northwest seemed an agricultural haven to farmers from the hilly East. The whole region had at one period in geological history lain beneath an ocean, gradually lifting to form a level lowland, comparable to the coastal plains of Virginia and the Carolinas. Over this, in the later Pleistocene period, moved the great glaciers that pushed slowly downward from the polar ice cap, grinding rocks into fertile soil, leveling the land, and leaving rugged moraines to mark their temporary or permanent stopping places. Two of those ice sheets played a particularly prominent role in shaping the surface features of the Lake Plains. One, the Illinoian Drift, covered the area north of the Ohio River with a deep layer of rock waste and glacial debris. The other, the Wisconsin Drift, moved southward over that barren mass at a later time, smoothing off hills and laying down an even layer of soil rich in the elements needed for agriculture. This beneficial glacier did not cover the whole Northwest; its extreme southern advance was marked by the Shelbyville Moraine which ran through central Illinois and across Indiana and Ohio. North of that line the gently rolling countryside was rich and good, with loam soils enriched by humus and lightened by sand; to the south jagged hills and a stubborn clay soil discouraged farming. Early settlers were quick to notice the difference; they referred to the rough southern country as "Egypt" and to the bountiful northern lands as "God's Country," where the yield was a third more and the price of land almost twice as high as in the south.

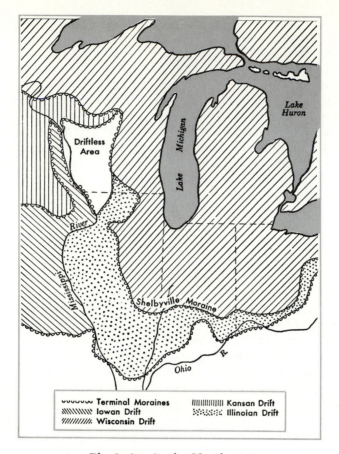

Glaciation in the Northwest

Important as were these soil differences in shaping the course of settlement, the first pioneers were influenced even more by the region's natural vegetation. This, in their minds, divided the countryside into three areas of varying desirability. One was the densely wooded section of southern Illinois and Indiana where a thick forest of hardwoods covered the land. Particularly prized were the silt-filled river bottoms, but even the hilly portions were eagerly sought after, for the plentiful timber promised profitable farming to westerners who judged the richness of land by the nature of its forests. The American Bottom, a seven-mile-wide plain stretching for forty miles along the Mississippi just north of the Kaskaskia River, was an especially choice spot that early attracted settlers.

Beyond the wilderness area lay a broad belt in central Indiana, Illinois, and southern Michigan where forests alternated with treeless prairies. In Michigan the open stretches resembled islands in a timbered sea. Some, known as Oak Openings, were sprinkled with tall oaks growing so far apart that a wagon could drive between them and were as free of underbrush as an English park. Others, the Prairie Rondes, were tiny prairies formed on beds of extinct glacial lakes where rich soil fostered such a luxurious growth of grass that trees could not take root. In western Indiana and central Illinois grasslands predominated, formed in some forgotten day by Indians who destroyed the forest with underbrush fires designed to drive game to a central point. The rolling prairie stretched for miles, broken only by occasional clumps of trees on some humid spot, or by sentinel-like rows of scrub growth along a meandering stream. Particularly impressive was the Grand Prairie of central Illinois. No traveler failed to be impressed by the magnitude of that vast plain, stretching away as far as eye could see, and covered with a six-foot growth of grass that billowed gently in the wind or, in the spring, dazzled onlookers with its color-splashed carpet of wildflowers. Yet the prairie country was shunned by the first settlers, whose frontier technique was adjusted to a wooded country. The grasslands were avoided until the pressure of increasing population forced pioneers to adapt to this newer environment. Even less hospitable was the third vegetation area of the Lake Plains, the belt of pine forests and conifers that grew in the sandy soil of northern Michigan and Wisconsin.

The wooded stretches of southern Indiana and Illinois, however, offered both adequate soil and familiar vegetation, and it was toward that area home-seekers turned just after the War of 1812. During this first period of Lake Plains settlement, between 1815 and 1830, immigrants came largely from the southern uplands. Disturbed social conditions there hurried them westward. Many were seasoned pioneers from Kentucky and Tennessee who, having been held back by a generation of Indian warfare, now resumed their advance. More were small farmers driven from their southern homes by the rapid extension of the plantation system, which engulfed the western Carolinas, Georgia, and eastern Tennessee during the postwar years. Some from those regions sought homes in the Northwest because their dislike of slavery made life amidst bonded labor unpleasant, others because the aristocratic social distinctions inherent in the plantation system were distasteful to their democratic instincts, and still more simply because their lands were absorbed by richer plantation owners. All these forces, operating in the fifteen years after the war, sent thousands of southerners across the Ohio.

They came in swarms. Some, from the back country of Virginia and Maryland, trekked westward along the National Road, a broad paved highway built across the mountains by the federal government. By 1818 this important route was opened as far as Wheeling where water transportation on the Ohio River was available; in 1833 its extension reached Columbus, Ohio. Others crowded along the crude roads built by southern states: the trail from Richmond to the Kanawha River, the pathways that utilized Ward's and Saluda gaps through the Blue Ridge to reach the western waterways, and especially the old Wilderness Road across Kentucky to Louisville, Cincinnati, and Maysville. From the embarkation points on the Ohio—Louisville and Shawneetown—they made their way northward along a network of territorial roads built between 1817 and 1822: to Lafayette and Vincennes in Indiana, to the Mississippi towns of Kaskaskia, Cahokia, St. Louis, and Alton, or to the farming lands bordering those forest trails. The roads were only crudely cut slashes through dense wilderness, dotted with stumps and interspersed with bottomless mudholes, but they did guide immigrants to their chosen destinations while tavern keepers along the way offered conveniences that helped speed the westward advance.

Over those rough trails came the settlers, bringing their few household belongings in Conestoga wagons or hand carts, and driving their hogs and cattle before them. Year after year the migration went on. "Old America seems to be breaking up and moving westward," wrote one traveler on the National Road in 1817. "We are seldom out of sight, as we travel on this grand track, towards the Ohio, of family groups before and behind us." Another, watching the steady procession of immigrant-laden flatboats down the Ohio, observed: "The numerous companies of immigrants who flock to this country, might appear, to those who have not witnessed them, almost incredible. But there is scarcely a day . . . but that there is a greater or less

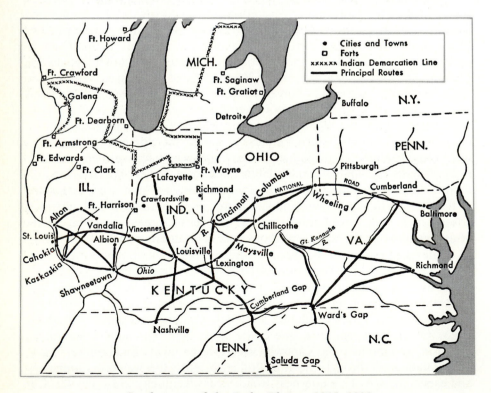

Settlement of the Lake Plains, 1815–1830

number of boats to be seen floating down its gentle current, to some place of destination."

The mecca of the first comers was the American Bottom and other river lowlands of Indiana and Illinois; after 1818 when these spots were filled, settlement spilled over into the uplands lying between the valleys. By that time land sales at Vincennes and Brockville, which had handled most of the public domain sold in Indiana, were declining as business shifted to the Crawfordsville office where interior lands were obtained. In Illinois half a million acres yearly passed into private hands. Not until 1830 did migration from the South diminish, and by that time the wooded hill-country of southern Indiana and Illinois was filled. Most newcomers found homes below a line—soon followed by the National Road—from Richmond, Indiana, through Indianapolis and Vandalia to St. Louis, although towns along the upper Wabash between Lafayette and Ft. Wayne testified to the attractiveness of the river lands. In Illinois the strip of lowlands bordering the Mississippi to a point well beyond the Illinois River was occupied, largely by veterans of the War of 1812 who were given bounty lands there. Nearly all pioneers avoided the prairies, although a group of several hundred English immigrants under a wealthy farmer, Morris Birkbeck, who arrived in 1818 without the prejudices of forest-trained American frontiersmen made their homes in the grasslands about Albion and Wanborough.

Most who came before 1830 purchased directly from government land offices, for the credit system used until 1820 and the set price of $1.25 an acre charged after that time discouraged speculators. A few companies did deal in farm lands, particularly in the Military Tract of western Illinois where 160-acre land warrants could be secured from the 18,000 veterans of the War of 1812, but their holdings seldom exceeded 10,000 acres. Two of the most important, the American Land Company and the Boston and Indiana Land Company, owned at the height of their activity 8,000 and 29,000 acres respectively. More speculative activity was concentrated on prospective town sites. Hundreds of favorable spots were snapped up by individual jobbers or small companies, converted into "paper towns," and sold to gullible easterners while the town itself was still an unbroken wilderness. Although a few—such as Terre Haute in Indiana—attracted settlers and paid their promoters dividends, more eventually were sold as farms for little more than their purchase price. Despite these activities, speculators played a less important role than on earlier frontiers.

While farmers spread over the timbered lands of the southern Lake Plains other pioneers from the South moved northward in search of a new source of wealth. Their goal was the Driftless Area of northwestern Illinois and southwestern Wisconsin, a region of rugged hills and deeply eroded streams bypassed by the glaciers, which smoothed the surrounding country. That rough area offered few agricultural possibilities, but lying beneath thin layers of eroded shale were outcroppings of rock containing rich veins of lead and other minerals. Both Indians and French traders had tapped this mineral wealth, but systematic exploitation did not begin until 1822 when a Kentucky promoter, Colonel James A. Johnson, arrived with supplies, miners, and 150 slaves. His success inspired a mining rush; by 1830 more than 10,000 miners had staked out claims, built the bustling town of Galena at the head of navigation of the Fever River, and were shipping 15,000,000 pounds of lead yearly to New Orleans. The lawlessness of the Fever River district—the saloons, gambling halls, bowie-knife fights, and vigilance committees that made violent mayhem a daily occurrence—was typical of all mining communities where the lure of sudden wealth drew settlers beyond the restraining forces of organized law.

The rapid peopling of the Driftless Area and the rush of settlers to the southern Lake Plains country convinced the federal government that more Indian lands must be opened to the swarming pioneers. From that belief stemmed an important change in Indian policy. In the immediate past American agents persuaded tribes to trade their hunting grounds for reservations where natives could subsist by farming. Now the rush of population indicated that even those tiny areas would soon be absorbed. The only solution was to transfer the Indians to unwanted lands beyond the Mississippi. By 1825 the federal government decided upon removal as a definite policy.

The first step was taken in August of that year when almost 1,000 representatives of all the northwestern tribes gathered at Prairie du Chien in response to an invitation from two agents of the War Department, Governor Lewis Cass of Michigan Territory and General William Clark. They had been called together, they were told, to agree on specific tribal boundaries as a means of maintaining peace; actually the United States wanted those divisions to facilitate land cessions. Some inkling of this made the Indians wary, but presents and annuities won most of them over and the Treaties of Prairie du Chien divided the Northwest among existing tribes. With that accomplished, agents turned at once to wresting land from the natives. In 1826 the Potawatomi ceded an enormous territory in Indiana, while the Miami turned over their remaining reservations in that state for $55,000 and an annuity of $25,000. For the next four years treaty making went grimly on, with tribes surrendering either their ancestral lands or their newly acquired reservations in Ohio, Indiana, and Illinois. Should the process go on unchecked, chieftains saw, every Indian in the Northwest would be forced to move beyond the Mississippi.

That realization, and the rise to tribal power of younger warriors who had forgotten the horrors of the War of 1812, was responsible for the last two native uprisings in the history of the Old Northwest. The first began in the spring of 1827 when the Winnebago chief, Red Bird, alarmed by the treaty making and the steady encroachment of Fever River settlers on his lands, led his tribe against the farmers around Prairie du Chien. Red Bird hoped his attack would lead to a general native uprising, but this failed to develop, largely because more farseeing Indians realized the hopelessness of resistance without British aid. The Winnebago, their hope of allies gone, retreated eastward along the Wisconsin River, pursued by a hastily gathered army of frontiersmen and regulars under General Henry Atkinson. At the Fox-Wisconsin portage another force from Ft. Howard awaited them. Caught between two armies, Red Bird surrendered at once. The outbreak, although not serious, convinced the United States a new fort was needed to guard the frontier. Ft. Winnebago, erected near the spot where Red Bird gave himself up, played a prominent role in the second Indian uprising.

This involved the Sauk and Fox tribes whose villages dotted the fertile river bottom just below the junction of the Rock and Mississippi rivers. Lawless miners from the Fever River District soon declared that no Indian should be allowed to hold such a choice spot. Acting on that frontier premise, the settlers formed a mob in the spring of 1829 and drove the peaceful Indians from their own corn field. The atrocity occurred when the Indians were sorely divided, the majority following the leadership of Keokuk who sought to avoid conflict and adjust to white institutions, the minority following an obscure war chief, Black Hawk, who favored retaining old Indian ways. There could be no united front against the Americans. Keokuk, accepting fate, led most of the Sauk and Fox across the Mississippi River, but Black Hawk decided to resist white pressure and remain. His position was hopeless from the start. In June, 1831, when Illinois authorities convinced themselves that the presence of the peaceful Indians endangered the frontier, a force of some 1,500 militia gathered, warned Black Hawk to leave, and then marched against his villages. The Indians, seeing that resistance would be suicidal, slipped across the Mississippi before the army reached them.

Black Hawk and his followers spent a miserable winter, having reached the Iowa country too late to plant corn or arrange shelter. As they shivered in icy blasts and wasted away with starvation, a vision rose in their minds—a vision of the peace and plenty of their homeland. If they could only return they would know contentment again! By spring Black Hawk had charted his course. He would lead his people back across the Mississippi, explain to Americans that they only wished to plant their crops and settle quietly on the fields of their ancestors. Certainly white men would not object if he moved openly and disavowed any warlike intentions. With that alluring prospect before him, he gathered hundreds of his fellow tribesmen and on April 6, 1832, returned to the Rock River Valley, crossing the Mississippi in full view of the garrison at Ft. Armstrong. His peaceful purpose was attested by the fact that almost 600 of his party were women and children who would never accompany a war party.

Black Hawk's return sent a wave of panic sweeping over the frontier. Rumors flew thick and fast: he had come back at the head of a bloodthirsty band, he had secured promises of help from other tribes, he was bent on driving the whites from the Illinois country. A call for volunteers brought 1,300 frontiersmen to Ft. Armstrong within a few weeks. On May 10, 1832, the imposing force with General Henry Atkinson at its head started up the

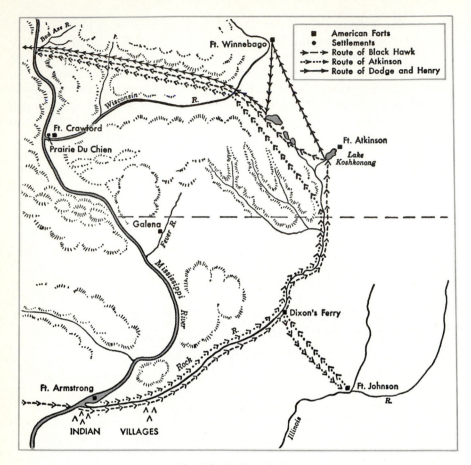

The Black Hawk War

Rock River, driving the bewildered Indians before them. Four days later the advance unit of 340 horsemen encountered a little party of forty Indians led by Black Hawk a few miles above Dixon's Ferry. Black Hawk tried to surrender, but, when his emissaries were fired upon by the inexperienced militiamen, decided to sell his life as dearly as possible. In the brief skirmish that followed his tiny band beat off the attackers. The saddened chief, knowing that war was now inevitable, moved his headquarters to the swamps about Lake Koshkonong where women and children could be hidden while warriors roamed the countryside. Between mid-May and the end of July the Indians killed nearly 200 whites, suffering equal losses themselves.

General Atkinson, in the meantime, was training new volunteers at Ft. Johnson, built for the purpose on the upper Illinois River. By June 19, 1832, he was ready to take up the chase once more, with an army of almost 4,500 men. His raw recruits moved so slowly through the tangled bogs that long before they reached Lake Koshkonong Black Hawk was on his way west, bound for the safety of the Iowa shore. Discouraged by the rough country, the white army paused to throw up new fortifications at Ft. Atkinson; while a small party under General James D. Henry and Major Henry Dodge pushed on to Ft. Winnebago for supplies. Black Hawk might have escaped entirely had not this party happened to cross his trail on its return trip. Henry and Dodge, realizing that the Indians were near, decided to take up the pursuit, at the same time sending word to Atkinson's main force to join them.

Black Hawk's doom was sealed. He managed to hold off his pursuers at the Wisconsin River while the main Indian party crossed the stream, but that was only a temporary reprieve. His warriors were so weakened with hunger that they dropped dead along the way as they stumbled doggedly westward. In that pitiful state they were set upon by Atkinson's army just as they reached the Mississippi. Black Hawk saw the hopelessness of the situation. Behind him were well-supplied Americans, ahead a gunboat floated on the broad surface of the Mississippi. Once more he tried to surrender, but his flag of truce was answered by a burst of fire from the vessel. For the next three hours a merciless slaughter went on as Indians were driven into the river at bayonet point, then shot as they struggled in the water. By nightfall only 150 of the embattled Indians who set out for the Rock River valley three months before remained alive and they were prisoners, including Black Hawk himself. The Bad Axe Massacre, as it was called, was one of the bloodiest tragedies in the sad history of American-Indian relations.

American ruthlessness in the Black Hawk War had its desired effect on other tribes of the Northwest. Resistance, they saw, meant only extermination; better to move west than be annihilated. Their cowed spirit was recognized by American agents, who went rapidly ahead with treaty making. Starting in 1832 when the Winnebago traded most of their Wisconsin lands for hunting grounds in the Far West, tribe after tribe succumbed to white pressure until by 1837 nearly all the Northwest was held by the United States. In those five years 190,879,937 acres were secured at a cost of $70,059,505 in gifts and annuities. Indians still remaining after 1840 despite those cessions were "escorted" to their trans-Mississippi lands by troops. Indian removal was badly mismanaged. By 1846 the last suffering tribe had departed for its unwanted new home; the few scattered bands remaining lived on marginal lands and were too weak to interfere with the advancing frontier.

The peopling of northern Indiana, northern and central Illinois, and southern Michigan began while Black Hawk's war still raged on the western borders of the Lake Plains. For twenty years—from 1830 to 1850—population moved steadily into the region, until the whole Northwest was filled. The source of this migratory stream was New England and the Middle States. Thrifty Yankees, driven westward by unsettled economic conditions at home and lured onward by improved transportation routes to the West, in those years filled the northern portion of the Lake Plains as solidly as their southern compatriots had the bottom lands of the Ohio Valley.

Better facilities for reaching the West shaped the course of the new migration. Some pioneers from the Middle States continued to use the old routes—the National Road, Forbes' Road, or the Catskill Turnpike—to reach the Ohio, then made their way down the river and northward to central Indiana or Illinois. More took advantage of a newly completed all-water route between East and West. The Erie Canal, opened to traffic in 1825 from the Hudson River to Lake Erie, offered the first really satisfactory means of reaching the Lakes country from New England. Travelers might complain of overcrowded canal boats, poor food, and swarming mosquitoes, but they were nevertheless able to travel cheaply, take their household goods with them, and be sure of reaching their destination without losing a wagon in a mudhole. Little wonder that the Erie Canal overnight became the most important route to the West, or that thousands of homeseekers made their way westward on its horse-drawn barges.

The principal effect of this waterway was to deflect the immigrant stream from the Ohio Valley to the Great Lakes. Passengers from the East, on reaching Buffalo, sought passage on lake steamers, particularly after 1833 when a packet line opened regular service between Buffalo and Detroit. Deck passage cost only about $3, allowing a traveler to secure fairly comfortable transportation from Massachusetts to Michigan for less than $10. Little wonder that few immigrants made the hazardous voyage down the Ohio; instead they followed this all-water route to the country about Lake Erie and Lake Michigan.

These new highways could not have played their role had not unsettled conditions in New England turned thousands of easterners toward the Northwest. An economic revolution was taking place there. Through the first two centuries of its existence New England was a region of small farms and selfsufficient agriculture, largely because the lack of markets discouraged the production of staples. By the 1830s, for the first time in the section's history, markets developed as non-food-producing communities sprang up around the factories that America's industrial revolution concentrated there. Between 1810, when the factory system was introduced, and 1860 urban dwellers increased from 7 to 37 per cent of the population. This potential market tempted farmers to abandon their old self-sufficient economy and specialize in the crops for which their soil was best suited. Some, in the Connecticut River valley, turned to tobacco growing, others to market gardening, and still more to the production of wool. This last crop caused the trouble, as the demand for wool remained steady at spawning textile mills and the breed of Saxony Merino sheep introduced into New England in 1824 proved ideally adapted to local conditions. A "sheep craze" swept over Massachusetts, Connecticut, and Vermont between 1825 and 1840 as farmer after farmer turned his cultivated fields into profitable pasture lands.

The effect was momentous. Sheep grazing required little manual labor but much land. Hence small farms gave way to sheep runs as the fortunates who switched to wool growing early bought out their neighbors. Dispossessed farmers could move into the valley towns seeking jobs in mills, or go west to the fertile Lake country. During the years of the "sheep craze" the rural population of New England steadily declined as immigrants trekked westward to begin life anew.

The end was not yet. After 1840 eastern agriculture staggered under a new blow: ruinous competition with cheaply produced farm goods from the West. Grain growers suffered first as Ohio Valley wheat and corn, moved eastward over the Erie Canal, invaded coastal markets. By 1845, when the cost of shipping a bushel of wheat from Chicago to New York was only twenty-five cents, nearly 1,500,000 bushels yearly passed through Buffalo, in addition to 700,000 barrels of flour. The flood of cereals from virgin western soils lowered prices so radically that thousands of New England farmers gave up the struggle, most of them moving west themselves. Others, who turned to wool growing, found their reprieve only temporary, for during the 1840s a "sheep craze" swept across Ohio. Again the eastern farmer was faced with importations of cheaply produced western goods, and again had no choice but surrender, as sheep could be fed more economically on the fertile fields of the Old Northwest than on the rock-strewn New England pastures. Thousands admitted defeat and, having no alternative now, turned their footsteps west, sometimes driving their flocks before them. Between 1840 and 1850 wool production in the Northeast declined 50 per cent. In vain did eastern farm journals, agricultural societies, and state politicians praise farming as the noblest of the professions. No campaign, not even one as extensive as this one, could still the migratory urge. Instead the exodus went on, as abandoned farms dotted the countryside in mute testimony to the rural decay of that once-prosperous section.

In the Middle States the same expelling forces were at work, although in somewhat modified form. The well-worked soils of New York and Pennsylvania proved incapable of competing with the virgin lands of the West in cereal production, forcing farmer after farmer into market gardening, cattle raising, or the dairy industry. This agricultural upheaval released thousands of families for the westward migration, just as had the "sheep craze" in New England. From both sections a stream of excess population made its way to the Lake Plains, there to produce more and more grain, ship greater quantities eastward, glut the market, and encourage others to follow in their footsteps. So rapid was the influx that the usual frontier lines were blurred; settlers transformed Michigan, Indiana, and Illinois from wilderness wastes to settled regions almost overnight.

Michigan, lying at the opposite end of Lake Erie from the terminus of the Erie Canal, felt the impact first. In 1830, when the movement began, the territory's settlements were confined to a ring of towns circling Detroit—Mt. Clemens, Pontiac, and Rochester in the Clinton River valley, Ann Arbor

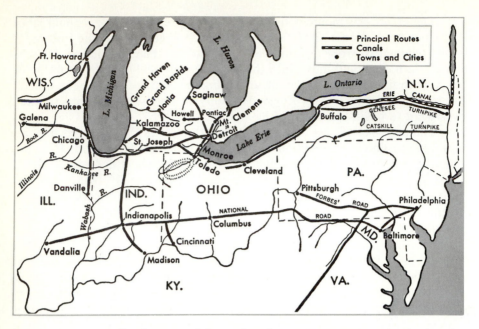

Settlement of the Lake Plains, 1830–1850

and Ypsilanti on the Huron River, and Monroe, Tecumseh, and Adrian along the Raisin River—all established by pioneers or speculators between 1817 and 1826. Beyond stretched the unbroken forest, for until the Erie Canal directed pioneers to the Lakes country, Michigan lay far from immigration routes. Michiganders believed that the territory's slow growth before 1825 could be blamed on the unfriendly picture painted by eastern guidebooks and geographies and by the hostile opinion of Edward Tiffin, an official surveyor, whose published report branded Michigan as a "poor barren, sandy land, on which scarcely any vegetation grows, except very small scrubby oaks." Actually the Tiffin report was little read; it was never mentioned by eastern guidebooks or newspapers; instead the guides used by immigrants universally praised the territory's agricultural prospects. Frontier settlers avoided the area at first simply because it lacked transportation outlets for their surpluses. By 1830, with the Erie Canal completed and steamboats navigating the Great Lakes, this was no longer true. The time was ripe for a rush of settlers.

Detroit felt their impact in 1831, as lake steamers deposited the first immigrants at its docks. "Almost every building that can be made to answer for a shelter is occupied and filled," the local newspaper reported that summer. More were hastily thrown together, and the sleepy little frontier village rapidly emerged as a new metropolis. By 1836 it boasted 10,000 inhabitants, a theater, a museum, a public garden, schools, churches, a library, a lyceum, a historical society, a ladies' seminary, a water and sewage system, and street lights of such remarkable inefficiency that—if the city's newspaper can be believed—only a few more were needed to produce total darkness.

Despite these improvements most newcomers did not stay in Detroit; instead they fanned out to people southern Michigan. Many went west along the two roads then available: the Chicago Road, which was completed in 1832, and the Territorial Road, which was authorized by the territorial legislature in 1829 and opened to St. Joseph in 1834. Those highways traversed a region of rolling hills, level plains, and fertile soils that held infinite promise to land-hungry easterners. By 1837, 25,000 people lived along the Chicago Road, and almost as many more in the Kalamazoo River valley. The latter, a particularly prized spot, was dotted with Prairie Rondes—some as large as eleven miles across—the deep black soil of which was ready for the plow without the backbreaking task of clearing. These, and the Oak Openings, were sought out first; then immigrants turned to the conquest of surrounding forests and to the building of towns at favorable sites along roads and rivers.

Other settlers moved north from Detroit to the valley of the Saginaw River where numerous Oak Openings offered tempting homesites. Although the town of Saginaw was laid out in 1832, mass migration did not set in until three years later when a highway was completed to Detroit. At the same time pioneers made their way to the forested lands along the Grand River, traveling northward first along Indian trails that crossed the Territorial Road, then following a highway opened between Marshall and Ionia in 1836. After 1838 they utilized the Grand River Road from Pontiac to Howell. By that time a sizeable town existed at Grand Rapids where an eighteen-foot fall in the river provided abundant water power. Another settlement was being nursed to maturity by speculators at Grand Haven. Most of the pioneers in the Grand River valley, as in the rest of southern Michigan, were transplanted New Englanders who had come westward with a song of hope upon their lips:

> Come all ye Yankee farmers who wish to change your lot,
> Who've spunk enough to travel beyond your native spot,
> And leave behind the village where Ma and Pa do stay,
> Come follow me and settle in Michigania,—
> Yea, Yea, Yea, in Michigania.

Another northwestern state, Indiana, fared less well during the 1830-50 migrations. While its northern counties were settled by the overflow from the Chicago Road its central portions were largely neglected until the 1850s. Two false impressions were responsible for this lag: the belief held by most immigrants that lands in the northeastern portion of the state were too wet to be attractive, and the hope of a handful of speculators that Indiana's prairies were so superior they would command a fabulous price.

The former illusion was fostered by travelers who journeyed westward through the tangled morass of the Black Swamp or picked their way among sluggish streams north of the Wabash. Their exaggerated tales of a whole countryside under water spread to editors of eastern newspapers and guide books who customarily referred to the "swamps and bogs of Indiana," while failing to mention the equally swampy regions of Illinois. That tradition, which persisted well into the 1830s, discouraged some settlers, but a more important deterrent was the engrossment of land by eastern speculators. This began in 1832 when a Connecticut businessman, Henry W. Ellsworth, visited Indiana as Indian commissioner. Struck by the beauty of the prairie country between the Wabash and Kankakee valleys, Ellsworth began buying land there in 1835, moving west a year later to settle on his 18,000 acres. His large scale agricultural methods and specially devised machinery proved so successful that he not only made additional purchases but also became a rabid advocate of prairie farming.

Ellsworth's enthusiasm was responsible for a speculative boom in Indiana land. His eastern friends began buying on his advice in 1836, but wholesale purchases did not begin until 1838 when he described the beauties and opportunities of the countryside in a widely circulated book, *Valley of the Upper Wabash*. He would, Ellsworth stated in that publication, gladly purchase prairie lands for any investor, manage estates for absentee owners, and guarantee a profit of 8 or 10 per cent, with anything above that figure divided between owner and operator. That attractive offer, coming just as the Panic of 1837 reduced investment opportunities in the East, led to a rush of speculative buying, with purchases ranging from a few hundred to many thousand acres. Within a few years most of northwestern Indiana was held by absentee owners, whose glorified conception of the value of their holdings led them to set prices of $5 or $10 an acre. Few buyers were willing to pay that much when good lands elsewhere were obtainable for $1.25 an acre. Northern Indiana remained largely without settlers until the 1850s when popular pressure and mounting taxes forced speculators to unload at more reasonable prices. Most of the purchasers at that time were from southern Indiana, a fact explaining the predominantly southern character of that state's population.

Illinois, suffering no handicaps such as these, gained population rapidly between 1830 and 1850. The rush to Chicago began in 1835, sending that tiny town, laid out only two years earlier, into a transformation similar to that which rocketed Detroit to a position of importance four years before. "Almost all vessels from the lower lakes are full of passengers," one editor wrote, "and our streets are thronged with wagons loaded with household furniture and the implements necessary to farming. Foot-passengers, too, with well-filled sacks on their shoulders come in large numbers." A year later 450 vessels disgorged their human cargoes, while the air rang with the sound of hammers as carpenters worked feverishly to keep pace with the growing demand for houses. The wood to build Chicago as well as the newly opened prairie farms came from the lumber camps in the pine forests of Michigan, Wisconsin, and Minnesota.

From Chicago settlers fanned out over northern Illinois, first seeking such choice spots as the Rock and Illinois river valleys, then filling in the forested uplands between. When these were occupied, later comers were brought face to face with an important problem. How could they make the transition from accustomed timber lands to the prairies of Illinois where alone cheap land remained? The task was formidable; to conquer the grasslands pioneers must discard their prejudices, abandon their traditions, and develop an entirely new frontier technique. They had, for generations, judged the richness of land by the density of its forest growth, used wood for everything from homes to fences, and obtained fuel, game, and water from the wilderness. Now they must settle on a barren waste apparently incapable of supporting forests, unprotected from winter blasts or summer heat, without logs for their cabins, rails for their fences, or fuel for their fires. They must dig wells, rather than depend on rippling forest streams, and provide drainage to carry spring rains from level lands. Worst of all, they must devise some means of breaking the tough prairie sod that shattered the fragile wooden plows to which they were accustomed.

Little wonder that settlers hesitated at the edge of the prairies before making the transition. Eventually, however, as each grassland was surrounded by homes, the conquest began. The shift was usually gradual; a farmer living near a prairie broke a little of the sod, using the rest for pasture. As others imitated his example a ring of fields spread around the edge of the grassy plot. Later comers pushed beyond to make their homes on the prairie itself, until eventually the whole area was under cultivation. This process was repeated again and again in northern Illinois, until by the end of the 1840s the entire state was settled. Only the central portions of the Grand Prairie were avoided until the 1850s when railroads brought them near enough to markets to make their cultivation profitable.

The development of new techniques made the conquest possible. Capital, prairie pioneers soon learned, was necessary, so they customarily worked for some other farmer for a year or so. Their carefully hoarded cash was then used to purchase a farm and pay for the initial sod breaking. This was done by itinerate prairie breakers with special equipment: a heavy plow built for the task and from three to six yokes of oxen. The plow broke only two acres a day; two dollars an acre was the usual price charged—more than the cost of the land—but then the principal expense was over. The first "sod crop" was planted by hacking the upturned furrows with an ax and dropping in a few kernels of corn; this usually produced about fifty bushels to the acre even without cultivation—enough to pay back part of the initial investment and finance more sod breaking the next year. In the meantime lumber for a home was hauled in, a well was dug, and fences constructed.

This last proved most difficult, as the split-rail fences that were alone available cost from $150 to $300 for a forty-acre farm. The heavy expenses, running as high as $1,000, did not alarm prairie farmers who knew two or three good crops would pay off the entire investment.

So attractive were the prospects that by the end of the 1830s enough of northern Illinois was filled to send an overflow spilling into Wisconsin. Some 30,000 pioneers lived in that pleasant land of rolling hills and small prairies in 1840, most of them in the farming communities around the Fever River District or along the federal road opened in 1837 between Chicago and Ft. Howard. In the next decade population increased to 305,000 as New Englanders flocked to the lake-front counties or marched northward along the Rock River valley. There they met other migrants, largely from the Middle States, advancing north and east along the Mississippi and Wisconsin rivers. To that region, too, came the vanguards of the European population streams that flooded the Old Northwest during the next decades. Some were Norwegians who built their Old World colonies about Lake Koshkonong, others were Irish laborers who turned to farming after completing the roads on which they had worked, but most were Germans. Driven from their homes by a potato famine and the disrupting effects of the unsuccessful uprisings of 1848, many refugees took passage on the cotton ships plying between European ports and New Orleans. They sought cheap, slave-free lands. In the 1840s Milwaukee was "all the rage" for Germans arriving in New York. By 1850, 640,000 foreign born lived in the Lake Plains area, forming about one-eighth of the population.

By that time the whole section was passing beyond the frontier stage, except for portions of Michigan and Wisconsin where less hospitable soils and dense pine forests discouraged settlement until the coming of the railroads. The 4,500,000 people whose homes dotted the Old Northwest in 1850 were drawn from a variety of older societies, as the following table of origins shows:

	New England	Middle States	South	Northwest	Native Born	Europe
Ohio	66,000	300,000	150,000	———	1,284,000	200,000
Indiana	11,000	76,000	175,000	130,000	500,000	55,000
Illinois	37,000	112,000	138,000	110,000	344,000	110,000
Michigan	31,000	150,000	4,000	18,000	140,000	55,000
Wisconsin	27,000	80,000	5,000	23,000	63,000	107,000

In the Lake Plains they met and mingled, blending the social mannerisms and economic habits of their homelands to create a unique society, distinct from those contributing to it and modified by the impact of the frontier. In Ohio, Michigan, and Wisconsin, where northerners predominated, the in-

stitutions of the Northeast held sway, in Indiana the social order was patterned on that of the South, while in Illinois the even balance between
northerners and southerners forced a compromise between disciples of the
two sections.

These divisions became apparent when the people of the Lake Plains
turned to erecting their governmental systems. Indiana in 1816 and Illinois
in 1818 entered the Union with constitutions that reflected both the prepon-
derantly southern nature of their populations and the liberalizing influence
of the frontier; property qualifications for voting were swept away, popularly
elected legislatures were made supreme, and the franchise was awarded all
adult males who had lived within the state for six months or a year—yet in
both slavery was allowed to continue under the guise of indentured servitude.
Michigan's frame of government was equally liberal when it applied for
statehood in 1837, and Wisconsin's outdid them all in guaranteeing unrestrained popular control: governor, legislators, and even judges were elected
for short terms, all native-born males were given the right to vote after one
year's residence and all foreign born when agreeing to a simple oath of
allegiance, small homesteads were exempted from seizure for debt, and
married women were allowed to control their own property. Wisconsin
became a state under this document in 1848.

These liberal innovations, however, did not extend to the free Negroes
who sought haven from slavery and eastern prejudice in the Old Northwest,
most as individuals, a few as groups such as those driven from North Carolina
who in 1832 founded the Roberts Settlement in Indiana. "Black Laws,"
rigidly restricting the freedom of Negroes, were adopted in most states;
Indiana led the way in 1803 with a statute forbidding blacks to testify in suits
involving whites. This was extended in 1807 to prohibit service in the militia,
and a few years later to bar all from voting. Between 1813 and 1815 the
lower house of the Indiana legislature three times voted to exclude all free
Negroes from the state, but in the end settled on a measure forcing black
males to pay a three-dollar annual poll tax. Ohio went so far as to force all
"colored" people who entered the state to post a $500 bond. These prej-
udices were mirrored in the state constitutions. A proposition before the
Indiana convention to grant Negroes the franchise was defeated by a vote
of 122 to 1; instead a clause excluding all black immigrants was approved
by the electorate by a six to one majority. Nor was Indiana, which was
more southern than most states of the Old Northwest, unique. Michigan and
Illinois forbade interracial marriages, while in the latter state any Negro
migrant who remained for ten days was fined $50 or threatened with the
public auction of his labor.

Tragic as were these laws, even more tragic was the failure of even the
liberally minded people o that day to recognize their own bigotry. To them,
even to many of the abolitionists, the Negro was simply excluded from
society; he could be ignored and his rights restricted without touching the
public conscience. Timothy Flint, an acute observer of the West, typified

this attitude when he could boast of a liberal social metamorphosis at a time when blacks were treated as little better than subhuman: "The society thus newly organized and constituted, is more liberal, enlarged, unprejudiced, and, of course, more affectionate and pleasant, than a society of people of *unique* birth and character, who bring all their early prejudices as a common stock, to be transmitted as an inheritance in perpetuity."

16

Settling the Gulf Plains
1815-1850

While Yankees, southerners, and immigrants transformed the Northwest into a land of fertile farms and bustling villages, another torrent of settlers inundated the Gulf Plains of the Southwest. That bountiful countryside of gentle hills and colorful red soils attracted, in the quarter-century after the War of 1812, the hordes of small farmers, lordly plantation owners, and docile slaves needed to erect a unique social order, built on black labor and white cotton.

The Southwest was opened to settlement in 1798 when Mississippi Territory was created, but only a handful of pioneers made their homes there in the next dozen years. Cheap and readily available lands in Georgia and Tennessee, Spanish control of the West Florida ports through which the region's produce must be exported, and the presence of the powerful Creek and Cherokee tribes in western Georgia, and of the Choctaw and Chickasaw in Mississippi and Alabama, all discouraged any mass movement to the territory. These obstacles might have been overcome had the region been capable of producing a valuable exportable crop, but the tobacco grown there was of an inferior quality, while the indigo that was feasible was messy to produce, attracting flies, and polluting streams. Equally important was the lack of direct communication with the settled areas of the Southeast. The two federally built roads opened before 1812 from Nashville to Natchez and from the Ocmulgee River to St. Stephens on the Tombigbee River were only crude trails utterly impassable during much of the year. Those obstacles kept migration at a minimum; in 1812 the white population of the territory consisted of 20,000 Spaniards, Loyalists, and Americans grouped about Natchez or spread along the lower Tombigbee River.

309

The metamorphosis of this backward frontier region into a prosperous land of farms and plantations can be explained in one word: cotton. Southern interest in that staple crop began to develop in the late eighteenth century when English inventors perfected the machinery needed to produce cotton cloth mechanically. Those epoch-making machines—James Hargreaves' "spinning jenny," Richard Arkwright's automatic carder, Samuel Crompton's "mule," and Edmund Cartwright's power loom—launched England on its industrial revolution. Before the turn of the century British mills produced cotton cloth more cheaply than the underpaid weavers of India who had long enjoyed a virtual monopoly in world production. The market was limitless; the whole world waited to be reclothed in cheaper fabrics than the expensive woolens traditional to Europe and America. Machines, workers, and power could be supplied in Britain; only raw cotton was needed.

News of these developments caused a flurry of excitement along the Atlantic seaboard during the 1790s. Plantation owners, struggling to make a profit by producing tobacco for an overcrowded world market, saw that fortunes awaited those switching to the promising new crop. They knew that two types of cotton could be grown in the South. One, Sea Island Cotton, which had been imported from Jamaica, had long silken fibres that could easily be separated from the glossy black seeds either by hand or by a simple machine known as a gin—two closely placed rollers which drew the lint through while the seeds popped out behind. Cultivation of this variety began in Georgia in 1786, but its commercial importance was limited by the fact that it could be grown only on the coastal islands and swampy lowlands between the St. John's and Santee rivers. The other, Upland Cotton, did not require the warm, moist climate of the Sea Island type and could be grown over most of the South. Its commercial production was impossible, however, because of the difficulty of separating its short fibres from their fuzzy green seeds. They clung so tenaciously that a slave could clean only a pound or two a day. Large scale cultivation would only be practicable if some mechanical means of cleaning Upland Cotton was devised.

There was much talk of such an invention among plantation owners during the early 1790s. Word of this fell on the ears of a young Yale graduate, Eli Whitney, when he arrived at a plantation near Savannah in the fall of 1792. Mrs. Nathanael Greene, who owned the plantation and had advanced ideas about a gin, encouraged Whitney to begin experimenting, and within a few weeks produced the first workable cotton gin. His invention consisted of a wooden cylinder bristling with stiff wires which revolved against the slatted sides of a box of cotton. The wires tore away bits of fibre while the slats held back the seeds, then the lint was brushed from the wire points by a second revolving cylinder set with brushes. This simple device, when harnessed to water power, cleaned 1,000 pounds of Upland Cotton a day; when saw-toothed iron disks were substituted for the wires the amount was doubled. Soon gins, located everywhere in the South, were ginning cotton for $1.50 a hundredweight.

Wherever soil and climate were suitable planters turned excitedly to the new crop. The price was high—forty cents a pound when production started —and profits fantastic. The Tidewater, where the plantation system was well established, made the transition first, but in 1800 the cotton plant started its march westward over the Virginia and Carolina Piedmont. During the next decade the economy of that section was revolutionized; small farms were engulfed by great estates, grains gave way before the new staple, and the free labor of the region was displaced by the expanding slave system. Between 1800 and 1810 the number of bonded servants in the lower Piedmont increased 70 per cent. By 1812, when war temporarily halted expansion, the cotton frontier was ready to advance across the Gulf Plains.

The War of 1812 paved the way, both by opening trade routes between the Southwest and the Gulf, and by preparing the Indians for removal. The routes were opened when Mobile and other Spanish Gulf cities fell to American forces during the fighting, thus assuring interior planters unmolested river shipments directly to the sea. At the same time Andrew Jackson's victory over the Creeks at the Battle of Horse Shoe Bend taught the United States that the southern tribes were so weak and torn by dissension they would be unable to resist forceful removal. The time was ripe to push them from their ancestral lands: the Creeks from the country between the Ocmulgee and Tombigbee rivers, the Cherokee from their mountain homes in northern Georgia and eastern Tennessee, the Choctaw from the wooded lands separating the Tombigbee and Natchez settlements, and the Chickasaw from northern Mississippi and western Tennessee.

That realization, and pressure from cotton planters eagers to invade the Gulf Plains, turned the government's attention to land cessions as soon as the war was over. A series of treaties forced on cowed tribes between 1816 and 1821 opened several tracts in central Georgia, western Alabama, and western Tennessee, but the rapidity with which these were overrun convinced the United States that something more was necessary. Nothing would satisfy land-hungry cotton growers but the removal of all Indians to lands beyond the Mississippi. Andrew Jackson, acting as agent for the war department, first attempted that solution when he gathered a handful of reluctant Cherokee together in July, 1817, and by threats and bribery forced them to exchange their tribal lands for an equal number of acres in the Far West. Every Cherokee had the choice, according to the treaty, of settling down in the East on 640 acres of land, or of moving to the West; those who chose the latter course were given free transportation, a gun, a blanket, a kettle, and a year's supplies. To Jackson's disgust virtually the entire tribe remained in the East; in fact, many Cherokees bought slaves and turned planters. Nor did a similar treaty with the Choctaw arranged by Jackson in October, 1820, convince that tribe to move beyond the Mississippi. A more aggressive policy was needed to open the Southwest.

This began in 1825 when President James Monroe publicly endorsed removal as a means of protecting Indians from the evils of white civilization.

This pronouncement signaled an about-face in national policy. Until this time assimilation had been the ideal; the Indian would be taught the white man's culture and fitted into the mainstream of American life. Now the principal purpose was expulsion; the nation's manifest destiny was to remove these troublesome occupants, making way for energetic Anglo-Americans equipped to exact a maximum yield from nature's bounties. This end justified any means. Although Monroe did not openly suggest the use of force, his agents were convinced he would condone more vigorous methods than the peaceful persuasion attempted in the past. Their first victims were the Creeks, whose presence in western Georgia long rankled officials of that frontier state. The farseeing Creek chieftains, anticipating the American policy, in 1824 decreed the death penalty for any chief selling or exchanging tribal lands. Undeterred by that threat, Monroe's agents determined to follow the usual practice of dealing with a bribed faction of the tribe. A meeting with a few greedy chiefs headed by Chief William McIntosh on February 12, 1825, resulted in the Treaty of Indian Springs, a scandalous document ceding all the Creek land and promising the tribe would leave for the Far West by September 1, 1826.

The majority of the Creeks, whose leader was the able Chief Big Warrior, met in council to decide on a policy suited to the emergency. Without hesitation, they pronounced the death penalty for the traitorous Chief McIntosh; a few weeks later his house was surrounded and he and two of his followers shot down. At the same time the Creeks refused to recognize the Treaty of Indian Springs or admit that any of their lands were sold. Their resistance bore some fruit. John Quincy Adams, who had replaced Monroe in the White House, was as sympathetic to the removal policy as his predecessor, but he was convinced that an injustice had been done and ordered a thorough investigation. When this not only disclosed the fraud used at Indian Springs but demonstrated that forty-nine out of every fifty Creeks opposed the treaty, President Adams did not hesitate. Authorized leaders of the tribe were requested to send a truly representative delegation to Washington where, in January, 1826, the Indians signed a new treaty slightly more to their liking. But the results were the same. Government pressure forced them to agree to removal, they were given until January 1, 1827, to begin their migration, and the rewards for those agreeing to go were substantially increased.

Georgia's governor, a hotheaded backwoodsman named George M. Troup, flew into a towering rage when he learned of the Treaty of Washington. His state, he loudly proclaimed, refused to recognize the new agreement and would begin occupying the Creek lands on September 2, 1826. President Adams was helpless before this determined resistance; even the United States marshal resigned when ordered to arrest intruders on Indian lands. The President had no choice but to urge the tribe to move as speedily as possible. The migration began in November, 1827, when the first large party made its way down the Tennessee and Mississippi rivers, then ascended the Arkansas River to the assigned territory. For the next two years the movement went on, as natives were rudely uprooted by Georgians who overran their villages or appropriated their fields. By the end of 1829 only a handful of Creeks remained in the state. The hurried and mismanaged departures and the failure of the United States to provide promised supplies meant untold suffering for the mistreated Indians many of whom failed to survive the journey.

The removal of the Creeks left only the Cherokee in possession of Georgia lands. The leaders of that powerful tribe, realizing their plight decided to use their advanced civilization as a cloak to guard their ancestral territories. Some were half-breeds, but even many of the full-bloods were well adjusted to the white man's way of life; the 15,000 members of the tribe owned 22,000 cattle, 1,300 slaves, 2,000 spinning wheels, 700 looms, 31 grist mills, 10 saw mills, 8 cotton gins, and 18 schools. Their written language, invented by Sequoya, was employed in a newspaper, *The Cherokee Phoenix*. Obviously they were not nomadic barbarians who could be easily pushed aside. Why not convince the Georgians of their stability, and at the same time solidify the tribe, by forming their own government? With this in mind delegates gathered at New Echota, Georgia, on July 4, 1827, to draft a constitution for a Cherokee Republic. Within a month the frame of government was ratified, Chief John Ross elected president, and a solid but non-violent front formed against white aggression.

Georgia's reaction was one of mingled fury and delight. The anger was aroused by the Cherokee's determination to retain lands coveted by the Georgians; they were delighted by the realization that the Indians had taken a step which would lead to the tribe's undoing. The Constitution of the United States forbade the erection of any new state within an existing state without the latter's consent. The New Echota constitution violated that provision. Therefore, Georgians reasoned, the federal government must punish the Cherokee by removing them from Georgia. This demand was voiced by the state legislature in December, 1827, when resolutions were adopted demanding national help in expelling the Indians. Congress responded by appropriating $50,000 for Cherokee removal. Armed with that sum, war department agents attempted to persuade the Indians to move peacefully, promising each lands in the West, transportation, a blanket, a rifle, a kettle, five pounds of tobacco, a year's supplies, and $50 in cash. During the summer of 1828 these inducements were dangled before the natives by skillful diplomats, but to little avail. The Indians were determined to cling to their lands at all costs.

The election of Andrew Jackson in 1828 ended the brief period of peaceful persuasion. That blunt frontiersman was not typical of those of his breed who considered a dead Indian to be the only good Indian; he had befriended many a native and during his military career upheld a rigid code of ethics in dealing with his enemies. His actions as President, however, were based on two beliefs. On the one hand Jackson was convinced that Indians were entitled only to the property they actually occupied as individuals, not the vast tribal tracts "on which they have neither dwelt nor made improvements, merely because they have seen them from the mountain or passed them in the chase." On the other Jackson held that the Indians enjoyed no special sovereignty that made them immune to congressional control; he saw them as subjects of the United States who must submit to the nation's laws. Treaties with tribes, in his eyes, had no more validity than treaties with any group of citizens. Moreover they usually benefited only a few tribal politicians at the expense of the members as a whole.

Building his policy on these notions, Jackson weighed the alternatives available to him. Three he dismissed at once: extermination offended his sense of human decency, assimilation had proven unworkable, and preservation of the natives under federal protection on ancestral lands was impossible given the social climate of the South. There remained only removal on liberal terms, with the Indians shifted to unwanted lands where they could preserve their native culture after generous compensation for their land holdings. Given the atmosphere of the time, Jackson probably followed the only alternative open to him. His policy might be judged cruel by later generations—and was—but given his prejudices, he could have followed no other. Jackson summed up his thoughts when he told the Senate: "Toward this race of people I entertain the kindest feelings, and am not sensible that the views which I have taken of their true interest are less favorable to them than those which oppose their emigration to the West."

This was the background of the stern pronouncements in Jackson's inaugural address. "I have," he wrote, "been unable to perceive any sufficient reason why the Red man more than the white, may claim exception from the municipal laws of the State within which they reside." Here was the green light to greedy Georgians who wanted the Cherokee lands. Spurred on by the discovery of gold in the Indian country, they hurried resolutions through the state legislature providing that after January 1, 1830, all state laws applied to Indians, who were also denied the right to be a witness or party in a legal suit where a white man was involved. Those two brutal measures not only broke down the tribal organization on which the red men depended, but placed them at the mercy of unscrupulous whites who appropriated their lands without fear of legal redress. Little wonder that the Cherokee appealed to Washington for the protection due them as wards of the government. Their answer came in May, 1830, when Congress passed a Removal Bill authorizing the President to move any eastern tribe to trans-Mississippi lands—by force if need be. In desperation they fell back upon their last hope; the Supreme Court was asked to issue an injunction restraining Georgia from carrying out its cruel laws. That body, in the case of *The Cherokee Nation vs. Georgia*, reluctantly decided the Indians did not constitute a foreign nation within the meaning of the Constitution and therefore had no right to bring suit before the Court.

The powerless Indians were now at the mercy of a helpless President and ruthless state officers who vied with each other in making life unpleasant for them. Payment of annuities was stopped, debts owed the Indians were declared cancelled, their lands were seized and their homes appropriated. Agents were sent among them to pit clan against clan and family against family in the hopes of breaking down tribal unity. When heartsick Christian missionaries among them protested these criminal acts they were sentenced to four years at hard labor as a reward for their pains. The clergymen's appeal to the higher authority of the Supreme Court gave the Indians a brief flurry of hope, for Chief Justice John Marshall held in the famous case of *Worcester vs. Georgia* that the Cherokee possessed the status of a "domestic dependent nation" under the protection of the federal government, and that Georgia had no right to molest them. This decision meant nothing, however, when Jackson held Marshall's opinion was too preposterous to be enforced. The stage was set for the final act in the sordid drama.

That was not long in coming. Chief Major Ridge, a wise leader since 1796, was by now convinced that factional pressures had so split the Cherokee that they were powerless to resist removal. Hence after twice forcing government agents to better their terms, he reluctantly signed the Treaty of New Echota in December, 1835. That document ceded all Cherokee lands to the United States in return for $5,600,000, guaranteed the Indians reimbursement for their improvements, and promised them free transportation to their new western homes. The majority renounced the agreement but realized it sealed their doom; now the United States could drive them from their homelands by force. For the next three years little bands straggled across the Mississippi, although the last did not depart until December, 1838, when troops were used to drive them west. About a quarter of the Indians perished in the cruel winter migration.

Georgia's example was imitated throughout the Southwest. Mississippi in 1830 and Alabama in 1832 extended their laws over all Indians within their borders and threatened to punish chiefs who tried to carry out the functions of their offices. The Indians fell easy prey to wily agents sent among them by Jackson. Those experienced land grabbers operated in the usual way: they sought out a few chiefs, bribed them into ceding all the tribe's lands, then forced the majority to accept and move beyond the Mississippi. The Choctaw succumbed in September, 1830, when a minority faction signed the Treaty of Dancing Rabbit Creek, giving up all eastern lands for a similar acreage in the West, annuities, moving expenses, and supplies. The remnant of the Creek tribe remaining in eastern Alabama accepted a similar agreement in March, 1832, and the Chickasaw followed with the Treaty of Pontotoc Creek in October of that year. The condition of their departure left the tribes divided and unable to adapt to life beyond the Mississippi.

During the next five years the members of the latter tribe drifted to their new homes, but the Choctaw and Creeks made more trouble. A provision in the Choctaw treaty allowing heads of families wishing to remain in the

East 640 acres each caused the difficulty with that tribe. By 1834 the 540 natives signifying their intention of staying held warrants entitling them to lands. Those "floating claims" attracted the attention of speculators, who descended upon the innocent Indians, bribed them into making false claims for more territory, and began a wholesale campaign designed to defraud the Indians. Within a few months one company amassed 1,280,000 acres; another land jobber secured 250 claims. A congressional commission which uncovered the whole sordid story soon sent the innocent Indian victims of white greed scurrying westward with nothing to show for their pains but an unpleasant experience.

The removal of the Creeks was even more disgraceful. Their treaty allowed each head of family to retain a half section which could either be sold or reserved for occupancy should the Indian decide to remain in the East. Surveys completed in December, 1833, showed the natives entitled to 2,000,000 acres; the remaining 5,000,000 acres formerly occupied by the tribe were thrown open to sale. This was an opportunity no speculator could resist—millions of acres of rich land in the hands of helpless Indians who could count on no protection from their wrecked tribal organization or an unsympathetic government. They swarmed from all over the South, those greedy land grabbers. The more honest cheated the natives of their lands by paying them in worthless bank notes, whipping them until they consented to sell, or buying when the natives were hopelessly drunk. The less scrupulous hired gangs of Indians to swear they owned lands that were not theirs, or set up stores selling only tobacco and whiskey where Indian landowners were encouraged to spend freely, then turn over their estates in payment. For months wholesale fraud went on until by 1835 the pitiful survivors were reduced to raiding settlements for food. That gave President Jackson his excuse; troops drove the last Alabama Creeks west at bayonet point.

Only one group remained in the South: the Seminole of Florida. Their presence had been resented for many years. Even before the United States secured that Spanish territory in 1821 wars had ravaged the Seminole country, encouraged by Negro slaves among the Indians who had escaped their masters and feared their freedom to be threatened, or by Georgia planters who hoped to close that escape route for their bondsmen. The Seminole were also stirred by the radical faction of the Creeks, the Red Sticks, who refused to accept the land cessions granted in the Treaty of Ft. Jackson. So turbulent was the situation there that in 1817 Andrew Jackson led an expedition into Spanish territory to subdue Pensacola and St. Marks, an episode known as the "First Seminole War."

Against this background of ill-feeling, the whites of Florida and Georgia lost no time in demanding that the Seminole surrender the reservation north of Lake Okeechobee that had been assigned them in 1823, charging that runaway slaves were being harbored there. In 1832 and 1833, minority factions were persuaded to sign treaties of cession and removal. The Indians, refusing to accept this fate, found a leader in Chief Osceola and took to the warpath in the "Second Seminole War." After six years of bloody fighting both sides were ready for a truce, the Seminole because they recognized an emerging humanitarianism among the American people as reaction to the heartlessness of the removal policy. But their hope of better treatment or at least delay in removal was in vain. Floridans wanted no Indian reservation in their territory and made it clear that they would be satisfied with nothing less than the extermination or migration of the entire tribe. Realizing their position, a band of more radical Seminole in July, 1839, fell on a detachment of dragoons on the Caloosahatchee River, killing many of them. This doomed hopes of an armistice. Atrocities multiplied on both sides as the war flamed anew. This time hostilities dragged on until 1842 when the last defeated band was driven across the Mississippi, or into the impenetrable depths of the Everglades. All the East was open to settlement; all the natives were rendered harmless in the distant lands of the Far West which were to be theirs "as long as trees grow and the waters run."

Long before the last embittered natives began their weary trek westward white settlers swarmed over the Southwest. The migration differed markedly from that to the Northwest; instead of being drawn from all parts of the United States and much of Europe the pioneers came from only one section: the seaboard states of the South Atlantic. That region sent its excess inhabitants to the frontier in such large numbers between 1815 and 1850 that its own population remained almost constant. By 1850, 40 per cent of all native-born South Carolinians then alive lived beyond the borders of their home state, 30 per cent of the North Carolinians, and 25 per cent of the Georgians. The remarkable exodus, which gave the Gulf Plains a strangely homogeneous population for a frontier area, was caused partly by unsatisfactory conditions in the Southeast, partly by the development of easily traveled routes between the two sections, and partly by the attractiveness of the western country toward which the pioneers turned their footsteps.

A major expelling force was the worn-out soil of the seaboard. Successive plantings of tobacco for more than a century, primitive agricultural methods, and the temptation normal in staple producing areas to "butcher" or "mine" the soil, left a monument of exhausted fields, gullied hillsides, and declining crops. Nor did the spread of cotton planting relieve the situation. While the older South momentarily benefited from a new plant that consumed existing minerals, the worn soils could not stand the abuse of repeated croppings long. That was especially the case as the cotton frontier spread over the hilly Piedmont, for high prices after the War of 1812 encouraged successive plantings, and the shallow humus soils were quickly washed away by the heavy southern rains once they were loosened by the plow. The whole country, one traveler complained, "is a scene of desolation that baffles description . . . farm after farm . . . worn out, washed and gullied; so that scarcely an acre could be found in a place fit for cultivation." Another commented upon the "dreary and uncultivated wastes, a barren and ex-

hausted soil, half-clothed negroes, lean and hungry stock, houses falling to
decay, and fences wind shaken and dilapidated.''

For a time, during the 1820s, southeastern planters tried to improve
their farms by adopting scientific methods; agricultural societies and farm
journals blossomed everywhere to tell farmers of improved plows, horizontal
furrowing, crop diversification, and fertilizers. The new hope was short-
lived, as most of the advice was based on inadequate information and failed
to improve fields worn beyond repair. At the end of the 1820s, when this
attempt at scientific agriculture proved a failure, a wave of despair swept
over the Southeast. One farm journal poet complained:

> No smiling pastures spread inviting here,
> But dry hot fields on ev'ry side appear.
> A sultry scene, a dismal waste, alas!
> Where man's great object is to kill the grass.

There was only one solution: trade the butchered lands of the East for the
virgin fields of the West. Thousands of farmers who reached that conclusion
swelled the population of the Gulf Plains.

Migration was made easier by the network of highways built by the
state and national governments in the years after 1815. Three roads led to
the Gulf Plains from the older South. Two, the Fall Line Road and the
Upper Road, converged at Columbus on the Chattahoochee River to form
the Federal Road to St. Stephens, Mobile, and Natchez. The third ran along
the Great Valley of the Appalachians to Knoxville where it divided, one
branch leading to Nashville and eventually on to Memphis, the other turning
southwest to Huntsville in the Tennessee Valley. From that junction a highway led settlers southward to the Black Warrior River valley while another
carried them west to Florence and the old Nashville-Natchez Road. An even
better route to southern Mississippi was provided in 1820 when Andrew
Jackson, as commander of the western army, opened the Military Road
between Florence and Lake Pontchartrain. The federal government was
responsible for another improvement, the Upper Federal Road across Alabama, which was authorized in 1833. Although all were only crude mud
tracks through the forest—bottomless quagmires in wet weather and rutted
horrors in dry—they provided sure if comfortless routes to important parts
of the Gulf Plains. Steamboats were also used by immigrants, for by 1820
they were ascending the Oconee to Milledgeville, the Tombigbee to Demopolis, and the Tennessee to Florence.

The magnet that drew men westward over those wilderness trails was
cotton land. This was rigidly defined by the natural conditions under which
cotton plants would thrive. One necessity, a long growing season with at
least 200 days between frosts, fixed the northern limit of the cotton belt at
a line extending from the northeast corner of North Carolina across northern
Georgia and Alabama, then sweeping northward to include western Tennessee. Beyond that point cotton could not be profitably produced except

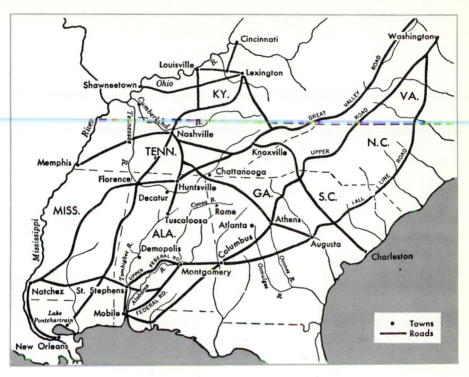

Settlement of the Gulf Plains, 1815–1850

in unusually favorable years, although the lowlands of the Tennessee River valley were an exception. On the south the boundary of the cotton belt was set by the autumn rainfall, for more than ten inches of precipitation during the fall interfered with the picking and ginning process.

Within that broad area the relative richness of the soil determined which lands should be absorbed by cotton-growing planters and which by corn-growing farmers. Pioneers moved first over the Georgia and Alabama Piedmont, a region of rolling hills and stiff red soils of average fertility, where inadequate subterranean drainage and the hilly countryside fostered rapid soil exhaustion. As gullied fields drove them on, frontier farmers found even less hospitable lands ahead. In northwestern Georgia and northern Alabama the Piedmont hills gave way to the rugged peaks of the Blue Ridge Mountains, the level reaches of the Coosa River valley, the ridges and narrow valleys of the mountainous Cumberland Plateau, and the gravelly wastes of the short-leaf pine belt. Only the Coosa Valley had the warm climate and deep limestone soil suitable to cotton growing, and there transportation difficulties stopped production. This upland region along the northern fringe of the cotton belt became a land of small farms occupied by yeoman farmers and poor whites who produced cereals for the larger plantations.

On either side of this unattractive area lay rich regions where plantations centered. One was the broad valley of the Tennessee River, a level plain fifteen miles wide where the calcareous limestone soil was fertile and deep. The other was the treeless Black Belt, which ran almost 300 miles across central Alabama and Mississippi. Its rotted-limestone earth, as productive as any in the South, supported magnificent plantations after pioneers overcame their prejudice against prairies. The southern edge of the Black Belt was bounded by a row of low hills, called the Pontotoc Ridge in Mississippi and the Chunnennuggee Ridge in Alabama, where the sandy loams were also extremely fertile and highly prized for cotton growing. Below this was a rugged red-soil belt of Red Hills, a country of varying soil richness that attracted both plantations and small farms. The Lime Sink area of Georgia, the Lime Hills of Alabama, and the Central Prairie of Mississippi were also suitable for plantations, especially the Central Prairie which resembled the Black Belt. The long-leaf pine country bordering the Gulf was less desirable; its gravelly soil, wire grass, and excessive rainfall combined to discourage most agricultural pursuits. That desolate region became the home of poor whites, small farmers, and cattle grazers.

Along the western edge of the Gulf Plains were two other regions that played an important role in the history of the Southwest. One was the forty-mile strip of Bluff Hills that ran through central Mississippi, an area so fertile that cotton planters sought land there despite the rugged character of the countryside. The other was the Mississippi Flood Plain, which stretched between the Gulf of Mexico and southern Missouri. That broad valley, formed by successive deposits of silt as the river flooded and receded, was among the richest areas in the United States. Although generally level except for the hills about Vicksburg and Natchez, the delta was avoided by early

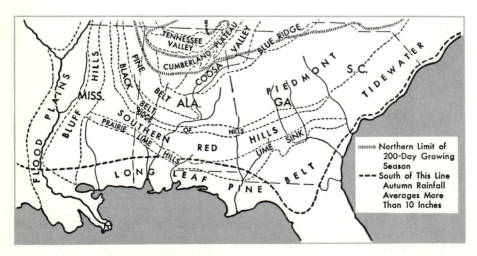

Soil Areas of the Gulf Plains

settlers who feared floods. Not until the 1840s when levees made life there reasonably safe was the region transformed into one of the South's prize agricultural areas. There, in the Tennessee Valley and in the Black Belt the large plantation system was most securely entrenched.

The prospect of finding such lands as these was one of the strongest forces driving men west in the years after 1815. In the vanguard, there as in the North, was the small farmer, driven from his eastern home by soil exhaustion. After selling his worn fields to a nearby planter whose large-scale methods allowed greater profits, he loaded his family and belongings on a wagon or two, and driving his livestock before him, began the trek westward. He timed his arrival for the early spring so he could girdle the trees and plant his first corn crop in April. By the time roasting ears were ready three months later he had built two square log cabins ten feet apart, connected by a covered passage where cooking was done during the hot months. Then, while his corn ripened, he cleared enough land to plant cotton the second year. If his farm was good, neighbors drifted in around him; within three or four years clearings dotted the wilderness and cotton exports were steadily increasing.

While the community was still in a primitive stage it was usually visited by a wealthy eastern planter seeking a favorable spot for settlement. That lofty individual probably owned a large plantation and many slaves in the East but he had decided to move, either because he was alert to the first signs of soil exhaustion in his old fields or because he recognized the chance for greater profits on the West's virgin land. His investment was too great, however, to risk any haphazard step; hence he was interested only in areas where pioneer farmers were testing the earth's fertility. When he found a likely site he either bought out several small frontiersmen or purchased adjacent land from the government, returned east to sell his old estate, and started to his new home with the elaborate retinue needed to move an entire plantation: several wagons filled with household goods, herds of livestock, a band of slaves marching together, and the planter's family in a horse-drawn buggy. Travelers along the Federal Road reported a constant stream of those migrating parties, moving westward by day and camping by the roadside at night.

On arriving at his newly purchased estate the planter directed his slaves into the many tasks needed to lay out a plantation; some were set to building log cabins that would serve the owner's family until a lordly frame house was constructed, others to clearing land and planting the first crop of cotton. As the remaining lands were cleared during the next few years the planter's profits steadily mounted, for his slave labor allowed him to extend his cultivated areas more rapidly than the small farmers around him, and his large-scale methods brought him a larger return on his investment. Profits were used to absorb his smaller competitors, one after the other, and to purchase slaves needed to operate their lands. Plantation expansion went on constantly, but most rapidly in periods of great prosperity or acute depression;

in good times high cotton prices favored the planter who specialized in that crop, in bad small farmers were less able to survive than their wealthier neighbors.

That process, repeated time and time again across the face of the Gulf Plains, explained the rapid expansion of the frontier. The plantation was a dynamic institution, constantly crowding out adjacent small farmers. As pioneers were displaced they moved west again, only to have planters reappear, buy out their lands, and send them on to new frontiers. An Alabama politician summed up the whole process when he complained: "Our small planters, after taking the cream off their lands, unable to restore them by rest, manures or otherwise, are going further west and south, in search of other virgin lands, which they may and will despoil and impoverish in like manner. Our wealthier planters, with greater means and no more skill, are buying out their poorer neighbors, extending their plantations, and adding to their slave force. The wealthy few, who are able to live on smaller profits, and to give their blasted fields some rest, are thus pushing off the many, who are merely independent." Slavery and the plantation system permitted wealth to perpetuate itself and combined to drive the less fortunate westward.

Expansion began as soon as the War of 1812 was over, spurred on by a combination of thirty-cent cotton, eastern lands worn thin by a generation of cotton planting, western territories newly cleared of Indians, and postwar prosperity, which sent a rush of farmers across western Georgia and Alabama in a "Great Migration" lasting until 1819. So numerous were the "come-outers" that they crowded the roads westward, some in wagons, some on horseback, some on foot. One traveler counted 4,000 persons plodding westward in nine days. Such was their demand for foodstuffs along the way that the price of corn rose from fifty cents to four dollars a bushel within a few months, and the supplies of bacon and salt pork were exhausted. Eastern newspapers did not seem to exaggerate when they mournfully predicted that within a decade the center of population would be beyond the mountains.

The Georgia Piedmont was engulfed first as population, dammed up behind the Ocmulgee River line for a generation, swept into each new block of Indian lands opened by cession, encouraged by the state's practice of granting 202½ acre plots free to those drawing lucky numbers at lotteries. The rapid growth of plantations there was illustrated by the increase in the number of slaves: from 14,064 in 1810 to 39,601 in 1820, 93,186 in 1830, 156,799 in 1840, and 232,193 in 1850. Others rushed into Alabama, lured by a burst of speculative activity. This began in March, 1817, when surveys of the ceded Choctaw and Cherokee lands were completed. These spelled opportunity for a group of influential Georgians who wanted to separate Alabama from Mississippi Territory, hoping then to monopolize the best lands and leadership roles in the new state. Their congressional tool was Senator George Tait of Georgia who piloted two bills through Congress in March, 1817, one authorizing the "Eastern Mississippi Territory" to form a government, the other creating the "Territory of Alabama." At the same time the ceded Chickasaw and Cherokee lands were assigned the land office at Huntsville for sale.

Only the honest commissioner of the federal land office, Josiah Meigs, stood in the way of a speculative spree, and he was soon pushed to one side by William H. Crawford of Georgia, who was then Secretary of the Treasury. Without even consulting Meigs, Crawford persuaded President Monroe to name his speculator-friends as officials of the new territory with authority to supervise land sales. So efficiently did they operate that surveyors gave them copies of plans and field notes long before they were made public, allowing them to purchase the best regions before they went on sale. Speculators even contrived to have these sales take place at Milledgeville, 150 miles from the area being settled, thus keeping actual settlers from attending and holding the bidding down. Not until they had secured the choice territories they wanted did they allow land offices to be opened at Catawba and Athens where small pioneers could buy what was left.

There were enough remaining to set loose an "Alabama Boom" of sizeable proportions. After 1817 hordes of farmers and would-be small speculators besieged the land offices at Huntsville, St. Stephens, and Catawba in such numbers that sales skyrocketed from 600,000 acres in 1816 to 2,278,045 three years later. At the Huntsville office alone returns totalled $5,500,000 in 1818. Bidding was so spirited that prices soared to $75 and even $100 an acre for good bottom lands and town sites. Tales of these fantastic sales brought an influx of speculators from all over the United States, bent on sharing the harvest. Their presence at Huntsville, where the prized Tennessee Valley lands were sold, accounted for sales that reached the amazing figure of $7,000,000 in 1818, the peak year. Even the wholesale engrossment of cotton land by jobbers failed to check migration; instead the nationwide excitement caused by the Alabama boom attracted even more settlers. One North Carolina planter wrote in 1817: "*The Alabama Fever* rages here with great violence and has carried off vast numbers of our citizens. I am apprehensive, if it continues to spread as it has done, it will almost depopulate the country."

By the close of 1819, when a serious panic slowed the westward march, 200,000 people lived in the Gulf Plains and one-half the nation's cotton was produced there. Western Georgia was comfortably filled, except for lands still occupied by Creeks and Cherokee. In Alabama one arm of settlement extended up the Tombigbee River as far as Demopolis, the head of steamboat navigation; another followed the Alabama River to Montgomery, a village laid out by speculators a short time before. From towns along those streams cotton was floated to Mobile in flat-bottomed barges or on primitive steamboats, to transform that sleepy Spanish port into a thriving American metropolis of 3,000 souls. Central Alabama gained less by the rush, partly because its water outlets were not satisfactory and partly because pioneers avoided the prairie lands of the Black Belt. A sprinkling of settlers who made their way west over the Great Valley Road from the Virginia and

Carolina back country were clustered about Tuscaloosa. Northern Alabama, where tempting lands of the Tennessee Valley beckoned settlers from Tennessee and Georgia, profited more. By 1820 most of the area's cotton country was under cultivation and a bustling commercial life developing at Tuscumbia and Decatur where cotton bales were stored until they could be floated over the Muscle Shoals rapids in periods of high water. In Mississippi the principal growth was about Natchez and along the Nashville-Natchez Road. Seventy-five thousand people, of whom 32,000 were slaves, lived there in 1820.

The "Great Migration" into the Gulf Plains made statehood possible for both Mississippi and Alabama. Mississippi acted first, for its concentrated population was able to apply greater pressure, and in 1817 entered the Union; Alabama followed two years later. Both adopted constitutions reflecting the leveling influence of the frontier. Neither required property for voting; both granted the franchise to all male whites residing there one year. Each made the legislature supreme over the governor—whose veto of any act could be overridden by a simple majority vote—and vested in that elective body power to appoint most state officials including judges. Representation in the assemblies was apportioned on the basis of free white population, thus giving the planter no advantage over the small farmer in government matters. The liberalism of the constitutions served as an additional inducement to settlers.

The migratory stream continued to flow through the 1820s, although in diminished volume. The few Indian cessions during the decade meant that most immigrants would direct their footsteps to the already settled areas of northern and southern Alabama and southwestern Mississippi, where population increased from 200,000 to 445,000. That many newcomers were planters was indicated by the mounting number of slaves: from 31 to 38 per cent of the Alabama population. Many small farmers displaced by growing plantations sought homes in two new regions opened during the 1820s. Those moving to Florida when that area was secured from Spain in 1821 were destined to disappointment; sandy soil and the Seminole War soon dashed their hopes of bountiful crops of cotton, sugar, coffee, oranges, almonds, olives, silk, and other semitropical products. Those entering western Tennessee were more fortunate, for rich alluvial soils produced large cotton crops. Settlement began in 1819 when speculators under Andrew Jackson laid out Memphis. During the rest of the decade the back country around that well-placed commercial town filled in rapidly.

The trickle of immigrants moving west during the 1820s swelled to flood proportions again in the prosperous 1830s. Prices and profits were fantastic during those boom years; returns of 35 per cent yearly were common, while one planter who equipped a plantation at a cost of $15,000 marketed a $50,000 crop two years later. Such fortunes proved an irresistible magnet, drawing settlers westward to the Indian lands obtained during Jackson's presidency. Some swept over the Creek and Cherokee lands of northern Georgia and eastern Tennessee to lay out farms and commercial towns: Atlanta, Rome, and Chattanooga. Others showed tardy appreciation for Alabama's Black Belt, bidding so enthusiastically for its lands that prices rose to $35 an acre. Still more carried the cotton frontier across central Mississippi, filling the Black Belt and northern Bluff Hills, and pushing on to unsettled portions of western Tennessee. A Huntsville newspaper correspondent, watching the migration, wrote in 1833: "It would seem as if North and South Carolina were pouring forth their population by swarms. Perhaps I have gone by in the Creek nation, over 3,000 persons, all emigrating, including negroes, of course. The fires of their encampments made the woods blaze in all directions." During the decade cotton exports from New Orleans doubled, while those from Mobile increased threefold.

By 1840 the boundaries of the cotton kingdom were marked out; only the fringes and a few bypassed wilderness islands remained to be settled. They were filled during the next twenty years as transportation improvements opened isolated areas. One was the Coosa Valley of western Georgia where small farmers were gradually replaced by cotton planters after railroads penetrated that region. Another was in east-central Mississippi, a rich-soil country formerly given over to cattle grazing due to the distance from water transportation. More important was the rush of planters to the Mississippi Flood Plains after 1842 when devastating floods brought home the need of cooperative efforts to protect the region. County supervisors were named to collect contributions, build levees, drain flooded areas, and convert the delta into a tempting agricultural country. The excellent silt soil soon attracted large planters, until by 1850 the Flood Plains rivaled the Black Belt in the size of holdings and concentration of slaves. By that time the fully settled Southwest produced nearly three quarters of the nation's cotton.

The social order created by this expansion differed from that developing in the Northwest at the same time. The Lake Plains by 1850 was a land of farmers producing a diversified list of cereal crops and livestock, a variety that marked the beginning of the expansion that would diversify the region's economy. This opportunity was denied the South by the rigidly drawn class lines that stratified the social order; a few fortunate individuals controlled most of the best land, and the concept of equality was in bad repute. Worst of all for the future, the deep South remained predominantly rural, lagging woefully behind in the industrial growth that after 1815 marked the emergence of the United States from its underdeveloped era. Not that planters lived in a precapitalist society but the glamor of cotton production was to blame; some 5 per cent of the Negro slaves in the South in 1850 did work in factories, and worked very well indeed, but cotton producers could outbid manufacturers for Negro labor, driving production costs to unprofitable heights. Nor would whites enlist as factory workers when all harbored the dream of becoming planters. The high profits of cotton growing in the Gulf Plains doomed the deep South to an agrarian economy that ran contrary to the national trend.

Within the social order that emerged under these conditions, class lines were tightly drawn. At the top of the social pyramid were the few great planters—never numbering more than 46,000—who owned one or more plantations, fifty or more slaves, and collectively three quarters of the wealth of the south. Those "cotton snobs" lived pleasure-packed lives; they wintered in great white-pillared houses at Montgomery or Mobile or Natchez, summered at popular watering places, read the best English literature or such polite native journals as *The Southern Literary Messenger*, dabbled in law and politics, and indulged in a constant round of parties, fox hunts, and horse racing. Those who sought a serious end in life served as justices of the peace, members of their state legislature, congressmen, or military leaders; those were the respectable professions alone acceptable in that highly stratified society. The majority were content to manage their estates or pursue pleasure with an avidity that suggested boredom.

They were supported by the several plantations that each owned in the Black Belt or Flood Plains. These estates contained at least 1,000 acres and 100 slaves—that being an efficient size which combined the economies of large-scale production with the compactness needed to keep workers from wasting too much time going to and from the fields—and were operated by a hired overseer. Dominating each plantation was the owner's great frame house with its spacious porches and classical colonnades. Around it were clustered the outbuildings, storage sheds, and log slave cabins. Near at hand was the cotton gin, a board structure set on pillars with a central hub reaching through to the ground level. Horses driven in a circle transmitted power to the gin on its raised platform, while the elevation allowed raw cotton to be fed directly into the machine from wagons. The cleaned lint was blown into another bin that reached to the ground in the rear. Close by was a bailing press, also operated by horsepower, where fibres were pressed into bales of standardized size and weight for shipping.

Most plantation overseers divided their crop about equally between cotton and corn, largely because slaves could plant and care for twice as much cotton as they could pick. Hence cotton acreage was determined by the picking capacity of the field hands and enough land was put into other crops to keep them employed the rest of the year. That was especially necessary as most of the planters' capital investment was in their slaves; their return depended on the efficiency with which the slaves were employed. For that reason planters often divided them into gangs under minor overseers, with one doing nothing but hoeing, another plowing, and the like. In that form the plantation system was one of the most efficient devised in the history of agriculture. Yet it depended for its success on exploitive methods, as neither the slaves nor overseers were interested in preserving the soil's fertility. Large-scale methods allowed plantation owners to buy out less effective neighbors, but doomed them to hard times once the initial fertility of their fields declined.

Influential as the great planters were, they were far outbalanced numerically by the social group next below them, the "one-horse" planters who operated their own estates with the help of from one to twenty bonded servants. About 20 percent of the southern whites were this class. Most of them lived hard lives on the less fruitful lands, either supervising their own Negroes or working beside the slaves in the fields. Their homes were log cabins or unkempt frame dwellings, their pleasures few, and their cultural interests confined to the bombastic outpourings of local newspaper editors whose concern was the moral and mental delinquency of rival publishers rather than conveying news. This miserable existence was forced upon the small planters by their all-consuming ambition: their one object was to multiply acres and slaves until they crossed the gulf into the planter class. A few saw their dream come true, but far more spent their lives in the hopeless pursuit of an unattainable ideal.

The middle-class group did much to popularize slavery among the non-slave owners who made up the bulk of the South's population. Small planters might spend their days in blue jeans and boots, sweating at the plow beside their black servants while their homespun-garbed wives tended to the dairying or labored over a spinning wheel, but on Sunday or election day they were transformed into the envied upper class in each Southern town. Clad in the distinctive broadcloth coat and high hat of the aristocracy, they voiced their opinions with an assurance becoming their exalted station. They naturally defended slavery, for only the perpetuation of the institution would allow them to become great planters, and their views helped win the masses of the people to support the system.

The small and large planters together, with their families, constituted about 23 per cent of the southern white population. The remaining 77 per cent were non-slave-holders. Most were yeomen farmers or herders whose tiny holdings dotted areas not suitable to plantation agriculture or the mountainous country, the pine barrens, and the northern and southern fringes of the cotton belt. There they lived in crude log cabins, dressed in dejected woolen hats, tow shirts, and blue jean breeches held up by a single "gallus," and spent their days in the backbreaking task of trying to scratch a living from a stubborn soil. Their appearance was deceiving, for most were earnest, honest folk. Pleasure and culture were equally unknown in their dreary lives. Some worked endlessly toward the day when they could buy a slave and begin the slow climb upward toward a position in the great planter class. Although they were the principal victims of the slave system, they were often among the institution's most violent defenders, believing its perpetuation would make their dreams of a planter's life come true.

Below the yeoman farmer in the South's social scale were poor whites and herdsmen. The poor whites—"crackers" or "sandhillers"—were scattered in small communities through the poorest Southern lands: Georgia's pine barrens, Mississippi's sandy-woods section, Alabama's piney forests, and the worn-out soils abandoned by cotton planters. Most of them made a pretence of farming, but they depended for food less on their weed-choked fields than on hogs that cared for themselves and on wild game. The herders, often descendants of Scotch-Irish frontiersmen familiar with tending livestock, also followed a lesiurely rather than a compulsive pursuit of wealth. They too appeared to be both shiftless and indolent, but they were part of the economic backbone of the region. They raised perhaps one third of the nation's hog supply, providing food for the deficit in the plantation economy. Herders and poor whites defended slavery, partly because they were frequently the victims of the petty thievery endemic in a slave society and partly because they realized that this barrier alone kept them from the bottom of the social scale.

That place was reserved for the slaves, who in 1850 numbered 1,841,000 for the lower South as a whole, as compared to 2,137,000 whites. Most were taken to the Gulf Plains by their masters, although a slave trade between the older seaboard states, where an excess supply existed, and the newer states of the Southwest developed as early as the 1820s. The majority worked as field hands on cotton plantations where they were fairly well treated, for owners soon found that workers declined in efficiency when discontented. Yet this modicum of security hardly compensated for the low living standard, lack of educational opportunity, and complete absence of individual freedom that slavery forced upon them. Slaves, however, developed complex and subtle mechanisms to control their own destinies, learn skills, and maintain family unity.

The southern social structure built upon a mudsill of bonded labor, was fully developed by 1850. Differing radically from that of the Northwest in basic crops, agricultural methods, form of labor, and social philosophy, the unique society reared in the South helped create the sectional conflicts that plagued the nation through the first half of the nineteenth century and eventually found expression in civil war.

The New West:
A National Problem
1815-1850

The peopling of the trans-Appalachian frontier brought the nation face to face with a troublesome problem. How could regions increasingly committed to economic specialization—the industrializing Northeast, the cotton-growing South, and the small-farm West—continue to coexist in harmony? An internal trade that would accentuate their interdependency was an obvious answer. Raw cotton for the Northeast's textile mills could come from the South; food for southern slaves from the West; manufactured goods for western and southern farmers from the Northeast. But such a trade depended on adequate transportation facilities, and these were far from sufficient to foster the interchange needed to keep sectional peace. Here was a challenge to American inventors. And here, too, was a supreme test for the nation's statesmen. Could they devise a formula that would provide each region with the governmental aid needed to support its own economic system without harming the economy of its neighbors? These were problems to test the wisdom of a Solomon, yet they must be solved amidst the mounting emotionalism of a country drifting toward civil war.

They stemmed from the West's mounting importance in the national economy. By the 1820s a tier of surplus-producing zones extended westward from the Appalachians to the Mississippi and beyond. Farthest south, stretching across the Gulf states from Georgia to Louisiana, was the cotton belt where the plantation system required the importation of some foods and most manufactured goods. North of this, in Kentucky, Tennessee, south Ohio, Indiana, and Illinois, corn and tobacco vied as the leading crops; much of the nation's tobacco and 56 per cent of its corn was grown there. Still farther north was a zone where wheat was king; northern Ohio and Indiana, southern Michigan and Wisconsin by 1840 produced one third of the country's supply; Ohio alone grew 17,000,000 bushels that year. Each of these areas must sell its surpluses to survive, and each needed to import items that it could not produce itself. Here was a challenge to the Northeast and South, each needing foodstuffs and each with a product to be sold. Which could capture the major share of the West's valuable trade?

The accident of technological progress gave the South an initial advantage, for the rapid evolution of the steamboat transformed the Mississippi River into an artery that united the South and West. The conquest of the western waterways began in 1811 when a 371-ton vessel, the *New Orleans*, was launched at Pittsburgh and sent off to New Orleans, with instructions to steam back up the river at each town to show that it could stem the current. By 1825, seventy-five steamboats plied the Mississippi and Ohio rivers, and by 1840, 187. Because the West frowned on monopoly, all were operated by individuals or small syndicates, creating a highly competitive system that lowered freight rates until the hundred pounds of produce that cost $5 for the New Orleans-Louisville trip by keelboat cost only $2 in 1820 and 25 cents in 1840.

Moreover steamboats could reach even the most remote parts of the Mississippi and Ohio valleys. Builders constantly increased their power and decreased their draft; the light, high-pressure engines that they developed were so powerful that their rhythmic strokes shook the entire vessel while the shallow hulls, surmounted by two or three upper decks, drew from two to four feet of water while carrying two tons of freight for every ton of boat. "Engines on a raft with $11,000 worth of jig-saw work," wags called them, but they could navigate anywhere; some captains insisted that their ships needed only a heavy dew. So efficient were they that by the 1830s every hamlet on a western creek deep enough to wade in dreamed of becoming a river port—and usually succeeded. Typical was Delphi, on the upper Wabash, which persuaded the captain of a light-draft vessel to make the attempt during high water in the spring of 1834. When the ship ran aground a few miles below town the whole citizenry turned out, drafted twenty yoke of oxen into use, and literally dragged the little steamboat through the mud to its destination. From that time on Delphi was, by its own boast, a "river port" directly connected with New Orleans.

Time soon showed that these efforts were wasted, for the steamboat only intensified the West's dependence on the East. The more westerners sold to the South, the more they must buy of eastern manufactures, expensively carried across the Appalachians by wagon freight. Too, steamboats were subject to the whims of the weather, operating largely in the high-water periods in spring and fall, thus glutting the New Orleans markets and driving prices down. If the mountains could be bridged, the city at the eastern terminus of that bridge would monopolize the West's lucrative trade. This was the incentive that plunged the seaboard commercial centers—Boston, New York, Philadelphia, and Baltimore—into a quarter-century of experimentation and competition that significantly altered the West's role in the national economy.

New York gained the first advantage. Stretching westward from the Hudson River was the Mohawk Valley, a natural pass through the mountains rising no more than 578 feet above sea level, and leading directly to the Great Lakes. Why not convert this into a waterway that would divert trade to New York? The Erie Canal, authorized by the state legislature in 1817 and opened in October, 1825, cost the state $7,000,000 but seldom had a better investment been made. Within nine years toll collections had paid for all costs, while the lowered freight rates—from $100 to $15 for the 363 miles between Buffalo and New York—funneled much of the West's commerce through New York City. Farms bordering the route doubled and quadrupled in value, undeveloped areas on either side boomed as feeder canals were built, and the whole state prospered.

The Erie's success set New York's rivals—Boston, Philadelphia, and Baltimore—to clamoring for their own western outlets. Boston, isolated by the Berkshire range that made canals prohibitively expensive, elected to pin its hopes on a railroad, even though that newfangled device was still in its early experimental stages. Two were chartered—the Boston and Worcester in 1830 and the Western Railroad Corporation in 1833—and by 1842 the rail link between Boston and Albany was operating. Not with outstanding success, however, for different gauge track required the transshipment of freight at West Stockbridge and Worcester, but still Boston was connected with the West.

Philadelphia's task was only slightly easier. In 1826 the Pennsylvania Legislature authorized the Pennsylvania Portage and Canal Company to begin construction, a monumental task that was completed eight years later. No better illustration could be found of the seaboard cities' eagerness for western trade than the cumbersome and impractical result. Goods destined for the West left Philadelphia on the horse cars of the Philadelphia and Columbia Railroad, were transshipped to canal barges at Columbia on the Cumberland River, followed the canal along the Juniata River through 108 locks to Hollidaysburg, were loaded on cars that hauled them ten miles up a series of inclined planes, coasted down to Johnstown, and were transferred again to canal boats that carried them the last 104 miles to the Ohio River. Those 320 miles cost $10,000,000 to build, but no one questioned the expenditure if western trade could be tapped.

Baltimore faced a still more difficult problem, for any waterway would have to scale a 2,754-foot elevation. Undaunted, the city's merchants chartered the Chesapeake and Ohio Canal Company, raised the millions needed, and began digging in 1827. Ten years later only a hundred miles had been built; when abandoned in 1850 the project had cost $11,000,000 and reached no farther than Cumberland at the base of the mountains. Nor was a second project—the Baltimore and Ohio Railroad—much more successful. The practicality of rail transporation had scarcely been tested in 1827 when building began, but by 1831 the tracks had reached Frederick and profits were sufficient to purchase three locomotives to replace the horse cars used at first. Litigation and financial troubles slowed construction, but in 1842 the railroad entered Cumberland and during the next decade crossed the mountains. Baltimore, like its rivals, had its connection with the West.

Scarcely had these projects been launched than the canal fever swept the western states. If the interior regions were to benefit from these outlets, they must be connected with the waterways that fed into the New York and Pennsylvania trade routes. Every list of commodity prices in the local press made this clear; corn that sold for 20 cents a bushel in Columbus or Indianapolis fetched 50 cents on the Ohio River. Farmers needed only a pencil and paper to realize what this meant: an additional profit of $18 a year on every acre they planted, of $2,840 on every quarter-section farm, of $408,960 on every township. Canals would pay for themselves a thousand times over as well as offering growers a choice of markets—in the East over the Erie or Pennsylvania outlets, or the South via the Mississippi River.

Ohio, nearest the Erie waterway, led the way in 1825 by authorizing two canals: the Ohio Canal which would use the Scioto, Muskingum, and Cuyahoga rivers to cross the state from Portsmouth to Cleveland, and the Miami and Erie Canal to follow the Miami River between Cincinnati and Toledo. Despite labor shortages, the ravages of malaria, and periodic shortages of cash, 2,000 workers labored for the next years, living in crude shantytowns and braving long hours in unhealthy swamps for the princely pay

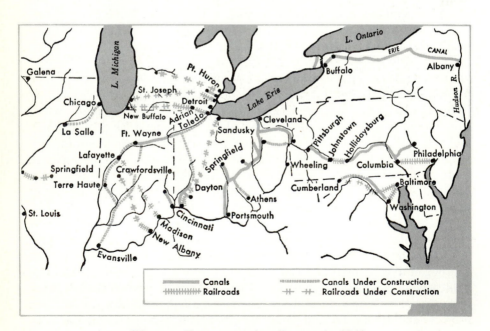

Western Transportation Routes in 1840

of $15 a month. The Ohio Canal was opened in 1833, the Miami and Erie a year later as far as Dayton where work ended until federal funds rescued the project a decade later. By this time small feeder canals connected much of the backcountry with these waterways, and thus with eastern or southern markets.

Indiana's grandiose plans dwarfed those of Ohio. These began modestly enough in 1832 when work started on a canal between Ft. Wayne and La-fayette to link the Wabash and Miami rivers, but not until 1836 was public sentiment ready to undertake a program that would benefit all the state. By that time the success of the Erie system, the tales of booming real-estate values in Ohio as the network there neared completion, and the availability of money in an inflationary economy had swept aside all reason. The Indiana Internal Improvement Act was a venture into fantasyland: a grid of canals and railroads and highways connecting virtually every hamlet in the state with the outside world at a cost of $13,000,000. This was one sixth of the total wealth of the state, but no one doubted the wisdom of borrowing such a sum, confident that tolls would retire the entire debt within a few years. Of this elaborate system, only the 458-mile long Wabash and Erie Canal was destined for completion, and that not until 1854.

Illinois plunged just as recklessly. The first phase—a canal between the Illinois River and Lake Michigan—was perfectly feasible, but no sooner was work begun in 1836 than every corner of the state began clamoring for similar favors. The resulting Internal Improvement Act adopted in January, 1837, dwarfed even the Indiana bill in utter impracticability: completion of the Illinois and Michigan Canal, 1,300 miles of railroads crisscrossing the state in every direction, a host of lesser lines connecting out-of-the-way villages, and even $200,000 for each county that was too remote to share in the largess. The 400,000 inhabitants of Illinois had been committed to an esti-mated expenditure of $10,500,000—a sum that had grown to $15,000,000 by the time the bubble burst with only one railroad—the Northern Cross from Quincy to Danville—advanced beyond the grading stage. Eventually this was completed in 1842 while the canal, after being taken over by creditors, was opened to traffic in 1848.

Even the new state of Michigan was infected with the internal-improve-ments virus. No sooner had statehood in 1837 removed federal restrictions on finances than a Board of Internal Improvements was authorized to borrow $5,000,000 to build three railroads—the Michigan Southern from Monroe to New Buffalo, the Michigan Central from Detroit to St. Joseph, and the Michigan Northern from Port Huron to Grand Rapids—as well as a number of canals and roads. By 1840 when financial troubles ended construction not one of these roads was half-way completed. Sadly the legislature disposed of its still-to-be-built canals, turned the roadbed of the Michigan Northern Railroad into a highway, and launched a half-hearted effort to raise funds to continue the remaining railways.

Underlying these giddy spending sprees by the western states was the easy money available during the inflationary 1830s. Any state launching an internal improvements program had only to issue bonds; these were readily marketable by New York bankers and British investment houses—that of Baring Brothers was most prominent—to wealthy English buyers who were happily unaware that state securities were backed by nothing more than a flimsy credit structure and could be repudiated at any time. So eagerly were they purchased that by 1835, $66,000,000 in English capital had been invested in the United States, and by 1837 another $108,000,000 had been added. The inflationary impact of these sums was multiplied by a vast increase in the domestic money supply. In those days any bank chartered by a state was allowed to issue its own currency, usually without proper supervision to assure adequate specie backing. Amidst the heady prosperity of the 1830's all did so; between 1832 and 1836 the volume of money in circulation sky-rocketed from $59,000,000 to $140,000,000. This encouraged wild speculation, not only by states on internal improvements, but in every form of investment. Much went into land along the frontiers; government sales that had averaged less than 4,000,000 acres a decade leaped to 38,000,000 between 1835 and 1837. Speculators were so active in laying out "town sites" in the West that one legislator seriously proposed setting aside two acres in each township for farming. Spending was getting out of hand; the time was ripe for a major crash.

That came with sickening suddenness in the spring of 1837 when tightened English credit forced southern cotton brokers, then the mercantile firms that handled their produce, then the banks that financed the traders, to face the realities of the situation. Their answer was to suspend specie payments on the bank notes that sustained the speculative bubble, then close their doors. By the close of 1837 half the Northeast's business establishments were bankrupt, unemployed workers begged for bread in every city, and Horace Greeley's *New York Tribune* was urging the poor to "Fly, scatter through the country, go to the Great West, anything rather than remain here."

His advice was sound—for the moment—for the full impact of the Panic of 1837 was not felt beyond the Appalachians until the autumn of 1839. Then the collapse came, and in exaggerated form. For the next two years prices slid downward, until by the end of 1841 flour sold at $2.50 a barrel, wheat at 40 cents a bushel, and corn at 25—prices below the cost of production. One by one banks closed their doors, until not one remained open in all the West. Their collapse plunged the states that had chartered them into financial chaos, for all had invested heavily in the banks' stocks, and all were hopelessly overcommitted with their internal improvement projects. The West awakened from its speculative spree with nothing but burdensome debts to show for its rosy dreams: Ohio owed its creditors more than $15,570,000, Indiana almost $15,000,000, Illinois a like sum, and Michigan some $5,000,000. These were impossible sums for thinly settled, impoverished states with no industrial resources. Why, westerners asked themselves, should they pay ruinous taxes solely for the benefit of wealthy easterners or Europeans who had loaned them money to build their now-stagnating internal improvements? In 1841 and 1842 nine states announced that they would pay no more interest on their debts, while others—including Michigan, Indiana, and Pennsylvania—repudiated portions of their obligations entirely. In all British investors lost some $100,000,000 in these ill-fated ventures.

Prospects for western farmers seemed dark as the decade of the 1840s dawned: an oppressive debt load that meant increased taxes, half-finished roads and canals and railroads that would never be completed, hopes of competitive markets that would have elevated prices forever shattered. If they could have peered into the future they would have taken heart, for the internal improvements already completed were to justify themselves within a remarkably short time by lowering the cost of imports, raising the price of exports, increasing real-estate values, and stimulating immigration. Wheat that sold for 20 cents a bushel in central Ohio or Indiana before canals were built brought 50 cents now, while the price of coffee, tea, sugar, salt, and other necessities was cut in half. More favorable economic conditions attracted immigrants; the population in counties touching the Indiana canals increased fivefold between 1835 and 1840, in those adjacent to the Illinois and Michigan Canal fortyfold. Other western regions grew more slowly; population increases near the Wabash and Erie Canal reached 400 per cent in the decade after it was opened, while the rest of the state gained at the rate of only 200 per cent. Westerners might grumble at debts and taxes, but the benefits they enjoyed were not insignificant.

This despite the fact that the internal improvements had not effected the commercial revolution anticipated. Western farmers did have three export routes available by 1835—south to New Orleans, east over the Pennsylvania system to Philadelphia, or northeast via the Erie canal to New York—but shipping costs varied so greatly that their choice was limited. To carry a ton of goods a mile by canal barge cost 1½ cents, by railroad 2½ cents, by lake steamer from 2 to 4 cents, and by river steamboat from ½ to 1½ cents. This differential, moreover, was accentuated by heavier transshipment costs on the eastern and northeastern outlets. Seemingly the result would be to funnel most goods, particularly bulky or heavy produce, southward to New Orleans.

Instead the newly built canals tended to divide the West into two trading areas, each shipping to its most profitable market. South of the Old National Road, where corn and its by-products were the principal staples, trade continued to follow the Mississippi route. North of this line the bulk of the exports flowed toward the Northeast via Lake Erie steamboats and the Erie Canal, deterred from using the southern outlet by the high transportation costs on the Ohio and Indiana canals. The result was shown in the percentage of western exports moving to the South, Northeast, and East:

		Volume Shipped	Percentage South	Percentage Northeast	Percentage East
Wheat	1835	150,000 bushels	17	83	—
	1840	2,000,000 bushels	2	97	1
Flour	1835	400,000 barrels	70	20	5
	1840	800,000 barrels	53	40	7
Corn	1835	1,000,000 bushels	98	2	—
	1840	1,000,000 bushels	98	2	—
Pork	1835	200,000 barrels	100	—	—
	1840	300,000 barrels	60	12	10

Obviously canal and road building before 1840 wrought no trade revolution in the West, nor did it alter significantly the sectional alignment that had persisted for a generation. Instead internal improvements fostered the growth of the northern areas of the New West, allowed the Northeast to make some inroads in the commercial monopoly earlier enjoyed by the South, and accentuated the interdependence of the three sections.

The boom-bust cycle of the 1830s that underlay the West's economic evolution had still another effect on the region, this one much to the liking of its inhabitants. For some time they had been complaining about the land system; the Land Law of 1820 which governed disposal of the public domain seemed advantageous enough—a settler could buy as few as 80 acres at a minimum price of $1.25 an acre—but it failed to check speculators from bidding the price beyond the reach of pioneers or from monopolizing the best sites. These objections reached a crescendo in the early years of the decade when the speculative fever sent land prices skyrocketing; they were renewed in a different tone after the Panic of 1837 when the $100 in specie needed to buy a farm was far beyond the reach of the average pioneer. Why, westerners asked, should the government exact such an exhorbitant sum from men who were willing to risk their lives to transform the wilderness into income-producing property that would benefit the entire nation? A land system designed to stimulate expansion rather than enrich speculators and the government was called for.

What the West wanted—and demanded—was a measure legalizing retroactive pre-emption: a law that would authorize a frontiersman to "squat" on the public site that pleased him, make certain improvements, and then be allowed to purchase at the minimum price without fear of being outbid by a speculator when the land came up for auction. This had long been a common practice—from one half to two thirds of the settlers in any new region were normally "squatters"—but the Panic of 1837 threatened to disrupt the whole system. Those who had not been able to accumulate the cash needed to bid for their farms at the public sales had in the past borrowed money from local banks at from 8 to 10 per cent interest; now the specie required for payment was obtainable only from "loan sharks" who bought the improved farm in their own names, then sold it back to its occupier on credit with interest charges of from 30 to 40 per cent a year. These ruinous practices would be ended if the settler was allowed to pre-empt the property that he was improving.

So westerners insisted, but easterners and southerners had other ideas. In their eyes, the public domain was the common property of all Americans and should be a continuing source of revenue; to dole out land to the "lawless rabble"—trespassers on the public domain—who lived along the frontiers would not only harm the nation's financial structure but unduly speed western expansion. Why, they asked, should Congress penalize the South and East by squandering their commonly held property and encouraging their citizens to leave factories and plantations by the promise of virtually free land? Better to maintain high land prices for the benefit of both the treasury and the national economy.

Westerners obviously faced an uphill battle to win a pre-emption act from Congress, but the end was worth the cost. In 1838, and again in 1840, bills allowing squatters already living on the public domain to pre-empt their lands were manipulated through House and Senate. This was encouraging but not enough; only a clearcut statement that all future squatters would be allowed to buy at the minimum price would satisfy the West. Such was the state of eastern and southern sentiment that such a bill seemed a remote possibility.

That one was adopted was due less to changing sentiment among easterners and southerners than to the maneuvers of office-hungry politicians in both the Whig and Democratic parties. The election of 1840 set the chain of events in motion. The Whigs, whose support came largely from northeastern industrialists, southern planters, and western mercantile leaders, captured the White House by parading their candidate, William Henry Harrison, as a coon-skinned, cider-guzzling frontiersman who would champion the cause of workers and farmers and pioneers rather than the upper classes he really represented. Knowing this, the Democrats decided to smoke Harrison and his cohorts into the open. In December, 1840, Democrat Thomas Hart Benton of Missouri introduced in the Senate a "Log Cabin Bill" authorizing all settlers on the public domain to build a cabin, make improvements, and purchase a quarter-section of land when it went on sale at $1.25 an acre. The Senate acted favorably two months later, with thirty-one Democrats voting "aye" and seventeen Whigs and two eastern Democrats "nay," but the measure passed too late for the House to act.

The Whigs, who controlled both houses of the new Congress that met in June, 1841, seemed highly unlikely to support pre-emption, but again the politics of necessity prevailed. Their legislative program was designed to placate two groups of their supporters; they promised a higher tariff wanted by northeastern manufacturers and the distribution of certain federal funds among the states to please southern planters. A nose-count soon showed that they could muster too few votes for their measures without help from western congressmen; this meant buying their support by more liberal land laws. The omnibus bill that finally passed in September, 1841, was a complex measure that related tariff, distribution, and land—but that included just the pre-emption provision that westerners wanted. Pioneer farmers now could settle where they wished, make a few improvements, and let the land pay for itself by selling their surpluses for the two or three years before it went on sale.

Westerners were delighted but their appetite for a liberalized land policy was only whetted. Why not the next logical step: granting free land to actual settlers who would improve their property? Why not reward those who gambled their futures to benefit the national economy by bringing the wilderness into use with the 160 acres that they needed? At first glance such a proposal seemed doomed at the outset; easterners and southerners would never favor squandering the public domain on the wastrels who lived on the fringes of settlement. Southerners, who had traditionally favored cheaper lands now changed their minds; they wanted high land prices to keep the treasury full so the tariff could be reduced. They were awakening to the fact that the rapid advance of the frontier threatened the plantation system to which they were committed. Further expansion of the cotton belt was limited by the rugged Ozark Plateau, the Indian Territory in Oklahoma, and the arid lands of Texas. No such barriers stood in the way of a northern advance across Iowa, Kansas, and Nebraska, all assured perpetual freedom by the Missouri Compromise. Liberal land laws would only multiply the number of free states, while the slave states remained static. They must be defeated.

This about-face was matched by a reversal of the Northeast's attitude. Industrialists there, traditionally opposed to cheap lands as a threat to their labor supply, increasingly recognized that every person who went west was a potential customer for their manufactured goods, every western enterprise a possible area for the investment of their surplus capital. They no longer needed to worry about a labor supply, for the flood of immigration from Ireland in the wake of the Potato Famine there assured an inexhaustible pool on which to draw. The growth of the West was no longer to be feared, but favored.

This view was supported by eastern wage-earners as they listened to the new breed of social reformers who rose to prominence during the 1840s. The message preached by these spokesmen was irresistible: low wages and miserable working conditions would persist as long as large numbers of workers competed for jobs. Only by draining away the surplus would employers be forced to pay higher wages and provide proper care for their employees. The most prominent of these spokesmen was George Henry Evans, a humanitarian long associated with bettering the lot of laborers, who in 1844 founded the National Reform Association to agitate for a liberal land policy. Within two years the association had branches in eight states, numbered such influential publicists as Horace Greeley of the *New York Tribune* among its members, and was winning the ears of politicians.

Workers, reformers, and industrialists agreed that the answer to the nation's problems was a Homestead Law offering free farms to settlers.

Westerners agreed heartily, for during the 1840s pre-emption was demonstrated to be less than the panacea anticipated. Speculators still monopolized the best lands by hiring armies of squatters to occupy choice spots or prospective town sites. Loan sharks still exacted excessive interest from farmers who had not saved enough to pay the minimum price when their lands went on sale. Western farmers, eastern industrialists, and the workers in the seaboard factories all agreed that these evils would persist until a Homestead Act was adopted; they were joined by abolitionists who saw that small farms created by such a law would block the expansion of the plantation system.

When Homestead emerged as a legislative issue in the middle 1840s sectional lines were not yet clearly drawn; the West was enthusiastic, the Northeast uncertain but increasingly interested, the New York-Pennsylvania region opposed, and the South divided with the Mississippi Valley in favor and the seaboard against. The first Homestead Bill was introduced in January, 1846, by Felix Grundy McConnell of Alabama; others followed regularly, usually sponsored by Andrew Johnson of Tennessee. None attracted national attention; not until 1850 did Congress discuss the issue, and not until 1852 was a vote taken. Then the measure was adopted in the House with 107 in favor and 56 opposed, but was never considered in the Senate. Clearly free land for the West must remain a dream until it could garner more support from the Northeast and Middle States.

That it did so eventually was due less to western propaganda or humanitarian agitation than to fundamental shifts in the sectional alliances that determined congressional policy during those years. These shifts, in turn, were the product of neither political manipulators nor governmental theorists; instead they stemmed from the urge for profits among hardheaded businessmen in the northeastern and western states. These were the realists who recognized that railroads were the wave of the future in the nation's transportation system, and that the experimentation done at state expense before the Panic of 1837 had developed railroad technology to the point that they now promised safe returns on investments. The success of these capitalists in forging a rail network during the two decades before the Civil War sharpened sectional divisions, shifted sectional loyalties, and brought that war into reality.

Railroad construction that began in the mid-1840s differed from that in the prepanic era in two significant ways. Then roads were seen simply as bridges between waterways, connecting the seaboard with the interior river system or with the Erie Canal; now they were viewed as independent arteries of trade, displacing rather than supplementing the water routes. Responsible were technological advances in England and the United States, improving rolling equipment and track-laying until railroads were not only faster but cheaper and more efficient than canal barges or steamboats. Now planners could build directly toward marketing areas, ignoring the rivers and lakes that had dominated their thinking in the past.

No less significant was a changed ownership pattern. Before the Panic of 1837 most railroads were either state-owned or subsidized; even the Baltimore and Ohio, although privately capitalized, depended largely on funds contributed by Baltimore, Washington, and other cities along the way. Now the trend was toward private ownership and operation, usually by corporations built on eastern capital. This shift was necessary; British capitalists who had earlier supplied the states with money for construction were so angered by debt repudiation that they were boycotting investment in the United States, while American voters burned in the collapse of the economic structure in 1837 would have no more of taxation for internal improvements. Private enterprise must assume such risks in the future.

Fortunately some capitalists were eager to do so. Most were in the Northeast where industrial recovery during the early 1840s created cash surpluses seeking investment opportunity. What better place to put those funds to work than in railroads? They had been nursed through the experimental stage at public expense and were now ready to yield extravagant returns. Too, they promised to return a double dividend, assuring eastern investors both high interest and an expanded market for the section's industrial surpluses. The roads most likely to produce this double benediction were those connecting seaboard cities with the emerging urban centers in the West: Cincinnati, Columbus, Cleveland, Indianapolis, Chicago, and St. Louis. This was the incentive that loosened the purse strings of investors in New England and the Middle States, resulting in a flow of capital westward that sent railroad construction into its boom period.

Improvement in the main east-west roads came first. Baltimore merchants, recognizing that the Chesapeake and Ohio Canal would never capture the traffic flowing over the Erie and Pennsylvania canal systems, began agitating in 1842 to extend the Baltimore and Ohio Railroad beyond Cumberland at the base of the mountains. Six years were needed to raise the capital necessary; but work was resumed in 1848, and by 1853 the tracks reached Wheeling on the Ohio River. This flurry of activity alarmed Philadelphia merchants, who recognized the deficiencies of the Pennsylvania canal system. When in 1843 promoters in the western part of the state chartered the Pittsburgh and Connellsville Railroad to connect Pittsburgh with the projected Baltimore and Ohio Railroad they recognized that they must act or lose the trade of their own backcountry to Baltimore. Their answer was the Pennsylvania Railroad, formed in 1846 to build westward along the route of the canal. By the end of September, 1850, construction reached Hollidayburg; bridging the rugged Juniata-Conemaugh Pass over the Alleghenies proved more difficult, but the whole line was in operation to Pittsburgh by December, 1852.

New York merchants had no such incentive, confident that the Erie Canal would give them a perpetual advantage over their rivals. Hence they made no such concentrated effort as did capitalists in Baltimore and Philadelphia, leaving railroad construction across the state to local promoters

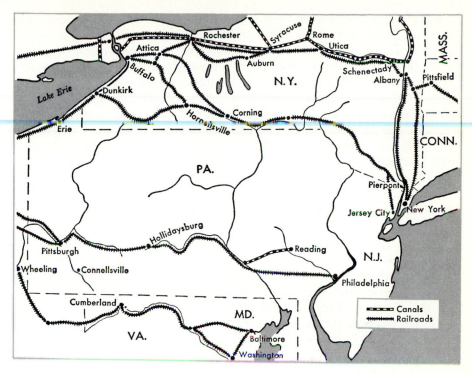

Principal East-West Trade Routes, 1840–1855

with limited funds. They began building short lines even before 1837, each designed to divert traffic from the Erie Canal by the promise of faster service, until by 1842 eight end-to-end lines connected Buffalo with Albany. The system was remarkably inefficient; goods must be transshipped from one line to another, while until 1848 none was allowed to carry goods that competed with the state-operated canal without paying toll charges. Consolidation was the obvious answer. The first step was taken in 1843 when passenger trains began operating over the entire route, and the last, nine years later, when an interchange of stock created the New York Central Railroad. At the same time an extension southward united Albany and New York, forging another all-rail route between the seaboard and Great Lakes. Still another followed, for merchants in the southern parts of the state, jealous of the growth of the Mohawk Valley, chartered the New York and Erie Railroad which by 1851 was completed between Pierpont on the Hudson River and Dunkirk on Lake Erie, 460 miles away. Connections with New York City and Buffalo soon followed.

The building of these major east-west lines centered the attention of eastern capitalists on railroad building in the West. Only by extensions that would tap every western population center could the full potential of the roads be realized by the Northeast, for so long as the western canal system (built to connect the Great Lakes and Ohio River) handled interior trade, a portion would be diverted to southern markets via river steamboats. Capital for these extensions must come from the seaboard states, for the West's scanty surpluses were being used to complete the canals projected there. By 1847 money was flowing westward from Boston, New York, Philadelphia, and Baltimore to launch the New West on its bonanza era of railroad building.

Ohio felt the effects first. One complex of roads designed to extend the marketing area of the New York Central and Erie lines pushed westward along the southern shore of Lake Erie between 1847 and 1853, one uniting Buffalo and Erie, another Erie and Cleveland, and the third Cleveland and Toledo. A second complex penetrated the area served by the Pennsylvania and Baltimore and Ohio railroads, one linking Pittsburgh with Cleveland, another—the Pittsburgh, Fort Wayne & Chicago Railroad—projected to reach Chicago. The former was completed in 1853; the latter reached Crestline that year where connections were made with Cleveland and Columbus. At the same time work began on two north-south lines, one between Sandusky and Springfield, the other between Cleveland and Cincinnati. By 1851 they had progressed to the point that all-rail shipment was possible from Cincinnati to either Sandusky or Cleveland, while feeder roads were being hurried to Newark, Springfield, Dayton, Mansfield, and Richmond. Ohio's rail network was still in its swaddling clothes at mid-decade, but most of the interior was within feasible rail distance of the seaboard.

Indiana's was still at the planning-board stage in 1850, but a pattern was already emerging. One minor line was completed that year between Indi-

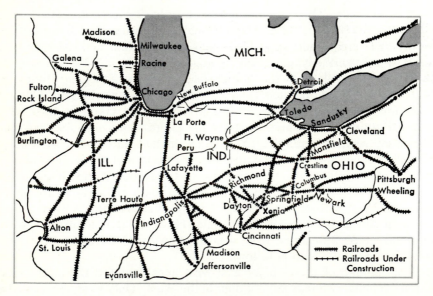

Principal Western Railroads in 1855

anapolis and Madison; others radiating out of Indianapolis toward Cincinnati, Jeffersonville, Peru, and Lafayette, were moving ahead rapidly. So rapidly, indeed, that within three years two important lines—the Bellefontaine and Indiana Railroad and the Terre Haute and Richmond Railroad—were in operation, allowing the shipment of eastern goods to the western border of the state, from the New York Central-Erie outlet via Crestline and Richmond to Terre Haute, from the Baltimore and Ohio-Pennsylvania terminus through Columbus, Springfield, and Richmond to the same destination.

Michigan, filling rapidly with settlers during these years, took its first step toward an eastern connection in 1846 when two of the ill-fated railroads launched during its internal-improvements boom—the Michigan Central and Michigan Southern—were sold for $2,500,000 to a group of Boston capitalists headed by John Murray Forbes. Construction was pushed so rapidly that in 1849 the Michigan Central's tracks reached New Buffalo where water connection was made with Chicago; two years later they had been extended to the Illinois border. By this time the Michigan Southern had built westward to La Porte, Indiana. Over the next year the two roads raced for the privilege of first entering Chicago, both reaching there in 1852.

Illinois, haunted by nightmares of its pre-1837 internal-improvements debacle, and lacking an important city to press for an eastern outlet, lagged behind its sister commonwealths. Not until 1848 did public interest begin to stir as towns and counties pledged funds to secure market connections and eastern capitalists awakened to the fact that the state was a fruitful field for investment. During the next two years a number of roads were launched: the Galena & Chicago Union to build westward to the lead mining districts, the Chicago, Burlington & Quincy and the Rock Island to link Chicago with the Mississippi River, the Chicago, Alton & St. Louis to connect the two most rapidly growing cities of the upper Mississippi Valley. By the early 1850s all had progressed to the point that goods from the East could be carried by rail as far as the Mississippi River.

Just as significant for the future was a project hatched by Stephen A. Douglas of Illinois, senator and Chicago booster. Hearing that a group of promoters were planning a north-south railroad to deflect the profitable lead trade of the Galena area southward to Cairo, and fearful lest this damage Chicago's future, Douglas proposed an Illinois Central Railroad that would build southward from both Chicago and Galena to Cairo. Eastern capital would not be attracted to a project that would drain commerce to the South; hence funds must be sought elsewhere. Douglas found the answer in government support; using his political influence he persuaded Congress in May, 1850, to grant the state the right of way along a route extending from Chicago and Galena to Cairo, together with alternate sections of land on either side to a distance of six miles. Thus was established the principle of railroad land grants, destined to be used a decade hence to finance the transcontinental lines of the 1860s and 1870s. The profits assured by this largess attracted the interest of John Murray Forbes and his fellow New England capitalists who in February, 1851, were awarded a contract to build the Illinois Central Railroad. Work progressed so rapidly that by 1855 the main line to Galena was opened, and that to Chicago a year later.

The flurry of railroad building that altered the map of the northern United States in the decade after 1843 was as significant politically as it was economically. Every mile of track laid, whether bridging the Appalachians or spanning the western states, not only brought West and Northeast into commercial interdependence but also reminded both sections of common interests and a common ideology that they shared in opposition to the South. They were, unbeknownst to both, being merged into one section: the North. As though sensing this threatening alliance, southerners were busily seeking independence from northern control and northern meddling. This could be secured only by severing the economic ties that had bound them to the other sections; now they would sell their cotton abroad rather than to New England, and produce their own food rather then relying on the Northwest. This was the theme of a giant "Commercial Convention" held in Memphis in 1845, that set in motion a number of railroad-building projects, all designed to accentuate the South's commercial autonomy. Their purpose was east-west connections that would allow the Southeast to be fed from the lower Mississippi Valley and Texas: roads between Charleston and Nashville, Charleston and Memphis, Richmond and Memphis, Savannah and Vicksburg. During the next two decades the South's money and energy were poured into these four railroads, all destined to widen the gulf between North and South.

Fortunately for the nation's future, the transportation revolution presaged by the burgeoning railroad network was far from completed in the early 1850s. Goods still flowed along the Mississippi artery in impressive quantities; some 740 steamboats and nearly 3,000 flatboats reached New Orleans yearly laden with farm products from the Ohio Valley. Yet the fact was clear each year western farmers sent a larger proportion of their surpluses eastward. River steamboats might be cheaper, but they were always in danger of blowing up or knocking out their bottoms on a river snag. Insurance underwriters, knowing this, charged higher rates on cargoes carried by boat than by rail, thus lowering the cost differential. By 1850 most passengers and light produce moved by rail, leaving the river boats only bulky freight. The Great Lakes-Erie Canal system remained competitive because it satisfied the needs of shippers of grain and forest products. Every western exporter who turned from the river to rail transportation helped cement the East-West alliance.

Nor was the end in sight; the contraction of southern markets for western foodstuffs resulting from the South's nationalistic urge to feed itself coincided with a remarkable expansion of the northeastern market as continuing industrialization and immigration multiplied the number of workers there. Figures for the per-capita production of food crops in 1850 showed what was happening:

	Wheat	Corn	Six Cereals
New England	0.4 bushels	3.70 bushels	7.99 bushels
Middle States	5.75 bushels	9.11 bushels	26.15 bushels
South	2.47 bushels	30.83 bushels	37.92 bushels
West	7.52 bushels	44.14 bushels	59.62 bushels

Those figures told an impressive story. The average American at this time consumed four bushels of wheat and 25 of corn yearly. Hence New Englanders had to import 3.6 bushels of wheat and 21.30 of corn per capita annually, the Middle States 1.75 bushels of wheat and 14.89 of corn, and the South only 1.53 bushels of wheat while it produced an excess of 19.14 bushels of corn. The West, on the other hand, must sell 3.25 bushels of wheat and 19.14 of corn for each inhabitant. Obviously its best market was not in the South, but in the Northeast where demand far exceeded supply.

The Northeast, moreover, offered far better facilities for overseas trade. Brokers soon found that grain destined for foreign markets kept much better in New York or Philadelphia than in humid New Orleans, lessening losses by spoilage. They discovered also that eastern wholesalers could advance funds that allowed them to hold foodstuffs in their warehouses for advantageous prices rather than dumping them immediately after the harvest. Most important, they were impressed by the widening overseas markets being developed by enterprising eastern exporters. Until the early 1840s most of the nation's grain surpluses had been sold in the West Indies and Latin America where corn meal and wheat flour were in demand, making New Orleans the logical export port. In 1846, however, England repealed the Corn Laws that had closed her ports to American grain since 1815, thus announcing that she would concentrate on industrial production while importing foodstuffs. High prices there accounted for the fact that during the next decade grain exports from the United States increased 170 per cent, nearly all due to English demand.

The result of this combination of circumstances—improved East-West transportation facilities, adequate credit, and expanding Northeastern and foreign markets—was a continuing increase in East-West trade. Figures on the percentage of western exports reaching the other sections in typical years tell the story:

		Amount exported	Percentage shipped to:		
			Northeast	East	South
Wheat	1844	4,000,000 bushels	96	—	4
	1849	5,500,000 bushels	92	—	8
	1853	11,000,000 bushels	99	—	1
Flour	1844	1,500,000 barrels	63	6	31
	1849	3,000,000 barrels	63	6	31
	1853	3,000,000 barrels	62	10	28
Corn	1844	1,500,000 bushels	10	—	90
	1849	6,000,000 bushels	60	—	40
	1853	8,000,000 bushels	63	—	37

For all who cared to read, those figures spelled the South's approaching isolation. By 1853, when the trading revolution was far from completed, the Northeast purchased 99 per cent of the West's wheat exports, 62 per cent of its flour, and 63 per cent of its corn. Exports fostered imports; by this time westerners bought only 28 per cent of the goods they needed from the South, in contrast with 35 per cent four years before.

These batteries of statistics revealed a significant trend in the nation's internal trade patterns. Better transportation facilities were weaning westerners from their traditional southern connections and building a commercial alliance between East and West. This was to be vastly strengthened over the next decade as railroad building, still in its infancy in the early 1850s, expanded to link the two sections ever more closely commercially. Vanishing now was the historic sectional pattern where Northeast, South, and West disputed among themselves or arranged the intersectional alliances that were translated into legislation by Congress. Instead two sections—North and South—were forming. Civil war was near now, but one more ingredient was needed before that holocaust began. Not until emotional convictions on both sides of the Mason-Dixon Line had reached such a fever pitch that further compromise was outmoded would the United States follow the road to war. The tinder box that touched off the conflict lay west of the Mississippi where new territories were already forming. Should they be slave or free? As Americans debated that all-important question emotions were stirred to the point that force must displace reason in shaping the nation's course. The expansion of the frontier over the trans-Mississippi West made the Civil War irrepressible.

THE TRANS-MISSISSIPPI FRONTIER

18

The Natural Setting

During the first half of the nineteenth century, while ax-swinging pioneers stripped away the virgin forests of the Lake Plains and transformed pine-filled woods along the Gulf into fields of snowy cotton, more adventurous Americans pressed beyond the Mississippi to begin the conquest of a new frontier. There, in a gargantuan land of rolling prairies, grass-blanketed plains, towering mountains, and parched deserts, they found what they sought: fertile farming country, lush green pastures, glittering pockets of precious metals, and a king's fortune in shining beaver peltry. News of this wealth set other Americans marching westward in an ever-growing migration that continued until the director of the census could announce, in 1890, that the unbroken frontier line was a thing of the past.

The rapid conquest of an area greater than that peopled during the two preceding centuries was evidence enough of the remarkable expansive power of Americans, but even more amazing was the fact that the advance into the Far West required a continuous adaptation to new and strange environments. No longer could the pioneers employ techniques learned by generations of forebears. They knew how to subdue the wilderness—by girdling trees, planting a crop of corn, building a cabin, clearing the land year by year—but in most of the trans-Mississippi West forests were absent. They knew how to conquer the prairie—by breaking the sod, planting an "ax-crop" of corn, and hauling in lumber needed for a home—but in the interminable plains the lessons of the past no longer applied. They knew how to manage a small farm, but beyond the Father of Waters they discovered that subhumid climates required extensive rather than intensive agriculture. Those obstacles, placed in the path of westward-marching pioneers by nature, must be surmounted before the continent was settled.

Westerners did not come face-to-face with those barriers until they passed beyond the first tier of states bordering the Mississippi. Southerners advancing into Louisiana or moving northward into Arkansas and Missouri found a familiar environment waiting them, where the verdant forests, good soils, and abundant rainfall of the Southern Lowlands encouraged the production of cotton or other semitropical crops. Only in northwestern Arkansas and southern Missouri did they encounter the first obstacle: the Ozark Plateau. That rugged upland of eroded hills and pine-covered highlands, guarded on the north by the dome-shaped St. Francis Mountains and on the south by the steep ridges of the Ouachita range, served as an effective barrier to frontier advance, for its rough topography and sterile soils discouraged settlement until better lands were exhausted. No such obstacle faced northern pioneers as they moved into the trans-Mississippi portion of the Central Lowlands. Instead they found a gently rolling prairie, covered with a luxurious growth of tall grass which stretched unbroken to the horizon except where belts of trees marked some river bed. To frontiersmen skilled in prairie farming the tall grass country of Iowa, northern Missouri, southern Minnesota, and eastern Kansas and Nebraska offered no difficulties. There, as in the southern Mississippi Valley, good soil and adequate rainfall promised profits to farmers.

Once frontier farmers passed beyond the western border of Missouri they entered the first of the unfamiliar regions which made pioneering in the trans-Mississippi West difficult. Stretching away before them was the giant physiographic province known as the Great Plains. That tilted plateau was formed over the course of centuries by streams flowing eastward from the Rocky Mountains into the Mississippi River. As rivers rushed down steep mountain slopes they picked up dirt and debris which was gradually deposited until a platform higher than the surrounding countryside was formed. Then the stream swung to right or left, seeking lower ground, which was in turn slowly elevated by continuous silt deposits. As this went on through geological age after geological age a great upland gradually took shape, sloping gently downward from its elevation of 5,000 feet at the foot of the Rockies to a point three or four hundred miles away where a sharp eastward-facing escarpment marked the junction of the Great Plains and the Central Lowlands.

Within the province the continued operation of natural forces created several regions, which affected the course of American settlement. North of the Platte River the many streams which formed the Missouri River system cut deeply into the gravelly soil, leaving a maze of eroded river beds and extensive badlands which made travel difficult and farming or grazing impossible. Dotting the Missouri Plateau were several groups of domed mountains such as the Black Hills of South Dakota, survivors of the erosive process that cut down the rest of the countryside to a lower level. Although mineral wealth buried beneath the forest-clad hills soon attracted settlers, most pioneers shunned the inhospitable region. ''The country,'' wrote one early traveler, "is here spread into wide and level plains, welling like the ocean, in which the view is uninterrupted by a single tree or shrub, and is diversified only by the moving herds of buffalo. The soil consists of a light-colored earth, intermixed with a large proportion of coarse gravel without sand, and is by no means as fertile as the plains . . . lower down the Missouri."

South of the Platte River the erosive action of wind and water shaped the Great Plains into three distinguishable regions. Along the eastern edge—in eastern Nebraska, central Kansas, and much of central Texas—was the Low Plains country, where rainfall wore away the light soils to leave a low-lying grassland, similar in some respects to the Central Lowlands. Just to the west, and separated from the Low Plains by a steep scarp known as the Break of the Plains, were the High Plains of western Kansas and the Texan Panhandle. Protected by a heavy grass matting from wind erosion and watered so infrequently that little soil washed away, the High Plains looked down upon the lower areas to either side. Beyond them, nestling beneath the foothills of the Rockies, a long Upland Trough stretched from New Mexico to Wyoming. There the scanty vegetation was insufficient to protect the light soil from blustery winds which carried away enough of the surface over the centuries to leave a chain of connected valleys—the Pecos Valley, the Colorado Piedmont, and Goshen Hole—which together separated the High Plains from the Rocky Mountains. Each region presented settlers with a different environmental problem which must be solved before settlement could go on.

Despite local variations the Great Plains province was distinguished by certain natural characteristics: a level or rolling surface, a complete lack of forest growth, and in most areas a subhumid climate. Of these the lack of adequate rainfall was most important. The phenomenon was explained by the mountain ranges lying to the west; easterly blowing winds from the Pacific were drained of moisture as they crossed the California ranges, picked up some water from the parched country between the coastal mountains and the Rockies, and were wrung dry again as they passed over that high range. Hence they blew, hot and dry, across the Great Plains, soaking up life-giving moisture as they passed, until they reached central Kansas or Nebraska where they deposited their burden in the form of rainfall. East of this "Line of Semiaridity" annual precipitation was normally the twenty inches or more needed for ordinary farming; to the west less than that amount fell each year. For the Great Plains as a whole the average was only fifteen inches—not enough to support agriculture. To make matters worse most rain fell between April and November when the glaring sun and hot summer winds quickly drained the water from the soil. The southern portions suffered most from evaporation, losing forty-six inches of moisture during the growing season while in the north the loss was only thirty inches.

The subhumid climate accounted for the types of vegetation that struggled for existence on the Great Plains. Forest growth was absent except

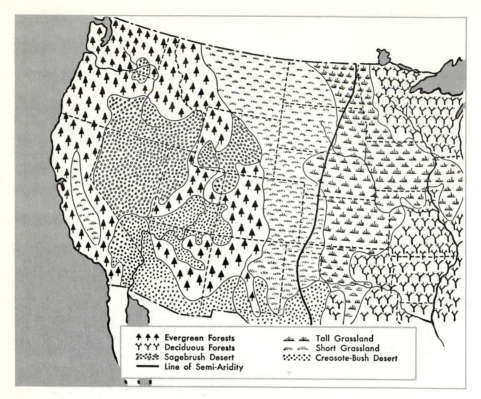

Natural Vegetation of the Trans-Mississippi West

along the streams or on such isolated elevations as the Black Hills. Instead the province was carpeted with the varieties of grass that could survive its semiarid climate. Along the eastern border was a "tall grass" country where waving stands of luxurious foliage three- to- six-feet high testified to the rich soil and adequate rainfall. In two places arms of prairie vegetation thrust well beyond the Line of Semiaridity; one in North Dakota where cold weather kept the earth moist by retarding surface evaporation, the other along the Platte River in central Nebraska. West of the "tall grass" grew a matting of short grass that, in the southern portions where rapid evaporation occurred, extended some distance east of the Line of Semiaridity. Still farther south on the plains of Texas, where precipitation was too scant to support a solid earth covering, the short grass gave way to desert grass or mesquite, growing in clumps, with bare patches of sun-baked soil between.

The Great Plains supported a wide variety of animal life which early lured trappers and hunters to the Far West. Beavers were plentiful in the many streams that coursed through the Missouri Plateau. Throughout the Plains lived other species whose remarkable speed enabled them to thrive in an open country where safety depended on ability to detect and escape enemies: keen-sighted and swift-legged antelope, donkey-eared jack rabbits whose powerfully developed hind legs could put an amazing distance between them and hunters in a short space of time, slinking wolf-like coyotes with an ability to scatter miles behind them that always amazed travelers. Those miserable, carrion-snatching creatures were everywhere present, ready to steal anything living or dead that could possibly be eaten. "The coyote," wrote Mark Twain after a trip across the Plains, "is a living, breathing allegory of want. He is *always* hungry. He is always poor, out of luck, and friendless. The meanest creatures despise him, and even the fleas would desert him for a velocipede." More abundant than the coyotes were the buffalos, who reproduced so rapidly amidst the favorable environment that millions existed, wandering in great herds covering as much as fifty square miles of prairie. The shaggy beasts were poorly equipped to defend themselves, for their poor eyesight, clumsy gait, and awkward movements made them easy prey for Indians or hunters. From them the nomads—red or white—who roamed the Plains secured all of the necessities of life: fresh or "jerked" (dried) meat, clothing, bedding, tents, skin boats, and even fuel in the form of dried dung or "chips."

The presence of buffalo accounted for the character of the Indian civilizations white men encountered when they entered the Great Plains. With plentiful food assured them, the grassland tribes lived nomadic lives rather than following the sedentary agricultural pursuits of natives east of the Mississippi. Their natural roving tendency was accentuated during the seventeenth century when Spanish traders supplied them with horses. By 1800 the animals were in general use among Plains Indians, who developed a remarkable skill on horseback which encouraged them to roam widely in pursuit of game or on warlike expeditions against enemy tribes. The natives' absolute dependence on the buffalo for food, shelter, and clothing, and their use of horses, not only marked them as a distinctive cultural group but made them formidable foes. No longer could white men strike at Indians by destroying their crops; now the natives must be fought on equal terms, with the Indians equipped to do battle or run away as circumstances dictated. The long period of nineteenth century warfare before the last Indian accepted defeat attested to their remarkable ability as warriors.

Within the Great Plains the many tribes developed differences in living habits that reflected the varying environments. The warlike Indian who occupied the High Plains were completely nomadic, with no permanent villages or gardens to bind them to any one locality, and with a culture dependent on the horse and buffalo. Of these the Blackfeet, Crows, Grosventres, and Teton-Dakota were most important on the northern High Plains, while to the south the Arapaho, Cheyenne, Comanche, and Kiowa were dominant. To the east and west of the central group of tribes were others whose living habits showed characteristics of both a plains and forest-land culture. Occupying the Low Plains east of the Line of Semiaridity were a number of "prairie Indians"—the Mandan, Iowa, Kansa, Missouri, Omaha,

Osage, Pawnee, Eastern Dakota, and Wichita—who planted maize and erected permanent villages of earth or bark lodges to which they returned each fall after summer excursions in pursuit of buffalo. West of the High Plains in the foothills and valleys of the Rockies, lived the Bannock, Nez Perce, Ute, and Shoshoni Indians who also hunted the buffalo during the summer, then returned to semipermanent winter camps. Unlike the eastern village groups they seldom grew corn, relying instead on wild roots and berries to supplement their diet of bison meat.

Despite differences in living habits, the material culture of the Plains Indians was much the same. All used stone knives, scrapers, and bone awls, all depended upon the bow and arrow in hunting and warfare, and all warriors carried into battle a long buffalo lance tipped with stone. Their remarkable skill with those weapons, particularly their short bows of wood or sinew-backed strips of mountain sheep horn, made them dangerous enemies. Until the introduction of the Colt revolver and repeating rifle, Plains Indians enjoyed a marked advantage over white men; a mounted warrior could send half a dozen arrows against his opponent while a white settler or soldier was cramming one bullet into his muzzle-loading gun. Their mobility also gave them strength in warfare. Their villages consisted of buffalo-hide tepees which could be folded quickly when an enemy approached, loaded on an A-shaped travois or carrying frame made from the tepee poles, and spirited away behind fast ponies before an attack was possible.

The Plains Indians were especially dangerous because physically they were among the finest types in all America. Their skin was a reddish chocolate, their hair black and straight, their eyes brown. Those who lived in the north were above average in height, with many six-footers among them, while the southern Indians were slightly smaller. The men dressed in a breechcloth, usually supplemented with long leggings which extended from hips to ankles, a buffalo robe thrown around the shoulders in winter, and among the northern Indians a "scalp shirt" of leather when on the warpath. Women wore sleeveless dresses of deer or elk skin, and both sexes used moccasins with a double rawhide sole for protection against hard ground.

The social organization of the Plains Indians was based on "bands" of three to five hundred people, under a "chief," who was usually the most influential and respected warrior of the group. Each was governed by a council of elder men meeting with the chief to decide all questions. Their decisions were enforced by small societies of warriors known as "soldier bands" which not only kept order, settled disputes, and punished offenders, but regulated hunts and ceremonies during peacetime and guarded against surprise attack when on the warpath. All Plains tribes had several "soldier societies," and a young brave normally advanced from one to another as his age and deeds justified promotion in the hierarchy they represented. Usually the societies had such names as Foxes, Crows, Bulls, or Dogs, which were adopted by the warriors as part of their names; the "Dog Soldiers," thus, might include braves called Crazy Dog, Mad Dog, Foolish Dog,

Young Dog, and Big Dog. Despite division into these "soldier societies," the bands maintained a high degree of autonomy and acted as individual units in both war and peace.

The only restrictions upon the independence of the bands were loose tribal organizations which united various groups of Plains Indians on the basis of similarity of language or customs, or through the happenstance of geographical distribution. Thus the Dakota Indians, the great Siouan-speaking group of the northeastern Plains, were divided into seven tribes, each containing several bands. Ordinarily the bands making up a tribe had little to do with each other, since the tribal unit was too large to obtain sufficient subsistence when hunting together, and the quest for food, as usual among hunting peoples was all-important. Occasionally, however, bands making up a tribe assembled for ceremonies or to agree upon some action. Thus the four bands of the Cheyenne tribe—the Aorta Band, the Hairy Band, the Scabby Band, and the Dogmen Band—met regularly at an appointed spot, camping about a central tepee where chiefs and elders of each band conferred. More often tribal unions failed to function; frequently several bands within a tribe were on the warpath while others remained at peace. This haphazard type of confederation complicated relations between the Indians and the United States government when the frontier advanced into the Plains region.

Less important to the Great Plains Indians than tribal organizations—but nevertheless essential to understanding their civilization—were the linguistic groups into which they were divided. Seven languages were spoken: *Siouan* by the Crows, Dakota, Iowa, Kansa, Mandan, Missouri, Omaha, Osage, and Oto; *Algonkian* by the Arapaho, Blackfeet, Cheyenne, and Grosventre; *Caddoan* by the Pawnee and Wichita; *Kiowan* by the Kiowa; *Shoshonean* by the Bannock, Comanche, and Shoshoni, and *Athapascan* and *Shahaptian* by smaller tribal units. Local dialects varied, but most tribes within a group were able to make themselves understood. In addition the Plains Indians developed a universal sign language which allowed natives of different stocks to communicate with each other, often at a distance.

Despite the complex hierarchy of tribes and linguistic stocks, the band was the all-important social and economic unit among Plains Indians. Within those tight-knit groups each warrior strove to gain social prominence and superiority over his fellow braves. That could be done by two means. He could secure a large number of horses which were the universal measure of wealth; stealing horses from other tribes or from whites was a practice which touched off many localized Plains wars. Or he could demonstrate his bravery in battle, for war deeds carried great weight in determining social rank. "Counting coup"—touching an enemy or capturing his weapons—was considered the greatest form of bravery and was far more widely practiced than killing and scalping. Those distinctions were widely sought not only to gain recognition but also because only the bravest and wealthiest warriors were allowed to enter into polygamous marriages. Numerous wives were an economic asset since the job of preparing hides or making clothes and tepees was a tedious one.

The principal economic function of the band was to engage in buffalo hunts. This important task required the cooperation of everyone. The usual method was the "surround," in which the herd was nearly encircled by warriors, then allowed to run while mounted men cut down the animals on flank and rear with bow and lance. Women, children, and older men followed to skin the slain beasts and cut up the meat. Unlike later white hunters, the Indians used nearly every part of the buffalo. The hide, after being fleshed and scraped, was treated with mixtures of fat and brains until cured and ready to use in clothing. The fresh meat was eaten raw, roasted, or boiled in a rawhide-lined earthen pit by dropping heated stones into the water. That not consumed on the spot was preserved; some by drying or "jerking" in the arid Plains air; some by cooking, shredding, and mixing with wild berries and fat to be stored in the rawhide bags as "pemmican," a lightweight emergency food highly prized by hunters for its nutritive value.

The religious ceremonies of the Great Plains Indians also focused on the band. Like most natives of North America, the western tribesmen believed in no single God but in a series of controlling powers that shaped the events of the universe. Of those the sun was paramount, but the earth, sky, moon, rocks, wind, and water were also felt to exert a continuous influence upon man and nature. Indians with special concessions from those powers were called "medicine men" or shamans, and were consulted in time of sickness, stress, or when members of the band were about to embark on the warpath. Hence the shamans were powerful men in each band, often able to decide between war and peace. They were not alone in possessing occult powers; the Plains Indians believed every young warrior, by fasting, prayer, and self-torture, could insure for himself a portion of divine wisdom. The lonely "vision quests" of youthful braves usually ended in semidelirious dreams which, when interpreted by the shaman, guided each man through his lifetime. Moreover every Indian constantly carried a "medicine bundle"—made by the shaman from bits of hair, stones, and animal teeth— supposed to give great power. The bundles were jealously guarded, for if one were lost doom inevitably followed.

The most important religious ceremony of the Plains natives was the Sun Dance, an eight-day-long ceremony held by united tribal bands during the summer months. Gathering around a central tree or "sunpole," the warriors of an entire tribe danced, sang, and performed ceremonial rites, gazing steadily at the sun as they moved through traditional patterns. The messiah enthusiasm induced by these rituals often inspired self-torture among the dancers, who dragged buffalo skulls attached to their flesh with leather thongs, ran skewers or ropes through the fleshy portions of their breasts or backs, and even sliced layers from their arms. Indians under the influence of religious excitement were particularly warlike, nor was the problem of negotiating with them made easier by the fact that Sun Dance rituals allowed bands to unite for tribal action against their enemies.

Wandering bands of warlike natives, drifting herds of bellowing buffalos, a seldom-veiled sun beating down upon parched earth from blue skies, endless vistas of grey-green grasslands stretching unbroken to the horizon— those were the impressions of the Great Plains carried away by Anglo-American frontier travelers who ventured upon their broad surface. On the whole, pioneers found little there to their liking. The cloudless heavens, the baked soil, the absence of timber, all created an impression of a desert unsuited for human habitation. Tales of a Great American Desert brought back by trappers and explorers were readily accepted by geographers. Across their maps they lettered in those discouraging words; until after the Civil War the impression persisted that the farming frontier could never invade that inhospitable region. For a generation the Great Plains were looked upon as a barrier standing between the Mississippi Valley and the fertile areas beyond, to be passed over as quickly as possible.

Nor did the next physiographic province to the westward prove more attractive. Along the rim of the Plains rose the towering peaks and rugged rock masses of the Rocky Mountains. That giant mountain chain, which stretched along the backbone of the continent from Alaska to central New Mexico, was divided into two distinguishable systems. In Idaho, western Montana, and northern Wyoming was a sprawling, ill-defined maze of north-south ranges and valleys which together comprised the Northern Rocky Mountain Province. The eastern edge of the mass was formed by the Lewis Range, the steep, glacier-cut walls of which marked the continental divide, and by the Big Horn Mountains which thrust an arm eastward into the Great Plains to enclose the fertile basin of the Big Horn River. Beyond those two ranges lay a valley, the Rocky Mountain Trench, where the level surface and forest-covered soil attracted farmers drifting westward to raise food for prospectors and miners. West of this lowland the Bitterroot Mountains rose precipitously. Although steep and high, the range was easy to cross along the many streams that drained westward into the Columbia River. Of these the Snake River was most important. Its level plain, extending eastward around the southern spur of the Bitterroots, served as a highway for Oregon pioneers making their way toward the Pacific. Just south of the Snake River plain lay the Wasatch Mountains on the eastern border of the Great Salt Lake. The mineral wealth hidden in the Northern Rockies made the region an early center in the advance of the mining frontier.

Below the Northern Rocky Mountain Province, in western Wyoming, was a broad plateau known as the Wyoming Basin. More truly a westward extension of the Great Plains than a part of the Rockies, that 250-mile-wide upland played a leading role in the American conquest of the Far West. Its level floor provided the single uninterrupted route through the mountains from the Plains to the intermontane lowlands beyond. Dotted with hills and covered with a sagebrush growth that offered no handicaps to travelers, the highway was discovered early in the nineteenth century by fur traders who gave it the name of South Pass. Through it passed the overland trails leading to the Pacific coast, but the tracks of the nation's first transcontinental railroad, the Union Pacific, were laid through the southern part of the Wyoming Basin.

South of the Wyoming Basin were the Southern Rockies, a wild and rugged mass of snow-clad peaks and high grassy valleys or "parks." Two ranges fringed the eastern border of the system, the Colorado Front Range which rose 6,000 feet above the Plains and was crowned by towering Pike's Peak, and the Sangre de Cristo Range which extended from the Arkansas River into central New Mexico. West of these interlacing systems and separated from them by a series of intermontane parks, were the Sawatch Range of western Colorado and the San Juan Range of Colorado and northern New Mexico. The Southern Rocky Mountain system was important in frontier history largely as a barrier to expansion, as its maze of majestic mountains and rock-strewn valleys contained few passes such as those penetrating the Northern Rockies. In one section—the region about Pike's Peak—gold discoveries attracted miners at an early date.

The vegetation and wild life of the Rocky Mountain Province was as much a product of the unique environment as that of the Great Plains. Precipitation was abundant, wrung from passing winds by the high peaks. Most fell during the late winter and early spring months in the form of snow which accumulated to a depth of twenty-five feet or more. The life-giving moisture encouraged a heavy growth of pine, fir, and spruce trees which grew so thickly that passage through them was difficult. Wild life abounded amidst those favorable conditions. Beaver were plentiful along the lower courses of the snow-streams, while bear were abundant in the higher altitudes, and mountain goats inhabited the rocky crags beyond the timberline. Although savage grizzlies and bloodthirsty mountain lions made life hazardous in the Rockies, trappers and traders were early lured there by the hope of obtaining beaver peltry and black bear skins. Indians also ventured into the forested valleys in search of game, but no tribe made its permanent home there.

Unattractive as the Rockies were, they were no more inhospitable than the physiographic region lying to their west, the Intermontane Province. That giant area, which comprised the whole country between the Rocky Mountains and the Pacific Ranges, was made up of three sections. To the north lay the Columbia Plateau, a high-lying upland of lava soil laid down in fairly recent geological times by the eruption of now extinct volcanoes. The weathering of the hardened mass left the country level except where rivers, cutting down through soft lava, gouged out deep gorges; the Snake River ran through a canyon 4,000 feet deep. Even those offered few obstacles to travelers, as routes followed by pioneers ran east and west along the stream's banks, making crossing unnecessary. Nor did the vegetation that covered the Columbia Plateau hinder migrations westward; most of the semiarid region was carpeted with sparse forest growth or with the plant indigenous to the northern deserts, the sagebrush. That dwarfed, drab-green shrub, which ranged in height from a few inches to four feet, offered poor fodder for horses, but its gnarled branches lighted many a cheery campfire for weary overland travelers. Only a lack of precipitation kept other types of vegetation from flourishing. Settlers found the rich lava soil produced abundantly on the few spots where rainfall was sufficient.

South of the Columbia Plateau was a depression known as the Great Basin, where scattered ranges of low-lying mountains were interlaced with level, desertlike valleys and plains. The distinguishing feature of the Great Basin Province was its lack of rainfall; over it swept westerly winds wrung so dry by the lofty Sierra Nevada ranges they actually picked up moisture from the already parched earth. The lack of rainfall and the high mountains which rimmed the region made it a basin in fact as in name; streams originating along its edges lost themselves in the sandy soil without ever reaching the sea. Of those the most important were the Humboldt, a river that meandered across northern Utah before disappearing in an alkaline lake bed known as Humboldt Sink, and the Carson, which flowed eastward from the Sierras to vanish in the great depression of Carson Sink. Along those two waterways marched the California pioneers on their way west. Sagebrush covered the northern half of the Great Basin; in the south where rainfall averaged only two inches a year arid deserts predominated: Death Valley and the Mojave Desert of California, the Gila Desert of Arizona. Even the hardy sagebrush could not survive there; the only vegetation was cacti and ugly creosote bushes, their dark leaves covered with an oily substance as protection against the beating rays of the sun.

In that harsh environment the life of the widely scattered Indian tribes—the Bannock, Shoshoni, Ute, Paiute, Gosiute, and Snake—was dominated by the food quest. A few, located on the richer Columbia Plateau or on the eastern fringes of the Great Basin, lived above the subsistence level on fish, bear, elk, and jack rabbits, but in the semidesert country of Nevada where game was scarce and vegetation scanty the rugged nomads were reduced to eating anything that could run, crawl, wriggle, or squirm—"anything," as Mark Twain remarked, "they can bite." Grasshoppers, snakes, reptiles, vermin, rodents, and such small game as they could capture formed a regular part of their meagre diet, usually supplemented with roots and tubers painfully dug from the dry ground, grass seed, and berries; their constant digging after food won them the contemptuous name of "Digger Indians" from the whites.

The culture of these hunter-gatherers was subtle in structure and content. Their homes were brush huts, lean-tos, or holes scooped in the earth; their clothing either a breechcloth or nothing at all; their implements such primitive devices as digging sticks and coiled baskets; their weapons the bow, club, and wooden lance. The basic social unit was the immediate family, for no larger group could be supported; only in rare periods of plenty did they gather in bands under the leadership of a chief. Ceremonies and religious activities were personal in a land where food was insufficient to support extensive gatherings, nor could the "Diggers" take time from their perpetual food quest to war on each other or on the whites. The hardships of Indian life were clear; an explorer left a vivid picture of their barren lives:

> In the Great Basin, where nearly naked he traveled on foot and lived in the sagebrush, I found him in the most elementary form; the men living alone, the women living alone, but all after food. Sometimes one man cooked by his home, his bows and arrows and bunch of squirrels by his side; sometimes on the shore of a lake or river where food was more abundant a little band of men might be found occupied in fishing; miles away a few women would be met gathering seeds and insects, or huddled up in a shelter of sagebrush to keep off snow.

Little wonder that Mark Twain called the "Goshoots" the "wretchedest type of mankind I have ever seen."

Between the Great Basin and the Southern Rockies was the broad plateau of the Colorado River, an extensive upland where the elevation ranged between 5,000 and 11,000 feet. Much of the province was so arid that only sagebrush existed on the gravelly soil, although greater rainfall at higher levels supported yellow pine, piñon, cedar, and juniper. Explorers who crossed the desolate highland were more impressed, however, with the hundreds of river gorges—such as the Grand Canyon of the Colorado— which cut the rough surface into an impassable maze. Most ranged from 500 to 5,000 feet deep and were impossible to cross; even today the Colorado Plateau is bypassed by all but two railroads which skirt its northern and southern edges. This unattractive region was avoided by all early pioneers except trappers who sought beaver along its streams, and miners who prospected for gold amidst its rocky hills.

Uninviting as the Colorado Plateau and southern Great Basin Provinces were, they supported a numerous Indian population when the invasion by Spanish and Americans began. Three types of native societies flourished in the southwestern culture area, each fully adjusted to local variations in environment. The central portion—western New Mexico and eastern Arizona—was the home of the Pueblo dwellers, a highly cultured group of tribes of which the Hopi, Zuñi, and Rio Grande Pueblos were most important. Living on a subdesert plateau which was bitterly cold in winter, and harassed constantly by powerful Ute Indians from the north and warlike Comanche from the east, these sedentary natives survived by building communal houses of adobe brick or dressed stone on inaccessible mesas or cavelike cracks in cliffs. Their elaborate dwellings could be entered only by ladders which reached a terraced second floor; access to the solidly walled first floor was gained by descending through holes left in the wooden ceiling. Within these fortlike homes the Pueblo lived their quiet lives, each family having two rooms for sleeping, eating, and grinding grain. Although they occasionally hunted antelope and deer with bows or throwing sticks, their principal food came from their own corn fields which, in that arid country, were sometimes as much as twenty miles from their homes. The Pueblo people not only won the struggle to stave off starvation but also developed the weaving of cotton or yucca fibres into cloth and the fashioning of handsome baskets and pottery. They were also a peaceful people, content to leave their neighbors alone. Seldom did the Pueblo take to the warpath against the whites.

Equally sedentary were the second group of Indians in the Southwest, the Village Dwellers who occupied the Gila and lower Colorado River valleys. Differing from the Pueblo in their dwellings—circular thatched huts covered with mud or straw—and emphasis on family living rather than communal groups, they nevertheless resembled their neighbors in their dependence on agriculture and in their remarkably developed culture. The Village Dwellers were sufficiently skilled to combat the arid climate by flood plain farming and by irrigation, while their woven baskets and mats were as skillfully made as those of any tribe in North America. They were, like the Pueblo, a peaceful people who did not interfere with the advance of the Spanish or American frontiers, although among themselves they practiced a highly ritualized warfare in which losses were slight. A few cracked skulls and bruises settled the most serious encounters to the satisfaction of all concerned, while no war was too serious to prevent frequent truces for meals or festivals. Most prominent among the several tribes making up the Village Dwellers were the Pima and Papago, and Mojave.

The third group of Indians in the Southwest were the Camp Dwellers, composed largely of Navaho and Apache who during the thirteenth or fourteenth century migrated from the Great Plains to homes in eastern New Mexico and western Texas. Their culture blended institutions adapted to both the Plains and Plateau environments; they lived in tepees, mud huts, or brush shelters, engaged in agriculture to supplement their principal food supply of game and wild berries or fruits, dressed in either the buckskin of the grasslands or the colorful two-piece cotton suits of the Navaho, and spent most of their lives in nomadic wanderings, although maintaining fields and storing food whenever possible. The Navaho especially showed tendencies to adopt the sedentary existence of the Pueblo; they herded sheep, produced intricate silver ornaments, wove color-splashed woolen blankets, and turned out beautifully designed baskets.

The Apache, on the other hand, were among the most warlike of all tribes. Excellent horsemen, skilled plains travelers, adept in the use of the short bow and lance, they raided whites and fellow Indians alike whenever possible. Like the warriors of the Plains their basic organization centered about the band, although constant losses through fighting prevented the groups from developing any stability; instead bands joined or broke apart according to the needs of the time. In the main, however, there were six tribal divisions—Jicarilla Apache, Mescalero Apache, Mimbreños, Chiricahua, San Carlos, and Coyotero—each subdivided into bands. Social organization reflected their seminomadic life; the highly complex controls usual among sedentary peoples were not needed. Tribal and band affairs were regulated by a chief, often elected by the elders for life. Separate chiefs were usually chosen for warfare and several bands sometimes joined under one leader when on the warpath. The warlike Apache made life in the Southwest even more unattractive to settlers than the obstacles strewn by nature across that wasteland.

More to the liking of pioneers than the Intermontane Province were the majestic peaks and fertile valleys of the Pacific Coast Province. Dominating that area was a formidable mountain range which stretched like a giant letter H across the western border of the continent. To the northeast were the Cascades, a chain of noble mountains sixty to eighty miles wide. Along their edges steep-walled valleys 3,000 feet deep provided well-watered farming land, while abundant passes allowed early travelers to reach the coastal lands beyond. In northern California the Cascades merged into the Sierra Nevadas, a towering mountainous wall from 12,000 to 14,000 feet high. They were difficult to cross, as their eastern slope was steep and their western cut by glacial gorges. The few passes were found only on the flanks of mountains 5,000 to 9,000 feet above sea level. Both the Cascades and Sierra Nevadas were heavily forested and deluged by heavy rainfall averaging more than seventy inches yearly, in contrast to the five or ten inches falling on the Great Basin a few miles east.

The Klamath Mountains of northern California, a rugged mass of wooded hills, joined the two interior chains with the coastal ranges which stretched northward and southward along the banks of the Pacific. These interlacing parallel ridges, broken by river gorges and plentifully watered by Pacific storms, encased a number of small valleys where good soil and adequate precipitation offered excellent farming opportunities. The Coastal Mountains descended precipitously to the very edge of the Pacific, forming a wall of forbidding cliffs broken by only a few good harbors—one at San Diego, a shallow inlet at Monterey Bay, a magnificent landlocked bay at San Francisco, and a well-protected harbor at Puget Sound. The paucity of good ports concentrated commercial activity along the Pacific coast in a few favored spots.

Embraced within the mountain ranges were four valleys destined to play a prominent role in the history of the frontier. North of the Columbia River, and nestled between the Cascades and the northern coastal ranges, was the 350-mile-long Puget Sound Trough—level, fertile, and well watered, with the nearby harbor at Puget Sound providing a convenient outlet. Even more tempting was the Willamette Valley south of the lower Columbia River. That broad alluvial plain, drained by the Willamette River and plentifully moistened by rain-bearing winds from the Pacific, proved extremely attractive to American pioneers; most of the immigrants who trekked westward along the Oregon Trail in the 1840s and 1850s sought farms on its fertile surface.

The remaining two valleys were in California—the Sacramento Valley to the north, the San Joaquin Valley to the south—both taking their names from rivers emptying into San Francisco Bay. Inadequate rainfall, evidenced in the sagebrush and bunch grass dotting their level floors, handicapped normal agriculture, although the lower Sacramento Valley could be farmed profitably. That region, where good soil and grasslands already shorn of trees made pioneering easy, was the mecca of the overlanders whose covered wagons cut the deep ruts of the California Trail during the 1840s.

When white men entered the Pacific Coast Province they found perhaps 300,000 Indians in possession, a large number for a California that was not the land of milk and honey modern imagination and irrigation have made it. The natives were notable for their linguistic and tribal diversity; they were broken into countless small bands or tribes that not only lived in semi-isolation but spoke their own local dialects of the linguistic stocks represented there: Athapascan, Shoshonean, and Yuman. Division was made necessary by the environment, for along the coast, as in the Great Basin, the paucity of natural foods forced Indians into small bands in their perpetual quest for subsistence. Their material culture was correspondingly low; they lived in brush shelters or lean-tos, wore only breechcloths, used simple weapons, and either dug roots from the ground or ate anything, living or dead, they could lay their hands on. Only in basketry did they show any degree of advancing civilization; their coiled and twined baskets were as skillfully constructed as those of any other North American Indians. In common with all nomadic peoples who roamed constantly in search of food, the social organization developed by the "Diggers" of California was at a low level. Controls were based largely on the family; on the rare occasions when they united in bands their leaders were little more than "talking chiefs" with no real power over the group. Unlike the Plains Indians, the California natives were short, stout, and dark skinned, with prominent Mongoloid features.

Variants of this culture were evident in northern California, Oregon, and Washington, where more abundant food supplies in the form of forest animals and salmon allowed the tribes to develop a richer life. Plank houses, canoes, and extensive woodworking, as well as a highly structured social and political organization, evidenced an advanced culture shared to some extent by the northern California Karok, Yurok, Shasta, and Hupa tribes. More warlike than less favored natives of the lower Pacific coast, who were virtually exterminated by the failure of Spain's mission system and cruel treatment at the hands of gold-rushing '49ers, the northern Indians gave up their lands to the whites only after a bitter struggle.

This was the panorama that lay before American pioneers as they crossed the Mississippi to begin the conquest of the Far West. A land of magnificent vistas, grass-tufted plains, soaring mountain peaks, parched deserts, subhumid climate, and varied Indian bands awaited the pioneers. But in that land were fortunes in buried mineral wealth, riches in beaver peltry waiting in every stream, green grasslands that offered ideal pasturage, and fertile valleys where good soil needed only the magic touch of man to yield up its rich bounty. Those garden spots lured adventurers westward during the nineteenth century until the conquest of the continent was completed.

The Spanish Barrier

1540-1776

The westward advance of the Anglo-American frontier was accomplished only by absorbing or pushing aside prior occupants of the continent. Some were natives; they were driven slowly backward, then crowded into reservations. Others were fellow Europeans. During the seventeenth century the Dutch of New York and the Spaniards of the Carolinas were thrust aside. In the eighteenth century the eastern Mississippi Valley was wrested from its French overlords. Now, in the nineteenth century, the same fate waited the Spanish-Americans whose ranches, mission stations, pueblos, and presidios dotted the trans-Mississippi West from Texas to California. Before American frontiersmen could reach the shores of the Pacific the Spanish barrier must be overrun.

Spain's advance toward the Southwest began in 1519 when Hernán Cortés led a band of stout-hearted followers into the heart of Mexico, convinced some of the Indians that he had come to deliver them from oppressive rulers, and with their help marched into lake-encircled Tenochtitlán, capital of the Aztec "empire." There Cortés found the wealth long sought by *conquistadors*, and there the delighted Spaniards established headquarters for their New World domains. From this Mexican city conquerors went forth to subdue neighboring provinces and press natives into service as laborers on ranch and in mine, or to fan out over the neighboring countryside in quest of new sources of wealth. By 1522 these adventurers were at Zacatula, on the Pacific, where a shipyard was built, vessels constructed, and the task of exploring the northern coast begun. Eleven years later a skilled navigator, Fortún Jiménez, discovered what he took to be a beautiful island far to the westward; California, he called it, after a mythical land which story tellers placed "at the right hand of the Indies . . . very close to the

Terrestrial Paradise.'' Not until 1539 did another follower of Cortés, Francisco de Ulloa, demonstrate that this landfall was a peninsula rather than an island. Sailing northward along the Lower California coast, he reached the head of the Gulf of California, ascended the Colorado River for a short distance, and returned after taking possession in the name of his ruler.

The barren wastes and arid deserts that greeted explorers should have convinced them that the northern country concealed no fortunes in precious metals, but more was needed to quench the ambitions of Cortés' rival and successor, Antonio de Mendoza, who arrived as first viceroy of New Spain in 1535. The coast might be inhospitable, but from the interior exciting tales poured into Mexico City. An Indian slave told of journeying forty days northward, where he saw "seven very large towns which had streets of silver workers." Mendoza listened, enchanted. Surely here was the wealth that had eluded Spain's explorers. Those rumors must be investigated.

Especially as an ideal guide for such an expedition was available. Stephen Dorantes, better known as Estevan the Black, had been one of the four survivors of the ill-fated expedition under Pánfilo de Narváez that reached Mexico City in 1536 after a harrowing journey across the continent. Estevan, a Negro slave, was purchased by Mendoza shortly afterward and was not reluctant to tell his master that he himself had seen great cities far to the northward during his wanderings. So it was that he was disguised as a medicine man and dispatched from Mexico City in 1539, accompanied by several Indian companions, and bearing instructions to send back wooden crosses whose size would indicate his distance from the goal. Behind him followed a sizeable expedition, headed by Fray Marcos de Niza, a Franciscan, with the usual retinue. Scarcely had the main force passed the boundaries of civilization than the crosses began to arrive from Estevan, each larger than the last, and with them word that he was now being escorted by almost 300 Indians who showered him with ornaments and jewels. Then, abruptly, no more crosses arrived. Fray Marcos, alarmed but undaunted, pressed ahead until he gazed across a valley at a great city that seemed larger than that of Mexico. Estevan, he learned, had tried to enter, and had been killed by the natives. Bearing this word, Marcos de Niza hurried back to tell Mendoza of the wonders he had seen. Surely he had discovered the fabled Seven Cities of Cibola, founded, according to hoary Spanish legend, by seven bishops who fled westward in the eighth century to a fabulously rich land beyond the Atlantic. Perhaps wealth would be found there to rival that of Mexico or Peru! Little wonder the viceroy burned with ambition to conquer the Seven Cities, or that *conquistadors* vied for the privilege of leading the expedition against them.

Francisco Vásquez de Coronado, a loyal follower of Mendoza, won the coveted post. He fitted out an elaborate retinue—225 mounted cavaliers, sixty-two foot soldiers, 800 Indians, 1,000 Negro and native slaves, herds of horses, oxen, cows, sheep, and swine, droves of laden mules—sent three supply ships up the coast with equipment, enlisted Fray Marcos as his guide, and on February 23, 1540, set out from the Spanish town of Compostela into the unknown northland. From the first bad luck dogged his footsteps. The supply ships entered the Colorado River safely but failed to locate the main party, which was struggling northward across the dry plateaus of northern Mexico amidst curses voiced by blue-blooded cavaliers as they painfully learned the difficulties of packing a mule or wringing subsistence from poverty-stricken Indians. In July the Spaniards reached their objective, the first of the Seven Cities, but they found no streets of silversmiths, no olive-skinned countrymen, no civilized domain. Instead a mud-walled pueblo of the Zuñi Indians, perched on the high plateau between the Little Colorado and Rio Grande rivers in New Mexico, awaited them. "Such were the curses that some hurled at Friar Marcos," wrote the awed chronicler, "that I pray God may protect him from them."

The heartbroken Coronado moved on to the banks of the Rio Grande to establish a winter camp. Small expeditions that roamed between the Grand Canyon of the Colorado and the southern Rockies brought back enough plundered food to keep the men alive, but of gold and silver they found none in all that plateau country. Nor did Coronado care. During the winter he stumbled upon a plains Indian, held as a Pueblo slave, who told marvelous lies of a city of Quivira, far to the north and east, where a noble lord "took his afternoon nap under a great tree on which were hung a great number of little gold bells, which put him to sleep as they swung in the air. . . . Everyone had their ordinary dishes made of wrought plate, and the jugs and bowls were of gold." With the first hint of spring the excited Spaniards were off once more, taking with them the slave, whom they called The Turk "because he looked like one." The vast expanse of the High Plains and the roving herds of buffalo amazed them; "the country is like a bowl, so that when a man sits down, the horizon surrounds him all around at the distance of a musket shot," wrote one, and another complained that for many leagues "they had seen nothing but cows and the sky." Across to the Pecos and the Brazos rivers they went, then northward for forty-two days until they reached Quivira—a collection of grass huts of the Wichita Indians on the Kansas River, where the chief wore a copper plate about his neck but there was no gold. Thoroughly discouraged, Coronado turned back to Mexico City which was reached early in 1542.

Mendoza was still not convinced that all the northland was barren. In June, 1542, he ordered two tiny ships and a nondescript crew under Juan Rodríquez Cabrillo to sail northward along the unexplored west coast of Lower California. Stopping frequently to take possession of the soil "in the name of His Majesty and of the most illustrious Señor Don Antonio Mendoza," Cabrillo pressed on until January, 1543, when an infected leg caused his death. His lieutenant, Bartolomé Ferrelo, continued until storms near the 42nd parallel turned him back. He sailed too far from land to discover the harbors at San Francisco and Monterey, but Cabrillo had located the bay at San Diego, later to become an important Spanish stronghold on the

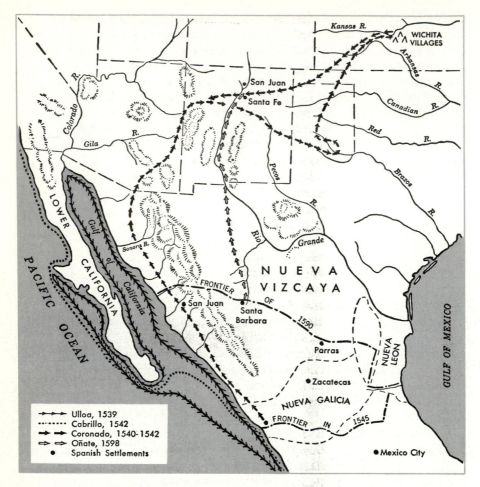

The Northern Mexican Frontier in the Sixteenth Century

California coast. The explorations of Ferrelo, Cabrillo, Coronado, and Ulloa vastly enlarged Spain's geographical knowledge and gave Spaniards a firm claim to the Southwest.

When Mendoza left the viceregal office in 1550 exploration beyond the northern fringes of New Spain was temporarily halted. His successors, realizing that no great wealth lay hidden in the heart of the continent, turned to developing resources nearer at hand. During the next half-century the Mexican frontier moved slowly northward, with miners, ranchers, and mission fathers as its trail-blazers. The advance began when discoveries of silver at Zacatecas in 1546 precipitated such a mining rush that the region north of Mexico City, the province of Nueva Galicia, was rapidly populated after 1548. During the next decade a number of mining sites still farther north were settled by adventuresome Spaniards and their Indian allies, who encountered great difficulties in subduing the nomadic natives and putting them to work in the mines. Bloody wars handicapped the extension of the new mining frontier; most labor was provided by sedentary southern tribes that were brought northward. By the early 1560s the country beyond Nueva Galicia was organized as the province of Nueva Vizcaya, with the energetic explorer and town-builder, Francisco de Ibarra, as governor. Mining towns and ranches grew rapidly there, while Ibarra himself led or inspired exploring expeditions which searched for new mining sites in such distant regions as the Sonora River Valley. His untiring efforts extended Mexico's northern frontier as far as southern Chihuahua before 1590.

If left to themselves, New Spain's miners and ranchers would have continued the slow movement northward until they engulfed all Mexico and the southwestern United States. Instead the threat of foreign intruders sent the frontiers forward in a series of spectacular thrusts which planted Spaniards in the American Southwest while great portions of northern Mexico remained unsettled. In Spanish eyes, rapid advance was necessary. By 1580 precious metals from Zacatecas, Nueva Vizcaya, Peru, and the mines of South America poured eastward through Panama or Mexico City to Spanish-bound ships waiting in the Caribbean. Through the same channel flowed wealth from the recently conquered Philippines, brought to Mexico in Manila galleons which regularly plied the Pacific with cargoes of spices, silk, china-ware, and gold. Officials realized the zone between Mexico City and southern Panama was a vulnerable spot in the empire's trade routes; should any foreign intruder reach that highway the wealth of New Spain would be his for the taking.

The first such intruder was Francis Drake, a bold son of England's Devonshire, who had learned to hate the Spaniards while an Elizabethan Sea Hawk and an audacious raider along the Spanish Main. Drake was no ordinary sea captain; his ambitions were grandiose: he would explore the Atlantic and Pacific coasts of South America from the Platte River to northern Chile, seeking harbors, cementing Indian alliances, and laying the basis for future colonies that would challenge possession of the very heartland of Spain's empire. How seriously Drake obeyed his instructions to search for the fabled Strait of Anian—the Northwest Passage—is unknown, but he was prepared to penetrate to the very heart of the Spanish empire in the Pacific. During the gloomy September of 1578 Drake's stout ship, the *Golden Hind*, beat its way through the Straits of Magellan "with its hell darke nights and the mercycles fury of tempestuous storms," to emerge on the broad Pacific where Spaniards gathered their treasure without thought of danger. From port to port he sailed, loading his vessel with gold, silver, and "goodly great emeralds" as long as one's finger. Off the coast of Peru he fell upon a treasure galleon, subdued its astonished crew (who no more expected to see an Englishman in the Pacific than in Heaven), and transferred to his own ship "great riches, as jewels and precious stones, thirteen chests full of reals of plate, fourscore pound weight of gold, and six and twenty tons of silver.'' The *Golden Hind* was loaded to the gunwales now; hence Drake sailed northward as far as the California bay bearing his name, nailed to "a faire great post" a brass plate proclaiming England's ownership of "New Albion," and on July 23, 1579, turned his vessel's prow westward to complete the circumnavigation of the globe. He returned to a hero's welcome; Queen Elizabeth knighted him and shared privately in the profits of the voyage.

Drake's accomplishments were more far-reaching, for he left a horrified New Spain behind him. If one Englishman could invade the Pacific, others might follow; the New World's wealth would never be safe until the approaches to Mexico were guarded. Colonies must be planted throughout the northern hinterland; the expense would be insignificant compared to the losses of another Drake's raid. Moreover still-hidden mines might be found there, or Indian workers to replace the worn-out natives of Mexico, or native souls for conversion. Those were the prospects that set Spain's officials to colony planning even before the *Golden Hind* reached England. For a time they could only plan—while the war with England that resulted in defeat for the Spanish Armada (1588) absorbed Spanish wealth and energy—but by 1595 they were ready to launch their projects.

One was the occupation of the California coast, both to guard the northern approach to Mexico and provide a haven for Manila galleons on their way back from the Philippines. The first necessity was a favorable harbor. A search for a site undertaken by the captain of a treasure ship in 1595 ended disastrously when the vessel was wrecked in Drake's Bay, but a second expedition in 1602 enjoyed more success. This was led by Sebastián Vizcaíno, a navigator of considerable experience but little skill, who commanded three ships and some 200 men. Sailing northward from Mexico around the stormy tip of Lower California, he reached a good harbor previously noted by explorers, giving it the name of "the glorious San Diego." The Santa Catalina Islands were discovered as he continued on to Monterey Bay, which Vizcaíno believed was the harbor sought by Spain. He carried on his search, however, as far as Drake's Bay, missing San Francisco Harbor once more. His enthusiastic reports convinced Spanish officials Monterey Bay was an ideal site for a colony, but before the settlement materialized the end of the English war made an outpost seem unnecessary.

The second colony planned to frustrate English intrusions in the Pacific fared better. This was in the interior, for Drake's raid convinced Spaniards that the Elizabethan seaman had discovered the fabled Northwest Passage. The fate of New Spain depended on forestalling England's occupation of that waterway. Selected to lay out the settlement was Juan de Oñate, a rich mine owner of Zacatecas, in whose veins flowed the blood of the *conquistadors*. Oñate was no stranger to that northern wasteland; no less than five minor expeditions had already penetrated its secrets and brought back helpful reports of farming possibilities there. By offering generous land bounties, he recruited a little force of 130 soldier-settlers; with them, an equal number of slaves, and eight Franciscan missionaries, he set out for his unpromising domain in February, 1598, driving 7,000 cattle and eighty-three loaded wagons. Marching northward from Santa Bárbara, the party crossed the Rio Grande below present-day El Paso, then followed the river northward to the mountain-rimmed valley of the Chama River. There Oñate called on friendly Indians to help build his town, which he called San Juan, and to construct a dam, an irrigation ditch, and a church. For a time things went badly; Oñate wanted to search for gold mines while his men preferred ranching or farming, but other settlers drifted in to lay out new towns such as Santa Fe (circa 1609). By this time the colonizers had found the key to their future prosperity. Oñate himself introduced the first sheep into New Mexico. They took naturally to the sparse grasses of that semiarid region, multiplying so rapidly that within a few years as many as 15,000 yearly were driven southward to Chihuahua and another 25,000 to Viscaya where they were in such demand that they were used as a medium for exchange. By 1620 when the Pilgrims landed in New England the province of New Mexico was established, with a population of 250 Spanish pioneers and 500 loyal Indians.

The burst of expansion that pushed New Spain's frontier northward into New Mexico ended in 1605 with the close of the Anglo-Spanish war. With England no longer feared, expenditures on profitless outposts did not seem justified. Neither were private adventurers attracted to a region whose meagre resources and wild Indians promised neither wealth nor an adequate labor supply. Spain's frontier advance might have halted in southern Nueva Vizcaya had not one type of pioneer been undeterred by unhospitable conditions. That was the missionary. For the next seventy-five years Dominican, Franciscan, and Jesuit priests moved steadily northward, until all northern Mexico was occupied and settlement ready to push on into Texas, Arizona, and California.

The mission as a frontier institution was not new; on every Spanish borderland cross and sword moved forward together. In the past, however, missionaries aided *conquistadors* and settlers by pacifying previously conquered natives. Now the role was reversed. Friars, advancing into the wilderness in their endless quest for souls, were followed by soldiers or ranchers who came to guard the mission stations or capitalize on wealth uncovered by mission fathers. The pattern became standardized. A lone friar with a few friendly natives set out from the mission frontier to seek a location for a new station. He chose an Indian village in some fertile valley, returned to his own mission, and led back a party of three to ten missionaries, as many families of Christianized Indians, and a handful of soldiers. Once on the chosen spot they urged tribesmen to help build crude habitations, then began the task of religious instruction. Within a year or two the faithful were set to work on a permanent church, often an elaborate structure of plastered adobe, richly ornamented to please the color-loving natives. Nearby were scattered a home for the missionaries, a blacksmith shop, flour mill, weaving rooms, carpentry shops, and the homes of Indians who had been persuaded to abandon their nomadic lives for Christianity and the ways of the white man.

There the friars labored mightily. Their task was not only to win souls, but to teach the agriculture and industries which would convert Indians into useful citizens. Hence each missionary was not only a religious instructor but a manager of a cooperative farm, a skilled rancher, and an expert teacher of carpentry, weaving, and countless other trades. The skill with which they executed these tasks attested to their considerable executive talents, just as the ease with which they pacified the most rebellious natives demonstrated their kindly personalities and diplomacy. Only rarely was the calm of a mission station marred by a native uprising; most Indians adapted slowly to Christian culture, when it did not conflict too directly with their closely held beliefs and practices, and substituted the religious pageantry of the Roman Catholic Church for the ceremonies of their own religions. Usually ten or more years were required to win over a tribe; then the station was converted into a parish church, the neophytes released from discipline and given a share of the mission property, and the friars moved on to begin the process anew. The mission station was a dynamic institution, forever intruding into new wildernesses, and leaving behind a civilized region.

When the mission frontier began its northern march at the opening of the seventeenth century the isolated New Mexican colony was separated from the Nueva Vizcaya settlements by almost 600 miles of arid wastes and rugged mountains. The physiographic features of northern Mexico determined the nature of the mission station advance by dividing the region into three areas. Along the west coast ran a coastal lowland separated from the rest of Mexico by the lofty Sierra Madre, a formidable barrier of towering peaks and deeply etched canyons almost impossible to cross. The advanced coastal tribes and primitive Indians who occupied the mountain valleys were selected by the Jesuits for salvation. East of the Sierra Madres was the central plateau of Mexico, rising 7,000 feet above the coastal plain and sloping gradually downward to join the tablelands of Arizona and New Mexico. That was the domain marked out for the Franciscan conquest. The Dominican stronghold lay along the east coast where mountain ranges not only cut them off from their fellow religionists but barred their path northward. They played little part in the settlement of the American Southwest.

The Jesuits were the first to begin the advance. Their pioneer on the northern frontier, Fray Gonzalo de Tapia, established the station of San Felipe on the Sinaloa River in 1591, and within a year reaped a harvest of 2,000 native souls. Success encouraged Fray Gonzalo to move on to the Fuerte River, where an Indian uprising not only won him the crown of martyrdom but led New Spain's officials to send a detachment of troops to protect the missionaries. For the next three decades the hard-bitten, bandy-legged commander of these soldiers, Captain Diego Martínez de Hurdaide, worked hand in hand with Jesuits to push the frontier northward. One by one the tribes of the Sinaloa frontier were subdued and Christianized. The

Fuerte Valley was entered and the station of Ahome founded, then the Mayo River valley where the Tesin mission was established and the Yaqui Valley where in 1617 the Jesuits built an imposing church at Tórin. Ahead lay the peaceful tribes of the upper Yaqui River; in 1620 the fathers founded the station of Batuco for their benefit. Ahead, too, lay the friendly Indians of the Sonora Valley who encouraged the Black Robes to found a group of stations about Pitic between 1638 and 1646. By that time the Jesuits maintained thirty-five missions along the coast, each caring for from one to four Indian towns. Although the advance slowed down as they entered the fringes of the hostile Apache country, they established the station of Cucurpe in the upper San Miguel Valley in 1687.

In the meantime other Jesuits moved northward along the eastern flank of the rugged Sierra Madre. Saving the primitive tribes of that semiarid upland proved difficult, for they were a wild, fleet-footed people, who did not take kindly to restraint. Obstacles only stirred the missionaries to greater

The Northern Mexican Frontier in the Seventeenth Century

efforts. Using the town of Parral as their headquarters, they extended their influence as far northward as the Tutuaca station by 1650. An Indian revolt that year wiped out these gains and discouraged Jesuit efforts for two decades, but in 1673 the northward march was resumed. Within five years stations at Tutuaca and Yepómera were established where eight Jesuits guarded the souls of Indians in thirty-two pueblos. By that time the Black Robes reigned over all the coastal plain and Sierra Madre country from central Mexico to a point near the present United States border.

While the Jesuits moved northward on lowlands and mountains, the Franciscans made spectacular gains on the central plateau. By 1645 their mission frontier reached the upper Conchos River and began to advance down that stream toward the Rio Grande. The most important gain was made in 1659 when a leading Franciscan, Fray García de San Francisco, led two companions overland to the Rio Grande ford near present-day El Paso to establish the station of Nuestra Señora de Guadalupe. The site proved so advantageous that within three years permanent buildings were completed, farmers drifted in, and the El Paso district assumed aspects of permanence. Its growth was hurried by the Pueblo Revolt of 1680. That uprising began along the upper Rio Grande when a giant Negro named Domingo Naranjo who had fled New Spain to join the Taos Pueblo a few years before proclaimed himself the spokesman for the god Pohe-yemo and ordered the Indians to slaughter their Spanish overlords. Dozens died in that attack, and hundreds more fled southward to the comparative safety of El Paso. The influx forced Spanish officials to establish a presidio there in 1683; at the same time a mission was founded where the Conchos joined the Rio Grande.

A third arm of the Mexican mission frontier reached out toward the Northeast. Its center was the province of Nuevo León, established in the late sixteenth century with its capital at Monterrey, and its pioneers Franciscan fathers seeking a harvest of souls in the country below the Rio Grande. Best known was Fray Lários, an earnest friar, who in the years just after 1670 founded the station of Monclova as a center for a group of four missions along the Salado River valley in the region later erected into the province of Coahuila. The fruits of these efforts were apparent by 1680. At that time the mission frontier stretched from Monterrey to the Conchos River, swept northward to include the numerous Franciscan stations in New Mexico, and reached the Pacific at the Sonora River. Behind lay a land of sedentary and Christianized natives, ahead a land of unsaved souls that soon lured missionaries into the present United States. To the northeast the road was blocked by hostile Apache, but to the north and northwest lay an unexplored domain known to the Spaniards as Pimería Alta. There the missionaries first entered the American Southwest.

In the van was an Italian-born priest who almost single handed won a new domain for Spain. Fray Eusebio Francisco Kino, a man "merciful to others but cruel to himself," reached the Sonora borderland in 1687, built the mission station of Dolores high on the San Miguel River, and threw himself into the task of winning heathen souls. For a time he was busy founding a chain of missions along the Altar and Magdalena rivers, but Fray Eusebio was never content as long as unsaved humans or unexplored lands lay ahead. In 1691 his religious wanderlust carried him into Arizona where, along the Santa Cruz and San Pedro valleys, he found natives eager for word of the Gospel. Nothing would do but to build a station among them; after cattle ranches were established to assure a food supply Father Kino in 1700 led a party northward to lay out the mission of San Xavier del Bac. The venture thrived from the first. Other stations were established in the vicinity; cattle ranches and farms followed as settlers moved in. Over them all the padre ruled with benevolent skill, although his real interest was that of the explorer. In all he made fourteen journeys of more than several hundred miles each, either alone or with a few companions, and on his death in 1711 left a series of excellent maps which added immeasurably to Spain's knowledge of the northern frontier.

If left to themselves the Franciscans would have occupied Texas just as Kino and his Jesuit companions settled Arizona. By the middle seventeenth century their stations were advancing steadily in that direction, some northward in the Nuevo León province, others eastward to the El Paso district or from New Mexico. By that time, too, Franciscan explorers searching for unsaved souls were investigating the possibilities of Texas. One group from New Mexico reached the upper waters of the Colorado River as early as 1632, another visited the Tejas Indians of the Trinity River valley in 1650, and a third from the mission station of Monclova baptized a number of Texan natives in 1675. Activities reached a near climax in 1683 when a delegation of Jumano Indians visited the El Paso district to ask the friars for spiritual guidance and the civil authorities for troops to protect them from threatening Apaches. The invitation sent the tiny Spanish outpost into a bustle of activity. Troops were raised, a delegation of missionaries selected, and a party formed to march northward as far as the junction of the Concho and Colorado rivers where a temporary altar was erected. The crop of souls and buffalo hides during a six-week stay proved so satisfactory that both church and civil authorities determined to seek permission for a permanent station in Texas. Before they could do so alarming news shocked the northern frontier. A new invader threatened that poorly guarded borderland.

France was the villain now, and its agent was Robert Cavelier, Sieur de La Salle. That visionary empire builder, hoping to connect the St. Lawrence and Mississippi river systems with a chain of trading posts, set sail from France in 1684, bound for the mouth of the Mississippi where he planned to build a stronghold. Missing the mouth of the river, he landed at Matagorda Bay on the Texas coast in January, 1685. After throwing up a rough fort, Ft. St. Louis, La Salle spent the next two years searching for the elusive Mississippi. On the last expedition, early in 1687, his overwrought followers rebelled, murdered their leader, and set out on foot for the French settlements in distant Canada. The few who remained at Ft. St. Louis were either slaughtered or enslaved by Texas Indians.

Word of these events, reaching New Spain in the form of exaggerated tales from the Indians, sent Spanish officialdom into a panic, for their fevered imaginations translated La Salle's venture into a threat against Mexico itself. Nine expeditions were hurriedly sent out to repel the invaders; one under Governor Alonso de León of Coahuila finally located the ruins of Ft. St. Louis and the charred bones of its murdered defenders in the spring of 1689. The welcome news of La Salle's failure, heard from the lips of two of his enslaved companions, did not quiet Spanish fears. The dread Frenchmen might try again; Mexico would never be safe until Texas was guarded. That warning, stated in emphatic language by de León, was echoed by the Franciscan missionary who accompanied him, Fray Damián Massanet. The Indians of Texas, the good friar reported to Mexico City, were ripe for conversion. Little wonder that the viceroy promptly consented to occupy Texas.

The expedition that set out from Monclova in the spring of 1690 under the joint command of de León and Father Massanet consisted of 110 soldiers and four Franciscan missionaries. They moved eastward to the headquarters of the Tejas tribe in the fertile Neches River valley where they labored the summer through building the station of San Francisco de los Tejas. That fall three missionaries and as many soldiers were left to guard the tiny outpost. A year later the garrison was increased to nine, for by that time the Indians were so warlike that even the stout-hearted Massanet admitted the need of a presidio to guard the missionaries. Before one could be built a native uprising in the autumn of 1693 forced the friars to retreat sadly to the Rio Grande. For the next two decades Texas remained unoccupied. During those years the Mexican frontier advanced to its southern edge when in 1699 the presidio of San Juan Bautista and three Franciscan missions were established at Eagle Pass on the west bank of the Rio Grande.

While New Spain slept, New France acted. La Salle's dreams came true in 1699 when the French built their colony of Louisiana at the mouth of the Mississippi. In vain Mexico's officials protested to Madrid; Spain's throne was occupied by Philip V, grandson of Louis XIV, who stood docilely by while his grandfather's legions overran a land that might have been his. One among the patriots of New Spain refused to be discouraged by official indifference. Fray Francisco Hidalgo, who served for a time among the Tejas Indians, was so eager to return to his former charges that he conceived a bold plan to stir his superiors into action. Early in 1713 he penned a veiled letter to the governor of Louisiana, hinting that French traders would be kindly received south of the Rio Grande. The delighted governor responded as Hidalgo hoped; an experienced trader, Louis de St. Denis, was dispatched westward with a supply of trading goods. Proceeding at a leisurely pace, St. Denis paused to found a post at the Indian village of Natchitoches on the Red River, then journeyed across Texas to emerge at the presidio of San Juan Bautista in July, 1714.

The effect on Mexican officials was that foreseen by Hidalgo. St. Denis and his followers were clapped into jail. While they languished there plans were formulated to forestall similar invasions. The reoccupation of Texas was the only answer. An expedition set out in June, 1716, with a soldier, Captain Domingo Ramón, in command, twenty-five soldiers, nine missionaries, and St. Denis as guide, for that glib-tongued Frenchman not only talked himself out of jail but into marriage with the presidio commandant's granddaughter. Reaching the Neches River in July, 1716, they fell to building the mission station of Nuestro Padre San Francisco de los Tejas and three minor stations, all east of the river. The presence of French trading goods among the Tejas Indians warned Captain Ramón that this outpost could be protected only by planting additional missions across the path used by natives in reaching St. Denis' post at Nachitoches. Before the year was out he built the Mission San Miguel only fifteen miles from the Red River, and the Mission Ais between the Neches and Sabine rivers. Six stations, all well equipped and guarded by a small presidio, then challenged French intruders. Two years later the *villa* of San Antonio was established in western Texas to guard the route between the frontier outposts and Mexico.

Spain established its northern frontier none too soon, for enemies began pressing upon its weakly guarded bulwarks even before the last outpost was completed. They came as French traders, moving out of Louisiana in quest of furs, hides, and gold. Their highways were the rivers that fringed Texas and New Mexico—the Red, Canadian, and Arkansas; their objective was the trade of the Plains tribes. For half a century they pressed upon New Spain's northern hinterland while Spaniards fought back with gun and Gospel to retain control of territories painfully won.

Skirmishing began in 1719 when three French expeditions used the outbreak of a European war between France and Spain as an excuse to test the Texas defenses. The first, a tiny force of seven soldiers from Natchitoches, captured the unguarded San Miguel mission in June, 1719, so alarming the friars of the Neches missions that all fled toward San Antonio near which one of the fathers, Antonio Margil, founded the Mission of San José y San Miguel de Aguayo a year later. The second, a band of traders commanded by the bold Claude Du Tisné, advanced overland from the Missouri River to the Jumano Indian villages on the Arkansas River where they audaciously plied their trade on New Spain's doorstep. The third struck even nearer. A trading party led by Bernard de la Harpe explored the middle Red River, crossed to the Arkansas and Canadian valleys, and attempted to open trade with the nomads of that open country. Neither Du Tisné nor de la Harpe won over the Indians they encountered, but the threat to Texas was nonetheless real. Clearly the fortifications must be strengthened or the borderland might fall to the French and their native allies.

The task was entrusted to two seasoned frontiersmen. The wealthy soldier-governor of Coahuila, the Marquis of Aguayo, raised 500 mounted troops and in November, 1720, led them out of Monclova along the road to

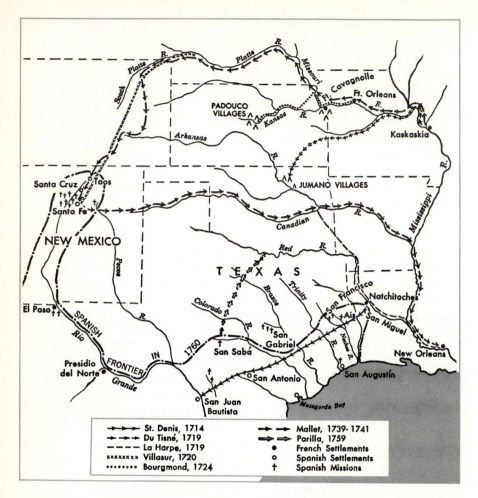

The Texas-New Mexico Frontier, 1700–1763

San Antonio. One by one the forsaken missions of eastern Texas were restored, then strengthened by the addition of a well-garrisoned presidio at Mission San Miguel. When Aguayo returned home during the winter of 1721–22 he paused to build a station and fort at Matagorda Bay. These distant outposts completed a chain of sixteen presidios that by this time stretched in a giant arc from East Texas to Sonora, manned by a total garrison of 806 men. Spain's northern rim was guarded, but the ramparts were none too strong.

They could be made safer, particularly in East Texas, if the Indians just north of the presidios were won from French to Spanish allegiance. This was the objective of the forty-five soldiers and sixty friendly natives under Pedro de Villasur who set out from Santa Fe during the summer of 1720.

They moved northward beneath the shadows of the Rockies without sighting a single Indian until they reached the Pawnee country near the junction of the North and South Platte rivers where they camped on August 12, 1720. All that night hostile Pawnee crept toward them under the protection of the tall grass, and at daybreak rushed pell-mell into the camp. The surprised Spaniards were unable to defend themselves against the sudden assault; Villasur was killed and only thirteen soldiers managed to escape. Seldom had a defeat cost so dearly. Spain's prestige was so low that every Plains tribe deserted to the French or sent its war parties to molest the enfeebled Spanish defenders.

The French were quick to take advantage of this golden opportunity. A skilled frontiersman, Étienne Veniard de Bourgmond, whose Indian wife and long career as a Missouri trader equipped him for the delicate task of tribal diplomacy, was hurried westward from Kaskaskia in the fall of 1723 with forty traders and a large store of trading goods. Moving swiftly up the Missouri, Bourgmond built a fortification, Ft. Orleans, in western Missouri, then pressed on along the Kansas River to the Padouca village on the upper reaches of that stream. There the skilled pioneer spread bale after bale of presents before the eager-eyed natives; all those and more, he said, would be theirs if they promised to trade only with Frenchmen. The Padouca chief readily agreed, assuring Bourgmond that although the Spaniards "bring us horses and bring us a few knives and a few awls and a few axes . . . they are not like you, who give us great quantities of merchandise, such as we have never seen before." Bourgmond's success seriously threatened New Spain's defenses; apparently the French were destined to make alliance after alliance until their native allies dominated the debatable land north of Texas. Yet the threat failed to develop when the outbreak of the Natchez and Fox wars east of the Mississippi during the 1720s forced New France to abandon its plans for a trading empire on the Plains country.

Not until the close of the 1730s could traders turn to molesting the Spanish borderlands once more. The leaders were two brothers, Pierre and Paul Mallet, who gained the idea that brought them fame while trading along the Mississippi. Why not, they reasoned, establish direct trade with the Spanish town of Santa Fe? Surely the Spaniards there, joined to Mexico by only a tortuous mountain trail, would pay well in peltry and silver for French goods; surely Indians along the way would welcome well-equipped traders. To test the idea the Mallets set out from Illinois in 1739, taking with them half a dozen companions and a plentiful supply of trading goods. Up the Missouri they went, until some Pawnee Indians corrected their hazy geographic notions, then out along the Platte and southward until they burst into Santa Fe on July 22, 1739. The reception waiting them reflected the eagerness of Spanish frontier settlers for manufactured goods; mission bells rang in welcome, splendid clothes were provided to replace their travel-stained garments, and comfortable homes were placed at their disposal. For nine months they lived luxuriously as guests of the New Mexican governor while a messenger hurried to Mexico City seeking permission for trade between Santa Fe and Louisiana. The answer, although not unexpected, was nonetheless disappointing; the Spanish empire, the New Mexicans were sternly reminded, was closed to all outside traders. The Mallets must be summarily deported.

This harsh decree meant little more to the inhabitants of Santa Fe than to the French traders themselves. Like all westerners they were more concerned with getting what they wanted than with abstract theories of empire. One thing they coveted was cheap manufactured goods. Hence they let the Mallets know they would violate the orders of their distant viceroy and welcome merchants from Louisiana. Bearing that welcome news, the jubilant brothers began their return journey on May 1, 1740, blazing a new trail along a river since known as the Canadian. During the next decade a number of traders journeyed regularly between the Mississippi Valley and New Mexico, bringing out implements, cloth, and other manufactured goods which were bartered for gold, silver, and furs. At first expeditions originated in New Orleans but by the middle 1740s French diplomats won over the Comanche and Jumano Indians and planted Ft. Cavagnolle in the midst of the Kansa tribe, thus opening a route to Santa Fe from the Illinois villages. The Santa Fe trade not only drained wealth from New Spain's northern province but gave the French a chance to establish friendly relations with the Plains Indians whose hunting grounds fringed the Texas-New Mexico frontier.

There, as on other American borderlands where Spanish, French, and English civilizations clashed, Spaniards failed to win the friendship of native tribes because their frontier institutions were little to the liking of the Indians. They offered the Indians salvation and discipline; the French promised brandy, guns, and knives. The Spanish urged natives to abandon nomadic ways for sedentary lives in mission villages; the Frenchmen followed the wandering Plains tribes across the vastness of the western prairies. Spaniards tried to recast natives in a Spanish mold and failed; Frenchmen learned to live as the natives did and succeeded. Only the French government's failure to exploit its advantage saved Spain's northern provinces during those years. But for royal indifference and the outbreak of King George's War, which cast the two nations as allies, both Texas and New Mexico would probably have fallen into the hands of French pioneers and their Indian allies.

By contrast, the efforts of Spaniards to defend their threatened domain were often inefficient and ineffective. On only one Texan frontier did they strengthen their position between 1740 and 1763 when the French made their spectacular gains. The southeastern coast of Texas, a neglected wilderness cut off from the rest of Mexico by the steep Sierra Gorda Range, was occupied by fragments of Indian tribes, renegades both white and native, and the outcasts found in any region beyond the law's pale. In 1746 that coastal lowland between the Pánuco and San Antonio rivers—was set aside as the province of Nuevo Santander under the governorship of an experienced Indian fighter, José de Escandón. After several exploring trips into his domain, Escandón set out in December, 1748, from the neighboring state of Querétaro, leading 500 colony planters secured by generous cash subsidies and promises of tax-free lands. At each favorable site he left a small garrison, missionaries, and a handful of "settlers and sojourners in the chaparral" until twenty settlements were scattered over the province. Most were south of the Rio Grande but two, Laredo and Dolores, were in Texas. An attempt to found a colony at the mouth of the Nueces failed when warlike Indians attacked Escandón's party, but during the next years settlers from lower Nuevo Santander drifted there, attracted by the ranching possibilities in that land of thick prairie grass, sparkling streams, and rolling countryside. By 1750 6,000 ranchers and miners in Nuevo Santander held southeastern Texas firmly for New Spain.

Less successful were Spanish efforts to expand the Texan frontier northward by winning over French-dominated tribes along the upper reaches of the Brazos and Colorado rivers. In 1746 several mission stations were established on the San Gabriel River, a tributary of the Brazos, at the request of minor tribes. Disease and raids by the fearsome Apache Indians forced the abandonment of the outposts nine years later. More enduring was the San Augustín mission, planted at the mouth of the Trinity in 1756 to hold back threatening French intruders. A final attempt to win the northern country was made that year when a delegation of Apache Indians visited Texas to ask for religious instruction and a presidio. The astonished Spaniards, who had battled those warlike tribesmen for a generation, seized the opportunity to found a mission on the San Sabá River a year later. Only after the station was established did the friars learn the reason for the Apache about-face; they wanted the Spanish to protect them from the dread Comanche. By 1758 bands of Comanche warriors were molesting the missionaries who sent out a call for aid. A punitive expedition of several hundred soldiers under Captain Parilla failed to ease the situation when it was decisively defeated by a Comanche war party on the Red River. Before the year was out the stations were withdrawn to the upper Nueces River and northern Texas abandoned to the Indians.

That was the last attempt to push the Texan frontier northward, as the transfer of Louisiana to Spain in 1763 removed the French menace. For the next generation Texas remained a neglected province, peopled by 2,000 Spaniards and a handful of Christianized Indians. Over it swept the Plains nomads on their buffalo hunts, scarcely aware of the scattered missions, presidios, and villages which symbolized Spain's half-hearted efforts to hold that isolated frontier.

In the meantime the attention of New Spain was directed to the Pacific coast where a new foreign menace threatened the borderlands of Mexico. Russia was the villain. After 1741, when a Danish navigator, Vitus Bering, sailing in the service of the czars, discovered Alaska and the Aleutian Islands,

Cossack traders pushed steadily southward along the North American coast in search of seal and sea otter peltry. By 1763 their vessels were cruising as far south as the Oregon country; near enough to threaten the California gateway to Mexico. So thought José de Gálvez, visitor-general of New Spain, a zealous administrator whose determination to revive the glories of New Spain amounted almost to fanaticism. Why not, he reasoned, forestall the Russians by seizing California at once? From the time that thought entered his mind he pursued the plan with remarkable singleness of purpose; every letter to the court of Charles III was filled with pleas for permission to extend Spain's empire northward. Such enthusiasm was infectious, and in 1767 consent came from across the sea. Gálvez, thoroughly delighted, hurried to Lower California to organize the colonizing party which would translate his dream into reality.

The time was ripe for such an enterprise. The Jesuits, who missionized Lower California, had recently been replaced by fourteen brown-robed Franciscans under Fray Junípero Serra, all inflamed with religious zeal and anxious to aid any enterprise promising a crop of souls. Their help allowed Gálvez to form two colonizing parties with unusual dispatch. One, composed of settlers under the skilled frontiersman Don Gaspar de Portolá and missionaries led by Father Serra, he planned to send overland. The other, made up of three vessels carrying additional colonists and supplies, would sail northward. They would meet at San Diego Bay, move on to Monterey Harbor, and there plant the flag and cross of Spain in the California wilderness.

By the early spring of 1769 all was ready. The ships set sail first and although one was lost at sea the other two reached San Diego Bay after a storm-plagued voyage which left the crews so weakened by scurvy they could scarcely launch the landing boats. The overland party fared better, despite the formidable task of crossing nearly 400 miles of unexplored desert with laden pack animals and several hundred head of cattle. An advance group of twenty-five frontier-seasoned soldiers moved ahead to break trail; behind them came the rest of the immigrants with Portolá and Serra in command. At times water was scarce, at others the road lay deep in sand or twisted across mountain heights, but more often the path lay "level, straight and happy" through flower-decked meadows where "willows, tule and a glad sky" greeted the travelers. Six weeks of journeying brought the 126 survivors to San Diego on July 1, 1769. After Father Serra sang the *Te Deum*, they watched Portolá take formal possession of Spain's newest outpost in the name of his king.

Two weeks of rest was all Portolá allowed his tired followers and those were devoted to building the mission station of San Diego Alcalá for Father Serra. On July 14 the hardy commander set out again, with twenty-seven soldiers, bound for Monterey. Their path lay through fertile valleys "so green that it seemed to us it had been planted" and over low-lying coastal mountains where curious Indians, "as naked as Adam in paradise before he

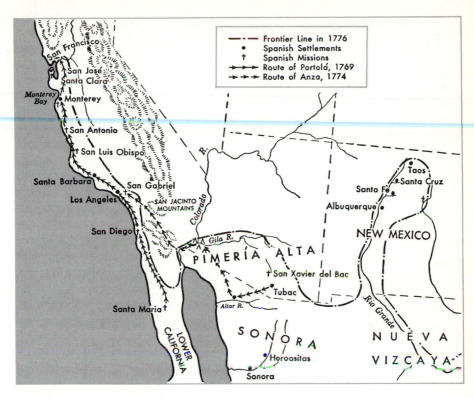

Spanish California, 1763–1776

sinned," offered them tributes of friendship. For a time the formidable Santa Luciá Mountains held them back, but on October 1, 1769, the party stood on the shores of Monterey Bay. The sight that met their eyes was disheartening. Instead of the broad, land-locked harbor described by early explorers, they saw a shallow, shelterless bay. The disappointed Portolá, convinced Monterey must lie somewhere ahead, led his men on for another month before they reached Drake's Bay, the landmarks of which they recognized. They started back, but their greatest discovery lay just ahead. On November 1 a scouting party stumbled upon a harbor so large that "not only all the navy of our most Catholic Majesty but those of all Europe could take shelter." San Francisco Bay, after eluding Spain's navigators for a century, yielded up its secret to an overland party! Portolá's men were too exhausted to take advantage of their find; instead they headed back to San Diego where they arrived on January 24, 1770, "smelling frightfully of mules."

No relief awaited them there. Fifty of the little band left behind with Father Serra were dead of scurvy, the rest sick, and supplies exhausted. For a time despair reigned, even in Portolá's stout heart, but the timely arrival of a supply ship from Mexico, just at the end of a nine-day vigil of prayer, rekindled hope. After waiting a short time for weakened bodies and crushed spirits to be restored, the courageous leader started northward again, reaching Monterey Bay in March, 1770. There he set his men to building the presidio of Monterey and the mission of San Carlos. During the next two years three more outposts were established: San Antonio mission at the southern tip of the Santa Lucíá Mountains, San Gabriel mission north of San Diego, and San Luis Obispo mission on the central coast of California. By 1773 California was guarded by five stations and two presidios, manned by a pitifully small force of sixty-one soldiers and eleven friars.

The feeble settlements could be strengthened in only one way; an overland route to the Mexican province of Sonora must be opened. Such a road would lure settlers northward and, even more important, allow food to reach California from the farms of northern Mexico. Part of the trail was already blazed by a wandering Arizona priest, Fray Francisco Garcés, who in 1771, with "no other escort than his guardian angel," explored the deserts of southern California to the foot of the San Jacinto Mountains. The possibility of extending Garcés' explorations northward occurred to Juan Bautista de Anza, captain of the Pimería Alta fortress of Tubac, a desert-toughened frontiersman who had spent an adventurous lifetime battling the Indians of northern Sonora. His request for permission to lead an overland expedition into California having been granted, he set out on January 8, 1774, followed by twenty leather-jacketed soldiers, a handful of servants and muleteers, Father Garcés, and herds of cattle and pack animals. The party reached the Yuma Indian villages at the junction of the Colorado and Gila rivers without difficulty, but then their trials multiplied. For eleven days they struggled across shifting dunes and parched deserts, only to be turned back when supplies ran out. Again they made the assault, and this time stumbled upon the Cocopa Mountains, a range of sparsely grassed hills that led them to the foot of the San Jacinto Mountains. After those were surmounted, on March 22, 1774, Anza and his party burst upon the surprised missionaries at the San Gabriel mission amidst a chorus of ringing bells, booming muskets, and shouted greetings. By May 26 the explorers were back in Tubac again, having covered more than 2,000 miles of inhospitable country.

The way was clear for the last step in the Spanish occupation of California: the establishment of an outpost on San Francisco Bay. The task was entrusted to Anza, who was placed in command of a motley crew of 240 colonists scraped from the slums and villages of Mexico. They set out from the Sonora village of Horoasitas on October 23, 1775, and by early January were at the San Gabriel mission where Anza allowed his followers a month's rest before pressing onward. When they reached the San Francisco harbor he set them to work, some on the presidio of San Francisco at the tip of the jutting Fort Point peninsula, others on the nearby mission stations of Arroyo de los Dolores and Santa Clara. When those were completed, Anza returned to his beloved desert fortress in northern Mexico, leaving the task of expanding the California settlements to other men. That went on slowly over the next years; San José mission was built in 1777, the town of Los Angeles laid out in 1781, and the presidio and mission of Santa Barbara a year later. The missions were beginning a process that was to make them almost indispensable to the civil and military population. As settlers drifted in, growing herds of cattle and orderly irrigated fields testified to the permanence of the new colony. And sturdy colonists they were, with Spanish, Indian, and Negro blood well mixed; 18 per cent of the Californians were of African descent, while of the forty-four first settlers of Los Angeles twenty-six traced their ancestry to Africa.

By the close of the 1770s New Spain's frontier stretched across the back country from eastern Texas to the shores of San Francisco Bay; a vast bulwark against intruders who threatened rich Mexico. Yet more than a thin line of presidios and mission stations was needed to repulse the enemies who soon hammered at the gates of Spain's fortress. Even as Anza's weary colonists fashioned the log walls of their tiny fort, a new and more aggressive nation was born in the East. The Philadelphia bells which proclaimed the independence of the United States in 1776 tolled the death knell of Spain's American empire. A chain reaction of revolution would soon follow, driving Spain from control of the vast colonies she had once established. As for the lands north of the Rio Grande, over the next decades the lusty young United States sent a stream of pioneers westward, to wrest away the lands won by two centuries of Spanish toil, until the boundaries of the infant Republic reached the Pacific.

20

The Traders' Frontier
1776-1840

For half a century after New Spain flung its protective wall across the northern approaches to Mexico, the feeble barrier underwent a constant assault. Pressing from the northwest were Cossack fur hunters from Russia's Siberia, New England ship captains seeking native trade, and wilderness-wise agents of England's powerful Hudson's Bay Company. From the northeast came Canadian traders and their Indian allies, bent on winning the allegiance and trade of the Plains tribes. Advancing from the east were arrogant American frontier invaders—explorers, trappers, pioneer farmers, ranchers, and missionaries—all determined to exploit the wealth of Spain's forbidden empire. Before those invincible forces the Spanish first fell back, then surrendered chunk after chunk of hard-won territory until all the Southwest was in alien hands. Of the aggressors the most dangerous were Americans, and their shock troops were the fur traders.

The attack began in the 1780s when agents of England's great trading companies—the Hudson's Bay Company and the North West Company—swarmed out of Mackinac and Prairie du Chien to barter with Indians as far west as the Mandan villages of the central Missouri River. In 1791 the seriousness of Britain's threat was demonstrated when Spanish traders along the Missouri were forcibly turned back by Indians who insisted that Englishmen supplied all the goods they needed; in the same year citizens of isolated Ste. Genevieve demanded protection from British-armed Osage tribesmen. Spain was in danger of losing all northern Louisiana unless it acted. Nor could mission stations tame the nomadic natives of the northern Plains country. In that emergency Spanish officials at New Orleans, turning instinctively to methods used effectively in the French frontier advance, determined to use the fur trade to guard their hinterland. They would, they

386

decided, win over the tribes along the Missouri with trading goods, establishing that river as the northern border of their domain.

The agents selected for the task were experienced French woodsmen acquired by Spain with Louisiana. Auguste Chouteau, a seasoned frontiersman who as a lad of fourteen helped found St. Louis, was dispatched in 1794 to build Ft. Carondelet among the Osage villages, partly to hold those hostile Indians in check, partly to win their allegiance by supplying them with goods. At the same time French traders at St. Louis were authorized to form a trading company, The Commercial Company for the Discovery of the Nations of the Upper Missouri, to win the friendship of tribes along the Big Muddy. As an additional incentive officials offered $3,000 to the first Spanish subject following the Missouri to the Pacific. Three expeditions sent out by the Commercial Company during 1794 and 1795 failed to accomplish much; one was led by a schoolmaster who proved a better teacher than explorer, another was turned back by unfriendly natives, and the third never went beyond the Mandan villages. The leader of the last, a Spanish subject named James Mackay, found the Dakota country teeming with British traders who were summarily ordered to leave the "Catholic Majesty's Dominions," but more than bluster was needed. For the next years the trading frontiers of the two nations clashed in the Plains country, with the British making steady gains. By 1802 they dominated the region as far south as the Omaha villages and west to the Yellowstone and Big Horn rivers.

That was bad enough in Spanish eyes, but worse was the assault on their eastern borderland which began in 1803 when the United States acquired Louisiana. For the first time the two countries destined to battle for the trans-Mississippi West stood face to face. One was old, royal, and weakened by European wars. The other was young, democratic, and arrogantly determined to expand. Both sought to control as much of the Southwest as possible; a decision fostered by the Louisiana Treaty which gave the United States title to "the colony or province of Louisiana, with the same extent that it now has in the hands of Spain and that it had when France possessed it." With no boundaries established, rambunctious American intruders felt free to enter any part of the West. For half a century they battered against Spain's outposts before they overran the defenses to sweep triumphantly to the Pacific.

Thomas Jefferson, President when Louisiana was purchased, mapped the strategy that opened the attack. For some time he had been interested in the unknown lands beyond the Mississippi. As a loyal patriot he felt the United States must locate unrevealed riches before any European power was tempted to settle uncomfortably close to the American borders. As a scientist he wanted to know what plants and animals abounded in the unexplored West, whether the fur trade could be developed there, and how the Missouri River might be used as a route across the continent. He had made a number of attempts to answer those questions before Louisiana was acquired. In 1786 he encouraged a colorful Connecticut wanderer, John Ledyard, to undertake a romantic foot journey that carried him almost across Siberia before Cossack police ended his hopes of crossing Bering Straits and exploring the North American interior. Again in 1792 Jefferson prodded the American Philosophical Society into financing the journey of a French scientist, André Michaux, who planned to "ascend the Missouri River, cross the Stony Mountains, and descend down the nearest river to the Pacific." That venture collapsed when the leader became involved with Citizen Genet in revolutionary intrigue. Jefferson's curiosity was still unsated when he became President in 1801.

Two years later, and before Napoleon even offered Louisiana to the United States, Jefferson tried again. This time he secured a secret appropriation from Congress for an exploring expedition westward "even to the Western Ocean, having conferences with the natives on the subject of commercial intercourse." His object was different now, for his program of pushing eastern Indians into small reservations necessitated the discovery of new trading areas for American trappers. That was the primary purpose in the President's mind when he selected as leaders for the expedition twenty-eight-year-old Meriwether Lewis, whose skill in wilderness ways dated from a boyhood spent beneath the shadows of the Blue Ridge, and William Clark—younger brother of George Rogers Clark—a thirty-two-year-old frontiersman and Indian fighter. Before they set out news of the Louisiana Purchase reached America. Exploration of the newly acquired domain was a major purpose of the expedition together with the search for fresh fur-trading areas and scientific observation.

That the Lewis and Clark expedition accomplished so much was due both to the quality of its leaders and the careful preparation that Jefferson supervised. The explorers were told to follow the Missouri River to its source, seek a water route to the Pacific, and make careful records of the geography, soils, minerals, and animal and vegetable life of the country they traversed. Their instructions from the President were detailed; they were to make observations on the latitude and longitude, temperature, rainfall, mountains, interlocking streams, animals, plants, and Indians. As part of his preparation Meriwether Lewis was sent to Philadelphia, the nation's scientific capital in those days, with letters of introduction to five leading scientists who were to brief him on their specialities. Thus Dr. Benjamin Rush provided expert advice not only on the care of the party's own sick, but on questions to be asked the Indians concerning native diseases. This careful preparation proved invaluable. Meriwether Lewis started on his journey so thoroughly educated in the natural sciences that his findings along the way, his classifications of animals, his herbarium specimens, and his voluminous field notes provided scholars with a mine of invaluable information.

Thus equipped, they set out from the East on July 5, 1803, gathered a crew of fifty-one strapping young frontiersmen along the way, and in late fall established winter quarters near St. Louis. Lewis and Clark spent the cold months drilling their men in frontier techniques. With the spring of 1804 the expedition started up the Missouri, traveling in an iron-reinforced keelboat and two pirogues. All summer they worried their way up the Big Muddy, stopping frequently to talk with Indians or make scientific observations, until the blasts of autumn found them at the Mandan villages. A blockhouse—Ft. Mandan—was built; there the explorers labored through the cold Dakota winter on six dugouts to replace the cumbersome keelboat they had used. By April, 1805, they were ready to start once more. The keelboat with a crew of sixteen men was sent back to St. Louis; the rest of the party turned their faces westward. With them went a talented Shoshoni Indian woman, Sacágawea, who had been a captive of the Dakota tribes and whom, as an unofficial member of the expedition, served as an interpreter. Her uncanny knowledge of edible berries and fruit, memory of parts of the country she had not seen since a child, the entertainment provided by the two-months-old papoose who made the journey strapped to her back, and the restraining influence that she exerted on the boisterous spirit of the half-tamed frontiersmen made her one of the party's most valuable members.

Scarcely less useful was the one Negro who accompanied the expedition, York, a slave belonging to William Clark. York was a giant of a man, standing well over six feet tall, and tipping the scales at slightly over 200 pounds. A superior hunter, a strong swimmer, an expert with the ax and setting pole, he was also a capable linguist who served as translator in the Indian country. York's principal value, however, was his reception by the Indian tribes encountered as the party moved westward. To all he was a delightful curiosity—"Great Medicine," they called him—and they came from miles to gape in wonder, or to rub his skin with moistened fingers to see if the black would come off. York played to his audience well, dancing with leaps and bounds that astounded all who saw him.

So the party pushed on, their light canoes slipping easily through the water, through country never before seen by Americans, where plentiful game kept the larder always full. Then up into the foothills of the Rockies they journeyed, through narrow canyons where the current raced swiftly, over rock-strewn portages, braving roaring rapids with the men "up to their armpits in the cold water." At the mouth of the Marias River they faced a difficult decision, for they had heard of no such stream and wondered if it would lead them to the Pacific. Fortunately they chose correctly and continued to ascend the Missouri to its Great Falls which they reached on June 13, 1805. The tired explorers were less awed by the magnificence of the spectacle than with the back-breaking task of portaging their goods around the obstacle. A month was needed before they could be on their way again, through wild mountain country, to Three Forks, where three small streams, which they named the Jefferson, Madison, and Gallatin, joined to form the Missouri. Lewis and Clark were anxious to find the Shoshoni Indians to replace supplies running dangerously low and secure horses for the journey across the Rockies. Hence they chose the northernmost of the streams, the

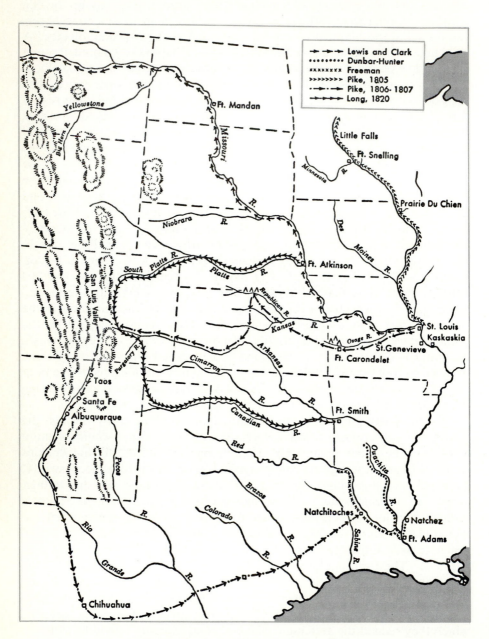

The Explorers' Frontier, 1776–1820

Jefferson, which Sacágawea told them led toward her country. Day after day the party toiled wearisomely onward without sighting a single native. Finally Lewis, fearful that the Indians were frightened into hiding by the size of his following, decided to go on ahead with only a small group. The little party passed Shoshoni Cove, crossed the continental divide at Lemhi Pass, and at last captured two terrified Shoshoni squaws who consented to lead them to the tribal camp near the headwaters of the Salmon River.

The worst was over. For a time the Indians were hostile but when a band of braves who went back to meet the main party returned with Sacágawea all fears were set at rest; she rushed forward "to dance and show every mark of extravagant joy . . . suckling her fingers to indicate that they were of her native tribe." A great council was held, the peace pipe passed about, and the Indians promised to provide Lewis and Clark with horses and guides to cross the mountains. Investigation showed the Salmon River was not the best route westward, for it tumbled through steep canyons where boats would surely be wrecked. Instead the travelers turned northward for a five day march into the Bitterroot Valley, then west again for ten days of weary plodding through snow flurries and drenching rain. On September 20, 1805, they finally emerged from the treacherous Lolo Pass into the open valley of the Clearwater River, where friendly Flathead Indians gave them food and shelter. A week of rest and the tired travelers were on their way once more, using canoes obtained from the natives to run the rapids of the Clearwater and Columbia, until finally in mid-November they stood on the banks of "that ocean, the object of all our labours, the reward of all our anxieties."

Winter camp was established on the banks of the Columbia a short distance from the sea. There the explorers camped for four months of drizzle,

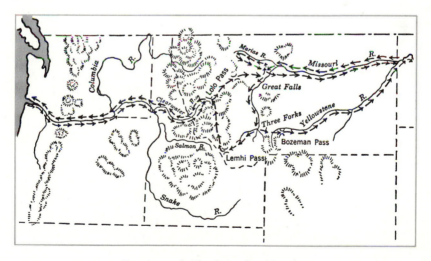

Lewis and Clark in the Northwest

rain, and fog which left bodies weak and nerves frayed. The return trip was begun in late March, 1806. Although forced to wait several weeks for the snows to melt from Lolo Pass, they were safely in the Bitterroot Valley by the end of June. There the expedition split in two. One party, led by Clark, retraced the outward trail to Three Forks where, under Sacágawea's guidance, it passed through mountainous Bozeman Pass to the upper Yellowstone River. On July 24, 1806, the group started downstream, taking careful note of the country traversed. In the meantime Lewis with nine followers crossed the continental divide through Lewis and Clark Pass, reached the Great Falls of the Missouri, then turned northward to explore the valley of the Marias River. That was dangerous country, roamed by hostile Blackfoot and Grosventre Indians, but all went well until July 27 when Lewis' men clashed with eight Blackfoot warriors, killing two of them. Realizing that the enraged tribe would be out in force for revenge, the explorers immediately started east, pushing their horses at full speed for more than 100 miles before they dared rest. They reached the Missouri safely, rejoining Clark's group a short distance below the mouth of the Yellowstone. On September 23, 1806, the Lewis and Clark expedition emerged at St. Louis to end one of the epic journeys in the history of exploration. They investigated thousands of miles of unknown country, found several usable passes through the Rockies, made important scientific observations, and established friendly relations with half-a-dozen Indian tribes, and all at a cost to the nation of $38,000 plus an additional $11,000 in bonuses and land warrants granted members of the expedition.

Thomas Jefferson saw to it, however, that they did not monopolize the plaudits of the grateful nation. Even as they battled their way across the continent other explorers were on their way westward to unlock other secrets of the Louisiana Territory. The President began planning expeditions as soon as America secured the trans-Mississippi West; one would ascend the Red River to its source and investigate the headwaters of the Arkansas, another would explore the Platte and Kansas rivers, a third the Des Moines, and a fourth the upper Mississippi and Minnesota rivers. Congress, lacking Jefferson's scientific and practical interest in Louisiana, granted him $3,000 rather than the $12,000 requested, but that was enough to equip one small party. William Dunbar, a noted scientist familiar with the Mississippi Valley, and George Hunter, a Philadelphia chemist, were placed in command of a seventeen-man force with orders to explore the Red River to its source. Soon after they set out from Natchez in October, 1804, they learned the Spaniards would resent their invasion of a borderland so near Texas, and rather than risk trouble, turned northward along the Ouachita River. Their thorough exploration of that stream was of scientific interest only, although they did go as far west as present-day Hot Springs, Arkansas.

Jefferson, instead of giving up hope, wrung another $5,000 from Congress for a second Red River expedition, this one commanded by Thomas Freeman, surveyor and astronomer. Starting from Ft. Adams in mid-April,

1806, the party of thirty-seven men made its way slowly up the log-choked stream in two flat-bottomed barges, stopping occasionally to hold councils with Indians along the way. The arduous labors came to naught; after almost 600 miles of effort they encountered a Spanish army from Texas whose commander ordered them to turn back. Freeman considered resistance for a time, but when common sense triumphed reluctantly retraced his steps. His expedition was hardly a success, as he traversed no ground not already explored by Spanish and French traders and brought back no word of the Red River's source.

With two failures in the South, Jefferson turned his attention to the less hazardous task of discovering the source of the Mississippi. His decision brought into prominence the explorer whose name has been forever associated with the conquest of the Far West, Lieutenant Zebulon Montgomery Pike. The twenty-six-year-old stripling began his discoveries in the fall of 1805 when he started northward from St. Louis with a well-stocked keelboat and twenty men. Stopping at the Falls of St. Anthony to purchase land for a government post, the party moved on to Little Falls where a small stockade was constructed for winter quarters. While most of the men settled down in cozy comfort, Pike and twelve companions pressed forward on sledges through the snow-blanketed Minnesota countryside. Here and there they found posts of the North West Company proudly flaunting the Union Jack, all occupied by cheerful Canadian traders who entertained the Americans royally and swore solemnly to display the Stars and Stripes in the future, knowing full well no one could punish them if they did not. At Leech Lake, which Pike mistakenly took to be the source of the Mississippi, the explorers started southward, reaching Little Falls on March 5. By the end of April, 1806, they were back in St. Louis.

That both the nation and Jefferson agreed with Pike's far-from-modest estimate of his accomplishments was shown when he was immediately sent out again, this time on the more difficult task of exploring the country between the Arkansas and Red rivers, winning the friendship of Indians there, and driving out unlicensed traders. By July, 1806, he was ready to take to the trail, leading twenty-three men up the Missouri and Osage rivers to the Osage villages, then across country to the Pawnee villages on the Republican River. He found the Indians ready to resist, having been recently visited by a Spanish army sent out to intercept the Americans, but Pike angrily told them the "warriors of his Great American Father were not women to be turned back by words," and pressed on. His trail led south now, to the Great Bend of the Arkansas River, then along that stream to the Rockies where a stout fortification was built on the site of today's Pueblo. For the next two months Pike explored the Colorado country, unsuccessfully tried to climb the peak bearing his name, and hunted in vain for the headwaters of the Red River.

Before snow left the mountain passes in the spring of 1807 he was on his way again, through the Royal Gorge of the Arkansas River, over the

Sangre de Cristo Mountains, and across the San Luis Valley, to emerge on the upper Rio Grande where he ordered his men to throw up a stockade. Pike either believed or pretended to believe he was still on American soil but an army of 100 mounted Spaniards from Santa Fe soon cured him of his illusion. He and his men were escorted into the New Mexican capital, questioned endlessly, hustled on to Chihuahua for more questioning, then marched across northern Mexico to Natchitoches where they were deposited on the American side of the border. Although his maps and papers were taken from him, Pike managed to remember enough of conditions along the southwestern border to prepare a report which brought him wide acclaim.

For a decade after the return of Pike's expedition, interest in western exploration waned as the United States fought the War of 1812 or grappled with the problems of reconstruction. When government attention was turned to the West once more in 1815 its objectives were different; parties went into the western country to found military posts that would hold the Indians in check, open the way for fur traders, and restrain British intruders. John C. Calhoun, the secretary of war, estimated that three forts on strategic waterways were needed first. Two, Ft. Smith on the Arkansas River, and Ft. Snelling at the junction of the Mississippi and Minnesota rivers, were begun between 1817 and 1819 by expeditions under Major Stephen H. Long and Colonel Henry Leavenworth—both strong blockhouses destined to play a prominent role in the advance of the frontier. Establishing the third proved more difficult. An elaborate expedition under Major Long and Colonel Henry Atkinson set out from St. Louis on July 4, 1819, bound for the Mandan villages, but the newfangled steamboats used broke down so regularly the party got no farther than Council Bluffs that year. There they built a log fort, Ft. Atkinson. Reports of mismanagement which reached the East during the winter so annoyed Congress that plans for an outpost at Mandan were abandoned.

Instead army officials decided on a last effort to seek the source of the Red River. Major Long, who was placed in charge of the nineteen soldiers assembled for the purpose, led the party out of Ft. Atkinson on June 6, 1820. Up the Platte and the South Platte they went, southward beneath the shadows of the Rockies where one of the men succeeded in climbing Pike's Peak, southward still to the Arkansas where the impressive Royal Gorge was re-explored. There they divided, one group to descend the Arkansas, the other under Major Long to press on in search of the Red River. The latter crossed the Purgatory and Cimarron rivers, then emerged on a large river which the leader took to be the Red. Thankfully he turned his men eastward along its banks, only to find he had hit upon the Canadian River which, to his great disgust, took him back to the Arkansas again. By mid-September, 1820, both branches of the expedition were safe at Ft. Smith, having accomplished almost nothing. The harmful effects of Long's fiasco were multiplied by the widely circulated report of his travels. Zebulon Pike had returned from his Red River expedition with word that the Great Plains were an arid desert, unfit for habitation by white men, but somehow his gloomy forebodings failed to make a national impression. Not so Long's equally unfavorable evaluation. "In regard to this extensive section of country between the Missouri River and the Rocky Mountains," he wrote, "we do not hesitate in giving the opinion that it is almost wholly unfit for cultivation, and of course uninhabitable by a people depending upon agriculture for their subsistence." The official map of his expedition labeled the whole Plains region as the "Great American Desert," a false designation destined to be copied by map makers for half a century. Major Long not only failed to unlock the secrets of the Far West; he nurtured a myth that denied what most frontier people believed, that the West was a fertile garden.

Two decades of official exploration accomplished little. The fringes of the Louisiana Purchase were explored, a few important rivers—the Missouri, Arkansas, and Canadian—traced to their sources, and a minute portion of the vast territory investigated. But the sources of such important streams as the Red, Platte, Osage, Republican, and Kansas rivers were still unknown, no usable pass through the Rockies was discovered, and the central portion of the Great Plains between the Missouri and Arkansas rivers still waited investigation. Jefferson's dream of a series of thorough explorations revealing every secret of the Louisiana country failed to materialize.

Fur traders succeeded where official explorers failed. Unsung and unheralded, too busy—or perhaps too uneducated—to seek fame by recording their wanderings, driven onward by the quest for generous profits rather than scientific curiosity, adventurous frontiersmen penetrated into every nook and corner of the Far West between 1807 and 1840. Spurring them on was the realization that peltry was cheapest among unsophisticated Indians who would barter bales of furs for a handful of trinkets. That commonsense point of view gave the trading frontier its remarkable mobility; the constant object of every trapper was to break through the fringe of sophisticated tribes to the richer regions beyond. Those unofficial explorers spied out the secrets of all the West, plotted the course of its rivers, discovered the passes through its mountains, and prepared the way for settlers by breaking down Indian self-sufficiency. No single group contributed more to the conquest of the trans-Mississippi region than those eager profit seekers who drew from the environment a valuable resource.

Their interest in the western country was aroused by the exciting news brought back by Lewis and Clark: tales of mountains teeming with beaver, of friendly Indians, and an all-water route along the Missouri River to the rich hunting ground. Through the winter of 1806–07 traders flocked into St. Louis, ready to start west as soon as ice broke in the Big Muddy, in a procession of barges, pirogues, and canoes, laden with knives, guns, whiskey, and knick-knacks. The most important party was headed by a Spanish trader, Manuel Lisa, and made up of forty-two unruly trappers. They worked their heavy keelboat up the Missouri and Yellowstone rivers to the mouth of the Big Horn where Lisa set the men to building a timbered blockhouse which, with typical frontier modesty, he named Ft. Manuel. There they spent the winter of 1807–08, trapping, hunting, trading, and roaming widely among tribes of the Northern Rockies. The most ambitious trip was made by John Colter who, with only a gun and a thirty-pound pack, tramped through the Yellowstone country, reached the Green River, and explored the valley of the Big Horn—500 miles of lonely mountain travel amidst icy winter blasts.

Lisa's party returned to St. Louis in the summer of 1808 with a wealth in furs and a store of sound advice. This boiled down to one salient fact: only large companies could trade successfully in the Northern Rockies, partly because hostile Indians along the Missouri would turn back small parties, partly because the time consumed reaching the heart of the fur country required more capital than individual traders commanded. That message, preached throughout St. Louis by Lisa, led to the formation of the Missouri Fur Company. Organized in February, 1809, to pool the resources of most of the city's leading traders, the company included in its ranks Manuel Lisa, William Clark, Auguste and Pierre Chouteau, Major Andrew Henry, Pierre Menard, and a host of others equally well known. For the next half-dozen years it dominated trade in the Northern Rockies.

The company's first expedition, which set out in the spring of 1809, included the partners, 172 men, a score of Indians returning to the Mandan villages at government request, nine large barges, and enough trading goods to stock five or six posts. The traders stopped at the mouth of the Knife River to build a stockade, Ft. Mandan, where some men were left to obtain beaver from the Plains Indians, then moved on to Ft. Manuel where a brisk trade with the Crow Indians was plied through the winter of 1809–10. Despite satisfactory profits, the partners divided on their future course. Some, led by Pierre Menard, a capable businessman who was more concerned with money than adventure, held that the costs of the Rocky Mountain trade in terms of human life and suffering were too high. He returned to St. Louis, and never again ventured into the mountains. Others, taking the opposite course, insisted that with only slightly greater risk better furs could be obtained from the less sophisticated Blackfeet, whose villages lay just to the west. That would be dangerous—the tribe hated Americans since two warriors had been killed by Meriwether Lewis on his return journey—but a large enough expedition could probably care for itself. That reasoning led one of the partners, Major Andrew Henry, to start for Three Forks in the spring of 1810 with a sizeable following. A log post was built first, then the traders moved cautiously into the forest in search of beaver peltry. The expected Blackfoot attack came on April 12 when a powerful war party swept down on the company fort, killed five men, and destroyed a large store of goods. Other raids cost three more lives before the traders rebelled and in July, 1810, returned to Ft. Manuel.

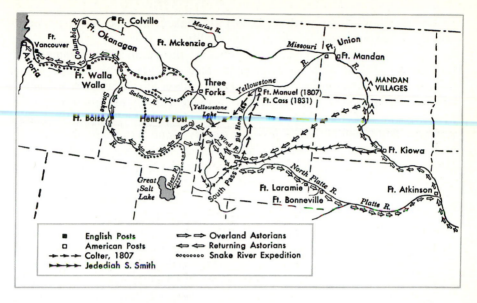

The Northern Traders' Frontier

Major Henry was unwilling to give up. With a party of volunteers he started south along the Madison River, crossed the continental divide, and on the upper Snake River built a few log cabins to serve as a trading post. The cold winter of 1810–11 brought few rewards; game was so scarce they returned to St. Louis in the spring of 1811 with only forty packs of beaver. That costly enterprise proved the undoing of the company; resources were so depleted Ft. Manuel was abandoned in 1813 and Ft. Mandan a year later. The Missouri Fur Company continued to operate on the lower Missouri but made no further effort to penetrate the Northern Rockies. Hostile Indians, poor management, and undercapitalization ended the first attempt to exploit the Far West's wealth.

Interest in the region did not die. As one company passed from the scene, another rose to take its place: the American Fur Company, organized in 1808 by the German-born financial genius, John Jacob Astor, whose grandiose schemes were breathtaking. He would, he planned, plant a chain of posts across the Far West from the Great Lakes to the Pacific. His headquarters would be at the mouth of the Columbia where furs from all the Rocky Mountain country could be shipped to the Orient. The trade promised not only fantastic profits (as New England ship captains already plying the China sea lanes demonstrated daily), but would strike a fatal blow at his hated Canadian rivals, the Hudson's Bay Company and the North West Company. Neither could send furs directly to the Far East, an area monopolized by the East India Company; hence his greater returns would eventually allow Astor to drive both into bankruptcy. So Astor hoped as he set about translating his dream into reality.

He first created a subsidiary company, the Pacific Fur Company, to take charge of the Columbia River post. That done, two expeditions set out for the Pacific. One group of thirty-three traders left New York by sailing vessel in September, 1810, and after an uneventful voyage entered the Columbia River in March, 1811, where work was begun on a blockhouse, named Astoria. The second party, known as the Overland Astorians, started from St. Louis in March, 1811, with an inexperienced New Jerseyan, Wilson Price Hunt, in charge. News of the Blackfoot attack on the Missouri Fur Company post at Three Forks convinced Hunt the route blazed by Lewis and Clark was unsafe, hence he struck out across the plains with his party of sixty-three men. Weeks of plodding across the interminable grassland followed, then the struggle upward into the Rockies, the discovery of a route across the continental divide along the Wind River, and the pleasure of emerging on the headwaters of the westward-flowing Snake River. Traveling was no easier along the rocky banks of that canyoned stream, but the travelers struggled on until they burst upon half-completed Astoria early in 1812.

All was well in the post, for the loss of one supply ship to hostile natives was forgotten when a second landed in May, deeply laden with food and trading goods. By June stacks of shining pelts were accumulating in the warehouses and barter was both brisk and profitable. That was the welcome news carried east by a party of "Returning Astorians" who set out on June 29, 1812, crossed the Rockies through South Pass, and followed the Platte River toward St. Louis—approximating the route later made famous as the Oregon Trail, and discovering the most important pass through the mountains. The promising start was deceptive. In January, 1813, news of the War of 1812 reached Astoria, together with the unpleasant information that a British warship was already on its way to capture the post. Astor's partners, knowing they could offer no resistance, sold the whole enterprise to the North West Company for the trifling sum of $58,000. The unfortunate accident of war ended American activity in the Northwest for a generation.

The withdrawal of the American Fur Company left two trading giants to dispute for the furs of the Pacific Northwest. The North West Company, expanding westward from its Great Lakes base, was the first to entrench itself, primarily because it devised a formula for blending the hard-fisted trading techniques of the European with an understanding of the cultural outlook of the Indian. The canoe that carried traders to native villages, the stockaded warehouse with abundant goods, and the *regale*, or treat of liquor as a preliminary to bargaining, were all the stock-in-trade of the North Westers, and they succeeded remarkably. The company's rival, the Hudson's Bay Company, made no such compromise with the environment; it constructed British-style forts, dispatched overpowering "brigades" of traders to overawe the natives, and shunned the use of liquor or gifts. So long as the two companies operated in the Great Lakes country each could cling to its own techniques, for Indians and furs were plentiful there, and distances to markets short.

As both vied for the trade of the Pacific Northwest, however, the superiority of the North West Company system demonstrated itself. For a time its successes were so complete that it seemed on the point of monopolizing the fur market there. Recognizing this, the Hudson's Bay Company came to the conclusion that it could endure only by cutting its rival's supply lines. Using its vast resources, it established settlements in the Red River area of Canada, a principal source of the foodstuffs needed by both. This move touched off a trade war between the two giants that raged for years, with prices slashed, traders murdered, and the Indians debauched. In the end the greater resources of the Hudson's Bay Company proved decisive; in 1821 the two signed a merger agreement to operate under the Hudson's Bay Company's name, in return for a twenty-one year monopoly in the Pacific Northwest granted by the crown. The task of wringing a profit from the Columbia Department was entrusted to an able administrator, George Simpson, who was given control in 1822 and four years later made Governor-in-Chief of the company's American domain. No better man could have been found. Simpson combined within his own small person boundless energy, rare diplomatic skill, limitless vision, administrative efficiency, and a love of empire which elevated him to a position of preeminence in the fur trade.

All those qualities were needed. The Columbia Department was so unprofitable the Hudson's Bay Company was on the verge of abandoning the region when Simpson reached there in 1824 after a grueling trip across the continent. Realizing a strong base was needed first of all, he set his men to building a large stockade, enclosing hundreds of yards, in which were clustered cabins, storehouses, and offices. About Ft. Vancouver he laid out fields where traders, idle during the summer, planted grain and potatoes, or pastured herds of sheep and hogs imported from California. Most important of all was the selection of a superintendent. Simpson's fortunate choice was Dr. John McLoughlin, a great hulk of a man who had learned the fur trade in eastern Canada. "He was," wrote Governor Simpson, "such a figure as I should not like to meet in a dark Night in one of the bye lanes in the neighbourhood of London, dressed in Clothes that had once been fashionable, but now covered with a thousand patches of different Colors, his beard would do honor to the chin of a Grizzly Bear, his face and hands evidently Shewing that he had not lost much time at his Toilette, loaded with arms and his own herculean dimensions forming a tout ensemble that would convey a good idea of the high way men of former days." That was the man whose abilities won the fond title of "White Eagle" from the Indians and the respectful salute of "King of the Oregon" from his comrades.

Dr. McLoughlin's chief concern was new trading areas. In quick succession abandoned forts were rebuilt at Walla Walla and Okanagan, and a new post opened at Ft. Colville to command the commerce of the Columbia

River. More important was the extension of the Hudson's Bay Company into the Snake River country, for there Dr. McLoughlin acted with imperialistic wisdom. The Oregon country, he knew, was in dispute between England and the United States. Ultimate ownership would go to the most securely entrenched nation; hence his duty was to keep Americans out. That could be done by stripping a zone east and south of the Columbia bare of all furs, creating a desert barrier to turn back traders from beyond the Rockies. Ruthless trapping there would not only help win Oregon but bolster the company's profits.

Exploitation of the Snake River country was entrusted to thirty-year-old Peter Skene Ogden. Gathering seventy-five trappers and several hundred pack animals, the skilled trader set out in December, 1824, pushing his way through the snow-choked passes to emerge at the Three Forks of the Missouri. The enmity of the Blackfeet turned him west along the Jefferson River, over the continental divide to the Salmon, and southward to the Snake, the men trapping and trading as they went. Exploration of the upper Snake and its tributaries led them along the Bear River to the point where it "discharged into a large Lake of 100 miles in length." Thus did Ogden record the discovery of Great Salt Lake. The expedition, retracing its steps to Three Forks, followed the Missouri almost to the Marias River before fear of the Blackfeet turned Ogden back to Ft. Vancouver which was reached after a year of wandering. The Snake Country Expedition opened a trading empire that was exploited by band after band of Hudson's Bay Company adventurers during the next dozen years. The Canadians, firmly entrenched, were truly lords of the Northwest.

Between the domain of the Pacific Northwest monopolized by the Hudson's Bay Company and the Mississippi Valley lay the richest prize of all: the beaver streams of the Northern and Central Rocky Mountains. The pioneers in the conquest of this last best West were Major Andrew Henry who had tasted the thrill of mountain life with the Missouri Fur Company, and William Henry Ashley, a Missourian whose ventures into business and politics had already won and lost him sizeable fortunes. Advertising in March, 1822, for 100 "enterprising young men," to "ascend the river Missouri," they formed a trading party that set out by keelboat for the upper Missouri, to build their headquarters post at the mouth of the Yellowstone River. Things went badly from the first. Hostile Arikara Indians in the Dakota country molested their boats as they passed, and in the mountains even more bloodthirsty Blackfeet pounced on stragglers and even engaged sizeable hunting parties in mortal combat. The losses incurred in 1823 when Ashley's principal expedition was attacked by the Arikara near the Mandan villages of Dakota finally convinced Ashley that trade in the Northern Rockies was impossible.

Instead he would shift his operations to the Central Rockies, where no Arikara lurked along the trade routes and no hostile Blackfeet waited to scalp his trappers. From Indians he had heard of a meadow stream just beyond the mountains that was teeming with beaver. To test this rumor he sent a small party westward from Ft. Kiowa in the autumn of 1823, with the remarkable Jedediah Strong Smith at its head. This skilled plainsman, who was destined to become America's greatest explorer, led his party across the blistering plains toward the Black Hills of the Dakotas, then around the Big Horns into the Wind River valley where they spent the winter in a village of friendly Crow Indians. Jed Smith was so anxious to test Indian tales of a pass through the mountains that loomed ahead that he started his followers on again amidst the deep snows of February. Always cold, often half-starved, but never faltering, the traders made their way along the Sweetwater until they made the effective discovery of South Pass, the broad portal through the Rockies that led them straight to the Green River, which they reached in March, 1824. Beaver were so plentiful that by June one of the trappers, Thomas Fitzpatrick, could start back to St. Louis with every pack-horse loaded with pelts.

News of these events so excited Ashley that he started west in November, 1824, despite the warnings of friendly Pawnee who told him that winter mountain travel was suicidal. Their prophecies were almost fulfilled; Ashley and his twenty-five followers chose to follow the South Fork of the Platte River into the Rockies rather than the North Fork route used by Smith and only reached the Green in April after terrifying months of frostbite and near-starvation. There he must decide how best to exploit the rich resources of this favored land. Should he set his men to building trading posts similar to those he and his predecessors had used in the Northern Rockies? Forts, he knew, aroused Indian ire by symbolizing the white occupation of their lands; moreover the Rocky Mountain natives were but poor trappers, preferring to hunt buffalo rather than search for beaver "in the bowels of the earth, to satisfy the avarice of the Whites." Swayed by these arguments, Ashley decided on a new method: one that revolutionized the fur trade for a generation to come. That spring he set his trappers free to roam far and wide, then meet at a rendezvous on Henry's Fork of the Green River to exchange their furs for the trading goods that Ashley had imported from St. Louis.

Thus was born the "rendezvous system" which from that day was a regular feature of the trade. Unitl 1840 most trappers settled in the mountains, to spend their days in an endless search for untrapped beaver streams. Each year at the end of the "spring hunt" they turned their steps toward the agreed-upon spot where they would meet a caravan from St. Louis loaded with luxuries and the few necessities that the forests could not provide: traps, guns, ammunition, knives, tobacco, and alcohol. The rendezvous system succeeded because it blended the white man's desire for furs with the traditions and customs of the Indians. A comparable trade fair had been staged annually by the Shoshoni Indians as a means of attracting white traders to their villages; indeed Ashley may well have known of the success of this venture when he planned his own gathering. Certainly the rendezvous was geared to the psychology of the western Indians; it elevated trading from a purely commercial to a social function.

The success of the first rendezvous assured others. Ashley sent out the 1826 caravan, earning such profits that he was able to retire a rich man at the end of the year. Three former associates under Jed Smith who bought out his interests earned comparable fortunes before 1830, when they sold out to Thomas Fitzpatrick, James Bridger, and Milton Sublette, organized as the Rocky Mountain Fur Company. This concern over the next years dominated the most colorful era in America's fur-trading history.

During that time some hundreds of trappers lived continuously in the mountains, all of them near-savages more at home amidst the silent forests or in Indian villages than in the haunts of their fellow men. Each year these "Mountain Men" emerged from their winter camps as soon as the spring sun thawed the beaver streams, trapped until July, then made their way to the rendezvous for their yearly contact with civilization. There an awesome sight awaited them: hundreds of bearded trappers in their fringed jackets and buckskin leggings, dozens of deserters from the Hudson's Bay Company, dark-skinned Mexicans from Taos and Santa Fe, and as many as 1,000 Indians who had gathered to watch the fun. Business came first as soon as the caravan from St. Louis arrived; trappers exchanged their "hairy bank notes," the beaver pelts, for the necessities of life and fineries for their squaws, then the flat casks of alcohol were opened and tin cups of the lethal fluid were passed about, turning the rendezvous into a scene of roaring debauchery. During the next few days the Mountain Men drank and gambled away their year's earnings before the caravan started eastward again, its owners richer by profits that sometimes reached 2,000 per cent, and the trappers stumbled away into the forest to rest a few weeks before the "fall hunt" began.

What a remarkable crew of robust, self-exiled individuals those Mountain Men were. Some were well educated; a few were hardened degenerates who crossed the Mississippi with a sheriff at their heels; most were under thirty; all preferred the forest solitudes to the regulated society of civilized America. Some were Negroes who found in the untamed West escape from the prejudices that made their lives miserable in the East. Such a man was Edward Rose who was as famed for his trading skills as he was for the shadowy reputation that had pursued him westward. Such a man was James P. Beckwourth, son of a white father and a black slave, who saw the Rocky Mountain country first in 1823 when he joined Ashley's brigade as a blacksmith. From that time on Beckwourth was wedded to a forest life, marrying a Crow Indian, and eventually joining the tribe where his prowess elevated him to a post as a principal chief. These men, and other Negroes like them whose names were unrecorded, played a yeoman task on this most risky of all frontiers.

The carefree days of the Mountain Men were numbered, for the profits of the Rocky Mountain Fur Company soon brought competitors into the field. Some were agents of small companies; present at the 1832 rendezvous were Nathaniel J. Wyeth who had come from New England with twenty-seven followers, Captain Benjamin L. E. Bonneville with New York capital and 110 trappers at his beck and call, traders of the newly formed St. Louis firm of Gantt and Blackwell, a brigade of Arkansans under Alexander Sinclair, and a party of eighty Mountain Men from Taos with "Old Bill" Williams in nominal control. This competition the well-heeled Rocky Mountain Fur Company could meet, but another rival at the 1832 rendezvous represented real danger. This was the venerable American Fur Company.

The American Fur Company entered the Rocky Mountain trade by the route that Ashley had followed a half-dozen years before. Slowly creeping westward after the collapse of its ill-fated Astoria venture, Astor's giant concern first ventured into the Upper Missouri Valley in 1827 when it bought out the small but ably manned Columbia Fur Company. Astor's business genius made it overnight a dangerous competitor for the established traders. He recognized that monopoly was distasteful to the public, hence he would nurture a few modest competitors while driving the bulk of them to the wall or absorbing their businesses. These plans were carried out with precise efficiency. A tightly knit establishment was set up, with operatives in the trading areas working under experienced managers, and with steamboats and improved means of travel developed to speed exchange between the rendezvous and markets. The American Fur Company saw, too, that the fur trade was not an instrument for moral reform, and that the government would be unable to punish those who defied its regulations by intruding on a rival's territory or peddling liquor to the Indians. It was after profits, whatever the harm done to its competitors or to the Indians.

Thus equipped, the company was able to take advantage of an unusual opportunity. Astor realized that its Ft. Union, built in 1828 at the mouth of the Yellowstone River, lay on the threshold of the forbidden Blackfoot country, the last virgin domain waiting exploitation by the trappers. If the American Fur Company could violate that native's sanctuary, its fortune would be made. The chance came in 1830 when it employed a Hudson's Bay Company deserter who had lived among these hostile tribesmen and won their friendship. He reluctantly agreed to enter the Blackfoot domain with a small band of adventurers who expected each step to be their last; instead the Indians recognized him as a friend and agreed to a trading contract. Ft. McKenzie was built on the Marias River in 1831 as a center for the new trade; that summer, too, a small steamboat reached Ft. Union. The natives were so impressed with the "Fire Boat that Walked on the Waters" that they shifted allegiance to the American Fur Company in droves.

These steps not only solidly planted the concern in the Northern Rockies but prepared it to invade the domain of the Rocky Mountain Fur Company. Ft. Cass was built at the mouth of the Big Horn in 1831 as the first step in this direction; from this outpost brigades of trappers were sent southward to seek out the Rocky Mountain Fur Company expeditions and follow them to good beaver country. Worse still was the decision to send two caravans of trading goods, one from Ft. Union and one from the East, to the 1832 rendezvous. Word of this threat reached the Rocky Mountain Fur Company leaders in time to allow them to win the race to the rendezvous and purchase most of the furs brought there, but they could take little solace in their victory. This contest between the two great rivals symbolized the dawn of an era where bitter competition was to mark the history of the fur trade, with its inevitable result—overtrapping and the extermination of the beaver.

This went on rapidly during the remaining years of the decade. Bands of hunters from the two principal contenders and their smaller rivals roamed the whole West, trapping streams that had been nearly exhausted, and searching everywhere in a vain quest for unexploited areas. To make matters worse, the Indians grew steadily more hostile in the face of this mass invasion of their hunting grounds. The Battle of Pierre's Hole, fought just after the 1832 rendezvous, cost the lives of five trappers, and was only a portent of more losses in the future. By 1834 the two companies were so discouraged by dwindling profits and the slaughter of their men that they attempted to come to terms. These negotiations could have only one outcome, for the American Fur Company could never surrender lest it lose prestige that would hamper its far-flung operations elsewhere. Before the year was out the Rocky Mountain Fur Company had sold out, assets, partners, and employees, to its rival. For a few more years of relative peace and declining returns the American Fur Company hung on, until a new and more dangerous rival entered the field.

This was the Hudson's Bay Company, which began sending its brigades farther and farther eastward from the Columbia River valley as the beaver supply of the Pacific Northwest disappeared. In 1837 it purchased Ft. Hall on the Snake River as a base for its new ventures; over the next two years its trapping brigades roamed the mountains freely, underbidding American traders for furs, and winning respect from the Indians by its just methods. As this giant firm monopolized the trade, the number of American Mountain Men steadily dwindled, until less than 120 attended the 1840 rendezvous. That was the end; the American Fur Company announced that it would no longer send a caravan into the mountains. The rendezvous era had ended.

The fur trade, however, showed a stubborn disinclination to die. Exports to Europe in 1840 were larger than in any prior year and both the volume and profit continued to mount steadily until after the Civil War. Responsible was the emergence of a number of small traders to fill the vacuum created by the end of the American Fur Company, and their realization that they must shift both their hunting grounds and products to capitalize on changing markets. The beaver trade that had sustained the rendezvous period and reached dynamic equilibrium between 1828 and 1834 continued to decline as overtrapping and changed European styles undermined that once-lucrative enterprise; the price of prime pelts that had averaged $5.99 a pound for some years dipped to $2.62 on the London market in 1841. Its place was taken by commerce in raccoon skins as a rage for Davy-Crockett-type hats swept Russia, Germany, and Poland. There was also a growing European demand for muskrat and otter skins, and for wolf, deer, and buffalo hides. Profits rivaled those garnered from the beaver trade; no less than 4,000,000 raccoon pelts were shipped to England during the 1840's and 9,000,000 during the 1850s and 1860s. The effect of these changes was to shift the operations from the Rockies to the fringes of the mountain country. Plains Indians rather than trappers provided the furs. Ft. Laramie became a thriving center for the export of deer skins, buffalo robes, and raccoon and muskrat pelts. Despite the demise of the beaver trade and the rendezvous, furs remained a valuable economic asset in the nation's trade.

The trapper's contribution to the opening of the West was matched by that of another group of traders who invaded the domains of New Spain to snatch wealth from under the noses of its jealous defenders. Some who braved Spanish wrath sought furs from the tribesmen of the southern Plains and Rockies. They began moving out along the Arkansas and Canadian rivers just before the War of 1812, with Manuel Lisa and Auguste Chouteau in the van, but not until the postwar years did trade assume sizeable proportions. Its principal organizer was Jules de Mun, a St. Louis merchant, who led parties of trappers into the upper Rio Grande Valley of New Mexico in 1816 and 1817, before Spain's aroused officials rallied to protect their borderland. De Mun paid $30,000 in confiscated furs to learn that Spaniards did not welcome traders from their northern neighbor.

More influential were the Santa Fe traders. Santa Fe in the opening years of the nineteenth century was a sleepy little town whose 2,000 inhabitants produced quantities of silver, furs, and mules. Its distance from Mexico—a tortuous mountain trail 1,500 miles long led to Mexico City—hampered the disposal of surpluses and doomed the New Mexicans to a perpetual shortage of manufactured goods. Direct trade between the Mississippi Valley and Santa Fe would benefit all concerned; Americans wanted furs and silver, Spaniards needed textiles, cutlery, and utensils. Why not use the short route between St. Louis and New Mexico to satisfy both? That was the ambition of the first bold traders who ventured into Santa Fe, all unmindful of the fact that Spain's laws rigidly excluded foreign merchants. They were sternly reminded of their oversight; party after party between 1804 and 1812 was hurried off to Chihuahua jails where the members were given ample time to lament their errors. Not until the Mexican Revolution of 1820 cast off the shackles of Spanish mercantilism was the Santa Fe trade opened to frontiersmen from the United States.

First to profit from this happy turn of events was William Becknell, a Missouri Indian trader whose good fortune won him the title of "Father of the Santa Fe Trade." The autumn of 1821 found him following the Arkansas River westward with some twenty plainsmen and a pack train of horses loaded with goods that he intended to barter for furs in the Southern Rockies. While working their way upward through the tortuous Raton Pass they

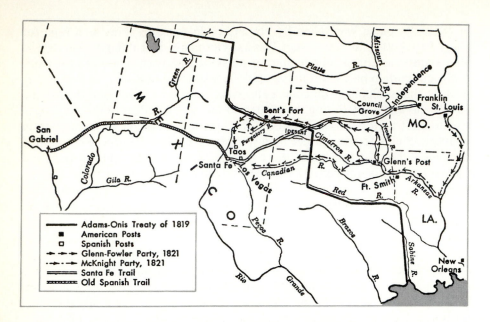

The Southern Traders' Frontier

stumbled upon an encampment of Mexican soldiers who told Becknell that Mexico was independent and would welcome American goods. The party started for Santa Fe at once, there to turn their merchandise into great bags of silver dollars with which Becknell returned to his home town of Franklin, Missouri, late in January, 1822. Two other traders were close on his heels. Thomas James, a St. Louis merchant seeking to unload a storeful of goods left on his hands after the Panic of 1819, reached Santa Fe on December 1, 1821, only two weeks after Becknell, and remained until June, vainly trying to dispose of his somber fabrics to the color-loving Mexicans. The third party, led by Jacob Fowler and Hugh Glenn, and comprised of eighteen trail-hardened frontiersmen including one Negro had also been bound for the mountains to trade with the Indians when it was visited by Mexican troops with news (as Fowler put it in his free-and-easy spelling) "that the mackeson province Had de Clared Independence of the mother Cuntry and is desirous of a traid With the people of the united States." Hurrying southward, they plied a brisk commerce until June, 1822, when they started homeward, well satisfied with their profits. William Becknell launched a second expedition from Franklin in June, 1822, with three heavily loaded wagons and twenty-one men. Knowing the difficulty of traversing the steep Raton Pass with his vehicles, he pioneered a shorter route across the dangerous Cimarron Desert. Thus was the Santa Fe Trail marked out by its innovator.

The first successful expeditions encouraged so many imitators that by 1824 the Santa Fe trade was well established. Eighty men, with twenty-five wagons, 159 pack horses, and $30,000 worth of goods, made the journey that year, returning safely with silver and furs worth $190,000. Such profits encouraged imitation; each year thereafter the number of traders and the volume of trade rose steadily. At the same time a demand for government protection resulted in a commission to mark out the trail and arrange treaties with the Osage and Kansa Indians guaranteeing caravans immunity from attack. When the Comanche and Kiowa, who refused to sign, raided a trading party in 1828, troops were sent to accompany the caravans across the plains. Until 1830, when congressional economy ended military escorts, the road to Santa Fe was comparatively safe. After that the traders were forced to protect themselves.

Turning to the task with typical frontier ingenuity, they soon developed the methods that elevated the Santa Fe trade into a thriving business. Each spring traders gathered at Independence, Missouri, a town founded in 1827 after Franklin was washed away by a shift in the Missouri's channel. For a month all was bustle in the tiny community—steamboats unloading, wagons rumbling through the dirt streets, traders haggling with local merchants over the price of goods. As soon as the grass turned green heavy Conestoga wagons began pulling out of Independence, each carrying some two tons of merchandise and pulled by five or six span of oxen under a colorful crew of mule skinners and bullwhackers clad in the leather jackets, flannel shirts, and blue jeans affected by plainsmen. The 150-mile journey to the Neosho River was made haphazardly. Beneath the towering hickory trees of Council Grove they prepared for the dangerous Indian country ahead. One seasoned trader was chosen captain by popular vote. He divided the wagons into four groups, each under a lieutenant familiar with the procedure the caravan must follow. All traders were sworn to obey the elected leaders unquestioningly.

The organization completed, the expedition set out about May 1 in a mile-long column that wound slowly south and west toward the Big Bend of the Arkansas. Ahead rode scouts, ready to signal the captain at the first hint of Indian "sign." If this indicated marauding bands were near, the leader ordered the wagons into four parallel columns, with lieutenants in charge of each. Then they were safe from any attack; if raiders approached the vehicles quickly formed a hollow square that no Indian war party could penetrate. Thus they marched at the rate of fifteen miles a day; across the Arkansas, over the desolate sixty-mile stretch of Cimarron Desert where Comanche and Kiowa lurked, through northern New Mexico, until the adobe houses of Santa Fe were sighted. Immediately all order was forgotten as each wagoner whipped up his oxen for a mad race to the town's gates. Within the New Mexican capital there was equal excitement, for the coming of *los Americanos* was the one event that broke the slumbering village's placid calm. Tavern keepers rushed to prepare beverages for parched wagoners, senoritas arrayed themselves in attractive garments, and every citizen who could walk or crawl crowded into the dusty streets to welcome the arrivals. All was bedlam during the next few days as dress goods, shawls, cutlery, guns, pans, beaver skins, mules, Spanish dollars, and silver bullion changed hands. The traders departed then, some who had been fortunate enough to dispose of their merchandise back along the 900 mile trail to Independence, others who had not to continue down into Mexico as far as Chihuahua or other commercial centers. Each year from 1830 to 1844 when Mexico closed Santa Fe to Americans, these scenes were repeated. The trade was revived after the War with Mexico and continued to thrive until it was displaced by the railroad.

The Santa Fe trade was never particularly important to the American economy; the value of merchandise carried to New Mexico rarely exceeded $130,000 and the number of persons involved was seldom more than eighty. Nevertheless the trade played a vital role in the advance of the frontier. The traders taught immigrants a safe and practical means of crossing the plains in wagon trains, provided the Mississippi Valley with needed specie, and brought back word of Mexico's feeble hold on her northern provinces. The pioneers who moved into Texas, New Mexico, and California risked conflict with the Mexicans because they were convinced little effort was needed to add the Southwest to the United States. Moreover the Santa Fe traders called attention to the possibility of trade with Indians whose villages bordered New Mexico. As early as 1828 three frontiersmen—Ceran St. Vrain, Charles Bent, and William Bent—built an adobe fortress, equipped with homes, warehouses, and an icehouse, on the upper Arkansas River. For the next fifteen years Bent's Fort dominated the trade of the Colorado country.

In the 1840s, when Santa Fe was closed to Americans and beaver diminishing in the central and northern Rockies, the day of the trader drew to a close. By that time Mountain Men and sun-darkened plainsmen had played their role. They deprived the Indians of self-sufficiency by accustoming them to white men's goods. They found South Pass, and discovered such important highways as the Snake River route to Oregon, the Humboldt River trail to California and the Gila River road to the Southwest. They brought back word of fertile valleys hidden beyond the mountains, of distant grasslands where cattle could be fattened, of tempting lands weakly held by despised neighbors. The traders opened the gates of the West to settlers who soon followed their trails across the continent.

The Mississippi Valley Frontier

1803-1840

The pioneer farmers who followed the traders into the Far West came largely from the Mississippi Valley frontier. There, in the tier of states bordering the Father of Waters, lived a hardier crew of frontier settlers than could be found elsewhere in the United States. Rich in experience but poor in cash, toughened by their experience in opening virgin land, alert to the main chance, indoctrinated with a restlessness inherited from generations of pioneering forefathers, they made ideal colonizers. Between 1825 and 1845 they elbowed their way into Texas, peopled the lush valleys of Oregon, settled the forbidding wastes of the Great Basin, and eased into Spanish California in such numbers that the Mexican War only climaxed an annexation movement well under way. Their life in the Mississippi Valley endowed them with the bumptious arrogance, the perpetual wanderlust, the awe-inspiring courage that allowed them to play a leading role in the history of American expansion.

Adventurous pioneers drifted into the area just west of the Father of Waters as soon as the Louisiana Purchase opened the way. The southern portion, set aside as the Territory of Orleans in 1804, filled first, for there the nucleus of French settlement about New Orleans promised attractive economic opportunities. Ten thousand immigrants arrived during the next two years, 4,000 more between 1807 and 1809, many of them French refugees from the war-torn West Indies. When the census of 1810 showed that the population justified statehood, Congress gave its blessing over New England's protests and in April, 1812, Louisiana entered the Union.

The 75,000 planters and merchants whose homes dotted the new commonwealth lived lives unlike those of other frontiersmen. Louisiana's social traditions were deeply rooted in the region's French and Spanish heritage. New Orleans, growing rapidly as trade down the Mississippi increased, set the pattern for all the state. There devout Catholics paid homage in an imposing cathedral which towered above iron-balconied homes, clumsy two-wheeled carts rumbled through dusty streets, hucksters shouted their wares from the public square in a medley of tongues, merchants in Parisian styles rubbed elbows with leather-clad traders, and Latin festivals enlivened existence in a way unknown to inhibited Americans. Beyond New Orleans were the plantations where slave laborers produced cotton, sugar, and other semitropical produce. By 1812 cleared fields extended along the Mississippi to the northern boundary, up the Red River as far as Natchitoches, and northward on either side of the Ouachita River. Eight years later 153,000 people lived in the state, which was thoroughly settled except for a few northern and western areas.

Outside of Louisiana progress was slower. The region was set aside in 1812 as the Territory of Missouri, but aside from the cluster of French towns about St. Louis and St. Genevieve and lead mining camps few settlers lived there. The agricultural frontier was so far east of the Mississippi that only the boldest pioneers would hurdle a pathless wilderness to seek such distant lands. Partly responsible also was the ownership of Arkansas and Missouri by Indians until just before the War of 1812. Their removal proved easy, as most natives had followed the buffalo herds westward to the Great Plains.The Osage surrendered their claims to Missouri and the northern half of Arkansas in 1808, while in 1817 the Quapaw Indians ceded the remainder of Arkansas together with a strip between the Arkansas and Red rivers in Oklahoma. All of Arkansas and Missouri were open to settlement.

Missouri felt the impact of immigration first in the period of prosperity following the War of 1812. By that time the eastern agriculture frontier touched the Mississippi in Kentucky and Illinois, the Indians were cowed into submission, and tales of rich Missouri lands reached the older settlements. Farmers came with a rush between 1815 and 1819; every day from thirty to fifty wagons loaded with homeseekers waited to cross the Mississippi at St. Louis. Tennesseans moved into the Ozarks while Kentuckians sought farms along the Missouri River where Boonville and Franklin were laid out in 1817. Latecomers ascended the tributaries of the Big Muddy to stake claims on the lower reaches of those streams. By 1820 an eighty-mile-wide strip along the Mississippi was settled and an arm of advancing population followed the Missouri half way across the territory.

The influx aroused the usual demands for statehood. Congress responded as soon as the census of 1820 showed sufficient population and the Missouri Compromise settled the troublesome slavery issue. Missouri entered the Union in August, 1821, with its golden era just ahead. Each yearthe tide of immigration grew larger, attracted by the rising prosperity of the

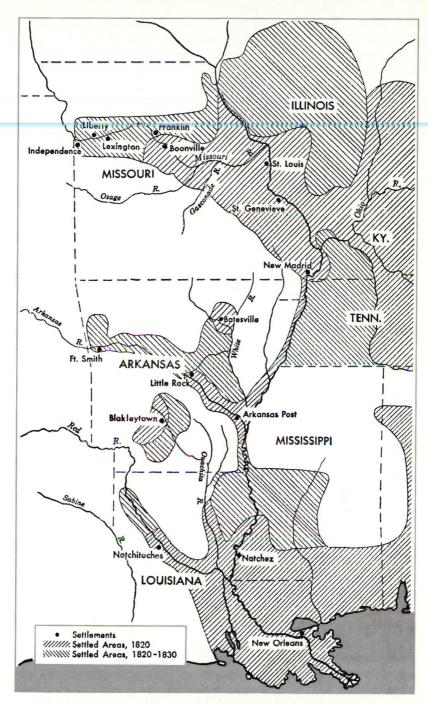

The Southern Mississippi Valley Frontier, 1815–1830

frontier state. The trade of all the Far West centered in Missouri; there caravans of covered wagons or river barges were formed to make their way to Three Forks, South Pass, and Santa Fe. Merchants were needed to supply traders with merchandise, farmers to feed both merchants and traders. The expanding market for agricultural produce attracted settlers whose westward advance along the Missouri Valley was marked by the founding of new towns: Lexington and Liberty in 1822, Independence in 1827. By 1830 all eastern Missouri was filled and settlements reached along the Big Muddy to the border.

In this settlement process, a pattern emerged that was to be typical in all the prairie states. The earliest newcomers occupied the prize spots: the rich-soil river bottoms, the loess hills, the most fertile grasslands. Nearby salt springs were also an attraction, as were timber stands needed for housing, fuel, and fencing. As these filled, the rate of occupation diminished while later-comers moved on to the better lands of the next adjacent region. This tended to drive down the price of the less-favored portions where the soils were less fertile and the terrain more rugged. As soon as speculators lowered the price to reflect the true value of the land, settlement began again, flowing over the hills and the less-fertile soil regions. This kept the per-acre population surprisingly stable. In one part of Missouri thirty-eight persons occupied each square mile in 1830, thirty-five in 1840, and thirty-six in 1850. The exceptions, of course, were the town sites. When a lucky speculator hit upon a plot favorable to urban growth—with adequate transportation facilities, the county seat, a prison, or a private educational institution— population mushroomed. This was particularly the case when two or more attractions coincided in one spot. Pioneers sought self-advancement by acquiring unusually favored lands or town lots that promised to escalate in value; when these were not available they moved on to a newer country beyond. Those who shied from such risks stayed on to buy the second allotments but only after the price reflected the true value.

The second state carved from the territory, Arkansas, grew more slowly. Until the War of 1812 only 1,500 white people lived in the region, most of them around the ancient French town of Arkansas Post on the lower Arkansas River. During the next decade population increased steadily, as pioneers laid out farms on the rich silt beds bordering the Mississippi, or pushed up the White River as far as Batesville, the Ouachita to Blakleytown, and the Arkansas to Little Rock. The frontier settlers insistence on self-rule led Congress to set Arkansas aside as a separate territory in 1819 when population numbered almost 14,000, an increase of 1,200 per cent in the decade. New settlers continued to trickle in. By the middle 1830s a thin line of farms extended westward as far as Ft. Smith on the territory's border and the people were thinking seriously of statehood. When an optimistic estimate in 1835 placed the population at 70,000, the territorial legislature called a constitutional convention to meet at Little Rock the following January. The resulting document fortunately reached Washington just as Michigan applied for admission, allowing Congress to dodge the slavery issue by admitting one free and one slave state. Under those terms Arkansas entered the Union in 1836.

While Missouri and Arkansas were filling with land-hungry farmers, other migrants from across the Mississippi moved into the area just west of those two states. The newcomers were driven to the frontier not by the hope of economic gain but by the bayonets of federal troops. They were the eastern Indians who, uprooted from their tribal lands, were forced to settle on unwanted vacant lands far from the haunts of white men. Between 1825 and 1840 they were driven westward by the national government, to establish a "permanent" Indian frontier beyond the 95th meridian. There the displaced tribes played a prominent part in the subsequent history of the trans-Mississippi frontier.

The concept of a "Permanent Indian Frontier," where Indians would be forever removed from the path of the advancing settlements, dawned on government officials soon after the United States acquired Louisiana and gained popularity after the War of 1812. By this time geographic knowledge was sufficient to allow careful planning. Just east of the Rocky Mountains, men of that day knew, lay a desolate region unfit for white habitation. Zebulon M. Pike, returning from his 1806 exploration, painted an unforgettable picture of its barrenness; "I saw in my route in various places," he reported, "tracts of many leagues where the wind had thrown up the sand in all the fanciful forms of the ocean's rolling waves and on which not a speck of vegetable matter existed." A later explorer, Stephen H. Long, fastened on the region the name that persisted for a generation: "The Great American Desert." This, officials agreed, was unfit as a foster home for transplanted eastern tribes, but should be reserved for the nomadic Indians already there. East of the desert, however, and stretching from the 95th to the 101st meridian, was a fertile land capable of supporting an Indian culture based on farming and the hunt, yet far enough from the settlements to be unwanted by frontiersmen for generations. If all Indians from east of the Mississippi could be removed there, valuable lands would be opened to pioneers, friction between the two races removed, and the natives protected from the sins and diseases of the white men.

The removal plan was formulated by John C. Calhoun, Monroe's secretary of war, in 1824. He proposed that the Indians of the Old Northwest, who supposedly numbered about 14,000, be shifted to either the headwaters of the Mississippi or the plains region west of the Missouri River. The southern tribes, estimated by Calhoun to include 79,000 natives, he suggested moving to the area south of the Missouri River lying between the 95th meridian and the "Great American Desert." Gifts and annuities totaling no more than $30,000, he thought, would induce the Indians to migrate. President Monroe laid his report before Congress on January 27, 1825.

The first step toward opening the reservations was to clear the Plains Indians from west of the 95th meridian. This was begun in June, 1825, when the Osage and Kansa tribes surrendered all of Kansas and northern Oklahoma save for two reservations: one for the Kansa along the Kansas River, one for the Osage on the northern boundary of Oklahoma. At the same time negotiations were opened with Choctaw and Cherokee who had been moved into Arkansas Territory between 1817 and 1820. That forested region was now considered too valuable for Indians; public opinion demanded that they exchange their reserves for others farther west. The Choctaw were the first to succumb; in 1825 they signed a treaty surrendering their Arkansas territories for a larger tract between the Canadian and Red rivers just beyond the 95th meridian. For a time this treaty seemed unenforceable; several hundred whites lived west of the boundary line and the Arkansas legislature violently objected to their removal. Threats of force were needed before the squatters were persuaded to abandon their claims. The next step was taken in 1828 when the Cherokee accepted a 7,000,000 acre reservation north of that assigned the Choctaw, together with a fifty-eight-mile-wide "Outlet" to the 100th meridian through which they could reach the buffalo country.

For the next fifteen years the work of "persuading" eastern tribes to accept homes along the Indian frontier went grimly on. Usually agents bribed some corrupt chief into signing a removal treaty, then forced the entire clan to move west. The Shawnee of Ohio came first, to a twenty-five-mile-wide strip south of the Kansas River, where they were joined in 1829 by their old neighbors, the Delawares, who accepted a reservation on the north bank of the stream together with an outlet to the buffalo country. In quick succession other tribes of the Old Northwest—the Kickapoo, Sauk, Fox, Chippewa, Iowa, Potawatomi, Ottawa, Peoria, and Miami—were crowded into small reserves just west of the 95th meridian or, in a few instances, onto lands in western Iowa. The Five Civilized Tribes of the South proved harder to uproot. The Choctaw came first in 1830 to lands just west of Arkansas; two years later the Chickasaw left Mississippi for a reservation adjoining that of the Choctaw. Both shared a Leased District through which they could reach the buffalo plains. The Cherokee followed in 1834 to occupy the territory north of the Canadian River already granted the tribe, while their neighbors, the Creeks, were assigned a large area still farther westward. They were compelled to share their holdings with the Seminole when those Florida Indians were finally driven to a strip of territory adjoining the Canadian River.

By 1840 the Permanent Indian Frontier was planted along the 95th meridian from the Red River to the Great Bend of the Missouri. In their reservations and on the Great Plains just beyond the Indians were, in theory, to spend the rest of time, free from molestation by whites. Basic to the removal policy was the belief that the natives would obtain food and clothing from buffalo hunts or farming without aid from the government. Congress sought to secure them economic isolation by two laws; one in 1834 created the Bureau of Indian Affairs entrusted with the task of establishing schools and superintendencies where the Indians could learn farming, the other—

the Indian Intercourse Act of 1834—forbade all white men except properly licensed traders to enter the reservations. Those measures signified official determination to let the Indians shift for themselves.

Two things doomed the policy to failure from the outset. One was the inability of eastern natives to adapt to the strange environment of the Plains. Accustomed as they were to a sedentary agricultural existence in the forested East, they were unable to adjust to the semiarid grasslands where differing farming techniques were required. Just as fatal was the failure of the two groups of natives living in the West—the intruded Indians and the Plains Indians—to live together peacefully. Easterners scorned their wandering

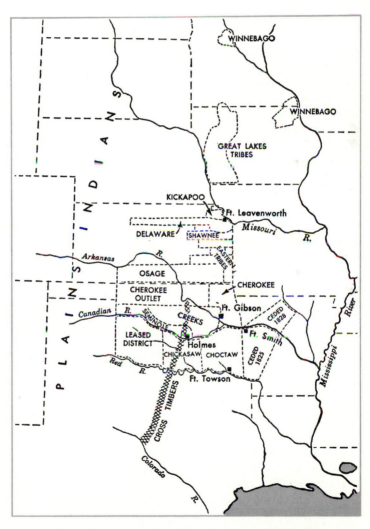

The "Permanent" Indian Frontier, 1820–1840

brethren of the prairies as primitive barbarians; westerners looked upon the newcomers as interlopers on lands rightfully theirs. Feeling was particularly strong in the Southwest, where the Osage blamed the intruders for the unpopular treaty that cost them their hunting grounds, and the Comanche, Kiowa, and Wichita tribes insisted that fully half the territory granted the Five Civilized Tribes was still their own. The United States, instead of being freed from Indian affairs, was not only forced to continue aiding the Indians but also was called upon to settle a series of near-wars which threatened to spread to the frontier settlements.

Conflicts began in 1823 when skirmishing between the Osage and the newly arrived Choctaw, Creek, and Shawnee tribes showed the stern hand of the Great White Father was needed to keep peace in the West. New forts, located strategically in the midst of the warring factions, seemed the answer. Two were established the next year—Ft. Towson on the Red River and Ft. Gibson on the Arkansas—and in 1827 a third, Ft. Leavenworth, was built on the Missouri River to control the intruded northern tribes. For the next half-dozen years those log and mud outposts stood guard over thousands of miles of Indian country, where constant efforts were needed to keep jealous Indians from flying at each others' scalp locks. Fear of federal troops rather than acceptance of the reservation system kept the hostile forces apart for a time.

In 1834 war began again, with Comanche and Kiowa as aggressors and traders and eastern Indians the victims. The secretary of war resorted first to diplomacy; commissioners were hurried west, presents gathered, and eight companies of dragoons marched out of Ft. Gibson to invite the hostile chiefs to a conference. The officer commanding the force, Colonel Henry Dodge, found the main Kiowa camp near the Washita Mountains in western Oklahoma. Skillful talk and good will engendered by the return of a Kiowa warrior who had been enslaved by the Osage persuaded a delegation of fifteen chiefs to accompany him eastward. The Comanche, fearful of being left to fight alone, hurriedly delegated eight leaders to join the party. All went well until they reached the Cross Timbers, a thirty-mile-wide belt of hardwoods running across the Plains between the Arkansas and Colorado rivers. The Comanche, whose grassland habits made them wary of all forested regions, refused to go any farther. Colonel Dodge was wise enough to accept their ultimatum. The party established a headquarters, Camp Holmes, on the Arkansas River while runners were dispatched to summon the federal commissioners and agents of the Creek, Cherokee, Choctaw, and Osage tribes.

Unfortunately the American negotiators took so long reaching the treaty grounds that the Comanche scattered for their usual spring buffalo hunt before they arrived. The early summer of 1835 was spent cutting a wagon road to Ft. Gibson so that supplies could be hauled in; then the delegates settled down to await the Indians who straggled into camp during July. In all, some 7,000 natives gathered, representing the Plains Indians of the Southwest, the Osage, and the Five Civilized Tribes. Negotiations duplicated those in dozens of similar meetings between the two races. In return for "a considerable supply of old flour and pork which," as one of the commissioners frankly stated, "if not consumed in this way, will be nearly a total loss," and an assortment of ornaments, knives, and gaudy gimcracks, the Comanche and Wichita accepted the eastern tribes as friends and allowed them to hunt the Plains east of Cross Timbers. Scanty as were the presents awarded the Indians, they were sufficiently alluring to bring the Kiowa, whose representatives failed to attend the conference, into line. A delegation from the tribe visited Ft. Gibson to ask similar treatment, which was accorded them in a separate agreement in May, 1837. If signed covenants meant anything, the southwestern frontier could expect a period of peace.

Yet the ink was scarcely dry on the four pages of marks made by chiefs on the Treaty of Camp Holmes before the Plains Indians grumbled they had not understood its meaning, that the presents given them were inferior, and that their hunting grounds must remain their own. Renewed skirmishing between eastern and western tribes followed, despite reminders from federal agents that the treaty was being violated; reprimands were shrugged away with the excuse that some other tribe was responsible or that younger warriors could not be restrained. Only the good sense of the intruded eastern Indians kept a major war from developing. A few battles with the Comanche and Kiowa convinced the easterners that safety depended on staying east of the Cross Timbers where Plains Indians dared not intrude. The peace that reigned in the Southwest for the next dozen years was due to that practical realization rather than the success of the United States.

Despite the failure of the American government to satisfy either the intruded or Plains Indians, the creation of the Permanent Indian Frontier greatly affected the course of white settlement. All unwittingly, the government had thrown a barrier across the path of advancing southern pioneers. As Louisiana, Arkansas, and Missouri filled, the adventurers who continually sought homes on the fringes of civilization found they could no longer drift ahead to adjacent lands as their venturesome forbears had done. Instead they must either bypass the Indians' reservation and the Great American Desert to seek farms in the fertile valleys of the Pacific coast or forsake their native land for the alien soil of Texas. That the pioneers who invaded Oregon, California, and Texas were predominantly from the lower Mississippi Valley was due largely to this situation.

That was the case especially as no similar land shortage developed in the upper half of the valley. The American invasion of Iowa's lush prairies and Minnesota's deep forests began so late there was no overcrowding there until after the Civil War. Before 1830 the whole region was controlled by native inhabitants—Sauk and Foxes along the Mississippi, Iowa on the banks of the Des Moines River, Oto, Missouri, and Omaha in the Missouri Valley, and Sioux and Chippewa in the northern wilds of Minnesota. Only whites able to win permission from the Indians could enter. Most prominent among the few who did was an ingratiating Frenchman, Julian Dubuque, who for twenty-two years before his death in 1810 commanded a colony of farmers and lead miners at the site of the Iowa city bearing his name. During the next twenty years only a handful of squatters managed to slip into the forbidden territory. Any mass invasion was impossible; miners who tried to exploit Dubuque's old lead mines in 1830 were rudely driven out by federal troops.

By that time the half-million people living in the adjacent states of Illinois, Missouri, and Indiana were demanding that the United States open Iowa to settlement. That their pleas did not fall on deaf ears was demonstrated in 1832 when the defeat of Chief Black Hawk and his Sauk followers gave the federal government a chance to act. Representatives of the beaten Sauk and Fox tribes were assembled at Ft. Crawford in August to learn the price they must pay for Black Hawk's audacity. The United States took a strip of Iowa land running along the west bank of the Mississippi from Missouri's northern boundary to the vicinity of Prairie du Chien. In return the Indians were granted a $20,000 annuity for thirty years, $40,000 more in the form of debt settlements, forty kegs of tobacco, and forty barrels of salt. On June 1, 1833, the "Black Hawk Purchase" was thrown open to settlement.

The rush began at once; all that summer land-hungry pioneers from Illinois, Indiana, Ohio, and Kentucky jammed the trails or waited days to cross the Mississippi on hand-rowed ferries. "The roads were literally lined with the long blue waggons of the emigrants wending their way over the broad prairies," wrote one who was moving west himself. Those arriving first staked out farms in the river bottoms where trees offered fuel, shelter, and a familiar environment; those coming later spilled out upon the rolling prairies where native grasses grew shoulder high. Others made their homes in towns that sprang up at the terminal points of the Mississippi ferries: Dubuque, Davenport, Burlington, and Keokuk. No one worried that the migration began too late for extensive planting that summer; a little starvation was worth enduring for such good land. There was suffering in Iowa during the winter of 1833–34 when heavy snows drove away game counted on for food, but with the spring of 1834 hard times were forgotten as cheerful pioneers broke the sod, planted their corn, and joined in the "play parties" that signaled the raising of each new cabin.

For the next few years the migration went on, drawn from an ever widening area as news of Iowa's good land spread eastward into New England and New York. One typical estimate of the frontier's possibilities appeared in a Buffalo newspaper:

> Taking into consideration the soil, the timber, the water and the climate, Iowa territory may be considered the best part of the Mississippi valley. The Indians so considered it, as appears from the name which they gave it. For it is said that the Sioux (Sac) and Fox Indians, on beholding the exceeding beauties of this region, held up their hands, and exclaimed in

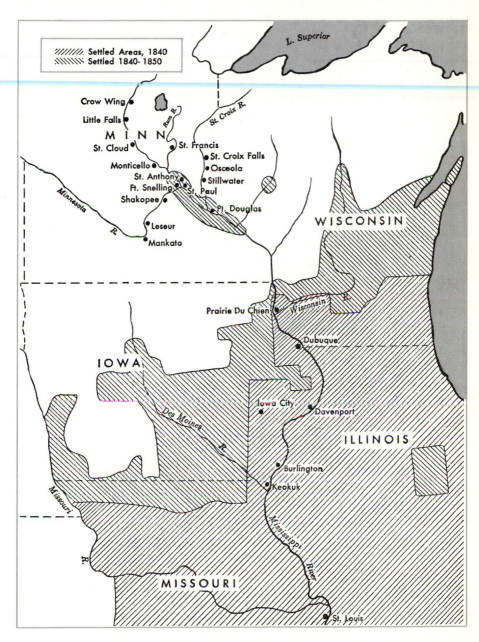

The Northern Mississippi Valley Frontier, 1830–1850

an ecstasy of delight and amazement, "I-O-W-A," which in the Fox language means, "this is the land."

Little wonder, when such paeans of praise attracted immigrants, that population was estimated at 10,000 in 1836, that a new strip of territory had to be purchased from the Indians in 1837, or that by 1840 43,000 people lived in Iowa. By that time the southern half of the Black Hawk Purchase was filled and the frontier advancing northward daily.

The growth was especially remarkable in a region with neither a land system nor a government. The lack of the former did not embarrass the pioneers; they were too accustomed to the dilatory habits of Washington's officialdom to be surprised when no land office was established in Iowa until 1838. Instead of bewailing the neglect, they fell back on the standard frontier practice of marking out the farms that they wanted, plus a sizeable additional plot for speculative sale to later comers, then squatting on them until the government was ready to sell. To protect themselves from speculators who might outbid them at government auctions, and to guard their own excessive holdings against newcomers until the price was high enough to justify sale, the squatters formed "Claim Associations" in Iowa as they had east of the Mississippi. By 1840 more than 100 of these extralegal organizations existed in the territory, their numbers sworn to eject outside speculators and to protect the speculative activities in which they themselves were engaged. Any jobber who bid above the minimum price at land sales, or any newcomer who tried to squat on the extra quarter-section that an association member had illegally usurped for resale, was risking a sound thrashing, and sometimes his life.

The checkerboard of claims associations that covered Iowa by the 1840s did not discourage land speculators, but did alter their business methods. The mere purchase of prize sites was hazardous; any attempt to monopolize the best regions might stir the associations into unwelcome activity. Hence they shifted to a form of investment known as "time-entry contracts." Under these the jobber purchased a farm in his own name, at the same time signing a bond guaranteeing its delivery to the would-be purchaser as soon as he had fulfilled the terms of the agreement. Interest rates on the contracts were high, ranging from 40 to 70 per cent a year, and profits to the speculators excessive. During Iowa's boom era they ranged up to 105 per cent a year and averaged 53.4 per cent. Yet the system operated with few complaints from purchasers. They knew that the jobber would never foreclose for nonpayment of interest during depression periods for the payments, even though late and less than agreed upon, provided a larger return on the investment than could be made without outright ownership. Too, Iowa's agricultural potentials were such that a good farm was worth an excessive tribute to a speculator; the soil was so rich that in good years it would pay several times the 100 per cent extracted by the time-entry contract. Better such a farm than no farm at all.

The problem of a satisfactory local government was less easily solved than that of a workable land system. Most settlers were law-abiding farmers, but the rough elements attracted to the Dubuque lead mining district and the "coarse and ferocious watermen" congregated about Keokuk made some law enforcement machinery necessary. At first farmers took matters into their own hands in typical frontier fashion, forming vigilance committees, setting up people's courts, and administering harsh but effective punishment to criminals. The rude system was properly looked upon as a temporary expedient to be supplanted whenever Congress provided a legal machinery. For a time congressmen refused to meet the responsibility, largely because southerners hesitated to take steps leading to the admission of another free state. In 1834 the area was attached to the territory of Michigan, then in 1836 added to Wisconsin Territory. Not until 1838 did local protests rise to such heights that the territory of Iowa was formed.

The first legislature, meeting in the fall of 1838, reflected the racial bias of its members by passing laws excluding Negroes and mulattoes from the territory, but more time was devoted to a furious debate over a site for the territorial capital. When legislators finally realized the intense local jealousies among existing villages would allow no compromise, they hit upon the device of a completely new town, which they called Iowa City. A commission selected the site in the spring of 1839, hired a farmer to plow a straight furrow 100 miles across the prairies from the Mississippi as a guide to immigrants, and in August marketed the first lots. When the cornerstone of the capitol building was laid a year later Iowa City boasted a population of twenty families.

Iowa was even more attractive with its self-governing legislature and territorial courts. So the rush went on. Little towns along the Mississippi blossomed overnight into proud cities, each boasting (in the words of a Burlington editor) of being "the largest, wealthiest, most business-doing and most fashionable city on, or in the neighborhood of the Upper Mississippi. . . . We have three or four churches, a theater, and a dancing school in full blast." Urban prosperity reflected the rapid settlement of the interior. By 1842 lands already obtained from the Indians were so well filled the government's treaty-making agencies were called into action once more, to wrest central and southern Iowa from the Sauk and Fox tribes. When the new purchase was officially opened at midnight of April 30, 1843, several thousand excited homeseekers were gathered for the first of the West's many rushes. At the deadline troops stationed along the border fired their guns into the air and the pioneers dashed pellmell forward to choice spots selected during earlier explorations. By daybreak of May 1, more than 1,000 farms were staked out and half a dozen towns established along the Des Moines River. So rapidly did the new area fill that four years later the rest of western Iowa was secured from the Potawatomi to make room for advancing pioneers.

The migration gave weight to a growing demand for statehood. When a referendum during the spring of 1844 showed a majority in favor, a constitution was drawn up for submission to Congress. Opposition there was strong, partly from Whigs who rebelled against its democratic provisions, partly from western congressmen who insisted Iowa's boundaries were too extensive. Continued admission of giant states, they pointed out, would diminish the political influence of the West at a time when that nationalistic region was needed to hold the warring North and South together. The result was a two-year delay, while Congress insisted on contracting Iowa's size, and the Iowans stubbornly refused. In the end a compromise was necessary. A new constitutional convention in 1846 drafted a document which made slight concessions; Congress reduced the boundaries slightly to their present form and in December, 1846, welcomed Iowa into the Union. As a state its rapid growth continued until by 1850 its inhabitants numbered 192,212 and its corn production touched 8,600,000 bushels. Already "I-o-way" was becoming famous as "the land where the tall corn grows."

While Iowa filled, the frontier moved northward into the wilderness of Minnesota's lakes and forests. The first pioneers in that clear-aired northland were traders whose cabins were built beneath the walls of Ft. Snelling after that outpost was established in 1819. Gradually others drifted into the primitive village of Mendota: agents of the American Fur Company, several dozen Swiss immigrants from the Hudson's Bay Company's Red River colony of Pembina, a few retired soldiers and trappers. Growth was necessarily slow, for all settlers were illegal squatters on either Indian lands or the federal military reservation about the fort. A new Indian cession was needed before the Minnesota country was ready to welcome a sizeable migration. That came in 1837 when treaties with the Sioux and Chippewa gave the United States the triangle between the Mississippi and St. Croix rivers as well as a chunk of northern Wisconsin. The rush to the new frontier could begin.

The first arrivals were lumbermen, attracted by the towering stands of virgin pine and hardwood that covered all the wild country south of Lake Superior. Within a few years sawmills operated at favored waterpower sites along the St. Croix River—Point Douglas, Stillwater, Osceola, and St. Croix Falls—while gangs of Irish woodsmen cut away the forests. Another arm of the lumbering frontier advanced along the upper Mississippi River. The prize spot there, the beautiful Falls of St. Anthony, was appropriated by a fortunate speculator in 1837; within a year his mill was in operation. Others established lumbering towns higher up the river: at Monticello, St. Cloud, and Little Falls, or in the Rum River Valley where St. Francis was the leading community. Many were temporary settlements, representing a brief halting place in the northern advance of the timber frontier.

Like trappers of an earlier day, lumbermen looked with disdain on farmers—prosaic individuals who appropriated lands better used for logging, or clogged streams with barges that hindered timber rafts bearing lumber to markets in the treeless prairies of Illinois or Iowa. Yet the logging camps themselves lured pioneer farmers into Minnesota by creating a demand for foodstuffs. At first supplies were brought in by keelboat, until news of high prices reached the ears of small farmers in Wisconsin, Illinois, and Iowa. They drifted in then, to till the acres cleared by foresters and sell their grain or pork to hungry loggers. Each lumbering town became the nucleus for a small agricultural settlement, with St. Anthony, St. Paul, and Stillwater soon outstripping the others in size.

As growth went on, year after year, the thoughts of pioneers turned to self-government. They had reason to complain; for a time their isolated triangle of settlements was a neglected part of Wisconsin Territory, then, after 1848, when Wisconsin became a state, was without any government whatsoever. A memorial praying for territorial status was prepared by a convention assembled at Stillwater in August, 1848, carried to Washington by an eloquent spokesman, and pushed through Congress in the spring of 1849. The new territory, although comprising all of Minnesota and most of the Dakotas, contained only 4,000 inhabitants, nor could more be expected so long as settlement was confined to the narrow area between the Mississippi and St. Croix rivers. The territorial government's first act was to press upon Congress the need for additional lands.

The response was gratifying. In 1851 the leading Sioux chieftains were brought together by Indian agents, lavished with presents, and persuaded to sign away their claims to most of western Minnesota. News of the treaty, spreading like wildfire along the frontier, attracted settlers from the whole north country to the new mecca. In vain federal troops at Ft. Snelling tried to hold them back until Congress ratified the agreement; as well as try to stop an irresistible force as an American frontier farmer when good lands lay ahead. They surged across the Mississippi, cut roads through the forest, staked out farms, and formed Claims Clubs for protection until government surveyors caught up with their fast-moving frontier. By the end of 1852, as many as 20,000 pioneers lived in the new cession, and the air rang with the sound of axes or the crash of falling trees as loggers cut down the virgin timber and farmers grubbed out their clearings.

Expansion continued at an ever-increasing pace during the next few years. Some newcomers strengthened the existing settlements along the St. Croix or pushed the frontier along the upper Mississippi Valley as far as Crow Wing. Others congregated in the cities taking shape on a few well-situated sites; St. Paul, located at the head of navigation of the Mississippi, skyrocketed from a few hundred to 8,000 in five years while a nearby rival, Minneapolis, laid out in 1852 on lands of the Ft. Snelling military reservation, gained even more rapidly. The mecca attracting most immigrants was the Minnesota River valley—in the words of one pioneer "the prettiest country lying wild that the world can boast of, got up with greatest care and effort by old Dame Nature ten thousand years or more ago, and which she has been improving ever since." The fertile lands bordering the stream were rapidly engulfed by farms or towns—Shakopee, LeSueur, Mankato—all little hamlets with a few log cabins and "enough imaginary public buildings, squares and streets for a moderately sized empire." In 1858 Minnesota became a state with a population that, according to the census of 1860, totalled 172,023.

Long before the last Mississippi Valley commonwealth joined its sister states in the Union, a new frontier was forming to the westward. Its pioneers were the small farmers of Missouri, Kentucky, Mississippi, Arkansas, and Louisiana, with a sprinkling from the upper-river country. Many restless drifters were ready to seek new homes by the close of the 1830s. A depression was upon them: the grim panic that paralyzed business and agriculture in the West from 1837 until the middle 1840s. In the Southwest especially the economic picture was dark. Most of the states there, with typical frontier optimism, had backed wildcat banks or plunged recklessly into internal improvement schemes. With the collapse of 1837 they were left with staggering debts and half-finished railroads which might take years to complete. As Mississippi Valley farmers surveyed the debacle, they asked themselves why they should linger amidst such desolation. State debts meant years of burdensome taxes. The unfinished transportation facilities doomed them to another decade of low produce prices. Why not escape to better lands?

For pioneers of the upper Mississippi Valley this meant only a shift to the virgin soil of Iowa or Minnesota, but southerners faced a more difficult problem. The good lands of the lower valley were already absorbed; only the hilly Ozark Plateau and a few isolated poor-soil regions remained unsettled. Ahead lay the Permanent Indian Frontier, beyond that the Great American Desert. Their only solution was to reach the far-western country described to them by traders and explorers. Discontent, overcrowding at home, and lack of opportunity for contiguous settlements accounted for the fact that many of the immigrants who peopled Texas, Oregon, and California were from the lower Mississippi Valley frontier.

They were ideal colonizers, those bold pioneers who blustered their way into the lands of Spain and England during the 1830s and 1840s. Life along the Father of Waters attracted a higher percentage of arrogant, foolhardy, cocksure, lionhearted, muscle-proud, bragging egotists than could be found on any other frontier. The work they did—manning keelboats, digging lead from the Fever River mines, clearing away forests, tilling the heavy soil—was a sort that placed a premium on brawn rather than brain. The one boast of westerners was that they daily performed tasks that would have broken lesser men. So they developed a boastful pride in their strength. Throughout the Mississippi Valley every man was as good as the next and considered himself a whole lot better.

When such arrogance was injected into an already turbulent frontier society the result was turmoil. Most of the settlers were orderly citizens, bent on improving their lot by legal means and as disapproving of lawlessness as their counterparts today. Yet the image that characterized this frontier more than any other is one of misfits, extroverts, brawlers, and gamblers. Most of this group went about heavily armed, despite laws in every community against carrying firearms, the lower classes with bowie knives or revolvers tucked in their boot tops, the elite with more dignified instruments of mayhem such as dirks and sword canes. The battles fought among these riffraff were rough and tumble affairs where the sole object was to incapacitate the opponent and no holds were barred. "When two men quarrel," wrote one shocked traveler, "they never have an idea of striking, but immediately seize upon each other, and fall and twist each other's thumbs or fingers into the eye and push it from the socket until it falls on the cheeks, as one of those men experienced today, and was obliged to acknowledge himself beat, although he was on top of the other—but he, in his turn had bit his adversary most abominably." Those who survived such eye-gouging, nose-chewing, ear-clawing battles felt proud of themselves.

They were insufferable braggarts, those Mississippi Valley frontiersmen. Their talk was of their skill with the rifle, their prowess in battle, their feats of inhuman strength. "I'm the darling branch of old Kentuck that can eat a painter, hold a buffalo out to drink and put a rifleball through the moon," one would shout, and another would reply: "I can wade the brown Mississippi, jump the Ohio, step across the Nolachucky, ride a streak of lightning, slip without a scratch down a honey locust tree, whip my weight in wildcats, and strike a blow like a falling tree." Those were the "ring-tailed roarers, half horse and half alligator," who boasted they lived on "churnbrain whiskey and bear's meat salted in a hailstorm, peppered with buckshot, and broiled in a flash of forked lightning." They boasted that they could outshoot, outride, outdrink, and outfight any man in all creation, and they could bluster their way into any man's nation with such bumptious assurance that no one dared stop them.

They made excellent colonizers, those ripsnorting, star-spangled pioneers from the Mississippi Valley. Respecting neither God nor man, proud of their country and disdainful of all other nations, as strong as the whiskey they drank and as brave as they pretended to be, they feared no "varmints," neither Indians nor the white-skinned Europeans who blocked their path westward. Brushing aside obstacles as casually as they bragged of gouging out eyes or biting off ears they carried the frontier westward in a series of dramatic moves that added Texas, Oregon, the Great Basin, and California to the United States.

22

The Annexation of Texas
1820-1845

The quarter-century following 1825 witnessed the most remarkable burst of expansion in the history of the United States. At the beginning of the period the nation's boundaries were apparently firmly established. The southwestern border, agreed upon in the Adams-Onís Treaty with Spain in 1819, began at the Sabine River, crossed to the Red River, zigzagged westward along the Red and the Arkansas, followed the crest of the Rockies to the 42nd parallel, then turned west to the Pacific. Ownership of the Oregon country was in dispute between England and the United States, but the Hudson's Bay Company's firm hold there indicated the final settlement would be in Britain's favor. For all practical purposes, the Rocky Mountains in 1825 marked the extreme western limit of American influence. Yet twenty-five years later not only Texas and Oregon but the vast territory between the mountains and Pacific was occupied by Americans. The amazing advance was accomplished by a series of thrusts westward from the Mississippi Valley frontier. The first was into Texas.

No aspect of the American settlement of the trans-Mississippi country has been more persistently misunderstood and misrepresented than the push of pioneers into that Mexican province. In the middle and later nineteenth century historians writing under the spell of the slavery controversy, were wont to view the penetration of Americans into Texas as part of a monstrous conspiracy on the part of the slave power to strengthen its hold upon the government of the United States by extending the area dedicated to slavery. Yet the extension of cotton culture into Texas was as natural a process as the creation of a wheat-growing empire in Minnesota and Dakota. The same inner urge which drove Missourians to Oregon in the 1840s impelled them to migrate to Texas in the 1820s. In short, Texas lay athwart the westward path from Tennessee as did Iowa and Nebraska from Ohio. The American colonization of Texas was a normal and natural feature of the age-old American tradition of pushing westward. That the heat engendered by the slavery issue was not necessary to attract American attention to Texas was shown by activities there long before the question of slavery became acute. By 1803 Americans were settled on the Ayish Bayou west of the Sabine; probably a few lived there long before that date. Traders and filibusterers were also interested. Philip Nolan, the well-known friend and associate of General James Wilkinson, apparently traded with San Antonio as early as 1785. He was certainly engaged there prior to 1797, when Wilkinson forwarded to Jefferson "specimens" discovered by Nolan during his travels in Texas. In 1800 he led a party of adventurers as far west as the Brazos where he rounded up several hundred wild horses. On the return trip Nolan lost his life in an attack by a Spanish force.

During the next decade ill-feeling between Americans and Spaniards along the border grew apace. Adventurers of all sorts were eager to participate in forays into Spanish territory. In 1812 Bernardo Guttierez, a Mexican refugee, and Augustus Magee, a onetime officer in the army of the United States, inspired by an abortive Mexican revolution to believe Texas might welcome freedom, led a force of several hundred men deep into the province. Possessing all the characteristics of a filibustering expedition to free Texas from the Spanish yoke, the invading force attracted to it many disaffected Spanish residents and won some fleeting successes before suffering almost complete butchery at the hands of vengeful loyalists. Only a handful of the Americans returned to tell the story.

Dissatisfaction on the lower Mississippi with the Adams-Onís Treaty of 1819, relinquishing Texas to Spain, was the signal for the last filibustering venture across the Sabine. At a public meeting held at Natchez that year a force was formed for an invasion, and James Long was placed in command. Forming a provisional government at Nacogdoches, the invaders proclaimed the independent Republic of Texas, prepared to use the land to attract immigrants, and unsuccessfully sought the support of Jean Lafitte, the pirate chieftain of the Gulf coast. Upon the outbreak of the Mexican revolution in 1821, Long, in alliance with liberal leaders of Mexico, marched far into Texas, where he captured the town of Goliad. His success was of brief duration. He was soon killed and Long's Republic of Texas vanished.

These ill-fated raids solidified a long-emerging decision among Mexico's officialdom. What Texas needed to save it from filibusters was a larger population. The inhabitants in 1821 were shockingly few; only 4,000 white persons were spread over that vast domain, a few of them in the presidial villa of San Antonio de Bexar or the other two small towns that had been planted by New Spain, most on ranchos where they raised long-horned cattle. Plans for attracting more had been discussed since 1801, but not until Mexico won its independence was action possible. Fear of the United States was at a low ebb then, thanks to American aid in the war of independence from Spain, while the Mexican rulers were well aware that the mounting strength of their northern neighbor was traceable to its favorable immigration policy. Their decision was made easier by the conduct of a few hundred Americans from Texas who had drifted across the Sabine River to appropriate homesites around Nacogdoches or across the Red River to occupy its southern bank. These formed an unruly crew, true, but they showed no inclination to dispute Mexico's authority. Officials were ready to swing open the gates to other Americans if ever the demand arose.

This came from a Missourian named Moses Austin whose career epitomized the westward movement. Born in Durham, Connecticut, in 1761, Austin engaged in mercantile business, first in Philadelphia, then in Richmond. Hearing favorable reports of the lead mines of southeastern Missouri he set out in 1796 for the Spanish province, where he at first prospered in the manufacture of shot and sheet lead, only to suffer financial disaster within a few years. As early as 1813 Austin entertained a vague idea of trading with Texas, a prospect which grew more pleasing as his business reverses became more acute. In 1820 he visited the province to investigate possibilities. Upon arrival at Bexar he announced that he desired to settle on Spanish soil, that he spoke for several hundred families who wished to do likewise, that he was a Catholic and a one-time subject to the Spanish monarch. His petition for a grant of land on which to locate his proposed colony was granted largely because of his proof of earlier Spanish citizenship in Louisiana.

Overcome by exposure and exhaustion on the return trip from Texas, Moses Austin died in June, 1821, his last request being that his son, Stephen Fuller Austin, should complete his unfinished task. The son hardly seemed to fit the role of empire builder. Slight of build, with the look and character of a scholar, he was little inclined to mingle with the rough characters who frequented the advanced frontiers. Yet he was also charitable, tolerant, affectionate, extremely loyal, and a born leader—traits essential to any successful colonizer. A native of Virginia where he had been well educated, young Austin had been seasoned for a year and a half on the Arkansas borderlands when his great opportunity came. His career there promised little for his future; he had speculated unsuccessfully in town sites, been narrowly defeated as a territorial delegate to Congress, and drifted from job to job in an unlikely variety of occupations. Nevertheless he had mingled with the ruling faction in Arkansas enough to learn a great deal about frontier politics, lessons that stood him in good stead when he learned of his father's death. Stephen Austin was twenty-seven years old at that time.

Taking with him from New Orleans eight or ten men, he set out for Texas on a tour of inspection with a view to selecting a location for the contemplated colony. He was well received by the governor at San Antonio, who recognized him as heir and successor to his father's plan of colonization. In the course of his reconnaissance he covered the area now included in twenty-three Texas counties. Although he planned to locate his settlement in the Colorado and Brazos valleys, he requested the reservation of a substantially larger area. Returning to New Orleans, Austin bought a small ship, the *Lively*, which he fitted out with a party of settlers who were to sound the coast, land at the mouth of the Colorado, build a fort, and plant a crop of corn. Austin himself was to lead a party overland to the colony. Mistaking the mouth of the Brazos for the Colorado, the *Lively* failed to keep the rendezvous. There was, therefore, no crop awaiting the overland party on its arrival in December, 1821, with the resulting hunger and hardship which usually attended first settlements on all frontiers. Despite the difficulties, the little band that accompanied Austin to the banks of the Brazos established the first organized Anglo-American settlement in Texas.

Thus far a letter from the Texan governor was the only authorization for Austin's plan of colonization, and he apparently assumed that no further confirmation was necessary. Great was his surprise, therefore, when he learned in March, 1822, that approval by the Congress of Mexico was necessary. Although he could ill afford the trip financially, and feared for the embarrassment which his settlers would suffer through delay, there was nothing for Austin to do but to proceed at once to Mexico City to seek official approval.

This proved difficult. He had no sooner reached the capital city in August, 1822, when a long-simmering conflict between Mexico's liberator, Agustín de Iturbide, and his opponents flamed into a minor rebellion; for almost a year Austin cooled his heels while the rival factions debated in Congress or clashed in bloodless engagements. Such was his skill that he managed to keep on good terms with all the quarreling groups and to improve his time by learning Spanish. Not until April 14, 1823—nearly a year after he arrived—was his patience rewarded with the generous grant that he sought. He was authorized to introduce 300 families of proper moral character who agreed to accept the Catholic faith; each family would be given one *labor* (177 acres) of farm land and seventy-four *labors* for stock raising, for a total of one *sitio* or square league. Austin was allowed to collect 12½ cents an acre for his services, and promised a bonus of 65,000 acres when 200 families were brought in. He must also found a town conveniently near the settlement.

During Austin's absence in Mexico City a trickle of immigration began, most of the newcomers coming in response to notices that he published in western and southwestern newspapers. They built their cabins in the bottom lands of the Brazos, Colorado, and Bernard rivers, all clustered about the little hamlet of San Felipe de Austin that Austin had marked as his headquarters. By the end of 1823 some 300 families lived in the colony—the "Old Three Hundred" in Texas history. Their presence attracted others, until by the end of 1825 a census showed 2,021 residents, of whom 443 were Negro slaves. Austin's venture had been launched on the road to success.

His duty was to dispense both land and government to his followers, an obligation complicated by his complete lack of defined powers. Especially annoying was the problem of distributing land, which affected every family in the colony. Some settlers were disgruntled when they found they were denied the particular location they desired, suspecting that Austin was holding it for himself or a friend. Others objected to what seemed excessive grants to certain individuals, overlooking the special equipment of men with many slaves or the compensations earned by building gins, sawmills, and gristmills. There was especial dissatisfaction with Austin's charge of 12½ cents per acre, a purely nominal sum designed to cover the expense which the administration and settlement of the land entailed. Realizing he could not please all, Austin pleased himself by administering justice impartially.

The drafting of a state constitution for the province of Texas-Coahuila in 1827 allowed Austin to divest himself of his political powers and relieved him of the painful duty of governing his band of "North American frontier republicans." In the autumn of that year an election was authorized for an *ayuntamiento*, whose jurisdiction was to extend from the Lavaca to the watershed east of the Trinity, and from the Gulf to the San Antonio road. On February 3rd and 4th, 1828, the first legally ordained balloting in Anglo-American Texas took place, an event of little novelty to Austin's colonists with their background of political experience in the United States. The establishment of the new government made Austin less responsible, but not less influntial in his colony. He operated in close harmony with the elected *ayuntamiento*, whose members always consulted him on any matter relating to contacts with Mexico or other colonies.

Meanwhile colonies and plans for colonies in Texas were being launched under other auspices. The colonization law of Mexico, an essential preliminary to any comprehensive scheme for settlement, was finally promulgated in August, 1824. It authorized the individual states, subject to certain stipulations, to dispose of the public lands within their confines and to supervise immigration thereto. The state laws must not, except with federal consent, allow the settlement of foreigners within ten leagues of the coast or twenty leagues of the international boundary. Not more than eleven square leagues could be held by any one person, nor were nonresidents of the Republic to hold land.

Acting under authority vested by this National Colonization Law, the State of Coahuila-Texas, of which Texas was a district, passed its own colonization act in March, 1825. This invited into the state immigrants who met the requirements of the federal law and provided for the needs of individual families and for colonies to be brought in by *empresarios*. An *empresario* must agree to establish 100 families on the land, receiving in return a bonus of five leagues of grazing land and five *labors* of farming land. Contracts with *empresarios* were to run for six years and were void, without claim to compensation, if the required 100 families were not settled within that period. Families brought in by the *empresario* were to receive one *labor* of farming land and twenty-four *labors* of grazing land, a total of a league,

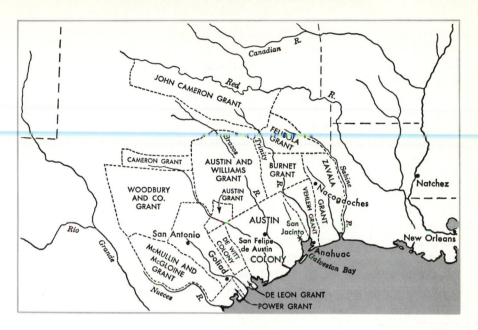

Texas in 1836

or 4,428 acres, for which a nominal payment of $30 a league was required in three installments. No better inducement for settlement could be offered.

The time was ripe for such a measure, for Americans in the southwestern borderland were eager to move. Texas promised two priceless commodities. One was cheap land; in the United States the after-effects of the Panic of 1819 deadened agricultural markets just at a time when the Land Act of 1820 required a cash payment of $1.25 an acre for the public domain. The other was good health. In the lower Mississippi Valley settlers constantly battled two diseases that made life miserable: bilious fever (or dysentery) and the ague (or malaria). Both were inevitable summer visitors, appearing with the first warm weather and lasting until frost, stalking about (as one traveler put it) "seeking whom they might destroy." They destroyed many; bilious fever afflicted whole towns while the ague was such a universal malady that church bells rang at a set hour to warn the people to take their doses of quinine. Why live in such agony when the pure air of Texas assured robust health? Perhaps a quarter of those who migrated at this time sought relief from illness, including three of the four men who later became presidents of the Republic of Texas.

Empresarios reaped the harvest of dissatisfaction in the American Southwest. Within six weeks after the enactment of the colonization law, four contracts were signed for the settlement of 2,400 families in Texas. A total of fifteen contracts were entered into by 1829, calling for the settlement of 5,450 families. Included in those was one with David G. Burnet, for 300 families, two with Joseph Vehlein, a German living in Mexico City, for 400 families, and one with Lorenzo de Zavala for the settlement of 500 families east of Nacogdoches. Those four contracts covered a compact area which seemed to offer an exceptional opportunity for large-scale settlement activities. In 1830 those *empresarios* pooled their resources with those of a group of New York and Boston capitalists under the name of the Galveston Bay and Texas Land Company. The organization planned to colonize its lands with Swiss and German settlers but its principal achievement was the introduction of several hundred American families into the area.

Of the fifteen contracts signed, not one was carried out to the letter. Under some not a single family was brought into Texas. Probably most *empresarios* entered into their agreements in good faith, with every intention of complying with the terms, but some were fly-by-night speculators who hoped to turn their contracts into profits by manipulation rather than colonization. Few of these succeeded; the only *empresarios* who garnered sizeable profits were those organized as the Galveston Bay and Texas Land Company whose holdings lay athwart the immigrant routes westward. Most eventually surrendered their grants with nothing to show save empty pockets.

Meanwhile Austin, whose original grant came directly from the national government rather than from the state, expanded the scope of his colonizing activities through additional contracts with Texas-Coahuila. Foreseeing the growth of an important cotton trade from Texas, he asked in February, 1825, for permission to settle another 300 families. In support of his request he shrewdly pointed out that numerous families of good character lived in the eastern part of Texas, where there was no local government and where they were unable to secure either title to the land or security against evil characters who preyed upon them. He proposed to settle those people on the Colorado and Brazos, above his original colony, where they would contribute their labor to the development of the country and serve as a buffer against Indian attacks. He also asked for a port on Galveston Bay, which he deemed essential to the successful development of cotton culture in the country. His request to settle 300 families was granted, a figure shortly increased to almost 500. That was the first of Austin's three contracts with the state. One in 1827 called for 100 families; another in 1828 authorized him to bring in 300 more, a total of 900 families for the three contracts. Then, in 1831 he and his secretary contracted to introduce more than 800 Mexican and European families.

Strong as was the tide of American settlement moving into Texas in 1825, it would have been even stronger but for the uncertainty of prospective immigrants regarding Mexico's attitude toward slavery and religious toleration. Despite Mexican opposition to slavery, Austin obtained a Texas-Coahuila law in 1828 recognizing labor contracts in which the immigrant, after liberating his slaves, promptly made them indentured servants for life. The question of toleration was one which Austin dared not take up in any formal way with Mexican officials. Nevertheless, a satisfactory arrangement was worked out. While Protestants were denied the privilege of worshipping in their own churches, they were not required to attend the Catholic church. Hence the problem of religion bulked larger in the mind of the would-be than the actual settler.

It was not surprising that pioneers going to Texas should turn to Austin's colony rather than those promoted by other *empresarios*. His settlement was well established. He had demonstrated his ability to get along with Mexican officialdom. His settlers had received title to the land and were conquering the wilderness. They had solved the problem of maintaining security from Indian attack, and advanced beyond the primitive stage of pioneering to that where at least a rude comfort was to be had. Controversies with other *empresarios* over contracts merely stressed to potential emigrants the comparative tranquility prevailing in Austin's zone of settlement. They were also aware that his was one of the garden spots of Texas, with soil of near-inexhaustible fertility, abundant rainfall, access to markets via sea routes, prairie lands with adequate timber nearby, and a mild climate where sea breezes modified the excessive heat of summer. Every visitor who returned to the United States was filled with enthusiasm for the natural advantages of Austin's colony and spread the word widely.

The steady growth of the colony attested to the effectiveness of this advertising campaign: from 2,021 in 1825 to 4,248 in 1831 and to 5,660 a year later. By the close of 1833 Austin had issued land titles to 1,065 families, including 755 in grants from the state and 310 in his original grant from the national government. The majority of Austin's settlers came to Texas from the region west of the Alleghenies and south of the Ohio, with a large number from Missouri, whose contributions to his original colony was proportionately greater than to the later ones. It was the nonslaveholder or small slaveholder from the southwest that colonized Texas during the first decade. In 1830 about 1,000 Negro slaves were owned by the nearly 8,000 Americans who lived in Texas, a little over half of them in Austin's colony.

While immigrants flocked to Texas under the auspices of *empresarios*, others arrived on their own initiative and expense. This was particularly true of the Nacogdoches area in the eastern part of the province. Many law-abiding pioneers, originally destined for Austin's colony, had settled in East Texas, built cabins, and raised crops without acquiring title to the land. Along with peaceful and respectable folk of this sort were an unusually high proportion of law breakers who had slipped across the border from Arkansas, unruly Spanish and French creoles, and Indians who refused to accept life on a reservation. All were little inclined to accept any form of discipline. In this region, and among these people, were heard the early rumblings of dissatisfaction that gave Mexican officials their first feeling of concern over the future of Texas.

They centered first in the *empresario* grant which had authorized one Haden Edwards to settle some 800 families near Nacogdoches, a large domain touching Austin's colony on the west at San Jacinto, and extending eastward to the "twilight zone" where lived squatters who acknowledged no superior authority. His contract required that he protect the prior rights of earlier settlers against claims of his own colonists, that he organize and command a militia to maintain order, and that after he introduced 100 families into his colony he must apply for the appointment of a commissioner to grant titles and lay out towns. Edwards proceeded in a peremptory manner with respect to the claims of earlier settlers, placing them on the defensive by calling upon them to show evidence of title to their land. The old inhabitants replied by a petition to the legislature asking that they be secured in their titles to the coast and border reservations, and to an additional twenty-five leagues around Nacogdoches. The uproar caused by the various indiscretions on the part of Edwards forced the Mexican officials to annul his contract and order him expelled from the country. The formal charges brought against him were "falsely styling himself military commander," compelling settlers to show title to their land under penalty of having it "sold to the highest bidder," depriving certain men of lands for the benefit of others, and pocketing the proceeds from land sales in the manner of an "absolute Lord and Master of those lands."

Despite the intercession of Austin in an effort to secure an inquiry into the merits of the controversy, the affair quickly got out of hand. Smarting under what he believed to be the unfair treatment accorded his brother, Benjamin Edwards on December 16, 1826, with less than a score of men, rode into Nacogdoches, unfurled a red and white banner inscribed with the words "Independence, Liberty and Justice," seized the old stone fort, and proclaimed the Republic of Fredonia. Although the border settlers were unsympathetic, exaggerated reports concerning the rebels' strength filled them with alarm. Believing they were forced to choose between strict neutrality and flight, many fled across the Sabine into American territory.

Edwards' one hope of success lay in the possibility of assistance from Austin's colony and the United States. Austin strove earnestly to persuade the rebels to ask for leniency at the hands of the government, to restrain men in his own colony from any radical move, and to induce officials to show moderation in dealing with the insurgents. The reply of the Edwards brothers was that they would accept nothing except complete "independence from the Sabine to the Rio Grande." Austin, however, not only succeeded in preventing his own men from casting their lot with the Fredonians but raised troops who marched with the Mexican forces against the insurrectionists. The rebellion collapsed with scarcely the firing of a shot, although Edwards made further unsuccessful attempts to enlist the support of American frontier settlers east of the Sabine.

This abortive Fredonian Uprising in 1826 should have been reassuring to the authorities in Mexico. It showed beyond possibility of doubt that the great mass of Anglo-American settlers in Texas, whether within or without Austin's colony, were loyal to the government and sincere in their resolve to be law-abiding Mexican subjects. Even the turbulent elements in the "twilight zone" along the eastern frontier had frowned upon the rebels. But the real significance of the affair was lost to Mexican officialdom. Instead of taking heart and regarding the experiment in American colonization of Texas as a success, they interpreted the insignificant incident as an indication of the aggressive designs of many Americans, in and out of Texas, upon the integrity of the Mexican Republic. The affair, affording additional proof that all-too-many Americans knew "no law but the sword," was one of numerous incidents which by 1830 convinced authorities in Mexico City of the need for a more cautious policy with respect to American settlement in Texas.

Among other factors arousing Mexican fears with respect to the security of Texas was the long-standing dissatisfaction in the United States with the boundary settlement of 1819. Not only had Thomas Hart Benton and other prominent individuals expressed disapproval of American relinquishment of claims to Texas, but John Quincy Adams, who became President in 1825, sought to rectify his earlier error in accepting the Adams-Onís treaty by instructing his minister to Mexico City, Joel R. Poinsett, to negotiate a boundary more acceptable to the Southwest. Poinsett made separate efforts in 1825 and 1827, offering Mexico $1,000,000 for Texas, but to no avail. In the end he signed an agreement confirming the 1819 boundary to facilitate completion of a commercial treaty. The sole result was to stir Mexican apprehensions that the United States was determined to acquire Texas, no matter by what means.

These fears were heightened when Andrew Jackson became President in 1829. Jackson was known as a dangerous expansionist; indeed Mexico had heard rumors that he intended to occupy Texas, then negotiate afterward. The President's actions seemed to confirm these rumors. He first raised the offer for Texas to $5,000,000, then when this was refused replaced Poinsett with the less savory Colonel Anthony Butler who for the next six years resorted to a variety of questionable tactics to persuade Mexico to change its mind. During this time Butler repeatedly tried to bribe Mexican officials, offered to take Texas as security for a loan, and urged Jackson to overrun the province by force. Butler's undiplomatic behavior further convinced the Mexican rulers that Texas could be saved from the hungry colossus of the north only if they acted at once.

To compound their problems, contemporaneously with Butler's sojourn in Mexico the administration press in the United States began a campaign for the annexation of Texas. Equally alarming were advertisements of a fraudulent land company which used the columns of the *National Intelligencer* to offer for sale 48,000,000 acres of land in Texas-Coahuila. Making use of an *empresario* contract authorizing the settlement of only 200 families, the company's advertising campaign gave the impression it could convey title to all Texas to American investors. Although such activities increased American interest in Texas and augmented the tide of immigration, they helped convince Mexico its northern provinces were in jeopardy.

The mounting tension was heightened by the political situation within Mexico. There, ever since that autumn day in 1810 when a parish priest named Manuel Hidalgo y Costilla raised the standard of revolt against Spain's rule, Mexico had been divided into two political camps. One, the "Federalists," adhered to Father Hidalgo's dream of an independent republic, democratically administered, and pledged to better the social and economic lot of the lower classes. The other, the "Centralists," also supported independence, but its *criollos* (men of pure Spanish blood born in Mexico) leaders shied from any social revolution that would elevate the lower classes. During the war against Spain these two parties forgot their differences, but once independence was won they divided sharply. The Centralists wanted a dictatorship headed by either an imported Bourbon prince or the local Agustín de Iturbide, the military hero who had led the revolutionary forces. The Federalists favored a republican democracy modeled on that of the United States. Their platform was a constitution written by Stephen F. Austin in 1824 while waiting confirmation of his grant, which adjusted the American frame of government to Roman law and Catholicism.

The tug-of-war between these two factions doomed Mexico to decades of turmoil before its people were able to secure and maintain an orderly and stable government. It also made inevitable a vacillating policy toward Texas. When the Federalists were in power they allowed their pro-American sympathies to shape their policies, favoring immigration from the United States into the province and a laissez-faire attitude toward its people. The Centralists reversed this pattern whenever they assumed office in Mexico, seeking to check the spread of American influence in Texas and installing autocratic controls there. The Federalists were first in command after independence was won in 1821—the generous land act of 1824 was one of the fruits of their regime—but when Centralists' guns upset the results of the first general election in 1828 Texan problems were certain to multiply.

The new rulers planned their moves carefully. They were aware of a report prepared in 1828 by General Manuel de Mier y Terán, who had visited Nacogdoches and expressed alarm at the "mixture of strange and incoherent parts" in the population there. A year later Terán was made commandant-general of the Eastern Provinces, including Texas, and asked to devise a program to save the area from American infiltration. His solution was three-fold: strengthen commercial ties with Mexico by stimulating coastal trade, settle Europeans and Mexicans in Texas as a counterweight to the Americans already there, and send sufficient Mexican troops to stifle any protest. These suggestions were expanded into a far more sweeping law adopted by the Centralists in 1830. Using the excuse that Texans had violated the Colonization Act of 1824 by refusing to become Catholics, the measure deprived the State of Coahuila-Texas of all authority over colonization, suspended existing *empresario* contracts, and vested complete control of immigration in the national government.

The Colonization Law of April 6, 1830, seemed deliberately designed to whet Texas resentment. "Citizens of foreign countries lying adjacent to the Mexican territory" were forbidden to settle there. No more slaves could be introduced, and all foreigners crossing the border must carry passports issued by Mexico. These restrictive rulings were no more annoying than a series of confused decrees governing *empresarios*. One article of the law guaranteed that "no change shall be made with respect to the colonies already established," while another stated that "those contracts of colonization . . . which are not yet complied with, shall subsequently be suspended." Which colonies were "established," and in which were the terms of the contract "not yet complied with"? Under a literal interpretation, all contracts, including Austin's, could be suspended. In practice officials allowed *empresarios* who had settled 100 families or more to retain their holdings. Those who failed to meet this standard saw their agreements cancelled, while even those who did not, realized that they were at the mercy of a dictatorial government that could exclude them at any time. They realized, correctly, that the Act of 1830 was a Centralist measure and by no means typical of public sentiment throughout Mexico; indeed most Federalists who were as numerous as their rivals were as opposed to the law as the Texans themselves. But they also knew that the Centralists would probably stay in power for some time, backed as they were by the money and guns of the anti-American *criollos* elite.

For a time these fears were stilled, for of the major objectives embodied in the 1830 law, only that calling for the military occupation of Texas was realized. The coastwise trade never materialized, colonization by Europeans failed, and the attempt to bar immigrants from adjacent countries (meaning the United States) backfired. Its effect was to ban industrious newcomers who had been selected by responsible *empresarios* while opening the gate to irresponsible squatters who came illegally with a chip on their shoulders. Among the uninvited who arrived at this time was one Sam Houston who appeared on the turbulent frontier of East Texas in 1832 after spending two years living among the Cherokee Indians.

As Americans increasingly outnumbered the 3,500 Mexicans in Texas, the gulf between them and their overlords widened. Blundering acts by the Centralists heightened ill-feeling, but the basic cause was a cultural gap that could never be bridged. Americans, with a heritage rooted in northern Europe and nurtured on the liberal doctrines of political democracy and Protestantism, were simply unable and unwilling to understand a Mexican culture that was rooted in ancient Rome and based on a belief in the duty of obedience to church and state. Feeling as they did that their beliefs and institutions were superior, their sense of isolation was accentuated by a compulsion to unite against all who threatened the basic premise on which their civilization had been built. Their ethnocentrism might have been kept under control had they been authorized to manage their local affairs, but the Centralists steadfastly refused to separate Texas from Coahuila as they wanted.

Instead the Texans were ruled from a capital at Saltillo, almost 700 miles away, where the one-house legislature of twelve admitted only one representative (later two) from the province. To accept continued domination by rulers who Texans scorned as an inferior people was unthinkable.

Underlying this prejudice were radically opposed concepts of government. In the United States legal power derived from the people, while individuals were protected from the state by written constitutions, federalism, and the separation of powers. In Mexico authority was vested in the country's rulers, who expected unquestioning obedience from their subjects. During their immediate post-revolutionary years, the Mexicans made exploratory gestures toward a federal system, but the tradition of absolutism was so strong that the constant trend was toward ever-greater centralization. This Americans feared, having been taught that the inevitable end-product of centralization was tyranny. Thus prejudiced, they were inclined to view every act of Mexican officialdom, no matter how innocent, as designed to rob them of their individual rights.

This alone explains their reaction when the Centralist government tried to implement Terán's report by planting military garrisons at San Antonio, Goliad, and Nacogdoches, and by strengthening the forces at Anahuac and other fortified towns. They saw these troops as instruments of oppression, not as guardians of their safety as they would have in the same situation in the United States. Even with the most tactful commanders, the presence of the garrisons would have bred trouble, but when authorities named an incompetent autocrat to command the force at Anahuac at the gateway to the unauthorized settlements in the "twilight zone," they were inviting trouble. This was an American, Colonel John Bradburn, who, in spite of sound advice by Terán, soon antagonized many of the settlers. He employed the colonists' slaves without compensation in building fortifications, incited Negroes to rebellion, and arrested for military trial several of the Americans. The latter action prompted a small force from Brazoria to march against Bradburn's garrison in June, 1832. Despite the commander's resignation under pressure and the release of the arrested settlers, a skirmish ensued between insurgents and troops in which the latter were defeated.

The uprising against Bradburn can be understood only in the light of political developments within Mexico. There the liberal Federalist Party seized control in 1832, elevating to the presidency a military chieftain named Antonio Lopez de Santa Anna. This bloodless revolution inspired the sympathy of most Americans in Texas, who knew that their future within the Mexican Republic could be secure only if Federalist doctrines triumphed. They honestly believed that their attack on Bradburn was a blow to restore the Constitution of 1824 and happy relationship between themselves and Mexico, a Mexico governed by Santa Anna and the Federalists. Their views were accurately mirrored in the "Turtle Bayou" resolutions that were adopted before the insurrectionists adjourned; the Texans would, the resolutions asserted, lay down their property and their lives to support "this distinguished leader" who was "so gallantly fighting in defense of civil liberty." Austin echoed those views when he wrote at the time that "the happiness and peace of the nation demand adherence to the plan of Santa Anna." Nor did Austin err when he recorded that in all Texas there was no hint of disloyalty, no sentiment for secession, no hostility to Mexican officials other than Bradburn. Texas did want separation from Coahuila and separate statehood, but that was all.

Having identified themselves with the successful Federalist Party and with Santa Anna, the Texans were in a strategic position to state their grievances and ask for a redress of the abuses which occasioned the recent difficulty. On August 22, 1832, therefore, they issued a call requesting each of the settlements to send five delegates to a convention at San Felipe on October 1, 1832. Although Austin doubted the wisdom of the convention, the wording of the invitation was no doubt his, and it was designed to give Mexican authorities a favorable view of the movement. It observed that with the spread of the civil war to Texas, the sporadic resistance in the province had been misinterpreted. Hence the convention was necessary to enable the Texans to affirm their support of the liberal movement led by Santa Anna.

The convention petitioned for a reform of the tariff which would allow the free importation of farm machinery, furniture, and clothing for another three years. The request for the repeal of the law excluding Americans from further settlement in Texas tactfully pointed out that it merely kept out law-abiding people, without restricting the more aggressive and turbulent elements. The convention asked for a more adequate Indian policy and for the appointment of a commissioner to adjust the land claims of the settlers in east Texas. Although Austin's proposal for a memorial against abuses in local government received scant consideration, approval was given to a petition requesting separation from Coahuila. It stressed the inequality of representation as well as the dissimilar soil, climate, and production in the two areas. William H. Wharton, leader of the more aggressive faction in Texas, was chosen to present the various petitions and memorials of the convention to the federal and state governments.

Before the 1832 convention adjourned, it resolved to meet again in San Felipe de Austin on April 1, 1833. The delegates who assembled that day were largely those who had met the year before—joined now by Sam Houston as a delegate from Nacogdoches—but their mood was far different. Their demands were the same—repeal of the American exclusion clause in the Act of 1830, continued freedom from tariff duties, a better mail service, separation from Coahuila—but this time the convention moved a step nearer independence by drafting a constitution for the "State of Texas"—a constitution, curiously enough, patterned after the Massachusetts constitution of 1780 with few changes adapted to the needs of a Mexican state. Stephen Austin had little sympathy for the more extreme demands, but he agreed to deliver the convention's petitions to Santa Anna in Mexico City. This was a futile gesture. Even the Federalists saw no reason why the Texans should be granted immunity from tariff restrictions, the right to own slaves, and exemption from military supervision. Nor were they willing to favor separate statehood for Texas, seeing that only as a first step toward secession. In the end Austin won only a single concession—repeal of the clause in the act of 1830 barring American migration into Texas—before he turned his steps toward home. At Saltillo he was arrested and hurried back to Mexico City where he learned that a letter written in anger during his negotiations—a letter urging his friends in Texas to form their own state government—had been apprehended by the police. Austin cooled his heels in a Mexican jail until July, 1835, when he was finally freed to return to Texas.

By this time the situation was changing rapidly, despite a series of conciliatory measures adopted by the Coahuila-Texas legislature extending greater control over local government, authorizing religious toleration and the use of English in public documents, and allowing an additional legislative delegate. These failed to turn the tide, for already a loosely-knit "war party" was beginning to coalesce. Responsible for this resurgence of revolutionary sentiment were changes within Mexico's political structure. Ever since taking office as president in 1832, General Santa Anna had moved steadily toward the political right and a union with the Centralist Party, revealing that he had donned the Federalist garb only long enough to win office. By 1834 he was openly the leader of the Centralists. With their support he proclaimed himself a permanent president, dismissed congress, and replaced the Constitution of 1824 with the *Siete Leyes* (the Seven Laws) that abolished the federal system and established a centralized dictatorship. Santa Anna added teeth to this document by placing his own puppets as governors of the provinces and removing most of the *ayuntamientos*, or town councils, that cared for local affairs. Within a year Santa Anna was the absolute dictator of all Mexico.

Federalists were so confounded by this defection of their leader that opposition emerged slowly, allowing him to tighten his controls until he was able to crush all opponents. This Federalist Party leaders in the provinces of Yucatán and Zacatecas discovered to their sorrow when they were ruthlessly punished for refusing to obey his orders to disarm. So did the governors of Coahuila-Texas when they tried to escape northward to create a Federalist stronghold at San Antonio; they were dispersed and arrested by Santa Anna's armies. Texans responded somewhat slowly, largely because they were confused by the rapidity of changes in the Mexican political scene. Santa Anna, they reasoned, could not be all bad since he had in 1833, as a Federalist, repealed the hated Colonization Act of 1830. So they hesitated to take sides until Santa Anna showed his true nature.

He did so when he decided to occupy Texas and disarm its inhabitants. Texans had their first hint at the course of events when the military commandant named for their province in January, 1835, sent a well-guarded collector to reopen the customs house at Anahuac. To have customs collected was bad enough, but when the collector began demanding bribes, opposition flared into a pocket-size local rebellion during which an American merchant was arrested. News of this reached San Felipe de Austin just as word also arrived that Santa Anna was leading an army northward to crush the Federalist uprisings that had flamed in many of the northern provinces. This was too much. On June 29, 1835, a band of forty hotheads led by W. B. Travis marched on Anahuac, forced the surrender of the small garrison there, and only dispersed after the commander had agreed to leave Texas with his troops.

Upon his return to San Felipe de Austin, Travis found strong disapproval of his actions. A meeting at Columbia condemned his course and affirmed the loyalty of the people to Mexico. Other communities emulated the example of Columbia and declared their desire for peace. But again Mexican officials played into the hands of the radical group. The military commandant ordered the arrest of Travis and others, making it clear at the same time that, with heavy reinforcements, he planned to take charge in person at San Antonio. That, the extremists averred, could mean only one thing—military rule in Texas.

Only a spark was needed to set off the conflagration now, and Santa Anna accommodated. Hearing exaggerated reports of events in Texas, he left his main army in northern Mexico and hurried ahead with a cavalry detachment to descend on the town of Gonzales and demand the surrender of cannon stored there. From all the surrounding countryside the Texans rallied. On October 2, 1835, they crossed the Guadalupe River to attack, sending the small Mexican force flying southward. Then, with Austin in command, they moved on to San Antonio where they laid siege to a sizeable Mexican detachment that had taken refuge there. Blood had been shed; a revolution was under way, but it was not at this stage a revolution against Mexico. Instead the Texans saw themselves as opposing only the Centralist dictatorship of Santa Anna. Nor were they rebelling alone, for their resistance was part of a general uprising in Mexico against the abrogation of the Constitution of 1824. Yucatán resisted so successfully that it remained virtually independent for a decade, while Federalists in portions of Tamaulipas, Neuvo León, and Coahuila sought to form the Republic of the Rio Grande as an independent nation. Santa Anna had stirred a hornet's nest of rebellion that must be crushed.

Realizing this, the Texans knew that they would not fight alone if they made their decision for independence. Armed with this consoling thought, they assembled at San Felipe de Austin on November 3, 1835, for a "Consultation." Austin was absent with the army when deliberations began, but fearing the group might go "too fast and too far" he forwarded a statement of what he thought they should attempt. Thanks to a sensible presiding officer, this plan became the agenda of the meeting. Austin's first suggestion was that the Consultation should issue a formal declaration of the reasons that impelled the Texans to take up arms. This, of course, raised the basic question whether they were seeking independence or merely the preservation of the federal system. Following several days of debate, it was voted, thirty-three to fifteen, to form a provisional government based "upon the principles of the Constitution of 1824." Although somewhat ambiguously worded, the Consultation had in effect only endorsed the Federalist Party's position against over-centralized authority. This created, the members drafted plans for a regular army, named three commissioners, including Austin, to solicit aid from the United States, and adjourned to meet again on March 1, 1836.

Before that date arrived events moved far and fast. In December, 1835, the garrison maintained by Santa Anna at San Antonio, for some months under siege by the Texans, surrendered. Its officers were made to swear that they would support the Constitution of 1824 and agree never to enter Texas again as a condition of their release. Those who chose to do so were given the alternative of remaining in Texas if they joined the Federalist cause. Santa Anna correctly interpreted these conditions as highly danger-ous; unless he acted at once Texas might become the rallying center for Federalists from all northern Mexico. Forming an army and placing himself in command, he started toward Texas. Unwittingly he had taken the one course that would convert the Texans from Federalists to revolutionaries.

For a time confusion reigned as Santa Anna with his almost 6,000 men advanced unmolested toward San Antonio. There a small force of 187 men waited behind the adobe walls of the Alamo Mission to bar his path. These brave Texans laid down their lives in the cause, but they killed 1,544 Cen-tralist soldiers before they succumbed. Their deaths touched off a spark of resentment everywhere; "Remember the Alamo" became a rallying cry that not even the most sluggish could resist. In this electrified atmosphere men of all shades of opinion agreed that independence was their only recourse; even Austin publicly declared for separation from Mexico. This spirit per-meated the fifty-nine delegates who assembled at the little village of Wash-ington on March 1, 1836, to decide the fate of their land. With one voice they agreed on a Declaration of Independence, then named Sam Houston commander-in-chief of the military force that would translate this intent into reality. A constitution for the Republic of Texas was also fashioned by a judicious borrowing of concepts and phrases from the constitution of the United States and the several states that the delegates knew. This provided for a president who would serve a three-year term and not be eligible for re-election, an elected congress, and a judicial system similar to that of the United States. Slavery was legalized, and each Texan granted a league and a *labor* of land.

To declare Texan independence was one thing; to win independence was quite another. True, Santa Anna's army was hardly a formidable foe. The makeshift crew of thousands of conscripted youths, old men, convicts, and Mayan Indians unfamiliar with either Spanish or firearms that he led into Texas dwindled rapidly as disease and desertion took their toll. Those who remained in the ranks were badly worn from the long march across the arid wastelands of northern Mexico, while the officers were so inefficient that discipline virtually vanished. The noisy caravan of women, children, muleteers, and curiosity seekers that tagged along used food supplies badly needed by the men themselves. By the time the army left San Antonio only 2,400 were fit to march, and most of these were desperately ill of dysentery. Rain fell almost constantly that spring, with swollen streams and dampened supplies intensifying the misery of the soldiers. Santa Anna was defeated before he actually met the Texans, a victim of inadequate supplies, faulty logistics, and poor planning.

None of this was known to Sam Houston as he retreated slowly eastward before the advancing Mexicans, at the same time welding his raw recruits into an army. From the Colorado, to the Brazos, to San Felipe de Austin, the Texans fell back. Each area that he abandoned added terror-stricken refugees to his retinue as the people fled eastward in a "runaway scrape" that crowded every road. Santa Anna, in hot pursuit, scented victory, and was impatient for his moment of triumph. Annoyed by the slowness of his ailing army, he decided to press ahead with only 900 picked men. Here was Houston's opportunity; Santa Anna had blundered by separating himself from his army and was fair game. On April 20, 1836, he closed in on the Mexican force which was camped on the banks of the San Jacinto River, leading his 800 Texans into camp only a short distance from the enemy. Santa Anna, confident that Houston would attack at dawn, kept his men up all that night building barricades and preparing for the assault. Dawn came, and no attack. In midmorning almost 500 reinforcements joined Santa Anna's force and the general began to breath a little easier. At noon he ordered a hot meal prepared, knowing his troops had had little sleep and less food for twenty-four hours. Only a skeleton force stood guard during the *siesta* that followed. This was the moment chosen by Houston to attack, his men slipping so noiselessly through the tall grass that they were not seen until they were only 200 yards from the Mexican lines. Then, shouting "Remember the Alamo! Remember Goliad!" they charged. Within seventeen minutes the battle was won, with 630 of the Mexican soldiers killed and 730 more, including Santa Anna himself, captured. Although the Mexican general soon repudiated the pledge to grant Texan independence that he made to win his release, Mexico was never again able to impose its authority on the newborn Republic.

Notwithstanding his undoubted interest in Texas and his earlier efforts to acquire it by purchase, President Jackson adopted a scrupulously proper attitude once there were forebodings of trouble in the province. As early as March, 1833, his secretary of state, Edward Livingston, wrote the American agent in Mexico, who was trying to purchase Texas, that the critical situation of affairs there made "it important that . . . negotiation on that subject should be brought to a speedy conclusion." In short, a revolt in Texas was the last thing Jackson desired, since it would interfere with his plans for peaceful acquisition. Once the revolution broke out the administration pursued a policy of strict neutrality, which, of course, was at variance with the sympathies of a large segment of the American public. That the neutrality laws were violated, and that extensive aid in American men and materials was supplied to Texas was in spite of, rather than because of, the federal government's course. On such a far-flung frontier nothing less than a substantial army could have enforced the neutrality laws.

After the defeat and capture of Santa Anna, Jackson's course was one of "watchful waiting" to see whether the Texans could maintain their independence and establish a stable government. The President's official conduct was the more notable because it was not in harmony with his private views. As an individual he favored recognition and probably desired annexation. He believed, however, that Congress should first express a view favorable to recognition and he desired to save his successor, Martin Van Buren, the inconvenience that might follow should the executive arm of the government be pledged to a course disapproved by the legislature. Jackson also privately pointed out to Texan officials that opposition of the commercial interests of the East to annexation might be allayed by Texan acquisition of California with its fine harbor of San Francisco Bay. On December 21, 1836, exactly eight months after San Jacinto, Jackson advised Congress that recognition at that time "could scarcely be regarded as consistent with that prudent reserve with which we have heretofore held ourselves bound to treat all similar questions."

By March 3, 1837, Jackson had changed his mind. Several events occasioned his reversal. Both houses of Congress, in response to a widespread popular desire, had voted funds for a diplomatic representative in Texas whenever the executive deemed it expedient to name one. The American minister to Mexico had arrived in Washington bringing word that another invasion of Texas was impossible. Santa Anna himself had confessed his country's inability to hold the rebellious province. Finally, if Texans were coldly disregarded by the United States, they might, by commercial concessions injurious to American business, purchase the assistance of England, which was much interested in the young republic. In view of those circumstances, Jackson, on the last day of his term, appointed a chargé d'affaires to the Republic of Texas. American recognition of Texas, coming more than ten months after San Jacinto, was considerably less precipitate than recognition of Mexico's independence from Spain.

Even before recognition was disposed of, the question of annexation arose. In November, 1836, following a Texan vote in favor of accession to the United States, the Texan representative in Washington was instructed to raise the issue. On August 4, 1837, the Texan minister submitted to the secretary of state a formal proposal for annexation of his country. Although employing both cogent argument and the threat that rejection of the proposition might impel Texas to throw herself into the arms of Britain and make commercial concessions injurious to American trade, the offer was politely but firmly rejected. The reasons, the minister explained to his government, were "party trammels," treaty obligations with Mexico, opposition of the free states, fear of involvement in a war that would be unpopular at home, and the danger of disruption of the union resulting from the raising of such an explosive issue. In the face of the avalanche of petitions against Texas which poured in from northern and eastern states, the Van Buren administration dared not waver from its earlier decision, with the result that in October, 1838, the Texan offer was withdrawn.

For the next three or four years the question of annexation was in abeyance, both in Texas and the United States. During that time the views of the administration in Washington gradually changed. John Tyler had scarcely succeeded to the presidency when his close political friend, Henry A. Wise of Virginia, suggested that he acquire Texas at the earliest possible moment. The idea was favorably received; Tyler reasoned that annexation would bring fame to him and advantage to the United States. However, because of his fear of hostility in the Senate, he withheld public announcement of his interest, giving rise to the impression beyond the Sabine that the American attitude toward Texas was what Sam Houston described as one of "habitual apathy."

Houston, the president of the Texan republic, countered by adopting a policy of studied indifference to annexation, ordering his representative in Washington to give the impression to American officials of a growing friendship between his country and England. In view of the fact that American expansion was always considerably motivated by suspicion of English designs, Houston was playing a clever game. Nor did he need to exaggerate the extent of British interest. Britain in the early 1840s was desirous of maintaining an independent Texas as a potential market for British goods, free from the annoying restrictions of the American protective tariff. She also wished, if possible, to see Texas develop as a cotton-producing rival of the southern states of the United States. But obviously Texas could compete with the South in cotton production only with the aid of slave labor, to which England was strongly opposed. Britain had withheld recognition of Texan independence until 1840 in the hope that Texas would abolish slavery as the price of recognition. She still hoped to bring about emancipation and would use a free Texas as a base to undermine slavery in the United States.

In March, 1843, England's design to injure American slavery by freeing the Texan slaves became known to Tyler. This intelligence produced such a reaction in Washington that the Texan minister thought if the government were aroused only a little more against the British it would move toward annexation. American opinion was further alarmed when in May the New York *Journal of Commerce* reported the existence in Texas of an abolition movement, believed to be backed and financed by England. In June at a World Anti-Slavery Convention in London further talk of a free Texas as "an asylum for runaways and a perpetual incitement to murder, insurrection and outrage by the slaves of the Southern States'' was not without its effect on the administration.

The impression of British designs on Texas was strengthened by a ruse of Houston, in which he made it appear that the truce between his country and Mexico had been entirely due to the good offices of England. Both official and unofficial circles, convinced of the seriousness of British purpose, reacted as the wily Texan president planned. On September 12, 1843, Andrew Jackson, living in retirement but still the most influential Democrat in the country, put aside his earlier caution to come out squarely for annexation. Now that the independence of Texas had been recognized by England and France, he said, the United States could negotiate with her as an independent nation. He declared the nation must acquire Texas, "peaceably if we can, forcibly if we must," as a means of checkmating English plans for an offensive and defensive treaty with that country.

The administration's reaction was made known to Texas on October 16, 1843, when Abel Upshur, Tyler's secretary of state, advised Isaac Van Zandt, the Texan representative in Washington, that recent developments in Europe had presented the question of annexation in "new and important aspects," and that he was prepared to make a proposition whenever he was assured Van Zandt had authorization to receive it. On the same day Van Zandt wrote the Texan secretary of state. He enclosed Upshur's note and expressed the belief that remarks of English officials had aroused the southern states, while fear that Britain might monopolize the carrying trade of Texas "seems to have touched the secret springs of interest" among manufacturers of the North. He believed that Texas and Oregon could be combined in a way to command widespread support in the United States, and added his opinion that if this opportunity were rejected by Texas she was not likely to have another so good.

After three months of waiting Van Zandt received a reply, dated December 13, 1843, which indicated that Houston was still playing the European powers against the United States. Texas, he stated, could not afford to compromise her good relations with Britain and France by staking all on an annexation proposal that Congress might reject. If, however, Congress would adopt a resolution authorizing the President to offer annexation, the proposition would receive the immediate consideration of the Texan government. In short, Houston would accept statehood in the Union but he could not afford to gamble. He must have assurance in advance.

In January, 1844, one of Tyler's aides asked Jackson to use his well-known influence with Houston to overcome the latter's opposition to annexation. This Jackson promptly did and his letters, combined with the undoubted eagerness in both Texas and Washington for incorporation, did much to overcome whatever opposition Houston still entertained. Nevertheless, Houston continued to be cautious and, before committing himself, submitted the proposition to the Texas Congress for consideration. His message to that body contained no specific recommendation. Although admitting that union was desirable, he stressed the threat of an unsuccessful effort to the good relations of his country with England and France. In any event, he thought, the attitude of the United States should be known in advance and Texas should avoid any appearance of eagerness.

In February, 1844, Upshur sent the Texas government a communication which forced Houston to take a more positive attitude. He argued at length the advantages to Texas of joining the United States and the disadvantages of continued independence. Texas might enjoy an alliance with Great Britain but, Upshur added, "the lamb can make no contract with the wolf, which will protect him from being devoured." How much better for Texas to join a rapidly growing nation such as the United States. Such an opportunity Texas now had, for, Upshur stated, "there is not in my opinion, the slightest doubt of the ratification of the treaty of annexation, should Texas agree to make one." In the Senate "a clear constitutional majority of two-thirds are in favor of the measure." Houston, convinced by this straightforward statement, appointed a special representative to aid Van Zandt at Washington in negotiating a treaty. In March, 1844, because of unsatisfactory relations with Mexico and the resulting fear of invasion, the Texan representatives were given even greater discretion in their negotiations; they were directed to conclude a treaty at once and on the best terms obtainable. As Upshur died before the conclusion of the treaty, the negotiations were continued by his successor, John C. Calhoun.

Tyler had consistently justified annexation on grounds of broad national interest, as a measure designed to benefit all sections of the country, and a move to aid the commercial interests of the North. But Calhoun, by injecting the slavery issue squarely into the discussion, made the question a bitterly sectional one. When he became secretary of state, he found on his desk a dispatch setting forth British policy with respect to Texas. In the communication was a frank statement of the already well-known fact that England was "constantly exerting herself to procure the general abolition of slavery throughout the world." Calhoun immediately seized upon that section. In a wholly disingenuous manner he sought to make it appear that for the first time the United States had learned of England's interest in universal emancipation, and that annexation was necessary for the protection of slavery in the United States against British designs.

Calhoun's ill-mannered remarks guaranteed defeat for the treaty by confirming northern suspicion that the movement for the acquisition of Texas was a slaveholders' "conspiracy." In his message transmitting the treaty to the Senate, Tyler tried hard to smoothe the troubled waters. He emphasized the benefits annexation would confer on American settlers already in Texas, on the commercial interests of North and East, on the western states by creating a market for their products, and on the South by giving it security and protection. His efforts were in vain. Added to the opposition of the antislavery elements was that of Henry Clay and Martin Van Buren, the expected nominees of their parties for the presidency. Clay's famous "Raleigh letter," appearing in the *National Intelligencer* on April 27th, opposed annexation because it would lead to war with Mexico, was not desired by public opinion, involved danger to the Union, and was not even in the interest of the South, since much of Texas was not suited to slavery. Van Buren's letter, published the same day in the Washington *Globe*, minimized the foreign danger in Texas and declared annexation was likely to involve the United States in war with Mexico. On June 8th the treaty came to a vote in the Senate. Its supporters could muster but sixteen votes as compared with thirty-five against. Seven Democratic Senators voted against it, while only one Whig was in favor.

Meanwhile the question of annexation invaded the campaign of 1844. When Van Buren's letter opposing the treaty appeared, Jackson, notwithstanding his friendship for the New Yorker, suggested that James K. Polk of Tennessee seek the Democratic nomination as a compromise candidate. Others within the party had the same idea and Polk was nominated on a platform calling for "re-annexation of Texas at the earliest practicable period." A united Democratic party was assured when Tyler, who had been nominated by a convention of his supporters, withdrew following the declaration for annexation. Although Clay was defeated because his conflicting statements on Texas proved unsatisfactory to a small antislavery minority in the North, Polk's victory was not due to support of the slave interest, but to the rampant expansionist sentiment in the West. Except for Ohio, he carried every state beyond the Appalachians.

Tyler was so determined to receive credit for acquiring Texas that, even before the defeat of the treaty, he decided his objective could be achieved by an act of Congress, which required merely a majority vote of the two Houses. Hence he promised the Texan negotiators that, should the treaty fail to be ratified, he would recommend admission of Texas as a state. Naturally, Tyler interpreted the outcome of the election as a mandate to proceed with his plan. In his annual message to Congress in December, 1844, he recommended that the terms of annexation contained in the defeated treaty be incorporated in a joint resolution to be "binding on the two countries when adopted, in like manner, by the government of Texas."

In pursuance of this recommendation a joint resolution was introduced in the House of Representatives. Although it was evident that a majority favored annexation, there was such difference of opinion over details as to threaten defeat. Despite this difficulty and the strong opposition of antislavery leaders, the resolution was adopted by the House on January 25, 1845, by a vote of 120 to 98. On February 27 the Senate accepted it in slightly amended form, 27 to 25. On the following day the House concurred in the Senate amendments by a vote of 132 to 76. The resolution was signed by Tyler on March 1.

The measure provided for the admission of Texas on condition that a popularly adopted state constitution be transmitted to the President of the

United States by January 1, 1846. Texas was to retain title to the lands within her borders but was to assume responsibility for the payment of her debts. With her consent, not more than four additional states might be carved from her territory. The Missouri Compromise line was applied to the new state.

Although unable to re-establish authority in Texas, Mexico had never recognized the province's independence. Too late now the Mexican government made a move designed to terminate the long-standing difficulties with the rebellious Texans. Through the good offices of the British and French governments Mexico agreed in May, 1845, to recognize their independence, provided they would not annex themselves to another country. Thus Texas was free to choose between incorporation in the American Union and recognition by Mexico in a form which would preclude admission to the United States. Texas had no difficulty in deciding in favor of annexation. When Congress convened in December, 1845, President Polk reported the province had accepted the conditions of annexation and submitted her state constitution. On December 10th a joint resolution was reported, declaring Texas a state, on a plane of equality with other states. The resolution passed the House by a vote of 141 to 56. The Senate accepted it 31 to 14. When the President signed the resolution on December 29, 1845, Texas became a state.

During the period of her independence Texas grew steadily in population, despite an uncertain future and the constant threat of further difficulties with Mexico. Immigration from the United States continued to increase, for bad times in the Mississippi Valley following the Panic of 1837 and the 1,280 acres of free land promised every newly arrived family by the Texan Republic proved an irresistible combination of forces. Why stay at home when a farm could be had for the asking in a land where the air was "as elastic as a morning zephyr," the growing season so favorable that two or three crops could be harvested yearly, and the climate so salubrious that men who wanted to die had to go elsewhere? No less than 6,000 persons jammed the road from Louisiana to Nacogdoches during the summer of 1837; seven years later 5,000 passed through the frontier town of Van Buren, Arkansas, on their way to the promised land. After 1841 when the Republic revived the *empresario* system to supplement individual grants, a sizeable migration from abroad swelled the moving tide. Many came from Germany, attracted by the advertising of the Society for the Protection of German Immigrants which settled 5,247 persons near the villages of New Braunfels and Fredericksburg. Others were from Holland or from France, where the wealthy Henri Castro squandered a fortune in transplanting 2,134 persons to his "Indian-infested" *empresario* grant which lay between the Nueces and Rio Grande rivers.

This influx sent the population figures skyrocketing, to 142,000 when Texas entered the Union, to 212,000 in 1850. That most were from Missouri,

Kentucky, and Tennessee was reflected in the fact that 58,000 slaves lived there in the latter year; actually the proportion of slave to white population was greater in Texas than in Kentucky or Tennessee. Yet less than 8,000 persons owned slaves, and of these more than half possessed fewer than five bonded servants. Texas was still in its small-farming, frontier stage, but was rapidly donning the garments of civilization.

23

The Occupation of Oregon

1825-1846

While one group of Mississippi Valley pioneers advanced into the Southwest to wrest Texas from its Mexican owners, another moved toward the Northwest to battle England's fur traders for possession of the Oregon country. That domain of snow-capped mountains, deserts, and forested valleys had long been an object of contention among the colonizing powers of the Old and New Worlds. Four nations—Spain, Russia, England, and the United States—claimed ownership at the dawn of the nineteenth century. During the next years the field was narrowed to two. Spain withdrew in 1819 when the Adams-Onís Treaty established the 42nd parallel as the northern boundary of California. Russia followed in 1824 and 1825 when English pressure forced the Czar to sign treaties with Britain and the United States ceding all claims south of latitude 54° 40'. Now the issues and contestants were clearly defined; English and American pioneers must decide which nation should win the region between the 42nd parallel and the line of 54°40'.

Actually the whole area was never in dispute. The United States was always ready to accept an extension of the 49th parallel Canadian boundary to the Pacific, and on several occasions offered to settle on those terms. Nor did England aspire to the whole region as far south as the 42nd parallel. Its ambition was to make the Columbia River the southern border of northwestern Canada, for ownership of the river was believed essential to control of the interior fur trade. Thus the region actually in dispute was the triangle between the 49th parallel and Columbia River. That was the "core" of the Oregon boundary controversy. Neither nation was ready to press for a settlement when the dispute first arose. Instead they signed a treaty of joint occupation in 1818. The agreement, which was to continue for ten years,

451

was renewed in 1827 with the understanding that either country might withdraw upon one year's notice. Each was content to let the future decide Oregon's fate.

Both England and the United States rested their claims to ownership on discovery and occupation. Britain justly said her explorers were first upon the scene. As early as 1778 Captain James Cook, a famous navigator, explored the North American coast between the 44th parallel and northern Alaska, seeking the fabled Northwest Passage. Captain Cook failed to find the legendary strait, but his men made another discovery equally important: sea otter furs secured from ambitious Oregon natives for a few pence sold readily in China for $100 each. That exciting news sent a swarm of British merchants into the Pacific during the next two decades, some of them independent traders, others agents of King George's Company which was formed in 1785 to exploit Oregon's wealth. The traders aroused such interest in the region that England sent another official expedition there in 1792. Captain George Vancouver, its commander, mapped the coast from San Diego to Alaska and was the first to circumnavigate the island bearing his name. Each expedition, whether seeking trade or scientific knowledge, bolstered England's claim to Oregon.

Other explorers carried Britain's flag into the Northwest by arduous overland journeys. Foremost among them was a daring agent of the North West Company, Alexander Mackenzie, whose perpetual search for new trading areas brought him to the shores of the Pacific long before Lewis and Clark crossed the continent. His first effort ended in failure when the river he followed west from Great Slave Lake veered northward to the Arctic Ocean. "River Disappointment" he christened the stream, a name changed by others with less painful memories to Mackenzie River. Three years later Mackenzie was back again, this time to ascend the Peace River, winter in the Canadian Rockies, and emerge in the spring of 1793 on the upper reaches of a river which he took to be the Columbia. Not until 1807 did a later explorer of the North West Company, Simon Fraser, prove that Mackenzie had discovered the Fraser River rather than the Columbia. This did not detract from his glory; he and his fellow adventurers who came by sea firmly established England's title to the Northwest.

The American claims were scarcely less impressive. The glory of planting the infant nation's flag on the Oregon coast belonged to two ship captains, Robert Gray and Benjamin Kendrick, sent out by a group of Boston merchants who learned of the possibilities of the China trade from the published journal of Captain Cook's voyage. They sailed from Boston in 1787, spent the winter of 1788-89 loading with sea otter skins, journeyed on to Canton, and finally completed the voyage around the world with a cargo of oriental luxuries which rewarded their backers handsomely. News of any new trade was important to seafaring Americans whose commerce had suffered greatly as a result of independence. A number of expeditions were immediately planned, the most important a second voyage undertaken by Captain Gray.

By the spring of 1791 he was off the Oregon coast once more, searching as usual for unsophisticated Indians willing to barter bales of peltry for handfuls of gimcracks. One spot investigated appeared to be a harbor guarded by a long sand bar over which breakers rolled continuously. For eleven days Captain Gray sought a pass through this barrier; when he finally succeeded he found himself not in a bay but on the bosom of a broad river to which he gave the name of his ship the *Columbia*.

Those pioneering efforts brought an influx of American traders to Oregon. Profits were high in the China trade; one shipowner bought 560 sea otter pelts worth $20,000 for $2 worth of trinkets, another traded a rusty chisel for furs valued at $8,000. Rewards such as those brought a stream of ships to the Pacific during the 1790s, just as England's merchants were forced to give up trade when their nation entered in the Napoleonic wars. By 1800 although Philadelphians who usually crossed the Atlantic rather than rounding Cape Horn shared the trade with New Englanders all white men were called "Bostons" by the natives.

American success on the sea was more than matched by British victories in the preliminary contest to occupy the interior. The vanguard was composed of fur traders. The initial advantage gained by the United States when John Jacob Astor's Pacific Fur Company founded Astoria was short-lived; after 1813 the forced sale of the post to the North West Company allowed Canadian trappers to roam freely over the whole Northwest, and from that time on Britain dominated the interior just as thoroughly as the United States controlled the coast. The advantage was increased in 1825 when the Hudson's Bay Company, strengthened by its merger with the North West Company four years before, established Ft. Vancouver on the north bank of the Columbia with Dr. John McLoughlin in charge. The English were so firmly planted in Oregon that the task of dislodging them seemed hopeless.

Still worse from the point of view of American hopes were the agricultural establishments reared by Dr. McLoughlin about his wilderness outpost. Necessity dictated his efforts, for the cost of transporting food to Oregon was so great Ft. Vancouver could never show a profit until made self-supporting. With that incentive, Dr. McLoughlin imported herds of cattle from California, pigs from Hawaii, and sheep from Canada; built a sawmill and a gristmill; and sent idle trappers out each summer to clear fields for wheat, corn, and oats. So successful were his efforts that by 1828 Hudson's Bay Company traders not only fed themselves but produced a surplus which was exported to Alaska and California by a subsidiary corporation, the Puget Sound Agricultural Company. Those activities not only helped the British maintain their strong position but directly influenced the controversy over the region. By the time Americans arrived 100 British and French Canadians were firmly entrenched on farms dotting the Puget Sound Valley— the only area actually in dispute. If possession was nine points of the law, England's position was secure and the American cause hopeless.

The United States was first made aware of the imminent loss of Oregon by the valiant efforts of a few visionary expansionists who deliberately set out to warn their countrymen. The first of these was Dr. John Floyd, a Virginia congressman. Through his friendship with William Clark, the explorer, through his cousin, Charles Floyd, a member of the Lewis and Clark expedition, and through his acquaintance with several prominent Astorians, Dr. Floyd developed an enthusiasm for Oregon which made him "The Father of the Oregon Country." On December 19, 1820, Dr. Floyd moved in Congress the appointment of a select committee to "inquire into the situation of the settlements upon the Pacific Ocean and the expediency of occupying the Columbia River." With the adoption of the motion, Floyd was made chairman of the committee, whose report has been compared, in Oregon annals, with Hakluyt's *Discourse on Western Planting* in the colonization of the New World. In the words of Thomas Hart Benton, with this report "the first blow was struck; public attention was awakened, and the geographical, historical and statistical facts [concerning Oregon] set forth in the report, made a lodgment in the public mind which promised eventual favorable consideration."

The committee's bill urging annexation received scant consideration, despite a speech by Floyd stressing the importance of the fur trade and venturing the opinion that Americans could establish lines of communication between the Columbia and the Mississippi more easily than the British across Canada. Undismayed, Floyd in 1822 introduced a substitute measure notable partly because it provided that when the settlement on the shores of the Pacific had a population of 2,000 it should become a territory of the United States, partly because the name of the territory was to be "Origon," marking the first American application of the name to that region.[1]

In debate upon his bill, Floyd reviewed the persistent westward push of population from colonial days by way of refuting the charge that it was fantastic to suppose the tide would continue to the western ocean. Even at the moment wagon trains were crossing the desert plains in the newly opened trade with Santa Fe, foreshadowing a new chapter in the epic of American expansion. To those who asserted that distance and the mountain barrier made certain a separate republic on the Pacific slope, Floyd replied that in 1775 Kentucky was considered "too far away even to be a part of the Union." But, if separation must prevail, it was far better that the settlers in the rival republic should be American emigrants, speaking the language and cherishing the ideals of liberty and democracy. Floyd found capable supporters from Maryland and Massachusetts, who observed that Russian

---

[1] William Cullen Bryant had applied the name to the Columbia River in the first edition of "Thanatopsis." He doubtless acquired the term in the writings of Jonathan Carver who in turn borrowed it from Major Robert Rogers. As early as 1765 Rogers used the spellings "Ouragon" and "Ourigon" in petitions asking authorization of the British government for explorations west of the Mississippi.

activity in the Pacific afforded convincing evidence of the valuable trade of the region. They not only stressed the importance of New England whaling in the North Pacific but showed an appreciation of Oregon's forest resources then quite unusual. On the basis of intelligence received from a New England ship captain, they predicted Oregon would supply South America with lumber.

Viewed in retrospect the arguments of the bill's opponents are of greater interest than those of its champions. Floyd's fellow Virginian, George Tucker, agreed that the westward-flowing tide of population could not be stemmed. Within less than half a century "Christian churches and temples of justice" would rear themselves in the wilderness along the Columbia. But, he contended, the people on the east and west side of the Rocky Mountains would have "a permanent separation of interests." East of the continental divide the country was held together by "the strongest and most indissoluble ties." It was "Atlantic country," and its commerce must forever remain tributary to that ocean. Not so with the population that would occupy the Pacific slope whose trade would be drawn within the orbit of Japan, China, and the Philippines. Tucker therefore opposed governmental encouragement to a settlement which must inevitably be lost to the nation. Equally pessimistic were New York congressmen who painted a dark picture of the obstacles to navigation at the mouth of the Columbia, and of the "bleak and inhospitable" climate which precluded the successful cultivation of cereal crops. The "impenetrable forests of hemlock, spruce and white cedar, of prodigious size" offered a further discouragement to the settler. Passage of the bill, they said, would result in the creation either of a colony or an independent state, neither of which would benefit the United States. Colonies were valuable only to manufacturing nations; moreover the possession of colonies was abhorrent to "the principles of our political institutions."

In January, 1823, the prolonged debate on Floyd's bill came to an end in the House and a vote was taken. The proposal was lost by a vote of 100 to 61. The idea of an American commonwealth on the Pacific was still too visionary for the average member of Congress to grasp. But Floyd's failure to achieve his immediate objective should not obscure his significant role in relation to the Oregon country. It was he who first stressed the possibilities of the region from the point of view of the immigrant. And it was the pioneer family, drawn to the attractive Willamette Valley, which ultimately made good the American claim to the far Northwest.

If American interest and activity in Oregon were to be kept alive, it must be through the exertions of private citizens actuated by any one of several different motives. Through accounts of official explorers and journals of fur traders there was available a substantial body of information regarding the region and its resources. All that was needed was a prophet, a champion of Oregon, endowed with sufficient imagination to extract from those works pertinent facts to arrest the attention of the people.

Such a promoter appeared in the person of Hall Jackson Kelley, a visionary Massachusetts school teacher, who soon replaced John Floyd as the nation's leading tubthumper for Oregon. Kelley became interested in the Pacific Northwest when reading reports of the Lewis and Clark expedition, and by 1826 was not only studying every publication that mentioned the region but bombarding Congress with letters urging that settlers be sent there at once. These demands were given substance when, in February, 1828, Kelley appeared with a "Memorial of Citizens of the United States" asking government support for a colony in the Oregon country, a memorial that was widely circulated. Assuming, as did most men of the time, the legal rights of the United States to the region, Kelley evolved a plan of colonization the success of which, he thought, was assured by the varied products of Oregon's soil and waters. Hampered by no great regard for accuracy of statement, he worked assiduously through speeches, broadsides, pamphlets, circulars, and letters in Boston newspapers to make Oregon known to the people of New England.

All this was a prelude to an expedition to settle Oregon. In 1831 Kelley incorporated the "American Society for Encouraging the Settlement of the Oregon Territory," with the avowed purpose of transplanting a New England town there which he hoped would become the nucleus of a state. He would, he announced, "repeat with appropriate variations the history of the Puritan Colony of Massachusetts Bay." Such was his appeal that by the spring of 1832 his society had recruited sufficient members that he could ask them to rendezvous at St. Louis for their overland trek. The few who appeared were disappointed, for Congress refused to provide the financial aid that was needed, and the whole grandiose scheme had to be abandoned. Kelley, however, made his way to San Diego where he met the trapper, Ewing Young, who volunteered to escort him to Oregon. There he was received with understandable frigidity by officials of the Hudson's Bay Company. Four months of their cold shoulders turned him toward New England again, his dreams shattered. Yet he had stirred interest that did not die.

Among those influenced by Kelley's propaganda was Nathaniel J. Wyeth, a successful Cambridge businessman, who saw in Oregon one of the few remaining opportunities to bring a portion of the wilderness under control, a task for which he believed himself qualified. Wyeth originally planned to unite a company of his own followers with Kelley's society, believing the greater strength secured would be an added guarantee of success. When it became evident that Kelley's group would not get beyond the discussion stage, he abandoned the idea of cooperation, deciding instead to form "a Joint Stock Trading Company of about 50 men to proceed to the Country, without positively settling the particular business in which they will engage but to be dictated by circumstances when there (probably the fur business will be selected)." The contract binding the company together was to endure for five years. Each member was required to furnish his own equipment and pay his own passage to Franklin, Missouri. He desired "especially coopers, blacksmiths, founders, and ingenious persons of any trade'' and would have ''nothing to do with any persons who are not industrious and temperate men, and of good constitutions and peacible [*sic*] dispositions.''

By December, 1831, thirty-one men had enlisted under Wyeth's banner. For weeks members of the company met at Wyeth's house on Saturday nights, to perfect plans and become acquainted. On March 1, 1832, the group assembled on an island in Boston harbor where they spent ten days inuring themselves to frontier hardships and displaying their ''showy and attractive uniform suits, a feature of which was a broad belt from which dangled bayonet, knife and ax.'' Rounding out their equipment was an ''amphibious machine'' which was alternately a wagon and a boat, depending upon the side which happened to be up at the moment. This was the butt of many jokes by the students of Harvard College, who christened it a ''Nat-Wyethium.''

Meanwhile, Wyeth had dispatched a vessel from Boston around the Horn to the mouth of the Columbia, where his overland party expected to meet the ship. He and his followers departed from Boston, in March, 1832, traveling by ship to Baltimore, whence they proceeded by way of Pittsburgh and Cincinnati to St. Louis, where the boat-wagon was abandoned. At Independence, Missouri, Wyeth was glad to attach his party to the yearly caravan of the Rocky Mountain Fur Company, under the experienced leadership of William L. Sublette.

Wyeth's *Journal* of the expedition across the continent constitutes one of the genuinely significant documents in the history of the Far West, recording as it does the experiences of the first Americans to make their way to the west coast by the historic route later christened the Oregon Trail. When the group arrived at Pierre's Hole, the rendezvous of the fur company, disaffection broke out among Wyeth's men, largely because they learned that Sublette would be unable to accompany them farther. Calling a meeting, at which he forbade discussion, Wyeth put the question of going on. Nine men voted to return, reducing the already depleted party to eleven. Milton G. Sublette, a mountain man, piloted them through the Blackfoot country, where Wyeth engaged in trapping with considerable success. After receiving kind treatment at Ft. Walla Walla, the Hudson's Bay Company post, he pushed on to Ft. Vancouver, where he arrived in October, only to learn that his ship and cargo had been lost. Unable to pursue his trading plans because of the misadventure of the ship, Wyeth began his return in February, 1833.

Upon reaching Boston, Wyeth organized the Columbia River Fishing and Trading Company, with a view to exploiting the salmon fisheries of the northwest coast. After persuading his Boston backers to fit out another ship, the *May Dacre*, he set out in 1834 on his second overland trip to Oregon. As the Rocky Mountain Fur Company refused to purchase the goods he had brought, he was forced to build Ft. Hall, at the confluence of the Pontneuf and Snake rivers, to store his merchandise. He reached Ft. Vancouver a day in advance of his ship. As the latter was to have arrived early to take advantage of the fishing season, Wyeth postponed salmon packing for the year. Instead he built Ft. William at the mouth of the Willamette, in the very shadow of the Hudson's Bay Company headquarters. Although Wyeth possessed undoubted business capacity, his plan was doomed to failure. The Great Company treated him kindly but checkmated his every move. As a contemporary remarked: "They preceded him, followed him, surrounded him everywhere and cut the throat of his prosperity with such kindness and politeness that Wyeth was induced to sell his whole interest, existent and prospective, in Oregon, to his generous, but too indefatigable, skillful and powerful antagonist." The company also purchased Ft. Hall, which long remained a landmark on the Oregon Trail. The activities of Kelley and Wyeth made the Columbia country comparatively well known to a substantial number of Americans, yet no permanent results of a tangible nature flowed directly from their efforts.

Far more important were the efforts of pious men and women interested in saving souls. The attention of missionaries was first directed to the region early in the century. In 1821 the Hawaiian station of the American Board of Commissioners for Foreign Missions had considered Oregon as a possible missionary field. Again in 1829 an agent of the American Board visited Oregon, by way of Hawaii, and recommended the founding of missions there. Because of the distance, expense, and preoccupation elsewhere the Board failed to act upon the suggestion. The actual beginnings of missionary activity in the Oregon country resulted from a chance journey made by some Northwest Indians out of sheer curiosity. In October, 1831, four Indians from the Oregon country—three Nez Perces and one Flathead—accompanied a group of traders on their return trip from the Rocky Mountains to St. Louis to satisfy their curiosity concerning the white man's way of life. There they were entertained at the home of General William Clark, Superintendent of Indian Affairs. While they were thus engaged, St. Louis was visited by William Walker, an educated Wyandot Indian from the East, who had arrived to arrange the migration of his people to a reservation nearby. Walker heard of the presence of the Oregon Indians in the city, but never met or saw them.

Fourteen months later, in January, 1833, Walker wrote a highly imaginative account of their visit to a friend, G. P. Disosway, agent among the Wyandot in Ohio, telling him that the Indians had made their wearisome trek to ask that the white man's "Book of Heaven" be sent to them and that ministers visit their tribes to show them the path to Heaven. This was pure fabrication; the Nez Perces and Flatheads had doubtless heard of Christianity from Iroquois visitors to their villages or from Spokane Indians who were being inducted into its mysteries by a converted fellow-tribesman, Spokane Garry, but their interest in the subject was completely casual. This made no difference to Disosway, who sent Walker's letter to the Methodist *Christian Advocate and Journal*, where it was published on March 1, 1833. Illustrating the letter was an imaginative drawing by Walker showing the manner in which the Flatheads deformed the shape of their children's heads in infancy.

Seldom has a letter so pricked the public conscience. Overnight the plea of the benighted heathen who had journeyed more than 2,000 lonesome miles to seek the word of God became the concern of the nation's religious community. Everywhere their plea for the "book containing directions how to conduct themselves in order to enjoy His favor and hold converse with Him" was hearkened to; everywhere congregations tearfully pledged that the Flatheads would have the divine guide they had requested, and with which "no one need go astray." Who could resist such an appeal from the "Wise Men of the West?" A letter from an imaginative Indian had done more to stir interest in the Oregon country than all the efforts of Wyeth and Kelley, and all the decade of pleading by agents of the American Board.

Contributions ranging from $10 to $2,000 began pouring into the *Christian Advocate*. The influential Wilbur Fisk, president of Wesleyan University, sprang into action and called for two men with the spirit of martyrs. The Reverend Jason Lee, a Canadian-born stripling of promise, earlier befriended by President Fisk, was clearly indicated as the leader of the mission. In November, 1833, Jason Lee, with his nephew Daniel Lee and Cyrus Shepard, was about to leave New York for St. Louis when he heard that Nathaniel Wyeth had just returned to Cambridge from his first expedition. He thereupon changed his plans and proceeded to Cambridge with a view to obtaining all possible information regarding the Northwest. He not only arranged with Wyeth for the shipment of mission goods on the latter's ship, the *May Dacre*, but agreed to cross the mountains with Wyeth and his company. Writing from the Missouri frontier on April 29, 1834, Lee announced that his party had been increased to five through the employment of P. L. Edwards and Courtney M. Walker, the latter not "a professor of religion," but a valuable addition because of his knowledge of Indian life.

After a not-too-difficult journey, in which they enjoyed the unfailing kindness and assistance of Wyeth's traders, they arrived at Ft. Vancouver, on September 15, where the usual hearty welcome was extended them by Dr. McLoughlin of the Hudson's Bay Company. On the 18th Jason and Daniel Lee, accompanied by men furnished by McLoughlin, departed on a tour of exploration of the Willamette Valley. They returned on the 27th, having been fifty miles up the river, well pleased with the countryside, and ready to listen to Dr. McLoughlin's persuasive eloquence. That canny administrator had no objection to missionaries, but only so long as they stayed out of the Indian country where they might disrupt the trade, south of the Columbia River where they would be in undisputed territory, and near Ft. Vancouver where they could be watched. Why, he asked them, should they risk their lives in the Flathead country where they would almost certainly be killed by marauding Blackfeet? Why not make their headquarters the pleasant—and safe—Willamette Valley? Those arguments carried the day. "A larger field of usefulness was contemplated as the object of the mission

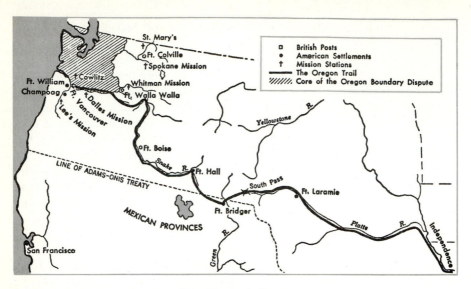

The Oregon Country

than the benefiting of a single tribe,'' wrote Daniel Lee. ''The wants of the whole country, present and prospective . . . were taken into account.'' With that comfortable rationalization the thoughts of a Flathead mission were forgotten. Two days later Jason Lee led his little party to the French Prairie, a grassy meadow some sixty miles up the Willamette, where they began building their mission.

With the aid of Dr. McLoughlin, who lent them horses, oxen, and cows, they built a log house near a settlement of some twenty families on the Willamette, the majority of them Roman Catholic French Canadians with Indian wives, and most of them onetime servants of the Hudson's Bay Company who had established themselves as farmers on the fertile and attractive valley lands. Although the area around the mission lacked a large Indian population, Lee was not disappointed because he saw the need for a strong support base from which to evangelize the tribes. The mission, therefore, was dedicated primarily to the improvement of social conditions within the agricultural settlement. The missionaries maintained a school, conducted religious services only imperfectly understood by the French, and formed a temperance society with which many of the men, through McLoughlin's encouragement, eventually affiliated.

This first agricultural community in the Oregon country was destined to provide the nucleus for further American settlement in the region. Although Jason Lee established a branch mission at The Dalles which became a religious station of importance, he was also concerned with encouraging evangelical Protestants to migrate to the Willamette Valley. His request for additional helpers was granted when in 1837 the Methodist Board of Missions sent out two parties with a total of twenty persons, including Dr. Elijah White, who was to become a conspicuous champion of American migration to the northwest coast. The following year Lee crossed the Rockies to the States. Accompanied by three half-breed children and two Indians, he lectured in the towns through which he passed. Although his primary purpose was to obtain funds to further his work, he succeeded in arousing a lively interest in Oregon on the part of potential emigrants. Lee also carried with him a petition, bearing the signatures of missionaries and settlers, asking Congress for legislation securing title to the lands they occupied, and for the extension of the laws of the United States over the region. The signers strongly asserted their belief that Oregon was to become a state of the Union.

Lee's tour of the East resulted in the appointment of twenty-one additional persons to the staff of the mission, of whom only five were ministers, but all of whom Lee considered essential to undergirding missionary activity. The others included mechanics, farmers, teachers, an accountant, and a physician. Supplemented by their families, the party numbered about fifty persons and became known as the "Great Re-enforcement." They arrived in 1839, bringing with them a grant of $42,000 to purchase machinery and equipment. With a well-rounded and trained personnel, and with so much to be done to better the economic life of the community, the religious purpose of the mission was firmly established. The newcomers laid out farms, built a sawmill at Willamette Falls, opened a store, and overnight transformed Lee's outpost into a typical frontier village. The efforts of a good-natured if not efficient evangelist had made him a colonizer. By the end of 1840 a traveler found 120 farms in the valley, operated by 500 farmers and 1,000 Indian servants, and pasturing 3,000 cattle, 2,500 horses, and "an infinite number of hogs."

All of this activity by the Methodists stirred other denominations to enter the Oregon mission field. Next on the scene was the Reverend Samuel Parker of Ithaca, New York, who in January, 1834, offered himself to the American Board for service among the Flatheads. When the Board was assured that the people of Ithaca would shoulder part of the expense, his offer was gladly accepted, the Board even appropriating funds to maintain his family during his absence. Parker then enlisted Samuel Allis, a minister, and John Dunbar, a divinity student, as associates. Due to faulty planning, his party arrived on the Missouri too late to accompany the fur traders on their annual trip. Allis and Dunbar occupied themselves with missionary work among the Indians of the Council Bluffs area, while Parker, in the face of the disapproval of his associates, returned to Ithaca, where the Board authorized him to spend the winter arousing missionary sentiment among the people of New York State. In the course of his winter's effort, Parker discovered the man who was to become the most noted of all Oregon missionaries, Dr. Marcus Whitman, of Wheeler, New York. On December 2, 1834, Whitman wrote the American Board offering himself as a companion to Parker. Then thirty-two years old, he had practiced medicine in Canada, but at the moment of his enlistment was associated with his brother in operating a sawmill at Rushville, New York.

Whitman and Parker arrived at St. Louis early in April, 1835. Proceeding up the Missouri River with the American Fur Company party to a point near the present Omaha, an overland caravan was formed at the trading ranch of Lucien Fontenelle. On June 22nd the trek began. Besides Fontenelle and the two missionaries, there were some fifty other men, six wagons, three yoke of oxen, and a large number of horses and mules. They arrived at Ft. Laramie on July 26th, crossed South Pass on August 10th, and reached the rendezvous on Green River on the 12th. There Whitman showed his medical skill by extracting an arrowpoint from the back of Jim Bridger. There, too, were assembled groups of Snake, Flathead, Nez Perce, and Ute Indians, who indicated their readiness to cooperate with a mission settlement in their country.

At this point it was decided that Whitman should return overland to New York for additional helpers, while Parker went on to the West with the Indians, gained their confidence, and spied out suitable locations for mission settlements. Although the latter made contacts at Ft. Walla Walla and Ft. Vancouver which ensured a friendly reception for the Whitman party when it came out the following year, he failed to return to the rendezvous with the information. Instead, he sailed for the States by way of Honolulu.

Upon his return to his native state, Whitman acquired a wife, Narcissa, and obtained authorization from the American Board to return to Oregon on a mission to the Flathead Indians. The Whitmans were authorized to take with them another married couple and two single men. Whitman's selection of his associates was not an altogether happy one. The Reverend Henry H. Spalding was not well balanced mentally and was unable to work easily with other people. In addition, he had been a schoolmate and disappointed suitor of Narcissa Whitman. To make matters worse, Mrs. Spalding was an invalid, although strong of spirit. The farmer-mechanic of the party was W. H. Gray.

The Whitman-Spalding party started from St. Louis on March 31, 1836, accompanied as far as the Green River rendezvous by the American Fur Company caravan. From this point they enjoyed the protection of Hudson's Bay Company traders. Their wagon was taken as far as Ft. Boise, being the first to travel west of Ft. Hall. The expedition claimed the added distinction of being the first in which white women crossed the continental divide. After recuperating at Ft. Walla Walla for a few days the party continued down the Columbia to Ft. Vancouver, where the accustomed hospitality of Dr. McLoughlin was shown them. Two mission stations were chosen in the interior of the Oregon country. One was at Waiilatpu, about twenty-five miles from Ft. Walla Walla, the other at Lapwai, Whitman going to the former, the Spaldings and Gray to the latter. Dr. McLoughlin provided the missions with bedding and clothing, allowed them to draw on Ft. Colville for grain and flour for two years, and permitted Narcissa Whitman to live as a guest at Ft. Walla Walla while her husband was preparing the mission building.

In the spring of 1837 Gray returned to the East for reinforcements, against the will of his associates. Despite misrepresentation and questionable practices on his part, of which Whitman advised the Board, the authorities in Boston decided to send additional helpers. Gray married while in the East and in 1838 returned to Oregon with his bride, three ministers and their wives, and a teacher. Of the three ministers—Cushing Eells, Elkanah Walker, and A. B. Smith—the first two became important figures in the annals of early Oregon. Smith was sent to a post on the Clearwater, where he failed, while Eells and Walker established a mission among the Spokane, near Ft. Colville.

While the Methodist Church and the American Board were inaugurating the missionary movement in Oregon, the Catholics were not idle. Insofar as the Indians visiting St. Louis in 1831 were inspired by a desire for the Gospel rather than mere curiosity, it was "black robes" and not Methodist parsons they were looking for, since they had gained some knowledge of the Catholic faith from fur traders, explorers, and Iroquois Indians who intermarried with the Flatheads. The first Catholic missionaries to the northwest coast, however, came by way of British North America and in response to an appeal from French Canadian settlers in the Willamette Valley. The Bishop of Quebec appointed the Abbe Francois Norbet Blanchet as Vicar General in Oregon and the Abbe Modeste Demers as his assistant.

Arriving at Ft. Vancouver in November, 1838, they received the usual assistance from Dr. McLoughlin, who himself became a Catholic a few years later. A mission was established at Cowlitz, while services were held from time to time in the Willamette Valley in a church built by the French settlers. Their work among the Indians was successful from the first, thanks largely to the "Catholic ladder" devised by Father Blanchet. This was a graphic presentation of world and Christian history—a square stick with marks indicating the years before and after Christ—that allowed Indians to understand their place in Christian time. Its use explains the marked success of Catholics, in contrast to their Protestant contemporaries, among the Indians of the Northwest.

In 1840 Jesuits entered the Oregon missionary field when Father Pierre De Smet was sent in response to an appeal of the Flatheads to the Jesuit novitiate at St. Louis. De Smet founded the pioneer Jesuit Mission of St. Mary's in the Bitterroot Valley in 1841. Within a short time his missions had increased to six and largely covered the interior portions of the Oregon country.

In contrast with the success of Catholics, the missions of the American Board proved a grave disappointment to their sponsors. By 1841 Walker and Eells in the Spokane country had found the natives largely indifferent to their efforts. Indian interest in the schools declined and the natives lapsed into their accustomed ways and traditional religious practices. The Indians admitted a lack of concern with their souls and expressed the opinion that a good supply of tobacco would bring greater success to the missionaries. In 1847 Mrs. Eells wrote: "we have been here almost nine years and have not yet been permitted to hear the cries of one penitent or the songs of one redeemed soul." The missions at Waiilatpu and Lapwai were equally discouraging, due largely to internal dissension resulting from the incompatibility of the staff members. Gray disliked Spalding, the latter was envious of the Whitmans, no one approved of Gray, and Smith recommended the recall of Spalding. In 1842 the Board members decided the Spokane mission was the only one worth saving. They accordingly ordered the closing of Waiilatpu and Lapwai, assigned Whitman and Rogers to the northern mission, and recalled Spalding, Gray, and Smith.

Whitman, angered by this act, started overland for Boston, which he reached on March 30, 1843. There he persuaded the Board to continue the two southern stations. While in the States he also visited Washington and conferred with the secretary of war regarding the establishment of supply stations along the Oregon route for the benefit of emigrants. This was Whitman's famous trip to the East that formed the basis of the legend that he saved Oregon for the United States. Whitman returned to Oregon with the overland emigrants of 1843.

Still the missions failed to prosper and the Whitmans were stalked by tragedy. In May, 1845, Whitman expressed to the Board his doubts concerning the future of the venture. Indian apathy toward the missionaries was being transformed into hostility. Whitman cited his experiences as a physician ministering to the needs of emigrants and aborigines. When his treatment of measles was followed by the recovery of white children and the death of Indians, due to the latter's lesser immunity, the natives were convinced he used poison rather than medicine, and that this was part of a settled policy. This was the immediate background of the massacre of Whitman, his wife, and twelve other persons at the hands of the Cayuse Indians in 1847.

Had the Oregon missions of the American Board been located in the area of American occupation, as was the Methodist mission of Jason Lee, their history might have been far different. They, too, might have become the nucleuses of American settlement and influence, which would have guaranteed them success among the pioneers regardless of the outcome of their labors among the Indians. Irrespective of success or failure, however, the missionaries, almost single-handed, kept alive a degree of American interest in the region. The first American settlement in the region, Jason Lee's station in the Willamette Valley, demonstrated the agricultural potentialities of the area and turned the tide of emigration in that direction. And the propaganda of the missionaries, carried on through various channels, helped swell the tide.

Not until 1836, when the American establishment in Oregon consisted of two areas of missionary activity and a handful of settlers in the Willamette

Valley, did the government take its first official cognizance of the country since the renewal of the treaty with Great Britain in 1827. In that year President Jackson sent W. A. Slacum to the Pacific coast to gather information about the area. Slacum made a careful survey of the region, mapped it, located Indian villages, studied the fur trade, visited Jason Lee's mission, and called upon most of the settlers in the Willamette Valley. His impressions were entirely favorable, while his enthusiasm for the country's grazing possibilities was especially pronounced. The settlers, however, were but meagerly provided with cattle, since the Hudson's Bay Company, although generous in lending oxen for work purposes, could not afford to deplete its own herds by selling breeding stock to the pioneers. With Slacum's encouragement, the pioneers organized the Willamette Cattle Company to import cattle from California, where Spanish breeds were plentiful. The Hudson's Bay Company, the Methodist Mission, individual settlers, and Slacum himself subscribed to the stock of the company. A delegation of settlers, headed by Ewing Young, who was thoroughly familiar with California, took passage on Slacum's ship in 1837 and brought back 600 head of livestock. Theirs was a noble sacrifice, for Mexican law forbade the export of cattle and the herd had to be driven over back trails that led across parched deserts and through dense forests. "Nearly every inch of progress," wrote a driver feelingly, "has been gained by the use of clubs, sticks, stones, and bawling." The sacrifice was handsomely rewarded, for the Willamette proved ideally suited to stock raising and the cattle multiplied rapidly. Tales of the drive, spread widely in eastern newspapers, also helped generate interest in Oregon.

So did Slacum's report when it was laid before Congress in December, 1837. His enthusiastic description of the country, his optimistic estimates of its future growth, and his insistence that the United States never surrender the area south of the 49th parallel, not only attracted national attention but brought into the arena a new congressional champion for the cause. Senator Lewis F. Linn of Missouri donned the mantle when he introduced into the Senate a bill to create the "Oregon Territory" with its doors open to all settlers. Accompanying his bill was a report reviewing the history of American claims to the region as well as a variety of colorful data on the overland trail. Distributed widely at government expense, this report did much to expand American knowledge of the northwest coast.

More was to come. During the summer of 1838 Jason Lee arrived in the East bearing a "Settlers' Petition" adopted by his fellow Oregonians demanding an immediate extension of governmental protection over their land. For the next months Lee traveled about, lecturing on the prospects of Oregon, collecting $40,000 for his mission, and visiting Washington to lay his petition before Congress. One of Lee's converts when he spoke at Peoria, Illinois, was Thomas J. Farnham, who then and there made a solemn pledge to raise the American flag over the Willamette Valley. Farnham made the journey westward, but his hopes of a one-man filibuster were frustrated by the Hudson's Bay Company's undisputable authority; in the end Farnham did little more than bring back another petition from the settlers demanding rule by the United States. His published account of his trip, however, was an effective piece of propaganda; so were the reports of Lieutenant Charles Wilkes who visited the northwest coast in 1841 in command of a governmental Pacific exploring expedition and wrote excitedly of what he saw. Gradually popular knowledge of the Oregon Country was increasing, and with it a mounting insistence that the region never be surrendered to England.

In the end, however, not governmental but population pressures were to tip the scales in favor of the United States. The flow of "emigrants" who braved the Oregon Trail for homes in the Northwest provided an argument that Great Britain never could answer. Underlying their migration was a combination of forces that sent thousands westward. Prolonged hard times in the Mississippi Valley following the Panic of 1837, inadequate transportation facilities in many parts of the Middle West, and depressed prices for farm products all tended to drive farmers from the interior valley. The undoubted attractions of the Willamette Valley, made more alluring by the vivid imaginations of Oregon champions, transportation facilities afforded by the river itself, favorable markets for Oregon products in the Orient and the Pacific, and high prices in Oregon, all tended to draw settlers in that direction. Another factor was the pioneer instinct, the "strong bent" of human spirits, the desire to blaze trails, to accept a difficult challenge, the thrill of opening a new country, as the long hunters had done in the Kentucky wilderness. And, finally, the Oregon fever was spread by a flood of propaganda literature: journals of traders and trappers, accounts of missionaries, descriptions of travelers, reports printed and circulated at government expense, and letters of earlier emigrants to friends back home describing their satisfaction with their new situation. By the close of the 1830s "Oregon Societies" were forming in town after town along the Mississippi Valley, with their members pledged to make the trek westward at the first opportunity. At least ten were recruiting converts by 1839.

The first sizeable migration began in 1842, the product of the organizing skill of Dr. Elijah White who had visited Lee's mission in the past and knew something of the Willamette Valley. Impressed with the extent of the "Oregon Fever" in Missouri, he determined to recruit a party of immigrants to accompany him westward where he was to become an Indian agent. Volunteers were plentiful—some 500 agreed to make the journey—but at the appointed time only 112 appeared at Independence, largely because the others could not sell their farms in the depression-plagued market. The trip was not a happy one. Scarcely had the party left Independence on May 16, 1842, in sixteen covered wagons when disputes began, climaxed by a near battle between dog owners and non-dog owners who charged that the animals were frightening away game and attracting Indians. Not until White was replaced by a more forceful leader, Lansford W. Hastings, did harmony return. The new captain drove the column so relentlessly that Ft. Vancouver was reached in December, the settlers having carried their belongings on their backs after leaving Ft. Hall.

Their expedition paved the way for a mass migration in 1843. No less than 1,000 people converged at Independence that spring, chose Peter H. Burnett of Missouri their captain, and on May 22 started west, driving 5,000 cattle and oxen. A military organization was agreed upon, with a corps of officials under Captain Burnett, and even an elected "Council" to settle disputes and pass laws needed by the traveling republic. Shortly after the start some complained that those with large herds were slowing the march. The Council, after proper deliberation, decided that the only solution was to divide the party into two parts, one column to move ahead rapidly, the other with the cattle to progress more slowly. The captain of the latter, Jesse Applegate, later penned one of the more popular accounts of the Oregon Trail in his "A Day with the Cow Column."

For a two-days' journey from Independence the Oregon and Santa Fe trails were one. Forty miles out a signboard pointed the way to the "Road to Oregon." At Ft. Laramie, where the trail left the plains for the mountain country, the emigrant had an opportunity to rest and redistribute his burden. On Independence Rock, 838 miles out, was the "register of the desert" on which family names were carefully inscribed. At South Pass, 947 miles, the pioneers crossed the continental divide through a broad valley of gentle slopes, at an elevation of 7,500 feet. Rest and repairs were to be had at Ft. Bridger, 1,070 miles from the starting point, which Jim Bridger, the famous Mountain Man, built in 1843 to accommodate the immigrants to come. After a journey of 1,288 miles the caravan reached Ft. Hall on the Snake River. Other milestones were Ft. Boise, a Hudson's Bay Company post on the Snake, and the Grand Ronde, a beautiful camping ground just east of the difficult Blue Mountains. After crossing the latter, the emigrants straggled across the barren plateau that sloped downward to the Columbia River, which in turn led them to Ft. Vancouver, 2,020 miles distant from their starting point.

As far as Ft. Hall the route was well marked but beyond that point it became a mere pack trail, unused by loaded wagons except the light vehicles of the Whitman-Spalding party. Finding the number of pack horses insufficient to carry families and goods to the Columbia, the emigrants had no choice but to continue by wagon. Being a large party, the men could be their own road makers, as the small parties preceding them could not. Furthermore, the 1843 caravan was accompanied by Marcus Whitman who, drawing upon his experience of 1836, was a skilled guide. Leaving Ft. Hall on August 30, they arrived at Ft. Boise twenty days later. On the last day of the month their eyes first rested upon the Grand Ronde whose tranquil beauty, after their desert experiences, elicited tears of joy. At Whitman's mission, Waiilatpu, they rested and obtained provisions for use at their destination. In late November they arrived in the Willamette Valley.

The caravan of 1843 employed the bivouac, familiar to plainsmen since wagons were first introduced on the Plains at the beginning of the Santa Fe trade. At night they drew the wagons up in a stockade or corral. In the words of Jesse Applegate the corral was "a circle one hundred yards deep, formed with wagons connected strongly with each other; the wagon in the rear being connected with the wagon in front by its tongue and ox chains. It is a strong barrier that the most vicious ox cannot break, and in case of attack from the Sioux would be no contemptible intrenchment." Fear of the Indians was misplaced, for in the early years of Plains travel the Indians proved more curious than dangerous. Bitter experience taught the members of the 1843 migration that baggage should be reduced to a minimum. The eastern portion of the trail was strewn with furniture and equipment discarded because too burdensome. They discovered that wagons must be rugged and durable, and that oxen were preferable to horses as draft animals and less attractive to the Indians. Cattle from Illinois and Missouri were best because accustomed to feeding upon prairie grass. Too few tools, and the wrong type of clothes embarrassed many, especially the women. The result was bare and bruised feet, and fine fabrics ruined by the dust and alkali of the desert. The older women adapted themselves to the requirements of the trek more readily than the younger ones, shortening their skirts to the danger point, while young ladies clung to eastern fashions. At the Snake River much of the finery went to the Indians in exchange for salmon, and the natives in their new raiment, "worn without regard to age or sex, were a costume picture only a trifle more fantastic than the emigrants themselves."

The great migration of 1843 proved a turning point in the history of Oregon. Skeptics had openly scoffed before departure; no less a person than Horace Greeley thought "this migration of more than a thousand persons in one body to Oregon wears an aspect of insanity." Their doubts were dispelled by the news that even loaded wagons had successfully traversed the entire route. Enthusiastic letters from emigrants to the folks back home, printed in local papers, and widely copied by the city press, soon made Oregon a household word and helped swell the tide. The substantial emigration of 1844, delayed by an unduly wet season, arrived at the Willamette very late, with provisions depleted and spirits dampened by the onset of the rainy season. Their gloom, however, was easily removed in the spring by "the kindling rays of a bright Oregon Sun." In 1845 a migration of some 3,000 almost doubled the population of the country. This time there were not one, but many caravans, comprising a dozen to twenty wagons, the better to preserve scarce fodder for the teams. The journey was comparatively uneventful, except for one party that started with 145 wagons and broke into a number of small units after quarrels disrupted its harmony. Abandoning the main trail beyond Ft. Boise for a cutoff that an old trapper assured them would save valuable time, they struggled through some of Oregon's most forbidding mountains and narrowly escaped complete extermination before finally reaching the Willamette Valley after great suffering and the loss of forty days. With the accession of 1845, the population of Oregon was increased to 6,000. The vast majority of the pioneers were located in the Willamette Valley, not only because of its natural attractions but also because Dr. McLoughlin, believing that Great Britain would ultimately acquire the region north of the Columbia, had been at pains to direct the Americans south of the river. In this effort he was not entirely successful, for a few of the immigrants, not to be discouraged, settled near the later Olympia in the Puget Sound country.

Once more American pioneers on a far distant frontier found themselves in a wilderness beyond the pale of statute law and organized society. In view of their remoteness from the States it was unlikely they would calmly await the extension of American sovereignty over them. In such a situation frontier settlers always showed themselves capable of dealing with the situation in their own way, and the Oregon pioneers were to be no exception.

Under the provisions of the joint occupation agreement, neither country could legally extend its jurisdiction over the Oregon settlers prior to a solution of the boundary difficulty. Great Britain authorized the Hudson's Bay Company to deal with minor infractions, but more serious cases were transferred to Canada for trial. American settlers were left to their own devices by the United States. Notwithstanding the uniform kindness and assistance which the American pioneers, whether missionaries or laymen, received at the hands of the Hudson's Bay Company, their feelings toward the Great Company were not sympathetic. The earliest American settlers were constantly aware of the company's hold, not only upon its retired employees settling in the country, but upon the Indians through its well-organized system of trade. This would give the company an advantage in the event of a clash between nationals of the two countries. It was only natural, therefore, that Americans should seek some counterweight to Hudson's Bay influence. This explains the memorial of Methodist missionaries to Congress in 1838, seeking recognition of land titles and the extension of American jurisdiction over Oregon. The next year proponents of the American viewpoint numbered seventy, a figure which was doubled by 1840 when a stronger petition warned against the Hudson's Bay Company. But still Congress remained indifferent.

In 1841 occurred an event which occasioned the first governmental action. Ewing Young, probably the most affluent of the pioneers, died intestate, leaving an estate which included some 600 head of cattle. The disposition of his estate was a matter of concern to his neighbors, who met at the Methodist Mission on the day following his funeral. An *ad hoc* probate court was created with a judge authorized to administer the estate according to the laws of the state of New York. As no copy of the statutes of the Empire State existed in the settlement, the judge had to recreate the laws from his imagination. At the same time a committee was appointed to frame a constitution and code of law. With a view to gaining the support of French

Canadian settlers, Father Blanchet was made chairman. The Father being unsympathetic and Dr. McLoughlin openly opposed to the idea, nothing was done.

The drive toward the creation of a frame of government was strengthened by the arrival of Elijah White's party of 120 immigrants in 1842. Further incentive resulted from the necessity of dealing with the menace of wild animals to the livestock of the settlers. This led to the so-called "Wolf Meetings," the first of which assembled in February, 1843, when a committee was appointed to consider the problem. At a second meeting on March 4, the committee's recommendation of a fund for bounties on the dead animals was approved, whereupon, W. H. Gray, one-time associate of Whitman but now residing in the valley, moved the appointment of a new committee to consider "the propriety of taking steps for the civil and military protection of the colony." The motion was carried, the committee appointed, and another meeting called for May 2 at Champoeg.

Pending this gathering a lively discussion revealed that not even all Americans were in agreement. Jason Lee, having petitioned for the extension of governmental authority over the settlement, approved action by the settlers themselves, but Elijah White counseled delay because he seemed to think he, as Indian agent, was authorized to govern the community. Americans generally, regardless of shades of opinion, sought to unite all nationalities against the Hudson's Bay Company. In this they were unsuccessful. When the meeting convened on May 2nd there was a full attendance of Canadians, who almost defeated a motion to organize a provisional government for Oregon. At that point most of the British faction withdrew. A legislative committee was allowed sixty days to frame a constitution and legal code, which were presented to the general meeting on July 5, 1843. On that day the assemblage adopted the "First Organic Law," based on the scanty legal lore to be found within the frontier community. The preamble, in the name of the people of "Oregon Territory," declared the laws were adopted "until such time as the United States of America extend their jurisdiction over us." Significant provisions were a plural executive, a legislative committee, voluntary subscription in lieu of taxation, and a prohibition upon slavery. Aversion to taxation seems to have been shared by the Oregon pioneers, in common with residents on other frontiers. Thus was a time-honored practice of the American frontier revived; another "compact" entered into by individualistic pioneers in a new homeland. The Oregon settlers were reacting to their wilderness setting as had the Watauga, the Transylvania, the Cumberland, and other frontier communities of an earlier day.

The great migration of 1843 was both an advantage and a disadvantage to the provisional government. It brought such able men as Burnett, Applegate, and Nesmith, whose talents were sorely needed by the new body politic. It also by sheer weight of numbers, removed all doubt as to American preponderance in Oregon. On the other hand, many of the newcomers were rough rural people from Missouri, with no religious leaning or preference, who resented the evident resolve of the Methodist mission crowd to retain control. Orderly Americans came to favor reconciliation with their British neighbors, and a government satisfactory to all concerned. The Canadians, on their part, now felt the need for protection against the turbulent and unruly elements among the new American immigrants.

In 1844 the more responsible leaders among the newcomers took matters into their own hands. They reformed the land laws, provided for a governor in lieu of the executive committee, and created a unicameral legislature to replace the legislative committee. Voluntary contributions for raising revenue gave way to optional taxation; if one refused to pay his taxes he had no vote and no recourse to the law for any purpose. He thus became an outcast. In July, 1845, the amended laws were accepted by the electorate.

The extent to which the interests of British and American elements in the population were reconciled was indicated by the election of a high official of the Hudson's Bay Company as treasurer of the territory, and by an oath of office which merely required that the individual support the provisional government only so far as its laws were consistent with his "duties as a citizen of the United States or a subject of Great Britain." In August, 1845, McLoughlin, in behalf of the company, recognized the provisional government. He wrote: "we decided upon joining the association both for the security of the Company's property and the protection of its rights."

While the Oregon pioneers temporarily solved their governmental problems, England and the United States wrangled over the boundary question. On three different occasions the United States had offered to accept the 49th parallel as the demarcation line and as often Great Britain had countered with the proposal that the Columbia should delimit the spheres of the two countries. From this position neither party had retreated a single step between 1824 and 1842. The area really in dispute, therefore, was that between the Columbia and the 49th parallel.

In 1843 there was considerable stiffening of the popular attitude in the United States with respect to Oregon. Disappointment at the failure of Linn's second Oregon bill in the Senate, and the belief that the United States had been ready to cede the area north of the Columbia in return for British aid in securing northern California, aroused indignation in various parts of the Mississippi Valley. Local meetings were followed by an Oregon Convention at Cincinnati in July, 1843, attended by about 100 delegates. The extreme American claim to the entire region between the 42nd parallel and 54°40′ advanced there became, under western influence, the Democratic rallying cry in the campaign of 1844. President Polk apparently adopted the frontier viewpoint when, in his inaugural address, he declared American title to "the whole of Oregon is clear and unquestionable."

Actually, however, the supreme object of the United States was still the 49th parallel boundary. The heavy migrations seemed to bring the goal nearer. Calhoun, secretary of state in 1844, told the British minister that 1,000 Americans had located in Oregon in 1843, estimated that the migration of 1844 would add another 1,500 to the American colony, and added that the forces that had driven the tide of population across the Alleghenies to the Mississippi would drive it on with increasing power across the Rockies to the banks of the Columbia, which were "destined to be peopled by us." The English government was sufficiently alarmed to send two military officers westward to inquire into the requirements for British defense of the country. In the same year the frigate *America* visited Puget Sound under the command of Sir John Gordon, brother of the British foreign secretary Lord Aberdeen, who sent an official to Vancouver to seek full information from Dr. McLoughlin on the relative strength of the American and British elements. The report was convincing; only 750 English faced nearly 6,000 Americans in the Oregon Country, and could never defend the region in case of attack.

Yet, the American settlements were confined almost entirely to the Willamette Valley, south of the Columbia. Only a handful of settlers from the States were located north of the river. The American argument of actual occupation, therefore, had validity only for the area which Britain was *always* prepared to concede—the area south of the Columbia. Why, then, did Britain accept the 49th parallel as the boundary, thereby relinquishing the region north of the Columbia, which its own nationals held securely? The answer is that the Hudson's Bay Company, alarmed at the aggressive and turbulent character of many American settlers in the Willamette Valley, feared for the safety of stores and other property at Ft. Vancouver, on the north bank of the Columbia. So real was the danger that Governor Simpson in 1845 directed that the headquarters of the company be moved to Ft. Victoria, on Vancouver's Island. Furthermore, the fur trade was declining along the Columbia, a victim of changed European styles that outmoded the beaver hat and tumbled the price of pelts. From the viewpoint of the Hudson's Bay Company, the Oregon Country was of so little value that it was not worth fighting for.

This was welcome news to Lord Aberdeen, the Tory foreign secretary. He had never had a high opinion of the Pacific Northwest—a "pine swamp" he called it—and as early as March, 1844, had been ready to deliver the core area to the United States rather than risk war. Yet to agree on the 49th parallel meant that Britain was surrendering, and surrender would mean political suicide for Aberdeen and his party. Before he could do so both the Whig opposition and public opinion must be won over. This miracle was accomplished by the spring of 1846 through a carefully planned campaign. By its close a reader of the London press would gain the impression that all Britain was clamoring for the 49th parallel boundary as a gesture of peace and good will toward the United States. With the road to a settlement nicely paved and the Hudson's Bay Company eager to rid itself of a costly territory, Aberdeen on June 6, 1846, offered the United States the 49th parallel as its northern boundary, with the line west of the coast to run between the shore and Vancouver Island, leaving that valuable property in British possession.

Only a few jingoistic senators objected; instead the Senate overwhelmingly urged President Polk to accept. On June 15, 1846, the treaty was formally ratified by a vote of forty-one to fourteen. The treaty was especially welcomed by the New England whaling interests that feared war with England; a conflict would not only leave their ships exposed to British attack but also cost them their freedom to hunt the waters of the Russian-American Fur Company for, once at war with England, the United States would doubtless court Russian neutrality. Polk, the New Englanders believed, was far too interested in acquiring land; the New Englanders were willing to settle for a good harbor or two on the Pacific from which to tap the China trade and for freedom to exploit the seas.

With the boundary settled, Americans in the Willamette Valley saw no reason why Congress could not create the Oregon Territory at once. The slavery issue doomed them to disappointment. The Oregonians were by no means abolitionists; their provisional constitution of 1844 barred all Negroes from the territory while a wealthy black who arrived that year, George W. Bush, was denied the right to settle and forced to move on to the Puget Sound country north of the Columbia where he prospered. Yet the provisional government had banned slavery, and a similar provision was now incorporated in the Oregon bill presented to Congress. This was sufficient to arouse such opposition from the proslavery forces that despite the friendly interest of President Polk and Senator Benton, the measure made no progress in 1846 and 1847. Not until the Whitman massacre in the latter year was it possible to secure action. This atrocity prompted the Oregon settlers to prepare a last memorial to Congress, earnestly praying that it take them under its protection. When this reached the East popular sympathy, already stirred by the butchery of the missionaries, forced the legislature to act. On August 13th, 1848, after a continuous session of twenty-one hours, the bill creating Oregon Territory was finally passed.

24

The Great Basin Frontier
1830-1846

For two centuries the frontier advance followed a well-defined pattern: whenever conditions at home held little promise and the regions ahead were sufficiently attractive a rapid westward movement took place. The migrations into Texas and Oregon ran true to that form. In each case overcrowding or instability in the Mississippi Valley uprooted pioneers; in each case they risked the uncertainties of wilderness travel to settle on rich lands which promised them the prosperity they had failed to find in the East. No such desires motivated the third company of immigrants who moved toward the Far West during those years. Their mecca was no black-soiled prairie or well-watered valley, but the arid desert of the Great Basin where sunbaked alkaline soils discouraged settlement by less hardy souls. Those newest pioneers were members of the Church of Jesus Christ of Latter-day Saints, and they sought the most isolated spot on all the continent where they could worship God as they chose. They found their haven beneath the shadows of Utah's Wasatch Mountains.

The wanderings that brought the Mormons to this desert Zion began many years before they made their last trek across the Plains. Persecution drove them onward, a persecution directed against their prophet, Joseph Smith. Smith was the child of Vermont parents who drifted westward until settling near the frontier village of Palmyra in upstate New York. There they were surrounded by other New Englanders, many of them steeped in the mystical, soul-searching traditions of evangelical Protestantism, and all susceptible to the highly charged atmosphere that prevailed in that day of religious controversy. In sparsely settled New York the social restraints that had inhibited their emotionalism in New England were relaxed. There the isolation of families one from another, the primitive schooling, the break-

474

down of orthodox religions, the lack of a stable political structure, the spatial mobility of the populace, all contributed to a psychosocial environment in which revelation was certain to thrive. This was the spiritual climate that nurtured young Joseph Smith's concern with the hereafter and that gave birth to Mormonism.

His first interest in religion was shown in 1820 when his parents were weighing the merits of the Methodist, Baptist, and Presbyterian revivalists then exhorting a local camp meeting. Joseph, who was fourteen years old, sought the answer in prayer, going alone into the forest to ask divine guidance. As he prayed, a dazzling light revealed God and the Savior standing before him. He should, they told him, concern himself with none of the existing churches; all had strayed from the true faith revealed to man when Christ was on earth. Joseph's mother, a mystical woman who was subject to visions, accepted her son's experience without question. From that day the family forsook other sects to await the revelation of a religion pleasing to the Almighty.

This came over the next years. In 1823 the Angel Moroni appeared before Joseph Smith to tell him that near Palmyra was buried a stone casket containing metal plates on which the story of the true belief was inscribed. Under Moroni's direction, Joseph unearthed the plates on September 22, 1823, but was not allowed to take them from their hiding place. In 1827, according to his own account, he was permitted to remove the plates and begin the task of translating the hieroglyphics in which God's revelation was written. For the next two years this task went on, with Smith sitting in a curtained alcove in a neighbor's farmhouse, reading aloud to a series of assistants who wrote as he dictated. In 1830 the transcription was completed and the Book of Mormon published. In the same year the Church of Jesus Christ of Latter-day Saints was organized with its first six members.

The Book of Mormon, which was destined to be accepted as the Gospel by thousands of the faithful, told the story of Lehi who about 600 B.C. was warned by the Lord to leave Jerusalem before the city's destruction. Lehi's party, related the Book of Mormon, journeyed along the Red Sea and eastward across Arabia to the ocean where they built a ship and sailed for the "promised land" in America. Arriving safely, Lehi died, after which his good sons–"Nephites"–separated themselves northward from the bad sons–"Lamanites"–who were later cursed with dark skins by the Lord and survived as ancestors of the American Indians. For a thousand years the Nephites and Lamanites fought, save for a period of peace from 34 A.D. to about 200 A.D. when Christ appeared among them to preach His sermons and organize His church. Although superior strategy and divine guidance allowed the Nephites to triumph in these wars, they finally sank into such wickedness that they lost God's grace, and were severely defeated at a great battle at "Cumorah" in the year 400 A.D. All were killed save Moroni, son of Mormon, who spent the remainder of his days inscribing the story of his people on metal plates to await the coming of a prophet worthy of revealing their truths to mankind. These were the plates found by Joseph near Palmyra.

Despite the appeal of the Book of Mormon to emotion-starved frontier families, the Church of Jesus Christ of Latter-day Saints grew slowly and was subjected to constant persecution. Taking to heart the adage that a prophet is forever without honor in his own country, Smith decided to lead his followers to a more congenial clime. The hamlet of Kirtland, in northeastern Ohio, was chosen as the new Zion on the advice of two Campbellite converts familiar with the region, and there Joseph and his followers moved in 1831. The Mormons enjoyed their first success in Kirtland; converts multiplied, fields were cleared, homes built, and an imposing temple begun. The prophet blossomed with this success, experiencing a series of revelations from which a body of church dogma emerged, one feature of which was a communal organization for the Mormon community. This economic system proved so efficient that the Saints prospered mightily and seemed destined to a tranquil future.

The Panic of 1837 punctured their dreams. The Mormons had been tempted by the speculative fever of the 1830s to launch a banking enterprise which collapsed with most of the other banks of the nation, leaving them heavily in debt and threatened by angry creditors. Many of the Saints turned against their prophet. He responded by reading them out of the church in language as inflammatory as their own, then fled westward with his remaining followers to join a small Mormon community recently established in the towns of Far West and DeWitt on the northwestern Missouri frontier. These experiences, which would have humbled a less-confident man, only embittered Joseph Smith. He arrived in Missouri convinced that Gentile persecution was the cause of all his troubles, and that peace could be won only by meeting force with force. "Our rights," one of his disciples told the people of Far West at a Fourth of July celebration in 1838, "shall no more be trampled with impunity. The man, or set of men, who attempt it, does it at the expense of their lives. And that mob which comes on to us to disturb us, it shall be between us and them a war of extermination, for we will follow them till the last drop of their blood is spilled, or else they will have to exterminate us."

Fighting words such as these only inflamed the Missouri pioneers. They already disliked the Mormons—as New Englanders, as suspected abolitionists, as prosperous landlords, as unorthodox believers. They suspected that Joseph Smith's prophecies of the day when his people would inherit the earth cloaked a Mormon plot to take over the community by force; when they saw bands of young Saints drilling their suspicions seemed confirmed. Little wonder that anti-Mormon mobs began forming about Far West during the summer of 1838 or that guerrilla warfare broke out in the fall. In vain Smith appealed to state officials for protection. "The Mormons must be treated as enemies," the governor of Missouri announced, "and must be exterminated or driven from the state, if necessary, for the public peace."

Through the winter gangs of inflamed Missourians struck again and again at the harassed Mormons of Far West, driving them from their homes into fields and forests where suffering was intense.

They could no longer stay in Missouri, Smith saw, nor could they move farther west where the Permanent Indian Frontier blocked their path. Hence he turned his steps eastward, followed by faithful Saints whose loyalty mounted with each setback. The site selected by the Prophet for their new homes was a swampy lowland near Quincy, Illinois, which had been avoided by earlier settlers. Reaching this unpromising spot in the spring of 1839, Smith sized up the situation shrewdly. Illinois, he saw, was ready to welcome newcomers who would help share the debt burden inherited from the state's collapsed internal improvement program. Moreover the two political parties, Whigs and Democrats, were so evenly matched that either would make concessions in return for a bloc of votes. Joseph Smith knew, too, that Illinois custom allowed liberal charters for new communities, granting an unusual degree of authority over local affairs to the town officials. This tradition allowed him to secure a charter that would allow the Mormon community to be virtually self-governing. Fifty of its fifty-seven sections were copied directly from the charters of other cities in the state, but they were so adroitly combined that they allowed the passage of any law not repugnant to the national constitution, granted local courts authority to try cases involving the interpretation of the charter, and authorized the creation of a local militia. This document was pushed through the state legislature, largely by the Whigs who were promised support in the 1840 election in return for their services. Joseph Smith was assured a largely independent commonwealth within Illinois where he could govern with a minimum of external interference.

Prosperity smiled on the Saints now. Ardent missionaries roamed the United States and Europe, winning converts who flocked to Nauvoo in such numbers that the city's population skyrocketed to 15,000 in 1844 when it dwarfed in size all other Illinois cities. By that time almost 2,000 tidy homes bordered its spacious streets, "almost all of them brick, built in the New England style, neat as well as substantial, surrounded by garden plats, . . . and without any of that unfinished temporary *makeshift* appearance that characterises the new settlements of the West." Over all towered the Mormon temple, a sturdy structure of stone and gilt. Farms were laid out nearby, small industries started, a quarry and brickyard opened, a sawmill set up in distant Wisconsin to provide lumber for homes and factories. Everyone was bustling, everyone happy. Each day religious pageants, athletic events, dances, song fests, or parades of the local militia company, the Nauvoo Legion, were staged to entertain the inhabitants. "I do not believe," one traveler wrote, "that there is another people in existence who could have made such improvements in the same length of time, under the same circumstances."

Joseph Smith was in his glory. His word was law in the Holy City, where he was mayor, commander of the Legion, and president of the church. Success seemed to breed success as the Prophet's plans went unchallenged; but as his strength increased his native shrewdness declined. Forgetting that anti–Mormon feeling persisted about Nauvoo, he went doggedly about the task of consolidating his hold. He issued an ordinance providing for the punishment of anyone using language disrespectful of the church, insisted that no Illinois law became valid in Nauvoo until it bore his signature, bargained overzealously with both parties before each election, and asked Congress to erect his city into a federal territory free of state control. Gentile grumbling that followed each dictatorial step rose to a crescendo when Smith announced himself a candidate for the presidency of the United States in 1844, on a platform that called for the freeing of all slaves and prisoners, a reduction in the number of congressmen, and the annexation of Mexico and Canada. The Whigs, who had supported the Mormons before, turned violently on Smith's followers, leaving them surrounded by a solid ring of enemies.

A united Nauvoo might still have held back the onslaught, but Smith's announced revelation in July, 1843, sanctioning polygamy for church leaders, ended all hope.[1] Many Mormons, refusing to accept the pronouncement, banded together against the Prophet. The newspaper founded to popularize their views, the Nauvoo *Expositor*, in its first issue of June 7, 1844, castigated Smith's views on both polygamy and economics, and demanded "the unconditional repeal of the city charter—to correct the abuses of the unit power."

Smith acted at once against the dissenters. A hurriedly called meeting of the city council declared the newspaper a nuisance that should be destroyed, an order carried out three days later when the marshal broke into the *Expositor*'s printing plant, smashed the press, and disposed of all available copies of the first issue. The editors fled to nearby Carthage, scattering flames of discontent along the way. There they swore out a warrant for Smith's arrest, listing the grievances which were rapidly arousing the countryside: suppression of the press, polygamy, and political dictatorship. As news of the dissension spread, mass meetings met to call for a "war of extermination" on the Mormons, mobs formed, feelings ran high. The state governor hurried from Springfield, but when he found the militia as rabidly anti-Mormon as the people, he realized peace could be preserved in only one way. Joseph Smith and his brother were persuaded to surrender, then lodged for their own protection in the Carthage jail. Even that proved futile. On June 27, 1844, a mob stormed into Carthage, battered its way into the prison, and brutally slaughtered the two Mormon leaders.

[1]One branch of the Mormon Church, the Reorganized Church of Jesus Christ of Latter-day Saints, with headquarters at Independence, Missouri, denies that Joseph Smith experienced this revelation or that he either practiced or sanctioned polygamy.

The handwriting on the wall was clear to the Saints now: they would never be safe within the United States. Despairingly, they prepared to begin their wanderings once more. Their first need was a modern Moses to lead them to a promised land. The choice was a happy one. Brigham Young, an early convert and head of the Council of Twelve Apostles, was a hardheaded realist whose organizational talents and outgoing nature equipped him for the difficult tasks ahead. All about Nauvoo angry Gentiles threatened mob action unless the Mormons left Illinois at once. Young managed to keep the peace for a year, but during the winter of 1845–46 he held the enemies in check only by promising that his people would be on their way "as soon as the grass grew and the water ran." Within the city broken-hearted Saints prepared to move, selling their property at ruinous prices to buy wagons, supplies, and live stock. In February, 1846, 1,600 Mormons crossed the frozen Mississippi to the little hamlet of Sugar Grove, Iowa, where temporary headquarters were established. During the next few months the rest of the Nauvoo population followed.

When the exodus began, Brigham Young planned to lead his people to some isolated spot beyond the Rocky Mountains, although his geographic knowledge was so hazy he had no exact location in mind. Hence he determined to make the journey in stages, sounding out each step in advance. The first stopping place selected was on the west bank of the Missouri opposite Council Bluffs. While the Saints waited at Sugar Grove, an advance party rode ahead to mark the trail, build bridges, lay out roads, establish permanent camp sites, erect cabins, and plant crops that the emigrants could harvest. By the time the vanguard reached Council Bluffs in June, 1846, the main party was ready to start. Young planned so efficiently that the migration was accomplished easily. All summer bands of Mormons trekked westward, stopping to eat bountifully of crops planted for them and sleep comfortably in well-equipped cabins. "We are happy and contented," one Saint wrote, "and the songs of Zion resounded from wagon to wagon, reverberating through the woods, while the echo was returned from the distant hills." By fall 12,000 were camped on the banks of the Missouri on Indian land at a spot called Winter Quarters.

The winter was one of suffering and hard work. Disease and icy blasts from the Plains took a toll of almost 600 lives, but the survivors spent no time mourning their dead. Brigham Young was teaching them the secrets of Plains travel. He divided them into parties of 100 with a captain over each, taught them how to drive their wagons in four parallel columns when danger threatened, showed them how to form their wagons into a solid corral at night, warned them never to forget their daily prayers, and cautioned them to obey orders blindly lest they fall prey to Indians. By spring the Mormons were as thoroughly disciplined as an army and as well versed in Plains lore as any one who had not actually traveled in the West.

The first party set out in mid-April, 1847—a well-organized Pioneer Band led by Brigham Young and made up of 146 young men and women, riding in 73 wagons and driving a large herd of livestock. Instead of following the Oregon Trail along the south bank of the Platte, Young blazed a new route just north of the stream, partly because the higher ground there was better suited to wagon travel, more because he wished to avoid rowdy Missourians who frequented the regular trail. From the first he enforced rigid discipline—prayers at five each morning, on the road two hours later, a twenty-mile march, a halt to form the nightly wagon corral with livestock within and sleeping tents without, evening prayers, bed at nine o'clock— that was the schedule followed day after day as the Pioneer Band plodded westward. Ft. Laramie was reached in early June. There the party halted to dry meat, fatten horses, and build ferry boats which were turned over to eight men left behind to carry later emigrants across the North Platte.

Then the difficult journey up into the mountains and through South Pass began. At Ft. Bridger, the trading post maintained by Jim Bridger, they heard discouraging advice. That seasoned old pioneer warned them only barren deserts lay ahead, so dry that neither animal nor vegetable life could possibly exist. He urged the Mormons to turn to the Willamette, Bear, or Cache valleys where white men and Indians produced crops as good as any grown in Kentucky. As for the Great Basin wasteland—he offered Brigham Young $1,000 for the first ear of corn raised there. The Mormons, seeking isolation as well as prosperity, refused to listen. They pressed on, over the rugged Uinta Range, across a sun-dried desert, into the eastern spurs of the Wasatch Mountains. There Brigham Young, struck down with mountain fever, took to a pallet in one of the wagons as they wended their way through steep passes where the men worked feverishly with picks and shovels to clear a path for the wagons until they crossed the summit to emerge in the narrow defile known as Emigration Canyon. As this broadened they had their first view of the mountain-fringed valley of the Great Salt Lake that was to be their future home.[2]

With joy in their hearts, the Mormons hurried on to their promised land, arriving on July 24, 1847, a day since celebrated as "Pioneer Day." The prospect would have brought despair to men of lesser faith. Above them towered the snow-capped peaks of the Wasatch Range, to the north and west was the glimmering surface of Great Salt Lake, but at their feet was a barren plain, cracked by the searing sun, dotted with a few straggling sagebrush plants, and inhabited by no living thing save a multitude of black crickets, lizards, and rattlesnakes. Members of the Pioneer Band, after shattering their plows in the dry soil, successfully dammed one of the two streams that gushed from the mountains, flooded a few acres until the ground was softened, then planted their first crops. Having supervised this exper- iment in irrigation and sent a party into California to buy cattle, Brigham

---

[2]According to Mormon legend, Young rose from his sick bed at the sight to say: "This is the place." This remark was first attributed to him by Wilford Woodruff in 1880; there is no contemporary evidence that it was ever made.

Young started east with a few followers to organize the 1848 migration. Not far from Great Salt Lake his heart was gladdened by the sight of a great Mormon company plodding westward: 1,553 people, 2,313 cattle, 887 cows, 358 sheep, 124 horses, 35 hogs, 716 chickens. All went smoothly for this mammoth party; by the time they joined the "Pioneer Band" a few weeks later no fewer than 1800 Saints were established about the southern tip of the Great Salt Lake.

There was suffering that first winter among the ill-fed, ill-clad, ill-housed Mormons. Food was so scarce they were reduced to meagre flour rations and to grubbing out the roots of the sego lily. Lumber—which had to be hauled in from distant forest slopes—was so hard to obtain many braved winter's blasts in covered wagons. Yet there was no despair among the shivering, hungry Saints; they knew Brigham Young would lead them to prosperity as surely as he had guided them to their Zion. Fortunately their childish faith was justified. Young worked frantically in the East that winter, gathering emigrants for the spring migration. "Come immediately and prepare to go West," he urged his people, "bringing with you all kinds of choice seeds, grains, vegetables, fruits, shrubbery, trees, and vines—anything that will please the eye, gladden the heart or cheer the soul of man." Eighteen hundred settlers responded during the summer of 1848 but their coming did not ease suffering, for the 5,000 acres cultivated that year were insufficient to provide all with food. Even the meagre harvest was threatened when myriads of black crickets descended on the growing grain; only a visitation by sea gulls who gobbled up the offenders saved part of the crop and when they left two weeks later the pests returned to the assault. Later visitations by gulls, particularly in 1849 and 1850, gave rise to the legend that they had been sent by God to save the Saints in 1848; the "Miracle of the Gulls," the Mormons then called it, and today a statue of a sea gull in Salt Lake City testifies to their faith in the Deity's concern with their safety. Those who endured the winter of 1848–49 were less sure; they knew that the crop had been badly damaged before the gulls arrived, that the crickets resumed their devastation as soon as the birds left, and that drought and frost took a heavier toll than the insects. The Saints had little occasion to believe in miracles as they suffered through the extremely cold winter of 1848-49—the "Starving Time" in Mormon history.

Amidst these hardships the work of rearing a permanent settlement went forward. In carrying out this task the Mormon church first exerted its great power to create a social order unique in the annals of the nineteenth-century frontier. Brigham Young prophesied the nature of society when he welcomed the pioneers of the 1848 migration to Great Salt Lake:

> No man can ever buy land here, for no one has any land to sell.

> But every man shall have his land measured out to him, which he must cultivate in order to keep it.

> Besides, there shall be no private ownership of the streams that come out of the canyons, nor the timber that grows on the hills.

> These belong to the people: all the people.

In those words Young laid down the principles that governed the planting of settlements, the development of irrigation, and the expansion of the Great Basin frontier.

The disciples' first need was a city to harbor emigrants soon to come. A site was chosen southeast of Great Salt Lake yet near enough mountain streams for irrigation. Church committees under Young's direction divided the area into square ten-acre plots separated by streets 130 feet wide. Each block was subdivided into eight lots of 1¼ acres which were assigned families, with the understanding that houses be built twenty feet from the front line and the intervening space planted to trees and shrubs. Irrigation ditches along each side of the streets provided water for vegetable gardens and fruit trees. In the center of the spacious city a large square was reserved for public buildings and a temple. On the outskirts the land was divided into five-acre plots for the use of artisans or other townsmen who wished to supplement their larders by raising small quantities of produce. Beyond were larger lots, ranging up to forty acres, assigned to farmers. All plots were granted free of charge, with the understanding that they might be sold or exchanged, but with all speculation forbidden.

The theory underlying the land system—that the welfare of the social group transcended the welfare of the individual—was equally well expressed in the agriultural methods devised by the Mormons. Holding to the concept that "land belongs to the Lord, and his Saints are to use so much as they can work profitably," church leaders assigned free farms to families in direct proportion to need. Thus a man with plural wives, numerous children, and some wealth might receive from forty to eighty acres, while a husband with one mate and less property would be given only ten or twenty acres. All fields adjoined an irrigation ditch connected with a stream from the Wasatch Mountains. The main ditches were planned by a committee and built jointly by all who used them, each providing labor in proportion to the amount of land he tilled. Each farmer then dug smaller trenches from the central trough to his own plot.

Rigid controls governed the use of water. Each main irrigation ditch was supervised by a church committee which saw to it that farmers received just enough precious fluid for efficient agriculture. Thus a farmer with forty acres might be given the right to use water from two to five o'clock on Monday, Wednesday, and Friday; one with only ten acres would be assigned the period from nine to ten o'clock on Tuesday, Thursday, and Saturday. Within two years after the Saints reached the Great Basin the system was functioning smoothly.

The methods devised by the Mormons for allotting both land and water represented a degree of cooperation rarely found among individualistic

American pioneers. Only once before in the history of the nation's expansion had a similar cooperative social order developed: among the Puritans of seventeenth-century Massachusetts. The similarity of the two groups of pioneers, although separated by two centuries and half a continent, explains their distinctive societies. Both Puritans and Mormons were an intensely religious people, governed by a closely knit hierarchy whose slightest whim was unquestioningly obeyed, and seeking isolation to worship as they pleased. The power of the church was one factor needed to assure social controls. Equally necessary were the inhospitable geographic environments in which both lived. The Saints were, in one sense, typical of all pioneers, who were less individualistic than opportunistic. The American settlers wanted wealth and security. If those ends were obtainable by speculation and exploitation, as in the humid East, they adopted a system of individual competiton; if harsh natural conditions made joint effort more satisfactory, as in rocky Massachusetts or barren Utah, they tried cooperation. The Mormons were simply wise enough to adopt an economic system suited to their unique environment. Thus a combination of religious and geographic forces weakened the centrifugal force of the frontier and made possible a Desert Zion that matched the Wilderness Zion of Massachusetts Bay.

Nevertheless, Brigham Young's wisdom in recognizing the need for joint effort cannot be overemphasized. Unity was needed especially for successful irrigation, and on that subject the Saints were completely without experience. Until they arrived at Great Salt Lake extensive irrigation was unknown anywhere in the Anglo-Saxon world. Yet within a brief period they not only devised a workable means of allotting water but developed a completely new legal concept to govern their enterprise. Rejecting the older common law system of "riparian rights" which forced every property owner who used water from a stream for power to return the same amount before the river reached his neighbor's lands, the Mormons adopted the Spanish "Doctrine of Appropriation." Brigham Young enunciated the revolutionary concept when he first reached Great Salt Lake, but not until 1852 was it given classic form by the territorial legislature: "The county court shall have control of all timber, water privileges, or any water course or creek, to grant mill sites, and exercise such powers as in their judgment shall best preserve the timber and subserve the interest of the settlement in the distribution of water for irrigation or other purposes." Young laid the basis for all subsequent irrigation law by evolving a doctrine that placed the good of the community above the interests of the individual.

The remarkable achievements in land distribution and desert agriculture assured permanence for the Mormon settlements, but their first prosperity was due to a happy accident. The California Gold Rush of 1849 sent a stream of miners pouring through Salt Lake City on their way west. Many inexperienced gold seekers who overloaded their wagons with clothes, tools, and machinery were anxious to sell before crossing the sandy deserts of the Great Basin and the precipitous trails of the Sierra Nevadas. They also needed fresh food and draft animals. The Saints found themselves in the fortunate position of being able to buy precious manufactured goods at prices lower than those of the New York wholesale houses, while selling mules at $200 apiece and flour at $25 a hundred pounds. Those not equipped to take advantage of this legalized robbery repaired broken wagons in return for unheard-of wages of $3 a day. Money, usually hard to get on the frontier, circulated freely in Salt Lake City by the close of 1849.

Continued prosperity was assured by a steady influx of new settlers over the next years. The Mormons were a zealous people; their missionaries roamed widely over the East, England, and the Baltic countries, preaching a message of hope to oppressed lower classes in industrial centers. Conversion, they promised, meant not only salvation but a chance to begin life anew in the church's desert utopia. Converts were won by the thousands, all of whom were urged to make their way to the Great Salt Lake. Those unable to pay their own expenses were aided by a Perpetual Emigrating Fund established in 1849; money obtained from the faithful was loaned to immigrants with the understanding that it be returned as soon as they were financially secure. A program of public works was set up in Salt Lake City to help others earn enough to defray travel costs.

Still more were helped by a system that Brigham Young devised in 1856 to cut down the expenses of wagon travel across the plains. Emigrants arriving at Iowa City, the jumping-off place for the Mormon Trail, were met by a crew of carpenters sent by the church to build two-wheeled hand carts large enough to carry a settler's belongings. The first "Hand Cart Brigade"— almost 500 men, women, and children—arrived in Salt Lake City during the summer of 1856, after pushing 100 carts across the 1,200 miles of trail in about the same time taken by prairie schooners. Two more parties reached Utah safely, but two others comprising more than 1,000 persons started so late that they were caught by early snows in Wyoming. Two hundred and twenty-five perished before a relief expedition rescued the remainder.

Despite that setback settlers continued to stream toward the Mormon Zion, many using hand carts until the method was abandoned in 1861. The steady influx brought the church leaders face-to-face with three major problems. How could they provide homes for the incoming thousands in that desert region? How could they continue their complete isolation from the Gentile world? How could they govern themselves? The skill shown by Brigham Young and his fellow churchmen in answering those perplexing questions not only testified to their ability but assured the Mormons a prosperous future.

The problem of providing newcomers with farms allowed the Mormons to demonstrate the remarkable efficiency of their cooperative social order. From the first they realized that colony planting in the Great Basin would differ from settlement in the humid East; each townsite must be selected with an eye to irrigation possibilities and the limited water supplies must be controlled in the interest of community welfare. Hence every step was carefully planned. A committee was sent out first to select a likely spot where a stream gushed from the Wasatch Mountains. Then the pioneers were selected—a bishop or elder as leader, a few experienced farmers and herdsmen, a blacksmith, a carpenter, a flour miller, a schoolmaster, a religious teacher, a number of inexperienced emigrants who could learn from the seasoned planters. The "Call" to join a colonizing expedition was looked upon as an honored opportunity to "build the Kingdom of God on earth" and never refused. All selected sold their goods, secured the implements and tools needed, and set out for their new homes. The combination of skilled leadership and selected personnel allowed the Mormons to plant new towns with none of the suffering usual on the frontier.

Equally important in explaining the rapid expansion of the Great Basin frontier was the unquenchable ambition of Brigham Young. He looked upon new settlements as one important means of achieving isolation for the desert nation that was his dream. Such a state could survive only with an outlet to the sea; hence he planned a string of towns across Utah, Nevada, and southern California to the Pacific. These would be connected with roads over which emigrants and supplies, brought in by ship, could reach Salt Lake City. In that way a strong, independent Mormon community would be built up, cut off from the United States by the Great American Desert. The "Mormon Corridor" from Great Salt Lake to San Diego was one of Young's great ambitions.

The Mormons directed most of their colonizing energies to the region south of Salt Lake City although three northern towns—Bountiful, Centerville, and Ogden—were planted between 1847 and 1850 on streams flowing into Great Salt Lake. Expansion southward along the "Mormon Corridor" began in 1849 when thirty families reached the shores of Utah Lake to lay out the town of Ft. Utah. Provo and Lehi were established on the edges of that large body of fresh water during the next year. Meanwhile other exploring parties, ranging farther afield, discovered the plentiful mountain streams that lost themselves in the arid San Pete Valley; there the villages of Nephi and Manti were settled in 1850. Still farther south in the valley of the Sevier River, Fillmore was founded in 1851, while in southern Utah Parowan and Cedar City were colonized during the next few years. Both were established with an eye to industrial developments, for they were located near beds of iron and coal. At Cedar City mines were opened, a wood-burning smelter capable of producing a ton of metal a day set up, and some 500 acres irrigated to provide food for workers. Still not content, Brigham Young in 1852 sent a company of colonizers into southern California with instructions to found a settlement near Cajon Pass where they could "cultivate the olive, grape, sugar-cane, and cotton, gather round them the saints, and select locations on the line of the proposed mail route." The 300 active Mormons entrusted with the task of founding this key town on the "Mormon Corridor" reached Cajon Pass in the spring of 1852, chose a favorable site, purchased land, and laid out a city called San Bernardino.

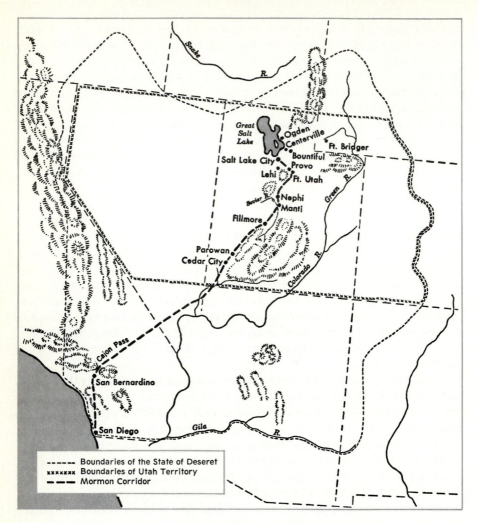

The Great Basin Frontier, 1846–1857

Two years later other small outposts were established along the corridor in the Nevada country. Into all moved new settlers as they came from the East or Europe; by 1856, 22,000 Saints lived about Great Salt Lake or in towns along the "Mormon Corridor." Their neat villages, well-irrigated fields, and prosperous industries were fitting tribute to Brigham Young's skill as a colonizer.

Closely allied with the program of expansion was the Mormons' attempt to achieve independence by diversifying their economy. Brigham Young believed this essential to the autonomous community he hoped to create; "seek diligently," he told his missionaries in Europe, "in every branch for wise, skillful and ingenious mechanics, manufacturers, potters, etc." When craftsmen arrived they were set to work at their trades. A sawmill and gristmill were erected at once, a salt works opened on the shores of Great Salt Lake, and a soda spring nearby turned to the use of the Saints. During the next half-dozen years small factories were constructed, usually with church funds, to produce pottery, leather goods, textiles, nails, cutlery, wooden bowls, soap, paper, guns, and glass. Typical was one enterprise devoted to finding a substitute for sugar, which could not be grown in the arid climate. Some of the disciples knew from Old World experience that beets and corn produced a saccharine product. They directed the construction of a small beet-crushing plant in 1855, fashioning the machinery from old wagon hubs, rims, and scrap iron. Those expedients, together with goods brought by emigrants along the California Trail, allowed the Mormons to approach that economic isolation which seemed necessary to religious independence.

Effective as were the Mormon colonizing and economic activities, their dream of autonomy was doomed from the outset. No expanse of Great American Desert could protect them from the grasp of their fellow-Americans; that they were left to their own devices for a few years was due only to American preoccupation with the Mexican War. When fighting ended in 1848 the alarming news reached Salt Lake City that the Mexican lands on which they lived were part of the United States. Brigham Young saw his Saints could be protected in only one way: immediate statehood alone would allow them to govern themselves, continue their religious practices unmolested, and guard their unpopular doctrine of polygamy. Hurrying into action, he issued a call for a convention which met at Salt Lake City in March, 1849, and adopted a typical frontier constitution, modeled after the frames of government in eastern states, but vesting complete power in popularly elected officials. Fear of outside aggression was reflected in a clause forcing all men between eighteen and forty-five to serve in the militia. The convention proposed the new state be called Deseret (a term taken from the Book of Mormon and meaning Honey Bee), and that it include all of present-day Utah, all of Arizona, most of Nevada, part of southern California, and portions of Idaho, Wyoming, and Colorado, with an outlet to the sea at San Diego.

While messengers carried the document east, the Mormons turned to creating a government that could function until statehood was granted. The election held that spring disclosed the close connection between church and state; Brigham Young was chosen governor, the lieutenant governor and secretary were his close associates, and the justices of the peace were all Mormon bishops. The State of Deseret was still a theocracy, although garbed in the regalia of civil government. The result was an extremely efficient rule which operated equitably for Mormons and Gentiles alike. Laws passed by the legislature which convened in July, 1849, provided for a system of courts and law enforcement officials that made Deseret a haven for overland emigrants seeking justice; non-Mormons stopping to smooth over differences or settle disputes universally praised the justices for their "fairness and impartiality." One grateful traveler wrote: "Appeals for protection from oppression, by those passing through their midst, were not made in vain; and I know of at least one instance in which the marshal of the State was dispatched, with an adequate force, nearly 200 miles into the western desert in pursuit of some miscreants who had stolen off with nearly the whole outfit of a party of emigrants. He pursued and brought them back to the city, and the plundered property was restored to its rightful owners."

The efficiency of the courts failed to influence congressmen called upon to create the State of Deseret. Even Mormon leaders saw the cause was hopeless as soon as Congress began debating their petition in the spring of 1850; from every corner came a chorus of attack and vituperation: population was insufficient to warrant statehood, territorial claims were overambitious, the Mormon church was anti-Christian, the practice of polygamy must be forbidden. Amidst clamor from the opposition the Mormon committee changed its request to one for territorial organization. Congress responded on September 9, 1850, when the Territory of Utah was established, with a name derived from the Ute Indians, and boundaries that included all Utah, most of Nevada, the western third of Colorado, and part of Wyoming.

Mormon fears of unsympathetic federal control were set at rest when President Millard Fillmore named Brigham Young governor and appointed four Saints and four Gentiles to the other administrative posts. This allowed the hierarchy to rule virtually unmolested; as the four non-Mormons cooled their heels with nothing to do, the theocracy continued to function smoothly with property disputes settled by the church courts, justice administered through ecclesiastical law, and affairs of state conducted with precious little attention to the statutes of the distant United States. So long as Gentile officials were content to collect their pay without working, all went well, but in 1855 three bitterly anti-Mormon judges were appointed to the territory, two of them apostates from the church, and the third a sworn enemy of the Saints. For a time they endured the sight of their empty courts with slowly rising tempers, then in the spring of 1857 returned to Washington shouting for revenge at every step. Utah Territory, they charged, was ruled by a ruthless dictator, Brigham Young, who used a band of "destroying angels" to stamp out all opposition and defied federal authority with every act. Lawful officials there, they said, were "constantly insulted, harassed and annoyed"; some had been killed and all government records destroyed.

The charges touched off a storm of protest against the Saints. Overland emigrants involved in the inevitable disputes over lost property or strayed cattle besieged Congress with complaints. The surveyor general of the United States charged that Mormons refused to let him operate in their territory. Indian agents claimed that "rude and lawless" young men from Utah were settling on Indian lands. Freighters and expressmen reported that "indiscriminate bloodshed" in the region about Great Salt Lake interfered with their business. No one in Washington bothered to determine that those reports were grossly exaggerated, for underlying the growing wave of antipathy for the Mormons was national contempt for polygamy. By the middle 1850s a score of books were in circulation branding plural marriage as lewd and immoral, newspapers filled their columns with vituperation, and ministers thundered from pulpits that the sinful practice must be stamped out. Amidst such an atmosphere every minor charge against the Mormons was magnified into a major offense; justice and principles of religious freedom were forgotten.

The Mormons, in turn, were in no mood to accept this criticism, for they were in the midst of a religious revival known as "The Reformation." Their zeal foreordained trouble when President James Buchanan in May, 1857, ordered 2,500 troops under Colonel Albert Sidney Johnston to Utah with instructions to enforce federal authority over the Saints. Word of their approach sent the Mormons into a panic. Knowing nothing of the army's purpose, and convinced that enemies in Washington were determined to kill their leaders and stamp out their faith, they rallied behind Brigham Young when he issued a call for volunteers to repel the invaders. As colonists from San Bernardino and other outposts abandoned their villages to rush to the defense of Zion, and as guerrilla bands hurried eastward to meet and delay the approaching soldiers, good Mormons everywhere prepared to burn their houses and retreat southward, to Mexico if necessary, for the privilege of worshipping as they chose. Exploring parties searching the Colorado River valley for good defensive sites to delay the attackers were the first to develop interest in that mighty stream's potentials. Fired by this zeal the guerrilla bands performed their duty with savage efficiency; draft animals in Johnston's army were stampeded, two wagon trains of supplies burned to ashes, and the grass fired for miles around until no fodder remained for the horses. First delayed and then halted by these tactics the troops finally gave up hope of reaching Utah that year and went into winter camp near Ft. Bridger.

The harm was done, however, for the threat of invasion had raised tempers so high among the Mormons that some irresponsible act was inevitable. This took the form of the Mountain Meadows Massacre of September, 1857. Its victims were 140 emigrants passing through southern Utah on their way to California. Most were respectable farmers, but some were "Missouri Wild Cats" who created constant trouble by insulting the Mormons they met, killing chickens with their bull whips, and harming crops. Feelings were high when, on September 7, the party was attacked by Indians near Cedar City; seven men were killed and the rest placed under siege. Serious trouble might still have been avoided had not one of the Missourians who slipped out to summon aid been murdered by a fanatical Mormon. His neighbors, smarting under the insults they had received from the party and fearful lest the whole community be punished for the murder, decided to kill every emigrant in the train. Word was sent to the doomed camp that the Indians had been pacified and that they could leave safely; as they marched out they were ruthlessly shot down. Within moments 120 persons lay dead, while the lives of only seventeen children were spared. Although the crime was inexcusable, the tensions on both sides made the massacre understandable.

Events such as the Mountain Meadows Massacre, forecasting bloodshed should Mormon legions and federal armies ever clash, convinced federal officials that they must seek a peaceful settlement of the Mormon War. The mediator selected for the delicate task was Colonel T. L. Kane, an old friend of the Saints, who was rushed overland to Salt Lake City during the winter of 1857–58. Only a few conversations with Brigham Young were needed for Kane to convince the harassed Disciples that the United States intended no interference with their religion and that they should admit the federal troops. Having paved the way, Kane crossed the Wasatch Mountains to the headquarters of the besieging army, where he persuaded the newly appointed territorial governor to accompany him into Utah without military protection. The peaceful gesture so allayed Mormon fears that they consented to accept Amerian officials without further resistance. From that time a non-Mormon sat in the governor's edifice at Salt Lake City, but for all practical purposes Brigham Young continued to rule the territory. Gentile governors soon discovered that they were, in the pained phrase of one of them, "sent out to do nothing"; Utah remained a Mormon territory during its frontier period, founded, governed, and developed by Saints.

The peopling of the Great Basin was well under way by the close of the 1850s. Laboring side by side in unique cooperative ventures, spurred on by bishops who praised industrious husbandmen from their pulpits or publicly blacklisted shirkers, skillfully guided by able leaders along a path toward economic and political independence, the Mormons succeeded where others might well have failed. Their indomitable energy and all-prevailing faith brought a desert Zion into bloom.

25

The Conquest of California

1830-1846

The chain of events that won the richest prize of all for the expanding American nation began when the worldwide spirit of rebellion that had sired the American and French revolutions sparked a revolt that ended in 1821 with the establishment of the Republic of Mexico under its popular leader, Agustín de Iturbide. The stirring scenes enacted about Mexico City as this revolution unfolded caused only a ripple of interest in the northern borderlands of New Spain; Californians watched indifferently as the new government was established, knowing that the vast distances isolating them from their mother country would not shrink, no matter who was in control. They did rebel against a singularly inept governor in 1828, but after the leader of that revolt had expended his ammunition and consumed his provisions peace returned. During the next fifteen years no less than nine rebellions were staged against the self-seeking incompetents sent from Mexico as governors. Mexico's failure to provide orderly government and the almost total lack of communication between Mexico City and Monterey did little to engender loyalty to the Republic of Mexico.

Nor was life in California the sort to produce hardy patriots capable of defending their land against threatening invaders from the United States. The secularization of the missions was responsible. Twenty-one of these imposing structures dominated the countryside between San Diego and San Francisco when Mexican independence was won, each an agricultural empire with a handful of Franciscans in command, an army of Indian neophytes to do the work, well-tilled fields, and gigantic herds of cattle and sheep. In all the missions owned 400,000 cattle, 60,000 horses, and 300,000 sheep and swine, in addition to hundreds of acres of vineyards and irrigated farmland. This prosperity spelled their downfall for by the early 1830s would-be land-

491

holders were eyeing their holdings with covetous greed. Their pressure triumphed in August, 1833, when the Mexican Congress adopted a secularization act that released the Indians from church control and threw the mission lands open to settlement. Governor José Figueroa pleaded in vain that this precipitous step would undo the patient labors of a half-century. In 1834 the thousands and thousands of acres under mission control were made available to those with enough influence to secure them.

Secularization ushered in California's *rancho* era. Under Mexico's Colonization Act of 1824, as amended in 1828, any qualified citizen who could prove that he had the means to stock his holdings could be granted a *rancho* of from one league (4,428 acres) to eleven leagues (48,708 acres). During the years just after 1834 roughly 700 *rancho* grants were made—the "Spanish Grants" as they came to be known—most of them in the coastal plains and hills between San Diego and San Francisco. Each was a minor principality, presided over by grandee *ranchero*, supervised by a *mayordomo*, and operated by crews of mestizo and Indian *vaqueros* who cared for the cattle. All this cost the owner almost nothing, for land and labor were almost free, fencing unknown, and the herds capable of multiplying rapidly in the favorable climate.

Life for the *rancheros* was easy during that pastoral period of California's history—too easy as events were to show. Indians, who were technically free but actually little better than slaves, performed all manual toil; they were the "tryers-out" of tallow and the tanners of hides who produced the two marketable products that the *ranchos* could export. The 4,000 Mexicans who lived on the *ranchos*, in the *pueblos* of San José and Los Angeles, or about the four *presidios*—San Diego, Santa Barbara, Monterey, and San Francisco—by all foreign accounts enjoyed a life of indolent ease. The *rancheros* dressed in barbaric splendor, spent the days riding about their lands, and squandered their nights and holidays in a constant pursuit of pleasure; gambling, horse-racing, bull-baiting, and gay dances were their everyday means of escaping boredom. No festival ended before all the wine was downed; no game played out until the last peso was gambled away. Food was so abundant that no stranger was turned away. Yet in all California there was not a school, a newspaper, a post office, a theater, or an art gallery. Why, they asked, should we train lawyers when there is no litigation, teachers when ignorance is bliss? Their life of ease had robbed them of initiative, of any desire for self-improvement. Even in the *pueblos* the strict military discipline sapped the people of their initiative. Everywhere men were contented, but they were also indolent, lazy, and backward. Theirs was not a life that would produce heroes.

Yet heroes were to be needed, for the remarkable burst of expansion that carried American pioneers into Texas, Oregon, and the Great Basin during the 1830s and 1840s led also to the peopling of Mexican California. There, as elsewhere in the Far West, the trader and settler were several jumps ahead of the government and its diplomacy. For more than half a century before the fortunes of war brought that Mexican province under the jurisdiction of the United States, there had developed a Yankee interest and influence in California which, sooner or later, must have made it American territory.

First on the scene were the sea-otter traders from New England—the "Bostons," the natives called them—who rapidly expanded their operations southward from the Oregon coast where they began their trade in the 1790s. They found a limitless supply; the California coast was so well-stocked with otters that in 1801 alone no less than 18,000 skins were exported. The risks were staggering but the returns from a fortunate voyage were phenomenal; New England ships of from 100 to 250 tons burden usually devoted two or three years to a voyage, rounding the Horn, loading with furs at ports along the coast, sailing to China once or twice to trade the skins for the exotic oriental goods prized in the United States, and finally reaching home after circumnavigating the globe. British merchants offered competition at first, but the trade was soon monopolized by Americans and Russians, the latter moving steadily southward from Alaska where the Russian-American Fur Company had begun operations in the 1780s. They posed a serious threat for a time when they built Ft. Ross not far above San Francisco, but inefficient management of the Russian-American Fur Company and the difficulty of transporting supplies across Siberia gave the Americans a healthy advantage. By the 1820s they dominated the trade, with a steady stream of ships visiting California. Their crews spread word of the riches of the land; the first published account of the region was William Shaler's *Journal of a Voyage from China to the Northwestern Coast of America* which appeared in 1808. Thanks to the sea-otter trade, the United States was beginning to learn of California's fine harbors, fertile soil, and balmy climate.

It was to learn still more over the next decades as the nation's economic activity expanded along the Pacific coast. After independence whalers from Nantucket and New Bedford resumed activity which the Revolution interrupted, rounded Cape Horn, and pushed their search into the North Pacific. Operating at such a distance from New England shores, a satisfactory voyage consumed three or four years, during which supplies must be acquired, rest for the crews obtained, and repairs made. For those purposes the harbors of Hawaii and California were ideally suited. A whaling ship normally carried a small supply of manufactured goods to exchange for necessary produce. Monterey and San Francisco were favorite ports of the whalers; as many as thirty ships frequently lay at anchor in the latter at one time. Their presence on California shores enlarged American acquaintance with the province's potentialities and whetted Yankees' appetites for the fine harbors there.

New England traders engaged in yet a third form of maritime activity in California—the hide and tallow trade. Cattle were abundant there, fattening on the mission lands first, then after secularization on the *ranchos* that blanketed the coastal region. Although meat from the lean, long-horned Spanish beeves was as famed for its toughness as its flavor, a ready market existed for the fat tallow and heavy hides that they produced. Tallow was prized in Peru and other South American countries where it could be made into the candles used in the silver mines. Hides commanded a steady price in New England and Europe, where they were needed for the shoe industry. So long as Spain's rigid mercantile system excluded foreign ships from her harbors, only a trickle of hides left California, carried by smugglers who risked official wrath for astronomical returns. After 1821, however, the Republic of Mexico opened its ports to merchants from all the world. The stage was set for the hide and tallow era of California's commercial history.

In one respect these traders had a significance not possessed by either sea-otter traders or whalers. Their business required dealings in the interior with mission authorities and ranchers. They, therefore, either established a resident agent in California or sent with their ship a supercargo who traveled about on a horse, purchasing hides from missions and ranches. In this way the traders acquired a better knowledge of California and its people than had their predecessors. Pioneers in this enterprise were the Boston mercantile houses of Bryant, Sturgis & Company and William Appleton & Company, but their example was imitated so widely that within a few years after 1827 when a British commercial concession expired, a number of American firms had established regular agents in California's ports, all authorized to buy hides and tallow, supervise their transportation to the nearest harbor, and arrange for their storage until a company vessel arrived. Alfred Robinson, one of Bryant, Sturgis & Company's resident agents, was among the many Americans to marry a Mexican beauty and settle down permanently to a business career.

The procedures of the trade were soon perfected. The first port of call for a hide and tallow trader was Monterey, location of the one custom house in the province and its civil, military, and social capital as well. Every ship received a trading license and paid a duty on its cargo ranging as high as $25,000. Payment entitled the ship to distribute its cargo along the entire California coast, a process that consumed from one to three years. The effects of the heavy duty were somewhat alleviated by taking on additional goods from unlicensed traders lurking along the shore. That practice, combined with bribery of customs officials and actual smuggling, rendered the duty less onerous. Even if duties were paid in full the trader shifted much of the burden to the California consumer, who obtained the goods at a profit of 300 per cent to the ship owner. Payment was either in silver or hides, better known as "California bank-notes," at an average of $1.50 to $2.00 apiece. Such returns attracted more and more traders until on at least two occasions more than fifty ships were in California harbors at one time, the majority flying the American flag. Under such conditions two or three years were necessary to secure a cargo of 20,000 to 40,000 hides.

The hide and tallow trade benefited both the Californians and the traders. For the former it provided abundant manufactured goods that were otherwise unobtainable, while customs duties supported such a government as California offered. To the New Englanders it brought modest pecuniary rewards which in good times could rise to spectacular heights. A typical ship might leave Boston with a cargo valued at $30,000, trade this in California for hides and tallow worth $69,000, and sell these in Boston for $84,000. The profits from the sale of Boston goods in California—the difference between $30,000 and $69,000—normally cared for the expenses of the two or three year voyage, leaving the margin between the cost of the hides and their price in Boston—the difference between $69,000 and $84,000—as the profit. This was governed by the current New England price for hides; if this happened to be low the returns from a voyage would be minimal but if it was high they could rise well above 10 per cent. The hide and tallow trade was no magic carpet to riches, but the traders played a role in history that transcended economic values. From them, for the first time, Americans learned of California's resources, its climate, and the weakness of the Mexican hold. The adventurous account of the experiences of one trader, Richard Henry Dana, told in his classic *Two Years before the Mast* (1840), taught the United States a great deal about California's riches and made Americans very much aware that California's destiny was their own.

While New England ship captains established commercial contacts in California, American fur traders blazed the overland trails to the Pacific which the emigrant would some day follow. The pioneers in that bold enterprise were members of the Rocky Mountain Fur Company, and their agent was Jedediah Strong Smith—the "Knight of the Buckskin" his companions called him—whose discoveries rivaled those of Lewis and Clark. With his Bible and rifle as constant companions (and he never allowed his belief in one to interfere with the use of the other) he traversed thousands of miles of mountains and deserts, opened countless trails, and marked the path across the Great Basin to the interior valleys of California: the Sacramento and the San Joaquin. The quest for new beaver country drove him on, but his discoveries far transcended commercial importance.

His first journey began in 1826 when he reached the company rendezvous at Great Salt Lake with a supply of trading goods from the East. Leaving Salt Lake on August 22, Smith and his party travelled southwest to Utah Lake, then by the Sevier River, across a mountain range to the Virgin River. Following that stream they came to the Colorado, which they descended for four days until they came to a valley occupied by Mohave Indians. After resting and obtaining food, fresh horses, and two Indian guides, the explorers proceeded on their way, probably by much the same route as that of the Santa Fe Railroad of today. By November 27 they were in camp a short distance from the San Gabriel mission. Thus they completed the overland journey to California, the first Americans to accomplish the feat.

Despite Mexican law, which forbade their presence in California, Smith and his men were hospitably received by the padres, fed and clothed, and allowed to rest. While his party remained at the mission, Smith visited San Diego to secure the governor's permission to journey through the province, a concession arranged by the gift of some fine beaver skins and the good offices of a hide and tallow trader. To Smith's disappointment, however, the most the governor would grant was the right to leave California over the route by which he had entered. Disregarding instructions, he led his men north into the San Joaquin Valley, down the valley to the Stanislaus or the Merced River, where he left all but two of his men, and up the middle fork of the Stanislaus to the crest of the Sierras. Once on the eastern slope of the latter Smith probably travelled along Walker River to Walker Lake. Then, following a northeasterly course, he arrived at the Great Salt Lake in June, 1827, after days of almost indescribable suffering and hardship.

On July 13, 1827, Smith set out again with nineteen men to join the hunters left in California. Travelling by the route of the previous year he arrived at the Mohave Indian settlement, where ten of his party were killed by natives. With considerable difficulty, Smith and the remainder arrived at Mission San Gabriel, whence he proceeded to the San Joaquin where he found the hunters left the previous spring. On this visit Smith was less hospitably received than the year before. At the Mission of San José he was arrested, thrown in jail, and for weeks denied the opportunity of seeing the governor. When he did, only the intervention of several American ship captains, who chanced to be in port, prevented Smith from being sent to Mexico as a prisoner. Instead, he was forced to post a $30,000 bond as a guarantee of his departure from California within two months. Traveling up the Sacramento Valley, Smith and his men failed to find a feasible pass through the Sierras. They then crossed the Coast Range Mountains and followed the coast to the Umpqua River in Oregon, from which they hoped to find the Willamette, which would lead them to the Columbia. While encamped on the Umpqua the party was surprised by previously friendly Indians who killed all except Smith and two of his men. The three survivors ultimately arrived at the Hudson's Bay post, Ft. Vancouver, where Dr. McLoughlin gave them his customary friendly greeting. He further sent a party to rescue the furs Smith had left on the Umpqua, which he agreed to purchase for $20,000. The latter action was the more notable since otherwise the furs would have been a total loss to Smith who had no means of transporting them to Salt Lake. In the spring of 1828 Smith made his way to Pierre's Hole. He had discovered two overland routes between California and the Great Salt Lake, revealed the matchless fertility of the inland valleys of California, traveled from the Mojave Desert to the Columbia, and made known to Hudson's Bay Company traders the route to the treasures of northern California. He, rather than Fremont, was the original California "Pathfinder."

If it was Jedediah S. Smith, the Puritan from New England, who first discovered an overland route to California, the southern uplander was not far behind. Among the Kentuckians who participated in the winning of the Far West, none was more genuinely a son of the frontier than Sylvester Pattie, who, finding life in his native state too tranquil, had sought adventure on the Missouri frontier as early as 1812. After a ten years' residence there he found the congestion so great he was again seized with an irresistible impulse to move on. In June, 1824, Sylvester Pattie, his twenty-year-old son James Ohio, and three other men set out on a trapping expedition to the Rocky Mountains. Foiled at Council Bluffs in their original plan to trade on the upper Missouri, they turned toward the Southwest, where they fell in with a party of Santa Fe traders on their way to New Mexico. Of the combined party of more than 100 men Sylvester Pattie became the leader. Although they arrived at Santa Fe in November, 1824, without incidents unusual to the Santa Fe trade, this was but the beginning of the Patties' career in the Southwest. That their adventures over the next years were more romantic, their escapes more miraculous and their suffering more awesome than those of any other traders in the region was due to the fact that James Ohio Pattie's *Personal Narrative* remains the principal source for knowledge of the southwestern trade. If Pattie ascribed to himself the adventures and discoveries of a dozen other men, as he certainly did, this does not detract from the charm of a book that is today as readable as on the day it was published.

During 1825 and 1826 the Patties, according to James Ohio's account, trapped on the Gila and operated copper mines at Santa Rita. The younger Pattie discovered a route from New Mexico to the eastern boundary of

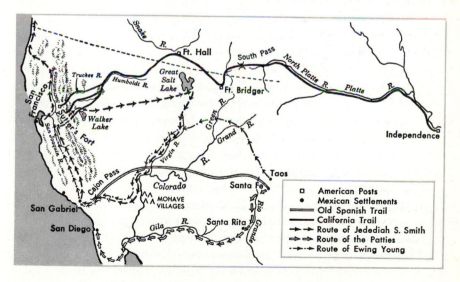

The American Occupation of California

California, explored much of the Colorado River (including the Grand Canyon), traversed the central Rocky Mountain region as far north as the Yellowstone and the Platte, and followed the Arkansas to the south, whence he crossed to the Rio Grande which brought him back to Santa Fe. Then, obtaining permission to trap in Chihuahua and Sonora, the Patties left Santa Fe on September 23, 1827, for the Gila, which they followed to the Colorado. They trapped along the lower stretches of the river until deterred by the strong tide. Turning upstream they found the swift current an equally great obstacle. Unable to proceed in either direction, they cached their furs and started across the Lower California desert for the settlements on the coast. In March, 1828, they arrived at Santa Catalina mission in Lower California, where they were received with scant hospitality. They were then sent under guard to San Diego where they arrived on March 27.

The Patties were placed in prison where the father died within a month. According to James Ohio's account, all efforts to secure his release, including the intercession of Yankee ship captains at San Diego, failed until he vaccinated the mission population of California against the ravages of small pox. But the facts are that there were no small-pox epidemics in Alta California during the mission period, and Pattie's story was just another tall tale, especially since he claimed to have inoculated 22,000 personns, some 6,000 more than the mission population. Pattie obviously romanticized and exaggerated something he really did see—an outbreak of measles—and made it into an exciting explanation of his release, which probably came about when authorities were convinced that he was harmless. James Ohio Pattie returned to the States by way of Mexico, arriving at his Kentucky birthplace in August, 1830. Other fur traders soon followed in the steps of Smith and the Patties, entering California by the clearly defined routes blazed by those pioneers.

If this were not bad enough for Mexican California, the trails pioneered by the fur trappers were soon expanded into commercial highways linking the New Mexican capital at Santa Fe with the coast. This was a natural development. For some time Santa Fe had been emerging as the center of a network of trading routes that covered much of the Southwest, some into Sonora and Chihuahua used by American miners seeking precious metals and by Santa Fe traders unable to dispose of their stock at Santa Fe itself, some northward to Taos and on into the fur-trapping country of the southern Rockies as far as the Green and Platte rivers, and now the most hazardous trail of all stretching westward into California. During the next few years this sustained a commerce of minor economic significance, but one that further threatened Mexico's ownership of its northern provinces.

Southern uplanders with a long frontier tradition behind them dominated the Santa Fe-California trade. A Tennessean, Ewing Young, was the one upon whom descended the mantle of the Patties. Departing from Taos in 1829, Young and his party traveled in a northwesterly direction to the Grand

River, crossed to the Green, and followed Smith's route to California. Returning to Taos in the summer of 1830, Young became a business partner of William Wolfskill, a Kentuckian who for several years had engaged in the trade to Santa Fe and Chihuahua. Their plan was to trap in the interior valleys of California. Following the San Juan, Grand, and Green rivers to the Colorado, they journeyed west to the Sevier River and southwest through the Mohave villages and Cajon Pass to Los Angeles. The Young-Wolfskill party blazed the "Old Spanish Trail" which became the regular caravan route for the Missouri-Santa Fe-Los Angeles trade.

The following year Young entered into another partnership under the name of Jackson, Waldo, and Young. The two companies sent by the new firm to California opened another route for the Los Angeles-Santa Fe trade. The first was designed to buy mules. Traveling by Pattie's trail through Albuquerque, Santa Rita, and the Gila to the Colorado, the party crossed the Imperial Valley and continued to San Diego and ultimately to San Francisco. The second led by Young, trapped along the Gila and Colorado, before journeying on to Los Angeles where they met the first party in the spring of 1832. The two commanders merged their groups for the return to the Colorado. There they separated, one party continuing on with the several hundred horses and mules acquired, while Young returned to California to trap. Young trapped in the San Joaquin and Sacramento valleys during the next two years, drove horses to Oregon in 1834, settled there, and became a regular dealer in mules between the Columbia and California.

Still another route to California opened in the 1830s was to become especially important in connection with later overland migrations. Joseph Reddeford Walker, a Tennessee native, after frontier experience as sheriff of a Missouri county, became a Santa Fe trader. When Captain Benjamin Bonneville planned his expedition, made memorable by the pen of Washington Irving, he chose Walker as one of his assistants. On July 24, 1833, Walker and his party departed from the Grand River to explore the vast desert area west of the Great Salt Lake. Finding the headwaters of the Humboldt River, they followed it "until they ascertained that it lost itself in a great swampy lake," then crossed the Sierras by either Truckee Pass or the Walker River valley. Walker's party was the first to cross the Sierras from east to west. Going up the San Joaquin Valley, they found Walker's Pass, through which they journeyed on their return to Bonneville on the Bear River in Utah.

Those were but a few of the many fur traders who found their way to California. One of the principal results of the expeditions was the inauguration of regular commercial intercourse between the western States and California—the well-known St. Louis-Santa Fe-California trade. Westbound, this traffic, which followed the "Old Spanish Trail" west of Santa Fe, carried American goods from St. Louis: blankets, woolen goods, and silver. In return there came silks from China—brought to the coast by trading ships—and horses and mules for the markets of western and southern states.

Strongly impressed by what they saw in California, a sizeable sprinkling of the fur traders decided to join the burgeoning American colony there. This had grown steadily since the first agents of the hide and tallow traders took up residence; by the 1830s its members, although far outnumbered, were a force to be reckoned with in the province's economy and politics. Some attained unusual prominence: Abel Stearns who was known as the wealthiest rancher in Southern California, William Heath Davis who played a leading role in the world of commerce, J. J. Warner whose giant ranch near San Diego was to become a haven for overland emigrants from the United States, John Marsh whose ranch in the lower San Joaquin valley played a similar part in the northern migrations, William Leidesdorff whose business skills elevated him to the top rank of the mercantile world despite the fact that he was the son of a white father and a Negro mother, Thomas O. Larkin of Monterey whose manipulations hurried the separation of California from Mexico. Dwarfing all these in future prominence was John Augustus Sutter, a rotund adventurer who blended bluff, deceit, and ability so expertly that no man ranked higher in influence. Having fled his native Switzerland in 1834 to escape arrest for bankruptcy, Sutter reached Monterey in June, 1839, armed with so many letters of introduction and boasting such a winning personality that he had no trouble convincing Governor Juan Bautista Alvarado to grant him citizenship and a princely domain on the American River near the Sacramento River. There he supervised the force of Kanakas who accompanied him from Hawaii as they built New Helvetia— or Sutter's Fort as it came to be known—an adobe-walled enclosure large enough to hold a thousand men. Its eighteen-foot walls, broken by towering bastions and cannon-studded turrets, surrounded a whole village of warehouses, mills, shops, and homes. Over all Sutter ruled like a king. He wrote, "I was everything—patriarch, priest, father, and judge." He was also to be the welcoming host for hundreds of Americans who reached California during the first years of the overland migrations.

Now, however, Sutter and his fellow-compatriots were increasingly sources of alarm for Mexican officialdom. Rumors flew that they planned to overthrow the governor, seize San Francisco, deliver the province to the United States. These were the more alarming because the leading Mexican-Californians were growing increasingly restless under Mexican misrule; they talked openly of wanting a native son as governor and greater autonomy for their state. This dissatisfaction came to a climax in 1836 when a minor rebellion elevated Juan Bautista Alvarado, a native Californian, to the governorship. Alvarado's revolution might have had little lasting importance save that it had been won by a comic-opera crew of American sailors, Mountain Men, and misfits enlisted by Isaac Graham, a raw-boned Tennessean who lived near San Juan. Graham, Alvardo promised, would be handsomely rewarded by a land grant for his services.

Alvarado, however, perhaps mindful of what Americans had done in Texas, lost much of his enthusiasm for his American compatriots once he was in power. Crimination and recrimination resulted, in which Graham asserted that Alvarado owed his elevation to the governorship to him. In such an atmosphere Alvarado was particularly sensitive to reports that Americans were plotting a revolution. When rumors continued, in April, 1840, about 100 British and American residents who lacked passports were arrested on the charge of participating in a plot to overthrow the government. Graham was alleged to be the leader. After rough treatment and a hurried trial at Santa Barbara, he and fifty conspirators were sent to Mexico, where the intercession of British officials secured pardon or acquittal for them. The so-called Graham affair of 1840 was symptomatic of trouble to come.

That trouble was brought nearer during the 1840s as the spirit of manifest destiny opened the floodgates of American expansion westward. Inevitably the migration that peopled Oregon during those years was also directed toward California. No mass movement focused there as it had in the Willamette Valley; the threat of bloodshed and the uncertainty of land titles in a Mexican province deterred all but the most adventurous. Yet the few thousand who invaded the province over the California Trail would have won the region for the United States, whether or not a Mexican War was fought, just as had their cousins won Texas and Oregon. They, not the military commanders who conquered California during that war, were the true heroes of expansionism. They were no self-sacrificing martyrs compelled westward by an urge to win new lands for their country. Instead they were uprooted farmers from the Mississippi Valley, moving ahead to find cheap lands and a favorable market for their goods. The California pioneers, in other words, were responding to the same impulses that drove frontier settlers across the Alleghenies or beyond the Mississippi. It mattered not to them that Oregon was claimed by Great Britain or that Texas and California were owned by Mexico. Good land lay ahead, and they must have their share.

Their appetite for expansion was whetted by tales heard from fur trappers, or the published words of hide and tallow traders and travelers who wrote of California. It had been stimulated still more by a group of self-appointed boosters who seemed driven by a compelling instinct to enlighten their countrymen on California's potential greatness. These propagandists told the truth as they saw it; California was a land of unsurpassed agricultural potential, of untapped natural resources, of unrivaled climate. By coupling their descriptions of the province's riches with exaggerated tales of its easy-going population and defenseless condition, these writers were extending an unrefusable invitation to Americans to come and take possession.

They were drawn from every group that touched Mexican California during its early years. One of the first was a sea-otter trader, Captain William Shaler, whose journal published in 1808 was a paean of unrestrained praise. "The climate of California," he wrote, "generally is dry and temperate, and remarkable healthy. . . . Most of the animals of Europe have been naturalized in California, where they have increased to a great degree; it is said that more than 80,000 cattle run wild in the mountains in the south part of the peninsula. This climate seems to be particularly favorable to horses and mules, as they retain their strength and vigor till past thirty years. . . . Most of the fruits and vegetables of Europe have been naturalized in California, where they come to great perfection." He added that "at great expense and considerable industry the Spaniards have removed every obstacle out of the way of an invading enemy. . . . The conquest of this country would be absolutely nothing; it would fall without an effort to the most inconsiderable force." James Ohio Pattie, whose *Personal Narrative* appeared in 1831, wrote that California "is no less remarkable for uniting the advantages of healthfulness, a good soil, temperate climate and yet one of exceeding mildness, a happy mixture of level and elevated ground and vicinity to the sea."

Hall Jackson Kelley of Oregon fame was also an enthusiastic advocate of American settlement in California. Much of his report on Oregon, presented to Congress in 1839, was devoted to California and expressed the belief that "at no very distant day a swarming multitude of human beings will again people the solitude, and that monuments of civilization will throng along those streams whose waters now murmur to the desert." Thomas Jefferson Farnham, another Oregon booster, was a California visitor whose *Life and Adventures in California* outdid all competitors in its fulsome praise of the province. After asserting that "no country in the world possesses so fine a climate coupled with so productive a soil" he referred contemptuously to the "miserable people who sleep, and smoke and hum some tune of Castilian laziness, while surrounding nature is thus inviting them to the noblest and richest rewards of honorable toil."

Probably the most influential single bit of California propaganda was Richard H. Dana's *Two Years before the Mast*, first published in 1840. Dana, a Harvard student, came to California in January, 1835, on board the *Pilgrim*, a hide and tallow trader, and remained until May, 1836. He repeatedly visited every California port and spent four months at the hide-houses of San Diego. After describing in lyrical vein the remarkable attractions of the land, Dana remarked: "In the hands of an enterprising people, what a country this might be!" Then added, "Yet how long would a people remain so in such a country? If the 'California fever,' laziness, spares the first generation, it is likely to attack the second."

These early California popularizers were merely visitors to the province. But permanent residents also aided materially in advertising the territory. Prominent among them was Alfred Robinson, resident agent of Bryant, Sturgis & Company, whose *Life in California* was published in 1846. His many years in the province, his obvious happiness with life there, and his familiarity with the commercial prospects that he had done so much to develop, gave his words an authenticity that was particularly convincing to the ambitious. Other Americans corresponded regularly with friends in the East, writing in a manner to ensure publication of their letters in local papers.

At least one wrote directly for newspaper publication. Thomas O. Larkin had arrived in California in 1832, built up a successful mercantile business at Monterey, and in 1843 became the United States consul. So well known was he that when interest in California began to evince itself in the States, prominent newspapers made him their correspondent, among them the *Sun*, *Herald*, and *Journal of Commerce* in New York, and the *Advertiser* in Boston. So eminently practical were Larkin's letters that they constituted a sort of settlers' guide, with advice on the equipment required by the prospective emigrant, descriptions of California crops, and counsel as to the procedure "on arriving on the banks of the Sacramento."

American settlers attracted to California by "boosters" and propagandists after 1841 differed markedly from those who arrived earlier. While the majority coming before 1840 had arrived by sea, those in the 1840s followed the overland route. They came chiefly from the Mississippi Valley, were attracted to the interior valleys rather than the coastal areas, were interested in agriculture rather than commerce, and avoided the native Californians. Few married native women, so they constituted a group apart. They were less welcome than their predecessors, since their agricultural economy competed with that of the natives instead of supplementing it as did the services of foreign merchants.

The point of origin of the first organized overland migration to California was Platte County, on the extreme western frontier of Missouri. Enthusiasm had developed there largely because of reports of a returned California trapper, Antoine Robidoux, a considerate man of such local repute that his words would be unquestioningly believed. "A perfect paradise, a perpetual spring," was his evaluation, bolstered by a wealth of information on the rich soil, the fertile valleys, the fortunes to be made in farming. His listeners could scarcely wait to depart; the Platte County Western Emigration Society was formed at once to enlist recruits for the journey. Robidoux's talks to the gatherings of this society did nothing to dim their enthusiasm; when asked about the chills and fever in California—the ague, or malaria, that plagued the Mississippi Valley—he replied that "there never was but one man in California who had the chills. He was from Missouri and carried the disease in his system. It was such curiosity to see a man shake with the chills that the people of Monterey went eighteen miles into the country to see him." Robidoux's efforts were reinforced by letters of Dr. John Marsh, of Mt. Diablo, a onetime resident of western Missouri, which appeared in many of the local newspapers of the state. The California fever was further disseminated by the Western Emigration Society which spread propaganda throughout the Mississippi Valley. As a result members of the society signed a pledge late in 1840, binding themselves to meet at Sapling Grove in eastern Kansas in May, 1841, prepared for the great trek. Five hundred signatures were obtained within one month.

Alarmed by the prospective removal of so many people, merchants and landed proprietors of Platte County launched a campaign of slander upon

California designed to discourage the migration. This was so effective that when the appointed day came in May, 1841, only sixty-nine persons appeared at Sapling Grove, and of those only one had signed the pledge the previous fall. What an unlikely group they were! Not a single one had experienced life on the trail, nor did any one have the haziest notion of where they were going or how to get there. "We only knew that California lay to the west," one of them wrote. All were poor, with total assets no more than a hundred dollars. Although they did not know it, their one priceless asset was the presence of John Bidwell, whose sterling qualities and skill as a leader were to earn the title "Prince of the California Pioneers."

No Mountain Men or experienced western travelers were present to serve as an antidote to the geographical ignorance of the group. Nor was the prospect of a successful journey increased by the choice, for reasons of expediency, of John Bartleson of Jackson County, Missouri, rather than Bidwell, as commander of the company. A further complication resulted from the presence of a number of women and children. Fortunately, for the earlier stages of the trip, they fell in with two very helpful men, Thomas Fitzpatrick, the well-known trapper, and Father De Smet, who was en route to the Flathead Indians. From the great bend of the Missouri the party followed the route of the Oregon migrations to the Platte, Ft. Laramie, Independence Rock, and the Sweetwater to the Rockies, through South Pass, and the Green River Valley to Soda Springs near the present Pocatello, Idaho. There Fitzpatrick and De Smet took the trail toward Oregon with thirty-two emigrants, who preferred the known route to the Columbia to the virtually unknown trail to California. The remainder—thirty-two men, one woman, and one child—turned westward to cross the desert that had so tested the stamina of Jedediah Strong Smith and Joseph Reddeford Walker.

With nothing to guide them save the admonition to bear due west from Salt Lake they plunged into the unknown, abandoning their wagons in favor of pack animals to gain time. On September 23 they came to the Humboldt which they followed to the Sink. Bearing southwest, they probably passed Humboldt and Carson lakes and came to the Walker River where they arrived on October 16. When a short reconnaissance revealed that "the mountains were barely passable" some members advised a return to Ft. Hall before winter's snow set in, but when the question was put to a vote the majority favored continuing. With their supply of beef exhausted and surrounded by "naked mountains whose summits still retained the snows of perhaps a thousand years," they struggled until October 29, when they despaired of reaching California. But the following day they discovered a westward-flowing river, the Stanislaus, which they followed to the site of Sonora. So exhausted were they when they arrived in the San Joaquin Valley that they could not believe they were in the promised land itself. California, some thought, must be 500 miles away. Soon they found antelope in abundance, along with "ripe and luscious wild grapes." With the assistance of an Indian guide they arrived at the ranch of Dr. John Marsh, near Mt. Diablo, on

November 4, 1841. Thus ended the first overland migration to California after a journey of six months.

Other parties followed. Within a few weeks the Workman-Rowland Company of twenty-five Americans and New Mexicans arrived from Santa Fe. In 1843 Lansford W. Hastings brought a group of forty pioneers by way of Oregon. The same year Joseph B. Chiles, one of the Bidwell-Bartleson party of 1841, led a large company from Missouri. Dividing at Ft. Hall, one group, proceeding by way of Oregon, arrived in the Sacramento Valley in November; the other, following the trail blazed by Joseph Walker a decade before, entered the San Joaquin Valley by way of Walker Pass. In 1844 Andrew Kelsey led thirty-six emigrants to California, while in the same year the larger Stevens-Murphy party earned the distinction of being the first group to bring wagons over the entire route from Missouri to California. Rumor had it that the immigrants of 1845 would be numbered in the thousands, but actually the total for the year was about 250, a large part of whom were included in the Grigsby-Ide party, who followed the Humboldt-Truckee route.

The outbreak of the war with Mexico in April, 1846, reduced, but failed to stop, the emigrant tide to California. That year was notable in the history of the overland migrations for the tragic fate that befell the Donner party. Organized largely in Illinois by George and Jacob Donner, this group left Independence in the spring of 1846 almost 100 strong. As other parties joined them along the way, their number was increased to about 200. All went well as far as Ft. Bridger. There they divided, the larger group following the usual route by Ft. Hall, the remaining eighty-seven taking the little-known Hastings' Cutoff on the south side of Salt Lake. The larger company arrived in California without undue suffering. The smaller was not so fortunate. They reached the south side of Salt Lake at the cost of a month's time and much of the strength of men and animals. Autumn was already upon them when they started across the desert. Late in the fall they arrived at the foot of the Sierra-Nevada barrier in a completely disorganized condition. Torn by factional discord, they began climbing upward, only to have an abnormally early winter break upon them. Snowbound near the shores of Donner Lake, they suffered acutely from cold and famine. Of the eighty-nine persons who started from Ft. Bridger, only forty-five survived, and some only by resorting to cannibalism. Along with the sordidness, inefficiency, and jealousy that brought tragedy to the party, there was bravery and heroism of a high order, without which the disaster would have been even more appalling.

While settlers were finding their way to California, officials in Washington were not indifferent to the fate of the province. Official interest dated from the time Andrew Jackson was made aware of the region's wealth by Anthony Butler, the American representative in Mexico City. In the course of his devious intrigues, Butler submitted a plan to acquire California, along with Texas and New Mexico, by placing $500,000 at the disposal of a Mexican priest, who would purchase Santa Anna's consent to the cession. Although

Jackson rejected Butler's scheme of bribery, his desire to obtain California was strengthened by the glowing account of the country which he received from William A. Slacum, a purser in the United States Navy. He accordingly instructed Butler to negotiate with Mexico for the cession of California north of the 37th parallel. As this area was north of the Missouri Compromise line, Jackson's objective was the acquisition of San Francisco Bay rather than the extension of slave territory. Nothing came of the plan; and Jackson, now convinced of Butler's dubious character, replaced him with another man.

When, after the battle of San Jacinto, Santa Anna sought American mediation between Mexico and Texas, Jackson formulated a plan to offer Mexico $3,500,000 for that part of California north of the 38th parallel. At the same time he suggested to W. H. Wharton, the Texan minister at Washington, that Texas should include California within its boundaries. By acquiring the great harbor of San Francisco Bay, Jackson thought the infant Republic would disarm the hostility of northern commercial interests to annexation.

After the failure of Jackson's various plans, Van Buren found himself too engrossed with financial problems to direct his attention to California. The Tyler administration, however, was quick to reaffirm American interest in the region. With Waddy Thompson, minister to Mexico, the acquisition of California amounted to an obsession. Profoundly impressed by the climatic, commercial, forest, and agricultural resources of the province, he hoped North and South would join hands to gain possession before France or England stepped in. Tyler, as well as Daniel Webster, the secretary of state, shared Thompson's views and authorized him to negotiate for the purchase of San Francisco and adjacent areas. It was hoped that Mexico might be induced to cede the region on condition of American assumption of claims against the country which the Mexican government was unable to satisfy.

Meanwhile Webster and Tyler formulated a more elaborate plan, the Tripartite Agreement, to which Great Britain, Mexico, and the United States were to be parties. Mexico was to cede Upper California to the United States for a sum not precisely stipulated. A portion of the money would be used to satisfy American claimants against Mexico, while the balance would liquidate claims of British creditors. The Oregon boundary was to be at the Columbia River. Webster and Tyler believed the acquisition of California would disarm northern hostility to the annexation of Texas, while the line of the Columbia would mollify more rabid western expansionists. For a time the Tyler administration pursued the plan with vigor. But with Webster's resignation as secretary of state, and the growing realization that no Mexican administration would dare sell California, lest it be immediately overturned, the plan lapsed.

The situation within California greatly affected the next stage in the negotiations. The passing years demonstrated repeatedly that the authorities in Mexico City lacked both the military and naval power necessary to defend the province. Communication between the colony and the mother country, whether by land or by sea, was far from satisfactory. Government was almost nonexistent. The administration of justice had broken down, finances were in a chaotic state, life and property were utterly insecure. As this anarchical state of affairs became progressively worse in the early 1840s California residents, whether native or foreign, realized that a change was necessary. Some natives favored annexation to the United States; some a protectorate under Britain or France; some independence. Of the foreigners, the majority wished to join the United States, a minority favored independence, and English residents desired British control.

Such was the situation when James K. Polk entered the White House in 1845. Polk was an ardent expansionist. Manifest Destiny "was as deep-rooted in his convictions as the rigid Calvinistic theology to which he subscribed." As to the imminent separation of California from Mexico, Polk had no doubt. Nor was he any less certain as to its ultimate fate. It must be annexed to the United States.

Among the considerations influencing Polk in his resolve to acquire California was the fear of British designs. That the government in London was never sufficiently interested in California to support any of the schemes for annexation in no way diminished the influence such reports exercised upon officials in Washington. Most of them had sufficient foundation in truth to warrant acceptance by the government and public in this country. One of the first manifestations of British interest in California was the publication in 1839 of Alexander Forbes' *History of California*. Although Forbes, a British consul in Mexico, had never set foot on California soil, he obviously had reliable sources of information regarding conditions in the province. As he freely admitted, the purpose of his book was to foster British settlement in California. He suggested cession to liquidate the debt of $50,000,000 held by British bond-holders in Mexico, and proposed that the creditors, organized as a company, play the role in California of a second East India Company. Forbes' words were interpreted by the Baltimore *American* as indicating a British plot to acquire California as a base for commerce with China and the East Indies. In the early 1840s newspapers in all sections of the country voiced similar opinions with respect to British designs. Britain's plans were believed by the press to be so inimical to the United States as to call for frustration at any cost.

Public concern over British schemes in California were shared by American officials. Waddy Thompson, the American minister in Mexico, constantly stressed the British menace in 1842 and 1843. Duff Green, whom Calhoun sent to Mexico as his confidential agent, wrote in similar fashion in 1844. Wilson Shannon, Thompson's successor in Mexico, reported negotiations for the sale of California to Britain. Reports from California were no more reassuring than those from Mexico. The Hudson's Bay Company was invading the province. Its trappers were active in the region, it had established a regular trading post at San Francisco, and it was asking for substantial grants of land from Mexican officials. In numerous ways the employees of the company showed a disposition to settle permanently there. The friendly attitude of some native leaders toward the company did not serve to quiet American fears.

The fund of information respecting British plans and activities in California available to Polk when he took office was soon amplified. In May, 1845, the President's agent in Mexico, William S. Parrott, reported the strengthening of British naval forces in the Pacific, with a view of taking over California in the event of war between the United States and Mexico. A short time later Parrott advised Polk of the plan of a youthful Irish priest, Eugene McNamara, to colonize California with settlers from his own country. McNamara, Polk was told, had received a grant of 3,000 leagues for this purpose, which constituted "a new feature in English policy and a new method of obtaining California." Polk's most pointed warning came from Thomas O. Larkin, the American consul in Monterey. On July 10, 1845, Larkin called the state department's attention to the activities of the Hudson's Bay Company in California, the financial assistance of two British firms in Mexico to a plan for suppressing any revolution Americans might instigate in the province, and the appointment of a British agent, in the guise of a consul, to work secretly against American plans in California. The degree to which Polk's moves to acquire California were influenced by concern over British designs can be—and have been—easily exaggerated, for he was wise enough to realize that the jingoistic ambitions of a few English empire-builders did not constitute official policy. He was also aware, however, that those ambitions provided him an effective tool to manipulate American opinion toward favoring peaceful annexation, and Polk used that tool well.

Polk's plan for the peaceful acquisition of California was a dual one. On the one hand, he would offer to purchase it outright from Mexico. Late in the autumn of 1845, he selected John Slidell of New Orleans to conduct this important negotiation. Slidell's acquaintance with Mexican conditions and his knowledge of the Spanish language seemed to qualify him for the mission. Polk instructed him to purchase both New Mexico and California. He supposed the two provinces might be had for $15,000,000 or $20,000,000 but was prepared to pay $40,000,000 if necessary.

Confronted with this offer, the Mexican government was torn between two emotions. The chronic need for money, the precarious nature of Mexican control in California, and a desire to appease the government in Washington made it favorably disposed toward the sale. National pride, the opposition of Britain, traditional hostility to the United States, and the knowledge that any territorial cession would be the signal for a revolutionary overturn in Mexico made compliance hazardous. When Slidell embarked upon his errand, a revolution had only recently occurred in Mexico, in which General José Maria Herrera was elevated to the presidency as successor to the deposed Santa Anna. Herrera in turn was being carefully watched by aspirants to his high office. In this situation Slidell's mission was kept secret, as a means of protecting the Herrera regime. News of his coming, however, preceded Slidell to Mexico, together with the ugly rumor that he carried a handsome bribe for President Herrera. Herrera had two alternatives. He could receive Slidell, at the almost certain cost of a revolution; or he could refuse him, at great financial loss and at the risk of offending the United States.

Faced with this difficult decision, Herrera declined to receive Slidell, assigning technical reasons for his action. Actually his refusal was dictated by fear of being overthrown. Before Slidell departed from Mexico City, however, a bloodless revolution removed Herrera from office. When his efforts to open negotiations with the new regime were curtly rebuffed, he asked for his passport and returned to Washington, convinced of the utter futility of attempting to deal with a country whose government was so lacking in stability. Thus ended Polk's plan for the purchase of California.

Meanwhile the President placed another scheme in operation. In October, 1845, James Buchanan, secretary of state, appointed Thomas O. Larkin, since 1843 United States consul in California, the confidential agent of the state department. Larkin was to inform himself on the affairs of California, to "exert the greatest vigilance" to prevent a European country from obtaining control of it, and to encourage Californians to turn to the United States for aid and counsel. While the United States would not incite the Californians to rebel, Larkin might let them understand his country would play the part of protector if they should seek separation from Mexico. "Whilest the President," he was told, "will make no effort and use no influence to induce California to become one of the free and independent States of this Union, yet if the people should desire to unite their destiny with ours, they would be received as brethren, whenever this can be done, without offering Mexico just cause for complaint." To gain the good will of the Californians, to engineer this union, and to foil the designs of European powers, Larkin was to rely largely on his own discretion.

As Larkin interpreted his instructions, he was to pave the way for the peaceful acquisition of California. With characteristic energy and thoroughness, he addressed himself to the task assigned him. To prominent Americans in the province, who had married California women and accepted Mexican citizenship, he wrote soliciting aid in winning the support of native Californians. Included in this number was Abel Stearns, whom he made his assistant in the Los Angeles area. Among Californians he found little love for Mexico, but some were predisposed to depend upon Britain for aid. Those known to be sympathetic to the American program he encouraged to affiliate with various juntos, which carried on active propaganda in support of his case.

Larkin's campaign showed distinct indications of success. Some of the leading Californians rallied to his support, including General José Castro, who drew up a plan for "declaring California independent in 1847 or 48 as soon as a sufficient number of foreigners should arrive." No less hopeful were reports from the Los Angeles region. In the spring of 1846 it appeared to be but a short time before California would go the way of Texas—declare her independence and join the United States. Two events, however, intervened to spoil Larkin's plan of peaceful acquisition. One was the Bear Flag Revolt; the other the outbreak of war with Mexico.

The genesis of the Bear Flag Revolt is to be found in the restlessness of a handful of American landowners, traders, and trappers in the Sacramento Valley who found a leader in the enigmatic John C. Frémont. In the spring of 1845 Frémont, an official explorer for the United States, left St. Louis with a picked group which included some of the most notable of the Mountain Men, among them Kit Carson and Joseph Walker. They ascended the Arkansas River, penetrated the Colorado Rockies, crossed the Nevada desert to the Humboldt River, and explored the region between the river and Walker Lake. Then the party divided. Frémont, with fifteen men, advanced by the Truckee River to the summit of the Sierra Nevada Range, then descended the American River into the Sacramento Valley. Walker, with the remainder of the party, followed his old trail into the San Joaquin Valley. Failing to meet the Walker group at the appointed rendezvous, Frémont visited Thomas O. Larkin at Monterey, where he met General José Castro, then in command of the post. Although suspicious of the entrance of Frémont's armed band into the province without permission, Castro's fears were somewhat allayed by Frémont's assurance that his interest in California was entirely of a scientific nature. It was agreed the Americans might winter in California on condition they keep away from the coast settlements.

In February, 1846, Frémont was joined by the Walker party and went into winter quarters near San José. Shortly, however, he moved across the Santa Cruz Mountains into the Salinas Valley, in violation of his pledge to keep away from the coast. When General Castro ordered him to leave the province, he denounced the order as a breach of faith and an insult to himself and his country. He thereupon moved his quarters to Hawk's Peak, an eminence overlooking the surrounding plain, where he defied Castro. For three days the forces of Castro and Frémont faced each other without shedding blood. Frémont then quietly abandoned his camp and advanced slowly up the Sacramento Valley to Oregon. The incident at Hawk's Peak doomed Larkin's plan for peaceful acquisition of California. It outraged the Californians and encouraged the restless settlers in the valley in their contempt for provincial authorities.

Nor was Frémont's role as an unwelcome troublemaker at its end. On May 8, when he and his men were camped at Klamath Lake, word reached him that a messenger from Washington was on his trail. Frémont, with ten men, started south at once, and after an all-night ride met the dispatch-bearer, Lieutenant Archibald H. Gillespie, at dawn on May 9. What passed between them will probably never be known. Gillespie had been sent west by Polk bearing secret instructions for Larkin and a packet of letters from Senator Thomas Hart Benton to his son-in-law, Frémont. In the best cloak-and-dagger tradition he destroyed the dispatches after memorizing them, crossed Mexico disguised as a merchant, and reached Monterey on April 17, 1846, where the Larkin messages were delivered before he started on Frémont's trail. Whatever Gillespie told him, Frémont gathered his men at once and started for the Sacramento Valley. His later claim—that the letters from Benton ordered him to stir up a revolution—seems highly unlikely; Benton was no expansionist and would certainly not have violated inter-national protocol to that degree. More likely Frémont made his decision on the basis of what Gillespie told him of happenings at Monterey; a United States warship was in port, he reported, bearing news that war had begun between the United States and Mexico. What better way for Frémont to don a hero's garb than by winning California for the United States? He would be the Sam Houston of the Pacific!

That decision made, Frémont hurried to Sacramento where the wildest rumors were rife as to the cruel fate American settlers were about to suffer at the hands of the California authorities. The settlers naturally turned to Frémont and his Mountain Men for protection. Regardless of whether Frémont instigated the revolt which followed, as Larkin and others alleged, his presence gave the insurgents the fortitude necessary for action. On June 10, 1846, a group of settlers led by Ezekiel Merritt, one of the more reckless frontiersmen in the valley, seized some horses intended for use by General Castro. A few days later a larger band invaded the village of Sonoma and carried Mariano G. Vallejo, California's wealthiest and most conspicuous citizen, a prisoner to Sutter's Fort, despite his well-known support of Larkin's plan of peaceful acquisition.

During the next few days the revolt in the Sacramento Valley became general. Disturbing news fanned the flames: General Castro was marching north from San Francisco to retake Sonoma and punish the rebels. The moment of final decision had come. Meeting together in the Sonoma plaza on June 15, the rebels listened to a fiery proclamation from the pen of one of their leaders, raised an unbleached cotton flag bearing the crude likeness of a grizzly bear, and declared independence for the Republic of California. All of this was more than Frémont could resist. Ten days later he marched into Sonoma, shouldered himself into command of the army, and at the head of 134 Mountain Men and Bear Flaggers started southward to engage General Castro's defenders. Pausing only to kill three Mexicans to avenge the deaths of two Americans who had lost their lives (these were the sole casualties of the Bear Flag Revolt), Frémont reached Monterey on July 19, 1846, to learn that the Mexicans were fleeing southward toward the border.

More important news also awaited him there. In the harbor lay the seven vessels of the American Pacific fleet, while the Stars and Stripes floated over the plaza and in the streets all was talk of the war between Mexico and the United States that had begun three months earlier. The glory of winning California was to fall upon the unnamed soldiers who a year later battered their way into Mexico City and dictated a peace adding all the Southwest to the United States.

Conquest and Controversy
1846-1850

That the frontier surge which carried American pioneers across Texas and into the valleys of California could go on without protest was unthinkable. Those were Mexican territories. Won by the blood and sweat of early conquerors, they had been viewed for generations as essential barriers against aggressive intruders from the United States. Public opinion in Mexico solidly insisted the northern provinces never be surrendered; public opinion north of the border was almost as united in support of annexing California. This was the basis for the conflict which began in 1846 and ended only when a triumphant United States wrested from its beaten opponent not only California but the whole region north of the Gila and Rio Grande rivers.

The causes that impelled both nations to welcome the Mexican War were far from simple. Historians a generation ago who maintained the United States was goaded into an imperialistic war by greedy slaveholders seeking more territory for their peculiar institution ignored both the psychology of the American people and the attitude of their government. Every patriot who clamored for Mexico's provinces would have indignantly denied any desire to exploit a neighbor's territory. The righteous but ill-informed people of that day sincerely believed their democratic institutions were of such magnificent perfection that no boundaries could contain them. Surely a benevolent Creator did not intend such blessings for the few; expansion was a divinely ordered means of extending enlightenment to despot-ridden masses in nearby countries! This was not imperialism, but enforced salvation. So the average American reasoned in the 1840s when the spirit of Manifest Destiny was in the air.

The impact of those intellectual currents on the American government was demonstrated repeatedly in the attitude of presidents from Jackson to

513

Polk. All wanted the northern Mexican provinces, and Polk at least was determined to secure them, but he looked upon war as a last resort. He and his predecessors tried bribery, purchase, and intrigue before reluctantly deciding the stubborn Mexicans could be convinced only by force. No one could condone the greedy determination to appropriate a neighbor's territory, yet Polk's most hostile critics were forced to concede that he tried every peaceful method before taking up arms, and that his reasons for coveting California were more humanitarian than mercenary.

Nor could anyone deny that the United States had grievances against Mexico which in the eyes of both American and European statesmen seemed irreconcilable. Those grew out of Mexico's turbulent governmental system. Its people, newly emerged from centuries of despotic rule, were ill-prepared to shoulder the burdens of democracy; its elected leaders, inexperienced in the republican tradition, were ill-equipped to guide a nation along the path to security and order. Hence Mexicans chose to settle their usual political differences with swords rather than ballots; the "Centralist Party" with its aim of centralized authority under a dictatorial leader alternated with the "Federalist Party" with its platform of democratic federalism in revolting against the regime in power. The inevitable result was a postrevolutionary era of periodic uprisings, chronic bankruptcy, property destruction, and utter failure to meet either national or international obligations. Neither the United States nor the European powers viewed that confusion as the product of immaturity rather than design. They saw in the frequent Mexican revolutions signs of anarchy rather than necessary steps in the evolution of a workable government, the failure of Mexico to pay its debts indications of fraud rather than a normal breakdown of the credit structure, the destruction of foreign life and property signs of international lawlessness rather than an example of chaos usual in periods of change. The Mexicans were guilty of being poor neighbors; the Americans were equally at fault for failing to excuse the sins of their inexperienced friends below the border.

Differences between the two powers began to develop as soon as Mexico's independence was won. The United States faced the problem of Mexican inefficiency first when it asked the new nation to reaffirm the Spanish Treaty of 1819 establishing western boundaries for the Louisiana Purchase. For seven years American ministers battled official indifference before an agreement was reached, and four more years were needed before that was ratified by the Mexican legislature in 1832. The treaty provided for a joint commission to survey the line, but despite American pleading, Mexico failed to name its representatives until the understanding lapsed and had to be renegotiated. Not until pressure was brought on the Mexican president did the new nation finally cooperate. Equally annoying was Mexico's failure to agree on a treaty of commerce and amity. Two treaties drawn up during the 1820s were rejected by the Mexican Congress, and no settlement reached until 1831. For that whole time American business men clamored in vain for the right to trade in their neighbor's ports.

Still worse in American eyes was Mexico's failure to protect life and property during the frequent revolutions that racked the infant republic. One shocking example occurred in 1835 when twenty-two American citizens accused of plotting with a revolutionary were executed without proper trial. More lost property during the periodic uprisings, and their strenuous efforts to recover created one of the most troublesome differences between the two nations. Their claims, as was usual in such circumstances, were directed first against Mexican officials who gave them no satisfaction, then the American government was called upon for aid. President Jackson responded to the creditors' pressure in 1829 when he asked the United States minister in Mexico City to intercede in their behalf. For the next seven years every request for payment was met with "cold neglect," until the fiery Jackson was convinced that Mexico's attitude "would justify in the eyes of all nations immediate war." He might, he wrathfully told Congress, make the next demand for settlement from the deck of a warship.

Jackson retired from office before making good his threat, but his successors were just as aroused by continued Mexican delays. Not until 1839 did they goad that nation into accepting a mixed arbitration commission with power to determine the justice of all claims and the amount due each creditor. That body, made up of two representatives from each country and an impartial commissioner named by the King of Prussia, met in August, 1840, and after several months of deliberation awarded American claimants $2,026,000 to be paid in five yearly installments. Three payments were made before Mexico announced her inability to continue. Little wonder that both disappointed creditors and government agents operating in their behalf became convinced Mexico was an irresponsible menace in the congress of nations. That their sentiment was shared elsewhere was shown by the attitude of England and France, whose nationals also lost heavily during the Mexican outbreaks. Both adopted a more belligerent tone than the United States, France going so far in 1838 as to fight the so-called "Pastry War" to collect defaulted debts. President Polk was not alone in believing Mexico's behavior left no room for peaceful settlement.

The grievances, however, were not all on one side. Viewed through Mexican eyes, the relations between the two powers during the twenty years before 1845 constituted one continuous aggression on the part of the powerful northern neighbor, directed toward dismembering Mexico and annexing its northern provinces. The history of Texas seemingly provided perfect proof. First the United States had disclosed its intentions by trying to buy, then when Mexico refused to sell, disguised troops were sent to wrest the province away by force! Everyone remembered the aid given Texan revolutionists by Americans who crossed the border to fight at San Jacinto, the half-hearted gestures of federal troops to stop those illegal excursions, and the joking manner in which newspapers condoned the invasion of a neighboring power. The United States, all Mexico believed, stooped to such unneutral conduct only because it engineered the revolution that made Texas free.

Additional proof was apparently provided by the "Gaines Affair" which occurred while Texan independence was being won. Major-General Edmund P. Gaines was sent to the Louisiana-Texas border in 1836 to protect American settlements from marauding Indians. Although ordered to maintain strict neutrality, he violated his instructions when a band of fleeing raiders took refuge in Texas, pursuing them across the international boundary as far as Nacogdoches. There he stayed through the summer, while irate Mexican officials bombarded Washington with complaints that he was aiding the revolutionists and must be withdrawn. For a time war threatened before Gaines returned to his own soil in the autumn and the differences were patched up. From that time on every Mexican was sure that an official American military expedition openly aided the Texan rebels.

America's imagined role in Texas was bad enough, but even worse from the Mexican standpoint was its identical activity in California. To their horror they saw the whole process repeated there: the early efforts to purchase the region, the infiltration of armed frontiersmen, growing differences between the invaders and the Mexican officials, the first clashes, and finally open rebellion and the proclamation of independence. The parallels between the Texan and Californian revolutions were too clear to be ignored; this was design rather than coincidence! Piece by piece Mexico was being dismembered. Better to resist than wait until the whole nation was gobbled up by the colossus of the north. There was some basis for alarm, of course, and every Mexican believed unquestioningly the lesson learned from the sequence of events.

An episode in 1842 capped the climax. In the fall of that year an American naval commander, Commodore Thomas Ap Catesby Jones, heard while cruising off the Peru coast that a Mexican war had begun and that California was to be surrendered to England to keep it from his own nation. Without pausing to test the truth of the rumor, Jones sailed northward to Monterey which he reached on October 18, 1842. Although the port was "quiet, peaceful, and normally dilapidated," he sent a landing party ashore, seized the surprised Mexican defenders, ran up the Stars and Stripes, and proclaimed California annexed to the United States. Not until two days later did he make the embarrassing discovery he had captured a city belonging to a friendly power. Commodore Jones made the best of a bad situation by elaborate apologies, while the Mexican governor, not to be outdone in courtesy, tendered the Americans a "well and brilliantly attended" ball. Then, having satisfied protocol, Jones settled into a month-long wait to prevent reprisals against Americans living in Monterey. When he finally sailed away after thirty-two days all Mexico was convinced that the United States expected war and had briefed its officers on the strategy to follow as soon as hostilities began. Tension was high from that time on.

A peaceful settlement might still have been possible save for the political situation in Mexico where the Centralists were plotting to oust the moderate Federalist, José de Herrera, who had held the presidency since 1843. Their weapon was public hatred of the United States. Herrera believed that international harmony would be hurried if Mexico resumed diplomatic relations with its northern neighbor—broken since 1836—but made the mistake of initiating a move toward that end just as Texas was being annexed in the spring of 1845. This was proof to Mexicans that the imperialistic colossus of the north was bent on dismembering their republic. Here was a situation made to order for the Centralists, who bombarded the nation with anti-Herrera propaganda during the summer, charging that he was truckling to American demands. Refusing to be overawed, Herrera persuaded the republic's congress in October, 1845, to declare that a representative from Washington would be welcomed in Mexico City "to settle the present dispute in a peaceful, reasonable and honorable manner"—phrasing generally interpreted to mean all issues dividing the two nations.

President Polk responded by hurrying John Slidell southward with instructions to purchase California and assume all claims against Mexico in return for an international boundary following the Rio Grande River to El Paso. His was a futile journey, for by the time he arrived in Mexico City in December 1845, the annexation of Texas had so enflamed public opinion that President Herrera did not dare open diplomatic relations with the United States, knowing that to do so would give the Centralists leverage to oust his party from power. Herrera's gesture accomplished nothing. On the very day that Texas was entering the Union a Centralist army under Mariano Parades stormed into the Mexican capital, drove Herrera into exile, and in a bloodless revolution seized control of the government. Slidell watched these events with mounting anger at his rebuff. "Be assured," he wrote Polk, "that nothing is to be done with these people until they shall have been chastised."

When Polk received Slidell's message on January 12, 1846, he knew that war was inevitable. If he had qualms of conscience at his role in precipitating the conflict he might have spared his doubts, for the situation in Mexico had brought that nation to the brink of conflict, whatever the United States might have done. Ever since the annexation of Texas the war spirit had flamed there, and with it a general acceptance of the political philosophy of the Centralists. When that party assumed control of the state with the overthrow of Herrera Mexico was committed to humbling the United States, and its leaders acted accordingly. The revolutionary junta that assumed control named as president the victorious general, Mariano Parades, who appointed as his secretary of war Juan N. Almonte, an avowed proponent of immediate hostilities. Mexico would fight, he declared, until Texas was restored to its true owners. Almonte began preparing at once, mobilizing troops, reorganizing the army, and unleashing a barrage of anti-American propaganda that would prepare public opinion. War existed in everything but name.

The decision of the Parades government to initiate hostilities was far more logical than it appears in retrospect. Mexican officialdom was con-

vinced that the nation would have powerful allies; the United States and
Britain were about to go to war over Oregon, while France had shown signs
of friendship that could easily be translated into aid. Geography was also
on Mexico's side. As Mexican forces marched northward across Texas
toward New Orleans and Mobile they would be aided by Indians anxious
to recover their lands and by slaves seeking freedom from bondage, forming
a giant army of conquest that would subdue Washington itself. If, on the
other hand, an American army did invade Mexico it would be stopped by
the arid deserts, barren mountains, and difficulty of obtaining supplies over
an ever-lengthening supply line. Such an invasion was unlikely, however,
for Mexicans were sure that northerners, and particularly abolitionists,
would refuse to support a conflict that would add more slave territory to the
Union. This would stifle the war effort; even a revolution against Polk was
possible.

Mexican Centralists were confident they could win a war even without
internal rebellion in the United States. They knew that their army was five
times as large as the American; they were also sure that man-to-man any
Mexican soldier could beat any American soldier, and a good many foreign
observers agreed with them. Had not Mexico been in almost continuous
state of war since 1821, training a whole generation in combat techniques?
Its military force was well disciplined, well armed, and thoroughly experienced; some Europeans rated it the best in the world in both manpower and
equipment. The United States, by contrast, would have to depend on an
untrained volunteer army and a poorly trained militia. Even such a well-
informed observer as the correspondent of the *London Times* was sure that
they would be no match for the Mexican soldiers. If the United States was
so strong, Centralist politicians asked each other, why had it failed to conquer
Canada in 1812? Why had Polk tried to buy California rather than taking it
by force? The United States was so torn by factionalism and so ill-prepared
that the Mexicans did not need to divide and conquer; the enemy was so
divided that conquest would be easy.

So the Mexicans reasoned, and every step in their reasoning brought
them nearer conflict. Little wonder that by the fall of 1845 public opinion
(ably fanned by Centralist propaganda directed against the Federalists) saw
war as not only inevitable but welcome. Polk was still seeking a peaceful
solution in August when circulars south of the Rio Grande commanded army
officers to recruit troops to wage war against the United States. "The time
to fight has come," President Parades told his people. "Soldiers! A rapa-
cious and grasping race have thrown themselves upon our territory and dare
to flatter themselves that we will not defend." Mexico wanted war by the
end of 1845, and Mexico was determined to have war.

The American people were not so sure, for they were of two minds.
Scientific studies, at that time, held the Indian incapable of assimilation, a
fact that made some politicians hesitate about taking Mexican lands. A
majority in the northeastern states were opposed because they looked upon

the struggle as a southern aggression to win more "slave pens," and feared the creation of new agricultural states when their own interests were industrial. The Massachusetts legislature reflected the section's attitude when it branded the war as "hateful in its objects . . . wanton, unjust and unconstitutional." Those sentiments were also expressed in the South and West, although there opposition came from Whig politicians. One told Congress the Mexicans should greet American troops with "bloody hands," and welcome them to "hospitable graves"; Abraham Lincoln gained momentary fame through his "Spot Resolutions" asking Polk to show the spot where American blood was spilled on "American soil." Wealthy southern planters were also inclined to distrust a war which might precipitate a controversy over slavery. For the most part, however, those two sections were the principal supporters of the war. The extent of sectional feeling was illustrated by the fact that the densely populated Northeast furnished only 7,930 volunteers, the expansionist West almost 40,000 and the South 21,000. The Northeast, the nation's richest region, also refused to aid the war financially.

Some Americans might be reluctant patriots, but the situation was beyond their control. After Mexico refused to receive John Slidell there was no turning back; the Centralists were in control there, and they wanted war. President Polk realized this, and realized also that the United States would benefit by maneuvering Mexico into striking the first blow. Hence on January 13, 1846 (the day after receiving news of Slidell's rejection), he ordered a detachment of troops under General Zachary Taylor into the area between the Nueces and Rio Grande rivers. This was the red flag to the bull, for while Texas claimed the whole area south to the Rio Grande, Mexico's claims to the Nueces boundary were based on far better authority. Polk, in effect, had ordered the occupation of a barren section of northern Mexico. For the next three weeks Taylor and his men waited there, hoping to goad the Mexicans into an attack, while tension mounted steadily. Polk succumbed to the pressure first. When Slidell reached Washington on May 8, 1846, with tales of his inhospitable treatment at the hands of the Mexicans, of war fever among the populace, and of the government's determination to fight, the President decided the time for action had come. The next day he called his cabinet together and announced his decision to recommend war to Congress, basing the demand on Mexico's refusal to meet its financial obligations, receive Slidell, or settle disputes by peaceful means. All agreed the step justified save George Bancroft, secretary of the navy, who advised delay until the Mexicans committed an act of aggression. When this suggestion was overruled, Polk left the meeting to begin work on a war message.

The message was never written, for electrifying news reached the capital that very night (May 9, 1846). A Mexican force under General Mariano Arista had crossed the Rio Grande from Matamoros on April 25, ambushed an American patrol, and killed or wounded sixteen men. This was the excuse Polk was waiting for. Hurriedly he drafted a new message which was read to Congress on May 11. The long-standing grievances between the two powers were scarcely mentioned in that amazing document. "Now, after reiterated menaces," Polk told Congress, "Mexico has passed the boundary of the United States, has invaded our territory and shed American blood upon the American soil. She has proclaimed that hostilities have commenced, and that the two nations are now at war. As war exists, and, notwithstanding all our efforts to avoid it, exists by the act of Mexico herself, we are called upon by every consideration of duty and patriotism to vindicate with decision the honor, the rights and the interests of our country." Two days later Congress declared that "by the Act of the Republic of Mexico a state of war exists," authorized the President to raise an army of 50,000 men, and appropriated $10,000,000 for military purposes.

Like it or not, the United States and Mexico were at war. The first blow was struck by the Mexican commander, General Mariano Arista, who on May 8, 1846—five days before war was officially declared—threw his army across the Rio Grande in the hope of opening the road to Louisiana by defeating Taylor. The American commander, too canny to be caught napping, met the invaders in two desperately fought battles at Palo Alto and Resaca de la Palma, defeating them in both and driving them back across the river. What Polk chose to define as American soil was freed of the enemy. The President could turn to a long-range plan for the defeat of Mexico.

Two objectives underlay the strategy mapped by Polk and his military advisers. One was to win the northern Mexican provinces. On the day war was declared he told his cabinet: "In making peace with our adversary, we shall acquire California, New Mexico, and other further territory, as an indemnity for this war, if we can." He planned to secure the territories by a joint operation; an army—large enough to conquer but small enough not to alarm the conquered—would march westward through Santa Fe into southern California where it would join a second sea-borne force in the conquest of that province. The second objective was to end the struggle quickly. For this another army would move south against Mexico City where, Polk hoped, the terms of surrender would be dictated. He believed the joint campaign would bring the war to a speedy close, an object greatly desired partly because a lengthy contest would prey on his conscience and lessen his popularity, partly because any prolonged war would play into the hands of the Whigs. Both ranking generals—General Zachary Taylor and General Winfield Scott—were members of that party, and Polk was determined to keep either from entering the White House as a military hero. "A peace," said his secretary of war, "must be conquered in the shortest space possible."

The "Army of the West," which was assigned the task of winning New Mexico and southern California, was placed in the capable hands of Colonel Stephen W. Kearny who assembled his force at Ft. Leavenworth on the Missouri River in the spring of 1846. His was a strange assortment of soldiers: 300 regular dragoons, about 1,000 Missouri frontiersmen, some 500

Mormon youths recruited from the camp at Council Bluffs where Brigham Young was preparing to lead his people westward, enough miscellaneous recruits to bring the total to 2,700 men. They set out from Ft. Leavenworth on June 30, 1846, across the nearly 800 miles of plains and deserts that led to Santa Fe. For days they were without adequate water or food, but the hardened plainsmen were so accustomed to hardships they frequently out-distanced the cavalry. By August 13, when almost within sight of Santa Fe disquieting news reached Kearny: 3,000 Mexicans lay in wait along the rim of a narrow canyon through which they must pass.

Rather than risk a frontal attack, Kearny resorted to diplomacy. James Magoffin, a wealthy Santa Fe trader taken along for just such an emergency, was sent ahead to plead with his good friends, the New Mexican officials, not to risk disaster by opposing the Americans. The governor of New Mexico, Manuel Armijo, a mountain of a man who had proven himself a capable administrator by surviving as governor since 1837 but whose tastes ran to food and commerce rather than fighting, recognized the inevitable. Hence he was easily persuaded by Magoffin to flee southward with most of his troops, leaving the city undefended. Five days later Kearny's army marched unmolested into Santa Fe. There he issued a proclamation which openly avowed the American intention to annex New Mexico, promised the citizens a democratic form of government as a prelude to territorial organization, and named a governor to administer the province. The liberal pronouncements won over most New Mexicans so completely that a detachment of troops which marched through southern New Mexico found the people generally loyal to the United States.

Kearny could turn to the next step in his program. He divided his army into three parts. One was left to administer New Mexico. That task proved difficult when a rebellion broke out in January, 1847, under the leadership of a disgruntled Mexican official who had failed to receive the extensive estates promised him for helping surrender the province. Not until scaling ladders were used to drive the rebels out of the adobe church at Taos was the uprising put down. A second small army of nearly 300 Missouri volunteers under Colonel A. W. Doniphan started south to take the Mexican city of Chihuahua. The undisciplined, tumultuous, profane crew of frontiersmen stormed into El Paso after defeating a Mexican force four times its size, crossed the deserts of northern Mexico, overwhelmed the 4,000 defenders of Chihuahua, and on March 2, 1847, took formal possession of that city of 14,000 inhabitants. Doniphan then turned his column of self-styled "ring-tailed roarers" eastward to Parras where they waited the army moving against Mexico City.

In the meantime the third segment of the force that took New Mexico, 300 mounted dragoons under Kearny, left Santa Fe on September 25, 1846, for California. Moving swiftly down the Rio Grande and westward toward the Gila River, they soon met a small party of scouts led by the famous Mountain Man, Kit Carson, bearing the welcome news that California was already won. Kearny, delighted at the prospect of a peaceful journey, sent most of his men back to Santa Fe and, pressing Kit Carson into service as a guide, started west with only 100 companions.

California had fallen before the assault of the United States Navy and the Bear Flaggers. The Pacific squadron which helped win victory was cruising off the coast of Mexico when word arrived on June 7, 1846, of the declaration of war. Its commander, Commodore John D. Sloat, acting under instructions dated a year earlier, sailed at once to Monterey which was occupied without much resistance on July 7. A few days later San Francisco was taken and California formally annexed to the United States. Word was hurried north to the Bear Flaggers who were only too glad to join in the conquest. Captain Frémont, with 150 mounted men, started south at once to join Commodore Robert F. Stockton, who had replaced the less-aggressive Commodore Sloat, at San Francisco. During the next few weeks the two officers commanded the bloodless occupation of northern California, while the Mexican General José Castro, knowing his cause was lost, fled southward.

The conquest of southern California proved almost as easy. Frémont and his "California company of mounted riflemen" were sent to San Diego by sea to cut off the retreating remnants of the Mexican army while Stockton followed more slowly along the coast. General Castro, caught between the two forces, elected to fight just south of Los Angeles. There he met a "gallant sailor army" which was landed by Commodore Stockton at San Pedro and marched overland to the enemy's positions. Before the Americans reached the battle ground the ill-trained Mexicans broke ranks to retreat pell-mell toward the border. On August 13, 1846, Frémont and Stockton entered Los Angeles where, four days later, the commodore formally annexed California to the United States with Frémont as its military governor.

The province proved easier to take than to hold. No sooner had the two commanders started north than Californians at Los Angeles rose in rebellion against the harsh military rule of subordinates left to control the city. By September, 1846, all southern California was in the hands of the rebels who could field an army of some 200 ill-equipped troops. Once more Stockton and Frémont hurried south, with Stockton going first and Frémont following more slowly by land. The naval force which landed at San Diego found itself so outclassed by the insurgents that only the timely arrival of Colonel Kearny from New Mexico saved the day. After fighting his way into San Diego by defeating the revolutionists at nearby San Pasqual, Kearny joined Stockton in a successful attack on Los Angeles where they waited the coming of Frémont. The rebels were waiting too, but with less heart, for their ammunition was nearly exhausted and their antiquated firearms beyond repair. When the blustering army officer appeared with an unruly following of about 400 Bear Flaggers, Mountain Men, and Indians they decided surrender was safer than battle. By mid-January, 1847, the counter-rebellion was over. A month later orders from Washington installed Kearny as governor of the new territory.

The conquest of California and New Mexico gave the United States Mexico's northern provinces only six months after war was declared. There remained the task of "conquering the peace" by inflicting such a decisive defeat that possession could be permanent. The task fell to General Zachary Taylor, whose army was poised on the banks of the Rio Grande ready to begin the decisive march on Mexico City. After spending several months whipping his raw recruits into shape, Taylor launched the invasion on August 19, 1846, with the city of Monterrey as his first objective. The town of Matamoros, just south of the river, fell without serious resistance, and Monterrey followed after three days of desperate fighting (September 21-23, 1846). There the Americans paused for eight weeks before advancing to Buena Vista where they were joined by a smaller force of Texas volunteers under General John E. Wool who had captured Monclova and Parras as they marched south. The combined armies settled down to wait the arrival of

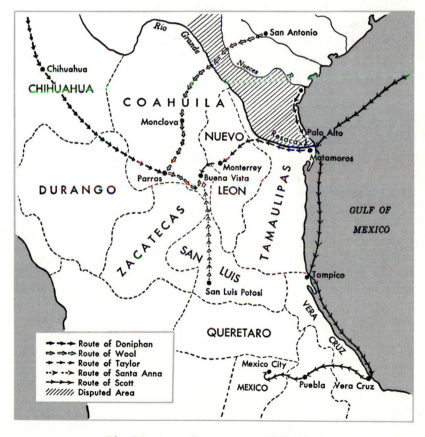

The Mexican Campaigns, 1846–1847

the 15,000 Mexicans General Santa Anna was leading northward. The expected attack came on February 22, 1847, when the Mexican force was hurled against the strong American position. For two days the battle raged before Santa Anna, despairing of dislodging the invaders from their mountain ravines, ordered a retreat.

This Battle of Buena Vista left the road to Mexico City open, but General Taylor was denied the glory of capitalizing on his triumph. By that time President Polk was growing alarmed at the mounting popularity of "Old Rough and Ready"; if Taylor was allowed to capture Mexico City the Whigs would be supplied with a military hero for the election of 1848. Hence the invasion plans were changed. The enemy capital would be taken, the President decided, not from the north but by an amphibious operation under General Winfield Scott, a pompous Whig with no popular appeal.

Sailing from New Orleans, General Scott's force landed just south of Vera Cruz on March 9, 1847. Guns were dragged ashore to begin an eighteen-day siege which ended when the strongly defended city capitulated. The road to Mexico City which lay ahead was a tortuous one, running steeply upward through mountain passes where Santa Anna with his defenders were prepared to resist every step. When General Scott reached the first canyon, the Cerro Gordo, he recognized the impossibility of a frontal attack and sent a subordinate, Captain Robert E. Lee, to seek an alternate route. When Lee returned with news of a rough woodland path around the Cerro Gordo, the main force was sent ahead at once, while a small party stayed behind to distract the Mexicans. Santa Anna learned of the maneuver in time to withdraw before being surrounded, but the pass was won.

Fighting constant small engagements, the invading army reached the large city of Puebla on May 15, 1847. There Scott, knowing the impossibility of keeping his supply lines open in a mountainous country where guerrilla bands operated freely, cut himself off from the coast and moved boldly ahead with 10,000 men, living off the country. Fighting upward over the rim of towering peaks that surrounded the Mexican plateau, the Americans burst at last into the lake-studded Valley of Mexico which sheltered their objective. By the end of August, 1847, they were at the gates of Mexico City.

That long-sought prize seemed almost impregnable. The Mexican capital stood in the midst of an extensive marsh that could be crossed only on stone causeways, all of them easily defended. Had its guardians chosen to resist they could have held off Scott's legions for weeks, if not forever. Instead they had no stomach for the task. The city *ayuntamiento* was dominated by members of the Federalist Party who saw in Santa Anna's dictatorial ambitions a greater threat to their freedoms than an American triumph. This conclusion reached, officials called off all preparations for the defense of the city, leaving it ready for the plucking. Of this the attackers were completely unaware; they knew only that dominating the two approaches to the city open to them was the towering hill of Chapultepec, whose precipitous walls bristled with soldiers. On September 13, 1847, the yelling Americans stormed over this barrier, then out upon the causeways, where pillars supporting aqueducts afforded some protection. Leaping from post to post in a manner reminiscent of Indian warfare, they reached the fortified city, burrowed under its stone walls, and on the evening of September 13 swept into its narrow streets. For three more days the defenders held out, contesting each foot in bitter hand-to-hand fighting, before Santa Anna ran up a white flag on September 17, 1847. The Mexican War was over; there remained the task of dictating the peace to a conquered people.

President Polk had anticipated the necessity. When General Scott invaded Vera Cruz he was accompanied by the chief clerk of the state department, Nicholas P. Trist, whose instructions authorized an immediate peace when Mexico City was taken. From the first Trist and Scott were at sword's point; the general resented the appointment of a "clerk" to carry on negotiations which he felt were within his own realm, while Trist's arrogant nature and blundering conduct did not ease the situation. For several weeks they kept up an angry correspondence—enlivened by one thirty-page note from Trist—and besieged their Washington superiors with such abusive messages that the President was finally forced to intercede. His decision was based on more than personal pique; Trist revealed in his negotiations before the armistice that he was willing to make such generous boundary concessions to the Mexicans that the state of Texas would have been dismembered. After one letter from Trist that lectured him on how to run the war and collect the tariff, a letter that Polk described as "arrogant, impudent, and very insulting to the government, and even personally offensive," his troublesome agent was recalled on October 6, 1847.

By the time news of the dismissal reached Mexico the whole situation had changed. Trist and Scott had patched up their differences and were bosom friends; Mexico City was in American hands; Santa Anna had abdicated as president; all was in confusion. Scott, fearful that unless peace were made at once all Mexico would be plunged into a state of anarchy, convinced Trist to violate his instructions and proceed with the peace treaty. This decision was as ill-conceived as it was audacious, for the Mexican government was in no danger of overthrow, the Mexican people were going about their business with revolution far from their minds, and ample time existed for Trist to communicate with Washington for updated instructions.

His ineptitude cost the United States heavily when he met the Mexican delegates at the nearby city of Guadalupe Hidalgo. His instructions were clear: the Rio Grande boundary for Texas, the acquisition of New Mexico and California, the right to transit across the Isthmus of Tehuantepec, payment of an indemnity to Mexico of no more than $15,000,000 and hopefully much less. All were violated by Trist who seemed bent on giving the Mexicans even more than they asked. He made no effort to secure access rights over the Isthmus of Tehuantepec or Baja California, ignored orders to run a boundary for New Mexico that would secure a railroad route along the

Gila River valley, surrendered American access to the Gulf of California by accepting the Gila-Colorado River boundary, failed to outlaw Mexican land grants made since May, 1846, as he was told (thus benefiting only a few speculators), and neglected to include a stipulated clause to the effect that the United States would "demand delivery" of Mexican citizens held by Indian tribes, an omission that later cost the nation $31,000,000. Trist's worse sin was to grant the full $15,000,000 indemnity instead of the lesser sum that could have been negotiated, and to commit his government to paying its own citizens $3,250,000 in claims against the Mexican government. In all his pig-headed refusal to cooperate with Polk meant that the victor in the Mexican War paid $22,140,053 in indemnity and claims, $31,000,000 in subsequent claims by Mexico, and $100,000,000 in military costs in return for 592,201 square miles of land—hardly a bargain for a winning nation.

In still another way Mexico benefited from Trist's refusal to resign. The terms he accepted were those acceptable to the United States at the beginning of the contest; in the year and a half that followed opinion in the United States changed radically. The ease with which American armies won victories apparently demonstrated to Americans something long suspected: the Mexicans were a misgoverned, misdirected people entirely unfit to develop the rich country where they lived. Hence the manifest destiny of the United States was clearly to annex all Mexico, that its downtrodden peons might have the advantage of democracy and enlightened rule! The demand gained weight with each passing month of the war. The New York *Evening Post* spoke for multitudes when it insisted Polk should never "resign this beautiful country to the custody of the ignorant cowards and profligate ruffians who have ruled it for the last twenty-five years." So did the Washington *Union* when it suddenly discovered Mexico was "a paradise blessed with every variety of climate, every capacity of soil, and almost every species of fruit and flower on the face of the earth."

As popular sentiment for the acquisition of all Mexico gained strength, politicians leaped upon the band wagon. One New York senator toasted an American Union "embracing the whole of the North American continent," and at least two of Polk's cabinet members—Robert J. Walker of Mississippi and James Buchanan of Pennsylvania—openly favored taking all Mexico. Their influence on the President was such that had Trist withdrawn gracefully the new commissioner would probably have insisted on complete annexation. Once the treaty was drafted, however, Polk did not dare repudiate his agent. Reluctantly, he submitted the document to the Senate for ratification, despite the "exceptional conduct of Mr. Trist." After a few minor amendments the peace party carried the day over the total-annexationists; on March 10, 1848, the treaty was accepted by a vote of thirty-eight to fourteen. Thus was the peace confirmed which had been "negotiated by an unauthorized agent, with an unacknowledged government, submitted by an accidental President to a dissatisfied Senate."

The expansionists who professed disappointment at the failure to take all Mexico could take solace as they surveyed the history of the years between 1845 and 1848. The territorial gains of that brief period were enough to satisfy all but the most rabid advocates of Manifest Destiny. The United States, by acquiring Texas, Oregon, the Southwest, and California, added 1,200,000 square miles to its domains, virtually doubled its territory and extended its boundaries to the Pacific. Only one more step was needed to complete the nation's expansion. The southern border established by the Mexican Treaty—along the Gila and Colorado rivers—was found unsatisfactory when transcontinental railroad routes were surveyed during the 1850s. To provide a right-of-way south of the Gila, the United States minister at Mexico City, James Gadsden, in December, 1853, arranged to buy an additional triangle of land for $10,000,000. The Gadsden Purchase gave the nation the continental boundaries of today.

The expansionist spree was not to pass without a sobering aftermath. For two decades before the Mexican War the spectre of sectional conflict increasingly haunted the United States as North and South drifted apart over the slavery issue; now the Treaty of Guadalupe Hidalgo brought the American people face to face with the whole terrifying question. What should happen to the lands acquired from Mexico? Should they be thrown open to slavery, or should Congress ban the southern institution there? Should they be divided into slave states to bolster the waning political strength of the South, or made into free states to increase the North's congressional supremacy? Four years of bitter debate, four years of frayed nerves and flaring tempers that brought the nation close to war, were needed before those pressing queries were temporarily answered.

The controversy was touched off by David Wilmot, a Pennsylvania Democrat who sat in the House of Representatives. Casting about for some means to regain local popularity lost by supporting his party's low tariff measures, Wilmot decided an appeal to his constituents' antislavery sentiments would be most effective. An appropriation bill before the House soon after war began gave him his opportunity. Rising to the occasion in August, 1846, he moved a proviso that slavery be forever barred from all lands obtained from Mexico. The Wilmot Proviso ended one era in the history of the United States. Gone was the day when cautious politicians could keep the slavery issue below the surface in their anxiety to preserve the Union and national parties. Southern Whigs and Democrats combined to denounce the Proviso as a gross invasion of sacred rights, while northerners of both parties united in its praise. From Congress the argument spread to the state legislatures, to street corners where angry men shouted insults or exchanged blows, to country stores where cracker-barrel antagonists pleaded for their sections, to farm gatherings, and to the teeming streets of cities. Everywhere men and women argued the merits of slavery with a conviction that boded ill for continued national harmony.

From the welter of words emerged a half-dozen solutions to the problem propounded by Wilmot's proviso. Northern extremists insisted Congress could and should bar slavery from the western territories. They maintained the legislature's constitutional power was adequate, for the Constitution authorized it to "make all needful rules and regulations respecting the territory or other property belonging to the United States." Moreover, they said, Congress was prohibited from placing more Negroes in bondage—and this would be the result of opening more land to slavery—by the Fifth Amendment forbidding the United States to deprive any person of his liberty without due process of law. Southern fire-eaters, on the other hand, held the government had no power to ban slavery in the West. The territories, they insisted, belonged not to the United States but to the states united; Congress simply administered each territory for its real owners—the states— as an attorney might administer property for a group of partners. Hence the final decision on the use of any territory rested with the states. If Mississippi decided its citizens could take their slave property into New Mexico, Congress had no legal right to interfere. Those were the extremist parties in the sectional debate, one demanding congressional action, the other insisting the legislature had no right to act.

Moderates on both sides of Mason and Dixon's line, seeking a solution that would avoid the dangerous constitutional issue, evolved other answers. Southerners of this hue favored extending the Missouri Compromise line of 36°30' to the Pacific, realizing this would give them most of the plundered Mexican lands for slavery. Northerners countered by insisting international law settle the issue; under accepted doctrine the region secured from Mexico, having been free under its former owner, would remain free until Congress acted specifically to allow slavery there. Other sincere compromisers, North and South, proposed throwing the whole question into the lap of the Supreme Court with the nation pledged to accept any decision, or favored "squatter sovereignty" to decide whether slaves could be taken into New Mexico and California. Proponents of the latter view came largely from the western border states, for that method—allowing settlers in each territory to decide whether they wanted slavery or freedom—appealed to the democratic instincts of the frontier.

The sharp division of opinion fed the flames of controversy but precluded any settlement before the election of 1848 offered an opportunity to test popular opinion. As usual in such a period of crisis, however, the people were not given a chance to express themselves; leaders of both parties were so anxious to keep northern and southern wings united they declined to meet the issue squarely. The Whigs, whose principal strength was in the North, nominated General Zachary Taylor, a Louisiana slave-holder, and went before the country without a platform, hoping that their glamorous candidate would attract enough southern votes to win him the office, and knowing that any statement of principles would offend one or the other of the strange bedfellows who made up the party. The Democrats, who looked to the South for support, chose a colorless northerner from Michigan, Lewis Cass, and in their platform avoided all mention of the one problem absorbing national attention. Only a minor party, the Free-Soil Party, took a definite stand in the election. Its members—abolitionists, northern Whigs, and Barnburning Democrats (so-called by enemies who accused them of being as anxious for reform as the Dutch farmer who burned down his barn to rid it of rats)—nominated Martin Van Buren and went before the nation with a platform pledge of "Free soil, free speech, free labor and free men" designed to appeal especially to the homestead-loving, slavery-hating West. Van Buren failed to win any electoral votes, but his Democratic followers in New York supported him so enthusiastically the state went Whig, and with it the nation. The result was no mandate on slavery; Cass carried eight free and seven slave states, Taylor seven free states and eight slave.

Zachary Taylor entered the White House in the spring of 1849 with few commitments and fewer ideas. He was a simple soldier, distrustful of politicians and inclined to view the slavery controversy as a teapot tempest that could best be quieted by compromise. If Congress had been able to pass any middle-of-the-road measure he would gladly have affixed his signature, but Congress wrangled instead, and while the argument went on the situation changed abruptly. Overnight the question of slavery in the Southwest was lifted from the realm of the academic to the point where a solution was imperative.

Workmen who discovered flakes of dull yellow metal in a mill race they were constructing on the lands of John A. Sutter were responsible. By mid-March of 1848 the exciting news was out, despite Sutter's efforts to keep the find a secret, and by mid-May San Francisco was deserted as the nation's greatest gold rush began. The East learned of the discovery in September, 1848, when alarmed reports arrived from Thomas O. Larkin, the consul at Monterey, accompanied by a little box of dust and nuggets from the territorial governor. The dispatches told an exciting story—of neglected shops and abandoned farms throughout California, of shiftless loafers washing out $50 worth of gold a day with nothing but a shovel and dishpan, of fabulous strike following fabulous strike, of the fortunes awaiting all who cared to pan the American River or the other streams that flowed westward from the Sierra Nevadas into the Sacramento Valley. When President Polk incorporated the reports in his December, 1848, message to Congress the whole country—the whole world—went mad. The rush to California was on.

Within a month sixty-one crowded ships were on their way around South America, many of them leaky tubs rescued from well-earned retirement to exact the scandalous fees fortune seekers willingly paid for passage to the "diggings." Those who could not afford the outrageous rates spent the winter gathering equipment for the overland journey. By the middle of May, 1849, 5,000 wagons were plodding westward along the California Trail; two weeks later an observer reported that 12,000 wagons had crossed the Missouri River and that 40,000 men were bound for the distant El Dorado.

Others made their way to Santa Fe, using the old trail or following the Arkansas River west from Ft. Smith, then struck out along Colonel Kearny's Gila River route or the Old Spanish Trail to the coast. Over those tortuous paths gold hunters poured by the tens of thousand that summer, as all America chanted:

> Oh Susanna, don't you cry for me,
> I'm off to California with my washbowl on my knee.

Suffering was intense among the ill-trained emigrants who knew nothing of plains travel save the little they learned from equally ignorant guidebook writers or newspaper editors. Indians stayed well away from the Forty-Niners, fearful of contracting diseases. On the trails across the Plains the cholera that lurked in every muddy waterhole took a toll of 5,000 lives; those who wandered from the popular paths frequently succumbed to starvation. In the Rocky Mountains more fell prey to dysentery or mountain fever as they struggled upward over steep trails with overloaded wagons. Beyond South Pass lay the dust and heat of alkali deserts, where the infrequent water-holes were often poisonous and the rare clumps of pasturage usually exhausted within a few weeks. By autumn, 1849, skeletons of dead horses and cattle lined the side of the road for hundreds of miles, while unmarked graves of humans were appallingly numerous. Yet the worst trials lay ahead where the steep, barren slopes of the Sierra Nevadas reared skyward across the path of the Forty-Niners. Weary emigrants often abandoned their wagons or ate their starving pack animals, as they sought strength to surmount the barrier. Others perished in snow-choked passes or, if they sought a route around the southern tip of the mountains, wandered into the dread Death Valley—a region of "dreadful sands and shadows . . . salt columns, bitter lakes, and wild, dreary, sunken desolation." A surprisingly large number of those who survived the ordeal were Negroes, some of them slaves. By 1850 almost 1,000 blacks lived in California, and by 1852 nearly 2,000, most of them concentrated in cities where prejudice was slightly less virulent than in the mining camps. They, like their white compatriots who reached the gold fields, fared better than cohorts left at home.

Miners needed their stamina in the roaring frontier communites that sprang up around the "diggings." In those ramshackle mining camps—appropriately labeled Poker Flat, Hangtown, Whiskey Bar, Placerville, Hell's Delight, Git-up-and-git, Skunk Gulch, Dry Diggings, Red Dog, Grub Gulch, and the like—where rooms rented for $1,000 a month and eggs cost $10 a dozen, were assembled the most colorful desperadoes ever gathered in one spot. Mingling together were Missouri farmers, Yankee sailors, Georgia crackers, English shopkeepers, French peasants, Australian sheepherders, Mexican peons, "heathen Chinee," and a liberal sprinkling of "assassins manufactured in Hell," all drawn to California by the magnet of gold. There fortunes were made in a day of grubbing and lost in a night of faro or red dog; there outlaws and women of easy virtue rubbed shoulders with ministers and sober farmers. About 100,000 people lived in California by the end of 1849, most of them respectable souls who wanted a better means of keeping order than the vigilance committees they set up themselves.

That was the situation that forced Congress to end its academic debate over slavery and come to grips with the problem. Some government must be provided before complete chaos reigned in California. President Zachary Taylor, gruff old militarist that he was, saw this and decided to act. His solution was to urge Californians to draw up a constitution and apply for admission as a state directly, thus dodging the question of congressional power over territories. A hint was all they needed; on August 1, 1849, a popular election named members of a constitutional convention which met in a Monterey schoolhouse in September, worked for six weeks, and emerged with an acceptable frame of government. A controversial clause barring slavery from the state was accepted unanimously and without debate. The document was overwhelmingly ratified by the people in mid-November, a governor and legislature chosen, and California was a state in everything but name. Congress must decide whether to accept the new commonwealth or face the wrath of Californians.

The question was placed squarely before the session which assembled in December, 1849, when a blunt message from President Taylor recommended that the new state be admitted and that New Mexico and Utah be organized as territories without reference to slavery. Congressional nerves were too frayed by years of argument to accept the proposals docilely. Southerners, horrified at the prospect of a free California upsetting the Senate balance between slave and free states, rose as a man to denounce Taylor's solution. John C. Calhoun, the intrepid old statesman of the section, led the attack; "I trust," he told his colleagues, "we shall persist in our resistance until the restoration of all our rights, or disunion, one or the other, is the consequence. We have borne the wrongs and insults of the North long enough." As northern extremists answered in equally fiery words, disunion seemed near. Never had the nation faced such grave peril.

Fortunately there were those in Congress who placed national interest above sectional passion. Why, they asked themselves, enflame the nation by debating slavery in California and New Mexico; in the former it had been abolished by popular decree; in the latter it might exist but showed little prospect of expanding. Congressmen were well aware that Negro servitude could and did exist in the Southwest; forty-eight of the ninety congressmen who went on record believed that staple crops could be grown in at least part of the territory acquired from Mexico, and where staples could be produced bonded labor could be used. But they also knew that the country was concerned more with constitutional issues than with the limits that nature had imposed on the extension of slavery, and surely they must find some compromise among the many problems revolving around the institution. That was the hope of two men in particular, Henry Clay of Kentucky and Stephen A. Douglas of Illinois, both senators from border states that would suffer greatly in any civil conflict. Together the strangely assorted pair—one a venerable Whig, the other a young Democrat—pieced together a legislative program designed to preserve the Union they both loved. California, they proposed, should be admitted as a free state. The remaining Mexican lands would be divided into the territories of New Mexico and Utah without mention of slavery, but with the understanding that the Supreme Court settle any disputes over the question during the territorial period and that the settlers themselves decide whether they should become slave or free states. The slave trade, they suggested, should be abolished in the District of Columbia but slavery be continued there. The Fugitive Slave Act should be strengthened. Texas must surrender its claim to a western boundary at the Rio Grande in favor of New Mexico, but in return the United States would assume the $10,000,000 debt acquired during the period of Texan independence.

The introduction of those proposals by Clay and Douglas launched the most superb debate in the Senate's history. Clay opened the contest on February 5, 1850, with a brilliant two-day speech that recalled "Young Harry of the West" to his enthralled listeners. From the North he asked acceptance of the substance of the Wilmot Proviso without demanding the principle; "You have got what is worth more than a thousand Wilmot Provisos," he told his northern colleagues. "You have nature on your side—facts upon your side—and this truth staring you in the face that there is no slavery in those territories." From the South he sought a promise of peace, reminding southerners of the benefits derived from the Union and warning them peaceful secession was impossible. His stirring words were echoed by Douglas and other moderates who saw compromise as the only means of avoiding a costly war.

The extremists refused to listen. John C. Calhoun, so old and weak his speech was read for him, warned that the South would accept nothing less than all the Mexican territories and a constitutional amendment protecting its institutions from the aggressions of the majority North. William H. Seward and Salmon P. Chase, speaking for northern extremists, denounced Clay's program in equally harsh terms as "radically wrong and essentially vicious." Congress, Seward said, might be willing to open the territories to slavery, "but there is a higher law than the Constitution," the law of God, which was broken by "all measures which fortify slavery or extend it." To those men, as to Calhoun, there could be no compromise.

Theirs was not the final word. This was spoken by a moderate northerner, Daniel Webster of Massachusetts, whose magnificent "Seventh of March" speech did much to shape congressional sentiment. "I speak today for the preservation of the Union," were his impressive opening words. "Hear me for my cause." They listened spellbound, the hundreds who crowded the benches and galleries of the Senate chamber, as his tired voice gained the strength of conviction. Northerners, he pleaded, should not attempt "to reaffirm an ordinance of nature, nor to reenact the will of God" by forbidding slaves in a region where none could exist; southerners should give up the dream of peaceful secession and escape from the "caverns of darkness" into the "fresh air of liberty and union." His stirring words, resounding throughout the nation, stirred up a ground swell of sentiment for compromise. "Union Meetings" were held in northern city after northern city, while in the South a convention that assembled at Nashville to talk secession adjourned after passing a few harmless resolutions. Clearly the majority preferred Clay's compromise to civil war.

This sentiment gained a champion in the White House when the death of President Taylor on July 9, 1850, elevated Millard Fillmore to the presidency. Taylor was a blunt old soldier whose bull-headed opposition to Clay's measures reflected the attitude of Seward whom he followed; Fillmore was a weak-kneed second-rater to whom compromise was second nature. His pressure upon congressmen, coinciding with growing popular support, convinced Clay and Douglas the time was ripe for a vote. One by one the bills were taken up and passed during the early weeks of September, to form the Compromise of 1850. California entered the Union as a free state, Utah and New Mexico were organized as territories with the understanding they become states with or without slavery as their constitutions dictated, the Texan boundary was placed at the 103rd meridian and the state's debt assumed by the United States, slavery was continued in the District of Columbia but the slave trade was abolished there, and a more stringent fugitive slave law was placed on the statute books.

When Millard Fillmore fixed his signature to the Compromise of 1850 he rolled back the clouds of war. Frantic efforts by Union-loving statesmen such as Clay and Webster temporarily dissolved the crisis created by Manifest Destiny. But the day of compromise was drawing to a close as an older generation passed from the scene and younger fire-eaters, bred in an atmosphere of conflict, assumed control of Congress. Those were the men who must meet the new crises created by the advancing frontier, and their failure led the nation straight along the road to civil conflict.

27

The West and Slavery

1850-1860

The decade of the 1850s brought the slavery controversy to the bloody climax of civil war. Every step taken during that fateful ten-year period—every political contest, every election, every congressional debate, every economic gain—carried the nation closer to the irrepressible conflict. For no compromise, such as the crazy-quilt fabric pieced together by Clay and Douglas in 1850, even if enacted, could do more than delay the separation of North and South. The economic and emotional gulf between the sections was so great that every minor irritant was magnified into a major difference by inflamed partisans on both sides of Mason and Dixon's line. So long as disputes arose the sections could know no peace, and so long as the frontier moved westward disputes must arise. Each advance of settlement reopened the sore question of slavery's status in the territories, until the nation's nerves were so frayed that war seemed a necessary balm.

A casual observer during the years just after the Compromise of 1850 was adopted would have noticed few surface indications of the widening sectional breach. Some southerners grumbled over the loss of California to free staters, some northerners harangued against the inhumanity of the fugitive slave act, but the majority pretended the compromise was a heaven-sent blessing which would settle the slavery issue for all time. National satisfaction was strengthened by the industrial boom launched by California's gold; the prosperous people wanted nothing to interfere with the pleasant task of money-making. In most southern elections held during 1851, union candidates triumphed decisively over secession-minded radicals, although in South Carolina and Mississippi the contest was close. In the North, too, abolitionists lost popularity. Throughout the country a grateful

534

people, worn by four years of controversy, returned thankfully to normal pursuits.

Beneath the surface calm, however, were indications of the brewing storm. The presidential election of 1852 provided the first warnings for those wise enough to see. Apparently both major parties followed their usual practices; the Democrats nominated a mediocre northerner, Franklin Pierce of New Hampshire, whose principal political virtues were a handsome face, a winning smile, and a well-publicized letter unequivocally endorsing the Compromise of 1850; the Whigs selected another military hero, General Winfield Scott of Mexican War fame, whose views on public issues were as obscure as his mental processes. The uninspired candidates devoted a spiritless campaign to praising the Compromise and swearing undying enmity to sectional discord. Only the Free-Soilers recognized that the slavery issue was dormant rather than dead, but their demands for congressional exclusion of bonded labor from the territories aroused little interest among a people who believed the western problem solved for all time.

To those who viewed the lackadaisical campaign as a sign of harmony the results came as a shock. The Democrats won a sweeping victory for their latest nonentity, losing only Massachusetts, Vermont, Kentucky, and Tennessee. The impressive triumph was made possible by two significant shifts within the ranks of the opposing parties. One was such a wholesale exodus of Barnburning Democrats from the Free-Soilers that the party's popular vote fell off by half as compared to 1848—an encouraging sign to those seeking sectional peace. The other and more important development was a movement of southern planters out of the Whig and into the Democratic Party. Wealthy cotton kings took that step partly because they could not reconcile their states' rights views with General Scott's military nationalism, partly because the growing conservatism of the Democrats appealed to them as men of property. In the end the Whigs carried only Kentucky and Tennessee among the border states, and none in the South. Their defeat sounded the death knell of the party below the Mason and Dixon line. The political spectrum was being reconstructed to preclude two viable national parties, just at a time when national institutions were needed to bind the nation together.

Before the year was out the Whigs suffered another telling blow in the deaths of Henry Clay and Daniel Webster. Those two grand old statesmen had held the party together through their personal influence; now younger leaders whose traditions were sectional rather than national assumed control. The result was complete disintegration. Some northern Whigs who had long seethed against a political alliance with slaveholders, began calling themselves "Conscience Whigs" and talking much as the Free-Soilers talked in 1848. Their leaders were men of the stamp of Charles Sumner of Massachusetts, William H. Seward of New York, and Abraham Lincoln of Illinois. Others in the North, organized as "Cotton Whigs," tried to carry on the tradition of compromise laid down by Clay and Webster. The remnants of the party in the South, the "Southern Whigs," had nothing to do with either faction. One political link was irreparably broken.

Although the shifting political allegiances apparently benefited the Democrats, the party was actually left weaker in everything but numerical strength. Its members had for some time been divided into northern and southern wings which were so evenly balanced that neither could dominate the other. With the migration of great planters into Democratic ranks, the southern faction gained enough strength to dictate the party's national strategy in the interests of the South. This was dangerous. For a time southerners might register some gains, but if they pressed their cause too vigorously northern Democrats would surely reach a point of rebellion. Then the last political bond uniting the sections would be severed. The history of the next half-dozen years amply demonstrated the reality of the peril, for the continued demands of southern Democrats finally led the nation into war.

The one thing the South wanted above all else was more land for slavery. Some they hoped to obtain beyond the borders of the United States; their attempts to secure Cuba, Nicaragua, and other bordering territories blackened the pages of American diplomacy during the periods of Democratic control in the 1850s. More would have to be secured within the country, and the Democrats' drive to obtain this renewed the sectional conflict. Northerners believed the status of slavery in the West settled for all time. The Missouri Compromise decreed that all lands east of the Rockies and north of the line of 36° 30′ should become free territories, all south of the line slave. The Compromise of 1850 cared for the matter in the domains taken from Mexico. That division, which satisfied all but the most northern extremists, was far from acceptable to the South. Slavery, they believed, was a dynamic institution that must expand to endure. This realization kept southern Democrats constantly alert for a chance to open more territory to their peculiar institution. Their opportunity came in January, 1854, when the Kansas-Nebraska bill was laid before Congress.

The act's sponsor was the idol of the northern Democrats, Senator Stephen A. Douglas of Illinois, whose faithful followers fondly dubbed him the "Little Giant" or the "Steam Engine in Britches." He proposed that the unorganized area of the Great Plains be divided into the two territories of Kansas and Nebraska, the boundaries of Kansas to be those of today extended to the Rockies, those of Nebraska to include all the region north to the 49th parallel. Both would be opened to slavery during the early territorial stages, but eventually the people of each would decide by popular vote whether they wanted the institution—a device Douglas called "Popular Sovereignty." He recognized that slavery could not legally exist in the area north of 36° 30′ so long as the Missouri Compromise remained on the statute books; hence the Kansas-Nebraska Act formally repealed the venerable ordinance, declaring instead that the true intent of Congress was "not to legislate slavery into any Territory or State, nor to exclude it therefrom, but to leave the people thereof perfectly free to . . . regulate their domestic institutions in their own way." That was the measure pushed through Congress on May 25, 1854, by a smoothly functioning Democratic machine.

Why did Douglas, a northerner, sponsor such a harmony-shattering bill? The answer can be found both in his own idealism and in the more sordid world of practical business and politics. Living as he did in a new land, the Illinois senator was a fervent believer in the frontier democracy that was entrenched there. Genuinely convinced that people should solve their own problems on the local level, he viewed popular sovereignty as a natural means of settling the slavery controversy according to the dictates of the majorities most concerned. In this his fellow-westerners agreed with him; from the Mississippi Valley to the Pacific coast the Kansas-Nebraska Act was hailed not as a disruptive measure or a triumph for the slave interests, but as an equitable means of allowing the territories to care for their own affairs. Douglas, and all the West, viewed his bill simply as a device to allow the self-rule that was the God-given right of all pioneers.

The more sordid world of practical politics also suggested the idea to him. Its medium was Douglas' good friend and fellow-Democrat, Senator David R. Atchison of Missouri. Atchison faced a bitter fight with his most formidable opponent, former Senator Thomas Hart Benton, to retain his seat in the 1854 election. The latter, casting about for some campaign issue particularly appealing to Missouri Democrats, had hit upon the idea of promising to open all lands lying to the west of the state to settlers. Atchison realized that this appeal would be effective unless he devised an even more attractive program. By the autumn of 1853 he had the answer: he would, he told his constituents, not only press for the organization of the western territories but insist that they be opened to slavery on the basis of popular sovereignty. In November, 1853, he persuaded Douglas to introduce such a bill in his capacity as chairman of the Senate Committee on Territories.

Douglas was delighted to do so, for the organization of the region fitted in well with his own ambitions. Both as a politician and an owner of extensive Illinois real-estate holdings, he was interested in the route of the transcontinental railroad then under discussion. Army surveys in 1853 had indicated that two routes were especially feasible, one through South Pass to connect San Francisco with either St. Louis or Chicago, the other uniting New Orleans and Los Angeles. Southerners were determined on the latter route and could rationalize their prejudices with sound reasons; they argued that a southern road would run through organized territory, that local traffic from settled areas along the way would reduce through transportation costs, and that easy contours would facilitate construction. Douglas, together with other northerners, was equally set on a railroad with an eastern terminus at Chicago. If he could persuade Congress to select the central route he would win the eternal gratitude of northerners and his own Illinois constituents, as well as improving himself financially by advancing the price of his extensive Chicago real estate holdings. The line could never be built, however, so long as the Louisiana Purchase was unorganized. Senator Atchison's proposed territory beyond Missouri and Iowa would answer the principal southern argument against the central route.

As Douglas mulled over the suggestion, however, he realized a bill to erect one territory there would never do. The first pioneers into the region would come from Missouri and Arkansas rather than thinly settled Iowa or distant Illinois, and would locate the territorial capital in the southern portion. A Pacific railroad through that city would emerge at St. Louis rather than Chicago, doing nothing for Douglas' political ambitions or financial hopes. The only answer was two territories rather than one, allowing the road to pass through the capital of the northern territory directly west of Chicago. That was in Douglas' mind when he recommended the organization of both Kansas and Nebraska on the basis of popular sovereignty.

No sooner was the bill framed than the Illinois senator realized he had arranged a masterful political *coup*. Kansas, he saw, would doubtless be won for slavery by immigrants from adjacent Missouri, while Nebraska, lying west of Iowa, would become a free territory. Thus both North and South would gain. The South would secure a new slave state and repeal of the Missouri Compromise. In return the section would give up hopes of a southern railroad, awarding the North that coveted concession together with an additional free state. Douglas believed a grateful people would hail him as the hero who solved the problem of sectionalism, saved the Union, and provided an orderly means of settling the slavery controversy for all time to come. The presidency, surely, would be the only fitting reward for such a service.

His error—natural in a practical politician—was the failure to understand the deep emotional conviction motivating both sections. To a majority of Americans the real issue was not a Pacific railroad—although southerners recognized the threat of the Kansas-Nebraska bill to their railroad ambitions—but "Southern Rights" versus "Northern Freedom." That alone accounted for the national reaction when news of the Kansas-Nebraska Act was flashed through the land. The South was overjoyed; Democratic politicians had won the thing southerners most wanted: more land for slavery. But the southern joy was more than matched by northern anger. The Missouri Compromise—a measure as inviolate as the Constitution—had been repealed by the hated slaveholders! "A violation of a sacred pledge," "a criminal betrayal of precious rights," "an enormous crime"—those were the epithets hurled by outraged northerners. Douglas, who had expected the worshipful thanks of his countrymen, found himself so unpopular in the North that he could, as he expressed it, travel from Boston to Chicago by the light of his burning effigies. Once more emotionalism ruled the United States, and this time there was no Henry Clay to lead the nation back to sanity.

The first result was a new shifting of party lines. The Democrats suffered least, despite the loss of some northerners who angrily withdrew from the party to take the name of Anti-Nebraska Democrats. The majority, however, even in the North, clung to the hope the Kansas-Nebraska Act would, as Douglas prophesied, reduce slavery from a national issue to a local problem. So long as they could follow Douglas and convince themselves they were pursuing a compromising course they were willing to stay in the party. The Whigs, who had been vainly trying to patch up their differences since 1852, were less fortunate. Southern Whigs, convinced the Democrats truly represented southern interests, abandoned their dying organization in droves, while Northern Whigs, left without a party, drifted into one or the other of the two new parties the Kansas-Nebraska Act helped create.

One, the American Party, had been gaining strength for some years before Douglas' measure brought an unexpected influx of members. Its objectives—to drive Papists and foreigners from the land—were no more truly American than the elaborate secret ritual which pledged its adherents to vote only for native-born Protestants. Yet the Know-Nothings (so named because they parried all queries about their order by saying "I know nothing about it") increased in power rapidly after 1850 when the Compromise, by apparently settling the slavery issue, allowed bigots to turn their invective against Popery and the foreign-born. The parade into the party's ranks assumed mass proportions after passage of the Kansas-Nebraska Act, for the order's stress on unity and stability indicated that it would rise above any sectional strife. The American Party carried six states in 1854 and 1855, and almost captured seven more, largely in New England and the border states. Fortunately its members split over slavery before the election of 1856, or the United States might have enthroned intolerance in the White House.

The second party to emerge from the political chaos created by the Kansas-Nebraska Act originated in the Middle West where indignation was particularly high. At a dozen places in the upper Mississippi Valley grumbling farmers met simultaneously to talk of the need for a new antislavery party that could combat the latest aggression of the slavocracy. One of the gatherings, held at Jackson, Michigan, on July 6, 1854, hit upon the happy device of reviving the name of Jefferson's old party and suggested they call themselves Republicans. The idea took hold at once; in community after community former Free-Soilers, Anti-Nebraska Democrats, and Conscience Whigs flocked together to form local units of the Republican Party, all of them pledged to prevent the extension of slavery into the territories. By the fall of 1854 the lusty new organization was firmly planted in the Old Northwest, although its strength elsewhere remained slight. Some emotional stimulus was needed before the young party could win northeastern conservatives.

This was provided by the disgraceful events taking place in Kansas. The Kansas-Nebraska Act brought no more peace to that unfortunate territory than to the nation. Perhaps popular sovereignty would have operated well applied to a well-settled region, but when inflicted on a newly opened territory it invited trouble. Northern abolitionists, angry at what seemed a deliberate southern attempt to rob them of Kansas, struck the first blow. Why not, they argued, frustrate the evil design by sending enough free-soilers into the territory to outvote the slaveholders who moved there? As the possibility dawned on abolitionists they hurriedly formed societies to collect funds, equip emigrants, and send them wholesale into the disputed region. Most prominent was the New England Emigrant Aid Society, chartered in April, 1854, by Eli Thayer, a Massachusetts free-soiler. By midsummer Thayer, enriched by contributions from a host of New England financiers, could boast that his society would have a thousand settlers in Kansas by the end of August and 20,000 by the first of the year.

Those extravagant claims had no basis in fact. During the critical years when the fate of Kansas hung in the balance only 4,208 pioneers moved there from New England, the center of abolitionism, and of those only 1,240 were aided by the Emigrant Aid Society. New Englanders were migrating during the 1850s, but to regions where life and property were secure; 90,000 settled in the free states of the Old Northwest and 5,799 in slave Missouri. This was also true of the other northeastern states. New York contributed 6,331 settlers to doubtful Kansas while sending 220,000 to the upper Mississippi Valley. Nor did southerners show any greater inclination to move there. The southeastern states sent only a handful of frontiersmen to Kansas, despite the efforts of one Jefferson Buford, a rabid proslavery man, who led one band of ruffians westward to offset the work of the Emigrant Aid Societies. Instead Kansas was peopled by pioneers from adjacent states. Ohio, Indiana, and Illinois sent 30,929 northern emigrants, while the southwestern states of Missouri, Kentucky, and Tennessee contributed 20,481. Obviously the forces which had led to the peopling of every frontier—proximity, overcrowding at home, the hope of gain—were responsible for the peopling of Kansas rather than any idealistic hope of saving the world. In all probability the threat of trouble over slavery kept settlers out rather than luring them in, particularly slaveholders who dared not risk their heavy property investment.

Certainly there was little abolitionist idealism represented there. Save for a few head-in-clouds reformers, most of the northern Republicans who settled in Kansas had little love for Negroes, fearing them as economic competitors and scorning them as a lower order of humanity unfit to mingle with whites. Their hostile attitude was distressingly common in the upper Mississippi Valley at that time; most northerners were so racially biased that they favored excluding blacks from the states or territories being opened in the West as they had in their native states. Slavery, they agreed, was an evil, but once the blacks were freed they should be confined to the South. Their prejudice was to shape their beliefs and action whenever a crisis emerged.

Despite the failure of the Emigrant Aid Societies to people Kansas with opponents of racial bigotry, several thousand farmers lived there by November, 1854, when the territorial governor, Andrew H. Reeder, a pro-

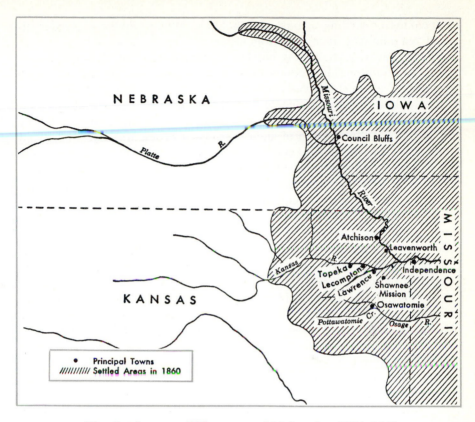

The Settlement of Kansas and Nebraska, 1854–1860

slavery Pennsylvania Democrat, summoned a convention to name a delegate to Congress. Missourians, operating through secret dens, crossed the border in such numbers that about half the votes cast for the successful candidate, a staunch proslavery advocate, were by nonresidents. The pattern was repeated on a more dramatic scale in the spring of 1855 when an election was staged to choose a legislature. Southerners, who had drifted across from Missouri to settle along the Missouri Valley, were in a majority at the time, but Missourians were unwilling to leave anything to chance. On the day of the election 5,000 "Border Ruffians," all armed to the teeth, swarmed into Kansas, took control of the voting booths, and cast four times as many ballots as there were registered voters in the territory. Governor Reeder, southern sympathizer though he was, protested in vain. Democratic officials in Washington turned a deaf ear as the solidly proslave legislature met at the town of Shawnee Mission to pass laws which limited office holding to believers in slavery, provided for the imprisonment of anyone declaring the institution did not legally exist in the territory, and inflicted punishment on all speaking or writing against slaveholding. When Governor Reeder objected again he was dismissed from office.

Free-staters, realizing the harsh measures would send half their members to jail, countered by holding an election of their own, this time to choose members of a constitutional convention which could seek admission for Kansas as a free state. Delegates selected in the one-sided contest met at Topeka in October, 1855, drafted a frame of government forbidding slavery, and authorized the election of state officials. Two months later the constitution was overwhelmingly ratified (as southerners abstained from voting) and a northern government set up. Kansas now had two separate communities, each with its own legislature, governor, and delegate to Congress. The proslave men were grouped around Leavenworth and Atchison in the Missouri Valley, the free-staters about Topeka and Lawrence on the Kansas River. Both contained an unhealthy sprinkling of cutthroats attracted by the promise of trouble, while southerners could count on support from Missouri "Border Ruffians" who were always spoiling to "clean out the abolition crowd." Civil conflict was inevitable.

It began in the spring of 1856 when a proslave sheriff visiting Lawrence was shot in the back by an unknown assassin. Although the cowardly act was disavowed by free-soilers, a southern grand jury handed down indictments for treason against half the leading citizens of Lawrence. The federal marshal appointed to deliver the warrants, correctly anticipating resistance, led 800 heavily armed bushwhackers and "Border Ruffians" into the free-state town in May, 1856. While northerners stood angrily aside the gang of ruffians destroyed the printing press of the local paper, tore down a hotel, burned the homes of several suspected abolitionists, and ransacked the town.

This wanton act profoundly impressed both North and South. Moderation vanished; Kansas overnight became a testing ground for the forces of slavery and freedom. Southern editors pictured the "Border Ruffians" as proud knights battling for a holy cause and demanded legislative appropriations to send armed bands into Kansas; northerners glorified the free-state bushwhackers as crusaders for freedom and requested renewed support for the Emigrant Aid Societies. The tense state of the nation's nerves was indicated by a meeting at a New Haven church to raise money for seventy Kansas-bound emigrants. The Reverend Henry Ward Beecher, in addressing the gathering, urged the settlers to go armed and boldly proclaimed that the dread Sharpe's rifle was a greater moral force for Kansas than the Bible. From that time on easterners entering the disputed territory carried "Beecher's Bibles," as the rifles were dubbed, and went prepared to fight for their rights. Open civil war was near.

Fighting began not long after the Lawrence raid. Old John Brown, a half-crazed religious fanatic whose Old Testament God demanded the spilling of blood for blood, touched off the conflict. Brooding over the sack of Lawrence, he convinced himself that he was divinely appointed to right the wrongs done by southerners. With his four sons and a few other deluded free-staters, John Brown slipped out of the frontier town of Osawatomie on the night of May 24, 1856, stole quietly upon the neighboring southern hamlet of Pottawatomie Creek, and hacked five southerners to death in cold blood. The "Pottawatomie Massacre" precipitated war in Kansas. For three months crops were neglected as bands of "Border Ruffians" or northern bushwhackers roamed the territory, burning, pillaging, and murdering, until the sky over the war-torn region was alight from flaming dwellings. Some $2,000,000 worth of property and 200 lives were sacrificed as "Bleeding Kansas" earned its name.

Just how much of the bloodshed was due to conflicts over slavery and how much to the activities of renegades in a frontier community can never be known. In all probability disputed land titles cost as many lives as the slave issue. Those stemmed from the negligence of government surveyors; not until the summer of 1856 were enough lands plotted to allow the first public sales. In the meantime thousands of pioneers squatted on farms and formed claims clubs to protect their holdings. Doubtless many of the battles were fought between squatters and later-comers who had purchased previously occupied land; that was indicated by the fact that the conflict reached a crisis in every region where surveys were just completed. Other minor wars were probably engineered by rival speculators in townsites, for overlapping grants to those prized spots were often made. Local residents were well aware that greed rather than idealism sparked most of the conflicts; army officers stationed in Kansas referred always in their reports to "armed bands," "plunderers," or "claim jumpers," and never to "free-staters" or "proslavery men." They were convinced, they told their superiors, that civilians promoted disorder and bloodshed to be able to profit from the turbulence. This was unknown to the rest of the nation. Every clash was magnified by the press into a struggle between the forces of slavery and freedom. The rampaging frontier was transformed into a testing ground for sectional conflict.

The effect was startling. "Bleeding Kansas" divided the nation as no other issue during the crucial decade. Southerners, reading distorted accounts of outrages committed upon their fellow slaveholders, came to believe all free-staters were fanatical ruffians who would be satisfied by nothing less than the annihilation of ever slaveholder. Northerners, learning from their papers of "bar-room rowdies . . . parading the country chopping single persons . . . to pieces, and frightening women and children," accepted rough-necked "Border Ruffians" as typical of all southerners. To men who believed in that way the day of compromise was past. The North, which had docilely accepted southern presidents, laws, and economic control for a generation, saw that the time had come to draw the line. From now on, grim free-staters told themselves, they would force their will on the minority South. A section that condoned the sack of Lawrence and the rape of Kansas deserved no compassion.

The spread of that sentiment among northerners proved a godsend to the Republican Party. Its principles were those gaining credence; the majority North, Republicans believed, should control the nation in its own interest without paying heed to the minority South. In the past sober men had refused to support an organization that proposed to substitute force for compromise, knowing the dangerous doctrine would breed disunion. Now caution was forgotten with each dispatch from "Bleeding Kansas"; through 1855 and 1856 thousands upon thousands of northerners flocked into Republican ranks. By the fall of 1856 the party could enter the presidential lists, with charismatic John C. Frémont as its candidate and the demand for free territories as its platform. Although the Democrats triumphed with their proslavery Pennsylvanian, James Buchanan, Frémont came closer to uniting North and West against the South than had any previous presidential aspirant. He carried every state north of Mason and Dixon's line save Indiana, Illinois, Pennsylvania, New Jersey, and California, to win 114 electoral votes. Sectional lines were drawing tighter and the end of the Union was in sight, for if ever the Republican principle of majority rule was accepted by the nation the South would certainly secede.

The event that swung northern opinion to that point occurred only two days after James Buchanan entered the White House: the Supreme Court's decision in the case of *Dred Scott* v. *Sanford*. The years of litigation that culminated in the momentous opinion began when Dred Scott, a Negro slave owned by an army surgeon named Dr. John Emerson, was taken from his Missouri home for brief residences at Ft. Armstrong in Illinois and Ft. Snelling in the unorganized territory later to become Minnesota. In 1838 master and slave returned to Missouri where, eight years later, Dr. Emerson died, leaving Dred Scott to his widow. Anxious to be rid of Scott but unable to free him under state law, Mrs. Emerson arranged for him to sue for his freedom in the Missouri courts, knowing that they had repeatedly held that residence in a free state or territory automatically freed a slave. To her disgust, the state supreme court reversed past precedents, largely because its pro-Atchison members were eager to embarrass Thomas Hart Benton, and ruled that Scott's status must be determined by Missouri law since he voluntarily returned there.

Mrs. Emerson, whose natural desire to free her troublesome servant had been bolstered by remarriage to a Massachusetts abolitionist, Dr. C. C. Chaffee, was unwilling to accept defeat. If, however, she appealed to the federal courts the problem of jurisdiction intervened, for their authority did not extend to suits arising between citizens of one state. That obstacle was overcome by the direct sale of Dred Scott to Mrs. Emerson's brother, J. F. A. Sanford of New York, and the case reopened in the United States Circuit Court of Missouri which held as had the state court. Appeal was then carried to the Supreme Court, where the suit was argued in February, 1856, and again in January, 1857. After listening to counsels' pleas the judges, in their mid-February conference, decided to brush aside the question of jurisdiction and decide the case against Scott on the grounds that the state supreme court's interpretation of Missouri law kept him in slavery.

At that point two northern members of the bench let it be known they intended to write dissenting opinions upholding the constitutionality of the Missouri Compromise—the statute under which Minnesota was free—using as an excuse Scott's brief residence there. Their motives were hardly laudable; Justice Benjamin R. Curtis of Massachusetts wished to popularize himself in Boston before retiring from the Court to resume private practice, and Justice John McLean of Ohio hoped to attract such favorable attention from Republicans that he could win the party's presidential nomination in 1860. Their selfish ambitions did the justices little good and the nation great harm, for the remaining judges—seven of whom were Democrats and five from the South—were unwilling to allow them to defend congressional exclusion of slavery from the territories without rebuttal. Abandoning their intention to dismiss the Dred Scott case on local grounds, the majority instructed the chief justice, Roger B. Taney of Maryland, to write an opinion denying Congress the power to ban slavery from federal territories.

The ingenious argument penned by Taney ran something like this: The Supreme Court, he wrote, could accept jurisdiction only in disputes arising between citizens of different states. Dred Scott was not entitled to become a litigant because he was not a citizen. He was not a citizen because he was a Negro, and at that point Judge Taney examined post-Revolutionary state laws to show that framers of the Constitution did not consider Negroes capable of citizenship. Moreover, the Chief Justice went on, Scott was not a citizen because he was still a slave. He had not been made free by his residence in Illinois; as a resident of Missouri the laws of any state in which he visited did not affect his status. Nor was he made free by his years in Minnesota Territory, for Minnesota was not legally free. Slaves, Taney held, were specifically protected from federal interference by the Fifth Amendment to the Constitution which prohibited Congress from depriving any person of his property without due process of law. To restrict the use of a man's property was to deprive that man of property. Therefore Congress could not legally bar slavery from the territories, and the Missouri Compromise was unconstitutional. Taney concluded the national legislature's only power over slavery "was the power coupled with the duty of guarding and protecting the owner in his rights."

The Dred Scott case was the most serious blow yet dealt to the ambitions of the North and the Republican Party. It was denounced in vitriolic language everywhere—"a wicked and false judgment," "willful perversion," "a new and atrocious doctrine," "the deadliest blow which has been aimed at the liberties of America since the days of Benedict Arnold," "entitled to just as much moral weight as would be the judgment of a majority of those congregated in any Washington bar-room"—those were some of the milder phrases hurled by indignant editors. Yet no amount of name-calling could disguise the fact that the judgment stood, and that a Democratic president was ready to enforce it. The sole Republican hope was to win control of the national government, pack the Supreme Court, and secure a reversal. Unless that was done the party was doomed, for it could no longer promise to ban slavery from the territories when the Supreme Court ruled Congress lacked power. Disgruntled Republicans found solace only in the outraged state of northern opinion. Even moderates believed themselves victims of a southern conspiracy to open territory after territory to slavery until bonded labor engulfed the nation. Fear for their own security, coupled with sympathy for the slaves, drove them into Republican ranks as never before. Each election through 1857 and 1858 showed the party's growing strength.

The Democrats, on the other hand, were grievously weakened by the Dred Scott decision. So long as the party advocated popular sovereignty it could retain a national organization, attracting to its fold southerners hoping to secure Kansas for slavery, westerners won over by the doctrine's democratic features, and easterners willing to embrace any compromise allowing them to continue business relations with the South. Now southern members renounced popular sovereignty in favor of the Dred Scott doctrine which promised all the West to slaveholders. Northern Democrats, unwilling to go that far, still hesitated to desert their party, knowing they must align themselves with the violently pronorthern Republicans. For a time they waited, still hoping for some middle-of-the-road solution which would save their southern trade and their beloved nation. In this crisis they turned naturally to their leader, Stephen A. Douglas. Could he find some way out of the dilemma? Upon the broad shoulders of the Little Giant rested the fate of the Democratic Party and the Union.

Douglas, realizing the importance of his decision, hesitated as long as possible before taking a stand, but was finally forced to declare himself when his Republican opponent in the Illinois senatorial election of 1858, Abraham Lincoln, pinned him down with a direct question: "Can the people of a United States territory in any lawful way exclude slavery from its limits prior to the formation of a State Constitution?" The Democratic leader had to decide between two unpleasant possibilities; if he answered "yes" he would please northern members of his party but offend the South, if he answered "no" he would satisfy southerners but lose his northern following. Douglas did not go back on his principles. His answer was known from the town in which it was delivered as the Freeport Doctrine. If the people of any territory wanted slavery, he said, they could choose a legislature pledged to enact laws necessary to protect the institution; if they were opposed they could elect free-state delegates who could by "unfriendly legislation" exclude it entirely. Popular sovereignty still existed, despite the Dred Scott decision!

The Freeport Doctrine re-elected Douglas to the Senate but split the Democratic Party in two. Southerners were horrified. Their former champion had threatened slavery by advising territorial legislatures not to enact "black codes"; he had defied the law of the land by urging citizens to violate the clear injunction of the Supreme Court. Every Democrat south of Mason and Dixon's line turned as a man from this Judas, leaving Douglas with only his northern supporters. The last political link binding the nation was severed.

Nor did events during the next two years strengthen Douglas' position in his own section. That rested on the success of popular sovereignty and every post from Kansas demonstrated the continued failure of the doctrine as a means of settling the slavery question. The aggressors in the troubled territory now were proslavery men who saw that drastic action was needed before continued migration from the more populous free states robbed them of their last chance to make Kansas slave. Taking advantage of the fact that a sympathetic Democratic government sat in Washington, they called a constitutional convention together at Lecompton in the fall of 1857, drafted a violently proslavery frame of government, arranged a ratification election which gave the people no chance to express themselves (they could only vote for the constitution with or without a provision to admit more slaves), and in the spring of 1858 asked that Kansas be admitted as a state. President Buchanan blindly submitted the Lecompton Constitution to Congress with the recommendation that it be accepted "to restore peace and quiet to the whole country."

The Republicans were solidly opposed; so was Douglas who courageously denounced the measure as not representative of majority will in Kansas, even though his words cost him the last hope of southern support. Democratic leaders, realizing the Lecompton Constitution was doomed to defeat, made a last desperate effort. Once more the people of the territory were asked to vote on the measure, this time with the promise of a sizeable land grant (of the sort usually given new states) if the constitution was accepted. When they marched to the polls in August, 1858, they overwhelmingly rejected the tempting offer rather than accept slavery. Kansas was destined now to enter the Union as a free state, but when? The Kansans wanted immediate action; meeting at Wyandotte early in 1860 they drew up a progressive, antislavery constitution which was submitted to Congress for approval. Its fate was sealed by the turbulent political scene; Democrats and Republicans, free-soil and proslavery men, all vied with each other in maneuvering for delay. Popular sovereignty had created a crisis so intense that the legislative process virtually halted. Kansas had to wait until 1861 for statehood, but its struggle for admission had hopelessly divided the Democrats.

The depth of the gulf was shown when party delegates met at Charleston to name the Democratic candidate for the election of 1860. The platform committee submitted two planks, one calling upon the federal government to protect slavery in the territories, the other upholding the right of the people to decide on their own institutions, subject to the decisions of the Supreme Court. When the latter was adopted by northern representatives the southern delegates stalked from the convention hall in open rebellion.

Adjourning to Baltimore, they named John C. Breckinridge of Kentucky as their standard bearer. In the meantime the northern Democrats selected Stephen A. Douglas as their candidate. The Democratic split was a reality.

This was a golden opportunity for the Republicans who met in a specially built "wigwam" in Chicago amidst an atmosphere of wild excitement. Yet the prospect of victory over a divided opposition did not stampede party leaders into any foolish moves. They realized northern moderates must be won over to insure a triumph, and that this could only be accomplished by nominating a middle-of-the-roader for the presidency and by drafting a platform with a wide popular appeal. Hence they passed over William H. Seward, whose outspoken references to a "higher law" and an "irrepressible conflict" made him unacceptable to all but radical free-staters, in favor of Abraham Lincoln of Illinois, who was known as a sincere lover of union. The platform was equally appealing; in place of the simple pledge to exclude slavery from the territories used in 1856, the document of 1860 promised homestead legislation to please the westerners, protective tariffs to win over eastern manufacturers, and an extensive program of government-supported internal improvements and railroads to attract business interests in both sections.

There remained in the United States a group of men satisfied with neither the Douglas Democrats, the Breckinridge Democrats, nor the Lincoln Republicans. Most were elderly individuals, bred in a tradition of union and compromise, who deplored without thoroughly understanding the sectional strife over slavery; others were former Know-Nothings who placed nationalism above all else. Their representatives met at Baltimore during the summer of 1860, organized themselves into a Constitutional Union Party, and selected a dull old antiquarian, John Bell of Tennessee, as their presidential candidate. The platform ignored slavery and urged the people to uphold the Constitution, the laws of the nation, and the Union.

The campaign between the four parties was one of the bitterest in the country's history, but the outcome was predestined. The South divided its vote between Breckinridge and Bell, the latter receiving his principal support in the rich-soil regions where wealthy planters shied from a sectional candidate who threatened secession. The border states cast their ballots for Bell and Douglas, for there too compromise seemed more expedient than civil war. The Northeast voted almost solidly for Lincoln, with a sprinkling of Douglas supporters among business men whose trade connections lay south of Mason and Dixon's line. If the final decision had rested among those three sections no one candidate could have secured a majority; the election would have been thrown into the House of Representatives where Democratic strength would probably have placed Breckinridge in the presidency. The outcome of the crucial contest hung on the vote of the Northwest.

A decade earlier that section would have voted for compromise, hanging as it did in the balance between North and South. Its strong union sentiment in 1850 had stemmed partly from a population drawn equally from southern and northeastern states, partly from a traditional legislative alliance with the agricultural cotton belt, and partly from trade connections maintained with both the other sections. So long as the upper Mississippi Valley divided its allegiance and commerce there could be no decision on the slavery question, for neither of the two major antagonists dared act while the unstable section balanced between them. As late as 1856 the Democratic Party registered thumping victories there; if those had been repeated in 1860 Lincoln would have been defeated and the Civil War postponed. Yet Lincoln carried the Northwest. The swing of that section from the Democratic to the Republican column—from divided allegiance to an open alliance with the North—made the irrepressible conflict inevitable. The shift in northwestern opinion between 1850 and 1860 was due to an influx of freedom-loving settlers, to growing realization that the section's legislative needs could best be secured by cooperating with the Northeast, and to a revolution in trade routes.

The new settlers who helped revise northwestern sentiment came partly from the Northeast, bearing with them strong antislavery concepts. More than 300,000 pioneers from New England and New York reached the upper Mississippi Valley during the 1850s. The South contributed few newcomers, for feeling over slavery was then so strong southerners hesitated to migrate to free states. More important than internal migration in explaining growing Republican strength in the Northwest was immigration from abroad. During the decade, over 1,000,000 Germans had landed on American shores, three quarters of whom settled in the upper Mississippi Valley. They brought with them a hatred of slavery and a love of freedom inspired by the ill-fated liberal revolutions of 1848 in Germany. Their first inclination was to join the Democratic Party whose name and traditions seemed to symbolize the freedoms they sought, but the rise of Republicanism gave them a clearer choice. They refused to follow ethnic guidelines in making up their minds; instead they divided along religious lines. German Catholics particularly were swayed by their fear of Know-Nothingism which was associated with the Republican Party in their minds; they tended to remain Democrats while German Protestants joined the Republican ranks. In several states of the Old Northwest, and in Illinois particularly, the religious factor played a less decisive role, for there the Republicans were less tainted by Know-Nothingism than in the Northeast. This allowed the Germans to vote as their consciences dictated on the slavery issue; in the seven northwestern states they cast 283,784 ballots for Lincoln, a figure gaining significance from the fact Lincoln's majority over Douglas there was only 149,807. Without the votes of northeasterners and immigrants, the Northwest would have been in the Democratic column when results were tabulated.

Equally important in explaining the section's swing was the growth of a Northeast-Northwest legislative alliance on all important national issues. Their traditional agreement on one public question—the tariff—was emphasized again in 1857 when a new Democratic-sponsored bill lowered customs duties even beyond the point reached in the Walker Tariff of 1846. The cry of anger from western and eastern newspapers indicated their common hatred of a cotton South which was attempting to strangle their economy for its own ends. They united, too, in denouncing the southern attack on federally supported internal improvements. Under the Democratic presidents who controlled the nation after 1852, appropriations for river and harbor bills were reduced to the vanishing point, to the disgust of both western farmers seeking outlets for their goods and eastern manufacturers looking for national markets.

The legislative issue that gave Northeast and Northwest the best chance to realize their common interests was Homestead. In the past they had sharply disagreed on land policy; the westerners favoring liberal laws, the easterners distrustful of measures that would drain laborers from factories. That division was forgotten as all classes in both sections united behind a measure to give settlers 160 acres of the public domain. Western support was consistent with its past policy, but eastern enthusiasm represented a break with precedent. This was due to the flood of Irish immigration that swept over the Northeast after 1845, creating an inexhaustible labor pool which convinced industrialists no amount of free land could deplete their supply of workers. No longer plagued by this fear, they looked upon Homestead as a device to build western markets for their manufactured goods. The South, on the other hand, was unalterably opposed, partly because land would be given in small units unsuited to slavery, partly because a free public domain would attract freedom-loving immigrants to the frontier. The clear sectional alignment on the issue was demonstrated in 1852, 1858, and 1859 when Homestead bills passed the northern-dominated House of Representatives, only to meet defeat in the Senate where the South's strength was greater. A measure squeezed through both houses in 1860 was vetoed by a Democratic president. On that issue, as on all others, North and West stood as one against a common enemy.

Even more important in explaining the swing of the Northwest were the section's shifting trade routes. Before 1850 its agricultural surpluses were exported southward along the Mississippi artery and to the East over the New York or Pennsylvania canal systems, with the bulk of the heavy goods reaching markets via New Orleans. The commercial alliance between South and West was broken during the 1850s by the railroad. For the first time the Appalachian Mountain barrier was bridged and the rich markets of the Atlantic seaboard opened to westerners. The steel network binding the North together in 1860 symbolized the section's new unity and provided an economic basis for the sectional realignment which found expression in war.

The race of eastern railroad promoters to tap markets in the Northwest began during the 1840s when roads were started westward from New York, Philadelphia, and Baltimore. Baltimore's venture, the Baltimore and Ohio Railroad, bogged down under financial difficulties in 1842 but was revived six years later and in 1853 emerged at Wheeling on the Ohio River. Philadelphia's western connection, the Pennsylvania Railroad, was opened as far as Pittsburgh a year later when the last difficult strip of mountain terrain was surmounted. From New York two lines were completed to Lake Erie during the decade. One was the result of a stock exchange among the numerous end-to-end roads which crossed the state from Albany to Buffalo; in 1853 they were brought together as the New York Central Railroad, with connections at Albany to New York City and Boston. The other was the New York and Erie Railroad, which was opened between New York City and Dunkirk on Lake Erie in 1852. By the middle 1850s four trunk lines were in operation between the principal coastal ports of the North Atlantic and the waterways of the Northwest. In addition two roads, the Grand Trunk and the Great Western, connected the Great Lakes with eastern Canada.

The railroads would have had little effect on western trade had not their construction been paralleled by a burst of road building in the upper Mississippi Valley states. During the decade nearly 10,000 miles of track were laid in that section. Many of the new lines were of only local importance, but more were built with an eye to extending eastern trunk lines and played an important role in developing trade with the seaboard. That was especially the case after 1857 when a depression forced many small roads into such financial difficulties that they were absorbed by the main east-west lines. By 1860 the New York Central Railroad and the Erie Railroad were connected with the Mississippi River by such lines as the Great Western Railroad, the Michigan Central Railroad, the Michigan Southern Railroad, and the roads skirting the southern shore of Lake Erie. The Pennsylvania Railroad was joined to Chicago by its subsidiary, the Pittsburgh, Ft. Wayne and

Transportation Routes in the Northwest, 1850

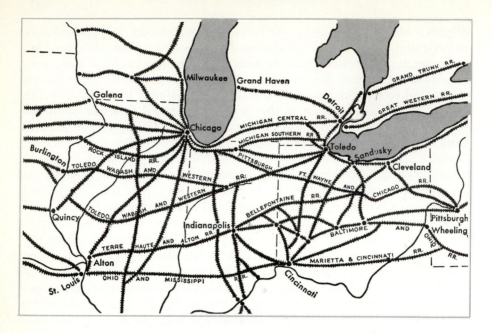

Transportation Routes in the Northwest, 1860

Chicago Railroad, and to the central sections of the Northwest by the Toledo, Wabash and Western Railroad. Direct shipments between St. Louis and the Wheeling terminus of the Baltimore and Ohio Railroad were possible over the Marietta and Cincinnati Railroad, the Ohio and Mississippi Railroad, and the Terre Haute and Alton Railroad. Competition between those lines was so intense, particularly after the Panic of 1857, that freight rates were often lower than by steamboat.

The result was a shift in western trade from the South to the Northeast. The extent of the revolution was revealed by commercial statistics showing the direction taken by the exports of the Northwest:

		To the East	*To the South*
Corn	1850	3,600,000 bushels	2,400,000 bushels
	1860	19,200,000 bushels	4,800,000 bushels
Pork	1850	300,000 barrels	1,200,000 barrels
	1860	930,000 barrels	570,000 barrels
Whiskey	1850	66,000 barrels	134,000 barrels
	1860	310,000 barrels	190,000 barrels
Wheat	1850	5,000,000 bushels	500,000 bushels
	1860	28,420,000 bushels	580,000 bushels
Flour	1850	2,070,000 barrels	930,000 barrels
	1860	4,345,000 barrels	1,155,000 barrels

The swing of the Northwest into the northern camp, brought about by the growth of a freedom-loving population, a fight for a common legislative program, and the cementing of commercial ties, proved decisive in the election of 1860. Had the section voted as it had a decade before Lincoln would have been defeated, for his margin of victory was small. His 190 electoral votes gave him a majority in the electoral college, yet his popular vote was only 40 per cent of the total cast and 1,000,000 less than that of his combined opponents. Lincoln owed his triumph to his impressive following in the Northeast and to a narrow victory over Douglas in each of the northwestern states. Shifting opinion in that crucial section placed a Republican in the White House.

The secession of the southern states was inevitable. South Carolina, where the tradition of rebellion was strong, led the way as soon as the election results were known. A Charleston convention in December, 1860, unanimously declared "the union now subsisting between South Carolina and the other states" forever at an end. One by one the other slave states of the lower South followed South Carolina into their newly formed Confederate States of America. Only Lincoln's decision not to let the "erring sisters depart in peace" was needed to touch off the Civil War.

That titanic four-year struggle touched the remote Far West only lightly. The states there cast their lot with one side or the other; Louisiana, Arkansas, and Texas with the Confederacy, Missouri and Iowa with the federal government. Most territories found the decision equally easy; Kansas and Nebraska were so strongly pro-Union they were rewarded with statehood during or just after the war, and although Utah had little liking for the United States, it too remained loyal. Only in New Mexico was there any question.

That thinly settled region was peopled by proslavery southerners who would doubtless have joined the Confederacy at once except for the garrison of 1,200 federal troops standing guard over them when war broke out. Their bias was expressed in March, 1861, when frontiersmen in the western portions of the territory met at Mesilla and after repudiating the government of both New Mexico and the United States, declared "the people of Arizona" a part of the Confederate States of America. Their action suggested a bold scheme to Confederate leaders. Why not send an army into the Southwest? The loyal southerners there would rise as a man to support such an expedition, making possible the conquest of the area between Texas and southern California. This would give the South an outlet in the Pacific, room for slavery expansion, and power needed for a place in the congress of nations. The Confederate attempt to carry out that plan accounted for the only military activity in the Far West.

The southerners dispatched a flying squad of mounted riflemen to the Arizona country before federal troops could put down the rebellion there. Those frontiersmen, after a dash across the Plains from Texas, reached Mesilla in late July, 1861, and quickly overwhelmed the few Union troops stationed there. In the meantime a larger Confederate force, led by Brigadier-

General Henry H. Sibley and made up of 1,750 men, started west to drive federal forces from the forts guarding eastern New Mexico. They reached Ft. Craig, the principal Union stronghold, in February, 1862, only to find the 1,000 soldiers there so strongly fortified that a long siege would be required. Rather than risk prolonged operations in an arid region where supplies were difficult to obtain, General Sibley bypassed Ft. Craig, moving on to Albuquerque and Santa Fe which were occupied without resistance. Starting northward toward Ft. Union where large quantities of goods were stored, he met his first serious opposition—a ragged army of grizzled Mountain Men and prospectors who had hurried south on its own initiative upon learning of the Confederate advance. The two forces met at Glorieta Pass near Santa Fe on March 28, 1862, and although the southerners held their ground their loss of supplies was so devastating that General Sibley was forced to retreat eastward. This move proved to be disastrous, for the desert heat and Union guerrilla bands took such a heavy toll of his men that his striking potential vanished. The Battle of Glorieta Pass involved only a few men, yet it was a watershed in the war in the Far West. Had Sibley triumphed and moved on westward California might have fallen into Confederate hands, with significant results in the final settlement. As it was, a federal force stationed there was freed by Sibley's retreat to drive Confederate invaders from Arizona.

That ended warfare in the Far West, but the fate of the Indian Territory was still in doubt. There factions within all of the Five Civilized tribes, conscious of their southern heritage, leaned strongly toward the Confederacy. The army recruited from among these sympathizers suffered a decisive defeat by a Union invading force at the Battle of Pea Ridge in March, 1862, but southern sentiment was still so strong among the Indians that more was needed. Campaigning continued there for the next year, reaching its first climax when a northern victory at Old Ft. Wayne brought the area north of the Arkansas River under Union control, and its second in April, 1863, when Ft. Gibson was occupied by federal forces. Using this well-placed outpost as a base for operations, northern armies dominated the Indian territory from that time on. Raids by Confederate guerrilla bands continued throughout the West; the notorious William C. Quantrill killed 150 persons in a raid on Lawrence, Kansas, during the summer of 1863, and attacked Ft. Gibson in April, 1864, but his campaigns were more annoying than decisive. The Civil War ended with the West firmly under federal control.

The Miners' Frontier

1858-1875

During the three decades following the Civil War wave after wave of pioneers swept over the trans-Mississippi West—miners, expressmen, Indian fighters, cowmen, pioneer farmers, and equipped farmers—all bent on stripping away wealth hidden in mountain canyons or spread temptingly in the form of lush green pasture lands and fertile prairies. The miners were first on the scene. Between 1858 and 1875 they carried their rough brand of civilization into the mountainous regions of Colorado and Nevada, across the deserts of Arizona, over the inland empire of Oregon, Washington, and Idaho, and through the wilds of Montana to the domed Black Hills of South Dakota. They found a fortune in gold and silver, and left behind ghost towns and a partly settled country.

To the westerner there was nothing remarkable in the fact that the mining frontier advanced rapidly while the United States was fighting a war for existence. That they should travel east or lend their weight to Union or Confederacy never occurred to them, or, if it did, the idea was dismissed as a fantastic notion. They were, like many frontier settlers, concerned not with distant events but with affairs close to home. Their provincialism rested partially on the isolation of pioneer settlements, but was due primarily to the limitless economic opportunities offered by the frontier; why bother with the outside world when a fortune lay on your own doorstep? Whenever chances for immediate economic betterment were greatest, preoccupation with local affairs mounted. That certainly was the case during the Civil War. What mattered that eastern streams ran red with blood when western streams concealed pockets of yellow gold? Westerners suffered no pangs of conscience as they ignored the war raging beyond the Mississippi to search for precious metals.

Although this attitude was typical, the miners differed from usual American frontier settlers. They occupied not fertile valleys or rich farmlands but often the unattractive portions of the Far West—steep mountainsides where roaring creeks covered deposits of precious metal, parched deserts where shifting sands hid beds of ore, arid highlands where jagged rock outcroppings shielded mineral-bearing lodes. The prospectors scoured thousands of square miles of mountain and desert that would have been avoided had farmers been the only pioneers. They were unusual, moreover, in that they moved not from east to west in the usual frontier pattern, but, initially, from west to east. For prospectors in most gold fields came from California rather than the settled areas of the Mississippi Valley.

Conditions within the far western state drove them out. They had gone there in the gold rush of 1849, at a time when gold nuggets or "dust" were relatively easy to obtain. Small quantities of the metal were present in rivers flowing westward into the Sacramento and San Joaquin valleys from the Sierra Nevadas, resting in pockets at the bottom of the streams. The particles were obtainable by a simple process called placer mining. A prospector needed only to throw a few shovelfuls of dirt into a "washing pan," twirl them about with water to wash gravel and stone away, and scrape away the grains of heavy gold left at the bottom. Where "pay dirt" was found in sufficient quantity to be "worked," one of two other devices was used. One was a "cradle," a crude contraption which the miner rocked with one hand while dipping in gravel and water with the other; the sand was washed away to leave particles of gold trapped against wooden cleats. Another was the "sluice box" or "long tom," a long wooden box fitted with cleats at its lower end, into which a stream was diverted while miners shoveled in pay dirt. The rushing water carried away the dirt, while the cleats captured the dust and nuggets. All those methods could be used by individuals or small groups, for they required neither capital nor experience. They were employed by the '49ers in the first exploitation of California's wealth.

By the middle 1850s, however, the day of the individual prospector was drawing to an end. Most rich "diggings" were already appropriated, and the region had been so thoroughly prospected there was no chance of finding more. Gold remained, but it was locked in lodes of quartz or buried deep beneath debris laid down by the passing centuries. To extract the precious metal crushing mills must be built, the stubborn quartz crumbled to the point where the gold could be dissolved in mercury, and the quicksilver evaporated in large retorts. Or shafts must be sunk to reach beds of ore fifty or one hundred feet below the surface. Both mills and tunnels were beyond the financial means of the average miner. Gold continued to be dug in California, but eastern capitalists provided the funds while, underground, hard-rock miners did the work. Thousands upon thousands of prospectors were left without any hope of making the "strike" that meant prosperity.

Any other form of life was unthinkable to most of them. They were inoculated with the feverish restlessness peculiar to the prospectors; in their eyes every rock outcropping, every cascading stream, might conceal a pocket of dull yellow metal worth a king's ransom. Nothing would satisfy them but a continuous quest for illusive fortune. Their needs were simple: a grub stake, a washing pan, a pack mule, endless hope. Their hunting ground was all the West, from the Pacific to the Rockies and from the mountains of British Columbia to the sun-dried valley of the Gila River. Throughout the late 1850s and 1860s they tramped over that domain, panning each likely stream and scanning each vein of rock for the telltale glint of yellow metal. Few operated alone, for the danger from Indians and outlaws was ever present; the solitary prospector with his mule and washing pan was an invention of twentieth-century Hollywood. On this frontier, as on all others, group cooperation was essential to both success and survival. Even then most failed to find enough gold to pay for their grub stakes, but a fortunate few stumbled upon rich pockets. Whenever such a strike was made a rush followed, with "yonder-siders" from California, "greenhorns" from the East, and grizzled prospectors from all the West, racing pell-mell to the spot. Those not drawn away by later rushes stayed to build the company mining towns in the Rocky Mountain country and much of the Great Basin.

The process began in 1858 with discoveries in Colorado, Nevada, and British Columbia. The Colorado strike was most exciting. Rumors of gold in the mountainous country below South Pass had persisted for years—kept alive by tales of trappers who emerged with handfuls of nuggets, or Indians who shot bullets of yellow metal—before a party of California-bound '49ers first investigated the region. The slight signs of "color" in their washing pans were not enough to detain them long, but when they returned to the East without any of California's riches, they fell to thinking of Colorado's possibilities. Two of the group, Captain John Beck of the Oklahoma country and W. Green Russell of Georgia, decided to return, readily persuading about 100 Indians and frontiersmen to accompany them. They started west along the Arkansas River in the spring of 1858, descended Cherry Creek to the headwaters of the South Platte, and there began panning streams. Ten days later they were joined by a party of prospectors from eastern Kansas who directed their search to the region about Pike's Peak. Findings were so few many drifted back East before late July when a member of the Beck-Russell party struck "pay dirt" near present-day Denver. Both groups then concentrated on that proven region, making a number of small strikes during the summer.

News of the discoveries, carried to the Mississippi Valley by travelers, found its way into Missouri newspapers in exaggerated form, for understatement was never a weakness of frontier editors. Moreover the Panic of 1857 was depressing business, and a gold rush would restore prosperity to pioneer towns where miners bought supplies. So writers filled their columns with feverish stories of prospectors whose daily take with a shovel and washing pan was $20, of an overland immigrant who used a hatchet and frying pan to wash three ounces of dust from Cherry Creek in an hour, of

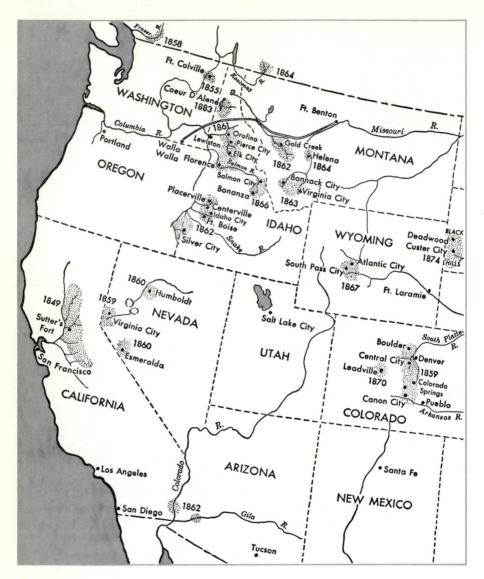

The Miners' Frontier, 1858–1875

riches dwarfing those of California in the new El Dorado. Those tall tales were eagerly accepted by poverty-ridden westerners; a youth seen collecting empty meal sacks at Council Bluffs only reflected the atmosphere of the day when he told questioners that he was going to stuff them with gold at Pike's Peak if he had to stay until fall to do it. That these signs presaged a major mining rush for the spring of 1859 was clear to the two parties of miners already in the Rocky Mountain country. Both they and the thousand other get-rich-quick enthusiasts who hurried to the spot that fall made no further pretense of mining, but spent the autumn and winter laying out the twin towns of Aurora and Denver City on either side of Cherry Creek. By the time that spring arrived they had thousands of lots surveyed in anticipation of a boom that seemed sure to come.

These preparations showed a sound knowledge of frontier psychology, for by the spring of 1859 conditions were ripe for one of the wildest and least rational rushes in the nation's history. All the ingredients were there—a depression in the East that unleashed a vast mobile population, exaggerated tales of the riches that lay ahead, relatively easy transportation routes to follow. Whenever this combination of forces operated a major rush took place, as it had to California in 1849. Now another was foreordained. All that winter western Missouri towns bustled with activity as storekeepers crammed shelves with sides of bacon, sacks of flour, cases of canned beans, and bundles of the shovels and pans needed by gold seekers. Horses and oxen were in such demand that prices soared. Wagonmakers labored long hours on every type of vehicle from roomy covered wagons to flimsy hand-carts that could be pushed across the Plains. And there was scarcely a Mississippi Valley barroom from Iowa to Arkansas not jammed with knots of men eagerly pouring over the *Pike's Peak Guide* which an enterprising printer had hurried from the presses. Those who knew the signs agreed all was in readiness for a rush rivaling that of 1849.

The first breath of spring started the hordes westward. Steamboats crowded to the rails poured throngs of immigrants ashore at every Missouri River town. "The streets," wrote one resident, "are full of people buying flour, bacon, and groceries, with wagons and outfits, and all around the town are little camps preparing to go west." All through April, May, and June they left the jumping-off places in a regular parade of Conestoga wagons, handcarts, men on horseback, men on foot—each with "Pike's Peak or Bust" crudely printed on their packs or wagon canvas. Most used the well-marked trail along the Platte and South Platte, others followed the Arkansas, or Kansas, or Smoky Hill rivers. By the end of June more than 100,000 "fifty-niners" were in the Pike's Peak country.

Their reception was disheartening. They spread out over the eastern Rockies, laying out mining camps as they went—Pueblo, Canon City, Boulder, and a host of others. They panned every stream, chipped every promising rock outcropping, and found nothing. This was not what the guide books led them to expect; the land was supposed to be yellow with gold. Disappointment spread among them. They had, in the phrase of the day, been "humbugged." In disgust they started east again, the hopeful slogan of "Pike's Peak or Bust" scratched from their wagons and the truthful "Busted, by God," scrawled in its place. By midsummer half of the 50,000 miners who actually reached Colorado were back in their eastern homes. The Pike's Peak gold rush of 1859 was one of the greatest fiascos in the history of the frontier.

Perseverance rewarded the several thousand miners who stayed on at Denver. In May, 1859, a wandering prospector, John H. Gregory, "struck it rich" on the north fork of Clear Creek. News of pay dirt yielding $2 a pan, proclaimed to the world by a frenzied extra of the newly started *Rocky Mountain News*, brought the usual rush of gold seekers from the whole Pike's Peak region converging on Gregory Gulch to stake out claims. By the middle of June 5,000 people lived there, most of them in a mining camp called Central City, and twenty sluice boxes were in operation. Disappointment soon replaced hope for the majority as the good claims were snapped up by the fortunate few, leaving the luckless many to wander on in their weary search. Their redoubled efforts, now they knew Colorado contained gold, led to a number of smaller strikes along the eastern front of the mountains. At each a mining camp sprang up, complete with an assortment of shacks made from flour sacks or old shirts, a dance hall, gambling dens, bawdy houses, and enough saloons to satisfy the insatiable thirst of hard-working miners.

Life in the mining camps—whether in California, the Pike's Peak country, or later communities—followed a unique pattern. Within their straggling borders the distinctive features of frontier existence were present in exaggerated form. On all frontiers men outnumbered women; in mining camps respectable ladies were so rare that men often gathered to gape admiringly at a woman's dress hung on a line. All western communities were cosmopolitan; at the diggings college graduates rubbed elbows with illiterates, ministers and rogues worked side by side over sluice boxes, slaveholders swung their picks beside Yankee abolitionists, drunken jailbirds mingled with pious deacons. Every frontier attracted lawless outcasts; in the gold fields the promise of easy money lured an unusually large number of desperadoes, gamblers, and harpies to prey on the physical or moral weakness of prospectors. Many frontier settlers squatted on government land; at the mines all were illegal trespassers on territory belonging to Indian tribes and the United States. Through the history of American expansion westerners had attempted to solve problems stemming from their unique environment by developing democratic institutions, casting off eastern control, and administering their own peculiar brand of justice. In the mining camps, frontier democracy, provincialism, and rough-and-ready legal practices were developed to the unusual degree required by unusual conditions .

The first miners in each new gold field were usually orderly men who were content to prospect without any social organization. With the initial strike and the rush of newcomers, some government was needed to protect the claims of those already there and provide for an equitable division of the remaining lands. As soon as the need became apparent a few leading miners issued a call for a mass meeting. This assembled in the camp's main street, a chairman was elected by voice vote, and laws were passed—regulating the size of the claim each prospector could stake out, outlining the procedure necessary to hold a claim, prescribing means for settling disputes and punishing crimes. Usually a committee of three or four "judges" to enforce the rough codes was named, but ultimate responsibility for their execution remained in the mass meeting, which might be summoned whenever an emergency arose. The simple democracy of the mining camps was typical of the frontier; from the days of the Mayflower Compact and the Watauga Association westerners had set up their own governments whenever they found themselves beyond the pale of the law.

The mass meeting, effective as it was in dealing with most problems rising in mining camps, failed to provide a satisfactory law-enforcement machinery. The miners were partly responsible, for they were hardened individualists who paid little attention to community affairs unless their own interests were threatened. Even more to blame were the roaring reprobates attracted to the diggings by the promise of easy money. They came by the score—shifty-eyed saloon keepers from the dives of New York, smooth-tongued gamblers from the East, fading harlots from the streets of Paris, Mexican outlaws from Sonora, "Sydney coves" from the penal colonies of Australia, gunmen and desperadoes from the wide-open towns of the Mississippi Valley—all lured by the prospect of helping themselves to dust and nuggets grubbed out by the miners. They flocked into each new mining camp in such numbers that they eventually challenged the leadership of the majority business group that was the stabilizing element in every community.

Whenever that occurred the law-abiding majority moved into action. A few citizens led the way; meeting secretly they organized a vigilance committee, complete with a written constitution pledging members to cooperate until order was restored. Others were quietly added until the committee was large enough to challenge the outlaws, then a few ringleaders among the desperadoes were selected for punishment, hunted down by the vigilantes, and after a brief trial, sentenced to "stretch hemp." Executions were carried out on the spot, usually from a limb of the nearest tree. Only a rare hanging was needed to send the camp's rogues scurrying to safety, nor were they likely to return, for once a vigilance committee established its authority a simple warning was enough to drive out the most hardened criminal. Organizations of that sort were formed in all the Colorado camps, as they had been in every gold field since 1851 when the first was set up at San Francisco.

Both vigilantes and mass meetings were looked upon as temporary stopgaps, to be disbanded as soon as governmental machinery was provided by the United States. Two things were necessary: laws regulating the use of the public domain by miners, and a stable government. The first could be provided only by Congress, which proved distressingly lax in dealing with the problem. As early as December, 1848, when the first reports of gold discoveries in California reached the East, President Polk recommended a law governing the disposal of gold-bearing lands which would "bring a large return of money to the treasury and at the same time . . . lead to the development of their wealth by individual proprietors and purchasers." His sensible proposal was completely ignored; not until 1853 was any measure passed and that only excluded mineral lands from pre-emption. Belatedly, in 1866, Congress ruled that mining territory was open to all citizens, "subject to such regulations as may be prescribed by law, and subject also to local customs or rules of miners in the several mining districts." This unusual measure, which simply recognized the right of miners to make their own laws, was one of the few congressional statues in the history of the frontier that did not try to inflict eastern institutions on the West.

The orderly government desired by miners was easier to obtain, for their pressure could prod indifferent Washington officials into action. The demand was usually voiced by the first prospectors on each new mining frontier; in the Pike's Peak country the few hardy souls who spent the winter of 1858-59 in Denver initiated the movement. Their thoughts turned to politics when an early snow in November, 1858, stopped all prospecting. Colorado was technically part of Kansas Territory at this time, and the legislature at Lawrence passed a good many sensible laws, laws which if enforced would have hurried the coming of orderly government to the Pike's Peak country. Notable among these was a measure setting up a perfectly workable system for regulating mining claims, another creating an efficient court system, and still another promulgating a code of civil law that would have operated successfully if applied. It never was. The Coloradoans wanted no control from a distant territorial capital and said so in a convention held late in November, 1858. Nothing would do but that delegates be sent to Washington, bearing a petition demanding immediate organization of the region as the State of Jefferson. "Making governments and building towns," wrote a visitor as he watched with amazement, "are the natural employments of the migratory Yankee. He takes to them as instinctively as a young duck to water. Congregate a hundred Americans anywhere beyond the settlements and they immediately lay out a city, frame a state constitution and apply for admission into the Union, while twenty-five of them became candidates for the United States Senate."

When Congress refused their request the miners took matters into their own hands. A meeting of delegates from six camps, held at Denver on April 15, 1859, put the issue squarely before the people: "Shall it be a government of the knife and revolver or shall we unite in forming here in our golden country, among the ravines and gulches of the Rocky Mountains, and the fertile valleys of the Arkansas and Plattes, a new and independent state?" Their answer was a call for a convention to draft a constitution for the State of Jefferson. By the time this assembled in June, 1859, the rush of '59ers was over and the prospects of maintaining a permanent population so uncertain that the delegates agreed to postpone action until autumn. They met again in October, after a popular referendum showed a majority favored immediate statehood, this time to draw up a frame of government for the proposed state. When this was ratified two weeks later a governor and legislature were chosen to govern the territory until Congress acted. That the interim government lacked any legal basis for existence did not bother a frontier community. "We claim," wrote the editor of the *Rocky Mountain News*, "that any body, or community of American citizens, which from any cause or any circumstance is cut off from, or from isolation is situated as not to be under, any active and protecting branch of the central government, have a right, if on American soil, to frame a government, and enact such laws and regulations as may be necessary for their own safety, protection and happiness."

Despite those bold words the temporary government did not work satisfactorily; its decrees were ignored by miners whose governmental needs were satisfied by local mass meetings and its officials soon tired of serving without pay. Only congressional action would save the situation, but Congress was in no mood to act. Each petition from the Territory of Jefferson was either brushed aside or hopelessly entangled in the raging slavery controversy; not until the southern states left the Union did Colorado achieve territorial organization with boundaries those of today. From that time on the region developed steadily. During the early 1860s shafts were sunk to the rich mother lodes near Boulder and Denver, machinery hauled in, labor and capital imported from the East, and precious metal extracted in fabulous quantities. Farmers drifted in, lured by high prices, attractive markets, and fertile mountain valleys. New mines were opened as prospectors uncovered beds of silver ore near Leadville in the 1870s and deposits of gold on Cripple Creek a few years later. Colorado entered the Union as a state in 1876, already well beyond the frontier stage.

While the Pike's Peak country was undergoing this transformation, other miners found fame and fortune in the mountains surrounding the Carson River valley of Nevada. Prospectors turned their attention to that region during the middle 1850s, acting under the sensible belief that if gold was found on the western slopes of the Sierra Nevadas it might also exist in the eastern foothills. Much activity was centered in two promising canyons that ran down the side of Davidson Mountain in the eastern Sierras: Gold Canyon and Six Mile Canyon. Gold had been found in these gulches as early as 1849, but results were so disappointing that most miners drifted away, leaving only a handful of ne'er-do-wells who hated to leave a country where they could work only three months a year. Only a happy accident transformed this decaying community into the West's wildest mining camp. In the spring of 1859 two prospectors, Peter O'Riley and Patrick McLaughlin, decided to test some likely looking dirt they had noticed near "Old Man Caldwell's" spring high up Six Mile Canyon. As they dug away under the June sun they uncovered a heavy, dark soil that proved to be rich in flake gold. Giddy with excitement, they spent the day feverishly digging and washing out the precious metal in a hastily devised cradle. While thus engaged they were visited by a drifter named Henry T. P. Comstock who was reputed to be the laziest man in the diggings. Seeing the $300 in gold that the partners had already washed out, the glib-tongued Comstock talked himself into a share of the claim, then talked so incessantly of "his" discovery and "his" claim that others began referring to the find as the "Comstock Lode." For the black dirt discovered by O'Riley and McLaughlin was actually the decomposed quartz of the Ophir vein of that richest of all mines.

The world knew nothing of this find until June 11, when the fortunate partners sent samples of a heavy bluish quartz that they unearthed in their digging across the mountains to Nevada City, California, to be assayed. The report was unbelievable: the "blue stuff" was almost pure silver and gold, and was worth $3,876 a ton. Overnight the nation learned of the fabulous riches of the Washoe District—so named for the Indians who lived there—and the rush was on. The first comers were well-to-do speculators from Nevada City who quietly staked out claims along the entire Comstock Lode where it outcropped between Gold Canyon and Six Mile Canyon, but the fact that the one proven mine was completely appropriated did not dampen the enthusiasm of the thousands of would-be miners who clogged the trails from California that summer. They blanketed the district with their claims and camps, although most stayed close to Davidson Mountain. There they concentrated in Virginia City, a nightmare assortment of smoky caves, leaky tents, and ramshackle saloons, where men paid a dollar a night for sleeping space on dirt floors wrapped in blankets rented from a shrewd trader for an additional dollar fee.

They lived in a fantastic world, the prospectors who reached Nevada during 1859 and 1860. Few of them could mine, for the gold was locked in quartz veins that could only be crushed with expensive machinery. So they spent their days staking out claims, their nights peddling shares in imaginary mines. Everyone was feverishly happy in that land of penniless millionaires. No one had enough money to pay his grocery bill, but everyone owned 30,000 or 40,000 "feet" in a dozen claims—the "Branch Mint," the "Root-Hog-or-Die," the "Let-Her-Rip," the "Treasure Trove," the "Grand Mogul"—that would soon be worth fortunes.

Gradually order replaced chaos as capital flowed in. Quartz mills were built at Gold Hill and Virginia City, lumber hauled in for homes, roads laid out across the mountains to California, express companies formed to carry out gold and bring in supplies needed by 15,000 people. The improvements helped translate the wild dreams of the miners into equally wild actuality. Fortune nodded to only a few—less than a dozen of the 3,000 mines staked out ever proved profitable—but their profits were unbelievable as each lode was followed deep into the earth. More than $15,000,000 worth of precious metal was taken from Davidson Mountain in the next four years; wealth that transformed Virginia City into a metropolis complete with five newspapers and a stock exchange; wealth that allowed rough miners who had lived on bacon and beans for years to revel in a diet of oysters, strawberries, squab, and champagne.

Prospectors who failed to strike it rich in the Washoe District sought a new Comstock Lode in other mountainous areas of western Nevada. By the end of 1860 news of strike after strike was sending Virginia City's miners off in a series of rushes that often emptied the city. One group of mines was opened in the Esmeralda Mountains southwest of Walker Lake, another in the Humboldt Mountains northeast of Washoe. Although neither proved as rich as the Davidson Mountain country every new discovery launched a period of wild trading in "feet" similar to that in Virginia City.

Expansion strengthened a demand for territorial organization which forced Congress to set aside western Utah as Nevada Territory in 1861. Governor James W. Nye, a New York politician, unwittingly brought himself undying fame by selecting as his secretary a young Missourian, Orin Clemens, who took west with him his younger brother, Samuel. Mark Twain's experiences in the mines of Washoe, Humboldt, and Esmeralda gave him material for *Roughing It*, a classic description of life in the Far West. Even that notable contribution failed to satisfy the Nevadians, who soon clamored for statehood. Under ordinary circumstances Congress would have brushed aside a request from a territory whose population of 20,000 was far below the standard, but in 1863 Republican leaders were willing to welcome any region which would assure Abraham Lincoln more electoral votes in 1864 and help ratify the Thirteenth Amendment. Although Democrats protested vehemently, Lincoln's support and the argument that any state with mines producing $24,000,000 yearly would soon attract a larger number of people, carried the day. On October 31, 1864, Nevada became a state; eight days later its voters rewarded Republicans by returning a thumping majority for the President's re-election.

The new state's palmiest days lay just ahead. During the next decade mine after mine was opened, as the Comstock Lode or similar veins were tapped at different subterranean spots by small companies. The greatest discovery came in 1873 when four miners, organized as the Consolidated Virginia, decided to test the theory that the Comstock grew wider deep within the bowels of the earth. Scraping together needed cash and equipment, they began the back-breaking task of boring through the flinty rock of Davidson Mountain. At 1,167 feet they struck the Big Bonanza; the lode at that point was fifty-four feet wide and filled with gold and silver. This richest find in the history of mining not only brought the prospectors a fortune of $200,000,000 but sent other miners to tunneling in the hope of striking similar hidden wealth. For the next years the air about Virginia City rang with the clank of metal drills and the boom of blasting powder as new mines were opened. Most proved fruitless but a few elevated their owners from paupers to millionaire "Kings of the Comstock" with ugly mansions on Virginia City's twisted streets or San Francisco's Nob Hill. For another ten years boring went on, until deepening shafts raised costs beyond the point where profits could be made. By 1890 the boom was over. Nevada sank into sleepy lethargy until its people discovered that gold was as plentiful in the pockets of tourists and divorce-seekers as in the pockets of streams or lodes.

While rich Washoe went through its evolution, prospectors carried the mining frontier into the Southwest. The first rush occurred in 1858 when dust was discovered along the lower Gila River. The find proved disappointing; but a new strike on the Colorado in 1862 led to a stampede from California, this time with permanent results. Tucson, the leading town, developed overnight into the "Sodom and Gomorrah" of the West, with such a colorful collection of cutthroats that sober citizens believed the influx due more to the San Francisco vigilance committee than to the attractiveness of the mines. Their demand for an orderly government forced Congress to create the Territory of Arizona in February, 1863. A year later the first crushing mills began the district's transformation into a stable mining region.

More important than the expansion of the miners' frontier into the South was its parallel movement northward into Washington, Canada, Idaho, and Montana. The first strikes were made in the "Inland Empire" of the Columbia Plateau where the Snake and Columbia rivers twisted their way to the sea through deep lava beds. Gold was discovered in 1855 near Ft. Colville, a former Hudson's Bay Company post on the upper Columbia, and although the find proved disappointing, prospectors were encouraged to wander over the region in the hopes of richer deposits. Some, pushing northward into the wilds of British Columbia with their washing pans, found "color" in the Fraser River during the fall of 1857. By the following spring all the West knew a new El Dorado waited exploitation, where Indians were friendly and miners could pan out from $10 to $50 worth of dust daily. The rush from California that followed dwarfed even the stampede to Washoe going on at the same time; roads to Stockton and Sacramento were jammed with prospectors making their way to the coast where they fought to board steamboats for the journey north. Thirty-five thousand people left the state for the Fraser River in 1858, most of them soon to return with the disappointing news that the gold-bearing sand bars of the river were so flooded mining was impossible.

They knew why. Not high water or shallow deposits doomed their efforts, but the dictatorial practices of James Douglas, a chief factor of the Hudson's Bay Company which controlled the area. Douglas and his superiors were determined that the disorder characteristic of American mining rushes should not be duplicated on the Fraser. Douglas laid down his rules in January, 1858: every miner would pay a monthly tax of twenty-one shillings (about five dollars) and all who refused to do so or who created trouble would not be allowed to mine. This rigid regulation was strictly enforced with the aid of the royal navy, especially after August 2, 1858, when the region became the colony of British Columbia with Douglas its first governor. Thereafter a "gold commissioner" stationed in each camp not only collected the monthly tax but administered justice with an iron hand. All who disobeyed lost their licenses, allowing anyone who wished to seize their claims. The result was the most orderly rush in American history—and the least productive. British and American miners alike grumbled that the fees, trade regulations, and moral codes stifled progress; if they could be abolished, the miners insisted, more workers would be attracted, competition would lower prices, and improved transportation would be provided. When their demands were ignored they showed their dissatisfaction by leaving the Fraser in droves; by the spring of 1859 when the mining season should have been at its height a mass exodus was under way. Flooded sandbars and the exhaustion of many deposits hurried their departure, but resentment against Britain's attempt to speed the coming of civilization played a part.

Those who stayed fanned out in two directions in their continuous hunt for the elusive yellow metal. Some prospected northward along the Fraser to Caribou Lake where they found enough gold to attract 1,500 miners during 1860 and 1861. More drifted southward into the Snake River valley where their spectacular strikes during the next four years lured the first permanent settlers to Idaho. The first was made by a party of a dozen miners under Captain E. D. Pierce who in August, 1860, found pockets of gold about twenty-five miles from the mouth of the Clearwater River. Exaggerated stories of their success inspired such a stampede during the spring of 1861 that several thousand miners occupied the district by the end of June, living in such camps as Orofino and Pierce City, and supplied from the nearby city of Lewiston which was founded by opportunistic merchants as an outfitting point. Although the Clearwater mines sent out $100,000 worth of dust monthly, most newcomers failed to find good sites not already pre-empted. After satisfying themselves the unworked streams nearby contained no hidden wealth they struck out southward once more, some to the South Fork of the Clearwater where the camp of Elk City was laid out, others to the Salmon River valley where the town of Florence was established. The pockets there were fabulously rich; one miner panned out $6,000 worth of dust in one day while another found shining scales worth $500 in the bottom of one pan.

Finds such as those brought a rush of population to the upper Snake River valley during 1862; all through the spring every steamer dumped hordes of "yonder-siders" from California on the Portland docks, every wagon train from the East brought throngs of "greenhorns" from the Missouri Valley or seasoned prospectors from the Pike's Peak country. Twenty thousand miners were at work in the Clearwater and Salmon River gold fields by the close of the year. Some who failed to find likely spots moved south, panning the tributaries of the Snake as they went. One found pay dirt on the Boise River during the autumn; during 1863 the stampede to that region scattered mines and camps—Placerville, Centerville, and Idaho City—along the valley. Another struck it rich on the Owyhee River; 2,500 miners followed him there to set up placers and sluice boxes around their camp at Silver City. The rushes to a region still held by Indians forced the government to build Ft. Boise as protection from the justly outraged natives.

On the heels of the prospectors, there as everywhere on the mining frontier, came permanent settlers. Mining camps attracted not only faro dealers, prostitutes of various races, and saloon keepers, but merchants, lawyers, clergymen, and editors willing to endure slovenly life for the high prices their services could command. Their purpose was to create in the gold country patent-office models of the cities they had known in the East, assuring themselves both safety and comfort. Each primitive camp, in their eyes, was the nucleus of a future metropolis, dominating the trade of the area about it. To hurry that day they turned themselves into typical "boosters," advertising for settlers, competing for colleges and court houses and jails, pressuring railroads to link them with other communities, and campaigning for sidewalks, street lights, sewers, and other amenities of city life. The influence of these solid citizens soon ended the lawlessness that marked the early stages of most new camps; all were transformed into orderly communities with well-functioning law-enforcement facilities within a few months. Even those that gained a reputation for mayhem and violence—towns such as Leadville and Tombstone and Deadwood—earned that dubious distinction only after they were reached by railroads, allowing the influx of big-city reporters who produced the lurid accounts that their readers wanted—and that have been inflicted on later generations as sober history.

This was the story of the urban centers that emerged as trade entrepots of the Inland Empire. Walla Walla especially rapidly developed pre-eminence, serving as an emporium for the Snake River mines and the gold fields opened along the Kootenay River of Canada in 1864. Lewiston, at the junction of the Snake and Clearwater rivers, was a lesser center, while in the southern Snake Valley, Idaho City forged ahead of competitors. In 1863 it boasted a population of 6,000 people, "elegant dance halls," roaring saloons, and thriving faro parlors, but Lewiston also was proud of a hospital, a theater, several churches, a fire department, and three newspapers, all symbols of its emergence as a metropolitan center. Underlying this development was the occupation of adjacent regions by farmers, lured by the high prices for food paid by the miners. Where else could they sell flour at $28 a hundredweight, cornmeal at $19, chickens at $5 apiece, butter at $1.20 a pound, and potatoes at twenty cents a pound? Gradually the region about Walla Walla filled up with industrious husbandmen.

Farmers, merchants, and miners united in demanding an orderly government, pointing out that the Idaho country could never be satisfactorily governed so long as it remained a part of Washington Territory. Petitions for separate organization were circulated in the mining camps as early as 1860, but Congress paid no heed until 1863 when the growing agricultural population and the introduction of mining machinery indicated the settlements were permanent. The Territory of Idaho, established in March of that year, included all of Montana and most of Wyoming.

Even as Congress acted, miners were stampeding into the eastern sections of the new territory. The pioneers on that frontier were two brothers, James and Granville Stuart, who in 1862 began prospecting the wild country near the headwaters of the Missouri River. On Gold Creek, a mountainous fork of the Clark's Fork River, they found enough pay dirt to justify building sluice boxes. News of their moderate success fell on the ears of a party of disappointed '59ers from Pike's Peak making their way overland to the Salmon River gold fields. Abruptly changing their plans, they started north from the Oregon Trail, panning streams as they went in true prospector style. On Beaverhead River, a tributary of the Jefferson River, they found a large pocket of gold. Others followed them in, until by the autumn of 1862 more than 400 prospectors were in the district, all building sluice boxes or throwing up the crude shacks of their camp, Bannack City.

Those pioneering achievements paved the way for the great Montana gold rush of 1863. The time was ripe for a new stampede. Favorable spots along the Snake River were already appropriated, releasing hundreds of prospectors who were ready to race to any new field. They could reach the Montana mines easily over a military highway, the Mullan Road, which was opened in early 1863 between Walla Walla and Ft. Benton, at the head of steamboat navigation on the Missouri. The combination of available population and easy transportation started the tide rolling as soon as snow melted that spring. Hundreds swarmed in to stake claims about Bannack City; others struck out over the neighboring mountain country in pursuit of wealth. The most fortunate stumbled upon gold in Alder Gulch, a tributary of the Gallatin River. Their attempt to keep the find a secret failed when one miner from the Gulch visited Bannack for supplies; he was followed back by 200 prospectors and the rush began. Virginia City, the camp established by the newcomers, within a year boasted a population of 4,000 men who amused themselves in eight billiard halls, five gambling establishments, three hurdy-gurdies, several bawdy houses, innumerable saloons, and two churches. Thirty million dollars worth of dust and nuggets were taken out of Alder Gulch during the next three years.

Even those riches were rivaled by those of the last great strike in the upper Missouri country. The fortunate miner responsible was a venerable Georgian, John Cowan, who worked his way down the Missouri during the spring of 1864 without detecting a trace of pay dirt. With supplies exhausted and on the point of turning back, he decided to test one last spot, which he called Last Chance Gulch. The pans of yellow nuggets that he found there attracted a rush of miners; Helena was laid out as a mining camp, sluice boxes built, new mines opened in a dozen gulches nearby, and the process begun of extracting the $16,000,000 worth of gold concealed in the region. Helena, conveniently situated on the trade route between Ft. Benton and Bannack and Virginia Cities, rapidly developed into one of the leading commercial emporiums of the mountain country.

The influx of merchants and farmers into fertile mountain valleys nearby, together with the discovery of mineral-bearing lodes which promised rich yields when quartz-crushing machinery could be brought in, testified to the permanence of the fields and accentuated the demand for a stable government. Petitions circulated among the mining camps were sympathetically received by Congress, which in May, 1864, created Montana Territory. The legislature, meeting in Bannack City in December, chose Virginia City as the territorial capital and adopted a seal depicting a miner's pick and shovel and a farmer's plow against a mountain background.

Despite those symbols of permanence, new gold rushes continued to thrill the prospectors of Idaho and Montana. One occurred in 1866 when pay dirt was found on the upper Salmon River; 5,000 miners stampeded to the spot during the summer, to lay out such camps as Salmon City and Bonanza. One famous spot there, the Charles Dickens Mine, yielded $1,000 a day in dust until the surface wealth was skimmed off. Another exciting strike was made a year later along the Sweetwater River of the Wyoming country; South Pass City and Atlantic City sprang up to hold the hordes who raced to the newest El Dorado. The pockets proved shallow, however, and by 1870 the Sweetwater boom was over, leaving behind no residue of farmers and merchants as a permanent population. The next rush was to the Coeur d'Alene Mountains of northern Idaho where pockets of gold were found in 1883. Those also proved so disappointing that by 1886 the prospectors were drifting away, leaving scarred hills, slashed gullies, and deserted ghost towns behind them.

The subsequent development of the northern Rocky Mountain mining country paralleled that of Nevada or Colorado. There as elsewhere early miners only captured a small portion of the surface wealth in their placers; the real riches lay far below the surface, encased in veins of quartz. During the 1870s and 1880s eastern capital moved into Idaho to extract the hidden fortunes; shafts were sunk, crushing mills built, and mine after mine opened. The most famous was the Bunker Hill and Sullivan Mine, discovered in 1885 by a wandering prospector who, pausing to rest on a pile of rock while chasing a runaway mule, found the stones streaked with lead and silver. Investigation disclosed his impromptu resting place to be part of a great dike of precious metals which eventually yielded $250,000,000 worth of silver and lead. Workers brought in to extract such wealth provided Montana and Idaho with permanent populations.

One region remained to be exploited by the drifting prospectors who were always on the fringes of the mining frontier—the Black Hills of Dakota. Rumors that those domed mountains cradled pockets of gold persisted among the mining camps. For years the West heard stories of Indians who appeared at Ft. Laramie with bags full of nuggets, of military commanders who found such wealth they kept their discoveries secret lest their men desert, of occasional prospectors who found pay dirt rivaling that about Sutter's Fort. The tales were not tested so long as gold fields farther west remained to be exploited, for the Black Hills country was occupied by warlike Sioux Indians and guarded by federal troops pledged to keep out all intruders. By 1874, however, the western mines were passing into the hands of eastern capitalists. Thousands of prospectors turned toward the Black Hills, certain that the forest-clad slopes concealed the riches fickle fate denied them elsewhere.

From Massachusetts to California expeditions were formed that spring to force their way past the soldiers ringing the promised land. Observers agreed that if they succeeded the stampede would dwarf the rush to Pike's Peak or the Washoe District.

The military authorities, aware the best way to stop the invasion was to disprove the rumors of Black Hills gold, decided upon official investigation. The expedition fitted out for the purpose—1,200 soldiers and scientists under General George A. Custer—returned in August with upsetting news; gold was present in payable quantities all through the district! The fat was in the fire. A proclamation from abashed army officials barring settlers from the territory did no good; from the entire West miners gathered, ready to defy the troops who barred their path. They concentrated especially at Sioux City, Iowa, where the editor of the Sioux City *Times* turned his paper into a screaming advertisement for the Black Hills' gold fields. Through the winter of 1874–75 they jammed the town's hotels and filled two large tents erected in the main street, ready to leave whenever the soldiers relaxed their vigilance. One party of twenty-eight prospectors broke through the cordon in December, made their way to the mines through the Dakota badlands, and pitched camp on French Creek where they panned gold until troops ejected them.

Their tales of Dakota wealth, magnified by every teller, ruined the government's last chance to hold the Black Hills for the Indians. Throughout the summer bands of miners filtered through the ring of guardians to pan gold furiously for a time before being driven out. In August, 1875, almost 600 miners were ousted, only to return again. As the game of hide-and-seek went on, military leaders realized no amount of force could hold back the miners indefinitely; the only solution was to extinguish the Indian title. When a nine-day conference with the Sioux in September failed to wring any concessions from the tribal leaders, disgusted federal agents decided to let the miners take their own chances. In October the Black Hills were thrown open to all comers who dared risk attack.

The rush began at once. From Iowa and the gold fields of the West prospectors came in droves, to swarm over the region with wash pans in hand, ready to set up placers at the first hint of yellow metal. Most of the 15,000 who entered that fall concentrated on the French Creek region where a town named Custer City was built, a mining district laid out, and laws governing the location of claims adopted. During the winter new discoveries in Deadwood Gulch sent a rush to that northerly valley. In April, 1876, Deadwood was founded, a ramshackle town of one saloon-filled street that twisted through the gulch, catering to the wide-open tastes of 7,000 miners "who had no Puritan prejudices to overcome." Custer City and Deadwood remained the leading cities during the mushroom stages of the rush, although camps were established at Lead City and Spearfish during 1876.

In the folklore of America, perpetuated by the authors of "westerns" that supply much of the motion picture and television fare enjoyed by the nation's viewers, Deadwood was not only the last but the most unrestrained of the "wild west" towns of the frontier era—a riproaring center of sin where the faro games were wilder, and the hurdy-gurdy dance halls noisier, and the shoot-outs more common, than in any other mining camp. For a time, true, Deadwood attracted a disproportionate percentage of the human scum usually found on remote frontiers—Wild Bill Hickok, California Jack, Bed Rock Tom, Poker Alice, Calamity Jane, and other psychopathic extroverts were there briefly. For a time, too, the wealth of the Black Hills lured desperadoes in such numbers that the local newspaper dismissed one holdup with: "We have again to repeat the hackneyed phrase, 'the stage has been robbed'." Yet Deadwood's wild-west era was brief; within a few months the orderly elements banded together to establish a provisional government and a police force that sent the desperadoes scurrying. In all during the city's early days only four killings occurred, and not a single lynching. The frontier might generate lawlessness, but the usual settlers wanted nothing less than to duplicate in a new home the orderly life of the old. They usually achieved that goal in a remarkably short time.

The eastward advance of the mining frontier ended with the Black Hills gold rush. Yet only the surface had been scratched; far more gold and silver remained locked in quartz lodes than had been removed by the primitive techniques of the prospectors. Now the day of the placer miner was ending, the day of the mining capitalist beginning. As the first-comers demonstrated the potential wealth of the Far West, eastern and particularly British capital began to flow westward to finance shaft drilling, quartz mills, hydraulic mining, strip mining, and the network of tunnels needed to bring that wealth into production. In the quarter-century after 1875 English investments grew by 2.3 billion pounds. This abundant capital financed the spectacular growth of copper and tin mining, operations that dwarfed the more glamorous gold and silver rushes. Even the gold deposits were exploited by corporate capital during this era; in the Black Hills the Homestake Mining Company began consolidating small claims as early as 1878, using such efficient methods to extract the precious metal that individual miners could not compete. The prospector and placer miner had left the stage, ousted by the giant enterprises that were to transform the Far West during the next generation into a thriving civilization.

The Transportation
Frontier
1858-1884

The rapidity of the mining frontier's advance greatly alarmed both East and West. In the past, easterners knew, pioneer communities were so near settled regions their economic and spiritual needs could be supplied by the older society. Now miners lived in isolated islands of settlement, scattered far and wide over the mountainous West, where they were distant from the civilization of the East. If left to themselves they might drift into lawless or pagan practices detrimental to the nation. Their salvation and the country's fate depended on the rapid development of transportation lines with the States. Prospectors in the Far West were equally insistent on better communications, knowing that roads would mean lower commodity prices for mining camps and more frequent news of happenings in the East. Both easterners and westerners agreed the improvements would require government support. Their pressure on Washington forced Congress to grant a series of subsidies between the middle 1850s and 1871 to express companies, stagecoach lines, telegraph corporations, and railroads. Federal aid not only gave the West needed economic outlets but opened vast portions of the continent to settlement.

The government's first attempts to provide communication facilities for westerners were hardly successful. In 1848 contracts were awarded for semimonthly mail service between New York and San Francisco by sea; under the arrangement letters were carried to Panama by the United States Steamship Company, carted across the isthmus, and sent northward on vessels of the Pacific Mail Steamship Company. The high costs (twelve to eighty cents an ounce) and the thirty days required for the roundabout journey only stimulated California's demand for overland service. Nothing would satisfy the miners but a direct route across the continent, with frequent way stations where horses could be changed often enough to assure the constant movement of the mails. Through the early 1850s western pressure on the government mounted, reaching a climax in 1856 when a giant petition, signed by 75,000 Californians, was laid before Congress. Daily mails over a road through South Pass, the signers agreed, were needed to quench the westerners' thirst for news.

No sooner was debate on the request begun than the sectional issue intruded. Southerners denounced the South Pass route, knowing that its eastern terminus at St. Louis or Chicago would not only benefit the North economically but presage a transcontinental railroad along the path pioneered by stagecoaches. This the South was bound to resist so effectually that a congressional decision on the issue was impossible. Instead the legislators in 1857 dodged the sectional question by appropriating money to survey and improve two roads, one from Ft. Kearney through South Pass to California, the other from El Paso to Ft. Yuma on the southern border of the state. Although unable to follow the same expedient in granting subsidies, congressmen hit upon an equally compromising device. The Post Office Appropriation Act of 1857 authorized the postmaster general to call for bids on a semi-weekly or weekly mail service from "such point on the Mississippi River as the contractors may select, to San Francisco." The company chosen must, according to the bill, guarantee delivery within twenty-five days in return for an annual subsidy of $600,000.

Southern congressmen supported the measure, which seemingly favored the short South Pass route over the longer roads across the Southwest, only because they knew their interests would be protected by the postmaster general, Aaron V. Brown of Tennessee. They were not disappointed. Brown, an ardent southerner, after throwing out all bids from northern companies, selected the offer of a firm headed by two seasoned expressmen, John Butterfield and William G. Fargo of New York, largely because they proposed to use a road from St. Louis or Memphis through Ft. Smith, El Paso, and Ft. Yuma to San Francisco. Objections to the roundabout "oxbow" route, as northerners derisively labeled it, were brushed aside with the assertion that the plentiful grasslands and healthy climate of the Southwest justified the greater distance!

A year of preparation was needed before the Butterfield Overland Mail started its first stagecoaches across the continent. First a "road" was marked out over the 2,812 miles between Tipton, Missouri, the western terminus of the railroad, and San Francisco. Along this "stations" of wood or adobe were scattered at intervals, where horses and mules could be sheltered, and food provided for passengers with stomachs strong enough to face the Plains fare of bacon, beans, bread, and what passed in the West for coffee. Each of the lonely outposts was placed under an "agent" who was usually a profane cutthroat wanted by half a dozen vigilance committees, and every 200 miles of road was entrusted to a "district agent" who differed from his unruly subordinates only in being quicker on the draw. Drivers, most of them swaggering bullies, were hired to handle the 1,000 mules and more than 500 horses purchased by the company.

The coaches introduced by the Butterfield Overland Mail revolutionized western travel. Known as Concord Coaches for their manufacturer—the Abbott-Downing Company of Concord, New Hampshire—they were far better suited to journeys across plains and deserts than any earlier vehicle. The wheels were heavy, with broad iron tires that would not sink in soft sand, and were set wide apart to keep the stage from tipping. The iron-reinforced wooden body was swung on leather thoroughbraces which absorbed some of the worst shocks, and was provided with leather curtains to protect the nine passengers from rain or cold. The driver and conductor, and sometimes a passenger or two, rode high up on the boxlike structure, while to the rear was a triangular "boot" which held mail sacks and luggage. The gaudily painted red or green vehicles were pulled by four galloping horses or half a dozen scampering mules.

They were used first on a large scale on September 15, 1858, when preparations for overland service were completed. That morning two coaches started on their lonely journey, one from the railroad terminus at Tipton, Missouri, the other from San Francisco. For three weeks they careened across the prairies, one racing east and the other west, as road-building crews stopped to cheer and settlers gathered from miles around to gape at the latest evidence of civilization. Hardships were many on the first run, but on the morning of October 10 one dust-stained coach swept into San Francisco, twenty-four days out of Missouri. "Had I not just come out over the route," wrote a tired correspondent who made the journey, "I

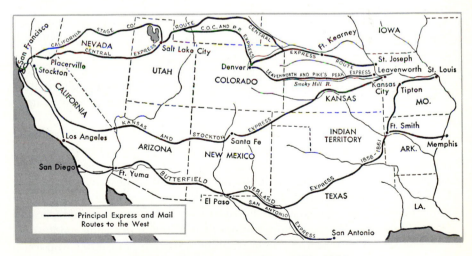

Overland Transportation, 1858–1875

would be perfectly willing to go back by it." In the meantime the east-bound coach reached St. Louis in a little less than twenty-one days. "I congratulate you on the result," President Buchanan wired Butterfield. "It is a glorious triumph for civilization and the Union."

For the next three years Butterfield Overland Mail coaches raced over the trails blazed by those pioneers, two each week in each direction, through rain and snow and desert heat, with scarcely a break in the service. Sometimes stations were raided by bands of Apache or Comanche who had not learned that the condemned army bacon provided by the company was not worth stealing. Sometimes coaches were attacked by marauding Indians; one overland driver complained to Mark Twain that he left the southern route because "he came as near as anything to starving to death in the midst of abundance, because they kept him so leaky with bullet holes that 'he couldn't hold his vittels.' " Usually passengers were few; the fare of $200 and the prospect of sitting for twenty-two days in a jolting coach did not attract pleasure seekers. But way traffic, generous government subsidies, and a steady increase in the amount of mail carried assured success for the venture. The company's prosperity encouraged the postmaster general to subsidize two alternate routes in the late 1850s, the Kansas and Stockton Express between Kansas City and Stockton, California, and the San Antonio Express connecting Texas with San Diego.

The support given southwestern routes by the Democratic officials who dominated national affairs under President Buchanan meant the early development of the central road across the continent would be left to private initiative. Interest in the possibility mounted during the middle 1850s as individual freighters, realizing that profits could be obtained by supplying Mormons and California miners with eastern goods, began plying the Platte River route with small wagon trains. Scarcely had trade begun when one freighter, an experienced Missourian named Alexander Majors, decided to monopolize the business. In 1855 he formed a partnership with two other plainsmen, William H. Russell and W. B. Waddell. The firm of Russell, Majors and Waddell, starting operations with about 300 wagons, grew so rapidly that by 1858 it operated 3,500 covered vehicles, employed 4,000 men, and owned 40,000 draft oxen. For the next few years it dominated freighting on the central Plains, carrying food and industrial produce to army camps or mining fields, and bringing out hides and precious metals.

Russell, Majors and Waddell prospered because they devised efficient methods for overland travel. Every wagon train they sent out from Missouri contained twenty-five covered wagons, each carrying three tons of goods and pulled by twelve oxen. A "bullwhacker" walked beside each wagon, controlling the animals with a twelve-foot bullwhip which cracked like a rifle when flicked against the oxen. Most drivers were rough-and-tumble laborers whose sulphurous profanity and fondness for drunken brawling made them known and feared along the whole frontier, although Alexander Majors, a pious man, tried to attract more orderly employees by promising each a

Bible and hymn book. Probably those inducements did less to keep bull-whackers in check than the wagonmaster who accompanied each train on its lonely march across the prairies. Those officials and their men, plodding along at the rate of fifteen miles each day, sleeping under the stars at night, supplied the isolated settlements of the Far West with necessities for almost a decade.

Profits from freighting encouraged the exuberant William H. Russell, the irrepressible plunger of the combination, to involve his partners in two fantastic ventures that vastly benefited the West but led inevitably to the company's downfall. One was a stagecoach line over the central route which, he hoped, would profit so enormously from the Pike's Peak gold rush that it would need no government subsidy. Majors and Waddell labored in vain to convince Russell that no line could succeed without federal aid; when they refused to back him he found a less conservative partner, John S. Jones, and formed the Leavenworth and Pike's Peak Express Company. Using vast sums of borrowed capital, the new concern laid out a route between Leavenworth and Denver that was ready for daily service by April 18, 1859. Despite the ten-day schedules and singularly efficient service, the project was doomed from the beginning, partly because the collapse of the Pike's Peak boom shrank anticipated revenue, partly because the expenses of $1,000 a day could only be borne with a government subsidy. Russell's answer was to extend operations to Salt Lake City where the California Stage Company provided connections with San Francisco. This was accomplished in July, 1859, by paying an excessive sum for the franchise of a small company already operating infrequently over the route.

Profits remained nonexistent, however, and Russell's partners were finally forced to come to his aid or risk the downfall of their own firm through his bankruptcy. In the autumn of 1859 they agreed to take over the stage-coaching venture and nurture it with funds from their freighting business until it could secure a lucrative mail contract. Reorganized as the Central Overland, California, and Pike's Peak Express, the new company operated triweekly coaches between Leavenworth and Placerville, but lost money so fast that its well-known initials were soon transformed to read "Clean Out of Cash and Poor Pay."

There was only one hope—a government subsidy—and only one slim chance of obtaining one. If the partners could convincingly demonstrate the superiority of the central route over the roundabout Butterfield route they might win the coveted mail contract. Only this faint hope induced Majors and Waddell to back Russell in another of his fantastic schemes: a Pony Express of relays of horsemen that would carry mails between Missouri and California in ten days. Surely, they reasoned, nothing would advertise the advantages of their stage service more dramatically than such breathtaking speed. So 190 way stations were built at ten-mile intervals between St. Joseph, Missouri, and San Francisco, 500 horses were selected for speed and stamina, and riders hired with courage and endurance needed for long hours in the saddle. The special equipment that was purchased caught the nation's imagination: close-fitting clothes for the riders, light racing saddles, mail pouches that could be tossed from horse to horse in a twinkling. By April 3, 1860, all was in readiness for the country's most spectacular experiment in lightning transportation.

Crowds cheered away the two riders who left St. Joseph and San Francisco that day. Each drove his horse at full gallop for ten miles, then came crashing into a station where another mount was held, saddled and ready to be away. In a flash the *mochila* holding the mail was flung across the new saddle, the rider leaped on it, and was off. Each rider rode seventy miles at this breakneck pace, then turned his pouches over to another and rested for the return trip. A few hours over ten days were required to cross the continent, ten days less than the fastest stagecoach. Here was something for the United States to celebrate. Eighty riders constantly in the saddle, day and night, forty of them flying east, forty of them west, over rolling prairies and tortuous mountain trails, with never a halt for snow or sleet or even Indian attack. Little wonder that one youngster who gained his first fame as a Pony Express rider, "Buffalo Bill" Cody, came to typify the wild-western frontier to generations of later Americans.

The Pony Express was richer in romance than in profits. Rates were high enough—$4 to $10 an ounce—and the number of letters carried increased from 49 on the first trip to 350 a year later, but each cost $38 to deliver and this was more of a drain than even the vast resources of Russell, Majors and Waddell could long endure. To make matters worse, a competitor was soon in the field. The electric telegraph was still in its infancy when the federal government endowed two companies, the Pacific Telegraph Company and the Overland Telegraph Company, to bridge the continent by wire. The first pole was set in July, 1861; from that date crews raced across the mountains and plains from west and east in a contest to enter Salt Lake City first and secure the business of that metropolis for their respective concerns. When the wires were joined on October 24, 1861, the time between the coasts was reduced from days to a fraction of a second and the Pony Express was doomed.

Its collapse also spelled doom for the harried partners. They had not only poured $500,000 into that hapless venture but had lost money steadily on their stagecoach line, for business failed to improve despite all the advertising received by the central route. Driven to desperation, Russell stooped to appropriating government securities with the cooperation of a good-hearted clerk in the Interior Department who was not above embezzlement to help a friend. This venture into low finance soon came to light; Russell vanished into a federal lockup and the firm of Russell, Majors and Waddell slid into bankruptcy. By a cruel irony of fate, this occurred just as its one chance occurred to secure a mail contract. With the outbreak of the Civil War, Congress was forced to shift the overland mail service northward, but it could scarcely award the contract to such a thoroughly discredited concern. Instead the Butterfield Overland Mail was shifted to the central route in March, 1861. Over the next few years this established company operated daily coaches between St. Joseph, Missouri, and Placerville, California, aided by the $1,000,000 annual subsidy that Russell, Majors and Waddell had ruined themselves to secure. On March 21, 1862, the few remaining assets of the Central Overland, California, and Pike's Peak Express were purchased at public auction by the man who dominated western transportation for the next five years: Ben Holladay.

Holladay was a coarse frontiersman, endowed by nature with shrewd cunning and an uncanny executive skill. Within a few months his smooth-running coaches were operating on schedule, attracting more passengers, and paying handsome dividends. Some of the revenue was used to buy improved Concord coaches, hire better drivers, and erect handsome stations where travelers could expect something better than the mouldy bread and spoiled pork inflicted on them in the past. More money went into lines to mining camps in Idaho, Montana, and Colorado, until Holladay controlled 5,000 miles of stage routes and was truly the "Napoleon of the Plains." Over this empire he ruled with an iron hand, riding constantly over his lines, goading his men on, and overawing the cutthroats who manned his stations, until he became a legendary figure in the West. Mark Twain caught the spirit of that frontier adulation in *Roughing It* when he recorded a conversation between an elderly pilgrim to the Holy Land and an impetuous young man who had once traveled in one of Holladay's coaches:

> "Jack, do you see that range of mountains over yonder that bounds the Jordan Valley? The mountains of Moab, Jack! Think of it, my boy— the actual mountains of Moab—renowned in Scripture history! We are actually standing face to face with those illustrious crags and peaks— and for all we know (dropping his voice impressively), *our eye may be resting at this very moment upon the spot* WHERE LIES THE MYSTERIOUS GRAVE OF MOSES! THINK OF IT, JACK!"
>
> "Moses *who?*" (falling inflection).
>
> "Moses *who!* Jack, you ought to be ashamed of yourself—you ought to be ashamed of such criminal ignorance. Why, Moses, the great guide, soldier, poet, lawgiver of ancient Israel! Jack, from this spot where we stand, to Egypt, stretches a fearful desert three hundred miles in extent —and across that desert that wonderful man brought the children of Israel!—guiding them with unfailing sagacity for forty years over the sandy desolation and among the obstructing rocks and hills, and landed them at last, safe and sound, within sight of this very spot; and where we now stand they entered the Promised Land with anthems of rejoicing! It was a wonderful, wonderful thing to do, Jack! Think of it!"
>
> *"Forty years? Only three hundred miles?* Humph! Ben Holladay would have fetched them through in thirty-six hours."[1]

---

[1]Samuel L. Clemens, *Roughing It* (New York, 1871), I, 58. Reprinted by special permission of the publishers, Harper and Brothers.

More than Holladay's genius was needed to keep western coaching alive, for by the middle of the 1860s the inevitability of progress placed the stamp of doom on his giant enterprises. He was wise enough to see the handwriting on the wall and sell out in 1866 to Wells, Fargo and Company, a New York concern which had served as a silent partner in the Overland Mail Company since its inception, and after March, 1860, had been in virtual control of operations, largely in the region west of the Rockies. Holladay acted none too soon. Within three years overland staging was relegated to a secondary place in frontier life by the coming of the railroad.

During the decade when stage coaching was at its heyday in the Far West, railways advanced slowly into the trans-Mississippi country. Construction was centered first in the humid regions adjacent to the Father of Waters, where thickening settlement and heavy agricultural yields promised adequate way traffic. During the 1850s the object of most promoters was to reach the Missouri River. First to be chartered were two Missouri roads, the Missouri Pacific Railroad which connected St. Louis and Kansas City (1851–1865), and the Hannibal and St. Joe Railroad between Hannibal and St. Joseph (1851–1859), but by the close of the decade activity shifted to Iowa continuations or railroads from Chicago. The pioneering line in that state was the Chicago and North Western Railroad; in 1855 its tracks reached the Mississippi opposite Clinton, Iowa, and during the next decade it pushed construction on to Council Bluffs on the Missouri. Close behind was the Rock Island Railroad which not only reached the Mississippi in 1854 but a year later opened the first bridge across the river, to the delight of awe-struck westerners. Its tracks entered Council Bluffs in 1860. The Chicago, Burlington and Quincy Railroad, building westward from Burlington through the Civil War decade, reached Council Bluffs in 1869 and Ft. Kearney, Nebraska, by 1873 when a depression stopped work. Northern Iowa was crossed by the Illinois Central Railroad, which completed its line from Dubuque to Sioux City in 1870.

Other railroad magnates turned their attention to the Minnesota country. A leading role there was played by the Chicago, Milwaukee and St. Paul Railroad, which by 1873 not only connected Chicago with Minneapolis and St. Paul, but operated a branch line half way across northern Iowa. Equally active was the Chicago and North Western Railroad which entered the territory in 1867 with the purchase of a defunct road that had attempted to build westward from Winona. When the Panic of 1873 ended construction, track extended across Minnesota and a short distance into Dakota Territory. Smaller lines, in the meanwhile, built northward from the Twin Cities; one, the Lake Superior and Mississippi Railroad, entered Duluth before 1873. By that time the northern tier of Mississippi states were crisscrossed by a number of east-west roads providing adequate transportation.

Less important in the development of the trans-Mississippi transportation network were the north-south lines begun just after the Civil War to connect points in Missouri or Kansas with the Gulf of Mexico. One, the

Missouri, Kansas and Texas Railroad, building south from Topeka, reached the Kansas border in 1870 after a race with a rival concern that was pushing its tracks out from Kansas City. Its reward was a generous land grant and a right of way across the Indian Territory; an inducement that speeded construction until the "Katy's" tracks crossed the Red River in 1872, to join with those of the Houston and Texas Central Railroad. Its only rival in the Gulf trade was the St. Louis, Iron Mountain and Southern Railroad. That line reached Texarkana in 1873 where it met the already completed International and Great Northern Railroad.

The imposing railway network laid down in the tier of states bordering the Mississippi was made possible by financial aid from hamlets through which the roads passed, the states in which they lay, and the federal government. The last source was most bountiful; from 1850 to 1871 Congress granted the public domain freely to western states with the understanding they pass the awards on to railroads in the form of land bounties. Every trans-Mississippi state but Texas (which controlled its own domain) shared in this largess, and each in turn doled out millions of acres in alternate sections which were sold by roads to meet construction costs. When promoters turned to railroad building in the Plains region west of the first tier of trans-Mississippi states, they faced a different situation. That giant grassland supported no settlers to provide roads with way traffic, no towns to offer aid, no states to pledge credit, no pioneers to purchase land grants. Building there was a task to try the skill of America's engineers and financiers.

That a transcontinental railroad must be built was acknowledged by all after the middle 1850s. The nation first began to visualize a Pacific road in January, 1845, when a New York business man and China trader, Asa Whitney, proposed to Congress that the government grant a sixty-mile strip between Lake Superior and the Oregon country to any company willing to risk construction. After this visionary plan was pigeonholed, Whitney launched a propaganda campaign to convince both congressmen and people that the project was feasible; for the next decade he spoke and wrote constantly in behalf of a Pacific railroad, showering Congress with petitions as he did so. Gradually public opinion was won to his side, partly by his arguments, but more by the realization that heavily populated California could be kept satisfied only with better transportation. By 1853 the most hardheaded realists agreed a transcontinental road was necessary and the most rugged individualists admitted government aid must be forthcoming for the project.

Unfortunately the conversion of public opinion coincided with the rise of sectional antagonism; by the time Congress admitted a railroad should be built no one could agree upon the route. Feeling was especially bitter because all believed one road to the Pacific would suffice forever, giving the section securing its eastern terminus a perpetual economic advantage. Southerners insisted the government support a line along the Butterfield Overland Mail route or one following the Canadian or Red rivers; northerners demanded a railway through South Pass. As Congress debated through the early years of the pre-Civil War decade, one group of realists concluded the problem might be settled by nature; perhaps one route was sufficiently superior to be used regardless of sectional feeling. To test that theory, Congress, in the spring of 1853, authorized the army to survey all feasible routes between the Mississippi Valley and the Pacific.

The findings, presented in ten bulky volumes in 1855, failed to still sectional clamor, for the surveys showed that four routes were practical: one between Lake Superior and Portland, another through South Pass to San Francisco, a third along the Red River to Southern California, and a fourth across southern Texas and the Gila Valley. Two northern and two southern possibilities did little to make a decision easier, but the great compromiser, Stephen A. Douglas, tried to find a solution. After preparing the way for his favored South Pass route by organizing the western territories in the Kansas-Nebraska Act, he proposed that Congress aid three railroads: a Northern Pacific Railroad from Wisconsin to Puget Sound, a Central Pacific Railroad from Missouri or Iowa to San Francisco, and a Southern Pacific Railroad from Texas to southern California. His catchall proposal might have satisfied the warring sections, but the expenses involved were too staggering to be considered. So long as sectionalism plagued the nation, no road could be built. The long debate, however, taught Congress that land grants and direct loans would be needed before private capitalists could be persuaded to undertake the project.

The opportunity to apply those lessons came with the secession of the Confederate states. Congress, controlled after 1861 by northerners who agreed on the central route, only needed prodding to act. That came from California in the person of Theodore D. Judah. Judah was a gifted engineer, chock-full of vision and energy, who had joined with four other promoters from his home state—Leland Stanford, Collis P. Huntington, Mark Hopkins, and Charles Crocker—to charter the Central Pacific Railroad of California. They proposed building eastward from San Francisco to the state border, and wanted both federal support and the promise of a line to connect their road with the Mississippi Valley. That was what Judah was after when he descended on Washington late in 1861, his valise jammed with plans and his head with grandiose schemes. His persistent lobbying was rewarded on July 1, 1862, when Congress passed a law launching the first Pacific railroad.

Two companies, the measure decreed, would build the road. The Central Pacific Railroad was assigned the difficult task of bridging the Sierra Nevadas in California. The other, incorporated by Congress as the Union Pacific Railroad, was authorized to build westward from the 100th meridian, climb the Rockies near South Pass, and meet the Central Pacific at the California-Nevada line. East of the 100th meridian five branches were to radiate out to Kansas City, Leavenworth, St. Joseph, Sioux City, and Omaha—a device used to forestall local jealousies. Each road was granted a 400-foot right-of-way, together with ten alternate sections of land for each mile of track laid. In addition the government agreed to loan the companies on a first-mortgage basis $16,000 for each mile built in level country, $32,000 a mile in the foothills, and $48,000 in the mountains. Generous as the terms were—one critic complained that "while fighting to retain eleven refractory states the nation permits itself to be cozened out of territory sufficient to form twelve new republics"—they failed to attract private capital needed by the Union Pacific. After two years of stalemate Congress came to the company's aid in July, 1864, by doubling the land grant, reducing the government loan to the status of a second mortgage, and increasing the number of $100 shares it was authorized to sell from 100,000 to 1,000,000. Money poured in then, and construction began.

The Central Pacific was off first in the race across the continent, spurred on by a loan of $1,659,000 from California, and President Lincoln's geographical legerdemain in shifting the Sierra Nevadas westward into the Sacramento Valley to allow the company to borrow $48,000 a mile when building across level country. The first track was laid in 1863 and inched forward slowly during the next years—twenty miles in 1864, twenty more in 1865, thirty in 1866, forty-six in 1867. The construction gangs were in the mountains then, battering their way over steep grades and around precipices of living rock, but the promoters had solved their worst problem—how to obtain labor in a frontier community—by importing gangs of Chinese coolies. Seven thousand pig-tailed workers hacked out the right-of-way, their broad straw hats and flapping trousers forming a picturesque sight as they trundled wheelbarrows of dirt or scampered away from charges of blasting powder. In the summer of 1867 the crest of the Sierras was crossed and only easier downgrades lay ahead. Anticipating that happy moment, the Central Pacific in 1866 wrung from Congress the right to lay its tracks on across the Nevada deserts "until they shall meet and connect with the Union Pacific Railroad."

By that time work on the Union Pacific was well under way. Construction was slow at first, as the company struggled to obtain workers and material from a war-burdened nation; only forty miles of track stretched west from Omaha at the close of 1865. During the next two years conditions improved rapidly. Gangs of Irish laborers drifted westward with the close of the war, seeking jobs on the construction crews. In 1867 the Chicago and North Western Railroad reached Council Bluffs, ending expensive steamboat transportation of rails and materials. Yet plentiful labor, adequate supplies, and an easy roadbed across the Plains did not solve the Union Pacific's construction problems. Everything needed had to be brought into that barren country; ties from the forests of Minnesota, stone from the quarries of Wisconsin, rails from the steel mills of Pennsylvania. Moreover the Indians were on the warpath, necessitating frequent halts while workers snatched rifles from "track trains" to beat off attacks.

Still the work went on. A 100 mile stretch would be surveyed, graded, bridges built. Then came the track layers. "A light car, drawn by a single horse, gallops up to the front with its load of rails. Two men seize the end of a rail and start forward, the rest of the gang taking hold by twos until it is clear of the car. They come forward at a run. At the word of command, the rail is dropped in its place, right side up, with care, while the same process goes on on the other side of the car. Less than thirty seconds to a rail for each gang, and so four rails go down to the minute. . . . The moment the car is empty it is tipped over on the side of the track to let the next loaded car pass it, and then it is tipped back again; it is a sight to see it go flying back for another load, propelled by a horse at full gallop at the end of 60 or 80 feet of rope, ridden by a young Jehu, who drives furiously. Close behind the first gang come the gaugers, spikers and bolters, and a lively time they make of it. It is a grand Anvil Chorus that these sturdy sledges are playing across the plains.'' So they swept across the continent in a mighty symphony of motion. Two hundred and sixty-six miles of track went down in 1866, 240 in 1867. In November of that year the gleaming rails reached Cheyenne and started their climb upward toward the pass that would span the Rockies.

Behind them they left a chain of ramshackle towns, sixty or seventy miles apart, that marked the temporary halting places of construction crews. Julesburg, Cheyenne, Laramie City—those are today the ghosts of that migrating ''Hell on Wheels'' which followed the Union Pacific across the continent. For a few months, or perhaps a whole winter, the gangs of workers would live in one of the outposts, going out to work each day on the ''track trains.'' Then, when the track had nosed out far ahead, the signal to move was given. All fell to work; in a few hours the town was dismantled, piled aboard flatcars, and on its way west, with inhabitants riding atop their dismantled homes. Sixty miles up the road they halted. Willing hands raised the ''Big Tent,'' a floored canvas structure 100 feet long and forty wide, which held a sumptuous bar, a dance floor, and elaborate gambling paraphernalia. Around it they threw up the ramshackle shacks or tents which held twenty-two more saloons, five dance halls, living quarters for the workers, and homes for the ''girls'' who were always ready to take away any portion of the workers' wages left by the faro dealers. Some 3,000 people drifted westward with that peripatetic Gomorrah—workers, bartenders, prostitutes, gamblers, speculators, outlaws, renegades, road agents, outcasts. ''Hell,'' one journalist observed, ''would appear to have been raked to furnish them.''

Nightly dissipation did not slow down the workers who, by the spring of 1868, realized they were not mere laborers on a railroad but participants in the greatest race in history. The Central Pacific was winging across the level deserts of Nevada. The Union Pacific was battling through the Rockies. Between them lay the plains of Utah, which an amiable government defined as mountain country, entitling builders to loans of $48,000 a mile as well as lucrative land grants. Each company spurred its men relentlessly in hope of grabbing off a major share of that prize. Five miles, seven miles, finally ten miles of track a day were laid by hustling crews, while far ahead graders worked feverishly to add government land and dollars to their companies' treasuries. The Central Pacific built 360 miles of road in 1868, the Union Pacific 425, accomplishments made possible by generous contracts with Brigham Young to supply highly efficient Mormon labor to supplement the Irish and Chinese crews. For a time, so bitter was the competition, they seemed destined never to meet. Congress had set no junction point and when the grading crews met they passed each other, laying out parallel roads a short distance apart. The farce only ended when Washington officials ruled the two roads must join at Promontory, Utah, a short distance from Ogden, Utah.

There, in mid-May, 1869, a little knot of workers and officials watched the placing of the last silver-bound laurel tie, the fixing of the last steel rail, the presentation of the golden spike which would bind the two roads together. "Hats off!" signaled a telegraph operator to all the listening nation. "Prayer is being offered." Thirteen minutes later, and with a sense of relief at getting down to business at last: "We have got done praying. The spike is about to be presented." A few well-aimed blows (after Leland Stanford missed with the first swing of his sledge), the tracks were joined, and two locomotives steamed forward until their pilots touched—

> "Facing on a single track,
> Half a world behind each back."

The United States celebrated that night; "Chicago made a procession seven miles long; New York hung out bunting, fired a hundred guns, and held thanksgiving services in Trinity; Philadelphia rang the old Liberty Bell; Buffalo sang the 'Star-Spangled Banner.'" Well might a war-torn people cheer the forging of a new bond of union.

Nor did they have long to wait before celebrating again. Long before the last golden spike sank firmly into the laurel tie at Promontory the nation, realizing one transcontinental railroad would never suffice, gave its blessing to half a dozen other projects designed to connect the two oceans. First to start westward was the Kansas Pacific Railroad, which was originally chartered to connect the Union Pacific with Kansas City. Its plans were changed in 1866 when financial difficulties beset the road; a revised charter authorized a direct line between Kansas City and Denver, with a branch extending on to the Union Pacific at Cheyenne. The prospect of securing both a generous land grant and the trade of the Colorado mines brought such a flood of support from investors that the Kansas Pacific was operating by the fall of 1870.

More important was the first of the southern lines, the Atchison, Topeka and Santa Fe Railroad. When the road was chartered in 1859 its president, Cyrus K. Holliday, hoped only to connect Atchison with the Kansas capital at Topeka, but a bountiful federal land grant in 1863 encouraged him to extend track on to Santa Fe. Five years were needed to find a construction company willing to undertake the task, then building progressed rapidly until 1873 when the Santa Fe reached LaJunta, Colorado. From that point Holliday decided to extend his line in two directions, one west through Pueblo and the Royal Gorge of the Arkansas River to the mining region about Leadville, the other south through Raton Pass to Santa Fe. Before either could be built he found he must displace a formidable rival.

The Santa Fe's competitor was the Denver and Rio Grande Railroad, which had been incorporated in 1870 by Denver business men. Their motives were understandable. The Kansas Pacific Railroad, they believed, would drain the trade of the entire Rocky Mountain country eastward through their city. The coming of the Santa Fe threatened to upset their plans, for southern Colorado would prefer to ship goods out by rail directly, rather than via Denver. Their answer was to challenge the interloper by building the Denver and Rio Grande which would not only tap the trade of southern Colorado but compete for New Mexico's commerce. Track was laid from Denver to Pueblo when the Panic of 1873 stopped construction for three years. That delay was fortunate for the Santa Fe. Speed was vital in reaching both Leadville and New Mexico, for both could be entered only through narrow passes holding only one line of track. While work on the Denver and Rio Grande was at a standstill, the better-financed eastern road usurped one of the routes, the Raton Pass into the territory by pushing its track southward toward Albuquerque in 1879. Its defeated rival, after a series of law suits and near battles between construction crews, captured control of the other; its right-of-way through the Royal Gorge of the Arkansas River prevented the Santa Fe from extending westward beyond Pueblo.

The end of the "Rio Grande War" left the Santa Fe's managers free to concentrate on newly aroused transcontinental ambitions. That was in their minds when, in 1880, they bought control of a defunct line, the Atlantic and Pacific Railroad, which had progressed no farther than the town of Vinita, Indian Territory, in its efforts to connect St. Louis with southern California. The purchase gave the Santa Fe a chance to enter St. Louis directly as well as the earlier line's federal land grant of twenty sections for each mile of track across New Mexico and Arizona. During the next three years work progressed rapidly at both ends of the expanded road. A branch from Wichita to Pierce City provided the St. Louis connection desired by the managers, while construction crews in the west reached Needles on the Arizona-California border, in 1883. There the Santa Fe joined another newly built road, the Southern Pacific Railroad, which was operated by the same group of financiers who controlled the Central Pacific. Extending from San Francisco to Needles and Yuma, the two points where the Colorado River could be crossed, the Southern Pacific dominated the commerce of southern California. By granting the Santa Fe trackage rights into San Francisco and Los Angeles, the Southern Pacific allowed the forging of a second transcontinental link.

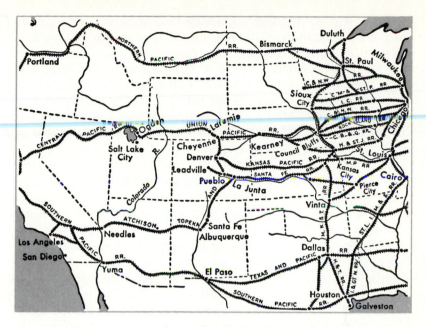

Principal Pacific Railroads in 1883

The third road completed was a rival of the Santa Fe for the trade of the Southwest. The Texas and Pacific Railroad was chartered in 1871 to build westward along the 32nd parallel to Yuma where it would meet the tracks of the Southern Pacific Railroad. Times were inauspicious for such a program; by 1877 the Texas Pacific was bankrupt after building no farther westward than Ft. Worth, Texas. The alarmed managers of the Southern Pacific realized that their expensive line, which was completed to Yuma that year, would pay no dividends without an eastern connection. After vainly pleading with Congress for the right to take over the land grant of the Texas and Pacific Railroad they decided to go ahead without congressional aid. Charters obtained from the Arizona and New Mexico territorial governments allowed construction to proceed rapidly eastward. In 1881 the directors of the Texas and Pacific, realizing they had lost the chance to build beyond Texas, transferred their western land grants to the Southern Pacific in return for an agreement that the two lines should meet in El Paso. Although Congress refused to sanction the transfer, the roads did join in 1882, completing another route across the continent. A year later the Southern Pacific secured its own line across Texas by purchasing the Galveston, Harrisburg and San Antonio Railroad.

While southern and central railroads were forging bonds between California and the Mississippi Valley, a fourth transcontinental line was pushing slowly across the northern plains and mountains. The Northern Pacific Railroad was chartered by the United States in 1864 to build from Lake Superior to Portland, Oregon. Although a generous land grant was provided—twenty sections to the mile in the states and forty in the territories—the failure of Congress to authorize mileage loans plunged the road into financial difficulties from the beginning. In 1869, with not a mile of track laid, the directors turned from the experienced railroaders who had managed the enterprise to seek the support of the nation's leading financial house, Jay Cooke and Company. After a thorough investigation Cooke, who was personally interested through his heavy investments in Minnesota land, agreed to act as the company's financial agent.

Money flowed in then. Construction began in 1870 and proceeded rapidly across Minnesota and Dakota to the Missouri River where the town of Bismarck was laid out; at the same time lines to Minneapolis and Duluth were added to the Northern Pacific's growing empire. Progress was short-lived, however, for the financial structure reared by Cooke was unsound. The heavy bonuses paid his banking house by the railroad, the large percentage exacted for selling bonds, and the generous blocks of stock distributed among influential politicians, left so little actual cash that construction could continue only as long as investors continued to buy stock. When rumors of mismanagement, extravagance, and corruption slowed down sales in the spring of 1873 Jay Cooke realized the cause was hopeless. On September 18, 1873, his banking house closed its doors, plunging the nation into a prolonged panic. For two years more the Northern Pacific struggled along, vainly seeking funds in a depression-ridden land, but in 1875 it too passed into bankruptcy.

Meanwhile, in Oregon developments were taking place which were to have a profound influence on the future of the Northern Pacific. One of the early railroads there was the Oregon and California, projected from Portland to the California boundary. Its bonds had been bought extensively by German investors. When the road became involved in financial difficulties in the 1870s, the German bondholders sent an agent to Oregon to investigate and report to them. This agent was Henry Villard, an immigrant from Germany who had made a reputation as a newspaper correspondent in his adopted country. Impressed by what he saw on his initial visit to Oregon in behalf of the bondholders, Villard decided to identify himself with transportation developments in the Pacific Northwest. In 1879 he acquired control of the Oregon Steam Navigation Company, a Portland enterprise which had dominated traffic on the Columbia between that city and the Inland Empire. He thereupon organized a new corporation, the Oregon Railway and Navigation Company, for the purpose of building a rail line along the water-level route on the south bank of the Columbia. This road would not only control rail traffic along the Columbia, but it would also serve as the outlet to tidewater for any transcontinental railway which might be built from the East to the Northwest Coast. In this way he would make Portland the commercial center of the Pacific Northwest.

Just as Villard was getting his plans under way the Northern Pacific was undergoing a financial renaissance after its bankruptcy of the middle seventies. In 1879 it began to push its rails west from Bismarck in Dakota Territory. Its objective was Tacoma, a terminal city which it planned to build on Puget Sound. Villard, well aware that Portland was handicapped by obstructions to navigation on the lower Columbia River and could not compete commercially with a rail terminus on a vastly superior harbor, was fearful that completion of the Northern Pacific would depreciate his extensive financial interests in the city. After vainly seeking to dissuade its managers from building across the Cascades or along the north bank of the Columbia, he offered to allow their trains to use the tracks of his Oregon Railway and Navigation Company on the south bank of that stream, hoping thus to divert their traffic through Portland. This they also spurned. Villard realized that he could protect his investments only by winning control of the Northern Pacific. For two months, between December, 1879, and January, 1880, he quietly purchased the road's stock, then when his own resources were exhausted, sent fifty of his friends a circular letter asking them to subscribe to an eight million dollar loan with no questions asked. Such was his reputation that not eight but twenty millions poured into the "blind pool."

Using this ample supply of cash, Villard purchased control of the Northern Pacific in the spring of 1881 and immediately assumed its presidency. Adequate funds allowed him to finish the line to Portland in the fall of 1883, although unexpectedly heavy construction costs more than exhausted his resources. These financial reverses forced Villard's resignation early in 1884, returning control to the group that wanted to build to Puget Sound. Reviving their original plan, they began construction at the confluence of the Snake and Columbia rivers, and laid track westward through the Yakima country and across the Cascades to Tacoma. By 1887 the Northern Pacific spanned the continent between Lake Superior and Puget Sound.

Transcontinental railroad construction ended temporarily with the completion of the Northern Pacific. East and West were now united not by the one railroad envisaged by Asa Whitney but by four, firmly binding the nation economically. Even more striking was their impact on the country they crossed in their long journey between the Mississippi and the Pacific. Their construction had cost the government heavily; in all, the roads were granted 181 million acres of land in the form of ten to forty alternate sections spanning the right of way, as well as sizeable interest-free loans. Westerners were soon to complain that this largess had a negative effect; its result, they argued, was to remove half of the best land adjacent to transportation from homesteading, and thus slow settlement. There was little justice in the claim. Studies show that the railroads sold land as fast or faster than the government would have. Westerners also claimed that railroad profits were large if not excessive and that the land grants were a "giveaway." Scholars disagree about the extent to which government aid allowed the major transcontinentals to earn high profits on their investments, although it now seems clear that the lines could and would have been built even without the land grants. But it is also true that the computed "social returns" on the federal funds allowed the railroads (measured by economic growth and output of man-power units in adjacent areas) was no less than 24.1 per cent. The region that benefited most immediately from this spurt was the Great Plains. With pioneers there assured access to the lumber and fuel needed for existence, and guaranteed an outlet for their produce, the conquest of this last unsettled frontier could begin. First, however, the native Americans whose villages dotted this giant grassland must be removed, whatever the promises made them that they could occupy the Plains country so long as trees grew and waters ran.

30

The Indian Barrier
1860-1887

The advance of the mining frontier and spread of a transportation network across the Great Plains brought the United States face to face with the recurrent Indian problem once more. What should be done with the natives who roamed prairies and hunted in mountain valleys coveted by whites? The blundering attempts of insensitive federal officials to answer that question plunged the West into a period of warfare which only ended when the beaten natives, their power and spirit broken, were crowded onto reservations where they no longer blocked the westward march of settlers. The Indian barrier was shattered in the post-Civil War years, but only at a cost of blood, wealth, and human decency so characteristic of the American frontier experience.

Geographical conditions divided the problem into two parts. The first—how to subdue Indians occupying the mountainous lands invaded by miners—proved easy to solve. The pattern followed everywhere on the mining frontier was established by the '49ers. The 150,000 "Digger" Indians who occupied California were a peaceful, pastoral people, subsisting upon grubs and roots, and living in small units which failed to give them the strength of numbers. During the 1850s the state government enacted a whole series of measures forbidding them to mingle with whites and denying them access to legal protection. This was an open invitation to the miners, who fell on them with savage fury, driving them from their homes, murdering their warriors, and using every feeble attempt at retaliation as an excuse to exterminate whole tribes. When the federal government belatedly intervened, only a handful of "Diggers" remained to be herded into reservations. A similar fate awaited the Snake and Bannock of the Oregon country and southern Idaho, and the Ute who occupied much of Utah and Nevada; most were docile peoples with neither inclination nor strength to resist the miners' assault on their homelands. Intermittent warfare between them and the whites went on between 1850 and 1855 when bribes and repeated defeats forced them to throw themselves on the mercy of the Americans. Six years later the Ute ceded most of their Utah lands to the United States in return for a small reservation northeast of Great Salt Lake.

The natives of the southwestern mountain country proved more troublesome, for that was the land of the powerful Apache and Navaho tribes. Their warlike reputation was sufficiently awe-inspiring to keep prospectors away until the 1850s when a number of federal forts—with Ft. Union guarding the eastern approaches to northern New Mexico the most prominent—were scattered through the region, manned by some 1,500 troops. Military invasion only inspired attack; haphazard fighting that began in 1851 reached a climax in 1860 when serious warfare broke out. For the next four years bands of Apache and Navaho, mounted and on foot and thoroughly at home in that wild country of canyons and deserts, fought so savagely that victory seemed near, but in the end government forces triumphed. During the campaigns of 1863-64, 664 Indians were killed and 8,793 captured—most of them by Colonel Kit Carson who pinned 7,000 in a canyon at one time—in a series of 143 battles which sapped native strength to the breaking point. By 1865 they were ready to submit to the fate awaiting them: crowding upon small reservations. Six thousand Navaho went first, on a tragic "long walk" to a reserve surrounding Ft. Sumner on the Pecos River, where they had the alternative of starving or irrigating 1,500 acres of inferior land. Starve many of them did, ignored by the Indian Office which claimed they were the army's responsibility, and unable to survive the cultural shock that came with a forced transition from herding to farming. They were followed by the Apache between 1871 and 1873 when they were assigned a number of small areas in New Mexico and Arizona. Many warriors, refusing to give up their nomadic ways, broke away to raid travelers and settlers for another decade.

Troublesome as were the mountain tribes, they were easier to handle than the second group challenging American authority during those years: the Indians of the Great Plains. All—from the Sioux and Cheyennes in the North to the Kiowa and Comanche of the Southwest—were skilled horsemen, able to sweep swiftly across the Plains, fall suddenly on their prey, and disappear with the speed of the wind. All fought with uncanny ability, dropping their bodies behind their galloping ponies, then rising unexpectedly to launch their weapons. All were equipped with stout ash bows, three feet or less long, so effective that a warrior could drive deadly barbed arrows clear through a buffalo while racing along at top speed. For Plains warfare their weapons were more effective than the muzzle-loading rifles issued to federal troops; a Comanche could send twenty arrows at a foe during the minute required to reload one of the cumbersome guns. Even the introduction of famed Colt "six-shooters" during the 1850s did not entirely offset the natives' advantage. The Indians of the Great Plains were dangerous antagonists in any war.

A conflict seemed remote when the invasion of the West by '49ers began. Everyone knew the central grassland was a Great American Desert, usable only by the primitive peoples—both native and intruded eastern Indians—who lived there. So long as the United States held to the concept of "One Big Reservation" the two races could live in peace, but any attempt to oust the Indians from their hunting grounds was sure to mean trouble. The advance of the mining and transportation frontiers launched the conflict. The mass migrations across the Plains, the development of freighting and express lines, the plans for transcontinental railroads, all demonstrated during the early 1850s that the policy of "One Big Reservation" was destined to speedy extinction. Gradually the demand grew for opening the central portion of the Indian country—the lands of Kansas and Nebraska where most transportation routes were concentrated—by pushing natives northward to unwanted lands beyond Nebraska, or south of the Kansas border. Frontier pressure for that highway forced the United States to abandon its policy of "One Big Reservation" for a system of "Concentration" which led directly to war.

The first step in applying the new policy was taken in 1851 when chiefs of the principal Plains tribes were assembled at Ft. Laramie by Thomas Fitzpatrick, the agent controlling that Platte River outpost. In return for gifts, annuities, and bounties, the Indians agreed to accept definite tribal limitations. These were carefully marked out for the visiting warriors. The Sioux were assured the Dakota country north of the Platte River, the Mandan and Grosventres a triangle just east of the Yellowstone, the Assiniboin the region west of that stream, the Crows a large area west of the Powder River, the Blackfeet the mountainous country about the headwaters of the Missouri, the Cheyenne and Arapaho the foothills of Colorado between the North Platte and Arkansas rivers. There, they were told, they could live unmolested for all time, each tribe secure in the knowledge its lands were clearly defined. Little did the chiefs realize they were victims of a device often used by the United States. Once their tribal territories were marked out, any one group could be forced to cede its holdings to the United States without arousing the others.

Only the Indians' failure to see the handwriting on the wall kept the frontier at peace for another decade. During those years the attention of the Indian Office was focused on intruded eastern tribes whose reservations bordered the western boundaries of Iowa and Missouri. With the organization of Kansas and Nebraska territories in 1854 their removal became necessary. Between 1854 and 1859 they were forced to give up their reserves in return for smaller reservations or the doubtful privilege of moving west to mingle with the Plains Indians. By 1860 most of Kansas and Nebraska and a corner of the Dakota country were freed of their native occupants. "By alternate persuasion and force," wrote a heartsick agent, "some of these tribes have been removed, step by step, from mountain to valley, and from river to plain, until they have been pushed halfway across the continent. They can go no further: on the ground they now occupy the crisis must be met, and their future determined.''

The crisis was not long in coming. The discovery of gold in the Pike's Peak country touched off the inevitable conflict. Some 100,000 miners crossed the Plains in 1859, elbowed their way into Cheyenne and Arapaho lands, and drove the Indians from their homes. Resentment bred of those outrages was infectious. The northern tribes were already restless; surveyors were among them with tales of iron horses soon to bring thousands of settlers into the West; prospectors were searching for precious metals in the beaver streams of the Rockies. Moreover a few farseeing chiefs realized they were caught in a vise between the mining frontier, advancing steadily from the west, and the agricultural frontier, pressing relentlessly from the east. They must resist or be exterminated. War talk was common among the Plains Indians by 1860.

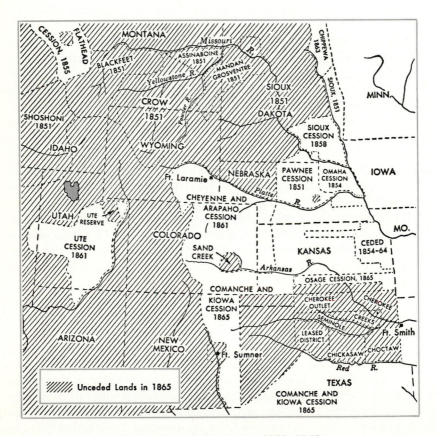

Indian Land Cessions, 1850–1865

Fighting began in the Colorado country. There Indian agents, all of them political hacks being rewarded for their services to the Republican Party, were so ignorant of native ways and psychology that they decided to forestall an attack by removing the Cheyenne and Arapaho from contact with the whites. Calling the chiefs of the two tribes into conference at Ft. Lyon on February 18, 1861, government officials tricked them into abandoning all claims to the area guaranteed them at Ft. Laramie in return for a small reservation between the Arkansas River and Sand Creek in eastern Colorado. That was going too far. Many warriors, refusing to abandon their nomadic ways, renounced the chiefs responsible for the treaty and took to the war path. For three years they raided mining camps and mail coaches while Colorado's territorial governor pleaded in vain for federal protection. When none was forthcoming from the war-rent East he took matters into his own hands. On June 24, 1864, all warring bands were ordered to proceed at once to Ft. Lyon; those refusing to obey were threatened with extermination. The harsh ruling only goaded the Indians into fiercer resistance. During the next few months they spread a path of desolation from the North Platte to the Arkansas, murdering settlers, burning homes, destroying overland mail stations, and pillaging travelers. By the autumn of 1864 all the Colorado countryside was in ruins and Denver isolated.

Fall, however, turned the Indians' thoughts toward peace, for tribal tradition dictated that fighting cease during cold winter months. Chief Black Kettle their leader, had that in mind when he sought out the federal commander at Ft. Lyon in late August, 1864, only to be told the official possessed no authority to end the war. The Colorado governor, Black Kettle was informed, must accept their surrender. A conference with that belligerent leader proved equally fruitless. After listening to the chieftain's plea for peace, Governor John Evans gruffly told him the war would go on; the white men, he said, were about to stop fighting among themselves "and the Great Father will not know what to do with his soldiers, except to send them after the Indians on the plains." His dire warning was echoed by the commander of the Colorado militia, Colonel J. M. Chivington, who glumly watched the Indians during the meeting. "My rule for fighting white men or Indians," he told Black Kettle bluntly, "is to fight them until they lay down their arms and submit."

Those threatening words should have convinced the chiefs that only more war would satisfy the Americans' lust for revenge, yet the yearning for peace was strong and they turned again to Ft. Lyon, hoping a new commander just appointed there would accept their surrender. That inexperienced leader was uncertain of his authority; at first he promised the Indians protection, then reversed himself and ordered them to leave the fort. Black Kettle, believing the war was over, led his almost 700 followers to a camp on Sand Creek, confident that federal troops would protect them from the Colorado militia. Scarcely had they departed when a regiment of 1,000 territorial volunteers under Colonel Chivington entered Ft. Lyon, hot on the

trail of the retreating tribe. The vacillating commander assured the militiamen he had not guaranteed the Indians protection and encouraged them to
attack at once. The stage was set for one of the bloodiest events in the
annals of Indian warfare.

Colonel Chivington and his men left Ft. Lyon after sundown on the
night of November 28, 1864. By daybreak of the next day they surrounded
the camp where some 500 unsuspecting natives slept peacefully. With the
first streak of light across the Plains the militia charged, rushing pell-mell
upon the confused Indians, firing and tomahawking as they went. In vain
did Black Kettle raise first an American flag, then a white flag. The disor-
dered Indians were driven across the camp, down into the dry bed of Sand
Creek, back against the high banks on the other side. Even women and
children who sought refuge in caves were dragged out to be shot or knifed.

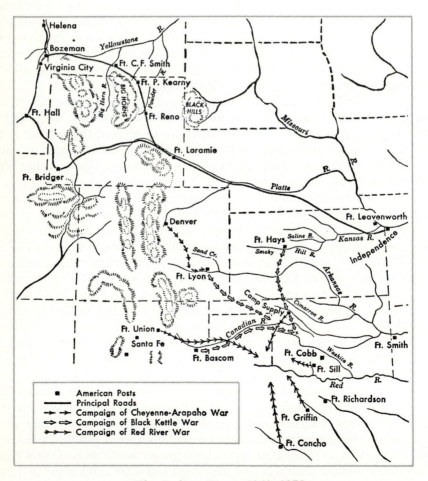

The Indian Wars, 1860–1875

"They were scalped," a watching trader later testified, "their brains knocked out; the men used their knives, ripped open women, clubbed little children, knocked them in the head with their guns, beat their brains out, mutilated their bodies in every sense of the word." Within a few hours the battered corpses of 450 Indians covered the battleground, although Black Kettle and a few younger warriors managed to escape.

The Chivington Massacre accomplished little. Word of the American brutality, carried across the Plains by survivors, inspired the remaining Cheyenne and Arapaho to greater resistance. Through the winter of 1864-65 raiding parties ranged the Platte Valley, sacking ranches, ripping down telegraph wires, raiding overland mail stations as far south as Julesburg and fighting pitched battles with troops sent against them. Yet the threat of another massacre could not be forgotten, and when peace commissioners arrived in October, 1865, the Indians were ready to lay down their arms. In conferences that followed the Cheyenne and Arapaho agreed to surrender unconditionally and to give up their Sand Creek Reservation in return for lands to be assigned them elsewhere. At the same time representatives of the Kiowa and Comanche tribes were forced to abandon all claims to central Texas, western Kansas, and eastern New Mexico, accepting instead a restricted hunting ground in the Panhandle country. With the end of Cheyenne-Arapaho War an armed truce prevailed in the Southwest.

Scarcely was the ink upon the treaty dry, however, before a new conflict broke out in the North—the Sioux War of 1865-67. The forces compelling the 16,000 Indians of the powerful confederation to take up the scalping knife were many. Some young braves were enflamed by tales of Indian gallantry carried northward from the scene of the Cheyenne-Arapaho War, or were angered by the Chivington Massacre. Others were aroused by news from the East; the Minnesota Sioux had gone on the warpath in 1862-63 and after their defeat had scattered among the Plains Indians urging revenge. Still more were alarmed by the American advance into Montana Territory; by 1865 Virginia City, Bozeman, and Helena were thriving mining communities. The final straw was a federal effort to connect Montana with the East by road. The inaccessibility of the region had long annoyed miners; their supplies had to be carted in by a roundabout trail through South Pass to Ft. Hall and Virginia City, or brought to Ft. Benton by steamboat for transportation overland along the Mullan Road. Neither route was satisfactory, for steamboats could reach Ft. Benton only during the few months when water was high on the Missouri, and the Ft. Hall road was circuitous and expensive. Their demand for a better outlet forced the United States to survey a new road during the summer of 1865, one that branched northward from Ft. Laramie, crossed the Powder River, skirted the foothills of the Big Horn Mountains, and emerged at Bozeman, Montana.

News that the United States planned to build the "Powder River Road" or "Bozeman Trail" goaded the Sioux into action. The proposed highway would ruin one of their favorite hunting grounds: the rolling foothills of the

Big Horns, where every slope was "covered with a fine growth of grass, and in every valley there is either a rushing stream or some quiet babbling brook of pure, clear snow-water filled with trout, the banks lined with trees— wild cherry, quaking asp, some birch, willow, and cottonwood." The Sioux loved to pitch their tepees beneath the sheltering mountains in that idyllic spot while replenishing their larders from nature's abundance; bear, deer, buffalo, elk, antelope, rabbits, and sage hens were so plentiful hunting was easy. They would never stand aside while white men usurped their treasured Utopia.

Their chief, Red Cloud, first protested, then warned that any attempt to build the Powder River Road would be resisted. His threat was met during the summer of 1865 when a column of troops marched through the Big Horn country, accomplishing little, but letting the Sioux know war was under way. A year later soldiers were again in the disputed region, with orders to secure the proposed road by building forts along the route. Three outposts were started—Ft. Reno on the Powder River, Ft. Phil Kearny somewhat north-ward, and Ft. C. F. Smith at the junction of the Big Horn and the Powder River Road. Through the summer of 1866 troops working on the fortifications were under almost constant attack; every straggler was cut down, every wagon train bringing in supplies raided, every wood-cutting party attacked. Skirmishing reached a climax in December when a wood train near Ft. Phil Kearny was assaulted. The relief party under Captain W. J. Fetterman foolishly pursued the Indians deep into the wilderness, was ambushed, and all eighty-two of its members slaughtered.

The Fetterman Massacre greatly affected both antagonists. The Sioux were overjoyed; the warriors carried on the attack so furiously that by the spring of 1867 the soldiers along the Powder River Road were virtually besieged in their forts. The Americans, on the other hand, were plunged into a period of gloomy soul-searching. Such slaughter, critics pointed out, called for a thorough investigation of the entire Indian administration. "Our whole Indian policy," proclaimed the *Nation*, "is a system of mismanage-ment, and in many parts one of gigantic abuse." Humanitarians agreed the causes were twofold. Partially to blame was the division of authority between the Department of the Interior and the Department of War. The former, through its Indian Office, attempted to placate the tribes with gifts, reser-vations, and annuities; the latter punished the Indians savagely for every infraction of rules. Equally responsible for the difficulties, eastern critics insisted, was the constant encroachment of whites on lands guaranteed na-tives, often with federal protection. They maintained war would cease only when the tribes were treated with justice and the "fire and sword" policy of the military brought to an end. Both criticisms pointed to one solution: let peace advocates settle the Indian problem in their own way without any war department meddling.

That viewpoint was brought home to Congress in March, 1867, by the report of a committee which used the Chivington Massacre as the basis for an attack on the army's role in the West. A bill "for establishing peace with certain Indian tribes now at war with the United States," was promptly introduced and as promptly passed. A Peace Commission of four civilians and three generals, the measure provided, should first bring the Sioux War to a close, then assure peace between the races by removing the causes for Indian wars. That could be done, Congress felt, by persuading the Indians to abandon their nomadic ways for protected lives on out-of-the-way reservations. Armed with those instructions, commissioners set out for the West in August, 1867.

Their coming heralded a new day in the dreary history of federal Indian policy. The old system of "One Big Reservation" was giving way to "Concentration"; but "Concentration" was doomed to succumb to the device of "Small Reservations." That, members of the Peace Commission agreed, was the only workable solution to the West's racial problem. Indians must be segregated at isolated points where, as wards of the government, they could be taught to live in fixed homes, till the soil, and begin a transition to the white man's way of life, a transition that would be completed when they could be assimilated into the social order as ordinary citizens. Both expansionist westerners and humanitarian easterners would certainly approve. Frontier farmers would be satisfied because sedentary tribesmen required less space than hunters, releasing thousands of acres for settlement. Friends of the Indians would be pleased because isolation would separate Indians from sinful white men, protect their territory from avaricious land grabbers, and assure them a chance to develop into assimilable citizens.

The Peace Commissioners in a preliminary conference at St. Louis agreed that two reservations would hold all the Plains Indians. One would be in the Black Hills country of Dakota Territory; there they planned to concentrate the 54,000 tribesmen who roamed the northern grasslands. The 86,000 southern Indians they hoped to settle in present-day Oklahoma. Each tribe, they decided, would be assigned definite lands where the natives could be supervised and instructed by agents of the Indian Office. Both districts would be provided with territorial governors "of unquestioned integrity and purity of character" who would plan a broad program of progressive civilization for their charges.

The sites selected for the reservations seemed ideal to the commissioners. The Black Hills country was far from the transcontinental transportation routes, and so hilly it would attract no settlers. The Oklahoma country was even better. The region had, in the 1830s, been divided among the Five Civilized tribes of the Southeast. The natural sympathy of the southern Indians for the Confederate cause during the Civil War allowed the United States to introduce charges of treason as an excuse to strip away some of their lands. Federal agents, meeting with the chiefs in the spring of 1866, forced them to surrender most of western Oklahoma; the Creek sold half their lands for thirty cents an acre, the Seminole turned their property in at fifteen cents an acre and were required to buy a smaller reservation at fifty cents an acre, the Chickasaw and Choctaw gave up their claims to a "leased district" west of their reserves, and the Cherokee abandoned rights to the "Cherokee Outlet" beyond the 96th meridian. With the five tribes assigned the eastern half of the district, the western was freed to receive the southern Plains Indians the Peace Commissioners hoped to place there. In both North and South the way was cleared for the inauguration of the "Small Reservation" system.

The commissioners met representatives of the southwestern tribes first at a great council on Medicine Lodge Creek. The Kiowa and Comanche were dealt with on October 21, 1867; after feasting, threats, and bribery they consented to accept a 3,000,000-acre reservation between the Red and Washita rivers in western Indian Territory where they would be fed and clothed until they learned how "to walk on the white man's road." A week later the Cheyenne and Arapaho succumbed to similar lures and accepted a reserve fringed by the Cimarron and Arkansas rivers. That grassy plain, where streams ran dry in summer and icy blasts whistled in winter, was a welcome haven to Indians who had roamed the open plains since the Sand Creek Reservation had been taken from them in 1865. At the same time other federal agents were busy with the peaceful tribes of the eastern Plains country, assigning lands taken from the Five Civilized tribes to the Osage, Pawnee, Oto, and Kansa tribes, and to eastern Indians ousted from Kansas or Nebraska.

Their principal task in the South accomplished, the Peace Commissioners turned to ending the Sioux War. They were wise enough to see the Indians would never cease fighting so long as the government insisted on the Powder River Road; by the time they reached the Ft. Laramie conference ground in the spring of 1868 they had decided to surrender on that point. Chief Red Cloud and his fellow warriors were so pleased that negotiations moved smoothly. In a treaty signed on April 29, 1868, the Sioux agreed to cease fighting and accept a permanent reservation in Dakota Territory west of the Missouri River. They were allowed to use their old hunting grounds so long as game justified the chase, while the country just east of the Big Horns was recognized as unceded Indian territory. The government, in turn, stopped work on the Powder River Road and abandoned the three forts guarding the highway.

The Ft. Laramie and Medicine Lodge treaties cleared the central Plains of Indians, but the Rocky Mountain country was still in Indian hands. Federal agents turned to the task of extending the "Small Reservation" policy there during the summer and fall of 1868. The Colorado Ute bowed before their demands first, accepting a large reserve in the western quarter of the territory. A few weeks later the Shoshoni and Bannock tribes ceded their lands in Wyoming and Idaho in return for annuities and two small reservations, one on the Wind River and the other near Ft. Hall. The Navaho and Apache of Arizona and New Mexico also agreed to settle down on small reservations scattered through those territories. "We have now selected and provided reservations for all, off the great road," wrote the western military commander in September, 1868. "All who cling to their old hunting-grounds are hostile and will remain so till killed off."

That estimate of the situation, grim as it was, was overoptimistic. Assigning Indians to reservations was one thing, but forcing them to live within narrow limits was quite another. A few old chiefs who were dulled by feasting and corrupted by bribes into signing away millions of acres of tribal lands could not force scores of braves to change their whole way of life. Rather than trooping docilely to their new homes, most younger warriors and many minor chiefs refused to abide by the treaties, denounced the leaders who signed them, and prepared to fight before surrendering their nomadic habits. By the fall of 1868 warfare along the borderland was in full swing, and this time a full decade of terrorism was required before the last beaten brave sullenly accepted the manner of living decreed by his white masters.

The struggle began in August, 1868, when bands of Cheyenne, Arapaho, Kiowa, and Comanche wrung an issue of new guns from a soft-hearted federal agent. Defying the orders of Chief Black Kettle, who since the Sand Creek Massacre had for many reasons sided with the whites, they started north to murder and pillage along the Smoky Hill and Saline valleys of Kansas. Their success inspired a general uprising in the Southwest; by early fall the countryside from Kansas to Texas was filled with 2,000 roving Cheyenne, Arapaho, Comanche, Kiowa, and Apache warriors.

General Philip H. Sheridan, who commanded part of the army in the West, realized his 2,600 troops could never track down the widely roaming raiders and spent the next few months training his men for a winter campaign. He planned three expeditions. Two would move eastward from Ft. Lyon, Colorado, and Ft. Bascom, New Mexico, driving the Indians into the Washita River valley where they would be crushed by the main army from Ft. Hays, Kansas. By mid-November all was in readiness. The two columns from the western forts set out at that time, while the principal force, commanded by Lieutenant-Colonel George A. Custer, drove to Camp Supply on the North Fork of the Canadian. There they were joined by a regiment of Kansas frontiersmen under the governor of the state who had resigned his post for a chance to "whup the redskins." The enlarged army, advancing slowly through hostile territory, soon stumbled across a fresh Indian trail in the foot-deep snow. Lieutenant-Colonel Custer, under orders to follow and attack the Indians took up the pursuit at once and on November 26, 1868, reached the native camp in the Washita Valley.

The flamboyant Custer had flushed important game: Chief Black Kettle and several hundred Cheyenne and Arapaho warriors were in the encampment. Custer arranged his attack carefully. That night four columns of soldiers slipped cautiously through trees fringing the river bank to surround the Indian position. At daybreak they rushed upon the Indians, who had not expected an attack and were taken completely by surprise. For a few hours furious hand-to-hand fighting raged along the banks of the Washita, but when the battle ended the bodies of 103 natives—including Chief Black Kettle—were strewn over the camp ground. Custer hurriedly slipped back to Camp Supply before braves from other camps along the valley could rally. His punishing victory weakened native resistance; when Custer's force returned two months later the surviving chiefs were escorted to Ft. Cobb, a federal outpost on the Washita, where they signed agreements accepting reservations. The Kiowa and Comanche were hurried away to lands assigned them in the Medicine Lodge Treaties, the Cheyenne and Arapaho to a reserve along the upper Washita River. In March, 1869, General Sheridan reported that most southwestern tribes were safely in the Indian Territory.

His estimate was also overoptimistic. Federal officials, who had discovered that settling Indians on reservations was more difficult than assigning them lands, soon learned that keeping the natives within the narrow confines of reserves was equally impossible. Within two years bands of braves

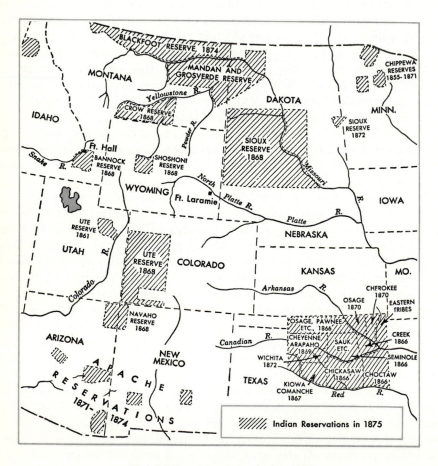

The Indian Frontier, 1866–1875

roamed the Texas Panhandle, stealing cattle, raiding isolated homesteads, and attacking overland freighters, until all the southwestern frontier clamored for relief. The volume of protest was so great by 1871 that General William Tecumseh Sherman, who had started an inspection tour of the western armies, felt called upon to act. Traveling northward from San Antonio to Ft. Richardson he found little evidence of Indian depredations—here a ruined home, there a scarred barn—but when he reached Ft. Richardson word waited him that set his blood boiling; a wagon train bound for the fort had just been ambushed and seven drivers killed. Indians who carried the attack to his doorstep, he vowed, must be punished.

While Sherman was still in that mood one of the raiders, Chief Satanta, boldly visited the fort to collect his annuities. He was arrested, and with two confederates sent to neighboring Jacksboro to stand trial for murder before a Texas civil court. One Indian was shot while trying to escape, but the other two were sentenced to be hanged after a dramatic trial which aroused national interest. General Sherman was greatly pleased; he believed he had discovered a more effective means of dealing with frontier marauders than turning them over to soft-hearted agents for a meaningless reprimand. His self-congratulations came too soon, for the clamor of eastern humanitarians forced the Texas governor to commute the sentences of the two chiefs to life imprisonment and finally to pardon them altogether. Sherman was outraged. "I believe Satanta and Big Tree will have their revenge," he wrote the governor, ". . . and if they are to have scalps, that yours is the first that should be taken."

Satanta and Big Tree did have their revenge. Their return to freedom encouraged Indian attacks that cost sixty Texans their lives in 1874 and plunged the Southwest into its last major conflict—the Red River War. This time the federal officials decided the natives must be so thoroughly crushed they would never again risk the wrath of their overlords. Three thousand troops were distributed among the forts surrounding the upper Red River valley—Ft. Union, Camp Supply, Ft. Sill, Ft. Griffin, and Ft. Concho. At an appointed time five formidable columns advanced upon the Indian stronghold. The natives struck back—fourteen pitched battles were fought—but by mid-November, 1874, the Americans were so successful General Sherman cautioned his men to "ease down on the parties hostile at present." All winter the Red River War went on, until June when resistance ended. Discouraged and worn, the half-starved Indians straggled back to their reservations, convinced at last they must accept the fate meted out by white masters.

One more war was needed to force the northern tribes into submission. The Sioux were the aggressors, although Americans had done little to placate their fears. Some natives were aroused by corruption in the Department of the Interior; they complained that supplies promised the Black Hills Reservation were too few and consisted of mouldy flour, spoiled beef, and moth-eaten blankets. Others were alarmed by the steady advance of the Northern

Pacific Railroad toward their territory. More were driven to rebellion by the Black Hills gold rush. By the summer of 1875 a thousand prospectors were tramping over their reservation while Indian Office officials sought in vain to buy the Sioux lands. When negotiations broke down in the autumn the United States washed its hands of the matter, opening the Indian lands to any miners who dared risk native wrath. They poured in by the tens of thousands that winter, all intent on staking claims without reference to the rights of the true owners. Little wonder the Indians were ready to rebel by the spring of 1876.

The conflict was touched off by the authorities. They knew that many younger braves were slipping away from the reservation to join bands of "non-treaty" Indians in the country east of the Big Horn. Fearing trouble, they ordered all Sioux, regardless of treaty guarantees that allowed them to hunt on the northern Plains, to return to the reserve by February 1, 1876. Two leaders of the Teton Dakota, Sitting Bull and Crazy Horse, not only refused but started collecting supplies on the Little Big Horn River with every indication that they meant to fight. When futile gestures by the Indian Office failed to win over the rebellious warriors, the problem was dumped on the army in March, 1876. A new Indian war was under way.

Once more General Sheridan sent three columns of converging troops against the enemy's headquarters in the Big Horn country; one under General George Crook moved northward from newly built Ft. Fetterman on the upper North Platte, a second commanded by General Alfred H. Terry started westward from Ft. Abraham Lincoln in Dakota Territory, and a third led by Colonel John Gibbon advanced eastward from Ft. Ellis in Montana. In

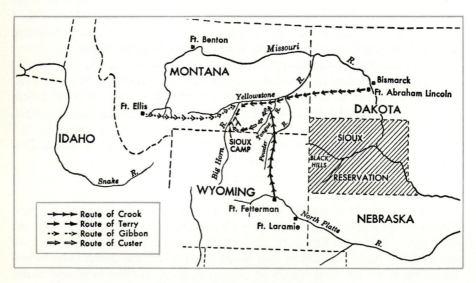

The Sioux War of 1875–1876

mid-June Terry reached the junction of the Rosebud and Yellowstone without having sighted any Sioux. Scouts, however, reported that a large band of Indians had crossed the Rosebud on its way to Sitting Bull's headquarters on the Little Big Horn. General Terry, commander of the united force, devised a sensible campaign at once. One of his subordinates, the irrepressible George A. Custer of southern Plains fame, was sent south along the Rosebud to track the Indians to their camp site, then swing his command around them so they could not retreat into the Big Horn Mountains. General Terry led the main army across country to the Big Horn River, planning to ascend that stream to the Sioux camp. His strategy would have succeeded but for one unpredictable factor: the recklessness of Custer.

That colorful commander was a vain and foolhardy leader, an immature personality beset with inner conflicts that could only be compensated by glory-seeking bravado and swagger. "Clad in buckskin trousers from the seams of which a large fringe was fluttering, red-topped boots, broad sombrero, large gauntlets, flowing hair, and mounted on a spirited animal," he loved to lead his men into dangerous exploits. Custer was smarting under an insult as he started along the Rosebud—he had been publicly rebuked by President Grant for testifying against the President's brother in a case involving fraudulent Indian trading practices—and longed to regain his self-esteem by some feat of valor. He was eager to repeat his Washita triumph. In that mood he approached the Sioux camp on the Little Big Horn. Could he risk allowing Sitting Bull and his band to escape before Terry could close in? Had he not been effective in using the surprise attack at Washita? He divided his small command into three columns and a pack train to march upon the Indians along either bank of the stream. On the morning of June 25, 1876, he ordered the advance.

Custer's own band of 265 men moved cautiously forward until skirmishing began at noon. When scouts reported many natives fleeing, he swung his command toward the village. As he did so the Sioux swept upon him. Instead of surprising a small Indian camp he had stumbled upon the Sioux's main encampment, where 2,500 warriors lay in wait! Quickly they surrounded his little force, pouring in a deadly fire as they surged around the thinning cluster of soldiers. Within a few hours all was over; Custer and his column lay dead on the battlefield. A similar fate for the remaining columns was averted by a hasty reunion with the pack train and the timely arrival of General Terry with the main army. The Battle of the Little Big Horn—"Custer's Last Stand" in the phrase of the day—was a dramatic and costly defeat.

The victory did the Sioux little good. They were driven slowly eastward during the summer, into the Tongue River valley, where they made the mistake of disclosing their position by attacking a wagon train bound for General Terry's forces. The troops closed in at once, rounding up 3,000 natives in a trap. On October 31, 1876, the Indians surrendered. Scattered bands still roamed the hills, but the decisive American victory and the approach of winter took the heart out of their attacks. Gradually they drifted back to the reservation, prepared to accept their fate. Only Chief Sitting Bull and a few die-hards refused to give up; they fled to Canada where they remained until 1881 when starvation forced them to plead for peace. The Northern Cheyenne were similarly rounded up and shipped to the Indian Territory where they were crowded into lands already occupied by the Southern Cheyenne. One group under Chief Dull Knife rebelled; starting northward toward their beloved hunting grounds in late 1878, they were overtaken by cavalry who slaughtered many, the remainder finally escaping to Pine Ridge where they became virtual prisoners on Red Cloud's reservation.

Although the Sioux War ended major Indian fighting in the West, sporadic outbreaks occurred for some years as fragments of tribes broke from their reservations for brief raids before being run down by troops. In 1877 the Nez Perce tribe of the Grand Ronde country of Oregon, led by Chief Joseph, carried on a running fight for four months before admitting defeat. Instead of being sent back to their old reserves, they were assigned barren lands in the Indian Territory where they rapidly succumbed to malaria and other diseases. The Apache of New Mexico also caused intermittent trouble between 1871 and 1888 when their great Chief Geronimo finally surrendered to a force under General Nelson A. Miles.

A final incident took place in 1890 when the Teton Sioux of South Dakota, poorly fed by an economy-minded Congress, facing the results of a serious drought, and with their reservations cut in half by a new treaty, became restless. While in this dissatisfied state, news reached them of a Paiute messiah, Wovoka, who promised all Indians that the performance of certain dances and rites would lead to the return of their lands and the disappearance of the whites. A large number of the despairing Sioux forsook all else to practice the "Ghost Dances," as the Americans disparagingly labeled the Wovoka ceremonies. This unusual activity alarmed whites into calling for troops, whose arrival only accentuated native fear of aggression. When military leaders tried to stop the dancing "craze," Indian resistance led to the death of a number of warriors including Sitting Bull, while an inept army attempt to disarm another band of Sioux resulted in the massacre of some 200 Dakota warriors, women, and children at the "Battle" of Wounded Knee. This ended the uprising, for the Indians realized they were helpless before the rapid-fire Hotchkiss guns of the soldiers.

Wounded Knee brought the military conquest of the Indians of the Far West to a tragic end. For thirty years the United States had seen fit to kill and subdue a segment of its people whose only crime was an insistence on maintaining their cultural identity rather than assimilate into the white social order. The Indians were victims of the age in which they lived. With the momentum of expansion well established, and with the nation's "Manifest Destiny" to control the continent clear, all who stood in the way of white conquest were doomed. Had the Indians managed to retain their life-pattern for a few more years, a more understanding generation of conquerors might have treated them less harshly but the end result would have been the same.

Ironically those conquerors were not only white soldiers and officers representing the dominant culture, but were themselves drawn from minority groups equally despised by the majority. Some were Indians. In 1866 Congress authorized the enlistment of 1,000 Indian "auxiliaries" for six-month terms at a salary of $13 a month. From that time on Indian scouts—drawn particularly from the Arikara and Grosventres tribes—played a vital role in the West, serving with every major force, and providing the information that cost the lives of hundreds of their ancient tribal enemies and saved the lives of even more soldiers. Particularly effective were the "Seminole Scouts," a band of thirty Indian-Negro mixed-bloods descended from runaway slaves who had joined the Seminole in Florida. Having demonstrated their skills there, they were transferred to the West in 1870 when the army was in desperate need of more scouts. For the next nine years they operated successfully on the Plains, fighting in a dozen major engagements, before fleeing to Mexico to escape discrimination and to protest the government's refusal to give them promised lands.

An even larger role was played by Negro troops. Congress in 1866 authorized the enlistment of two regiments of Black Cavalry—the 9th and 10th—and two of infantry—the 24th and 25th—to aid in the "pacification" of the West as they had in the defeat of the Confederacy. Both cavalry units were formed that year, the 9th at New Orleans under Colonel Edward Hatch, the 10th at Leavenworth under Colonel Benjamin Grierson, both whites who were thoroughly sympathetic with their troopers. Not until four years later were the Negro infantry regiments formed, and then from remnants of earlier black regiments that had seen service in the Civil War. From the beginning they operated under untold handicaps; they suffered constantly from discrimination, were subjected to far harsher punishment than meted out to other soldiers, and were forced to use broken-down horses, second-hand equipment, and cast-off guns. Yet recruitment proved easy, for the army offered Negroes status and dignity denied them in the closed society of that day.

They played an important role. The infantry regiments were used primarily for guard duty and construction tasks, but the cavalry, the "Buffalo Soldiers" they were called by the Indians because of their short curly hair, patrolled the whole West from the Canadian border to the Rio Grande, chasing Indians back to their reservations, arresting rustlers, guarding stage coaches, and escorting surveying parties. They also fought valiantly in a series of campaigns against the Apache, Sioux, Kickapoo, and Comanche, took part in the Red River War, and had a hand in bringing Geronimo to bay. In all the Buffalo Soldiers compiled a record at least as good as that of their white comrades in arms, while their desertion rate was far lower; in 1876 the 9th Regiment had six absentees and the 10th eighteen, compared with 170 for the white 3rd Regiment and 224 for the 5th.

The whites and blacks who fought the Native Americans were bound to win not because of superior valor or military skill, but because they were aided by an unforseen circumstance that tipped the scales. This was the extermination of the buffalo by professional hunters. Those shaggy beasts were food and shelter for Plains Indians; so long as giant herds roamed the West the Indians could continue their nomadic ways, drifting across the grasslands in the hunt. Once the buffalo vanished the Indians' livelihood was gone and they had no choice but to accept federal bounty. The slaughter of the giant herds that grazed the plains—one north and the other south of the central overland route—began when the Union Pacific was built in 1867 and lasted until 1883 when the bison were virtually exterminated.

Probably millions of buffalo lived in the West when the first hunters arrived with their powerful, long-range rifles. They fell mercilessly upon the stupid beasts, shooting them from train windows, pursuing them on horseback, and butchering them as they forded streams. Thousands of "sportsmen" took advantage of the opportunity to kill indiscriminately between 1867 and 1872, with no other reward than the sight of dying animals. The herds might have survived that onslaught, but their fate was sealed when a Pennsylvania tannery discovered in 1871 that buffalo hides could be used for commercial leather. With every bison worth from $1 to $3, professional hunters swarmed over the Plains to exploit the new source of wealth. Between 1872 and 1874 3,000,000 beasts were killed yearly; after that the rate of slaughter increased as companies sent bands of hired hunters into the field. Groups of eight or nine plainsmen, armed with long-range rifles and accompanied by wagons to carry out the hides, could kill and skin fifty or more bison daily. By 1878 the southern herd was exterminated; in 1883 the buffalo vanished from the northern Plains. A museum expedition seeking specimens that year found less than 200 in all the West, while by 1903 the number had dwindled to thirty-four. Little wonder that the Indians, their staff of life gone, were forced to accept a servile fate as wards of the government.

But the problem of dealing with the Native Americans was not settled when they abandoned their nomadic ways. A policy that would allow the two races to live together was needed. The old system failed, all agreed, because it emphasized tribal units; since the beginning of settlement tribes had been treated as sovereign nations capable of enforcing treaty obligations, when actually they were dependent social groups without national rights. Treaties between Indians and the United States bound only the natives, yet whenever the federal government broke a covenant war resulted. The solution, reformers conceded, was to treat natives as individuals while training them to assume the responsibilities of citizenship.

A few earlier experiments suggested that the method would be successful. These had been arranged by both Indian agents and military commanders who had been sickened by the brutality of Plains warfare and felt a genuine compassion for their foes. Such a general was John Pope, who saw in the end of warfare on the southern Plains an opportunity to test his belief that the Indians were capable of fitting into the social order of the whites. For the next half-dozen years he used his post in the Indian Territory to instruct his charges in farming techniques and other skills that would make assimilation possible. Pope operated under impossible handicaps; Congress refused to appropriate funds needed, while Indian Bureau agents insisted on selling guns to the braves for hunting rather than encouraging them to adopt a sedentary life. By 1883 the experiment had to be abandoned with little accomplished. Yet some of the more sympathetic observers in and out of the army realized that with proper support Pope had found a solution to the "Indian Problem."

Even before he launched his experiment, Congress had taken the first step toward a new policy in 1871 when it decreed that no Indian tribe "shall be acknowledged or recognized as an independent nation, tribe or power, with whom the United States may contract by treaty." This encouraged the Indian Office to weaken tribal organization by breaking down the power of chiefs. Agents were told to help their wards establish councils to usurp governmental powers formerly exercised by leaders; such units were formed among the Apache in the early 1880s and copied elsewhere. An Indian Office order of 1883 went a step further by setting up court systems to relieve chiefs of judicial functions. Two years later a congressional decree extended the jurisdiction of federal courts over Indians on reserves. Step by step the tribal organization disintegrated until the Indians were treated as individuals, their traditional culture shattered.

At the same time natives were trained to assume new responsibilities. Federal education began in 1879 when the Carlisle Indian School of Carlisle, Pennsylvania, threw open its doors to fifty Pawnee, Kiowa, and Cheyenne brought east for the experiment. Their success convinced Congress the Indians, despite what science at that time saw as their racial limitations, were capable of improvement and encouraged the first sizeable appropriations for Indian schools during the early 1880s. From that time on sums annually set aside for the purpose increased, some for eastern boarding schools such as Carlisle, but more for day schools on the western reservations. Emphasis was placed on mechanical and agricultural subjects which would fit Indians for the white men's way of life, as well as on courses designed to train Indians for citizenship.

The final step in formulating the new policy was to carry the principle of individualism into land ownership by giving each native a farm. Agitation for division of tribal lands developed rapidly during the 1880s, with support from two strangely divergent groups. One was made up of land-hungry frontier settlers who recognized that any splitting of the reservations would release thousands of acres for white settlers. The other was composed of eastern humanitarians—the "Lo! the Poor Indian" reformers as westerners dubbed them—who sincerely believed assimilation the only answer to the West's racial problem and sought to hasten the mingling by turning natives from the chase to agriculture. Organized in such societies as the Indian Rights Association, and aided by such publications as the magazine *Council Fire* (1878), they were in a position to propagandize both the government and the people. Their campaign was effective; thousands of Americans were won to the cause of reform by Helen Hunt Jackson's *A Century of Dishonor* (1881) and other sentimental distortions sponsored by humanitarians. By the middle 1880s reforming pressure on Congress was too strong to resist.

Within that body the Indians were championed by Henry L. Dawes, senator from Massachusetts and chairman of the Senate Indian Committee. Long a friend of the Indian, and convinced by 1885 that severalty would solve the racial problem, he threw himself into the contest with the vigor of a reformer. His reward came on February 8, 1887, when he watched President Grover Cleveland sign the Dawes Severalty Act. That important measure authorized the President to divide the lands of any tribe, giving each head of a family 160 acres, with lesser amounts to bachelors, women, and children. The plots, rather than going directly to the Indians, were to be held in trust by the government for twenty-five years, a device deemed necessary to prevent untrained natives from disposing of their holdings immediately. All those receiving grants were to be made citizens of the United States. Reservation lands remaining after the division were to be sold by the government, with profits deposited in a trust fund for educational purposes.

The Dawes Act was not the panacea envisaged by its backers; later congresses altered its provisions and in the twentieth century overthrew its basic premise by returning to a policy that respected Indians' cultural traditions rather than attempting to recast them in the white man's mold. But frontier settlers and humanitarians of the post-Civil War era, confident their solution was final, were satisfied. The last page was written on the saga of western warfare; the two races would live forever in peace. At last the restless pioneer could advance unmolested across the Great Plains where once the shaggy buffalo and tawny native had long held sway. There had been no national policy of genocide but the attitudes shared by frontier militiamen, most army officers, settlers, miners, and humanitarians resulted in an attack on the social and religious fabric of Indian life. That Indians as a people survived at all is a testimony to their vitality and to their capacity to nurture their heritage in a hostile world. It also indicates that once the land issue was settled few whites concerned themselves with the Indian issue.

31

The Ranchers' Frontier
1865-1887

Indian removal paved the way for the conquest of America's last frontier—the Great Plains province. That gargantuan grassland had halted the westward march of farmers, who found its arid climate, sparse vegetation, and unfamiliar soils unsuited to pioneering techniques acquired in the humid East. Their reluctance to assault the unfamiliar plains environment provided an opportunity for another group of westerners—the ranchers. In the two decades after the Civil War great herds of bellowing longhorns, guarded by colorfully garbed cowboys on spirited ponies, spread over the whole pastureland, bringing fortunes to their owners and romance to the annals of the frontier. That was the day of the cattleman, the day when the longhorn steer was King of the West.

The giant industry had its beginnings in southern Texas. Cattle introduced there by Spaniards in the eighteenth century—scrawny, tough beasts bred by Moorish herdsmen—multiplied rapidly, especially in the triangle formed by the junction of the Rio Grande and the Gulf of Mexico. Conditions were ideal in that spot; the climate warm, the grass green all year, water plentiful from tributaries of the Nueces, the range so open that cattle drifted from feeding ground to feeding ground without encountering trees. Moreover few Indian raiders ventured south of San Antonio. In that ideal setting Mexican ranchers learned how to care for cattle on the open range. They learned to herd on horseback, to identify their own beasts by brands, to use a "roundup" to mark newborn calves. By the time Americans invaded Texas the Nueces Valley was a great cattle range, where thousands of steers roamed freely over the unfenced grassland under the watchful eye of vaqueros.

611

Some American intruders were ranchers whose practices as well as animals contributed to the growth of the infant Texan cattle industry. Their eastern milch cows, breeding with the Mexican herds, produced a variety of strains more suitable to the American market than the original Moorish type. One clearly distinguished breed was the "Texas-Mexican," tall and gaunt, splashed with patches of white, and with enormous horns twisting back toward the body. Another was the "Spanish," which resembled the crossbreed but was somewhat smaller with shorter horns and gentler spirit. A third, the "Long-haired Texans," were round, well-formed beasts with long legs, heavy body, medium horns, and a heavy coat of brownish color. The "Wild Cattle" of western Texas were thin, blue-horned, mealy-nosed, and brown in color. All were tough and wiry, able to care for themselves on parched summer prairies or during winter blizzards.

The Americans who controlled Texas after its independence paid little attention to the increasing herds, largely because almost no market for beef was near enough to make sales profitable. A few were driven to Austin or Galveston, a few more to New Orleans, some even to the Ohio Valley where an adventurous herdsman sold a thousand head in 1846. Others were marketed in the gold fields of Colorado, Arizona, and California during the late 1850s, but in each case the expenses of the drive and the difficulties of overland herding discouraged any large-scale attempts. For the most part the cattle were allowed to roam wild over the lush grasslands, drifting northward in search of new feeding grounds as they increased in numbers until they blanketed western Texas between the Rio Grande and the upper Panhandle. They multiplied especially during the Civil War years when drives to market were stopped by Union control of the Mississippi, until by the close of the war some 5,000,000 longhorns roamed Texas. Most were "mavericks" that could be claimed by anyone bothering to affix a brand, although a few were held on ranches in the belt of open country east of the Cross Timbers.

By 1865 a few astute Texans recognized that the millions of cattle might be turned into tidy profits. They knew good steers could be had for the asking in their own state, or could be purchased for $3 or $4 a head from ranchers. They learned that the upper Mississippi Valley, its livestock supplies depleted by war, was willing to pay up to $40 a head for marketable beasts. Only a little arithmetic was required to demonstrate the fortunes to be made from that price differential. If a rancher could get a herd of 3,000 longhorns to the northern markets the profits would amount to $100,000; if all 5,000,000 Texas cattle could be driven north the state would be enriched to the extent of $180,000,000! Nor was this simply a fantastic dream. Texans were aware that the hardy animals could be driven overland without difficulty so long as the journey lay through open prairie. They knew, too, that railroads were jutting westward into the central Plains; the Missouri Pacific Railroad reached Sedalia, Missouri, in 1865 and could be used as a shipping point to eastern markets. Why not capitalize upon the happy combination of circumstances to amass King Midas' own wealth for themselves?

The "Long Drive" was the result. During the winter of 1865–66 a number of Texans and a few prudent investors from Iowa and Kansas quietly rounded up herds, laid in equipment, and hired cowhands. In late March, when the grass on the northern Plains began to green, they started. Each band of a thousand or more cattle was driven by half a dozen cowhands, all adept in the use of the lasso and six-shooter, and paid $25 to $40 a month. A chuck wagon carrying food and equipment, with the cook at the reins, broke trail, followed by the horse wrangler and his horses; then came the longhorns, strung out over a mile of prairie. At the "point" or head of the column two riders kept the cattle on their course, others guarded the flank, and two more rode at "drag" in the rear to spur on halting beasts. The whole "outfit" was commanded by a trail boss who received a salary of $125 a month.

Experience soon taught the bosses to drive the cattle slowly at first and to watch them carefully at night, but within a week the steers were "road broken" enough to move ahead more rapidly. After that the larger herds were guarded by only two hands at night, they drifted slowly away from the bedding ground at daybreak, grazing as they went. After an hour or so the pace was speeded up until noon when a halt was made at some stream where the cook, who had galloped ahead in the chuck wagon, had dinner waiting. The cattle grazed for a few hours while the crew ate, then were driven rapidly on until nightfall. That was the pattern followed by the dozens of herds that left Texas in the spring of 1866; in all some 260,000 head started for the Missouri Pacific railheads at Sedalia.

Nevertheless the Long Drive was far from successful. Bad luck plagued drovers from the beginning. Heavy rains in Texas muddied trails, swelled streams, and made life so unpleasant that many hands deserted their jobs. Beyond the Red River where the Sedalia Trail crossed a corner of the Indian Territory herds were frequently stampeded by Indians who then demanded a reward for returning the beasts to their owners. Still farther north the wooded hills of the Ozark Plateau terrified the cattle; longhorns accustomed to the open range bolted rather than enter forested regions. When that obstacle was passed another was encountered in the irate farmers of Missouri, who were out in force to repel herds that might infect their own cattle with the dread Texas Fever. At every county line armed bands of backwoodsmen halted drovers, shot cattle, or fought it out with cowhands. The successive barriers kept all but a few steers from reaching Sedalia, but the $35 a head received for those convinced Texas ranchers and drovers the Long Drive would be successful if they could find a less hazardous route to market.

The honor of laying out a better trail went not to a drover but to Joseph G. McCoy, an Illinois meat dealer, who realized a fortune awaited anyone controlling the spot where southern sellers and northern buyers could meet most advantageously. That point, he reasoned, must lie on the Kansas Pacific Railroad, then building westward from Kansas City; this would allow herders to avoid wooded areas and settlements while driving cattle northward. Officials of the line proved so enthusiastic McCoy was able to exact promises of low freight rates from them, but the president of the road connecting Kansas City with St. Louis and the markets of the East, the Missouri Pacific Railroad thought the plan fantastic and refused to cooperate. Undaunted, McCoy turned to a second railroad having eastern connections from Kansas City, the Hannibal and St. Joe Railroad. Before the winter of 1866–67 was over he signed a contract assuring him favorable shipping terms for cattle between the Plains and Chicago.

McCoy's next task was to select the point on the Kansas Pacific tracks where the Long Drive would end. After careful study he chose the little hamlet of Abilene, Kansas, because, as he wrote, "the country was entirely unsettled, well watered, excellent grass and nearly the entire area of country was adapted to holding cattle." Abilene—a drowsy little village with a handful of settlers and so little business the one saloon keeper spent part of his time raising prairie dogs for tourists—was transformed overnight by his decision. During the spring of 1867 McCoy imported lumber for stockyards, pens, loading chutes, barns, a livery stable, and a hotel to house the cowhands. All was bustle and confusion as the building program was rushed to completion; by July, McCoy was able to send riders southward to intercept Sedalia-bound herds with welcome news of a new market at Abilene. Unfortunately most of the drovers had gone too far to be turned back, but 35,000 Texas steers passed through McCoy's loading chutes that fall. The banquet held on September 5, 1867, to celebrate the first shipment of cattle east was a gala affair, where southern drovers and northern dealers toasted the wedding of their sections and talked joyfully of the profits that would be theirs in the future.

Abilene assured success for the Long Drive. The drovers who reached there in 1868 with 75,000 head were enthusiastic over the trail northward—the Chisholm Trail, they called it—and carried word to Texas of the ease with which steers could be driven where there were no settlements, hills, or wooded areas. Their advertising started the tide rolling; between 1868 and 1871 nearly 1,500,000 Texan beeves were loaded in the Abilene yards. By that time the advance of settlement in eastern Kansas and the march of railroads across the Plains conspired to shift the cattle trail farther westward. Ellsworth, lying sixty miles west of Abilene on the Kansas Pacific Railroad, and Newton on the newly built Atchison, Topeka and Santa Fe Railroad, were the terminal points for the Long Drive between 1872 and 1875, receiving about 1,500,000 head. After 1875 the center was Dodge City, Kansas, which shipped 1,000,000 Texas beeves eastward in the next four years. In all 4,000,000 cattle reached the Kansas railroads during the years when the Long Drive was a feature of the cattle frontier.

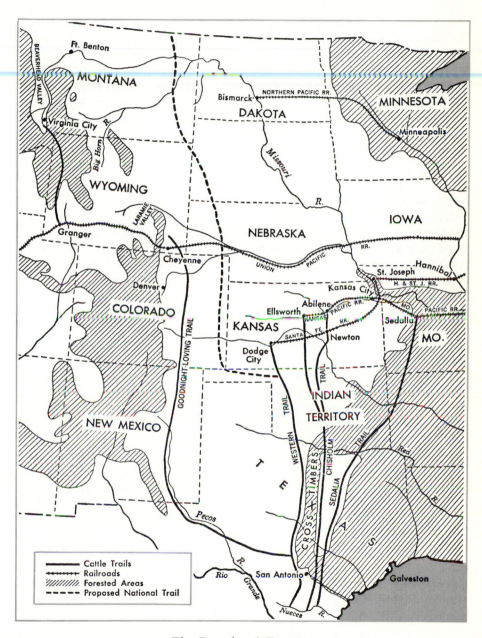

The Ranchers' Frontier

The "Cattle Towns" at the heads of the trails (the term *cow town* was not used until well into the 1880s and then in a slightly derogatory sense) have been glorified in film and fiction as models of unbridled corruption where hurdy-gurdy dance halls, bawdy houses, and gambling saloons lined the streets and shoot-outs were of such common occurrence that the local "boot hills" received new customers daily. Two of them—Ellsworth and Dodge City—did gain an unenviable reputation for lawlessness, but only during their early years before the cattle trade began, when buffalo hunters and bad men concentrated there. This changed as soon as the trade attracted a business entrepreneurial group of hard-headed merchants interested in profits and with a major investment to protect. They wanted law enforcement, but they recognized also that cowhands needed relaxation at the end of the long drive, and that unduly harsh punishment for wrongdoers would cause ill-feeling among the drovers, and with it a possible loss of trade. Hence saloons and dance halls were allowed, but not in excessive numbers; Abilene during its busiest season boasted no more than eleven taverns, Ellsworth ten, and Dodge City eight. Most were miserable holes-in-the-wall dispensing cheap whiskey, although Dodge City was proud of its tastefully decorated "Long Branch" saloon and Abilene of its celebrated "Alamo" where triple doors gave easy access to the long bar and gaming tables. Dance halls and brothels were even less common; Abilene had only three houses of prostitution in 1869 with twenty-one whores, but the city boasted not a single dance hall until 1871 when one flourished for a single season. Dodge City in its heyday claimed only two dance halls, one for whites and one for blacks.

Within these establishments order was the rule of the day—and night. Vigilantism was tried by the business leaders—once in Ellsworth in 1873 and once in Dodge in 1881—but they disliked such primitive justice and saw to it that the towns were incorporated as soon as possible and provided with efficient law-enforcement machinery. This always took the form of a small police force supported by high license fees and by fines paid by saloons, gambling houses, and brothels; the glamorous "cow town" marshal was only a police captain who also served as street commissioner. These officers saw to it that the laws were rigidly enforced; ordinances against carrying guns were in force in all cattle towns, and homicides kept at a minimum; between 1870 and 1885 only forty-five men were killed (including sixteen by police), and of these thirty-nine died of gunshot wounds, not six-shooters. Only twice were as many as five men killed during a single year—in Ellsworth in 1873 and in Dodge City five years later. The "shootout" glorified in "western" stories and motion pictures was unheard of. Justice was admittedly lenient lest the cattlemen take offense and take their herds elsewhere, but in all the cattle towns only three men were executed for crimes and one was lynched; not one of these was a cowhand, and none were convicted of gun fighting or a shooting affair. Those who endured the hardships of the Long Drive were hardly treated as saints when they reached their destinations, but neither were they plunged into the tinseled palaces of sin that have become a part of the national legend.

Nor did they enjoy unusual profits, for the drive was found from its very beginning to be economically hazardous. The difficulties which beset drovers were many. Their cattle lost so much weight in the 1,500 mile journey northward that few could be sold to eastern stockyards at good prices; most went as "feeders" to some Nebraska or Iowa farmer for fattening on corn. Their expenses increased steadily, especially after 1867 when natives in the Indian Territory discovered that an ancient congressional statute forbade traffic across their lands without special permission. First the Cherokee, then the tribes farther west, capitalized on the situation by charging ten cents a head for all steers driven through their reservations. Far worse, from the drovers' point of view, was the hostility of the Kansans. Irate farmers, knowing Texas Fever was carried by disease-transmitting ticks which infected Texas cattle, were always out in force to repel northward-bound herds. At first they resorted to shooting, but that was outmoded when their control of state legislatures allowed them to erect legal barriers. Both Missouri and Kansas passed quarantine laws in 1867, forbidding the entrance of cattle during the summer and fall when ticks were most active, and Kansas in 1884 ruled that no Texas steers could be driven into the state except in December, January, and February. Although drovers often evaded the laws the growing agricultural population demanded and secured better enforcement. Texans, faced with a loss of profitable markets, spent a great deal of money and energy between 1884 and 1886 propagandizing for a "National Cattle Trail" that would be immune to state interference—for a time the Texas Live Stock Association kept two full-time lobbyists in Washington to carry on the agitation—but northern opposition and congressional indifference ended that hope. By 1885, however, the Long Drive had become uneconomic. Ranchers on the northern Plains near railroads were well stocked with cattle. That not only allowed cattle growers to evade barriers erected by farmers and Indians but also placed them in a better position to bargain with buyers who dictated prices in the Kansas cattle towns.

In Texas railroads came to the cattle country. During the 1870s the Missouri, Kansas and Texas Railroad, the Texas and Pacific Railroad, and numerous other lines opened communication with St. Louis, New Orleans, and Memphis. The possibility of direct marketing encouraged dozens of ranchers to stake out claims on the grassland between the Cross Timbers and the Pecos Valley where nutritive bunch grass, mesquite, and grama grass provided adequate fodder. Within a decade the whole Panhandle was carved into enormous ranches, some of them so large that cowhands rode scores of miles from their homes to reach their front gates.

The problem of growing cattle near the northern railroads was just as easily solved. The climate was harsh, with roaring winter gales and occasional ice storms, but cattle could weather most blizzards so long as they drifted before the wind with their rumps to the tempest. Only when ice blanketed the ground was there any real danger, and that happened infrequently. During most of the year steers could feast on short prairie grass or scrape away snow to munch winter-cured fodder. The longhorns' ability to thrive on the northern Plains was demonstrated long before the close of the Civil War by traders who bartered sleek oxen for worn-out livestock along the immigrant trails, and by small ranchers who supplied the Montana gold fields with fresh beef. By 1868 herds dotted the High Plains country from the Rio Grande Valley to the Big Horn Basin, amply demonstrating that cattle could be grown anywhere. Only two things were needed to transform the local industry into a mammoth enterprise: adequate markets and improved steers to satisfy the discriminating taste of eastern consumers.

Both were provided during the 1870s. Railroads pushed steadily across the northern Plains during the decade: the Union Pacific, the Kansas Pacific, the Santa Fe, the Northern Pacific, the Burlington, and other smaller lines. At the same time mechanical improvements in meat handling and slaughtering—modern killing methods, refrigerator cars, and cold storage—widened the market for western beef. From the open range to the kitchen range was an easy step, and the demand for American meat mounted until all the East and much of Europe was fed by Plains ranchers. The quality of western beef was improved at the same time. As tough Texas cows were brought north, they were bred with heavier Hereford and Angus bulls to produce round-bellied, white-faced cattle which combined the stamina of longhorns and the weight and tenderness of eastern breeds. Able to survive cold winters and fetch an excellent price at the Chicago stockyards, the hybrids proved an ideal stock for the northern range.

The distinctive breed was developed in Kansas, for there Texas longhorns and eastern cattle first met. From the beginning of the Long Drive enterprising ranchers were on hand to purchase cows that were too scrawny or sickly to be sold; they were then fattened on prairie grass, bred with Hereford bulls, and used to build up herds of healthy cattle that showed little trace of their rangy Texas ancestors. As the ventures proved profitable, more and more cattle were diverted from the cattle towns to stock the northern range, while the brisk demand for Hereford bulls drove their price up to $1,000. By the end of the 1860s ranches covered most of Kansas and Nebraska as well as portions of the Indian Territory where land was leased from the natives. Many drovers from Texas, finding they must compete with sleek steers from the nearby range when selling their herds, moved to Kansas themselves or laid out ranches there where they could fatten and hybridize their stock before sale.

From Kansas ranching spread into Colorado as soon as the Kansas Pacific and Union Pacific railroads joined that area to the outside world. Most of the cows needed to stock the range came from Texas, driven northward over the Goodnight-Loving Trail after that route was laid out in 1866. By 1869 1,000,000 longhorns grazed within the borders of Colorado Territory, and the herds were improving so rapidly that stock raisers clamored for laws against further Texas importations lest stray bulls corrupt their Hereford-crossed strains. Statutes authorizing ranchers to shoot any loose Texan bull on sight testified to the regard with which they held their herds.

The advance of the cattle frontier into Wyoming began in 1868 when a Colorado rancher, J. W. Iliff, drove one of his herds to the plains near Cheyenne. His exorbitant profits from sales of beef to construction crews on the Union Pacific Railroad and miners prospecting the South Pass country, called attention to the richness of the range; others followed until by 1871 perhaps 100,000 cattle pastured there, most of them under the watchful eye of ranchers who owned only a few hundred head. The number increased rapidly after 1873 when the panic hurried the stocking of the northern range by lowering the price of Texan cattle. The center of the industry in Wyoming was the Laramie Valley, a region of rolling bench lands where grass and water abounded, and in the plateau country just west of the Laramie Mountains. After those regions filled ranchers spread their herds over most of the territory.

Extensive cattle raising in Montana began in 1871 when a herd of 800 Texas longhorns were driven into the Beaverhead River valley by an enterprising herder with an eye on the rich market in nearby mining camps. Plentiful grass in that mountainous upland and the failure of Montana's mining population to increase as rapidly as expected allowed the herds to multiply rapidly; by 1874 the surplus above local needs reached 17,000 head and good beef steers sold for as low $10. Those depressed prices transformed Montana ranching from a local to a national enterprise; eastern buyers, hearing sleek beeves could be purchased for a low sum, flocked in during the autumn, ready to pay up to $18 a head. The herds were driven south to the Union Pacific tracks at Granger, Wyoming—a difficult route through sparsely grassed country—but profits were great enough to convince Montana ranchers they must look to the East rather than to mining camps for future markets.

With plentiful sales promised, the cattle frontier could move out of the mountain valleys into the broad plains of eastern Montana where rich grass, plentiful streams, and protecting hills offered ideal pasturage. For a few years the advance was slow; Sitting Bull was on the warpath and neither man nor beast was safe until after 1878 when the last band of Sioux was driven onto a reservation. Then great herds were driven north from Colorado or Wyoming to stock the promising grassland. "Eastern Montana has suddenly awakened," wrote an editor. ". . . Stock is pouring in from every hand." Marketing remained difficult—cattle must be driven south to the Union Pacific Railroad or east to the Northern Pacific tracks at Bismarck—but no amount of isolation could discourage a stock raiser in that day of expansion. Ranches filled Montana, then spilled over into Dakota territory during the 1870s.

By 1880 the cattle industry was firmly planted throughout the Great Plains. A traveler riding northward from lower Texas would seldom be out of sight of herds of white-faced longhorns, grazing under the watchful eye of bronzed cowhands; he would find them in the Panhandle country, along the Pecos Valley of New Mexico, on the sun-baked plains of the Indian Territory, among the rolling prairies of western Kansas and Nebraska, scattered through the high grasslands of eastern Colorado and Wyoming, and dotting the wind-swept plains of Montana and Dakota. Prosaic census figures described the expansion of the cattle frontier:

	Cattle in 1860	Cattle in 1880
Kansas	93,455	1,533,133
Nebraska	37,197	1,791,492
Wyoming	none	521,213
Montana	none	428,279
Dakota	none	140,815

Texas longhorns, Kansas Herefords, and adventurous ranchers from all the West had created a new empire—the Cattle Kingdom. "Cotton was once crowned king," wrote an exuberant editor, "but grass is now."

From the Great Plains the cattle industry spread westward into the unlikely grazing lands of Arizona and New Mexico. Arizona blossomed into a drovers' haven during the 1870s when herdsmen found that cattle on their way to California markets (where $5 beeves fetched a profitable $150) could pasture in the river valleys where grass was ample, particularly the valleys of the San Pedro and Santa Cruz rivers. Other ranchers at about the same time began experimenting with herds on the plateau country of northern Arizona, along the Little Colorado River and about the mining town of Prescott. This infant industry expanded remarkably during the late 1870s and early 1880s when a number of new army posts were established in the region, offering a market for beef, and when steady pressure on the Apache Indians opened more and more grazing land. Arizona's boom period as a ranching territory began in the 1880s when the defeat of Geronimo ended the Apache menace and the exhaustion of the Texas range sent dozens of ranchers westward. By 1890 beef cattle were so numerous in Arizona that the grasslands there were in danger of overstocking. By this time Oregon was also attracting ranchers, who found good pasturage on the plains in the eastern part of that state during wet years. There, too, the industry dominated the economy.

Underlying the remarkable expansion which engulfed an area half the size of Europe within a single generation was the age-old hope for sudden wealth. Conditions on the Great Plains seemed to promise fabulous profits. The land was free—millions of acres of it—all carpeted with rich grass and safe from meddlesome government agents. Cattle to stock the range were cheap; longhorns could be purchased in Texas at $7 or $8 a head, driven north to a likely spot, crossed with an imported eastern bull, and allowed to multiply as nature dictated. The rancher had only to sit back and watch his wealth increase, knowing every healthy steer would fetch from $50 to $60 at the nearest railroad. A few years of frugal living, while profits were turned back into the herd, would allow any pioneer to pyramid a modest investment into a handsome fortune.

There was no lack of adventurers to people the ranchers' frontier. Most were young men and women who had scraped necessary capital together, bought their herds, and started out in search of a likely grazing spot. Because grass and water were necessary, a site was always selected on the bank of a stream. There the prospective rancher either homesteaded 160 acres or simply appropriated the land. Then, if a few straggly trees grew nearby, a cabin was raised; if not a tent of buffalo skin was put up or a dugout was scooped from the muddy bank of the river. With that simple equipment, a supply of beans, bacon, and coffee, and a horse or two, the rancher was ready to watch cattle graze, watch them fatten, watch them multiply. When beef animals were cut away to be sold the proceeds were used to buy more stock, build a ranch house, and erect corrals for horses. Three or four good years were enough to put the business on a paying basis, with herds so large cowhands were hired to watch them.

By that time other ranchers were moving in nearby, along the same stream or across the divide on the banks of the next waterway. They were not near neighbors in the eastern sense of the words—they might be fifteen or twenty miles away—but they were close enough to cause trouble unless a system of frontier law was devised. How could ranchers keep their cattle separated from those of a neighbor? How could a rancher sustain a claim to a portion of the public domain? How could newcomers be kept from overcrowding the range? Distant legislatures could not solve those problems; like earlier frontier settlers throughout America's history ranchers must make their own laws. The body of custom and rule they worked out allowed expansion to go on with a minimum of disorder.

Basic to the system was the concept that control of a stream included control of adjacent lands. Thus ranchers staking out a claim to one bank of a creek secured a "range right" to as much of the river as they preempted and all the land running back to the "divide," or highland separating the stream from the one lying beyond. This was the claim, although the ranchers did not own a foot of it legally; public opinion, backed by the effective argument contained in six-shooters, gave them a right to use it without fear. The usual ranches in the Great Plains contained thirty or forty square miles.

The imaginary "range lines" between holdings were respected by humans, but cattle drifted from ranch to ranch in their search for better pasturage until herds of several owners were frequently hopelessly intermingled. Ranchers' attempts to keep their steers separate from those of their neighbors gave prominence to two customs—"line-riding" and the "roundup." In line-riding, cowhands were stationed along the borders of each ranch, usually in groups of two, ten or twenty miles apart, with a dugout to protect them in winter and the open sky as their canopy in summer. Each morning they set out from their lonely posts, riding in opposite directions until they met the range hand from the nearest camp on either side. Herds belonging to their employer were driven back from the border; those of neighbors were "drifted" in the direction of their own ranch.

Vigilant as line-riders might be, animals did intermingle. Twice each year, in the spring and fall, "roundups" were held to separate mixed herds and identify newborn calves. At the time agreed upon, each rancher sent a chuck wagon and "outfit" to a designated spot. Then the crews fanned out over the range, driving all cattle in the vicinity toward camp, until a herd of several thousand was assembled. While the milling mass of animals was held together, riders of the ranch where the roundup was held made the first "cut," riding skillfully through the herd to single out animals bearing their employer's brand. Those brands—distinctive marks burned into the flanks with red-hot branding irons—were registered to avoid confusion; some symbols of better-known ranches became as famous as baronial symbols of feudal days. As calves always followed the mothers, they could now be lassoed, thrown, and marked with the iron.

After the first division, workers from other ranches cut out their own cattle; a process repeated until the last cow was branded. Then the owner of the ranch where the roundup took place held back his herd while the rest were driven to the next ranch, where the procedure was duplicated. That went on until the last range was visited and the cattle of the whole region branded and returned to their owners. The work was hard—cowhands spent eighteen or twenty hours a day in the saddle for weeks at a time—but the roundup was one of the most colorful institutions in the history of the frontier. The thousands of bellowing cattle, blazing branding fires, scores of range hands, and scattered chuckwagons, all hazy with dust and drenched by a brilliant sun, caught the imagination of easterners as did nothing else in the Far West.

Eastern imagination in turn, has given the nation one of its most enduring legends: the myth of the glamorous "cowboy." Actually the clean-cut heroes of Hollywood and the television screen bear little resemblance to the hardworking men who tended cattle in the heyday of the open range. "Cowboys," as one of them put it, were simply hired hands on horseback, doomed to a life of dull routine as they "rode line" separating the unfenced ranches, doctored sick animals, or drifted herds from pasturage to pasturage. Little wonder that when they "hit town" on rare occasions they indulged in the riotous conduct that has come to typify them for cinema addicts the world over. There was little romance in their lonely lives; even the widely publicized "ten-gallon" hats, chaps, knotted handkerchiefs, and colorful shirts that they sometimes wore to charm strangers were often displaced by a working garb of overalls, a cast-off army overcoat that had seen service in the Civil War, and a derby hat. Even their individualism has been exaggerated; many joined a labor union, the Knights of Labor, and a group struck one ranch during the 1884 roundup.

Nor were cowhands all the sturdy Anglo-Saxons popularized on film. A good many of them were Negroes. When the cattle drives began many former slaves who had lived in Texas were accustomed to life in the saddle and to handling the longhorns traditionally produced in that state; they would logically be hired as drovers now, as would other blacks who moved westward in search of employment after the Civil War. Of the cowhands who participated in the long drives, many were blacks and Mexican-Americans. A trail outfit could include two or three black cowhands; some even became trail bosses. Negroes also worked for ranchers over the entire Great Plains area as the cattle kingdom spread. Men along the ranching frontier were more likely to be judged by their skills than by their color but black cowhands were usually assigned unpleasant tasks. Mexican-American cowhands—vaqueros—were even more at home in the Southwest than were the blacks. Many of their customs, tools, and institutions were a vital part of the industry. Unlike whites and blacks, they tended to work on one ranch in crews under Spanish-speaking bosses. Although cowhands were usually male, many ranchers were women, often as skilled in the ways of the cattle frontier as the men they employed.

The ranchers' days, and the days of the open range, were numbered, for by the middle 1880s astute observers began to recognize trouble ahead. Overstocking was responsible. During the early 1880s the whole western world awakened to the possibilities of the Cattle Kingdom. Markets were expanding as railroads pushed into the Great Plains and steamships brought European customers closer to the United States. Soon the entire world would be willing to pay handsomely for western beef! Any doubting scoffer could be convinced by the steady price rise at the Chicago stock yards, an advance that carried choice steers to a high of eight or nine cents a pound. Anyone could reap a fortune by doing nothing more than watch his animals multiply on virtually free government or railroad land.

Even the unvarnished truth would have started a rush to the Plains, but that was not the literary diet fed Americans by magazines and newspapers. Western editors, never notable for understatement, filled their columns with statistics proving that anyone investing $25,000 in cattle could run his fortune to $80,000 in five years, or stated authoritatively that profits of 40 and 50 per cent annually were the rule rather than the exception. Those tall tales were spread wholesale through the eastern farm journals. Typical was an item in the *Breeder's Gazette*:

A good sized steer when it is fit for the butcher market will bring from $45.00 to $60.00. The same animal at its birth was worth but $5.00. He has run on the plains and cropped the grass from the public domain for four or five years, and now, with scarcely any expense to its owner, is worth forty dollars more than when he started on his pilgrimage. A thousand of these animals are kept nearly as cheaply as a single one, so with a thousand as a starter and an investment of but $5,000 in the start, in four years the stock raiser has made from $40,000 to $45,000. Allow $5,000 for his current expenses which he has been going on and he still has $35,000 and even $45,000 for a net profit. That is all there is to the problem and that is why our cattlemen grow rich.

Struggling farmers in the East, reading those statements, developed such a feverish state of mind that many accepted as true the sly tale given wide circulation by Bill Nye, the Laramie *Boomerang* humorist: "Three years ago a guileless tenderfoot came into Wyoming, leading a single Texas steer and carrying a branding iron; now he is the opulent possessor of six hundred head of fine cattle—the ostensible progeny of that one steer."

Propaganda such as that could have only one effect; by the summer of 1880 the rush to the new El Dorado was on. Trains were jam-packed with youngsters from eastern farms and factories, some with savings strapped about their waists, others ready to borrow at interest rates which varied from 2 per cent a month to 1 per cent a day. What did those fantastic charges matter when beef sold at the Chicago yards for $9.35 a hundred! Their frantic bidding on cattle to stock the range sent prices skyrocketing; ordinary stock that sold for $8 a head in 1879 brought $35 in Texas by 1882 and were resold in Wyoming at $60. So great was the demand that between 1882 and 1884 the eastern cattle shipped westward as range stock balanced the number sent east to market! While the boom lasted, between 1880 and 1885, the whole Plains country was inundated with thousands of ranchers and millions of cattle without stamina or experience to survive there.

More disastrous than the rush of men was the flow of capital from the East and Europe. Investors caught the fever in 1882 when they read in financial journals of the Prairie Cattle Company's 42 per cent dividend or the 49 per cent profits of Montana ranchers. Before the year was out businessmen, bankers, lawyers, and politicians were forming companies to share in those fortunes. Their recipe for prosperity was simple; they put up capital, a few ranchers were taken in to furnish experience, and the government provided land. During 1883 twenty stock-raising corporations, capitalized at $12,000,000 were formed in Wyoming alone. Some staked out range rights, but more consolidated smaller ranches already in existence; typical was the Swan Land and Cattle Company which used $3,750,000 raised by stock sales in the East to combine three eastern Wyoming ranches into a hundred-mile estate containing 100,000 head of cattle. All over the West grizzled cowhands who had "ridden the line" for years found themselves seated about directors' tables where eastern bankers listened respectfully to their opinions.

From the East the mania spread to abroad. British capitalists became interested when a parliamentary committee soberly reported in 1880 that profits of 33⅓ per cent could be expected in American ranching, an estimate that appeared less fantastic after an Edinburgh corporation, the Prairie Cattle

Company, declared a dividend of 28 per cent in 1881. For the next four years British investors, with the vision of 40 per cent profits before them, and with little understanding of western ranching and its problems, poured their money into corporations to compete with American companies for range rights and cattle. One enterprising Indianapolis broker, Francis Smith, catapulted into sudden wealth by establishing an office in London where trusting Britishers could deposit their money, then scattering agents through the South and West to seek out borrowers for the ample funds acquired. All over London "drawing rooms buzzed with stories of this last of bonanzas; staid old gentlemen, who scarcely knew the difference between a steer and heifer, discussed it over their port and nuts." The flow of wealth from across the Atlantic hurried overstocking and brought the day of reckoning nearer.

Experienced ranchers were thoroughly alarmed by 1885. They knew the arid plains could support the thousands of steers pastured there only when weather conditions were exceptionally favorable. They realized pasturage was wearing thinner each year, and that herds could no longer be driven to green feeding grounds when grass gave out, for all the Plains were pre-empted. In their panic they sought to insure themselves against the hard times ahead. Some fenced the range to protect their ranches from rival claim and farmers, and their cows from inferior bulls; by the end of 1885 the Plains country was entangled in a barbed-wire network. One Colorado company had 1,000,000 acres enclosed, while a group of Texas Panhandle ranchers stretched a steel barrier from the Indian Territory to the Rio Grande to keep out Kansas cattle. Few bothered to purchase the land they fenced; most simply enclosed part of the public domain, then stood ready to protect their holdings by "gun law."

Equally indicative of the fears besetting experienced ranchers during the cattle boom was the way in which they rushed into stock-breeders' associations. Those cooperative enterprises offered many advantages; they kept intruders out of full-stocked ranges, supervised roundups, ran down "rustlers," fought for lower railroad rates, offered bounties for wolves, and protected the brands of members. Usually they began as local groups, formed when stockmen of one region met, drew up articles of agreement to protect the range, and in typical frontier fashion agreed to abide by the will of the majority. As they multiplied several combined to form territorial associations which prescribed the roundup districts for a whole territory, formulated rules for branding and drives, restricted the number of cattle allowed on the range, and even set up courts to settle disputes between members. Livestock associations blanketed the Great Plains by 1885, typifying both the frontier tendency toward self-government and the rancher's fear of range overstocking.

More than fencing and organization were needed to keep the cattle boom alive. By the summer of 1885 hundreds of ranchers felt the squeeze of mounting costs and falling prices. Each year more profits went into fencing, dues to livestock associations, and increasingly expensive cattle; each year after 1882 sums paid them at the Chicago stock yards diminished as over-production drove beef prices downward. The experienced among them realized the downward spiral had begun; some sold their herds rather than risk wintering cattle insufficiently fattened on the overcrowded range, further depressing prices. To make matters worse a presidential order in August, 1885, forced stockmen who had leased lands in the Indian Territory to leave that region. Some 200,000 beeves were driven into the crowded ranges of Colorado, Kansas, and Texas that fall. Only a cycle of bad years was needed to prick the inflationary bubble and deflate the whole Cattle Kingdom.

That began during the winter of 1885–86, a cold blustery winter which took a frightful toll on the northern Plains. Few cattle were driven to the northern range after 1885. The summer of 1886 was hot and dry, withering grass and drying up streams. Stock owners became panicky as fall approached. Some cattle were driven into Canada or onto leased lands on the Crow Reservation in Montana; others were sent east to be boarded by farmers along the agricultural frontier. Still more were dumped on the market. Prices tumbled amidst the selling spree, until steers worth $30 a year before went begging at $8 or $10 each. "Beef is low, very low, and prices are tending downward, while the market continues to grow weaker every day," complained the *Rocky Mountain Husbandmen*. "But for all that, it would be better to sell at a low figure, than to endanger the whole herd by having the range overstocked."

Those who sold, even at low prices, were wise. The winter of 1886–87 was long famous in western annals. Snow blanketed the northern Plains in November, so deep that starving animals could not paw down to grass. In early January a warm "chinook" wind brought some relief, but late in the month the worst blizzard ever experienced by ranchers howled across the West from Dakota to Texas. In the past cattle had withstood tempests by drifting before them; now they piled up against fences to die by the thousands. On the heels of the storm came a numbing cold which drove temperatures to sixty-eight degrees below zero. Ranchers, huddled about their stoves, did not dare think of what was happening on the range—of helpless cattle pawing at frozen snow in search of a little food or fighting to strip bark from willows and aspens along streams, "dogies" and unseasoned eastern cattle foundering in drifts, whole herds jammed together in ravines to escape the frosty blast and dying by the thousands. When spring finally came cattlemen saw a sight they spent the rest of their lives trying to forget. Carcass piled upon carcass in every ravine, gaunt skeletons staggering about on frozen feet, heaps of dead animals along the fences, trees stripped bare of their bark—those were left as monuments to the thoughtless greed of ranchers.

The cold winter of 1886–87 ended the "open range" phase of the cattle industry. A few small ranchers struggled on, encouraged by excellent grazing conditions during the summer of 1887; a few more drifted farther westward to the grasslands of Arizona and eastern Oregon where their herds joined those of the pioneer ranchers who were already established there. But for most the only answer was bankruptcy. With creditors clamoring at their doorsteps they dumped steers on the market so rapidly the Chicago price for grass-fed beef tumbled from $2.40 a hundred in the spring of 1887 to $1.90 in the fall. Nor did conditions improve during the next half-dozen years as Texas growers unloaded stock no longer needed on the northern Plains, and farmers depressed the market by selling heavily during a cycle of dry years which depleted supplies of feed corn. Under those conditions company after company slid over the line into bankruptcy; the giant Swan Land and Cattle Company of Wyoming succumbed in May, 1887, and the Niobrara Cattle Company of Nebraska soon followed. The few that persisted faced constant criticism from those who remembered the suffering of 1886–87. "A man who turns out a lot of cattle on a barren plain without making provision for feeding them," wrote one western editor, "will not only suffer a financial loss but also the loss of the respect of the community in which he lives." In Wyoming alone the number of cattle declined from 9,000,000 head in 1886 to 3,000,000 nine years later.

Hostile public opinion and financial necessity both dictated that in the future cattle and grass be kept in even balance. That could not be done on the open range; the only solution was for each rancher to fence his lands, restrict his herds to a reasonable size, and insure adequate winter food by growing hay. Fencing went on rapidly in the High Plains country through the later 1880s—with ranchers buying some land, leasing more, and enclosing all they dared in addition—until mowing machines and hay rakes were as common a sight in the West as chuck wagons in former days. And the cowhand, that romantic knight of the saddle, spent his days digging post holes, jacking up wagon wheels as fence tighteners, and haying. "I remember," reminisced one sadly, "when we sat around the fire the winter through and didn't do a lick of work for five or six months of the year, except to chop a little wood to build a fire to keep warm by. Now we go on the general roundup, then the calf roundup, then comes haying—something that the old-time cowhand never dreamed of—then the beef roundup and the fall calf roundup and gathering bulls and weak cows, and after all this a winter of feeding hay. I tell you times have changed." The day of the open range was gone; the West was becoming a land of big pastures, stocked with carefully bred, carefully sheltered beeves.

Oldtimers who sorrowed at those changes had another cause for alarm, for during the 1880s two dangerous invaders pressed upon the borders of the Cattle Kingdom. From the west came the sheepherders. Those unromantic individuals moved into the trans-Mississippi country during the 1870s, driven from their Ohio Valley pasturages by low prices for wool and high prices for feed. Some moved as far as California, others to the mountain parks of southern Colorado, but New Mexico was the mecca for most. During the 1880s the industry boomed there, with a wool crop of 4,000,000 pounds in 1880 skyrocketing to 9,000,000 a decade later and some 5,500,000 woolies pasturing. At the same time sheep growers began shifting eastward into the Great Plains country. Ranchers scoffed at first, but when they learned that sheep could be raised with half the effort and twice the profit of steers, many made the transition. Others fought back. They claimed sheep ruined the grass by close cropping, and were ready to back their argument with "shooting irons." Open warfare between sheepherders and cowhands raged along the western border of the cow country for years, accounting for twenty deaths, a hundred injuries, and 600,000 sheep destroyed (most of them driven over cliffs) on the Wyoming-Colorado range alone. Yet no force could hold back such a profitable enterprise, and herds of bleating "woolies" encroached steadily on the cattle ranchers' domain.

More dangerous were the invaders pressing upon the eastern fringes of the Cattle Kingdom—the pioneer farmers. Their advance onto the Great Plains began just as ranchers staked out their empire, and for the next years they pressed westward, despite the bitter hostility of stock growers. The stubborn advance of homesteaders against gun-toting cowhands, sullen sheepherders, and the terrifying obstacles of nature wrote the last epic chapter in the history of the American frontier.

32

Opening the Plains
1870-1890

The unfamiliar environment of the Great Plains could be utilized by American frontier settlers in two different ways. One was to devise an economic enterprise adapted to the section's unusual features; the cattle ranchers did that by perfecting grazing methods suited to an unfenced range. The other was to conquer nature's obstacles by applied technology. The Great Plains were opened to pioneers during the 1870s not by adventurous trailblazers but by inventors toiling over drafting boards, laborers sweating over whirring machines, and production managers struggling with the complexities of factory production, for those were the men who applied the techniques of the industrial revolution to the unique problems of America's last frontier. Their success made expansion possible.

The task facing them—and the farmers who depended on their skill—was formidable. The Plains country was a vast grassland which stretched away to lonely horizons, unbroken except where straggling trees followed the course of some meandering stream. Nowhere could pioneers find materials and living conditions with which they were familiar. There was no lumber for homes, barns, or split-rail fences. There was no water save the muddy gruel in occasional rivers. There were no belts of trees to shelter them from the baking sun of summer or raging winter blizzards. And worst of all there was in all the province seldom enough rainfall; annual precipitation west of the 98th meridian was normally below the twenty inches required for agriculture. The frontier farmers, to succeed in that subhumid region, must devise new farming methods or be provided with farm machinery that would allow the cultivation of tracts large enough to offset the low yield per acre. Those were the needs that must be filled by prophets of the industrial revolution.

Farmers did not have long to wait. The United States in the postwar years was entering upon its machine age; everywhere in the East smoke-belching factories multiplied as the nation, awakening to the possibilities of mechanization, enshrined mechanical efficiency as its new god. The atmosphere was conducive to rapid development in any industrial field that promised profits; let it be known a new gadget was needed and a dozen manufacturers set to work to satisfy the demand. Few fields promised better financial rewards than supplying western farmers. Thousands of pioneers were ready to advance into the Great Plains when provided with the mechanical means for doing so; the lucky artisan producing something they could use would reap a fortune. That was the incentive that set the wheels of industry turning; in a brief decade inventors perfected the wire fences, well-drilling machinery, and farm implements that allowed the Plains to be subdued.

Efficient fencing material was required first of all. Farmers realized that when the agricultural frontier touched the eastern fringes of the Cattle Kingdom in Kansas and Nebraska. Struggling to keep milling steers from trampling new-planted corn, they demanded that ranchers fence the range; ranchers answered with equal venom that farmers should protect their own fields. Western newspapers bristled with letters arguing the question during the early 1870s, but no solution was possible until a good fencing material was devised. Wood, carted in from distant Wisconsin forests, was prohibitively priced. A Department of Agriculture report in 1871 estimated a 160-acre homestead which cost its owner $20 in land-office fees would require $1,000 worth of wooden fence "for protection against a single stock-grower, rich in cattle, and becoming richer by feeding them without cost on the unpurchased prairie." Sums such as that were unknown among pioneer farmers, let alone the additional amounts needed for repairs. The nation was sobered when the secretary of agriculture revealed in 1871 that its fences cost $2,000,000,000 and that the annual interest and upkeep cost was $2,000,000. The market for any manufacturer producing cheap fencing was unlimited.

That inventors rose to the challenge was shown by Patent Office records; while only one or two patents for new types of fences were issued yearly before the Civil War, in the decade afterward the number leaped to 122 annually. The fortunate individual who hit upon the best solution was Joseph F. Glidden, a farmer of De Kalb, Illinois. Faced with the problem of enclosing his own 600-acre prairie farm, Glidden devised a practical fence by twisting together two strands of wire in such a way they would hold pointed wire barbs at short intervals. After convincing himself the "barbed wire" fence could be produced cheaply, he patented his invention on November 24, 1874, rented a small factory in De Kalb, hired a crew of boys to string the barbs on the twisted strands, and began manufacturing his product as the Barb Fence Company. Within a few months Glidden's fencing was selling so well steam machinery was installed and production stepped up to five tons a day. Eager buyers took all he manufactured at eighteen cents a pound.

Eastern capitalists soon became interested. The nation's leading producer of ordinary wire, the Washburn and Moen Manufacturing Company of Worcester, Massachusetts, noticed the unusually large orders for its product arriving from De Kalb. An agent sent west to investigate during the summer of 1875 returned with samples which were turned over to a machine designer with orders to develop a mechanical method for producing barbed wire. When that was perfected early the following year, representatives of the Worcester firm approached Glidden with an offer to buy out his patent. He consented to sell a half interest to Washburn and Moen for $60,000 and a royalty of twenty-five cents on every 100 pounds manufactured. The way was cleared for the large-scale production of the first practical fencing the world had known.

Work began in April, 1876, when a power machine was set up in De Kalb, and so brisk was demand that by the end of the year fifteen more were operating. Nearly 3,000,000 pounds of barbed wire fence were sold in 1876, 12,000,000 in 1877, 50,000,000 in 1879 and 80,000,000 in 1880. Three years later the Glidden factory was a giant two-story structure where 202 automatic machines transformed 1400 miles of plain wire into 600 miles of fencing every ten hours. Mass production methods lowered the price steadily, from $20 for 100 pounds in 1870 to $10 in 1880 and less than $4 in 1890. The decline brought decent fences within the reach of all, and after the first skepticism was surmounted, its use spread like wildfire. Cattle ranchers and farmers both bought extravagantly, but barbed wire was primarily a farmer's weapon against trespassers.

As essential to Plains agriculture as good fencing was adequate water. Nature failed to provide enough except in eastern Texas, Kansas, and Nebraska. Over the Great Plains, moreover, the constant glare of the sun, the rapid runoff of sporadic rains on hard-packed soil, and ever-blowing winds which sucked up surface moisture, contributed to the section's aridity. Before the province could be utilized means must be found to bring water to the land, or farming techniques suitable to a subhumid environment devised.

The first task proved difficult. Water could be brought to the soil by tapping surface accumulations through irrigation, or by elevating subsurface deposits through wells. Irrigation was feasible only along the western fringes of the Great Plains where streams gushing from the Rocky Mountains could be utilized. Projects of that sort, usually of a cooperative nature, were attempted in Colorado during the 1870s and in Wyoming a decade later, but the number of usable rivers was few and the amount of land brought under cultivation negligible. The West had yet to learn that private enterprise lacked the resources and the overall viewpoint needed in such a gigantic undertaking. Some few westerners, notably William N. Byers, editor of the *Rocky Mountain News* of Denver, did realize that only federal support and national planning would allow irrigation projects to succeed, and as early as 1864 begin preaching that doctrine. Their pleas fell on deaf ears for a generation; not until 1894 did Congress pass the Carey Act, which set aside the proceeds from certain land sales to supply water, and not until 1902 did it adopt the Newlands Reclamation Act authorizing the governmental construction of irrigation projects. These measures operated most successfully in mountain areas where water could be impounded behind government-built dams. Elsewhere on the Plains irrigation experiments failed; even where storage facilities were provided by damming rivers the infrequent rains failed to keep pools filled, and dams silted up so rapidly they proved useless. The sole results of numerous attempts were flattened pocketbooks and broken spirits.

Efforts to utilize the "ground water" which underlay the Great Plains proved almost as disheartening. Subterranean pools could be tapped only when conditions were favorable; the "water plane" which caught surface moisture as it seeped downward had to be near enough to make well drilling practicable, and soil texture sufficiently porous to allow pipe to penetrate. That was possible only where an impervious rock layer collected water in beds of gravel, and such spots were rare on the Plains. In some places eastward-flowing rivers cut so deeply that their beds lay below the water plane and drained away the deposits; in others loose-textured soils were lacking. Even where ground water existed the subsurface pools were too small and the rate of replacement too slow for extensive irrigation. How to secure water needed for farming was the most pressing problem in the Plains region.

The early pioneers, unaware of the difficulties awaiting them, turned first to methods used in the East; they tried to dig open wells from which water could be raised with the traditional oaken bucket and well sweep. The odds were seemingly insurmountable: a heavy prairie soil that made digging difficult, a water table so low that shafts of from 100 to 500 feet were necessary, the uncertainty of locating subsurface pools with nothing more accurate than a divining rod. Too, open wells were a hazard on the level plains, as many an unwary night traveler found. Yet water must be had, and thousands were dug by the farmers themselves or by professional diggers; one, a legendary figure named "Dutch Joe" Grewe, was reputedly able to dig at the rate of thirty feet a day. Such performances were rare, however, and common sense decreed that a better method be sought. Pipes driven into the ground by mechanical driving equipment were the obvious answer, but these did not solve the problem. To reach the deposits was one thing; to raise water to the surface was another. Old-fashioned hand methods were outmoded in a region where wells must be several hundred feet deep to tap subterranaen pools. Some mechanical device must be substituted.

Windmills promised to provide the solution. Constantly blowing winds swept the level surface of the Great Plains; the average wind velocity ranged from twelve to fourteen miles an hour in contrast with the eight or ten miles average in the eastern half of the United States. Why not use the free power to pump the subsurface water needed by the pioneers? That possibility occurred to several windmill manufacturers who moved their plants to Illinois and Wisconsin during the late 1860s. There they developed an instrument suited to western conditions; fragile blades used in the East were reduced in size, the complex mechanism employed to keep the mill headed into the wind replaced by a simple vertical fin, and a governor added to reduce the pitch of the blades when high winds revolved them too rapidly. By 1873 when the improvements were perfected a number of small plants were located along the eastern fringes of the prairie country, ready to meet the expected demand.

That this did not develop was due to the manufacturers' failure to solve one problem: how to lower the price to a level within the reach of the small farmer. Well drillers charged from $1.25 to $2 a foot for wells which in the Plains country ranged between fifty and 500 feet deep. When a $100 windmill was added, the cost was more than $1,000, an impossible sum. Industrialists found a ready market for their products—in 1879 sixty-nine small plants produced $1,000,000 worth of windmills yearly—but most of the buyers were railroads, towns, and ranchers. Not until the late 1890s did mounting farm incomes and reduced production costs allow small farmers to enjoy the luxury of a mechanical water supply.

With irrigation impossible and wells expensive, the only alternative was a method of tillage that would preserve the scant supplies of moisture in the ground. Once more farmers called upon scientists for help. The problem, the experts saw, was to devise a manner of cultivation which would bring subsurface water to plant roots by capillary action, then hold it in the ground by checking evaporation. Their answer was "dry farming." Farmers were advised to plow furrows twelve to fourteen inches deep, thus loosening the soil and allowing water to move upward as the principle of capillarity operated. They were told to harrow their fields after each rainfall, creating a dust mulch of fine soil particles that would stop the evaporation common in crusted earth where water escaped through tiny pores. In that way every drop of the precious liquid was stored near the plant roots. Dry farming was no panacea—the results were often uncertain and the method failed altogether in unusually dry years—but it did open sections of the West normally closed to agriculture.

Neither dry farming nor normal agriculture could have succeeded on the Great Plains without a further contribution from eastern inventors. Farm machinery, on a scale undreamed of in the humid East, was essential in the semiarid West. The dry farmer, faced with the necessity of harrowing his fields within forty-eight hours after each rainfall, needed mechanical help. The ordinary farmer was equally dependent on machinery in a land where large holdings were required to assure an adequate income. The subnormal rainfall was responsible; in the East 80 acres of properly drenched land provided a family with a comfortable living, but in the parched West 360 acres or more were needed to produce the same capital return. Large-scale methods were essential, based on the substitution of machines for men.

Before the conquest of the Plains could proceed the industrial revolution must provide pioneers with farm machinery.

All the machines needed in the West—chilled-iron and steel plows, grain drills, reapers, disk harrows, straddle-row cultivators, and threshing machines—were in use before the Civil War. The slight demand for labor savers on eastern farms kept prices high and the machines were not perfected because improvements based on actual use were slow in coming; a greater demand was needed to encourage the development of cheap, durable farm implements. That developed during the war years; most men were drained away by enlistments, leaving only a few workers to produce grain needed for eastern laborers, warring armies, and a Europe beset by crop failures. They could meet the responsibility—and take advantage of skyrocketing prices—only by mechanizing production; the number of mowing machines in use increased fourfold between 1861 and 1865 and the manufacture of other farm machinery increased in proportion. After the war good markets abroad encouraged increased output through investment in mechanical devices.

Their demand encouraged improvements in farm machinery that made the conquest of the Great Plains possible. The plow was one instrument that evolved rapidly. James Oliver of Indiana began the process in 1868 when he built a chilled-iron plow equipped with a smooth-surfaced moldboard that slipped through humus prairie soils without clogging; other inventors improved his basic implement by covering wearing surfaces with steel. By 1877 thoroughly modern plows were in use. The next step was to lift the farmer from the furrow to a seat on the machine, vastly speeding plowing. Patents for a sulky plow were taken out as early as 1844 but not until agriculture invaded the Plains was the need great enough to inspire improvements. These followed so rapidly that sixteen practical plows were manufactured by 1873. Other manufacturers, conscious of the need for speed on extensive western farms, provided the sulkies with additional shares, allowing a farmer to turn over two or three furrows at once.

Similar improvements speeded planting. The spring-tooth harrow, perfected by a Michigan mechanic in 1869, proved more usable on prairie soils than disk and spike-tooth implements, for its flexible teeth bounced over obstacles and automatically dislodged debris. When a farmer had prepared the ground, he could plant his grain with end-gate seeders, introduced in the early 1870s to scatter seed from the end of a wagon. By 1874 they were displaced by grain drills—machines equipped with small disks to open seed furrows in the soil and a battery of pipes which fed the grain from a large box into the ground. Scientific corn planting was made possible by the checkrower—an implement that spaced the corn in equidistant hills and made possible alternate cultivation horizontally and transversely across a field. One was patented by two Illinois inventors in 1864 and was in general use ten years later. Even more useful in the West was the lister (1880), a double-moldboard planting-plow which dug a deep furrow by casting the earth up on either side, planted corn at the bottom, and covered the seed, all in one operation. This allowed the deep planting needed in semiarid regions; as plants grew the ridges of earth between the rows were dragged back until a level field awaited the harvest.

The handling of hay, an essential crop on all western farms, was speeded by a number of inventions. The mowing machine was in use before the Civil War but the tripping, spring-tooth rake was a product of the 1860s, the harpoon fork which carried hay into barns along carrier tracks fitted to the ridge pole was perfected in 1864, and the hay loader was patented in 1876. The first practical baling press, with power provided by horses attached to a rotating sweep, was built by an Illinois mechanic in 1866.

Harvesting machinery was even more essential in a region where the crop might suffer from storms or heat if not gathered at just the moment of maturity. Reapers used in the past would not do; they simply cut wheat or oats and deposited the stalks on a platform where men riding there could tie them into bundles. The grain was then shocked to wait pickup wagons. This method not only caused constant grumbling among hired hands who were forced to tie furiously to keep up with the machine, but required a larger number of workers than could be obtained on the usual farm. Only a "binder," which would both cut and tie bundles of grain, would satisfy the Plains farmers. Ingenious automatic wire binders were developed by several inventors during the 1870s but proved unsatisfactory; the stiff wires had to be cut by hand before grain could be threshed or fed to cattle. Not until 1878 was the first successful cord binder perfected. That laborsaving machine, which allowed two laborers and a team of horses to harvest twenty acres of wheat a day, was in general use by 1880.

Even that was not fast enough to satisfy owners of the West's vast grain fields. Their demand for more efficient harvesters led to the development of the header during the 1880s. This large machine, which was pushed by a team of six horses, cut heads from stalks in a swath twice as wide as that left by a binder, then carried them over an endless belt to a specially built wagon driven alongside, its far side built high to catch the heads as they tumbled in. They were then stacked to wait the thresher, while the standing straw was either used for pasturage or plowed under. The combine, which cut and threshed grain in one operation, was introduced in the great grain fields of California in the 1880s but did not come into general use on the Plains until a generation or more later.

The evolution of the thresher was equally rapid. Two models were in use in 1870, one a cumbersome affair which drew its power from ten horses, employed nine workers, and threshed 300 bushels daily, the other using only two horses and capable of separating 135 bushels each day. The first important improvement was made in 1882 when a blower was added to stack the straw; during the next few years inventors developed self-feeders, band-cutters, and automatic weighers. Steam power gradually replaced horse power. With the improved machines a smaller crew could handle twice or three times the amount of grain threshed at the close of the Civil War. Efficient corn-harvesting implements were harder to perfect; the first practical cornhusker was not patented until 1890, and the first workable corn binder not until 1892. The silo, a barrel-like structure for storing feed corn, was invented in 1875 by a University of Illinois scientist and was soon in general use throughout the northern Plains.

The United States commissioner of labor, surveying improvements in farm machinery in the 1890s, reduced the story of time and money saved in the production of each acre of produce to simple tabular form:

	Time worked		Labor cost	
Crop	Hand	Machine	Hand	Machine
Wheat	61 hours	3 hours	$3.55	$0.66
Corn	39 hours	15 hours	3.62	1.51
Oats	66 hours	7 hours	3.73	1.07
Loose hay	21 hours	4 hours	1.75	0.42
Baled hay	35 hours	12 hours	3.06	1.29

Those figures told a dramatic story. The industrial revolution freed American farmers from time shackles which had bound them since land was first tilled. They no longer needed to limit planting to the amount they could reap by hand in the ten-day period when grain was prime. A single farmer in the past knew he could plant no more than 7½ acres of wheat, for that was all he could cut during the limited harvesting season. The same farmer in 1890 could devote 135 acres to wheat, knowing his efficient binder could care for that amount without danger of spoilage. Machinery gave farmers the tools needed for extensive agriculture.

Yet the pioneer farmer, indebted as he was to the industrial revolution, lost as much as he gained from the forces that ushered America into its machine age. For he needed not only fences and steel plows; he needed land as well. That must come from the government. In former years farmers were sufficiently powerful to win congressional support for a succession of laws liberalizing the land system, first by reducing the acreage obtainable, then by lowering the price, and finally by recognizing pre-emption and homestead. With the machine age control of the government slipped from the hands of farmers into those of eastern industrialists. Whether the effect of earlier large-scale investors in public lands—holders rather than users—seriously retarded the farming frontier and whether eastern influence on federal land policy increased or diminished efficiency in agriculture remains a hotly debated topic among historians.

When settlement of the Great Plains began, two Homestead acts, one passed in 1862 and the other in 1866, governed the disposal of land. The act of 1866, the "Southern Homestead Act," proved a tragic failure. Designed to provide free 160-acre farms to freed slaves in five states of the Southwest, it was systematically sabotaged by southern administrators who granted only inferior lands in an effort to keep the Negroes on plantations where they could be hired cheaply. Moreover the high cost of filing a claim eliminated all but a few freedmen. By 1870, when the whole program collapsed, only 4,000 black families had been given lands. The better known "Homestead Act of 1862" seemed destined to a better fate. That measure, passed with the best of intentions after a generation of agitation by eastern workers and western pioneers, seemed foolproof. Any adult citizen or any alien who had filed his first papers could, for a $10 fee, claim 160 acres of the public domain. After he had "resided upon or cultivated the same for a term of five years immediately succeeding the time of filing" and paid a few fees, he secured final title. The law apparently assured every underpaid laborer, every expansionistic westerner, a chance to secure a free farm.

In practice, however, the farmer benefited only slightly from the Homestead Act, and the laborer not at all. The latter, whose annual wages frequently did not exceed $250, had neither the entry fees to file a claim, the considerable sum necessary to move his family to the frontier, nor the money to buy expensive tools and farm equipment. Even in rare cases where a worker scraped enough together he lacked the experience needed to homestead virgin territory and the resources to support himself for two or three years before his farm became self-supporting. Possibly the Homestead Act could have served as a "safety valve" for laborers if the government provided free transportation and machinery as well as free land, although even that beneficence would not have endowed city dwellers with the desire to change their mode of life. Actually most pioneers who invaded the interior grasslands came from adjacent states and were drafted from the ranks of men already skilled in agriculture.

That the Homestead Act failed to benefit western farmers was due partly to deficiencies in the law and partly to successful efforts of speculators to circumvent the will of its authors. The inadequacies of the original law were accidental; its framers, whose experience was gathered in the humid East, drafted a measure that was unworkable in the semiarid West. In the Mississippi Valley a unit of 160 acres was generous; few frontier settlers bought more than 80 acres and a free grant of twice that amount seemed certain to satisfy the most avaricious. A farmer on the Great Plains needed far more or much less—2,000 to 50,000 acres as a rancher, 360 to 640 acres for extensive agriculture, 40 to 60 acres to practice irrigation. Nowhere west of the 98th meridian was 160 acres a workable agricultural unit. The Homestead Act prevented pioneers from acquiring the best amount of land for their needs.

Bad as it was, the measure was made worse as amendments were adopted by Congress, often under pressure of groups seeking means of engrossing the West's resources. The first, the Timber Culture Act of March 13, 1873, was a sincere attempt to adjust the Homestead Act to western conditions. It allowed homesteaders to apply for an additional 160 acres, if they would plant at least one-fourth to trees within four years. During the fifteen years the law was on the statute books, 65,292 individuals patented 10,000,000 acres. Few were speculators; the expense of planting trees and the long wait before final ownership did not appeal to those seeking a quick turnover. The Timber Culture Act not only encouraged needed forestation but allowed thousands of homesteaders to expand their holdings to a workable size.

A second amendment, the Desert Land Act of March 3, 1877, although ostensibly designed to benefit the pioneer, was actually lobbied through Congress by cattle ranchers. Those wealthy individuals, sensing the end of the open range, were constantly seeking some means of purchasing government land at the minimum price. Under existing laws that was impossible; a rancher could homestead 160 acres, add another 160 under the Timber Culture Act, and buy an additional quarter section under the Pre-emption Act of 1841. Even if all cowhands served as dummy entrymen the rancher was unable to build up a sufficient acreage for extensive grazing. Ranchers, seeking a means of securing more, were largely responsible for the Desert Land Act. The measure provided that individuals could secure tentative title to 640 acres in the Great Plains or Southwest by an initial payment of twenty-five cents an acre. After three years, if they had irrigated a portion of the land and were willing to pay an additional dollar an acre, the tract became theirs. In the interim they could transfer the claim if they wished.

The act was an open invitation to fraud. Cattle ranchers could take out a claim, round up a few witnesses to swear they "had seen water on the claim" (which usually meant a bucket of water dumped on the ground), and secure title by paying $1.25 an acre. Cowhands could be hired to repeat the process, transferring their claims to employers after making the first entry. That the framers intended misuse of the law was clear in its terms, for no one could cultivate 640 acres of irrigated soil. Unfortunately not all settlers saw through the subterfuge. Claims for 9,140,517 acres were filed under the Desert Land Act, but final patents were issued on only 2,674,695 acres. Threequarters of the claimants gave up the struggle to irrigate worthless lands before the three-year period expired; probably most of the remainder were ranchers.

The lumber interests, quick to learn a lesson from the ranchers, assured themselves a chance to raid natural resources with the Timber and Stone Act of June 3, 1878. That amazing measure, which applied only to lands "unfit for cultivation" and "valuable chiefly for timber" or stone in California, Nevada, Oregon, and Washington, allowed any citizen or first-paper alien to buy up to 160 acres at $2.50 an acre—about the price of one good log. It invited corruption; any timber magnate could use dummy entrymen to engross the nation's richest forest lands at trifling cost. Company agents rounded up gangs of alien seamen in waterfront boardinghouses, marched them to the courthouse to file their first papers, then to the land office to claim their quarter section, then to a notary public to sign over their deeds to the corporation, and back to the boardinghouses to be paid off. Fifty dollars was the usual fee, although the amount soon fell to $5 or $10 and eventually to the price of a glass of beer. By 1900 almost 3,600,000 acres of valuable forest land were alienated under the measure.

The homesteaders, angered though they might be at the shameless exploitation of the nation's resources, reserved their greatest wrath for other representatives of eastern capitalism—the speculators. That unpopular group was as active in the West as it had been through the history of the frontier, gobbling up choice lands, engrossing town sites along streams and railroads, usurping river bottoms and irrigable areas, and piling up giant holdings to be held for high prices. The average small farmer, lured to the West by the hope of a free homestead, was forced to accept an inferior farm far from transportation or pay the exorbitant fees demanded by jobbers. The story of settlement under the Homestead Act was not one of downtrodden laborers rising to affluence through governmental beneficence, but more often a tale of fraud and monopoly which only ended with seven eighths of the public domain in the hands of a favored few.

The methods used by speculators to acquire land were necessarily ingenious in a period when free farms were supposedly available to all. Some took advantage of deficiencies in federal laws. The Pre-emption Act of 1841 still remained on the statute books and after 1862 applied to unsurveyed lands, while the Homestead Act governed only surveyed lands. Astute jobbers, moving west in advance of surveying crews, pre-empted and purchased the best spots at $1.25 an acre. Others took advantage of the Homestead Act's failure to provide for cancellation of patent if the grant was sold or transferred. Dummy entrymen were used to secure quarter section after quarter section. The practice was encouraged by a "commutation clause" which allowed any homesteader not wishing to wait five years to purchase 160 acres for $1.25 an acre after six months' residence and certain rudimentary improvements. Jobbers employed gangs of hirelings to spend a summer on some favored spot, then bought the land at a price far below its actual worth.

Speculators were equally inventive in developing devices to circumvent the law's insistence on a suitable habitation. Some built miniature houses, then swore they had erected a "twelve by fourteen dwelling"—failing to specify they meant inches rather than feet. Others rented portable cabins which were wheeled from claim to claim for a $5 rental. Witnesses were hired to swear they had seen a dwelling on the property—omitting the fact the "dwelling" would be on a neighbor's homestead the next day. More threw up crude shacks that let in more climate than they kept out, or solemnly testified they lived in a shingled residence after precariously fastening two shingles to the sides of a tent. Land Office agents who should have detected those frauds could not; districts in the West were so large—some contained 20,000 square miles—that adequate inspection was impossible. Moreover poorly paid clerks who depended on fees for a living would not ferret out violations too scrupulously.

While thousands of acres passed into speculators' hands through fraudulent use of the Pre-emption and Homestead Acts, millions were engrossed by other means. By far the largest land jobbers in the West were the railroads, whose giant holdings did more than anything else to upset the homestead principle of "land for the landless." Those were secured between 1850 and 1871 when Congress freely awarded the public domain to induce construction; 181,000,000 acres were granted railroad corporations during those years, in addition to 3,000,000 acres given road and canal companies. Of the amount going to railroads 131,350,534 acres were given directly, largely to the transcontinental lines in the form of ten to forty alternate sections for each mile of track laid. The remaining 49,000,000 acres were granted through states or, in the case of Texas, by the state itself. In addition the roads were given 840,000 acres by local governments, towns, and individuals. Railroads were the nation's largest landowners when the settlement of the Great Plains began.

To make matters worse, from the settlers' point of view, the form in which grants were made withheld additional millions of acres from pioneers. Usually Congress gave each railroad a right-of-way together with alternate sections in a strip from twenty to eighty miles wide—twenty if the road was given ten sections to the mile, forty if the grant was for twenty sections, and eighty if forty sections were awarded. Usually the whole strip was withdrawn from settlement for several years while the road selected its right-of-way and decided which alternate sections to keep. Frequently even larger tracts were withheld; if lands within the grant were already occupied, the railroad could choose its acreage from nearby territory and the Land Office sometimes set aside strips 60 to 120 miles wide in which corporation officials could make their choice. Until they decided homesteaders were forced to stake their claims from thirty to sixty miles from transportation. Even when that was not done, alternate sections retained by the government near railroads were either sold at $2.50 an acre or limited to homesteads of eighty acres. Settlers wanting choice land adjacent to communication had to buy from railroads at a price which in 1880 averaged $4.76 an acre.

While large portions of the public domain went to railroads, equally vast amounts were given the states under the Morrill Land-Grant Act of 1862. That measure, which was designed to encourage agricultural education, granted each state 30,000 acres of western land for each of its senators and representatives in Congress, with the understanding the proceeds be used to endow colleges where young men could be trained in scientific farming. The older states, which benefited most because of their large population, were authorized to locate their acreage anywhere in the West. Thus New York selected forest lands in Wisconsin and prairie lands scattered through the western Mississippi Valley to utilize its 990,000-acre allotment. In all the states received 140,000,000 acres through the Morrill Act and similar measures. None was given to homesteaders; nearly all passed through the hands of speculators on its way to final users. Often jobbers purchased thousands of acres at fifty cents an acre, then resold to pioneers at prices ranging from $5 to $10 an acre.

Speculating companies also secured western territory by direct purchase. Although sales of that sort contradicted the spirit of the Homestead Act, Congress made no move to stop them and underpaid Land Office clerks could usually be persuaded to part with plots at $1.25 an acre. Lumbering and mineral interests were especially active in arranging sales; typical was the Higgins Land Company which obtained 11,000 acres of Minnesota iron land—some worth $50,000 an acre a few years later—for $14,000. Some of the best prairie land of Kansas, Nebraska, Dakota, and the Pacific states was sold to speculators in blocks of 10,000 to 600,000 acres before Congress ended the practice in 1889 by limiting purchases to 320 acres. Until that time more land was sold yearly after 1862 than before the Homestead Act was passed. Other jobbers secured western tracts by buying land warrants issued as bounties to veterans from the nation's many wars. Revolutionary scrip was still in circulation in the 1880s, as well as bounty warrants from all conflicts since that time, and could be bought for less than face value. Antique deeds and direct sales allowed speculators to secure about 100,000,000 acres between 1862 and the close of the century.

Another source of land for jobbers was the shrinking Indian reservations. As tribe after tribe surrendered its holdings during the period of concentration after the Civil War, the reserves were either sold by the Indians or disposed of by the government. In either case speculators benefited; natives were anxious to sell in large blocs and the United States, which was pledged to compensate tribes for confiscated lands, could not open the regions to homesteaders. Nearly all the plundered reservations were sold in giant tracts to investors eager to purchase lands already improved by Indians. Not until 1887, when the Dawes Severalty Act stipulated that reservation land be sold to actual settlers in 160-acre units, was that source closed to jobbers, who in the meantime secured more than 100,000,000 acres of Indian territory.

Land office officials, summing up the amounts given or sold to speculators and corporations, found the results impressive:

Grants to railroads	181,000,000 acres
Grants to states	140,000,000 acres
Direct sales by Land Office	100,000,000 acres
Indian lands sold	100,000,000 acres
Total	521,000,000 acres

Half a billion acres were surrendered to investors in an era when orators boasted the United States was giving land free to its poverty-stricken masses! While the wealthy few engrossed those princely estates, only 600,000 patents to homesteads were issued, totaling 80,000,000 acres. If every homesteader was a bona fide farmer, only one acre out of every six was given away; actually many were dummy entrymen, ranchers, and representatives of mining or lumbering companies. Probably not more than one acre in every nine went directly to pioneers, the supposed beneficiaries of the Homestead Act!

The results of the incongruous land system were clear to every new settler who reached the West. He could, he found, either accept an isolated homestead on poor soil distant from transportation, or buy his farm from one of the speculators there before him. If the pioneer happened to arrive in Kansas between 1868 and 1872 he was confronted with a dozen advertisements for land that was "Better Than A Homestead"; the Union Pacific Railroad offered 1,200,000 acres at from $1 to $15 an acre, the Kansas Pacific Railroad 5,000,000 acres at $1 to $6, the Kansas and Neosho Valley Railroad 1,500,000 acres at $2 to $8, the Capital Land Agency 1,000,000 acres at comparable prices, the state of Kansas 500,000 acres of school and college lands at $3 to $5, the federal government 6,000 acres of Indian lands at the same rate, and smaller jobbers 350,000 acres at $3 to $10. That was typical of all the Great Plains country. Frontier settlers could get good land in the West, but they had to pay heavily for it.

Yet the Homestead Act, although failing to provide "free land for the homeless," did make farms available for a sizeable proportion of would-be farmers who could not otherwise have become independent producers. Case studies of the operation of the measure in Nebraska have shown that the cold statistics on homestead entries do not tell the whole story. They fail to show that settlers, by a judicious selection of claims and by the cooperative purchase of adjacent land from speculators, were able to build up farms of the proper size and shape to be best suited to the environment, even to the point of following the topography of river bottoms or divides. Neither do they reveal that while only 57 per cent of the homesteaders made good their claims (in contrast to 80 per cent of those who purchased college land-grant farms and 90 per cent of those who bought on time from the Union Pacific Railroad), many who abandoned their holdings sold out to nearby homesteaders or followed a family decision to develop another entry of the several taken out with the understanding that only one would be used. Actually the attrition rate among homesteaders reflected the normal hazards of pioneering and was not much greater than among those who purchased on credit.

Statistical studies similarly fail to reveal the economic and social benefit of homesteading to pioneer communities. A case study of one Nebraska county—Gage County where the nation's first homestead was patented—reveals a typical pattern: only 15.4 per cent of the land was granted under the Homestead Act while 40 per cent passed into private hands through the Agricultural College Act and much of the remainder through speculators. Yet the homesteaders were able to improve their farms more rapidly than purchasers, largely because they could use their property for mortgaged loans for capital improvements, not to pay off the seller. The resulting development of homesteaded properties at a faster rate than those that had been bought from speculators or railroads not only stimulated the economic progress of the region, but operated as a democratizing influence, elevating the former poor who could not initially afford property more rapidly than those of greater wealth who had sunk their capital assets into land instead of improvements.

Still more significant was the Homestead Act's role in advertising the trans-Mississippi West. All the world knew that a bountiful government would award honest enterprise with priceless grants, and if hopeful home-seekers found only sordid speculation at the end of their rainbow, they nevertheless stayed on to break the Plains. They had the tools needed for the conquest—fences, windmills, and farm machinery—and if they sometime entered upon their task with bitterness in their hearts, they were still effective pioneers. The way was open for the advancing agriculture frontier.

33

The Farmers' Frontier
1870-1890

The waning years of the nineteenth century witnessed the greatest movement of peoples in the history of the United States. Millions of farmers, held back for a generation by the forbidding features of the Great Plains, surged westward between 1870 and 1890. They filled Kansas and Nebraska, engulfed the level grasslands of Dakota, occupied the rolling foothills of Wyoming and Montana, and in a desperate bid for vanishing lands, elbowed Indians from the last native sanctuary in Oklahoma. A larger domain was settled in the last three decades of the century than in all America's past; 407,000,000 acres were occupied and 189,000,000 improved between 1607 and 1870; 430,000,000 acres peopled and 225,000,000 placed under cultivation between 1870 and 1900. Surveying that breathtaking advance, the director of the census announced in 1890 that the country's "unsettled area has been so broken into by isolated bodies of settlement that there can hardly be said to be a frontier line."

The forces which sent men and women westward through the nation's history operated during those years—dissatisfaction at home, alluring prospects ahead, the hope of sudden wealth. Three groups felt their influence. One was made up of former slaves driven from their plantation homes by economic turmoil and the vicious persecution of blacks as federal troops were withdrawn from the South. A former slave turned land promoter from Louisiana, Henry Adams, help to organize the "Exodus of 1879"; during that year between 20,000 and 40,000 Negroes followed his advice to take out a farm in Kansas, some walking, some coming by boat on the Mississippi. Plantation owners, alarmed at this departure of cheap contract workers, stationed armed guards at river ports and threatened to sink any steamer carrying blacks up the river. Still others were turned back by discouraging

644

reports from the first black settlers to reach Kansas. Penniless, inexperienced, and friendless, many encountered hostility from white Kansans or were unable to afford land worthy of farming. Those who survived spent a miserable winter but went on to establish many small Negro communities in the state. Their suffering brought its just reward, for southern blacks eventually owned some 20,000 acres of Kansas farmland. Blacks also settled in Oklahoma, where they were led by Edward P. McCabe, a former "Exoduster," who hoped to create a black state.

The second, and far more populous group, lived in the Mississippi Valley where population had been increasing so regularly for thirty years that overcrowding was driving the pioneer fringe to move on. During the decade of the 1870s every state bordering the Mississippi except Arkansas and Minnesota lost population, and they remained static. Kansas gained 347,000 new settlers during that ten-year period, while increases in Nebraska, Texas, and other Plains states were proportional. The trend continued between 1880 and 1890 when Iowa, Missouri, and the states of the Old Northwest contributed more than 1,000,000 pioneers to the advancing frontier. The greatest gains were registered in the area just west of the Minnesota-Louisiana tier, with Nebraska increasing its population by 240,000 people. The end of the westward movement was indicated during the next decade when Kansas, Nebraska, Iowa, Missouri, and Arkansas all lost settlers as hard times and the lure of the city turned men eastward once more.

The third group that helped people the Plains came from abroad. Some were Irish peasants who drifted westward as railroad laborers, then stayed to till the soil. Nebraska boasted six predominantly Irish colonies in 1890 (one named O'Neill), Minnesota had four, and Dakota Territory numbered 20,000 natives of Ireland among its inhabitants. Canada also contributed heavily in the post-Civil War period when the inflated American currency gave Canadian dollars twice their normal buying power. Still more came from northern Europe. Germans, already well established in the upper Mississippi Valley, continued to migrate by the thousands to Kansas, Nebraska, Dakota, Minnesota, and Texas. Peasants from the Scandinavian countries were even more numerous. The "America Fever" lured 10,000 immigrants from Norway, Sweden, and Denmark in 1865, and the number increased yearly until 1882 when 105,362 arrived. The rugged climate of Minnesota and Dakota appealed to those sturdy farmers; 400 Minnesota towns bore Swedish names by 1890, while travelers in eastern Dakota reported that anyone speaking Norwegian could find companionship sooner than one whose sole language was English.

Both natives and foreigners who peopled the Great Plains were attracted by the most effective advertising campaign ever to influence world migrations. Steamship companies, anxious to reap a harvest of passenger fares, invested heavily in European newspaper space, marred the walls of half the Continent with their posters, and provided free transportation for immigrants wishing to revisit the old country providing they urged others to return.

Western states maintained immigration bureaus in the East and Europe, where hired agents scattered propaganda and urged farmers to migrate to the land of plenty. Minnesota established its bureau in 1867, Iowa followed in 1870, and the other states fell into line during the next years. When compared with the Far West pictured by those expert boosters, even the Garden of Eden seemed unattractive.

Their efforts were surpassed by those of the West's principal colonizers—the land-grant railroads. They stood to benefit doubly from western settlement; newcomers would not only buy their land but create way traffic previously lacking in the sparsely settled region. Hence every western road set up both a Land Department, entrusted with selling the alternate sections granted by the government, and a Bureau of Immigration. The former priced the land—usually at from $2 to $8 an acre—arranged credit terms needed by immigrants, and supervised numerous devices to attract prospects: reduced round-trip tickets for possible buyers, land-viewing expeditions where purchasers were lavishly entertained, free transportation for settlers' household effects, elaborate "reception houses" along the right of way where buyers and land viewers were accommodated. This cost the railroads heavily—the budget of the Union Pacific Land Office touched nearly $815,000,000 during its decade of operation—but the results were spectacular. Areas in which advertising was concentrated, in both the eastern United States and Europe, contributed almost twice as many settlers to Nebraska's population as other regions. Although the Burlington's boast that "better terms than these have never been offered to purchasers of land and probably never will be," was exaggerated, land departments did yeoman service in attracting settlers. They also provided a higher type of immigrant than normal; in 1869 the Burlington adopted a policy of advertising only in selected areas in Britain where farm income was exceptionally high, at the same time ordering its agents to screen out those who seemed unlikely to keep up the payments on their lands. Areas settled by immigrants of this type usually progressed more rapidly than less favored areas near them.

The Bureaus of Immigration were just as active. Their task was to advertise the Great Plains until all the rest of the world contributed a share of its population to the area. If some who came settled on railroad lands so much the better; those who did not were equally welcome as producers of goods which the roads could carry. All railroads maintained agents in eastern seaports to greet immigrants, arrange their transportation west, and see to it that no rival company lured away prospective settlers. Agencies were also set up in Europe; the Northern Pacific Railroad's pattern—a central office in London with branches in Liverpool, Germany, Holland, and the Scandinavian countries—was typical of most lines. Agents were usually returned immigrants with outstanding persuasive powers, or the leading personages in their communities. Ministers were often employed in Scandinavian countries in the hope they could influence many to migrate through personal appeal.

The agents' principal task was to let every European know the American West was a land of milk and honey. Their brochures, newspaper advertisements, and posters were glossy examples of overstatement. The Northern Pacific Railroad assured possible settlers the country it served was so healthy every known malady was cured there, while the Platte Valley became, in the language of a Union Pacific agent, "a flowery meadow of great fertility clothed in nutritious grasses, and watered by numerous streams." Even Dakota was transformed by imaginative boosters into a paradise where "mocking birds and gorgeous paroquets and cockatoos warble musical challenges to each other amid the rich foliage of the sweet-bay and mango trees." Usually the leaflets stressed profits awaiting settlers on the Great Plains; "many fields of properly cultivated wheat," one Burlington advertisement declared, "have yielded *over thirty bushels of grain per acre, and many fields of corn over seventy.*" Stories of personal success were often cited— of one immigrant who reached the West in poverty seven years before and was worth $10,000, of another whose $8,000 investment in Kansas lands yielded $11,000 a year. Nor did such fortunes mean backbreaking toil; "settling on the prairie which is ready for the plow," a Union Pacific writer pointed out, "is different from plunging into a region covered with timber. Nature seems to have provided protection for man and beast; all that is required is diligent labor and economy to ensure an early reward." The women were not forgotten. One Burlington brochure reminded them men so outnumbered ladies in the West that "when a daughter of the East is once beyond the Missouri she rarely recrosses it except on a bridal tour." Some women took up land themselves. Homes and wealth awaited everyone in the Shangri La pictured by the railroads!

The results of the advertising, and of promotional work carried on among veterans' organizations by company agents, cannot be assessed accurately. Occasionally agents could point to tangible examples—colonies of several hundred settlers from Germany or New England who moved west in a body— but most newcomers arrived as individuals. Undoubtedly thousands were influenced by the Bureaus of Immigration; propaganda campaigns on such a scale—both the Burlington and Union Pacific spent $1,000,000 on advertising—were certain to have some effect. No region in the history of the frontier benefited as did the Great Plains from induced colonization.

Effective as the appeals were, they succeeded only because western farming promised unusual profits. Every pioneer knew that steadily expanding markets awaited his produce. Native population increased rapidly in the prosperous postwar years, both by natural growth and the influx of 14,000,000 immigrants. More and more must be fed, for in that day of industrialization, non-food-producing city dwellers multiplied faster than the population as a whole. Americans were hearty eaters; two and one-half acres of farm and ten acres of pasture were required to provide the meat, eggs, poultry, and grain consumed by each yearly, in contrast to the quarter-acre needed in such a low-subsistence-level country as Japan. That meant a steady domestic market for everything the farmer grew, while any surpluses could be shipped abroad. England's consumption of American wheat increased yearly during the 1870s, reaching a high point in 1880 when 153,000,000 bushels were sold there for $191,000,000. Pioneers believed the demand would keep prices high forever. In proof they pointed to the fact that between 1866 and 1881 wheat seldom slumped below the dollar a bushel which meant prosperity for the producer. With profits virtually assured, a farm in western Kansas or Dakota seemed an absolutely safe investment.

Moreover scientists and industrialists were opening new markets for homesteaders. Their greatest contribution was an improved milling process which allowed the wheat frontier to extend into the Great Plains. That section, experiment showed, was ill suited to the soft winter wheat grown by eastern farmers; the cold winters of the northern Plains killed seed before it sprouted, while wide seasonable variations of heat and cold in Kansas or Nebraska destroyed the tender kernels. Only "hard" wheat could be grown there. Trial and error soon demonstrated that the hard spring variety grown in northern Europe thrived in the Minnesota-Dakota country, while the Kansas-Nebraska region was ideally suited to hard-kerneled "Turkey Red" wheat introduced by Mennonite settlers from Russia. Neither could be grown commercially, however, until a satisfactory milling method was evolved. The older process—grinding between two grooved millstones set close together—would not do; the brittle husks splintered into such fine fragments they could not be sifted out, leaving the flour dirty and rancid. Moreover chunks of the glutinous kernel clung to the shattered husks and were lost. Hard wheat could never be marketed until those defects were overcome.

Minneapolis millers, anxious for profits that would be theirs if they found a means of milling spring wheat, solved the problem by developing the "New Process" method of making flour. This called for a series of successive grindings. First the hard kernels were cracked between two smooth grindstones, revolving slowly and set wide apart, which broke the berries into coarse particles without scorching them. The resulting mixture— half flour and half "middlings"—was then sifted through cloth to "bolt out" the flour, while the "middlings" passed to a "purifier" of moving sieves fanned by a strong air current that separated husks and bran from the white chunks of wheat kernel. Those were reground into a rich flour which, because of its higher gluten content, produced more bread per unit than ordinary starch flour. "New Process" flour was in such demand that the Washburn Mills of Minneapolis, the first to perfect the method in 1871, amassed profits of $650,000 in three years before competition lowered the price to a reasonable level. Within a short time the "gradual reduction" system was not only generally adopted but improved by substituting revolving rollers for millstones, a device copied from Hungary where hard wheat was also grown. After experiments with metal and porcelain rollers, millers in 1879 perfected a corrugated, chilled-iron roller that was tough, long-lasting, and nonbreakable. When seven or eight were arranged in series, each grinding more finely than the last and with purifiers and sieves between, pure white flour was produced more rapidly and with one-third less power than with millstones. By 1881 the mills of Minneapolis, St. Louis, and Kansas City were ready to turn any quantities of hard wheat into "New Process" flour.

Improved methods for handling grain also broadened farmers' markets by reducing middlemen's fees. They were developed rapidly during the postwar years when national prosperity placed a premium on efficiency; in such an era older practices of moving bagged wheat by hand seemed outmoded. By the beginning of the 1870s a farmer could take his wagonload of wheat to an "elevator"—wood or concrete warehouses built along railroads—knowing that from then on it would be handled mechanically. Conveyor belts lifted the grain into a bin within the elevator, chutes carried it to waiting freight cars, locomotives pulled the loaded cars to lake ports where the golden kernels were cascaded directly into the holds of eastern-bound steamers, or to Minneapolis where moving belts unloaded the trains at the door of flour-mills. The thousands of bushels hourly handled by mechanical methods saved millions of dollars for farmers and consumers.

The vision of limitless markets conjured up in the minds of pioneers by these inventions was needed to hold them on the Great Plains when they learned the discrepancy between the promises of railroad advertisements and grim reality. Life was hard in a land where nature provided few comforts needed by man; every necessity must be painfully fashioned from inadequate materials by back-breaking toil. How to build a house where there was no timber, how to obtain water where there were no springs, how to keep warm where there was nothing to burn, how to battle the elements where there was no shelter—those were the problems faced by farmers on the Great Plains. Many failed to solve them and fled back east; those who stayed on conquered obstacles that would have defeated people of lesser stamina.

Adequate housing was the most pressing need. Pioneers usually built a dugout first, scooping a hole in the side of a hill, blocking the front with a wall of cut sod, and covering the top with a few poles which held up a layer of prairie grass and dirt. Although the flimsy dwellings were often washed away by rains and were always dirty, they housed whole families for months or even years before giving way to a more permanent structure— the sod house. That was made by turning over even furrows in a half-acre plot where turf was particularly thick. The long strips were then cut into three-foot sections, carted to the building site, and laid into walls, with joints broken as in brick laying and space provided for two windows and a door. If lumber was available the settler built a frame roof; if not he set a ridge pole on two forked sticks, laid more poles as rafters, and covered his house with a layer of prairie grass topped by another of thick sod. Ambitious farmers plastered their dwellings with a mixture of clay and ashes or smoothed the walls with a spade, but most left the rough sod where it was placed. A wooden door made from packing boxes, a cloth over the windows, a blanket hung down the center to make two rooms, a few chairs fashioned from such nail kegs and drygoods cases as were available, and the sod house was ready for occupancy.

The rough dwellings had some advantages—they were warm in winter and cool in summer, never blew down, and were safe from prairie fires— but life within their dank walls was thoroughly unpleasant. Even in dry weather dirt and straw which dropped from the ceiling was the despair of tidy eastern housewives. During rainy periods sod roofs became soggy quagmires that poured rivulets upon the homesteader, then dripped dismally for three days before drying. In those trying times the mud floors were too swampy to walk upon and wives could cook only with an umbrella held over the stove; after they were over every stitch of clothing must be hung out to dry. Little wonder that every family built a frame dwelling as soon as possible, or that a few years in a sod house convinced many a pioneer family the Great Plains were no place for them.

The search for water was just as difficult. The frontier farmer who lived near a stream hauled the precious fluid home in barrels; the farmer who did not depended on rainwater collected in swampy buffalo wallows or in dug cisterns. Freezing in winter, hot and swarming with insects in summer, the ground water was a source of "prairie fever"—or typhoid—which ravaged Plains settlers. The only alternative was a hand-dug well. That difficult task was accomplished with the help of a spouse or neighbor; while one dug, the other hauled the dirt to the surface in a bucket operated by a windlass until a hole several feet across reached down to water level. In lowlands near streams wells were only forty or fifty feet deep, but on higher table lands they extended downward 200 or 300 feet before water was reached. The days of back-breaking work with pick and shovel that went into digging exemplified the difficulties of life on the Plains, yet not until the 1880s was well-drilling machinery sufficiently common to relieve pioneers of the task.

Fuel was as hard to get as water. Those who lived within forty or fifty miles of a stream gladly hauled wood that distance so long as the supply lasted; others depended on dried buffalo excrement which was gathered by the wagonload and piled in ricks for winter use. As the herds were eliminated even buffalo "chips" became so rare travelers usually carried a bag to salvage dung found along their way. Cow manure was also burned near the cattle trails; farmers encouraged drovers to bed down herds nearby, knowing several hundred pounds of fuel would be left behind. Those expedients were only temporary, and most plainsmen had to fall back on their own ingenuity to keep warm. Some grew sunflowers, cut the woody stalks while green, and seasoned them against the coming winter. More used hay, twisting the dried grass into "cats" so it would burn slowly, and piling it about the door of their sod houses. Special stoves for hay burning were widely sold during the 1870s; one common type contained two long cylinders which were filled alternately, then fed into the firebox by a spring device until emptied. None of the ingenious contraptions worked well. They required constant refueling, filled sod houses with noxious gases, and constantly threatened to ignite the piles of flammable hay nearby. Later farmers burned corncobs or dried cornstalks, but no satisfactory fuel was found until railroads brought coal into the Great Plains.

If the Plains environment made life difficult, the procession of the equinoxes made living intolerable. Every season brought new hardships for the pioneer. In the spring, floods often surged across the countryside as bank-level streams, swelled into torrents by the sudden runoff of winter snows, swept houses and livestock before them. Summer usually ushered in a searing wave of heat and drought that withered grass, cracked the parched soil, and burned young crops to a crisp. With the temperature hovering about the 110-degree mark for weeks at a time and south winds blowing across the baked countryside like blasts from hell, streams dried up, animals died, and men staggered through their tasks, their faces chalk-white with dried perspiration. Kansans might jest that sinners were always buried in overcoats to protect them from temperature changes, but in their hearts they knew the heat was no joking matter; one scorching summer sent 30,000 newcomers back to the more comfortable East.

During more temperate years a worse plague threatened plainsmen—a grasshopper invasion. They came without warning, those myriads of insects, flying before north winds in mile-wide clouds that blotted out the sun. When they settled they pelted the sides of houses like hailstones, covered trees so densely limbs broke, and buried the whole countryside under a living mass several inches deep. Chickens and hogs ate until they were sick; men with strings tied about their pant legs to keep pests from their clothing rushed to cover the well before the water was polluted. Nothing else could be saved. The hoppers ate everything: cornstalks, young grain, vegetables under the ground, leaves and bark from trees, sweaty wood from plow handles or pitchforks, weathered lumber on house walls, mosquito netting in the windows, and clothes within the cabins, leaving, as one settler put it, "nothing but the mortgage." There was no living in the desolation they left behind. Heartsick farmers slaughtered their livestock and headed east, with signs on their wagons proclaiming they came "From Kansas, where it rains grasshoppers, fire and destruction." Invasions did not come every year—the worst was in 1874 when the whole Great Plains country from Dakota to northern Texas was devastated—but no pioneer felt safe until autumn winds signaled the end of summer.

Then a new danger threatened. The tinder-dry grass, if ignited by a chance spark, would send prairie fires raging across miles of countryside. Few people lost their lives in conflagrations—farmers soon learned to keep a circle of land around their homes burned over as protection, and travelers carried matches to start backfires—yet property losses and discomfort were common. Even those were preferable to the hardships facing settlers when autumn gave way to winter. Storms that swept the open grasslands during that season were awesome things; ice, dust, and snow particles were whipped before a raging wind with such force they sifted into the snuggest dwellings. Settlers, awakening after an all-night blizzard, found their furniture covered by inches of snow and their houses so cold food froze on the table, jars of preserves burst even near the stove, and bread was so frigid it could be sliced only after warming. Animals suffered more than humans. Ice covered cattle until their heads, as big as bushel baskets, had to be rested on the ground; smaller animals could only survive in settlers' houses. Often a pioneer family lived for days with horses, pigs, calves, and chickens cooped within a crowded sod house while the thermometer rested at twenty or thirty degrees below zero.

Although these intolerable conditions did not endure always, there was little in the environment of the Great Plains to attract pleasure seekers. But the pioneers who went west were after wealth rather than fun. What mattered a few discomforts when opportunity beckoned? Winter blizzards and summer droughts could be endured so long as the West held cheap lands, ready markets, and the thrill of pioneering. Every newcomer was sure nature would treat him kindly or that he was strong enough to battle the elements until prosperity smiled. That hope sent the farmers' frontier surging westward in the post-Civil War years.

When the movement began settlements planted during the prewar era fringed eastern Kansas and Nebraska. Atchison and Leavenworth on the Missouri, Topeka and Lawrence on the Kansas River, Omaha in Nebraska, and the dozen farming communities between, were all small, all nestled in river bottoms, and all in the primitive stage where new arrivals absorbed most local produce. With the close of the Civil War the influx began. Pioneers moved out along streams first of all, where rich alluvial soils and timber awaited them, then after 1870 advanced onto the rolling plains. Every railroad building across Kansas or Nebraska drew settlers westward; along the tracks of the Kansas Pacific the frontier advanced 100 miles between 1870 and 1872. "Settlements," wrote a passenger, "are springing up rapidly. Even the lapse of a few months makes a perceptible difference to the eye of the passing traveler." After 1875 when the Red River War cleared southwestern Kansas of Indians the tide swung in that direction, following the Santa Fe Railroad and scattering such towns as Wichita, Wellington, and Dodge City in its wake. Other settlers built their homes along the Union Pacific right-of-way in Nebraska. By 1880 agriculture in both states was reaching levels of productivity greater than the national average, and adventurous farmers, misled by a cycle of unusually wet years, were pushing into semiarid regions beyond. Kansas boasted nearly 850,000 inhabitants that year and Nebraska more than 450,000.

The peopling of Kansas and Nebraska during the 1860s and 1870s established a rural-urban settlement pattern that was roughly maintained in the occupation of all the Great Plains states. The small towns on the Plains relied on the same promotional devices as the developers of Chicago and

St. Louis. This varied from the image of the West as the "land of the long furrow" where farming was the sole activity. As early as 1860, when both territories were in their beginning pioneer stage, Kansas boasted two cities with more than 2,500 inhabitants—Leavenworth with 7,429 and Atchison with 2,616—but it also contained fourteen other towns with populations of over 1,000, forty-six over 500, and ninety with from fifty to 500. With only 2,000,000 acres in private hands at this time, and with many of these held by speculators, the urban dwellers clearly were almost as numerous as the farm dwellers. In Nebraska the situation was comparable; only 38 per cent of the 11,581 persons living there in 1860 were engaged in agriculture. During the next decade the urbanization trend accelerated; by 1870 the city population had increased by 416.6 per cent and the farm by only 221.7 per cent. In these two areas, an urban frontier advanced side-by-side with a rural frontier, shaping the character and economy of the region. Merchants no less than farmers were demanding favorable land legislation, urging Indian removal, and providing the aggressive leadership that hurried the coming of civilization.

While Kansas and Nebraska were welcoming town and country dwellers, other frontier settlers turned northward to the Dakota country. The peopling of that region began in the late 1850s when settlers from Minnesota and Nebraska, lured by the advertising of two speculating concerns—the Western Town Company of Iowa and the Dakota Land Company of Minnesota—crossed the Missouri River to lay out the towns of Flandreau, Sioux Falls, Vermillion, Yankton and Bon Homme. The Dakota Land Company lobbied successfully enough to win organization for Dakota Territory in 1861, although migration did not assume sizeable proportions until 1868 when the Sioux Indians were driven to a reservation west of the Missouri River. The result was the first "Dakota Boom" between 1868 and 1873. Favorable weather and excellent crops contributed to the rush, but equally important were railroad connections that assured farmers decent markets. The Illinois Central Railroad brought southeastern Dakota within selling distance of Chicago when its tracks reached Sioux City in 1879, while branch lines to Yankton and Sioux Falls built during the next years made marketing even easier. Other roads opened the northeastern fringes of the territory at about the same time; the Chicago and North Western Railroad reached Watertown in 1873, the Northern Pacific Railroad extended to Bismarck, and the St. Paul and Pacific Railroad touched Wahpeton.

Each line attracted settlers. The region about Yankton and Vermillion received the first influx; by the end of 1868 almost 10,000 pioneers were breaking sod there, and others continued to come in such numbers land prices skyrocketed to $20 an acre. More moved northward along the Big Sioux River, or laid out such towns as Fargo and Grand Forks in the Red River valley; the latter hamlet contained eight houses, a store, a hotel, and two saloons in 1872. More adventurous pioneers advanced across Dakota with the Northern Pacific Railroad, to found islands of settlement about

Jamestown, Bismarck, and other outposts. Before the Panic of 1873 slowed the westward movement, Dakota boasted a population of more than 20,000.

Between 1873 and 1878, when the second "Dakota Boom" began, the territory grew slowly, but during those years the basis for a new rush was laid. Partially responsible was the Black Hills gold rush of 1875; the 10,000 prospectors who flocked to the mines created an unparalleled market for farm produce. Equally important was activity forced on the Northern Pacific Railroad by the Panic of 1873. Officials of that bankrupt line, realizing their road could never prosper until lands bordering its right of way were settled, decided on an experiment to demonstrate the area's fertility. An expert wheat grower from Minnesota, Oliver Dalrymple, was provided with eighteen sections of Red River valley land and adequate capital for its development. Scorning traditional farming methods, Dalrymple hired gangs of workers, bought machinery by the carload, and launched a large-scale experiment that startled the whole West. The result was phenomenal: a yield of twenty-five bushels to the acre on a 4,500 acre plot that cost only $9.50 an acre to cultivate. With wheat selling at ninety cents a bushel profits were well over 100 per cent. Eastern capital, quick to sense opportunity, flowed in at once as syndicates bought up estates of from 5,000 to 100,000 acres along the Red River, a broad bottomland ideal for wheat growing. By 1878 "bonanza farms" covered the 300-mile length of the valley.

The demonstrated success of these ventures, the chance of selling food to Black Hills miners, and the advertising of a territorial Bureau of Immigration established in 1875, all contributed to the "Dakota Boom" that set in after 1878, but more important was railroad activity in the northern Plains country. The westward-building lines from Iowa and Minnesota which stopped construction with the Panic of 1873 were fully revived by the end of the decade and ready to extend their tracks across Dakota Territory. Two, the Chicago, Milwaukee and St. Paul Railroad and the Chicago and North Western Railroad, reached the Missouri River in 1880, opening most of southeastern Dakota to settlement. The northern portions were served by the Northern Pacific Railroad which used the postdepression years to construct branches from its Bismarck line to La Moure and other pioneer towns. Both those roads were anxious to sell their federal land grants and build up way traffic; their advertising lured thousands of immigrants to the territory.

An even more energetic role was played by a newcomer among western lines, the Great Northern. The Great Northern Railroad was formed in 1879 by James J. Hill, a financial genius who recognized a profitable field for exploitation in the belt of Plains country lying north of the Northern Pacific tracks. After learning railroading as an employee of the St. Paul and Pacific Railroad, Hill used the Panic of 1873 to win control of the company that employed him, interested eastern capital, and by 1879 was ready to begin construction. Rails were laid northward to Fargo and Grand Forks, then the road turned west and built slowly across Dakota, reaching Devil's Lake in

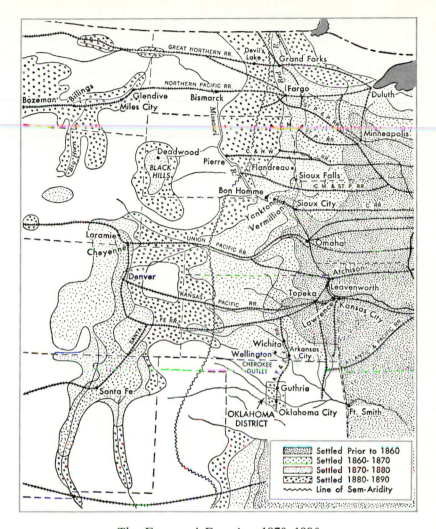

The Farmers' Frontier, 1870–1890

1883 and Seattle in 1893. Its creeping progress was carefully planned by Hill. Realizing the Great Northern had no land grant and must depend on traffic for revenue, he made every effort to develop the country as construction went on; feeder lines were built, immigrants brought from Europe, model farms laid out, blooded cattle imported, money loaned to farmers, and free transportation offered homeseekers. The thousands of pioneers who broke the plains of northern Dakota were brought west by the road's colonization program.

With transportation provided and returning prosperity in the air, the way was open for the "Dakota Boom" of 1878–85. Settlers came by the thousands to the new El Dorado, from Europe and from the Mississippi Valley states. They filled the river bottoms, then pushed out across the Plains in the wake of railroads. "You may," wrote one observer, "stand ankle deep in the short grass of the uninhabited wilderness; next month a mixed train will glide over the waste and stop at some point where the railroad has decided to locate a town. Men, women and children will jump out of the cars, and their chattels will tumble out after them. From that moment the building begins." All was bustle and excitement amidst such scenes—streets jammed with homesteaders, railroad cars trundling westward at a rate of hundreds a week loaded with immigrants' goods, crowds jamming land offices. Even the figures for homestead grants in the territory reflected the feverish expansion:

1877	213,000 acres	1883	7,317,000 acres
1878	1,377,000 acres	1884	11,083,000 acres
1879	1,657,000 acres	1886	3,075,000 acres
1882	4,360,000 acres	1888	1,881,000 acres

Nor did the grants include millions of acres sold by railroads or acquired through other means than homesteading. So rapidly did land pass into private hands that by 1885 all Dakota east of the Missouri River was settled and the population was 550,000—a 400 per cent increase over 1880. Crop failures during dry years at the close of the decade ended the boom and drove some pioneers back east, but the census of 1890 showed 500,000 people still in the territory, occupying most of the lands suitable for agriculture.

While Dakota boomed, the mountainous regions farther west gained population more slowly. Wyoming's development began in early 1867 when speculators, anticipating the coming of the Union Pacific tracks, laid out such towns as Cheyenne and Laramie along the right of way. Those pioneer outposts grew so rapidly—Cheyenne contained a motley crew of 6,000 track layers, cattle rustlers, freighters, prospectors, trappers, ranchers, gamblers, and dispensers of assorted vice by the end of the year—that Wyoming won territorial organization in 1868. Farmers, however, avoided the semiarid High Plains until the early 1880s when a few pioneers sought homes along the eastern fringes of the Big Horn Mountains where streams could be used for irrigation. Their success launched a mild rush to northern Wyoming; 2,000,000 acres, irrigated by 5,000 miles of ditches, were placed under cultivation during the decade. Yet only 62,255 people lived there in 1890. Wyoming, with its vast stretches of arid or mountainous countryside, was destined to remain sparsely settled for many years.

That was also the fate of Montana. Farmers began drifting in during the 1870s, attracted by the prospect of feeding the permanent mining population in Butte and other mountain towns, but not until 1881 when the Northern Pacific tracks entered the territory was there any sizeable influx. The newcomers followed the railroad westward, laying out such towns as

Glendive, Miles City, and Billings, and spread their farms across the Yellowstone Valley. Montana gained 100,000 settlers during the decade, reaching a population of 132,000 in 1890, yet most of the territory was too arid or mountainous to attract farmers.

The "Dakota Boom" and the development of Wyoming and Montana during the 1880s created the usual demand for statehood. Throughout the decade petitions from the territories were ignored, largely because all three were predominantly Republican, and the Democrats, who controlled one or the other houses of Congress, refused to consider their admission. Not until 1888 when the election that placed Benjamin Harrison in the White House gave Republicans a slim majority in both House and Senate was action possible. The triumphant members of the party, after assuring themselves even greater strength by dividing Dakota Territory in two and heeding the pleas of rapidly growing Washington Territory, in February, 1889, authorized North Dakota, South Dakota, Montana, and Washington to frame constitutions. All were admitted in an "Omnibus Bill" adopted in November of that year. Wyoming and nearby Idaho, indignant at the slight, lost no time in drawing up their own frames of government and demanding statehood. Congress responded in 1890 by making the last of the northwest territories into states.

As the frontier swept across the northwestern Plains, another stream of pioneers moved into the Southwest. Texas was the mecca that lured many; during the 1870s the number of farms in the state increased from 61,125 to 174,184 and the line of settlement reached almost to the line of semiaridity. The rapid advance, which paralleled the peopling of Kansas, set the stage for one of the most dramatic events in the history of American expansion. Ahead of the advancing arms of settlement were sterile lands unfit for farming; between them were millions of acres of good soil assigned to the twenty-two tribes that occupied the Indian Territory. Why, pioneers asked, should that rich domain be left in the hands of 75,000 primitive red men? Why should industrious Americans seek land in vain while each square mile of the West's finest garden spot was held by only one "redskinned varmint"? Why not open the Indian Territory to farmers who could make its treeless wastes blossom? That demand sent thousands of lawless intruders into the Indian Territory during the 1880s, forced the United States to recast its Indian policy, and culminated in the rush of "Oklahoma Boomers" onto the nation's last public domain.

The first interest in opening the Indian Territory was shown not by pioneers but by the railroads that crossed the region or planned to build there: the Atlantic and Pacific Railroad, the Missouri, Kansas and Texas Railroad, and the Atchison, Topeka and Santa Fe Railroad. Officials of those lines, aware that prosperity depended on developing way traffic, petitioned Congress to open some Indian lands as early as 1874, but a few years of halfhearted agitation convinced them Washington would never act until their pleas were backed by popular pressure. If that was needed, the railroads must produce it. They apparently found an instrument for their purpose in Elias C. Boudinot, a disgruntled Cherokee who had broken with his tribe and was working as a clerk in the national capital. Boudinot, after receiving several financial favors from the Missouri, Kansas and Texas Railroad, showed his gratitude by publishing a long article in the Chicago *Times* during the spring of 1879. The Indian country, he declared in his widely reprinted letter, contained 13,000,000 unsettled acres that belonged to no tribe and were really a part of the public domain. He told westerners the area could only be opened by public demand and offered to supply all interested with maps and full instructions. Although proof is lacking, the expensive literature Boudinot sent out to questioners was probably supplied by railroads.

Like most effective propaganda, Boudinot's exaggerated statements contained a kernel of truth. Lying in the heart of the Indian Territory were 2,000,000 acres of good land which had been ceded to the United States by the Creeks and Seminole, and not yet assigned to any tribe. That was the mecca to which frontier eyes turned as railroad advertising centered western attention on the Indian country. All through the summer of 1879 camp fires of Kansas pioneers buzzed with talk of the "Oklahoma District"—its mild climate, its sparkling streams, its fertile soil. Editors in Missouri and Kansas, catching the fever, filled their columns with glowing descriptions, or apoplectically denounced the government for closing such a Garden of Eden to settlers. Excitable homesteaders, reading those tales, decided to take matters into their own hands. Little bands of them drifted into the Oklahoma District during the early summer, bent on staking out farms. Federal troops managed to check the invasion by barricading the Kansas border with six army camps, but no feeble barrier could keep frontier farmers from lands they wanted as their own.

That was demonstrated during 1880 when the "Boomers" found a leader. David L. Payne, who led the assault on the Oklahoma District for the next four years, was an Indian fighter, an unsuccessful homesteader, a congenital drifter, "a giant physically, tough as a pine knot, courageous as a lion, with a perfect ignorance of fear." He reached Kansas early in 1880, still smarting from his dismissal as assistant doorkeeper of the House of Representatives, and immediately led a party of eleven frontiersmen into the district. When they were discovered by troops and unceremoniously escorted back across the border, Payne was not discouraged; in June he started south again, this time with twenty followers. Once more soldiers found them, ushered them out of the Indian country, and fined them $1,000—a sentence that meant nothing because neither Payne nor his ragged disciples owned any property. By October, 1880, he was in Kansas once more, organizing a force of several hundred homeseekers for a new invasion. Soldiers held them back by shooting their horses until an early autumn forced them to scatter, but Payne was undaunted. For the next two years he and his fellow "Boomers" played a game of hide-and-seek along the Kansas borderland; one indignant officer complained life there was reduced to chasing Payne into Oklahoma and driving him out again.

The preliminary invasions prepared the way for the first organized assault on the Indian Territory. David Payne fathered the attack. During the spring of 1883 he welded the Kansas homeseekers into a compact society— the Oklahoma Colony—with a set of officers (including Payne as president), dues of $2.50 a year, and an oath binding members to defy the government until Oklahoma District was theirs. Within a year the law-defying group boasted 40,000 members and a treasury balance of $100,000. The Oklahoma Colony gave Payne his last chance to open the Indian country by force. Gathering between 500 and 600 heavily armed members at Hunnewell on the Kansas line, he led them south in the spring of 1884, publicly proclaiming his intention to shoot it out with any soldiers who tried to stop them. For a time this seemed a possibility when a white officer in charge of the Negro cavalry guarding the region ordered his men to fire. Fortunately the well-trained "Buffalo Soldiers" delayed long enough to allow their hotheaded leader to regain his composure. For a time the invaders clung to an outpost in the district, until pressure from troops whittled down their numbers to a point where Payne and a few followers could be arrested. Taken to Ft. Smith for trial, Payne was soon released to return to Kansas, where he was welcomed by a parade of "Boomers" carrying banners that proclaimed "On To Oklahoma," and "We Go This Time To Stay."

When Payne died in November his mantle descended to one of his lieutenants, W. L. Couch, who proved to be as aggressive as his predecessor. Bands of "Boomers" were sent into the territory through the winter of 1884–85, and while many were driven back, enough escaped the cordon of troops to build up a camp of some 400 men on Stillwater Creek. There they were discovered in January by a strong cavalry force. Couch refused to leave; he told the commander his followers were well armed and determined to fight for their land. Bloodshed was only avoided when the officers, wisely deciding against a frontal assault, threw a ring of soldiers around the "Boomer" camp. Unable to get supplies from Kansas, the 400 isolated invaders straggled back, muttering they would return.

With that fiasco, the scene of conflict shifted to Washington. Since the opening of the decade western congressmen, railroad lobbyists, and "Boomer" spokesmen had bombarded Congress with petitions, bills, and resolutions demanding the Indian Territory be opened. Their first victory came on March 3, 1885, when an appropriation act authorized the Indian Office to extinguish all native claims to the two unoccupied portions of the region—the Oklahoma District and the Cherokee Outlet. For the next three years Indian agents did nothing, knowing that any settlement would doom the whole reservation system. During that time Couch led party after party into Oklahoma whenever the border patrols turned their backs, while westerners in Washington urged the Indian Office to act. The pressure was too strong to be denied; in January, 1889, the Creeks and Seminole were forced to surrender their rights to the Oklahoma District in return for cash awards of $4,193,799. Two months later Congress officially opened the district to settlers under the Homestead Act, and authorized the chief executive to locate two land offices there. Acting under those instructions, President Harrison on March 23, 1889, announced the Oklahoma District would be thrown open at noon on April 22.

The month between March 23 and April 22, 1889, was one of feverish excitement. Kansas businessmen and bankers who had worked to open Oklahoma were delighted. From all the West the homeless, the speculators, the adventurers, jammed roads with their wagons, fought for space in towns, and scattered their rude shacks along the southern border of Kansas and the northern boundary of Texas. A few days before the opening all were allowed to surge across the Cherokee Outlet on the north and the Chickasaw reservation on the south to the borders of the promised land. There they waited, eager and impatient, for noon of April 22. On that sunny morning 100,000 persons surrounded the Oklahoma District, most of them strung along the northern border where for miles on end horsemen, wagons, hacks, carriages, bicycles, and a host of vehicles beggaring description stood wheel to wheel, awaiting the signal. At Arkansas City fifteen trains, so jammed with sweating humanity that platforms and roofs overflowed, were lined up, ready to steam forward along the Santa Fe tracks that crossed the district. Ahead were troops, stationed at regular intervals to hold back "Sooners" unwilling to wait the deadline.

Slowly the minutes ticked away toward the zero hour. Officers, their watches synchronized, waited with guns in air, ready to fire the shots that signaled the opening. At last the revolvers barked, and along the line pandemonium broke loose. Men whipped up their horses, wagons careened wildly forward, horses freed from overturned vehicles galloped madly about—all was hurrah and excitement. The Santa Fe trains, steaming slowly forward at a regulated pace which would not give their passengers an undue advantage, disgorged riders along the route as men leaped from roofs or platforms and rushed about in search of a claim. Noise and confusion reigned as the shouts of successful "Boomers," the crash of hammers on stakes, the clatter of wagons, the crash of overturned vehicles, and the curses of disappointed homeseekers mingled to create a bedlam unique in the annals of the nation.

Within a few hours the 1,920,000 acres of the Oklahoma District were settled. Everywhere homesteaders labored to erect shelters, while among them wandered the unsuccessful, still seeking some overlooked spot. Others marked out city lots; Oklahoma City had a population of 10,000 tent dwellers that night and Guthrie nearly 15,000. Within a few weeks the newborn cities were fully equipped with local governments—W. L. Couch was mayor of Oklahoma City—and the demand was mounting for territorial organization. Congress bowed to the pressure on May 2, 1890, when Oklahoma Territory was set up. Its population was increased during the next few years by a series of reservation "openings" as the Dawes Severalty Act was applied to tribe after tribe. The Sauk, Fox, and Potawatomi lands—900,000 acres in all—were thrown open in September, 1891; the 3,000,000 acres of the Cheyenne-Arapaho reservation in April, 1892. A more dramatic rush occurred at noon on September 16, 1893, when 100,000 homeseekers re-enacted the "Boomer" invasion of 1889 on the 6,000,000 acres of the Cherokee Outlet. Smaller openings during the next years gradually extended the settled areas, until by 1906 the territory embraced the area covered by the state today and contained 500,000 inhabitants, in addition to scattered remnants of Indian tribes, now living on the 160 acre plots allotted them by the government. Oklahoma became a state in 1907.

The admission of Oklahoma left only the territories of New Mexico and Arizona outside the Union. Both were sparsely settled by ranchers, irrigation farmers, and townsmen who lived in villages fringing the Santa Fe and Southern Pacific Railroads' tracks; Arizona's population in 1900 was only 125,000 and New Mexico's 300,000. Yet the demand for statehood grew steadily during the early twentieth century. Congress tried to solve the problem in 1905 by admitting them as a single state, a suggestion which was indignantly rejected in both territories—Arizona because its small native population feared domination by mixed-blood Mexicans and Americans who controlled its neighbor, New Mexico because the move threatened its distinctive Spanish institutions. Not until 1912 did Washington back down and admit New Mexico and Arizona as separate states. Their constitutions, like those of the other western commonwealths, reflected the liberal political concepts of the frontier in clauses accepting initiative and referendum, direct primaries, short terms for elected officials, women's suffrage, limited executive power, and even—in the case of Arizona—the popular recall of judges.

With the entrance of those two states into the Union, the political organization of the West was completed. Forty-eight commonwealths stood as monuments to the frontier men and women who in three centuries carried the banner of civilization from the Atlantic to the Pacific. Yet the last chapters were still to be written in the epic of the advancing frontier. The economic and social problems created by the remarkable agricultural expansion of the post-Civil War years were destined to plague the nation for a half-century to come.

The Agrarian Revolt
1873-1896

The unprecedented expansion of the post-Civil War frontier had far-reaching repercussions. Never before had so many Americans faced the hardships of pioneer life; never before had such a sizeable segment of the population paid the social cost of frontier development. Earlier pioneers accepted deprivation, poverty, and isolation as a price worth paying for land and a chance to gain economic independence, but now the situation was different because the opening of the Plains was a function of commercial rather than subsistence farming. From the 1870s to the 1890s farmers' complaints resounded through the nation's legislative chambers, voiced by westerners whose blunt speech and Lincolnesque garb startled orthodox easterners no less than their heretical economic doctrines. The agrarian revolt shattered political traditions, dramatized the shortcomings of the nation's financial structure, and provided the social criticism that served as a basis for the improvement of American society during the twentieth century.

The forces driving the western farmers into open rebellion were both social and economic. They knew their living conditions were miserable. The large-scale agriculture suited to the Plains doomed them to a lifetime of semi-isolation, separated from his nearest neighbor by half a mile of bleak prairie, and cut off entirely from the rest of the world in a day when automobiles, telephones, radios, and even rural mail deliveries were undreamed of. The work was drudgingly monotonous. For the woman there were endless routine tasks: baking, sewing, cleaning, tending chickens and the garden plot, hauling water and fuel, helping out with the harvest, and bearing children amidst medieval conditions. For the man there was only the variety of a country where nature dictated specialization rather than diversification; he plowed his ground, planted his wheat or corn, cultivated his fields, harvested his crop, shivered through the winter, and started all over again. Day after day, year after year, the farmer plodded through that drudgery, seldom seeing a new face, hearing of the changes in city life, and paying close heed to the price of cotton or wheat or corn as set in Chicago or Liverpool.

Farmers had known hardship in the past, but then their lot was endurable because farming was seen as a noble calling. Now they contrasted their miserable existence with the joys of the city dweller. That was the era of the rise of the city when the nation buzzed with tales of newborn metropolitan splendors. Every magazine was studded with breathless articles describing the wonders of newfangled trolley cars and street lights, the gaiety of theaters and parties, the opportunities offered by museums, libraries, and schools. Even books designed to scare country youths from urban pitfalls—*The Spider and the Fly; or, Tricks, Traps, and Pitfalls of City Life by One Who Knows* (1873), *Metropolitan Life Unveiled; or the Mysteries and Miseries of America's Great Cities* (1882), and a host of others—painted sin in such glowing colors that farm living seemed less attractive. The city so dazzled America's imagination that the farmer, long the "bone and sinew of the nation," became a "hayseed" or a "rube" scorned by his urbane countrymen.

Gibes might have been endurable if profits had been high, but agricultural prices receded steadily between the Civil War and 1897 except for a brief boom during the early 1880s. The Department of Agriculture recorded the dismal story of the collapse in its annual record of amounts paid for major crops:

Year	Wheat	Corn	Cotton
1870–1873	$106.7 bushel	$43.1 bushel	$15.1 pound
1874–1877	94.4 bushel	40.9 bushel	11.1 pound
1878–1881	100.6 bushel	43.1 bushel	9.5 pound
1882–1885	80.2 bushel	39.8 bushel	9.1 pound
1886–1889	74.8 bushel	35.9 bushel	8.3 pound
1890–1893	70.9 bushel	41.7 bushel	7.8 pound
1894–1897	63.3 bushel	29.7 bushel	5.8 pound

Farmers also knew that these prices were paid after carriers, handlers, and commission agents took their fees. What farmers received will never be known—they were poor bookkeepers—but the sum was small enough to convince them they were operating at a loss through most of the period. Wheat, they pointed out, cost sixty-five cents a bushel to grow and sold for forty-two cents; corn that cost them twenty cents a bushel went begging at ten cents. Regardless of what economists told them, such returns did not justify the hardships of frontier life. "There is," one of them concluded, "something radically wrong in our industrial system. There is a screw loose."

Eastern experts could tell them what was wrong. The trouble, according to those seers, was overproduction; the industrial revolution had opened grain- and cotton-producing areas in Canada, Australia, Argentina, Russia, India, and other underdeveloped countries as well as in the American West, flooding the world with more goods than could be consumed. Farmers were unimpressed by that explanation. The cause of their suffering, they insisted, was not overproduction but underconsumption. They pointed out that eastern workers starved because bread prices were too high, while western farmers burned their grain because wheat prices were too low. Why, they asked, should makers of clothes be underfed while makers of food were underclad? The answer was clear. Between producer and consumer were a number of "thieves in the night" who exacted too high a toll—railroads, grain elevator operators, bankers, and tax makers. If they could be eliminated or regulated, food prices would be so low easterners could buy according to their full capacity to consume and there would be no farm surpluses.

Railroads were the principal offenders in the farmers' eyes. Lines west of the Mississippi charged rates that seemed exorbitantly high to shippers, who were impressed by such figures as those illustrating ton-mile charges for typical years:

Year	Pennsylvania RR east of Chicago	Burlington RR Chicago to Missouri River	Burlington RR west of Missouri River
1873	$1.26	$1.61	—
1877	.95	1.32	$4.80
1881	.86	1.16	3.20
1885	.70	.96	2.25
1889	.69	.87	1.59
1893	.62	.82	1.33
1897	.56	.78	1.28

The roads explained the discrepancies logically. Western railroads, they pointed out, ran through sparsely settled areas where way traffic was insignificant, hauls short, and traffic moved only in one direction; freight cars had to be "deadheaded" westward to carry out grain during the harvest season and eastward during the rest of the year when farmers had nothing to export. That cost money which shippers must pay.

None of the arguments impressed westerners. Railroads were unpopular anyway, as land monopolists and political dictators, and when wealthy directors tried to justify a system that forced shippers to pay the same amount to send a bushel of wheat from Fargo to Minneapolis as from Minneapolis to New York, farmers refused to listen. Their own explanations seemed more logical. Western railroads, they charged, were giant monopolies determined to charge all the traffic would bear. In proof they cited two damning practices. One was the manner in which lines paralleling the Great Lakes raised rates during the winter when water competition vanished; the other the device of "transit rates" adopted in the West to eliminate competitors. No road would accept produce for any point short of its easternmost terminal. Thus a Dakota farmer wishing to sell wheat in Minneapolis was forced to pay the full rate to Chicago before a railroad would take his load, then sell his unused transit rights between Minneapolis and Chicago at a heavy discount. Practices such as those convinced westerners the roads were deliberately robbing farmers for the benefit of overpaid officials and eastern stockholders.

Grain-elevator operators were viewed with equal distrust. The elevators—great storage bins for grain that were scattered through the West by eastern corporations—were as monopolistic as the railroads; the roads refused to lay sidings for more than one in each community. As direct loading on freight cars was also forbidden by western lines, farmers could sell only to the local elevator operator, accepting any price he cared to pay. Most merchants were too wary to abuse their position openly, knowing their price must bear some relation to the Chicago quotations farmers read in their papers, but the system of "grading" universally employed offered chances for fraud that few could resist. Spring wheat which was "sound, plump and well-cleaned" and weighed at least fifty-eight pounds a bushel was to be graded No. 1, wheat that was "reasonably clean and of good milling quality" which tipped the scales at fifty-seven pounds No. 2, and "all inferior, shrunken, dirty" grain weighing between fifty-three and fifty-six pounds No. 3. Less ethical operators misgraded grain flagrantly, paying farmers for No. 2 when a load was of No. 1 quality; those with better-developed consciences resorted to "mixing." A wagon of No. 1 weighing fifty-nine pounds and a wagon of No. 2 weighing fifty-seven would be dumped together to form two loads of No. 1 at fifty-eight pounds. Grain growers, watching profits that should have been theirs vanish into the overstuffed pockets of elevator owners, were convinced the problem of underconsumption could not be solved so long as those middlemen stood between them and consumers.

Farmers believed monopolies raised the price of goods they bought as well as lowering the price of foods they sold. They knew that in the postwar industrial era the nation's manufacturing concerns were combining through trusts and pools into monopolistic giants capable of setting artificial prices on any commodity; a 100 per cent increase in the cost of plows following one merger told them that. Why, they asked themselves, should they be forced to pay unjust tribute to corporations producing the clothing they wore, the machinery they used, the fertilizer for their fields, and the fuel for their homes? Why not call upon the government to regulate robber-baron industries in the public interest? If private enterprise would not price goods fairly the people should step in!

Surveying the whole situation, the farmer in the early 1870s concluded he was a badly abused individual, cheated by elevator owners, robbed by railroads, and overcharged by manufacturers. His one chance to restore prosperity was through political action; if he gained control of the government he could pass laws designed to dissolve monopolies, control prices, and wipe out the barriers between him and eastern consumers. That was the rallying cry that broke down the farmers' traditional barrier of isolation, and united them in a succession of crusading political and economic efforts.

First to emerge was a fraternal organization, the National Grange of the Patrons of Husbandry, which was formed in 1867 by Oliver Hudson Kelley, a former Minnesota farmer and post-office clerk, and by William Saunders, both of whom were experienced organizers and were well aware of the plight of the farmer. Their purpose was twofold: to funnel farm discontent into a reform organization where its demands for change would be heard, and to ease the loneliness of farm life by providing means of cooperative social gatherings. They believed that local branches, or Granges, would help minimize the drudgery of farming; members could meet monthly, listen to talks on agriculture, partake of community pleasures, and enjoy the ritualistic mumbo jumbo with which Kelley and Saunders endowed their society. With this in mind Kelley forsook his government post to travel through the West organizing Granges. For a time he enjoyed indifferent success—members were few in the nine states where branches were founded before 1870—but by the close of 1871 the time for expansion was at hand. Prices were tobogganing downward, competition mounting, resentment against monopolies growing. Farmers, looking about for some medium to express their discontent, turned to the Patrons of Husbandry. Overnight the rivulet of new members swelled to flood proportions; 1,105 lodges were formed in 1872, 8,400 more in the panic year, and 4,700 in the first two months of 1874. By that time 1,500,000 men and women belonged to the Grange.

Here was a force of vast potential power, both economically and politically. Their economic pressure could best be applied by a rebellion against middlemen dealers in farm implements and other necessities, and even against the manufacturers of those items. This took two forms. On the one hand they sought to use cooperative buying as a means of bypassing dealers who exacted excessive profits. "We propose," they declared in their 1874 national convention, "meeting together, talking together, working together, buying together, and in general acting together for our mutual protection and advancement." That was done by appointing state agents to negotiate with manufacturers, promising them large orders in return for low prices; when one willing to cooperate was found all Granges pooled their orders and bought directly. Farmers found they could affect amazing economies; reapers were purchased for $175 rather than $275, wagons for $90 instead of $150, sewing machines for half their usual cost of $100. Although some corporations refused to deal with the agents, others sprang up to capitalize on the vogue of direct selling. Notable was Montgomery Ward and Company which declared on opening its doors in 1872 that its purpose was to "meet the wants of the Patrons of Husbandry." Cooperative buying not only saved farmers thousands of dollars directly but forced local merchants to meet competition by lowering prices.

Encouraged by those successes, the Patrons of Husbandry entered the more hazardous field of production. In most western states local Granges purchased or founded grain elevators, packing plants, flour mills, banks, insurance companies, and other small businesses catering to the farmer; in Iowa alone thirty elevators were operated by the society. A more important experiment began in 1874 when the Iowa Grange began manufacturing reaping machines for sale at half the established price, later expanding to include three plow factories. Most experiments failed, partly because inexperienced management and inadequate capitalization handicapped production, but more because of the cutthroat competition of other manufacturers. Thoroughly alarmed by early Granger successes, corporations lowered prices to such impossible levels that the society's factories, which had sold at too low a cost to build up reserves, were forced into bankruptcy. The collapse of cooperative enterprises hastened the end of the Patrons of Husbandry, but not before they demonstrated that cooperation was an effective weapon against middlemen.

The Grangers' second objective—to curb monopolistic railroads and grain elevators—was harder to achieve. Their own constitution prohibited direct political action, yet these giant corporations could be forced to charge equitable prices only by some countervailing power, which meant the state or national governments. This, in turn, required the election of legislators bold enough to devise regulatory legislation. Grangers first entered the political arena in 1873 and 1874 when they united behind legislative candidates from the major parties who favored their programs, or cast their ballots for Reform or Anti-Monopoly Party officeseekers. Their views were best represented in the governments of Illinois, Wisconsin, Iowa, and Minnesota, not because the Grange was strongest there—Kansas and Nebraska had the highest proportion of members—but because the Republican and Democratic parties were so evenly balanced that they held the balance of power. In those four upper-Mississippi Valley states agrarian protest was ready to make itself heard in the legislative chambers and state capitols, with significant implications for the future.

Even then, however, those who spoke most effectively for reform were not Grangers and in most cases were not even farmers; the former were denied active political participation by their constitution and the latter were too thinly spread to serve as a meaningful pressure group. Instead the burden of change was carried by the town merchants and small businessmen in the Granger states. They, as much as the farmers, suffered from the railroads' pricing practices, for they were the ones who paid the excessive freight rates and who most felt the impact of discriminatory acts. Particularly were merchants resentful of the lower rates charged by railroads on longhaul merchandise, a practice favoring competitors in terminal market cities and hurting the small town distributors. The railroads must be brought to their senses.

But how? Creating competitors was not the answer; any efficient transportation system in the thinly settled West must be monopolistic. The only solution was government regulation: state agencies setting maximum rates railroads and elevators could charge for transporting and storing grain. No other agrarian demand aroused more controversy than this, and none embodied such significant long-term implications for the nation's future. The Grangers were asking the states to interfere with private enterprise for the public good, even to the point of depriving capitalists of complete control over their own property. For those with long memories this was no heretical doctrine; before the Civil War most states had exercised the numerous regulatory functions needed to keep the capitalistic system on an even keel. Few recalled those days, however; the generation of the 1870s had been reared in a laissez-faire world where both state and national politicians enshrined private property as a holy untouchable, well beyond the reach of the masses. Little wonder that the old order quaked with fear as the agrarian demands were heard.

The four upper-Mississippi Valley states of Illinois, Iowa, Wisconsin, and Minnesota led the way. Illinois acted first in 1873 when its legislature, prodded by smalltown businessmen and merchants and with agrarian interests strongly represented, adopted a carefully framed law establishing a commission with authority to set maximum rates on both freight and passenger traffic. Railroads were allowed to seek increases when they could show any rate was discriminatory, but the measure expressly stated that the presence of competition at some points and not at others would not be considered justification for a charge of discrimination. Minnesota followed a year later when the legislature established uniform rates for the entire state. Wisconsin and Iowa set maximum rates, then named a commission to enforce the laws and collect information. In each state the issue of public welfare versus private enterprise was before the people by the close of 1874.

The faulty structure of the Granger Laws—any flat rate set by a legislature could readily be proven discriminatory—and the vicious campaign waged against them by the railroads through intentionally poor service and the malicious raising of all rates to the legal maximum, soon led to their repeal in Minnesota, Iowa, and Wisconsin. In Illinois, however, where the 1873 law was too well drawn to be attacked, the railroads sought to avoid regulation by appealing to the courts. The measure, they contended, violated the clause of the Fourteenth Amendment which forbade a state to deprive any person of life, liberty, or property without due process of law. Rate setting, by denying corporations the free use of their property, deprived them of property. That was the argument used by railroads and elevator owners to carry their case along the tortuous legal paths which finally ended in the United States Supreme Court in October, 1876.

Of the eight so-called "Granger Cases," the most significant was *Munn vs. Illinois*, which involved a statute setting rates for storing and handling grain. The Court, taking note of the fact that wheat from seven or eight states passed through only fourteen Chicago warehouses, propounded a vital question: should the nine corporations owning those elevators be allowed unrestrained control over the millions of farmers living in the Upper Mississippi Valley? The majority held they should not. Property, the justices agreed, ceased to be completely private whenever it was "affected with a public interest." This occurred when it was "used in a manner to make it of public consequence, and affect the community at large. When, therefore, one devotes his property to a use in which the public has an interest, he, in effect, grants to the public an interest in that use, and must submit to be controlled by the public for the common good, to the extent of the interest he has thus created." Grain elevators, railroads, gristmills, ferries, and other essential industries were defined by the Court as "clothed in a public interest" which justified state regulation without violating the Fourteenth Amendment.

The Granger Cases opened a new era in the relations of government and industry but the organization which gave them its name barely survived to enjoy its triumph. Farmers were losing interest by 1877. In some states, notably Wisconsin where agrarians played a larger role in reform agitation than any other, the railroads fought back, raising rates, curtailing service, and discriminating against Grange members until the people were convinced the transportation octopus was too powerful to be challenged. In others, such as Illinois, monopolies were frightened into such good behavior by the threat of further legislation that farmers believed the battle won and deserted the Grange. In still others, principally Iowa, the collapse of cooperatives embittered many who lost financially. After 1880 the Patrons of Husbandry continued to gain membership, but purely as a social and educational organization, centered in the agricultural states of the East, and emphasizing adult education in the form of reading programs, debates, literary discussions, and fraternal events.

During the next few years agrarian discontent waned. An attempt was made to enlist westerners in the Greenback Party, an eastern organization which urged currency inflation by demanding the government continue greenbacks (unbacked paper currency issued during the Civil War) in circulation. Although Greenbackers polled 1,000,000 votes in the congressional elections of 1878—two thirds of them from the Middle West—their political impotence was demonstrated a year later when the Resumption Act went into operation; this measure provided that after January 1, 1879, the number of greenbacks in circulation be reduced from $431,000,000 to $346,681,016 and that these be made redeemable at face value in gold. The deflationary measure proved so popular in the increasingly conservative East that the Greenback Party was doomed when it entered the election of 1880. Despite the valiant campaign waged by its presidential candidate, James B. Weaver of Iowa, and despite a forward-looking platform which called for women's suffrage, a graduated income tax, congressional regulation of interstate commerce, and a more flexible currency, the party polled only 308,578 votes.

The Greenbackers failed to become a major medium for western discontent only because times were inauspicious for a party promising currency inflation. Such a program appealed largely to debtors struggling to meet their obligations, while between 1880 and 1887 farmers were so pleasantly engrossed in acquiring debts that they gave no thought to repayment. The West was booming during those years. The weather was good; unprecedented rains turned semiarid lands of western Kansas and Nebraska into flowering gardens. The market was steady; the effects of the Panic of 1873 were forgotten as factories hired food-consuming workers to manufacture products demanded by a newly prosperous nation. Most important of all, money was plentiful, money for farm machinery, new lands, and better homes, which could be had almost for the asking.

Eastern investors were responsible. Where, capitalists asked themselves amidst the returning prosperity of the late 1870s, was the safest place for savings? Certainly not the banks and industries of the East; they were shown to be unsound during the panic. Western lands seemed the answer. Interest rates were high; farmers willingly paid from 6 to 8 per cent on mortgages and from 10 to 18 on chattels. The money was safe; prices were sure to increase steadily with free lands running out. No Gibraltar could be more secure than a juicy 8 per cent mortgage on a choice bit of Kansas property! So reasoned the nation's businessmen, and they rushed to capitalize before it was too late. Hundreds of mortgage companies were formed between 1875 and 1877, all with eastern headquarters, western branches, and agents scattered widely through the rural districts. For a small fee they would find western borrowers for eastern capital. Their task was not to raise money. Investors fought for that privilege; "my desk," wrote the leader of one company, "was piled high each morning with hundreds of letters, each enclosing a draft and asking me to send a farm mortgage from Kansas or Nebraska." Instead their principal energies went into convincing farmers to borrow money. Agents roamed the prairie states in horse and buggy, pleading with westerners to accept a loan. Never in the memory of pioneers was cash so plentiful.

Few farmers could resist the pressure. The specialized farming on the Plains required capital, and newcomers to the West mortgaged their homesteads to buy farm machinery, mortgaged the farm machinery to provide money until the first crop was harvested, mortgaged the first crop to carry the family through the winter. Oldtimers, even though in no pressing need, succumbed to the blandishments of agents, reasoning that improved implements or an additional quarter-section of land would mean higher profits. New mortgage debts incurred in Kansas during 1885 were double—and in 1887 triple—those of 1880; in other western states the story was the same. By 1887 the per capita debt in the Plains country was the highest in the nation, despite the region's comparative poverty. In Kansas and North Dakota there was one mortgage for every two persons; in Nebraska, South

Dakota, and Minnesota one for every three; in the five states as a whole at least one for each family.

As eastern capital flowed into the farm belt, land values skyrocketed. Kansas farms that cost $15 an acre a few years before changed hands at $270 an acre; open Colorado range which had been pastured free sold at $10 or $20 an acre. Speculation was especially rampant in western towns. Every tiny hamlet pictured itself as a future metropolis and planned accordingly, borrowing heavily from eastern capitalists to build courthouses, jails, schoolhouses, waterworks, electric light plants, and sewage systems. Fifteen Kansas towns installed streetcars during the boom, all with capital from the East. "Don't be afraid to go into debt," one exuberant editor counseled. "Spend money for the city's betterment as free as water. . . . Let the increase of population and wealth take care of taxes." Even that fantastic advice seemed reasonable. Wealth was increasing; town lots in Omaha, Wichita, Lincoln, Atchison, and dozens of other villages pyramided in price from $200 to $2,000 in a year, while forty-two sections of prairie adjoining Wichita were subdivided and sold during the spring of 1887 for $35,000,000! The West was in the midst of a speculative spree unrivaled since the 1830s.

Then came the day of reckoning. Poor weather heralded the end. The cold winter of 1886-87 ruined ranchers and closed one market for farm goods. The summer of 1887 was hot and dry. Day after day a blistering sun and searing south winds withered crops, then chinch bugs swarmed in to devour the few green stalks that survived. A few farmers gave up the struggle when they viewed their parched fields at harvest time, but most had enough faith in the future to stay on. But the next year was no better, nor the next. For a dismal decade rainfall in the Plains country failed to reach the twenty inches needed for agriculture. Every harvest season brought new disasters. Along the arid western fringes of the farming frontier homesteaders gave up the struggle and retreated east, their covered wagons proclaiming "In God We Trusted, in Kansas We Busted." Between 1888 and 1892 half the population of western Kansas moved out and 30,000 left South Dakota; 18,000 prairie schooners entered Iowa from Nebraska in 1891 alone. Many who remained became tenants. Just east of the deserted zone farmers, with a larger stake in lands and improvements, were unable to flee—only one in every eight moved east. They remained on overmortgaged farms, going deeper into debt each year, to form the group that expressed itself most violently during the agrarian revolt of the 1890s. Still farther east, along the Missouri River, was a belt where rainfall, although inadequate, was still sufficient for normal agriculture. The farmers there, although not so desperate as those farther west, were burdened with debts accumulated during the boom years.

All the frontier was ripe for revolt. The farmer realized his perpetual hard times were not, as he formerly believed, caused entirely by railroads or elevator operators, but in part by the nation's financial structure. He had been encouraged to borrow money for expansion during the boom; now he needed cash desperately and none was forthcoming. Easterners closed their purses with the collapse of 1887, leaving him no alternative but to borrow from loan sharks who charged from 20 to 40 per cent interest, then took his entire crop as payment. Under those conditions he was unable to keep up interest payments on his mortgage and faced the threat of foreclosure. In Kansas alone 11,000 farm mortgages were foreclosed between 1889 and 1893. That meant an alarming increase in farm tenancy; by 1890 one quarter of the farmers of Kansas were tenants or share-croppers, 17 per cent of those of Nebraska, 11 per cent of South Dakota, and 5 per cent of North Dakota. The West, it appeared, was becoming an area of landless peasants where absentee landlords and corporations owned the soil. Even those who escaped were burdened with interest payments and staggering taxes inherited from the overambitious expansion of the boom period. One thing seemed clear. There was too little money in the nation. More was needed, to raise the tumbling prices of farm goods, to ease the weight of taxes, to lift the mortgage load from western shoulders. The currency supply of the United States, the westerner held, was both too inadequate and too inelastic to meet the needs of an expanding economy.

To debtors the inadequacy of the monetary system seemed obvious; the $2,000,000,000 in gold and greenbacks that served the nation in 1865 were still in circulation in 1890, caring for the needs of a doubled population and a tripled business activity. That meant a steady increase in the purchasing power of each dollar. A dollar that had bought one bushel of wheat in 1865 paid for two bushels in 1890. Even that could have been endured if debts had declined proportionately, but the opposite was true. Every increase in the value of the dollar—each fall in the price level—made repayment more difficult. Supposing a farmer borrowed $1,000 in 1885 when No. 1 hard wheat sold at $1 a bushel, agreeing to pay the sum back in five years with 8 per cent interest. As far as he was concerned he had borrowed 1,000 bushels of wheat. But in 1890 when the loan was due, wheat sold at only fifty cents a bushel. He must pay back not 1,000 bushels but 2,000 bushels, plus interest which amounted not to $400 but to $500. Actually the dollar appreciation rate was so rapid during the 1880s that a loan contracted in 1880 increased 12 per cent in the next five years and another 12 per cent by 1890. The farmer saw no reason why he should be penalized for the sins of the nation; if the dollar was being overworked, currency should be increased proportionately with business activity so he could pay back his debts at a just figure.

The monetary system also suffered, westerners insisted, because of its inelasticity; money was never available at the time and place it was most needed. That not only hurt farmers whenever they marketed crops but threatened to keep them in economic thralldom for a generation. The immediate deficiencies were apparent with every harvest; when millions of dollars worth of produce were dumped on the nation's markets within a few weeks the currency system was so overburdened that interest rates shot upward, driving prices down. After the crop was disposed of dollars, no longer in such demand, declined in value, prices edged upward just as farmers started buying. Those fluctuations, although not large, often made the difference between poverty and prosperity during bad years.

More serious were the long-term results of monetary inelasticity; the nation's money supply, instead of increasing when the need was greatest, actually declined. Three principal types of currency were in circulation: gold dollars which increased in volume slowly as bullion was mined, redeemable greenbacks to the set sum of $346,681,016, and National Bank Notes issued by federally chartered banks on the basis of their government bonds. The banknotes, although designed to make the currency system elastic, failed to do so, partly because the retirement of the national debt steadily reduced the number of bank-owned government bonds on which they were issued (the number decreased from $339,000,000 in 1873 to $168,000,000 in 1891) and partly because variations in the business cycle removed banknotes from circulation when they were needed most. That unhealthy situation was due to the tendency of nonbanker holders of government securities to sell heavily in periods of prosperity, driving the price down as they took their money into the stock market for speculation. The more conservative banks bought bonds heavily during such periods, thus increasing the supply of banknotes and speeding the inflationary trend. Then when a depression era began, former stock buyers hurried to purchase government bonds as a safer investment. That drove bond prices upward to a point where banks sold widely, reducing the number of banknotes in circulation and hurrying deflation. Even economists realized their country's inelastic currency made each depression more serious and each speculative splurge more dangerous.

The average westerner, although unfamiliar with the intricacies of monetary theory, was wise enough to see that the way to relieve a money shortage was to place more money in circulation. That would increase the demand power of eastern buyers, raise prices, and allow farmers to pay off their loans at a reasonable figure. In casting about for some safe medium that would bring a stable currency system and an expanding national economy into more equitable relationship without disastrous inflation, many agrarians hit upon silver dollars. Silver bullion, they knew, was pouring from western mines in large but controllable amounts. They realized, too, that through most of this nation's history, silver coins circulated freely along with gold coins, despite the difficulty of keeping the amount of precious metal in each balanced. That obstacle finally ended the system of bimetallism just before the West's need for additional currency became acute. The ratio of sixteen to one—sixteen times as much silver in silver dollars as gold in gold dollars—proved unsatisfactory after the '49 rush lowered the price of gold; so much was mined that it became less valuable, in relation to silver, than in the past. Silver dollars disappeared from the market as their owners, realizing the precious metal in them was worth more than its face value, melted them down for commercial sale. At the urging of treasury officials who wanted to remain on a gold standard Congress in 1873 when it abolished the coinage of silver dollars, set up a limited legal-tender value for lesser silver coins and placed the nation on a gold basis.

As knowledgeable treasury agents anticipated, the situation changed. The large quantities of silver from the mines of Nevada, Arizona, and Colorado that poured into money markets during the 1870s drove down that metal's price in relation to gold; whereas the ratio in 1873 was 15.72 to 1 by 1878 the values stood at 17.72 to 1, and each year thereafter the discrepancy increased. Too late western farmers and silver miners wakened to the realization that the "Crime of 1873" deprived them of the cheaper currency they needed—a circulating medium that would bear a closer relationship to the price level than gold. Their protests, voiced most effectively at first by an urban East-Midwest coalition of reformers who recognized the national advantage of a more flexible currency, gained them a slight concession in 1878 when Congress passed the Bland-Allison Act, authorizing the secretary of the treasury to buy not less than $2,000,000 nor more than $4,000,000 worth of silver bullion each month for coinage into silver dollars of full legal tender. The presidents who administered the measure during the next twelve years kept purchases at the legal minimum, buying $308,000,000 worth of bullion which was coined into $370,000,000—the $70,000,000 profit going to the government. That dribble of new currency scarcely replaced banknotes retired by debt payments. Something more drastic was needed to ease the financial burdens of the West. The "free and unlimited" coinage of silver at a ratio of 16 to 1 was the only answer!

The organization seized upon by embattled farmers to express this demand was the Farmers' Alliance, which through the late 1880s played the same role the Grange had performed a decade earlier. Formed originally in 1874 by Texas cattlemen seeking a medium to combat horse thieves, the Alliance grew slowly in the Southwest until 1886 when it claimed 50,000 members. A division in the ranks that year opened the way to greater success; when a faction split away to protest the injection of political issues into the society's creed, its leaders decided to heal the breach by a program of expansion "so that the whole world of cotton raisers might be united for self-protection." The time was ripe for such a step. During 1887 two similar organizations in neighboring states—the Farmers' Union of Louisiana and the Agricultural Wheel of Arkansas—were merged with the older body under the name of the Farmers' and Laborers' Union of America. Within two years the Union reached into all southern states and boasted a membership of nearly 1,000,000. There, ready made, was an organization through which farmers of the Southwest could demand currency reform and promote a more democratic America.

In the meantime a similar alliance took shape in the Northwest. Its patron saint was Milton George, editor of a Chicago farm journal called the *Western Rural*, and staunch opponent of railroads and monopolies. Casting about for some means of reviving agitation carried on by the Grange, George in 1880 conceived a Farmers' Alliance for his own section. The idea, well publicized by the *Western Rural*, took hold at once; by adopting a militant stand on political questions the Northwest Alliance won 100,000 members by the middle 1880s and was ready to capitalize on discontent that followed the collapse of the boom. Members came flocking in after 1886. "The people are aroused at last," wrote George in 1887. "Never in our history has there been such a union of action among farmers as now." The thousand new members a week who joined through 1890 allowed the secretary to boast, with pardonable enthusiasm, that the organization would soon number 2,000,000. Tailored to the needs of the Northwest as the Farmers' and Laborers' Union was to the Southwest, Milton George's creation gave farmers of the upper Plains a chance to carry their grievances into the political arena.

Their opportunity came in December, 1889, when leaders of the northern and southern alliances met at St. Louis in an effort to unite the two bodies. Although local jealousies prevented a merger, both seized the chance to draw up platforms which were found to be virtually identical; they favored a graduated income tax, government ownership of railroads, laws against excessive land holdings, strict government economy, the abolition of national banks, and the substitution of greenbacks for banknotes as currency, with the Southern Alliance asking also for free silver coinage at 16 to 1. Sectional lines had disappeared on fundamental issues; for all practical purposes western and southern farmers were united in a powerful organization which, if employed politically, might move the mountains of eastern conservatism. That heady realization sent farmers into the elections of 1890 with the fervor bred of resentment against low prices, crushing debts, and burdensome taxes.

That they had no party through which to voice their grievances made no difference. In the Southwest they gained control of local Democratic machines; in the Northwest they held local conventions of Alliance delegates to form parties of their own—the People's Party, Independent Party, Industrial Party, and Alliance Party. The campaign they waged was not truly a campaign at all but, in the words of one observer, "a religious revival, a crusade, a pentecost of politics in which a tongue of flame sat upon every man, and each spake as the spirit gave him utterance." The people were wild with zeal as they rallied behind the holy cause. They drove for miles across the hot countryside to jam picnic grounds, churches, and opera houses; 1,600 teams converged on Hastings, Nebraska, in one day; crowds of 25,000 were reported in Kansas. They unfurled banners—"We Are Mortgaged, All But Our Votes," "Vested Rights Will Go Down Forever And Human Rights Will Prevail"—and they sang their songs:

> I was raised up in the kind of school,
> Good-bye, my party, good-bye.

> That taught to bow to money rule,
>   Good-bye, my party, good-bye.
> And it made of me a "Kansas Fool,"
>   Good-bye, my party, good-bye.
> When they found I was a willing tool,
>   Good-bye, my party, good-bye.

But mostly they listened to orators.

The evangelists of the crusade were primarily horny-handed sons and daughters of toil who needed no inspiration but fervent belief in their cause. Mary Elizabeth Lease was one, an eccentric thirty-seven-year-old lawyer, whose emotional outbursts gave rise to the legend that she urged on her audiences: "What you farmers need to do is to raise less corn and more *Hell*." Jerry Simpson was another. Sailor, soldier, Kansas farmer, his rumpled clothes inspired a political opponent to remark that he probably wore no socks, winning him the nickname of "Sockless Jerry Simpson." Quite different was Ignatius Donnelly, a brilliant orator and inspired debater, whose impassioned pleas won thousands of Minnesota farmers. Different too was James B. Weaver, of Iowa, greenbacker and politician, whose serenity in the midst of tumult proved as effective as the roaring enthusiasm of his contemporaries. But the real heroes were not spotlighted orators; they were the farmers who spoke against monopoly and gold with an effectiveness born of conviction. "The farmers, the country merchants, the cattle-herders, they of the long chin-whiskers, and they of the broad-brimmed hats and heavy boots," wrote an observer, "had also heard the word and could preach the Gospel of Populism. The dragon's teeth were sprouting in every corner of the land. Women with skins tanned to parchment by the hot winds, with bony hands of toil and clad in faded calico, could talk in meeting, and could talk right straight to the point."

This was a slightly romanticized appraisal. True, the majority of the Populists were drawn from rural areas, but they differed little from their Republican or Democratic opponents save for their more precarious financial condition or isolation from towns and railroads. Those on the lower rungs of the ladder—most Negroes and recent immigrants—were conspicuously absent from the Populist ranks; they preferred the Republican Party not because they were intimidated, but because they felt that at this stage of their entrance into the social order their interests were better served by affiliating with the ruling majority.

Their absence did not quench the zeal for reform. Throughout the West agrarians marched grimly to the polls in the election of 1890. The results were impressive. Southern Alliance candidates won gubernatorial contests in four states, secured control of eight legislatures, and captured forty-four seats in the House of Representatives and three in the Senate. In the Northwest the victories, although less startling, were still decisive. Kansans gave Alliance nominees control of the lower house of the state legislature, placed five of them in the House of Representatives, sent the bewhiskered William

A. Peffer to the Senate, and chose a state legislature with ninty-one Populists, twenty-six Republicans, and eight Democrats. In Nebraska independents won both legislative houses and one of the state's three congressional seats. South Dakota elected an independent senator, and in other states Alliance candidates took so many votes from Republicans that an unusually large number of Democrats were placed in state and national offices. The embattled farmers, without even a political organization, seemed on the road to national success.

Alliance leaders, elated by victory and hopeful for the future, turned at once to the task of welding their followers into a united party. A meeting of 1,400 delegates from Southern and Northwestern Alliances held at Cincinnati in May, 1891, showed the time was not yet ripe; southerners were too hopeful of winning control of the Democratic Party to risk supporting a third party. When representatives met again on February 22, 1892, all doubts were dispelled; the continued conservatism of Democratic officeholders convinced even middle-of-the-road delegates from the South that independent action was needed to save the farmer. Realization that a new party was to be formed lent enthusiasm to the thousands of "grey-haired, sunburned and roughly clothed men" who gathered beneath fluttering flags in the St. Louis Exposition Music Hall on the anniversary of the first President's birth. A parade of speakers came first—Ignatius Donnelly, Mary Lease, "Sockless Jerry" Simpson, Terence Powderly of the Knights of Labor. Then resolutions were adopted and a committee of fifteen named to set the time and place for a convention to nominate candidates for the 1892 election. Thus was born the People's Party. Nominations would be made, the fifteen committeemen decided, at Omaha on July 4, 1892.

The 1,300 delegates who assembled for that epoch-making meeting first drafted the new party's platform. After a ringing preamble based upon the proposition that "wealth belongs to him who creates it," the remarkable document listed the demands of the farmers: free and unlimited coinage of silver "at the present legal ratio of 16 to 1," a circulating medium of at least $50 a person, honesty and economy in government, a graduated income tax, postal savings banks, government ownership of railroads and telegraph lines, abolition of alien land holdings, and the reclamation of all lands held by "railroads and other corporations in excess of their actual needs." Other resolutions, not included in the platform but submitted at the same time, urged shorter working hours for labor, laws forbidding the admission of undesirable aliens, the direct election of senators, a single term for the President, and the general use of the initiative and referendum. When that forward-looking program was laid before the cheering delegates they roared their approval for forty minutes before enthusiasm was stemmed. Well they might. The "Omaha Platform" promised to lift the West from its economic doldrums and usher in an era of justice, equality, and prosperity for common men throughout the nation.

Winning the election proved harder than formulating a progressive program. The People's Party nominee, James B. Weaver of Iowa, was a seasoned campaigner, but his long association with agrarian reform stamped him as a radical in the eyes of many moderates. Nor could the Populist workhorses—Mary Lease, Ignatius Donnelly and all the rest—arouse the same enthusiasm for shopworn issues they had two years before. The result became clear when ballots were counted. The Populists cast 1,000,000 votes—about 9 per cent of the total—and carried Kansas, Nevada, Colorado, and Idaho, as well as securing one electoral vote each from North Dakota and Oregon. The center of agrarian discontent was in the Plains states rather than the states bordering the Mississippi; in Minnesota the Populists, who had almost won in 1890, ran a poor third.

Far from discouraged, leaders of the People's Party looked eagerly toward the election of 1896, confident that the nation's unsound economy and the stupidity of the older parties would work in their favor during the four intervening years. They were not disappointed. Drought-withered crops, falling prices, and mounting debts continued to win converts, but even more effective were the blundering efforts of Republicans and Democrats to solve the West's problems. The former took the first step; in 1890 a Republican-dominated Congress, seeking to salve western wounds, passed the Sherman Silver Purchase Act, which authorized the Treasury Department to purchase 54,000,000 ounces of silver yearly—about double the amount prescribed by the Bland-Allison Act—for coinage into silver dollars, paying the miners in legal-tender certificates redeemable "in gold or silver." The carefully phrased measure not only preserved the gold standard by allowing the secretary of the treasury to redeem silver certificates in gold (a practice universally followed), but plunged the nation into a panic which brought agrarian discontent to a climax.

The causes underlying the Panic of 1893 were largely psychological. Locked in the treasury building at Washington was a reserve of gold bullion established in 1879 as backing for redeemable greenbacks in circulation. Popular fancy decided the reserve was the Gibraltar of American finance; so long as it remained large the currency system was safe, but should it fall below $100,000,000 (a meaningless figure fixed by the public as a safety line) money would be worthless. Until 1890 the fund was well over $200,000,000; then it began to decline as inept Republican tariffs cut down federal revenue and cautious financiers started hoarding gold. Year after year the reserve dwindled, until shortly after Grover Cleveland became President in the spring of 1893, it slipped below the $100,000,000 mark. Fear swept the nation. Industrialists cut payrolls, merchants ended purchases, brokers dumped stocks, banks closed to escape runs, workers marched on Washington demanding relief. For the farmer, depression meant low prices would slide even lower; corn sank below fifteen cents a bushel, cotton sold for less than five cents a pound. Only one thing failed to decline during the summer of 1893—the debts.

The farmers knew how to restore prosperity. Throughout the West their anguished cry arose: stop deflation by restoring the free and unlimited coinage of silver! Everywhere prophets rose to drive the message home to the people. William H. Harvey was most prominent; his booklet, *Coin's Financial School*, argued for bimetallism in a language the ordinary person could understand. "Give the people back their favored primary money!" Harvey urged. "Give us two arms with which to transact business! Silver the right arm and gold the left arm! Silver the money of the people and gold the money of the rich!" But President Cleveland refused to listen. Fundamentally conservative, he believed the panic would end only when public confidence was restored by checking the drain on the government's gold reserve. Hence he called Congress into special session, used his patronage to secure support, and won repeal of the Sherman Silver Purchase Act. His futile gesture satisfied no one—continued redemption of greenbacks kept the bullion reserve below the $100,000,000 mark—while westerners were left apoplectic with rage. The Democrats, they believed, had sold out to the bankers; the Republicans were hopelessly reactionary. The common man's only hope was the People's Party.

The hue and cry for "free silver" which followed the Panic of 1893 did Populists an injustice. Until that time their platform was built on a broad foundation of reform in which monetary policy played but one part; the delegates at the Omaha convention of 1892 cheered the railroad plank more than free silver and gave the land plank "a regular Baptist camp meeting chorus." Now other issues were forgotten as party leaders, sensing the popular demand for inflation, staked their hope for success on silver coinage. Their tactics not only pushed other reforms into the background and cost Populists the support of men who wanted railroad regulation or a democratized government structure, but allowed the older parties to steal some of their thunder. After 1893 the nation divided along sectional rather than political lines, with western Democrats and Republicans as rabid for free silver as Populists, and easterners of every complexion in favor of the gold standard. Yet inflationary sentiment was growing, and on that the People's Party pinned its hope for victory in 1896.

The party's leaders agreed upon an apparently foolproof strategy as the crucial contest drew near; they would delay their convention until after the older parties came out against free silver, then sweep up silverites and reformers who rebelled against such archaic conservatism. The wisdom of the course seemed justified when the Republicans met in June. Under the influence of their genial dictator, Marcus Hanna, they nominated the reactionary William McKinley of Ohio on a platform containing an unequivocal gold plank, whereupon thirty-four western delegates, led by Senator Henry M. Teller of Colorado, walked out in disgust. Delighted Populists, confident the rebels would bolster their own ranks, congratulated themselves on their tactics as they waited for Democrats to follow a similar course.

Unfortunately the Democratic Party refused to follow the expected pattern. When its convention assembled at Chicago, silverites from South and West shouted down the gold minority from the East and adopted a monetary plank demanding "the free and unlimited coinage of both gold and silver at the present legal ratio of sixteen to one." Then, still flushed with victory, Democratic inflationists sat spellbound as a thirty-six-year-old delegate from Nebraska, William Jennings Bryan, praised their action. They thrilled to his opening words as he proclaimed his intention to speak "in defense of a cause as holy as the cause of liberty—the cause of humanity"; they hung breathlessly on each syllable as he castigated Republicans in his magnificent conclusion: "If they dare to come out in the open field and defend the gold standard as a good thing, we will fight them to the uttermost. Having behind us the producing masses of the nation and the world, supported by the commercial interests, the laboring interests, and the toilers everywhere, we will answer their demand for a gold standard by saying to them: You shall not press down upon the brow of labor this crown of thorns, you shall not crucify mankind upon a cross of gold." Oratory carried the day; Democrats brushed aside preconvention contenders to make Bryan their presidential candidate.

Populists were in a quandary. Should they submerge their own party, cast their lot with the Democrats, and win free silver for the nation? Or should they retain their identity, split the silverite vote, and hand the United States over to gold-standard Republicans? For the pragmatic politicians who headed the People's Party, political suicide was preferable to national suicide; better to surrender hope of glory than burden the United States with "a cross of gold" for another four years. Fusionists dominated the convention which assembled at Chicago in late July 1896. Bryan was selected as the party's presidential candidate without serious opposition, but the Maine banker chosen by the Democrats for the vice-president's office, Arthur Sewall, was passed over in favor of Thomas Watson, a Georgia Populist. The platform advocated reform in transportation, the land system, and other matters dear to farmers, as well as free silver.

The "Battle of the Standards"—silver and gold—was one of the most bitterly contested elections in history. Bryan, instilled with some of the Populists' crusading zeal, staged a spectacular campaign in which he traveled 13,000 miles, visited two thirds of the states, and gave 400 impassioned speeches. Behind him, he insisted, were the common people; against him the forces of wealth and industry. "There are but two sides in the conflict that is being waged in this country today," declared a Populist Manifesto. "On the one side are the allied hosts of monopolies, the money power, great trusts and railroad corporations, who seek the enactment of laws to benefit them and impoverish the people. On the other are the farmers, laborers, merchants, and all other people who produce wealth and bear the burdens of taxation. . . . Between these two there is no middle ground."

This was a complex election with the nation divided in part along sectional, class, and ethnic lines. Party loyalty and particularly religious differences played a role in voter decision-making second only to economic status. In Wisconsin, for example, Democrats triumphed less because of their demand for free silver than because German Catholics shifted en masse into that party to protest a Republican-sponsored state law to require all public instruction in the schools to be in English. Yet monetary issues transcended all others. On this basis Populism tended to polarize western society, with the merchants and business men of Main Street who had favored railroad regulation in the days of the Grangers swinging into the Republican column. Farmers and rural elements at the same time moved toward Populism, and after the fusion, into the Democratic Party.

For the moment the political readjustments, with their class-conflict overtones, meant that Bryan and his cohorts faced insurmountable obstacles. Employers used threats of wage cuts or layoffs to force workers into the Republican column; newspapers reflected the conservatism of their owners by solidly supporting McKinley. A worse handicap was confusion resulting from the separate vice-presidential candidates of Populists and Democrats. The result was a victory for McKinley, with a majority of 600,000 popular votes, and 271 electoral votes to 176 for Bryan. His strength lay north of the Ohio and east of the Mississippi where the Granger states of the Old Northwest were now in the Republican column; Bryan carried all the West except Minnesota, Iowa, North Dakota, California, and Oregon, and won most of the South. McKinley's victory—and a Gold Standard Act adopted in 1900—sounded the death knell of the People's Party. In 1900 they fused with the Democrats once more, even though Bryan subordinated free silverism to anti-imperialism, but in 1904 and 1908 their own candidates were in the field. The disheartening showing—only 29,000 votes in 1908—forced the party's dissolution.

Even in defeat the Populists were in part vindicated in later years. They wanted prosperity; after 1897 good times descended on the West in the wake of plentiful rains. They wanted inflation; gold discoveries in Alaska, Africa, and Australia poured such quantities of bullion into parched channels of trade that between 1897 and 1906 the money per capita increased from $22.92 to $32.77, and in 1920 passed the $50 mark set by farmers as their ideal. They wanted relief from debt; rising prices after 1897 allowed them to meet creditors' demands. They wanted progressive government reform; the conservative Theodore Roosevelt gave them railroad regulation, the reactionary William Howard Taft postal savings banks, and the liberal Woodrow Wilson a more flexible currency through the Federal Reserve System. The initiative and referendum the Populists desired, and the recall they considered too radical to ask, were in general use by 1912. One by one the principles of the "Omaha Platform" were accepted, until farmers' demands that seemed radical in the 1890s appeared conservative in the 1970s.

The agrarians fought a brave fight, and cannot be blamed if they mistook temporary relief for permanent victory. When high prices in the early twentieth century convinced them, falsely, that their battle was won, they furled their banners with the relief all men feel when a conflict ends. They could not know that the plight of the family farmer in a settled, industrialized continent was one of the most perplexing problems bequeathed to future generations by the passing of the frontier.

35

The Frontier Heritage

What was the frontier's bequest to the future? How did the continuous rebirth of civilization in successive geographic areas, which went on during the three centuries required to settle the continent, affect the characters and the institutions of the pioneers and their children? Are the traits that supposedly distinguish Americans from other peoples of today's world traceable to this unique experience in their history? And, if this is the case, how can the nation—a nation that has been expanding through most of its existence and utilizing almost limitless resources—adjust itself to the necessity of living within closed borders in an era of limited resources? Only an answer to these questions will demonstrate America's debt to the frontier men and women who fought their way from Atlantic to Pacific, leaving behind a residue of national characteristics and unsolved problems which were the pioneers' most important bequest to later generations.

That the frontiering experience helped reshape the American character is easy to understand. In at least two ways expansion altered individual and institutional behavior.

First, pioneering was a selective process. The frontier appealed less to the secure, the contemplative, and the cautious than to the restless, the men and women of action, and the venturesome; those who traded the known comforts of the East for the hazards of the unknown West were men and women who were willing to gamble against nature for the chance of self-betterment. Neither wealth nor poverty determined who made the move. Although the very poor usually did not have the resources needed to migrate in the nineteenth century and the very rich lacked the urge, a sizeable sprinkling from both groups could be found among the pioneers. Most, however, were recruited from the middle class; most, too, were individuals

683

whose drive for self-improvement was often stronger than in those left behind. The concentration on successive frontiers of men and women of this nature meant that the "go-ahead" spirit would be higher there than in the East. Along the frontiers an atmosphere of progress prevailed, influencing men and women and their institutions.

Second, and more important, was the impact of the distinctive *social* environment that existed in the newer settlements. This resulted from a complex equation involving the physical environment and human aspirations. The principal distinguishing feature of the physical environment was the altered "man-land" ratio; in older communities men and women were many and land scarce; in the newer, the opposite was true. This meant that in the successive Wests, the relatively propertyless individual had a better chance to gain social and economic status than in the heavily populated Easts, whether as farmer, merchant, professional man, or speculator. There a newcomer found comparatively unutilized resources as well as a plastic social order that had not yet been solidified by the passage of time. One gave the settler an improved opportunity to amass wealth and property, the other, a chance to rise in society on a scale unrivaled elsewhere. Class lines existed along the frontiers, but they were less firmly drawn, and more easily breached, than in older communities.

As important as physical conditions in shaping the social environment was the inherited culture of the Anglo-American pioneers. That they were uniquely equipped to capitalize on frontier opportunity for self-betterment is realized when we compare the institutions in Spanish and English America. Latin American development was slower and different because the settlers came from lands that were still emerging from their medieval past; they were accustomed to absolutism in government and religion, to a semifeudal economic system, and to a society in which a variety of restraints curbed individual self-advancement. Pioneers in the English colonies migrated from one of the more advanced countries of that day; they had been bred in the traditions of an expanding capitalistic system, of private ownership of property, and of a considerable amount of political and economic freedom for the individual. They were equipped by training and tradition to capitalize on the relatively greater opportunity for self-betterment provided by the physical environment of the frontier. This combination of resources awaiting use and a people with a built-in incentive to use them shaped the social environment of frontier communities. Later immigrants with equally progressive views shared in the opportunities created on the frontier.

Unlike the physical environment which was rapidly altered by the pioneers, this social environment extended its influence over both space and time. The frontier set a high level of human expectation. Attitudes instilled into pioneers by residence in a land where unusual opportunity for social and economic progress whetted men's ambitions and shaped their behavior inevitably spread eastward, first to areas adjacent to the frontier, and ultimately in ever-diluted form to the most remote Easts. This was accomplished in two ways. First, contact between westerners and easterners was constant, as visitors, travelers, letters, and returning emigrants transmitted word of the West's riches and inspired imitation of westerners' traits. Second, and more important, was the effect of the continuing flow of frontier material goods over the older portions of the continent. As virgin resources were exploited, and as the new wealth generated by their exploitation spread eastward, a relatively greater opportunity for individual self-advancement was created everywhere in the nation, and even in Europe. The "go-ahead" spirit was quickened over a wide area, but was greatest at the source of supply, the frontier.

The social environment persisted in time as well as space, although gradually diminishing with the passing years. This was due in part to the continuing impact of frontier wealth as successive layers of virgin resources were made available through technological innovation. Even today the nation's abundance is traceable in part to the relative newness of the natural riches that it is exploiting; older countries whose resources have been tapped for hundreds or thousands of years have no such bounty to encourage enterprise among their peoples. The persistence of a frontier social environment may be explained in part also by the natural tendency of traits and attitudes to perpetuate themselves. Children reared in a pioneer environment where they moved often would have a greater tendency toward mobility than Europeans, who had been tied through childhood to an ancestral home, and would in turn infect their children with a desire for change. Similarly young people reared in families where material values were enshrined or where social democracy was considered a natural right, or where women had independently achieved success or won favor, were more likely to accept materialism, equality, and active females as normal and desirable than youths from other lands where standards differed. Frontier traits were passed along from generation to generation, and still influence American behavior today. Moreover, popular culture in Europe as well as America depicted the West as a land of promise. The social environment persisted long after the frontier from which it emerged.

The key feature of this environment, it must be emphasized, was the stimulus provided to upward social mobility. The pioneers who went west carried with them the Anglo-American belief in progress; the sifting process that occurred with each move concentrated in the successive Wests individuals among whom this urge was especially strong. In their new homes examples of spectacular success were everywhere apparent: the farmer whose fertile fields brought overnight affluence, the speculator who had reaped a fortune by the sale of his town lots, the miner who had "struck it rich" with the turn of his shovel. Economic success was the ordained lot of frontiers and frontier settlers. Incentive and opportunity were there; men and women had only to apply themselves to achieve wealth and an elevated social status.

This was the atmosphere that accentuated certain characteristics and value judgments until they became a lasting part of the American character. These changes, it should be stressed, were of degree only; the frontiering experience did not create new characteristics in individuals or remake all institutions. Instead it tended to strengthen certain behavioral patterns and weaken others, and always in slight degree. This was natural. Human nature tends to cling to traditional practices and be skeptical of the new. The purpose of frontier settlers was to build in the West a replica of the social order they had known in the East, but with a higher place on the scale reserved for themselves. That their attitudes and practices were altered in the slightest is testimony to the powerful impact of the frontier environment.

Among these none bulked larger than the changed political philosophy and practices of the frontier settlers. In this realm the role of the successive Wests was to accelerate the trend toward democracy long apparent in the western world, not to innovate new theory and institutions. Parts of Europe were well along the road toward political equalitarianism when the settlement of America began; the frontier simply provided a congenial environment for a continuation of this trend. There the wide dispersal of land ownership, the absence of a prior leadership structure, and the need for self-rule to solve unique local problems mitigated against control by the few or the distant. The men who drafted the constitutions of newly created western states mirrored these forces (in a sense the wheel was not reinvented on each frontier, it was merely improved upon); they proved themselves to be imitative rather than creative when they copied clauses from the constitutions of eastern states with which they were familiar, but they revealed themselves to be more democratic than their counterparts in the East by borrowing the most liberal features of these documents. Nearly all vested unusual power in the legislatures, which were considered more responsive to public opinion than the governors, and most provided for a rapid rotation of legislators by limiting office-holding to short terms. The Wests also showed a tendency to extend the elective process to a wide range of officials; governors, legislators, school-board members, and even judges—who were not required to be lawyers—were chosen by the people. Later in the nineteenth century the newer states of the West pioneered in bringing legislation under popular control with such devices as the initiative, referendum, and recall. Even more pronounced was the tendency of frontier communities to award governing posts to ordinary citizens who had risen from the ranks.

With the dispersal of political power went a broadening of the franchise as property qualifications and religious tests for voters and office holders were swept away. Here, as in other areas, a trend was set; during the Revolutionary period six eastern states liberalized their voting laws, with Pennsylvania going so far as to open the ballot box to any taxpayer. Yet not until the first frontier state—Vermont—entered the Union was complete manhood suffrage achieved. The next three states to be formed—Tennessee, Kentucky, and Ohio—contained aristocratic restrictions, largely because their constitutions were written by members of an elite class that retained many prejudices normal among upper-class easterners. Beginning with Indiana and Illinois, western states regularly entered the Union with manhood suffrage and a governmental structure that reflected complete faith in the people; western states also first extended the suffrage to women. The West did not originate political democracy, but westward expansion expanded belief in popular rule.

If the pioneering experience fostered political participation, it also accelerated the emergence of a social democracy that was even more typically American. This came naturally to a frontier people who lived amidst daily examples of the potential equality of all men. Class lines based on old wealth meant little in a land where the local ne'er-do-well might be transmuted into the town's richest citizen by a fortunate mining strike, the humble landowner transformed into a millionaire with a lucky real-estate speculation, or the local barmaid elevated to the peak of society's pyramid by marrying the village banker. Examples of differences based on status persisted, but with all men and women potentially wealthy amidst frontier opportunity, all individuals should be treated as equals. Servants in the traditional sense were unknown in the West; they not only demanded to be called "helpers," but insisted on dining with the family and mingling with guests as equals. These attitudes have persisted; the taxicab driver who addresses his well-to-do passenger as "Mac" is mirroring an extreme in social democracy that would be unthinkable in older and less fluid societies.

American attitudes toward political and social democracy were based on the faith that all men could achieve success by utilizing nature's untapped resources. The presence along the frontiers of unique opportunities for self-improvement similarly accentuated other traits that are today considered typically American. One was the distinctive form of individualism that Europeans still associate with those reared in the United States. To the pioneer, every person was a self-dependent individual, fully capable of sucess without the aid of society. If people fell by the wayside they had only themselves to blame, for they had not taken proper advantage of their opportunities. Hence the frontier was distrustful of governmental meddling with affairs of the individual. The successful person should be let alone to achieve greater success; the unsuccessful should not be pampered. There was nothing irreconcilable between this brand of individualism and the cooperative enterprise that flourished on every frontier. Aid from neighbors for defense, cabin raisings, corn huskings, and road building was to be expected in a land where division of labor was unknown and manpower scarce. The aid of the government could be recruited for public enterprises such as railroads, canals, and irrigation systems, for government had an obligation to open land for development. But neither society nor government was entitled to sprinkle roadblocks in the way of an individual's accumulation of wealth in that same land where wealth was so easy to acquire. The "rugged American individualism" of the late nineteenth century was simply frontier individualism, mouthed now by economic elites whose philosophy paralleled that of the pioneers but who had isolated themselves from competition through monopoly.

The unique opportunity for self-betterment in the successive Wests similarly helped shape the attitude of Americans toward material goods. The creation of wealth by the continuing exploitation of successive layers of natural resources, and the steady flow of that wealth eastward, helped engender a state of mind in which material progress became the sole measure of many people. Money was the talisman that would open the door to elevated social status, the key to political influence, the portal to cultural magnificence. Money, to many frontier settlers and to many Americans after them, was the primary objective in life. Materialistic attitudes, long associated with the United States by the citizens of other lands, are traceable in part to frontier affluence.

So also are a number of other traits that have been identified as typical of the United States. Hard work was the gospel of the frontier. With wealth the certain destination of all who labored, and with every pioneer community measuring its progress toward civilization by the dedication of its inhabitants, there was little regard in pioneer life for the sluggard or the lazy. All must labor for the common good no less than the personal good; those who would not had no place in the social order and were left behind. Although machines and automation have in the twentieth century usurped many of the tasks formerly assigned to men and women, this attitude persists in the United States. The prolonged siesta of other lands, the leisurely luncheons, the hour-long teas, are frowned upon; only the recently introduced "coffee break" has intruded on the routine of dedicated labor. When Americans do forsake their tasks, they turn to the no less arduous pursuit of pleasure on the golf course, ski trails, or bowling alleys. Unhurried leisure in the European sense is anathema to the hard-working citizenry.

The American tradition of wastefulness is also traceable to the westering experience. The pioneers had a dual reason to scorn conservation of the natural wealth about them: resources were so plentiful that not even the most fevered imagination could picture their depletion, and wealth could be gained more rapidly by their exploitation than by their preservation. So pioneers raped the virgin forests, gutted the land of mineral wealth, and mined the fertility from the soil with no thought of posterity; this was the open road to fortune, not scrimping and conserving. The conservationist cause has been preached with some success in the twentieth-century United States, but even as the number of conservationists grows the habit of wastefulness persists. The United States is today the land of the no-deposit-no-return bottle, the beer can, and the plastic cup. American industry bases its production on planned obsolescence, with everything from children's toys to automobiles cunningly contrived to disappear within a distressingly short time. The thrift natural to Europeans is scorned in the United States.

Improvisation is another American characteristic that stems in part from the pioneering past. Pioneers were faced with a succession of unique problems where past precedent did not apply; only by devising new techniques and gadgets were they able to exploit the riches about them fully. So they were quick to experiment, and scornful of traditional practices. This did not mean that the West was the mother of invention; the leisure, the training, and the materials needed to create new products were lacking there. But the Wests did create a demand for changed methods that offered an incentive to eastern inventors. The result was to encourage experimentation throughout the land, to lessen reliance on traditionalism, and to encourage modernization. The mechanical innovations on which the nation's industrial expansion has been built were encouraged by the willingness of its people to try the new rather than be bound by the old.

The relative ease with which individuals could better themselves in the West bred the habit of moving about, for physical mobility is often a manifestation of social mobility. With progress the order of the day, men and women were tempted to shift their homes often as they sought more abundant opportunity. Had the social order been static, there would have existed no such temptation, and the extent of internal migration would have been no greater than in the Europe of the eighteenth and nineteenth centuries. But opportunity did knock, and so they responded—moving from East to West, from farm to town, from town to city. Others followed to fill the places they vacated, some from Europe as immigrants, others from the East, but all attracted by the dream of self-improvement. This repeated moving lessened the sense of attachment to place that was normal in more stabilized societies. Even today Americans are a mobile people, less bound to the family homestead than their counterparts in older lands.

The frontiering experience also endowed Americans with certain attitudes that persist down to the present. The rosy optimism and rising level of expectation with which the people of the United States contemplate the future has long been recognized as distinct. The pioneer was a confirmed optimist and with good reason; life in a new land where progress was the order of the day, where continuous improvement was inevitable, encouraged the belief that tomorrow would surely be better than today. Nowhere was the "go-ahead" spirit better exemplified than in the successive Wests of the nineteenth century; with unbounded resources awaiting exploitation, with a continent to be robbed of its riches, with speculation in the air, westerners were cockily confident of a better future as they hurried to reach the pot that they knew to be at the end of the rainbow. Until recently most Americans believed theirs was the "great nation of futurity," and President Ronald Reagan insisted during his campaign that the future could be as bright as the past if government taxation and regulation levels were reduced. Faith in the future was a built-in byproduct of frontier abundance.

This extended to the pioneers' faith in nation as well as in themselves. They raised material wealth to a national value and equated material success with national culture. To them this country was destined to become the greatest power in all creation. How could it fail with a hardy people and the world's most richly endowed land! So westerners boasted tiresomely of the rosy future when the United States would have the strongest army, the mightiest navy, the most extensive territories on the globe. This aggressive nationalism was heightened by the frontier habit of moving about, which lessened local attachments, and by the partnership between state and national governments needed to build roads and canals, dispose of the public domain, and in many other ways care for the needs of an expanding people. The ardent, spread-eagle nationalism that characterized the United States during the nineteenth century, and that persists today in more sophisticated form, was in part a product of the pioneering experience.

The composite westerners who emerged from the frontier process defy accurate description, partly because their habits and attitudes varied with time and place, partly because their conduct was governed no less by the inherited traits that they carried west than by the social environment in which they lived. In general, however, that environment endowed them with identifiable characteristics. The westerners were materialistic, mobile, versatile, innovative, wasteful, optimistic, and nationalistic. They believed in democracy, and shaped their governments and social attitudes to conform to that belief. They scorned precedent and tradition. They were individualistic and resented governmental interference in economic affairs, but willing to cooperate with neighbors for the public good. Above all, the westerners were practical opportunists, little concerned with the past or with theory, and concerned primarily with devising habits and institutions that would allow them to utilize most efficiently the abundant resources amidst which they lived.

This attitude meant trouble when the frontier passed from the American scene. For the three centuries needed to settle the continent, generation after generation had looked to the receding area of free land in the West as a region of potential opportunity. Actually fewer and fewer easterners could go there; a declining number had the skills or wealth or spirit of adventure needed to grapple with a primitive wilderness. Yet all solaced themselves with the belief that in time of stress that secure harbor awaited them or their neighbors. All thought too that the United States was great because newly tapped resources turned the wheels of industry, prosperous because the continuous westward drain of surplus manpower kept wages up and the living standard high. Whether true or false, these concepts were so often voiced by orators, writers, and politicians that they were accepted by a majority of nineteenth-century Americans. Belief in the frontier as a source of opportunity, strength, and wealth was rooted in the national tradition.

To make matters even worse, most Americans were confident that the area of free land would last forever. Every school book provided them with staggering statistics concerning the public domain: the United States, they knew, acquired 1,465,000,000 acres of land between 1783 and 1860; enough, when made into 160 acre farms, to provide homes for 9,000,000 families. Not even the most feverish imagination could picture such a supply being exhausted in a mere half-century; surely the secretary of war had been right in 1827 when he confidently reported that 500 years would be required to fill the West. Lulled by such prospects, and unaware as were western "boomers" that most of the lands beyond the Mississippi were unsuitable for habitation, the great mass of the people in the 1880s still looked to a rosy future of continuous expansion. To them the announcement of the superintendent of the census in 1890 that the country's "unsettled area has been so broken into by isolated bodies of settlement that there can hardly be said to be a frontier line" remaining, came as a distinct shock. Since that time they have been adjusting themselves—economically, psychologically, and politically—to life in a nonexpanding land.

The economic impact of the passing of the frontier was comparatively slight, largely because the westward movement continued after 1890 as before. Good land still waited newcomers in the West, for despite the pronouncement of the Census Bureau, only a thin film of population covered that vast territory. All the Far West, with the exception of California, contained fewer farms in 1890 than the single state of Mississippi, and only half as many as Ohio. Even the tiny state of Delaware which, as one of its citizens once remarked, had three counties at low tide and two at high, boasted more farms than Idaho or Montana, three times as many as Wyoming, and seven times as many as Arizona or Montana. Nor was this discrepancy due entirely to the larger farms of the semiarid trans-Mississippi country; in the entire area, again omitting California, only twice as many acres were under cultivation as in the single state of Ohio. Seekers after economic betterment could still follow Horace Greeley's advice in the first years of the twentieth century as they had in the nineteenth.

They did so. Through the history of man's migrations population has tended to flow away from regions of excessive competition and declining opportunity to newer areas where lands are cheaper, competitors fewer, and the chances for speculative gain greater. To thousands of Americans, reacting in this normal way, the West was still the land of promise. They continued to move there; some to fill the gaps between widely scattered farms in previously settled lands; others to new frontiers in Montana and Idaho. The lands were not the best in the West—those had been claimed by the first comers—but that did not deter homeseekers in a day when such scientific improvements as irrigation and dry farming promised to transform deserts into fertile fields. The persistence of the westward movement during the twentieth century was shown by the continuing demand for government land; four times as many acres were homesteaded after 1890 as before, and twice as many since 1910 as in the prior fifty years. The continued drift westward was also demonstrated by the steady movement of the nation's center of population; in 1890 this median point was central Indiana; in 1920 it lay sixty-two miles farther westward; by 1940 it had advanced another thirty-five miles; by 1960 it had reached the vicinity of Salem in Illinois and by 1970 was Illinois' St. Clair County near the town of Mascoutan. The "westward tilt" of the continent was still draining people toward the Pacific, as it had through the country's adolescent years.

Nor was the trans-Mississippi area the only frontier attracting Americans during the opening decades of the twentieth century. Pioneers, never respecters of international boundaries, found a new land of opportunity in the Prairie Provinces of Canada. Canadians were eager to receive them; an extensive advertising campaign designed to lure immigrants was launched in 1897. Americans were equally eager to listen as the supply of cheap lands diminished in the United States and farm tenancy increased; a direct correlation existed between the regions that contributed most heavily to the Canadian migration and the percentage of farm tenants. The tide began to flow in the late 1890s, and between 1900 and 1920 almost 300,000 Americans made their way northward to homestead in Manitoba, Alberta, or Saskatchewan. So great was the rush that the scenes were reminiscent of some of the earlier migrations to the western frontier: thousands crowded on trains of the "Soo Line" from St. Paul to Portal, thousands of others moved north in caravans of covered wagons. The lure was cheap land, accentuated as always by the speculative profits waiting immigrants. A farmer who could sell a 320-acre Dakota farm in 1910 for $50 an acre, then purchase a similar homestead in Saskatchewan for $2 an acre, could count on a profit of some $14,000 even after deducting his moving expenses. Moreover that new farm would yield equally large speculative returns. "There is," one explained, "no way people can pick up $3,000 easier than to come up and homestead here for three years. There will be 160 acres for nothing, and if the land is any good, at the end of three years you can sell it for $20 an acre." Those were the prospects that lured opportunity-seekers to the "last best West."

Continued expansion into the Canadian Northwest and the submarginal lands of the American Far West softened the impact of the frontier's closing on the nation's economy but had little influence on the popular mind. The psychological effects of the dramatic Census Bureau announcement of 1890 far outweighed the material. Gradually, unexpectedly, the nation realized that its age of expansion was over, its age of adjustment to closed boundaries at hand. To thousands of thinking citizens the implications seemed staggering. Overnight they must answer a dozen difficult questions. Could the farmer, who had traditionally produced cash crops with little capital expenditure on permanent improvements, adjust to the European habits of soil conservation and stability? Could the worker, who (in popular belief at least) had been able to escape economic storms by fleeing westward to take up land, maintain the high wages on which the nation's living standard was based? Could the government, which (it was fondly believed) had been kept on an even keel by the escape of discontented elements through a frontier "safety valve," prevent "radicals" from gaining control? Could the national economy, which had been geared for three centuries to continuous expansion, survive without new natural resources to exploit? Little wonder that the American people, asking themselves these questions and others like them, succumbed to doubts that helped transform their rural economy, their foreign policy, and their theories of government.

Their concern was no better shown than in the rising prices for farm commodities during the first two decades of the twentieth century. To the farmer this was a delightful—and unaccountable—phenomenon. Since the Panic of 1873 they had watched the cash return from their crops sink lower and lower, as debts mounted and political discontent grew in proportion. Then, suddenly, in 1897 the tide turned. Buyers offered decent prices for wheat, corn that had not been worth marketing began to flow eastward once more, and livestock was in steady demand. For the next years prices moved rapidly upward. Taking the year 1899 as a standard with commodity values at 100, the price index during the following decade was: 1900, 106.4; 1905, 133; 1910, 189.2. The upward spiral was arrested somewhat after 1910, only to climb again with the outbreak of World War I and the mounting demand for American foodstuffs in warring Europe. During all those years, and until 1920 the farmer experienced a prosperity that he had almost forgotten how to enjoy.

The reasons for this inflationary trend in agricultural prices were many. Partly responsible was the general upward swing of the price index as new gold discoveries in Alaska, Africa, and Australia increased the world's supply of money. Partly to blame, too, was the working of the law of supply and demand; lagging farm production during the drought and low-price years between 1887 and 1896 had failed to keep pace with the needs of the growing population. New industrial uses for corn and other farm produce also increased demand just at a time when the supply was short. No doubt, also, increasing productivity because of mechanization played a part in profit making. Those were the real reasons for agricultural prosperity in the early twentieth century, but to the average American another seemed even more important. The connection between mounting prices and the close of the frontier was inescapable. American farm lands were running out!

Popular reaction to this grim realization was expressed in several ways. Scholars wrote warnings to future generations in which the term, "law of diminishing returns," frequently figured. Beyond a certain limit of productiveness, they pointed out, an increased application of labor and capital to natural resources would not result in a proportionate increase in yield. The United States had reached that point with the end of the frontier; the virgin fertility of the soil was skimmed off and production in the future would be more halting and expensive. Hence, the prophets insisted, the era of cheap food had passed forever; no longer would American grains allow the world's population to increase as it had in the nineteenth century; no longer could people concentrate in cities and be assured a cheap living. Ahead lay a period of mounting prices, growing scarcity, and a declining standard of living. In the future natural resources must not be squandered; salvation depended on saving and conservation.

Other less responsible seers were even more calamitous as they viewed the end of the era of free land. "With our increasing population," wrote Theodore Roosevelt, "the time is not far distant when the problem of supplying our people with food will become pressing." Said another public leader: "We must increase production per acre by more intelligent methods, or we must face the relentless certain day when we shall not produce enough to supply our own necessities." Even James J. Hill, president of the Great Northern Railroad and thorough student of western conditions, reflected the general alarm: "in twenty-five years," he wrote, "we shall have a nation-wide famine."

When prophets and public spokesmen voiced such alarming sentiments, little wonder that the ordinary people succumbed to hysterical fear. This was best shown in the skyrocketing of land prices between 1900 and 1920. Everyone wanted farm land, to hold against the day when real famine would send values to even more stratospheric levels. So they rushed to buy; retired farmers bought farm after farm with assurance that their savings were safer than in a bank; eastern capitalists shipped their money westward to share in the virtually guaranteed profits; owners of small farms mortgaged their paid-for acres to buy still more. With demand unlimited and the supply restricted the resulting price rise was inevitable. Lands six miles from a railroad that had sold for $3 an acre in the 1870s went freely in 1910 at $150 an acre. Between 1900 and 1910 prices for farm lands throughout the United States increased 118.1 per cent; in Nebraska the increase was 231.8 per cent, in North Dakota 321.3 per cent, in Idaho 353 per cent, in South Dakota 377.1 per cent. During the next decade prices continued to rise, but at a less rapid pace.

This upward spiraling of land values inevitably affected the farmers. Their immediate reaction was one of delighted approval. Never had they known such prosperity; not only did high commodity prices assure them a comfortable living, but the rapid increase in the value of their property transformed them into a wealthy group through no effort of their own. Had they but known, however, those high land prices forecast a troubled future. They meant, for one thing, that farmers would have to resort to increasing crop specialization to secure an adequate return on invested capital. By 1920 the one-crop system was as firmly planted in the West as in the South, with hard spring wheat grown almost exclusively in the northern Plains country, hard winter wheat between northern Texas and southern Nebraska, corn in the area about Iowa, and dairy products in the urbanized regions of Illinois, Wisconsin, eastern Iowa, and southern Minnesota. Farmers whose future was mortgaged to one crop were less well equipped to withstand periods of drought or low prices than those practicing diversified agriculture. Even more dangerous was the increase in farm tenancy as farmers leased lands from their neighbors, and as eastern investors and western syndicates rushed to secure land in that day of rising prices. By 1920, 40 per cent of the farms of Iowa and 50 per cent of the farms of Illinois were owned by absentee landlords. Although tenancy was as low as 20 per cent in some of the newer regions of the West, the trend was clearly toward a system of absentee ownership, share cropping, and suitcase farming where lands were plowed, sowed, and reaped by migrating labor.

American agriculture could have withstood the risks of specialization and the disadvantages of tenancy if the demand for produce had continued high, and if no new competitors had appeared. Unfortunately for the farmer, fate decreed that neither should be the case. Demand steadily declined as the population, which had been growing rapidly in Europe and America during the nineteenth century, leveled off in the twentieth, a victim of modern warfare and a lowered birth rate. Moreover the restrictive immigration laws of the 1920s further restricted the farmers' markets by cutting down the number of food-consuming aliens reaching the East. Equally damaging was the intrusion of new competitors into the world's markets. New hitherto-undeveloped lands brought under cultivation during the prosperous years of the early twentieth century—in Canada, Australia, South America, and Russia especially—were by the mid-1920s pouring their cheap produce into the food baskets of the western world. Now American farmers must compete with them, as well as with the improved yields of their own neighbors, made possible by technical improvements and increased care in cultivation.

The result was far from that envisaged by the seers of the early twentieth century. Instead of having too little food, the nation found itself with too much. The artificial demand created by World War I kept prices up until 1920, then the break came. The total farm income of the United States, which had touched a high point of $17,600,000,000 in 1919, slumped to only $10,260,000,000 that year. Six years later it had crept up to $12,985,000,000, but with the industrial depression of 1929 it started down again, reaching $6,900,900,000 in 1931. During the next decade, and until a second world war provided temporary relief, the American farmer existed only through federal bounty. Such were the results of overexpansion in land and prices that followed the closing of the frontier.

The end of the era of westward expansion, although most notable in its effect on the farmer, was not without influence on other aspects of American life. One immediate result was to strengthen popular support for the nation's newly launched imperialistic foreign policy. To say that the vanishing frontier was alone responsible for the jingoism of the 1890s would be a gross exaggeration; improved transportation facilities, the demand of industrialists for markets, the export of surplus capital abroad, and the example set by European nations were all equally important. Yet, for the man on the street, there was a direct connection between the Census Bureau's announcement of 1890 and the need for overseas possessions. With opportunity drawing to a close within the nation's borders, many Americans reasoned, the government's duty was to provide areas for exploitation elsewhere. Hence they gave enthusiastic approval to the leaders who grabbed Puerto Rico and the Philippines from Spain in 1898, added the Hawaiian Islands and other Pacific possessions, muscled Panama from Colombia in 1903, and extended American hegemony over the Caribbean during the next decades. To many Americans these lands were new frontiers, waiting development by a new type of pioneer from the United States.

More thoughtful men, realizing that no amount of external expansion could replace the vanishing lands of the West, recognized that the nation must learn to live within its fixed borders. This, they saw, would require a new and more positive role for the federal government. In the past the limitless opportunity awaiting everyone in the expanding United States minimized the need for governmental interference in the affairs of individuals. Men could look after themselves; Congress could stand aside while the citizens worked out their own economic destiny amidst the plentiful natural resources available in the nineteenth century. In the future chances for that kind of individual success would lessen as free lands vanished. Instead competition for the limited resources remaining would inevitably increase as the continent filled in. Only positive government action would prevent the development of a dog-eat-dog social order in which the few would gain at the expense of the many.

This realization has shaped the political philosophy of progressive American statesmen virtually since the beginning of the twentieth century. It underlay the conservation and regulatory policies of Theodore Roosevelt's "Square Deal," which was rooted in the belief that competition for the nation's dwindling resources must be controlled by the federal government. It shaped Woodrow Wilson's "New Freedom," which sought to assure continued economic opportunity for the individual by checking industrial monopoly. It inspired Franklin D. Roosevelt's "New Deal," with its understanding that government must offer the people security and opportunity formerly provided by the "safety valve" of the frontier. It governed the "Fair Deal" of Harry S. Truman and the "New Frontier" of John F. Kennedy, both designed to provide a better world through legislation rather than through the completely free enterprise possible in an expanding social order. And it was implicit in the "Great Society" of Lyndon B. Johnson with its acceptance of the belief that the state must care for a variety of needs formerly provided by frontier opportunity. Franklin D. Roosevelt summed up not only his own but the nation's post-frontier philosophy when he declared in a radio address in 1935: "We can no longer escape into virgin territory: we must master our environment. . . . We have been compelled by stark necessity to unlearn the too comfortable superstition that the American soil was mystically blessed with every kind of immunity to grave economic maladjustments, and that the American spirit of individualism—all alone and unhelped by the cooperative efforts of government—could withstand and repel every form of economic disarrangement or crisis."

Acting upon this premise, these and other statesmen of the twentieth century worked diligently to awaken a reluctant American people to the necessities of a closed-space existence. They sought to curb industrial monopolies, made suddenly more dangerous in a land where opportunity for competition in new areas had diminished. They tried to regulate the country's distribution facilities, lest excessive profits for middlemen lower the standard of living. They encouraged workers and farmers to act cooperatively in an effort to wring a more equitable share of the nation's wealth from industry. They set up social security systems to provide old-age pensions, unemployment relief, and disability payments for those temporarily or permanently unable to cope with the problems of society. They attempted, in other words, to secure for individuals through positive governmental action the social welfare and economic opportunity that was once provided by free land.

That the West itself opposed rather than aided this adjustment is not surprising. There the frontier traditions of individualism, surface-skimming waste, brash overconfidence, and reckless speculation were best perpetuated; the pioneer had always been too absorbed in his own pursuit of wealth to pay much attention to the needs of society. Moreover the West had, throughout its history, been a stronghold of political conservatism, despite outraged cries of easterners against western "radicalism." Its periodic protests were really leveled against change, and its fundamental desire was to maintain the democratic, agrarian, social order of the eighteenth century, in the increasingly industrialized world of the nineteenth and twentieth centuries. This was the purpose of the wild "men of the western waters" who in Jackson's day lifted their voices against the financial policies of New England manufacturers. This was the ambition of the Grangers who in the 1870s urged an end to monopolies and a return to free competition. This was the hope of the Populists, who in the 1890s pleaded for the easier money supply that the nation had known before a capitalistic creditor class took over the reins of government. And this was the dream of the farmers who in the 1930s shifted the center of conservative Republicanism to the upper Plains states in their vain effort to check a "New Deal" that promised to adjust the entire nation to the needs of a modern industrial world, of the Southerners and Southwesterners who in 1964 and 1980 embraced presidential candidates whose refusal to accept the realities of post-frontier life won the enthusiastic support of those who shared with them the belief that economic growth was unlimited, energy independence simply a matter of opening more lands for exploitation, and who gave solid support to conservative presidents Richard M. Nixon and Ronald Reagan, who believed that private enterprise could solve all national problems.

The passing of the frontier has important implications for the future. The hardy self-reliant men and women who through three centuries conquered the continent have played their role in the drama of American development; the new generation must escape the prejudices of an outworn past and build on the lasting values of the frontier experience. It is now clear that social democracy, economic opportunity, and political freedom are not contingent on national expansion, nor must the ecological structure be permanently damaged to maintain a satisfactory standard of living for the American people. There are more rational long-term solutions to the problems faced by this generation and those to come. There must be a recognition that the strong desires of individuals do not transcend the requirements of society. The pioneers of the future will need more than primitive tools and ambitions to blaze the trail into the newer world of a cooperative democracy that is America's future; they must retain their sense of optimism, their profound faith in themselves, their willingness to innovate, and their abiding trust in democracy, for on the new frontier men and women shall go forward together or they shall not go forward at all.

Bibliography

The following bibliography is highly selective. Only works valuable for their additions to knowledge or their synthesis of periods of history are included, and only those bearing upon topics discussed in the text. Moreover the vast proliferation of books and articles on frontier history over the past years has decreed that older studies must give way to newer treatments. Many monographic works listed in prior editions of this book have been excluded in this edition. Any student seriously interested in any topic is advised to use prior editions as well as this one to compile a proper bibliography in the area he proposes to study. Because so much valuable material is contained in historical journals, many of which are referred to repeatedly, their titles have been abbreviated. The following key lists the abbreviations that have been used:

A. Americas
A.A. American Anthropologist
A.A.A.G. Annals of the Association of American Geographers
A.A.A.P.S.S. Annals of the American Academy of Political and Social Science
A.A.S., Proceedings American Antiquarian Society Proceedings
A. and W., Arizona and the West
A.B.E. American Bureau of Ethnology
A.E.R. American Economic Review
A.H. Agricultural History
A.H.A., Annual Report American Historical Association, Annual Report
A.H.Q., Arkansas Historical Quarterly
Al.H.Q. Alabama Historical Quarterly
A.H.R. American Historical Review
A.H.S. Alabama Historical Society
Am.H. American Heritage
A. of I. Annals of Iowa
A. of W. Annals of Wyoming

A.P.S., Proceedings   American Philosophical Society, Proceedings
A.P.S.R.,   American Political Science Review
A.Q.   American Quarterly
A.R.   Alabama Review
A.R.C.S.   American Review of Canadian Studies
Ariz.H.R.   Arizona Historical Review
A.S.   American Studies
A.W.   American West
B.A.G.S.   Bulletin of the American Geographical Society
B.H.M.   Bulletin of the History of Medicine
B.H.R.   Business History Review
B.H.S., Publications   Buffalo Historical Society, Publications
B.M.H.S.   Bulletin of the Missouri Historical Society
B.R.   Bucknell Review
Ca.H.R.   Catholic Historical Review
C.A.   Current Anthropology
C.H.   Church History
C.H.R.   Canadian Historical Review
C.H.A., Report   Canadian Historical Association, Report
C.H.S.B.   Connecticut Historical Society, Bulletin
C.H.S., Collections   Chicago Historical Society, Collections
C.H.S.Q.   California Historical Society Quarterly, and California Historical Quarterly
Ci.H.S.B.   Cincinnati Historical Society, Bulletin
C.M.   Colorado Magazine
C.O.   Chronicles of Oklahoma
C.S.   Capital Studies
C.S.H.S.   Comparative Studies in History and Society
C.S.M., Publications   Colonial Society of Massachusetts, Publications (Transactions)
C.W.H.   Civil War History
D.   Dialogue
E.   Ethnohistory
Ec.H.R.   Economic History Review
E.E.H.   Explorations in Economic History
E.G.   Economic Geography
E.H.R.   English History Review
E.I.H.C.   Essex Institute Historical Collections
E.T.H.S., Publications   East Tennesee Historical Society, Publications
F.C.H.Q.   Filson Club Historical Quarterly
F.H.Q.   Florida Historical Quarterly
F.S.   Feminist Studies
G.H.Q.   Georgia Historical Quarterly
G.P.J.   Great Plains Journal
G.R.   Geographical Review
H.   Historian
H.A.H.R.   Hispanic American Historical Review
H.L.Q.   Huntington Library Quarterly
H.O.   Historical Outlook
H.Q.   History Quarterly
H.S.   Historical Studies, Australia
H.T.   History and Theory
I.H.B.   Indiana Historical Bulletin
I.H.S., Publications   Indiana Historical Society, Publications

I.J.H.P. Iowa Journal of History and Politics
I.M.H. Indiana Magazine of History
I.S.H.A., Transactions Illinois State Historical Society, Transactions
I.Y. Idaho Yesterdays
J.A.C. Journal of American Culture
J.A.H. Journal of American History
J.Ar.H. Journal of Arizona History
J.A.S. Journal of American Studies
J.E.B.H. Journal of Economic and Business History
J.E.H. Journal of Economic History
J.E.S. Journal of Economics and Sociology
J.H.M. Journal of the History of Medicine
J.Et.S. Journal of Ethnic Studies
J.F.H. Journal of Forest History
J.I.C.H. Journal of Imperial and Commonwealth History
J.I.S.H.S. Journal of the Illinois State Historical Society
J.L.C.H.S. Journal of the Lancaster County Historical Society
J.L.P.U.E. Journal of Land and Public Utility Economics
J.M.F. Journal of Marriage and the Family
J.M.A.H. Journal of Mexican American History
J.M.H. Journal of Modern History
J.Miss.H. Journal of Mississippi History
J.Mo.H. Journal of Mormon History
J.N.H. Journal of Negro History
J.P.C. Journal of Popular Culture
J.P.E. Journal of Political Economy
J.P.H. Journal of Presbyterian History
J.S.D.H. Journal of San Diego History
J.Q. Journalism Quarterly
J.S.H. Journal of Southern History
J.So.H. Journal of Social History
J.W. Journal of the West
K.H. Kansas History
K.H.Q. Kansas Historical Quarterly
K.H.S., Collections Kansas Historical Society, Collections
K.S.H.S.R. Kentucky State Historical Society Register
L.H. Louisiana History
La.H. Labor History
L.H.Q. Louisiana Historical Quarterly
L.S. Louisiana Studies
M. Montana
M.A. Mid-America
Ma.H. Maryland Historian
Ma.H.M. Maryland Historical Magazine
M.H. Minnesota History
M.H.B. Minnesota Historical Bulletin
M.H.M. Michigan History Magazine
M.H.R. Missouri Historical Review
M.H.S., Collections Minnesota Historical Society, Collections
M.H.S., Proceedings Massachusetts Historical Society, Proceedings
M.H.S.Q. Maine Historical Society Quarterly
M.H.S., Publications Mississippi Historical Society, Publications
Mich.A. Michigan Academician
Mil.A. Military Affairs

Mil.R. Military Review
M.P.H.S., Collections Michigan Pioneer and Historical Society, Collections
M.V.H.A., Proceedings Mississippi Valley Historical Association, Proceedings
M.V.H.R. Mississippi Valley Historical Review
N. The Nation
N.C.H.R. North Carolina Historical Review
N.D.H. North Dakota History
N.D.H.Q. North Dakota Historical Quarterly
N.E.Q. New England Quarterly
N.F. Niagara Frontier
N.H. Nebraska History
N.H.B. Nebraska Historical Bulletin
N.H.S.Q. Nevada Historical Society Quarterly
N.L.B. Nebraska Law Bulletin
N.M.H.R. New Mexico Historical Review
N.M.Q. New Mexico Quarterly
N.O.Q. Northern Ohio Quarterly
N.R. New Republic
N.Y.H. New York History
N.Y.H.S.Q. New York Historical Society Quarterly
N.Y.S.H.A., Proceedings New York State Historical Association, Proceedings.
O.A.H.Q. Ohio Archaeological and Historical Quarterly
O.H. Ohio History
O.H.Q. Oregon Historical Quarterly
Ohio H.Q. Ohio Historical Quarterly
O.N. Old Northwest
O.V.H.A., Proceedings Ohio Valley Historical Association, Proceedings
P. Palimpsest
Pac.H. Pacific Historian
P.A.H. Perspectives in American History
P.H. Pennsylvania History
P.H.R. Pacific Historical Review
P.M.H.B. Pennsylvania Magazine of History and Biography
P.N.Q. Pacific Northwest Quarterly
Pro. Prologue
P.S.Q. Political Science Quarterly
Q.H. Quaker History
Q.J.U.N.D. Quarterly Journal of the University of North Dakota
Q.J.N.Y.S.H.A. Quarterly Journal of the New York State Historical Association
Q.J.S. Quarterly Journal of Speech
R.E.S. Review of Economic Statistics
R.I.H. Rhode Island History
R.R.V.H.R. Red River Valley Historical Review
S.A.C. South Atlantic Quarterly
S.C.Q. Southern California Quarterly
S.D.H. South Dakota History
S.D.H.C. South Dakota Historical Collections
S.E.J. Southern Economic Journal
S.H.Q. Southwestern Historical Quarterly
S.H.S.N.D., Collections State Historical Society of North Dakota, Collections
S.H.S.W., Proceedings State Historical Society of Wisconsin, Proceedings.
Sm.J.H. Smithsonian Journal of History
S.R. Southwest Review
S.R.L. Saturday Review of Literature

S.S. Social Studies
S.S.H. Social Science History
S.S.J. Social Science Journal
S.S.Q. Social Science Quarterly
St.H.S. Studies in History and Science
T.H.M. Tennessee Historical Magazine
T.S.H.A.Q. Texas State Historical Association Quarterly
U.H.Q. Utah Historical Quarterly
U.of K., Bulletin University of Kansas, Bulletin
V. Ventures
V.H. Vermont History
V.M.H.B. Virginia Magazine of History and Biography
W.A.S.A.L., Transactions Wisconsin Academy of Science, Arts and Letters, Transactions
We.H.Q. Western Historical Quarterly
W.H.Q. Washington Historical Quarterly
W.H.R. Western Humanities Review
W.H.S., Proceedings Wisconsin Historical Society, Proceedings
W.M.C.Q. William and Mary College Quarterly, and William and Mary Quarterly
W.M.Q. Wisconsin Magazine of History
W.P.H.M. Western Pennsylvania Historical Magazine
W.R.H.S., Report Western Reserve Historical Society, Report
W.V.H. West Virginia History
Y.R. Yale Review

1 The Frontier Hypothesis

The Turner Thesis. Any study of the American frontier should begin with the stimulating essay by Frederick Jackson Turner, "The Significance of the Frontier in American History," in the same author's *The Frontier in American History* (New York, 1920). This volume contains numerous other essays dealing with aspects of the problem, while still more are in Turner's *The Significance of Sections in American History* (New York, 1932). His earlier essays, several of which reveal the evolution of the frontier concept in his mind, are in *The Early Writings of Frederick Jackson Turner* (Madison, 1938). Essays dealing specifically with the theory of the frontier have been assembled in Ray A. Billington, ed., *Frontier and Section: Selected Essays of Frederick Jackson Turner* (Englewood Cliffs, 1961). Previously unpublished lectures, essays, and letters by Turner have been published in two volumes by Wilbur R. Jacobs, ed., *Frederick Jackson Turner's Legacy: Unpublished Writings in American History* (San Marino, 1965), and *The Historical World of Frederick Jackson Turner* (New Haven, 1966). Ray A. Billington, ed., *Dear Lady: The Letters of Frederick Jackson Turner and Alice Forbes*

Perkins Hooper, 1910–1932 (San Marino, 1970), sheds light on Turner's historical concepts as well as other aspects of his thought. A penetrating introduction to a modern edition of Turner's, master's thesis, *The Character and Influence of the Indian Trade in Wisconsin: A Study of the Trading Post as an Institution* (Norman, 1977), by David H. Miller and William W. Savage, sheds new light on the significance of that work in frontier historiography.

Ray A. Billington, *Frederick Jackson Turner* (New York, 1973) is the first full-length biography; the book is criticized for not sufficiently stressing Turner's role as a teacher in Vernon E. Mattson, "Frederick Jackson Turner: A Study in Misplaced Priorities," *N.H.S.Q.*, XXII (Summer, 1979). Brief and factual is James D. Bennett, *Frederick Jackson Turner* (Boston, 1975). Aspects of Turner's career are explored in articles by Ray A. Billington, particularly "Frederick Jackson Turner: The Image and the Man, *We.H.Q.*, III (April, 1972), and "Frederick Jackson Turner: Non-Western Historian," *W.A.S.A.L., Transactions,* LIX (1971). A number of articles on Turner published originally in the *Wisconsin Magazine of History* have been collected in Lawrence Burnette, Jr., ed.,

Wisconsin Witness to Frederick Jackson Turner (Madison, 1961), while Richard Hofstadter, *The Progressive Historians* (New York, 1968), is a sparkling intellectual portrait.

Ray A. Billington, *The Genesis of the Frontier Thesis: A Study in Historical Creativity* (San Marino, 1971), explores Turner's early life and thought as the frontier hypothesis emerged in his mind. Earlier articles on the same theme are Fulmer Mood, "The Development of Frederick Jackson Turner as a Historical Thinker," C.S.M., *Transactions,* XXXIV (December, 1939); and Rudolph Freund, "Turner's Theory of Social Evolution," *A.H.,* XIX (April, 1945). Earlier writers who partially explored the frontier concept are discussed in Fulmer Mood, "The Concept of the Frontier, 1871–1898: Comments on a Select List of Source Documents," *A.H.,* XIX (January, 1945) and especially John T. Juricek, "American Usage of the Word 'Frontier' from Colonial Times to Frederick Jackson Turner," A.P.S. *Proceedings,* CX (February, 1966). Turner's influence as a teacher is described in Wilbur R. Jacobs, "Frederick Jackson Turner—Master Teacher," *P.H.R.,* XXIII (February, 1954). William Toll, "W. E. B. DuBois and Frederick Jackson Turner: The Unveiling and Preemption of America's 'Inner History'," *P.N.Q.,* LXV (April, 1974), explains the social forces that popularized Turner's theories while repressing those of DuBois dealing with minorities, while Alazar Weinryb, "The Justification of a Causal Thesis: An Analysis of the Controversies over the Theses of Pirenne, Turner, and Weber," *H.T.,* XIV (1975), discusses three theses that have touched off major historical controversies.

Numerous scholars have explored Turner's methodology and historical concepts. The best of the resulting studies are: Merle Curti, "The Section and the Frontier in American History: The Methodological Concepts of Frederick Jackson Turner," in Stuart A. Rice, ed., *Methods in Social Science* (Chicago, 1931), and Norman D. Harper, "Frontier and Section, a Turner 'Myth'?" *Historical Studies, Australia and New Zealand,* No. 18 (May, 1952). Of value in this connection are studies by Carl Becker, "Frederick Jackson Turner," in Howard W. Odum, ed., *American Masters of Social Science* (New York, 1927), Avery Craven, "Frederick Jackson Turner," in William T. Hutchinson, ed., *Marcus W. Jernegan Essays in American Historiography* (Chicago, 1937), Avery Craven, "Frederick Jackson Turner, Historian," *W.M.H.,* XXV (June, 1942), and Avery Craven, "The 'Turner Theories' and the South," *J.S.H.,* V (August, 1939). Gilman M. Ostrander, "Turner and the

Germ Theory," *A.H.,* XXXII (October, 1958), demonstrates Turner's acceptance of a historical concept popular at the time he wrote. Two excellent articles by Lee Benson are "Achille Loria's Influence on American Economic Thought: Including His Contributions to the Frontier Hypothesis," and "The Historical Background of Turner's Frontier Essay," both published in that author's *Turner and Beard* (Glencoe, 1960).

Scholars in other disciplines have found Turner's presentation of his theories as challenging as the theories themselves. His use of rhetorical devices as they influenced his theories is explored in two articles by Merrill Lewis, "The Art of Frederick Jackson Turner: The Histories," *H.L.Q.,* XXXV (May, 1972), and "Language, Literature, and the Shaping of the Historical Imagination of Frederick Jackson Turner," *P.H.R.,* XLV (August, 1976). In a similar vein, three excellent studies by Ronald H. Carpenter discuss the relationship between his ideas and his oratorical styles: "The Rhetorical Genesis of Style in the 'Frontier Hypothesis' of Frederick Jackson Turner" *So. Speech Comm. Journal,* XXXVII (Spring, 1972), "Frederick Jackson Turner and the Rhetorical Impact of the Frontier Thesis," *Q.J.S.,* LXII (April, 1977), and "Style and Discourse as an Index of Frederick Jackson Turner's Historical Creativity," *H.L.Q.,* XL (May, 1977).

Criticisms of the Hypothesis. Bibliographies of the principal critical essays published during the attack on Turner's theories are Gene M. Gressley, "The Turner Thesis— a Problem in Historiography, *A.H.,* XXXII (October, 1958), and Walter Rundell, Jr., "Concepts of the 'Frontier' and the 'West'," *A. and W.,* I (Spring, 1959). The entire controversy is surveyed and the attacks and defense summarized in Ray A. Billington, *The American Frontier Thesis: Attack and Defense* (Washington, 1971). The principal articles in the controversy are published in the same author's *The Frontier Thesis: Valid Interpretation of American History?* (New York, 1966), Richard Hofstadter and Seymour M. Lipset, eds., *Turner and the Sociology of the Frontier* (New York, 1968), and George R. Taylor, ed., *The Turner Thesis* (Lexington, 1972 edn.). Criticism began in the 1920s with John C. Almack, "The Shibboleth of the Frontier," *H.O.,* XVI (May, 1925), which attacked the thesis from a Marxian point of view. The assault was continued by Charles A. Beard, "Culture and Agriculture," *S.R.L.,* V (October, 1928), which charged that the frontier thesis explained the American past less accurately than economic forces; and by Louis

M. Hacker, "Sections—or Classes," *N.*, CXXXVII (July, 1933), which condemned Turner for ignoring the class conflict.

More serious were the attacks levied by Benjamin F. Wright, Jr., in two essays: "American Democracy and the Frontier," *Y.R.*, XX (December, 1930), and "Political Institutions and the Frontier," in Dixon R. Fox, ed., *Sources of Culture in the Middle West* (New York, 1934). Both refuted Turner's claim that American democracy originated on the frontier, holding instead that it had developed in Europe and that western political institutions were imitative rather than original. Turner's assertion that the frontier acted as a "safety valve" for oppressed eastern workers was challenged in Carter Goodrich and Sol Davison, "The Wage Earner and the Western Movement," *P.S.Q.*, L (June, 1935), and LI (March, 1936), and Murray Kane, "Some Considerations on the Safety Valve Doctrine," *M.V.H.R.*, XXIII (September, 1936). They were answered by Turner's staunchest defender, Joseph Schafer, in three articles: "Some Facts Bearing on the Safety-Valve Theory," *W.M.H.*, XX (December, 1936), "Concerning the Frontier as Safety Valve," *P.S.Q.*, LII (September, 1937), and "Was the West a Safety Valve for Labor," *M.V.H.R.*, XXIV (December, 1937). Schafer's meager statistics were questioned in Carter Goodrich and Sol Davison, "The Frontier as Safety Valve: A Rejoinder," *P.S.Q.*, LIII (June, 1938).

The failure of the frontier to attract eastern workers was demonstrated in Fred A. Shannon, "The Homestead Act and the Labor Surplus," *A.H.R.*, XLI (July, 1936), while Rufus S. Tucker, "The Frontier as an Outlet for Surplus Labor," *S.E.J.*, VII (October, 1940), analyzed population trends to reach the same conclusion. That eastern workers could not afford to move to the frontier was demonstrated in Clarence H. Danhof, "Farm-Making Costs and 'Safety Valve', 1850–60," *J.P.E.*, XLIX (June, 1941). A "final" word on the subject was voiced by Fred A. Shannon, "A Post Mortem on the Labor-Safety-Valve Theory," *A.H.*, XIX (January, 1945), which argued that the frontier after the 1840s was not even an outlet for potential wage earners.

During the 1940s various other aspects of the Turner thesis came under attack. Murray Kane, "Some Considerations on the Frontier Concept of Frederick Jackson Turner," *M.V.H.R.*, XXVII (December, 1940), contended that Turner was at fault for explaining migration solely in geographic terms, rather than as a complex social phenomenon. James

C. Malin, *Essays in Historiography* (Lawrence, 1946), similarly deplored Turner's emphasis on a "space concept" to the exclusion of other forces. More devastating were two articles by George W. Pierson, "The Frontier and Frontiersmen of Turner's Essays," *P.M.H.B.*, LXIV (October, 1940), and "The Frontier and American Institutions," *N.E.Q.*, XV (June, 1942), the first questioning that American traits stemmed largely from the frontier experience, the second that the country's institutions derived from the western environment. A later critic, Sterling Kernek, "Pierson versus Turner: A Commentary on the Frontier Thesis," *H.S.* (October, 1969), finds Pierson more guilty than Turner of romanticism and questionable reasoning. Most of the early criticisms were repeated in Richard Hofstadter, "Turner and the Frontier Myth," *A.S.*, XVIII (Autumn, 1949).

More recent scholarship has tended in two directions. One is to test aspects of the frontier thesis on its own merits, rather than to belabor Turner's statement of the thesis. The findings of the many investigators who have contributed to this literature are appraised in Ray A. Billington, *America's Frontier Heritage* (New York, 1966), which re-examines the hypothesis in the light of modern social-science theory. Among the notable contributors to this school, some have weighed Turner's political concepts. Stanley Elkins and Eric McKitrick, "A Meaning for Turner's Frontier," *P.S.Q.*, LXIX (September, 1954), and (December, 1954), advanced proof that the frontier experience did accelerate the democratic trend. More significant was the careful study by Merle Curti, *The Making of an American Community* (Stanford, 1959), which employed statistical evidence to demonstrate the impact of the frontier environment on the democratic social and political structure of Trempealeau County, Wisconsin, as it emerged from wilderness to civilization. John D. Barnhart, *Valley of Democracy: The Frontier versus the Plantation in the Ohio Valley, 1775–1818* (Bloomington, 1953), examines the emergence of political institutions in this area to reveal the extent of imitation and democratic innovation.

Other students have re-examined aspects of the frontier thesis to determine their validity. Allan Bogue shows that pioneers were prone to innovate in "Pioneer Farmers and Innovation," *I.J.H.P.*, LVI (January, 1958). Gould P. Colman, "Innovation and Diffusion in Agriculture," *A.H.*, XLII (July, 1968), suggests statistical devices for testing the speed of acceptance of new farming techniques, a subject well discussed in H. J. Habakkuk,

American and British Technology in the Nineteenth Century: The Search for Labour Saving Devices (Cambridge, 1962). Irwin Feller, "The Urban Location of United States Invention," *E.E.H.*, VIII (Spring, 1971), explores the location of inventions between 1860 and 1910.

That the pioneering experience was a spur to nationalism is maintained in Daniel J. Elazar, *The American Partnership* (Chicago, 1962), and Henry E. Fritz, "Nationalistic Response to Frontier Expansion," *M.A.*, LI (October, 1969). David W. Noble, *Historians Against History: The Frontier Thesis and the National Covenant in American Historical Writing since 1830* (Minneapolis, 1966) deplores the nationalizing impact of the thesis itself. Warren I. Susman, "The Useless Past: American Intellectuals and the Frontier Thesis: 1910–1930," *B.R.*, XI (March, 1963), shows that intellectuals of the predepression years revolted against the frontier concept because of its nationalistic implications.

Recent scholarship has also demonstrated that earlier critics of the safety-valve doctrine were not entitled to the last word. This reevaluation began with Norman J. Simler, "The Safety-Valve Doctrine Reevaluated," *A.H.*, XXXII (October, 1958), and was continued in two convincing studies: George G. S. Murphy and Arnold Zellner, "Sequential Growth, the Labor-Safety-Valve Doctrine and the Development of American Unionism," *J.E.H.*, XIX (September, 1959), and Ellen von Nardroff, "The American Frontier as Safety Valve—The Life, Death, Reincarnation, and Justification of a Theory," *A.H.*, XXXVI (July, 1962). George R. Woolfolk, "Turner's Safety-Valve and Free Negro Westward Migration," *J.N.H.*, L (July, 1965), demonstrates the manner in which the frontier served as a safety valve for Negroes fleeing from oppressive orthodoxy and conformity in older societies. In another setting, Duane A. Smith, "Colorado's Urban-Mining Safety Valve," *C.M.* XLVII (Fall, 1971), shows that labor unrest before the 1890s was minimized by the drainage of miners to new sites or urban centers. Even a basic argument of the antisafety-valve theorists has been attacked in Robert E. Ankli, "Farm Making Costs in the 1850s," *A.H.*, XLVIII (January, 1974), which uses computerized techniques to demonstrate that the cost of new farms was within the reach of transplanted wage-earners.

The arguments favorable to the frontier thesis advanced in recent times are admirably summarized in Jackson K. Putnam, "The Turner Thesis and the Westward Movement: A Reappraisal," *We.H.Q.*, VII (October, 1976).

Historians have paid increasing attention to the "urban frontier" of the nineteenth century. A pioneer work, Richard C. A. Wade, *The Urban Frontier* (Chicago, 1959), demonstrates that town-planting began early in the westering process and that the orderly migration process envisaged by Turner should be refined. Wade's conclusions have been questioned in Howard J. Nelson, "Town Founding and the American Frontier," *Year Book of the Association of Pacific Coast Geographers*, XXXVI (1974), which maps towns in relation to the frontier zone and shows that they normally were planted as adjuncts to a rural frontier.

The study of the frontier as a legend has also demonstrated its influence in later American thought. The ground-breaking work in this field was Henry Nash Smith, *Virgin Land* (Cambridge, 1950), which showed that many aspects of the frontier thesis were grounded in American folklore at the time Turner developed his thesis. Edwin Fussell, *Frontier: American Literature and the American West* (Princeton, 1965), reveals how the image of the frontier has influenced American writers; more searching is Richard Slotkin, *Regeneration through Violence: The Mythology of the American Frontier, 1600–1860* (Middletown, 1973). Lawrence M. Hauptman, "Mythologizing Westward Expansion: Schoolbooks as the Image of the American Frontier before Turner," *We.H.Q.*, VIII (July, 1977), shows that many aspects of the frontier myth were embodied in a thousand school books used during the nineteenth century. The evolution of the frontier hero-type in American writing is traced in J. A. Leo LeMay, "The Frontiersman from Lout to Hero," *A.A.S.*, LXXXVIII (1979), while Ray A. Billington, *Land of Savagery/Land of Promise: The European Image of the American Frontier* (New York, 1981), explores the myth in European fiction and promotional literature.

The Reorientation of Frontier Studies. Modern scholars recognize that both traditional and environmental forces have played roles in shaping American culture, but have argued over which exercised the greater influence. This problem is explored in such works as Earl Pomeroy, "Toward a Reorientation of Western History: Continuity and Environment," *M.V.H.R.*, XLI (March, 1955); Howard R. Lamar, "Historical Relevance and the American West," *V*, VIII (Fall, 1968); and Richard D. Batman, "The California Political Frontier: Democratic or Bureaucratic?" *J.W.*, VII (October, 1968), a case study of California politicians, concluding that most were eastern oriented and that a "political frontier" existed; Ben M. Vorpahl, "Presbyterian and the Frontier Hypothesis: Tradition and Modification in the American Garden," *J.P.H.*, VL (June, 1967). Two articles that suggest the future of frontier studies are Harry N. Scheiber, "Turner's Legacy and the Search for a Reorientation of Western History," *N.M.H.R.*, XLIV (July, 1969), and Mary Young, "The West and American Culture Identity: Old Themes and New Variations," *We.H.Q.*, I (April, 1970). Eight scholars in as many essays suggest fresh approaches toward an understanding of the influence of the frontier on American life in Jerome O. Steffen, ed., *The American West: New Perspectives, New Dimensions* (Norman, 1979).

Historians have also turned to the computer to analyze aspects of Turner's frontier theory, with mixed results. Demographic studies have shown that the marriage age on the frontier was higher than anticipated, and that other features of Turner's frontier thesis required modification. Typical of such studies are: Sherman L. Ricards, "A Demographic History of the West: Butte County, California, 1850," M.A.S.A.L., *Papers*, XLVI (1961), George Blackburn and Sherman L. Ricards, "A Demographic History of the West: Manistee County, Michigan," *J.A.H.*, LVII (December, 1970), Sherman L. Ricards and George M. Blackburn, "A Demographic History of the West: Nueces County, Texas," *Pro.*, IV (Spring, 1972), William G. Robbins, "Opportunity and Persistence in the Pacific Northwest: A Quantitative Study of Early Roseburg, Oregon," *P.H.R.*, XXXIX (August, 1970), Lowell E. Gallaway and Richard K. Vedder, "Mobility of Native Americans," *J.E.H.*, XXXI (September, 1971), and John Modell, "Family and Fertility on the Indiana Frontier, 1820," *A.Q.*, XXIII (December, 1971). Other statistical studies have explored social mobility in various frontier communities. Typical of these works, which generally substantiate the findings of Merle Curti in his pioneering work listed above, are: Martha M. White, "Factors of Nationality in Frontier Mobility in San Diego County," *J.S.D.H.*, XX (Spring, 1974), Paul G. Merriam, "Urban Elite in the Far West: Portland, Oregon, 1870–1890," *A. and W.*, XVIII (Spring, 1976), D. Aidan McQuillan, "The Mobility of Immigrants and Americans on the Kansas Frontier," *A.H.*, LIII (July, 1979), and Gordon W. Kirk, Jr., *The Promise of American Life: Social Mobility in a Nineteenth-Century Immigrant Community, Holland, Michigan, 1847–1994* (Philadelphia, 1978). More general essays dealing with social mobility on the frontier are in Edward Pessen, "Social Mobility in American

History: Some Brief Reflections," *J.S.H.*, XLV (May, 1979), and Edward Pessen, ed., *Three Centuries of Social Mobility in America* (Lexington, Mass., 1974). Expert analyses of the changing social structure in early frontier communities are: Carl Nordstrom, *Frontier Elements in a Hudson River Village* (Port Washington, 1973), Philip L. White, *Beekmantown, New York: Forest Frontier to Farm Community* (Austin, 1979), and Don H. Doyle, "Social Theory and New Communities in Nineteenth-Century America," *We.H.Q.*, VIII (April, 1977), the latter an impressive analysis of the social structure of pioneer Jacksonville, Illinois.

Democracy, or lack of democracy, and lawlessness on the frontier are considered in such studies as David J. Bodenhamer, "Law and Order on the Early Frontier: Marion, Indiana, 1823–1850," *We.H.Q.*, X (July, 1979), Ronald C. Woolsey, "Crime and Punishment: Los Angeles County, 1850–1856," *S.C.Q.*, LXI (Spring, 1979), and Michael S. Corey, " 'Democracy' on the Frontier: A Case Study of Nevada Editorial Attitudes on the Issue of Non-White Equality," *N.H.S.Q.*, XXI (Fall, 1978). The latter finds a high incidence of racial intolerance, particularly directed against blacks. Ray M. Shortridge, "An Assessment of the Frontier's Influence on Voter Turnout," *A.H.*, L (July, 1976), finds voter turnout in frontier communities no different from those in established regions.

The effect of family relationships on migration patterns is studied in Robert E. Bieder, "Kinship as a Factor in Migration," *J.M.F.*, II (August, 1973), while Nicholas O. Hardeman, *Wilderness Calling: The Hardeman Family in the Westward Movement, 1750–1900* (Knoxville, 1977), traces one family's migration westward. Gilbert C. Fite, "The Pioneer Farmer: A View Over Three Centuries," *A.H.*, L (January, 1976), sees pioneering as a major force in the creation of national traits.

Equally promising as a device to appraise the frontier's influence is the study of comparative frontier areas. The extensive literature on this subject is listed in Marvin Mikesell, "Comparative Studies in Frontier History," *A.A.A.G.*, I (March, 1960). The problems involved in the study of comparative frontiers are considered in Paul F. Sharp, "Three Frontiers: Some Comparative Studies of Canadian, American, and Australian Settlement," *P.H.R.*, XXIV (November, 1955). Among the many studies of frontiers beyond the United States the following will be found especially useful: Donald W. Treadgold, "Russian Expansion in the Light of Turner's Study of the American Frontier," *A.H.*, XXVI

(October, 1952), Peter J. Coleman, "The New Zealand Frontier and the Turner Thesis," *P.H.R.*, XXVII (August, 1958), Fred Alexander, *Moving Frontiers: An American Theme and its Application to Australian History* (Melbourne, 1947), H. C. Allen, *Bush and Backwoods: A Comparison of the Frontier in Australia and the United States* (East Lansing, 1959), William H. McNeill, *Europe's Steppe Frontier* (Chicago, 1964), Martin T. Katzman, "The Brazilian Frontier in Comparative Perspective," *C.S.H.S.*, XVII (July, 1975), Earl T. Glauert, "Ricardo Rojas and the Emergence of Argentine Cultural Nationalism," *H.A.H.R.*, XLIII (February, 1963), and Joseph L. Wieczynski, *The Russian Frontier: The Impact of Borderlands upon the Course of Early Russian History* (Charlottesville, 1976). All, but particularly the latter, find that the Turner thesis applies to greater or less degree in the countries under study. An excellent series of suggestions for comparative studies is in W. Turrentine Jackson, "A Brief Message for the Young and/or Ambitious: Comparative Frontiers as a field for Investigation," *We.H.Q.*, IX (January, 1978). Two volumes of essays offer excellent guidance as well as impressive results: David H. Miller and Jerome O. Steffen, eds., *The Frontier: Comparative Studies* (Norman, 1977), and William W. Savage, Jr. and Stephen I. Thompson, eds., *The Frontier: Comparative Studies. Volume II* (Norman, 1979). Jerome O. Steffen, *Comparative Frontiers: A Proposal for Studying the American West* (Norman, 1980), suggests the study of internal frontiers to appraise the relative influence of parent and frontier cultures, while Ray A. Billington, "Frontiers," in C. Vann Woodward, ed., *The Comparative Approach to American History* (New York, 1968), argues that the uniqueness of the American frontier experience makes comparisons difficult.

A remarkably stimulating application of the Turner Thesis to world history is in Walter P. Webb, *The Great Frontier* (Boston, 1952). His thesis is criticized in Archibald R. Lewis and Thomas F. McGann, eds., *The New World Looks at its History* (Austin, 1963), and explained in two biographical studies: Necah S. Furman, *Walter Prescott Webb: His Life and Impact* (Albuquerque, 1976), and Gregory M. Tobin, *The Making of a History: Walter Prescott Webb and the Great Plains* (Austin, 1976). Kenneth R. Philip and Elliott West, eds., *The Walter Prescott Webb Memorial Lectures: Essays on Walter Prescott Webb* (Austin, 1976), contains four essays by experts analyzing his life and thought.

Historians and geographers have recently rediscovered Turner's works on sectionalism, which were long considered unimportant. Robert H. Block, "Frederick Jackson Turner and American Geography," *A.A.A.G.*, LXX (March, 1980), appraises Turner's role as the father of modern geography, while Michael C. Steiner, "The Significance of Turner's Sectional Thesis," *We.H.Q.*, X (October, 1979), shows that his views on sectionalism were far more accurate than previously believed. Richard Jensen, "On Modernizing Frederick Jackson Turner: The Historiography of Regionalism," *We.H.Q.*, XI (July, 1980), holds on the other hand that his views on regionalism have restrained more imaginative approaches to the subject.

Women and Minorities on the Frontier. Only recently have historians recognized that blacks, Mexican Americans, and women played a major role in the advance of the American frontier. Specific notes on the roles played by Negroes are included in later chapter bibliographies, but three general works on their contributions deserve mention: W. Sherman Savage, *Blacks in the West* (Westport, 1977), Kenneth W. Porter, *The Negro on the American Frontier* (New York, 1971), a collection of germinal essays, and William L. Katz, *The Black West* (New York, 1971), a popular condensation of some of the major literature on the subject.

The role of women has attracted greater attention, but has only recently been subjected to critical study. Typical of older works that pictured women as docile drudges, or as principally important for bringing culture to the Wests were: William F. Sprague, *Women and the West: A Short Social History* (Boston, 1940), Nancy W. Ross, *Westward the Women* (New York, 1944), and Dee A. Brown, *Gentle Tamers: Women of the Old Wild West* (Lincoln, 1958). More detailed, but reflecting this same viewpoint is Eugenie A. Leonard, *The Dear-Bought Heritage* (Philadelphia, 1965), which deals with women on the colonial frontier.

Today's studies usually see women not as stereotypes such as those popularized by western films and novels, but as human beings performing a variety of tasks and being of essential service in the westward advance of population. This viewpoint is mirrored in such works as Paula Treckel, "An Historiographic Essay," *O.N.*, I (December, 1975), a review of several older works and a statement of the newer viewpoint, June Sochen, "Frontier Women: A Model for all Women," *S.D.H.*, VII (Winter, 1976), Lillian Schlissel, "Women's Diaries on the Western Frontier," *A.S.*, XVIII (Spring, 1977), and especially three stimulating studies by Glenda Riley, "Images of the Frontierswoman: Iowa as a Case Study," *We.H.Q.,* VIII (April, 1977), "Not Gainfully Employed": Women on the Iowa Frontier, 1833–1870," *P.H.R.,* XLIX (May, 1980), and "Women in the West," *J.A.C.* III (Summer, 1980). In the same vein is Beverly J. Stoeltje, " 'Helpmate for Men Indeed,' The Image of the Frontier Woman," *J.M.F.,* LXXXVIII (January, 1975). A pioneering book reflecting the modern viewpoint on frontier women is Julie R. Jeffrey, *Frontier Women* (New York, 1979), which is concerned largely with the trans-Mississippi West. Other works on frontier women on the overland trails are described in the bibliography to Chapter XXIII below.

2 The Land and Its People

The Geographic Setting. Wallace W. Atwood, *The Physiographic Provinces of North America* (Boston, 1940), is still standard; this may be supplemented with C. Langdon White and Edwin J. Foscue, *Regional Geography of North America* (New York, 1943), and Ralph H. Brown, *Historical Geography of the United States* (New York, 1948). A series of excellent essays on the nature and definition of sectionalism are in Merrill Jensen, ed., *Regionalism in America* (Madison, 1951), while Wilbur Zelinsky, *The Cultural Geography of the United States* (Englewood Cliffs, N.J., 1973), provides additional information. The entire issue of the *Annals of the Association of American Geogaphers,* LXII (June, 1972), is devoted to articles on the geographic regions of the United States.

The Native Americans—General Works. Books and articles dealing with 280 Indian tribes published before 1958 are listed in George P. Murdock, *Ethnographic Bibliography of North America* (New Haven, 1960). More recent bibliographical studies include William T. Hagen, *The Indian in American History* (Washington, 1971); Wilbur R. Jacobs, "Revising Revisions on the American Indian and Frontier in American History," *We.H.Q.,* V (January, 1973), which discusses recent anthropological studies; Dwight L. Smith, ed., *Indians of the United States and Canada: A Bibliography* (Santa Barbara, 1974), which lists 1,687 works: and three excellent collections by Francis P. Prucha, "Books on American Indian Policy: A Half-Century of Important Work 1970-1975," *J.A.H.,* LXIII (December, 1976), *A Bibliographical Guide to the History of Indian-White Relations in the United States* (Chicago, 1977), a massive and important compilation, and *United States Indian Policy: A Critical Bibliography* (Bloomington, 1977). The latter is one of a series of critical bibliographies dealing with aspects of Indian history being published by the Newberry Library.

Several collections of documents dealing with the Indian and Indian-white relations have appeared. Jack D. Forbes, *The Indian in America's Past* (Englewood Cliffs, 1964), is brief and openly pro-Indian. More balanced are two volumes edited by Francis P. Prucha, *The Indian in American History* (New York, 1971), and *Documents of American Indian Policy* (Lincoln, 1975). Wilcomb E. Washburn, ed., *The Indian and the White Man* (Garden City, 1964), assembles source documents that stress the injustice of Indian displacement, while the same editor has compiled a massive collection of congressional documents touching on Indian relations in *The American Indian and the United States: A Documentary History* 4 v. (New York, 1973). A documentary collection is Virgil J.Vogel, ed., *This Country Was Ours: A Documentary History of the American Indian* (New York, 1972).

The essential reference book on American Indians has long been Frederick W. Hodge, *Handbook of American Indians North of Mexico,* 2 v. (Washington, 1907, reprinted 1959), but this is now being displaced by a monumental series of volumes edited by Bruce G. Trigger, *Handbook of North American Indians* (Washington, 1976—) to be published over the next years. Both contain basic information on the location, numbers, and culture of all tribes.

General histories of the Native Americans are numerous. Perhaps the most useful to historians is William Brandon, *The Last Americans* (New York, 1974), a brilliantly written book; others of comparable usefulness are: D'Arcy McNickle, himself an Indian, *Indians and Other Americans: Two Ways of Life Meet* (New York, rev. edn., 1970); Ruth M. Underhill, *Red Man's America: A History of Indians in the United States* (Chicago, rev. edn., 1971); Clark Wissler, *Indians of the United States* (rev. edn., 1966), the latter two by anthropologists; Harold E. Driver, *Indians of North America* (Chicago, rev. edn., 1969), another competent anthropological treatment; Alvin M. Josephy, Jr., *The Indian Heritage of America* (New York, 1968), Wilcomb E. Washburn, *The Indian in America* (New York, 1975), an excellent overall treatment by a skilled historian; George P. Castile, *North American Indians* (New York, 1979); Jennings C. Wise, *The Red Man in the New World*

Drama (New York, 1971), a strongly pro-Indian study; and Roger L. Nichols, *The American Indian: Past and Present* (New York, rev. edn., 1981).

Number of Native Americans A pioneering attempt to determine the number of Indians in North America when the white conquest began is S. F. Cook, *The Conflict Between the California Indian and White Civilization* 4 v. (Berkeley, 1943). His figures were dramatically upgraded in a groundbreaking article by Henry Dobyn, "Estimated Aboriginal American Population," *C.A.*, VII (April, 1966), which placed the number in North America between nine and ten million. Sherburne F. Cook and Woodrow W. Borah, *Essays in Population History, I. Mexico and the Caribbean* (Berkeley, 1971), to *III. Mexico and California* (Berkeley, 1979), concluded that even this estimate was too low, and held that the number in both Americas was nearer a hundred million. These figures are held as grossly exaggerated in William Peterson, "A Demographer's View of Prehistoric Demography," *C.A.*, XVI (June, 1975). This literature is surveyed from the viewpoint of a historian in two essays by Wilbur R. Jacobs "The Indian and the Frontier in American History—a Need for Revision," *We.H.Q.*, IV (January, 1973), and "The Tip of the Iceberg: Pre-Columbian Indian Demography and Some Implications for Revisionism," *W.M.C.Q.*, XXXI (January, 1974). A number of articles stemming from the controversy over numbers are in William M. Denevan, ed., *The Native Population of the Americas in 1492* (Madison, 1976), while a bibliography of the subject is in Henry F. Dobyns, *Native American Historical Demography: A Critical Bibliography* (Bloomington, 1976).

The startling decrease in the number of Native Americans since the conquest by Europeans has called attention to disease as a factor in reducing Indian populations. This subject is the theme of such pioneering studies as Henry F. Dobyns, "An Outline of Andean Epidemic History to 1720," *B.H.M.*, XXXVII (November, 1963), Calvin Martin, "Wildlife Diseases as a Factor in the Depopulation of the North American Indian," *We.H.Q.*, VII (January, 1976), Alfred W. Crosby, "Virgin Soil Epidemics as a Factor in the Aboriginal Depopulation of America," *W.M.H.Q.*, XXXIII (April, 1976), and Clyde D. Dollar, "The High Plains Smallpox Epidemic of 1837–38," *We.H.Q.*, VIII (January, 1977).

Native American Culture. Modern historians and anthropologists recognize that Indian culture was highly sophisticated. A pioneer work on the subject was A. L. Kroeber,

Anthropology, Race, Language, Culture, Psychology, Prehistory (New York, 1948), summarizing the findings of his generation. This should be supplemented by two more recent works: Wendell H. Oswalt, *This Land Was Theirs: A Study of the North American Indian* (New York, 1966), which deals with specific cultural areas, and Peter Farb, *Man's Rise to Civilization as Shown by the Indians of North America* (New York, 1968), a broadly imaginative treatment of the subject. Equally valuable is Carl O. Sauer, *Sixteenth Century North America: The Land and the People as Seen by Europeans* (Berkeley, 1971), which describes Native American culture before the changes wrought by European contacts. Aspects of that culture are treated in such works as: Julia M. Seton *American Indian Arts* (New York, 1962), Ruth M. Underhill, *Red Man's Religion* (Chicago, 1965), and Virgil J. Vogel, *American Indian Medicine* (Norman, 1970). Irving Hallowell, "The Backwash of the Frontier: The Impact of the Indian on American Culture," in Walker D. Wyman and Clifton B. Kroeber, *The Frontier in Perspective* (Madison, 1957), is a classic essay.

Other cultural investigations have shed light on many aspects of life among Native Americans. The extent of agricultural as opposed to hunting among eastern tribes is the theme of Gregory Waselkov, "Prehistoric Agriculture in the Central Mississippi Valley," *A.H.*, LI (July, 1977), while the ability of Indians to adopt the white man's fighting habits is shown in Patrick M. Malone, "Changing Military Technology among the Indians of Southern New England, 1600–1677," *A.Q.*, XXV (March, 1973), James Axtell and William C. Sturtevant, "The Unkindest Cut, or Who Invented Scalping," *W.M.C.Q.*, XXVII (July, 1980), argues that scalping was not introduced into America by the British but was an established pre-Columbian custom. Other myths concerning the drinking habits of Native Americans are set at rest in Joy Leland, *Frontier Myths: North American Drinking and Alcohol Addiction* (New Brunswick, 1976). The sophisticated legal system of the Cherokee has been studied in Rennard Strickland, *Fire and the Spirits: Cherokee Law from Clan to Court* (Norman, 1975), and particularly in John P. Reid, *The Law of Blood: The Primitive Law of the Cherokee Nation* (New York, 1970), and *A Better Kind of Hatchet: Law, Trade, and Diplomacy in the Cherokee Nation during the Early Years of European Contact* (University Park, 1976), which show how the failure of Carolinians to understand Cherokee law and customs hindered relationships.

The widespread use of slavery among the

tribes of the Southeast is shown in R. Halliburton, Jr., *Red Over Black: Black Slavery among the Cherokee Indians* (Westport, 1977), the first competent study of the subject, Theda Perdue, *Slavery and the Evolution of Cherokee Society, 1540–1866* (Knoxville, 1979), and Daniel F. Littlefield, *Africans and Creeks: From the Colonial Period to the Civil War* (Westport, 1979). That white captives of Indians often preferred the Indian way of life and refused to return to "civilization," is shown in Norman J. Heard, *White into Red: A Study of the Assimilation of White Persons Captured by Indians* (Metuchen, 1973), James Axtell, "The White Indians of Colonial America," *W.M.C.Q.*, XXXII (January, 1975), which stresses the reasons for their choice, and Richard Van Der Beets, ed., *Held Captive by Indians: Selected Narratives, 1642–1836* (Knoxville, 1973), which reprints eighteen narratives written by captives.

Regional and Tribal Histories. Useful regional histories include: George E. Hyde, *Indians of the Woodlands: From Prehistoric times to 1725* (Norman, 1962), W. Vernon Kinietz, *The Indians of the Western Great Lakes, 1615–1760* (Ann Arbor, 1965), Ruth Y. Wetmore, *First on the Land: The North Carolina Indians* (Winston-Salem, 1975), Charles Hudson, *The Southeastern Indians* (Knoxville, 1976) an excellent study of prehistoric culture, and Howard S. Russell, *Indian New England before the Mayflower* (Hanover, 1980).

Tribal histories are more numerous, and essential in understanding both Native American culture and the Indians' contacts with the whites. Among the most valuable of these are: Anthony F. C. Wallace, *The Death and Rebirth of the Seneca* (New York, 1970), Anson Bert, *The Miami Indians* (Norman, 1970), William T. Hagen, *The Sac and Fox Indians* (Norman, 1958), James A. Clifton, *The Prairie People: Continuity and Change in Potawatomi Indian Culture, 1665–1965* (Lawrence, 1977), R. David Edmunds, *The Potowatomi: Keepers of the Fire* (Norman, 1978), Bruce G. Trigger, *The Children of Aataentsic: A History of the Huron People to 1660* (Montreal, 1976), Jerry E. Clark, *The Shawnee* (Lexington, 1977), Patricia K. Ourada, *The Menominee Indians: A History* (Norman, 1979), Edmund J. Danziger, *The Chippewas of Lake Superior* (Norman, 1978), Gary C. Goodwin, *Cherokees in Transition: A Study of Changing Culture and Environment Prior to 1775* (Chicago, 1977), Duane H. King, *The Cherokee Indian Nation: A Troubled Nation* (Knoxville, 1979), Jesse O. McKee and Jon A. Schlenker, *The Choctaws: Cultural Evolution of a Native American Tribe* (Jackson, 1980), Jerald Milanich and Samuel Procter, *Tacachale: Essays on the Indians of Florida and Southeastern Georgia during the Historic Period* (Gainesville, 1978), which deals with the Calusa, Tocobaga, Timuca, Seminole and Guale tribes, and Karen I. Blu, *The Lumbee Problem: The Making of an American Indian People* (New York, 1980), which describes the Lumbee of North Caorlina.

Indian-White Relations: The Early Contacts. Historians have recently begun to investigate the prejudices and attitudes of whites and Indians in their relationships as a basis for an understanding of white-Indian contacts and conflicts. An exhaustive treatment of British writing during the early years of contact to reveal British attitudes is H. C. Porter, *The Inconstant Savage: England and the North American Indian, 1500–1600* (London, 1979). Far more interpretive are Bernard Sheehan, *Savagism & Civility: Indians and Englishmen in Colonial Virginia* (Cambridge, 1980), Gary B. Nash, *Red, White, and Black: The Peoples of Early America* (Englewood Cliffs, 1974), a stimulating appraisal of attitudes of whites, blacks, and Indians in their interrelationships, and Robert F. Berkhofer, Jr., *The White Man's Indian: Images of the American Indian from Columbus to the Present* (New York, 1977). J. E. Chamberlin, *The Harrowing of Eden: White Attidues toward Native Americans* (New York, 1975), contrasts the differing views of the Indian in the American and Canadian colonies. Karen O. Kupperman, *Settling with the Indians: The Meeting of English and Indian Cultures in America, 1580–1640* (Totowa, 1980), holds that Europeans saw Indians as humans, but sufficiently inferior to be treated as menials. All of these studies show that both the British people and the colonists divided Native Americans into "good" and "bad" Indians, and that these fixed stereotypes greatly altered relations with the various tribes.

Modern scholarship has also begun to probe the impact of the Indians' own cultural beliefs and practices on their relations with whites. Two classic treatments of this subject are P. Richard Metcalf, "Who Should Rule at Home? Native American Politics and Indian-White Relations," *J.A.H.*, LXI (December, 1974), which demonstrates that intertribal conflicts played a major role in tribal attitudes toward whites, and Calvin Martin, *Keepers of the Game: Indian-Animal Relationships and the Fur Trade* (Berkeley, 1978), a study of the Micmac Indians of Maritime Canada demonstrating that contacts with the whites upset delicate spiritual relationships between the Indians and their environment. The difference in attitudes of the French in Canada toward the Indians, and the effect of these differences on relationships, is admirably explored in Cornelius J. Jaenen, *Friend and Foe: Aspects of French-Amerindian Cultural Contact in the Sixteenth and Seventeenth Centurys* (New York, 1976). The cultural borrowing and their effect on both Indian and white agriculture are shown in Helen C. Rountree, "Change Came Slowly: The Case of the Powhatan Indians of Virginia," *J.Et.S.*, III (Fall, 1975), and Thomas R. Wessel, "Agriculture, Indians, and American History," *A.H.*, L (January, 1976). Alden T. Vaughan and Daniel K. Richter, "Crossing the Cultural Divide: Indians and New Englanders, 1605–1763," *A.A.S.*, *Proceedings* XC (1980), challenges the traditional view that more whites adopted Indian ways than the opposite. Robert F. Berkhofer, *Salvation and the Savage* (Lexington, 1965), appraises the impact of contact with missionaries on the Indians' beliefs.

A brief survey of the early relationships between the two cultures is in William T. Hagen, *American Indians* (Chicago, 1961). More detailed for the early contacts is Francis Jennings, *The Invasion of America: Indians, Colonialism, and the Cant of Conquest* (Chapel Hill, 1975). James Axtell, "The Scholastic Philosophy of the Wilderness," *W.M.C.Q.*, XXIX (July, 1972), explores early contacts in the northern colonies, while Leslie F. S. Upton, *Micmacs and Colonists: Indian-White Relations in the Maritimes, 1713–1867* (Vancouver, 1980), tells the tragic story of the relationships of one tribe with their French and English conquerors. Wilbur R. Jacobs, *Dispossessing the American Indian* (New York, 1972), is a stimulating collection of essays based partly on anthropological findings, while Wilcomb E. Washburn, *Red Man's Land—White Man's Law* (New York, 1971), describes the legal expedients on which this dispossession was based. A pioneering essay by an anthropologist, Nancy O. Lurie, "Indian Cultural Adjustment to European Civilization," in James M. Smith, ed., *Seventeenth-Century America, Essays in Colonial History* (Chapel Hill, 1959), makes clear the problems of assimilation.

3   Europe's First Frontier, 1492–1615

Spain in America. An excellent brief survey is in Charles Gibson, *Spain in America* (New York, 1966). This may be supplemented by two searching studies: Louis B. Wright, *Gold, Glory, and the Gospel: The Adventur-* *ous Lives and Times of the Renaissance Explorers* (New York, 1970), which attempts to appraise the motives of the Spanish pioneers with strong emphasis on the religious impulse. Silvio Zavala, *New Viewpoints on the Spanish Colonization of America* (Philadelphia, 1943), describes Spanish colonizing methods.

The narratives of the principal explorers are in Frederick W. Hodge and Theodore H. Lewis, *Spanish Explorers in the Eastern United States, 1528–1543* (New York, 1907). Cleve Hallenbeck, *Álvar Núñez Cabeza de Vaca* (Glendale, 1940), reproduces documents dealing with de Vaca's journey, while de Soto's wanderings are described by contemporaries in James A. Robertson, ed., *True Relation of the Hardships Suffered by Governor Fernando de Soto*, 2 v. (De Land, 1932). The chronicles of Don Tristán de Luna Y Arellano's ill-fated attempt to settle Florida are in Herbert I. Priestley, ed., *The Luna Papers*, 2 v. (De Land, 1928). Herbert E. Bolton, ed., *Arredondo's Historical Proof of Spain's Title to Georgia* (Berkeley, 1925), prints documents on the origins of the mission system.

Early Spanish exploration and attempts at settlement are described in two books by Woodbury Lowery, *Spanish Settlements within the Present Limits of the United States, 1513–1561* (New York, 1901) and *Spanish Settlements within the Present Limits of the United States. Florida, 1562–1574* (New York, 1905). Herbert E. Bolton, *The Spanish Borderlands* (New York, 1921), a pioneering interpretative survey of the Spanish thrust northward, has been displaced by John F. Bannon, *The Spanish Borderlands Frontier, 1513–1821* (New York, 1971), a thorough appraisal based on recent scholarship. Jack D. L. Holmes, "Interpretations and Trends in the Study of the Spanish Borderlands: The Old Southwest," *S.H.Q.*, LXXIV (April, 1971), provides a critical bibliography and suggestions on areas deserving further research.

The careers of two early explorers are thoroughly investigated in Edward W. Lawson, *The Discovery of Florida and Its Discoverer Juan Ponce De Leon* (St. Augustine, 1946), and T. Maynard, *De Soto and the Conquistadores* (New York, 1930). Charles E. Burgess, "The De Soto Myth in Missouri," *B.M.H.S.*, XXIV (July, 1968), uses anthropological evidence to argue that the expedition never entered Missouri. A popular general account by Timothy Severin, *Explorers of the Mississippi* (New York, 1968), also deals with the De Soto expedition. Still reliable for all Spanish exploration is John B. Brebner, *Explorers of North America, 1492–1806* (New York, 1933), while F. A. Kirkpatrick, *The*

Spanish Conquistadores (New York, 1934) is a standard survey. Carroll L. Riley, "Blacks in the Early Southwest," *E.,* XIX (Summer, 1972), catalogues blacks in the Southwest in the sixteenth and seventeenth centuries.

Spanish Settlement in the Southeast. J. G. Johnson, "A Spanish Settlement in Carolina, 1526," *G.H.Q.,* (December, 1923), deals with the Aylón expedition to San Miguel de Guadalupe. The establishment of Spain's Florida Settlements is briefly described in John Tracy Ellis, *Catholics in Colonia America* (Baltimore, 1965), and Michael V. Gannon, *The Cross in the Sand: The Early Catholic Church in Florida* (Gainesville, 1965). Bartoloé Barrientos, *Pedro Menéndez de Avilés, Founder of Florida* (Gainesville, 1965), reprints documents describing his activities.

Menéndez's attempts to found interior forts are described in J. G. Johnson, "The Spaniards in Northern Georgia during the Sixteenth Century," *G.H.Q.,* IX (June, 1925), while the beginnings of Port Royal are described in Mary Ross, "Spanish Settlement of Santa Elena," *G.H.Q.,* IX (December, 1925). A thorough account of the founding of St. Augustine and the scattering of outposts through Florida over the next years is in Eugene Lyon, *The Enterprise of Florida: Pedro Menéndez de Avilés and the Spanish Conquest of 1565–1568* (Gainesville, 1976), a book based on sound research and thoughtful interpretation. A statistical analysis of the population of St. Augustine, demonstrating its reliance on Spain for survival, is in Theodore G. Corbett, "Population Structure in Hispanic St. Augustine, 1629–1763," *F.H.Q.,* LIV (January, 1976).

The study of the Spanish mission frontier should begin with Herbert E. Bolton, "The Mission as a Frontier Institution in the Spanish-American Colonies," *A.H.R.* XXIII (October, 1917). The impact of this article on later writing is discussed in John F. Bannon, "The Mission as a Frontier Institution: Sixty Years of Interest and Research," *We.H.Q.,* X (July, 1979). The two standard works on the missions in eastern North America are Herbert E. Bolton and Mary Ross, *The Debatable Land* (Berkeley, 1925), and John T. Lanning, *The Spanish Missions of Georgia* (Chapel Hill, 1935). Paul Quattlebaum, *The Land Called Chicora: The Carolinas under Spanish Rule with French Intrusions, 1520–1670* (Gainesville, 1956), deals with the expansion of Spanish missions into the Carolinas, while Clifford M. Lewis and Albert J. Loomie, *The Spanish Jesuit Mission in Virginia, 1570–1572* (Chapel Hill, 1953), describes the brief expansion into that distant frontier. Two attempts

to expand the mission frontier are the theme of Micheal V. Gannon, "Sebastian Montero, Pioneer American Missionary, 1566–1572," *Ca.H.R.,* LI (October, 1965), which describes an expedition into Orista, and L. A. Vigneras, "A Spanish Discovery of North Carolina," *N.C.H.R.,* XLVI (October, 1969), dealing with a company that moved northward in 1566 under Pedro de Coronas. That the missions were ineffective as agencies of defense and that they were but poorly supported economically, partly because the Franciscans discouraged agriculture as a means of keeping control of their converts, is demonstrated in two articles by Robert A. Matter, "Economic Basis of the Seventeenth-Century Florida Missions," *F.H.Q.,* (July, 1973) and "Missions in the Defense of Spanish Florida, 1566–1710," *F.H.Q.,* LIV (July, 1975). Excellent accounts of mission life as seen through the eyes of several different *visitas* are in two studies by Fred L. Pearson, Jr., "The Florencia Investigations of Spanish Timucua," *F.H.Q.,* LI (October, 1972), which deals with the inspection of Captain Joaquin de Florencia in 1694 and 1695, and "Spanish-Indian Relations in Florida, 1602–1675; Some Aspects of Selected *Visitas*," *F.H.Q.,* LII (January, 1974).

A competent retelling of the story of French invasions of Spain's Florida empire is Charles E. Bennett, *Laudonniere and Fort Caroline: History and Documents* (Gainesville, 1964), with additional documents in the same author's *Three Voyages* (Gainesville, 1975). A briefer summary of the French invasion is in Madele F. Gorman, "Jean Ribault's Colonies in Florida," *F.H.Q.,* XLIV (August, 1965). Paul E. Hoffman, "The Narrow Waters Strategies of Pedro Menéndez," *F.H.Q.,* XLV (July, 1966), explains Spanish strategy; the standard work on the conflict between the two frontiers is Verne E. Chatelain, *The Defences of Spanish Florida, 1565–1763* (Washington, 1941); a brief but reliable version is Henry Folmer, *Franco-Spanish Rivalry in North America, 1542–1763* (Glendale, 1953). Eugene Lyon, "The Captives of Florida," *F.H.Q.,* L (July, 1971), explores the fate of the captives taken in Menéndez's attack on Ribault's force. Aspects of the subject are considered in Mary Ross, "French Intrusions and Indian Uprisings in Georgia and South Carolina, 1577–1580," *G.H.Q.,* VII (September, 1923), J. G. Johnson, "The Yamasee Revolt of 1597 and the Destruction of the Georgia Missions," *G.H.Q.,* VII (March, 1923), Mark F. Boyd, et al., *Here They Once Stood: The Tragic End of the Apalachee Missions* (Gainesville, 1951), and Mary Ross, "The Restoration of the Spanish Missions in Georgia, 1598–1606," *G.H.Q.,* X (September, 1926). Charles W. Spellman, "The 'Golden Age' of the Florida Missions, 1632–1674," *Ca.H.R.,* LI (October, 1965), argues convincingly that this was a period of decline and decay rather than growth, with the mission frontier dying by the 1670s. This viewpoint is bolstered by the findings of James W. Covington, "Apalachee Indians, 1704–1763," *F.H.Q.,* L (April, 1972), which shows how the extermination of this tribe by the English ended the food supply for Spain's missions. A scholarly work by Paul E.Hoffman, *The Spanish Crown and the Defense of the Caribbean, 1535–1585* (Baton Rouge, 1980), demonstrates that Spain's defense system was adequate against the French, but broke down after Drake's raid in 1586; the same author summarizes his findings in "A Study of Florida Defense Costs, 1565–1585: A Quantification of Florida History," *F.H.Q.,* LI (April, 1973), which shows that Florida absorbed 52 per cent of the total sums spent on the defense of the Caribbean. Barbara A. Purdy, "Weapons, Strategies, and Tactics of the Europeans and Indians in Sixteenth- and Seventeenth-Century Florida," *F.H.Q.,* LV (January, 1977), is more a catalogue of weapons used by the Indians than an apprisal of their effectiveness in defense.

France in America. Collected documents on the Cartier voyages are in three volumes edited by H.P. Biggar: *The Precursors of Jacques Cartier* (Ottawa, 1911), *The Voyages of Jacques Cartier* (Ottawa, 1924), and *A Collection of Documents Relating to Jacques Cartier and the Sieur de Roberval* (Ottawa, 1930). The Champlain narratives have been collected in six volumes edited by H.P. Biggar and others, *The Works of Samuel de Champlain* (Toronto, 1922–1936).

Among the secondary works dealing with French expansion, the best and most recent is W.J. Eccles, *The Canadian Frontier, 1534–1760* (New York, 1969), a revisionist work that challenges many long-accepted beliefs. Among earlier histories of the region, none is more readable than Francis Parkman, *Pioneers of France in the New World* (Boston, 1885). William B. Munro, *Crusaders of New France* (New Haven, 1918), deals with the same period, while fuller accounts are in George M. Wrong, *The Rise and Fall of New France,* 2 v. (New York, 1928), and Gustave Lanctot, *A History of Canada,* Vol. I: *From Its Origins to the Royal Regime, 1663* (Cambridge, 1963). A readable and scholarly study of Champlain is Morris Bishop, *Champlain: The Life of Fortitude* (New York, 1948). A chatty sound biography that is Samuel E.

Morison, *Samuel de Champlain: Father of New France* (Boston, 1972), particularly when dealing with the voyages.

Early French exploration is discussed in Lawrence J. Burpee, *The Discovery of Canada* (New York, 1926), and John B. Brebner, *Explorers of North America, 1492–1806* (New York, 1933). The influence of trade on French expansion is described in H. A. Innis, *The Fur Trade in Canada* (New Haven, 1930), and Clarence Vandiveer, *The Fur-Trade and Early Western Exploration* (Cleveland, 1929). The effect of early French activity on the Indians of the St. Lawrence Valley is expertly described in Bernard G. Hoffman, *Cabot to Cartier: Sources for a Historical Ethnography of Northeastern North America, 1497–1550* (Toronto, 1961). Warfare among those tribes in terms of trade rivalry is explored in Bruce G. Trigger, "Trade and Tribal Warfare on the St. Lawrence in the Sixteenth Century," *E.,* IX (Summer, 1962). Cornelius Jaenne, Jr., *Friend and Foe: Aspects of French-Amerindian Cultural Contacts in the Sixteenth and Seventeenth Centuries* (New York, 1976) demonstrates that the deteriorating relationship between the two races was based on deep cultural differences that could not be reconciled.

4 The Southern Frontier, 1600–1700

English Exploration and Settlement. Brilliant accounts of the British voyages that led to the occupation of North America are in Samuel E. Morison, *The European Discovery of America: The Northern Voyages* (New York, 1971), and *The European Discovery of America: The Southern Voyages* (New York, 1974). For a scholarly version of the explorations the two standard works by the great master of the subject are: David B. Quinn, *England and the Discovery of America, 1481–1620: From the Bristol Voyages of the Fifteenth Century to the Pilgrim Settlement of Plymouth* (New York, 1974), and *North America from the Earliest Discovery to the First Settlements* (New York, 1977). A brief overview of the subject is in K. G. Davies, *The North Atlantic World in the Seventeenth Century* (Minneapolis, 1974). A pioneering work that is still useful is James A. Williamson, *The Voyages of the Cabots and English Discovery of North America under Henry VII and Henry VIII* (London, 1929). John T. Juricek, "John Cabot's First Voyage," *Sm.J.H.,* II (Winter, 1967–68), uses recently discovered documents to conclude that Cabot explored both Cape Berton and Newfoundland. Ernest A. Strathmann, *Sir Walter Raleigh* (New York, 1951), is an interpretative biography of a leading promoter of colonization; equally valuable is a newer study by Willard M. Wallace, *Sir Walter Raleigh* (Princeton, 1959). A. L. Rowse, *The Elizabethans and America* (New York, 1959), is a readable interpretation of early English expansion into America.

By far the most useful work on colony planting and expansion in the Southeast is W. Stitt Robinson, *The Southern Colonial Frontier, 1607–1763* (Albuquerque, 1979), a work that expertly synthesizes the vast literature on the subject. Also useful are John E. Pomfret, *Founding the American Colonies, 1583–1660* (New York, 1970), Daniel J. Boorstin, *The Americans: The Colonial Experiment* (New York, 1958), which is an original interpretation, and R.C. Simmons, *The American Colonies: From Settlement to Independence* (New York, 1976), an expert synthesis of the entire period. Colony founding and institutional development are treated fully in such classic works as Charles M. Andrews, *The Colonial Period of American History. The Settlements,* 3 v. (New Haven, 1934–37), and Herbert L. Osgood, *The American Colonies in the Seventeenth Century,* 3 v. (New York, 1904–07). The latter contains chapters on the land system, defense, and Indian relations. Works concerned more specifically with the southern colonies include William E. Dodd, *The Old South, Struggles for Democracy* (New York, 1937), Thomas J. Wertenbaker, *The Old South: The Founding of American Civilization* (New York, 1942), and especially Wesley F. Craven, *The Southern Colonies in the Seventeenth Century* (Baton Rouge, 1949). Thomas J. Wertenbaker, *The First Americans, 1607–1690* (New York, 1927), Louis B. Wright, *The Atlantic Frontier* (New York, 1947), and Louis B. Wright, *The Cultural Life of the American Colonies, 1607–1763* (New York, 1957), deal with social and intellectual life.

Virginia and Maryland. Documentary materials dealing with settlement and expansion are in Lyon G. Tyler, ed., *Narratives of Early Virginia, 1606–1625* (New York, 1907), and Clayton C. Hall, ed., *Narratives of Early Maryland, 1633–1684* (New York, 1910). C. M. Andrews, ed., *Narratives of the Insurrections, 1675–1690* (New York, 1915), contains the records of Bacon's Rebellion. The early history of the Chesapeake colonies is also treated in histories of Virginia and Maryland, of which the latest are Louis D. Rubin, Jr., *Virginia: A Bicentennial History* (New York, 1977), Richard Walsh and William L. Fox,

eds., *Maryland: A History, 1632–1974* (Baltimore, 1974), a fine collaborative work by ten experts, and Carl Bode, *Maryland, A Bicentennial History* (New York, 1978).

The Virginia Colony. Carl Bridenbaugh, *Vexed and Troubled Englishmen, 1590–1642* (New York, 1968), is a highly readable analysis of social conditions in England that does much to explain the eagerness of some to migrate to America. The advertising that attracted their attention to Virginia is appraised in Hugh T. Lefler, "Promotional Literature in the Southern Colonies," *J.S.H.,* XXXIII (February, 1967). Secondary works concerned largely with seventeenth-century Virginia include the first volume of Richard L. Morton, *Colonial Virginia,* 2 v. (Chapel Hill, 1960). Mathew P. Andrews, *The Soul of a Nation: The Founding of Virginia* (New York, 1943), deals in detail with the first twenty years of Virginia history. Two volumes by Philip A. Bruce, *Economic History of Virginia in the Seventeenth Century,* 2 v. (New York, 1910), contain accounts of agricultural development, Indian defense, and the land system. The early settlement of Jamestown has inspired many historical works, of which the best is Carl Bridenbaugh, *Jamestown, 1544–1699* (New York, 1980), a popularly written but scholarly work. Philip L. Barbour, *The Jamestown Voyages under the First Charter, 1606–1609* (Cambridge, 1969), describes and documents the early settlement, while the same author's "The Earliest Reconnaissance of the Chesapeake Bay Area: Captain John Smith's Map and Indian Vocabulary," *V.M.H.B.,* LXXIX (July, 1971), identifies spots visited by the famous explorer. Biographies of that glamorous pioneer include Philip L. Barbour, *The Three Worlds of Captain John Smith* (Boston, 1964), and Alden T. Vaughan, *American Genesis: Captain John Smith and the Founding of Virginia* (Boston, 1975), the latter a readable summary of modern information on the early settlement. The Indian maiden whose name has been so often associated with that of John Smith has been studied in Grace S. Woodward, *Pocahontas* (Norman, 1969), and Philip L. Barbour, *Pocahontas and Her World: A Chronicle of America's First Settlement* (Boston, 1970), both of which throw light on Indian-white relations. Two important revisionist articles by Edmund S. Morgan question earlier authors. In "The Labor Problem at Jamestown, 1607–18," *A.H.R,* LXXVI (June, 1971), Morgan shows that the reluctance of the first settlers to work followed a British pattern and was not due to the company system; in "The First American Boom: Virginia 1618–1630," *W.M.C.O.,* XXVIII (April, 1971), he shows that the colony's problems multiplied rather than diminished with the introduction of private ownership as the rich used their power to hoard food supplies while less fortunate colonists starved. The colony's problems are further explored in Karen O. Kupperman, "Apathy and Death in Early Jamestown," *J.A.H.*, LXVI (June, 1979), which explains the high death rate in the settlement partly in terms of apathy brought on by malnutrition, partly by the psychology of despair that prevailed.

Historians have increasingly seen the 1622 Massacre as a turning point in the colony's history. Before that time Indians were seen as prospective agriculturists and allies; after the massacre they were viewed as fit only for extermination. This is the thesis convincingly developed in Alden T. Vaughan, " 'Expulsion of the Savages'; English Policy and the Massacre of 1622," *W.M.C.Q.*, XXXV (January, 1978), and in Bernard W. Sheehan, *Savagism & Civility: Indians and Englishmen in Colonial Virginia* (Cambridge, 1980). Nicholas P. Canny, "The Ideology of English Colonization: From Ireland to America," *W.M.C.Q.*, XXX (October, 1973), argues cogently that England's experiences in subduing the Irish in the sixteenth century helped convince the colonists that the Indians were an inferior people, fit only for extermination.

On early Maryland Mathew P. Andrews, *The Founding of Maryland* (Baltimore, 1933), has not completely displaced Bernard C. Steiner, *Beginnings of Maryland* (Baltimore, 1903). The findings of these authors have been challenged in Aubrey C. Land, "The Planters of Colonial Maryland," *Ma.H.M.*, LXVII (Summer, 1972), which shows that only 2 per cent of the colony's planters in the seventeenth century were affluent while the remainder lived near the subsistence level. John D. Krygler, "Sir George Calvert's Resignation as Secretary of State and the Founding of Maryland," *Ma.H.M.*, LXVIII (Summer, 1973), shows that Calvert's resignation, and the subsequent founding of Maryland, was for political rather than religious causes.

The agricultural expansion of Virginia and Maryland over the Tidewater awaits a historian, although Thomas P. Abernethy, *Three Virginia Frontiers* (University, 1941), shows the possibility of such a study. Scattered information is in histories of agriculture, from the scholarly work of L. C. Gray, *History of Agriculture in the Southern United States to 1860*. 2 v. (Washington, 1933), to such modern surveys as Willard W. Cochrane, *The Development of American Agriculture: A Historical Analysis* (Minneapolis, 1980). The ev-

olution of farming techniques in the Chesapeake area is expertly studied in Susie M. Ames, *Studies of the Virginia Eastern Shore in the Seventeenth Century* (Richmond, 1940), and Paul G. E. Clemens, *The Atlantic Economy and Colonial Maryland's Eastern Shore* (Ithaca, 1980). Two case studies of communities shed light on the larger problem of agricultural expansion: Paul G. E. Clemens, "The Settlement and Growth of Maryland's Eastern Shore during the English Restoration," *Ma.H.*, V (Fall, 1974), which studies the evolution of Talbot County, and Carville V. Earle, *The Evolution of a Tidewater Settlement System: All Hallow's Parish, Maryland, 1650–1783* (Chicago, 1975). Other historians have investigated aspects of the problem in such studies as: Harold B. Gill, Jr., "Wheat Culture in Colonial Virginia," *A.H.*, LII (July, 1978), showing that wheat was a valuable export crop to the West Indies by the 1730s, Russell R. Menard, "Farm Prices of Maryland Tobacco, 1659–1712," *Ma.H.M.*, LXVIII (Spring, 1973), a valuable listing compiled from estate inventories, and Russell R. Menard, "From Servant to Freeholder: Status Mobility and Property Accumulation in Seventeenth-Century Maryland," *W.M.C.Q.*, XXX (January, 1973), a revealing case study of social mobility in relation to land holdings.

One important expelling force that drove settlers westward is examined in Avery O. Craven, *Soil Exhaustion as a Factor in the Agricultural History of Virginia and Maryland* (Urbana, 1925), while Vertrees J. Wyckoff, *Tobacco Regulation in Colonial Maryland* (Baltimore, 1936), explores another aspect of the same problem.

The effect of the land system on southern expansion still awaits study. A few scholars have demonstrated the rich returns awaiting those who delve into the land office records of Virginia and Maryland: Abbot E. Smith, "The Indentured Servant and Land Speculation in Seventeenth Century Maryland," *A.H.R.*, XL (April, 1935), V.J. Wyckoff, "Land Prices in Seventeenth-Century Maryland," *A.E.R.*, XXVII (March, 1938), V.J. Wyckoff, "The Size of Plantations in Seventeenth-Century Maryland," *Ma.H.M.*, XXXII (December, 1937), and Aubrey C. Land, "A Land Speculator in the Opening of Western Maryland," *Ma.H.M.*, XLVIII (September, 1953).

A volume essential to understanding the relationships between the economy, social structure, and expansion in the early southern colonies is Edmund S. Morgan, *American Slavery-American Freedom* (New York, 1975), a brilliant analysis of the shift from indentured to slave labor, and the effect of this shift on thought and the social structure. Some of Morgan's conclusions are questioned in Virginia Bernhard, "Poverty and the Social Order in Seventeenth-Century Virginia," *V.M.H.B.*, LXXXV (April, 1977). Of comparable importance in understanding the society of the early southern colonies is Thad W. Tate and David L. Ammerman, eds., *The Chesapeake in the Seventeenth Century: Essays on Anglo-American Society* (Chapel Hill, 1980), a series of ten essays by as many experts. Allan Kulikoff, "The Origins of Afro-American Society in Tidewater Maryland and Virginia, 1700–1790," *W.M.C.Q.*, XXXV (April, 1978), shows that a community life among the slaves developed slowly during the 1680–1740 period when a heavy black immigration caused disruptions, only to be revitalized in the 1740–1790 period. An immensely valuable work that provides the best and most accurate estimates of colonial populations between 1623 and 1775 is Robert V. Wells, *The Population of the British Colonies in America before 1776: A Survey of Census Data* (Princeton, 1976). Marcus W. Jernegan, *Laboring and Dependent Classes in Colonial America* (Chicago, 1931), is still valuable for its findings on the relationship between labor conditions and expansion.

The story of Virginia's fur trade and Indian relations remains to be told. A general treatment is in Paul C. Phillips, *The Fur Trade* (Norman, 1961), the first volume of which deals with the early period. More satisfactory is the excellent account of the first massacre in William S. Powell, "Aftermath of the Massacre: The First Indian War, 1622–1632," *V.M.H.B.*, LXVI (January, 1958).

Bacon's Rebellion. The causes of this uprising have long been debated by historians. The older view, set forth by Thomas J. Wertenbaker, *Give Me Liberty: The Struggle for Self-Government in Virginia* (Philadelphia, 1958), held that Bacon was a champion of democratic reform and that his insurrection was a landmark in the history of liberty. This was challenged in Wilcomb E. Washburn, *The Governor and the Rebel: a History of Bacon's Rebellion in Virginia* (Chapel Hill, 1957), which demonstrated that Bacon was primarily interested in killing Indians to obtain their land. This interpretation in turn was questioned by Bernard Bailyn, "Politics and Social Structure in Colonial Virginia," in James M. Smith, ed., *Seventeenth-Century America: Essays in Colonial History* (Chapel Hill, 1959), who traced unrest to the competition of rival elite groups for favor and power within the social order. Warren M. Billings, "The Causes of Bacon's Rebellion: Some Suggestions,"

V.M.H.B., (October, 1970), revealed political instability and deteriorating economy as a cause for dissent and showed that the General Assembly of June, 1676, mirrored popular opinion rather than being radical. Helpful in understanding the social structure are the lectures by Wesley F. Craven, *White, Red, and Black: The Seventeenth Century Virginian* (Charlottesville, 1971). Edmund S. Morgan, "Headrights and Head Counts: A Review Article," *V.M.H.B.*, LXXX (July, 1972), questions Craven's methodology in using headrights to determine the volume of migration, holding that in many cases the rights were not exercised until many years after arrival.

The continuing impulse of the democratic reforms generated by the forces that bred Bacon's rebellion is demonstrated in John C. Rainbolt, "The Alteration in the Relationship between Leadership and Constituents in Virginia, 1660–1720," *W.M.C.Q.*, XXVII (July, 1970). The author demonstrates that in the years after Berkeley's departure the ruling class was frequently subservient to the wishes of the common planters. Wilcomb E. Washburn, "The Effect of Bacon's Rebellion on Government in England and Virginia," *Contributions from the Museum of History and Technology, United States National Museum Bulletin 225* (Washington, 1962), 135–152, argues convincingly that the movement toward self-government in Virginia began not during the rebellion but as a result of the heavy handed actions of the royal commission sent to investigate.

The Carolina Frontier. An excellent history of early North Carolina is Hugh T. Lefler, *Colonial North Carolina: A History* (New York, 1973). South Carolina's beginnings are admirably explored in Eugene M. Sirmans, *Colonial South Carolina: A Political History, 1663–1763* (Chapel Hill, 1966), and Converse D. Clowse, *Economic Beginnings in Colonial South Carolina, 1670-1730* (Columbia, 1971); Louis B. Wright, *South Carolina: A Bicentennial History* (New York, 1976), is brief but excellently written. The earliest promotional activities that lured settlers to Albemarle Sound are described in Lindley S. Butler, "The Early Settlement of Carolina: Virginia's Southern Frontier," *V.M.H.B.*, LXXIX (January, 1971), and the first attempts at settlement detailed in William S. Powell, "Carolina and the Incomparable Roanoke: Explorations and Attempts at Settlement, 1620–1663," *N.C.H.R.*, LI (January, 1974). That the social structure of early North Carolina was based on a small-farmer society is admirably demonstrated in Jacquelyn H. Wold, "Patents and

Tithables in North Carolina, 1663–1729,'' *1607–1763* (New York, 1966). Details on in-
N.C.H.R., LVI (July, 1979). The influence of stitutional and political development in the
migration from Barbados on the class struc- books by Andrews and Osgood cited in the
ture of early South Carolina is explored in previous chapter are essential to understand-
Richard Waterhouse, "England, the Carib- ing the settlement, land system, defense, and
bean, and the Settlement of Carolina, *J.A.S.,* other aspects of New England expansion.
IX (December, 1975). That diseases common Useful also is Thomas J. Wertenbaker, *The*
to swampy areas helped alter the settlement *Puritan Oligarchy* (New York, 1947). Of par-
pattern in the Carolinas is the theme of St. ticular importance to students of the frontier
Julian R. Childs, *Malaria and Colonization in* is Lois K. Mathews, *The Expansion of New*
the Carolina Low Country, 1562–1692 (Balti- *England* (Boston, 1909). R. A. East, "Puri-
more, 1940). That the quitrent system was tanism and Settlement," *N.E.Q.,* XVII (June,
largely ineffective in raising revenue is dem- 1944), deals with the expelling effect of reli-
onstrated in Alan D. Watson, "The Quitrent gious conflicts, as does Emery Battis, *Saints*
System in Royal South Carolina," *W.M.C.Q.,* *and Sectaries: Anne Hutchinson and the An-*
XXXIII (April, 1976), while Robert K. Aker- *tinomian Controversy in the Massachusetts*
man, *South Carolina Colonial Land Policies* *Bay Colony* (Chapel Hill, 1962). That Anne
(Columbia, 1977), shows that the land policy Hutchinson was motivated by the frustations
under the proprietors and royal government arising from life in a completely male-domi-
was effective in encouraging settlement and nated society is the theme of Lyle Koegler,
discouraging speculation. "The Case of the American Jezebels: Anne
  The most informative history of the Car- Hutchinson and Female Agitation during the
olina fur trade and the conflicts that it bred Years of Antinomian Turmoil, 1636–1640,"
with Spain is Verner W. Crane, *The Southern* *W.M.C.Q.,* XXXI (January, 1974).
Frontier, 1670–1732 (Durham, 1928). Other   **Studies of Specific Colonies.** A useful ac-
aspects of the international struggle on the count of early Plymouth is George F. Willison,
southern borderland are considered in Herbert *Saints and Strangers* (New York, 1945). More
E. Bolton and Mary Ross, *The Debatable* thorough, particularly in tracing relations with
Land (Berkeley, 1925), and J. G. Johnson, England, is George D. Langdon, Jr., *Pilgrim*
"The Spanish Period of Georgia and South *Colony: A History of New Plymouth, 1620–1691*
Carolina History, 1566–1702," *University of* (New Haven, 1966). A ground-breaking study
Georgia Bulletin, XXIII (May, 1923). Two that helps explain the nature of Pilgrim society
histories of one of the leading tribes involved is John Demos, *A Little Commonwealth: Fam-*
have been written; Mrs. Douglas S. Brown, *ily Life in Plymouth Colony* (New York, 1970).
The Catawba Indians: The People of the River Less original, but still a competent picture of
(Columbia, 1966), is encyclopedic; Charles M. the colony's economic life, is Darrett B. Rut-
Hudson, *The Catawba Nation* (Athens, 1970), man, *Husbandmen of Plymouth: Farms and*
adds little to the story but is brief and well *Villages in the Old Colony* (Boston, 1967).
documented. James W. Covington, "Apala- Michael Zuckerman, "Pilgrims in the Wilder-
chee Indians, 1704–1763," *F.H.Q.,* L (April, ness: Community, Modernity, and the May-
1972), explores the fate of the tribe after its pole at Merry Mount," *N.E.Q.,* L (June,
devastation by forces under Governor James 1977), speculates that the Pilgrims disliked
Moore. The trade in whitetail deer hides, Morton and his fellow-traders not because of
which centered in Savannah and Charlestown, their competition, but because they personified
is admirably described in Don LaFave, "Time the authoritarianism of England that they were
of the Whitetail: The Charles Town Indian trying to escape.
Trade, 1690–1715," *St.H.S.,* V (Fall, 1973).   Among the many books on the early de-
A sketchy account of the expansion of the velopment of the Massachusetts Bay Colony
Charles Town trade into Alabama is Louis R. the most useful is Benjamin W. Labaree, *Co-*
Smith, Jr., "British-Indian Trade in Alabama, *lonial Massachusetts: A History* (Millwood,
1670–1756," *A.R.,* XXVII (January, 1974). 1979). The beginnings of one of the earliest
settlements are described in Richard P. Gild-
rie, *Salem, Massachusetts, 1626–1683: A Cov-*

5   The Northern Frontier,

1600–1700

enant Community (Charlottesville, 1975), while
Darrett B. Rutman, *Winthrop's Boston: Por-*
trait of a Puritan Town, 1630–1649 (Chapel
Hill, 1965) analyzes the economic and social

  The Settlement of New England. A good developments in Boston during its pioneer
general account is in John E. Pomfret, *Found-* period. Helpful biographies include: Samuel
ing the American Colonies, 1583–1600 (New E. Morison, *Builders of the Bay Colony* (Bos-
York, 1970), but far more specific is Douglas ton, 1930), Lawrence S. Mayo, *John Ende-*
E. Leach, *The Northern Colonial Frontier,*

cott: A Biography (Cambridge, 1936), and Frances Rose-Troup, *John White* (New York, 1930).

Recent scholarship dealing with Massachusetts has used statistical techniques to analyze the social structure and voting patterns. One such study, Philip J. Greven, Jr., *Four Generations: Population, Land and Family in Colonial Andover, Massachusetts* (Ithaca, 1970), reveals the surprising longevity and fertility of early generations in contrast with later comers. Michael Zuckerman, *Peaceable Kingdoms: New England Towns in the Eighteenth Century* (New York, 1970), argues that town governments assumed more and more authority at the expense of the central government during the seventeenth century. His thesis is disputed by David G. Allen, "The Zuckerman Thesis and the Process of Legal Rationalization in Provincial Massachusetts," *W.M.C.Q.*, XXIX (July, 1972). Edward M. Cook, Jr., *The Fathers of the Towns: Leadership and Community Structure in Eighteenth Century New England* (Baltimore, 1976), analyzes the leadership structure in seventy-four New England towns in the post-pioneer period to find that elite groups were most strongly established in older communities; a statistical study of one community, Stephen Innes, "Land Tenancy and Social Order in Springfield, Massachusetts, 1652–1702," *W.M.C.Q.*, XXXV (January, 1978), reveals that one third of the residents were renters with a resulting class stratification. Two stimulating articles by T. H. Breen and Stephen Foster, "Moving to the New World: The Character of the Early Massachusetts Immigration," *W.M.C.Q.*, XXX (April, 1973) and "The Puritans' Greatest Achievement: A Study of Social Cohesion in Seventeenth-Century Massachusetts," *J.A.H.*, LX (June, 1973), show that the nuclear family was the normal unit of settlement, helping explain the social stability that prevailed, and that the resulting town structure was sufficiently authoritarian to maintain this stability. T. H. Breen, "Persistent Localism: English Social Change and the Shaping of New England Institutions," *W.M.C.Q.*, XXXII (January, 1975), ascribees many of the institutions of early New England to the enduring conflict in England between religious factions rather than to the unique qualities of Puritanism, an important revisionist interpretation. The physical life of early Bostonians as shaped by their living conditions is admirably described in Carl Bridenbaugh, "Yankee Use and Abuse of the Forest in the Building of New England, 1620–1660," *M.H.S., Proceedings*, LXXXIX (1977).

Since the publication of Robert E. Brown, *Middle Class Democracy and the Revolution in Massachusetts* (Ithaca, 1955), scholars have argued over the degree of voter participation in Massachusetts politics. The early stages of this controversy are admirably summarized in Bernard Bailyn, *The Origins of American Politics* (New York, 1968). Brown's contention that the poiltical base was steadily broadened to bring virtual democracy has been challenged and supported. Kenneth A. Lockridge, *A New England Town the First Hundred Years. Dedham, Massachusetts, 1636–1736* (New York, 1970), holds that the basis of political power shifted from the selectmen to the town meeting after the passing of the first generation. Similarly Robert E. Wall, Jr., "The Massachusetts Bay Colony Franchise in 1627," *W.M.C.Q.*, XXVII (January, 1970), shows that by 1647 in most towns 50 per cent of the adult males could vote, while Richard C. Simmons, "Godliness, Property, and the Franchise in Puritan Massachusetts: An Interpretation," *J.A.H.*, LV (December, 1968), holds that after 1664 political rights were generally held not only by church members but by most propertied classes. On the other hand Timothy H. Breen, "Who Governs: The Town Franchise in Seventeenth-Century Massachusetts," *W.M.C.Q.*, XXVII (July, 1970), shows that social and legal limitations kept far more people from the polls than had been assumed. This is also the conclusion of Michael Zuckerman, "The Social Context of Democracy in Massachusetts," *W.M.C.Q.*, XXV (October, 1968), which intelligently appraises the literature on the subject to that time.

The westward movement into the Connecticut Valley is admirably described in Albert E. Van Dusen, *Puritans Against the Wilderness: Connecticut History to 1763* (Chester, 1975), and Robert J. Taylor, *Colonial Connecticut: A History* (Millwood, 1979). Robert C. Black III, *The Younger John Winthrop* (New York, 1966), is a competent biography of the founder of Saybrook and New London, while Frank Shuffelton, *Thomas Hooker, 1586–1647* (Princeton, 1977), deals expertly with this important pioneer. Harral Ayres, *The Great Trail of New England* (Boston, 1940), traces the routes followed in migrations to the Connecticut Valley. The standard work on the New Haven colony is Isabel M. Calder, *The New Haven Colony* (New Haven, 1934). The early history of the Connecticut colony is best told in Mary J. A. Jones, *Congregational Commonwealth: Connecticut, 1636–1662* (Middletown, 1968), which describes the migration but is largely concerned with the interlocking governmental-religious structure. That New Haven strongly supported Oliver Cromwell and was handsomely rewarded during the Commonwealth interlude is deomonstrated in Francis J. Bremer, "The New Haven Colony and Oliver Cromwell," *C.H.S.B.*, XXXVIII (July, 1973). The social structure of Connecticut towns has attracted recent historical study. Among the results are: Linda A. Bissell, "From One Generation to Another: Mobility in Seventeenth-Century Windsor, Connecticut," *W.M.C.Q.*, XXXI (January, 1974), which argues that the large amount of land discouraged mobility; Estelle F. Feinstein, *Stamford from Puritan to Patriot: The Shaping of a Connecticut Community* (Stamford, 1976), which is principally valuable for its use of local materials, and Bruce C. Daniels, *The Connecticut Town: Growth and Development, 1635–1790* (Middletown, 1979), which admirably synthesizes modern research on New England towns. Richard L. Bushman, *From Puritan to Yankee: Character and the Social Order, 1690–1765* (Cambridge, 1967), shows that rising economic ambitions shattered the world of order and piety that had been inherited from the seventeenth century.

Expansion southward from the Massachusetts Bay Colony is brilliantly portrayed in Carl Bridenbaugh, *Fat Mutton and Liberty of Conscience: Society in Rhode Island, 1636–1690,* (Providence, 1974). Two other modern histories of the colony also have much information: Sydney V. James, *Colonial Rhode Island: A History* (New York, 1975), and william G. McLoughlin, *Rhode Island: A Bicentennial History* (New York, 1978). A meticulous study of one area in Rhode Island is Carl W. Woodward, *Plantation in Yankeeland: The Story of Cocumscussoc, Mirror of Colonial Rhode Island* (Chester, 1972). Biographies of Rhode Island's founder also contain essential information; of these the latest and best is Edmund S. Morgan, *Roger Williams: The Church and the State* (New York, 1967), although S. H. Brockunier, *The Irrepressible Democrat: Roger Williams* (New York, 1940), is still useful. The wanderings of another Rhode Island pioneer are described in Kenneth W. Porter, "Samuell Gorton. New England Firebrand," *N.E.Q.*, VII (March, 1934). The role of Indians in shaping Roger Williams' beliefs is the theme of Jack L. Davis, "Roger Williams among the Narragansetts," *N.E.Q.*, XLIII (December, 1970). Joel A. Cohen, "Democracy in Revolutionary Rhode Island: A Statistical Analysis," *R.I.H.* (Winter & Spring, 1970), concludes that elitist Whig groups controlled the colonial government.

Expansion into northern New England is expertly and delightfully traced in Charles E. Clark, *The Eastern Frontier: The Settlement of Northern New England, 1610–1763* (New

York, 1970). The same author's *Maine: A Bicentennial History* (New York, 1977), deals briefly with the early occupation. Edwin A. Churchill, "The Founding of Maine, 1600–1640: A Revisionist Interpretation," *M.H.S.Q.*, XVIII (Summer, 1978), argues that no fishermen settled the coast before 1660, while the operations of a Massachusetts-based speculative company responsible for Maine's early occupation are expertly examined in Gordon E. Kershaw, *'Gentlemen of Large Property and Judicious Men': The Kennebeck Proprietors, 1749–1775* (Sommersworth, 1975). A massive and ill-digested study of another aspect of expansion northward from Massachusetts is David E. Van Deventer, *The Emergence of Provincial New Hampshire 1623–1741* (Baltimore, 1976); brief and interpretive is Elizabeth F. and Elting B. Morison, *New Hampshire: A Bicentennial History* (New York, 1976).

Any study of the Middle Colonies should begin with Van Cleaf Bachman, *Peltries or Plantations: The Economic Policies of the Dutch West India Company in New Netherland, 1623–1629* (Baltimore, 1969), a work of sound scholarship on the changing economic ambitions of the company, and Thomas J. Condon, *New York Beginnings: The Comerical Origins of New Netherland* (New York, 1968), which admirably describes the shift from a trading-post to a colonial philosophy. Briefer, but containing usable summaries, are the accounts of settlement in the many histories of the colonies involved. Among these, the most recent and useful are: A. C. Flick, ed., *History of the State of New York,* 10 v. (New York, 1932–37); Michael Kamman, *Colonial New York: A History* (New York, 1975); Philip S. Klein and Ari Hoggenboom, *A History of Pennsylvania* (New York, 1973); Joseph E. Illick, *Colonial Pennsylvania: A History* (New York, 1976); Thomas C. Cochran, *Pennsylvania: A Bicentennial History* (New York, 1978); John E. Pomfret, *Colonial New Jersey: A History* (New York, 1973); Thomas Fleming, *New Jersey: A Bicentennial History* (New York, 1977); Peter O. Wacker, *Land and People: A Cultural Geography of Preindustrial New Jersey* (New Brunswick, 1975), an excellent study by a geographer showing the evolution of settlement patterns; John A. Munroe, *Colonial Delaware: A History* (Millwood, 1979); and the several biographies of William Penn that stress his role as Pennsylvania's founder, Harry E. Wildes, *William Penn* (New York, 1974), a factual record lacking in interpretation, Gary B. Nash, *Quakers and Politics* (New York,

1968), Joseph E. Illick, *William Penn the Politician: His Relations with the English Government* (Ithaca, 1965), Edwin B. Bronner, *William Penn's 'Holy Experiment': The Founding of Pennsylvania, 1681–1701* (New York, 1962), and Mary M. Dunn, *William Penn: Politics and Conscience* (Princeton, 1967). A searching study of the social and economic development of the early Middle Colonies is Carl Bridenbaugh, "The Old and New Societies of the Delaware Valley in the Seventeenth Century," *P.M.H.B.,* C (April, 1976).

The early Dutch and Swedish settlements have been extensively studied. The Swedish occupation of the Delaware Valley is exhaustively studied in Amandus Johnson, *The Swedish Settlements on the Delaware, 1638–1664,* 2 v. (New York, 1911), and more readably in Christopher Ward, *The Dutch and Swedes on the Delaware, 1609–64* (Philadelphia, 1930). Evelyn Page, "The First Frontier—The Swedes and Dutch," *P.H.,* XV (October, 1948), provides proof of the environmental impact on these colonies. A thorough treatment of the Dutch settlements is in C. A. Weslager, *Dutch Explorers, Traders, and Settlers in the Delaware Valley, 1609–1664* (Philadelphia, 1961); briefer and less thoroughly researched are the accounts in Gerald F. DeJong, *The Dutch in America, 1609–1974* (Boston, 1975), and Henry Van der Zee and Barbara Van der Zee, *A Sweet and Alien Land: The Story of Dutch New York,* (New York, 1978).

Modern views on the system of patroonship are found in such works as Oliver A. Rink, "Company Management or Private Trade: The Two Patroonship Plans for New Netherland," *N.Y.H.,* LIX (January, 1978), which shows that the proprietors had planned to establish the patroon system as early as 1628, and Donna Merwick, "Dutch Townsmen and Land Use: A Spatial Perspective on Seventeenth-Century Albany, New York," *W.M.C.Q.,* XXXI (January, 1980), which explains that the Dutch, in contrast with the English, were more interested in town-living and trade than in landed estates. Harry M. Ward, *The United Colonies of New England, 1643–90* New York, 1961), is a solid work on the reaction of New England to the Dutch threat. The first well-documented history of a basic event in the rivalry is Ronald D. Cohen, "The Hartford Treaty of 1650: Anglo-Dutch Cooperation in the Seventeenth Century," *N.Y.H.S.Q.,* LIII (October, 1969). Philip J. Schwartz, *The Jarring Interests: New York's Boundary Maker, 1664–1776* (Albany,

1979), expertly explores the settlement of boundary disputes with other colonies after the conquest of New York by England.

The New England Land System. The origin of the town system of settlement is explained in John F. Sly, *Town Government in Massachusetts (1620–1930)* (Cambridge, 1930). Important studies that throw light on the land system within the towns are Roy H. Akagi, *The Town Proprietors of the New England Colonies* (Philadelphia, 1924), Florence M. Woodard, *The Town Proprietors in Vermont* (New York, 1936), and William Haller, *The Puritan Frontier: Town-Planting in New England Colonial Development, 1630–1660* (New York, 1951). The latter reveals the diversified motives that led to town planting. A model case study of Sudbury, Massachusetts, is Sumner C. Powell, *Puritan Village: The Formation of a New England Town* (Middletown, 1963). The emergence of speculative activity in Maine, Rhode Island, and the Middle Colonies still awaits study.

Indians and the Fur Trade. No subjects in colonial history deserve investigation more than the fur trade, Indian relations, and defense. The first volume of Paul C. Phillips, *The Fur Trade,* 2 v. (Norman, 1961), deals generally with the trade and serves to illustrate the need for additional research. Francis X. Moloney, *The Fur Trade in New England, 1620–1676* (Cambridge, 1931), is thoughtful but brief; Arthur H. Buffinton, "New England and the Western Fur-Trade, 1629–1675", *C.S.M., Publications,* XVIII (Boston, 1917), deals only with international conflicts arising from the trade. A comprehensive work is needed, as well as special studies of phrases and leaders. Daniel S. Updike, *Richard Smith: First English Settler of the Narragansett Country, Rhode Island* (Boston, 1937), shows the possibility of the latter type of work.

The Puritan attitude toward the Indian underlay both the fur trade and white-native relations. Some light is shed on Puritan prejudices in Peter N. Carroll, *Puritanism and the Wilderness: The Intellectual Significance of the New England Frontier, 1629–1700* (New York, 1969), a work that explores the way in which the Puritan viewed the wilderness around him. More useful is the penetrating analysis of the Puritans' image of the Indian, showing their sense of decency and concern, in Alden T. Vaughan, *New England Frontier: Puritans and Indians, 1620–1675* (Boston, 1965), G. E. Thomas, "Puritans, Indians, and the Concept of Race," *N.E.Q.,* XLVIII (March, 1975), argues on the other hand that the Puritans were racists and followed policies designed to exterminate the Indians. Their failure to understand the function of the Indian shamans, and the effect of this misunderstanding on relations between the races, is the theme of Frank Shuffelton, "Indian Devils and Pilgrim Fathers: Squanto, Hobomok, and the English Conception of Indian Religion," *N.E.Q.,* XLIX (March, 1976). Lloyd C. M. Hare, *Thomas Mayhew, Patriarch to the Indians* (New York, 1932), deals with Puritan mission efforts, as does the sensitive biography by Ola E. Winslow, *John Eliot, 'Apostle to the Indians'* (Boston, 1928), Neal Salisbury, "Red Puritans: The 'Praying Indians' of Massachusetts Bay and John Eliot," *W.M.C.Q.,* XXXI (January, 1974), argues on the other hand that the missionaries deliberately upset the Indians' cultural patterns to force them to adopt the ways of civilization. The successful efforts of one tribe to adapt to the needs of their conquerors is described in Timothy J. Sehr's excellent "Ninigret's Tactics of Accommodation—Indian Diplomacy in New England, 1637–1675," *R.I.H.,* XXXVI (May, 1977). Of major importance in understanding the relations between the Iroquois and Dutch and English settlers in New York is Allen W. Trelease, *Indian Affairs in Colonial New York: The Seventeenth Century* (Ithaca, 1960). The author maintains that the Iroquois wars were caused not by that tribe's determination to serve as middlemen between Europeans and Great Lakes Indians, but because they wanted new hunting grounds and to rob their neighbors of furs. Books on the militia system and on defense are needed.

More attention has been paid to the Indian wars. A usable account of the first major struggle is Howard Bradstreet, *The Story of the War with the Pequots, Re-Told* (New Haven, 1933); this should be balanced by Alden T. Vaughan, "Pequots and Puritans: The Causes of the War of 1637," *W.M.C.Q.,* XXI (April, 1964), which lays hostilities to the quarrelsome nature of the Indians rather than to Puritan land hunger. Kenneth M. Morrison, "The Basis of Colonial Law: English Paranoia and the Abenaki Arena of King Philip's War, 1675–1678," *N.E.Q.,* LIII (September, 1980), finds the Indians driven to war by unresolved tensions among the colonists. Douglas E. Leach, *Flintlock and Tomahawk: New England in King Philip's War* (New York, 1958), is an excellent survey that thoroughly covers that important subject. Leach has edited a useful contemporary account of the war in *A Rhode Islander Reports on King Philip's War* (Providence, 1963). The way in which Cotton Mather used the war to increase his own power in Massachusetts in described in Anne

K. Nelson, "King Philip's War and the Hubbard-Mather Rivalry," *W.M.C.Q.,* XXVIII (October, 1970), while Richard R. Johnson, "The Search for a Useable Indian: An Aspect of the Defense of Colonial New England," *J.A.H.,* LXIV (December, 1977), examines the methods by which the Puritans used divisions among the Indians to their advantage during the war. Kathryn Whitford, "Hannah Dustin: The Judgment of History," *E.I.H.C.,* CVIII (October, 1972), examines the manner in which that well-known story of the war has changed over the years to reflect changing attitudes toward the Native Americans.

Seven narratives illustrating the manner in which the Puritans' views of Indians changed as a result of King Philip's war are assembled in Richard Slotkin and James K. Folson, eds., *So Dreadful a Judgment: Puritan Response to King Philip's War, 1676–1677* (Middletown, 1978). That many Narragansett warriors survived the struggle demonstrated in Paul R. Campbell and Glenn W. LaFantasie, "Scattered to the Winds of Heaven—Narragansett Indians, 1676–1880," *R.I.H.,* XXXVII (August, 1978), while John A. Sainsbury, "Indian Labor in Early Rhode Island," *N.E.Q.,* XLVIII (September, 1975), examines the menial tasks to which the defeated red men were subjected after the war.

6   The Old West, 1700–1763

General Works. Frederick Jackson Turner, "The Old West," *The Frontier in American History* (New York, 1920), is the best comprehensive account, although fuller information on the land system, fur trade, defense, and colonial wars is in Herbert L. Osgood, *American Colonies in the Eighteenth Century,* 4 v. (New York, 1924–25). The period is expertly surveyed in Wesley F. Craven, *The Colonies in Transition, 1660–1713* (New York, 1968).

Exploration and Settlement of the Piedmont. Harry R. Merrens, "Historical Geography and Early American History," *W.M.C.Q.,* XXII (October, 1965), reveals that the concept of the Appalachians as a barrier has been exaggerated. The standard work on exploration is Clarence W. Alvord and Lee Bidgood, *The First Explorations of the Trans-Allegheny Region by the Virginians, 1650–1674* (Cleveland, 1912). This should be supplemented with Lyman Carrier, "The Veracity of John Lederer," *W.M.C.Q.,* XIX (October, 1939). Leonidas Dodson, *Alexander Spotswood, Governor of Colonial Virginia, 1710–1732* (Philadelphia, 1932), explores the career of a leading advocate of expansion. Delma R. Carpenter, "The Route Followed by Governor Spotswood in 1716 Across the Blue Ridge Mountains," *V.M.H.B.*, LXXIII (October, 1965), traces and maps the route followed on a principal exploring expedition. A revisionist study showing that Edward Bland's party explored the region southwest of Virginia, not to the westward as has been assumed, is Alan V. Briceland, "The Search for Edward Bland's New Britain," *V.M.H.B.*, LXXXVII (April, 1979).

Information on the westward movement from Virginia and the Carolinas is scattered. Three studies by Robert D. Mitchell illuminate the migration from Virginia: "The Shenandoah Valley Frontier," *A.A.A.G.*, LXII (September, 1972), an excellent account of the three migratory streams into that frontier area, "Content and Context: Tidewater Characteristics in the Shenandoah Valley," *Ma. H.*, V (Fall, 1974), an analysis of the similarities and differences of the parent and new societies, and *Commercialism and Frontier: Perspectives on the Early Shenandoah Valley* (Charlottesville, 1977), a masterful survey of the entire settlement. Paula H. Anderson-Green, "The New River Frontier Settlement on the Virginia-North Carolina Border, 1760–1820," *V.M.H.B.*, LXXXVI (October, 1978), shows that "plain folk" predominated among the pioneers. Two competent accounts of expansion westward from North Carolina are: Harry R. Merrens, *Colonial North Carolina in the Eighteenth Century: A Study in Historical Geography* (Chapel Hill, 1964), a challenging study by a geographer, and Robert W. Ramsey, *Carolina Cradle: Settlement of the Northwest Carolina Frontier, 1747–1762* (Chapel Hill, 1965). The latter is a detailed study of the southern Piedmont, and especially of Rowan County. Robert I. Meriwether, *The Expansion of South Carolina, 1729–1765* (Kingsport, 1941), is valuable, although poorly digested. A well-researched local study that is broader than its title implies is Thomas H. Pope, *The History of Newberry County, South Carolina, Volume I, 1749–1860* (Columbia, 1973). A painstakingly researched biography of the governor who served between the Yamassee War and 1719, and again between 1730 and 1735 is Richard P. Sherman, *Robert Johnson: Proprietare & Royal Governor of South Carolina* (Columbia, 1967). An important study showing that ranching in the usual sense developed in the Old West only on the South Carolina frontier is Gary S. Dunbar, "Colonial Carolina Cowpens," *A.H.*, XXXV (July, 1961).

The Middle Colonies. Useful for an understanding of the New York frontier is Ruth

L. Higgins, *Expansion in New York with Especial Reference to the Eighteen Century* (Columbus, 1931). A traditional story of the New York land system is Charles W. Spencer, "The Land System of Colonial New York," *N.Y.S.H.A. Proceedings,* XVI (1917), but this must be supplemented with the revisionist volume by Sung Bok Kim, *Landlord and Tenant in Colonial New York: Manorial Society, 1664–1775* (Chapel Hill, 1978), which shows that tenants were generally sufficiently prosperous to be satisfied, and that the rebellions of 1766 were sparked by the demands of land-hungry speculators from outside the colony. This view is substantiated by a case study of a German immigrant who arrived in 1636, Morton Wagman, "The Rise of Pieter Claessen Wyckoff: Social Mobility on the Colonial Frontier," *N.Y.H,* LIII (January, 1972). More general but valuable is Edith M. Fox, *Land Speculation in the Mohawk Valley* (Ithaca, 1949). The current belief among historians that large land-holders made few profits and contributed much to the expansion of the settlements is bolstered by the study of one such New York group in Armand La Potin, "The Minisink Grant: Partnerships, Patents, and Processing Fees in Eighteenth Century New York," *N.Y.H.,* LVI (January, 1975).

An excellent study of an early Pennsylvania frontier by a geographer is James T. Lemon, *The Best Poor Man's Country: A Geographic Study of Early Southeastern Pennsylvania* (Baltimore, 1972), which traces population movements and urban trends. An older work, marred by its ill-digested information but still useful on migration into the Susquehanna Valley of Pennsylvania is Charles A. Hanna, *The Wilderness Trail,* 2 v. (New York, 1911), but this must be supplemented by Gary B. Nash, "The Quest for the Susquehanna Valley: New York, Pennsylvania, and the Seventeenth-Century Fur Trade," *N.Y.H.,* XLVIII (January, 1967), which describes Penn's attempt to secure the valley. Three articles by Francis Jennings deal with the treatment of the Indians of western Pennsylvania: "The Indian Trade of the Susquehanna Valley," *A.P.S., Proceedings,* CX (December, 1966), an excellent study describing the trade and attempted settlement between 1682 and 1732, "The Scandalous Indian Policy of William Penn's Sons: Deeds and Documents of the Walking Purchase," *P.H.,* XXXVII (January, 1970), a careful examination of the ethics of the Walking Purchase, and "Incident at Tulpehocken," *P.H.,* XXXV (October, 1968), dealing with the illegal use of Indian lands by James Logan after Penn's death. The best biography of Logan is Frederick B. Tolles, *James Logan and the Culture of Colonial Pennsylvania* (Boston, 1957). Errol T. Elliott, *Quakers on the American Frontier* (Richmond, 1969), traces the establishment of individual new meetings to show their role in the peopling of interior Pennsylvania and the West. Specialized studies that throw light on Pennsylvania expansion are: Jerome H. Wood, Jr., *Pennyslvania Crossroads: Lancaster, Pennsylvania, 1730–1790* (Harrisburg, 1979), an excellent example of the manner in which the study of a community can illuminate the history of a region, and Charles Morrison, "Early Land Grants and Settlers along Patterson Creek," *W.V.H.,* XL (Winter, 1979), a detailed study of surveys and land grants. Marvin F. Russell, "Thomas Barton and Pennsylvania's Colonial Frontier," *P.H.,* XLVI is an able biographical sketch of a prominent frontiersman.

The best work on early German migration to the Middle Colonies is Walter A. Knittle, *Early Eighteenth Century Palatine Emigration* (Philadelphia, 1937), which deals with immigration to New York, 1708–10. The history of the Palatines in Pennsylvania is treated in Ralph Wood, ed., *The Pennsylvania Germans* (Princeton, 1942). The German advance into the Great Valley is the theme of John W. Wayland, *The German Element of the Shenandoah Valley of Virginia* (Charlottesville, 1907). Homer T. Rosenberger, "Migrations of the Pennsylvania Germans to Western Pennsylvania," *W.P.H.M.,* LIII (October, 1970, and January, 1971), is antiquarian, but does trace several families to the West. The diary kept by one migrant is the basis of a case study by Theodore Thayer, "An Eighteenth-Century Farmer and Pioneer: Sylvanus Seely's Early Life in Pennsylvania," *P.H.,* XXXV (January, 1968).

Ian C. C. Graham, *Colonists from Scotland: Emigration to North America, 1707–1783* (Ithaca, 1956), is an admirable study of Scotch-Irish migration and settlement; a more limited treatment is in R. J. Dickson, *Ulster Immigration to Colonial America, 1718–1775* (New York, 1966). Material on economic conditions inducing migration is in E. R. R. Green, "Scotch-Irish Emigration: An Imperial Problem," *W.P.H.M.,* XXXV (December, 1952). The same author has edited an excellent volume of essays dealing with aspects of the migration, *Essays in Scotch-Irish History* (New York, 1969). A valuable work tracing the migrations of the Scotch-Irish is James G. Leyburn, *The Scotch-Irish: A Social History* (Chapel Hill, 1962). Studies of the westward migration of particular groups of Scotch-Irish within America include : E. R. R. Green,

"Queensborough Township: Scotch-Irish Emigration and the Expansion of Georgia, 1763–1776," *W.M.C.Q.,* XVII (April, 1960), Charles W. Bryan, Jr., "Morgan Bryan, Pioneer on the Opequon and Yadkin," *V.M.B.H.,* LXX (April, 1962), and Hubertis M. Cummings, *Scots Breed and Susquehanna* (Pittsburgh, 1964), the latter a history of the Scotch-Irish who settled along the Susquehanna River. A geographer traces this movement by studying church locations between 1730 and 1790 in Robert D. Mitchell, "The Presbyterian Church as an Indicator of Westward Expansion in 18th Century America," *Professional Geographer,* XVIII (September, 1966).

Settlement of the New England Back Country. In addition to the works cited in Chapter V, James T. Adams, *Revolutionary New England, 1691–1776* (Boston, 1923), is helpful. The works of Akagi and Woodard on the land system deal also with the eighteenth century. Expansion into western Connecticut is studied in Albert L. Olson, *Agricultural Economy and Population in Eighteenth-Century Connecticut* (New Haven, 1935), and into Vermont in Matt B. Jones, *Vermont in the Making, 1750–1777* (Cambridge, 1939) and Charles M. Thompson, *Independent Vermont* (Boston, 1942). The traditional story of the notorious New Hampshire Grants is challenged in John F. Looney, "Benning Wentworth's Land Policy: A Reappraisal," *Historical N.H.,* XXIII (Spring, 1968), and Allan R. Raylond, "Benning Westworth's Claims in the New Hampshire-New York Boundary Controversy: A Case of Twenty-Twenty Hindsight," *V.H.,* XLIII (Winter, 1975). The conflict between New York and Massachusetts over their borders is described in Oscar Handlin, "The Eastern Frontier of New York," *N.Y.H.,* XVIII (January, 1937). Julian Boyd, *The Susquehanna Company: Connecticut's Experiment in Expansion* (New Haven, 1935), describes attempted expansion into Pennsylvania. The lure of land speculation among New Englanders is demonstrated by Theodore B. Lewis, "Land Speculation and the Dudley Council of 1686," *W.M.C.Q.,* which shows that many leading men in Massachusetts were eager to serve on the Council for New England, a royal agency that had revoked the colony's charter, simply because of the opportunity for speculation that the post provided.

Significance of the Old West. Theodore Roosevelt, *The Winning of the West,* 6 v. (New York, 1889), is a classic description of social life, while Thomas J. Wertenbaker, *The Founding of American Civilization. The Middle Colonies* (New York, 1938), stresses foreign contributions. A modern account of life in the back country is D. Huger Bacot, "The South Carolina Up Country at the End of the Eighteenth Century," *A.H.R.*, XXVIII (July, 1923). The evolution of a distinctive frontier architecture is traced in C. A. Weslager, *The Log Cabin in America* (New Brunswick, 1969). Studies of the evolution of the frontier's chief weapon are in John G. Dillin, *The Kentucky Rifle* (Washington, 1924), and Felix Reichmann, "The Pennsylvania Rifle: A Social Interpretation of Changing Military Techniques," *P.M.H.B.*, XLIX (January, 1945), while James C. King, "The Frontier Gunsmith and Indian Relations," *W.P.H.M.*, L (January, 1967), describes how the Indians became dependent on the gunsmiths to repair weapons furnished them. Another frontier artifact that was developed in the Old West is described in Michael J. Herrick, "The Conestoga Wagon of Pennsylvania," *W.P.H.M.*, LI (April, 1968).

An excellent introduction to the conflicts within the colonies during the eighteenth century is George R. Adams, "The Carolina Regulators: A Note on Changing Interpretations," *N.C.H.R.*, XLIX (October, 1972), which summarizes the extensive literature and changing interpretations. Brooke Hindle, "The March of the Paxton Boys," *W.M.C.Q.*, III (October, 1946), is the best account of this uprising, although the literature collected in John R. Dunbar, ed., *The Paxton Boys* (The Hague, 1957), throws additional light on the subject. So also does the collection of modern writings edited by Wilbur R. Jacobs, *The Paxton Riots and Frontier Theory* (Chicago, 1967). Hubertis M. Cummings, "The Paxton Killings," *J.P.H.*, XLIV (December, 1966), comes to the conclusion that the killings were justified by the treatment received by Presbyterian frontiersmen during the war. That religious divisions rather than class or sectional underlay the Paxton uprising is cogently argued in Peter A. Butzin, "Politics, Presbyterians, and the Paxton Riots, 1763–1764," *J.P.H.*, (Spring, 1975), while David Sloan, " 'A Time of Sifting and Winnowing:' The Paxton Riots and Quaker Non-Violence in Pennsylvania," *Q.H.*, LXVI (Spring, 1977), deals with the lasting impact of the struggle on the Quakers.

Historians are divided over the question: were the conflicts in the colonies inspired by class or regional differences. The older view, represented by such works as Archibald Henderson, "The Origin of Regulation in North Carolina," *A.H.R.*, XXI (January, 1916), held that sectional differences were solely responsible; this is answered by Marvin L. M. Kay, "The North Carolina Regulation, 1766–1776: A Class Conflict," in Alfred F. Young, ed.,

The American Revolution (DeKalb, 1976). Still other causal forces are discussed in: James P. Wittenberg, "Planters, Merchants, and Lawyers: Social Change and the Origins of the North Carolina Regulation," *W.M.C.Q.*, XXXIV (April, 1977), which holds the uprisings were fueled by local issues and represented neither a broad sectional nor class conflict, and A. Roger Ekirch, "The North Carolina Regulators on Liberty and Corruption, 1766–1771," *P.A.H.*, XI (1977–1978), which argues that the Regulators were basically conservative and wanted only to end corruption in government. Basic documents for North Carolina are in William S. Powell, et. al., eds., *The Regulators in North Carolina: A Documentary History, 1759–1776* (Raleigh, 1971). An excellent account of the conflict in South Carolina is Richard M. Brown, *The South Carolina Regulators* (Cambridge, 1963). Problems that stirred conflict in Virginia are considered in E. Lee Shepard, " 'The Ease and Convenience of the People': Courthouse Locations in Spotsylvania County, 1720–1840," *V.M.H.B.*, LXXXVII (July, 1979), a discussion of the problem of locating courthouses near the people in large frontier counties, and Richard R. Beeman, "Social Change and Cultural Conflict in Virginia: Lunenburg County, 1746 to 1774," *W.M.C.Q.*, XXXV (July, 1978), which shows that Anglican elite groups did not emerge in the interior because the socioeconomic structure had not stabilized. Alonzo T. Dill, "Sectional Conflict in Colonial Virginia," *V.M.H.B.*, LXXXVII (July, 1979), analyzes the conflicts in Virginia between the wealthy planters of the York and James River basins and the poorer farmers of the Northern Neck and Southside.

7 The French Barrier, 1615–1763

Two volumes by W. J. Eccles reflect modern understanding of French expansion and conflict in America. The more general of these is *France in America* (New York, 1972); The same author's *The Canadian Frontier, 1534–1760* (New York, 1969), focuses more directly on expansion and challenges many basic assumptions of the older histories. John A. Caruso, *The Mississippi Valley Frontier: The Age of French Exploration and Settlement* (Indianapolis, 1966), tells a more traditional story but is readable.

Older histories that describe the founding and growth of French Canada provide useful data not found in the interpretative volumes by Professor Eccles: Herbert I. Priestley, *France Overseas through the Old Régime*

(New York, 1939); Adam Shortt and Arthur G. Doughty, *Canada and Its Provinces*, 23 v. (Toronto, 1914–17); and Gustave Lanctot, *A History of Canada*, 3 v. (Cambridge, 1963–66), which covers the period from 1660 to 1763. Arthur R. M. Lower, *Canadians in the Making: A Social History of Canada* (Toronto, 1958), is also useful. Many of the histories of Indian-white relations listed in the bibliography to Chapter II contain important information, as does Harold A. Innis, *The Fur Trade in Canada* (New Haven, 1930).

Early Explorers and Missionaries. John B. Brebner, *The Explorers of North America* (New York, 1933), is brief and convenient, but may be supplemented with Paul L. Haworth, *Trailmakers of the Northwest* (New York, 1921), which deals specifically with French explorers. The best biography of the early explorer is Jean Delandlez, *Life and Voyages of Louis Jolliet (1645–1700)* (Chicago, 1948), while a controversial work on his principal discovery is Francis B. Steck, *The Jolliet-Marquette Expedition 1673* (Washington, 1927), which holds that Jolliet was not a Jesuit and could not have written the narratives ascribed to him. Both of these points are successfully challenged in Joseph P. Donnelly, *Jacques Marquette, S.J., 1637–1675* (Chicago, 1968), an excellent biography, which proves Marquette was an ordined priest and did write the 1673 journal. His argument is substantiated in Raphael N. Hamilton, *Marquette's Explorations: the Narratives Re-examined* (Madison, 1970), a work of meticulous scholarship. The explorations of Radisson and Groseilliers are expertly described in Grace L. Nute, *Caesars of the Wilderness* (New York, 1943). A brief history of mission activity is in J. H. Kennedy, *Jesuit and Savage in New France* (New Haven, 1950). An excellent biography of a leading Jesuit missionary is Joseph P. Donnelly, *Jean de Brébeuf, 1593–1649* (Chicago 1976), which tells the story of the whole Huronia mission effort. Wilfried and Elsie M. Jury, *Sainte-Marie Among the Hurons* (Toronto, 1954), locates and describes an important mission station. Raphael N. Hamilton, "Jesuit Mission at Sault Ste. Marie," *M.H.*, LII (Summer, 1968), describes in detail the founding of the first mission at that strategic point in 1668. Missionary activities in Maine are the theme of Sister Mary G. Legar, *The Catholic Indian Missions in Maine (1611–1820)* (Washington, 1929), in Michigan in George Paré, "The St. Joseph Mission," *M.V.H.R.* (June, 1930), and in the Illinois country in Sister Mary B. Palm, *The Jesuit Missions of the Illinois Country, 1673–1763* (St. Louis, 1931).

The Period of Expansion, 1670–1690. Louise P. Kellogg, *The French Règime in Wisconsin and the Northwest* (Madison, 1925), and Clarence W. Alvord, *The Illinois Country, 1673–1818* (Springfield, 1920), describe the French occupation of the Northwest. The same story is more popularly told in the classic volumes of Francis Parkman; *La Salle and the Discovery of the Great West, The Old Règime in Canada under Louis XIV*, and *Count Frontenac and New France under Louis XIV* (Boston, 1898). These older works should be balanced by reading W. J. Eccles, *Canada Under Louis XIV, 1663–1701* New York, 1964), a fresh interpretation. Thomas Chapis, *The Great Intendent* (Toronto, 1914), deals with Talon, while an outstanding revisionist biography of Frontenac is by W. J. Eccles, *Frontenac: The Courtier Governor* (Toronto, 1959), which questions Frontenac's military skill and finds him guilty of benefiting himself more than the colony with his trading policies. The history of the fort that Frontenac built is told in Richard A. Preston, Ed., *Royal Fort Frontenac* (Toronto, 1958).

Frances Krauskopf, "The Documentary Basis for La Salle's Supposed Discovery of the Ohio River," *I.M.H.*, XLVII (June, 1951) argues convincingly that this explorer under Frontenac did not reach the Ohio.

Documents on the French occupation of the Northwest are in Theodore C. Pease and Raymond C. Werner, eds., *The French Foundations, 1680–1693* (Springfield, 1934). Local studies touching on the expansion include: Peter L. Scanlon, *Prairie du Chien: French, British, American* (Prairie du Chien, 1937), John McDermott, *Old Cahokia: A Narrative and Documents Illustrating the First Century of Its History* (St. Louis, 1949), and Natalia M. Belting, *Kaskaskia Under the French Regime* (Urbana, 1948).

Two useful books deal with the role of the Iroquois Indians in the emerging French-English conflict: George T. Hunt, *The Wars of the Iroquois* (Madison, 1940), and Allen W. Trelease, *Indian Affairs in Colonial New York: The Seventeenth Century* (Ithaca, 1960). The former argues that the Iroquois sought to serve as middlemen between the Europeans and the Great Lakes tribes; the latter that they wanted to subdue those tribes to extend their own hunting grounds. Bruce G. Trigger, "The Jesuits and the Fur Trade," *E.*, XII (Winter, 1965), holds that Jesuit missionary activity among the Iroquois was governed by religious and economic factors, operating in concert, while Bruce G. Trigger, "The French Presence in Huronia: The Structure of Franco-Huron Relations in the First Half of the Seventeenth Century," *C.H.R.*, XLIX (June, 1968), argues that the Iroquois wars were designed not to secure new fur-hunting lands but to force the Huron to share the northern trade. A history of the wars between the Iroquois, Hurons, and the Great Lake tribes by Robert F. Bowman is in *N.O.Q.*, XXX (Autumn, 1958) to XXXV (Spring, 1963). A brief analysis of military tactics is in Keith F. Otterbein, "Why the Iroquois Won: An Analysis of Iroquois Military Tactics," *E.*, XI (Winter, 1964). The best history of the Hudson's Bay Company is E. E. Rich, *The History of the Hudson's Bay Company, 1670–1870*, 2 v. (London, 1958–1962); Arthur J. Ray and Donald S. Freeman, *'Give us Good Measure': An Economic Analysis of the Relations between the Indians and the Hudson's Bay Company before 1763* (Toronto, 1978), uses the company's ledgers, hitherto unseen by historians, to show that the Indians thought first of profits and were always open to roles as middlemen.

The Imperial Wars. A survey of the international relations underlying the French-English wars is Max Savelle, *The Originals of American Diplomacy: The International History of Anglo-America, 1492–1763* (New York, 1968); equally essential to an understanding of the roots of this struggle are the early volumes of Lawrence H. Gipson, *The British Empire Before the American Revolution*, 14 v. (New York, 1936–69), a work of immense scholarship, and Douglas E. Leach, *Arms for Empire: A Military History of the British North American Colonies in North America, 1607–1763* (New York, 1973). Modern viewpoints on the French-English wars are to be found in the brief but scholarly work by Howard R. Peckham, *The Colonial Wars, 1689–1762* (Chicago, 1964). The same author offers interesting sidelights in "Speculations on the Colonial Wars," *W.M.C.Q.*, XVII (October, 1960). The munitions and supplies used by both antagonists are described in Edward P. Hamilton, "Colonial Warfare in North America," M.H.S., *Proceedings*, LXXX (1968). W. J. Eccles, "The Social, Economic, and Political Significance of the Military Establishment in New France," *C.H.R.*, LII (March, 1971), is a brilliantly interpretative discussion of the French military force as a surprisingly effective body. Deficiencies in British policies are appraised in James A. Henretta, *'Salutary Neglect'; Colonial Administration Under the Duke of Newcastle* (Princeton, 1972).

Conflict on the Northern Borderland. An important article that helps set the stage for the later struggle is Bruce G. Trigger, "The Mohawk-Mahican War (1624–28): The Establishment of a Pattern," *C.H.R.*, LII (September,

ber, 1971); the author shows why the English-Iroquois alliance developed. The role of the New York fur traders in the beginnings and during the course of the French and Indian wars is admirably described in Thomas E. North, *The Fur Trade in Colonial New York, 1686–1776* (Madison, 1975), an important volume that relates the trade to political and economic factors. The reasons for Iroquois neutrality in Queen Anne's War are examined in Anthony F. C. Wallace, "Origins of Iroquois Neutrality: The Grand Settlement of 1701," *P.H.*, XXIV (July, 1957), while efforts to win over the Five Nations are described in Richmond P. Bond, *Queen Anne's American Kings* (New York, 1952). The vain efforts of Massachusetts to secure aid from Connecticut during the early wars is described in Richard A. Marcus, "The Connecticut Valley: A Problem in Intercolonial Defense," *Mi.A.*, XXXIII (April, 1969).

Warfare in New York is discussed in Ruth L. Higgings, *Expansion in New York with Especial Reference to the Eighteenth Century* (Columbus, 1931), and in New England in James T. Adams, *Revolutionary New England, 1691–1776* (Boston, 1923). The latter should be supplemented with Ronald O. MacFarlane, "The Massachusetts Bay Truck-Houses in Diplomacy with the Indians," *N.E.Q.*, XI (March, 1938), and Arthur H. Buffinton, "The Isolationist Policy of Colonial Massachusetts," *N.E.Q.*, I (April, 1938). Documents and a scholarly history of one of the major expeditions of the war are in Gerald S. Graham, ed., *The Walker Expedition to Quebec, 1711* (Toronto, 1954). Yves F. Zoltvany, "New France and the West," *C.H.R.*, XLVI (December, 1965), shows that resistance in New France to orders from Paris to check expansion between 1701 and 1713 weakened the colony on the eve of another major war. G. M. Waller, *Samuel Vetch: Colonial Enterpriser* (Chapel Hill, 1960), is a biography of the promoter who sought to encourage British expansion into Nova Scotia, Cape Breton, and Quebec between 1709 and 1712.

Conflict on the Southern Borderland, 1690–1715. The French-Spanish-English conflicts are described in Verner W. Crane, *The Southern Frontier, 1670–1723* (Durham, 1928). The expansion of the English trading frontier is the theme of Mary Rothrock, "Carolina Traders among the Overhill Cherokees, 1690–1760," E.T.H.S., *Publications*, I (1929), and W. Neil Franklin, "Virginia and the Cherokee Indian Trade, 1673–1752," E.T.H.S., *Publications*, IV (1932). Leitch J. Wright, Jr., "Spanish Reaction to Carolina," *N.C.H.R.*, XLI (Autumn, 1964), describes Spanish countermeasures against the encroaching English frontier in the 1680s and 1690s, while the effort of southern frontiersmen to capture Spanish Florida in Queen Anne's War is the theme of Charles W. Arnade, *The Siege of St. Augustine* (Gainesville, 1959). The origins and course of the French conflict with the Alabama Indians, a small tribe at the junction of the Coosa and Tallapoosa rivers, is the theme of Jay Higginbotham, "Origins of the French-Alabama Conflict, 1703–1704," *A.R.*, XXXI (April, 1978). A near-rebellion in St. Augustine in July 1712, is explained in William R. Gillaspie, "Sergeant Major Ayala y Escobar and the Threatened St. Augustine Mutiny," *F.H.Q.*, XLVII (October, 1968).

The conflict over the founding of Louisiana is treated in William E. Dunn, "French and Spanish Rivalry in the Gulf Region of the United States, 1678–1702," University of Texas, *Bulletin* (Austin, 1917). An excellent biography of the successful contestant is Nellis M. Crouse, *Lemoyne d'Iberville: Soldier of New France* (Ithaca, 1954). R. G. Mc-Williams, "Iberville and the Southern Indians," *A.R.*, XX (October, 1967), describes Iberville's relations with the Indians while exploring the lower Mississippi between 1699 and 1701. Jay Higginbotham, *Old Mobile: Fort Louis de la Louisiana, 1702–1711* (Mobile, 1977) is voluminous and detailed. Material is also plentiful in the several histories of Louisiana, of which the most useful are Charles Gayarré, *History of Louisiana*, 4 v. (New Orleans, 1932), and Marcel Giraud, *A History of French Louisiana Volume I : The Reign of Louis XIV, 1698–1715* (Baton Rouge, 1974). The latter, translated from the French edition of 1953, is scholarly but lacks modern interpretations. Marshall Sprague, *So Vast So Beautiful a Land: Louisiana and the Purchase* (Boston, 1974), is a popular history to 1803, and Joe G. Taylor, *Louisiana: A Bicentennial History* (New York, 1976) is brief but sound. The colony's expansion is described in Stanley Faye, "The Contest for Pensacola Bay and Other Gulf Ports, 1698–1722," *F.H.Q.*, XXIV (January, 1946). The early development of Louisiana is described in N. M. Miller Surrey, *The Commerce of Louisiana during the French Régime, 1699–1763* (New York, 1916).

The Southern Frontier, 1715–1740. The Franco-Spanish conflicts on the western borders of Louisiana are described in William E. Dunn, "Spanish Reaction against the French Advance toward New Mexico, 1717–1727," *M.V.H.R.*, II (December, 1915). The occupation of Georgia is well covered in an excellent state history, Kenneth Coleman, *Colonial*

Georgia: A History (New York, 1976), and in such specialized works as Phinizy Spalding, *Oglethorpe in America* (Chicago, 1977), which is the best discussion of Oglethorpe's role in the founding, James E. Callaway, *The Early Settlement of Georgia* (Athens, 1948), and Paul S. Taylor, *Georgia Plan: 1732–1752* (Berkeley, 1972), the latter a thorough discussion of the plans of the founders for a compact colony of poorer Englishmen, and the reasons for its failure. That such colonies were common in the projects of the day is shown in Milton Ready, "The Georgia Concept: An Eighteenth Century Experiment in Colonization," *G.H.Q.*, LV (Summer, 1971). Both Albert W. Saye, *New Viewpoints in Georgia History* (Athens, 1943), and E. Merton Coulter, "Was Georgia Settled by Debtors?" *G.H.Q.*, LIII (December, 1969), argue convincingly that not more than a dozen of the early colonists came from debtor prisons; the remainder were largely poor peasants. Gerald L. Cates, " 'The Seasoning'; Disease and Death among the First Colonists of Georgia," *G.H.Q.*, LXIV (Summer, 1980), shows that the death rate was far higher among colonists on charity than those who had paid their own way. The life of the people during the early years is depicted in Harold E. Davis, *The Fledgling Province: Social and Cultural Life in Colonial Georgia, 1733–1776* (Chapel Hill, 1976). Milton L. Ready, "Land Tenure in Trusteeship Georgia," *A.H.*, XLVIII (July, 1974), demonstrates that the trustees' policy of small grants discouraged settlement, while Netty Wood, "Thomas Stephens and the Introduction of Black Slavery in Georgia," *G.H.Q.*, LVIII (Spring, 1974), shows that the secretary of the colony violated the wishes of the proprietors in heeding popular will for the introduction of slaves in 1742–1743. Verner W. Crane, *The Southern Frontier, 1670–1732* (Durham, 1928), is the best account of the conflict in the Southwest, while the story is continued in less satisfactory form in John P. Corry, *Indian Affairs in Georgia, 1732–1756* (Philadelphia, 1936), and James G. Johnson, *The Colonial Southeast, 1732–1763: An International Contest for Territorial and Economic Control* (Boulder, 1932). Georgia-Creek relations are considered, in John T. Lanning, *The Diplomatic History of Georgia: A Study of the Epoch of Jenkin's Ear* (Chapel Hill, 1936). The latter should be supplemented by Trevor R. Reese, "Georgia in Anglo-Spanish Diplomacy, 1736–1739," *W.M.C.Q.*, XV (April, 1958), which examines the background of the controversy from the English point of view, and Trevor R. Reese, "Britain's Military Support of Georgia in the War of 1739–1748,"

G.H.Q., XLIII (March, 1959), which shows British aid to be inadequate and Georgians primarily responsible for victory, Larry E. Ivers, *British Drums on the Southern Frontier: The Military Colonization of Georgia, 1733–1749* (Chapel Hill, 1974), contains a mass of ill-digested information. William S. Willis, "Divide and Rule: Red, White, and Black in the Southeast," *J.N.H.*, XLVIII (July, 1963), examines Georgia's frontier policy of pitting Indians against slaves to prevent either minority from uniting with the other against the whites.

The Northwestern Frontier, 1715–1740. In addition to the standard volumes by Kellogg and Alvord cited above, information is contined in Murray G. Lawson, *Fur: A Study in English Mercantilism, 1700–1775* (Toronto, 1943). The Fox Wars are capably described in Louise P. Kellogg, "The Fox Indian Wars during the French Régime," *S.H.S.W., Proceedings* (1907). The best critical biography of a leading explorer is Nellis M. Crouse, *La Vérendrye: Fur Trader and Explorer* (Ithaca, 1956). The explorer's journals are expertly edited, with fresh commentary by Ray Woods, in G. Hubert Smith, *The Explorations of the La Vérendryes in the Northern Plains, 1738–43* (Lincoln, 1980).

The Northern Frontier, 1715–1740. In addition to the works listed above on the New York–New England region, information may be found in Frank H. Severance, *An Old Frontier of France; the Niagara Region and Adjacent Lakes Under French Control*, 2 v. (New York, 1917). Yves F. Zoltvany, "The Frontier Policy of Philippe de Rigaud de Vaudreuil, 1713–1725," *C.H.R.*, XLVIII (September, 1967), not only explains French strategy, but shows Vaudreuil to be a far abler strategist than formerly supposed. The best biography of Sir William Johnson is Milton W. Hamilton, *Sir William Johnson: Colonial America, 1715–1763* (Port Washington, 1976) eventually to be completed in two volumes. An account of relations between New York and the Iroquois, based on papers of the Society for the Propagation of the Gospel, is John W. Lydekker, *The Faithful Mohawks* (New York, 1938). Books previously cited on New England's northern frontier, may be supplemented by a valuable reinterpretation of Lovewell's War: Fannie H. Eckstorm, "The Attack on Norridgewock: 1724," *N.E.Q.*, VII (September, 1934). That Massachusetts interest in Nova Scotia was not expansionist is shown in George A. Rawlyk, *Nova Scotia's Massachusetts : A Study of Massachusetts-Nova Scotia Relations, 1630–1784* (Montreal, 1973). New England's role in the warfare of the 1740s is well told in G. A. Rawlyk, *Yankees at Louisbourg* (Orono, 1967), a readable history of the siege, Louis E. de Forest, ed., *Louisbourg Journals, 1745* (New York, 1932), and Fairfax D. Downey, *Louisbourg: Key to a Continent* (Englewood Cliffs, 1966). Reasons for the fort's surrender, explained in terms of its inadequate defenses, are in Robert E. Wall, Jr., "Louisbourg, 1745," *N.E.Q.*, XXXVII (March, 1964), while the reasons that the fort was returned to France after King George's War are satisfactorily explained for the first time in Jack M. Sosin, "Louisbourg and the Peace of Aix-la-Chapelle, 1748," *W.M.C.Q.*, XIV (October, 1957). Douglas E. Leach, "Brothers in Arms? Anglo-American Friction at Louisbourg, 1745–1746," *M.H.S., Proceedings*, LXXXIX (1977), demonstrates that mutual distrust and dislike between the New England provincials and British regulars was intensified during the siege, contributing to the dissatisfaction that underlay the Revolution.

The Ohio Valley Frontier, 1720–1754. The westward movement of the Pennsylvania trading frontier is studied in Robert L. D. Davidson, *War Comes to Quaker Pennsylvania, 1682–1756* (New York, 1957). Edward G. Everett, "Pennsylvania's Indian Diplomacy, 1747–1753," *W.P.H.M.*, XLIV (September, 1961), ably analyzes the use of gifts and diplomacy by Pennsylvania to keep peace among the Ohio and western Pennsylvania Indians, while James C. King, "Indian Credit as a Source of Friction in the Colonial Fur Trade," *W.P.H.M.*, XLIX (January, 1966), shows the manner in which trading firms used credit to establish supremacy over the Indians. That Pennsylvania deliberately humiliated the Shawnee to win the support of the Miami is shown in Lyle L. Rosenberger, "The Lancaster Treaty of 1748," *J.L.C.H.S.*, LXXVI (Trinity, 1972). One path used by the traders is exactly located in Niles Anderson and Edward G. Williams, "The Venango Path as Thomas Hutchins Knew It," *W.P.H..M.*, XLIX (January and April, 1966). Biographies of the leading protagonists include: Paul A. W. Wallace, *Conrad Weiser, 1696–1760* (Philadelphia, 1945), Arthur D. Graeff, *Conrad Weiser, Pennsylvania Peacemaker* (Fogelsville, 1946), Anthony F. C. Wallace, *King of the Delawares: Teedyuscung* (Philadelphia, 1949), and especially Albert T. Volwiler, *George Croghan and the Westward Movement, 1741–1782* (Cleveland, 1929). A more personal biography of this important frontiersman is Nicholas B. Wainwright, *George Croghan, Wilderness Diplomat* (Chapel Hill, 1959). An excellent account of the events leading to Charles Langlade's attack on Fort

Pickawillany in 1752 and of the attack itself is David Edmunds, "Pickawillany: French Military Power versus British Economics," *W.P.H.M.*, LVIII (April, 1975). One result of Croghan's activity is shown in John R. Sahli, "The Growth of British Influence among the Seneca to 1768," *W.P.H.M.*, IXL (April, 1966). The activities of a leading Pennsylvania trading firm are described in Nicholas B. Wainwright, "An Indian Trade Failure: The Story of Hockley, Trent and Croghan Company," *P.M.H.B.*, LXXII (October, 1948). French activities in the region are the theme of Charles W. Dahlinger, *The Marquis Duquesne, Sieur de Menneville* (Pittsburgh, 1932), and Norman W. Caldwell, *The French in the Mississippi Valley, 1740–1750* (Urbana, 1941). A useful case study of a Canadian firm active in the western trade at this time is Dale Miquelon, "Havy and Lefebvre of Quebec: A Case Study of Metropolitan Participation in Canadian Trade, 1730–60," *C.H.R*, LVI (March, 1975).

The Seven Years War. Among the dozens of general accounts of the war, which range from Francis Parkman's vivid *Montcalm and Wolfe*, 2 v. (Boston, 1898), to laborious monographs, the most thorough is Lawrence H. Hipson, *The British Empire Before the American Revolution*, Vols. V through VIII (New York, 1942–54). These cover the period from 1748 to 1763. The war as viewed from outside the United States is considered in Walter L. Dorn, *Competition for Empire, 1740–1763* (New York, 1949). Patrice L. Higonnet, "The Origins of the Seven Years' War," *J.M.H.*, XL (March, 1968), explores the European origins of the conflict, holding that both nations blundered into an unwanted confrontation. A popular history of the conflict that stresses vivid writing and military events is Harrison Bird, *Battle for a Continent. The French and Indian War, 1754–1763* (New York, 1965). Biographies of leaders include: J. C. Long, *Mr. Pitt and America's Birthright* (New York, 1940), F. E. Whitton, *Wolfe and North America* (Boston, 1929), J. C. Long, *Lord Jeffery Amherst* (New York, 1933), and Stanley M. Pargellis, *Lord Loudoun in America* (New Haven, 1933). Reed Browning, "The Duke of Newcastle and the Financing of the Seven Years' War," *J.E.H.* XXXI (June, 1971), is a revisionist study showing that the Newcastle ministry handled the war's finances well and was popular with England's business community. Alan Rogers, *Empire and Liberty: American Resistance to British Authority, 1755–1763* (Berkeley, 1975), argues that American resistance to British authority during the war sowed the seeds of rebellion

that blossomed in the Revolution.

The part played by the Ohio Company in opening the struggle is traced in Kenneth P. Bailey, *The Ohio Company of Virginia and the Westward Movement, 1748–1792* (Glendale, 1939), while a special aspect of that company's activity is explored in Lois Mulkearn, "Why the Treaty of Logstown, 1752," *V.M.H.B.*, LIIIX (January, 1951). Biographical sketches of two frontiersmen are: Lilly L. Nixon, *James Burd, Frontier Defender* (Philadelphia, 1941), and Howard G. Clark, "John Fraser, Western Pennsylvania Frontiersman," *W.P.H.M.*, XXXVIII (Fall-Winter, 1955) to XXXIX (Summer, 1956). Virginia's role in precipitating the conflict is traced in the standard biography of the colonial governor, John R. Alden, *Robert Dinwiddie: Servant of the Crown* (Charlottesville, 1974), while Washington's expeditions of 1753 and 1754 are described in Bernhard Knollenberg, *George Washington: The Virginia Period, 1732–1775* (Durham, 1964), and James T. Flexner, *George Washington: The Forge of Experience (1732–1775)* (Boston, 1965). The most detailed history of Washington's expedition to the Forks of the Ohio is Paul A. W. Wallace, "George Washington's Route from Venango to Fort Le Boeuf, 1753," *P.H.*, XXVIII (October, 1961). Washington's own accounts of his journeys, together with other useful documents, are in Hugh Cleland, ed., *George Washington in the Ohio Valley* (Pittsburgh, 1955).

Two books deal with the history of the region about the Forks of the Ohio during this period, one in encyclopedic detail, the other in popular fashion: Alfred P. James and Charles M. Stotz, *Drums in the Forest* (Pittsburgh, 1958), and Walter O'Meara, *Guns at the Forks* (Englewood Cliffs, 1965). A sound biography of the fated English general is Lee McCardell, *Ill-Starred General: Braddock of the Coldstream Guards* (Pittsburgh, 1958), but by far the best account of Braddock's expedition to the Forks of the Ohio is Paul E. Kopperman, *Braddock on the Monongahela* (Pittsburg, 1977), which blames defeat on a panic among the regulars and the failure of Colonel Thomas Gage to secure the flanks. Peter E. Russell, "Redcoats in the Wilderness: British Officers and Irregular Troops in Europe and America, 1740 to 1760," *W.M.C.Q.*, XXXV (October, 1978), substantiates this view by showing that British troops had been trained at home in wilderness tactics. John K. Lacock "Braddock Road," *P.M.H.B.*, XXXVIII (January, 1941), exactly traces the route of Braddock's Road; this has been corrected for one portion by Paul A. W. Wallace, " 'Blunder Camp': A

Note on Braddock's Road," *P.M.H.R.*, LXXXVII (January, 1963). Two contemporary journals of the expedition by British members are published as Charles E. Hamilton, ed., *Braddock's Defeat* (Norman, 1959). Additional light is thrown on fighting in Pennsylvania by Howard H. Peckham, ed., "Thomas Gist's Indian Captivity, 1758–1759," *P.M.H.B.*, LXXX (July, 1956). War along the northern borderlands is the theme of such works as John B. Brebner, *New England's Outpost: Acadia before the Conquest of Canada* (New York, 1927), and J. Clarence Webster, *The Forts of Chignecto; A Study of the Eighteenth Century Conflict between France and Great Britain in Acadia* (St. John, 1930). Dominick Graham, "The Planning of the Beauséjour Operation and the Approaches to War in 1755," *N.E.Q.*, (December, 1968), demonstrates that the attack was planned by Governor Shirley without authority from England and forced on a reluctant Newcastle ministry. Richard G. Lowe, "Massachusetts and the Acadians," *W.M.C.Q.*, XXV (April, 1968), describes the fate of the displaced Acadians when they were exported to New England. Fighting on the New York frontier is considered in John R. Cuneo, *Robert Rogers of the Rangers* (New York, 1959), and Edward P. Hamilton, *Fort Ticonderoga: Key to a Continent* (Boston, 1964), while Brian L. Dunnigan, "Vauban in the Wilderness: The Siege of Fort Niagara, 1759" *N.F.*, XXI (Summer, 1974), shows that both attackers and defenders relied on the tactics of an early eighteenth century military theorist.

The best work on frontier defense in Pennsylvania following Braddock's defeat is William A. Hunter, *Forts on the Pennsylvania Frontier, 1753–1758* (Harrisburg, 1960). Benjamin Franklin's role on the frontier during this period is colorfully described in Leonard W. Labaree, "Benjamin Franklin and the Defense of Pennsylvania, 1754–1757," *P.H.*, XXIX (January, 1962). Other works dealing with aspects of the subject include: C. Hale Sipe, *Fort Ligonier and Its Times* (Harrisburg, 1932), John S. Fisher, "Colonel Armstrong's Expedition against Kittanning," *P.M.H.B.*, LI (January, 1927), and Mary C. Darlington, *History of Colonel Henry Bouquet and the Western Frontiers of Pennsylvania, 1747–1764* (n.p., 1920). Jack D. Marietta, "Conscience, the Quaker Community, and the French and Indian War," *P.M.H.B.*, XCV (January, 1971), describes the split among Quakers over support for the war. Albert P. James has edited *The Papers of Henry Bouquet. The Forbes Expedition* (Harrisburg, Pa., 1951). Niles Anderson, "New Light on the 1758 Forbes Campaign," *W.P.H.M.*, L (April, 1967), sets the record straight on aspects of the campaign; the same author describes the conflict between Forbes and Washington in "The General Chooses a Road: The Forbes Campaign of 1758 to Capture Ft. Duquesne," *W.P.H.M.*, XLII (June, 1959), to (December, 1959). The aid given by one state is admirably described in Nellie Norkus, "Virginia's Role in the Capture of Fort Duquesne, 1758," *W.P.H.M.*, VL (December, 1962). West Virginia's role in the war is the theme of Otis Rice, "The French and Indian War in West Virginia," *W.V.H.*, XXIV (January, 1963), and Virginia's in Louis K. Koontz, *The Virginia Frontier, 1754–1763* (Baltimore, 1925), and Roy B. Cook, "Virginia Frontier Defenses, 1719–1795," *W.V.H.*, I (January, 1940). Gwenda Morgan, "Virginia and the French and Indian War: A Case Study of the War's Effect on Imperial Relations," *V.M.H.B.*, LXXXI (January, 1973), reveals that England's dissatisfaction with Virginia's aid in the war underlay the future ill treatment of the colony by the mother country. Efforts to guard the Forks of the Ohio after the capture of Ft. Duquesne are described in Ann Quattrocchi, "Thomas Hutchins: Provincial Soldier and Indian Agent in the Ohio, Valley, 1758–1761," *W.P.H.M.*, VL (September, 1962).

The best study of the Cherokee war is David H. Corkran, *The Cherokee Frontier: Conflict and Survival, 1740–62* (Norman, 1962). Briefer treatments of aspects of the subject are Philip M. Hamer, "Anglo-French Rivalry in the Cherokee Country, 1754–17757," *N.C.H.R.*, II (July, 1925), Philip M. Hamer, "Fort Loudoun in the Cherokee War, 1758–1761," *N.C.H.R.*, II (October, 1925), and Samuel C. Williams, "Fort Robinson on the Holston," *E.T.H.S.*, *Publication*, IV (1932). Also pertinent to an understanding of the war on the southern borderlands are David R. Chesnutt, "South Carolina's Penetration of Georgia in the 1760s: Henry Laurens as a Case Study," *S.C.H.M.*, LXXIII (October, 1972), which deals with an intercolonial contest over ownership of the area between the St. Johns and Altamaha rivers, and Alan Calmes, "The Lyttelton Expedition of 1759: Military Failure and Financial Success," *S.C.H.M.*, LXXVII (January, 1976), which described Governor William H. Lyttelton's expedition against Fort Prince George on the Keowee River. Commercial activities along the southern coast are the theme of Joyce E. Harman, *Trade and Privateering in Spanish Florida, 1732–1763* (St. Augustine, 1969).

The French exodus from the interior after defeat is described in Louise P. Kellogg, "La Chapelle's Remarkable Retreat Through the

Mississippi Valley, 1760–1761," *M.V.H.R.*, XXII (June, 1935). Documents on the diplomacy of the peace are in Theodore C. Pease, ed., *Anglo-French Boundary Disputes in the West, 1749–1763* (Springfield, 1936). The establishment of the western boundary is considered in Theodore C. Pease, "The Mississippi Boundary of 1763: A Reappraisal of Responsibility," *A.H.R.*, XL (January, 1935), and Arthur S. Aiton, "The Diplomacy of the Louisiana Cession," *AH.R.*, XXXVI (July, 1931). Spain's initial efforts to take over Louisiana are the theme of Gilbert Din, "Early Spanish Colonization Efforts in Louisiana," *L.S.*, XI (Spring, 1972), while Andrew S. Walsh and Robert V. Wells, "Population Dynamics in the Eighteenth-Century Mississippi River Valley: Acadians in Louisiana," *J. So.H.*, XI (Summer, 1978), examines the nature of the Acadian society that was established there.

British occupation of the Floridas is described in C. N. Howard, "The Military Occupation of British West Florida, 1763," *F.H.Q.*, XVII (January, 1939). A thorough history of the transfer of the Floridas from Spain and France to England is Robert L. Gold, *Borderland Empires in Transition: The Triple-Nation Transfer of Florida* (Carbondale, 1969).

8 British Western Policy, 1763–1776

General Works. The best single treatment of British western policy in the pre-Revolutionary era is Jack M. Sosin, *Whitehall and the Wilderness: The Middle West in British Colonial Policy, 1760–1775* (Lincoln, 1961), although the same author's *The Revolutionary Frontier, 1763–1783* (New York, 1967) expertly surveys the subject more briefly. An older work on the subject, long a classic, is Clarence W. Alvord, *The Mississippi Valley in British Politics*, 2 v. (Cleveland, 1917). The latter volume is overlaudatory of Lord Shelburne, a view that can be balanced by reading R. A. Humphreys, "Lord Shelburne and the Proclamation of 1763," *E.H.R.*, XLIX (April, 1934), R. A. Humphreys, "Lord Shelburne and British Colonial Policy, 1766–1768," *E.H.R.*, L (April, 1935), and John A. Schutz, *Thomas Pownall, British Defender of American Liberty* (Glendale, 1951). Another sound biography of a leading British statesman of the period is Lewis Namier and John Brooke, *Charles Townshend* (New York, 1964). By far the most comprehensive treatment of the entire period, from the empire point of view, are

the concluding volumes of Lawrence H. Gipson's monumental *The British Empire before the American Revolution: Volumes IX through XII* (New York, 1956–1965). These cover the period from 1763 to 1776. Another sweeping survey of the European impact on America during these years is Max Savelle, *Empires to Nations: Expansion in America, 1713–1824* (Minneapolis, 1974).

The Iroquois Frontier. Although unduly sensitive to the Indian cause, Georgiana C. Nammack, *Fraud, Politics, and the Dispossession of the Indians: The Iroquois Land Frontier in the Colonial Period* (Norman, 1969) is a valuable case study in the manner in which speculators and politicians robbed the red men of their lands. Sir William Johnson's role in this process is admirably described in Milton W. Hamilton, *Sir William Johnson: Colonial American, 1715–1763* (Port Washington, 1976), although the full treatment must await the second volume of this excellent biography. James T. Flexner, *Mohawk Baronet: Sir William Johnson of New York,* (New York, 1959), deals with this period but neglects Johnson's business and speculative activities. This deficiency is partially remedied by two thorough studies of his lieutenant by Albert T. Volwiler, *George Croghan and the Westward Movement, 1741–1782* (Cleveland, 1926), and Nicholas B. Wainwright, *George Croghan, Wilderness Diplomat* (Chapel Hill, 1959). Johnson's published papers are in James Sullivan, Milton W. Hamilton, et. al., eds., *The Sir William Johnson Papers*, 13 v. (Albany, 1921–1962). Essential to an understanding of the period is the scholarly biography of John R. Alden, *John Stuart and the Southern Colonial Frontier* (Ann Arbor, 1944). An important document bearing on the evolution of policy in the South is Wilbur R. Jacobs, ed., *Indians of the Southern Frontier: The Edmund Atkin Report and Plan of 1755* (Columbia, 1954). Additional light on Indian relations on the southern frontier is thrown by such studies as: Helen L. Shaw, *British Administration of the Southern Indians, 1756–1783* (Lancaster, 1931), Merritt B. Pound, "Colonel Benjamin Hawkins—North Carolinian—Benefactor of the Southern Indians," *N.C.H.R.*, XIX (January and April, 1942), and Grace S. Woodward, *The Cherokees* (Norman, 1963). David H. Corkran's well-researched volume, *The Creek Frontier, 1540–1783* (Norman, 1967), is also essential. A revisionist approach to the Proclamation of 1763, Eugene M. De Papa, "The Royal Proclamation of 1763: Its Effect upon Virginia Land Companies," *V.M.H.B.*, LXXXIII (October, 1975), finds the proclamation a success, for it was considered only temporary and did restrain speculative activities between 1763 and 1768. The standard work on redrawing the southern boundary line is Louis De Vorsey, Jr., *The Indian Boundary in the Southern Colonies, 1763–1775* (Chapel Hill, 1966). Minor points are corrected in the same author's later "Indian Boundaries in Colonial Georgia," *G.H.Q.*, LIV (Spring, 1970). An older work may still be used for the northern treaty-making, Max Farrand, "The Indian Boundary Line," *A.H.R.*, X (July, 1905), but this should be supplemented with Peter Marshall, "Sir William Johnson and the Treaty of Fort Stanwix, 1768," *J.A.S.*, I (October, 1967). Howard Lewin, "A Frontier Diplomat: Andrew Montour," *P.H.*, XXXIII (April, 1966), traces the career of a minor diplomatic figure who participated in the Ft. Stanwix conference.

Land Speculation. The principal study of speculation in pre-Revolutionary years, Thomas P. Abernethy, *Western Lands and the American Revolution* (New York, 1937), is as essential to the understanding of this period as the books by Jack M. Sosin previously cited. Sosin's research in British documents not used by Abernethy has also led to corrections such as those contained in the excellent article: Jack M. Sosin, "The Yorke-Camden Opinion and American Land Speculators," *P.M.H.B.*, LXXXV (January, 1961). In addition several monographs deal with specific speculating companies. On the Ohio Company see; Kenneth P. Bailey, *The Ohio Company of Virginia and the Westward Movement, 1748–1792* (Glendale, 1939), Alfred P. James, *The Ohio Company: Its Inner History* (Pittsburgh, 1959), and Alfred P. James, *George Mercer of the Ohio Company: A Study of Frustration* (Pittsburgh, 1963). Other speculating activities are described in George E. Lewis, *The Indiana Company, 1768–1798* (Glendale, 1941), Archibald Henderson, "Dr. Thomas Walker and the Loyal Land Company of Virginia," *A.A.S., Proceedings*, n.s., XLI (1931), and Clarence W. Alvord, ed., *The Illinois-Wabash Company* (Chicago, 1915). A usable account of the last great company is James D. Anderson, "Vandalia: The First West Virginia," *W.V.H.*, XL (Summer, 1979). Washington's many speculative enterprises are considered in Charles H. Ambler, *George Washington and the West* (Chapel Hill, 1936), Roy B. Cook, *Washington's Western Lands* (Strasburg, 1930), and Cecile E. Goode, "Gilbert Simpson: Washington's Partner in Settling His Western Pennsylvania Lands," *W.P.H.M.*, LXII (April, 1979).

Pontiac's Rebellion. The thesis that the rebellion was a well-organized conspiracy, set forth in classic form in the vivid *Conspiracy of Pontiac*, 2 v. (Boston, 1910) by Francis Parkman, has been disproven in Howard H. Peckham, *Pontiac and the Indian Uprising* (Princeton, 1947). Peckham's contention that Pontiac acted alone and without the support of a confederacy is disputed, not too convincingly, in Wilbur R. Jacobs, "Was the Pontiac Uprising a Conspiracy?" *O.A.H.Q.*, LIX (January, 1950). Norman G. Holmes, "The Ottawa Indians of Oklahoma and Chief Pontiac," *C.O.*, XLV (Summer, 1967), uses Indian legend to date Pontiac's birth in 1714. Bernard Knollenberg, "General Amherst and Germ Warfare," *M.V.H.R.*, XLI (December, 1954), and a rejoinder by Donald H. Kent in *ibid.*, XLI (March, 1955), discuss Amherst's plan to poison Indians with smallpox infected blankets. A vivid description of Pontiac's siege of Detroit is Myles M. Platt, "Detroit under Siege 1763," *M.H.*, XL (December, 1956). Studies of the principal military leader include E. Douglas Branch, "Henry Bouquet: Professional Soldier," *P.M.H.B.*, LVII (January, 1938), and Mary C. Darlington, *History of Colonel Henry Bouquet and the Western Frontiers of Pennsylvania, 1747–1764* (n.p., 1920). A day-by-day journal of Bouquet's march of 1764 to Fort Pitt, reproduced from his orderly book, is in Edward G. Williams, ed., *Bouquet's March to the Ohio: The Forbes Road* (Pittsburg, 1975). Charles S. Grant, "Pontiac's Rebellion and the British Troop Movements of 1763," *M.V.H.R.*, XL (June, 1953), demonstrates that the redistribution of British Troops in America had no relationship to the rebellion.

British Occupation of the Illinois Country and the Northwest. Alterations in British policy after Pontiac's Rebellion are expertly analyzed in Peter Marshall, "Colonial Protest and Imperial Retrenchment: Indian Policy, 1764–1768," *J.A.S.*, V (April, 1967), which deals with the Plan of 1764 and its abandonment. B. D. Bargar, *Lord Dartmouth and the American Revolution* (Columbia, 1965) is a careful study of the 1772–1775 period when Dartmouth was secretary of state. An older secondary work on the Illinois country is Clarence E. Carter, *Great Britain and the Illinois Country, 1763–1774* (Washington, 1910). These books should be supplemented by two studies of trading activity in Illinois: Max Savelle, *George Morgan, Colony Builder* (New York, 1932), and William V. Byars, *B. and M. Gratz, Merchants in Philadelphia, 1754–1798* (Jefferson City, 1916). Reasons for the failure of Morgan's concern are discussed in Charles M. Thomas, "Successful and Unsuccessful Merchants in the Illinois Country," *J.I.S.H.S.*,

XXX (January, 1938). That the evacuation of Fort Pitt in 1772 was made inevitable by the abandonment of Ft. Chartres in the Illinois Country is argued persuasively in John W. Huston, "The British Evacuation of Fort Pitt, 1772," *W.P.H.M.*, XLVIII (October, 1965). The British expedition that took over Fort Chartres and the Illinois Country is expertly described in Robert R. Rea, "Assault on the Mississippi—The Loftus Expedition, 1764," *A.R.*, XXVI (July, 1973).

The standard works on the British occupation of the Northwest are Louise P. Kellogg, *The British Régime in Wisconsin and the Northwest* (Madison, 1935), and Nelson V. Russell, *The British Régime in Michigan and the Old Northwest* (Northfield, 1939). Wayne E. Stevens, *The Northwest Fur Trade, 1763–1800* (Urbana, 1928), deals with that important subject, while the effect of the trade on British western policy is considered in Marjorie G. Reid, "The Quebec Fur-Traders and Western Policy," *C.H.R.*, VI (March, 1925). Efforts of the British to cement their hold in the Northwest after their occupation are described in David R. Farrell, "Anchors of Empire: Detroit, Montreal, and the Continental Interior, 1760–1775," *A.R.C.S.*, VII (1977), which deals with the establishment of garrisoned towns, and John C. Guzzardo, "The Superintendent and the Ministers: The Battle for Oneida Alliances," *N.Y.H.*, LVII (July, 1976), an excellent case study of the manner in which one Iroquois tribe was fragmented. The trade network that had spread through the Northwest by the time of the Revolution is described in Walter S. Dunn, Jr., "The Frontier on the Eve of the Revolution," *N.F.*, XX (Winter, 1973).

British Occupation of Florida. Conditions in Florida at the time of the British occupation are admirably described in John J. TePaske, *The Governorship of Spanish Florida, 1700–1763* (Durham, 1964). The fullest study is Cecil Johnson, *British West Florida, 1763–1783* (New Haven, 1943). The standard work on East Florida is Charles L. Mowat, *East Florida as a British Province, 1763–1784* (Gainesville, 1943, reissued 1964). Articles that reflect current views on the British in Florida include Robert R. Rea, "Lieutenant Colonel James Robertson's Mission to the Floridas, 1763," *F.H.Q.*, LIII (July, 1974), describing the journey of an agent of Amherst's who visited the region to recommend occupation tactics, R. F. A. Fabel, "Governor George Johnstone of British West Florida," *F.H.Q.*, LIV (April, 1976), dealing with the governor who served between 1764 and 1767, and Robert R. Rea, "John Eliot, Second Gov-

ernor of British West Florida," *A.R.*, XXX (October, 1977), on the brief career of his successor. Also of use are Wilbur H. Siebert, "The Departure of the Spaniards and Other Groups from East Florida, 1763–1764," *F.H.Q.*, XIX (October, 1940), Charles L. Mowat, "The Land Policy in British East Florida," *A.H.*, XIV (April, 1940), and Robert R. Rea, "'Graveyard for Britons,' West Florida, 1763–1781," *F.H.Q.*, XLVII (April, 1969), which vividly describes the miserable conditions under which British troops lived. Claude C. Sturgill, "John Bull's Stinginess in East Florida," *F.H.Q.*, L (January, 1972), disputes the commonly held view that British appropriations for the Florida garrison were insufficient due to a desire of British officials to lower taxes at home. An admirable account of Spain's problems in trying to maintain control in Louisiana, where the French were in sometimes open revolt, is John P. Moore, *Revolt in Louisiana: The Spanish Occupation, 1766–1770* (Baton Rouge, 1976).

The Quebec Act. The role of the Illinois villages in the formulation of this measure is admirably considered in Jack M. Sosin, "The French Settlements in British Policy for the North American Interior, 1760–1774," *C.H.R.*, XXXIX (September, 1958). The two most recent histories of the act are: Reginald Coupland, *The Quebec Act* (Oxford, 1925), and Charles H. Metzger, *The Quebec Act, a Primary Cause of the American Revolution* (New York, 1936). The administration of the act is considered in Hilda M. Neatby, *The Administration of Justice under the Quebec Act* (Minneapolis, 1937). Hilda Neatby, *The Quebec Act: Protest and Policy* (Scarborough, 1972), describes how historians over the years have dealt with the measure. That the act was viewed favorably in Pennsylvania where it was seen as a restraint on the activities of Virginia traders is argued in Robert F. Oaks, "The Impact of British Western Policy on the Coming of the American Revolution in Pennsylvania," *P.M.H.B.*, CI (April, 1977).

9 Settlement Crosses the Mountains, 1763–1776

General Works. The most essential work on the subject is Jack M. Sosin, *The Revolutionary Frontier, 1763–1783* (New York, 1967), but John A. Caruso, *The Appalachian Frontier* (Indianapolis, 1959) is also useful and is particularly well written. Francis S. Philbrick, *The Rise of the West, 1754–1830* (New York, 1965), also deals with the first settlements, but in excessive detail. Many aspects of settlement are considered in Thomas P. Abernethy, *Western Lands and the American Revolution* (New York, 1937).

Expansion of the Northern Frontier. Solon J. Buck and Elizabeth H. Buck, *The Planting of Civilization in Western Pennsylvania* (Pittsburgh, 1939) is essential. Other accounts are in Kenneth P. Bailey, *Thomas Cresap, Maryland Frontiersman* (Boston, 1944). An excellent biography of a leading frontiersman is Kenneth Bailey, *Christopher Gist: Colonial Frontiersman, Explorer and Indian Agent* (Hamden, 1976). Social conditions are described in J. E. Wright and Doris S. Corbett, *Pioneer Life in Western Pennsylvania* (Pittsburgh, 1940), while sources are collected in Sylvester K. Stevens and Donald H. Kent, eds., *Wilderness Chronicles of Northwestern Pennsylvania* (Harrisburg, 1941). George D. Wolf, *The Fair Play Settlers of the West Branch Valley, 1769–1784: A Study of Frontier Ethnology* (Harrisburg, 1969) is a case study of the 150 settlers who lived on the West Branch of the Susquehanna River during this period, to show how well they adapted to frontier conditions.

The occupation of western Virginia is briefly summarized in John A. Williams, *West Virginia: A Bicentennial History* (New York, 1976), and fully in Otis K. Rice, *The Allegheny Frontier: West Virginia Beginnings, 1730–1830* (Lexington, 1970), a fine use of local history to illuminate the national scene. Older works on the region that are still useful include Ruth W. Dayton, *Pioneers and Their Homes on the Upper Kanawha* (Charleston, 1948), and Lucullus McWhorter, *The Border Settlers of Northwest Virginia from 1767 to 1795* (Hamilton, 1915). John E. Stealey, "George Clendinen and the Great Kanawha Valley Frontier," *W.V.H.,* XXVII (July, 1966), is a case study of a successful pioneer.

The Holston and Watauga Frontiers. A thorough account is Samuel C. Williams, *Dawn of Tennessee Valley and Tennessee History* (Johnson City, 1937), and a briefer study is Thomas P. Abernethy, *From Frontier to Plantation in Tennessee* (Chapel Hill, 1932). Information will also be found in Philip H. Hamer, ed., *Tennessee, a History, 1673–1932,* 4 v. (New York, 1933), Wilma Dykeman, *Tennessee: A Bicentennial History* (New York, 1975), Mary F. Caldwell, *Tennessee: The Dangerous Example, Watauga to 1849* (Nashville, 1974), a book that is more entertaining than analytical, and John P. Arthur, *Western North Carolina* (Raleigh, 1914). Sam B. Smith, ed., *Tennessee History: A Bibliography* (Knoxville, 1974), lists more than 6,000 items. One important settlement is described in William

A. Pusey, "The Location of Martin's Station, Virginia," *M.V.H.R.,* XV (December, 1928). The standard biography of a leader of the settlement is Carl S. Driver, *John Sevier, Pioneer of the Old Southwest* (Chapel Hill., 1932). The career of a pioneer in Augusta County, Virginia, is well told in Patricia G. Johnson, *James Patton and the Appalachian Colonists* (Verona, 1975). James W. Hagy, "The Frontier at Castle's Woods, 1769–1786," *V.M.H.B.,* LXXV (October, 1967), describes the founding of a small settlement on the Clinch River by Jacob Castle, in 1769.

Lord Dunmore's War. The history of the war may be traced in Randolph C. Downes, "Dunmore's War: An Interpretation," *M.V.H.R.,* XXI (December, 1934), and Percy B. Caley, "Lord Dunmore and the Pennsylvania-Virginia Boundary Dispute," *W.P.H.M.,* XXII (June, 1939). Richard O. Curry, "Lord Dunmore and the West: A Re-evaluation," *W.V.H.,* XIX (July, 1958), argues that speculative pressure was only one of several forces leading to the war; the author repeats his arguments with slight additional evidence in "Lord Dunmore—Tool of Land Jobbers or Realistic Champion of Colonial 'Rights'?: An Inquiry," *W.V.H.,* XXIV (April, 1963). That the Indian superintendents not only did not cooperate with Dunmore in fomenting the war but did their best to protect the colonists from an expanded conflict is amply demonstrated in Jack M. Sosin, "The British Indian Department and Dunmore's War," *V.M.H.B.,* LXXIV (January, 1966). The military campaigns are described in Robert L. Kerby, "The Other War in 1774: Dunmore's War," *W.V.H.,* XXVI (October, 1974), and the principal battle in two articles that contribute little but brevity: Kenneth R. MacDonald, Jr., "The Battle of Point Pleasant: First Battle of the American Revolution," *W.V.H.,* XXXVI (October, 1974), which shows that the battle was not the first, and Elizabeth M. Fels, "The Battle of Point Pleasant: Its Relation to the American Revolution and to Tennessee," *T.H.Q.,* (Winter, 1974). Still useful is Virgil A. Lewis, *History of the Battle of Point Pleasant* (Charleston, 1909).

The Kentucky Frontier. Histories of the state have much information on the settlement period. Steven A. Channing, *Kentucky: A Bicentennial History* (New York, 1977), devotes the first of five chapters to the pioneer period; full accounts are in Thomas D. Clark, *Kentucky: Land of Contrast* (New York, 1968), and Otis K. Rice, *Frontier Kentucky* (Lexington, 1975), while a valuable interpretative essay is in Thomas P. Abernethy, *Three Virginia Frontiers* (University, 1941).

The career of Dr. Thomas Walker is described in Ann W. Burns, *Daniel Boone's Predecessor in Kentucky* (Frankfort, 1930), while Lucien Beckner, "John Findley: The First Pathfinder of Kentucky," *H.Q.*, I (April, 1972), deals with another pioneer. More useful are Charles A. Talbert, *Benjamin Logan: Kentucky Frontiersman* (Lexington, 1962), a work of extensive scholarship that reveals for the first time Logan's major contributions to the founding of Kentucky, and Kathryn H. Mason, *James Harrod of Kentucky* (Baton Rouge, 1951). Of the more than fifty biographies of Daniel Boone, the most complete is John Bakeless, *Daniel Boone* (New York, 1939). Boone's Wilderness Road is described in Robert L. Kincaid, *The Wilderness Road* (Indianapolis, 1947). Much useful information is in Thomas L. Connelley, "Gateway to Kentucky: The Wilderness Road, 1748–1792," *K.S.H.S.R.*, LIX (April, 1961), which describes the parties passing over the road. James W. Hagy, "The First Attempt to Settle Kentucky; Boone in Virginia," *F.C.H.Q.*, XLIV (July, 1970), demonstrates that Boone was only a guide for the 1773 party that entered Kentucky from Castle Woods, and that William Russell was the real leader. The activities of another early settler are described in Anna M. Cartlidge, "Colonel John Floyd: Reluctant Adventurer," *K.S.H.S.R.*, LXVI (October, 1968); Lloyd entered Kentucky as a surveyor in 1770 and was frequently in the area thereafter. The activities of another group of surveyors sent westward in 1774 are described in two articles by Neal O. Hammon: "The Fincastle Surveyors in the Bluegrass, 1774," *K.S.H.S.R.*, LXX (October, 1972), and "The Fincastle Surveyors at the Falls of the Ohio," *F.C.H.Q.*, XLVII (January, 1973).

The best account of the Transylvania Company's ill-fated venture is in William S. Lester, *The Transylvania Company* (Spencer, 1935). The composition of the company is studied in Archibald Henderson, "The Transylvania Company: A Study in Personnel," *F.C.H.Q.*, XXI (January, 1947 to October, 1947). A little known phase of the company's history is described in Samuel C. Williams, "Henderson and Company's Purchase Within the Limits of Tennessee," *T.H.M.*, V (April, 1919).

Among the many histories of pioneer settlements in Kentucky are: Willard R. Jillson, *Harrod's Old Fort* (Frankfort, 1929), and Calvin M. Fackler, *Early Days of Danville* (Danville, 1941). Neal O. Hammon, "Captain Harrod's Company, 1774: A Reappraisal," *K.S.H.S.R.*, LXXII (July, 1974), traces the route westward used by the settlers of Har-rodsburg, and lists members of the party. Readable contemporary accounts include Lewis H. Kilpatrick, ed., "Journal of William Calk," *M.V.H.R.*, VII (March, 1921), and Louise P. Kellogg, "A Kentucky Pioneer Tells Her Story of Early Boonesborough and Harrodsbuurg," *F.C.H.Q.*, III (October, 1929).

10   The West in the American Revolution, 1776–1783

General Accounts. No history of the West in the Revolutionary war has been written, although the subject is admirably studied in Jack M. Sosin, *The Revolutionary Frontier, 1763–1783* (New York, 1967). Dale Van Every, *A Company of Heroes: The American Frontier, 1775–1783* (New York, 1962), is a popular history. Most modern histories of the war devote proper space to its western phases. Among these, the most useful are: Marshall Smelser, *The Winning of Independence* (Chicago, 1972), a capable summary of recent scholarship, and two volumes by John R. Alden, *The American Revolution, 1775–1783* (New York, 1954), and *A History of the American Revolution* (New York, 1969). The latter is probably the best single account of the conflict. The best history of the military campaigns is Don Higginbotham, The War of American Independence: Military Attitudes, Policies, and Practice 1763–1789 (New York, 1971); also useful for this phase of the war are Willard M. Wallace, *Appeal to Arms* (New York, 1951), Howard H. Peckham, *The War for Independence* (Chicago, 1958), and E. James Ferguson, *The American Revolution: A General History, 1763–1790* (Homewood, 1974). Two specialized studies of aspects of the military story are Arthur R. Bowler, *Logistics and the Failure of British Arms in America, 1775–1783* (Princeton, 1975), and David R. Palmer, *The Way of the Fox: American Strategy in the War for America, 1775–1783* (Westport, 1975). Much material is also in Thomas P. Abernethy, *Western Lands and the American Revolution* (New York, 1937). Some information is in the biographies of two of the English leaders, Alan Valentine, *Lord North*, 2 v. (Norman, 1967), and Franklin and Mary Wickwire, *Cornwallis: The American Adventure* (Boston, 1970), a sympathetic analysis, which refutes the charge that Cornwallis was responsible for the British defeat at the Battle of King's Mountain.

The War in the South. The thorough survey, John R. Alden, *The South in the Revolution, 1763–1789* (Baton Rouge, 1957), provides an excellent overall picture. More specialized is Kenneth Coleman, *The American Revolution in Georgia, 1763–1789* (Athens, 1959). The principal story of the war in the Southwest is told in the scholarly study by James H. O'Donnell, III, *Southern Indians in the American Revolution* (Knoxville, 1973), while the war in backcountry South Carolina is the theme of Robert D. Bass, *Ninety-Six: The Struggle for the South Carolina Back Country* (Lexington, 1978), which carries the story to the destruction of Fort Ninety-Six. Monographic studies that together tell the detailed story include Philip M. Hamer, "The Wataugans and the Cherokee Indians in 1776", *E.T.H.S., Publications*, III (1931), Randolph C. Downes, "Cherokee-American Relations in the Upper Tennessee Valley, 1776–1791," *E.T.H.S., Publications*, VIII (1936), Hugh F. Rankin, "The Moore's Creek Bridge Campaign, 1776," *N.C.H.R.*, XXX (January, 1953), describing the defeat of Tories who rose prematurely, Robert L. Ganyard, "Threat from the West: North Carolina and the Cherokee, 1776–1778," *N.C.H.R.*, XLV (January, 1968), recounting the war against the Cherokee that began in April, 1776, and Gary D. Olson, "Loyalists and the American Revolution: Thomas Brown and the South Carolina Backcountry, 1775–1776," *S.C.H.M.*, LXVIII (October, 1967) and LXIX (January, 1968) telling of a leading planter's efforts to recruit a Loyalist force in the backcountry. The role of the Creeks is admirably described in David H. Corkran, *The Creek Frontier, 1540–1783* (Norman, 1967), and Edward J. Cashin, "Nathaniel Greene's Campaign for Georgia in 1781," *G.H.Q.*, LXI (Spring, 1977). Walter T. Durham, "Kasper Mansket: Cumberland Frontiersman," *T.H.Q.*, XXX (Summer, 1971), examines the career of a pioneer who settled in the Cumberland Valley in 1780.

A thorough study of the Virginia frontier is Freeman H. Hart, *The Valley of Virginia in the American Revolution, 1763–1789* (Chapel Hill, 1942); that of Tennessee is Samuel C. Williams, *Tennessee During the Revolutionary War* (Knoxville, 1974 edn.). No adequate biography of James Robertson has been written, but his role in the founding of Nashville is appraised in such works as William H. McRaven, *Life and Times of Edward Swanson* (Nashville, 1937), Katherine R. Barnes, "James Robertson's Journey to Nashville: Tracing the Route of Fall, 1779," *T.H.Q.*, XXXV (Summer, 1976), Anita S. Goodstein, "Leadership on the Nashville Frontier, 1780–1800," *T.H.Q.*, XXXV (Summer, 1976) which analyzes the leaders who controlled the colony, and Walter T. Durham, *Daniel Smith: Frontier Statesman* (Gallatin, 1976), the biography of a surveyor

who helped settle the area. Anita S. Goodstein, "Black History on the Nashville Frontier, 1780–1810," *T.H.Q.*, XXXVIII (Winter, 1979), deals expertly with the introduction and spread of slavery in the Nashville area.

The role of westerners in the final campaigns in the South is appraised in M. F. Treacy, *Prelude to Yorktown: The Southern Campaign of Nathaniel Green, 1780–1781* (Chapel Hill, 1963), and such biographical studies of western leaders as Alice N. Waring, *The Fighting Elder: Andrew Pickens* (Columbia, 1962), and Don Higginbotham, *Daniel Morgan: Revolutionary Rifleman* (Chapel Hill, 1961). The role of Loyalists in these campaigns, and in the war in general, is admirably appraised in two modern works: North Callahan, *Royal Raiders: The Tories of the American Revolution* (Indianapolis, 1963), and Paul H. Smith, *Loyalists and Redcoats: A Study in British Revolutionary Policy* (Chapel Hill, 1964).

Two scholarly books deal with the war in the Floridas: J. Leitch Wright, *Florida in the American Revolution* (Gainesville, 1975) and J. Barton Starr, *Tories, Dons, and Rebels: The American Revolution in British West Florida* (Gainesville, 1976); a far briefer account is in Gloria Jahoda, *Florida: A Bicentennial History* (New York, 1976). Eight essays by as many experts are in Samuel Proctor, ed., *Eighteenth-Century Florida: The Impact of the American Revolution* (Gainesville, 1978). Special aspects are treated in a number of scholarly studies: J. Barton Starr, " 'The Spirit of What Is There Called Liberty': The Stamp Act in British West Florida," *A.R.*, XXIX (October, 1976), which explains why West Florida opposed the Stamp Act which was accepted in East Florida, Albert W. Haarman, "The Spanish Conquest of British West Florida, 1779–1781," *F.H.Q.*, XXXIX (October, 1960), Lucille Griffith, "Peter Chester and the End of the British Empire in West Florida," *A.R.*, XXX (January, 1977), a competent biography of the wartime governor, George E. Buker and Richard A. Martin, "Governor Tonyn's Brown-Water Navy: East Florida during the American Revolution, 1775–1778," *F.H.Q.*, LVIII (July, 1979), an able description of the manner in which Governor Patrick Tonyn used a small flotilla to defend East Florida from attacks from Georgia and South Carolina, Bettie J. Conover, "British West Florida's Mississippi River Posts, 1763–1779," *A.R.*, XXIX (July, 1976), showing that British policy prevented the erection of forts needed to defend the province, W. Calvin Smith, "Mermaids Riding Alligators: Divided Command on the Southern Frontier,

1776–1778," *F.H.Q.*, LIV (April, 1976), arguing that the warfare between Florida and Georgia was indecisive because of divided command on each side, and Eric Beerman, " 'Yo Solo' not Sole: Juan Antonio de Riaño," *F.H.Q.*, LVIII (October, 1979), demonstrating that Riaño played as essential a role in the forced entrance to Pensacola Bay as his more famous brother-in-law, Bernardo de Gálvez.

The War in the Northwest. Important essays by experts are assembled in David C. Skaggs, ed., *The Old Northwest in the American Revolution: An Anthology* (Madison, 1977); Skaggs presents a useful overview in "Between the Lakes and the Blue Grass: An Overview of the Revolution in the Old Northwest," *N.O.Q.*, XLVIII (Summer, 1976). Especially useful for the war in Kentucky is John Bakeless, *Daniel Boone* (New York, 1939). The siege of Boonesborough is described in George W. Ranck, *Boonesborough* (Louisville, 1939), and the discontent that underlay the Clark expedition in Patricia Watlington, "Discontent in Frontier Kentucky," *K.S.H.S.R.*, LXV (April, 1967). This stemmed not only from the dangers endured, but from the failure of Virginia to give the pioneers adequate protection or land.

George Rogers Clark has inspired as much authorship as Daniel Boone. A full account is in August Derleth, *Vincennes: Portal to West* (Englewood Cliffs, 1968). The most useful biography, and the best history of the war in the West, is James A. James, *The Life of George Rogers Clark* (Chicago, 1928), although Temple Bodley, *George Rogers Clark* (Boston, 1926), is also useful and Lowell H. Harrison, *George Rogers Clark and the War in the West* (Lexington, 1976) brief and readable although adding nothing new to the story. Documents ably edited by John D. Barnhart, *Henry Hamilton and George Rogers Clark in the American Revolution with the Unpublished Journal of Lieut. Gov. Henry Hamilton* (Crawfordsville, 1951), show that Clark's own accounts of his Vincennes campaign denied Hamilton much credit due him. The maps used by Clark to find his way westward are described in George M. Waller, "George Rogers Clark and the American Revolution in the West," *I.M.H.*, LXXII (March, 1976). Clarence W. Alvord, ed., *The Illinois-Wabash Land Company* (Chicago, 1915), suggests that land speculation was one factor encouraging Clark to undertake his Illinois campaigns, Joseph P. Donnelly, *Pierre Gibault, Missionary, 1737–1802* (Chicago, 1971), tells the story of a priest who reached Kaskaskia in 1768, aided Clark on his military campaigns, and served in the West until his death.

A controversial literature has developed over the influence of Clark's campaigns on the peace commissioners who in 1783 awarded the Northwest to the United States. James A. James insists that Clark won the Northwest in his article "The Northwest: Gift or Conquest?" *I.M.H.*, XXX (March, 1934). The opposite point of view, that Clark no longer controlled the West in 1783, is defended by Clarence W. Alvord, "Virginia and the West; An Interpretation," *M.V.H.R.*, III (June, 1916). That the American peace commissioners knew of Clark's conquest is shown in a letter edited by Lewis J. Carey, "Franklin is Informed of Clark's Activities in the Old Northwest," *M.V.H.R.*, XXI (December, 1934). David C. Skaggs, "Lord Shelburne's Gift: The Old Northwest," *Mil.R.* LVI (September, 1976), holds that Shelburne was willing to exchange the Old Northwest for strategic areas needed to house Loyalists.

A brief but informed survey of the Revolution in the Illinois Country is Reginald Horsman, "Great Britain and the Illinois Country in the Era of the American Revolution," *J.I.S.H.S.*, LXIX (May, 1976). Fuller accounts are in Clarence W. Alvord, *The Illinois Country, 1673–1818* (Springfield, 1920), and Robert L. Schuyler, *The Transition in Illinois from the British to American Government* (New York, 1909). Donald Chaput, "Treason or Loyalty? Frontier French in the American Revolution," *J.I.S.H.S.*, LXXI (November, 1978), concludes that the French inhabitants divided as their self-interest dictated between the British and American causes.

The Revolution in the upper Northwest is described in Louise P. Kellogg, *The British Régime in Wisconsin and the Northwest* (Madison, 1935), and Nelson V. Russell, *The British Régime in Michigan and the Old Northwest* (Northfield, 1939). Nelson V. Russell, "The Indian Policy of Henry Hamilton, a Revaluation," *C.H.R.*, XI (March, 1930), exonerates the Detroit commander of the charge of being a "hair buyer." British policy concerning the use of Indians is explained, and justified, in Jack M. Sosin, "The Use of Indians in the War of the American Revolution: A Re-Assessment of Responsibility," *C.H.R.*, XLVI (June, 1965). The career of a leading Tory who operated with Indians is traced in Thomas Boyd, *Simon Girty, The White Savage* (New York, 1928). A scholarly history of an important fort is told in Thomas I. Pieper and James B. Gidney, *Fort Laurens, 1778–1779: The Revolutionary War in Ohio* (Kent, 1976), while the background of Britain's problems in holding the Detroit are explained in Peter Marshall, "Imperial Policy and the Government of Detroit: Projects and Problems, 1760–1774," *J.I.C.H.*, II (January, 1974). Britain's attempt to hold the Grand Portage area as a means of retaining control of the western fur trade are described in Nancy L. Woodworth, "Grand Portage in the Revolutionary War," *M.H.*, XLIV (Summer, 1975).

The history of the war in the Old Northwest may be pieced together from monographs dealing with aspects of the story. Max Savelle, *George Morgan, Colony Builder* (New York, 1932), and Randolph C. Downes, "George Morgan, Indian Agent Extraordinary, 1776–1779," *P.H.*, I (October, 1934), deal with the early years, as does Percy B. Caley, "The Life-Adventures of Lietuenant-Colonel John Connolly," *W.P.H.M.*, XI (January, 1928), and following issues. The later period is studied in Randolph C. Downes, "Indian War on the Upper Ohio, 1779–1782," *W.P.H.M.*, XVII (June, 1934), which concludes that the American hold on the region gradually declined. Other accounts of events in the area are: Charles G. Talbert, "Kentucky Invades Ohio—1780," *K.S.H.S.R.*, LII (October, 1954), Charles G. Talbert, "Kentucky Invades Ohio—1782," *K.S.H.S.R.*, LIII (October, 1955), and Louis E. Graham, "Fort McIntosh," *W.P.H.M.*, XV (May, 1932). Warfare in Pennsylvania is described in Edward G. Williams, *Fort Pitt and the Revolution on the Western Frontier* (Pittsburgh, 1978), which is overlaudatory in tone.

The New York Frontier During the Revolution. A thorough account of the war in western New York is Howard Swiggett, *War Out of Niagara* (New York, 1933). Warfare along the northern fringes is described in Charles A. Jellison, *Ethan Allen: Frontier Rebel* (Syracuse, 1969), an objective biography that also serves as a history of the beginnings of Vermont. By far the best study of the ill-fated Canadian invasion of 1775–1776 is Robert M. Hatch, *Thrust for Canada. The American Attempt on Quebec in 1775–1776* (Boston, 1979). The vital role of the British navy in this campaign is revealed in W. H. Whiteley, "The British Navy and the Siege of Quebec," *C.H.R.*, LXI (March, 1980), while Sir Guy Carleton is exonerated from blame for not destroying the retreating Americans in R. Arthur Bowler, "Sir Guy Carleton and the Campaign of 1776 in Canada," *C.H.R.*, LV (June, 1974), and Paul D. Nelson, "Guy Carleton versus Benedict Arnold: The Campaign of 1776 in Canada and Lake Champlain," *N.Y.H.*, LVII (July, 1976), both of which blame Carleton's failure on the terrain, logistical problems, and hard luck.

The struggle of the Americans and New York State to convince the Iroquois to remain neutral is admirably described in Barbara Graymont, *The Iroquois in the American Revolution* (Syracuse, 1972), a book that views events from both the white and Indian perspectives. American efforts are appraised in James F. and Jean H. Vivian, "Congressional Indian Policy During the War for Independence: The Northern Department," *Ma.H.M.*, LXIII (September, 1968), and Ralph T. Pastore, "Congress and the Six Nations, 1775–1778," *N.F.*, XX (Winter, 1973), which shows that Congress was unable to provide needed gifts and aid. British activities are the theme of Jonathan G. Rossie, "The Northern Indian Department and the American Revolution," *N.F.*, XX (Autumn, 1973), a capable description of the work of the department in retaining Iroquois loyalty.

Three recent biographical studies of Burgoyne's defeat at Saratoga exonerate him of blame and paint him as the scapegoat of Britain's incompetent military leaders: James Lunt, *John Burgoyne at Saratoga* (New York, 1975), Gerald Howson, *Burgoyne of Saratoga: A Biography* (New York, 1979), and Michael Glover, *General Burgoyne in Canada and America: Scapegoat for a System* (London, 1976).

A thorough history of the most important campaign fought in western New York is Alexander C. Flick, *The Sullivan-Clinton Campaign in 1779* (Albany, 1929), but this should be supplemented with the fine biography of the commander, Charles P. Whittemore, *A General of the Revolution: John Sullivan of New Hampshire* (New York, 1961). A revisionist study of the expedition, Donald R. McAdams, "The Sullivan Expedition: Success or Failure?" *N.Y.H.S.Q.*, LIV (January, 1970), concludes that the campaign was immediately successful in bolstering American morale and forcing Britain to pour more troops into Canada, but failed to damage the Iroquois sufficiently to discourage further raiding. Don R. Gerlach, "Philip Schuyler and the New York Frontier in 1781," *N.Y.H.S.Q.*, LII (April, 1969), describes the activities of an upstate New Yorker who used his wealth and credit to supply the American forces.

The War on the Mississippi River. The subject is surveyed in general terms in Lawrence Kinnaird, "The Western Fringe of the Revolution," *We.H.Q.*, VII (July, 1976), and in the latter chapters of Buchanan P. Thomson, *Spain: Forgotten Ally of the American Revolution* (North Quincy, 1976). Far fuller is the account in John W. Caughey, *Bernardo de Gálvez in Louisiana, 1776–1783* (Berkeley, 1934). A perceptive study of an important area is Robert V. Haynes, *The Natchez District and the American Revolution* (Jackson, 1976). The career of the Spanish captain in charge of Natchez's defenses is described in Jack D. L. Holmes, "Juan de la Villebeuvre: Spain's Commandant of Natchez during the American Revolution," *J.Miss.H.,* XXXVII (February, 1975). Other important studies are: John W. Caughey, "Willing's Expedition Down the Mississippi," *L.H.Q.,* XV (January, 1932), Kathryn Abbey, "Peter Chester's Defense of the Mississippi After the Willing Raid," M.V.H.R., XXII (June, 1935), and D. C. Corbitt, "James Colbert and the Spanish Claims to the East Bank of the Mississippi," *M.V.H.R.,* XXIV (March, 1938). The activities of the leading American in the region are described in James A. James, *Oliver Pollock: The Life and Times of an Unknown Patriot* (New York, 1937). Joseph G. Tregle, Jr., "British Spy Along the Mississippi: Thomas Hutchins and the Defenses of New Orleans, 1773," *La.H.,* VII (Fall, 1967), deals with a leading British informer.

Studies of the relations between Spain, England, and the United States on the upper Mississippi include: Abraham P. Nasatir, "The Anglo-Spanish Frontier in the Illinois Country during the American Revolution, 1778–1783," *J.I.S.H.S.,* XXI (October, 1928), and Don Rickey, Jr. "The British-Indian Attack on St. Louis, May 26, 1780," *M.H.R.,* LV (October, 1960), a detailed history of the expedition led by Emanuel Hess.

Revolutionary Diplomacy and the Peace. An able general treatment is in Lawrence S. Kaplan, *Colonies into Nation: American Diplomacy, 1763–1801* (New York, 1972). The only history of the frontier in Revolutionary diplomacy, now badly out of date, is Paul C. Phillips, *The West in the Diplomacy of the American Revolution* (Urbana, 1913), but two more recent books, although not dealing specifically with the West, shed much light on the subject: Richard B. Morris, *The Peacemakers: The Great Powers and American Independence* (New York, 1965), and Richard W. Van Alstyne, *Empire and Independence: the International History of the American Revolution* (New York, 1965). An older general history which is still of use is Samuel F. Bemis, *The Diplomacy of the American Revolution* (New York, 1935). The same author's *Pinckney's Treaty* (rev. edn., New Haven, 1960), devotes considerable space to the diplomacy of the peace settlement, as does a modern biography of the British leader: John Norris, *Shelburne and Reform* (New York, 1963). The background and social views of the leading French negotiator are admirably

presented in Orville T. Murphy, "Charles Gravier de Vergennes: Profile of an Old Regime Diplomat," *P.S.Q.,* LXXXIII (September, 1968), while the major role played by another issue is recognized for the first time in Orville T. Murphy, "The Comte de Vergennes, the Newfoundland Fisheries, and the Peace Negotiations of 1783: A Reconsideration," *C.H.R.* XLVI (March, 1965). The effect of the fur trade on the peace conference needs further study, although the subject is touched on in Wayne E. Stevens, *The Northwest Fur Trade, 1783–1800* (Urbana, 1928).

11   The Western Problem, 1783–1790

General Works. The best single survey of frontier problems during these years is Reginald Horsman, *The Frontier in the Formative Years, 1783–1815* (New York, 1970). The new nation's attempt to develop a western policy is treated in no one book, although scattered chapters in Thomas P. Abernethy, *Western Lands and the American Revolution* (New York, 1937) are helpful. More useful is Francis S. Philbrick, *The Rise of the West, 1754–1830* (New York, 1965), which is detailed but contains essential information, and Curtis P. Nettels, *The Emergence of a National Economy, 1775–1815* (New York, 1962), which is a thorough study of economic developments.

Land Cessions. A thorough study of the land cessions is needed. The older standard account, Herbert B. Adams, *Maryland's Influence upon Land Cessions to the United States* (Baltimore, 1885), has been challenged by the studies of Merrill Jensen: "The Cession of the Old Northwest," *M.V.H.R.,* XXIII (June, 1936), "The Creation of the National Domain, 1781–1784," *M.V.H.R.,* XXVI (December, 1930), *The Articles of Confederation* (Madison, 1940), and *The New Nation* (New York, 1950), which emphasize the influence of land speculators. The same theme is stressed in St. George L. Sioussat, "The Chevalier De La Luzerne and the Ratification of the Articles of Confederation in Maryland, 1780–1781," *P.M.H.B.,* LX (October, 1936). Jean H. Vivian, "Military Land Bounties during the Revolutionary and Confederation Periods," *Ma.H.M.,* LXI (September, 1966), concludes that the holders of bounties influenced land legislation, but that other forces were far more important.

A detailed history of Connecticut's cession is Larry R. Gerlach, "Firmness and Prudence: Connecticut, the Continental Congress, and the National Domain," *C.H.S.B.,* XXXI

(July, 1966), which shows that the state tried to retain control of the Wyoming Valley before shifting its interest to the Western Reserve. Peter Onuf, "Toward Federalism: Virginia, Congress, and the Western Lands," *W.M.C.Q.*, XXXIV (July, 1977), argues that Virginia's primary motive in ceding her vast holdings was to strengthen the Union by removing a basic cause of friction between the states. The standard work on the South Carolina cession is R. S. Cotterill, "The South Carolina Cession," *M.V.H.R.*, XII (December, 1925). Works on the Georgia cession, which was not completed until 1802, are listed in Chapter XII.

North Carolina's Cession and the State of Franklin. The fullest history is Samuel C. Williams, *History of the Lost State of Franklin* (New York, 1933), but more interpretative accounts are in Thomas P. Abernethy, *From Frontier to Plantation in Tennessee* (Chapel Hill, 1932), and Walter F. Cannon, "Four Interpretations of the History of the State of Franklin," *E.T.H.S., Publications*, XXII (1950). Also valuable are chapters in Carl S. Driver, *John Sevier* (Chapel Hill, 1932). Local problems facing the Franklin leaders are ably described in Paul M. Fink, "Some Phases of the History of the State of Franklin," *T.H.Q.*, XVI (September, 1957). Eric R. Lacy, "The Persistent State of Franklin," *T.H.Q.*, XXIII (December, 1964), traces the history of the concept of eastern Tennessee as a separate state from the Franklin era to the Civil War.

Indian problems related to the state are described in Randolph C. Downes, "Cherokee-American Relations in the Upper Tennessee Valley, 1776–1791," *E.T.H.S., Publications*, VIII (1936). Additional information is in George D. Harmon, *Sixty Years of Indian Affairs, 1789–1850* (Chapel Hill, 1941).

Organization of the Land System. Still the most thorough account is Payson J. Treat, *The National Land System, 1785–1820* (New York, 1910), although more recent books dealing with the land system as a whole provide more up-to-date interpretations. Among the most useful of these are Benjamin H. Hibbard, *A History of the Public Land Policies* (2nd edn., Madison, 1965), Roy M. Robbins, *Our Landed Heritage* (rev. edn., Lincoln, 1976), Paul W. Gates and Robert B. Swenson, *History of Public Land Law Development* (Washington, 1968), and Everett Dick, *The Lure of the Land: A Social History of the Public Lands from the Articles of Confederation to the New Deal* (Lincoln, 1970). Many articles essential to an understanding of the origins of the land system are gathered in Vernon Car-

stensen, ed., *The Public Lands* (Madison, 1963). Marshall Harris, *Origin of the Land Tenure System in the United States* (Ames, 1953), appraises the influence of colonial precedents on the Ordinance of 1785, while Rudolf Freund, "Military Bounty Lands and the Origins of the Public Domain," *A.H.*, XX (January, 1944), shows that pressure from war veterans helped shape the land policy. This may be supplemented by the detailed survey of state and national laws on the subject in Paul V. Lutz, "Land Grants for Service in the Revolution," *N.Y.H.S.Q.*, XLVIII (July, 1964). The importance of right of occupancy laws in the evolution of the land system is examined in Paul. W. Gates, "Tenants of the Log Cabin," *M.V.H.R.*, XLIX (June, 1962). Useful also is Henry Tatter, "State and Federal Land Policy during the Confederation," *A.H.*, IX (October, 1935). William D. Pattison, *The Beginnings of the American Rectangular Land Survey System, 1784–1800* (Chicago, 1957), describes the Ordinance of 1785 and the surveys made under it. William D. Pattison, "The Survey of the Seven Ranges," *Ohio.H.Q.*, LXVIII (April, 1959), demonstrates that the slowness of these surveys was an important factor in stimulating the organization of the Ohio Company.

The Northwest, 1783–87. A brief history of Indian relations and settlement in the Northwest is in Randolph C. Downes, *Frontier Ohio, 1778–1803* (Columbus, 1935). Even more essential is James A. James, *Life of George Rogers Clark* (Chicago, 1928), which describes Indian and military affairs thoroughly. More light is thrown on an important treaty in Henry S. Manley, *The Treaty of Fort Stanwix, 1784* (Rome, 1932), and on the Treaty of Ft. McIntosh by Louis E. Graham, "Fort McIntosh," *W.P.H.M.*, XV (May, 1932). The most important military expedition is exhaustively studied in Leonard C. Helderman, "The Northwest Expedition of George Rogers Clark, 1786–1787," *M.V.H.R.*, XXV (December, 1938).

Events in regions adjacent to the Ohio country may be traced in: Solon J. Buck and Elizabeth H. Buck, *The Planting of Civilization in Western Pennsylvania* (Pittsburgh, 1939), Louise P. Kellogg, *The British Régime in Wisconsin and the Northwest* (Madison, 1935), Nelson V. Russell, *The British Régime in Michigan and the Old Northwest* (Northfield, 1939), and Clarence W. Alvord, *The Illinois Country, 1673—1818* (Springfield, 1920).

The Ohio Company. An excellent history of the company is in the introduction to Archer B. Hulbert, ed., *The Records of the Original Proceedings of the Ohio Company,*

2 v. (Marietta, 1917). Biographies of the leading members include: James Woodress, *A Yankee's Odyssey: The Life of Joel Barlow* (Philadelphia, 1958), Charles S. Hall, *Life and Letters of General Samuel Holden Parsons* (Binghamton, 1905), Mary Cone, *Life of Rufus Putnam* (Cleveland, 1886), and W. P. and J. P. Cutler, *The Life, Journals and Correspondence of Rev. Manasseh Cutler*, 2 v. (Cininnati, 1888).

The Ordinance of 1787. Fifteen essays dealing with aspects of the origin and functioning of the American territorial system are in John P. Bloom, ed., *The American Territorial System* (Athens, 1974). One of these, Arthur Bestor, "Constitutionalism and the Settlement of the West: The Attainment of Consensus, 1754–1784," is a brilliant legalistic discussion of the evolution of the principle that territories should evolve into states. This same theme is stressed in Chad J. Wozniak, "The New Western Colony Scheme: A Preview of the United States Territorial System," *I.M.H.*, LXVIII (December, 1972), which finds the roots of the concept of eventual equality in the plans for Vandalia and other speculative colonies. George M. Dennison, "An Empire of Liberty: Congressional Attitudes Toward Popular Sovereignty in the Territories, 1787–1867," *Ma.H.*, VI (Spring, 1975), traces the concept of territorial self-rule in the years after the Ordinance of 1787 was adopted.

The most usable study of the adoption of the ordinance is Jack E. Eblen, "Origins of the United States Colonial System: The Ordinance of 1787," *W.M.H.*, LI (Summer, 1968), a documented history of the steps leading to the adoption of the ordinance. The same author expertly surveys the territorial system created by the ordinance in *The First and Second United States Empires: Governors and Territorial Government, 1784–1912* (Pittsburgh, 1968). Western influences on the Ordinance of 1787 were first demonstrated in Frederick J. Turner, "Western State-Making in the Revolutionary Era," *A.H.R.*, I (October, 1895, and January, 1896), while an example of the separatist tendency is described in Randolph C. Downes, "Ohio's Squatter Governor: William Hogland of Hoglandstown," *O.A.H.Q.*, XLIII (April, 1934). Robert E. Berkhofer, "Jefferson, the Ordinance of 1784, and the Origins of the American Territorial System" *W.M.C.Q.*, XXIX (April, 1972), argues convincingly that the 1787 ordinance was merely an extension of congressional thinking as embodied in the earlier measure, and not the reversal that most historians have claimed.

Land Speculation in the Ohio Country,

1787–90. A thorough history of the Symmes Purchase is in the introduction of Beverley W. Bond, Jr., *The Correspondence of John Cleves Symmes, Founder of the Miami Purchase* (New York, 1926). Bond has also edited *The Intimate Letters of John Cleves Symmes and His Family* (Cincinnati, 1956). John Walton, "The Men of Losantiville," *F.C.H.Q.*, XLVII (October, 1973), is a scholarly study of the several founders of the Cincinnati colony, showing what each contributed to the project. A detailed biography of one of these founders by the same author is *John Filson of Kentucky* (Lexington, 1956). The Scioto speculation is studied in Archer B. Hulbert, "The Methods and Operations of the Scioto Group of Speculators," *M.V.H.R.*, I (March, 1915), and II (June, 1915), and in Joseph S. Davis, *Essays in the Earlier History of American Corporations* (Cambridge, 1917). The career of a man who figured prominently in the speculation is described in Archer B. Hulbert, "Andrew Craigie and the Scioto Associates," *A.A.S., Proceedings*, n.s., XXIII (1913). The democratizing influence of surveyor activity and the land system in the Virginia Military Tract are described in Ellen W. Denney, "Surveyor Speculation in the Virginia Military Tract, the Territorial Period," *Ci.H.S.B.*, XXXIV (Fall, 1976).

Early Settlement and Government in the Ohio Country. Establishment of the first government in Ohio is described in Beverly W. Bond, Jr., "An American Experiment in Colonial Government, *M.V.H.R.*, XV (September, 1928), and Elbert J. Benton, "Establishing the American Colonial System in the Old Northwest," *I.S.H.S., Transactions*, XXIV (1918). Documents dealing with the subject are in the second and third volumes of Clarence E. Carter and John P. Bloom, eds., *The Territorial Papers of the United States* (Washington, D.C., 1934–in progress). A careful study of the government of the Ohio Territory as represented in its three governors is in Jo Tice Bloom, "The Congressional Delegates from the Norhtwest Territory, 1799–1803," *O.N.*, III (March, 1977).

12   The West in American Diplomacy, 1783–1803

General Works. An excellent general survey of western diplomacy during these years is Reginald Horsman, *The Frontier in the Formative Years, 1783–1815* (New York, 1970). The best study of British-American relations is the balanced treatment in Charles R. Ritcheson, *Aftermath of the Revolution:*

British Policy Toward the United States, 1783–1795 (Dallas, 1969), while an equally valuable work on relations with France is Albert H. Bowman, *The Struggle for Neutrality: Franco-American Diplomacy during the Federalist Era* (Knoxville, 1974). Frederick W. Marks, III, *Independence on Trial: Foreign Affairs and the Making of the Constitution* (Baton Rouge, 1973), relates foreign problems emerging in the West with the collapse of the Confederation. A sweeping but sound survey, based on modern interpretations, is in John R. Howe, *From the Revolution through the Age of Jackson: Innocence and Empire in the Young Republic* (Englewood Cliffs, 1973). More detailed for this period is the excellent study by Alexander DeConde, *Entangling Alliance: Politics and Diplomacy Under George Washington* (Durham, 1958); Paul A. Varg, *Foreign Policies of the Founding Fathers* (East Lansing, 1963) is also searching and sound. Light on problems in the Southwest is thrown by Thomas P. Abernethy, *The South in the New Nation, 1789–1819* (Baton Rouge, 1961), and in the Northwest by two volumes by Randolph C. Downes, *Council Fires on the Upper Ohio* (Pittsburgh, 1940), and *Frontier Ohio, 1788–1803* (Columbus, 1935). The latter region is also considered extensively in A. L. Burt, *The United States, Great Britain, and British North America, 1783–1815* (New Haven, 1940).

Information is also to be found in the biographies of the leading political figures of the day. Among the most useful of these are: James T. Flexner, *George Washington and the New Nation (1783–1793)* (Boston, 1970), Forrest McDonald, *The Presidency of George Washington* (Lawrence, 1974), which is brief and interpretative, Dumas Malone, *Jefferson and His Times,* 5 v. (Boston, 1948–1974), a monumental work of scholarship; Forrest McDonald, *The Presidency of Thomas Jefferson* (Lawrence, 1976), a decidedly anti-Jefferson interpretation; Merrill D. Peterson, *Thomas Jefferson and the New Nation: A Biography* (New York, 1970), a better balanced treatment; Broadus Mitchell, *Alexander Hamilton: A Concise Biography* (New York, 1976), which compresses a larger work by the same author; Gilbert L. Lycan, *Alexander Hamilton & American Foreign Policy: A Design for Greatness* (Norman, 1970), an unabashedly pro-Hamilton interpretation; and Ralph A. Brown, *The Presidency of John Adams* (Lawrence, 1975), a narrative treatment.

Diplomatic Problems in the Old Northwest. An excellent overall view of all aspects of the relationships, incorporating modern scholarship, is J. Leitch Wright, Jr., *Britain and the American Frontier* (Athens, 1976). The problem of the Northwest Posts was first presented in proper historical perspective by Andrew C. McLaughlin, "The Western Posts and British Debts," *A.H.A., Annual Report for 1894* (Washington, D.C., 1895). The view that England retained the posts to prevent an Indian war is ably argued by A. L. Burt, "A New Approach to the Problem of the Western Posts" *C.H.A., Report for 1931* (Ottawa, 1932), while G. S. Graham, "The Indian Menace and the Retention of the Western Posts," *C.H.R.,* XV (March, 1934), presents documentary evidence to support this thesis. The influence of the fur trade on British policy is discussed in Wayne E. Stevens, *The Northwest Fur Trade, 1763–1800* (Urbana, 1928), Ida Johnson, *The Michigan Fur Trade* (Lansing, 1919), and the first volume of Paul C. Philips, *The Fur Trade,* 2 v. (Norman, 1961).

An excellent study of the origins of American Indian policy during this period is Francis P. Prucha, S.J., *American Indian Policy in the Formative Years: The Indian Trade and Intercourse Acts, 1790–1835* (Cambridge, 1962). Briefer, but still essential, is Reginald Horsman, "American Indian Policy in the Old Northwest, 1783–1815," *W.M.C.Q.,* XVIII (January, 1961), which argues that the basic purpose of American policy was to acquire all Indian land, for the benefit of the red men no less than the white.

A convenient and up-to-date survey of events that shaped British-American-Indian relationships on the Northwestern frontier is Joyce G. Williams and Jill E. Farrelly, *Diplomacy on the Ohio-Indiana Frontier, 1783–1791* (Bloomington, 1976). Indian contacts in the Northwest are treated in Louise P. Kellogg, *The British Régime in Wisconsin and the Northwest* (Madison, 1935), Nelson V. Russell, *British Régime in Michigan and the Old Northwest* (Northfield, 1939), George D. Harmon, *Sixty Years of Indian Affairs, 1789–1850* (Chapel Hill, 1941), and Philip M. Hamer, "The British in Canada and the Southern Indians, 1790–1794," *E.T.H.S., Publications,* II (1930).

Warfare in the Ohio Country. Excellent for this period is Francis P. Prucha, *The Sword of the Republic, The United States Army on the Frontier, 1783–1846* (New York, 1969). Harrison Bird, *War for the West, 1790–1813* (New York, 1971), tells the story with greater detail but is less well documented. These accounts may be supplemented with Harry E. Wildes, *Anthony Wayne* (New York, 1941). An excellent account of James Wilkinson's efforts to oust Wayne from his command is in Richard H. Kohn, "General Wilkinson's Vendetta with General Wayne: Politics and Command in the American Army, 1791–1796," *F.C.H.Q.*, XLV (October, 1971). That Wilkinson served ably as commander of the Western Department between 1792 and 1793 is demonstrated in David A. Simmons, "The Military and Administrative Abilities of James Wilkinson in the Old Northwest, 1792–1793," *O.N.*, III (September, 1977). A brief biography of another general serves as a history of relationships during this regime: Alan S. Brown, "The Role of the Army in Western Settlement: Josiah Harmar's Command, 1785–1790," *P.M.H.B.*, XVIII (April, 1969). Other military leaders are described in F. Clever Bald, "Colonel John Francis Hamtramck," *I.M.H.*, XLIV (December, 1948), and Patricia Jahns, *The Violent Years: Simon Kenton and the Ohio-Kentucky Frontier* (New York, 1962). Events during the Indian wars are touched upon in Paul A. Hutton, "William Wells: Frontier Scout and Indian Agent," *I.M.H.*, LXXIV (September, 1978) which deals definitively with a frontiersman who fought in the Ohio campaigns; Gerard Clarfield, "Protecting the Frontiers: Defense Policy and the Tariff Question in the First Washington Administration," *W.M.C.Q.*, XXXII (July, 1975), demonstrating that Hamilton secured passage of his 1792 tariff act by linking it with additional troops for the Northwest; and two competent studies by R. David Edmunds, "Wea Participation in the Northwest Indian Wars, 1790–1795," *F.C.H.Q.*, XLVI (July, 1972), and " 'Nothing Has Been Effected' : The Vincennes Treaty of 1792," *I.M.H.*, LXXIV (March, 1978), on a successful treaty with the Wabash Indians. Patrick J. Furlong, "The Investigation of General Arthur St. Clair, 1792–1793," *C.S.*, V (Fall, 1977), describes in detail the congressional investigation into St. Clair's defeat in 1791.

Two excellent articles by Reginald Horsman provide insights into the events leading to the Battle of Fallen Timbers: "The British Indian Department and the Abortive Treaty of Lower Sandusky," *Ohio H.Q.*, LXX (July, 1961), and "The British Indian Department and the Resistance to General Anthony Wayne, 1793–1795," *M.V.H.R.*, XLIX (September, 1962). The battle itself is expertly described in Thomas R. Case, "The Battle of Fallen Timbers," *N.O.Q.*, XXXV (Spring, 1963). Letters of Wayne that shed light on his campaign are in Richard C. Knopf, ed., *Anthony Wayne, a Name in Arms* (Pittsburgh, 1960). Additional documents on military affairs are in Richard C. Knopf, ed., "Wayne's Western Campaign: The Wayne-Knox Correspondence," *P.M.H.B.*, LXXVIII (July, 1954, and

October, 1954), and Gayle Thornbrough, ed., *Outpost on the Wabash, 1787–1791: Letters of Brigadier General Josiah Harmar and Major John Francis Hamtramck* (Indianapolis, 1958).

The most recent study of Jay's Treaty is Jerald A. Coombs, *The Jay Treaty: Political Battleground of the Founding Fathers* (Berkeley, 1970), which is particularly useful on the political background. An excellent biography is by Richard B. Morris, *John Jay, The Nation, and The Court* (Boston, 1967), which stresses his judicial career. Two older works still may be used: Samuel F. Bemis, *Jay's Treaty* (New York, 1924), and Frank Monaghan, *John Jay* (New York, 1935), which devotes much space to Jay's diplomatic activities. The best account of the Treaty of Greenville is in two articles by Dwight L. Smith, "Wayne's Peace with the Indians of the Old Northwest, 1795," *O.S.A.H.Q.*, LIX (July, 1950), and "Wayne and the Treaty of Greene Ville," *O.S.A.H.Q.*, LXIII (January, 1954). Gerard Clarfield, "Postscript to Jay's Treaty; Timothy Pickering and Anglo-American Relations, 1795–1797," *W.M.C.Q.*, XXIII (January, 1966), describes Anglo-American relations in the years just after the treaty. A highly critical account of Lieutenant-Governor John G. Simcoe's efforts to build a defense system for upper Canada while governor there between 1792 and 1796 is in Malcolm MacLeod, "Fortress Ontario or Forlorn Hope? Simcoe and the Defense of Upper Canada, *C.H.R.*, LIII (June, 1972).

Diplomacy in the Southwest. An essential book to understanding this period is J. Leitch Wright, Jr., *Anglo-Spanish Rivalry in North America* (Athens, 1971); equally important are two earlier works that have not been supplanted: Arthur P. Whitaker, *The Spanish-American Frontier, 1783–1795* (Boston, 1927), and E. Wilson Lyon, *Louisiana in French Diplomacy, 1759–1804* (Norman, 1934), which describes the role played by France in the complex negotiations. The opening chapters of Samuel F. Bemis, *Pinckney's Treaty* (New Haven, 1960), stress diplomatic aspects. Two excellent biographies of Spanish governors are essential: Caroline M. Burson, *The Stewardship od Don Esteban Miró, 1772–1792* (New Orleans, 1924), and Jack D. L. Holmes, *Gayoso: The Life of a Spanish Governor in the Mississippi Valley, 1789–1799* (Baton Rouge, 1965). Gayoso served as governor at Natchez until 1797, then for two years as governor-general of Louisiana. An excellent description of the methods used by Miró to induce the Spanish government to open Louisiana to American Protestants is Gilbert C. Din,

"The Immigration Policy of Governor Esteban Miró in Spanish Louisiana," *S.H.Q.*, LXXIII (October, 1969); the author shows that Miró, not Floridablanca, was the true father of this policy. James H. Mast, "Hugh Henry Brackenridge and the Mississippi Question, 1786–1787," *W.P.H.M.*, LIV (October, 1971), tells how one frontier lawyer opened his political career by attacking Spain's Mississippi policy. Special aspects of the Spanish-American dispute are discussed in Abraham P. Nasatir, "The Anglo-Spanish Frontier on the Upper Mississippi, 1786–1796," *I.J.H.P.*, XXIX (April, 1931), and Lawrence Kinnaird, *New Spain and the Anglo-American West*, 2 v. (Los Angeles, 1932). Thomas D. Watson, "Continuity in Commerce: Development of the Panton, Leslie and Company Trade Monopoly in West Florida," *F.H.Q.*, LIV (April, 1976), examines the manipulations through which this trading company maintained its position under Spanish rule in East Florida.

The efforts of both Spanish and Americans to secure Indian allies in the Southwest are described in Craig Symonds, "The Failure of America's Indian Policy on the Southwestern Frontier, 1785–1793," *T.H.Q.*, XXXV (Spring, 1976), Thomas D. Watson, "A Scheme Gone Awry: Bernardo de Galvez, Gilberto Antonio de Maxent, and the Southern Indian Trade," *L.H.*, XVII (Winter, 1876), David H. White, "The Indian Policy of Juan Vicente Folch, Governor of Spanish Mobile," *A.R.*, XXVIII (October, 1975), Randolph C. Downes, "Creek-American Relations, 1782–1790," *G.H.Q.*, XXI (June, 1937), Kenneth Coleman, "Federal Indian Relations in the South, 1781–1789," *C.O.*, XXXV (Winter, 1957–58), Merritt B. Pound, *Benjamin Hawkins, Indian Agent* (Athens, 1951), Lawrence Kinnaird, "International Rivalry in the Creek Country," *F.H.Q.*, X (October, 1931), Jane M. Berry, "The Indian Policy of Spain in the Southwest, 1783–1795," *M.V.H.R.*, III (March, 1917), and Arthur P. Whitaker, "Spain and the Cherokee Indians, 1783–98," *N.C.H.R.*, IV (July, 1927). Two careful studies of the principal Creek chief are Arthur P. Whitaker, "Alexander McGillivray," *N.C.H.R.*, V (April, 1928), and John W. Caughey, *McGillivray of the Creeks* (Norman, 1938). The manner in which McGillivray rose to a position of leadership in his tribe is expertly described in J. H. O'Donnell, "Alexander McGillivray: Training for Leadership," *G.H.Q.*, XLIX (June, 1965). His motives in drafting the Treaty of New York, and his desire to obtain a free port in Florida for the import of munitions, are explored expertly in J. Leitch

Wright, Jr., "Creek-American Treaty of 1790: Alexander McGillivray and the Diplomacy of the Old Southwest," *G.H.Q.*, LI (December, 1967). The Loyalist firm which supplied McGillivray with ammunition is studied in Marie T. Greenslade, "William Panton," *F.H.Q.*, XIV (October, 1935), and Robert S. Cotterill, "A Chapter of Panton, Leslie and Company," *J.S.H.*, X (August, 1944). Janice B. Miller, "The Struggle for Free Trade in East Florida and the Cédula of 1793," *F.H.Q.*, LV (July, 1976), shows that Spain's refusal to break the trade monopoly of the Panton, Leslie and Company stirred such resentment that the country's hold on Florida was doomed. The later history of the company, which changed its name to The Forbes Company, is well covered in David H. White, "The Forbes Company in Spanish Florida, 1801–1806," *F.H.Q.*, LII (January, 1974). Spain's diplomatic squabbles are also considered in Jack D. L. Holmes, "Spanish Treaties with the West Florida Indians, 1784–1802," *F.H.Q.*, XLVIII (October, 1969); J. Leitch Wright, Jr., "British Designs on the Old Southwest: Foreign Intrigue on the Florida Border, 1783–1803," *F.H.Q.*, XLIV (April, 1966), and Gilbert L. Lycan, "Alexander Hamilton's Florida Policy," *F.H.Q.*, L (October, 1971), which discloses Hamilton's continuing interest in securing Florida and his plan to lead an army there in 1798–1800.

The Spanish Conspiracy. The first modern account of the conspiracy in Kentucky was William R. Shepherd, "Wilkinson and the Beginnings of the Spanish Conspiracy," *A.H.R.*, IX (April, 1903), which demonstrated that the intrigue originated with Wilkinson rather than the Spaniards. Other scholars have added much to the original story: Arthur P. Whitaker, "James Wilkinson's First Descent to New Orleans in 1787," *H.A.H.R.*, VII (February, 1928) and Thomas R. Hay, "Some Reflections on the Career of General James Wilkinson," *M.V.H.R.*, XXI (March, 1935). The latter argues that Wilkinson was never serious in his intrigues with Spain. Two biographies add detail to the story: James R. Jacobs, *Tarnished Warrior: Major-General James Wilkinson* (New York, 1938), and Thomas R. Hay and M. R. Werner, *The Admirable Trumpeter: A Biography of General James Wilkinson* (New York, 1941). Patricia Watlington, "John Brown and the Spanish Conspiracy," *V.M.H.B.*, LXXV (January, 1967), uses new evidence to prove conclusively that Brown did negotiate with Spain for the separation of Kentucky from the Union. The history of Kentucky just after the conspiracy is told in Patricia Watlington, *The Par-*

tisan Spirit: Kentucky Politics, 1779–1792 (New York, 1972), an excellent discussion of the factionalism that persisted long after the conspiracy was over.

The Spanish Conspiracy in Tennessee is described in Arthur P. Whitaker, "Spanish Intrigue in the Old Southwest: An Episode, 1788–89," *M.V.H.R.*, XII (September, 1925). The same author shows the connection between the intrigue and land speculation in "The Muscle Shoals Speculation, 1783–1789," *M.V.H.R.*, XIII (December, 1926), a thesis carried a step further by Thomas P. Abernethy, *From Frontier to Plantation in Tennessee* (Chapel Hill, 1932). William H. Masterson, *William Blount* (Baton Rouge, 1954) is a sound biography, while papers relating to land promotion are in Alice B. Keith and William H. Masterson, eds., *The John Gray Blount Papers, 1764–1802*, 3 v. (Raleigh, 1952–1965). Sevier's role is examined in Carl S. Driver, *John Sevier* (Chapel Hill, 1932). One aspect of Spanish immigration policy is explored in Max Savelle, "The Founding of New Madrid," *M.V.H.R*, XIX (June, 1932).

International Conflict and the Genet Mission. The effect of the Nootka Sound Controversy on diplomacy in the Southwest is described in William R. Manning, "The Nootka Sound Controversy," *A.H.A., Annual Report for 1904* (Washington, 1905), and Frederick J. Turner, "English Policy Toward America in 1790–1791," *A.H.R.*, VII (July, 1902). A sound and readable story of the Genet Mission is Harry Ammon, *The Genet Mission* (New York, 1973). Special aspects are studied in: E. Merton Coulter, "The Efforts of the Democratic Societies of the West to Open the Navigation of the Mississippi," *M.V.H.R.*, XI (December, 1924), and E. Merton Coulter, "Elijah Clarke's Foreign Intrigue and the 'Trans-Oconee Republic,' " *M.V.H.A.* Proceedings, X (1919-20). Thomas J. Farnham, "Kentukcy and Washington's Mississippi Policy of Patience and Persuasion," *K.S.H.S.R.*, LXIV (January, 1966), demonstrates that Washignton's delaying tactics allowed James Innes and other Kentukcy leaders to recognize that his aims were the same as theirs and thus checked an uprising; Donald S. Spencer, "Appeals to the People; The Later Genet Affair," *N.Y.H.S.Q.*, LIV (July, 1970), describes the Federalists' use of Genet's incautious statements for their own political ends.

Spanish intrigue in Kentucky after the Genet mission is treated in the biographies of Wilkinson and in Arthur P. Whitaker, "Harry Innes and the Spanish Intrigue: 1794–1795," *M.V.H.R.*, XV (September, 1928). The problems of Spain in holding the region after 1795

are made the subject of a case study of one post near Memphis in David H. White, "Commandant Folch at San Fernando de las Barrancas, 1795–1796," *T.H.Q.*, XXXIII (Winter, 1974).

The Yazoo Land Companies. The Attempt of Georgia speculators to expand westward is considered in Samuel B. Adams, "The Yazoo Fraud," *G.H.Q.*, VII (June, 1923), and Arthur P. Whitaker, ed., "The South Carolina Yazoo Company," *M.V.H.R.*, XVI (December, 1929). The career of the South Carolina Yazoo Company's agent is traced in John C. Parish, "The Intrigues of Dr. James O'Fallon," *M.V.H.R.*, XVII (September, 1930). In a scholarly article, Donald A. MacPhee, "The Yazoo Controversy: The Beginning of the 'Quid' Revolt," *G.H.Q.*, XLIX (March, 1965), the split in the Jeffersonian Party in Georgia is traced to the Yazoo grants. C. Peter Magrath, *Yazoo: Law and Politics in the New Republic. The Case of Fletcher v. Peck* (Providence, 1966), is badly organized and based on inadequate research, but it casts light on the sectional divisions that governed the congressional vote on the question of compensation for the Yazoo claimants, The activity of one of the claimants the New England-Mississippi Land Company is the subject of Jane Elsmere, "The Notorious Yazoo Land Fraud Case," *G.H.Q.*, LI (December, 1967).

Indian problems arising from the attempted expansion are considered in Randolph C. Downes, "Creek-American Relations, 1790–1795," *J.S.H.*, VIII (August, 1942), and George D. Harmon, *Sixty Years of Indian Affairs, 1789–1850* (Chapel Hill, 1941). The romantic career of William Augustus Bowles in the Southwest is described in an excellent biography, J. Leitch Wright, Jr., *William Augustus Bowles: Director General of the Creek Nation* (Athens, 1967); aspects of his career are discussed in Lyle N. McAlister, "William Augustus Bowles and the State of Muskogee," *F.H.Q.*, XL (April, 1962), and David H. White, "The Spaniards and William Augustus Bowles in Florida, 1799–1803," *F.H.Q.*, LIV (October, 1975).

The Treaty of San Lorenzo. That frontier concern over navigation of the Mississippi was a primary force leading to the treaty is demonstrated in Stuart S. Sprague, "Kentucky and the Navigation of the Mississippi: The Climactic Years, 1793–1795," *K.S.H.S.R.*, LXXI (October, 1973). The treaty itself is admirably described in Arthur P. Whitaker, *The Mississippi Question, 1795–1803* (New York, 1934), and Samuel F. Bemis, *Pinckney's Treaty* (rev. edn., New Haven, 1960). Bemis maintains that Godoy had no knowledge of the terms of Jay's Treaty and that he acquiesced to Pinckney's demands because of fear of an Anglo-American alliance. Whitaker argues that Godoy had a copy of Jay's Treaty during the latter stages of the negotiations, and explains the Spanish surrender in terms of the failure of the nation's frontier policy and the critical European situation. Whitaker proves his case in two articles: "New Light on the Treaty of San Lorenzo: An Essay in Historical Criticism," *M.V.H.R.*, XV (March, 1929), and "Godoy's Knowledge of the Terms of Jay's Treaty," *A.H.R.*, XXXV (July, 1930).

Spanish-American Conflicts After Pinckney's Treaty. The period is thoroughly covered in Whitaker, *The Mississippi Question.* Isaac J. Cox, *The West Florida Controversy* (Baltimore, 1918) also surveys the era in its opening chapters. Efforts of the United States to win over the southwestern Indians is the theme of Ora B. Peake, *A History of the United States Indian Factory System, 1795–1822* (Denver, 1954). Isabel Thompson, "The Blount Conspiracy," *E.T.H.S., Publications,* II (1930), deals with that subject. The futile efforts of Governor Claiborne to keep peace between the Indians and whites along the Florida border is discussed in an able biography, Joseph T. Hatfield, *William Claiborne: Jeffersonian Centurian in the American Southwest* (Lafayette, 1976), and in such articles as Jared W. Bradley, "William C. C. Claiborne: The Old Southwest and the Development of American Indian Policy," *T.H.Q.,* XXXIII (Fall, 1974), Joseph T. Hatfield, "Governor William Claiborne, Indians, and Outlaws in Frontier Mississippi, 1801–1802," *J.Miss.H.,* XXVII (November, 1965), and W. Jared Bradley, "W. C. C. Claiborne and Spain: Foreign Affairs Under Jefferson and Madison, 1801–1811," *L.H.,* XII (Fall and Winter, 1971). A little-known aspect of Spain's policy is explained in Abraham P. Nasatir, *Spanish War Vessels on the Mississippi, 1792–1796* (New Haven, 1968), an account of a small fleet that patrolled the river to hold back the aggressive Americans before the 1795 treaty.

The Louisiana Purchase. A searching examination of the steps leading to the purchase, and the purchase itself, is Alexander DeConde, *The Affair of Louisiana* (New York, 1976), which argues that the acquisition was the result of a long-sustained effort for imperial expansion on the part of the new nation. Essential to the story also are Whitaker, *The Mississippi Question,* and E. Wilson Lyon, *Louisiana in French Diplomacy, 1759–1804* (Norman, 1934). The same author has written a sound biography of François Barbe-Marbois, *The Man Who Sold Louisiana* (Norman,

1942). The efforts of France to secure Louisiana from Spain are described in Mildred S. Fletcher, "Louisiana as a Factor in French Diplomacy from 1763 to 1800" *M.V.H.R.,* XVII (December, 1930). An explanation of Spain's retention of the province in 1795 is in Arthur P. Whitaker, "Louisiana in the Treaty of Basel," *J.M.H.,* VIII (March, 1936). André LaFargue, "The Louisiana Purchase: The French Viewpoint," *L.H.Q.,* XXIII (January, 1940), argues that the cession of the province to the United States benefited France.

The closing of deposit at New orleans in 1802 is studied in E. Wilson Lyon, "The Closing of the Port of New Orleans," *A.H.R.,* XXXVII (January, 1932), and Arthur P. Whitaker, "France and the American Deposit at New Orleans," *H.A.H.R,* XI (November, 1931). Stuart S. Sprague, "Jefferson, Kentucky, and the Closing of the Port of New Orleans, 1802–1803," *K.S.H.S.R.,* LXX (October, 1972), deals with Jefferson's effort to check Kentuckians from attacking New Orleans after the French acquisition. The early years of the new American province are viewed in Philip C. Brooks, "Spain's Farewell to Louisiana, 1803–1821," *M.V.H.R.,* XXVII (June, 1940). John L. Allen, "Geographical Knowledge & American Images of the Louisiana Territory," *We.H.Q.,* II (April, 1971), concludes on the basis of examining travel accounts and newspapers that the American people pictured Louisiana as a vast garden ideal for settlement. Jefferson's attempt to fasten the American legal system on the new province, which succeeded in criminal law, is examined in George Dargo, *Jefferson's Louisiana: Politics and the Clash of Legal Traditions* (Cambridge, 1975). Efforts of Spaniards to reoccupy the area after the purchase are surveyed in Thomas P. Coffey, "Spanish Intrigue in the Territory of Orleans," *R.R.V.H.R.,* III (Fall, 1978). That Federalists still condemned the purchase until it became more popular is shown in Jerry W. Knudson, "Newspaper Reaction to the Louisiana Purchase," *M.H.R.,* LXIII (January, 1969). A superior history of the principal city, stressing its economic growth in French and Spanish hands, and its significance to the American economy is John G. Clark, *New Orleans, 1718–1812: An Economic History* (Baton Rouge, 1970).

13 Settling the Appalachian Plateau, 1795–1812

General Works. Reginald Horsman, *The Frontier in the Formative Years, 1783–1815*

(New York, 1970), is particularly valuable in its description of the settlement of this region and the nature of the society that developed there. John A. Caruso, *The Appalachian Frontier: America's First Surge Westward* (Indianapolis, 1959) supplies colorful information as well as a rounded story of the earlier developments. The portions of Malcolm J. Rohrbough, *The Trans-Appalachian Frontier* (New York, 1978), that deal with this area are excellent on social and institutional development, while James E. Davis, *Frontier America, 1800–1840: A Comparative Demographic Analysis of the Settlement Process* (Glendale, 1977), uses statistical techniques to exmaine the changing nature of frontier households in North and South. For the South, Thomas P. Abernethy, *The South in the New Nation, 1789–1819* (Baton Rouge, 1961), is both scholarly and well-rounded. Economic developments concerning the West are treated in Curtis P. Nettels, *The Emergence of a National Economy, 1775–1815* (New York, 1962).

Sources and Routes of Westward Migration. The only satisfactory study of the expelling forces driving easterners westward during the period is Lewis D. Stilwell, *Migration from Vermont (1776–1860)* (Montpelier, 1937), although the problem is touched upon in Harold F. Wilson, *The Hill Country of Northern New England* (New York, 1936), Avery O. Craven, *Soil Exhaustion as a Factor in the Agricultural History of Virginia and Maryland, 1606–1860* (Urbana, 1925), and John D. Barnhart, "Sources of Southern Migration into the Old Northwest," *M.V.H.R.,* XXII (June, 1935). Studies similar to Stilwell's for other regions would be welcomed.

Equally neglected is the subject of road building between East and West. Works dealing with transportation in general scarcely touch upon the subject: Balthasar H. Meyer, ed., *History of Transportation in the United States before 1860* (Washington, 1917), and Malcolm Keir, *The March of Commerce* (New Haven, 1972). Scattered information is also in Archer B. Hulbert, *Historic Highways of America,* 16 v. (Cleveland, 1902–05). A thorough study of travel routes would help explain the nature of western settlement. An able work for a nearby region is William J. Wilgus, *The Role of Transportation in the Development of Vermont* (Montpelier, 1945).

Growth of Settlement in Kentucky and Tennessee. The works cited in Chapter IX contain information, especially Thomas P. Abernethy, *From Frontier to Plantation in Tennessee* (Chaple Hill, 1932), Stanley J. Folmsbee, et. al., *Tennessee: A Short History* (Knoxville, 1969), and Robert S. Cotterill,

History of Pioneer Kentucky (Cincinnati, 1917). The well-researched biography of a leading Kentuckian at this time, Lowell H. Harrison, *John Breckinridge: Jeffersonian Republican* (Louisville, 1969), provides an excellent account of life in the region. A popular but sound history of the settlement of the region between 1781 and 1794 is Dale Van Every, *Men of the Western Waters* (Boston, 1956). William B. Hamilton, "The Southwestern Frontier, 1795–1817: An Essay in Social History," *J.S.H.,* X (November, 1944), is interpretative. The surveying and occupation of one region is treated in James A. Ramage, "The Green River Pioneers: Squatters, Soldiers, and Speculators," *K.S.H..S.R.,* LXXV (July, 1977), and the career of one successful settler who arrived in Lexington in 1795 and was a leading merchant for the next half-century is in the same author's *John Wesley Hunt: Pioneer Merchant, Manufacturer, Francier* (Lexington, 1974). Joan W. Coward, *Kentucky in the New Republic: The Process of Constitution Making* (Lexington, 1979), expertly examines Kentucky's first two state constitutions and its early government.

Tennessee's development during these years is considered in Stanley J. Folmsbee and Lucile Deaderick, "The Founding of Knoxville," *E.T.H.S., Publications,* XIII (1941), and Samuel C. Williams, "The Admission of Tennessee into the Union," *T.H.M.,* IV (December, 1945). While growth in the area south of Tennessee was slow during this period, important beginnings were made. Two solidly researched articles by Alan V. Briceland explore the establishment of the land system on the Tombigbee frontier: "The Mississippi Territorial Land Board East of the Pearl River, 1804," *A.R.,* XXXII (January, 1979), and "Land, Law, and Politics on the Tombigbee Frontier, 1804," *A.R.,* XXXIII (April, 1980). Two pockets of settlement that emerged are considered in James F. Doster, "Early Settlements on the Tombigbee and Tensaw Rivers," *A.R.,* XII (April, 1959), and E. Merton Coulter, *Old Petersburg and the Broad River Valley of Georgia: Their Rise and Decline* (Athens, 1965). The latter expertly deals with a settlement on the upper Savannah River which flourished briefly in the late 1700s and early 1800s. A similar small settlement on the Broad River in Georgia is described in G. Melvin Herndon, "Samuel Edward Butler of Virginia Goes to Georgia, 1784," *G.H.Q.,* LII (June, 1968). The efforts of an agent sent by Jefferson to settle land claims east of the Pearl River in Mississippi Territory as a prelude to settlement are discussed in Alan V. Briceland, "Ephraim Kirby: Mr. Jefferson's Emissary on the Tombigbee-Mobile Frontier in 1804,'' *A.R.*, XXIV (April, 1971). Somewhat shallow, but still of some use, is Charles D. Lowery, "The Great Migration to the Mississippi Territory, 1789–1819," *J.M.H.*, XXX (August, 1968), which shows that a trickle of population was entering the territory between 1798 and 1812. A contrast between the treatment of blacks under Spanish and American rule is revealed in Jack D. L. Holmes, "The Role of Blacks in Spanish Alabama: The Mobile Districts, 1780–1813," *Al.H.Q.*, XXXVII (1975).

The Occupation of Central and Western New York. General works include: Alexander C. Flick, ed., *History of the State of New York*, 10 v. (New York, 1932–37), Ruth L. Higgins, *Expansion in New York with Especial Reference to the Eighteenth Century* (Columbus, 1931), David M. Ellis, *Landlords and Farmers in the Hudson-Mohawk Region, 1790–1850* (Ithaca, 1946), Dixon R. Fox, *Yankees and Yorkers* (New York, 1940), and Lois K. Mathews, *The Expansion of New England* (Boston, 1909). The settlement of the Massachusetts boundary dispute and removal of the Indians is described in Thomas C. Cochran, *New York in the Confederation* (Philadelphia, 1932), while the occupation of the Susquehanna region is considered in James A. Frost, *Life on the Upper Susquehanna, 1783–1860* (New York, 1951). Factors encouraging land speculation are assessed in Dixon R. Fox, *Decline of Aristocracy in the Politics of New York* (New York, 1918), and less satisfactorily in two books by Aaron M. Sakolski, *The Great American Land Bubble* (New York, 1932), and *Land Tenure and Land Taxation in America* (New York, 1957). Speculative influences in the settlement of another northeastern region, a portion of northern New Hampshire, are surveyed in Roger H. Brown, *The Struggle for the Indian Stream Territory* (Cleveland, 1955). Vivian C. Hopkins, "De Witt Clinton and the Iroquois," *E.* VIII (Spring, 1961), shows that the New York governor's interest in the Indians was of some importance in the state's removal policies.

The occupation of the region east of the Genesee River is treated in George H. Humphrey, *Nathaniel Gorham* (Rochester, 1927), and Eleanor Young, *Forgotten Patriot: Robert Morris* (New York, 1950). None probe deeply into their subjects' speculative activities. More useful for a small phase of Morris' career as speculator is Norman B. Wilkinson, "Robert Morris and the Treaty of Big Tree," *M.V.H.R.*, XL (September, 1953), and particularly Barbara A. Chernow, "Robert Morris: Genesee Land Speculator," *N.Y.H.*, LVIII

(April, 1977), which is a thorough discussion of his speculative activities to 1796. Some material is also found in Neil A. McNall, *An Agricultural History of the Genesee Valley, 1790–1860* (Philadelphia, 1952).

The standard work on the Pulteney Estates is Paul D. Evans, "The Pulteney Purchase," *Q.J.N.Y.S.H.A.*, III (April, 1922), although additional material is in Helen I. Cowan, *Charles Williamson: Genesee Promoter* (Rochester, 1941), and John O. Van Deusen, "Robert Troup: Agent of the Pulteney Estates," *N.Y.H.*, XXIII (April, 1942). Equally valuable is Jeannette B. Sherwood, "The Military Tract," *Q.J.N.Y.S.H.A.*, VII (July, 1926). A biography of an early settler is Herbert B. Howe, *Jedediah Barber, 1787–1876: A Footnote to the History of the Military Tract of Central New York* (New York, 1939).

A thorough study of the settlement of western New York is in Paul D. Evans, *The Holland Land Company* (Buffalo, 1924). This should be supplemented with William Chazanof, *Joseph Ellicott and the Holland Land Company* (Syracuse, 1970), an excellent case study of the use of political influence by an agent of the company to secure low land prices, roads, and other necessities for settlement. The conflict between the Holland Land Company and the New York Genesee Company is described in Julian P. Boyd, "Attempts to Form New States in New York and Pennsylvania in 1786–1796," *Q.J.N.Y.S.H.A.*, XXIX (July, 1931). The role of Dutch capital in this entire process is shown in a recently translated work of vast learning: Pieter J. Van Winter, *American Finance and Dutch Investment, 1780–1805: With an Epilogue to 1840)* (New York, 1977). The early history of a leading city is told in Blake McKelvey, *Rochester: The Water Power City, 1812–1854* (Cambridge, 1945), and more briefly in the same author's *Rochester on the Genesee: The Growth of a City* (Syracuse, 1973).

The Occupation of Northern New York and Western Pennsylvania. In addition to the works cited above, several studies deal with northern New York: Dorothy K. Cleaveland, "Trade and Trade Routes of Northern New York," *N.Y.S.H.A., Proceedings*, XXI (1923), Charles H. Leete, "The St. Lawrence Ten Towns," *Q.J.N.Y.S.H.A.*, X (October, 1929), and Alta M. Ralph, "The Chassanis or Castorland Settlement," *Q.J.N.Y.S.H.A.*, X (October, 1919). An excellent history of a principal city, which sheds a great deal of light on the settlement of the region, is Charles M. Snyder, *Oswego: From Buckskin to Bustles* (Port Washington, 1968).

The occupation of western Pennsylvania is described in Solon J. Buck and Elizabeth H. Buck, *The Planting of Civilization in Western Pennsylvania* (Pittsburgh, 1939), and Stevenson W. Fletcher, *Pennyslvania Agriculture and Country Life, 1640–1840* (Harrisburg 1950). John E. Winner, "The Depreciation and Donation Lands of Pennsylvania," *W.P.H.M.*, VIII (January, 1925), deals with the settlement of the military reserves, while conflicts between the state and speculators over land titles are described in Walter J. McClintock, "Title Differences of the Holland Land Company in Northwestern Pennsylvania," *W.P.H.M.*, XXI (June, 1938), and Elizabeth K. Henderson, "The Northwestern Lands of Pennsylvania, 1790–1812," *P.M.H.B.*, LX (April, 1936). The activities of a leading speculating concern are described in R. Nelson Hale, "The Pennsylvania Population Company," *P.H.*, XVI (April, 1949), and Robert D. Arbuckle, "John Nicholson and the Pennsylvania Population Company," *W.P.H.M.*, LVII (October, 1974). The latter particularly is an excellent account of the company's operations until its collapse in 1815.

Extension of Settlement in the Old Northwest. A readable description of the Ohio Valley as seen by travelers, with sections on travel routes, farms, towns, and other aspects of settlement, is in John A. Jakle, *Image of the Ohio Valley: A Historical Geography of Travel* (New York, 1977). Two books that describe the occupation of the region are Beverley W. Bond, Jr., *The Civilization of the Old Northwest* (New York, 1934), and Randolph C. Downes, *Frontier Ohio, 1788–1803* (Columbus, 1935). Biographies of leaders include Julia P. Cutler, *Life and Times of Ephraim Cutler* (Cincinnati, 1890), David M. Massie, *Nathaniel Massie, A Pioneer of Ohio* (Cincinnati, 1896), and Freeman Cleaves, *Old Tippecanoe, William Henry Harrison and His Times* (New York, 1939). Essential documents are in Clarence E. Carter, ed., *The Territorial Papers of the United States* (Washington, D.C., 1934—in progress). Payson J. Treat, *The National Land System, 1785–1820* (New York, 1920), describes the Land Act of 1800; the operation of the land laws in the Old Northwest is admirably treated in Malcolm J. Rohrbough, *The Land Office Business. The Settlement and Administration of American Public Lands, 1789–1837* (New York, 1968). That the land system discouraged a wide dispersal of ownership is shown in a statistical study based on the 1810 census, Lee Soltow, "Inequality Amidst Abundance: Land Ownership in Early Nineteenth Century Ohio," *O.H.*, LXXXVIII (Spring, 1979). This reveals that while the median farmer owned 150 acres, a few great landlords monopolized thousands of acres while nearly 50 per cent of the adult population were landless.

A thorough account of the Connecticut Land Company is in Claude L. Shepard, "The Connecticut Land Company and Accompanying Papers," *W.R.H.S., Annual Report*, XCVI (1916), while the settlement of the western portion of the Western Reserve is considered in Helen M. Carpenter, "The Origin and Location of the Fire Lands of the Western Reserve," *O.A.H.Q.*, XLIV (1935), and Karl F. Geiser, "New England and the Western Reserve," *M.V.H.A., Proceedings*, VI (1912–13).

Most of the books cited on Ohio contain material on the evolution of a governmental system. They should be supplemented with: Randolph C. Downes, "The Statehood Contest in Ohio," *M.V.H.R.*, XVIII (September, 1931), William Utter, "Saint Tammany in Ohio: A Study of Frontier Politics," *M.V.H.R.* XV (December, 1928), and especially Alfred B. Sears, *Thomas Worthington: Father of Ohio Statehood* (Columbus, 1958). An essential interpretive study of the evolution of democratic institutions in both Ohio and the Old Northwest is John D. Barnhart, *Valleys of Democracy: The Frontier versus the Plantation in the Ohio Valley, 1775–1818* (Bloomington, 1953). The same author explores aspects of governmental origins in: "The Southern Influence in the Formation of Ohio," *J.S.H.*, III (February, 1937), and "The Southern Element in the Leadership of the Old Northwest," *J.S.H.*, I (May, 1935). The lengthy introduction in Francis Philbrick, ed., *The Laws of the Illinois Territory, 1809–1818* (Springfield, 1950), is a pioneering study of the growth of frontier legal institutions.

Economic developments in the Northwest during the period are surveyed in the interpretive article by Randolph C. Downes, "Trade in Frontier Ohio," *M.V.H.R.*, XVI (March, 1930). Water transportation is considered in W. Wallace Carson "Transportation and Traffic on the Ohio and Mississippi before the Steamboat," *M.V.H.R.*, VII (June, 1920), and especially Leland D. Baldwin, *The Keelboat Age on Western Waters* (Pittsburgh, 1941). No satisfactory history of land travel exists, although Clement L. Martzolff, "Zane's Trace," *O.A.H.Q.*, XIII (1904), contains some information.

The nature of the unique social order developing in the Ohio Valley can only be understood against its urban background; this theme is explored in Richard C. Wade, *The Urban Frontier* (Cambridge, 1959) an important study.

The civilization itself is described in such works as Beverley W. Bond, Jr., *The Civilization of the Old Northwest* (New York, 1934), and James M. Miller, *The Genesis of Western Culture: The Upper Ohio Valley, 1800–1825* (Columbus, 1938). Interpretative essays on the subject are in Dixon R. Fox, ed., *Sources of Culture in the Middle West* (New York, 1934), and Joseph Schafer, "Beginnings of Civilization in the Old Northwest," *W.M.H.,* XXI (December, 1937). A sensitive and understanding study of the occupation, growth, and cultural and social progress of a typical pioneer area is in two books by Harriette S. Arnow, *Seedtime on the Cumberland* (New York, 1960), and *Flowering on the Cumberland* (New York, 1963).

14   The West in the War of 1812, 1812–1815

General Works. A classic account, still worth reading, is in Henry Adams, *History of the United States during the Administrations of Jefferson and Madison,* 9 v. (New York, 1881–91). Among recent general histories of the period surveying the war and its results, the most useful are Reginald Horsman, *The Frontier in the Formative Years, 1783–1815* (New York, 1970), and Marshall Smelser, *The Democratic Republic, 1801–1815)* (New York, 1968). The best of several one-volume histories of the conflict is Reginald Horsman, *The War of 1812* (New York, 1969); a single chapter summarizes the causes while the rest of the volume deals with military and naval events. Military history is also stressed in J. Mackay Hitsman, *The Incredible War of 1812: A Military History* (Toronto, 1965), and James R. Jacobs and Glenn Tucker, *The War of 1812: A Compact History* (New York, 1969). Harry C. Coles, *The War of 1812* (Chicago, 1965) is also a first-rate general account, as is John K. Mahon, *The War of 1812* (Gainesville, 1972), which stresses the southern theater. Patrick C. T. White, *A Nation on Trial: America and the War of 1812* (New York, 1965) is interpretative.

Much information may also be gleaned from biographies of the political leaders. The appropriate volumes in the multi-biography of James Madison by Irving Brant contain the fullest account: *James Madison: The President, 1809–1812* (Indianapolis, 1956) and *James Madison: Commander in Chief, 1812–1816* (Indianapolis, 1961). A one-volume abridgment of this six-volume biography by the same author is *The Fourth President: A Life of James Madison* (Indianapolis, 1970). A good survey is Harold S. Schultz, *James Madison* (New York, 1970). Political manipulations in the years before the war are the theme of Noble E. Cunningham, Jr., *The Jeffersonian Republicans in Power: Party Operations, 1801–1809* (Chapel Hill, 1963). Philip P. Mason, ed., *After Tippecanoe: Some Aspects of the War of 1812* (East Lansing, 1963) contains six lectures on various phases of the conflict. Lawrence S. Kaplan, "France and the War of 1812," *J.A.H.,* LVII (June, 1970), is a valuable revisionist article, showing that France did play a role in American plans in 1812, and that only Napoleon's fall prevented it from playing a larger part in the contest.

Causes of the War. For a number of years historians have disagreed on the causes of the War of 1812. The earlier literature on the subject is summarized in Warren H. Goodman, "The Origins of the War of 1812: A Survey of Changing Interpretations," *M.V.H.R.,* XXVIII (September, 1941), the later in Clifford L. Egan, "The Origins of the War of 1812: Three Decades of Historical Writing,"*Mil.A.,* XXXVIII (April, 1974), which begins the story where Goodman ends. Among the early explanations advanced by monograph writers, one of the most plausible is that set forth in two articles by George R. Taylor, "Agrarian Discontent in the Mississippi Valley Preceding the War of 1812," *J.P.E.,* XXXIX (August, 1931), and "Prices in the Mississippi Valley Preceding the War of 1812," *J.E.B.H.,* III (November, 1930). These hold that the West blamed a depression on Britain's interference with neutral shipping, and demanded war to restore good times. His findings are bolstered by Thomas S. Berry, *Western Prices Before 1861* (Cambridge, 1943). Julius W. Pratt, *Expansionists of 1812* (New York, 1925), holds that a desire for expansion into Canada and the Floridas drove the West to war. The expansionist argument is carried a step farther by Louis M. Hacker, "Western Land Hunger and the War of 1812: A Conjecture," *M.V.H.R.,* X (March, 1924), who argues that the need for more land as settlement approached the prairies underlay the western desire for Canada. This is refuted by Julius W. Pratt, "Western Aims in the War of 1812," *M.V.H.R.* XII (June, 1925), which emphasizes the Indian menace as a motive for the acquisition of Canada.

The expansion southward which preceded the outbreak of the war is studied in Rembert W. Patrick,*Florida Fiasco: Rampant Rebels on the Georgia-Florida Border, 1810–1815* (Athens, 1954). The role of one American, a Baton Rouge merchant, in these borderland activities is explored in Henry E.

Sterk and Brooks Thompson, "Philemon Thomas and the West Florida Revolution," *F.H.Q.*, XXXIX (April, 1961).

The argument that maritime factors were primarily responsible for engendering a war spirit in the West and South has gained increasing support in recent years. The theme was admirably developed in A. L. Burt, *The United States, Great Britain, and British North America, 1783–1815* (New Haven, 1940). Additional evidence is provided in an interpretative article by Reginald Horsman, "Western War Aims, 1811–1812," *I.M.H.*, LIII (March, 1957). These exploratory investigations have been given mature status in two excellent monographic studies: Bradford Perkins, *Prologue to War: England and the United States, 1805–1812* (Berkeley, 1961), and Reginald Horsman, *The Causes of the War of 1812* (Philadelphia, 1962). Both stress the maritime factor as basically important. So does Paul A. Varg, *Foreign Policies of the Founding Fathers* (East Lansing, 1963), an interpretative treatment of the period before 1812.

Modern scholars have attempted to weigh these factors by an analysis of congressional and state behavior. The first attempt in this direction was John S. Pancake, " 'The Invisibles'; A Chapter in the Opposition to President Madison," *J.S.H.*, XXI (February, 1955), who held that a group of senators joined with the War Hawks in 1811 to push the President into strong measures against England; this view was bolstered by Margaret K. Latimer, "South Carolina: A Protagonist of the War of 1812," *A.H.R.*, LXI (July, 1956), which argued that three South Carolina congressmen— John C. Calhoun, William Lowndes, and Langdon Cleves—arrived in Washington with nationalistic biases and persuaded others to back the vigorous foreign policy they desired. That these special interest groups were primarily responsible was disputed by Norman K. Risjord, "1812: Conservatives, War Hawks, and the Nation's Honor," *W.M.C.Q.*, XVIII (April, 1961), who joined with Bradford Perkins, *Prologue to War,* cited above, in contending that the majority of the Republicans were motivated not by selfish or anti-Madison motives, but by a desire to preserve the national honor. A third interpretation was added by Roger H. Brown, *The Republic in Peril: 1812* (New York, 1964), and "The War Hawks of 1812: An Historical Myth," *I.M.H.*, LX (June, 1964); he insisted that party loyalty was basically responsible, and that most votes on war issues were along party rather than sectional lines. A statistical analysis of the congressional votes supports Brown's view;

Reginald Horsman, "Who Were the War Hawks?" *I.M.H.*, LX (June, 1964), analyzed the sectional loyalties of the sixty-one Representatives without conclusive results; Leland R. Johnson, "The Suspense was Hell: The Senate Vote for War in 1812," *I.M.H.*, LXV (December, 1969), and particularly Ronald L. Hatzenbuehler, "Party Unity and the Decision for War in the House of Representatives, 1812," *W.M.C.Q.*, XXIX (July, 1972), and "The War Hawks and the Question of Congressional Leadership in 1812," *P.H.R.*, XLV (February, 1976). The latter concludes that partisan loyalty rather than bloc sectional voting determined the attitude of congressmen, and that only eight Republicans played key roles in whipping their fellow-Republicans into favoring the War.

These findings are substantiated by studies of individual states. William A. Walker, Jr., "Martial Sons: Tennessee Enthusiasm for the War of 1812," *T.H.Q.*, XX (March, 1961), William R. Barlow, "Ohio's Congressmen and the War of 1812," *O.H.*, LXXII (July, 1963), Martin Kaufman, "War Sentiment in Western Pennsylvania: 1812," *P.H.*, XXXI (October, 1964), and William Barlow, "The Coming of the War of 1812 in Michigan Territory," *M.H.*, LIII (Summer, 1969), all conclude that the urge to defend the national honor rather than territorial ambitions governed prowar sentiment. The most elaborate state study is of Pennsylvania. Victor Sapio, *Pennyslvania and the War of 1812* (Lexington, 1970), shows that sentiment favored war solely to preserve the national honor and maintain Republican Party solidarity. These findings are bolstered in Norman K. Risjord, "The War Hawks and the War of 1812," *I.M.H.*, LX (June, 1964), which concludes that most of the War Hawks had supported war measures in earlier congresses, and that they were dedicated to preserving the nation's honor and party unity. The latest study supporting this interpretation is Harry W. Fritz, "The War Hawks of 1812: Party Leadership in the Twelfth Congress," *C.S.*, V (Spring, 1977), Ronald L. Hatzenbuehler and Robert L. Ivie, "Justifying the War of 1812: Behavior in Early War Crisis," *S.S.H.*, IV (Fall, 1980), uses quantitative techniques to show that war would have come earlier had Republican congressmen developed their rhetoric of justification.

Current scholarship disputes the traditional view of the War Hawks as responsible for the war, shifting the blame instead to President Madison. This view was advanced by Irving Brant, "Madison and the War of 1812," *V.M.H.B.*, LXXIV (January, 1966), which holds that Madison was not a reluctant militarist but had assured France as early as 1809 that he would go to war against England unless that country ceased its attacks on American shipping. It is substantiated by a statistical study by J. C. A. Stagg, "James Madison and the 'Malcontents': The Political Origins of the War of 1812," *W.M.C.Q.*, XXXIII (October, 1976), a path-breaking study showing that war came when it did largely because of Madison's partisan leadership rather than because of pressure from the War Hawks. This viewpoint is substantiated by two articles, James H. Broussard, "Party and Partisanship in American Legislatures: The South Atlantic States, 1800–1812," *J.S.H.*, XLIII (February, 1977), which studies key roll-call votes of the legislatures of Virginia and the Carolinas to reveal that partisan feeling was strongest on party issues, and especially Rudolph M. Bell, "Mr. Madison's War and Long-term Congressional Voting Patterns," *W.M.C.Q.*, XXXVI (July, 1979), which analyzes 602 roll-call votes between 1789 and 1812 to show that partisan unity was so strong that Madison could count on solid support when he chose to lead the country into war.

While Jeffersonian Republicans were united under Madison in favoring war, Federalists were equally opposed. The growing unity of the party as war neared is described in Donald R. Hickey, "The Federalists and the Coming of the War, 1811–1812," *I.M.H.*, LXXV (March, 1979). The same author demonstrates statistically that the legend that only New England Federalists opposed the conflict is wrong in "Federalist Party Unity and the War of 1812," *J.A.S.*, XII (March, 1978), demonstrating that more than 90 per cent of the congressmen voted against war measures, whatever their section. That Connecticut Federalists were true to their party tradition in opposing the conflict is shown in Donald Yacovone, "Connecticut Against the Tide: Federalism and the War of 1812," *C.H.S.B.*, XL (January, 1975). William Gribbin, *The Churches Militant: The War of 1812 and American Religion* (New Haven, 1973) finds New England Congregationalists strongly opposed to the war with Methodists and other dissenting sects in favor. That trade with the enemy was carried on by New England Federalists is shown in H. N. Muller, III, " 'A Traitorous and Diabolical Traffic': The Commerce of the Champlain-Richelieu Corridor During the War of 1812," *V.H.*, XLIV (Spring, 1976).

The Outbreak of Indian Fighting. Essential to understanding the outbreak of Indian warfare is Reginald Horsman, *Expansion and American Indian Policy, 1783–1812*

(East Lansing, 1967), an invaluable background work. This should be supplemented by the searching study of one phase of the nation's emerging Indian policy: Francis P. Prucha, S.J., *American Indian Policy in the Formative Years: The Indian Trade and Intercourse Acts, 1790–1834* (Cambridge, 1962). Harrison's treaty–making activities which drove the Indians to the war path are discussed in Freeman Cleaves, *Old Tippecanoe: William Henry Harrison and His Times* (New York, 1939), and James A. Green, *William Henry Harrison: His Life and Times* (Richmond, 1941). A special aspect is treated in scholarly fashion in Dwight L. Smith, "Indian Land Cessions in Northern Ohio and Southeastern Michigan (1805–1808)," *N.O.Q.*, XXIX (Winter, 1956–57). Special aspects of Harrison's activity are considered in Elmore Barce, "Governor Harrison and the Treaty of Fort Wayne," *I.M.H.*, XI (December, 1915).

The best biography of the Indian leader is Glenn Tucker, *Tecumseh: Vision of Glory* (Indianapolis, 1956); John M. Oskison, *Tecumseh and His Times: The Story of a Great Indian* (New York, 1938) is overlaudatory. His visit to the Creek nation and its important results is appraised in Mary J. McDaniel, "Tecumseh's Visit to the Creeks," *A.R.*, XXXIII (January, 1980). A provocative article by Reginald Horsman, "British Indian Policy in the Northwest, 1807–1812," *M.V.H.R.*, XLV (June, 1958), demonstrates that while British agents did not incite the Indians, they did seize on Indian unrest to foment discontent among the tribes to the end that Canada might be saved. The same author has written a lively biography of one of the leading British agents who engaged in these activities: *Matthew Elliott: British Indian Agent* (Detroit, 1964).

The clash of fur trading interests which helped precipitate war has not been adequately studied. Kenneth W. Porter, *John Jacob Astor, Business Man*, 2 v. (Cambridge, 1931), deals with the leading American trader. This may be supplemented by the discussion of the interrelationship of Canadian and American companies in Wayne E. Stevens, "Fur-Trading Companies in the Northwest, 1760–1816," *M.V.H.A., Proceedings*, IX (1916–17). American efforts to win Indian allegiance are the theme of Edgar B. Wesley, "The Government Factory System among the Indians," *J.E.B.H.*, IV (May, 1922), and Ora B. Peake, *A History of the United States Indian Factory System, 1795–1822* (Denver, 1954).

That women were engaged in the trade is shown in John E. McDowell, "Therese Schindler of Mackinac: Upward Mobility in the Great Lakes Fur Trade," *W.M.H.,* XLI (Winter, 1977–78).

The Military Phase of the War. An excellent survey is Francis P. Prucha, *The Sword of the Republic. The United States Army on the Frontier, 1783–1846* (New York, 1969); the histories of the war cited above also deal with military events. Alec R. Gilpin, *The War of 1812 in the Old Northwest* (East Lansing, 1958) is more thorough, but antiquarian in tone. That the failure of the militia system used in the war was due more to the incompetence of the leaders than the system itself is argued in Robert L. Kerby, "The Militia System and the State Militias in the War of 1812," *I.M.H.,* LXXIII (June, 1977), while the inefficiency of the Quartermaster General's office is shown in Robert C. Vitz, "James Taylor, the War Department, and the War of 1812," *O.N.,* II (June, 1976). A principal seat of conflict is described in Paul J. Woehrmann, *At the Headwaters of the Maumee: A History of the Forts of Fort Wayne* (Indianapolis, 1971). Brereton Greenhous, "A Note on Western Logistics in the War of 1812," *M.I.,* XXXIV (April, 1970), has important information. The biographies of Harrison cited above have much information on military events, as does William T. Utter, *The Frontier State, 1803–1825* (Columbus, 1942). Works on General Hull include Milo M. Quaife, "General William Hull and His Critics," *Q.A.H.Q.,* XLVII (April, 1938), a vigorous defense of Hull. The career of another American leader is briefly studied in Thomas W. Parsons, "George Croghan in the War of 1812," *N.O.Q.,* XX (Autumn, 1948). David D. Anderson, "The Battle of Fort Stephenson: the Beginning of the End of the War of 1812 in the Northwest," *N.O.Q.,* XXXIII (Spring, 1961), describes the British defeat at this fort near Sandusky in August, 1813. The reason for this and comparable defeats is traced to uninformed decisions by the British high command in John K. Mahon, "British Command Decisions in the Northern Campaigns of the War of 1812," *C.H.R.,* LXVI (September, 1965). A readable story of Harrison's Canadian campaigns, together with other aspects of the warfare on the Canadian borderland, is in Pierre Berton, *The Invasion of Canada, 1812–1813* (Boston, 1980); also useful is Paul J. Woehrmann, "The American Invasion of Western Upper Canada in 1813," *N.O.Q.,* XXXVIII to XL (Autumn, 1966 to Winter, 1967–68). Howard S. Miller and Jack A. Clarke, "Ships in the Wilderness: A Note on the Invasion of Canada in 1813," *O.H.,* LXXI (July, 1962), treat the contributions to

victory of Thomas Jessup who built the ships that carried Harrison across Lake Erie on his way to the Battle of the Thames.

The Battle of Lake Erie is described in Theodore Roosevelt, *The Naval War of 1812* (New York, 1882), and the biographies of Perry, of which the best is Charles J. Dutton, *Oliver Hazard Perry* (New York, 1935). An excellent biographical sketch of the British commander and the fate that he suffered for losing the Battle of Lake Erie is in Howard H. Peckham, "Commodore Perry's Captive," *O.H.,* LXXII (July, 1963).

The war in the Wisconsin country is described in Louise P. Kellogg, *The British Régime in Wisconsin and the Northwest* (Madison, 1935), and Julius W. Pratt, "The Fur Trade Strategy and the American Left Flank in the War of 1812," *A.H.R.,* XL (January, 1935). The career of the leading British agent in the region is recounted in Louis A. Tohill, "Robert Dickson, British Fur Trader on the Upper Mississippi," *N.D.H.Q.,* III (October, 1928–April, 1929). David Edmunds, "The Illinois River Potawatomi in the War of 1812," *J.I.S.H.S.* LXII (Winter, 1969), is an able history of relations with one tribe.

A detailed history of war on the Niagara frontier is L. L. Babcock, "The War of 1812 on the Niagara Frontier," *B.H.S., Publications,* XXIX (Buffalo, 1927); documents are in Ernest A. Cruikshank, *Documentary History of the Campaign upon the Niagara Frontier in the Years 1812, 1813, 1814,* 7 v. (Welland, 1899–1905).

The War on the Southern Frontier. That Britain planned to make the Gulf Coast a major theater in the war, but was unable to do so until 1814 is demonstrated in John K. Mahon, "British Strategy and the Southern Indians: War of 1812," *F.H.Q.,* XLIV (April, 1966). Frank L. Owsley, "The Role of the South in the British Grand Strategy in the War of 1812," *T.H.Q.,* XXXI (Spring, 1972), underlines this judgment and surveys fighting there. The same author's "British and Indian Activities in Spanish West Florida During the War of 1812," *F.H.Q.,* XLVI (October, 1967), broadens our knowledge of activity on this front, while Clifford L. Egan, "United States, France, and West Florida, 1803–1807," *F.H.Q.,* XLVII (January, 1969), argues that Jefferson had counted on French aid to secure West Florida from Spain and that the urge for war accentuated when Napoleon refused to abide by his promises. J. H. Alexander, "The Ambush of Captain John Williams, U.S.M.C.; Failure of the East Florida Invasion, 1812–1813," *F.H.Q.,* LVI (January, 1978), holds that the ambush of a small supply train near St. Augustine forced the "People's Army" from Georgia that had besieged that port to withdraw, thus saving East Florida for Spain.

Two modern studies of the reaction of southern states to the War of 1812 shed light on the problems of the region: Sarah M. Lemmon, *Frustrated Patriots: North Carolina and the War of 1812* (Chapel Hill, 1973), a careful study of enlistment, financial support, and use of troops, and James W. Hammack, Jr., *Kentucky and the Second American Revolution: The War of 1812* (Lexington, 1976), which reveals the high expectations of the people as contrasted with the scant results of the military expeditions originating there.

The outbreak of fighting in the South and the principal massacre there are described in Frank L. Owsley, "The Fort Mims Massacre," *A.R.*, XXIV (July, 1971). James W. Holland, "Andrew Jackson and the Creek War: Victory at the Horseshoe," *A.R.*, XXI (October, 1968), is a thorough history of that important campaign. This campaign and the later warfare on the gulf coast are briefly treated in the standard biographies of Andrew Jackson, of which the latest and best is Robert V. Remini, *Andrew Jackson and the Course of American Empire, 1767–1821* (New York, 1977), the first of a projected multivolume study. More detailed is D. Rowland, *Andrew Jackson's Campaign Against the British* (New York, 1926). Aid given to Jackson by Georgia in his 1813 Creek campaign is described in Hugh M. Thomason, "Governor Peter Early and the Creek Indian Frontier, 1813–1815," *G.H.Q.*, XLV (September, 1961). New light is thrown on the last phases of the war in the South by John K. Mahon, "British Command Decisions Relative to the Battle of New Orleans, *L.H.*, VI (Winter, 1965), but far more thorough is Wilburt S. Brown, *The Amphibious Campaign for West Florida and Louisiana, 1814–1815: A Critical Review of Strategy and Tactics at New Orleans* (University, 1969); this may be supplemented with Willard B. Robinson, "Maritime Frontier Engineering: The Defense of New Orleans," *L.H.*, XVIII (Winter, 1977). Two popular histories of the Battle of New Orleans are Samuel Carter, III, *Blaze of Glory: The Fight for New Orleans, 1814–1815* (New York, 1971), and Robin Reilly, *The British at the Gates: The New Orleans Campaign in the War of 1812* (New York, 1974). The importance of one of the steps taken by Jackson before the battle is shown in Frank L. Owsley, "Jackson's Capture of Pensacola," *A.R.*, XXXI (July, 1966).

Two popular works on American naval victories in the North are Charles G. Muller, *The Proudest Day: Macdonough on Lake Champlain* (New York, 1960), and Harrison Bird, *Navies in the Mountains: The Battles on the Waters of Lake Champlain and Lake George, 1609–1814* (New York, 1962).

The West in the Peace Negotiations. The standard account of the negotiations is Fred L. Engleman, *The Peace of Christmas Eve* (New York, 1962). Chester G. Dunham, "Christopher Hughes, Jr., at Ghent, 1814," *M.H.M.*, LXVI (Fall, 1971), deals with the secretary of the American peace mission.

15 Settling the Lake Plains, 1815–1850

General Works. Excellent interpretative chapters are in Frederick J. Turner, *The United States, 1830–1850* (New York, 1935), but essential to knowledge of the area is the monumental compilation by R. Carlyle Buley, *The Old Northwest: Pioneer Period, 1815–1840*, 2 v., (Indianapolis, 1950), and Malcolm J. Rohrbaugh, *The Trans-Appalachian Frontier* (New York, 1978), which uses modern techniques to analyze community growth and economic development. Eleven essays explaining the remarkable growth of the region's economy are in David V. Klingaman and Richard K. Vedder, eds., *Essays in Nineteenth Century Economic History: The Old Northwest* (Athens, 1975). A popular story of the settlement of the region is John A. Caruso, *The Great Lakes Frontier* (Indianapolis, 1961), Lois K. Mathews, *The Expansion of New England* (Boston, 1909) traces the migration of a leading population group. Significant in understanding the emerging civilization of the region is Daniel J. Elazar, *Cities of the Prairie: The Metropolitan Frontier and American Politics* (New York, 1970), a historical analysis of the cultural, economic, and political growth of seventeen cities in the five midwestern states. Modern analyses of social groups in the Old Northwest during its pioneer period add insights into the effect of pioneering on society: James E. Davis, "'New Aspects of Men and New Forms of Society': The Old Northwest, 1790–1820," *J.I.S.H.S.*, LXIX (August, 1976), which ascribes creativity and egalitarianism to the pioneering experience, and Don Harrison Doyle, *The Social Order of a Frontier Community: Jacksonville, Illinois, 1825–70* (Urbana, 1878), which shows that the intent of the settlers was not egalitarianism but a nascent capitalism.

Removal of the Indians. Basic is Francis P. Prucha, *American Indian Policy in the Formative Years* (Cambridge, 1962), Robert W. McCluggage, "The Senate and Indian

Land Titles, 1800–1825," *We.H.Q.*, I (October, 1970), studies the establishment of senate policies for Indian removal and shows that the government at no time favored granting land titles to the red men. Studies of the removal of individual tribes from the Northwest are Robert L. Fisher, "The Treaties of Portage des Sioux," *M.V.H.R.*, XIX (March, 1933), Ronald N. Satz, "Indian Policy in the Jackson Era: The Old Northwest as a Test Case," *M.H.*, LX (Spring, 1976), which deals with removal of the Winnebago: R. David Edmunds, "Potawatomis in the Platte Country: An Indian Removal Incomplete," *M.H.R.*, LXVIII (July, 1974), Larry L. Leach, "Final Journey," *I.H.B.*, LII (April, 1975), which also deals with the Potawatomi; Robert A. Trennert, "The Business of Indian Removal: Deporting the Potawatomi from Wisconsin, 1851," *W.M.H.*, LXIII (Autumn, 1979), a particularly capable account; David Edmunds, "The Prairie Potawatomi Removal of 1833," *I.M.H.*, LXVIII (September, 1972), and Robert E. Smith, "The Wyandot Exploring Expedition of 1839," *C.O.*, LV (Fall, 1977), which deals with the removal of the last of the Wyandot Indians from Ohio. Dorothy V. Jones, "A Preface to the Settlement of Kansas," *K.H.Q.*, XXIX (Summer, 1963), tells the tragic story of the removal of one band of Indians from Ohio to Kansas. A battle that occurred in Indiana in 1824 over removal is described in George Chalou, "Massacre on Fall Creek," *Pro.*, IV (Summer, 1972). That Indians living in areas where population pressures were not great could retain their lands is shown in Elizabeth Neumeyer, "Michigan Indian Battles Against Removal," *M.H.*, LV (Winter, 1971); the author shows that the Potowatomi in southern Michigan were forced to move but that those in the north were unmolested.

The forts that were scattered through the Old Northwest to provide defense are located and described in Francis P. Prucha, *A Guide to the Military Posts of the United States, 1789–1895* (Madison, 1964). Frontier defense is also the theme of Edgar B. Wesley, *Guarding the Frontier: A Study of Frontier Defense from 1815 to 1825* (Minneapolis, 1935), and Henry P. Beers, *The Western Military Frontier, 1815–1846* (Philadelphia, 1935). Francis P. Prucha, *Broadax and Bayonet: The Role of the United States Army in the Development of the Northwest, 1815–1860* (Madison, 1953), deals with army activities in the Upper Mississippi Valley; the same author has edited a series of reports from officers in the region in, *Army Life on the Western Frontier: Selections from the Official Reports* (Norman, 1958).

The most important forts are described in: Louise P. Kellogg, "Old Fort Howard," *W.M.H.*, XVIII (December, 1934), Bruce E. Mahan, *Old Fort Crawford and the Frontier* (Iowa City, 1926), Evan Jones, *Citadel in the Wilderness: The Story of Fort Snelling and the Old Northwest Frontier* (New York, 1966), and Thomas Friggens, "Fort Wilkins: Army Life on the Frontier," *M.H.*, LXI (Fall, 1977), the latter dealing with a little known fort established on Copper Harbor in 1844. Roger L. Nichols, "The Army and the Indians 1800–1830—A Reappraisal: The Missouri Valley Example," *P.H.R.*, XLI (May, 1972), holds that the military policy was a failure, and that the Indians were in complete possession of the region until the pressure of advancing settlement drove them out.

An excellent account of the Black Hawk War is in Cyrenus Cole, *I Am A Man—The Indian Black Hawk* (Iowa City, (1938); even more valuable for its portrayal of the tensions that led to the conflict is Cecil Eby, *"That Disgraceful Affair": The Black Hawk War* (New York, 1973). Military campaigns are thoroughly studied in Joseph I. Lambert, "The Black Hawk War: A Military Analysis," *J.I.S.H.S.*, XXII (December, 1939). William T. Hagan, *The Sac and Fox Indians* (Norman, 1958) tells the story from the Indian point of view, as does the autobiography of Black Hawk, the best edition of which is Donald Jackson ed., *Ma-ka-tai-me-she-kia-kiak—Black Hawk: An Autobiography* (Urbana, 1955). Other documents are in Ellen M. Whitney, ed., *The Black Hawk War, 1831–1832*, 2 v. (Springfield, 1970–1975). The career of one of Black Hawk's principal opponents is described in Louis Pelzer, *Henry Dodge* (Iowa City, 1911), and another in Roger L. Nichols, *General Henry Atkinson: A Western Military Career* (Norman, 1965). A contemporary account of the major battle is printed in Roger L. Nichols, ed., "The Battle of Bad Axe: General Atkinson's Report," *W.M.H.*, L (Autumn, 1966). The removal of the defeated Indians is described in Grant Foreman, *The Last Trek of the Indians* (Chicago, 1946); additional details are revealed in Ronald A. Rayman, "Joseph Monfort Street: Establishing the Sac and Fox Indian Agency in Iowa Territory," *A.of I.*, XLIII (Spring, 1976), dealing with the Indian agent assigned to the tribe, and Michael D. Green, "The Sac-Fox Annuity Crisis of 1840 in Iowa Territory," *A. and W.*, XVI (Summer, 1974), a story of the vain effort of the deposed Indians to obtain annuities due them.

Sources and Routes of Westward Migration. General histories of transportation, such as B. H. Meyer, ed., *History of Transportation in the United States before 1860* (Washington, 1917), have only scattered information on the turnpikes of this period. The story of the Old National Road is told in Philip D. Jordan, *The National Road* (New York, 1948). The extension of the road into Illinois is the theme of Thomas L. Hardin, "The National Road in Illinois," *J.I.S.H.S.*, LX (Spring, 1967).

Transportation on the Great Lakes is popularly described in Walter Havighurst, *The Long Ships Passing: The Story of the Great Lakes* (New York, 1942). The inns in which the travelers stayed are expertly described in Paton Yoder, *Taverns and Travelers: Inns of the Early Midwest* (Bloomington, 1969).

The expelling factors driving immigrants from New England are discussed in Lewis D. Stilwell, *Migration from Vermont (1776–1860)* (Montpelier, 1937), and more popularly but less thoughtfully in Stewart H. Holbrook, *The Yankee Exodus* (New York, 1950). The changes in farming techniques that undermined New England agriculture are described in Clarence H. Danhoff, *Changes in Agriculture: The Northern United States, 1820–1870* (Cambridge, 1969), and histories of American agriculture, of which the two most recent and best are John T. Schlebecker, *Whereby We Thrive: A History of American Farming, 1607–1972* (Ames, 1975), and Willard W. Cochrane, *The Development of American Agriculture: A Historical Analysis* (Minneapolis, 1980). An earlier article applying specifically to New England is Percy W. Bidwell, "The Agricultural Revolution in New England," *A.H.R.*, XXVI (July, 1921). Robert Balivet, "The Vermont Sheep Industry, 1811–1880," *V.H.*, XXXIII (January, 1965), and Caroll W. Pursell, Jr., "E. I. du Pont and the Merino Mania in Delaware, 1805–1815," *A.H.*, XXXVI (April, 1962), reveal the role played by introducing merino sheep into the United States. A case study of one state to reveal the emerging forces that drove settlers westward is Norman V. Smith, "A Mature Frontier: The New Hampshire Economy, 1790–1850," *H.N.H.*, XXIV (Fall, 1969). Efforts of farm journals and other eastern publications to keep the farmers from migrating are expertly described in Donald B. Marti, "In Praise of Farming: An Aspect of the Movement for Agricultural Improvement in the Northeast, 1815–1840," *N.Y.H.*, LI (July, 1970). A more thorough study of the forces inducing migration, and of migration itself is needed.

The Settlement of Indiana. Particularly useful is the first of a projected five-volume history of the state: John D. Barnhart and Dorothy L. Riker, *Indiana to 1816: The Colonial Period* (Indianapolis, 1971). The same story is told briefly but well in William E. Wilson, *Indiana: A History* Bloomington, 1966), and Howard H. Peckham, *Indiana: A Bicentennial History* (New York, 1978). These works may be supplemented with two interpretative articles that explain the lateness of the settlement process there: Richard L. Power, "Wet Lands and the Hoosier Stereotype," *M.V.H.R.*, XXII (June, 1935), which ascribes the state's unpopularity to its reputation for wet lands, and Paul W. Gates, "Land Policy and Tenancy in the Prairie Counties of Indiana," *I.M.H.*, XXXV (March, 1939), which demonstrates the effect of land speculation on settlement. Three learned articles by Elfrieda Lang analyze the movement of peoples into northern Indiana: "An Analysis of Northern Indiana's Population in 1850," *I.M.H.*, XLIX (March, 1953), "Southern Migration to Northern Indiana before 1850," *I.M.H.*, L (December, 1954), and "Ohioans in Northern Indiana before 1850," *I.M.H.*, XLIX (December, 1953). Less analytical, are two studies by Leon M. Gordon of the same area: "Effects of the Michigan Road on Northern Indiana, 1830–1860," *I.M.H.*, XLVI (December, 1950), and "Settlements in Northwestern Indiana, 1830–1860," *I.M.H.*, XLVIII (March, 1951). Logan Esarey, *The Indiana Home* (Crawfordsville, 1943), is a classic description of social conditions.

The Settlement of Illinois. Two recent histories describe the settlement process: Robert P. Howard, *Illinois: A History of the Prairie State* (Grand Rapids, 1972), which is thorough but pays little attention to the pre-statehood period, and Richard J. Jensen, *Illinois: A Bicentennial History* (New York, 1978), a compact but useful volume. The situation at the time of statehood is described in Solon J. Buck, *Illinois in 1818* (2nd edn. Urbana, 1967). Also helpful for describing the occupation of the region about Chicago is Bessie L. Pierce, *A History of Chicago, The Beginning of a City, 1673–1848* (New York, 1937). Dealing more specifically with the settlement process are Arthur C. Boggess, *The Settlement of Illinois, 1778–1830* (Chicago, 1908), and William V. Pooley, *The Settlement of Illinois from 1830 to 1850* (Madison, 1908). Charles Boewe, *Prairie Albion: An English Settlement in Pioneer Illinois* (Carbondale, 1962), deals with an early prairie settlement in the southern portion of the state, while Alice E. Smith, *George Smith's Money* (Madison, 1966) is a biography of an early migrant from Scotland. The omission of any discussion of land speculation in these two books is partially offset by Paul W. Gates, "Disposal of the Public Domain in Illinois, 1848–1856," *J.E.B.H.*, III (February, 1931), and a challenging collection of nine essays by the same author: *Landlords and Tenants on the Prairie Frontier: Studies in American Land Policy* (Ithaca, 1973). Case studies of speculative activity include three articles by Patrick E. McLear, "Speculation, Promotion and the Panic of 1837 in Chicago," *J.I.S.H.S.*, LXII (Summer, 1969), "William Butler Ogden: A Chicago Promoter in the Speculative Era and the Panic of 1837," *J.I.S.H.S.*, LXX (November, 1977), and "John Stephen Wright and Urban and Regional Promotion in the Nineteenth Century," *J.I.S.H.S.*, LXVIII (November, 1975). Also important are Theodore L. Carlson, *The Illinois Military Tract: A Study of Land Occupation, Utilization and Tenure* (Urbana, 1951), and Larry Gara, "Yankee Land Agent in Illinois," *J.I.S.H.S.*, XLIV (Summer, 1951). An important revisionist study showing large profits made by speculators is Robert P. Swierenga, "Land Speculator 'Profits' Reconsidered," *J.E.H.*, XXVI (March, 1966). Robert F. Severson, et. al., "Mortgage Borrowing as a Frontier Developed: A Study of Mortgages in Champaign County, Illinois, 1836–1895," *J.E.H.*, XXVI (June, 1966), reveals that the average rural loan was $1,500, about the same as in urban areas, and that 75% of the money borrowed came from local sources, not eastern capitalists. The career of one alien landlord who eventually owned 250,000 acres peopled by 1,500 tenants is described in Homer P. Socolofsky, *Landlord William Scully* (Lawrence, 1979).

The development of agricultural techniques suitable to prairie farming are described in Danhoff, *Changes in Agriculture,* referred to above, and in Paul W. Gates, *The Farmer's Age: Agriculture 1815–1860* (New York, 1960), an invaluable work. In addition a number of monographic studies deal with pioneer farming in the state. Paul C. Henlein, "Early Cattle Ranches of the Ohio Valley," *A.H.*, XXXV (July, 1961), describes the spread of ranching on Illinois' Grand Prairie. Even more useful is James W. Whitaker, *Feedlot Empire: Beef Cattle Feeding in Illinois and Iowa, 1840–1900* (Ames, 1975), which despite its title is a fine history of cattle growing on the prairies of the two states. The transition from forest to prairie agriculture is described in David E. Schob, "Sodbusting on the Upper Midwestern Frontier, 1820–1860," *A.H.*, XLVII (January, 1973), which describes equipment used, and Terry G. Jordan, "Between the Forest and the Prairie," *A.H.*, XXXVIII (October, 1964), and Martin L. Pri-

mack, "Land Clearing under Nineteenth-Century Techniques: Some Preliminary Calculations," *J.E.H.*, XXII (December, 1962). The latter analyzes the relative costs of clearing under differing conditions. Allan G. Bogue, *From Prairie to Corn Belt: Farming on the Illinois and Iowa Prairies in the Nineteenth Century* (Chicago, 1963), is a brilliant study of corn-belt settlement that frequently challenges accepted interpretations. A case study of eight Illinois counties, revealing both the nature of land speculation and land use there, is Margaret B. Bogue, *Patterns from the Sod: Land Use and Tenure in the Grand Prairie, 1850–1890* (Springfield, 1959). David E. Schob, *Hired Hands and Plowboys: Farm Labor in the Midwest, 1815–1860* (Urbana, 1975), expertly describes workers and working conditions in midwestern farms of this period. Another important study of one rural town, Paris, Illinois, between 1820 and 1840 is Richard S. Alcorn, "Leadership and Stability in Mid-Nineteenth Century America: A Case Study of an Illinois Town," *J.A.H.*, LXI (December, 1974), an analysis of the leadership structure. Richard Bardolph, *Agricultural Literature and the Early Illinois Farmer* (Urbana, 1948), discusses the influence of farm journals on agricultural techniques.

The development of the Galena lead mining district is described in several monographs: John A. Wilgus, "The Century Old Lead Region in Early Wisconsin History," *W.H.M.*, X (June, 1927), and William J. Peterson, "The Lead Traffic on the Upper Mississippi, 1823–1848," *M.V.H.R.*, XVII (June, 1930). James E. Wright, *The Galena Lead District: Federal Policy and Practice, 1824–1847* (Madison, 1966), is a legalistic description of the leasing system used in the mines after 1807, and its failure. The Lewistown Road from Springfield to Galena is described in Russell C. Birk, "Shortest Route to the Galena Lead Mines: The Lewistown Road," *J.I.S.H.S.*, LXVI (Summer, 1973), while the inability of Indian agents to protect tribal lands from miners is the theme of Ronald A. Rayman, "Confrontation at the Fever River Lead Mining District: Joseph Montfort Street vs. Henry Dodge," *A. of I.*, XLIV (Spring, 1978). Arthur C. Todd, *The Cornish Miner in America* (Glendale, 1967), thoroughly explores the activities of one of the most prominent mining groups there.

The Settlement of Michigan. Alec R. Gilpin, *The Territory of Michigan* (East Lansing, 1970) is a detailed history of the period from 1805 to 1837. More general are the surveys in F. Clever Bald, *Michigan in Four Centuries* (New York, 1954), Willis F. Dunbar,

Michigan: A History of the Wolverine State (Grand Rapids, 1965), George S. May, *Michigan: A History of the Wolverine State* (rev. edn., Grand Rapids, 1980), and Bruce Catton, *Michigan: A Bicentennial History* (New York, 1976). The career of an early settler in Detroit is told in Frank B. Woodford and Albert Hyma, *Gabriel Richard: Frontier Ambassador* (Detroit, 1959). Andrew D. Perejda, "Sources and Dispersal of Michigan's Population," *M.H.*, XXXII (December, 1948), is a statistical survey. Madison Kuhn, "Tiffin, Morse, and the Reluctant Pioneer," *M.H.,L* (June, 1966), shows that the hostile report on Michigan's farming possibilities issued by Edward Tiffin in 1815 had nothing to do with the slowness of the settlement process there. Three useful articles by Bernard C. Peters explain the settlement pattern in western Michigan: "Early Town-Site Speculation in Kalamazoo County," *M.H.*, LVI (Fall, 1972), "The Fever Period of Land Speculation in Kalamazoo County, 1817–1837," *Mich.A.*, VII (Winter, 1976), and "Michigan's Oak Openings: Pioneer Perceptions of a Vegatative Landscape," *J.F.H.*, XXII (January, 1978). The history of one urban center is told in Floyd R. Dain, *Every House a Frontier: Detroit's Economic Progress, 1815–1825* (Detroit, 1956).

The Settlement of Wisconsin. Two volumes in a multivolume history of the state provide an excellent survey embodying the latest research: Alice E. Smith, *The History of Wisconsin, Vol. I: From Exploration to Statehood* (Madison, 1973) and Richard N. Current, *The History of Wisconsin, Vol. II: The Civil War Era, 1848–1873* (Madison, 1976). Robert C. Nesbit, *Wisconsin: A History* (Madison, 1973), is a fine survey, while Richard N. Current, *Wisconsin: A Bicentennial History* (New York, 1977) is interpretive. These should be supplemented with the accounts of regional settlement prepared by Joseph Schafer under the general title of the Wisconsin Domesday Book: *Town Studies* (Madison, 1924), *Four Wisconsin Counties* (Madison, 1927), *The Wisconsin Lead Region* (Madison, 1932), and *The Winnebago-Horicon Basin* (Madison, 1937). Also useful is the biography of a leading land agent: Larry Gara, *Westernized Yankee: The Story of Cyrus Woodman* (Madison, 1956). Alice E. Smith, *Millstone and Saw, The Origins of Neenah-Menasha* (Madison, 1966), expertly describes the founding and growth of the twin cities at the falls of the Fox River. Economic developments near the close of the pioneer era are the theme of two important books: Vernon Carstensen, *Farms or Forest: Evolution of a State Land Policy for Northern Wisconsin, 1850–1932*

(Madison, 1958), and James W. Hurst, *Law and Economic Growth: The Legal History of the Lumber Industry in Wisconsin, 1836–1915* (Cambridge, 1964).

The Foreign-Born in the Northwest. General accounts are in the standard histories of immigration. More detailed studies of the role of Scandinavians in the Northwest are: Kendric C. Babcock, *The Scandinavian Element in the United States* (Urbana, 1914), Theodore C. Blegen, *Norwegian Migration to the United States*, 2 v. (Northfield, 1931–1940), and other specialized studies of immigrant groups. One such group in the West is discussed in Lawrence M. Larson, "The Norwegian Element in the Northwest," *A.H.R.*, XL (October, 1934). An excellent regional study of racial mingling is in Kathleen N. Conzen, *Immigrant Milwaukee, 1836–1860: Accommodation and Community in a Frontier City* (Cambridge, 1976). Several of the essays in Melvin G. Holli and Peter d'A. Jones, ed., *The Ethnic Frontier: Essays in the History of Group Survival in Chicago and the Midwest* (Grand Rapids, 1977), are pertinent.

Political Conflicts in the Old Northwest. The antagonisms that developed when northerners, southerners, and the foreign born tried to erect political institutions are fully explored in two important books: John D. Barnhart, *Valley of Democracy: The Frontier versus the Plantation in the Ohio Valley, 1775–1818* (Bloomington, 1953), and Richard L. Power, *Planting Corn Belt Culture: The Impress of the Upland Southerner and Yankee in the Old Northwest* (Indianapolis, 1953). Bayard Still, "State Making in Wisconsin, 1846–48," *W.M.H.*, XX (September, 1936), and Frederic L. Paxson, "A Constitution of Democracy—Wisconsin, 1847," *M.V.H.R.*, II (June, 1915), deal with special aspects.

16 Settling the Gulf Plains, 1815–1850

General Works. No history of southern migration into the Gulf Plains has been written. Scattered information is in R. S. Cotterill, *The Old South* (Glendale, 1939), as well as in more recent general histories of the South. Among the best of these are Clement Eaton, *A History of the Old South, The Emergence of a Reluctant Nation* (3rd edn., New York, 1975), I. A. Newby, *The South: A History* (New York, 1978), Monroe L. Billington, *The American South: A Brief History* (New York, 1971), and Francis B. Simkins and Charles P. Roland, *A History of the South* (New York, 1972). Particularly useful are three volumes in the *History of the South Series:* Thomas P. Abernethy, *The South in the New Nation, 1789–1819* (Baton Rouge, 1961), Charles S. Sydnor, *Development of Southern Sectionalism, 1819–1848* (Baton Rouge, 1948), and Avery Craven, *The Growth of Southern Nationalism, 1848–1861* (Baton Rouge, 1953). Two books by Frederick J. Turner are still essential to an understanding of the regions of the United States in this era: *Rise of the New West, 1819–1828* (New York, 1906), and especially *The United States, 1830–1850* (New York, 1935). Everett Dick, *The Dixie Frontier* (New York, 1948), deals with social aspects. Two interpretative essays are: Frank L. Owsley, "The Pattern of Migration and Settlement on the Southern Frontier," *J.S.H.,* XI (May, 1945), and William O. Lynch, "The Westward Flow of Southern Colonists before 1861," *J.S.H.,*IX (August, 1943).

Additional information on the southern frontier can be gleaned from histories of slavery and agriculture. John Hope Franklin, *From Slavery to Freedom: A History of Negro Americans* (5th edn., New York, 1980), and Kenneth M. Stampp, *The Peculiar Institution: Slavery in the Ante-Bellum South* (New York, 1956), are standard accounts based on modern scholarship. They may be supplemented with recent ground-breaking studies of slave life that question traditional stereotypes: Eugene D. Genovese, *Roll, Jordan, Roll: The World the Slaves Made* (New York, 1974), showing that slaves both accommodated to and resisted white culture; Philip S. Foner, *History of Black Americans: From Africa to the Emergence of the Cotton Kingdom* (Westport, 1975), the first of a four-volume study of slavery; John W. Blassingame, *The Slave Community: Plantation Life in the Ante-Bellum South* (rev. edn., New York, 1980), a statement of the slaves' retention of their own culture; Leslie S. Owens, *This Species of Property: Slave Life and Culture in the Old South* (New York, 1976), a well-documented analysis of slave life, and C. Duncan Rice, *The Rise and Fall of Black Slavery* (New York, 1975), which summarizes recent scholarship. Basic documents are in Willie Lee Rose, ed., *A Documentary History of Slavery in North America* (New York, 1976), while the free Negro in the South is pictured as enjoying fairly high social status in Ira Berlin, *Slaves Without Masters: The Free Negro in the Antebellum South* (New York, 1974).

The most useful account of southern agriculture for this period is in Paul W. Gates, *The Farmer's Age: Agriculture, 1815–1860* (New York, 1960). This may be supplemented with such useful monographs as James C.

Bonner, *A History of Georgia Agriculture, 1732–1860* (Athens, 1964), and John H. Moore, *Agriculture in Ante-Bellum Mississippi* (New York, 1958). Two of the South's leading crops are discussed in Donald L. Kemmerer, "The Pre-Civil War South's Leading Crop: Corn," *A.H.,* XXIII (October, 1949), Harry B. Brown, *Cotton* (New York, 1927), David L. Cohn, *The Life and Times of King Cotton* (New York, 1956) and S. G. Stephens, "The Origins of Sea Island Cotton," *A.H.,* L (April, 1976). An important revisionary study by Forrest McDonald and Grady McWhiney, "The Antebellum Southern Herdsmen: A Reinterpretation," *J.S.H.,* XLI (May, 1975), shows that hog and cattle grazing played a far more important role in the southern economy than historians have believed.

Indian Removal. Dale Van Every, *Disinherited. The Last Birthright of the American Indian* (New York, 1966), is an account of Indian removal, as is Gloria Jahoda, *The Trail of Tears* (New York, 1975). Collected essays on aspects of the removal story are in Charles M. Hudson, ed., *Four Centuries of Southern Indians* (Athens, 1975), and Arrell M. Gibson, ed., *America's Exiles: Indian Colonization in Oklahoma* (Oklahoma City, 1976).

The racial concepts that underlay Indian removal are expertly explored in Bernard W. Sheehan, *Seeds of Extinction: Jeffersonian Philanthropy and the American Indian* (Chapel Hill, 1973), which traces the evolution of the belief that Indians must be "civilized" to survive. This theme is continued in Robert A. Trennert, Jr., *Alternatives to Extinction: Federal Indian Policy and the Beginnings of the Reservation System* (Philadelphia, 1975). Two leaders who helped further this belief are described in George A. Schultz, *An Indian Canaan: Isaac McCoy and the Vision of an Indian State* (Norman, 1972), and Herman J. Viola, *Thomas L. McKenney: Architect of America's Early Indian Policy, 1816–1830* (Chicago, 1974). The changing beliefs of one early advocate of the removal policy are described in Lynn H. Parsons, " 'A Perpetual Harrow Upon My Feelings': John Quincy Adams and the American Indian,"*N.E.Q.,* XLVI (September, 1973). The failure of one reform group to aid the Indian cause is explained in Linda K. Kerber, "The Abolitionist Perception of the Indian," *J.A.H.,* LXII (September, 1975), which shows that abolitionists failed to understand the Indians' desire to maintain their own culture.

Biographies of Andrew Jackson cited earlier contain much information on the emergence of the removal policy during his administrations. The emergence of this policy is studied in Francis P. Prucha, *American Indian Policy in the Formative Years: The Indian Trade and Intercourse Acts, 1790–1835* (Cambridge, 1962), and the policy itself in Ronald N. Satz, *American Indian Policy in the Jacksonian Era* (Lincoln, 1975). Michael P. Rogin, *Fathers and Children: Andrew Jackson and the Subjugation of the American Indian* (New York, 1975), argues that Jackson's fatherless childhood led him into a parental attitude toward the Indians and a desire to remove them from dangerous contact with whites. That Jackson had the interest of the Indians at heart and is ill-deserving of the criticisms of his policy is the theme of Francis P. Prucha, "Andrew Jackson's Indian Policy: A Reassessment," *J.A.H.*, LVI (December, 1969), a view also maintained in Richard H. Faust, "Another Look at General Jackson and the Indians of Mississippi Territory," *A.R.*, XXVIII (July, 1975). The opposite case is argued in Wilcomb E. Washburn, *Red Man's Land—White Man's Law: A Study of the Past and Present Status of the American Indian* (New York, 1971), an excellent legal analysis. Richard W. Barsness, "John C. Calhoun and the Military Establishment, 1817–1825," *W.M.H.*, L (Autumn, 1966), is sympathetic toward a man who helped inaugurate the removal policy. The shift in American attitude toward the Indian from one favorable to assimilation between 1780 and 1840 to one favoring conquest and expulsion is traced in Reginald Horsman, "American Indian Policy and the Origins of Manifest Destiny," *U. of Birmingham Hist. Quarterly* XI No. 2 (1968).

The removal process is described in the general books cited above and in numerous monographs. Despite its title, Mary E. Young, *Redskins, Ruffleshirts, and Rednecks: Indian Allotments in Alabama and Mississippi* (Norman, 1961) is a scholarly study of treaty making with the Creek, Choctaw, and Chickasaw tribes that forced their remove; Robert S. Cotterill, *The Southern Indians: The Story of the Civilized Tribes before Removal* (Norman, 1954), deals with these tribes and others. A series of volumes by Grant Foreman tell the story of the removal of the five southern tribes: *Indians and Pioneers* (New Haven, 1930), *Indian Removal: The Emigration of the Five Civilized Tribes of Indians* (Norman, 1932), *Advancing the Frontier* (Norman, 1933), and *The Five Civilized Tribes* (Norman, 1934). Briefer accounts are in George D. Harmon, *Sixty Years of Indian Affairs* (Chapel Hill, 1941), and William C. MacLeod, *The American Indian Frontier* (New York, 1928). Brad Agnew, *Fort Gibson: Terminal on the Trail of Tears* (Norman, 1980), ably describes the history of the western terminal of the removal routes and the peace that was maintained there.

Removal of the Cherokee has inspired a considerable literature. General treatments are in Kenneth P. Davis, "The Cherokee Removal, 1835–1838," *T.H.Q.*, XXXII (Winter, 1973), a survey, and Samuel Carter III, *Cherokee Sunset: A Nation Betrayed* (New York, 1976), an emotional popularization. That the Cherokee were adjusting well to white society in the South is shown in Henry T. Malone, *Cherokees of the Old South: A People in Transition* (Athens, 1956), an understanding study of the tribal attempts to adopt the American culture; John P. Reid, *The Law of Blood: The Primitive Law of the Cherokee Nation* (New York, 1970), and *A Better Kind of Hatchet: Law, Trade and Diplomacy in the Cherokee Nation during the Early Years of European Contact* (University Park, 1976), which describe the sophisticated legal system which underlay tribal unity; William G. McLoughlin, "Thomas Jefferson and the Beginnings of Cherokee Nationalism, 1806 to 1809," *W.M.C.Q.*, XXXIII (October, 1975), a scholarly study of the emergence of tribal statues and police system; and William G. McLoughlin and Walter H. Conser, Jr., "The Cherokees in Transition: A Statistical Analysis of the Federal Cherokee Census of 1835," *J.A.H.*, LXIV (December, 1977), an analysis of the tribe's social and economic activities that shows how deeply its roots were planted in southern soil. This is illustrated also in works dealing with the slaves owned by the Cherokee: William G. McLoughlin, "Red Indians, Black Slavery and White Racism: America's Slaveholding Indians," *A.Q.*, XXVI (October, 1974), a legal examination of Cherokee slaveholding, and R. Halliburton, Jr., "Origins of Black Slavery among the Cherokee," *C. of O.*, LII (Winter, 1974–75). Tim Gammon, "Black Freedmen and the Cherokee Nation," *J.A.S.*, XI (1977), reveals that the Cherokee were sufficiently "civilized" to discriminate against black freemen.

That divisions within the tribe allowed the federal government to carry through its removal policy is demonstrated in a sizeable literature. Thurman Wilkins, *Cherokee Tragedy: The Story of the Ridge Family and the Decimation of a People* (New York, 1970), holds that outside pressures had so divided the tribe that it could not resist removal; the book tells the tragic story of John Ridge who led the faction that signed the Treaty of New Echota in 1836. Biographies of the two principal leaders are Kenny A. Franks, *Stand Watie and The Agony of the Cherokee Nation*

(Memphis, 1979), an able story of the manner in which Watie and Elias Boudinot emerged as leaders of the "Treaty" faction of the tribe, and Gary E. Moulton, *John Ross: Cherokee Chief* (Athens, 1978), an excellent account of his political career. Ross' personal life is dealt with in the same author's "Chief John Ross: The Personal Dimension," *R.R.V.H.R.,* II (Summer, 1975). Details of the financial disputes involving Ross and his opponents are in Gerald A. Reed, "Financial Controversy in the Cherokee Nation, 1839–1846," *C. of O.,* LXX (Spring, 1974), and Gary E. Moulton, "Chief John Ross and Cherokee Removal Finances," *C. of O.,* LII (Fall, 1974). Ross' efforts to organize a nonviolent campaign to resist removal are described in Walter H. Conser, Jr., "John Ross and the Cherokee Resistance Campaign, 1833–1838," *J.S.H.,* XLIV (May, 1978). Mary W. Clarke, *Chief Bowles and the Texas Cherokee* (Norman, 1971) is concerned with members of the tribe in North Carolina and Tennessee who were moved to Arkansas and East Texas. Ralph H. Gabriel, *Elias Boudinot, Cherokee, and His America* (Norman, 1941) is useful. Legal aspects of Cherokee removal are summarized in the standard biography of Chief Justice Marshall: Albert J. Beveridge, *The Life of John Marshall,* 4 v. (Boston, 1916–19), and in Edwin A. Miles, "After John Marshall's Decision: *Worcester* v. *Georgia* and the Nullification Crisis," *J.S.H.,* XXXIX (November, 1973), which is concerned with the aftermath of the famous case. B. B. Lightfoot, "The Cherokee Emigrants in Missouri," *M.H.R.,* LVI (January, 1962), describes the Indians forced march across the state in the winter of 1837–38.

The removal of other tribes is surveyed in numerous books and articles. Among these studies by Richard J. Hryniewici explain two important Creek treaties: "The Creek Treaty of Washington, 1826," *G.H.Q.,* XLVIII (December, 1964), and "The Creek Treaty of November 15, 1827," *G.H.Q.,* LII (March, 1968). An excellent account of their removal is in Angie Debo, *The Road to Disappearance: A History of the Creek Indians* (Norman, 1980), while Kenneth L. Valliere, "The Creek War of 1836: A Military History," *C. of O.* LVII (Winter, 1979–80), describes the brief war that followed Indian resistance to speculative pressure to absorb their land. James F. Doster, *The Creek Indians and Their Florida Lands, 1740–1823,* 2 v. (New York, 1974), deals with legalistic problems of land ownership in a fragment of the tribe that had moved to Florida in 1740. An excellent study of an important tribe is Arthur H. DeRosier, *The Removal of the Choctaw Indians* (Knoxville,

1970); the same author explores one aspect more deeply in "Andrew Jackson and Negotiations for the Removal of the Choctaw Indians," *H.,* XXIX (May, 1967), a study of factionalism in negotiations leading to the Treaty of Dancing Rabbit Creek in 1830. Arrell M. Gibson, *The Chickasaws* (Norman, 1971) has a fine account of Chickasaw removal, while one important step in that removal is described in Thomas D. Clark, "The Jackson Purchase: A Dramatic Chapter in Southern Indian Policy and Relations," *F.C.H.Q.,* L (July, 1976). Two recent studies of the Choctaw as well as histories of that tribe are important: Rex Syndergaard, "The Final Move of the Choctaws, 1825–1830," *C. of O.,* LII (Summer, 1974), and H. Glenn Jordan, "Choctaw Colonization in Oklahoma," *C. of O.,* LIV (Spring, 1976). This issue is devoted to numerous articles on the removal of the southern tribes. The forced removal of one small tribe is studied in W. David Baird, "The Reduction of a People: The Quapaw Removal, 1824–1834," *R.R.V.H.R.,* I (Spring, 1974). Eleven essays dealing with small fragments of tribes that remained in the East after removal are in Walter L. Williams, ed., *Southeastern Indians since the Removal Era* (Athens, 1979).

The attempts to remove the Seminoles, and the three Seminole Wars that resulted, have attracted much historical attention. Material is in Edwin C. McReynolds, *The Seminoles* (Norman, 1957), but a more thorough account is in Virginia B. Peters, *The Florida Wars* (Hamden, 1979), which deals with the entire period between 1810 and 1858. Despite its title, George Walton, *Fearless and Free: The Seminole Indian War, 1835–1842* (Indianapolis, 1977), adds little to John K. Mahon, *History of the Second Seminole War* (Gainesville, 1967). A readable biography of the Indian leader is William and Ellen Hartley, *Osceola: The Unconquered Indian* (New York, 1973). Naval warfare in the Everglades is surveyed in George E. Bucker, *Swamp Sailors: Riverine Warfare in the Everglades, 1835–1842* (Gainesville, 1975), while the role played by black slaves among the Seminoles is examined in Daniel F. Littlefield, Jr., *Africans and Seminoles: From Removal to Emancipation* (Westport, 1977).

A number of specialized studies deal with aspects of the wars and removal. Among these the most valuable are: Wayne B. Lollar, "Seminole-United States Financial Relations, 1825–1866," *C. of O.,* L (Summer, 1972), which describes the treaties of Camp Moultrie and Payne's Landing; James W. Covington, "Federal Relations with the Apalachicola Indians, 1823–1838," *F.H.Q.,* XLII (October,

1963); Michael E. Welsh, "Legislating a Homestead Bill: Thomas Hart Benton and the Second Seminole War," *F.H.Q.*, LVII (October, 1978), dealing with Benton's efforts in 1842 to secure free land for Seminoles to remain in florida; Michael G. Schene, "Fort Foster; A Second Seminole War Fort," *F.H.Q.*, LIV (January, 1976), describing the building of a fort near Tampa in 1836; Gary E. Moulton, "Cherokees and the Second Seminole War," *F.H.Q.*, LIII (January, 1975), which shows how John Ross was used by the government as a negotiator in the Second Seminole War; George C. Bittle, "The First Campaign of the Second Seminole War." *F.H.Q.*, XLVI (July, 1967), Kenneth W. Porter, "Billy Bowlegs (Holata Micco) in the Seminole Wars," *F.H.Q.*, XLV (January and April, 1967), and James W. Covington, "An Episode in the Third Seminole War," *F.H.Q.*, XLV (July, 1966), which despite its title is a brief history of the war. Episodes in the conflicts are described in Frank Laumer, *Massacre!* (Gainesville, 1968), a romanticized version of the massacre of 108 regulars from Fort Brooke in 1835; E. Merton Coulter, "The Chehaw Affairs" *G.H.Q.*, XLIX (December, 1965), describing the burning of an Indian village in the First Seminole War, and George R. Adams, "The Caloosahatchee Massacre: Its Significance in the Second Seminole War," *F.H.Q.*, XLVIII (April, 1970), which shows that the killing of a detachment of dragoons in July, 1839, negated peace efforts then under way. Kenneth W. Porter, "Negroes and the Seminole War, 1835–1842," *J.S.H.*, XXX (November, 1964), demonstrates that former slaves were so numerous among the Seminoles that they sometimes outnumbered Indians during the conflicts with government troops. Two articles by John K. Mahon study the treaties that ended the war and consigned the Indians to reservations: "The Treaty of Moultrie Creek, 1823," *F.H.Q.*, XL (April, 1962), and "Two Seminole Treaties: Payne's Landing, 1832, and Ft. Gibson, 1833" *F.H.Q.*, XLI (July, 1962). The aftermath of the wars is the theme of L. Edward Carter, "The Seminole Nation After Leaving Florida," *C. of O.*, LV (Winter, 1977–78).

The activity of land speculators in the wake of Indian removal has aroused the interest of investigators. Mary E. Young, "Indian Removal and Land Allotment: The Civilized Tribes and Jacksonian Justice," *A.H.R.*, LXIV (October, 1958), shows that the removal policy was designed to benefit the Indians, but had the opposite effect by making them prey to speculators. The activity of speculators in various regions from which Indians had been removed is discussed in James W. Silver,

"Land Speculation Profits in the Chickasaw Cession," *J.S.H.*, X (February, 1944), Dennis East, "New York and Mississippi Land Company and the Panic of 1837," *J.M.H.*, XXXIII (November, 1971), dealing with a company formed in 1835 to exploit the Chickasaw cession, Mary E. Young, "The Creek Frauds: A Study in Conscience and Corruption," *M.V.H.R.*, XLII (December, 1955), and Gordon T. Chappell, "Some Patterns of Land Speculation in the Old Southwest," *J.S.H.*, XV (November, 1949), the latter dealing with the Tennessee Valley.

Causes of the Migration. The decaying agriculture of the Southeast which drove settlers westward is studied in Avery O. Craven, *Soil Exhaustion as a Factor in the Agricultural History of Virginia and Maryland, 1606–1860* (Urbana, 1926). The part played by the plantation system in causing soil exhaustion has been disputed among historians. W. H. Yarbrough, *Economic Aspects of Slavery in Relation to Southern and Southwestern Migration* (Nashville, 1932), holds wasteful slave labor largely responsible, while Ulrich B. Phillips, "Plantations with Slave Labor and Free," *A.H.R.*, XXX (July, 1925), contends that free labor exhausted the soil as rapidly as slave. Phillip's point is examined in two articles by Robert R. Russel, "General Effects of Slavery upon Southern Economic Progress," *J.S.H.*, IV (February, 1938), and "The Effects of Slavery upon Nonslaveholders in the Ante Bellum South," *A.H.*, XV (April, 1941). This whole controversy is examined in Gavin Wright, "New and Old Views on the Economics of Slavery," *J.E.H.*, XXXIII (June, 1973). Modern mathematical techniques have been used to shed new light on the subject, as shown in such studies as Richard K. Vedder and David C. Stockdale, "The Profitability of Slavery Revisited: A Different Approach," *A.H.*, XLIX (April, 1975), which shows that slavery and cotton production were highly profitable in the years before the Civil War, and Ralph V. Anderson and Robert E. Gallman, "Slaves as Fixed Capital: Slave Labor and Southern Economic Development," *J.A.H.*, LXIV (June, 1977), which uses statistics to show that planters were forced to diversity to assure full employment for their slaves, thus assuring a more staple economy and a higher per capita income. Works on the nature of plantation society listed later in this chapter also shed light on this problem.

The efforts of the Southeastern states to check migration through agricultural reform is the theme of such studies as G. Melvin, "Agricultural Reform in Antebellum Virginia: William Galt, Jr., A Case Study," *A.H.*, LXI

(July, 1978), Charles W. Turner, "Virginia Agricultural Reform, 1815–1860," *A.H.*, XXV (July, 1952), Charles W. Turner, "Virginia State Agricultural Societies, 1811–1860," *A.H.*, XXXVIII (July, 1964), Cornelius O. Cathey, *Agricultural Developments in North Carolina, 1783–1860* (Chapel Hill, 1956), and Vivian Wiser, "Improving Maryland's Agriculture, 1840–1860," *M.H.M.*, LXIV (Summer, 1969). Edward C. Papenfuse, Jr., "Planter Behavior and Economic Stability in a Staple Economy," *A.H.*, XLVI (April, 1972), argues that by the 1790s eastern planters knew how to preserve soils but still migrated because of fear of future soil exhaustion.

Development of Transportation Routes. General Books on transportation, such as Thomas H. MacDonald, *History and Development of Road Building in the United States* (Washington, 1926), contain only scattered information on roads between Southeast and Southwest. The scant information unearthed by scholars is contained in specialized articles: Julian P. Bretz, "Early Land Communications with the Lower Mississippi Valley," *M.V.H.R.*, XIII (June, 1926), Yancey M. Quinn, Jr., "Jackson's Military Road," *J. Miss. H.*, XLI (November, 1979), Peter J. Hamilton, "Early Roads in Alabama," *A.H.S., Transactions*, II (1897–98), and R. S. Cotterill, "The Natchez Trace," *T.H.M.*, VII (April, 1921). A thorough study of the subject is needed.

The Course of Settlement. The movement of population into western Georgia was led by gold seekers, whose adventures are described in E. Merton Coulter, *Auraria: The Story of a Georgia Gold-Mining Town* (Athens, 1956), and James W. Covington, ed., "Letters from the Georgia Gold Region," *G.H.Q.*, XXXIX (December, 1955). A major rush into the North Carolina back country in 1830–31, in which as many as 5,000 slaves were employed to dig gold, is described in Edward W. Phifer, "Champagne at Brindletown: The Story of the Burke County Gold Rush, 1829–1833," *N.C.H.R.*, XL (October, 1963). The expansion of the agricultural frontier in Georgia is described in Ralph B. Flanders, *Plantation Slavery in Georgia* (Chapel Hill, 1933). Reba S. Biehle, "Edward Oxford: Pioneer Farmer of Middle Georgia, *G.H.Q.*, LII (June, 1968), is an excellent case study of a farmer who moved to Georgia in the early nineteenth century. The role of the state in controlling migration is discussed in Milton S. Heath, *Constructive Liberalism: The Role of the State in Economic Development in Georgia to 1860* (Cambridge, 1954). Douglas C. Wilms, "Georgia's Land Lottery in 1832," *C.*

of O., LII (Spring, 1974), describes one of six lotteries held by the state to dispose of land taken over from the Indians.

The only adequate study of migration into any portion of the Southwest is Thomas P. Abernethy, *The Formative Period in Alabama, 1815–1828* (rev. edn., University, 1965), but this must be supplemented with Grady McWhiney, "The Revolution in Nineteenth-Century Alabama Agriculture," *A.R.*, XXXI (January, 1978), which for the first time pays proper attention to the role of livestock in the early settlement of the state. A case study of one successful immigrant in the region is Darrel E. Bigham, "From the Green Mountains to the Tombigbee: Henry Hitchcock in Territorial Alabama, 1817–1819," *A.R.*, XXVI (July, 1973), and another is Ray Mathis, *John Horry Dent: South Carolina Aristocrat on the Alabama Frontier* (University, 1979). Reliance must also be placed on the scattered information in such studies as Charles S. Davis, *The Cotton Kingdom in Alabama* (Montgomery, 1939), and histories of the state, of which the most recent is Virginia V. der V. Hamilton, *Alabama; A Bicentennial History* (New York, 1977), which is brief on the settlement period. A case study in migration to Alabama is Hugh H. Wooten, "Westward Migration from Iredell County, 1800–1850," *N.C.H.R.*, XXX (January, 1935). Even more revealing is the detailed description of an Alabama settlement in Blount County, showing the effect of the 1819 speculation and the nature of the migrants: Chriss H. Doss, "Early Settlement of Bearmeat Cabin Frontier," *A.R.*, XXII (October, 1969). The influence of speculators who secured choice lands and elitist social positions through the favoritism of William H. Crawford and other Georgia politicians is described in Frances C. Roberts, "Politics and Public Land Disposal in Alabama's Formative Period," *A.R.*, XXII (July, 1969). Chase C. Mooney, *William H. Crawford, 1772–1834* (Lexington, 1974), is an excellent biography of a Georgia pioneer.

A brief survey of Mississippi's early settlement is in Charles D. Lowery, "The Great Migration to the Mississippi Territory, 1789–1819," *J.M.H.*, XXX (August, 1968). Two articles in a special issue of the *Journal of Mississippi History* devoted to the 150th anniversary of statehood are especially useful: Richard A. McLemore and Nannie P. McLemore, "The Birth of Mississippi," and W. B. Hamilton, "Mississippi in 1817: A Sociological and Economic Analysis," *J.M.H.*, XXIX (November, 1967). The same issue has a capable article by Winbourne M. Drake, "The Framing of Mississippi's First Constitution." Some information on these events is also in the histories of the state, of which the best is Richard A. McLemore, ed., *A History of Mississippi,* 2 v. (Hattiesburg, 1973), a collaborative work by forty-one specialists. An able brief account showing the problems of land disposal caused by Spanish and British claims is Robert V. Haynes, "The Disposal of Land in the Mississippi Territory," *J.Miss.H.,* XXIV (October, 1962), Robert Nesbit, "The Federal Government as Townsite Speculator," *E.E.H.,* VII (Spring, 1970), describes the manner in which speculators used the act of 1817 authorizing the naming of a surveyor for Mississippi Territory to accumulate holdings. An excellent history of one principal community is D. Clayton James, *Antebellum Natchez* (Baton Rouge, 1968). Other works on the occupation of Tennessee include Harriet C. Owsley, "Westward to Tennessee," *T.H.Q.,* XXIX (Spring, 1965), and Samuel C. Williams, *Beginnings of West Tennessee, in the Land of the Chickasaws, 1541–1841* (Johnson City, 1930). That the new settlers, at least in the Nashville area, were about equally divided between Democrats and Whigs, regardless of their social status, is statistically demonstrated in Burton W. Folsom II, "The Politics of Elites: Prominence and Party in Davidson County, Tennessee, 1831–1861," *J.S.H.,* XXXIX (August, 1973).

Sidney W. Martin, *Florida during the Territorial Days* (Athens, 1944) has information on migration into that state, as does Charlton W. Tebeau, *A History of Florida* (Coral Gables, 1971). These may be supplemented with special studies of Florida's settlment. Louis R. Bisceglia, "The Florida and the Gallatin-Vives Misunderstanding," *F.H.Q.,* XLVIII (January, 1970), shows that Francisco Vives, the Spanish commissioner who came to negotiate the cession in 1820, was authorized to yield Florida if that would check American expansion into Texas. The workings of the commission set up in 1822 to decide conflicting land claims are described in George C. Whatley and Sylvia Cook, "East Florida Land Commission: A Study in Frustration," *F.H.Q.,* L (July, 1971), while John C. Upchurch, "Aspects of the Development and Exploration of the Forbes Purchase," *F.H.Q.,* XLVIII (October, 1969), deals with the occupation of a large tract east of the Apalachicola River developed by the Apalachicola Land Company in the 1830s and 1840s. An important work by Julia F. Smith, *Slavery and Plantation Growth in Antebellum Florida, 1821–1860* (Gainesville, 1973), argues successfully that on this frontier, at least, a precapitalistic frontier never emerged and that planters carved

large capitalistic enterprises from the territory with the use of borrowed money. The biography of a commission merchant which illustrates this philosophy is Jerrell H. Shofner, *Daniel Ladd: Merchant Prince of Frontier Florida* (Gainesville, 1978).

Plantation Society on the Southern Frontier. Modern scholarship, based on quantitative data studies, has altered the picture of southern plantation life that existed for generations. One significant contrast concerns the yeoman farmer; the classical article by Paul H. Buck, "The Poor Whites of the Ante-Bellum South," *A.H.R.,* XXXI (October, 1925), has been challenged by Eugene D. Genovese, "Yeoman Farmers in a Slaveholder's Democracy," *A.H.,* XLIX (April, 1975), which questions that their loyalty to the slave system was based on fear of slaves and the need to have someone below themselves in the social order. A thorough study for one region is Blanche H. Clark, *The Tennessee Yeoman, 1840–1860* (Nashville, 1942). A reinterpretation of the place of the overseer in southern society is attempted in William K. Scarborough, *The Overseer: Plantation Management in the Old South* (Baton Rouge, 1966), which shows that most were well trained and capable. A brief statement of the thesis of the book by the same author is "The Southern Plantation Overseer: a Re-evaluation," *A.H.,* XXXVIII (January, 1964). Another aspect of the overseer system is considered in William L. Van DeBurg, *The Slave Drivers: Black Agricultural Labor Supervisors in the Antebellum South* (Westport, 1979), an able study showing that black supervisors served as intermediaries between owners and slaves, and played a role in lessening the harshness of the system. A revisionist view of the slave trade is in Michael Tadman, "Slave Trading in the Ante-Bellum South: an Estimate of the Extent of the Inter-Regional Slave Trade," *J.A.S.,* XIII (August, 1979), which shows that the trade accounted for well over half of the inter-regional slave movements.

The productivity and treatment of slaves has inspired a particularly interesting controversy among historians. This began with the publication of Robert W. Fogel and Stanley L. Engerman, *Time on the Cross: The Economics of American Negro Slavery* (Boston, 1974), which used computerized analysis of mass data to show that blacks achieved a significant culture under slavery, that they were harder working and more efficient than white workers, that they were well treated and happy, and that the slave labor system was 35 per cent more efficient than the northern free-labor system. These findings have been harshly attacked in such books as Herbert G. Gutman, *Slavery and the Numbers Game: A Critique of Time on the Cross* (Urbana, 1975) and Paul A. David, et al., *Reckoning with Slavery: A Critical Study of the Quantitative History of American Negro Slavery* (New York, 1976), in which five scholars dispute everything in *Time on the Cross* from its statistical techniques to its conclusions.

Other scholars have disputed specific themes in the Fogel-Engerman volume. Richard Sutch, "The Treatment Received by American Slaves: A Critical Review of the Evidence Presented in *Time on the Cross*," *E.E.H.*, XII (October, 1975), uses statistical evidence to show that slaves were treated harshly; Gavin Wright, *The Political Economy of the Cotton South: Households, Markets and Wealth in the Nineteenth Century* (New York, 1978), argues that slave labor was profitable only because it allowed greater crop diversification than in the North; Leslie H. Owens, *This Species of Property: Slave Life and Culture in the Old South* (New York, 1976), maintains that slaves were discontented with their status and presents a convincing analysis of the system to prove this point; Gaven Wright, "Slavery and the Cotton Boom," *E.E.H.*, XII (October, 1975), presents evidence to show that while cotton prices were high in the 1850s, they would have declined radically over the next years, thus disputing the "efficiency" of the slave system.

These careful studies have altered the traditional view of the slave system. The newer concepts are embodied in such interpretative works as Herbert G. Gutman, *The Black Family in Slavery and Freedom, 1750–1925* (New York, 1976), an important study of family structure which concludes that slave families were stable and maintained a two-parent relationship for the most part; and Raimondo Luraghi, *The Rise and Fall of the Plantation South* (New York, 1878), a sweeping survey by a mildy Marxist Italian historian.

Other students of slavery have probed the economics of the system. The earlier literature may be surveyed in Harold D. Woodman, "The Profitability of Slavery: A Historical Perennial," *J.S.H.*, XXIX (August, 1963), and Stanley L. Engerman, "The Effects of Slavery Upon the Southern Economy: A Review of the Recent Debate," *E.E.H.*, IV (Winter, 1967). A series of papers on the subject are presented in William N. Parker, ed., "The Structure of the Cotton Economy of the Antebellum South," *A.H.*, XLIV (Janaury, 1970). Modern scholars generally agree that slavery was moderately profitable to planters, and sufficiently viable to be consistent with the

growing economy. Eugene D. Genovese, *The Political Economy of Slavery* (New York, 1965), brilliantly relates the economy of the slave system to the social fabric of the antebellum south. A careful study by Robert S. Starobin, *Industrial Slavery in the Old South* (New York, 1970), concludes that some 5 per cent of the slave population worked at industrial jobs and that slavery and industrialism were not considered incompatible at that time. His views are supported in Charles B. Dew, "Disciplining Slave Ironworkers in the Antebellum South: Coercion, Conciliation, and Accommodation," *A.H.R.*, LXXIX (April, 1974), which shows that slaves hired as ironworkers were properly treated and enjoyed amiable relations with their employers and fellow workers.

17   The New West: A National Problem, 1815–1850

The Maturing of Western Agriculture. An essential work is Paul W. Gates, *The Farmer's Age: Agriculture, 1815–1860* (New York, 1960). Recent histories of agriculture also provide general information; the best of these are John T. Schlebecker, *Whereby We Thrive: A History of American Farming, 1607–1972* (Ames, 1975), and Willard W. Cochrane, *The Development of American Agriculture: A Historical Analysis* (Minneapolis, 1980). David E. Schob, *Hired Hands and Plowboys: Farm Labor in the Midwest, 1815–1860* (Urbana, 1975), although dealing largely with the Old Northwest, sheds light on farm practices in the entire West. The westward migration of wheat and corn growing is traced in Louis B. Schmidt, "The Westward Movement of the Wheat Growing Industry in the United States," *I.J.H.P.*, XVIII (July, 1920), and "The Westward Movement of the Corn Growing Industry in the United States," *I.J.H.P.*, XXI (January, 1923). A general history of livestock raising is James W. Thompson, *A History of Livestock Raising in the United States, 1607–1860* (Washington, 1942), while specialized studies for the Old Northwest include Charles R. Leavitt, "Transportation and the Livestock Industry in the Middle West to 1860," *A.H.*, VIII (January, 1934), Robert L. Jones, "The Beef Cattle Industry in Ohio Prior to the Civil War," *O.A.H.Q.*, LXIV (April, 1955 and July, 1955), and two excellent monographs: James W. Whitaker, *Feedlot Empire: Beef Cattle Feeding in Illinois and Iowa, 1840–1900* (Ames, 1975), which is broader than its title indicates, and Paul C. Henlein, *The Cattle Kingdom in the Ohio Val-*

ley (Lexington, 1959), a scholarly study. The same author has written "Early Cattle Ranches of the Ohio Valley," *A.H.*, XXXV (July, 1961). A similar study of sheep raising is in the well-documented work of Stephen L. Stover, "Early Sheep Husbandry in Ohio," *A.H.*, XXXVI (April, 1962).

Transportation: The Steamboat Era. Of the several histories of transportation, by far the best for this period is George R. Taylor, *The Transportation Revolution, 1815–1860* (New York, 1951), Louis C. Hunter, *Steamboats on the Western Rivers* (Cambridge, 1949) is a classic history of all phases of steamboat transportation in the West. Steamboating on the Great Lakes is popularly treated in Walter Havighurst, *The Long Ships Passing* (New York, 1942). Special studies of transportation on western rivers include: for the upper Mississippi, Mildred L. Hartsough, *From Canoe to Steel Barge* (Minneapolis, 1934), and for the Ohio River, Charles H. Ambler, *History of Transportation in the Ohio Valley* (Glendale, 1932). The technological improvements that allowed flatboats to survive in the steamboat era are described in James Mak and Gary M. Walton, "The Persistence of Old Technologies: The Case of Flatboats," *J.E.H.*, XXXIII (July, 1973). The origin and building of the canal around the Falls of the Ohio are described in Stuart S. Sprague, "The Louisville Canal: Key to Aaron Burr's Western Trip of 1805," *K.S.H.S.R.*, LXXII (January, 1973), which argues that Burr's purpose was not the conquest of Mexico but a speculative enterprise centering around the canal, Stuart S. Sprague, "The Canal at the Falls of the Ohio and the Three Cornered Rivalry," *K.S.H.S.R.*, LXXII (January, 1974), an able account of the building of the canal, and Martha Kreipke, "The Falls of the Ohio and the Development of the Ohio River Trade, 1810–1860," *F.C.H.Q.*, LIV (April, 1980). Louis Hunter, "Studies in the Economic History of the Ohio Valley," *Smith College Studies in History*, XIX (1933–34), discusses the effect of weather on the economy of transportation. A statistical analysis of the profits available from keelboats, flatboats, and steamboats in Erik F. Haites and James Mak, "Ohio and Mississippi River Transportation," *E.E.H.*, VIII (Winter, 1970–71), explains the dominance of the steamboat by the 1840s. William A. McKay, "The Packet Boat Era on the Ohio," *F.C.H.S.Q.*, XL (October, 1966), is a nostalgic account of the old packet boats that operated out of Louisville. Lawrence H. Larsen, "New Orleans and the River Trade: Reinterpreting the Role of the Business Com-

munity," *W.M.H.*, LXI (Winter, 1977–78), describes the shift in opinion among New Orleans merchants to railroad promotion when they realized that distance from European ports and the uncertainties of the river trade handicapped them economically.

The relative costs of steamboat transportation, and the impact of shipping on the economy, have attracted the attention of quantitative-minded historians. In Erik F. Haites, et al., *Western River Transportation: The Era of Early Internal Development, 1810–1860* (Baltimore, 1975), three scholars deal expertly with these questions and others connected with the economy of transportation. Jeremy Atack, et. al., "The Profitability of Steamboating on the Western Waters," *B.H.R.*, XLIX (Autumn, 1975), demonstrates that profit rates in steamboating were about the same as in other investments, and were much higher in tributary than in trunk transportation, while Erik F. Haites and James Mak, "Economies of Scale in Western River Steamboating," *J.E.H.*, XXXVI (September, 1976), holds to the opposite view that trunk lines operated at a higher utilization rate because of fewer navigation hazards and larger markets. A statistical study showing that steamboats led to a great productivity surge in the areas they tapped during the 1840s, but that this declined thereafter is James Mak and Gary M. Walton, "Steamboats and the Great Productivity Surge in River Transportation," *J.E.H.*, XXXII (September, 1972).

The Canal Era. Two important studies by Carter Goodrich and others deal with the economic basis and impact of the western canals: *Government Promotion of American Canals and Railroads, 1800–1890* (New York, 1960), and *Canals and American Economic Development* (New York, 1961). The former reveals the extent to which canals depended on government subsidy; the latter studies the manner in which they stimulated the economic growth of adjacent areas. A popular history of canal construction is Madeline S. Waggoner, *The Long Haul West: The Great Canal Era, 1817–1850* (New York, 1958). Valuable is the excellent study by Ronald E. Shaw, *Erie Water West: A History of the Erie Canal, 1792–1854* (Lexington, 1966). The problem of financing the Erie Canal is dealt with in Nathan Miller, *The Enterprise of a Free People: Aspects of Economic Development in New York State during the Canal Period, 1792–1838* (Ithaca, 1962), while Ronald W. Filante, "A Note on the Economic Viability of the Erie Canal," *B.H.R.*, XLVIII (Spring, 1974), uses statistical techniques to show that the canal was able to compete with other forms of transportation by reducing tolls and concentrating on bulky freight.

The reaction of other eastern cities to the success of the Erie Canal is the theme of Julius Rubin, *Canal or Railroad? Imitation and Innovation in the Response to the Erie Canal in Philadelphia, Baltimore, and Boston* (Philadelphia, 1961). A similar study on a less broad scale is James W. Livingood, *The Pennsylvania-Baltimore Trade Rivalry, 1780–1860* (Harrisburg, 1947). The beginning of the canal movement in Pennsylvania is traced in Robert E. Carlson, "The Pennsylvania Improvement Society and Its Promotion of Canals and Railroads, 1824–1826," *P.H.*, XXXI (July, 1964), which deals in detail with the organization that had so much to do with launching the canal movement. The building of the Pennsylvania system is described in Theodore B. Klein, *The Canals of Pennsylvania and the System of Internal Improvements* (Harrisburg, 1900), an older work that is still useful. Books that deal with the origins and development of the Maryland system include: Walter S. Sanderlin, *The Great National Project* (Baltimore, 1947), and the opening chapters of Edward Hungerford, *The Story of the Baltimore and Ohio Railroad, 1827–1927*, 2 v. (New York, 1928).

Economists differ over the economic benefits gained by the states financing the east-west canal systems. Carter Goodrich, "Internal Improvements Reconsidered," *J.E.H.*, XXX (June, 1970), expertly surveys the recent literature on the subject. Two typical articles are Roger L. Ransom, "Interregional Canals and Economic Specialization in the Antebellum United States," *E.E.H.*, (Fall, 1967), which measures the economic impact of the Erie and Pennsylvania systems, and Albert W. Niemi, Jr., "A Further Look at Interregional Canals and Economic Specialization, 1820–1840," *E.E.H.*, VII (Summer, 1970), which shows that canals encouraged diversification of the economy and stimulated manufacturing at the expense of agriculture. This assertion was answered by Ransom in "A Closer Look at Canals and Western Manufacturing in the Canal Era," *E.E.H.*, VIII (Summer, 1971), showing that areas not adjacent to canals diversified more rapidly than those adjoining; this in turn inspired Niemi to reply in "A Closer Look at Canals and Western Manufacturing in the Canal Era: A Reply," *E.E.H.*, IX (Summer, 1972), with further arguments to support his position. This and comparable questions relating the growth of the economy to transportation are in David C. Klingaman and Richard K. Vedder, eds., *Essays in Nineteenth Century Economic History: The Old Northwest* (Athens, 1975).

Internal Improvements in the Northwest. The standard work on the Ohio canal system is the excellent monograph by Harry N. Scheiber, *Ohio Canal Era: A Case Study of Government and the Economy, 1820–1861* (Athens, 1969) that shows Ohio more successful in completing than in operating its system. Chester E. Finn, "The Ohio Canals: Public Enterprise on the Frontier," *O.A.H.Q.*, LI (January, 1942, and March, 1942), is a sound interpretation stressing the role of government in the construction. John S. Still, "Ethan Allen Brown and Ohio's Canal System," *Ohio H.Q.*, LXVI (January, 1957), is the best history of the surveys that located the canal routes. Construction of the two principal canals is described in Arthur H. Hirsch, "The Construction of the Miami and Erie Canal," *M.V.H.A.*, *Proceedings*, X (1919–20), and John J. George, "The Miami Canal," *O.A.H.Q.*, XXXVI (January, 1927). Harry B. Scheiber, "Land Reform, Speculation, and Government Failure: The Administration of Ohio's State Canal Lands, 1836–60," *Pro.*, VII (Summer, 1975), shows that the state's failure to develop a long-range plan led to waste and confusion, while the same author examines the effect of the system on the state's economy in "Public Canal Finance and State Banking in Ohio, 1825–1837," *I.M.H.*, LXI (June, 1969). Richard T. Farrell, "Internal-Improvement Projects in Southwestern Ohio, 1815–1834," *O.H.*, LXXX (Winter, 1971), the growth of Cincinnati to its trade outlets. Charles R. Poinsatte, *Fort Wayne During the Canal Era, 1828–1855* (Indianapolis, 1969), studies the growth of one canal-located city.

Indiana's canal system is described in Paul Fatout, *Indiana Canals* (West Lafayette, 1972). Lee Newcomer, "Construction of the Wabash and Erie Canal," *O.A.H.Q.*, XLVI (April, 1937), tells the story of the principal canal, while the same author discusses financial aspects in "A History of the Indiana Internal Improvement Bonds," *I.M.H.*, XXXII (June, 1936).

An excellent history of the Illinois system is John H. Krenkel, *Illinois Internal Improvements, 1818–1848* (Cedar Rapids, 1958), while the operation of its canals is pleasantly described in John M. Lamb, "Canal Boats on the Illinois and Michigan Canal," *J.I.S.H.S.*, LXXI (August, 1978). Daniel J. Elazar, "Gubernatorial Power and the Illinois and Michigan Canal: A Study of Political Development in the Nineteenth Century," *J.I.S.H.S.*, (Winter, 1965), relates the growth of gubernatorial authority in the state to their insistence on the canal's completion. The one railroad built at the time is described in H. J. Stratton, "The Northern Cross Railroad," *J.I.S.H.S.*, XXVIII (July, 1935).

The only special works on Michigan internal improvements are: Lew A. Chase, "Michigan's Share in the Establishment of Improved Transportation between the East and the West," M.P.H.S., *Collections*, XXXVIII (1912), and Leo Van Meer, "Clinton-Kalamazoo Canal," *M.H.M.*, XVI (Spring, 1932).

Sectionalism and Land Policy. The extent to which sectional antagonisms, created by economic specialization in the Northeast, West, and South, and accentuated by the expanding transportation network, influenced congressional legislation on the land system and other issues is still disputed among historians. Using computerized techniques of qunatitative data analysis, two have reached opposite conclusions. Joel H. Silbey, *The Shrine of Party: Congressional Voting Behavior, 1841–1852* (Pittsburgh, 1967), shows that party rather than sectional loyalties determined congressional votes during this period. Taking the opposite view as a result of analyzing 120 House votes on major issues between 1835 and 1861, Thomas B. Alexander, *Sectional Stress and Party Strength* (Nashville, 1967), concludes that sectional divisions were apparent by 1836 and steadily intensified over the next decades. Ronald P. Formisano, *The Birth of Mass Political Parties: Michigan, 1827–1861* (Princeton, 1971), shows, on the other hand, that ethnoreligious alignments rather than economic divisons determined the nature of political conflicts in one state, while Gene W. Boyett, "Quantitative Differences between the Arkansas Whig and Democratic Parties, 1836–1850," *A.H.Q.*, XXXIV (Autumn, 1975), reveals that in another the exact opposite was true. The vast historical literature on this subject, and on the nature of political alignments during the Jackson era, is summarized in Ronald P. Formisano, "Toward a Reorientation of Jacksonian Politics: A Review of the Literature, 1959–1975," *J.A.H.*, LXIII (June, 1976).

The impact of these divisions on the formulation of land policy during these years has attracted much interest. The most useful of the several books on the subject is Paul W. Gates and Robert W. Swenson, *History of Public Land Law Development* (Washington, 1968), while the operation of the system is described in Hildegard B. Johnson, *Order Upon the Land: The U.S. Rectangular Land Survey and the Upper Mississippi Country* (New York, 1976). Everett Dick, *The Lure of the Land: a Social History of the Public*

Lands from the Articles of Confederation to the New Deal (Lincoln, 1970) is narrative and anecdotal rather than analytical. Older histories that are still useful include Roy M. Robbins, *Our Landed Heritage* (Lincoln, 1976 edn.), and Benjamin H. Hibbard, *A History of Public Land Policies* (rev. edn., Madison, 1965). More important for this period is Raynor G. Wellington, *Political and Sectional Influence of the Public Lands, 1828–1842* (n.p., 1924), which is a detailed study of the relationship of land, tariff, and financial questions. William S. Hoffman, "The Downfall of the Democrats: The Reaction of North Carolinians to Jacksonian Land Policy," *N.C.H.R.*, XXXIII (April, 1956), shows that North Carolina remained Whig for fifteen years in protest against Jackson's land policies. Hugh C. Bailey, "John W. Walker and the Land Laws of the 1820s," *A.H.*, XXXII (April, 1958), deals with the origins of the land laws, while Zane L. Miller, "Senator Nathaniel Macon and the Public Domain, 1815–1828," *N.C.H.R.*, XXXVIII (October, 1961), describes the career of a southern politician who consistently opposed their liberalization. The history of "right of occupancy" laws is expertly told in Paul W. Gates, "Tenants of the Log Cabin," *M.V.H.R.*, XLIX (June, 1962). That the popularity of more liberal land laws helped Benton win office is the theme of Donald J. Abramoske, "The Public Lands in Early Missouri Politics," *M.H.R.*, LIII (July, 1959).

The influence of speculators on land sales during the 1830s still awaits a historian. Aaron M. Sakolski, *Land Tenure and Land Taxation in America* (New York, 1932), deals generally with the subject, but three articles by Paul W. Gates probe far deeper: "The Role of the Land Speculator in Western Development," *P.M.H.B.*, LXVI (July, 1942), "Southern Investments in Northern Lands Before the Civil War," *J.S.H.*, V (May, 1939), and "Frontier Landlords and Pioneer Tenants," *J.I.S.H.S.*, XXXVIII (June, 1945).

Understanding of the background of the Homestead Act, and of developing land policy during the 1940s, must begin with George M. Stephenson, *The Political History of the Public Lands from 1840 to 1862* (Boston, 1917), an older work which accepts the thesis that sectional forces transcended all others. A more detailed study of one important law is Roy M. Robbins, "Pre-emption—a Frontier Triumph," *M.V.H.R.*, XVIII (December, 1931). Studies of the growing sentiment for homestead among eastern workers are: Helen S. Zahler, *Eastern Workingmen and National Land Policy, 1829–1862* (New York, 1941), and Roy M. Robbins, "Horace Greeley: Land

Reform and Unemployment, 1837–1862," *A.H.*, VII (January, 1933). Two studies of a reformer who made free land a principal plank in his platform are Patrick W. Riddleberger, *George Washington Julian, Radical Republican: A Study in Nineteenth Century Politics and Reform* (Indianapolis, 1966), and James L. Roark, "George W. Julian: Radical Land Reformer," *I.M.H.*, LXIV (March, 1968). Irving Mark, "The Homestead Ideal and Conservation of the Public Domain," *J.E.S.*, XXII (April, 1963), shows the persistence of the ideal of free land for the needy. Forces leading toward a South-West alliance in the 1840s are described in Henry C. Hubbart, "Pro-Southern Influences in the Free West, 1840–1860," *M.V.H.R.*, XX (June, 1933). That southern opposition to the Homestead Act was far from unanimous, and that other forces helped defeat a Homestead bill during the 1850s is ably demonstrated in Gerald Wolf, "The Slavocracy and the Homestead Problem of 1854," *A.H.*, XL (April, 1966), which analyzes the roll call vote on an 1854 bill.

Railroads and the Western Economy. The sectional alignments that took shape during the 1830s and 1840s with the spread of a canal network were upset during the 1840s and 1850s by the building of the nation's railroad system. Among the standard histories of railroad transportation, two books by John F. Stover are excellent surveys: *The Life and Decline of the American Railroad* (New York, 1970), and *Iron Road to the West: American Railroads in the 1850s* (New York, 1978). An important book is Carter Goodrich, *Government Promotion of American Canals and Railroads, 1800–1890* (New York, 1960), which proves the importance of government aid in railroad building. One aspect of this subject, the role of the army in early railroad construction, is thoroughly studied in Forest G. Hill, *Roads, Rails and Waterways: Army Engineers and Early Transportation* (Norman, 1957). The railroad is related to the whole transportation network in George R. Taylor, *The Transportation Revolution, 1815–1860* (New York, 1951).

East-West Railroads. A classic study of one phase is Edward C. Kirkland, *Men, Cities and Transportation, A Study in New England History, 1820–1900*, 2 v. (Cambridge, 1948). Harry H. Pierce, *Railroads of New York: A Study of Government Aid, 1826–1875* (Cambridge, 1953) is an excellent history. Useful are two studies of railroad financing: Arthur M. Johnson and Barry E. Supple, *Boston Capitalists and Western Railroads* (Cambridge, 1967), and Dorothy R. Adler, *British Investment in American Railroads, 1834–1898*

(Charlottesville, 1970). Stephen Salsbury, *The State, the Investor, and the Railroad: The Boston and Albany, 1825–1867* (Cambridge, 1967) shows that the principal source of capital for this East-West line was Boston merchants who wanted to open new interior markets for their goods.

Among histories of individual lines, Edward Hungerford, *The Story of the Baltimore and Ohio Railroad, 1827–1927*, 2 v. (New York, 1928) is the best general work on that line, while the history of the roads that were united into the New York Central system is told in Frank W. Stevens, *The Beginnings of the New York Central, 1826–1853* (New York, 1926), Edward Hungerford, *Men and Iron: The History of the New York Central* (New York, 1938), and Alvin F. Harlow, *The Road of the Century* (New York, 1947). An important aspect of the New York Central's history is discussed in David M. Ellis, "Rivalry Between the New York Central and the Erie Canal," *N.Y.H.*, XXIV (July, 1948). Edward Hungerford, *Men of Erie* (New York, 1946), describes that road. That small towns were as eager for government subsidies to finance railroads as large cities is shown in James A. Hijiya, "Making a Railroad: The Political Economy of the Ithaca and Oswego, 1828–1842," *N.Y.H.*, LIV (April, 1973). An overly detailed history of a principal East-West Pennsylvania line across Pennsylvania is Homer T. Rosenberger, *The Philadelphia and Erie Railroad: Its Place in American Economic History* (Potomac, 1976), while the Pennsylvania system as a whole is described in W. H. Schotter, *The Growth and Development of the Pennsylvania Railroad Company* (Philadelphia, 1927). No separate study of Boston's attempts to reach the interior has been written, but an excellent brief account is in George R. Taylor, *The Transportation Revolution, 1815–1860* (New York, 1951).

Railroads in the Northwest. An excellent work, referred to above, is John R. Stover, *Iron Road to the West: American Railroads in the 1850s* (New York, 1978), which deals extensively with the Northwest. No account of Ohio's railroad builders has been written, but aspects of the story are considered in such works as Walter R. Marvin, "The Steubenville and Indiana Railroad: The Pennsylvania's Middle Route to the Middle West," *O.A.H.Q.*, LXVI (January, 1957), and John E. Pixton, Jr., *The Marietta and Cincinnati Railroad, 1845–1883: A Case Study of American Railroad Economics* (University Park, 1966). Frank A. Hargraves, *A Pioneer Indiana Railroad: The Origin and Development of the Monon* (Indianapolis, 1932), Roger H.

Van Bolt, "Hoosiers and the Western Program, 1844–1848," *I.M.H.*, XLVIII (September, 1952), and Victor M. Bogle, "Railroad Building in Indiana, 1850–1855," *I.M.H.*, LVIII (September, 1962) touch on railroad construction in that state. William F. Raney, "The Building of the Wisconsin Railroads," *W.M.H.*, XIX (June, 1936), is brief; August Derleth, *The Milwaukee Railroad* (New York, 1948) is popularly written. The inadequacies of such works are demonstrated by such well-researched studies of a principal Illinois railroad as John F. Stover, *History of the Illinois Central Railroad*, (New York, 1975), and Paul W. Gates, *The Illinois Central Railroad and Its Colonization Work* (Cambridge, 1934), which deals expertly with the disposal of the road's land grant. Richard C. Overton, *Burlington Route. A History of the Burlington Lines* (New York, 1865) is another masterful history, with a fine discussion of construction in Illinois and the Midwest. The efforts of midwesterners to encourage railroad building are described in two articles by Mentor L. Williams: "The Background of the Chicago River and Harbor Convention, 1847," *M.A.*, XXX (October, 1948), and "The Chicago River and Harbor Convention, 1847," *M.V.H.R.*, XXXV (March, 1949). A thorough, competent history of Michigan railroads is Willis F. Dunbar, *All Aboard! A History of Railroads in Michigan* (Grand Rapids, 1969), while the economic aspects of construction are treated in Robert J. Parks, *Democracy's Railroads: Public Enterprise in Jacksonian Michigan* (Port Washington, 1972), which demonstrates that Michigan's roads were the product of public rather than private enterprise.

Shifting Trade Routes. Economists disagree on the impact of the new railroads on the nation's economy. Robert W. Fogel, *Railroads and American Economic Growth* (Baltimore, 1964), uses complex econometric techniques to demonstrate that the effect was minimal or nonexistent; Albert Fishlow, *American Railroads and the Transformation of the Ante-Bellum Economy* (Cambridge, 1965), employs equally sophisticated mathematical devices to show that the railroads had a measurable effect on the economy. Peter D. McClelland, "Railroads, American Growth, and the New History: A Critique," *J.E.H.*, XXVIII (March, 1968), criticizes the methodology of both Fogel and Fishlow. Similar differences exist among scholars who try to determine the effect of railroad building on economic growth of the various sections. Merl E. Reed, *New Orleans and the Railroads: The Struggle for Commercial Empire, 1830–1860* (Baton Rouge, 1966), shows that

the city fell behind other ports such as New York due to unfavorable railroad connections; Donald Markwalder, "The Ante-Bellum South as a Market for Food—Myth or Reality," *G.H.Q.*, LIV uses statistics to argue that the South produced nearly all the food that it needed, and that its supposed dependence on the Old Northwest was a myth. This thesis is substantiated in a careful study by Sam B. Hilliard, *Hog Meat and Hoecake: Food Supply in the Old South, 1840–1860* (Carbondale, 1972), which concludes that the region was not nearly so dependent on outside suppliers as supposed. These findings cast doubt on the validity of a long-held thesis that shifting trade routes helped shatter the alliance between the South and the Upper Mississippi Valley, leading to the sectional realignment between North and South that made the Civil War inevitable. This shift and its impact are analyzed in a long-standard work: A. L. Kohlmeier, *The Old Northwest as the Keystone of the Arch of American Federal Union: A Study in Commerce and Politics* (Bloomington, 1938). Additional interpretative material is in Henry C. Hubbart, *The Older Middle West, 1840–1880* (New York, 1936), and R. R. Russel, "A Revaluation of the Period before the Civil War: Railroads," *M.V.H.R.*, XV (December, 1928).

18   The Natural Setting

Geographic Conditions in the Far West. A helpful discussion of physiographic regions in the United States is Nevin M. Fenneman, *Physiography of Western United States* (New York, 1931). Brief special studies include: William J. Peterson, "Geography of Iowa Territory," *P.*, XIX (July, 1938), and Chessley L. Posey, "Influence of Geographic Factors in the Development of Minnesota," *M.H.*, II (August, 1918). Eugene W. Hollon, *The Great American Desert: Then and Now* (New York, 1966) has excellent chapters on the geography and ethnohistory of the Southwest. An attempt to define this region, more successful in stating than in solving the problem, is R. Laurence Moore, "The Continuing Search for a Southwest: A Study in Regional Interpretation," *A. and W.*, VI (Winter, 1964). A significant work on the Northwest is D. W. Meinig, *The Great Columbia Basin: A Historical Geography, 1805–1910* (Seattle, 1968), which relates land forms and soil to the settlement pattern. Robert Dunbier, *The Sonoran Desert: Its Geography, Economy, and People* (Tucson, 1968) is a classic descriptive work showing the manner in which various peoples have adapted to the arid environment of the Southwest. Walter Prescott Webb, *The Great Plains* (Boston, 1931) is a classic description of the environmental impact of the semiarid West on imported cultures. Essays dealing with aspects of the story are collected in Brian W. Blouet and Frederick C. Luebke, eds., *The Great Plains: Environment and Culture* (Lincoln, 1979). The generally hostile view of the plains reported by early army expeditions is explained in Roger L. Nichols, "The Army and Early Perceptions of the Plains," *N.H.*, LVI (Spring, 1975), while Elwyn B. Robinson, "An Interpretation of the History of the Great Plains," *N.D.H.*, XLI (Spring, 1974), isolates four factors responsible for the area's unique history. D. W. Meinig *Southwest: Three Peoples in Geographical Change, 1600–1970* (New York, 1971) is a thoughtful analysis of the effect of environments on intruding cultural groups.

The Western Indian: General Works. All of the surveys of Indian culture listed in Chapter II contain information on the Indians of the Trans-Mississippi country, and provide excellent introductions to the subject. They may be supplemented by general histories concentrating on the tribes of the Far West. Edward H. Spicer, *Cycles of Conquest* (Tucson, 1964) is a fine work by an anthropologist dealing primarily with the Southwest, while John C. Ewers, *Indian Life on the Upper Missouri* (Norman, 1968) brings together fifteen articles on the subject from the pen of this leading anthropologist, while Erna Gunther, *Indian Life: On the Northwest Coast of North America, As Seen by the Early Explorers and Fur Traders during the Last Decades of the Eighteenth Century* (Chicago, 1972), throws light on early Indian-European contacts in that region. Changes in Indian culture wrought by the introduction of the horse from Europe are described in Robert M. Denhardt, *The Horse of the Americas* (Norman, 1975 edn.), Frank G. Roe, *The Indian and the Horse* (Norman, 1955), and Preston Holder, *The Hoe and the Horse on the Plains: A Study of Cultural Development among North American Indians* (Lincoln, 1970), which uses the Caddoan peoples as an example of agricultural culture and the Sioux of a horse-hunting culture. Early Indian patterns of settlement as determined by climate and topography are discussed in L. S. Cressman, *Prehistory of the Far West: Homes of Vanished Peoples* (Salt Lake City, 1977). The manner in which tribes shifted locations as the Spanish frontier advanced is described and mapped in Albert H. Schroeder, "Shifting for Survival in the Spanish Southwest," *N.M.H.R.*, XLIII (October, 1968). Tony McGinnis, "Economic Warfare on the North-

ern Plains," *A. of W.*, XLIV (Spring, 1972), shows how the tribes fought among themselves to preserve hunting grounds, and how these conflicts complicated Indian-white relations. That this internal warfare dictated relations of tribes with the whites is admirably demonstrated in Richard White, "The Winning of the West: The Expansion of the Western Sioux in the Eighteenth and Nineteenth Centuries," *J.A.H.*, LXV (September, 1978), an important study. A case study of the changes in Indian life necessitated by white contacts is in the same author's "Indian Land Use and Environmental Change: Island County, Washington, A Case Study," *A. and W.*, XVII (Winter, 1975).

Cultural Areas and Linguistic Stocks. Histories of cultural groupings and linguistic families are numerous. A classic study of the Plains Indians is George E. Hyde, *Indians of the High Plains* (Norman, 1959); also useful are Francis Haines, *The Plains Indians* (New York, 1976), an excellent history from earliest times to the present, and Thomas E. Mails, *The Mystic Warriors of the Plains* (Garden City, 1972), which is a popular account for the period 1825–1875. Bertha P. Dutton, *Indians of the American Southwest* (Englewood Cliffs, 1975) is a competent overview of the desert tribes of the Four Corners region, while Pliny E. Goddard, *Indians of the Southwest* (New York, 1931), deals with the southern Plains country. For the Intermontane Province, Julian H. Steward, *Basin-Plateau Sociopolitical Groups* (Washington, 1938) is a study of all groups on an ecological basis. The Indians of California, and particularly estimates of their numbers, are discussed in Sherburne F. Cook, *The Population of the California Indians, 1769–1970* (Berkeley, 1976), and Sherburne F. Cook and Woodrow Borah, *Essays in Population History: Mexico and California* (Berkeley, 1979). George Woodcock, *Peoples of the Coast: The Indians of the Pacific Northwest* (Bloomington, 1977) and Pliny E. Goddard, *Indians of the Northwest Coast* (New York, 1934), treat the native groups of the Pacific Northwest. Of particular value is Muriel H. Wright, *A Guide to the Indian Tribes of Oklahoma* (Norman, 1951), which contains histories of the sixty-five tribes that have lived in the region. C. Gregory Crampton, "Indian Country," *U.H.Q.*, XXXIX (Spring, 1971), introduces a special issue of the journal with a number of articles on Utah's Indians. W. W. Newcomb, ed., *Indian Tribes of Texas* (Waco, 1971), brings together a similar collection of essays on Texas Indians. Donald J. Hughes, *American Indians in Colorado*

(Boulder, 1977) is concerned largely with the Utes.

Among histories of individual tribes, George E. Hyde, *A Sioux Chronicle* (Norman, 1956), George E. Hyde, *Spotted Tail's Red Folk: A History of the Brulé Sioux* (Norman, 1961), and James C. Olson, *Red Cloud and the Sioux Problem* (Lincoln, 1965), are all classic works on the Sioux. More recent works on this tribal group include Ernest L. Schusky, *The Forgotten Sioux* (Chicago, 1975), which is actually a study of the Lower Brulé, and two works by Roy W. Meyer, *The Village Indians of the Upper Missouri: The Mandans, Hidatsas, and Arikaras* (Lincoln, 1977), and *History of the Santee Sioux: United States Indian Policy on Trial* (Lincoln, 1980). Two of the eastern plains tribes are admirably studied in Martha R. Blaine, *The Ioway Indians* (Norman, 1979), and W. David Baird, *The Quapaw Indians: A History of the Downstream People* (Norman, 1979). John C. Mathews, *The Osages: Children of the Middle Waters* (Norman, 1961), William E. Unrau, *The Kansa Indians: A History of the Wind People, 1673–1873* (Norman, 1971), and George E. Hyde, *Pawnee Indians* (Boulder, 1951), are standard on those plains tribes. Virginia C. Trenholm, *The Arapahoes, Our People* (Norman, 1970), is most useful for the early period. George B. Grinnell, *The Cheyenne Indians,* 2 v. (New Haven, 1923), is still a standard work, but must be supplemented with Stan Hoig, *The Peace Chiefs of the Cheyennes* (Norman, 1980), a serious examination of the motives and techniques of those who sought to avoid warfare. Also useful are John C. Ewers, *The Blackfeet: Raiders of the Northern Plains* (Norman, 1958), and the same author's *The Horse in Blackfoot Indian Culture* (Washington, 1955). Peter J. Powell, *Sweet Medicine,* 2 v. (Norman, 1969), is a masterful description of the culture and religion of the Northern Cheyenne; excellent on the Southern Cheyenne is Donald J. Berthrong, *The Southern Cheyennes* (Norman, 1963). Ernest Wallace and E. Adamson Hoebel, *The Comanches: Lords of the South Plains* (Norman, 1953), is excellent; T. R. Fehrenbach, *Comanches: The Destruction of a People* (New York, 1974), deals with the near-extermination of the tribe in warfare with the whites. Two sound works on the Kiowa are Wilbur S. Nye, *Bad Medicine and Good: Tales of the Kiowas* (Norman, 1962), and Mildred P. Mayhall, *The Kiowas* (Norman, 1963). Virginia C. Trenholm and Maurine Carley, *The Shoshonis: Sentinels of the Northern Rockies* (Norman, 1964) is a sound history. Tribes of the Northern Rockies and Pacific Northwest are described in Brigham D. Madsden, *The Bannock of Idaho* (Caldwell, 1958), John Fahey, *The Flathead Indians* (Norman, 1974), Brigham D. Madsen, *The Lemhi: Sacajawea's People* (Caldwell, 1979), Robert H. Ruby and John A. Brown, *The Cayuse Indians: Imperial Tribesmen of Old Oregon* (Norman, 1972), the same authors' *The Chinook Indians: Traders of the Lower Columbia River* (Norman, 1976), Francis Haines, *The Nez Perces: Tribesmen of the Columbia Plateau* and Alvin M. Josephy, *The Nez Perce Indians and the Opening of the Northwest* (Lincoln, 1980 edn.). Olga W. Johnson, *Flathead and Kootenay: The Tribes and the Region's Traders* (Glendale, 1969), and Robert H. Ruby and John A. Brown, *The Cayuse Indians: Imperial Tribesmen of Old Oregon* (Norman, 1972), deal with the tribes of the Pacific Northwest. H. B. Cushman, *History of the Choctaw, Chickasaw and Natchez Indians* (Stillwater, 1962) is concerned with the history of those transplanted tribes in the West.

Ruth M. Underhill, *The Navajos* (Norman, 1956), Clyde Kluckhohn and D. C. Leighton, *The Navaho* (Cambridge, 1946), and Clyde Kluckhohn, et. al., *Navajo Material Culture* (Cambridge, 1971), deal expertly with a leading tribe of the Southwest. Expert studies of the several divisions of the Apaches include C. L. Sonnichsen, *The Mescalero Apaches* (Norman, 1959), Dan L. Thrapp, *Victorio and the Mimbres Apaches* (Norman, 1974), and Dolores A. Gunnerson, *The Jicarilla Apaches: A Study in Survival* (DeKalb, 1974). A readable general history of the more than twenty bands constituting the Apaches is Donald E. Worcester, *The Apaches: Eagles of the Southwest* (Norman, 1979).

Excellent studies of another southwestern group of Indians include Joe E. Sando, *The Pueblo Indians* (San Francisco, 1976), written by a member of the tribe and a sound and well-researched study, Harry C. James, *Pages from Hopi History* (Tucson, 1974), a popular account, C. Gregory Crampton, *The Zunis of Cibola* (Salt Lake City, 1978), and John L. Kessell, *Kiva, Cross and Crown: The Pecos Indians and New Mexico* (Washington, 1979). Both of the latter are superior studies by competent scholars. Ward A. Minge, *Acoma: Pueblo in the Sky* (Albuquerque, 1976) is a fine history of this famed pueblo from 1540 to the present.

Additional works that contain much information on the Indian, but are principally concerned with Indian-white relationships, are listed in the bibliography to Chapter XXX.

19 The Spanish Barrier, 1540–1776

General Works. Essential is John F. Bannon, *The Spanish Borderlands Frontier, 1513–1821* (New York, 1971), which incorporates the findings of modern scholarship and is the best single study of the borderlands. Charles Gibson, *Spain in America* (New York, 1966), is a brief survey which concentrates more fully on Spanish America itself. These works have displaced Herbert E. Bolton, *The Spanish Borderlands* (New Haven, 1921). Herbert I. Priestley, *The Coming of the White Man* (New York, 1930), describes social and economic conditions on the southwestern frontier. Two books by W. Eugene Hollon throw light on the whole history of the Southwest: *The Southwest: Old and New* (New York, 1961), and *The Great American Desert: Then and Now* (New York, 1966). Sixteen of Herbert E. Bolton's most important essays have been collected by John F. Bannon, ed., *Bolton and the Spanish Borderlands* (Norman, 1964). More useful are eighteen essays by modern experts gathered by David J. Weber, ed., *New Spain's Far Northern Frontier: Essays on Spain in the American West, 1540–1821* (Albuquerque, 1979). Donald E. Worcester, "The Significance of the Spanish Borderlands to the United States," *We.H.Q.,* VII (January, 1976), is interpretative. Agents and agencies of expansion are discussed in two excellent modern studies: Max L. Moorhead, *The Presidio: Bastion of the Spanish Borderlands* (Norman, 1975, and Oakah L. Jones, Jr., *Los Paisanos: Settlers on the Northern Frontier of New Spain* (Norman, 1979). Works on a third instrument of the frontier, the mission station, are listed later in this chapter.

Early Spanish Exploration. The two most recent biographies of Cortés are Salvador de Madariaga, *Hernán Cortés, Conqueror of Mexico* (New York, 1941), and Henry Wagner, *The Rise of Fernando Cortés* (Los Angeles, 1944). The standard biography of the first viceroy is Arthur S. Aiton, *Antonio de Mendoza, First Viceroy of New Spain* (Durham, 1927).

Brief accounts of Spanish exploration are in John B. Brebner, *The Explorers of North America, 1492–1806* (New York, 1933). Carl Sauer, *The Road to Cibola* (Berkeley, Calif., 1932) traces in detail the land route northward used by the expeditions. The most recent collection of narratives of the Coronado expedition is George P. Hammond and Agapito Rey, eds., *Narratives of the Coronado Expedition, 1540–1542,* 2 v. (Albuquerque, 1940). The standard secondary account is Herbert E. Bolton, *Coronado Knight of Pueblos and Plains,* (New York, 1950). Angelico Chavez, *Coronado's Friars* (Washington, 1968) is a work of meticulous scholarship that identifies the five Franciscans who accompanied Coronado. The route followed by the expedition is made clearer in Clevy L. Strout, "Flora and Fauna Mentioned in the Journals of the Coronado Expedition," *G.P.J., XI* (Fall, 1971) and "The Coronado Expedition: Following the Geography Described in the Spanish Journals," *G.P.J., XIV* (Fall, 1974). Two explorers connected with Coronado are discussed in Cleve Hallenbeck, *The Journey of Fray Marcos de Niza* (Dallas, 1949), Mabel Farnhum, *The Seven Golden Cities* (Milwaukee, 1943), which also deals with Niza, and Adolph F. Bandelier, *The Discovery of New Mexico by the Franciscan Monk Friar Marcos de Niza in 1539* (Tucson, 1981), a newly translated account by a French historian. The excavation of possible sites of the villages Coronado visited in Kansas is described in Waldo R. Wedel, "After Coronado in Quivera," *K.H.Q., XXXIV* (Winter, 1968).

Early Advance of the Mexican Frontier. The movement of population northward across Mexico still awaits study. The subject is touched upon in Hubert H. Bancroft, *History of the North Mexican States and Texas,* 2 v. (San Francisco, 1884–89), and in the introductions to Charles W. Hackett, ed., *Historical Documents Relating to New Mexico, Neuva Vizcaya, and Approaches Thereto,* 3 v. (Washington, 1923–37). An account of the frontier thrust into one northern Mexican province is J. Lloyd Mecham, *Francisco de Ibarra and Neuva Vizcaya* (Durham, 1927). Three scholarly volumes explore the early advance of settlement northward: P. J. Bakewell, *Silver Mining and Society in Colonial Mexico: Zacatecas, 1540–1700* (New York, 1971), Philip W. Powell, *Soldiers, Indians and Silver: North America's First Frontier War* (Tempe, 1975 edn.), and Philip W. Powell, *Mexico's Miguel Caldera: The Taming of America's First Frontier, 1548–1597* (Tucson, 1977), a brilliantly written biography of the soldier who opened Zacatecas and other silver frontiers in northern Mexico.

The impact of Francis Drake's voyage on New Spain's expansion northward is the subject of extensive historical investigation. That his purpose was to explore the South America coast from the Platte River to the thinly occupied region of northern Chile as a site for possible colonies is argued in K. R. Andrews, "The Aims of Drake's Expedition of

1577–1580," *A.H.R.*, LXXIII (February, 1968). The effect of his voyage on Spanish interest in the northern provinces is assessed in Henry R. Wagner, *Sir Francis Drake's Voyage around the World, Its Aims and Achievements* (San Francisco, 1926), while the same author describes the resulting activity along the California coast in *Spanish Voyages to the North-West Coast of America in the Sixteenth Century* (San Francisco, 1929). Basic documents describing the voyage of Drake are in John Hampden, ed., *Francis Drake, Privateer: Contemporary Narratives and Documents* (University, 1972), while the extensive literature on his landing site in California is surveyed in N. B. Martin, "*Portus Novae Albionis:* Site of Drake's California Sojourn," *P.H.R.*, XLVIII (August, 1979). Later voyages along the California coast are described expertly in such works as W. Michael Mathes, "The Discovery of Alta California: João Rodrígues Cabrillo or Juan Rodrígues Cabrillo," *J.S.D.H.*, XIX (Summer, 1973), an attempt to learn whether the explorer was Spanish or Portuguese, *Vizcaíno and Spanish Expansion in the Pacific Ocean* (San Francisco 1968), and "Don Pedro Porter y Casanate, Admiral of the South Seas, 1611–1662," *S.C.Q.*, LIV (Spring, 1972). The ships used on the Cabrillo expedition are expertly described in Harry Kelsey, "The California Armada of Juan Rodrígues Cabrillo," *S.C.Q.*, LXI (Winter, 1979). A well-researched book telling the whole story of New Spain's frontier in the Pacific is L. Warren Cook, *Flood Tide of Empire: Spain and the Pacific Northwest, 1543–1819* (New Haven, 1973).

The Founding of New Mexico. By far the best work on this period is George P. Hammond and Agapito Rey, eds., *The Rediscovery of New Mexico, 1580–1594* (Albuquerque, 1966), which reproduces the narratives of all expeditions prior to Oñate. The expertly prepared introductions give the history of the region for these years. The standard account of Spanish settlement there is George P. Hammond, *Don Juan de Oñate and the Founding of New Mexico* (Santa Fe, 1926). George P. Hammond and Agapito Rey, eds., *Don Juan de Oñate, Colonizer of New Mexico, 1595–1628,* 2 v. (Albuquerque, 1953) is an admirable documentary collection, while the same two authors in "The Crown's Participation in the Founding of New Mexico, *N.M.H.R.*, XXXII (October, 1957), show the unusual efforts of the government to sustain the colony to 1621. The role of Oñate's son in New Mexico's founding is discussed in Agapito Rey, "Cristóbal de Oñate," *N.M.H.R.*, XXVI (July, 1951). That Oñate himself died not in Mexico but at Guadalcanal, Spain, in 1626, is dem-

onstrated in Eric Beerman, "The Death of an Old Conquistadore: New Light on Juan de Oñate," *N.M.H.R.*, LIV (October, 1979). That Albuquerque was founded by settlers who drifted to the site rather than by an expedition supposedly sent by Governor Francisco Cuervo in 1706 is demonstrated in Marc Simmons, "Governor Cuervo and the Beginnings of Albuquerque: Another Look," *N.M.H.R.*, LV (July, 1980). Among the histories of New Mexico, one that deals solely with the Spanish period is Cleve Hallenbeck, *Land of the Conquistadores* (Caldwell, 1950).

The Northern Mexican Frontier Advances. A principal instrument for Spanish expansion was the mission station. Herbert E. Bolton, "The Mission as a Frontier Institution in the Spanish-American Colonies," *A.H.R.*, XXIII (October, 1917), first called attention to the mission station as a device for advancing the frontier. A later article by the same author, "The Black Robes of New Spain," *Ca.H.R.*, XXI (October, 1935), surveys their northern progress in Mexico in general terms. More detailed treatments are in William E. Shiels, *Gonzalo de Tapia (1561–1594)* (New York, 1934), and in the studies of Peter M. Dunne, *Pioneer Black Robes on the West Coast* (Berkeley, 1940), *Pioneer Jesuits in Northern Mexico* (Berkeley, 1944), *Early Jesuit Missions in Tarahumara* (Berkeley, 1948), and *Black Robes in Lower California* (Berkeley, 1952)). The failure of the Indian policy in northern Mexico to subdue some tribes is described in Max L. Moorhead, "Spanish Deportation of Hostile Apaches: The Policy and the Practice," *A. and W.*, XVII (Autumn, 1975) and Thomas E. Sheridan, "Cross and Arrow: The Breakdown of Spanish-Seri Relations, 1729–1750," *A. and W.*, XXI (Winter, 1979).

The New Mexican Revolt that halted the advance of that frontier, and the revolt's aftermath, are described in numerous studies. Angelico Chavez, "Pohé-Yemo's Representative and the Pueblo Revolt of 1680," *N.M.H.R.*, XLII (April, 1967), advances the thesis that an able mulatto who posed as the representative of the god Phoé-Yemo plotted and directed the 1680 revolt. On the revolt itself a satisfactory history is Charles W. Hackett, *Revolt of the Pueblo Indians of New Mexico and Otermin's Attempted Reconquest, 1680–1682* (Albuquerque, 1942). The basic conflict between the Pueblo's religious beliefs and Catholicism as a factor underlying the revolt is the theme of Henry W. Bowden, "Spanish Missions, Cultural Conflict and the Pueblo Revolt in 1680," *C.H.*, XLIV (June, 1975). The composition of the Juan Paez Hurtado expedition that resettled the area in 1795 is analyzed in Clevy L. Strout, "The Reset-tlement of Santa Fe, 1695: The Newly Found Muster Role," *N.M.H.R.*, LIII (July, 1978), while the standard account of the reconquest is J. Manuel Espinosa, *Crusaders of the Rio Grande* (Chicago, 1942). Oakah L. Jones, Jr., *Pueblo Warriors & Spanish Conquest* (Nor-man, 1966), learnedly discusses the use of Pueblo Indians by Mexican authorities in the subsequent defense of the region.

Herbert E. Bolton, *Rim of Christendom* (New York, 1936), is still the best study of the initial occupation of Arizona, while essential documents are in Fay J. Smith, et. al., eds., *Father Kino in Arizona* (Phoenix, 1966), and Herbert E. Bolton, ed., *Kino's Historical Memoir of Pimería Alta, 1683–1711*, 2 v. (Cleveland, 1919). A sound account is also in Jay J. Wagoner, *Early Arizona: Pre-History Civil War* (Tucson, 1975). The exact route of one of Kino's explorations is traced in Ronald L. Ives, "Father' Kino's 1697 Entrada to the Casa Grande Ruin in Arizona: A Reconstruc-tion," *A. and W.*, XV (Winter, 1973). John A. Donohue, *After Kino: Jesuit Missions In Northwestern New Spain, 1711–1767* (St. Louis, 1969) is a carefully researched book on the latter period of Spain's mission activity in Arizona; a still later period is described in Sidney R. Brinckerhoff, "The Last Years of Spanish Arizona, 1786–1821," A. and W., IX (Spring, 1967). John L. Kessell, *Mission of Sorrows: Jesuit Guevavi and the Pimas, 1691–1767* (Tucson, 1970), is a well-written history of the Mission of Los Santos Angeles de Guevavi in southern Arizona.

The Occupation of Texas.   The best ac-count of the mission frontier in Texas is Carlos E. Castañeda, *Our Catholic Heritage in Texas*, 4 v. (Austin, 1936–39), which describes mis-sionary activity between 1519 and 1782. La Salle's intrusion is best described in Robert S. Weddle, *Wilderness Manhunt: The Spanish Search for La Salle* (Austin, 1972), and more generally in Henry Folmer, *Franco-Spanish Rivalry in North America, 1542–1763* (Glen-dale, 1953). A good account of La Salle', sur-vivors who left his fort in 1687 is in Robert S. Weddle, "La Salle's Survivors," *S.H.Q.*, LXXV (April, 1972).

The Spanish recovery of Texas is treated in Ross Phares' sound biography of Louis St. Denis, *Cavalier in the Wilderness* (Baton Rouge, 1952). Briefer accounts are in Char-mion C. Shelby, "St. Denis's Second Expe-dition to the Rio Grande, 1716–1719," *S.H.Q.*, XXVII (January, 1924), and Charles W. Hack-ett, "The Marquis of San Miguel de Aguayo and His Recovery of Texas from the French, 1719–1723," *S.H.Q.*, XLIX (October, 1945).

The founding and history of two important missions is described in Marion A. Habig, "Mission San José y San Miguel de Aguayo, 1720–1824," *S.H.Q.*, LXXI (April, 1968), and Robert S. Weddle, *San Juan Bautista: Gate-way to Spanish Texas* (Austin, 1968). Rea-sons for Spain's failure to hold the area firmly are explored in Odie B. Faulk, "The Coman-che Invasion of Texas, 1743–1846," *G.P.J.*, IX (Fall, 1969), a history of successful raids there, and James M. Daniel, "The Spanish Frontier in West Texas and Northern Mex-ico," *S.H.Q.*, LXXI (April, 1968), showing how Indian raiding parties swept through the "Despoblado," to raid Texas, and New Spain's efforts to guard the region.

Conflict on the French-Spanish Border-land.   In addition to the general history by Henry Folmer listed above, excellent ac-counts of this border warfare are in Elizabeth A. H. Jones, *Storms Brewed in Other Men's World: The Confrontation of Indians, Span-iards, and the French in the Southwest, 1540–1795* (College Station, 1975). Essays dealing with the subject are collected in John F. McDermott, ed., *The Spanish in the Mis-sissippi Valley, 1762–1804* (Urbana, 1974). A thoughtful interpretation of the entire conflict by its most thorough student is Abraham P. Nasatir, *Borderland in Retreat: From Spanish Louisiana to the Far Southwest* (Albuquer-que, 1976). The invasion of French traders that touched off the conflict is described in Frederick W. Hodge, "French Intrusion to-ward New Mexico in 1695," *N.M.H.R.*, IV (January, 1929), Mildred M. Wedel, "Claude–Charles Dutisné: A Review of His 1719 Journeys," *G.P.J.*, XII (Spring, 1973), Charmion C. Shelby, ed., "Projected French Attacks upon the Northeastern Frontier of New Spain, 1719–1721," *H.A.H.R.* XIII (No-vember, 1933), Milton Reichart, "Bourg-mont's Route to Central Kansas: A Reexam-ination," *K.H.*, II (Summer, 1979), and Gilbert J. Garraghan, *Chapters in Frontier History* (Milwaukee, 1934). Spanish attempts to repel the invaders are the theme of Charles W. Hackett, "Policy of the Spanish Crown Re-garding French Encroachments from Louisi-ana, 1721–1762," *New Spain and the Anglo-American West* (Los Angeles, 1932). The de-feat of one Spanish expedition is discussed in Alfred B. Thomas, "Massacre of the Villasur Expedition," *N.H.*, VII (July, September, 1924). French trade with Santa Fe is de-scribed in Herbert E. Bolton, "French Intru-sions into New Mexico, 1749–1752," *The Pacific Ocean in History* (New York, 1917), and the history of one French outpost told in Charles E. Hoffhaus, "Fort de Cavagnial: Imperial France in Kansas, 1744–1764," *K.H.Q.*, XXX (Winter, 1964). The inability of Spain to deal with the Louisiana tribes that had been under French influence is shown in Lawrence Kinnaird, "Spanish Treaties with Indian Tribes," *We.H.Q.*, X (January, 1979).

Herbert E. Bolton, *Texas in the Middle Eighteenth Century* (Berkeley, 1915), contains the classic account of Spanish activity following the French threats. A more detailed story of the occupation of the coast is in Lawrence F. Hill, *José de Escandón and the Founding of Nuevo Santander* (Columbus, 1926), while expansion northward into the Apache country is considered in Robert S. Weddle, *The San Sabá Mission: Spanish Pivot in Texas* (Austin, 1964). The latter is an excellent history of the region, as well as of the mission and presidio. A popular book that deals with one of the supply routes to the area is Hodding and Betty W. Carter, *Doomed Road of Empire: The Spanish Trail of Conquest* (New York, 1963), which tells the story of the Spanish Road connecting Saltillo and Natchitoches. A well-told story of Spain's attempts to strengthen its Texan outposts is in Robert S. Weddke and Robert H. Thonhoff, *Drama & Conflict: The Texas Saga of 1776* (Austin, 1976). The effect of these conflicts on population distribution in Texas is shown in Alicia V. Tjarks, "Comparative Demographic Analysis of Texas, 1777–1793," *S.H.Q.*, LXXVII (January, 1974).

Last Days of the Northern Frontier in New Mexico and Sonora. A well-researched study of the use of Spanish engineers to aid settlement and defense on the northern frontiers in the latter part of the eighteenth century is Janet R. Fireman, *The Spanish Royal Corps of Engineers in the Western Borderlands: Instruments of Bourbon Reform, 1764 to 1815* (Glendale, 1977). The northward extension of New Mexico's trading frontier is described in Frances L. Swadesh, *Los Primeros Pobladores: Hispanic Americans of the Ute Frontier* (Notre Dame, 1974), while continued defensive measures used in New Mexico are described in such works as Max L. Moorhead, "Rebuilding the Presidio of Santa Fe, 1789–1791," *N.M.H.R.*, XLIX (April, 1974), Donald J. Lehmer, "The Second Frontier: The Spanish," in Robert G. Ferris, ed., *The American West: An Appraisal* (Santa Fe, 1963), an interpretative essay on the Mexican northward-moving frontier, Ted J. Warner, "Frontier Defense," *N.M.H.R.*, XLI (January, 1966), and particularly Max L. Moorhead, *The Apache Frontier: Jacob Ugarte and Spanish-Indian Relations in Northern New Spain, 1769–1791* (Norman, 1968). Marc Simmons, "Spanish Government and Colonial

Land Practices," *N. M. Quart.*, XXXVIII (Spring, 1968), shows that Spain tried to protect its borderlands by insisting on compact settlements along the frontier. The economic development of northern Mexico in its early stages is the theme of Lesley B. Simpson, *The Encomienda in New Spain: The Beginning of Spanish Mexico* (Berkeley, 1966), while cattle ranches as staging areas for the advance northward are briefly appraised in Donald D. Brand, "The Early History of the Range Cattle Industry in Northern Mexico," *A.H.*, XXXV (July, 1961). Marc Simmons, *Spanish Government in New Mexico* (Albuquerque, 1968) is a capable history of the period from 1772 to 1821. Aspects of the story are told in Noel M. Loomis and Abraham P. Nasatir, *Pedro Vial and the Roads to Santa Fe* (Norman, 1967), which is based on extensive documentation on the 1780s and later periods, John L. Kessell "Campaigning on the Upper Gila, 1756," *N.M.H.R.*, XLVI (April, 1971), an account of the Bustamante expedition of that year, and Ronald L. Ives, "Retracing the Route of the Fages Expedition of 1781," *A. and W.*, VIII (Spring, 1966). An excellent account of the northern Sonoran frontier from the failure of the Jesuit missions to the American invasion is John L. Kessell, *Friars, Soldiers, and Reformers: Hispanic Arizona and the Sonora Mission Frontier, 1767–1856* (Tucson, 1976). In "Friars versus Bureaucrats: The Mission as a Threatened Institution on the Arizona-Sonora Frontier, 1767–1842," *We.H.Q.*, the same author shows that the missions survived the Napoleonic Wars only because the government had no workable alternatives. Albert Stagg, *The First Bishop of Sonora: Antonio de Los Reyes, O.F.M.* (Tucson, 1976) is a biography of the bishop who was sent to the frontier on the expulsion of the Jesuits in 1767. The attempts to open a direct road between the Sonora and New Mexican frontiers are described in Marc Simmons, "Spanish Attempts to Open a New Mexico-Sonora Road," *A. and W.*, XVII (Spring, 1975). New Spain's final years in Texas are described in Odie B. Faulk, *The Last Years of Spanish Texas, 1778–1821* (The Hague, 1974), and Felix D. Almaráz, Jr., *Tragic Cavalier: Governor Manuel Saledo of Texas, 1803–1813* (Austin, 1971). The merging of white and Indian cultures along the northern frontiers during the late Spanish period is the theme of such works as Edward H. Spicer, *Cycles of Conquest: The Impact of Spain, Mexico, and the United States on the Indians of the Southwest, 1533–1960* (Tucson, 1962), Jack D. Forbes, *Apache, Navaho, and Spaniard* (Norman, 1960) and Feranando

Benìtez, *Century After Cortèz* (Chicago, 1965).

The Mexican Borderland, 1821–1846. The story of the borderlands after Mexican independence is yet to be told. The importance of the subject is amply revealed in David J. Weber, "Mexico's Far Northern Frontier, 1821–1854: Historiography Askew," *We.H.Q.*, VII (July, 1976); the same author has compiled an excellent bibliography for the subject in "Mexico's Far Northern Frontier, 1821–1845: A Critical Bibliography," *A. and W.*, XIX (Autumn, 1977). Aspects of the economic history of the area are studied in such works as Alvin R. Sunserim, "Agricultural Techniques in New Mexico at the Time of the Anglo-American Conquest," *A.H.*, XLVII (October, 1973), Marc Simmons, "Spanish Irrigation Practices in New Mexico," *N.M.H.R.*, XLVII (April, 1972), showing that Spanish and Pueblo customs were both used; Richard E. Greenleaf, "Land and Water in Mexico and New Mexico, 1700–1721," *N.M.H.R.*, XLVII (April, 1972), and Billy D. Walker, "Copper Genius: The Early Years of Santa Rita del Cobre," *N.M.H.R.*, LIV (January, 1979), a well-researched study of the copper mines of southwestern New Mexico. The demographic structure of countryside and town along the northern frontier during its last days has also been studied in several articles. Robert Archibald, "Acculturation and Assimilation in Colonial New Mexico," *N.M.H.R.*, LIII (July, 1978), a description of the fluid class structure, Alicia V. Tjarks, "Demographic, Ethnic and Occupational Structure in New Mexico, 1790," *A.*, XXXV (July, 1978), a solid statistical work providing an excellent picture of the population on the basis of the 1790 census; Henry F. Dobyns, *Spanish Colonial Tucson: A Demographic History* (Tucson, 1976), which uses a variety of sources to construct a demographic profile of the community; and two articles by W. H. Timmons, "The Population of the El Paso Area—a Census of 1784," *N.M.H.R.*, LII (October, 1977), and "The El Paso Area in the Mexican Period, 1821–1848," *S.H.Q.*, LXXXIV (July, 1980), a history of the region and its economy.

The Occupation of California. General histories of the state devote proper attention to the Spanish period; of these the most recent are Walton Bean, *California: An Interpretative History* (2nd. ed., New York, 1973), David Lavender, *California: A Bicentennial History* (New York, 1976), and Andrew F. Rolle, *California: A History* (New York, 1981), an excellent brief account. Fuller treatments are in two older works by Charles E. Chapman, *The Founding of Spanish California, 1678–1783* (New York, 1916), and *A History of California: The Spanish Period* (New York, 1921).

The Russian threat is summarized in James R. Gibson, *Imperial Russia in Frontier America: The Changing Geography of Supply of Russian America, 1784–1867* (New York, 1976), a searching study of Russia's efforts to supply its posts, and the failure of the company and particularly Howard I. Kushner, *Conflict on the Northwest Coast; American-Russian Rivalry in the Pacific Northwest, 1790–1867* (Westport, 1975). A contemporary history by a Russian agent of the company, recently translated, is P. A. Tikhmenev, *A History of the Russian-American Company* (Seattle, 1978). Two reports by Russian agents who spent time in America have been published by James R. Gibson, "Russian America in 1833: The Survey of Kirill Khlebnikov," *P.N.Q.* LXIII (January, 1972), and "Russian America in 1821," *O.H.Q.*, (June, 1976), which also is based on the reports of Khlebnikov. The career of the Spanish agent who capitalized on fears of Russia is discussed by Herbert I. Priestley, *José de Gálvez, Visitor-General of New Spain* (Berkeley, 1916). Michael E. Thurman, *The Naval Department of San Blas*, (Glendale, 1967), studies the port from which expeditions sailed northward. An excellent survey of Spain's activities in the region is in Warren L. Cook, *Flood Tide of Empire: Spain in the Pacific Northwest* (New Haven, 1971). The effect of the Russian activities in the Northwest on Spanish Indian policy is the theme of Christon Archer, "The Making of Spanish Indian Policy on the Northwest Coast," *N.M.H.R.*, LI (January, 1977).

The career of a largely forgotten early explorer is described in Janet R. Fireman and Manuel P. Servin, "Miguel Costansó: California's Forgotten Founder," *C.H.S.Q.*, XLIX (March, 1970), which deals with the life of a navigator who spent three years after 1764 mapping the coast. A full account of an important expedition is Theodore E. Treutlein, "The Portalá Expedition of 1769–1770," *C.H.S.Q.*, XLVII (December, 1968); less full is Donald A. Nuttell, "Gaspar de Portalá: Disenchanted Conquistador of Spanish Upper California," *S.C.Q.*, LIII (September, 1971). Narratives of the Portalá expeditions are in Ray Brandes, ed., *The Costansó Narrative of the Portalá Expedition* (Newhall, 1970), Herbert E. Bolton, *Fray Francisco Palóu's Historical Memoirs of New California*, 4 v. (Berkeley, 1926), and Douglas S. Watson, *The Spanish Occupation of California* (San Francisco, 1934). The standard biography of Portolá's chronicler is Herbert E. Bolton, *Fray Juan Crespi, Missionary Explorer of the Pacific*

Coast, 1769–1774 (Berkeley, 1927). Early propaganda activities that publicized California are described in W. Michael Mathes, "Early California Propaganda: The Works of Fray Antonio de la Ascension," *C.H.S.Q.,* L (June, 1971), and Daniel J. Garr, "A Rare and Desolate Land: Population and Race in Hispanic California," *We.H.Q.,* VI (April, 1975). Edwin A. Beilharz, *Felipe de Neve, First Governor of California* (San Francisco, 1971) is a scholarly study of the man who became governor in 1777 and supervised the founding of the first settlements.

The most thorough study of the California mission frontier is still Zaphyrin Englehardt, *The Missions and Missionaries of California,* 4 v. (San Francisco, 1908–1915), although John A. Berger, *The Franciscan Missions of California* (New York, 1941), is more readable. Maynard Geiger, *The Life and Times of Fray Junipero Serra, O.F.M.,* 2 v. (Washington, 1959), is a work of monumental scholarship. The same author's *Franciscan Missionaries in Hispanic California, 1769–1848* (San Marino, 1969), identifies and describes all missionaries. His *Mission Santa Barbara, 1782–1965* (Santa Barbara, 1965), is a classic description of one mission, and his "New Data on Mission San Juan Capistrano," *S.C.Q.,* XLIX (March, 1967), adds details to the story of that outpost. The route followed by Serra between Lorato and San Diego is exactly defined in Ronald L. Ives, "Problems of the Serra Route," *J.S.D.H.,* XXI (Fall, 1975). The treatment of the Indians by missionaries is discussed by Florian F. Guest, "The Indian Policy Under Fermín de Lasuén, California's Second Father President," *C.H.S.Q.,* XLV (September, 1966), who concludes that Serra's successor inaugurated a firm but kindly policy. That the Indians were effectively converted is disputed by Martha Voght, "Shamans and Padres: The Religion of the Southern California Mission Indians," *P.H.R.,* XXXVI (November, 1967), who shows that they carried from the missions a religion that blended Catholicism with their own traditional religion. Sherburne F. Cook examines this argument and other aspects of the mission system in a volume of essays: *The Conflict Between the California Indian and White Civilization* (Berkeley, 1976), and is in turn answered in Francis F. Guest, O.F.M., "An Examination of the Thesis of S. F. Cook on the Forced Conversion of Indians in the California Missions," *S.C.Q.,* LXI (Spring, 1979), which holds that after 1790 conversion was largely voluntary. Manuel P. Servin, "The Secularization of the California Missions: A Reappraisal," *S.C.Q.,* XLVII (June, 1965), blames

the troubles of the missions on the overzealous nature of the branch of the Franciscan order that operated in California, the Fernandinos.

Recent scholarship has been devoted to the broader impact of the mission system in Spanish California. Their economic impact is the theme of Robert Archibald, *The Economic Aspects of the California Missions* (Washington, 1978), which shows that by 1810 they had developed an almost self-dependent economy for the region. That the system disrupted the Indians' own social structure is demonstrated in George H. Phillips, *Chiefs and Challengers: Indian Resistance and Cooperation in Southern California* (Los Angeles, 1975), an in-depth analysis of three tribes near San Diego. A capable modern account of one mission is Robert S. Smilie, *The Sonoma Mission, San Francisco Solano de Sonoma* (Fresno, 1975), while two church leaders are described in Franics F. Guest, *Fermin Francisco de Lasuén (1736–1803): A Biography* (Washington, 1973), an account of the second head of the Franciscans in California, and Francis J. Weber, *Francisco Garcia Diego: California's Transition Bishop* (Los Angeles, 1971), an able biography of the bishop sent to restore order after the Mexican Revolution. An ethnic survey of the missions at this time is reprinted in Maynard Geiger and Clement W. Meighan, eds., *As The Padres Saw Them: California Indian Life and Customs as Reported by the Franciscan Missionaries, 1813–1815* (Santa Barbara, 1976).

The founding of San Francisco as a Spanish outpost has been much studied. A brief study of one explorer is Raymond F. Wood, "Francisco Garcés Explorer of Southern California," *S.C.Q.,* LI (September, 1969); the same author's "Juan Crespi: The Man who Named Los Angeles, *S.C.Q.,* LIII (September, 1971), is based on the Crespi diaries. Useful is Theodore E. Treutlein, *San Francisco Bay: Discovery and Colonization, 1769–1776* (San Francisco, 1968), a thorough study. Raymond F. Wood, "The Discovery of the Golden Gate: Legend and Reality," *S.C.Q.,* LVIII (Summer, 1976), expertly reappraises the evidence to show that the Fages party was the first to sight the bay in 1770. Pedro Fages has inspired other recent investigations into aspects of his career, with the results embodied in Donald A. Nuttall, "Light Cast Upon Shadows: The Non-California Years of Don Pedro Fages," *C.H.S.Q.,* LVI (Fall, 1977), Joseph P. Sanchez, "Pedro Fages in Sonora, 1767–1768, and 1777–1782," *R.R.V.H.R.,* II (Winter, 1975), and particularly Theodore E. Treutlein, "Fages as Explorer, 1769–1772," *C.H.S.Q.,* LI (Winter,

1972), a translation of a diary kept in 1772 while exploring the San Francisco Bay.

Documents on the Garcés and allied expeditions are in John Galvin, ed., *A Record of Travels in Arizona and California, 1775–1776* (San Francisco, 1965), a new translation well edited, John Galvin, ed., *The First Spanish Entry into San Francisco Bay, 1775* (San Francisco, 1971), which prints for the first time the narratives of Fray Vicente Santa Maria, and Herbert E. Bolton, ed., *Anza's California Expeditions*, 5 v. (Berkeley, 1930). The first volume of the latter is a scholarly history of Anza's activities. The narrative of his second expedition has been edited by Herbert E. Bolton, *Font's Complete Dairy, a Chronicle of the Founding of San Francisco* (Berkeley, 1933), while the same author has written the standard account of the second Anza expedition in *Outpost of Empire* (New York, 1931). The routes followed by the Anza expeditions are accurately described in Jack D. Forbes, "The Development of the Yuma Route before 1826," *C.H.S.Q., XLIII* (June, 1964). Efforts to open routes connecting California with other portions of New Spain are described in Lowell J. Bean and William M. Mason, eds., *The Romero Expeditions, 1823–1826* (Los Angeles, 1963), Walter Briggs, *Without Noise of Arms: The 1776 Domingues-Escalante Search for a Route from Santa Fe to Monterey* (Flagstaff, 1976), and Ted J. Warner, ed., *The Dominguez-Escalante Journal: Their Expedition through Colorado, Utah, Arizona and New Mexico in 1776* (Provo, 1976), a new and accurate translation of the journals.

20   The Traders' Frontier, 1776–1840

American Exploration of the Far West. Two general accounts are Bernard DeVoto, *The Course of Empire* (Boston, 1952), and Ray A. Billington, *The Far Western Frontier, 1830–1860* (New York, 1956). By far the best account of the exploration of the West is William H. Goetzmann, *Exploration and Empire. The Explorer and the Scientist in the Winning of the American West* (New York, 1966), which weaves together the story of official and private exploration. Gloria G. Cline, *Exploring the Great Basin* (Norman, 1963) is a competent treatment of one area. Popular histories of exploration that are both readable and accurate include Gerald Rawlings, *The Pathfinders: The History of America's First Westerners* (New York, 1964), and Henry Savage, Jr., *Discovering America* (New York, 1979), which describes major expedi-

tions from Lewis and Clark to John Wesley Powell. An older work that is useful is E. W. Gilbert, *The Exploration of Western American, 1800–1850* (Cambridge, 1933), written by a geographer.

The narratives of the Lewis and Clark expedition are in Reuben G. Thwaites, ed., *Original Journals of the Lewis and Clark Expedition, 1804–1806*, 8 v. (New York, 1904–1905); a useful one-volume condensation is Bernard DeVoto, *The Journals of Lewis and Clark* (Boston, 1953). Invaluable correspondence concerning the expedition has been collected in Donald Jackson, ed., *Letters of the Lewis and Clark Expedition, With Related Documents, 1783–1854* (Urbana, 1979 edn.), while notes kept by William Clark on the journey have been edited by Ernest S. Osgood, *The Field Notes of Captain William Clark* (New Haven, 1964). Among the many secondary accounts of the expedition, those by John Bakeless, *Lewis and Clark* (New York, 1947), Richard Dillon, *Meriwether Lewis: A Biography* (New York, 1965), which is primarily a history of the expedition, and David F. Hawke, *Those Tremendous Mountains: The Story of the Lewis and Clark Expedition* (New York, 1980), are readable and based on scholarly studies. These may be supplemented by biographical works on members of the party. Charles G. Clarke, *The Men of the Lewis and Clark Expedition* (Glendale, 1970), lists and describes the fifty-one members. M. O. Skarsten, *George Drouillard: Hunter and Interpreter for Lewis and Clark* (Glendale, 1964), adds details, while Jerome O. Steffen, *William Clark: Jeffersonian Man on the Frontier* (Norman, 1977), fits Clark into the intellectual atmosphere of his day, showing that he was a competent naturalist and self-educated. Sacágawea, the Indian guide, has inspired a surprising amount of scholarship: Harold P. Howard, *Sacajawea* (Norman, 1971), Ella E. Clark and Margot Edmonds, *Sacagawea of the Lewis and Clark Expedition* (Berkeley, 1980), and Anna L. Waldo, *Sacajawea* (New York, 1979). The latter is vigorously attacked in Blanche Schroer, "Boat-Pusher or Bird-Woman? Sacagawea or Sacajawea?" *A. of W., LII* (Spring, 1980). Irving W. Anderson, "Probing the Riddle of the Bird Woman," *M., XXIII* (October, 1973), shows that Sacágawea did not die in the 1850s as some have maintained, but on December 20, 1802, at Ft. Manuel. Two expert biographical sketches of her husband are Dennis R. Ottoson, "Toussaint Charboneau, a Most Durable Man," *N.D.H., VI* (Spring, 1976), and Irving W. Anderson, "A Charbonneau Family Portrait," *A.W., XVII* (March–April, 1980).

Roy E. Appleman, "Joseph and Reuben Field, Kentucky Frontiersman of the Lewis and Clark Expedition and their Father, Abraham," *F.C.H.Q.*, IXL (January, 1975), tells of two of the nine Kentuckians on the expedition.

These accounts may be supplemented with special studies of aspects of the expedition's history. Donald Jackson, "Ledyard and Lapérouse: A Contrast in Northwestern Exploration," *We.H.Q.*, IX, (October, 1978), explains why Lewis and Clark rather than Ledyard led the expedition, while John L. Allen, *Passage Through the Garden: Lewis and Clark and the Image of the American Northwest* (Chicago, 1975), links the purposes of the explorers with the collapse of hopes that a Northwest Passage might be found. The preparations for the trip, including the rigorous training received by Meriwether Lewis, are described in Rochonne Abrams, "Meriwether Lewis: Two Years with Jefferson the Mentor," *M.H.S.B.*, XXXVI (October, 1979), and in Paul R. Cutright, *Lewis and Clark: Pioneering Naturalists* (Urbana, 1969). Comparable studies of the medical training received by the explorers are Donald Snoddy, "Medical Aspects of the Lewis and Clark Expedition," *N.H.*, LI (Summer, 1970), Drake W. Will, "Lewis and Clark: Westering Physicians," *M.* XXI (October, 1971), and particularly E. G. Chuinard, *Only One Man Died: The Medical Aspects of the Lewis and Clark Expedition* (Glendale, 1979), the latter a competent study written by a medical doctor. A geographer, John L. Allen, "Lewis & Clark on the Upper Missouri: Decision at the Marias," *M.*, XXI (July, 1971), reveals how the explorers were handicapped by their lack of geographical knowledge, and the problem they faced in deciding whether to follow the Marias or Missouri where the two rivers meet. Donald Jackson, "The Public Image of Lewis and Clark," *P.N.Q.*, LVII (January, 1966), speculates on the reasons for the continuing interest in the explorers, while Rochonne Abrams, "A Song of the Promise of the Land: The Style of the Lewis and Clark Journals," *M.H.S.B.*, XXXII (April, 1976), finds that the prose in the journals was typically American in its pragmatic views. A history of the various editions of those journals is in Paul R. Cutright, *A History of the Lewis and Clark Journals* (Norman, 1976). The forty-one sites associated with the expedition are located, and the expedition itself well described in a National Park Service publication: Roy E. Appleman, *Lewis and Clark: Historic Places Associated with The Transcontinental Exploration (1804–06)* (Washington, 1975).

The several expeditions that continued the exploration of the Far West after Lewis and Clark have been described in numerous books and articles. Dan L. Flores, "Rendezvous at Spanish Bluff: Jefferson's Red River Exploration," *R.R.V.H.R.*, IV (Spring, 1979), deals with an expedition under Thomas Freeman and Peter Custic along the Red River valley that was turned back by the Spaniards in 1806. The best account of Pike's explorations is in W. Eugene Hollon, *The Lost Pathfinder: Zebulon Montgomery Pike* (Norman, 1949), while documents are in Donald Jackson, ed., *Journals of Zebulon Montgomery Pike: With Letters and Related Documents* (Norman, 1966). Donald Jackson, "Zebulon Pike and Nebraska," *N.H.*, XLVII (December, 1966), describes an expedition led by Pike into Nebraska to make peace with the Pawnee in 1806–1807. Richard G. Wood, *Stephen Harriman Long, 1784–1864: Army Engineer, Explorer, Inventor* (Glendale, 1966), is based largely on printed documents but is the only biography. Long's expeditions of 1819 and 1820 are described in Rober L. Nichols, "Stephen Long and Scientific Exploration on the Plains," *N.H.*, LII (Spring, 1971), which stresses his scientific contributions. Useful narratives of the Long expeditions are in Lucile M. Kane, et. al., eds., *The Northern Expeditions of Stephen H. Long: The Journals of 1817 and 1823 and Related Documents* (Minneapolis, 1978), and Harlin M. Fuller and LeRoy R. Hafen, eds., *The Journal of Captain John R. Bell, Official Journalist for the Stephen H. Long Expedition to the Rocky Mountains, 1820* (Glendale, 1957), while the expedition's route is traced in John M. Tucker, "Major Long's Route from the Arkansas to the Canadian River, 1820," *N.M.H.R.*, XXXVIII (July, 1963). A sound biography of a later explorer is W. Eugene Hollon, *Beyond the Cross Timbers: The Travels of Randolph B. Marcy, 1812–1887* (Norman, 1955), while his expedition into the upper Red River country in 1852 is described in Michael Tate, "Randolph B. Marcy, First Explorer of the Wichitas," *G.P.J.*, XV (Spring, 1976). Martha C. Bray, ed., *The Journals of Joseph N. Nicollet: A Scientist on the Mississippi Headwaters* (St. Paul, 1970), and Edmund C. and Martha C. Bray, eds., *Joseph N. Nicollet on the Plains and Prairies: The Expeditions of 1838–39 with Journals, Letters and Notes on the the Dakota Indians* (St. Paul, 1976), deals expertly with that explorer. Roger L. Nichols, *The Missouri Expedition, 1818–1820* (Norman, 1969), deals with an expedition under John Gale, which was sent west in 1818 to establish posts but never went beyond Council Bluffs.

General Works on the Fur Trade. Paul C. Phillips, *The Fur Trade,* 2 v. (Norman, 1961), is essential, but has not completely displaced the older work by Hiram M. Chittenden, *The American Fur Trade of the Far West,* 3 v. (rev. edn., New York, 1935). A significant work by a geographer, David J. Wishart, *The Fur Trade of the American West, 1807–1840: A Geographical Synthesis* (Lincoln, 1979) surveys the history of the trade in terms of a geographical framework, arguing that overtrapping led to a decline in the trade and created an ecological desert. That the traders themselves have been overly glamorized, and that they made an important contribution to the mercantile frontier, is the theme of a stimulating essay by Howard R. Lamar, *The Trader on the American Frontier: Myth's Victim* (College Station, 1977). Everett Dick, *Vanguards of the Frontier* (New York, 1941), and Bernard DeVoto, *Across the Wide Missouri* (Boston, 1947), are semipopular accounts. A brief general view of the significance of the trade is Doyce B. Nunis, Jr., "The Fur Men: Key to Westward Expansion, 1822–1830," *H.,* XXII (February, 1961). A revisionist article of major importance, James L. Clayton, "The Growth and Economic Significance of the Fur Trade, 1790–1890," *M.H.,* XL (Winter, 1966), proves that profits steadily increased during most of the trade, despite the near-extermination of the beaver. Wilcomb E. Washburn, "Symbol, Utility, and Aesthetics in the Indian Fur Trade," *M.H.,* XL (Winter, 1966), shows that successful traders had to know Indian customs thoroughly. Dale L. Morgan, "The Fur Trade and its Historians," *M.H.* (Winter, 1966) deals with writings on the subject and the areas needing exploration.

The Fur Trade of the Northern Rockies. Two excellent works of impeccable scholarship survey this subject: John E. Sunder, *The Fur Trade on the Upper Missouri, 1840–1865* (Norman, 1965), which deals with the last years of the trade, and Richard E. Oglesby, *Manuel Lisa and the Opening of the Missouri Fur Trade* (Norman, 1963), which narrates the beginning of the trade. An able biography of Lisa's most famous trader is Burton Harris, *John Colter: His Years in the Rockies* (New York, 1952). Two of Lisa's competitors are treated in articles by William E. Foley and Charles D. Rice, "Compounding the Ricks: International Politics, Wartime Dislocations and Auguste Chouteau's Fur Trading Operations," *M.H.S.B.,* XXXIV (April, 1978), and "Pierre Chouteau; Entrepreneur as Indian Agent," *M.H.R.,* LXXII (July, 1978). Rhoda R. Gilman, "The Fur Trade in the Up-

per Mississippi Valley, 1630–1850," *W.M.H.,* LVIII (Autumn, 1974), briefly surveys that topic. Trading methods on this frontier are competently described in Ray H. Mattison, "The Upper Missouri Fur Trade: Its Method of Operation," *N.H.,* XLII (March, 1961). Government attempts to control the trade by limiting the use of liquor are described in David C. Rowe, "Government Relations with the Fur Trappers of the Upper Missouri, 1820–1840," *N.D.H.,* XXV (Spring, 1968). Competent on the subject of its title is Rhoda R. Gilman, "Last Days of the Upper Missouri Fur Trade," *M.H.,* XLII (Winter, 1970). That posts there carried on important farming projects to increase their self-sufficiency is demonstrated in David Washart, "Agriculture at the Trading Posts on the Upper Missouri Prior to 1843," *A.H.,* XLVII (January, 1973).

A popular but sound history of the American Fur Company is David Lavender, *The Fist in the Wilderness* (New York, 1964). The biography by Kenneth W. Porter, *John Jacob Astor, Business Man,* 2 v. (Cambridge, 1931), devotes several chapters to its activities. The company's conflict with Canada's North West Company on the Pacific Coast, immortalized in Washington Irving's *Astoria* (New York, 1846 and later edns.), is described in these works. The North West Company's early trade with the Far West through the use of Russian contacts is described in Barry M. Gough, "The North West Company's 'Adventure to China'," *O.H.Q.,* LXXVI (December, 1975), while the adventures of two rival agents bound for Astoria are told in Barry M. Gough, "The 1813 Expedition to Astoria," *Beaver,* XX (Autumn, 1973), which deals with an English voyage, and Gabrial Franchère, *Adventure at Astoria, 1810–1814* (Norman, 1967), the journal of a trader who went west on the *Tonquin.* Lisa's dramatic efforts to overtake the Overland Astorians is described by a member of the party in John C. Luttig, *Journal of a Fur-trading Expedition on the Upper Missouri, 1812–1813* (rev. edn., New York, 1964). The narratives of the Returning Astorians, proving that they discovered South Pass, are in Philip A. Rollins, ed., *The Discovery of the Oregon Trail* (New York, 1935). David Lavender, "Some American Characteristics of the American Fur Company," *M.H.,* XL (Winter, 1966), ascribes Astor's failure to his attempt to imitate trading techniques of the North West Company rather than recognizing the American distaste for monopoly.

A searching interpretation of the Hudson's Bay Company's expansion into the northern Rockies and California is in John S.

Galbraith, *The Hudson's Bay Company as an Imperial Factor, 1821–1869* (Berkeley, 1957). An equally essential work is the monumental history of the company by E. E. Rich, *The History of the Hudson's Bay Company, 1670–1870*, 2 v. (London, 1958–62). The best of many biographies of its principal agent, although still not satisfactory, remains Frederick V. Hollman, *Dr. John McLoughlin, The Father of Oregon* (Cleveland, 1907), but this should be supplemented with William R. Sampson, ed., *John McLoughlin's Business Correspondence, 1847–48* (Seattle, 1973), which reveals the extent of the company's economic activities. Another agent who served as trader and guide between 1841 and 1856 is described in D. Geneva Lent, *West of the Mountains: James Sinclair and the Hudson's Bay Company* (Seattle, 1963). The introduction by Richard Glover to *David Thompson's Narrative, 1784–1812* (Toronto, 1962) provides a history of the trade in the early period. Modern interpretations of the merger with the North West Company include W. L. Morton, "The Northwest Company: Peddlars Extraordinary," *M.H.*, XL (Winter, 1966), which ascribes the success of the company to its combining familiar British business tactics with an intimate knowlege of Indian customs, and K. G. Davis, "From Competition to Union," *M.H.*, XL (Winter, 1966), an account of the events leading to union. The most complete story of the company's expansion is in the introduction to Frederick Merk ed., *Fur Trade and Empire, George Simpson's Journal* (2nd edn., Cambridge, 1968). The efforts of the company to expand into the northern Rockies are described in Frederick Merk, "Snake Country Expedition, 1824–25: An Episode of Fur Trade and Empire," *M.V.H.R.*, XXI (June, 1934). The records of the principal expeditions are in E. E. Rich, ed., *Peter Skene Ogden's Snake Country Journals, 1824–25 and 1825–1826* (London, 1950), K. G. Davies, ed., *Peter Skene Ogden's Snake Country Journal, 1826–27* (London, 1961), and Glyndwr Williams, ed., *Peter Skene Ogden's Snake Country Journals, 1827–28 and 1828–29* (London, 1971). Francis D. Haines, ed., *The Snake Country Expedition of 1830–1831: John Work's Field Journal* (Norman, 1971) is the narrative of a brigade that traveled through Idaho, Utah, and Nevada that winter, while Doyce B. Nunis, Jr., ed., *The Hudson's Bay Company's First Fur Brigade to the Sacramento Valley: Alexander McLeod's 1829 Hunt* (Los Angeles, 1968), is a well-edited journal of an expedition into California. David E. Miller, "Peter Skene Ogden's Trek into Utah, 1828–29," *P.N.Q.*, LI (January, 1960), is ex-

cellent on the Ogden expedition of 1828–29, and the John Work expedition of 1831. Gloria G. Cline, *Peter Skene Ogden and the Hudson's Bay Company* (Norman, 1975), is an excellent biography of one of the company's principal agents, while Richard Dillon, *Siskiyou Trail: The Hudson's Bay Company Route to California* (New York, 1975), is a popular account of the extension of its trade southward.

The success of the Hudson's Bay Company's relationship with the Indians is explained in the fine study by Arthur J. Ray, *Indians in the Fur Trade: Their Role as Trappers, Hunters and Middlemen in the Lands Southwest of Hudson Bay, 1660–1870* (Toronto, 1974), which shows how the Assiniboine, Cree and western Ojibwa developed their trapping and trading skills, and how their own tribal culture was altered as a result. Other comparable investigations are reported in Peter W. Dunwiddie, "The Nature of the Relationship between the Blackfeet Indians and the Men of the Fur Trade," *A.of.W.*, XLVI (Spring, 1974), and John A. Alwin, "Pelts, Provisions and Perceptions: The Hudson's Bay Company Mandan Indian Trade, 1795–1812," *M.*, XXIX (July, 1979).

The Fur Trade in the Central Rockies. An excellent history of this trade is in Dale L. Morgan, *Jedediah Smith and the Opening of the West* (Indianapolis, 1953), which is in effect a history of the trade in that region. This may be supplemented with Richard M. Clokey, *William H. Ashley: Enterprise and Politics in the Trans-Mississippi West* (Norman, 1979), the first full-scale biography of this important figure. John C. Ewers, "The Indian Trade of the Upper Missouri before Lewis and Clark: An Interpretation," *M.H.S.B.*, X (July, 1954), shows that the Shoshoni had developed the rendezous system of trading long before Ashley, and that he probably imitated them when he worked out his techniques. A well-researched history of the system that Ashley introduced, locating each rendezvous, is Fred R. Gowans, *Rocky Mountain Rendezvous: A History of the Fur Trade Rendezvous, 1825–1840* (Provo, 1976). W. J. Rorabaugh, *The Alcoholic Republic* (New York, 1980), includes some colorful accounts of drinking on these occasions. Important documents are in Dale Morgan, ed., *The West of William H. Ashley* (Denver, 1964), Harrison C. Dale, ed., *The Ashley-Smith Explorations and the Discovery of a Central Route to the pacific, 1822–1829* (rev. edn., Glendale, 1941), and Maurice S. Sullivan, ed., *The Travels of Jedediah Smith* (Santa Ana, 1934). Donald M. Frost, "Notes on General Ashley, the Overland Trail, and South Pass," *A.A.S., Proceedings,* CIV (1944), contain important observations and documents. A popular history of one expedition launched by Ashely is Alson J. Smith, *Men Against the Mountains: Jedediah Smith and the South West Expedition of 1826–1829* (New York, 1965); another is described in Charles L. Camp, "Jedediah Smith's First Far Western Expedition," *We.H.Q.,* IV (April, 1973) which traces the explorer's exact route on his 1823 expedition to the Wind River country.

Among the more authentic impressionistic sketches of the Mountain Men is William Brandon, "The Wild Freedom of the Mountain Men," *Am.H.,* VI (August, 1955). Lewis O. Saum, *The Fur Trader and the Indian* (Seattle, 1965), appraises the attitude of fur trappers toward Indians, and describes their treatment of the red men. An extremely valuable article by William H. Goetzmann, "The Mountain Man as Jacksonian Man," *A.Q.,* XV (Fall, 1963), analyzes data available on 446 Mountain Men to show that the majority clung to the hope of returning to civilization, and that most of them did so. These findings are disputed in Harvey L. Carter and Marcia C. Spencer, "Stereotypes of the Mountain Men," *We.H.Q.,* VI (January, 1975), which holds that most were adventure-seekers rather than questers after profits, and by William R. Swagerty, "Marriage and Settlement Patterns of Rocky Mountain Trappers and Traders," *We.H.Q.,* XI (April, 1980), a statistical profile of 322 trappers showing that these were neither expectant capitalists nor social outcasts, but sought to rise to entrepreneurial positions with little success. Harry H. Anderson, "Fur Traders as Fathers: The Origins of the Mixed-Blooded Community among the Rosebud Sioux," *S.D.H.,* III (Summer, 1973), shows that the offspring of trappers provided a leadership elite for this tribe. A major contribution to fur-trade scholarship is the multivolume encyclopedia of the Mountain Men edited by LeRoy R. Hafen, *The Mountain Men and the Fur Trade of the Far West,* 10 v. (Glendale, 1965–1972). Carl P. Russell, *Firearms, Traps & Tools of the Mountain Men* (New York, 1967), deals expertly with their weapons and artifacts, while Walter O'Meara, *Daughters of the Country: The Women of the Fur Traders and Mountain Men* (New York, 1968), describes their Indian companions and shows how much they contributed to the success of the trade.

Of the dozens of biographies of these colorful characters, the most reliable are: Alpheus H. Favour, *Old Bill Williams, Mountain Man* (Chapel Hill, 1936), Harvey L. Carter,

"Dear Old Kit: The Historical Christopher Carson (Norman, 1968), an honest and skilfull attempt to separate fact from fiction, LeRoy R. Hafen and W. J. Ghent, *Broken Hand, the Life Story of Thomas Fitzpatrick* (Lincoln edn., 1980), Charles Kelly and M. L. Howe, *Miles Goodyear, First Citizen of Utah* (Salt Lake City, 1937), John E. Sunder, *Bill Sublette: Mountain Man* (Norman, 1959), Charles Kelly and Dale L. Morgan, *Old Greenwood, The Story of Caleb Greenwood: Trapper, Pathfinder, and Early Pioneer* (Georgetown, 1965), Sardis W. Templeton, *The Lame Captain: The Life and Adventures of Pegleg Smith* (Los Angeles, 1965), Forbes Parkhill, *The Blazed Trail of Antoine Leroux* (Los Angeles, 1966), Iris H. Wilson, *William Wolfskill, 1798–1866: Frontier Trapper to California Ranchero* (Glendale, 1965), Raymond W. Thorp and Robert Bunker, *Crow Killer,* Bloomington, 1961), John M. Myers, *Pirate, Pawnee and Mountain Man: The Saga of Hugh Glass* (Boston, 1963), George P. Hammond, ed., *The Adventures of Alexander Barclay, Mountain Man: A Narrative of His Career, 1810 to 1855: His Memorandum Diary, 1845–1850* (Denver, 1976), which is largely a fine biography by the editor, Howard L. Conrad, *Uncle Dick Wootton: The Pioneer Frontiersman of the Rocky Mountain Region* (Lincoln, 1980), M. Morgan Estergreen, *Kit Carson: A Portrait in Courage* (Norman, 1962), Richard E. Oglesby, "Pierre Menard, Reluctant Mountain Man," *M.H.S.B.,* XXIV (October, 1967), LeRoy R. Hafen, "Etienne Provost, Mountain Man and Utah Pioneer," *U.H.Q.,* XXXVI (Spring, 1968), Elinor Wilson, *Jim Beckwourth: Black Mountain Man and War Chief of the Crows* (Norman, 1972), and Kenneth L. Holmes, *Ewing Young: Master Trapper* (Portland, 1967).

Among works dealing with some of the business leaders in the fur trade, light on the confusing Sublette family is thrown by three articles by Doyce B. Nunis, Jr., "The Sublettes: A Study of a Refugee Family in the Eighteenth Century," *V.M.H.B.,* LXIX (January, 1961), "Milton Sublette. Thunderbolt of the Rockies," *M.,* XIII (July, 1963), and "The Enigma of the Sublette Overland Party, 1845," *P.H.R.,* XXVIII (November, 1959). The same author has written an excellent brief biography of one of the brothers: *Andrew Sublette, Rocky Mountain Prince, 1808–1853* (Los Angeles, 1960). Another brief but capable biography of a Sublette brother is John E. Sunder, "Solomon Perry Sublette: Mountain Man of the Forties," *N.M.H.R.,* XXXVI (January, 1961). Louis Pfaller, "Charles Larpentuer," *N.D.H.,* XXXII (January, 1965), deals with a less well-known trader, John E. Sunder,

Joshua Pilcher: Fur Trader and Indian Agent (Norman, 1968), is a sound biography of a small St. Louis businessman who entered the trade where he enjoyed little success.

Among the more accurate and readable diaries or journals kept by the traders are: Dale L. Morgan and Eleanor T. Harris, eds., *The Rocky Mountain Journals of William Marshall Anderson: The West in 1834* (San Marino, 1967), David Meriwether, *My Life in the Mountains and On the Plains* (Norman, 1965), Osburne Russell, *Journal of a Trapper, or Nine Years in the Rocky Mountains* (Boise, 1921), Warren A. Ferris, *Life in the Rocky Mountains* (Salt Lake City, 1940), Zenas Leonard, *Narrative of the Adventures of Zenas Leonard* (rev. edn., Norman, 1959), Charles L. Camp, ed., *James Clyman, American Frontiersman* (rev. edn., Portland, 1960), and LeRoy R. Hafen and Ann W. Hafen eds., *Rufus B. Sage, His Letters and Papers, 1836–1847* (Glendale, 1956). That the literary qualities of many journals have been lost in rewriting by editors is shown in Don D. Walker, "The Mountain Man Journal: Its Significance in a Literary History of the Fur Trade," *We.H.Q.*, V (July, 1974).

Accounts of trading posts and forts that played their role in the western trade include: LeRoy R. Hafen and Francis M. Young, *Fort Laramie and the Pageant of the West, 1834–1890* (Glendale, 1938), Richard G. Beidleman, "Nathaniel Wyeth's Fort Hall," *O.H.Q.*, LVIII (September, 1957), Frank C. Robertson, *Fort Hall: Gateway to the Oregon Country* (New York, 1963), Ray H. Mattison, "Fort Union: Its Role in the Upper Missouri Trade," *N.D.H.*, XXVIII (January–April, 1962), David Lavender, *Bent's Fort* (New York, 1954), and Fred R. Gowans and Eugene E. Campbell, *Fort Bridger: Island in the Wilderness* (Provo, 1975). A detailed account of the excavation of one fort, showing that the trappers lived very well with French wines and even a clock, is Jackson W. Moore, Jr., *Bent's Old Fort: An Archeological Study* (Boulder, 1975).

The Santa Fe Trade. An excellent bibliography of all books and articles dealing with the trade is Jack D. Rittenhouse, *The Santa Fe Trail: A Historical Bilbiography* (Albuquerque, 1971). Hobart E. Stocking, *The Road to Santa Fe* (New York, 1971), describes the adventures of a modern geologist as he retraced the route and provides accurate maps of the trail. Among the many popular histories of the trade, the best are R. L. Duffus, *The Santa Fe Trail* (New York, 1930), Stanley Vestal, *The Old Santa Fe Trail* (Boston, 1939), and Seymour V. Connor and Jimmy M. Skaggs,

Broadcloth and Britches: The Santa Fe Trade (College Station, 1977). Early attempts to open the trade are described in Alfred B. Thomas, "The First Santa Fe Expedition, 1792–1793," *C.O.* IX (June, 1931), Isaac J. Cox, "Opening the Santa Fe Trail," *M.H.R.*, XXV (October, 1930), and George S. Ulibarri, "The Chouteau-Demun Expedition to New Mexico, 1815–17," *N.M.H.R.*, XXXVI (October, 1961). Narratives of the three expeditions of 1821 are. Walter B. Douglas, ed., *Three Years Among the Indians and Mexicans by Thomas James* (St. Louis, 1916), Elliott Coues, ed., *The Journal of Jacob Fowler* (New York, 1898; new edn. with notes by Raymond W. and Mary L. Settle, Lincoln, 1970), and Archer B. Hulbert, ed., *Southwest on the Torquoise Trail; the First Diaries on the Road to Santa Fe* (Denver, 1933). Harry R. Stevens, "A Company of Hands and Traders: Origins of the Glenn-Fowler Expedition of 1821–1822," *N.M.H.R.*, XLVI (July, 1971), expertly describes the beginnings of the party. A later expedition is discussed in Kenneth L. Holmes, "The Benjamin Cooper Expeditions to Santa Fe in 1822 and 1823," *N.M.H.R.*, XXXVIII (April, 1963). The classic description of the trade by a trader is Josiah Gregg, "Commerce of the Prairies," in Reuben G. Thwaites, ed., *Early Western Travels*, 32 v. (Cleveland, 1904–06). Doubts on Gregg's authorship are cast by John T. Lee, "The Authorship of Gregg's 'Commerce of the Prairies,'" *M.V.H.R.*, XVI (March, 1930).

Other useful accounts of travel over the trail include: F. F. Stephens, ed., "Major Alphonse Wetmore's Diary of a Journey to Santa Fe in 1828," *M.H.R.*, VIII (July, 1914), James J. Webb, *Adventures in the Santa Fé Trade, 1844–1847* (Glendale, 1931), and John E. Sunder, ed., *Matt Field on the Santa Fe Trail* (Norman, 1960). Donald Chaput, *François X. Aubry: Trader, Trailmaker, And Voyageur in the Southwest, 1846–1854* (Glendale, 1975), and William C. McGaw, *Savage Scene: The Life and Times of James Kirker, Frontier King* (New York, 1972), are biographies of traders during the later period of the trail, while Franz Huning, *Trader on the Santa Fe Trail: Memoirs of Franz Huning* (Albuquerque, 1973), are the reminiscences of a trader who operated after the American conquest.

The extension of the trade southward into Mexico is studied in Max L. Moorehead, *New Mexico's Royal Road: Trade and Travel on the Chihuahua Trail* (Norman, 1958), while the federal government's efforts to protect the traders are described in Kate L. Gregg, ed., *The Road to Santa Fe* (Albuquerque, 1952), which deals with surveys and treaty-making,

Thomas Hart Benton's role in providing surveys and protection is described in Stephen Sayles, "Thomas Hart Benton and the Santa Fe Trail," *M.H.R.*, LXIX (October, 1974), and the surveys are described accurately in T. Lindsay Baker, "The Survey of the Santa Fe Trail, 1825–1827," *G.P.J.*, XIV (Spring, 1975). The importance of military protection is made clear in Otis E. Young, *The First Military Escort on the Santa Fe Trail* (Glendale, 1952), Robert M. Utley, "Fort Union and the Santa Fe Trail," *N.M.H.R.*, XXXVI (January, 1961), and Leo E. Olive, "Fort Atkinson on the Santa Fe Trail, 1850–1854," *K.H.Q.* XL (Summer, 1974). Leo E. Olivia, *Soldiers on the Santa Fe Trail* (Norman, 1967) is a straight forward account of efforts by troops to guard the trade. Robert A. Trennert, "Indian Policy on the Santa Fe Road: The Fitzpatrick Controversy of 1847–1848," *K.H.*, L (Winter, 1978), deals with protection for traders after American annexation, and the efforts of Thomas Fitzpatrick, Indian agent at Bent's Fort, to provide such protection. Business aspects of the trade are considered in Lewis E. Atherton, "Business Techniques in the Santa Fe Trade," *M.H.R*, XXXIV (April, 1940), while Janet Lecompte, "La Tules and the Americans," *A.and W.*, XX (Autumn, 1978), is a pleasant account of a woman, Dina Gertrudis Barceló, who operated Santa Fe's largest gambling establishment.

The Fur Trade in the Southwest. The classic description is Robert G. Cleland, *This Reckless Breed of Men: The Trappers and Fur Traders of the Southwest* (New York, 1950), but this should be supplemented by David J. Weber, *The Taos Trappers: The Fur Trade in the Far Southwest, 1540–1846* (Norman, 1971), an excellent scholarly account of the rise of the trade in the southern Rockies, its spread over the trails radiating north of Santa Fe, and its decline. The pioneering study of American penetration is Thomas M. Marshall, "St. Vrain's Expedition to the Gila in 1826," *The Pacific Ocean in History* (New York, 1917); of equal importance is Joseph J. Hill, "Ewing Young in the Fur Trade of the Far Southwest, 1822–1834," *O.H.Q.*, XXIV (March, 1923). The two most important narratives are Charles L. Camp, ed., *George C. Yount and His Chronicles of the West* (Denver, 1966), and James Ohio Pattie, The *Personal Narrative of James O. Pattie of Kentucky* (Cincinnati, 1831, and later edns.). The latter should be used only after reading the critical evaluation by Joseph J. Hill, "New Light on Pattie and the Southwest Fur Trade," *S.H.Q.*, XXVI (April, 1923); and the study of Pattie's evidence concerning the route he followed in A.

L. Kroeber, "The Route of James Ohio Pattie on the Colorado in 1826: A Reappraisal," *A. and W.*, VI (Summer, 1964). Janet Lecompte, "Brent, St. Vrain & Co. among the Comanche and Kiowa," *C.M.*, XLIX (Fall, 1972), deals with a fort established by the company on the south fork of the Canadian river in 1842. Jack D. Forbes, *Warriors of the Colorado: The Yumas of the Quechan Nation and Their Neighbors* (Norman, 1965), recounts the contacts between the traders and a principal Indian tribe. Two articles by Wayne Morris deal with the trade along the Arkansas River: "Traders and Factories on the Arkansas Frontier, 1805–1822," *A.H.Q.*, XXVIII (Spring, 1969), and "Auguste Pierre Chouteau, Merchant Prince of the Three Forks of the Arkansas," *C.O.*, XLVIII (Summer, 1970).

21 The Mississippi Valley Frontier, 1803–1840

Peopling the Lower Mississippi Valley. Carnie W. McGinty, *A History of Louisiana* (New York, 1949), and Edwin A. Davis, *Louisiana: The Pelican State* (Baton Rouge, 1959), provide good surveys of the settlement of that state. A study of the failure of the rectangular survey system to meet the needs of the region is Harry L. Coles, Jr., "Applicability of the Public Land System to Louisiana," *M.V.H.R.*, XLIII (June, 1956). That Jefferson named James Wilkinson the first territorial governor because he believed that his military experience was needed to keep order there is shown in William E. Foley, "James A. Wilkinson: Territorial Governor," *M.H.S.B.*, XXV (October, 1968), which also is an excellent history of his administration. The early economic history of the region is admirably described in John G. Clark, *New Orleans 1718–1812: An Economic History* (Baton Rouge, 1970).

Margaret Ross, *Arkansas Gazette: The Early Years, 1819–1866* (Little Rock, 1969), is both a significant contribution to the history of frontier journalism and a capable history of the territory and state during those years. An history of pioneer Arkansas is Lonnie J. White, *Politics on the Southwestern Frontier: Arkansas Territory, 1819–1836* (Memphis, 1964). The same author has explored the creation of the territory in "Dividing Missouri: The Creation of Arkansas Territory," *M.H.S.Bull.*, XVII (April, 1961). Migration into the territory is the theme of Robert B. Walz, "Migration into Arkansas, 1820–1880: Incentives and Means of Travel," *A.H.Q.*, XVII (Winter, 1958), and Henry K. Swint,

"Ho For Arkansas," *A.H.Q.,* XXIV (Autumn, 1965). Orville W. Taylor, *Negro Slavery in Arkansas* (Durham, 1958), has some information on the pioneer period, while Daniel F. Littlefield, "The Salt Industry in Arkansas Territory, 1819–1839," *A.H.Q.,* XXXII (Winter, 1973), explores one phase of early economic activity.

The most thorough modern history of Missouri is in the three volumes by William E. Foley, Perry McCandless, and William E. Parish, *A History of Missouri* (Columbia, 1972–73), carrying the story from 1673 to 1873. Briefer but useful are David D. March, *A History of Missouri* (West Palm Beach, 1967), Paul C. Nagel, *Missouri: A Bicentennial History* (New York, 1977), and Edwin C. McReynolds, *Missouri: A History of the Crossroads State* (Norman, 1962). The story of the settlement of the state is told in James F. Ellis, *The Influence of Environment on the Settlement of Missouri* (St. Louis, 1929), Hattie M. Anderson, "Missouri, 1804–1828: Peopling a Frontier State," *M.H.R.,* XXXI (January, 1937), and Russell L. Gerlach, "Population Origins in Rural Missouri," *M.H.R.,* LXXI (October, 1976), while Randall C. Manring, "Population and Agriculture in Nodaway County, Missouri, 1850 to 1860," *M.H.R.,* LXXII (July, 1978), is a case study of the manner in which the economy diversified as the population matured. Lewis E. Atherton, "Missouri's Society and Economy in 1821," *M.H.R.,* LXV (July, 1971), capably surveys the territorial social order, while preparations for statehood are considered in Jerome O. Steffen, "William Clark: A New Perspective" of Missouri Territorial Politics, 1813–1820," *M.H.R.,* LXVII (January, 1973), and William E. Foley, "The American Territorial System: Missouri's Experience," *M.H.R.,* LXV (July, 1971). The difficulties encountered by settlers who moved in at this time are stressed in Roger L. Nichols, "Martin Cantonment and American Expansion in the Missouri Valley," *M.H.R.,* LXIV (October, 1969). Excellent statistical studies of the occupation of the Boonslick region are Walter A. Schroeder, "Spread of Settlement in Howard County, Missouri, 1810–1859," *M.H.R.,* LXIII (October, 1968), and Stuart F. Voss, "Town Growth in Central Missouri, 1815–1860: An Urban Chaparral,"*M.H.R.,* LXIV (October, 1969 to January, 1970). Early urbanization there is also explored in J. Christopher Schnell and Patrick E. McLear, "Why the Cities Grew: A Historiographic Essay on Western Urban Growth, 1850–1880," *M.H.S.B.,* XXVII (April, 1972). Arvarh Strickland, "Aspects of Slavery in Missouri, 1821," *M.H.R.,* .LXV

(July, 1971), surveys the situation at the time of statehood. Capable studies of mining activity there are A. M. Gibson, "Lead Mining in Southwest Missouri to 1865," *M.H.R.,* LIII (April, 1959), James D. Norris, *Frontier Iron: The Maramex Iron Works, 1826–1876* (Madison, 1964), and particularly Arrell M. Gibson, *Wilderness Bonanza: The Tri-State District of Missouri, Kansas, and Oklahoma* (Norman, 1972), a scholarly work that traces the history of lead mining in the region from its beginnings to modern times. Transportation as a factor in one lead-mining area is discussed in Milan J. Kedro, "The Three Notch Road Frontier: A Century of Social and Economic Change in the St. Genevieve District," *M.H.S.B.,* XXIX (April, 1973). That grist mills played a major role in the frontier era in Missouri is proven in Priscilla A. Evans, "Merchant Gristmills and Communities, 1820–1880: An Economic Relationship," *M.H.R.,* LXVIII (April, 1974).

Two of the conflicts that divided pioneer St. Louis are described in Ronald L. F. Davis, "Community and Conflict in Pioneer St. Louis, Missouri," *We.H.Q.,* X (July, 1979), dealing with the antagonisms between representatives of the old French and new American cultures as personified in William C. Lane who arrived from Pennsylvania in 1818, and Maximilian Reichard, "Black and White on the Urban Frontier: The St. Louis Community in Transition, 1800-1830," *M.H.S.B.,* XXXIII (October, 1976), a study of the increasingly repressive slave codes within the city. An important book dealing with the planning of St. Louis and other cities in the trans-Mississippi West is John W. Reps, *Cities of the Urban West: A History of Frontier Urban Planning* (Princeton, 1979).

Establishing a Permanent Indian Frontier. An illuminating article, Ralph C. Morris, "The Notion of a Great American Desert East of the Rockies," *M.V.H.R.,* XIII (September, 1926), traces the growth of the desert concept, but Francis P. Prucha, "Indian Removal and the Great American Desert," *I.M.H.,* LIX (December, 1963), demonstrates that this concept had nothing to do with shaping Indian policy; the boundaries of the desert were well known and the government had no intention of sending displaced Indians there. That much of the West including the most fertile parts were seen as desert by easterners at that time is amusingly demonstrated in Roger L. Welsch, "The Myth of the Great American Desert," *N.H.,* LII (Fall, 1971), while J. Christopher Schnell, "William Gilpin and the Destruction of the Desert Myth," *C.M.,* XLVI (Spring, 1969), explores the role of Gilpin and other land speculators who wished to induce settlement by breaking down the legend.

The books cited in Chapter XVI on Indian removal apply also to the settlement of the tribes in the West. Grant Foreman, *The Last Trek of the Indians* (Chicago, 1946), deals with the movement of Indians from the Old Northwest into Kansas and Nebraska. An important specialzed study is Donald J. Berthrong, "John Beach and the Removal of the Sauk and Fox from Iowa," *I.J.H.P.*, LIV (October, 1956). Bruce E. Mahan, *Old Fort Crawford and the Frontier* (Iowa City, 1926), also touches on the removal of the northern tribes, as do William E. Lass, "The Removal from Minnesota of the Sioux and Winnebago Indians," *M.H.*, XXXVIII (December, 1963), Roy W. Meyer, "The Iowa Indians, 1836–1885," *K.H.Q.*, XXVIII (Autumn, 1962), and Gary C. Anderson, "The Removal of the Wdewakanton Dakota in 1837: A Case for Jacksonian Paternalism," *S.D.H.*, X (Fall, 1980), which holds that removal benefited the tribe. A well-researched study of the removal of one Minnesota tribe is in Edmund J. Danzinger, Jr., "They Would Not be Moved: The Chippewa Treaty of 1854," *M.H.*, XLIII (Spring, 1973), while Robert A. Trennert, "A Trader's Role in the Potawatomie Removal from Indiana: The Case of George W. Ewing," *O.N.*, IV (March, 1978) explains how one trader was encouraged by the government to contract such heavy debts for the tribesmen that they were forced to move.

The standard works on the southeastern tribes that were moved to the Indian Territory are by Grant Foreman: *Indians and Pioneers* (Norman, 1936), traces the history of the Oklahoma country to 1830: *Indian Removal* (Norman, 1932), deals with the transfer of the Indians to the region; and *Advancing the Frontier* (Norman, 1933), continues their story to 1860. An excellent history of the western terminal to which Indians were moved is Brad Agnew, *Fort Gibson: Terminal on the Trail of Tears* (Norman, 1980). Other military posts in the region and their role in keeping peace on the frontier are considered in William B. Morrison, *Military Posts and Camps in Oklahoma* (Oklahoma City, 1936), and in specialized studies of individual posts. An excellent history of one fort that was established in 1817 to keep order between the Osage and Cherokee and played a major role in Indian affairs for a generation is Edwin C. Bearss and Arrell M. Gibson, *Fort Smith: Little Gibraltar on the Arkansas* (Norman, 1969). Details on the construction of this fort are in James N. Maskett, "The Final Chapter in the Story of the First Fort Smith," *A.H.Q.*, XXV (Spring, 1966). Problems rising from the Treaty of Doak's

Stand and the role of Ft. Smith in solving them are explored in Edwin C. Bearss, "Fort Smith as the Agency for the Western Choctaws," *A.H.Q.*, XXVII (Spring, 1968). Dorothy J. Cadwell, "The Big Neck Affair: Tragedy and Farce on the Missouri Frontier," *M.H.R.*, LXIV (July, 1970), deals with an episode that arose in 1828 when displaced Iowa Indians returned to Missouri and skirmished with the settlers.

Other forts along the borderland have also been described by historians. Richard E. Mueller, "Jefferson Barracks: The Early Years," *M.H.R.*, LXVII (October, 1972), is a study of operations out of a post built just south of St. Louis in 1826, while George Walton, *Sentinel of the Plains: Fort Leavenworth and the American West* (Englewood Cliffs, 1973) is a modest study of that Kansas outpost. Eloise F. Robbins, "The Original Military Post Road between Fort Leavenwoth and Fort Scott," *K.H.*, I (Summer, 1979), describes a section of the road that was designed to connect all western posts. Another principal post built in 1838 near modern Watts, Oklahoma, is expertly studied in two articles by Daniel F. Littlefield, Jr., and Lonnie E. Underhill, "Fort Wayne and the Arkansas Frontier, 1838–1840," *A.H.Q.*, XXXV (Winter, 1976), and "Fort Wayne and Border Violence, 1840–1847," *A.H.Q.*, XXXVI (Spring, 1977). That these forts did little to keep the peace is explained partly by the hostile attitude of their officers toward Indians as demonstrated in William B. Skelton, "Army Officers' Attitudes Toward Indians, 1830–1860," *P.N.Q.*, LXVII (July, 1976).

The more sympathetic attitude of missionaries and government agents toward the Indians is demonstrated in such studies as Courtney A. Vaughn, "Job's Legacy: Cyrus Byington, Missionary to the Choctaws in Indian Territory," *R.R.V.H.R.*, III (Fall, 1978), Richard H. Faust, "William Medill: Commissioner of Indian Affairs, 1845–1849," *O.N.*, I (June, 1975), showing how Medill sought to build schools and suppress the liquor trade in Indian Territory, and William G. ,McLaughlin, "Indian Slaveholders and Presbyterian Missionaries, 1837–1861," *C.H.*, XLII (December, 1973), Leslie Hewes, *Occupying the Cherokee Country of Oklahoma* (Lincoln, 1978) is a brief history of the land allotment system attempted by the Cherokee in Indian Territory.

The reaction of the Plains Indians to the intrusion of eastern tribes is considered in Rupert N. Richardson, *The Comanche Barrier to South Plains Settlement* (Glendale, 1933), and in the histories of tribes cited in Chapter

XVI. Bert Anson, "Variations of the Indian Conflict: The Effects of the Emigrant Indian Removal Policy, 1830–1854," *M.H.R.*, LIX (October, 1964), demonstrates that the intruded Indians spread disease and vice among the Plains Indians just as did contact with the whites. An excellent account of an expedition into the southern Plains led by Colonel Henry Dodge to sign peace treaties between tribes of that area is Brad Agnew, "The Dodge-Leavenworth Expedition of 1834," *C. of O.*, LIII (Fall, 1975).

The Settlement of Iowa. An excellent history of the state is Leland L. Sage, *A History of Iowa* (Ames, 1974); Joseph F. Wall, *Iowa: A Bicentennial History* (New York, 1978) is brief but sound. Essays dealing with the early culture of the state are in John J. Murray, ed., *The Heritage of the Middle West* (Norman, 1958). Works dealing specifically with settlement are: Cardinal Goodwin, "The American Occupation of Iowa, 1833–1860," *I.J.H.P.*, XVII (January, 1910), and J. A. Swisher, "The First Land Sales," *P.*, XIX (November, 1938). Allan G. Bogue, *From Prairie to Corn Belt: Farming on the Illinois and Iowa Prairies in the Nineteenth Century* (Chicago, 1963), upsets many long-accepted interpretations. Equally revisionist is Donald L. Winters, *Farmers Without Farms: Agricultural Tenancy in Nineteenth-Century Iowa* (Westport, 1978), which shows that farmers used tenancy willingly to accumulate funds for purchase. Of value is a statistical analysis of Wapello County to show the origins of the Iowa population: Mildred Throne, "A population Study of an Iowa County in 1850," *I.J.H.*, LVII (October, 1959). An even more important study, Robert P. Swierenga, *Pioneers and Profits: Land Speculation on the Iowa Frontier* (Ames, 1968), analyzes land sales in thirty-four counties during the pioneer period to show that speculators both made handsome profits and played a valuable role in the occupation of the area. The same author discusses a later type of speculator in "The Tax Buyer as a Frontier Investor Type," *E.E.H.*, VII (Spring, 1970). In an additional study of sixteen Iowa counties, Swierenga shows that speculators played a valuable role in the settlement process, and that farmers borrowed their techniques to avoid high interest rates: *Acres for Cents: Delinquent Tax Auctions in Frontier Iowa* (Westport, 1976); some of the principal conclusions of this book are summarized in the author's "Acres for Cents: Delinquent Tax Auctions in Frontier Iowa," *A.H.*, XLVIII (April, 1974). Swierenga also demonstrates that large Iowa speculators enjoyed a higher rate of return on their investments than small operators in "The Equity Effects of Public Land Speculation in Iowa; Large versus Small Speculators," *J.E.H.*, XXXIV (December, 1974). Some of Swierenga's conclusions are questioned in Peter D. McClelland, "New Perspectives on the Disposal of Western Lands in Nineteenth Century America," *B.H.R.*, XLIII (Spring, 1969). A case study of one Iowa speculating concern is admirably presented in Robert P. Swierenga, "The 'Western Land Business': The Story of Easley & Willingham, Speculators," *B.H.R.*, XLI (Spring, 1967). A move of one family from Pennsylvania to Iowa is described in Bertha R. Leaman, "An Early Settler in Iowa: Westward Expansion in Microcosm," *A. of I.*, XLI (Summer, 1971). A case study of one group of urban speculators who ended in failure is William Silag, "Sioux City: An Iowa Boom Town," *A. of I.*, XLIV (Spring, 1979).

The influence of transportation routes on settlement is considered in W. Turrentine Jackson, "The Army Engineers as Road Builders in Territorial Iowa," *I.J.H.P.*, XLVII (January, 1949). Allan G. Bogue, "The Iowa Claim Clubs: Symbol and Substance," *M.V.H.R.*, XLV (September, 1958), shows that the clubs were more often used by than against speculators. The beginnings of government are the theme of Kenneth E. Colton, "Iowa's Struggle for a Territorial Government," *A. of I.*, XXI (April, 1938).

The Settlement of Minnesota. Theodore C. Blegen has written two excellent brief histories of the state: *Building Minnesota* (Boston, 1938), and *Minnesota: A History of the State* (Minneapolis, 1963). Brief but sound is William E. Lass, *Minnesota: A Bicentennial History* (New York, 1977). Indian relations are discussed in Willoughby M. Babcock, Jr., "Major Lawrence Taliaferro, Indian Agent," *M.V.H.R.*, XI (December, 1924), and Evan Evans, *Citadel in the Wilderness: The Story of Fort Snelling and the Old North-West Frontier* (New York, 1966). Life at another Minnesota fort, Ft. Ridgely, during the 1850s is described in Hubert G. Smith, "A Frontier Fort in Peacetime," *M.H.*, VL (Fall, 1976). The role of water power in early urban development is discussed in Lucile M. Kane, *The Waterfall That Build a City: The Falls of St. Anthony in Minneapolis* (St. Paul, 1966). That guidebooks played an important role in directing settlers to Minnesota is demonstrated in Carlton C. Qualey, "A New Eldorado, Guides to Minnesota, 1850's and 1860's," *M.H.*, XVII (Summer, 1971), while Lars Ljungmark, *For Sale—Minnesota: Organized Promotion of Scandinavian Immigration,*

1866–1873 (Chicago, 1971), describes efforts to attract one group of immigrants.

The advance of the farm frontier is described in Cardinal Goodwin, "The Movement of American Settlers into Wisconsin and Minnesota," *I.J.H.P.,* XVII (July, 1919). The early settlement of the Red River valley is considered in John P. Pritchett, *The Red River Valley, 1811–1849* (New Haven, 1942). Biographies of early settlers include: Solon J. Buck, *William Watts Folwell* (Minneapolis, 1933), George M. Stephenson, *John Lund of Minnesota* (Minnapolis, 1935), and Merlin Stonehouse, *John Wesley North and the Reform Frontier* (Minneapollis, 1965). Rodney C. Loehr, ed., *Minnesota Farm Diaries* (St. Paul, 1939) is an important collection, while valuable sketches are in Theodore C. Blegen, *The Land Lies Open* (Minneapolis, 1949).

Governmental beginnings are described in William Anderson and A. J. Lobb, *History of the Constitution of Minnesota* (Minneapolis, 1921), and Lucile M. Kane, "Governing a Frontier City: Old St. Anthony, 1855–72," *M.H., XXXV* (September, 1956). An aspect of state-federal relations is treated in F. Paul Prucha, S.J. "The Settler and the Army in Frontier Minnesota," *M.H., XXIX* (September, 1948).

22 The Annexation of Texas, 1820–1845

General Works. A recent history of Texas is Seymour V. Connor, *Texas: A History* (New York, 1971), a convenient summary incorporating modern scholarship. The same author is the editor of a multivolume history of the state; the two volumes pertinent to this period are David M. Vignes, *The Revolutionary Decades: The Saga of Texas, 1810–1836* (Austin, 1965), and Seymour V. Connor, *Adventure in Glory: The Saga of Texas, 1836–1849* (Austin, 1965). Rubert N. Richardson, *Texas: The Lone Star State* (2nd edn., New York, 1958) is a standard book that is still useful, while Joe B. Frantz, *Texas: A Bicentennial History* (New York, 1976), is brief and witty. H. H. Bancroft, *History of the North Mexican States and Texas,* 2 v. (San Francisco, 1884–89) contains a mass of information, as does Louis J. Wortham, *A History of Texas: from Wilderness to Commonwealth,* 5 v. (Fort Worth, 1924), which is journalistic, but embodies the results of much research. A brief but competent survey is in W. Eugene Hollon, *The Southwest: Old and New* (New York, 1961). David G. McComb, *Houston: The Bayou City* (Austin, 1969), sheds light on social and economic development in one important area.

American Colonization of Texas. A basic monograph is Mattie A. Hatcher, *The Opening of Texas to Foreign Settlements, 1801–1821* (Austin, 1927). This may be supplemented with Rie Jarratt, *Gutiérrez de Lara, Mexican-Texan* (Austin, 1949), a brief account of filibustering. Eugene C. Barker, *Mexico and Texas, 1821–1835* (Dallas, 1928) is the best description of the governmental system. The series of events that led to the union of Texas and Coahuila is described in Florence C. Lister and Robert H. Lister, *Chihuahua: Storehouse of Storm* (Albuquerque, 1966). Two massive books by Thomas L. Miller, *Bounty and Donation Land Grants of Texas, 1835–1888* (Austin, 1967), and *The Public Lands of Texas* (Norman, 1972), are more factual than interpretative, but contain a mine of information on the land system and land grants.

Essential to the story of American settlement is Eugene C. Barker, *Life of Stephen F. Austin* (Nashville, 1925), which is not only a biography but a history of the era. Barker's "The Government of Austin's Colony, 1821–1831," *S.H.Q.,* XXI (January, 1918), is the best work on the subject. Austin's early and thoroughly undistinguished career is the theme of Robert L. and Pauline H. Jones, "Stephen F. Austin in Arkansas," *A.H.Q.,* XXV (Winter, 1966), while his unsuccessful effort to obtain a land grant in the city of Austin is described in Sam A. Suhler, "Stephen F. Austin and the City of Austin: An Anomaly," *S.H.Q.,* LXIX (January, 1966). A capable biography of his principal lieutenant who was to remain prominent in Texan history is Margaret S. Henson, *Samuel May Williams: Early Texas Entrepreneur* (College Station, 1976).

The *empresario* system and early colonization may be studied in the histories of the several colonies. One monumental work of modern scholarship is Malcolm D. McLean, ed., *Papers Concerning Robertson's Colony in Texas,* 7 v. to date (Fort Worth, 1974–1979). Volumes published to date carry the story of the colony and region from 1788 to 1831. Less comprehensive is Edward A. Lukes, *De Witt Colony of Texas* (Austin, 1976), a localized study. Other useful accounts include Lois Carver, "Benjamin Rush Milam," *S.H.Q.,* XXXVIII (October, 1934, and January, 1935), Mary V. Henderson, "Minor Empresario Contracts for the Colonization of Texas," *S.H.Q.,* XXXI (April, 1928, and July, 1928), and Leo Hershkowitz, " 'The Land of Promise': Samuel Swartwout and Land Speculation in Texas, 1830–1838," *N.Y.H.S.Q.,* XLVII

(October, 1964). Seymour V. Connor, *The Peters Colony of Texas: A History and Biographical Sketches of the Early Settlers* (Austin, 1959), not only tells the story of a principal colonizing venture, but uses mass data to reveal the nature of the typical Texan pioneer. A competent biography of an early settler is W. J. Hughes, *Rebellious Ranger: Rip Ford and the Old Southwest* (Norman, 1964), while C. Alan Hutchinson, "General José Antonia Mexía and His Texas Interests," *S.H.Q.*, LXXXII (October, 1978), is an excellent account of an agent for the Galveston Land Company and Zavala interests who played a later role in the Revolution. That a desire for health motivated between 20 and 25 per cent of the Texas pioneers is the theme of Billy M. Jones, "Health Seekers in Early Anglo-American Texas" *S.H.Q.*, LXIX (January, 1966).

The Texan Revolution. A learned interpretation of the entire revolutionary process is in William C. Binkley, *The Texas Revolution* (Baton Rouge, 1952). The cultural conflicts that underlay Texan revolutionary sentiment are explored in Samuel H. Lowrie, *Culture Conflict in Texas, 1821–1835* (New York, 1932), Gerald Ashford, "Jacksonian Liberalism and Spanish Law in Early Texas," *S.H.Q.*, LVII (July, 1953), and Cecil Robinson, "Flag of Illusion," *A.W.*, V. (May, 1968). Diplomatic differences are described in detail in William R. Manning, *Early Diplomatic Relations between the United States and Mexico* (Baltimore, 1916), and Eugene C. Barker, "The United States and Mexico, 1835–1837," *M.V.H.R.*, I (June, 1914). Mounting tensions are made clear in a dispatch from the first American minister to Mexico to Henry Clay in 1825, Ralph E. Weber, "Joel R. Poinsett's Secret Mexican Dispatch Twenty," *S.C.H.R.*, LXXV (April, 1974). Barker's contention that land speculators were not primarily responsible for revolutionary agitation, "Land Speculation as a Cause of the Texas Revolution," *T.S.H.A.Q.*, X (July, 1914), is more convincing than the opposite view in Elgin Williams, *The Animated Pursuit of Speculation: Land Traffic in the Annexation of Texas* (New York, 1949). The conflict over colonization that contributed to the revolution is discussed in Ohland Morton, *Terán and Texas: A Chapter in Texas-American Relations* (Austin, 1948). Lonnie J. White, "Disturbances on the Arkansas–Texas Border, 1827–1831," *A.H.Q.*, XIX (Summer, 1960), shows that border troubles contributed to the unrest that underlay the revolution. A detailed study of the final step leading to independence is in R. Henderson Shuffler, "The Signing of Texas' Declaration of Independence: Myth and Record,"

S.H.Q., LXV (January, 1962). James M. Day, *Black Beans and Goose Quills: Literature of the Texan Mier Expedition* (Waco, 1970) is the best work on one of the early conflicts that helped foment the Revolution. Revealing accounts by two contemporaries are: Marilyn M. Sibley, ed., *Samuel H. Walker's Account of the Mier Expedition* (Austin, 1978), and Joseph D. McCutchan, *Mier Expedition Diary: A Texan Prisoner's Account* (Austin, 1978).

Military events are described in John H. Jenkins, ed., *The Papers of the Texas Revolution, 1835–1836*, 10 v. (Austin, 1973). Gerald S. Pierce, *Texas Under Arms, 1836–1846* (Austin, 1969), is detailed and poorly organized. Much information is also in biographies of the military leader, Sam Houston. These include Donald Braider, *Solitary Star: A Biography of Sam Houston* (New York, 1974), which is popular and laudatory; and M. K. Wisehart, *Sam Houston: American Giant* (Washington, 1962). Llerena Friend, *Sam Houston, the Great Designer* (Austin, 1954) emphasizes his later career. Houston's own story is told in Amelia W. Williams and Eugene C. Barker, eds., *The Writings of Sam Houston, 1813–1863*, 8 v. (Austin, 1938–1943), and Donald Day and Harry H. Ullon, eds., *The Autobiography of Sam Houston* (Norman, 1954). Fuller on one period of his life is Jack Gregory and Rennard Strickland, *Sam Houston and the Cherokees, 1829–1833* (Austin, 1967), which argues that he lived among the Indians before going to Texas to recruit a force to be used there. On the other hand Robert L. and Pauline H. Jones, "Houston's Politics and the Cherokees, 1829–1833," *C.O.*, XLVI (Winter, 1968–69), holds that he joined the tribe to find solace for his personal turmoil and had no plans for the future. Biographies of Houston's military confederates include Martha A. Turner, *William Barret Travis: His Sword and His Pen* (Waco, 1972), Archie P. McDonald, *Travis* (Austin, 1976), and Cleburne Huston, *Deaf Smith: Incredible Texas Spy* (Waco, 1973), a colorful history of a scout for Houston's army. That many Mexicans fought with Houston and received bounty lands in payment is shown in Thomas L. Miller, "Mexican Texans in the Texas Revolution," *J.M.A.H.*, III (1973).

Santa Anna's invasion, which touched off fighting, is well described in James Presley, "Santa Ann's Invasion of Texas: A Lesson in Command," *A. and W.*, X (Autumm, 1968); the author shows that poor planning and the difficulties of campaigning with such overdrawn supply lines doomed his effort. A well-researched work by Walter Lord, "Myths &

Realities of the Alamo," *A.W.*, V (May, 1968), corrects several misstatements in the standard work on the subject, Amelia W. Williams, "A Critical Study of the Seige of the Alamo and the Personnel of Its Defenders," *S.H.Q.*, XXXVI (April, 1933, to April, 1934). See, for the victory at San Jacinto, Sam H. Dixon and Louis W. Kemp, *The Heroes of San Jacinto* (Houston, 1932). Border troubles between the United States and Texas are discussed in James W. Silver, *Edmund Pendleton Gaines, Frontier General* (Baton Rouge, 1949), and between Texas and its Indian foes in David M. Vigness, "Indian Raids on the Lower Rio Grande, 1836–1837," *S.H.Q.*, LIX (July, 1955). The role of a battalion of troops from Georgia that was supported by that state through the Revolution is described in Jewel D. Scarborough, "The Georgia Battalion in the Texas Revolution: A Critical Study," *S.H.Q.*, LXIII (April, 1960). George L. Charlton, "Vince's Bridge: Question Mark of the San Jacinto Campaign," *S.H.Q.*, LXVIII (January, 1965), is a critical study of the last battle of the war. A little-known subject is the theme of Tom H. Wells, *Commodore Moore and the Texas Navy* (Austin, 1960) and J. Jack Bauer, "The United States Navy and Texas Independence: A Study in Jacksonian Integrity," *Mil.A.*, XXXIV (April, 1970). Gene Brack, "Mexican Opinion of the Texas Revolution," *S.H.Q.*, LXXII (October, 1968), shows that Mexicans first became fully aware of the United States during the conflict, and that the hostility that helped touch off the Mexican War began to develop at that time. The views of one Mexican who fought with Santa Anna are recorded in José Enrique de la Pena, *With Santa Anna in Texas: A Personal Narrative of the Revolution* (College Station, 1975).

The Texan Republic. The story of Texan politics during the ear of independence is told in Stanley Siegel, *A Political History of the Texas Republic, 1836–1845* (Austin, 1956), and in the scholarly biographies of its presidents: Stanley Siegel, *The Poet President of Texas: The Life of Mirabeau B. Lamar, President of the Republic of Texas* (Austin, 1977), which is brief and factual, Mary W. Clarke, *David C. Burnet* (Austin, 1969), and Herbert P. Gambrell, *Anson Jones: The Last President of Texas* (rev. edn., Austin, 1964). Mary W. Clarke, *Thomas J. Rusk: Soldier, Statesman, Jurist* (Austin, 1971) is a competent biography of another politician who fought at San Jacinto, served in Congress, and became justice of the Texas supreme court.

The continued influx of settlers during the Republic period is touched on in such works as Richard B. Hughes, "Old School Presby-terians: Eastern Invaders of Texas, 1830–1865," *S.H.Q.*, LXXIV (January, 1971), which shows that many conservative members of this sect who came west did not vary their beliefs or institutions, and William Seale, "San Augustine, in the Republic of Texas," *S.H.Q.*, LXXII (January, 1969), the story of the birth and death of a pioneer community. The large German migration of the period is surveyed in Gilbert G. Benjamin, *The Germans in Texas: A Study in Immigration* (Austin, 1974), an unrevised reprint of an earlier work. Irene M. King, *John O. Meusebach: German Colonizer of Texas* (Austin, 1967), tells the story of the *Adelsverein* which during the 1840s brought some seven thousand Germans to Texas. Terry G. Jordan, *German Seeds in Texas Soil: Immigrant Farmers in Nineteenth–Century Texas* (Austin, 1966), uses statistical techniques to demonstrate that these newcomers failed to adopt wasteful American ways in their farming. A well-researched study of another immigrant group is T. Lindsay Barker, *The First Polish Americans: Silesian Settlements in Texas* (College Station, 1979). Barnes F. Lathrop, *Migration into East Texas, 1835–1860* (Austin, 1949), is a thorough account of the occupation of one region.

The nature of the Texas social order has concerned several historians. Mark. E. Nackman, "Anglo-American Migrants to the West: Men of Broken Fortunes? The Case of Texas, 1821–46," *We.H.Q.*, V (October, 1974), concludes that the majority of the settlers were poor and came following the panics of 1819 and 1837. That the slaveholding aristocracy far outnumbered yeomen farmers in the elite governing group is demonstrated in Randolph B. Campbell, "Planters and Plain Folk: Harrison County, Texas, as a Test Case, 1850–1860," *J.S.H.*, XL (August, 1974), a point made even more convincingly in Randolph B. Campbell and Richard G. Lowe, *Wealth and Power in Antebellum Texas* (College Station, 1977). Alwyn Barr, *Black Texans: A History of Negroes in Texas* (Austin, 1973), devotes a small space to the Republican period, while James Smallwood, "Blacks in Antebellum Texas: A Reappraisal," *R.R.V.H.R.*, II (Winter, 1975), presents proof that Negroes were treated no better there than in the Lower South. George R. Woolfolk, *The Free Negro in Texas, 1800–1860* (Ann Arbor, 1976), shows that the complex ethnic mix there allowed a more rapid assimilation than elsewhere. A collection of diaries and letters from women who settled on the Texan frontier is in Crystal S. Ragsdale, *The Golden Free Land: The Reminiscences and Letters of*

Women on an American Frontier (Austin, 1976). That the era of the Republic was a period of urban beginnings is amply shown in Kenneth W. Wheeler, *To Wear a City's Crown: The Beginnings of Urban Growth in Texas, 1836–1865* (Cambridge, 1968), which describes the beginning of Houston, Galveston, San Antonio, and Austin. William R. Hogan, *The Texas Republic. A Social and Economic History* (Norman, 1946), is excellent.

Border troubles that plagued Texas during its Republic era are examined in excessive detail in Joseph M. Nance, *After San Jacinto: The Texas-Mexican Frontier, 1836–1841* (Austin, 1963), and *Attack and Counterattack: The Texas-Mexican Frontier, 1842* (Austin, 1965). One episode in this conflict is examined in Ralph A. Wooster, "Texas Military Operations Against Mexico, 1842–1843," *S.H.Q.*, LXVII (April, 1964), while documents are in Dorman H. Winfrey, ed., *Texas Indian Papers, 1825–1843* (Austin, 1959). A scholarly history of Texan expansionist ambitions during independence is William C. Binkley, *The Expansionist Movement in Texas, 1836–1850* (Berkeley, 1925). This should be supplemented with the detailed history of the 1841 expedition against Santa Fe: Noel M. Loomis, *The Texas-Santa Fé Pioneers* (Norman, 1958). This should be balanced with a revisionist article based on Mexican archival documents, Charles R. McClure, "The Texan-Santa Fe Expedition of 1841," *N.M.H.R.*, XLVIII (January, 1973), which pictures Governor Manuel Armijo not as an incompetent bungler but as a victim of tragic circumstances. The career of the American consul at Santa Fe at the time is described in Thomas E. Chavez, "The Trouble with Texans: Manuel Alverez and the 1841 Invasion," *N.M.H.R.*, LIII (April, 1978). On the less well-known Mier expedition see David M. Vigness, "A Texas Expedition into Mexico, 1840," *S.H.O.*, LXII (July, 1958), and Frederick C. Chabot, ed., *Texas Expeditions of 1842* (San Antonio, 1942).

Texas Annexation. A survey of Texan diplomatic relations during this period is Joseph W. Schmitz, *Texan Statecraft, 1836–1845* (San Antonio, 1945). Priscilla Benham, "Diplomatic Correspondence of the United States Charge d'Affairs to the Republic of Texas," *R.R.V.H.R.*, V (Winter, 1980), is, despite its title, a competent history of relations between the two countries during the years that Texas was seeking annexation. The development of a spirit of nationalism within Texas that influenced negotiations is the theme of Mark E. Nackman, *A Nation Within a Nation: The Rise of Texas Nationalism* (Port Washington, 1975).

The influence of the slave question on annexation is particularly well examined in Frederick Merk, *Slavery and the Annexation of Texas* (New York, 1972), which holds that the story of British involvement was invented by proslavery politicians to hurry annexation. William J. Cooper, Jr., "The Cotton Crisis in the Antebellum South: Another Look," *A.H.*, XLIX (April, 1975), examines planter opinion to find that there was no fear of land exhaustion and that they did not see Texas necessary for the expansion of cotton growing. Other aspects of the story are treated in Harriet Smither, "English Abolitionism and the Annexation of Texas," *S.H.Q.*, XXXII (January, 1929). Madeleine B. Stern, "Stephen Pearl Andrews, Abolitionist, and the Annexation of Texas," *S.H.Q.*, LXVII (April, 1964), examines the career of a Texan abolitionist who carried on negotiations with England for annexation. In an important article, Frederick Merk, "A Safety Valve Thesis and Texan Annexation," *M.V.H.R.*, XLIX (December, 1962), appraises the "Safety-valve" argument of Robert Walker that Texas should be annexed to attract slaves from the older South.

Relations with France during the Republic and annexation eras are described in Nancy N. Barker, ed., *The French Legation in Texas*, 2 v. (Austin, 1971–73), which combines a sound narrative with basic documents from the French archives. The same author has studied the activities of the principal French agent in Texas in "Devious Diplomacy: Dubois de Saligny and the Republic of Texas," *S.H.Q.*, LXXII (January, 1969), and "In Quest of the Golden Fleece: Dubois de Saligny and French Intervention in the New World," *We.H.Q.*, III (July, 1972). She explores Saligny's later career in "The Republic of Texas: A French View," *S.H.Q.*, LXXI (October, 1967). The older view expressed in Ephraim D. Adams, *British Interests and Activities in Texas, 1838–1846* (Baltimore, 1910), that Britain actively sought annexation and that her attitudes played a prominent role in stirring American interest, has been partially discredited by later scholarship.

Norman E. Tutorow, in two excellent articles, "The Whigs of Ohio and Texas Annexation," *N.O.Q.*, XLIII (Winter, 1971), and "Whigs of the Old Northwest and Texas Annexation, 1836–April, 1844," *I.M.H.*, LXVI (March, 1970), shows that until 1842 opposition to annexation in the Old Northwest was bipartisan and based on dislike of slavery; after that date the Whigs solidified on the issue as a means of preserving the party. The efforts of a Massachusetts committee to check annexation is studied in Kinley J. Brauer, "The Massachusetts State Texas Committee: A Last Stand Against the Annexation of Texas," *J.A.H.*, LI (September, 1964). That the South was not united on annexation is demonstrated in Elizabeth H. West, "Southern Opposition to the Annexation of Texas," *S.H.Q.*, XVIII (July, 1914), while George H. Gibson, "Opinion in North Carolina Regarding the Acquisition of Texas and Cuba, 1835–1855," *N.C.H.R.*, XXXVII (January and April, 1960), shows that the issue was of little interest in one southern state and had but slight effect on the election of 1844. Claude H. Hall, *Abel Parker Upshur. Conservative Virginian, 1790–1844* (Madison, 1964), is a capable biography of the secretary of state who managed annexation negotiations. Frederick Merk, *Fruits of Propaganda in the Tyler Administration* (Cambridge, 1971), uses newly discovered documents to show that Tyler used a secret fund to win domestic support for his annexation of Texas. Rupert N. Richardson, *Frontier of Northwest Texas* (Glendale, 1963), is an expert study of Texan frontier problems after annexation, while Ralph A. Wooster, "Membership in Early Texas Legislatures, 1850–1860," *S.H.Q.*, LXIX (October, 1965) is also concerned with the post-annexation period.

23   The Occupation of Oregon

General Works. Of the histories of the Pacific Northwest, the most recent and readable are Dorothy O. Johansen and Charles M. Gates, *Empire of the Columbia: A History of the Pacific Northwest* (rev. edn., New York, 1967), and Oscar O. Winther, *The Great Northwest. A History* (New York, 1947). An excellent modern interpretation is Earl Pomeroy, *The Pacific Slope: A History* (New York, 1965). The standard history of the state of Washington is Mary W. Avery, *Washington: A History of the Evergreen State* (Seattle, 1965), while Gordon B. Dodds, *Oregon: A Bicentennial History* (New York, 1977), provides an extensive brief history of the pioneer period.

The establishment of British interests in the Northwest is treated in E. E. Rich, *The History of the Hudson's Bay Company, 1670–1870*, 2 v. (London, 1958–62), and in the works on Dr. John McLoughlin and other company officials cited in the bibliography to Chapter XX. These may be supplemented with a collection of McLoughlin, documents dealing especially with the Oregon problem:

Burt B. Barker, ed., *The McLoughlin Empire and Its Rulers* (Glendale, 1959). A sound biography of another Hudson's Bay Company factor influential in diversifying the economic activities in the Oregon Country is Jean M. Cole, *Exile in the Wilderness: The Biography of Chief Factor Archibald McDonald, 1790–1853* (Don Mills, 1979).

British maritime activity in the Pacific Northwest is the theme of Robert B. Whitebrook, *Coastal Exploration of Washington* (Palo Alto, 1959), Bern Anderson, *Surveyor of the Sea: The Life and Voyages of Captain George Vancouver* (Seattle, 1960), and particularly Barry M. Gough, *The Royal Navy and the Northwest Coast of North America, 1810–1815: A Study of British Maritime Ascendency* (Vancouver, 1971), a scholarly appraisal of the influence of British sea power on Anglo-American relations. Two important source books show the importance of one of Britain's overland pioneers in establishing early control over the area: T. H. McDonald, ed., *Exploring the Northwest Territory: Sir Alexander Mackenzie's Journal of a Voyage by Bark Canoe from Lake Athabasca to the Pacific Ocean in the Summer of 1789* (Norman, 1966), and W. Kaye Lamb, ed., *The Journals and Letters of Sir Alexander Mackenzie* (Cambridge, 1970). Other books dealing with English expansion into the region are listed in the bibliography to Chapter XX.

Early American Interest in Oregon. The American approach to Oregon from the sea is studied in several excellent monographs. Derek Pethick, *First Approaches to the Northwest Coast* (Seattle, 1976, and J. Wade Caruthers, *American Pacific Ocean Trade: Its Impact on Foreign Policy and Continental Expansion, 1784–1860* (New York, 1973), expertly survey American voyages and exploration in the half-century before Vancouver's expeditions. A more detailed account of one group of commerical enterprises there, centering around Robert Morris and the Philadelphia capitalists that he enlisted in the cause, is in Jonathan Goldstein, *Philadelphia and the China Trade, 1682–1846: Commercial, Cultural, and Attitudinal Effects* (University Park, 1978). David B. Tyler, *The Wilkes Expedition: The First United States Exploring Expedition (1838–1842)* (Philadelphia, 1968) is a sound study; William Stanton, *The Great United States Exploring Expedition of 1838–1842* (Berkeley, 1975) adds details from the expedition 's own reports and notes.

Early American Activity in Oregon. Awakening congressional interest in Oregon is best described in Charles H. Ambler, "The Oregon Country, 1810–1830: A

Chapter in Territorial Expansion," *M.V.H.R.*, XXX (June, 1943). The designs of leading congressional expansionists are explored in Charles H. Ambler, *Life and Diary of John Floyd* (Richmond, 1918), and Michael B. Husband, "Senator Lewis F. Linn and the Oregon Question," *M.H.R.*, LXVI (October, 1971). Thomas B. Jones, "Henry Clay and Continental Expansion, 1820–1844," *K.S.H.S.R.*, LXXIII (July, 1975), deals with the efforts of a leading expansionist in Congress to stir interest in Oregon. The career of the leading propagandist, Hall Jackson Kelley, is described in Fred W. Powell, *Hall Jackson Kelley–Prophet of Oregon* (Portland, 1917), while the same author has edited most of Kelley's writings on Oregon in *Hall J. Kelley on Oregon* (Princeton, 1932).

The Coming of the Missionaries. Nard Jones, *The Great Command: The Story of Marcus and Narcissa Whitman and the Oregon Country Pioneers* (Boston, 1960) is a popular history of the mission movement in Oregon; the same may be said of Cecil P. Dryden, *Give All to Oregon! Missionary Pioneers in the Far West* (New York, 1968). In greater detail is Cornelius J. Brosman, *Jason Lee, Profit of the New Oregon* (New York, 1932). This should be supplemented by a revisionist work of major importance: Robert J. Loewenberg, *Equality on the Oregon Frontier. Jason Lee and the Methodist Mission, 1834–43* (Seattle, 1976), which argues that Lee's efforts to "civilize" the Indians was only a step toward their salvation and that his political maneuvers were directed toward the same end. His points are sharpened in, "New Evidence, Old Catagories: Jason Lee as Zealot," *P.H.R.*, XLVII (August, 1978). Other missionaries are treated in carefully researched books by Clifford M. Drury, *Marcus and Narcissa Whitman and the Opening of Old Oregon* (Glendale, 1973), *Henry Harmon Spaulding: Pioneer of Old Oregon* (Caldwell, 1936), and *Elkanah and Mary Walker, Pioneers among the Spokanes* (Caldwell, 1940). The diaries and journals of the six women who accompanied the early missionary parties westward have been published by Clifford M. Drury, ed., *The First White Women Over the Rockies,* 2 v. (Glendale, 1963), and *The First White Women Over the Rockies: Diaries, Letters, and Biographical Sketches* (Glendale, 1966). The same author has analyzed one of the missionary papers to determine the reasons for its effectiveness as a propaganda device attracting immigrants in "The Oregonian and Indian's Advocate," *P.N.Q.*, XLVI (October, 1965). Extensions of the mission system are described in Clifford M. Drury, "The

Spokane Indian Mission at Tshimakain, 1838–1848," *P.N.Q.*, LXVI (January, 1878), and Robert J. Loewenberg, " 'Not by Feeble Means': Daniel Lee's Plan to Save Oregon," *O.H.Q.*, LXXIV (March, 1973), which deals with the mission at the Dalles. Robert F. Berkhofer, Jr., *Salvation and the Savage: An Analysis of Protestant Missions and American Indian Response, 1787–1862* (Lexington, 1965), is an excellent appraisal of missionary influence, concluding that most failed because of unsurmountable obstacles and inadequate support. A popular biography is John U. Terrell, *Black Robe: The Life of Pierre-Jean De Smet—Missionary, Explorer and Pioneer* (Garden City, 1964). The diaries of a young man who accompanied De Smet westward in 1841 are printed in Nicolas Point, *Wilderness Kingdom: Indian Life in the Rocky Mountains: 1840–1847* (New York, 1967).

The Overland Migration. By far the best book on the overland trails is John D. Unruh, Jr., *The Plains Across: The Overland Emigrants and the Trans-Mississippi West, 1840–60* (Urbana, 1979), a monumental work dealing with the first twenty years of the overland migration. David Lavender, *Westward Vision: The Story of the Oregon Trail* (New York, 1963), is based on wide reading popularly presented. W. J. Ghent, *The Road to Oregon* (New York, 1929) describes the journey westward, while George Shumway, Edward Durell, and Howard C. Frey, *Conestoga Wagon, 1750–1850* (York, 1964), is crammed with information on the wagons used by the overland migrants. James C. Bell, *Opening a Highway to the Pacific, 1838–1846* (New York, 1921) is concerned with the forces leading to migration. Two excellent books describe the trail and its users: Merrill J. Mattes, *The Great Platte River Road; the Covered Wagon Mainline Via Fort Kearny to Fort Laramie* (Lincoln, 1969), which is based on an examination of seven hundred diaries for this portion of the road, and Louise Barry, *The Beginnings of the West: Annals of the Kansas Gateway to the American West* (Topeka, 1972), which chronicles all expeditions passing through Kansas on the way west. Erwin N. Thompson, *Shallow Grave at Waiilatpu: The Sagers' West* (Portland, 1969), describes the migration of Henry and Naomi Sager and their seven children. Among the dozens of diaries or memoirs left by those who followed the Oregon Trail, the classis is Jesse Applegate, "A Day with the Cow Column," *O.H.Q.*, I (December, 1900), which describes the 1843 migration; an excellent collection of overland diaries has appeared as Dale Morgan, ed., *Overland in 1846: Diaries and Letters of the*

California-Oregon Trail, 2 V. (Georgetown, 1963) while others are in Maude A. Rucker, ed., *The Oregon Trail and Some of Its Blazers* (New York, 1930). The role of two key forts in the migration is examined in Frank C. Robertson, *Fort Hall, Gateway to the Oregon Country* (New York, 1963), and David W. Lupton, "Fort Bernard on the Oregon Trail," *N.H.*, (LX (Spring, 1979). The improvement of the trail is considered in such studies as Robert A. Murray, "Trading Posts, Forts and Bridges of the Casper Area—Unraveling the Tangle of the Upper Platte," *A. of W.*, XLVII (Spring, 1975), and Leah C. Menefee and Lowell Tiller, "Cutoff Fever," *O.H.Q.*, LXXVII (December, 1976) to LXXIX (Spring, 1978), which tells the story of the Elliott Cutoff in the upper Willamette Valley. The effect of guide books on the migration is explored in Helen B. Kroll, "The Books That Enlightened the Emigrants," *O.H.Q.*, XLV (June, 1944), while Thomas F. Andrews, " 'Ho! for Oregon and California!' An Annotated Bibliography of Published Advice to the Emigrant, 1841–47," *Princeton Univ. Library Chronicle*, XXXIII (Autumn, 1971), is an excellent guide.

Two aspects of life on the Oregon and other trails have, until recently, been neglected by historians. One of these—the impromptu legal institutions that provided for law and order on the road is superbly treated in a trail-blazing book by John P. Reid, *Law for the Elephant: Property and Social Behavior on the Overland Trail* (San Marino, 1980). Less searching, and dealing primarily with the trials held on the trail, is David J. Langum, "Pioneer Justice on the Overland Trails," *We.H.Q.*, V (October, 1974). The other neglected area—the role of women in the migrations—has inspired more writing. Some is directed toward the role of women in the Far West, with only sections devoted to their experiences during migration; the best of such works is Julie R. Jeffrey, *Frontier Women: The Trans-Mississippi West, 1840–1880* (New York, 1979), an excellent study. So also is Christine Fischer, ed., *Let Them Speak for Themselves: Women in the American West, 1849–1900* (Hamden, 1977), a well-selected collection of contemporary narratives showing the way in which women responded to various environments.

Works about or by women pertaining directly to the overland trails include John M. Faragher, *Women and Men on the Overland Trail* (New Haven, 1979), which uses trail diaries to reconstruct the nature of midwest frontier families, Georgia W. Read, "Women and Children on the Oregon-California Trail in the Gold Rush Years," *M.H.R.*, XXXIX (October, 1944), an anecdotal summary, Helen H. Smith, "Pioneers in Petticoats,' *Am.H.*, X (February, 1959), with examples of the ways in which women reacted to the trails experience, Robert L. Mankers, "Wives, Mothers, Daughters: Women's Life on the Road West," *A. of W.*, XLII (October, 1970), a competent survey of many diaries, Ruth B. Moynihan, "Children and Young People on the Overland Trail," *We.H.Q.*, VI (July, 1975), which is episodic but still presents a good picture of life on the trails, and John M. Faragher and Christine Stansell, "Women and Their Families on the Overland Trail to California and Oregon, 1842–1867," *F.S.*, II (1975), a solid account of the role of the family during migrations.

The Oregon Colony. A statistical survey of the Oregon population, based on census returns, is in William A. Bowen, *The Willamette Valley: Migration and Settlement on the Oregon Frontier* (Seattle, 1978). A study of social conditions within the valley should begin with the stimulating article by Dorothy O. Johansen, "A Working Hypothesis for the Study of Migrations," *P.H.R.*, XXXVI (February, 1967), which shows that the different characteristics of the Oregon and California populations can be explained by the "pull-factors" attracting them to the two regions. A competent social history of the area is Sidney Warren, *Farthest Frontier: The Pacific Northwest* (West York, 1949). The evolution of a provisional government is explained in revisionist terms in Robert J. Loewenberg, "Creating a Provisional Government in Oregon: A Revision," *P.N.Q.*, LXVIII (January, 1977), which shows that Lee opposed the formation, and that it was not formed to "save" Oregon. More traditional views are in the biography of one of the leaders, Kenneth L. Holmes, *Ewing Young. Master Trapper* (Portland, 1967), and in several articles: J. Neilson Barry, "The Champoeg Meeting of March 4, 1844," *O.H.Q.*, XXXVIII (December, 1937), Russell B. Thomas, "Truth and Fiction of the Champoeg Meeting," *O.H.Q.*, XXX (September, 1922), and Kent D. Richards, "The Methodists and the Formation of the Oregon Provisional Government," *P.N.Q.*, LXI (April, 1970). A full account of the early meetings is in John A. Hussey, *Champoeg, Place of Transition* (Portland, 1967). Arthur L. Throckmorton, *Oregon Argonauts: Merchant Adventurers on the Western Frontier* (Portland, 1961) is, despite its title, a sober and enlightening study of business activity among the Oregon pioneers for the period 1839–1869.

The Oregon Boundary Dispute. An excellent survey of British policy in the dispute over the ownership of the Oregon Country is Wilbur D. Jones, *The American Problem in Britrish Diplomacy* (Athens, 1974), while American strategy is expertly analyzed in David M. Pletcher, *The Diplomacy of Annexation: Texas, Oregon, and the Mexican War* (Columbia, 1973), and the several biographies of President Polk, of which the best for this period is Charles Sellers, *James K. Polk, Constitutionalist, 1843–1846* (Princeton, 1966). A full account is in Melvin C. Jacobs, *Winning Oregon* (Caldwell, 1938), although this should be supplemented with the interpretation by Richard W. Van Alstyne, "International Rivalries in Pacific Northwest," *O.H.Q.,* XLVI (September, 1945). Norman A. Graebner, *Empire on the Pacific* (New York, 1955), holds that commercial factors were a principal influence in the annexation of both Oregon and California. This view is attacked in Shomer S. Zwelling, *Expansion and Imperialism* (Chicago, 1970). William A. Hansen, "Thomas Hart Benton and the Oregon Question," *M.H.R.,* LXIII (July, 1969), adds nothing to our knowledge of Oregon diplomacy but is a convenient summary of one prominent senator's view. That the slavery issue was involved in the debate over Oregon is revealed in R. Alton Lee, "Slavery and the Oregon Territorial Issue: Prelude to Compromise of 1850," *P.N.Q.,* LXIV (July, 1973).

The most convincing story of the diplomacy of Oregon is told in a series of articles that have been collected in Frederick Merk, *The Oregon Question: Essays in Anglo-American Diplomacy and Politics* (Cambridge, 1967). The view that Lord Aberdeen was influential in the surrender, as set forth in these articles, is challenged, not too convincingly, in Wilbur D. Jones, *Lord Aberdeen and the Americas* (Athens, 1958); Stuart Anderson, "British Threats and the Settlement of the Oregon Boundary Dispute," *P.N.Q.,* LXVI (October, 1975), also holds that Merk is wrong in saying that British threats to use naval power had no influence. Pressure by whaling interests to protect their rights in the Pacific from British naval threats is discussed in Howard I. Kusher, " 'The Oregon Question Is . . . a Massachusetts Question'," *O.H.Q.,* LXXV (December, 1974), James O. McCabe, "Arbitration and the Oregon Question," *C.H.R.,* XLI (December, 1960), demonstrates that England favored arbitration as a means of settling a troublesome dispute over a territory that she really did not want, and that American pressure prevented this. Equally enlightening is a study by Richard S. Cramer, "British Magazines and the Oregon Question," *P.H.R.,* XXXII

(November, 1963), which shows that British magazines generally opposed surrender for political reasons, and not because of any genuine interest in the territory. The impact of the Oregon question on American politics is expertly discussed in Frederick Merk, "Presidential Fevers," *M.V.H.R.,* XLVII (June, 1960), and Norman Graebner, "Politics and the Oregon Compromise," *P.N.Q.,* LII (January, 1961). Keith Murray, *The Pig War* (Tacoma, 1968), describes a minor war that broke out in 1859 over ownership of the San Juan Islands after a faulty survey of the Oregon Treaty line left them in dispute.

24 The Great Basin Frontier, 1830–1846

General Works. A searching examination of recent writing on Mormonism is in Rodman W. Paul, "The Mormons as a Theme in Western Historical Writing," *J.A.H.,* LIV (December, 1967). A complete listing of all books and articles dealing with Mormonism is in Chad J. Flake, ed., *A Mormon Bibliography, 1830–1930* (Salt Lake City, 1978), while 2,900 diaries and autobiographies are described in Davis Bitton, *Guide to Mormon Diaries and Autobiographies* (Provo, 1977). Probably the best history of Mormonism by objective Mormon scholars is Leonard J. Arrington and Davis Bitton, *The Mormon Experience: A History of the Latter-day Saints* (New York, 1979); another competent study by two Mormon scholars is James B. Allen and Glen M. Leonard, *The Story of the Latter-day Saints* (Salt Lake City, 1976), which devotes 286 pages to the pioneer period. Equally sound is Thomas F. O'Dea, *The Mormons* (Chicago, 1957), an impartial and thorough study by a sociologist. Of merit is the biography of the founder of the church: Fawn M. Brodie, *No Man Knows My History. The Life Story of Joseph Smith* (New York, 1945); Donna Hill, *Joseph Smith: The First Mormon* (Garden City, 1977) is also an insightful biography by a non-Mormon. Brigham Young has been less fortunate in a biographer than Joseph Smith. Preston Nibley, *Brigham Young, the Man and His Work* (Salt Lake City, 1936) is too openly biased in favor of Young to be reliable and Stanley P. Hirshson, *The Lion of the Lord. A Biography of Brigham Young* (New York, 1969), too strongly opposed. A useable collection of documents dealing with all phases of Mormon history is William Mulder and A. R. Mortensen, *Among the Mormons. Human Accounts by Contemporary Observers* (New York, 1958). A challenging work on the origins of Mormonism is Mario S. De Pillis, "The Social Sources of Mormonism," *Church Hist.*, XXXVII (March, 1968), which argues that many of its doctrines and practices stemmed from the frontier environment of western New York where it originated and the pioneer conditions of the Mississippi Valley where it developed. Material on the later pioneer period is in the several histories of Utah, of which the latest are Charles S. Peterson, *Utah: A Bicentennial History* (New York, 1977), which is an excellent brief study, and Richard D. Poll, ed., *Utah's History* (Provo, 1978), a collaborative work by twenty-eight scholars. That women played a larger role than ordinarily supposed in the early occupation of Utah is shown in the twelve essays in Claudia L. Bushman, ed., *Mormon Sisters: Women in Early Utah* (Cambridge, 1976).

Persecution and the Early Migrations. The persecutions that drove the Mormons from Missouri are reviewed in Warren A. Jennings, "Factors in the Destruction of the Mormon Press in Missouri, 1833," *U.H.Q.*, XXXV (Winter, 1967), Warren A. Jennings, "The Expulsion of the Mormons from Jackson County, Missouri," *M.H.R.*, LXIV (October, 1969), and Warren A. Jennings, "The Army of Israel Marches into Missouri," *M.H.R.*, LXII (January, 1968). Events that followed the Missouri persecutions are studied in George R. Gayler, "Attempts by the State of Missouri to Extradite Joseph Smith, 1841–1843," *M.H.R.*, LVIII (October, 1963). Robert B. Flanders, *Nauvoo: Kingdom on the Mississippi* (Urbana, 1965) is an objective and well-written history of the Mormon residence in Illinois. David E. Miller and Della S. Miller, *Nauvoo: The City of Joseph* (Santa Barbara, 1974), tells much the same story but adds an understanding of the people's faith in Joseph Smith. Stanley B. Kimball, "The Mormons in Illinois, 1836–1846: A Special Introduction," *J.I.S.H.S.*, LXIV (Spring, 1971), introduces a special issue of the journal on this subject. James L. Kimball, Jr., "The Nauvoo Charter: A Reinterpretation," *J.I.S.H.S.*, LXIV (Spring, 1971), shows that the charter did not favor the Mormons unduly as historians have believed. Reasons for their growing unpopularity are examined in George R. Gayler, "The Mormons and Politics in Illinois, 1839–1844," *J.I.S.H.S.*, XLIX (Spring, 1956), and Hamilton Gardner, "The Nauvoo Legion, 1840–1845—A Unique Military Organization," *J.I.S.H.S.*, LIV (Summer, 1961). That Joseph Smith was probably defending polygamy as early as 1842 is shown in Lawrence Foster, "A Little-Known Defense of Polygamy from

the Mormon Press in 1842," *D.*, IX (No. 4, 1974). Eight letters from the *Warsaw [Illinois] Signal*, revealing the depth of anti-Mormon sentiment in that nearby town are in Annette P. Hampshire, "Thomas Sharp and Anti-Mormon Sentiment in Illinois, 1842–1845," *J.I.S.H.S.*, LXXII (May, 1979). A learned discussion by a lawyer of the trial of Smith assassins by Dallin H. Oaks and Marvin S. Hill, *Carthage Conspiracy: The Trial of the Accused Assassins of Joseph Smith* (Urbana, 1975), concludes that four of the five acquitted conspirators were guilty. The divisions within the church that followed Smith's death are expertly described in F. Mark McKiernan, ed., *The Restoration Movement: Essays in Mormon History* (Lawrence, 1973), while Mormon folk tales of the sufferings experienced by the assassins in their later lives are shown to be part of American legend in Richard C. Poulsen, "Fate and the Persecutors of Joseph Smith: Transmutations of an American Myth," *D.*, XI (Winter, 1978).

The Utah Migration. The Mormon exodus across Iowa after the flight from Nauvoo is described in R. E. Harvey, "The Mormon Trek Across Iowa Territory," *A. of I.*, XXVIII (July, 1946). That the Mormons in establishing their Winter Quarters illegally usurped Indian lands, and that government efforts to remove them were not the result of anti-Mormon prejudice is shown in Robert A. Trennert, Jr., "The Mormons and the Office of Indian Affairs: The Conflict Over Winter Quarters, 1846–1848," *N.H.*, LIII (Fall, 1972). Their experiences at Winter Quarters are the theme of E. W. Shumway, "Winter Quarters, Nebraska, 1846–1848," *N.H.*, XXXV (June, 1954). A. R. Mortensen, "Mormons, Nebraska, and the Way West," *N.H.*, XLVI (December, 1965), also stresses the fact that the period at Winter Quarters was a watershed in Mormon history.

The Mormon migration to Utah is skillfully described in Wallace Stegner, *The Gathering of Zion: The Story of the Mormon Trail* (New York, 1964), a book that combines sound scholarship, objectivity, and a sparkling literary style and in Joseph E. Brown, *The Mormon Trek West* (New York, 1980), a heavily illustrated popular account. The organization of the migrating parties is expertly described in Philip A. M. Taylor, "The Mormon Crossing of the United States, 1840–1870," *U.H.Q.*, XXV (October, 1957). For the important 1847 migration to Utah, *William Clayton's Journal* (Salt Lake City, 1921), is a revealing document; *Appleton Milo Harmon Goes West* (Berkeley, 1946), is another excellent journal of that trip. One of the finest

Mormon overland diaries, which also describes life in pioneer Utah, is Juanita Brooks, ed., *On the Mormon Frontier: The Diary of Hosea Stout, 1844–1861*, 2 v. (Salt Lake City, 1965). Documents on the handcart migration, together with an excellent account of that subject, are in LeRoy R. Hafen and Ann W. Hafen, *Handcarts to Zion* (Glendale, 1960). Biographies of the pioneers are: John H. Evans, *Charles Coulson Rich, Pioneer Builder of the West* (New York, 1936), Reva Stanley, *A Biography of Parley P. Pratt; the Archer of Paradise* (Caldwell, 1937), Harold Schindler, *Orrin Porter Rockwell: Man of God, Son of Thunder* (Salt Lake City 1966), Samuel W. Taylor, *The Kingdom or Nothing: The Life of John Taylor, Militant Mormon* (New York, 1976), and two books by Leonard J. Arrington, *From Quaker to Latter-day Saint: Bishop Edwin D. Woolley* (Salt Lake City, 1976), and *Charles C. Rich: Mormon General and Western Frontiersman* (Provo, 1974).

The first settlements are well described in Andrew L. Neff, *History of Utah, 1847–1869* (Salt Lake City, 1940). C. D. Harris, *Salt Lake City, a Regional Capital* (Chicago, 1940), tells the story of the principal city. William Hartley, "Mormons, Crickets, and Gulls: A New Look at an Old Story," *U.H.Q.*, XXXVIII (Summer, 1970), shows that few crickets were killed by gulls during the first year, and reasons that the legend of the "Miracle of the Gulls" was a later creation. Davis Bitton and Linda P. Wilcox, "Pestiferous Ironclads: The Grasshopper Problem in Pioneer Utah," *U.H.Q.*, LXIV (Fall, 1978), charts the plagues of grasshoppers between the 1840s and 1969.

Expansion of Mormon Settlements. Early expansion is admirably described in L. H. Creer, *The Founding of an Empire: The Exploration and Colonization of Utah, 1776–1856* (Salt Lake City, 1947). Milton R. Hunter, *Brigham Young the Colonizer* (Salt Lake City, 1940) is an excellent account of expansion within the Great Basin area and beyond, as is Nels Anderson, *Desert Saints: The Mormon Frontier in Utah* (Chicago, 1942). Brigham Young's role, made clear in these volumes, is further defined in Leonard J. Arrington and Ronald K. Esplin, "Building a Commonwealth: The Secular Leadership of Brigham Young," *U.H.Q.*, LXV (Summer, 1977), which paints a vivid picture of Young as a human being, and two selections from his letters, accurately transcribed: Dean C. Jessee, ed., *Letters of Brigham Young to His Sons* (Salt Lake City, 1974), and Dean C. Jessee, "The Writings of Brigham Young," *We.H.Q.*, IV (July, 1973). The assumption of most writers on colonization—that Young planned a cordon of settlements to repel invaders—is disputed in Eugene E. Campbell, "Brigham Young's Outer Cordon—a Reappraisal," *U.H.Q.*, XLI (Summer, 1973), arguing that the colonies were established for a variety of reasons.

The histories of several of the colonies have been written. Among the best are two excellent studies by Charles S. Peterson, *Take Up Your Mission: Mormon Colonization Along the Little Colorado River, 1870–1900* (Tucson, 1973), which is of broader scope than its title indicates, and *Look to the Mountains: Southeastern Utah and the La Sal National Forest* (Provo, 1975). The later period of colonization treated in these books is the theme also of studies of northward expansion and resulting hostility: A. J. Simminds, "Southeast Utah as a Pioneer Mormon Safety Valve," *I.Y.*, XXIII (Winter, 1980), Leonard J. Arrington, "The Mormon Settlement of Cassia County, Idaho, 1873–1921," *I.Y.*, XXIII (Summer, 1979), and Merle W. Wells, *Anti-Mormonism in Idaho, 1872–92* (Provo, 1978). The hostility that developed at Mormon intrusion into Nevada is explained in Leonard Arrington and Richard Jensen, "Panaca: Mormon Outpost Among the Mining Camps," *N.H.S.Q.*, XVIII (Winter, 1975).

Helpful biographies of leaders in the expansion include: Juanita Brooks, *Dudley Leavitt, Pioneer to Southern Utah* (St. George, 1942), Paul Bailey, *Jacob Hamblin, Buckskin Apostle* (Los Angeles, 1948), John H. Krenkel, ed., *The Life and Times of Joseph Fish, Mormon Pioneer* (Danville, 1970), and Andrew K. Larson, *Erastus Snow, Missionary and Pioneer for the Early Mormon Church* (Salt Lake City, 1971). Robert G. Cleland and Juanita Brooks, eds., *A Mormon Chronicle: The Diaries of John D. Lee, 1848–1876*, 2 v. (San Marino, 1955) is a rewarding document. Brigham Young's continuing role as a colonizer is shown in Gordon Irving, "Encouraging the Saints: Brigham Young's Annual Tours of the Mormon Settlements," *U.H.Q.*, XLV (Summer, 1977).

The reliance of Mormons on attracting converts from abroad is described in Philip A. M. Taylor, *Expectations Westward* (Edinburgh, 1965), which makes clear the elaborate machinery devised by Brigham Young to care for immigrants at every stage of their journey. Ronald W. Walker, "The Stenhouses and the Making of a Mormon Image," *J.Mo.H.*, I (1974), is an excellent account of two early agents of the church in England, while the diary of another missionary there has been published in James B. Allen and Thomas G. Alexander, ed., *Manchester Mormons: The Journal of William Clayton, 1840–1842* (Santa

Barbara, 1974). William Mulder, *Homeward to Zion: The Mormon Migration from Scandinavia* (Minneapolis, 1957) is a scholarly history of mission activities in that area.

The emphasis of the Mormons on group activity is partially explained in Leonard J. Arrington and Feramorz Y. Fox, *Building the City of God: Community and Cooperation among the Mormons* (Salt Lake City, 1976), an honest book explaining failures as well as successes, and Ephraim E. Ericksen, *The Psychological and Ethical Aspects of Mormon Group Life* (Chicago, 1923). James B. Allen, "Ecclesiastical Influence on Local Government in the Territory of Utah," *A. and W.,* VIII (Spring, 1966), reveals the extent to which the church regulated and controlled the political and social life of the community, as does Klaus J. Hansen, *Quest for Empire: The Political Kingdom of God and the Council of Fifty in Mormon History* (East Lansing, 1967). The latter examines the role of a council created in 1842 to serve as the political arm of Mormonism. That the spirit engendered by the influence of religion stimulated rather than repressed the intellectual life of Utah is convincingly demonstrated in Leonard J. Arrington, *The Intellectual Tradition of Mormon Utah* (Logan, 1968), while its effect on social life is the theme of William J. McNiff, *Heaven on Earth: A Planned Mormon Society* (Oxford, 1940), and Joseph Heinerman, "Early Utah Pioneer Cultural Societies," *U.H.Q.,* XLVII (Winter, 1979). Its importance in the economic realm is discussed in Leonard J. Arrington, *Great Basin Kingdom: An Economic History of the Latter-Day Saints, 1830–1900* (Cambridge, 1959), a monumental work of scholarship. The remarkable cohesiveness of the Mormons is explained in terms of personal loyalty to Brigham Young in Philip A. M. Taylor, "Early Mormon Loyalty and the Leadership of Brigham Young," *U.H.Q.,* XXX (Spring, 1962), and as a result of the unusual combination of geographic and religious forces in Philip A. M. Taylor and Leonard J. Arrington, "Religion and Planning in the Far West: The First Generation of Mormons in Utah," *Ec.H.R.,* XI (August, 1958). That the Mormons did respond to frontier forces by moving toward greater democracy is argued in Alexander Evanoff, "The Turner Thesis and Mormon Beginnings in New York and Utah," *U.H.Q.,* XXXIII (Spring, 1965).

Mormon-Indian Relations. That conflicts between the Great Basin Indians and the Mormons were inevitable is shown in Beverly P. Smaby, "The Mormons and the Indians: Conflicting Ecological Systems in the Great Basin," *A.S.,* XVI (Spring, 1975). Floyd A.

O'Neil and Stanford J. Layton, "Of Pride and Politics: Brigham Young as Indian Superintendent," *U.H.Q.* XLVI (Summer, 1978), explains why the Mormons' land-grabbing tendency was restricted by Young's religious beliefs; that this policy was greatly different from that of other frontiersmen is challenged in Howard A. Christy, "Open Hand and Mailed Fist: Mormon-Indian Relations in Utah, 1847–52," *U.H.Q.,* XLVI (Summer, 1978). Charles S. Peterson, "Jacob Hamblin, Apostle to the Lamanites, and the Indian Mission," *J.M.O.H.,* II (1975), deals with a prominent Indian missionary of the 1850s, while a minor war with one band of Indians in 1853 is described in Howard A. Christy, "The Walker War: Defense and Conciliation as Strategy," *U.H.Q.,* XL (Fall, 1979).

Mormon Conflicts with the United States. An excellent, scholarly survey of the mounting tensions and conflict is in Norman F. Furniss, *The Mormon Conflict, 1850–1859* (New Haven, 1960), although one author objects that the volume pays too little attention to President Buchanan's role: William P. Mackinnon, "The Gap in the Buchanan Revival: The Utah Expedition of 1857–58," *U.H.Q.,* XLV (Winter, 1977). Dale L. Morgan, "The State of Deseret," *U.H.Q.,* VIII (April–July, 1940), is a thorough account of governmental beginnings. The anti-Mormon spirit that was stirring in the United States by 1856 is discussed in Richard D. Poll, "The Mormon Question Enters National Politics, 1850–1856," *U.H.Q.,* XXV (April, 1957), while the religious revivalism that stirred the Mormons to the point of bloodshed is described in Gustive O. Larson, "The Mormon Reformation," *U.H.Q.,* XXVI (January, 1958). Gustive O. Larson, "Land Contest in Early Utah," *U.H.Q.,* XXIX (October, 1961), shows that hostility of federal surveyors was a principal cause of Mormon opposition. The account of the episode that touched off the conflict by Juanita Brooks, *The Mountain Meadows Massacre* (rev. edn., Norman, 1962), is objective and scholarly, as is the same author's biography of a principal fomenter of that outbreak, *John Doyle Lee; Zealot—Pioneer Builder—Scapegoat* (Glendale, 1961). William Wise, *Massacre at Mountain Meadows: An American Legend and a Monumental Crime* (New York, 1976) is little more than an anti-Mormon polemic. That the Mormons were able to acquire the latest weapons for the conflict is shown in Harry W. Gibson, "Frontier Arms of the Mormons," *U.H.Q.,* XLII (Winter, 1974). Recent scholarship has also demonstrated that the Mormons were able to acquire Ft. Bridger in 1855, before the outbreak of the war: Fred R. Gowans, "Fort Bridger and the Mormons," *U.H.Q.*, XLII (Winter, 1974).

Military events of the Mormon War are described in Richard D. Poll and Ralph W. Hansen, " 'Buchanan's Blunder'—The Utah War, 1857—1858," *Mil.A.*, XXV (Fall, 1961). Melvin T. Smith, "Colorado River Exploration and the Mormon War," *U.H.Q.*, XXXVIII (Summer, 1970), shows that the Mormons sent expeditions along the Colorado River as war approached to seek Indian aid, spy out defensive positions, and locate avenues of retreat. A competent brief biography of a Mormon who led raiding parties during the war is Charles S. Peterson, " 'A Mighty Man Was Brother Lot': A Portrait of Lot Smith, Mormon Frontiersman," *We.H.Q.*, I (October, 1970). Thomas G. Alexander and Leonard J. Arrington, "Camp in the Sagebrush: Camp Lloyd, Utah, 1858–1861," *U.H.Q.*, XXXIV (Winter, 1966), describes the occupation of Salt Lake City by Union troops after the war, and their relations with the people. Documents on the war are in LeRoy R. Hafen and Ann W. Hafen, eds., *The Utah Expedition, 1857–1858* (Glendale, 1958). Letters sent eastward from the American expeditionary army have been skillfully edited in Harold D. Langley, ed., *To Utah with the Dragoons and Glimpses of Life in Arizona and California, 1858–1859* (Salt Lake City, 1974). The career of the mediator who ended the conflict is traced in Oscar O. Winther, ed., *The Private Papers and Diary of Thomas Lieper Kane, A Friend of the Mormons* (San Francisco, 1937).

One reason for the continued national apprehension after the Mormon War is explored in Leonard J. Arrington and Jon Haupt, "Intolerable Zion: The Image of Mormonism in Nineteenth Century American Literature," *W.H.R.*, XXII (Summer, 1968); the authors show that from the 1850s on most books damned Mormonism. The effect of this attitude on Utah's relations with the nation is expertly appraised in Gustive O. Larson, *The 'Americanization' of Utah for Statehood* (San Marino, 1971). Howard R. Lamar, "Statehood for Utah: A Different Path," *U.H.Q.*, XLX (Fall, 1971), traces the history of Utah's statehood efforts.

25   The Conquest of California, 1830–1846

General Works. The most voluminous single work on California is H. H. Bancroft, *History of California*, 7 v. (San Francisco, 1884–90), which has been the foundation of a large part of the subsequent work on the subject. Of the many more modern histories of the state, the most useful are listed under Chapter XIX. A pioneer work, now out of date, on the role of Negroes in the occupation of California is Delilah Beasley, *The Negro Trail Blazers of California* (Los Angeles, 1919). Valuable insights on the state's history are also in Earl Pomeroy, *The Pacific Slope* (New York, 1965). A detailed older study is Irving B. Richman, *California Under Spain and Mexico, 1235–1847* (Boston, 1911). Warren A. Beck and Ynez D. Haase, *Historical Atlas of California* (Norman, 1975), locate trail routes, missions, ranches and other features.

The Coming of the Traders. Excellent general surveys are Derek Pethick, *First Approaches to the Northwest Coast* (Seattle, 1976), and J. Wade Caruthers, *American Pacific Ocean Trade: Its Impact On Foreign Policy and Continental Expansion, 1784–1860* (New York, 1973). The standard account of the important sea otter trade is Adele Ogden, *The California Sea Otter Trade, 1784–1848* (Berkeley, 1941, reprinted 1975), while two special groups of maritime traders are the theme of Jonathan Goldstein, *Philadelphia and the China Trade, 1682–1846: Commercial, Cultural, and Attitudinal Effects* (University Park, 1978), and Robin W. Doughty, "The Farallones and the Boston Men," *C.H.S.Q.*, LIII (Winter, 1974). The latter deals with the Farallon Islands near San Francisco, centers for the early seal trade. Three articles by Sister Magdalen Coughlin shed light on early American relations with the coast: "The Entrance of the Massachusetts Merchant into the Pacific," *S.C.O.*, XLVIII (December, 1966), describing economic conditions in Massachusetts during the 1780s and the first contacts; "Boston Smugglers on the Coast (1797–1821): An Insight into the American Acquisition of California," *C.H.S.Q.*, XLVI (June, 1967), showing that a thriving trade existed long before 1821 when it was officially opened; and "Commercial Foundations of Political Interest in the Opening Pacific, 1789–1829," *C.H.S.Q.*, L (March, 1971), revealing the government aid to merchants who were looked on as heralds of empire. Two contemporary narratives of the trade are William Shaler, *Journal of a Voyage between China and the North-Western Coast of America, made in 1804* (Claremont, 1935), and D. Mackenzie Brown, ed., *China Trade Days in California; Selected Letters from the Thompson Papers, 1832–1863* (Berkeley, 1947). An excellent analysis of the mechanics of the trade, based on a statistical study of the records of William Appleton &

Company, is Bruno Fritzsche, " 'On Liberal Terms': The Boston Hide Merchants in California," *B.H.R.*, XLII (Winter, 1968); the author shows that profits depended on the California goods sold in Boston. A sound biography of a leading trader is Andrew F. Rolle, *An American in California: The Biography of William Heath Davis, 1822–1909* (San Marino, 1956). The best contemporary descriptions are in Richard H. Dana, *Two Years Before the Mast* (New York, 1840), Doyce B. Nunis, Jr., ed., *The California Diary of Faxton Dean Atherton, 1836–1839* (San Francisco, 1964), the diary of a clerk for the hide firm of Alpheus B. Thompson, and Alfred Robinson, *Life in California* (New York, 1846). The spread of the cattle ranching on which the trade was built is described in L. T. Burcham, "Cattle and Range Forage in California: 1770–1880," *A.H.*, XXXV (July, 1961).

Two excellent articles describe relationships between the American traders and those from Russia who were advancing southward along the coast from Alaska: James R. Gibson, "Sables to Sea Outters: Russia Enters the Pacific," *Alaska Rev.*, III (Fall and Winter, 1968), which traces expansion across Siberia and into the northern Pacific during the eighteenth century, and Mary E. Wheeler, "Empires in Conflict and Cooperation: The 'Bostonians' and the Russian-American Fur Company," *P.H.R.*, XL (November, 1971), which shows that the Russian traders were dependent on those from New England for supplies. John A. Harrison, *The Founding of the Russian Empire in Asia and America* (Miami, 1971), adds little to the story told in Donald W. Treadgold, *The Great Siberian Migration* (Princeton, 1957). That the American traders looked down on the Chinese with whom they dealt rather than being awed by their cultural heritage is shown in Stuart C. Miller, "The American Trader's Image of China, 1785–1840," *P.H.R.*, XXXVI (November, 1967)..

Early trade between Santa Fe and California is expertly described in David J. Weber, *The Taos Trappers: The Fur Trader in the Far Southwest, 1540–1846* (Norman, 1971). Particular aspects are touched upon in Alice B. Maloney, "The Richard Campbell Party of 1827," *C.H.S.Q.*, XVIII (December, 1939), and Eleanor Lawrence, "Mexican Trade between Santa Fe and Los Angeles, 1830–1848," *C.H.S.Q.*, X (March, 1931). Documents are in LeRoy R. Hafen and Ann W. Hafen, eds., *Old Spanish Trail: Santa Fé to Los Angeles* (Glendale, 1954).

The early fur traders are described in Hiram M. Chittenden, *The American Fur Trade in the Far West*, 3 v. (rev. edn., New York, 1935), David J. Wishart, *The Fur Trade of the American West, 1807–1840: A Geographical Synthesis* (Lincoln, 1979), and especially Robert G. Cleland, *This Reckless Breed of Men: The Trappers and Fur Traders of the Southwest* (New York, 1950). James Ohio Pattie, *The Personal Narrative of James O. Pattie of Kentucky* (Cincinnati, 1831, and later edns.), is colorful rather than reliable. Pattie's tales of inoculating the Indians against smallpox have been debunked in Rosemary K. Valle, "James Ohio Pattie and the 1827–1828 Alta California Measles Epidemic," *C.H.S.Q.*, LII (Spring, 1973), and Robert J. Moes, "Smallpox Immunization in Alta California: A Story Based on José Estrad's 1821 Postscript," *S.C.Q.*, LXI (Summer, 1979), showing that inoculation was common after 1821 when it was first used by a Russian doctor there. On the important exploration of Jedediah Smith the classic work is Dale L. Morgan, *Jedediah Smith and the Opening of the West* (Indianapolis, 1953). Documents describing Smith's California journeys are in Harrison C. Dale, ed., *The Ashley-Smith Explorations and the Discovery of the Central Route to the Pacific, 1822–1829* (Cleveland, 1919), Maurice S. Sullivan, ed., *The Travels of Jedediah Smith* (Santa Ana, 1934), Dale Morgan, ed., *The West of William H. Ashley* (Denver, 1964), and especially George R. Brooks, ed., *The Southwest Expedition of Jedediah S. Smith: His Personal Account of the Journey to California, 1826–1827* (Glendale, 1977). The last is a newly discovered journal kept by Smith. A popular history of Smith's California explorations is Alston J. Smith, *Men Against the Mountains: Jedediah Smith and the South West Expedition of 1826–1829* (New York, 1965). An able biography of an early California trader is Douglas S. Watson, *West Wind: The Life of Joseph Reddeford Walker* (Los Angeles, 1934), while Robert V. Hine, *Edward Kern and American Expansion* (New Haven, 1962), tells the story of an American artist who visited California with one of Frémont's expeditions.

California Life at the Close of the Mexican Era. The efforts of the Franciscan president of the missions to care for his Indian charges after secularization is shown in Michael C. Neri, "Narciso Durán and the Secularization of the California Mission," *Am.*, XXXIII (January, 1977), while Daniel Garr, "Planning, Politics, and Plunder: The Missions and Indian Pueblos of Hispanic California," *S.C.Q.*, LIV (Winter, 1972), describes efforts to turn missions into urban units after secularization.

Social conditions in California during its

so-called "Pastoral Period" between 1821 and 1846 are delightfully described in Nellie V. Sánchez, *Spanish Arcadia* (Los Angeles, 1929); the lack of democratic institutions during that era is discussed in Francis M. Guest, "Municipal Government in California," *C.H.S.Q.*, XLVI (December, 1967). That the American image of the Californios as lazy was not solely due to nationalistic prejudice but was held by Russian, French, and even Spanish visitors is shown in David L. Langum, "Californios and the Image of Indolence," *We.H.Q.*, IX (April, 1978). That Los Angeles was a trade center, not a sleepy village, by 1822 is argued in Howard J. Nelson, "The Two Pueblos of Los Angeles: Agricultural Village and Embryo Town," *S.C.Q.*, LIX (Spring, 1977). A history of one group of twenty-two Mexicans who settled near Fort Ross in 1834 is told in A. Alan Hutchinson, *Frontier Settlement in Mexican California: The Híjar-Padrés Colony, and Its Origins, 1769–1835* (New Haven, 1969).

Material on Americans who settled in California before the overland migrations began may be found in Doyce B. Nunis, Jr., *The Trials of Isaac Graham* (Los Angeles, 1967), which is actually a fine biography; George D. Lyman, *John Marsh, Pioneer* (New York, 1930), Reuben L. Underhill, *From Cowhide to Golden Fleece* (Stanford, 1939), a biography of Thomas O. Larkin, Sheldon G. Jackson, *A British Ranchero in Old California: The Life and Times of Henry Dalton and the Rancho Azusa* (Glendale, 1977), and Richard Dillon, *Fool's Gold: A Biography of John Sutter* (New York, 1967). The latter, although making no pretense of original scholarship, is based on the latest findings and must be rated the best available study of Sutter. John A. Hawgood, "John Augustus Sutter: A Reappraisal," *A. and W.*, IV (Winter, 1962), is an excellent pen portrait. Documents are in George P. Hammond, ed., *The Larkin Papers*, 10 v. (Berkeley, 1951–64), John A. Hawgood, ed., *First and Last Consul. Thomas Oliver Larkin and the Americanization of California* (2nd edn., Palo Alto, 1970), and Douglas S. Watson, ed., *The Diary of Johann Augustus Sutter* (San Francisco, 1932). William H. Davis, *Seventy-Five Years in California* (San Francisco, 1929), is valuable.

The Overland Migrations. Popular, but sparklingly written and based on research, is George R. Stewart, *The California Trail: An Epic with Many Heroes* (New York, 1962). Essential also is the monumental history of the overland trails by John D. Unruh, Jr., *The Plains Across: The Overland Emigrants and the Trans-Mississippi West, 1840–1860* (Urbana, 1979). Harlan Hague, *The Road to Cal-*

ifornia: The Search for a Southern Overland Route, 1540–1848 (Glendale, 1978), describes the attempts to open the southern route from the earliest days to the Gold Rush. A detailed study of the eastern portion of the trail and the parties that followed it is Merrill J. Mattes, *The Great Platte River Road: The Covered Wagon Mainline via Fort Kearny to Fort Laramie* (Lincoln, 1969), while Louise Barry, *The Beginnings of the West: Annals of the Kansas Gateway to the American West, 1540–1854* (Topeka, 1972) lists every party that crossed the state.

Doyce B. Nunis, Jr., "California Why We Came: Myth or Reality," *C.H.S.Q.*, XLIV (June, 1965), discusses the literature that has helped promote migration to California. A graphic account of the adventures of the first overland party to reach California is in the biography of its leader: Rockwell D. Hunt, *John Bidwell, A Prince of California Pioneers* (Caldwell, 1942). Bidwell's own account has been reprinted as John Bidwell, *Journey to California* (San Francisco, 1937). George R. Stewart, ed., *The Opening of the California Trail* (Berkeley, 1953), contains the records of the leading immigrant party of 1844, while the chronicler of an important group of 1846 was Edwin Bryant, *What I saw in California* (Santa Ana, 1936). Nearly all contemporary records and reminiscences concerning the tragic Donner party are in Charles F. McGlashan, *History of the Donner Party* (latest edn., Standord, 1947). An excellent modern study is George R. Stewart, *Ordeal by Hunger. The Story of the Donner Party* (rev. edn., Boston, 1960). That the party was warned not to take the trail that led to its tragedy is shown in Albert Shumate, "A Note on the Donner Party Tragedy," *Pac.H.*, XXIII (Spring, 1979). A revisionist article by Thomas F. Andrews, "Lansford W. Hastings and the Promotion of the Salt Lake Desert Cutoff: A Reappraisal," *We.H.Q.*, IV (April, 1973), shows that the Donners did not take the Hastings Cutoff because of the guidebook, as often stated, but due to other advice. The same author expertly examines Hastings' career in "The Ambitions of Lansford W. Hastings: A Study in Western Myth-Making," *P.H.R.*, XXXIX (November, 1970), and "The Controversial Hastings Overland Guide: A Reassessment," *P.H.R.*, XXXVII (February, 1968); the former shows that he had no intention of becoming the "Sam Houston of California," and the latter that his guidebook, while erroneous, was no worse than others issued at the same time.

American Acquisition of California. The standard work on the growth of annexation sentiment in the United States is Robert G.

Cleland, "The Early Sentiment for the Annexation of California: An Account of the Growth of American Interest in California, 1835–1846," *S.H.Q.*, XVIII (July, 1914 to January, 1915). E. D. Adams, "English Interest in the Annexation of California," *A.H.R.*, XIV (July, 1909), shows that American fears of English annexation were groundless. That they existed was due in part to the outspoken statements by the British consul in California, Alexander Forbes, *California: A History of Upper and Lower California* (London, 1839). The elevation of Forbes to his post is described in A. P. Nasatir, "International Rivalry for California and the Establishment of the British Consulate," *C.H.S.Q.*, XLVI (March, 1967). That large numbers of British nationals, many of them Irish, did live in southern California is demonstrated by Robert A. Burchell, "British Immigrants in Southern California, 1850–1870," *S.C.Q.*, LIII (December, 1971). Sheldon G. Jackson, "Two Pro-British Plots in Alta California," *S.C.Q.*, LV (Summer, 1973), and "The British and the California Dream: Rumors, Myths and Legends," *S.C.Q.*, LVII (Fall, 1975), demonstrate that while the British government had no interest in California a number of private promoters hatched schemes to add it to the empire. John A. Hawgood describes an abortive German plan to buy California in 1842 in "A Projected Prussian Colonization of Upper California," *S.C.Q.*, XLVIII (December, 1966), while A. P. Nasatir, "French Activities in California before Statehood," *A.H.A., Pacific Coast Branch, Proceedings*, III (1928), explores the fears aroused by alleged French designs on the region. Standard diplomatic accounts are in Eugene I. McCormac, *James K. Polk: A Political Biography* (Berkeley, 1922), and especially Charles Sellers, *James K. Polk, Constitutionalist, 1843–1846* (Princeton, 1966). Norman Graebner, *Empire on the Pacific* (New York, 1955), argues that eastern commercial interests were primarily responsible for the demand for both California and Oregon; he is answered in Shomer S. Zwelling, *Expansion and Imperialism* (Chicago, 1970).

Society in Transition. Theodore Grivas, *Military Governments in California, 1846–1850* (Glendale, 1963), is concerned with the adjustment of govenmental agencies to the new regime, while the manner in which these agencies stimulated economic activity is discussed in Gerald D. Nash, *State Government and Economic Development: A History of Administration Policies in California, 1849–1933* (Berkeley, 1964), while religious readjustments are the theme of Michael C. Neri,

"González Rubio and California Catholicism, 1846–1850," *S.C.Q.*, LVIII (Winter, 1976), a history of the diocesan administrator during the transition, and John B. McGloin, *Jesuits by the Golden Gate: The Society of Jesus in San Francisco, 1849–1969* (San Francisco, 1972). The effect of the change on several types of communities is studied in Mary Tucey and David Hornbeck, "Anglo Immigration and the Hispanic Town: A Study of Urban Change in Monterey, California, 1835–1850," *S.S.J.*, XIII (April, 1976), Daniel J. Garr, "Los Angeles and the Challenge of Urban Growth, 1835–1849," *S.C.Q.*, LXX (Summer, 1979), and particularly Roger W. Lotchin, *San Francisco, 1846–1856: From Hamlet to City* (New York, 1974). Kevin Starr, *Americans and the California Dream, 1850–1915* (New York, 1973), is a brilliant social and intellectual history. The opening chapters of Douglas H. Daniels, *Pioneer Urbanites: A Social and Cultural History of Black San Francisco* (Philadelphia, 1980), and Robert L. Carlton, "Blacks in San Diego County: A Social Profile, 1850–1880," *J.S.D.H.*, XXI (Fall, 1895), are sound introductions to the important study of blacks in the state. Christiane Fischer, "Women in California in the early 1850s," *S.C.Q.*, LX (Fall, 1978), is a pioneering investigation of another neglected subject. Leonard Pitt, *The Decline of the Californios: A Social History of the Spanish-American Californians, 1846–1890* (Berkeley, 1966), deals expertly with the passing of a prominent group, although Charles Hughes, "The Decline of the Californios: The Case of San Diego, 1848–1856," *J.S.D.H.*, XXI (Summer, 1975), shows that in that area the "arcadian era" of the 1846–1856 period described by Pitt did not develop. That literacy varied with the ethnic background in Los Angeles just after American acquisition is demonstrated in Michael Weiss, "Education, Literacy and the Community of Los Angeles in 1850," *S.C.Q.*, LX (Summer, 1978). The impact of the early governors on society is the theme of Benjamin F. Gilbert, *The Governors of California* (Georgetown, 1965).

The transition of California from Mexican to American rule gave rise to a variety of problems concerning land ownership. These are admirably described in Paul W. Gates, *California Ranchos and Farms, 1846–1862* (Madison, 1968), and in several important articles: "Pre-Henry George Land Warfare in California," *C.H.S.Q.*, XLVI (June, 1967), dealing with conflicts between squatters and speculators for land, "The Fremont-Jones Scramble for California Land Claims," *S.C.Q.*, LVI (Spring, 1974), which describes the scramble among politicians for 813 Mexican land claims, "The Land Business of Thomas O. Larkin," *C.H.S.Q.*, LIV (Winter, 1975), showing that Larkin was involved in many land deals, and "Carpetbaggers Join the Rush for California Land," *C.H.S.Q.*, LVI (Summer, 1977), revealing that American military, naval, and political leaders were able to secure vast acreages. Gordon M. Bakken, "The Development of Landlord and Tenant Law in Frontier California, 1850–1865," *Pa.H.*, XXXI analyzes sixty legal cases dealing with landlord-tenant relations, while the broader legal implications are discussed in Richard R. Powell, *Compromises and Conflicting Claims: A Century of California Law, 1760–1860* (Dobbs Ferry, 1977). The career of a surveyor who marked out many of the claims in preparation for the American take-over is surveyed in Geoffrey P. Mawn, " 'Agrimensor y Arquitecto': Jasper O'Farrell's Surveying in Mexican California," LVI (Spring, 1974). The career of a leading politician active in the transition to American rule is David A. Williams, *David C. Broderick: A Political Portrait* (San Marino, 1969).

26 Conquest and Controversy, 1846–1850

American-Mexican Relations. Essential background for understanding the outbreak of war is Frederick Merk, *The Monroe Doctrine and American expansion* (New York, 1966), which shows that Tyler and Polk mirrored the national viewpoint when maintaining that expansion was necessary to secure the national interest. Relations between the two countries are described in Karl M. Schmitt, *Mexico and the United States, 1821–1973* (New York, 1974), which is brief on this period, but competent. Such older works as George L. Rives, *The United States and Mexico, 1821–1848*, 2 v. (New York, 1913), provide details but little adequate interpretation. This is supplied in the best biography of the President, Charles G. sellers, Jr., *James K. Polk, Constitution—1843–1846* (Princeton, 1966), and in the competent study of annexation by DAvid M. Pletcher, *The Diplomacy of Annexation: Texas, Oregon, and the Mexican War* (Columbia, 1973). Charles A. McCoy, *Polk and the Presidency* (Austin, 1960), examines the internal policies and conflicts of the Polk administration, while Claude H. Hall, *Abel Parker Upshur: Conservative Virginian, 1790–1844* (Madison, 1963), is the biography of his secretary of state. Polk's papers will eventually

appear in Herbert Weaver and Paul H. Bergeron, Eds., *The Correspondence of James K. Polk* (Nashville, 1969—).

A number of brief histories of the war have been published in recent years. The best of these is K. Jack Bauer, *The Mexican War, 1846–1848* (New York, 1974), which is excellent on the military campaigns. Readable also is John E. Weems, *To Conquer a Peace: The War Between the United States and Mexico* (Garden City, 1974), which considers the campaigns in terms of ten military leaders. Ronnie C. Tyler, *The Mexican War: A Lithographic Record* (Austin, 1974), reproduces forty-nine illustrations. Useful also are Otis A. Singletary, *The Mexican War* (Chicago, 1960), Charles L. Dufour, *The Mexican War: A Compact History, 1846–1848* (New York, 1968), and Seymour V. Connor and Odie B. Faulk, *North America Divided: The Mexican War, 1846–1848* (New York, 1971).

Causes of the Mexican War. Few subjects have been so vigorously debated among historians. The traditional nineteenth-century view—that the war was a product of southerners' desire for more slave territory—was first challenged by Justin H. Smith, *The War with Mexico*, 2 v. (New York, 1919), Smith's thesis, that Mexican inefficiency justified war on the part of the United States, has been modified by later scholars studying specific phases of the problem. H. Donaldson Jordan, "A Politician of Expansion: Robert J. Walker," *M.V.H.R.*, XIX (December, 1932), holds Polk and his cabinet at least as responsible as Mexico. Richard R. Stenberg, "The Failure of Polk's Mexican War Intrigue of 1845," *P.H.R.*, IV (March, 1935), goes beyond by charging that Polk tried to precipitate the war in 1845. This same thesis is argued with little success in Glenn W. Price, *Origins of the War with Mexico: The Polk–Stockton Intrigue* (Austin, 1967). Neither Stenberg nor Price have been able to locate evidence for their views, which rest on conjecture. More responsible historians have suggested that neither the traditional interpretation nor that of Justin Smith was adequate, finding instead that a variety of factors operated. In a challenging study, Frederick Merk, *Manifest Destiny and Mission in American History: A Reinterpretation* (New York, 1963), suggests that historians have overemphasized the strength of expansionist sentiment, and that "manifest destiny" was not the force they have assumed. William H. Goetzmann, *When the Eagle Screamed: The Romantic Horizon in American Diplomacy, 1800–1860* (New York, 1966), stresses the role of the romantic impulse in expansionist sentiment and argues that expansionism was the product of a variety of external pressures.

More recently historians have sharply divided in assessing blame. One school holds Mexico primarily responsible, stressing the disorders that prevented its complying with proper standards of international behavior. Prominent in this group are Connor and Faulk cited above, and Sanford H. Montaige, *Blood Over Texas* (New Rochelle, 1976). Others see the war as the product of a variety of factors. Gene M. Brack, *Mexico Views Manifest Destiny, 1821–1846: An Essay on the Origins of the Mexican War* (Albuquerque, 1976), in a heavily documented study, asserts that Mexican fear of cultural extinction at the hands of the United States inclined that nation to take up arms. That Polk was forced to take up arms by the failure of the missions that he sent to Mexico, and that he desired peace, is the theme of Ward McAfee, "A Reconsideration of the Origin of the Mexican-American War," *S.C.Q.*, LXII (Spring, 1980); on the opposite side Ramón E. Ruiz, "A Commentary on Morality: Lincoln, Justin H. Smith, and the Mexican War," *J.I.S.H.S.*, LXIX (February, 1976), holds that Polk goaded Mexico into war with his policy on the Mexican boundary. William H. Mullins, "The British Press and the Mexican War: Justin Smith Revised," *N.M.H.R.*, LII (July, 1977), presents substantial evidence to show that Justin Smith was wrong when he pictured the British press as strongly anti-American on the war issues, while Raymund A. Paredes, "The Mexican Image in American Travel Literature, 1831–1869," *N.M.H.R.*, LII (January, 1977), shows that the image of the Mexicans as indolent and inefficient contributed to American desires for the country. Two extremely helpful articles that survey this recent literature and add important contributions are Benjamin Tomas, "Recent Historiography of the Origins of the Mexican War," *N.M.H.R.*, LIV (July, 1979), and Norman A. Graebner, "The Mexican War: A Study in Causation," *P.H.R.*, XLIX (August, 1980). Somewhat less current, but still valuable, is Peter T. Harstad and Richard W. Resh, "The Causes of the Mexican War: A Note on Changing Interpretations," *A. and W.*, VI (Winter, 1964). Earlier American expeditions into Mexico that inflamed that country against the United States are described in Charles H. Brown, *Agents of Manifest Destiny: The Lives and Times of the Filibusters* (Chapel Hill, 1980).

American Opinion and the Mexican War. The traditional view that southerners and Democrats favored the war while Whigs and northerners were opposed has been subjected to rigid scrutiny in recent historical studies. A general study of the subject that summarizes many of the findings is in John H. Schroeder, *Mr. Polk's War: American Opposition and Dissent, 1846–1848* (Madison, 1973). National opinion as measured in Congress is studied in such works as John R. Collins, "The Mexican War: A Study in Fragmentation," *J.W.*, XI (April, 1972), an analysis of roll-call votes showing that the war promoted sectional divisions rather than being caused by them, and G. S. Borit, "Lincoln's Opposition to the Mexican War," *J.I.S.H.S.*, LXVII (February, 1974), which shows that Lincoln's popularity in Illinois was not significantly lessened by his opposition to the war. Northern opinion is also tested in David L. Paulus, "Rhode Island and the Mexican War," *R.I.H.*, XXXVII (August, 1978), which finds opposition mounting steadily, and Hal W. Bochin, "Caleb Smith's Opposition to the Mexican War," *I.M.H.*, LXIX (1973), picturing an Indiana politician as walking a middle road to continued popularity. Opinion in the Old Northwest is carefully weighed in Norman E. Turorow, *Texas Annexation and the Mexican War: A Political Study of the Old Northwest* (Palo Alto, 1978).

Similar studies have also revealed the divisions in the southern states. B. H. Gilley, " 'Polk's War' and the Louisiana Press," *L.H.*, XX (Winter, 1979), shows that the war lost popularity in that state during its course, while Royce C. McCrary, "Georgia Politics and the Mexican War," *G.H.Q.*, LX (Fall, 1976), is a careful examination of the way in which Whigs and Democrats used the war to their own advantages. An important study of opinion in South Carolina is Ernest M. Lander, Jr., *Reluctant Imperialists: Calhoun, the South Carolinians, and the Mexican War* (Baton Rouge, 1980).

California and the Bear Flag Revolt. All histories of California cited earlier deal extensively with the Bear Flag Revolt. Frémont's role is assessed in Allan Nevins, *Frémont: Pathmarker of the West* (New York, 1939) and Ferol Egan, *Frémont: Explorer for a Restless Nation* (New York, 1977), the latter a popular biography that adds a few new materials. A fine account of his role is also in the introductions to Mary Lee Spence, and Donald Jackson, eds., *The Expeditions of John Charles Frémont. Vol. II The Bear Flag Revolt and the Court Martial* (Urbana, 1973). The future careers of three of his fellow explorers are described in Harvey L. Carter, "The Divergent Paths of Frémont's 'Three Marshals'," *N.M.H.R.*, XLVIII (January, 1973). Historians have been unable to agree on whether

Frémont knowingly precipiated the revolt. Ernest A. Wiltsee, *The Truth About Frémont: An Inquiry* (San Francisco, 1936), and Richard R. Stenberg, "Polk and Frémont, 1845–1846," *P.H.R.*, VII (September, 1938), hold that he acted on secret instructions from Polk; more convincing is the opposite conclusion reached by George Tays, "Frémont Had No Secret Instructions," *P.H.R.*, IX (June, 1940), and John A. Hussey, "The Origin of the Gillespie Mission," *C.H.S.Q.*, XIX (March, 1940). Additional light is thrown on the problem, which is probably insoluble, in a competent biography of the officer who delivered messages to Frémont: Werner H. Marti, *Messenger of Destiny: The California Adventures, 1846–1847, of Archibald H. Gillespie, U.S. Marine Corps* (San Francisco, 1960). The laudatory history of a leading Californian is Myrtle M. McKittrick, *Vallejo, Son of California* (Portland, 1944). Lawrence C. Allin, "Log of Conquest," *P.H.R.*, XXXVIII (May, 1968), shows that Commodore Jones stayed thirty-two days in Monterey after his premature capture of that town to prevent reprisals against Americans in the city. Two aspects of the military phase of the Bear Flag Revolt are treated in Sally C. Johns, "Viva Los Californios! The Battle of San Pasqual," *J.S.D.H.*, XIX (Fall, 1973), and Donald C. Biggs, *Conquer and Colonize: Stevenson's Regiment and California* (San Rafael, 1977), the latter the history of a regiment raised in New York by Colonel Jonathan D. Stevenson to fight in California. The introduction to Doyce B. Nunis, ed., *The Mexican War in Baja California: The Memorandum of Captain Henry W. Halleck Concerning His Expeditions in Lower California, 1846–1848* (Los Angeles, 1977), is the best history of the war in Lower California.

The Military Phase. The several histories of the war cited earlier have solid descriptions of the military campaigns. The best biography of the Mexican commander is Oakah L. Jones, Jr., *Santa Anna* (New York, 1968), a revisionist work that shows Santa Anna as generally a patriot and always a product of his background. For the two American leaders the student may consult: Holman Hamilton, *Zachary Taylor* (New York, 1942), Silas B. McKinley and Silas Bent, *Old Rough and Ready: The Life and Times of Zachary Taylor* (New York, 1946), Brainerd Dyer, *Zachary Taylor* (Baton Rouge, 1946), Arthur D. H. Smith, *Old Fuss and Feathers: The Life and Exploits of Lt.-General Winfield Scott* (New York, 1937), and Charles W. Elliott, *Winfield Scott: The Soldier and the Man* (New York, 1937). Charles P. Roland, *Albert Sidney Johnson: Soldier of Three Republics* (Austin, 1964),

describes the military exploits of a Texan volunteer commander at the Battle of Monterey; an excellent biography of another professional soldier who fought with General Taylor is Grady McWhiney, *Braxton Bragg and Confederate Defeat. Volume I, Field Command* (New York, 1969). Particularly valuable is the excellent biography of the commander of the Army of the West, Dwight L. Clarke, *Stephen Watts Kearny: Soldier of the West* (Norman, 1961).

Special studies deal with aspects of the American campaigns. George M. Brooke, Jr., "The Vest Pocket War of Commodore Jones," *P.H.R.*, XXXI (August, 1962), capably describes the ill-timed attack of Jones on Monterey, while William H. Ellison, "San Juan to Cahuenga: The Experiences of Frémont's Battalion," *P.H.R.*, XXVII (August, 1958), is a clear account of Frémont's role in the suppression of the uprising in the southern part of the region. A detailed treatment of one aspect of Frémont's campaign is John D. Tanner, Jr., "Campaign for Los Angeles—December 29, 1846, to January 10, 1847," *C.H.S.Q.*, XLVIII (September, 1969). The story of the recruitment and services of a unit active in California is in W. Ray Luce, "The Mormon Battalion: A Historical Accident?" *U.H.Q.*, XLII (Winter, 1974). That Mexico's Indian policy was so faulty that New Mexico was left with little defense is shown in Daniel Tyler, "Mexican Indian Policy in New Mexico," *N.M.H.R.*, LV (April, 1980). The role of Apache and other Indians in weakening northern Mexico is the theme of Ralph A. Smith, "Indians in American-Mexican Relations before the War of 1846," *H.A.H.R.*, XLIII (February, 1963). Two studies throw light on Doniphan's expedition: Ralph A. Smith, "The 'King of New Mexico' and the Doniphan Expedition," *N.M.H.Q.*, XXXVIII (January, 1963), which describes the exploits of James Kirker who served as scout for Doniphan, and Thomas L. Karnes, "Gilpin's Volunteers on the Santa Fe Trail," *K.H.Q.*, XXX (Spring, 1964), which explains the role of Doniphan's men after returning from Mexico.

Articles dealing with the Army of the West and the occupation of New Mexico include Daniel Tyler, "Gringo Views of Governor Manuel Armijo," *N.M.H.R.*, XLV (January, 1970), which proves that American traders who saw the governor as a cowardly and inefficient tyrant were wrong; George W. Smith and Charles Judah, "Manifest Destiny: War in the West," *N.M.Q.*, XXXVIII (Spring, 1968), describing Kearny's entrance into Santa Fe; Frank McNitt, "Navaho Campaigns and the Occupation of New Mexico, 1847–1848,"

N.M.H.R., XLIII (July, 1968), describing attacks on the army of occupation by Indians; Lawrence R. Murphy, "The United States Army in Taos, 1847–1852," *N.M.H.R.*, XLVII (January, 1972), on the Taos Rebellion and the American effort to restore order over the next years; and Lee Myers, "Illinois Volunteers in New Mexico, 1847–1848," *N.M.H.R.*, dealing with an Illinois force that took over guard duty at Taos after the rebellion there.

A thorough and delightful history of General Taylor's campaigns in northern Mexico is David Lavender, *Climax at Buena Vista. The American Campaigns in Northeastern Mexico, 1846–1847* (Philadelphia, 1966). A controversy growing out of the retreat of an Indiana regiment at the Battle of Buena Vista is thoroughly explored In Herman J. Viola, "Zachary Taylor and the Indiana Volunteers," *S.H.Q.*, LXXII (January, 1969). The internal factionalism that allowed General Scott to take Mexico City is admirably described in Dennis E. Berge, "A Mexican Dilema: The Mexico City Ayuntamiento and the Question of Loyalty, 1846–1848," *H.A.H.R.*, L (May, 1970). Henry O. Whiteside, "Winfield Scott and the Mexican Occupation: Policy and Practice," *M.A.*, LII (April, 1970), describes Scott's successful effort to devise a policy that would end the war rapidly without alienating the inhabitants.

The naval history of the war is told in K. Jack Bauer, *Surfboats and Horse Marines: U.S. Naval Operations in the Mexican War, 1846–1848* (Annapolis, 1969), and Samuel E. Morison, *'Old Bruin': Commander Matthew C. Perry, 1794–1858* (Boston, 1967), a superior biography of the commander of the American forces in the Gulf of Mexico.

Henry W. Barton, "Five Texas Frontier Companies during the Mexican War," *S.H.Q.*, LXVI (July, 1962), sheds light on the operations of the volunteer system for raising troops, while Thomas M. Davies, Jr., "Assessments During the Mexican War: An Exercise in Futility," *N.M.H.R.*, XLI (July, 1966), reveals the failure of an attempt to pay for the war by levies against Mexican business men and industries. The unpopularity of the war nationally is the theme of Frederick Merk, "Dissent in the Mexican War," *M.H.S., Proceedings*, LXXXI (1969), and its popularity in the South in Robert A. Brent, "Mississippi and the Mexican War," *J.M.H.*, XXXI (August, 1969).

A number of soldier's letters have been collected in George W. Smith and Charles Judah, eds., *Chronicles of the Gringos: The U.S. Army in the Mexican War, 1846–1848* (Albuquerque, 1968). Other important collections,

all well edited, are Ralph P. Bieber, ed., *Marching With the Army of the West, 1846–1848* (Glendale, 1936), and Ralph P. Bieber, ed., *Exploring Southwestern Trails, 1846–1854* (Glendale, 1938). Journals of individual soldiers or officers who provide particularly good pictures of the times are: Ross Calvin, ed., *Lieutenant Emory Reports* (Albuquerque, 1951), Dwight L. Clarke, ed., *The Original Journals of Henry Smith Turner with Stephen Watts Kearny to New Mexico and California, 1846* (Norman, 1966), John Galvin, ed., *Western America in 1846–1847. The Original Travel Diary of Lieutenant J. W. Abert* (San Francisco, 1966), and Robert V. Hine and Savoie Lottinville, eds., *Soldier in the West: Letters of Theodore Talbot During His Services in California, Mexico and Oregon, 1845–53* (Norman, 1972). Most of the latter deals with experiences under Frémont and in the California campaigns. The memoirs of two men who later attained fame are: William S. Myers, ed., *The Mexican War Diary of George B. McClellan* (Princeton, 1917), and T. Harry Williams, ed., *With Beauregard in Mexico: The Mexican War Reminiscences of P.G.T. Beauregard* (Baton Rouge, 1956).

The Diplomacy of the War and Peace. The standard account is Jesse S. Reeves, *American Diplomacy under Tyler and Polk* (Baltimore, 1907), an older work that has never been completely replaced, but should be supplemented by special studies that deal with aspects of the problems. Jack Northrup, "The Trist Mission," *J.M.A.H.*, III (1973), capably describes the negotiations between Scott, Trist, and Santa Anna, while two articles illuminate further: Thomas J. Farnham, "Nicholas Trist & James Freaner and the Mission to Mexico," *A. and W.*, XI (Autumn, 1969), and Jack Nortrup, "Nicholas Trist's Mission to Mexico: A Reinterpretation," *S.H.Q.*, LXXI (January, 1968); the former shows that Trist's decision to ignore his recall was influenced by Freaner, a newspaperman; the latter that Trist's blunders resulted in a far worse and more costly treaty than the United States could have negotiated. That Polk's peace efforts were frustrated by the ability of the press to reveal his secret designs is shown in Anna K. Nelson, "Secret Agents and Security Leaks: President Polk and the Mexican War," *J.Q.*, LII (Spring, 1975). Reginald Horsman, "Scientific Racism and the American Indian in the Mid-Nineteenth Century," *A.Q.*, XXVII (May, 1975), demonstrates that the image of the Indian created by scientists was of such an inferior race that some statesmen hesitated to acquire the Mexican territories with their native populations. Polk is shown to have welcomed the treaty, faulty as it was, to end a war that had created so many dilemmas for his administration in Norman A. Graebner, "Lessons of the Mexican War," *P.H.R.*, XLVII (August, 1978). The standard work on changing American sentiment toward Mexico during the war is John D. P. Fuller, *The Movement for the Acquisition of All Mexico, 1846–1848* (Baltimore, 1938). Divided attitudes on expansion in the South are examined in John Hope Franklin, "The Southern Expansionists of 1846," *J.S.H.*, XXV (August, 1959), while Eugene K. Chamberlin, "Nicholas Trist and Baja California," *P.H.R.*, XXXII (February, 1963), shows that the United States could have obtained Lower California if Trist had obeyed his instructions. Problems created by the treaty are discussed in Donald E. Cutter, "The Legacy of the Treaty of Guadalupe Hidalgo," *N.M.H.R.*, LIII (October, 1978), and Van Hastings Garner, "The Treaty of Guadalupe Hidalgo and the California Indians," *I.H.*, IX (Winter, 1976). The chaotic situation in New Mexico following the treaty is well described in Alvin R. Sunseri, *Seeds of Discord: New Mexico in the Aftermath of the American Conquest, 1846–1861* (Chicago, 1979), and in Paul Horgan, *Lamy of Santa Fe* (New York, 1975), a brilliant biography of Bishop Juan Bautista Lamy who took office in 1850. That the 1848 treaty did not quiet the expansionist urge is shown in Howard I. Kushner, "Visions of the Northwest Coast: Gwin and Seward in the 1850s," *We.H.Q.*, IV (July, 1973).

The thorough study of the Gadsden Purchase by Paul N. Garber, *The Gadsden Treaty* (Philadelphia, 1923), may be supplemented with J. Fred Rippy, "The Negotiation of the Gadsden Treaty," *S.H.Q.*, XXVII (July, 1923). Joseph F. Park, "The Apaches in Mexican-American Relations, 1846–1861: A Footnote to the Gadsden Treaty," *A. and W.*, III (Summer, 1961), demonstrates that American failure to stop Apache raids into Mexico after 1848 was responsible for certain clauses in the treaty. A detailed history of the boundary surveys that followed the Mexican War is in Odie B. Faulk, "The Controversial Boundary Survey and the Gadsden Treaty," *A. and W.*, IV (Autumn, 1962), showing that the Gadsden Treaty was necessary to rectify their mistakes.

Odie B. Faulk, *Too Far North . . . Too Far South* (Los Angeles, 1967), is a history of the commission that between 1848 and 1853 ran the boundary line agreed upon in the Treaty of Guadaloupe Hidalgo. A biography of the principal commissioner is Robert V. Hine, *Bartlett's West: Drawing the Mexican Boundary* (New Haven, 1968); the commis-

sioner's own account of the expedition is in John R. Bartlett, *Personal Narrative of Explorations and Incidents in Texas, New Mexico, California, Sonora, and Chihuahua*, 2 v. (Chicago, 1965).

The Origins of the Slavery Controversy. The question of slavery in the territories acquired from Mexico began to stir the nation even before the Treaty of Guadaloupe Hidalgo was signed. Kinley J. Brauer, *Cotton versus Conscience: Massachusetts Whig Politics and Southwestern Expansion, 1843–1848* (Lexington, 1967), analyzes that conflict between the Cotton and Conscience Whigs of Massachusetts as the latter moved into the Free Soil Party. That Taylor was the Whig candidate in the 1848 election was due to the need of the Whigs to win crucial areas in the South is argued in Brian G. Walton, "The Elections for the Thirtieth Congress and the Presidential Candidacy of Zachary Taylor," *J.S.H.*, XXXV (May, 1969). The natural conflict between "Free Soilers" and proponents of manifest destiny is explored in Major L. Wilson, "Manifest Destiny and Free Soil: The Triumph of Negative Liberalism in the 1840s," *H.*, XXXI (November, 1968), and Major L. Wilson, "The Free Soil Concept of Progress and the Irrepressible Conflict," *A.Q.*, XXII (Winter, 1970).

The origins of the Wilmot Proviso are considered in Charles B. Going, *David Wilmot, Free Soiler* (New York, 1924). Chaplain W. Morrison, *Democratic Politics and Sectionalism: The Wilmot Proviso Controversy* (Chapel Hill, 1967), holds that the Proviso resulted from conflicts within the Democratic Party and the need of the Van Burenites to strengthen their position in the party councils. Eric Foner, "The Wilmot Proviso Revisited," *J.A.H.*, LVI (September, 1969), agrees that Democratic divisions underlay the measure, but holds that the Van Burenites were trying to protect themselves in face of the growing antislavery sentiment in their own constituencies. The constitutional arguments used are weighed in Jesse T. Carpenter, *The South as a Conscious Minority, 1789–1861* (New York, 1930). The part of the Free Soil Party in the elections of 1848 is treated in Joseph G. Rayback, *Free Soil: The Election of 1848* (Lexington, 1970), a scholarly study.

The best study of the Compromise of 1850 is Holman Hamilton, *Prologue to Conflict: The Crisis and Compromise of 1850* (Lexington, 1964). The role of Stephen A. Douglas in drafting the compromise measures is explained in an excellent biography by Robert W. Johannsen, *Stephen A. Douglas* (New York, 1973), while the same author has edited important documents in *The Letters of Stephen A. Douglas* (Urbana, 1961). Two other biographies that shed light on the compromise are Gerald M. Capers, *John C. Calhoun—Opportunist: A Reappraisal* (Gainesville, 1960), and Robert J. Rayback, *Millard Fillmore: Biography of a President* (Buffalo, 1959). Information will also be found in biographies of Henry Clay, and especially George R. Poage, *Henry Clay and the Whig Party* (Chapel Hill, 1936). Holman Hamilton, "Texas Bonds and Northern Profits: A Study in Compromise, Investment, and Lobby Influence," *M.V.H.R.,* XLIII (March, 1957), presents convincing proof that Texan bondholders helped lobby the Compromise through Congress, while the same author's "The 'Cave of the Winds' and the Compromise of 1850," *J.S.H.,* XXIII (August, 1957), is the best analysis of the actual votes on the measure. Southern reaction to the compromise is considered in Richard H. Shryock, *Georgia and the Union in 1850* (Philadelphia, 1926). The effect of the measure on a midwestern state is appraised in Morton M. Rosenberg, "Iowa Politics and the Compromise of 1850," *I.J.H.P.,* LVI (July, 1958), and on a southern state in John Meador, "Florida and the Compromise of 1850," *F.H.Q.,* XXXIX (July, 1960). Both stress the political disintegration that followed passage of the measure. The impact of the compromise on a prominent religious group is explored in Wesley Norton, "The Presbyterian Press and the Compromise of 1850," *J.P.H.,* XL (December, 1962).

The California Gold Rush. Any study of this subject should begin with the excellent interpretative volume by Rodman W. Paul, *Mining Frontiers of the Far West, 1848–1880* (New York, 1963). The same author tells the story in greater detail in his *California Gold: The Beginnings of Mining in the Far West* (Cambridge, 1947). Paul's *The California Gold Discovery* (Georgetown, 1966) assembles and expertly analyzes all contemporary accounts of this event. John W. Caughey, *Gold Is The Cornerstone* (Berkeley, 1948) is a comprehensive general survey, as is Donald D. Jackson, *Gold Dust* (New York, 1980). The latter is a popular account, but based on solid research and perhaps the best history of the rush. The best biography of the discoverer is Theressa Gay *James W. Marshall, the Discoverer of California Gold* (Georgetown, 1967), and of his employer Richard Dillon, *Fool's Gold: A Biography of John Sutter* (New York, 1967).

The routes westward followed by the Forty-Niners have been often described by historians. The most readable account of

travel over the several overland routes is Jackson's *Gold Dust*. This may be supplemented with the fine introductions in David M. Potter, ed., *Trail to California: The Overland Journey of Vincent Geiger and Wakeman Bryarly* (New Haven, 1945), and Dale L. Morgan, ed,. *Overland Diary of James A. Pritchard* (New York, 1959). Both are based on the reading of a large number of diaries, and together constitute an excellent history of the overland trail. Leslie L. D. Shaffer, "The Management of Organized Wagon Trains on the Overland Trail," *M.H.R.,* LV (July, 1961), is based on emigrant diaries. The fact that most migrants found the deserts easy to cross and that an unusually heavy rainfall allowed them to spread the impression that much of the West was fertile is stressed in Watson Parker, "Wading to California: The Influence of the Forty-Niners on the Notion of a Great American Desert," *G.P.J.,* III (Spring, 1964). Essential to an understanding of life on the trail is John P. Reid, *Law for the Elephant: Property and Social Behavior on the Overland Trail* (San Marino, 1980), and John M. Faragher, *Women and Men on the Overland Trail* (New Haven, 1979), a pioneering study of family life. Journals kept by travelers on the overland trail are too numerous to list, numbering into the hundreds. Journals of travelers who branched from the main trail to enter southern California are collected in LeRoy R. Hafen and Ann W. Hafen, eds., *Journals of Forty-Niners, Salt Lake to Los Angeles* (Glendale, 1954); Ralph P. Bieber, ed., *Southern Trails to California in 1849* (Glendale, 1937), performs the same service for the southern trails. Two recently published diaries of particular merit are Thomas D. Clark, ed., *Off at Sunrise: The Overland Journal of Charles Glass Gray* (San Marino, 1976), and Bruce L. McKinstry, ed., *The California Gold Rush Overland Diary of Byran N. McKinstry, 1850–1852* (Glendale, 1975). Herbert Eaton, *The Overland Trail to California in 1852* (New York, 1974), assembles eighty diaries of emigrants for that year. Particularly important is Sandra L. Myres, ed., *Ho for California! Women's Overland Diaries from the Huntington Library* (San Marino, 1980), which prints five revealing diaries by women.

Usable accounts of the sea routes to California are in John H. Kemble, *The Panama Route, 1844–1869* (Berkeley, 1943), and Raymond A. Rydell, *Cape Horn to the Pacific: The Rise and Decline of an Ocean Highway* (Berkeley, 1952). Recently published journals of those who followed the sea routes include June A. Reading, ed., *Consignments to El Dorado: A Record of the Voyage of the Sutton*

(New York, 1972), a record of a trip around the Horn in 1849; Lonnie J. White and William R. Gillespie, *By Sea to San Francisco, 1849–1850: The Journal of Dr. James Morison* (Memphis, 1977), which describes the same route; and Duane A. Smith and David J. Weber, eds., *Fortunes Are for the Few: Letters of a Forty Niner* (San Diego, 1977), dealing with a trip over the Panama Route. Albert Shumate, *The California of George Gordon and the 1849 Sea Voyages of His California Association* (Glendale, 1976), is an excellent biography of an Englishman who became a successful San Francisco merchant.

The first thorough account of the route across Nicaragua which was traveled by some eighty thousand would-be miners is David I. Folkman, Jr., *The Nicaragua Route* (Salt Lake City, 1972). Popular, but based on wide reading in the sources, is Ferol Egan, *The El Dorado Trail: The Story of the Gold Rush Routes across Mexico* (New York, 1970). Two well-written accounts of travel over the southern trails are Odie B. Faulk, *Destiny Road: The Gila Trail and the Opening of the Southwest* (New York, 1973), and Bertha S. Dodge, *The Road West: Saga of the 35th Parallel* (Albuquerque, 1980), both of which deal with a longer period but devote proper space to the California rush.

The coming of one large alien group to California is described in Charles Bateson, *Gold Fleet for California: Forty Niners from Australia and New Zealand* (East Lansing, 1964), and particularly in Jay Monaghan, *Australians and the Gold Rush: California and Down Under, 1849–1854* (Berkeley, 1966). The same author has dealt with another group from Latin America in *Chile, Peru, and the California Gold Rush of 1849* (Berkeley, 1973), while narratives of Chileans who participated have been collected in Edwin A. Beilharz and Carlos U. López, *We Were 49ers: Chilean Accounts of the California Gold Rush* (Pasadena, 1976). Abraham P. Nasatir, "Chileans in California During the Gold Rush Period and the Establishment of the Chilean Consulate," *C.H.S.Q.,* LIII (Spring, 1974), makes clear the difficulties of foreign miners. So also does Sister M. Colette Standart, O.P., "The Sonora Migration to California, 1848–1856: A Study in Prejudice," *S.C.Q.,* LVIII (Fall, 1976). Excellent studies of two other ethnic groups are Robert E. Levinson, *The Jews in the California Gold Rush* (New York, 1978), which shows that most of the 300 who took part played prominent mercantile roles, and Rudolph M. Lapp, *Blacks in Gold Rush California* (New Haven, 1977), a careful appraisal of the roles of the 500 blacks who participated.

That discrimination against blacks in California led many to migrate to the British Columbia mining camps is shown in Malcolm Edwards, "The War of Complexional Distinction: Blacks in Gold Rush California and British Columbia," *C.H.S.Q.,* LVI (Spring, 1977).

The prejudices stirred by the presence of blacks and aliens are examined in Richard H. Peterson, *Manifest Destiny in the Mines: A Cultural Interpretation of Anti-Mexican Nativism in California, 1848–1853* (San Francisco, 1975), Harry H. L. Kitano, and Roger Daniels, *American Racism* (Englewood Cliffs, 1970), and Robert F. Heizer and Alan F. Almquist, *The Other Californians: Prejudice and Discrimination under Spain, Mexico and the United States* (Berkeley, 1971). The latter deals especially with the treatment of the Indians by the miners, as does Ferdinand F. Fernandez, "Except a California Indian: A Study in Legal Discrimination," *S.C.Q.,* L (June, 1968), and particularly Robert F. Heizer, ed., *The Destruction of the California Indians: A Collection of Documents from the Period 1847–1865* (Santa Barbara, 1974). James J. Rawls, "Gold Diggers: Indian Miners in the California Gold Rush," *C.H.S.Q.,* LV (Spring 1976), shows that while nearly half the miners in 1848 were Indians, prejudice soon drove them from the mines. The sufferings of another group that felt the lash of discrimination are described in Gunther Barth, *Bitter Strength: A History of the Chinese in the United States, 1850–1870* (Cambridge, 1964).

Some 4000 mining camps in California are located and described in Edwin G. Gudde, *California Gold Camps: A Geographical and Historical Dictionary of Camps, Towns, and Localities Where Gold Was Found and Mined* (Berkeley, 1975). That many of the mining techniques used were introduced by miners who had gained experience in the Appalachian gold mines is shown in Otis E. Young, Jr., "The Southern Gold Rush: Contributions to California and the West," *S.S.Q.,* LXII (Summer, 1980). Life in the mines is described in popular fashion in Joseph H. Jackson, *Anybody's Gold. The Story of California's Mining Towns* (New York, 1941). That all life was not pleasant is brought home vividly in George W. Groh, *Gold Fever* (New York, 1966), a medical history of California during the rush.

The manner in which Americans in California organized a state government even before congressional authorization is told in George Tennis, "California's First State Election November 13, 1849," *S.C.Q.,* L (December, 1968). William H. Ellison, *A Self-Governing Domain* (Berkeley, 1950) is a history of California's political development during and after the gold rush, a subject also explored in Gerald D. Nash, *State Government and Economic Development: A History of Administration Policies in California, 1849–1933* (Berkeley, 1964).

27   The West and Slavery, 1850–1860

General Works. The most recent general interpretation of the 1850s is from the pen of Allan Nevins: *Ordeal of the Union*, 2 v. (New York, 1947), and *The Emergence of Lincoln*, 2 v. (New York, 1950). A brief and orthodox account is in Jay Monaghan, *Civil War on the Western Border, 1854—1865* (Boston, 1955). A convenient summary is in Henry H. Simms, *A Decade of Sectional Controversy, 1851–1861* (Chapel Hill, 1942). A useful summary of modern interpretations, briefly presented, is Peter J. Parish, *The American Civil War* (New York, 1975); another helpful synthesis is Robert H. Jones, *Disrupted Decades: The Civil War and Reconstruction Years* (New York, 1973). Perhaps the most original interpretation of the period is in David M. Potter and Don E. Fehrenbacher, *"The Impending Crisis, 1848–1861* (New York, 1976), a brilliantly written book. Shelby Foote, *The Civil War: A Narrative*, 3 v. (New York, 1958–1974), is a solid study, stressing military history. That southerners favored the war to save their region from "Africanization" as whites moved away and the racial balance could be preserved only by sending slaves westward is the thesis of William Barney, *The Road to Secession: A New Perspective on the Old South* (New York, 1972). Major L. Wilson, *Space, Time, and Freedom: The Quest for Nationality and the Irrepressible Conflict* (Westport, 1974), argues that the ideas held by Americans concerning slavery and expansion were themselves ingredients in the decision for separatism and war. Helpful in understanding the decade of controversy are such biographical studies as Robert W. Johannsen, *Stephen A. Douglas* (New York, 1973), David Donald, *Charles Sumner and the Coming of the Civil War* (New York, 1960), the same author's *Charles Sumner and the Rights of Man* (New York, 1970), William E. Parrish, *David Rice Atchison of Missouri: Border Politican* (Columbia, 1961), Albert D. Kirwan, *John J. Crittenden: The Struggle for the Union* (Lexington, 1962), and Elbert B. Smith, *The Presidency of James Buchanan* (Lawrence, 1975).

The Period of Calm, 1850–1854. A challenging survey is in Michael F. Holt, *The Political Crisis of the 1850s* (New York, 1978),

which maintains that slavery did not play a major role in disrupting the second party system, but that the collapse of that system opened the way to the debate over slavery. Less controversial and providing an excellent survey are the two volumes by Roy F. Nichols, *Franklin Pierce: Young Hickory of the Granite Hills* (Philadelphia, 1931), which like all good biographies is a history of a period as well as a man and *The Democratic Machine, 1850–1854* (New York, 1923). A case study of one southern state, demonstrating that the swing of northern Whigs into the antislavery camp doomed the party in the slave states by 1852 is James R. Merrill, "The Presidential Election of 1852: Death Knell of the Whig Party of North Carolina," *N.C.H.R.*, XLIV (October, 1967). The beginnings of internal conflict within the political parties in other southern states is studied in John McCardell, "John A. Quitman and the Compromise of 1850 in Mississippi," *J. Miss. H.*, XXXVII (August, 1975), Brian G. Walton, "Arkansas Politics during the Compromise Crisis," *A.H.Q.*, XXXVI (Winter, 1977), and particularly Michael B. Dougan, *Confederate Arkansas: The People and Politics of a Frontier State in Wartime* (University, 1976), which is devoted largely to the course of Arkansas to secession. The widening division as mirrored in the various constitutional theories expressed in congressional debate is studied in Robert R. Russel, "Constitutional Doctrines with Regard to Slavery in Territories," *J.S.H.*, XXXII (November, 1966). The move of the North toward a more militant antislavery attitude is shown in Eric Foner, *Free Soil, Free Labor, Free Men: The Ideology of the Republican Party before the Civil War* (New York, 1970), and Major L. Wilson, "The Repressible Conflict: Seward's Concept of Progress and the Free-Soil Movement," *J.S.H.*, XXXVII (November, 1971). That this trend was not sparked by a belief in racial equality is shown in Eugene H. Berwanger, *The Frontier Against Slavery: Western Anti-Negro Prejudice and the Slavery Extension Controversy* (Urbana, 1967), which shows a general sentiment against allowing blacks to move into the western states. The southern swing to a stauncher defense of slavery is revealed in such studies as Ronald T. Takaki, *A Pro-Slavery Crusade: The Agitation to Reopen the African Slave Trade* (New York, 1971), and in the careers of southern firebrands described in Laura A. White, *Robert Barnwell Rhett, Father of Secession* (New York, 1931), and Henry H. Simms, *Life of Robert M. T. Hunter: A Study in Sectionalism and Secession* (Richmond, 1935). The pressures on

Congress resulting from these increasing tensions are described in Glen M. Leonard, "Southwestern Boundaries and the Principles of Statemaking," *We.H.Q.,* VIII (January, 1977), which deals with attempts to define the boundaries created in the Compromise of 1850.

The Kansas-Nebraska Act. Historians have quarreled for years over Douglas' motive for introducing the Kansas-Nebraska Act into Congress, holding that he was seeking southern votes for his bid for the presidency, that he was responding to political pressures from friends in Missouri, or that he was attempting to secure a Chicago terminal for a transcontinental railroad that would enhance the value of his real-estate holdings. This whole subject is well discussed in Johannsen, *Stephen A. Douglas,* cited earlier. James C. Malin, *The Nebraska Question, 1852–1854* (Lawrence, 1953), contends that Douglas was responding to democratic forces originating on the Kansas frontier. The author presents this same viewpoint more briefly in "The Nebraska Question: A Ten Year Record, 1844–1854," *N.H.,* XXXV (March, 1954). He is substantiated by two stimulating articles by Robert W. Johannsen, "The Kansas-Nebraska Act and the Pacific Frontier," *P.H.R.,* XXII (May, 1953), which concludes that the pioneers viewed popular sovereignty as a democratic instrument, not a device to extend slavery, and "Stephen A. Douglas, 'Harper's Magazine,' and Popular Sovereignty," *M.V.H.R.,* XLV (March, 1959), which employs Douglas' own words to substantiate this viewpoint. The problem of Douglas' motivation is carefully examined in Roy F. Nichols, "The Kansas Nebraska Act: A Century of Historiography," *M.V.H.R.,* XLIII (September, 1956), which shows that political manipulation in Congress helped shape the measure in its final form. That the act was primarily a creation of Douglas or any other politician is challenged in Robert R. Russel, "The Issues in the Congressional Struggle over the Kansas-Nebraska Bill, 1854," *J.S.H.,* XXIX (May, 1963), which shows that the slavery provisions were hammered out as compromise measures in committee and caucus meetings between northern Democrats and southerners of all political hues. The manipulations in Congress that led to the act's adoption are the theme of Dennis Thavenet, "Governor William A. Richardson: Champion of Popular Sovereignty in Territorial Nebraska," *N.H.,* LIII (Winter, 1972), while Gerald W. Wolff, *The Kansas Nebraska Bill: Party, Section, and the Coming of the Civil War* (New York, 1977), concludes on the basis of a statistical study of 396 congressional roll-call votes that party loyalties played a larger role in the decision than hitherto supposed. That the concept of popular sovereignty as a solution to the slavery question was introduced as early as 1847 is shown in Bruce I. Ambacher, "The Pennsylvania Origins of Popular Sovereignty," *P.M.H.B.,* XCVIII (July, 1974).

The political results of the Kansas-Nebraska Act are considered in Michael F. Holt, "The Politics of Impatience: The Origins of Know Nothingism," *J.A.H.,* LX (September, 1973), Ray A. Billington, *The Protestant Crusade, 1800–1860* (New York, 1938), which deals with the Know-Nothings, Andrew W. Crandall, *The Early History of the Republican Party, 1854–1856* (Boston, 1930), and George H. Mayer, *The Republican Party, 1854–1964* (New York, 1964). The Republican role in the election of 1856 is described in Ruhl J. Bartlett, *John C. Frémont and the Republican Party* (Columbus, 1930), and in the various biographies of Frémont, of which the latest is Allen Nevins, *Frémont, Pathmarker of the West* (New York, 1939). A case study of the political chaos that followed passage of the act is ably presented in Morton M. Rosenberg, *Iowa on the Eve of the Civil War: A Decade of Frontier Politics* (Norman, 1972).

Bleeding Kansas. The older interpretation that the New England Emigrant Aid Society saved Kansas for freedom has long since been disproven in such studies as Ralph V. Harlow, "The Rise and Fall of the Kansas Aid Movement," *A.H.R.,* XLI (October, 1935). A thorough study of the company is in Samuel A. Johnson, "The Genesis of the New England Emigrant Aid Society," *N.E.Q.,* III (January, 1930), while Robert E. Moody, "The First Year of the Emigrant Aid Company," *N.E.Q.,* IV (January, 1931), adds additional information. That the company did play a significant role in the contest for Kansas is argued in the first full-length, scholarly history of its activities: Samuel A. Johnson, *The Battle Cry of Freedom: The New England Emigrant Aid Company in the Kansas Crusade* (Lawrence, 1954). The rescue of a New England Aid Society agent who had been captured by a proslavery mob is dramatically described in Stan Hoig, "Silas S. Soule: Partisan of the Frontier," *M.,* XXVI (January, 1976). The Society's post-1854 history is surveyed in Horace Andrews, Jr., "Kansas Crusade: Eli Thayer and the New England Emigrant Aid Company," *N.E.Q.,* XXXV (December, 1962).

The Kansas warfare that followed the initial settlements is briefly considered in Philip S. Klein, *President James Buchanan: A Biography* (University Park, 1962), a work generally sympathetic to the President. Alice Nichols, *Bleeding Kansas* (New York, 1954), is more colorful than reliable. The traditional views reflected in this book have been challenged by James C. Malin, *John Brown and the Legend of Fifty-Six* (Philadelphia, 1942). This suggests that skirmishing over land was responsible for much of the warfare, and indicates that a thorough restudy of the whole episode is needed. This is made even clearer by the careful study of land disposal during the period by Paul W. Gates, *Fifty Million Acres: Conflicts over Kansas Land Policy, 1854–1890* (Ithaca, 1954). This view is substantiated by William H. Beezley, "Land Office Spoilsmen in 'Bleeding Kansas'," *G.P.J.,* IX (Spring, 1970), which shows that the inefficient politicians who administered the land system were guilty of faulty surveys, corruption, and delays that bred discontent. Another, and more questionable, interpretation of the warfare, advanced by James A. Rawley, *Race & Politics: 'Bleeding Kansas' and the Coming of the Civil War* (New York, 1969), is that Republicans acted as they did because they were determined to keep Negroes out of the territory.

The efforts of both North and South to win Kansas have been carefully investigated. Information on southern activities is in Granville D. Davis, "Arkansas and the Blood of Kansas," *J.S.H.,* XVI (November, 1950), Floyd C. Shoemaker, "Missouri's Proslavery Fight for Kansas, 1854–1855," *M.H.R.,* XLVIII (April, 1954)—XLIX (October, 1954), and Lester B. Baltimore, "Benjamin F. Stringfellow: the Fight for Slavery on the Missouri Border," *M.H.R.,* LXII (October, 1967). The career of the North's leading agitator is studied in the Malin biography of John Brown cited earlier, Richard O. Boyer, *The Legend of John Brown: A Biography and a History* (New York, 1973), and Stephen B. Oates, *To Purge This Land With Blood: A Biography of John Brown* (New York, 1970), a scholarly work that provides a well-rounded picture but refuses to come to grips with Brown's psychiatric problems. Brown's relations with blacks and their impact on his raid are the theme of Benjamin Quarles, *Allies for Freedom: Blacks and John Brown* (New York, 1974).

Clarification of the conflicts within Kansas and their background is provided in Keith Sutherland, "Congress and the Kansas Issue in 1860," *K.H.Q.,* XXXV (Spring, 1969), which analyzes the congressional debate over the Wyandotte Constitution, Russel K. Hickman, "The Reeder Administration Inaugurated," *K.H.Q.,* XXXVI (Autumn, 1970), an excellent description of the 1854 election of

a territorial delegate using statistical techniques, Harvin Ewy, "The United States Army in the Kansas Border Troubles, 1855–1856," *K.H.Q.,* XXXII (Winter, 1966), a well-documented study of the efforts of the army to end warfare, and the biographies of two politicians active during the territorial period: Mark A. Plummer, *Frontier Governor: Samuel J. Crawford of Kansas* (Lawrence, 1971), and Burton J. Williams, *Senator John James Ingalls: Kansas' Iridescent Republican* (Lawrence, 1972). The political reshuffling in one western state that followed Bleeding Kansas is described in Gerald Stanley, "Slavery and the Origins of the Republican Party in California," *S.C.Q.,* LX (Spring, 1978).

The Dred Scott Case. Two excellent books deal authoritatively with the Dred Scott case: Don E. Fehrenbacher, *The Dred Scott Case: Its Significance in American Law and Politics* (New York, 1978), a superior treatment showing that Taney distorted legal history to create a proslavery constitution, and Walter Ehrlich, *They Have No Rights: Dred Scott's Struggle for Freedom* (Westport, 1979), a fine history of the progress of the case through the courts and its impact on society. The case is also analyzed in biographies of Justice Taney: Carl B. Swisher, *Roger B. Taney* (New York, 1935), Charles W. Smith, *Roger B. Taney, Jacksonian Jurist* (Chapel Hill, 1936), Walter Lewis, *Without Fear or Favor. A Biography of Chief Justice Roger Brooke Taney* (Boston, 1965), and in Carl B. Swisher, *History of the Supreme Court of the United States. Volume V: The Taney Period, 1836–64* (New York, 1974), an encyclopedic study.

The modern interpretation of the decision began with an article by Frank H. Hodder, "Some Phases of the Dred Scott Case," *M.V.H.R.,* XVI (June, 1929), which demonstrated that the majority opinion was forced on the Democratic judges by the ambitions of the two Republican justices on the bench. The political aspirations of one of these northerners are surveyed in Francis P. Weisenburger, *The Life of John McLean* (Columbus, 1937). E. I. McCormac, "Justice Campbell and the Dred Scott Case," *M.V.H.R.,* XIX (March, 1933), shows that one of the southern justices reversed a former opinion to agree with his colleagues.

Two studies of the case in the Missouri courts show the impact of the slavery controversy on changing legal opinions. Helen T. Catterall, "Some Antecedents of the Dred Scott Case," *A.H.R.,* XXX (October, 1924), demonstrates that in eight previous cases the Missouri Supreme Court held a slave was freed by residence in a free state. Walter Ehrlich, "Was the Dred Scott Case Valid?" *J.A.H.*, LV (September, 1968), uses legal evidence to show that Sanford was not the legal owner of Dred Scott, even though he thought that he was, and had no right to arrange for the case as he did. William M. Wiecek, "Slavery and Abolition before the United States Supreme Court, 1820–1860," *J.A.H.*, LXV (June, 1978), traces the evolution of the court's ruling on slavery to show how the Dred Scott case fitted into the pattern, while Marvin L. Winitsky, "Roger B. Taney: A Historiographical Inquiry," *Ma.H.M.*, LXIX (Spring, 1974), demonstrates that the image of Taney as reflected in historical works has changed often since 1860.

The Triumph of Sectionalism, 1857–1860. An excellent study of the election of 1858, casting some doubts on the traditional roles assigned Lincoln and Douglas in that contest, is Richard A. Heckman, *Lincoln v. Douglas: The Great Debates Campaign* (Washington, 1967). The election is also treated at length in Damon Wells, *Stephen Douglas: The Last Years. 1857–1861* (Austin, 1971), an able account of Douglas' final political activities. An important revisionist argument is in David E. Meerse, "The Northern Democratic Party and the Congressional Elections of 1858," *C.W.H.*, XIX (June, 1973), which uses statistical techniques to show that the election was not the political debacle pictured by most historians and that both Douglas and Buchanan could interpret the results as favorable. The origins of the feud between these two leaders is analyzed by the same author in "Origins of the Buchanan-Douglas Feud Reconsidered," *J.I.S.H.S.*, LXVII (April, 1974), which demonstrates that their falling-out did not come until 1858 and was over popular sovereignty. An excellent account of the debates themselves is Saul Sigelschiffer, *The American Conscience: The Drama of the Lincoln-Douglas Debates* (New York, 1973), a dramatic and well researched study. A challenging article by D. E. Fehrenbacher, "Lincoln, Douglas, and the 'Freeport Question'," *A.H.R.*, LXVI (April, 1961), reveals that the Freeport Doctrine was far less important than usually pictured by historians. Additional material is in the numerous biographies of Lincoln, of which the best multivolume treatment is J. G. Randall and Richard Current, *Lincoln the President*, 4 v. (New York, 1945–1955), and the best one-volume study, Stephen B. Oates, *With Malice Toward None: The Life of Abraham Lincoln* (New York, 1977). Political events following the debates are discussed in Roy F. Nichols, *The Disrup-*

tion of American Democracy (New York, 1948).

No modern interpretation of the election of 1860 has been written, but five essays by as many competent historians present aspects of recent interpretations in Norman A. Graebner, ed., *Politics and the Crisis of 1860* (Urbana, 1961). Of particular importance is Paul W. Gates, "The Struggle for Land and the 'Irrepressible Conflict'," *P.S.Q.*, LXVI (June, 1951), which reveals the effect of Buchanan's land policy in weakening the Democratic Party in the West just before the election. This is also touched upon in James C. Malin, "Thomas Jefferson Sutherland, Nebraska Boomer," *N.H.*, XXXIV (September, 1953).

Keith Sutherland, "The Structure of Congress as a Factor in the Legislative Crisis of 1860," *M.A.*, LI (October, 1969), argues that the congressional system had so stagnated by 1860 that it could function only with strong political parties; as they collapsed in 1860 so did the legislative process, creating the crisis solved by the election. That Douglas was too committed to national unity to take the sectional stand needed to win support for the presidency is the theme of Robert W. Johannsen, "Stephen A. Douglas and the South," *J.S.H.*, XXXIII (February, 1967), while John T. Hubbell, "The Douglas Democrats and the Election of 1860," *M.A.*, LV (April, 1973), describes the struggle for delegates by the Douglas Democrats. Several articles review sectional aspects of the contest. David L. Porter, "The Mississippi Press and the Election of 1860," *J. Miss. H.*, XXXIV (August, 1972), examines seven of the state's newspapers and argues that they correctly mirrored sentiment for the several candidates; more revealing is William L. Barney, *The Secession Impulse: Alabama and Mississippi in 1860* (Princeton, 1974), which shows that turbulent conditions within the state contributed to the triumph of the Breckinridge Democrats. That a Whig politician, Alexander K. McClure, was primarily responsible for Pennsylvania's support for Lincoln rather than Seward is disputed in Early R. Curry, "Pennsylvania and the Republican Convention of 1860: A Critique of McClure's Thesis," *P.M.H.B.*, XCVII (April, 1973). The existence of a conservative region within Indiana is explained in E. Duane Elbert, "Southern Indiana in the Election of 1860," *I.M.H.*, LXX (March, 1974). Another statistical study, William Roed, "Secessionist Strength in Missouri," *M.H.R.*, LXXII (July, 1978), questions the usual assumptions concerning the 1860 vote in that state, while Walter D. Kamphoefner, "St. Louis Germans and the Republican Party, 1848–1860," *M.A.*,

LVII (April, 1975), presents figures to show that the slavery issue, not nativism and temperance, determined the German vote. In the same vein, Gerald Stanley, "The Slavery Issue and the Election in California, 1860," *M.A.*, LXII (January, 1980), shows that the relatively moderate stand of the Republicans on slavery won over many Democratic voters. The career of one compromiser is described in Joseph H. Parks, *John Bell of Tennessee* (Baton Rouge, 1950), and of another in Jack Kelly, "John J. Crittenden and the Constitutional Union Party," *F.C.H.Q.*, XLVIII (July, 1974), a brief history of the party in Kentucky.

The swing of the Northwest to the Republican column has long interested historians. That changing transportation routes due to railroad building in the Midwest helped cement a Northeast-Midwest sectional alliance is the theme of Robert R. Russel, A "Revaluation of the Period before the Civil War: Railroads," *M.V.H.R.*, XV (December, 1928). An excellent account of the railroad building in the Midwest that altered economic ties is John F. Stover, *Iron Horse to the West: American Railroads in the 1850s* (New York, 1978). The important role of British capital in building the western railroads is admirably explained in Ralph W. Hidy and Muriel E. Hidy, "Anglo-American Merchant Bankers and the Railroads of the Old Northwest, 1848–1860," *B.H.R.*, XXXIV (Summer, 1960), which is based on the records of Baring Brothers and Company and George Peabody and Company.

The economic impact of railroad construction on the sections has not been fully explored. The traditional view, that the South remained dependent on the West for its foodstuffs and that its economy was threatened by the cementing of an East-West alliance is developed in John G. Clark, "The Antebellum Grain Trade of New Orleans: Changing Patterns in the Relation of New Orleans with the Old Northwest," *A.H.*, XXXVIII (July, 1964), and especially in A. L. Kohlmeier, *The Old Northwest as the Keystone of the Arch of American Federal Union: A Study in Commerce and Politics* (Bloomington, 1938). This has been challenged by scholars using statistical techniques. James Mak, "Interregional Trade in the Antebellum West: Ohio, a Case Study," *A.H.*, XLVI (October, 1972), demonstrates that in Ohio most of the state's trade was internal to provide food for the non-producing areas. Stimulating articles show that southern agriculture was both more diversified and productive than hitherto believed, and that the region virtually fed itself are: Donald Markwalder, "The Antebellum South

as a Market for Food—Myth or Reality?" *G.H.Q.*, LIV (Fall, 1970), and William K. Hutchinson and Samuel H. Williamson, "The Self-Sufficiency of the Ante-Bellum South: Estimates of Food Supply," *J.E.H.*, XXXI (September, 1971).

The traditional view that foreign-born voters, and particularly Germans, shifted into the Republican Party in 1860 and carried the Old Northwest for Lincoln is argued in Donald V. Smith, "The Influence of the Foreign Born of the Northwest in the Election of 1860," *M.V.H.R.*, XIX (September, 1932). More sophisticated testing techniques allow modern scholars to question this. Paul J. Kleppner, "Lincoln and the Immigrant Vote: A Case of Religious Polarization," *M.A.*, XLVIII (July, 1966), shows that both Germans and Irish divided along religious lines. The same author substantiates these divisions in a broader time period in *The Cross of Culture: A Social Analysis of Midwestern Politics 1850–1900* (New York, 1970). Eleven articles on this theme have been collected in Frederick C. Luebke, *Ethnic Voters and the Election of Lincoln* (Lincoln, 1971), an important compilation.

The West in the Civil War. An adequate survey is in Jay Monoghan, *Civil War on the Western Border, 1854–1865* (Boston, 1955). G. Thomas Edwards, "Holding the Far West for the Union: The Army in 1861," *C.W.H.*, XIV (December, 1968), shows how General Edwin V. Sumner's able administration of Union forces kept the peace in California. The conflict in the Pacific Northwest is described in Robert W. Johannsen, *Frontier Politics and the Sectional Conflict: The Pacific Northwest on the Eve of the Civil War* (Seattle, 1955), and James E. Hendrickson, *Joe Lane of Oregon: Machine Politics and the Sectional Crisis, 1849–1861* (New Haven, 1967).

Military operations west of the Mississippi are touched on in the monumental work by Allan Nevins, *The War for the Union*, 4 v. (New York, 1959–1971), and are briefly interpreted in Robert G. Athearn, "West of Appomattox," *M.*, XII (Spring, 1962). This issue contains a number of articles by scholars on aspects of the war in the West. Ray C. Colton, *The Civil War in the Western Territories: Arizona, Colorado, New Mexico, and Utah* (Norman, 1959), is overdetailed, but contains useful information, as does Robert H. Jones, *The Civil War in the Northwest: Nebraska, Wisconsin, Iowa, Minnesota, and the Dakotas* (Norman, 1960). LeRoy H. Fischer, ed., *The Western Territories in the Civil War* (Manhattan, 1977), assembles seven essays, most concerned with economic and social conditions.

Warfare in the Southwest is competently described in Robert L. Kerby, *Kirby Smith's Confederacy: The Trans-Mississippi South, 1863–1865* (New York, 1972), which describes campaigns between the Mississippi River and Indian Territory. The Confederate general who operated there late in the war is described in Bobby L. Roberts, "General T. C. Hindman and the Trans-Mississippi District," *A.H.Q.*, XXXII (Winter, 1973). Stephen B. Oates, *Confederate Cavalry West of the River* (Austin, 1961), stresses warfare in Arkansas and Missouri, as does William E. Parrish, *Turbulent Partnership: Missouri and the Union, 1861–1865* (Columbia, 1963). Particularly useful for much of the western conflict is the capable description of a leading Confederate general's activities: Albert Castel, *General Sterling Price and the Civil War in the West* (Baton Rouge, 1968). An aspect of the subject is competently treated in James L. Nichols, *The Confederate Quartermaster in the Trans-Mississippi* (Austin, 1964).

Warfare in Kansas is described in Albert Castel, *A Frontier State at War: Kansas, 1861–1865* (Ithaca, 1958). Guerrilla activity there and in Missouri is described in Burton J. Williams, "Quantrill's Raid on Lawrence: A Question of Complicity," *K.H.Q.*, XXXIV (Summer, 1968), which casts doubt on the long-held belief that the raiders were aided by a local banker; LeRoy H. Fischer and Lary C. Rampp, "Quantrill's Civil War Operations in Indian Territory," *C.O.*, XLVI (Summer, 1968), describing an attack on Ft. Gibson; W. Wayne Smith, "An Experiment in Counterinsurgency: The Assessment of Confederate Sympathizers in Missouri," *J.S.H.*, XXXV (August, 1969), on efforts to control guerrillas by assessing their property; and especially in two well-researched books: Albert Castel, *William Clarke Quantrill: His Life and Times* (New York, 1962), and Richard S. Brownlee, *Gray Ghosts of the Confederacy: Guerrilla Warfare in the West, 1861–1865* (Baton Rouge, 1958). An excellent study of Charles R. Jennison and the Seventh Kansas Volunteer Cavalry is Stephen Z. Starr, *Jennison's Jayhawkers: A Civil War Cavalry Regiment and Its Commander* (Baton Rouge, 1973).

The war in the Indian Territory and the Southwest has been extensively studied. An inadequate work on the war in the Indian Territory is Donald A. and Kary C. Rampp, *The Civil War in the Indian Territory* (Austin, 1975), which utilizes only a small portion of the archival materials available. David A. Nichols, *Lincoln and the Indians: Civil War Policy and Politics* (Columbia, 1978), also deals with a topic that deserves more searching treatment. A series of brief essays on the subject, many of them inadequately researched, are in LeRoy H. Fischer, ed., *The Civil War Era in Indian Territory* (Los Angeles, 1974). That Lincoln paid too little attention to Indian affairs is shown in Edmund J. Danziger, Jr., "The Indian Office During the Civil War: Impotence in Indian Affairs," *S.D.H.*, V (Winter, 1974). Tom Holman, "William G. Coffin, Lincoln's Superintendent of Indian Affairs for the Southern Superintendency, *K.H.Q.*, XXXIX (Winter, 1973), reveals the efforts of a capable administrator to deal with refugees from Indian Territory who fled into Kansas, while relations of Confederates within the territory are described in T. Paul Wilson, "Delegates of the Five Civilized Tribes to the Confederate Congress," *C. of O.*, LIII (1975). Kenny A. Franks, "An Analysis of the Confederate Treaties with the Five Civilized Tribes," *C. of O.*, L (Winter, 1972–73), shows that the Confederate commissioner, Albert Pike, awarded the Indians unusually generous terms to win their allegiance.

Various engagements in the Southwest have also been appraised by historians. Prominent among these is a battle fought in northern Arkansas in 1862: Walter L. Brown, "Pea Ridge: Gettysburg of the West," *A.H.Q.*, XV (Spring, 1956), and the same author's "Albert Pike and the Pea Ridge Atrocities *A.H.Q.*, XXXVIII (Winter, 1979). The latter describes northern reaction to the rumor that Union soldiers killed in the battle had been scalped by Cherokee. This engagement is also touched upon in Gary N. Heath, "The First Federal Invasion of Indian Territory," *C.O.*, XLIV (Winter, 1966–67), and William J. Willey, "The Second Federal Invasion of Indian Territory," *C.O.*, XLIV (Winter, 1966–67). The warfare about Ft. Smith in the last years of the war is the theme of Edwin C. Bearss, "General Cooper's CSA Indians Threaten Fort Smith, *A.H.Q.*, XXVI (Autumn, 1967), and Edwin C. Bearss, "Federal Generals Squabble over Fort Smith, 1863–1864," *A.H.Q.*, XXIX (Summer, 1970). Mike Fisher, "The First Kansas Colored Massacre at Poison Springs," *K.H.*, II (Summer, 1907), describes the massacre by Confederate troops of black Union soliders sent south from Ft. Smith in 1864.

Warfare in the Far West has been described in numerous works. A detailed discussion of the small bands of Confederate raiders operating between 1861 and 1864 is Morris F. Taylor, "Confederate Guerrillas in Southern Colorado," *C.M.*, XLVI (Fall, 1969). The role of Colorado volunteers in New Mexico and elsewhere is described in Martin H. Hall, "Colorado Volunteers Save New Mexico for the Union," *M.A.*, XXXVIII (October, 1956). Martin H. Hall, *The Confederate Army of New Mexico* (Austin, 1978), expertly retells much of the same story, with additional details, told by the same author in his *Sibley's New Mexico Campaign* (Austin, 1960), the standard history of the Confederate invasion of that territory. David Westphall, "The Battle of Glorieta Pass: Its Importance in the Civil War," *N.M.H.R.*, XLIV (April, 1969), argues convincingly that the significance of the battle that climaxed this invasion has never been properly recognized. The influence of a staunch Republican politician in suppressing Confederate activities in New Mexico is discussed in Lawrence R. Murphy, "William F. M. Arny: Secretary of New Mexico Territory, 1862–1867," *A. and W.*, VIII (Winter, 1966). Clashes along the Texan borderlands are the theme of L. W. Horton, "General Sam Bell Maxey: His Defense of North Texas and the Indian Territory," *S.H.Q.*, LXXIV (April, 1971), and Michael L. Tate, "The Frontier of Northwest Texas during the Civil War," *C. of O.*, L (Summer, 1972). The war on the Pacific Coast is well-described in Aurora Hunt, *The Army of the Pacific* (Glendale, 1951). Ronnie C. Tyler, *Santiago Vidaurri and the Southern Confederacy* (Austin, 1973), is a sound biography of the governor of Coahuila-Nuevo Leon during the Civil War years, stressing the aid that he provided the Confederacy by extensive trade with Texas in firearms.

The effect of the Civil War on western agriculture is brilliantly examined in Paul W. Gates, *Agriculture and the Civil War* (New York, 1965). The degree to which the war affected technological change and economic growth has been argued by historians and economists, many of whose views are presented in David T. Gilchrist, ed., *Economic Change in the Civil War Era* (Greenville, 1965). Wayne D. Rasmussen, "The Civil War: A Catalyst of Agricultural Revolution," *A.H.*, XXXIX (October, 1965), argues convincingly that the war did stimulate changes in western farming and production.

28   The Miners' Frontier, 1858–1875

General Works. The best history of western mining, and the first to show both the commercial and technological relationships between the many mining districts, is Rodman W. Paul, *Mining Frontiers of the Far West,* 1848–1880 (New York, 1963). Another competent survey is William S. Greever, *The Bonanza West: The Story of the Western Mining Rushes, 1848–1900* (Norman, 1963). Two books by Otis E. Young emphasize technological developments on the mining frontier: *How They Dug the Gold: An Informal History of Frontier Prospecting, Placering, Lode Mining, and Milling in Arizona and the Southwest* (Tucson, 1967), and *Western Mining: An Informal Account of precious-Metals Prospecting, Placering, Lode Mining and Milling on the American Frontier from Spanish Times to 1893* (Norman, 1970). A useful collection of readings from contemporary newspapers and other sources is Marvin Lewis, ed., *The Mining Frontier: Contemporary Accounts from the American West in the Nineteenth Century* (Norman, 1967). Two excellent studies of mining technology are Otis E. Young, Jr., *Black Powder and Hand Steel: Miners and Machines on the Old Western Frontier* (Norman, 1976), and Clark E. Spence, *Mining Engineers and the American West: The Lace-Boot Brigade, 1849–1933* (New Haven, 1970). The miners themselves have been thoroughly studied in Mark Wyman, *Hard Rock Epic: Western Miners and the Industrial Revolution, 1860–1910* (Berkeley, 1979), which shows the effect of technological change on the miners, John Rowe, *The Hard-Rock Men: Cornish Immigrants and the North American Mining Frontier* (New York, 1974), Arthur C. Todd, *The Cornish Miner in America* (Glendale, 1967), which is readable, Richard E. Lingenfelter, *The Hardrock Miners: A History of the Mining Labor Movement in the American West, 1863–1893* (Berkeley, 1974), the first capable history of labor organization among the miners, and Ronald C. Brown, *Hard-Rock Miners: The Intermountain West, 1860–1920* (College Station, 1979), an excellent survey of living and working conditions. One important social institution is studied in Elliott West, *The Saloon on the Rocky Mountain Mining Frontier* (Lincoln, 1979), and Ann Burk, "The Mining Camp Saloon as a Social Center, *R.R.V.H.R.*, II (Fall, 1975). That mining practices were borrowed from Spanish America is shown in Otis E. Young, "The Spanish Tradition in Gold and Silver Mining," *A. and W.*, (Winter, 1965).

Two excellent studies of investment in western mining are Clark C. Spence, *British Investment and the American Mining Frontier, 1860–1901* (Ithaca, 1958), and W. Turrentine Jackson, *The Enterprising Scot: Investors in the American West after 1873* (Edinburgh, 1968). About half of the latter deals with investment in copper mining. The career of one mining promoter, Theodore J. Lamoreaux, is traced in Lewis Atherton, "The Mining Promoter in the Trans-Mississippi West," *WeH.Q.*, I (January, 1970), while techniques used by speculators to dupe investors are explained in Otis E. Young, " 'Salting' and 'High-Grading': Vices of the Mining Frontier," *S.C.Q.*, LI (September, 1969). A fine study of the most successful mining entrepreneurs, showing that the rate of upward mobility among them was higher than in other business enterprises, is Richard H. Peterson, *The Bonanza Kings. The Social Origins and Business Behavior of Western Mining Entrepreneurs, 1870–1900* (Lincoln, 1977). That American miners who migrated to fields abroad carried with them practices that sometimes succeeded is shown in E. Daniel and Annette Potts, *Young America and Australian Gold: Americans and the Gold Rush of the 1850s* (St. Lucia, Australia, 1974). Watson Parker, "The Causes of American Gold Rushes," *N.D.H.*, XXXVI (Fall, 1969), argues that rushes occurred during periods of turbulence when the gold region had received exceptional publicity.

The Mining Frontier in Colorado. Robert G. Athearn, *High Country Empire: The High Plains and the Rockies* (New York, 1960), contains a good brief survey. Of the histories of the state that contain the most useful information are LeRoy R. Hafen, ed., *Colorado and Its People*, 4 v. (New York, 1948), Carl Abbott, *Colorado: A History of the Centennial State* (Boulder, 1976), and Robert G. Athearn, *The Coloradans* (Albuquerque, 1976). Joseph E. King, *A Mine to Make a Mine: Financing the Colorado Mining Indstury, 1859–1902* (College Station, 1977), is a solid contribution, demonstrating that much of the capital needed came from England. A useful history of Denver and its relations to the mining camps is Lyle W. Dorsett, *The Queen City: A History of Denver* (Boulder, 1977).

The beginnings of the 1859 rush are traced in two articles by Calvin W. Gower, "Aids to Prospective Prospectors: Guidebooks and Letters from Kansas Territory, 1858–1860," *K.H.Q.*, XLIII (Spring, 1977), and "Gold Fever in Kansas Territory: Migration to the Pike's Peak Gold Fields, 1858–1860," *K.H.Q.*, (Spring, 1973). A brief survey of the rush is Agnes W. Spring, "Rush to the Rockies, 1859: Colorado's Gold Rush of 1859," *C.M.*, XXXVI (April, 1959). LeRoy R. Hafen, "Cherokee Goldseekers in Colorado, 1849–1850," *C.M.*, XV (May, 1938), is the best account of the initial discoveries, while Caroline Bancroft, "The Elusive Figure of John Gregory," *C.M.*, XX (July, 1943), is the best biography of the

miner who made the first large "strike." A useful, but restricted, biography of an early miner is in Elma D. R. Spencer, *Green Russell and Gold* (Austin, 1966). Special studies of mining areas add a great deal of information. Three of the best of these are from the pen of Duane A. Smith: *Silver Saga: The Story of Caribou, Colorado* (Boulder, 1974), "The Promoter, the Investor, and the Mining Engineer: A Case Study," *H.L.Q.*, XXXIX (August, 1976), dealing with Parrott City and reproducing the diary of James D. Hague, an early promoter and mining engineer, and *Rocky Mountain Boom Town: A History of Durango* (Albuquerque, 1980). A fine study of another Colorado area is in Janet Lecompte, *Pueblo, Hardscrabble, Greenhorn: The Upper Arkansas, 1832–1856* (Norman, 1978), which deals with early settlement.

Among the usable biographies of prominent miners are Duane A. Smith, *Horace Tabor: His Life and the Legend* (Boulder, 1973), the best of the many studies of this glamorous character; H. William Axford, *Gilpin County Gold: Peter McFarlane, 1848–1929: Mining Entrepreneur in Central City, Colorado* (Chicago, 1976), a life of a mining engineer and foundry operator; James E. Fell, Jr., "Nathaniel P. Hill: A Scientist-Entrepreneur in Colorado," *A. and W.*, XV (Winter, 1973); Robert M. Horne, "James Fergus in the Colorado Gold Fields," *C.M.*, L (Winter, 1973), tracing the career of a Scot who began mining in 1860; and Frank Waters, *Midas of the Rockies. The Story of Stratton and Cripple Creek* (New York, 1937).

The story of one rush is well told in Robert L. Brown, *An Empire of Silver: A History of the San Juan Silver Rush* (Caldwell, 1965). That mining techniques developed in Colorado were widely exported is shown in Rodman W. Paul, "Colorado as a Pioneer of Science in the Mining West," *M.V.H.R.*, XLVII (June, 1960), while another searching study by Duane A. Smith, "Decade of Frustration: Colorado and California Silver Mining in the 1860s," *S.C.Q.*, LVI (Summer, 1974), grapples with the problem of why silver mining succeeded in Colorado and did not in California. A biography of a Colorado freighter who operated between the mining camps is Frances and Dorothy Wood, *I Hauled These Mountains In Here* (Caldwell, 1977), the life of David Wood.

Contemporary accounts of the Pike's Peak rush have been edited by LeRoy R. Hafen in three volumes of the *Southwest Historical Series: Pike's Peak Gold Rush Guide Books of 1859* (Glendale, 1941), *Overland Routes to the Gold Fields, 1859, from Con-*

temporary Diaries (Glendale, 1942), and *Colorado Gold Rush; Contemporary Letters and Reports, 1858–1859* (Glendale, 1941). Another contemporary description by a competent observer, also edited by LeRoy R. Hafen, is Henry Villard, *The Past and Present of the Pike's Peak Gold Regions* (Princeton, 1932). Daniel E. Conner, *A Confederate in the Colorado Gold Fields* (Norman, 1970), contains the reminiscences of a prospector who joined the 1859 rush and spent some time in Colorado.

The Mining Frontier in Nevada. Grant H. Smith, *History of the Comstock Lode* (Reno, 1943), is standard. Capable accounts are to be found in recent histories of the state, of which the most useful is Russell R. Elliott, *History of Nevada* (Lincoln, 1973). Robert Laxalt, *Nevada: A Bicentennial History* (New York, 1977), is brief, while Gilman M. Ostrander, *Nevada: The Great Rotten Borough, 1858–1964* (New York, 1966), contains colorful information. Of the many popular histories of Nevada mining, G. D. Lyman, *Ralston's Ring: California Plunders the Comstock Lode* (New York, 1937), is especially readable.

The life of one miner in California and Nevada as recorded in his extensive journals is in Walter Van Tilburg Clark, ed., *The Journals of Alfred Doten, 1849–1903* (Reno, 1973). Dan De Quille, *The Big Bonanza* (New York, 1947), is a reprint of a fine contemporary account; others have been collected in Duncan Emrich, ed., *Comstock Bonanza* (New York, 1950). Biographies of men prominent in early mining are Robert E. and Mary F. Stewart, *Adolph Sutro: A Biography* (Berkeley, 1962), Francis P. Weisenburger, *Idol of the West: The Fabulous Career of Rollin Mallory Daggett* (Syracuse, 1965), and Otis E. Young, Jr., "Philip Deidesheimer, 1832–1916: Engineer of the Comstock," *S.C.Q.,* LVII (Winter, 1975), describing the contributions of the engineer who developed the cube system for holding back earth in the Comstock mines. One of the most able histories of a mining district ever written is W. Turrentine Jackson, *Treasure Hill. Portrait of a Silver Mining Camp* (Tucson, 1963), a history of the White Pine Mining District in central Nevada. Lewis Atherton, "Structure and Balance in Western Mining History," *H.L.Q.,* XXX (November, 1966), deals with the promoter who developed the Tonopah district of Nevada.

The emerging social order in the Nevada mines has recently attracted the interest of historians. One segment of society is studied in a statistical examination of the Virginia City prostitutes, Marion Goldman, "Sexual Commerce on the Comstock Lode," *N.H.S.Q.,*

XXI (Summer, 1978), and George M. Blackburn and Sherman L. Ricards, "The Prostitutes and Gamblers of Virginia City, Nevada, 1870," *P.H.R.,* XLVIII (May, 1979). The racist attitudes of two leading newspapers are examined in Michael S. Coray, " 'Democracy' on the Frontier: A Case Study of Nevada Editorial Attitudes on the Issue of Nonwhite Equality," *N.H.S.Q.,* XXXI (Fall, 1978), while the forty-five blacks who lived in Nevada in 1860 are described in Elmer Rusco, *'Good Times Coming?' Black Nevadans in the Nineteenth Century* (Westport, 1976). One aspect of the movement for statehood is examined in David A. Johnson, "A Case of Mistaken Identity: William M. Stewart and the Rejection of Nevada's First Constitution," *N.H.S.Q.,* XXII (Fall, 1979), proving that Stewart was a principal advocate, not opponent, of the 1864 constitution. The conflict with Mormon settlers as the population moved into the Reese River county is described in John M. Townley, *Conquered Provinces: Nevada Moves Southeast, 1864–1871* (Provo, 1973).

The Mining Frontier in Arizona. No history of Arizona mining has been written. Brief accounts are in Rufus K. Wyllys, *Arizona: The History of a Frontier State* (Phoenix, 1951), and Jay J. Wagoner, *Early Arizona: Prehistory to Civil War* (Tucson, 1975). Life during the rush is vividly described in a diary edited by Clement Eaton, "Frontier Life in Southern Arizona, 1858–1861," *S.H.Q.,* XXXVI (January, 1933). A colorful contemporary record of the mines is Daniel E. Conner, *Joseph Redderford Walker and the Arizona Adventure* (Norman, 1957), the journal of an early trader. Contemporary accounts are also in Constance W. Altschuler, ed., *Latest from Arizona! The Hesperian Letters, 1859–1861* (Tucson, 1969), reproducing the correspondence of a journalist, Thomas M. Turner, and Lonnie E. Underhill, ed., "The Tombstone Discovery: The Recollections of Ed. Schieffelin and Richard Gird," *A. and W.,* XXI (Spring, 1979).

Studies of early miners are often colorful. Frank Love, "Poston and the Birth of Yuma: The Father of Arizona Invents a Story," *J. Ar.H.,* XIX (Winter, 1978), tells of the founding of that important crossroads city, while two articles by Constance W. Altshuler, "The Case of Sylvester Mowry: The Charge of Treason," *A. and W.,* XV (Spring, 1973), and "The Case of Sylvester Mowry: The Mowry Mine," *A. and W.,* XV (Summer, 1973), describe the treasonable activities of this leading citizen during the Civil War and the federal confiscation of his mine. C. L. Sonnichsen, *Colonel Green and the Copper Skyrocket* (Tucson,

1974), is a spritely biography of a leading mining magnate. An excellent survey of economic progress in Arizona during the early stages of capital accumulation there is William H. Lyon, "The Corporate Frontier in Arizona," *J. Ariz. H.*, IX (Spring, 1968). The difficulties of supplying the Arizona mines are explored in Henry P. Walker, "Freighting from Guyamus to Tucson, 1850–1880," *W.H.Q.*, I (July, 1970). Mining in two important areas of the territory is described in Odie B. Faulk, *Tombstone: Myth and Reality* (New York, 1972), a sober antidote to the lurid tales told of this frontier town, and Harwood Hinton, "Frontier Speculation: A Study of the Walker Mining Districts," *P.H.R.*, XXIX (August, 1960). Two informative studies of important mining areas are Robert L. Spude, "A Land of Sunshine and Silver: Silver Mining in Central Arizona, 1871–1885," *J.Ar.H.*, XVI (Spring, 1975), describing the silver rushes between 1871 and 1875, and Gregory P. Dowell, "The Total Wreck: Arizona's Forgotten 'Bonanza' Mine," *A. and W.*, XX (Summer, 1978), telling the story of a mine opened in 1881 that produced $500,000 worth of metal.

The Mining Frontier in the Northwest. The standard account, now out of date, is William J. Trimble, *The Mining Advance into the Inland Empire* (Madson, 1914). More general descriptions of the rushes are in Dorothy O. Johansen and Charles M. Gates, *Empire of the Columbia: A History of the Pacific Northwest* (New York, 1967), Earl Pomeroy, *The Pacific Slope* (New York, 1965), and Hubert H. Bancroft, *History of Washington, Idaho, and Montana, 1845–1889* (San Francisco, 1890). The economic aspects of the mining advance are considered in a scholarly work by Oscar O. Winther, *The Old Oregon Country* (Stanford, 1950).

The Fraser River rush still awaits its historian, but the extensive description in Margaret A. Ormsby, *British Columbia: A History* (n.p., 1958), is both scholarly and penetrating. Of use also are Donald Sage, "Gold Rush Days on the Fraser River," *P.N.Q.*, XLIV (October, 1953), and the biography of the Hudson's Bay Company official who maintained order, Walter N. Sage, *Sir James Douglas and British Columbia* (Toronto, 1930). Barry M. Gough, " 'Turbulent Frontiers' and British Expansion: Governor James Douglas and the Royal Navy, and the British Columbia Gold Rushes," *P.H.R.*, XLI (February, 1972), shows how Douglas used the navy to keep order, and served as an unwitting agent for British expansion. The same author, on the other hand, concludes in "Keeping British Columbia British: The Law-and-Order Question on a Gold

Mining Frontier," *H.L.Q.*, XXXVIII (May, 1975), that the attempt to hurry civilization kept many miners away. A little known aspect of the rush is told in Crawford Kilian, *Go Do Some Great Thing: The Black Pioneers of British Columbia* (Vancouver, 1978), which tells the story of Archy Lee, a fugitive slave, who established a community of sixty-five blacks on Vancouver Island in 1858.

The Mining Frontier in Idaho. A thorough account is in the work by Trimble listed above. The same author, "A Reconsideration of the Gold Discoveries in the Northwest," *M.V.H.R.*, V (June, 1918), deals more fully with the first strikes. Later phases of Idaho mining are popularly treated in Angus Murdock, *Boom Copper* (New York, 1943). The most recent history of the state, F. Ross Peterson, *Idaho: A Bicentennial History* (New York, 1976), gives a brief summary. Betty Derig, "Celestials in the Diggings," *I.Y.*, XVI (Fall, 1972), tells of the 4,000 Orientals in the Idaho mines. A scholarly analysis of the economic effects of mining in Idaho is in August A. Bolino, "The Role of Mining in the Economic Development of Idaho Territory," *O.H.Q.*, LIX (June, 1958), while the governmental organization that followed the advent of the miners is treated in Merle W. Wells, "The Creation of the Territory of Idaho," *P.N.Q.*, XL (April, 1949).

The Mining Frontier in Montana. The account in Trimble may be supplemented with the thorough study in Merrill G. Burlingame, *The Montana Frontier* (Helena, 1942), and the numerous versions in the histories of the state, of which the latest and best is Michael P. Malone and Richard B. Roeder, *Montana: A History of Two Centuries* (Seattle, 1976). Reminiscences of the Stuart brothers who made the first strikes are in Paul C. Phillips, ed., *Forty Years on the Frontier as Seen in the Journals and Reminiscenses of Granville Stuart*, 2 v. (Cleveland, 1925). S. Lyman Tyler, ed., *The Montana Gold Rush Diary of Kate Dunlap* (Salt Lake City, 1969), is that of an excellent observer who arrived at Bannack City in 1865.

Special studies of the Montana fields include a careful analysis of the food supply problem: H. A. Texler, *Flour and Wheat in the Montana Gold Camps, 1862–1870* (Missoula, 1918). An excellent account of the overland route from Minnesota used by some 1,400 miners between 1862 and 1867 is Helen M. White, ed., *Ho! For the Gold Fields. Northern Overland Wagon Trains of the 1860s* (St. Paul, 1966), which reproduces important documents. Dorothy M. Johnson, *The Bloody Bozeman* (New York, 1971), is a popular account of one trail, while special studies of road building include Oscar O. Winther, "Early Commercial Importance of the Mullan Road," *O.H.Q.,* XLVI (March, 1945), and Alexander C. McGregor, "The Economic Impact of the Mullan Road on Walla Walla, 1860–1883," *P.N.Q.,* LXV (July, 1974). Helen M. White, "Minnesota, Montana, and Manifest Destiny," *M.H.,* XXXVIII (June, 1962), deals with efforts to establish communications between Minnesota and Montana, while a searching study by Alton B. Oviatt, "Pacific Coast Competition for the Gold Camp Trade of Montana," *P.N.Q.,* XLVI (October, 1965), shows the manner in which Pacific coastal towns vied for connections with interior mining districts. Robert L. Housman, "The First Territorial Legislature in Montana," *P.H.R.,* IV (December, 1935), deals with governmental beginnings, as does James L. Thane, Jr., "An Ohio Abolitionist in the Far West: Sidney Edgerton and the Opening of Montana, 1863–1866," *P.N.Q.,* LXVII (October, 1976), which deals with the first chief justice of the territorial court. The manner in which a group of dedicated citizens saved Helena from the fate of most temporary mining camps is described in Joan Bishop, "A Season of Trial: Helena's Entrepreneurs Nurture a City," *M.,* XXVIII (July, 1978).

One of the few works dealing with the South Pass gold rush is Robert A. Murray, "Miner's Delight, Investor's Despair," *A. of W.,* XLIV (Spring, 1972), a history of the three stages of mining development there.

The Mining Frontier in the Dakotas. An excellent history of the Black Hills gold rush, covering the years between 1874 and 1879 in meticulous detail is Watson Parker, *Gold in the Black Hills* (Norman, 1966). Newspaper accounts of the expedition are reprinted in Herbert Kraus and Gary D. Olson, eds., *Prelude to Glory* (Sioux Falls, 1974). Donald Jackson, *Custer's Gold: The United States Cavalry Expedition of 1874* (New Haven, 1966), is a solid study; so also are Max E. Gerber, "The Custer Expedition of 1874: A New Look," *N.D.H.,* XL (Winter, 1973), and Lawrence A. Frost, "The Black Hills Expedition of 1874," *R.R.V.H.R.,* IV (Fall, 1979). An earlier expedition is described in Grant K. Anderson, "Black Hills Sooners: The Davy Expedition of 1868," *A. of W.,* XLIX (Spring, 1977), which tells of a group under a well-known scout, Peter B. Davy, that was turned back by the army. The role of the Episcopalian missionary who served as interpreter and treaty-maker with the Santee Sioux is recounted in Grant K. Anderson, "Samuel D. Hinman and the Opening of the Black Hills,"

N.H., LX (Winter, 1979). A series of five articles dealing in depth with the exploration of the Black Hills is James D. McLaird and Lesta V. Turchen, "Exploring the Black Hills, 1855–1875. Reports of Government Expeditions," *S.D.H.,* III (Fall, 1973) to IV (Fall, 1974). A pioneering article demonstrating that tin mining was as essential as gold mining in developing the Black Hills region is W. Turrentine Jackson, "Dakota Tin: British Investors at Harney Peak," *N.D.H.,* XXXIII (Winter, 1966). That Deadwood far from deserved its reputation as a center of lawlessness, with only four killings and no lynchings during its pioneer period, is demonstrated in Harry H. Anderson, "Deadwood: An Effort at Stability," *M,* XX (January, 1970). The career of a leading Black Hills freighter is exhaustingly studied in Agnes Wright Spring, *Colorado Charley, Wild Bill's Pard* (Boulder, 1968).

The Mining Camps. The best study of the camps as embryo urban areas is Duane A. Smith, *Rocky Mountain Mining Camps: The Urban Frontier* (Bloomington, 1967), which traces their emergence from primitive settlements to miniature cities, faced with all the problems of major cities. The same author argues that the camps served as a safety valve in drawing off miners and other workers from older cities, thus keeping labor unrest at a minimum, in his "Colorado's Urban-Mining Safety Valve," *C.M.,* XLVIII (Summer, 1971).

The problem of maintaining order in the camps has interested many scholars. Rodman W. Paul, "Patterns of Culture in the American West," in *Frontier Alaska: A Study in Historical Interpretation and Opportunity* (Anchorage, 1968), contrasts the manner in which this was solved on the Mormon, mining, cattle, and foresting frontiers. Ann M. Keppel, "Civil Disobedience on the Mining Frontier," *W.M.H.,* XLI (Spring, 1958), while dealing with the lead mines, illustrates the universal refusal of miners to obey laws imposed from above. Their efforts to create their own legal machinery and institutions are described in Jim D. Hill, "The Early Mining Camp in American Life," *P.H.R.,* I (September, 1932), while the organization of such legal districts and the laws that they enacted are the theme of Percy S. Fritz, "The Constitutions and Laws of Early Mining Districts—in Boulder County, Colorado," *C.U.S.,* XXI (Boulder, 1934). Charles H. Shinn, *Land Laws of Mining Districts* (Baltimore, 1885, Reprinted, New York, 1948) is a pioneering study of the same problem.

That miners sought as rapidly as possible for the orderly rule of traditional American institutions is demonstrated in several studies of state-making in Nevada and Colorado. Kent D. Richards, "Washoe Territory: Rudimentary Government in Nevada," *A. and W.,* XI (Autumn, 1969), describes efforts to set up territorial and state governments even before 1861. That Colorado early resented rule by Kansas, despite the excellence of many laws passed in its behalf, is shown in Calvin W. Gower, "Kansas Territory and the Pike's Peak Gold Rush: Governing the Gold Region," *K.H.Q.,* XXXII (Autumn, 1966), while John D. W. Guice, in an important study, explores the impact of the court system throughout the Rocky Mountain mining country in his Rocky Mountain Bench: The Territorial Supreme Courts of Colorado, Montana, and Wyoming, 1861–1890 (New Haven, 1972). How relations with Kansas hurried separate territorial status for Colorado is the theme of Calvin W. Gower, "Gold Rush Governments," *C.M.,* LXII (Spring, 1965). That the Colorado constitution served as model for those of other Rocky Mountain states is shown in Gordon M. Bakken, "The Impact of the Colorado State Constitution on Rocky Mountain Constitution Making," *C.M.,* XLVII (Spring, 1970). The evolution of an urban atmosphere in developing mining camps is expertly studied in Gunther Barth, *Instant Cities: Urbanization and the Rise of San Francisco and Denver* (New York, 1975), while Frank Mazzi, "Harbingers of the City: Men and Their Monuments in Nineteenth Century San Francisco," *S.C.Q.,* LV (Summer, 1973), applies the same techniques to a study of San Francisco.

A good introduction to vigilante justice is in the popular but reliable book by Wayne Gard, *Frontier Justice* (Norman, 1949). Hubert H. Bancroft, *Popular Tribunals,* 2 v. (San Francisco, 1887), records virtually every instance of vigilante activity in California mining camps. These local studies should be supplemented by the broader treatment in two modern studies of frontier violence: W. Eugene Hollon, *Frontier Violence: Another Look* (New York, 1974), and Richard M. Brown, *Strain of Violence: Historical Studies of American Violence and Vigilantism* (New York, 1975). The latter treats violence in its broadest psychological and sociological sense. The origins of the most famous of the vigilante committees in California are authoritatively treated in Mary F. Williams, *History of the San Francisco Committee of Vigilance of 1851* (Berkeley, 1921). Records of the committee, edited by Mary F. Williams, have been published as *Papers of the San Francisco Committee of Vigilance of 1851* (Berkeley, 1919). A popular history of the San Francisco Committee of 1856, which defends its work, is Stanton A. Coblentz, *Villains and Vigilantes* (New York, 1936). That religion played an important role in the emergence of the 1856 committee is the theme of Robert M. Senkewicz, "Religion and Non-Partisan Politics in Gold Rush San Francisco," *S.C.Q.,* LXI (Winter, 1979), while the career of one of its principal critics is told in Clifford M. Drury, *William Anderson Scott: "No Ordinary Man,"* (Glendale, 1967). A brief history of a vigilance committee that operated in Colorado in 1860 is Calvin W. Gower, "Vigilantes," *C.M.,* XLV (Spring, 1964).

29 The Transportation Frontier, 1858–1884

General Works. Any study of the subject should begin with the comprehensive survey by Oscar O. Winther, *The Transportation Frontier. Trans-Mississippi West, 1865–1890* (New York, 1964). W. Turrentine Jackson, *Wagon Roads West* (rev. edn., Lincoln, 1980), is an important book that not only surveys early road building but demonstrates the close cooperation between private enterprise and federal aid in spanning the West. One important but often neglected phase of western transportation history is treated in William E. Lass, *A History of Steamboating on the Upper Missouri River* (Lincoln, 1962), and Richard E. Lingenfelter, *Steamboats on the Colorado River, 1852–1916* (Tucson, 1978).

Establishing a Mail Service. Water communication between the East and California is described in three articles by John H. Kemble: "Pacific Mail Service between Panama and San Francisco, 1949–1851," *P.H.R.,* II (December, 1933). The standard work on the overland mail is LeRoy R. Hafen, *The Overland Mail 1849–1869* (Cleveland, 1926), a scholarly study. One phase of the subject neglected by Hafen was the use of the Santa Fe Trail as a mail route, this has been admirably remedied by Morris F. Taylor, *First Mail West: Stagecoach Lines on the Santa Fe Trail* (Albuquerque, 1971). Curtis Nettels, "The Overland Mail Issue in the Fifties," *M.H.R.,* XVIII (July, 1924), surveys steps leading to the establishment of the Butterfield Overland Mail Company, while the definitive history of that concern is in Roscoe P. Conkling and Margaret B. Conkling, *The Butterfield Overland Mail, 1857–1869,* 3 v. (Glendale, 1947). Waterman L. Ormsby, *The Butterfield Overland Mail* (San Marino, 1942), and William Tallack, *The California Overland Express, the Longest Stage-Ride in the World* (Los Angeles, 1935), are the best contemporary accounts by travelers; these and other reminiscences of the journey are collected in Walter B. Land, ed., *The First Overland Mail: Butterfield Trail* (n.p., 1940). Attempts to keep new mining camps in Colorado provided with a mail service are described in Joel Barker, "Colorado Mail Service," *C.M.*, XLIX (Summer, 1972).

Freighting on the Plains. An excellent history of freight transportation over the Central Route between 1848 and 1869 is William E. Lass, *From the Missouri to the Great Salt Lake: An Account of Overland Freighting* (Lincoln, 1972), while the leading freighting company is expertly described in Raymond W. and Mary L. Settle, *War Drums and Wagon Wheels: The Story of Russell, Majors and Waddell* (rev. edn., Lincoln, 1966). An important aspect neglected by the Settles, the proliferation of small freighting companies, is admirably surveyed in Henry P. Walker, *The Wagonmasters: High Plains Freighting from the Earliest Days of the Santa Fe Trail to 1880* (Norman, 1966). Carol Gendler, "Territorial Omaha as a Staging and Freighting Center," *N.H.*, XIL (Summer, 1968), adds local detail. A local study is Harold E. Briggs, "Early Freight and Stage Lines in Dakota," *N.D.H.Q.*, III (July, 1929). Memoirs of early drivers of freight wagons are William F. Hooker, *The Prairie Schooner* (Chicago, 1918), and William F. Hooker, *The Bullwhacker: Adventures of a Frontier Freighter* (Yonkers-on-Hudson, 1925).

Overland Expressing. Excellent studies of the express and stagecoaching businesses on the west coast are in Oscar O. Winther, *Express and Stagecoach Days in California* (Stanford, 1936), and *The Old Oregon Country. A History of Frontier Trade, Transportation, and Travel* (Stanford, 1950). Ralph Moody, *Stagecoach West* (New York, 1967), is a popular history of coaching in the 1858–1868 period. Alvin F. Harlow, *Old Waybills: The Romance of the Express Companies* (New York, 1934), is the best general history of the express business, while the beginnings of expressing in California are admirably described in Charles Outland, *Stagecoaching on El Camino Real: Los Angeles to San Francisco, 1861–1901* (Glendale, 1973), a thorough discussion of coaching along that route.

A popularly written history of the leading coaching concern is Edward Hungerford, *Wells Fargo: Advancing the American Frontier* (New York, 1949), but this should be supplemented with a number of careful studies of that company. Ruth Teiser and Catherine Harroun, "Origins of Wells, Fargo and Company, 1841–1852," *B.M.H.S.*, XXII (June, 1948),

has to do with the company's early operations in California, while two excellent articles by W. Turrentine Jackson reveal a far wider role of the company in overland expressing than had earlier been realized: "A New Look at Wells Fargo, Stagecoaches and the Pony Express," *C.H.S.Q.*, XLV (December, 1966), and "Wells Fargo: Symbol of the Wild West," *We.H.Q.*, III (April, 1972). This author expertly appraises the company's role in California during the 1850s and 1860s in "Stages, Mail and Express in Southern California: The Role of Wells, Fargo & Co. in the Pre-Railroad Period," *S.C.Q.*, LVI (Fall, 1974), "Racing from Reno to Virginia City by Wells Fargo and Pacific Union Expresses," *N.H.S.Q.*, XX (Summer, 1977), telling of the rivalry between the company and the Pacific Union Express Company over this route, and four articles on "Wells Fargo Stagecoaching in Montana," *M.*, XXIX (January to October, 1979). An encyclopedic account of Wells Fargo in Arizona is John and Lillian Theobald, *Wells Fargo in Arizona Territory* (Tempe, 1978).

The standard work on stagecoaching over the central route is the history of the firm of Russell, Majors & Waddell: Raymond W. Settle and Mary L. Settle, *Empire on Wheels* (Stanford, 1949). This should be supplemented with two scholarly essays by George R. Root and R. K. Hickman: "Pike's Peak Express Companies: Solomon and Republican Routes," *K.H.Q.*, XIII (August, 1944, and November, 1944), and "Pike's Peak Express Companies: The Platte Route," *K.H.Q.*, XIII (November, 1945) and XIV (February, 1946). The career of the company's most famous agent is depicted in Lew L. Callaway, "Joseph Alfred Slade: Killer or Victim," *M.M.H.*, III (January, 1953). Samuel L. Clemens, *Roughing It* (Hartford, 1872), is a classic description of travel over this route. Calvin W. Gower, "The Pike's Peak Gold Rush and the Smoky Hill Route, 1859–1860," *K.H.Q.*, XXV (Summer, 1959), is a capable history of an alternate route to Denver. The standard work on coaching in the 1860s is J. V. Frederick, *Ben Holladay* (Glendale, 1940). Agnes W. Spring, *The Cheyenne and Black Hills Stage and Express Routes* (Glendale, 1949), is a scholarly history of stagecoaching north of Cheyenne after the building of the first railroad. This same theme is further explored in Oscar O. Winther, "The Persistence of Horse-Drawn Transportation in the Trans-Mississippi West, 1865–1900," in *Probing the American West* (Santa Fe, 1962). The history of the last of the stage lines to operate on the overland route when its role was confined to connecting rail terminals is Morris F. Taylor, "The Barlow and Sanderson Stage Lines in Colorado, 1872–1886," *C.M.*, L (Spring, 1973).

The best work on the Pony Express is Raymond W. Settle and Mary L. Settle, *Saddlers and Spurs: The Pony Express Saga* (Harrisburg, 1955). Several articles make important contributions: Olaf T. Hagen, "The Pony Express Starts from St. Joseph," *M.H.R.*, XLIII (October, 1948), examines the factors that led to the selection of St. Joseph as the eastern terminus; Louise P. Hauck, "The Pony Express Celebration," *M.H.R.*, XVII (July, 1923), identifies the first rider as Johnson W. Richardson. Merrill Mattes and Paul Henderson, "The Pony Express: Across Nebraska from St. Joseph to Fort Laramie," *N.H.*, XLI (June, 1960), traces the exact route followed by the riders. W. Turrentine Jackson, "Wells Fargo's Pony Express," *J.W.*, XI (July, 1972), continues the story of the Pony Express after the demise of the parent firm. An interesting account of a pony express that operated from the Red River to Helena between January, 1867 and March, 1868 is in John S. Gray, "The Northern Overland Pony Express," *M.*, XVI (October, 1966). The extension of telegraph service westward is expertly described in Robert L. Thompson, *Wiring a Continent* (Princeton, 1947).

Building the Railroads. The general histories of railroad building cited in Chapter XVII may be supplemented by special studies of the western lines. Of these the most recent is still Robert E. Riegel, *The Story of the Western Railroads* (New York, 1926). Technical, but important for the understanding of western railroading, is Julius Grodinsky, *Transcontinental Railway Strategy, 1869—1893: A Study of Businessmen* (Philadelphia, 1962). Carter Goodrich, *Government Promotion of American Canals and Railroads, 1800–1890* (New York, 1960), deals with the subsidies to the transcontinental lines, and shows the continuous dependence of transportation systems on government aid. John F. Stover, *Iron Road to the West: American Railroads in the 1850s* (New York, 1978), provides essential background in discussing road building in the Mississippi Valley as the transcontinental lines were being launched.

Early agitation for a Pacific Railroad receives scholarly treatment in Robert R. Russel, *Improvement of Communication with the Pacific Coast as an Issue in American Politics, 1783–1864* (Cedar Rapids, 1948). Margaret L. Brown, "Asa Whitney and His Pacific Railroad Publicity Campaign," *M.V..H.R.*, XX (September, 1933), and Jere W. Robertson, "To Build a Pacific Railroad: Congress, Texas, and the Charleston Convention of 1854,"

S.H.Q., LXXVIII (October, 1974), deal with the promotional efforts that helped launch the railroad project, while the latter author in "The South and the Pacific Railroad, 1845–1855," *We.H.Q.*, V (April, 1974), shows that delays in launching the road were caused partly by disputes within the South over the eastern terminus. The standard history of the government surveys is George L. Albright, *Official Explorations for the Pacific Railroads, 1853–1855* (Berkeley, 1921). This should be supplemented with the biographical study of one of the surveyors, Paul W. Golad, "Frederick West Lander and the Pacific Railroad Movement," *N.H.*, XXXV (September, 1954), and especially by the narratives of members of the surveying parties collected in LeRoy R. Hafen and Ann W. Hafen, *Central Route to the Pacific* (Glendale, 1957). The planning and survey of an important route is explored in H. Craig Miner, *The St. Louis-San Francisco Transcontinental Railroad: The Thirty-Fifth Parallel Project, 1853–1900* (Lawrence, 1972). David E. Conrad, "The Whipple Expedition in Arizona," *A. and W.*, XI (Summer, 1969), and "Whipple's Pacific Railroad Survey in the Indian Territory," *R.R.V.H.R.*, I (Winter, 1974), deal with the exploration of a portion of the route.

Railroad construction in the tier of states adjacent to the Mississippi River and beyond is described in Riegel, *Story of the Western Railroads,* cited earlier, in such specialized treatments as Leonard F. Ralston, "Railroad Interests in Early Iowa," *A. of I.*, XLI (Winter, 1973), which shows that suspicion of the roads' monopolistic practices originated in the 1850s and 1860s, and in studies of individual lines. Among the latter David G. Taylor, "Thomas Ewing, Jr., and the Origins of the Kansas Pacific Railroad Company," *K.H.Q.*, deals with the promoters who launched that line in 1855, while Richard C. Overton, *Burlington Route: A History of the Burlington Lines* (New York, 1965), is a model to which all writers of railroad history should aspire. The same author has studied the activity of the Burlington as a colonizing agency in *Burlington West* (Cambridge, 1941). Unfortunately other roads have not been so kindly treated by historians. The only history of the Chicago and North Western Railroad is the dated study by William H. Stennett, *Yesterday and Today* (Chicago, 1910). Thorough investigations of these and similar roads are needed. An important aspect of their history in one state is explored in Earl S. Beard, "Local Aid to Railroads in Iowa," *I.J.H.P.*, L (January, 1952). A major problem of early railroad builders—the hostility of river men who resented any bridging of streams—is the theme of Benedict K. Zobrist, "Steamboat Men versus Railroad Men: The First Bridging of the Mississippi River," *M.H.R.*, LIX (January, 1965).

By far the best history of the Union Pacific Railroad is Robert G. Athearn, *Union Pacific Country* (Chicago, 1971), which focuses on the building of the road and its impact on the settlement and development of the West. Charles E. Ames, *Pioneering the Union Pacific: A Reappraisal of the Builders of the Railroad* (New York, 1969), attempts to shift blame for the financial scandals that marked the road's construction from Oliver and Oakes Ames to Thomas C. Durant. James McCague, *Moguls and Iron Men: The Story of the First Transcontinental Railroad* (New York, 1964), and Wesley S. Griswold, *A Work of Giants: Building the First Transcontinental Railroad* (New York, 1962), are popularly written and describe construction. The economics of road-building are stressed in Robert W. Fogel, *The Union Pacific Railroad: A Case in Premature Enterprise* (Baltimore, 1960). Wallace D. Farnham, "The Pacific Railroad Act of 1862," *N.H.*, XLIII (September, 1962), is an excellent analysis of the measure that created the Union Pacific, while the same author explores the road's relations with the federal government in " 'The Weakened Spring of Government': A Study in Nineteenth-Century History," *A.H.R.*, LXVIII (April, 1963). Construction problems are emphasized in the biography of the chief engineer: Stanley P. Hirshson, *Grenville M. Dodge: Soldier, Politician, Railroad Pioneer* (Bloomington, 1967). Wallace D. Farnham, "Grenville Dodge and the Union Pacific: A Study of Historical Legends," *J.A.H.*, LI (March, 1965), shows that Dodge was more efficient as a diplomat and organizer than as a construction engineer. The impact of a rival road on the planning for the Union Pacific is explored in William R. Petrowski, "The Kansas Pacific Railroad in the Southwest," *A. and W.*, XI (Summer, 1969).

How the building of the road was viewed by the people of Kansas is the theme of Joseph W. Snell and Robert W. Richmond, "When the Union and Kansas Pacific Built Through Kansas," *K.H.Q.*, XXXII (Summer, and Autumn, 1966). That the Mormon community contributed heavily in skill and manpower to construction in Utah is shown in two excellent articles by Robert G. Athearn: "Opening the Gates of Zion: Utah and the Coming of the Union Pacific Railroad," *U.H.Q.*, XXXVI (Fall, 1968), and "Contracting for the Union Pacific," *U.H.Q.*, XXXVII (Winter, 1969).

The same author explores a spur road built by the Mormons as a result of the coming of the Union Pacific in: "Railroad to a Far Off Country: The Utah & Northern," *M.*, XVIII (October, 1968). That Utah's economy was vastly benefited by the railroad construction is shown in Leonard J. Arrington, "The Transcontinental Railroad and the Development of the West," *U.H.Q.*, XXXVII (Winter, 1969). Richard E. Kotter, "The Transcontinental Railroad and Ogden City Politics," *U.H.Q.*, XLII (Summer, 1974), deals with the destructive impact of construction on control by the elite Mormon governors in one community.

The effect of the road on communities along the way is described in Robert A. Murray, "Fort Fred Steele: Desert Outpost on the Union Pacific," *A. of W.*, XLIV (Fall, 1972), Gilbert A. Stelter, "The Birth of a Frontier Boom Town: Cheyenne in 1867," *A. of W.*, XXXIX (April, 1967), and Nyle H. Miller and Robert W. Richmond, "Sheridan, a Fabled End-of-Track Town on the Union Pacific Railroad, 1868–1869," *K.H.Q.*, XXXIV (Winter, 1968). Gilbert Stelter, "The City and Westward Expansion: A Western Case Study," *We.H.Q.* IV (April, 1973), deals with the growth of Cheyenne. How Chinese laborers were recruited, and their major role in building the Central Pacific across the Sierras, is described in Alexander Saxton, "The Army of Canton in the High Sierra," *P.H.R.*, XXXV (May, 1966), and George Kraus, "Chinese Laborers and the Construction of the Central Pacific," *U.H.Q.*, XXXVII (Winter, 1969). Robert M. Utley, "The Dash to Promontory," *U.H.Q.*, (April, 1961), deals with the last phases of construction. David E. Miller, ed., *The Golden Spike* (Salt Lake City, 1973), assembles ten essays celebrating the centennial of the Union Pacific's construction.

Much of the history of the Union and Central Pacific railroad is told in biographies of its founders. David Lavender's *Collis P. Huntington, The Great Persuader* (Garden City, 1970), is the best study of that leader, while Norman E. Tutorow, *Leland Stanford: Man of Many Careers* (Menlo Park, 1971), adds information. A popular history is Oscar Lewis, *The Big Four: The Story of Huntington, Stanford, Hopkins, and Crocker, and the Building of the Central Pacific* (New York, 1938).

Economic historians have attempted to determine with statistical techniques whether the land grant to the Union Pacific was essential to its financial success. Stanley L. Engerman, "Some Economic Issues Relating to Railroad Subsidies and the Evaluation of Land Grants," *J.E.H.*, XXXII (June, 1972), raises more questions than it answers, while Lloyd J. Mercer, "Taxpayers or Investors: Who Paid for the Land Grant Railroads?" *B.H.R.*, XLVI (Autumn, 1972), concludes that the grants paid only a portion of the construction costs. The difficulty of appraising profits is shown in William R. Petrowski, "Kansas City to Denver to Cheyenne: Pacific Railroad Construction Costs and Profits," *B.H.R.*, XLVIII (Summer, 1974), while two articles by Heywood Fleisig, "The Union Pacific Railroad and the Railroad Land Grant Policy," *E.E.H.*, XI (Winter, 1973–74), and "The Central Pacific Land Grant Policy," *J.E.H.*, XXXV (September, 1975), argue that profits were sufficiently high to show that grants were not necessary and represented excessive subsidization.

Railroad building in the Rocky Mountain country is expertly described in the excellent histories of two principal railroads: Robert G. Athearn, *Rebel of the Rockies: A History of the Denver and Rio Grande Western Railroad* (New Haven, 1962), and Richard C. Overton, *Gulf to Rockies: The Heritage of the Fort Worth and Denver-Colorado and Southern Railways, 1861–1898* (Austin, 1953). George L. Anderson, *Kansas West* (San Marino, 1963), studies the construction of Denver's railroad connections to the transcontinental lines, while railroading in the northern Rockies during the 1870s and 1880s is explored in Merrill D. Beal, *Intermountain Railroads: Standard and Narrow Gauge* (Caldwell, 1962). Herbert O. Brayer; *William Blackmore: A Case Study in the Economic Development of the West,* 2 v. (Denver, 1939), tells the story of an important railroad promoter, while miscellaneous documents are collected in E. O. Davis, comp., *The First Five Years of the Railroad Era in Colorado* (Golden, 1948).

Several works touch on the extension of the railroad network into the Indian Territory and Texas. James R. Fair, Jr., *The North Arkansas Line: The Story of the Missouri and North Arkansas Railroad* (Berkeley, 1969), tells the story of a minor road from Joplin, Missouri to Helena, Arkansas. Road building in the Indian Territory is touched on in Craig Miner, "Border Frontier: The Missouri River, Fort Scott and Gulf Railroad in the Cherokee Neutral Lands, 1868–1870," *K.H.Q.*, XXXV (Summer, 1969), and Nancy H. Self, "The Building of the Railroads in the Cherokee Nation," *C.O.*, XLIX (Summer, 1971). Virginia H. Taylor, *The Franco-Texan Land Company* (Austin, 1969), tells of a speculating company formed by bondholders of the Memphis, El Paso, and Pacific Railroad, while the career of a Texan railroad promoter is traced in Vernon G. Spence, *Colonel Morgan Jones: Grand*

Old Man of Texas Railroading (Norman, 1971).

A solid history of the Santa Fe is Keith L. Bryant, Jr., *History of the Atchison, Topeka and Santa Fe Railway* (New York, 1974), but this should be supplemented with the scholarly work on the road's land grant and its disposal: William S. Greever, *Arid Domain. The Santa Fe Railway and Its Western Land Grant* (Stanford, 1954). George A. Hamm, "The Atchison Associates of the Santa Fe Railroad," *K.H.Q.*, XLII (Winter, 1976), deals with the group that until 1869 was assigned the task of building the road. Joseph W. Snell and Don W. Wilson, "The Birth of the Atchison, Topeka and Santa Fe Railroad," *K.H.Q.*, XXXIV (Summer, 1968), is a capable history of the road's formation. An extension of the Santa Fe into southern California is described in Frank Hoyt, "San Diego's First Railroad, the California Southern," *P.H.R.*, XXIII (May, 1954). The best work on the early history of another southern road is A. B. Armstrong, "Origins of the Texas and Pacific Railway," *S.H.Q.*, LVI (April, 1953). Ralph N. Traxler, Jr., "Collis P. Huntington and the Texas and Pacific Railroad Land Grant," *N.M.H.R.*, XXXIV (April, 1959), describes the efforts of Huntington to secure the Texas and Pacific grant for the Southern Pacific Railroad, while Craig Miner, "The Colonization of the St. Louis and San Francisco Railway Company, 1880–1882: A Study of Corporate Diplomacy," *M.H.R.*, LXIII (April, 1969), continues the story as it affected the Atlantic and Pacific's successor. The Southern Pacific lacks a modern historian, but its early career is capably reviewed in Ward McAfee, *California's Railroad Era, 1850–1911* (San Marino, 1973). That the Southern Pacific was not a greedy "octopus," and that its interests paralleled those of the state is the theme of Richard J. Orsi, "The *Octopus* Reconsidered: The Southern Pacific and Agricultural Modernization in California, 1865–1915," *C.H.S.Q.*, LIV (Fall, 1975). The southern railroads that crossed Arizona are admirably treated in David F. Myrick, *Railroads of Arizona. Volume I, The Southern Railroads* (Berkeley, 1975).

The standard work on the Northern Pacific is James B. Hedges, *Henry Villard and the Railways of the Northwest* (New York, 1930), but this should be supplemented with Dietrich G. Russ, *Henry Villard: A Study of Transatlantic Investments and Interests, 1870–1895* (New York, 1978), which shows that Villard owed his success to his skill in mediating between the German and American capital markets. Information on the road is also in the biography of its financier, Henrietta M. Larson, *Jay Cooke, Private Banker* (Cambridge, 1936). Thomas A. Clinch, "The Northern Pacific Railroad and Montana's Mineral Lands," *P.H.R.*, XXXIV (August, 1965), describes the contest between the road and mining interests for mineral lands. The contributions of a topographical engineer to the surveys of the route are demonstrated in Vincent J. Flanagan, "Gouverneur Kemple Warren, Explorer of Nebraska Territory," *N.H.*, LI (Summer, 1970). Kenneth Hammer, "Territorial Towns and the Railroad," *N.D.H.*, XXXVI (Fall, 1969), and John L. Harnsberger and Robert P. Wilkins, "New Yeovil, Minnesota, a Northern Pacific Colony in 1873," *A. and W.*, XII (Summer, 1970), deal with the effect of the road on settlement. That it vastly benefited the economy of the region it traversed is argued in John S. Cochran, "Economic Importance of Early Transcontinental Railroads: Pacific Northwest," *O.H.Q.*, LXXI (March, 1970).

An excellent history of one of the Northern Pacific's competitors, the Canadian Pacific Railway, is a three-volume study by Pierre Berton, *The National Dream: The Great Railway, 1871–1881* (Toronto, 1970), *The Last Spike* (Toronto, 1971), and *The Impossible Railway: The Building of the Canadian Pacific* (New York, 1972). Briefer, but solidly researched, is W. Kaye Lamb, *History of the Canadian Pacific Railway* (New York, 1977). Other Canadian lines are well treated in George R. Stevens, *History of the Canadian National Railways* (New York, 1963).

30 The Indian Barrier, 1860–1890

General Works. The histories of Indian tribes listed in the bibliographies to Chapters II and XVIII are essential to understanding the final stages of the tragic epic of the Native Americans' struggle for survival. A popular rendition of this story, not free from errors, is Dee Brown, *Bury My Heart at Wounded Knee* (New York, 1971). That the Indians were doomed as a result of their own intertribal conflicts has been argued; John C. Ewers, "Intertribal Warfare as the Precursor of Indian-White Warfare on the Northern Plains," *We.H.Q.*, VI (October, 1975), shows that four major alliances among the western tribes underlay these conflicts, while W. W. Newcomb, Jr., "A Re-examination of the Causes of Plains Warfare," *A.A.*, LII (July–September, 1950), demonstrates the seriousness of these wars. Gary C. Anderson, "Early Dakota Migration and Intertribal War:

A Revision," *We.H.Q.*, XI (January, 1980), deals with conflicts between the Chippewa and Sioux. The white-Indian conflicts were intensified by the changing image of the Indian in the white man's eyes. William W. Savage, ed., *Indian Life: Transforming an American Myth* (Norman, 1977), assembles thirteen essays revealing that Americans who earlier had pictured "good" and "bad" Indians, now ranked all "bad," fit only for extermination. The changing attitude of army officers is traced in Thomas C. Leonard, "Red, White and the Army Blue: Empathy and Anger in the American West," *A.Q.*, (May, 1974). This viewpoint is related to racism in essays in Howard Peckham and Charles Gibson, eds., *Attitudes of Colonial Powers Toward the American Indian* (Salt Lake City, 1969), and prevailed in Europe as in America as shown in Ray A. Billington, *Land of Savagery, Land of Promise: The European Image of the American Frontier* (New York, 1981).

The men who fought the Indians are described in Oliver Knight, *Life and Manners in the Frontier Army* (Norman, 1978), and Don Rickey, Jr., *Forty Miles a Day on Beans and Hay: The Enlisted Soldier Fighting the Indian Wars* (Norman, 1963). One group, Confederate prisoners who were released from northern jails to fight between 1864 and 1866, are described in D. Alexander Brown, *The Galvanized Yankees* (Urbana, 1963). That some of the most valiant fighting was done by Negro soldiers has only recently been recognized. William H. Leckie, *The Buffalo Soldiers: A Narrative of the Negro Cavalry in the West* (Norman, 1967), is a masterful account of the role of two black cavalry regiments, while Arlen L. Fowler, *The Black Infantry in the West, 1869–1891* (Westport, 1971), describes the activities of the 24th and 25th infantry. John M. Carroll, ed., *The Black Military Experience in The American West* (New York, 1971), is a convenient collection of documents dealing with Negro troops, while the experiences of one group of Buffalo Soldiers in Utah are described in Donald G. Coleman, "The Buffalo Soldiers: Guardians of the Uintah Frontier," *U.H.Q.*, XLVII (Fall, 1979). The unique problems faced by troops engaged in Indian warfare are expertly analyzed in Robert M. Utley, "A Chained Dog: The Indian Fighting Army." *A.W.*, X (July, 1973), and in the reminiscences of participants collected in Lonnie J. White, ed., *Hostiles and Soldiers* (Boulder, 1972). The difficulty of supplying the armies are described in such studies as Robert W. Frazer, "Purveyors of Flour to the Army: Department of New Mexico, 1849–1861," *N.M.H.R.*, XLVII (July, 1972), and "Army Agriculture in New Mexico, 1852–53," *N.M.H.R.*, L (October, 1975), and in Jerome A. Greene, "Army Bread and Army Mission on the Frontier: With Special Reference to Fort Laramie, Wyoming," *A. of W.*, XLVII (Fall, 1975). Problems faced by those accompanying the armies are discussed in Patricia Y. Stallard, *Glittering Misery: Dependents of the Indian Fighting Army* (Fort Collins, 1978), and Sandra L. Myres, ed., *Cavalry Wife: The Diary of Eveline N. Alexander, 1866–1867* (College Station, 1977), the latter the journal of an army wife who was stationed at Ft. Gibson. The correspondents who followed the soldiers are described in Oliver Knight, *Following the Indian Wars: The Story of the Newspaper Correspondents among the Indian Campaigners* (Norman, 1960).

Early Indian Policy in the Far West. A serious study of the emerging Indian policy is Edmund J. Danziger, *Indians and Bureaucrats: Administering the Reservation Policy During the Civil War* (Chicago, 1974). The application of this policy in the Indian Territory is treated in M. Thomas Bailey, *Reconstruction in Indian Territory: A Story of Avarice, Discrimination, and Opportunism* (Port Washington, 1972), for the period from 1866 to 1877, while the efforts of one tribe to adjust to the situation are the theme of Sue Hammond, "Socioeconomic Reconstruction in the Cherokee Nation," *C. of O.*, LVI (Summer, 1978). The fate of this tribe's Negro slaves after emancipation is described in Daniel F. Littlefield, Jr., *The Cherokee Freedmen: From Emancipation to American Citizenship* (Westport, 1978). The role of Indian agents is appraised in LeRoy M. Fischer, "The United States Indian Agents to the Five Civilized Tribes," *C. of O.*, L (Winter, 1972–3), and other articles in this issue which is entirely devoted to the subject. Their relations with the half-blood and Indian clerks who carried on the administration is discussed in H. Craig Miner, " 'A Corps of Clerks': The Bureaucracy of Industrialization in Indian Territory, 1866–1907," *C. of O.*, LIII (Fall, 1975). William D. Pennington, "Government Policy and Indian Farming on the Cheyenne and Arapaho Reservation, 1869–1880," *C. of O.*, LVII (Summer, 1979), describes the failure of attempts to teach farming to the Indians on another reservation, while a sound biography of one of the agents is Lawrence R. Murphy, *Frontier Crusader—William F. M. Arny* (Tucson, 1972). Although Michael A. Sievers, "Malfeasance or Indirection? Administration of the California Indian Superintendency's Business Affairs," *S.C.Q.*, LVI (Fall, 1974), deals only with California; it serves as a case

study of the difficulties of administering Indian policy in the period just after the Civil War.

The Ft. Laramie Treaties of 1851 are considered in LeRoy R. Hafen and F. M. Young, *Fort Laramie and the Pageant of the West* (Glendale, 1938), LeRoy R. Hafen and W. J. Ghent, *Broken Hand: the Life Story of Thomas Fitzpatrick* (Denver, 1973 edn.), and LeRoy R. Hafen, "Thomas Fitzpatrick and the First Indian Agency of the Upper Platte and Arkansas," *M.V.H.R.*, XV (December, 1928). Burton S. Hill, "The Great Indian Treaty Council of 1851," *N.H.*, XLVII (March, 1966), provides more local color than fresh information on the 1851 treaty. Stan Hoig, *The Western Odyssey of John Simpson Smith: Frontiersman, Trapper, Trader and Interpreter* (Glendale, 1974), is a biography of the colorful trader who served as interpreter at Ft. Laramie.

The best survey of frontier defense and military operations for the period is in two fine volumes by Robert M. Utley, *Frontiersmen in Blue: The United States Army and the Indian, 1848–1865* (New York, 1967), and *Frontier Regulars: The United States Army and the Indians, 1866–1891* (New York, 1974). Recent histories of important forts include: Lawrence R. Murphy, "Cantonment Burgwin, New Mexico, 1852–1860," *A. and W.*, XV (Spring, 1973), William L. Chapel, "Camp Ricker: Outpost in Apacheria," *J.Ar.H.*, XIV (Summer, 1973), David E. Kyvig, "Policing the Panhandle: Fort Elliott, Texas, 1875–1890," *R.R.V.H.R.*, I (Autumn, 1974), Mary O. Handy, *History of Fort Sam Houston* (San Antonio, 1951), Carl C. Rister, *Fort Griffin on the Texas Frontier* (Norman, 1956), Roger T. Grange, "Fort Robinson, Outpost on the Upper Plains," *N.H.*, XXXIX (September, 1958), Chris Emmett, *Fort Union and the Winning of the Southwest* (Norman, 1965), Donald W. Whisenhunt, "Fort Richardson: Outpost on the Texas Frontier," *Southwestern Studies*, V (No. 4, 1968), David K. Strate, *Sentinel on the Cimarron: The Frontier Experience of Fort Dodge, Kansas* (Dodge City, 1970), and Robert C. Carriker, *Fort Supply Indian Territory: Frontier Outpost on the Plains* (Norman, 1970). Important regional studies include Robert A. Murray, *Military Posts in the Powder River Country of Wyoming, 1865–1894* (Lincoln, 1968), Lee Myers, "Military Establishments in Southwestern New Mexico: Stepping Stones to Settlement," *N.M.H.R.*, (January, 1968), and especially Robert G. Athearn, *Forts of the Upper Missouri* (New York, 1967). These and other forts are listed in Francis P. Prucha, *Guide to the Military Posts of the United States, 1789–1895* (Madison, 1964), and in more detail in Herbert M. Hart, *Old Forts of the Far West* (Denver, 1965).

William E. Unrau, "The Civilian as Indian Agent: Villain or Victim," *We.H.Q.,* III (October, 1972), questions the inefficiency of Indian agents and argues that most played a valuable role. His conclusions are generally substantiated by such studies of particular agencies as Lee Cutler, "Lewis Tatum and the Kiowa Agency, 1869–1873," *A. and W.,* XIII (Autumn, 1971), Ernest L. Schusky, "The Upper Missouri Indian Agency," *M.H.R.,* LXV (April, 1971), and Michael A. Sievers, "The Administration of Indian Affairs on the Upper Missouri, 1858–1865," *N.D.H.,* XXXVIII (Summer, 1971).

Early Warfare in the Southwest. The subject is placed in proper historical perspective in Edward H. Spicer, *Cycles of Conquest: The Impact of Spain, Mexico, and the United States on the Indians of the Southwest, 1533–1890* (Tucson, 1962). The standard work on the Navajo wars is Frank McNitt, *Navajo Wars: Military Campaigns, Slave Raids, and Reprisals* (Albuquerque, 1972); useful also is L. R. Bailey, *The Long Walk: A History of the Navajo Wars, 1848–68* (Los Angeles, 1964). The fate of the defeated Indians is traced in Gerald Thompson, *The Army and the Navajo: The Bosque Redondo Reservation Experiment, 1863–1868* (Tucson, 1976), a sad tale of the conflict between government agencies that doomed the Native Americans to tragic lives. One Indian fighter active in the war is glorified in a well-written book: Marc Simmons, *The Little Lion of the Southwest; A Life of Manuel Antonio Chaves* (Chicago, 1973). Frank D. Reeve, "Navaho Foreign Affairs, 1795–1846," *N.M.H.R.,* XLVI (April and July, 1971), is a detailed history of New Mexican-Indian relations before the conquest, essential as background. Important material on a principal campaign against the Navajo is in Lawrence C. Kelly, ed., *Navajo Roundup: Select Correspondence of Kit Carson's Expedition against the Navajo, 1863–1865* (Boulder, 1971). The controversy over treatment of the defeated Navajo after the "Long Walk" is described in Edmund J. Danziger, Jr., "The Steck-Carleton Controversy in Civil War New Mexico," *S.H.Q.,* LXXIV (October, 1970).

Warfare on the fringes of the Southwest during this period is touched on in such works as Ferol Egan, *Sand in the Whirlwind: the Paiute Indian War of 1860* (New York, 1972), on a minor war at Pyramid Lake, Nevada, in which 160 Indians were killed; Leslie G. Hunter, "The Mohave Expedition of 1858–59," *A. and W.,* XXI (Summer, 1979), dealing with an expedition against the Mohave after they

attacked a wagon train that ended resistance by that tribe; and John M. Carroll, *Custer in Texas: An Interrupted Narrative* (New York, 1975), tells of Custer's six-month's experiences there.

The early wars against the Apache are best described in Dan L. Thrapp, *The Conquest of Apacheria* (Norman, 1967), which deals with the fifty years before 1887. James T. King, "George Crook: Indian Fighter and Humanitarian," *A. and W.,* IX (Winter, 1967), shows that Crook's humanitarian policy toward the Indian was developed during his early campaigns against the Apache. Those campaigns are discussed in Morris F. Taylor, "Campaigns Against the Jicarilla Apache, 1854," *N.M.H.R.,* XLIV (October, 1969), and Ralph H. Ogle, *Federal Control of the Western Apaches 1848–1886* (Albuquerque, 1970), although the latter does little more than list engagements. One campaign against the Ute and Apache is described in Morris F. Taylor, "Action at Fort Massachusetts: The Indian Campaign of 1855," *C.M.,* XLII (Fall, 1965). The career of a leading scout in the Apache wars is described in Dan L. Thrapp, *Al Sieber, Chief of Scouts* (Norman, 1964). Frank McNitt, *The Indian Traders* (Norman, 1962), is a history of trade with the Navajo, Hopi, and Zuni Indians during this and later periods, and Ralph A. Smith, "The Scalp Hunter in the Borderlands, 1835–1850," *A. and W.,* VI (Spring, 1964), is concerned with professional hunters of Apache scalps such as James Kirker.

Relations on the southern borderland with the Comanche, with stress on trade between the two peoples, are explored in Charles L. Kenner, *A History of New Mexican-Plains Indian Relations* (Norman, 1969). Michael L. Tate, "Frontier Defense on the Comanche Rangers of Northwest Texas, 1846–1860," *G.P.J.,* XI (Fall, 1971), and Brad Agnew, "The 1858 War against the Comanches," *C.O.,* XLIV (Summer, 1971), are concerned with aspects of the relationships. Douglas C. Jones, *The Treaty of Medicine Lodge* (Norman, 1966), discusses the treaty made in October, 1867, in which the Comanche, Kiowa, and other tribes of the area agreed to retreat to Indian Territory. This treaty and its background are also discussed in Ralph A. Smith, "The Fantasy of a Treaty to End Treaties," *G.P.J.,* XII (Fall, 1972).

Warfare on the Plains. A useful survey, carrying the story from 1851 to Wounded Knee, is S. L. A. Marshall, *Crimson Prairie: The Wars Between the United States and the Plains Indians during the Winning of the West* (New York, 1972). Sound biographies of the leading military commanders are Richard N. Ellis, *General Pope and United States Indian Policy* (Albuquerque, 1970), and Robert G. Athearn, *William Tecumseh Sherman and the Settlement of the West* (Norman, 1956). Competent studies of two other commanders are Marvin E. Kroeker, *Great Plains Command: William B. Hazen in the Frontier West* (Norman, 1976), and Langdon Sully, *No Tears for the General: The Life of Alfred Sully, 1821–1879* (Palo Alto, 1974). That these and other leaders showed an increasingly humanitarian attitude toward their foes is shown in Richard N. Ellis, "Humanitarian Generals," *We.H.Q.,* III (April, 1972).

Warfare on the Southern Plains. A comprehensive book on warfare on the southern plains between 1864 and 1875 is William H. Leckie, *The Military Conquest of the Southern Plains* (Norman, 1963). Documents dealing with these campaigns are in LeRoy R. Hafen and Ann W. Hafen, *Relations with the Indians of the Plains, 1857–1861: A Documentary Account of the Military Campaigns, and Negotiations of Indian Agents* (Glendale, 1959).

The episode that touched off the plains warfare has been much discussed by historians. Michael Sievers, "Sands of Sand Creek Historiography," *C.M.,* XLIX (Spring, 1972), correctly points out that none has emerged with a synthesis that recognizes the multiple forces creating this outbreak. That a primary reason for the massacre was the political pressure leading to the appointment of inferior Indian agents is cogently argued in Harry E. Kelsey, "Background to Sand Creek," *C.M.,* XLV (Fall, 1968); the same author has written a useful biography of the man who was Colorado's governor at the time in *Frontier Capitalist: The Life of John Evans* (Boulder, 1969). A popular but useful history is Stan Hoig, *The Sand Creek Massacre* (Norman, 1961). Raymond C. Carey sheds light on this affair in "The Puzzle of Sand Creek," *C.M.,* XLI (Fall, 1964), a judicious appraisal of the blame for the massacre. Savoie Lottinville, ed., *Life of George Bent: Written from His Letters by George E. Hyde* (Norman, 1968) tells the story of the outbreak and subsequent conflict from the Indian viewpoint. That the congressional investigation that followed was biased in favor of the Indians is argued in Harry Kelsey, "The Doolittle Report of 1867: Its Preparation and Shortcomings," *A. and W.,* XVII (Summer, 1975).

The spread of warfare over the southern plains after Sand Creek is expertly studied in Wilbur S. Nye, *Plains Indian Raiders: The Final Phases of Warfare from the Arkansas to the Red Rivers* (Norman, 1968). The failure of the Kiowa to enter into the war is explained in Forrest D. Monaghan, "Kiowa-Federal Relations in Kansas, 1865–1868," *C.O.,* XLIX (Winter, 1971), and Timothy A. Zwink, "E. W. Wynkoop and the Bluff Creek Indian Council, 1866," *K.H.Q.,* XLIII (Summer, 1977). The latter describes peace negotiations with the nontreaty tribes, as does Thomas D. Isern, "The Controversial Career of Edward W. Wynkoop," *C.M.,* LVI (Winter–Spring, 1979). Lonnie J. White, "Indian Raids on the Kansas Frontier, 1869," *K.H.Q.,* XXXVIII (Winter, 1972), describes the spread of hostilities into that area, while the conflict in western Nebraska is the theme of James T. King, "Forgotten Pageant—The Indian Wars in Western Nebraska," *N.H.,* XLVI (September, 1965). Defensive efforts in southern Colorado are described in Morris F. Taylor, "Fort Stevens, Fort Reynolds, and the Defense of Southern Colorado," *C.M.,* XLIX (Spring, 1972). The same author in "Plains Indians on the New Mexico-Colorado Border: The Last Phase," *N.M.H.R.,* XLVI (October, 1971), is over detailed in listing engagements fought in the vicinity. Duane Gage, "Black Kettle: A Noble Savage?" *C.O.,* XLV (Autumn, 1967), demonstrates that Black Kettle was not present during the raid that bears his name, and instead maintained a friendly attitude toward the United States.

The story of the Cheyenne-Arapaho War is told in Donald J. Berthrong, *The Southern Cheyennes* (Norman, 1963). Lonnie J. White, "The Cheyenne Barrier on the Kansas Frontier," *A. and W.,* IV (Spring, 1962), concentrates on the period from June, 1868 to June, 1869, while the same author has collected essays dealing with the Cheyenne War in *Hostiles and Horse Soldiers: Indian Battles and Campaigns in the West* (Boulder, 1972). Rupert N. Richardson, *The Comanche Barrier to South Plains Settlement* (Glendale, 1933), is still useful, but should be supplemented with Stan Hoig, *The Battle of the Washita: The Sheridan-Custer Indian Campaign of 1867–69* (Garden City, 1976). Even more valuable is Robert M. Utley, *Life in Custer's Cavalry: Diaries and Letters of Albert and Jennie Barnitz, 1867–1868* (New Haven, 1977), a firsthand account of a participant at Washita. Morris F. Taylor, "The Carr-Penrose Expedition: General Sheridan's Winter Campaign, 1868–1869," *C. of O.,* LI (Summer, 1973), deals with an expedition from Ft. Lyon under Captain William H. Penrose. Carl P. Tyson, "Highway of War," *R.R.V.H.R.,* III (Summer, 1978), describes an early expedition up the Red River under Nathaniel P. Banks that failed. The career of an agent to the Ute Indians in the 1870s is described in Robert Emmitt, *The Last War Trail: The Utes and the Settlement of Colorado* (Norman, 1954). Ernest Wallace, *Ronald S. Mackenzie and the Texas Frontier* (Lubbock, 1964), is the biography of an army officer who commanded troops in Texas during these campaigns; Jean L. Zimmerman, "Colonel Ronald S. Mackenzie at Fort Sill," *C.O.*, XLIV (Spring, 1966), traces his career after 1875 when he was transferred to Fort Sill. General William R. Shafter, who commanded Negro troops in Texas during the 1870s, is studied in Robert M. Utley, " 'Pecos Bill' on the Texas Frontier," *A.W.*, VI (January, 1969).

O'Nell Pate, "The Battle of Adobe Walls," *G.P.J.*, deals at length with the episode that touched off the Red River War. The war itself is described in James L. Haley, *The Buffalo War: The History of the Red River Indian Uprising of 1874* (Garden City, 1976), and in William H. Leckie, ed., "The Red River War, 1874–1875," *R.R.V.H.R.*, III (Spring, 1978), a collection of essays on the war. An important expedition is detailed in Robert C. Carriker, "Mercenary Heroes: The Scouting Detachment of the Indian Territory Expedition, 1874–1875," *C. of O.*, LI (Fall, 1973) which deals with three columns under Pope. Benjamin Capps, *The Warren Wagon Train Raid* (New York, 1974), is a full history of the raid that led to the arrest of Satanta.

The fate of the defeated Indians is the theme of Donald J. Berthrong, *The Cheyenne and Arapaho Ordeal: Reservation and Agency Life in the Indian Territory, 1875–1907* (Norman, 1977), Virginia Shaw, "The End of the Cheyenne-Arapaho Alliance," *R.R.V.H.R.*, V (Winter, 1980), shows that the cultural gap between the two tribes made it impossible for them to occupy the one reservation assigned them, while Virginia R. Allen, "The White Man's Road: The Physical and Psychological Impact of Relocation on the Southern Plains Indians," *J.H.M.*, shows that the defeat and insecurity created an emotional climate detrimental to both mental and physical health. That conflicts between military and civilian authority on the reservations contributed to the fatal climate there is shown in John B. Harte, "Conflict at San Carlos: The Military-Civilian Struggle for Control, 1882–1885," *A. and W.*, XV (Spring, 1973). Val J. McClellan, *This Is Our Land* (New York, 1977), contains a hodge-podge of ill-digested information on the Meeker Massacre, a minor episode involving the White River Ute that occurred in 1879.

Warfare on the Northern Plains. General

accounts of the Sioux wars are in George E. Hyde, *A Sioux Chronicle* (Norman, 1956), and James C. Olson, *Red Cloud and the Sioux Problem* (Lincoln, 1965). A Brief general history of the Sioux wars in Minnesota during the 1860s is Willoughby M. Babcock, "Minnesota's Indian War," *M.H.*, XXXVIII (September, 1962). More complete is C. M. Oehler, *The Great Sioux Uprising* (New York, 1959). Principal expeditions in the war are described in Edward Noyes, "Neighbors 'To the Rescue': Wisconsin and Iowa Troops Fight Boredom, Not Indians, in Minnesota in 1862," *M.H.*, XLVIII (Winter, 1979), which describes the lack of activity of troops from Iowa and Wisconsin; Clair Jacobson, "The Battle of Whitestone Hill," *N.D.H.*, describing a battle fought in North Dakota in 1863, and Geraldine Bean, "General Alfred Sully and the Northwest Indian Expedition," *N.D.H.*, XXXIII (Summer, 1966). Robert H. Jones, "The Northwestern Frontier and the Impact of the Sioux War, 1862," *M.A.*, XLI (July, 1959), stresses the fact that this was one of the most destructive Indian wars in history, while Roy W. Meyer, "The Establishment of the Santee Reservation, 1866–1869," *N.H.*, XLV (March, 1964), traces the transfer of the Santee Sioux to a Nebraska reservation after the uprising. The broader effect of the Sioux War on the West as a whole is the theme of Edmund J. Danziger, Jr., "The Crow Creek Experiment: An Aftermath of the Sioux War of 1862," *N.D.H.*, XXXVII (Spring, 1970). Two articles by Michael A. Sievers, "Westward by Indian Treaty: The Upper Missouri Example," *N.H.*, LVI (Spring, 1975), and "The Administration of Indian Affairs on the Upper Missouri, 1858–1865," *N.D.H.*, XXXVIII (Summer, 1971), deal with problems created by the war's heritage. The Canadian-American problems resulting from the wars are the theme of Alvin C. Gluek, Jr., "The Sioux Uprising: A Problem in International Relations," *M.H.*, XXXIV (Winter, 1955). Early Indian relations in the Dakota country are described by a contemporary observer in Lucile M. Kane, ed., *Military Life in Dakota. The Journal of Philippe Régis de Tribriand* (St. Paul, 1951). Robert G. Athearn, "The Fort Buford 'Massacre,' " *M.V.H.R.*, XLI (March, 1955), ably demonstrates that this 1867 episode in the Dakotas was not a massacre as believed at the time.

Several of the sites of battles are exactly located in J. W. Vaughn, *Indian Fights: New Facts on Seven Encounters* (Norman, 1966). Scholarly, but still failing to grasp the significance of the cultural change taking place among the northern tribes, is Roy W. Meyer,

History of the Santee Sioux: United States Indian Policy on Trial (Lincoln, 1967).

The Powder River Road controversy that touched off the most serious phase of the Sioux warfare is admirably described in Grace R. Hebard and A. R. Brininstool, *The Bozeman Trail*, 2 v. (Cleveland, 1922). E. A. Brininstool, *Crazy Horse* (Los Angeles, 1949), deals largely with the death of this chief. Burton S. Hill, "John Bozeman and the Bozeman Trail," *A. of W.*, XXXVI (October, 1964), is a brief biography, while documents are in LeRoy R. Hafen and Ann W. Hafen, eds., *Powder River Campaigns and Sawyers Expedition of 1865: A Documentary Account* (Glendale, 1961). Two episodes in the warfare along the trail are treated in Robert A. Murray, "The Wagon Box Fight: A Centennial Appraisal," *A. of W.*, XXXIX (April, 1967), and Brian Jones, "John Richard, Jr., and the Killing at Fetterman," *A. of W.*, XLIII (Fall, 1971). The tense state of nerves on the frontier at the time is illustrated in James L. Thane, Jr., "The Montana 'Indian War' of 1867," *A. and W.*, X (Summer, 1968), describing the military preparations, costing over a million dollars, made when a false rumor of an Indian invasion of Montana spread. On the other hand, reasons for Sioux discontent are explained in Carol A. Ripich, "Joseph H. Wham and the Red Cloud Agency," *A. and W.*, XII (Winter, 1970), which describes efforts of a government agent to move Red Cloud and his Sioux from Wyoming to the Dakota reservation in 1871, and Wesley C. Wilson, "The U.S. Army and the Piegans: The Baker Massacres on the Marias, 1870," *N.D.H.*, XXXII (January, 1965), which describes the merciless killing of 173 Indians. Another massacre that could have been avoided, that of a band of Pawnee by the Sioux in 1873, is described in Paul D. Riley, "The Battle of Massacre Canyon," *N.H.*, LIV (Summer, 1973). A battle on the site of modern Casper, Wyoming, is pictured in J. W. Vaughn, *The Battle of Platte Bridge* (Norman, 1963). Vaughn has also written *With Crook on the Rosebud* (Harrisburg, 1956).

Biographies of military leaders have much to say about the northern Plains warfare. A classic work by Crook's lifetime aide that is still essential is John G. Bourke, *On the Border with Crook* (Chicago, 1891). Charles King, *Campaigning with Crook* (Norman, 1964), is also a classic. Essential, too, is R. G. Carter, *On the Border with Mackenzie* (New York, 1961). Useful also are John W. Bailey, *Pacifying the Plains: General Alfred Terry and the Decline of the Sioux, 1869–1890* (Westport, 1979), Virginia M. Johnson, *The*

Unregimented General (Boston, 1926), a competent study of General Nelson A. Miles, and James T. King, *War Eagle: A Life of General Eugene A. Carr* (Lincoln, 1963). General Crook's autobiography has been made available in Martin F. Schmitt, ed., *General George Crook: His Autobiography* (Norman, 1960). James T. King, "Needed: A Re-evaluation of General George Crook," *N.H.*, XLV (September, 1964), charges that Crook has been overrated by earlier biographies and needs to be given a lesser place in history.

Custer and the Little Big Horn. Few episodes in American history have inspired such voluminous historical writing. This is examined in Robert M. Utley, *Custer and the Great Controversy: The Origin and Development of a Legend* (Los Angeles, 1962), and Michael Sievers, "The Literature of the Little Big Horn: A Centennial Historiography," *A. and W.*, XVIII (Summer, 1976). The best history of the campaign in which Custer died is John S. Gray, *Centennial Campaign: The Sioux War of 1876* (Ft. Collins, 1976), while the best biography, although too favorable to Custer, is Jay Monaghan, *Custer: The Life of General George Armstrong Custer* (Boston, 1959). Robert Ege, *Curse Not His Curls* (Ft. Collins, 1974), is also strongly pro-Custer, but tells the story of his battle well. James Willert, *Little Big Horn Diary: Chronicle of the 1876 Indian War* (La Mirada, 1977), is a day-by-day chronicle of the campaign. Custer's two principal opponents are appraised in Alexander B. Adams, *Sitting Bull: An Epic of the Plains* (New York, 1974), and Stephen E. Ambrose, *Crazy Horse and Custer: The Parallel Lives of Two American Warriors* (Garden City, 1975). One of Custer's subordinates is the theme of John U. Terrell and George Walton, *The Life and Trial of Major Reno* (New York, 1966), which is designed for a popular audience; another who fought with him is described in Ben Innis, *Bloody Knife! Custer's Favorite Scout* (Ft. Collins, 1973). Contemporary accounts of the campaign are in James H. Howard, trans., *The Warrior Who Killed Custer: The Personal Narrative of Chief Joseph White Bull* (Lincoln, 1968), W. A. Graham, ed., *The Custer Myth: A Source Book of Custeriana* (Harrisburg, 1953), Daniel O. Magnussen, ed., *Peter Thompson's Narrative of the Little Big Horn Campaign, 1876* (Glendale, 1974), Kenneth Hammer, ed., *Custer in '76: Walter Camp's Notes on the Custer Fight* (Provo, 1976), and Benjamin F. Cooling, III, ed., *Soldering in the Sioux Country* (San Diego, 1971), a diary kept by Charles H. Springer in an 1865 campaign. John M. Carroll, ed., assembles government documents dealing with the campaign in *Gen-*

eral Custer and the Battle of the Little Big Horn: The Federal View (New Brunswick, 1976). Custer's own autobiography has been reprinted as *My Life on the Plains* (Norman, 1962). That Indian scouts played a major role in the campaign is ably demonstrated in John S. Gray, "Arikara Scouts with Custer," *N.D.H.,* XXXV (Spring, 1968). That all of the commanders in the campaign had been taught Napoleonic tactics at West Point, and that Custer violated these rules is shown in Archer Jones, "The United States in the Little Big Horn Campaign," *N.D.H.,* XLIII (Spring, 1975). Edgar I. Stewart, *Custer's Luck* (Norman, 1955), is a usable history of the battle. Harry H. Anderson has shed new light on two aspects of the campaign: in "Cheyennes at the Little Big Horn—A Study of Statistics," *N.D.H.,* XXVII (Spring, 1960), he demonstrates that 1,500 Indians were at the battle, not the 3,000 usually stated, and in "Indian Peace-Talkers and the Conclusion of the Sioux War of 1876," *N.H.,* XLIV (December, 1963), he shows that diplomacy rather than military prowess ended the war in the late winter of 1877.

The aftermath of the defeat of Custer is described in Peter M. Wright, "The Pursuit of Dull Knife from Fort Reno in 1878–1879," *C.O.,* XLVI (Summer, 1968), dealing with the capture of a band of Northern Cheyenne who left the reservation, and Gary Pennanen, "Sitting Bull: Indian Without a Country," *C.H.R.,* LI (June, 1970), which traces the flight of the defeated Sioux to Canada and their sad plight there. The anxiety that gripped the West while waiting for Crazy Horse to surrender is described in Oliver Knight, "War or Peace: The Anxious Wait for Crazy Horse," *N.H.,* LIV (Winter, 1973). The attempts to disarm the Sioux and herd them on reservations following Custer's defeat are described in Richmond L. Clow, "General Philip Sheridan's Legacy: The Sioux Pony Campaign of 1876," *N.H.,* LVII (Winter, 1976), and Forrest W. Daniel, "Dismounting the Sioux," *N.D.H.,* XLI (Summer, 1974). Harold Umber, "Interdepartmental Conflict Between Fort Yates and Standing Rock: Problems of Indiaan Administration, 1870–1881," *N.D.H.,* XXXIX (Summer, 1972), discusses the conflict between military commanders at Ft. Yates and the government agents on Standing Rock Reservation, largely after the 1876 campaign. An attempt to move the Sioux to Indian Territory is described in Richmond L. Clow, "The Sioux Nation and Indian Territory: The Attempted Removal of 1876," *S.D.H.,* VI (Fall, 1976). The relative quiet that fell over Fort Custer after the war is reflected in a series of

newspaper articles reprinted in Richard Upton, ed., *Fort Custer on the Big Horn, 1877–1898: Its History and Personalities as Told and Pictured by Contemporaries* (Glendale, 1973).

The response of the nation to the defeat is touched on in two articles by Brian W. Dippie, " 'What Will Congress Do About It?' The Congressional Reaction to the Little Big Horn Disaster," *N.D.H.,* XXXVII (Summer, 1970), and "The Southern Response to Custer's Last Stand," *M.,* XXI (April, 1971). Robert A. Murray, "The Custer Court Martial," *A. and W.,* XXXVI (October, 1964), describes the court martial of Custer in 1867 that may have influenced his later behavior; the records of that hearing are in Lawrence A. Frost, *The Court-Martial of General George Armstrong Custer* (Norman, 1968). His widow's role in transforming Custer into a legendary character is explained in Michael L. Tate, "The Girl He Left Behind: Elizabeth Custer and the Making of a Legend," *R.R.V.H.R.,* V (Winter, 1980), while the growth of that legend in the years since 1876 is described in Brian W. Dippie, *Custer's Last Stand: The Anatomy of an American Myth* (Missoula, 1976), and explained in Bruce A. Rosenberg, *Custer and the Epic of Defeat* (University Park, 1974).

A thorough study of the extermination of the buffalo that so affected the Plains Indians is Wayne Gard, *The Great Buffalo Hunt* (New York, 1959); excellent accounts of the herds from the ice age to the 1890s are in David A. Dary, *The Buffalo Book: The Full Saga of the American Animal* (Chicago, 1974), and Tom McHugh, *The Time of the Buffalo* (New York, 1972). Francis Haines, *The Buffalo,* (New York, 1970), is also helpful. Carl C. Rister, "The Significance of the Destruction of the Buffalo," *S.H.Q.,* XXXIII (July, 1929), deals with the southern herd, while the slaughter of the northern herd is considered in H. A. Trexler, "The Buffalo Range of the Northwest," *M.V.H.R.,* VII (March, 1921). John R. Cook, *The Border and the Buffalo* (Topeka, 1907), is a memoir of a buffalo hunter, while the profits to be obtained from trade in buffalo bones are described in LeRoy Barnett, "The Buffalo Bone Commerce on the Northern Plains," *N.D.H.,* XXXIX (Winter, 1972).

The Last Indian Wars. Excellent accounts of the Modoc War in the Oregon Country in 1872–1873 are in Keith A. Murray, *The Modocs and Their War* (Norman, 1959), a general account, Erwin N. Thompson, *Modoc War: Its Military History and Topography* (Sacramento, 1972), which deals with military events as influenced by topography, and Richard Dillon, *Burnt-Out Fires* (Englewood Cliffs, 1973), a description of the war in northern California designed for popular reading. The better-known Nez Perce War is admirably treated in John D. McDermott. *Forlorn Hope: The Battle of White Bird Canyon and the Beginning of the Nez Perce War* (Boise, 1978), which describes the defeat of two cavalry units in June, 1877, that launched the conflict, and Alvin M. Josephy, Jr., *The Nez Perce Indians and the Opening of the Northwest* (New Haven, 1965). Merrill D. Beal, *I Will Fight No More Forever: Chief Joseph and the Nez Perce War* (Seattle, 1963), is also a balanced account. Information may also be found in two histories of the tribe: L. V. McWhorter, *Hear Me, My Chiefs! Nez Perce History and Legend* (Caldwell, 1952), and Francis Haines, *The Nez Perces: Tribesmen of the Columbia Plateau* (Norman, 1955). Mark H. Brown, *The Flight of the Nez Perce* (New York, 1967), is a scholarly account of the retreat of the Indians, showing that Chief Joseph played only a minor role in this. Other works that deal with Indian conflict in the Pacific Northwest are Robert H. Ruby and John A. Brown, *Half-Sun on the Columbia: A Biography of Chief Moses* (Norman, 1965), and Stephen D. Beckham, *Requiem for a People: The Rogue Indians and the Frontiersmen* (Norman, 1971). John A. Carpenter, "General Howard and the Nez Perce War of 1877," *P.N.Q.*, IL (October, 1958), describes peace making in the Northwest after the wars, while Alan Osborne, "The Exile of the Nez Perce in the Indian Territory, 1878–1885," *C. of O.*, LVI (Winter, 1978–79), chronicles the sad history of the tribe after its surrender.

The role of Catholic missionaries in helping bring peace to the Northwest is discussed in Harrod L. Howard, *Mission Among the Blackfeet* (Norman, 1971), and especially in Robert I. Burns, *The Jesuits and the Indian Wars of the Northwest* (New Haven, 1965). For the Bannock War see George F. Brimlow, *The Bannock War of 1878* (Caldwell, 1938), and for the Dull Knife Raid, Dennis Collins, *The Indian's Last Fight, or the Dull Knife Raid* (Girard, n.d.).

The Apache Wars of the 1880s are seen from the Indian viewpoint in Woodworth Clum, *Apache Agent: The Story of John P. Clum* (Boston, 1936), while the best biography of the Apache leader is Angie Debo, *Geronimo: The Man, His Time, His Place* (Norman, 1976). Alexander B. Adams, *Geronimo: A Biography* (New York, 1971), is an attempt to see Geronimo's exploits through his own eyes. A popular account of the campaign itself is Odie B. Faulk, *The Geronimo Campaign*

(New York, 1969). Dan L. Thrapp, *General Crook and the Sierra Madre Adventure* (Norman, 1972), describes a campaign in which Crook invaded the Indians' Sierra Madre hideout in 1882–1883, while Jack C. Gale, "Hatfield Under Fire, May 15, 1886: An Episode in the Geronimo Campaigns," *J.Ar.H.*, XVIII (Winter, 1977), deals with another invasion of Apache territory that ended in disaster for the invader, Captain Charles P. Hatfield. Joseph A. Stout, Jr., *Apache Lightning: The Last Great Battles of the Ojó Calientes* (New York, 1974), is a popular version that adds little. Reminiscences of participants include Dan L. Thrapp, ed., *Dateline Fort Bowie: Charles Fletcher Lummis Reports on an Apache War* (Norman, 1978), Jack C. Lane, ed., *Chasing Geronimo: The Journal of Leonard Wood, May–September, 1886* (Albuquerque, 1970), and John Bigelow, Jr., *On the Bloody Trail of Geronimo* (Los Angeles, 1958), as well as the classic descriptions of George Crook, *Résumé of Operations Against the Apache Indians from 1882 to 1886* (Washington, 1886), and Nelson A. Miles, *Personal Recollections of Nelson A. Miles* (Chicago, 1896).

An excellent account of the final wars on the northern plains is Robert M. Utley, *The Last Days of the Sioux Nation* (New Haven, 1963); Ralph K. Andrist is less scholarly and covers a wider time-span. Episodes in the final wars are described in Anthony McGinnis, "Intertribal Raiding on the Northern Plains after the Surrender of Sitting Bull," *R.R.V.H.R.*, II (Fall, 1975), showing that tight controls after 1881 stopped the intertribal raiding that had been a major cause of conflict, and Stephen D. Youngkin, "Prelude to Wounded Knee: The Military Point of View," *S.D.H.*, IX (Summer, 1974), a study of the criticisms of government policy by military leaders. A popular but objective account of the Battle of Wounded Knee is Rex A. Smith, *Moon of Popping Trees,* (New York, 1975), which traces the background of the massacre. The relation of the massacre to the Ghost Dance is made clear in Elaine G. Eastman, "The Ghost Dance War and Wounded Knee Massacre of 1890–1891," *N.H.*, XXVI (January, 1945) and (March, 1945). Henry F. Dobyns and Robert C. Euler, *The Ghost Dance of 1889 among the Pai Indians of Northwestern Arizona* (Prescott, 1967), describes the outbreak at that spot; the influence of the new religion on the Indians is explored in Joseph G. Jurgensen, *The Sun Dance Religion: Power for the Powerless* (Chicago, 1972).

Development of Indian Policy. A brief general history is S. Lyman Tyler, *A History of Indian Policy* (Washington, 1973), but far better for this period is Loring B. Priest, *Uncle Sam's Stepchildren: The Reformation of United States Indian Policy, 1865–1887* (New Brunswick, 1942). This should be supplemented with the careful study by Henry E. Fritz, *The Movement for Indian Assimilation, 1860–1890* (Philadelphia, 1963), and Alban W. Hoopes, *The Road to the Little Big Horn—and Beyond* (New York, 1975), which describes the wars and developing policy between 1864 and 1881 in popular fashion.

The role of reformers in shaping the emerging policies is treated in Robert W. Mardock, *Reformers and the American Indian* (Columbia, 1971), and in the pioneering studies by Francis P. Prucha: *American Indian Policy in Crisis: Christian Reformers and the Indian, 1865–1900* (Norman, 1976), a revealing view of the reformers as they sought to achieve Indian assimiliation, and *The Churches and Indian Schools, 1888–1912* (Lincoln, 1979), a fine account of the conflict between Catholic and Protestant reformers over the right to teach the Indians. Francis P. Prucha, ed., *Americanizing the American Indians* (Cambridge, 1973), is a useful collection of documents on the Indian reformers. Robert I. Burns, *The Jesuits and the Indian Wars of the Northwest* (New Haven, 1965), deals expertly with the reforming activities of that group, while the role of the Bureau of Catholic Indian Missions is described in Peter J. Rahill, *The Catholic Indian Missions and Grant's Peace Policy, 1870–1884* (Washington, 1953). The influential part of another sect is shown in Michael C. Coleman, "Not Race, but Grace: Presbyterian Missionaries and American Indians, 1837–1893," *J.A.H.,* LXVII (June, 1980), which shows that these missionaries refused to accept the racist views of the day and held that the Indians could be fitted into society.

Special studies of the developing federal policy are many. The inauguration of the Indian policy under Grant is studied in Henry G. Waltmann, "Circumstantial Reformer: President Grant and the Indian Problem," *A. and W.,* XIII (Winter, 1971), which pictures Grant as more sympathetic to the Indians than supposed but so politically inept that he could do nothing to help them, and in Donald Chaput, "Generals, Indian Agents, and Politicians: the Doolittle Survey of 1865," *We.H.Q.,* III (July, 1972), on the effort of Senator James R. Doolittle to secure a proper policy after heading an investigating commission in 1865, and particularly Lawrie Tatum, *Our Red Brothers and the Peace Policy of President Ulysses S. Grant* (Lincoln, 1970). Kenneth E. Davison, "President Hayes and the Reform

of American Indian Policy," *O.H.,* LXXXII (Summer–Autumn, 1973), deals with changes in the key period 1879–1881 when Carl Schurz was Secretary of the Interior. Two of the perennial conflicts that hampered the evolution of a policy are discussed in Francis P. Prucha, "The Board of Indian Commissioners and the Delegates of the Five Civilized Tribes, *C. of O.,* LVI (Fall, 1978), describing the lobbying efforts of Indian delegates in Washington, while H. Craig Miner, *The Corporation and the Indian: Tribal Sovereignty and Industrial Civilization in Indian Territory, 1865–1907* (Columbia, 1976), deals with the pressure brought by industrial corporations to disrupt the tribal system. The role of the Interior Department in these conflicts is demonstrated in Thomas G. Alexander, *A Clash of Interests: Interior Department and Mountain West, 1863–96* (Provo, 1977).

A competent study of the attempt to transfer control of Indian affairs to civilian hands in the period before 1875 is in Donald J. D'Elia, "The Argument over Civilian and Military Indian Control, 1865–1880," *H.,* XXIV (February, 1962). Other works that deal with aspects of the policy include William T. Hagan, *Indian Police and Judges: Experiments in Acculturation and Control* (New Haven, 1966), and Ray H. Mattison, "The Indian Reservation System on the Upper Missouri, 1865–1890," *N.H.,* XXXVI (September, 1955).

The effect of the Dawes Act on the Indians is admirably treated in Francis P. Prucha, ed., *The Dawes Act and the Allotment of Indian Lands* (Norman, 1973), a government report prepared by D. S. Otis of the Bureau of Indian Affairs, and a searching discussion of the act and its consequences. The operation of the Dawes Act in specific reservations is tested in Burton M. Smith, "The Politics of Allotment: The Flathead Indian Reservation as a Test Case," *P.N.Q.,* LXX (July, 1979), Ross R. Cotroneo, "A Time of Disintegration: The Coeur d'Alene and the Dawes Act," *We.H.Q.,* V (October, 1974), and Donald J. Berthrong, "Legacies of the Dawes Act: Bureaucrats and Land Thieves at the Cheyenne-Arapaho Agencies of Oklahoma," *A. and W.,* XXI (Winter, 1979). An excellent study by William T. Hagan, *United States-Comanche Relations: The Reservation Years* (New Haven, 1976), describes the waning fortunes of that tribe between 1867 and 1906.

Historians have also examined the reasons for the failure of Indian policy during these years. Frederick E. Hoxie, "The End of the Savage: Indian Policy in the United States Senate, 1880–1900," *C. of O.,* LV

(Summer, 1977), examines the views of senators and concludes that they had been coverted to the belief that the Indians were not "savages," and could be made to conform to the ways of the white men. On the other hand, the failure is blamed on the racial bias of westerners in Robert. W. Mardock, "The Plains Frontier and the Indian Peace Policy, 1865–1880," *N.H.*, XIL (Summer, 1968). Case studies of this failure include A. Glen Humphreys, "The Crow Indian Treaties of 1868; An Example of Power Struggle and Confusion in United States Indian Policy," *A. of W.*, XLIII (Spring, 1971), Berlin B. Chapman, *The Otoes and Missourias: A Study of Indian Removal and the Legal Aftermath* (Oklahoma City, 1965), and William T. Hagan, "Kiowas, Comanches, and Cattlemen, 1867–1906: A Case Study of the Failure of U.S. Reservation Policy," *P.H.R.*, XL (August, 1971), the latter an excellent account of the manner in which cattlemen bilked the Indians of their lands.

31 The Cattlemen's Frontier, 1865–1887

Three standard books tell the story thoroughly: Ernest S. Osgood, *The Day of the Cattlemen* Minneapolis, 1929), Edward E. Dale, *The Range Cattle Industry* (Norman, 1930), and Louis Pelzer, *The Cattlemen's Frontier* (Glendale, 1936); all are readable and have stood the test of time. They should, however, be balanced with more modern works that strip the cattle frontier of its legendary glamour. Lewis Atherton, *The Cattle Kings* (Bloomington, 1961) demonstrates that the true heroes were the cattle ranchers rather than the cowboys, and that these hard-headed business men really developed the West. The business side of ranching is also the theme of the excellent study by Gene M. Gressley, *Bankers and Cattlemen* (New York, 1966), which stresses the flow of capital to the West and shows that important events occurred in the plush Cheyenne Club rather than on the open range. That cattle-raising was a business that attracted hard-fisted investors is amply demonstrated in modern studies of its financial structure, and particularly in the flow of foreign capital. A classic work in this category is W. Turrentine Jackson, *The Enterprising Scot: Investors in the American West after 1873* (Edinburgh, 1968). Gene M. Gressley, "Broker to the British: Francis Smith and Company," *S.H.Q.*, LXXI (July, 1967), is the case study of a man who made a fortune by soliciting British money to be loaned in the West. The trade itself is described in Richard

Perren, "The North American Beef and Cattle Trade with Great Britian," *E.H.R.*, XXIV (August, 1971). Important articles are Herbert O. Brayer, "The Influence of British Capital on the Western Range-Cattle Industry," *Tasks of Economic History, Supplement*, IX (1949), J. Fred Rippy, "British Investment in Texas Lands and Livestock," *S.H.Q.*, LVIII (January, 1955), William W. Savage, Jr., "Cows and Englishmen: Observation on the Investment by British Immigrants in the Western Range Cattle Industry," *R.R.V.H.R.*, I (Spring, 1974), speculating on why British invested in ranching rather than in other parts of the empire, Jimmy M. Skaggs, "Pecuniary Man: Attitudes of British Investors Toward the Western Range Cattle Industry," *R.R.V.H.R.*, I (Spring, 1974), which concludes that investors were interested only in high interest rates, and Harmon R. Mothershed, "The British Investment Public and the Swan Land and Cattle Company, Limited," *A. of W.*, XLVIII (Fall, 1976), which shows that investors in this company received few dividends but were properly compensated through the rise of land prices. W.G. Kerr, *Scottish Capital on the American Credit Frontier* (Austin, 1976), is an excellent account of investment, with proper attention to that in cattle.

A usable guide to the vast literature on cattle raising is Henry E. Fritz, "The Cattlemen's Frontier in the Trans-Mississippi West. An Annotated Bibliography," *A. and W.*, XIV (Spring and Summer, 1972). Useful essays are in E. E. Dale, *Cow Country* (rev. edn., 1965), and Maurice Frink, et. al., *When Grass Was King: Contributions to the Western Range Cattle Industry Study* (Boulder, 1956). Chapters in Walter P. Webb, *The Great Plains* (Boston, 1931), and Fred A. Shannon, *The Farmers' Last Frontier* (New York, 1945), are also essential to an understanding of the range cattle industry.

The Origins of Texas Ranching. Odie B. Faulk, "Ranching in Spanish Texas," *H.A.H.R.*, XLV (May, 1965), traces the history of ranching in Texas from 1721 when the first herds arrived to the Texan Revolution. The impact of this Spanish period on the institutions and artifacts of ranching are described in Sandra L. Myres, "The Ranching Frontier: Spanish Institutional Backgrounds of the Plains Cattle Industry," in Harold M. Hollingsworth, ed., *Essays on the American West* (Austin, 1969). This view is successfully disputed in two important studies, Terry G. Jordan, "The Origin of Anglo-American Cattle Ranching in Texas: Documentation of Diffusion from the Lower South," *E.G.*, VL (January, 1969), and John D. W. Guice, "Cattle Raisers of the Old Southwest: A Reinterpretation," *We.H.Q.*, VIII (April, 1977). These demonstrate that the major characteristics of western ranching had developed east of the Mississippi in the early nineteenth century and moved westward with the frontier. A brief description of early ranching during the American period is Francis L. Fugate, "Origins of the Range Cattle Era in South Texas," *A.H.*, XXXV (July, 1961); a good brief account is in Ernest Wallace, *Texas in Turmoil: The Saga of Texas, 1849–1875* (Austin, 1965). J. Frank Dobie, *A Vaquero of the Brush Country* (Dallas, 1929), delightfully describes wild cattle roundups along the Rio Grande.

The Long Drive. The best work on the subject is Wayne Gard, *The Chisholm Trail* (Norman, 1954). Harry S. Drago, *Great American Cattle Trails* (New York, 1965), is a sober, scholarly study of all cattle trails from those of colonial Massachusetts to those of the Great Plains. That cattle driving was feasible long before the Long Drive was developed is shown in J. H. Atkinson, "Cattle Drives from Arkansas to California Prior to the Civil War," *A.H.Q.*, XXVIII (Autumn, 1969), a discussion of three drives in the 1850s. William E. Unrau, "Joseph G. McCoy and Federal Regulation of the Cattle Trade," *C.M.*, XLIII (Winter, 1966) demonstrates McCoy's dislike of all regulation of the drives that he launched on the Chisholm Trail. Kansas and Nebraska farmers used English principles of herd law, modified to fit the local need, in keeping herds from their fields; this is demonstrated in Rodney O. Davis, "Before Barbed Wire: Herd Law Agitation in Kansas and Nebraska," *J.W.*, IV (January, 1967). The wider effect of the trails is explored in Wayne Gard, "The Impact of the Cattle Trails," *S.H.Q.*, LXXI (July, 1967), an article introducing an issue of that journal devoted to the 100th anniversary of the Chisholm Trail. Life along the trail is described in Sam B. Ridings, *The Chisholm Trail* (Guthrie, 1936). Reminiscences and diaries of herders are collected in J. Marvin Hunter, ed., *Trail Drivers of Texas* (Nashville, 1925), and Baylis J. Fletcher, *Up the Trail in '79* (Norman, 1968). An account of one drive over the Chisholm Trail is in William L. Urban, "The Juvenal Cattle Drives of 1870," *K.H.Q.*, XXXIX (Summer, 1973).

Trails that displaced the Chisholm Trail have attracted less attention, Jimmy M. Skaggs, "Northward Across the Plains: The Western Cattle Trail," *G.P.J.*, XII (Fall, 1972), deals with the trail from Texas through Dodge City that emerged in the 1870s. That Goodnight laid out the trail named after him when driving a herd to a specific market at the ranch of the Patterson Brothers rather than to an unknown Colorado destination is shown in Charles Kenner, "The Origins of the 'Goodnight' Trail Reconsidered," *S.H.Q.*, LXXVII (January, 1974); that drive itself is described in Sue Flanagan, "Charles Goodnight in Colorado," *C.M.*, XLIII (Winter, 1966). Theodore B. Lewis, "The National Cattle Trail, 1881–1886," *N.H.*, LII (Summer, 1971), shows that Texas ranchers were the principal promoters of this trail.

The economics of the Long Drive have attracted attention from economic historians. Jimmy M. Skaggs, *The Cattle Trailing Industry: Between Supply and Demand* (Lawrence, 1873), studies the middlemen who arranged and financed the drives, while David Galenson, "The End of the Chisholm Trail," *J.E.H.*, XXXIV demonstrates that trail driving ended not because of quarantine laws but because the northern ranges were fully stocked. A statistical study showing that profits were high enough to justify the risks of the Long Drive is in David Galenson, "The Profitability of the Long Drive," *A.H.*, LI (October, 1977). This view is disputed in R. Taylor Dennen, "Cattle Trailing in the Nineteenth Century," *J.E.H.*, XXXV (June, 1975), which holds that the quarantine laws played a major role.

The Cattle Towns. Any study of these end-of-trail communities must begin with the excellent revisionist work by Robert R. Dykstra, *The Cattle Towns,* (New York, 1968), which examines their socioeconomic structure and shows them to be business-oriented with little of the lawlessness attributed to them. Two of the more famous towns are examined in this light by the same author in "The Last Days of 'Texan' Abilene: A Study in Community Conflict on the Farmer's Frontier," *A.H.*, XXXIV (July, 1960), and "Ellsworth, 1869–1875: The Rise and Fall of a Kansas Cow Town," *K.H.Q.*, XXVII (Summer, 1961). Dykstra's conclusions are bolstered in Carol Leonard and Isidor Wallimann, "Prostitution and Changing Morality in the Frontier Cattle Towns of Kansas," *K.H.*, II (Spring, 1979), a well-researched study showing that opposition to prostitution mounted rapidly as the populations increased. Philip D. Jordan, "The Town Marshal: Local Arm of the Law," *A. and W.*, XVI (Winter, 1974), describes the functions of law officers in cattle towns, as does Larry D. Ball, *The United States Marshals of New Mexico and Arizona Territories* (Albuquerque, 1978). The subject is briefly surveyed in W. Eugene Hollon, *Frontier Violence: Another Look* (New York, 1974). Histories of other cattle towns are Norbert R.

Mahnken, "Ogallala—Nebraska Cowboy Capital," *N.H.*, XXVIII (April–June, 1947), and Burton S. Hill, "Buffalo—Ancient Cow Town. A Wyoming Saga," *A. of W.*, XXXV (October, 1963).

Recent studies of the so-called "Bad Men" of the West tend to substantiate the findings of Dykstra that they were few, inconspicuous, and largely the invention of newspaper correspondents and fiction writers. Both Dale T. Schoenberger, *The Gunfighters* (Caldwell, 1971), and Joseph G. Rosa, *The Gunfighter: Man or Myth* (Norman, 1969), amply prove this to be the case. So does Frank R. Prassel, *The Western Peace Officer: A Legacy of Law and Order* (Norman, 1972), which reveals the western marshal as an unglamorous character who spent his time arresting drunks or rounding up stray dogs and almost never engaged in gun battles. Unglamorous descriptions of some of the famed western "gunmen" include Nyle H. Miller and Joseph W. Snell, *Why the West Was Wild* (Topeka, 1963), dealing with Kansas fighters and lawmen who gained undeserved reputations, Joseph G. Rosa, *They Called Him Wild Bill: The Life and Adventures of James Butler Hickok* (rev. edn., Norman, 1974), and Leon C. Metz, *Pat Garrett: The Story of a Western Lawman* (Norman, 1974). Julian Samora, et. al., *Gunpowder Justice: A Reassessment of the Texas Rangers* (Notre Dame, 1979), pictures this group as less romantic than its image suggests.

Development of the Northern Range. The spread and retreat of the northern range is described in geographic terms in Terry G. Jordan, "The Origin and Distribution of Open Range Cattle Ranching," *S.S.Q.*, XLIII (June, 1972). The extension of the cattle frontier over the Northwest is described in Harold E. Briggs, *Frontiers of the Northwest* (New York, 1940), and Robert G. Athearn, *High Country Empire: The High Plains and the Rockies* (New York, 1960). The Colorado industry is thoroughly treated in O. B. Peake, *The Colorado Range Cattle Industry* (Glendale, 1939), and Wyoming ranching in W. E. Guthrie, "The Open Range Cattle Business in Wyoming," *A. of W.*, V (July, 1927), Dan W. Greenburg, *Sixty Years, . . . The Cattle Industry in Wyoming* (Cheyenne, 1932), and especially T. A. Larson, *History of Wyoming* (Lincoln, 1978 edn.), an excellent history of the state. The same author includes a chapter on range cattle in his briefer *Wyoming: A Bicentennial History* (New York, 1977), while Clark C. Spence, *Montana: A Bicentennial History* (New York, 1978), and other histories of Montana devote proper space to ranching. Studies of pioneer cattlemen who helped de-

velop the Wyoming phase of the industry are B. W. Allred, "George Morgan, Pioneer Importer and Breeder of American Herefords," *A. of W.*, XLII (April, 1970), and James D. McLaird, "Ranching in the Big Horns: George T. Beck, 1856–1894," *A. of W.*, XXXIX (October, 1967), and "Building the Town of Cody: George T. Beck, 1894–1942," *A. of W.*, XL (April, 1968). A thorough study of the Johnson County War in Wyoming between squatters and large ranchers is told in Helena M. Smith, *The War on Powder River* (New York, 1966). Aspects of the conflict are considered in Lewis L. Gould, "A. S. Mercer and the Johnson County War: A Reappraisal," *A. of W.*, VII (Spring, 1965), Lewis L. Gould, "Francis E. Warren and the Johnson County War," *A. and W.*, IX (Summer, 1967), Lewis L. Gould, "Willis Van Devanter and the Johnson County War," *M.*, XVII (October, 1967), M. Paul Holsinger, "Willis Van Devanter: Wyoming Leader, 1884–1897," *A. of W.*, XXXVII (October, 1965), and Frank N. Schubert, "The Suggs Affray: The Black Cavalry in the Johnson County War," *We.H.Q.*, IV (January, 1973). The latter describes Buffalo Soliders assigned to the town of Suggs and their mistreatment.

For the Montana phase of the industry consult Robert H. Fletcher, *From Grass to Fences: The Montana Range Cattle Story* (New York, 1960), which is based on the records of the Montana Stock Growers Association. The career of a prominent Montana ranch is explored in Walt Coburn, *Pioneer Cattleman in Montana: The Story of the Circle C Ranch* (Norman, 1968), written by the son of a rancher, Robert Coburn, who began operating in 1886. The best work on South Dakota ranching is Bob Lee and Dick Williams, *Last Grass Frontier: The South Dakota Stock Grower Heritage* (Sturgis, 1964). D. Jerome Tweton, *The Marquis de Morés: Dakota Capitalist, French Nationalist* (Fargo, 1972), is more critical of Morés than Donald Dresden, *The Marquis de Mores: Emperor of the Badlands* (Norman, 1970).

The Extension of the Range Cattle Industry. The spread of ranching westward into Utah is treated in Don D. Walker, "From Self-Reliance to Cooperation: The Early Development of the Cattleman's Association in Utah," *U.H.Q.*, XXXV (Summer, 1967), and in the same author's "The Cattle Industry in Utah, 1850–1900," *U.H.Q.*, XXXII (Summer, 1964). Excellent on its extension into the Pacific Northwest is Orin J. Oliphant, *On the Cattle Ranges of the Oregon Country* (Seattle, 1968). Arizona ranching is well protrayed in J. J. Wagoner, "Development of the Cattle

Industry in Southern Arizona, 1870s and 1880s,'' *N.M.H.R.*, XXVI (July, 1951), and Jane W. Brewster, ''The San Rafael Cattle Company. A Pennsylvania Enterprise in Arizona,'' *A. and W.*, VIII (Summer, 1966), the history of a successful concern founded in the 1880s. Lowell H. Harrison, ''Thomas Simpson Carson, New Mexico Rancher,'' *N.M.H.R.*, XLII (April, 1967), deals with a Scot who ranched successfully in Arizona and New Mexico; the spread of the industry in the latter state is also described in Gerald Baydo, ''Cattle Ranching in the Pecos Valley of New Mexico,'' *Rocky Mt. Soc. Science Jour.*, VIII (April, 1971). New Mexico's Lincoln County War is best described in Robert N. Mullin, ed., *Maurice G. Fulton's History of the Lincoln County War* (Tucson, 1968). The diary and letters of the young Englishman whose murder touched off the war are in Frederick W. Nolan, comp., *The Life and Death of John Henry Tunstall* (Albuquerque, 1965).

The extension of the cattle frontier into West Colorado is told in Morris F. Taylor, ''Ranching on the Outboundaries of the Las Animas Grant in Colorado, 1884–1899,'' *A. and W.*, XVI (Summer, 1974), and into West Texas in Frederick W. Rathjen, *The Texas Panhandle Frontier* (Austin, 1974), Robert M. Utley, ''The Range Cattle Industry in the Big Bend of Texas,'' *S.H.Q.*, LXIX (April, 1966), and Richard Graham, ''The Investment Boom in British-Texas Cattle Companies, 1880–1885,'' *B.H.R.*, XXXIV (Winter, 1960). Two prominent Texas ranches are described in Dulcie Sullivan, *The LS Brand: The Story of a Panhandle Ranch* (Austin, 1968), which has a full account of the seventy-nine cowboys who struck the 1883 roundup, and William C. Holden, *The Espuela Land and Cattle Company A Study of a Foreign-Owned Ranch in Texas* (Austin, 1970). Thadis W. Box, ''Range Deterioration in West Texas,'' *S.H.Q.*, LXXI (July, 1967), tells how overcropping brought the industry to the brink of disaster by the end of the 1880s. One result was a shift of grazing northward into Canada. This is described in Paul Sharp, *Whoop-up Country: The Canadian-American West, 1865–1885* (rev. edn., Helena, 1960).

Histories of stockmen's associations have been listed above in connection with ranching in the several states. In addition the associations have been treated in a number of monographic studies. For the Wyoming Stock Growers' Association, the story is told in detail in a series of articles by W. Turrentine Jackson: ''Railroad Relations of the Wyoming Stock Growers' Association,'' *A. of W.*, XIX (January, 1947), ''The Wyoming Stock Grow-

ers' Association: Political Power in Wyoming Territory, 1873–1890,'' *M.V.H.R.*, XXXII (March, 1947), and ''The Wyoming Stock Growers' Association: Its Years of Temporary Decline, 1886–1890,'' *A.H.*, XXII (October, 1948). The same association's history is popularly told in Maurick Frink, *Cow Country Cavalcade: Eighty Years of the Wyoming Stock Growers;' Association* (Denver, 1954). Lewis Nordyke, *Great Roundup: The Story of Texas and Southwestern Cattlemen* (New York, 1955), is a journalistic history of the Texas and Southwestern Cattle Raisers Association. The career of one of the leaders of this organization is traced in Jimmy M. Skaggs, ''John Thomas Lytle: Cattle Baron,'' *S.H.Q.*, LXXI (July, 1967). The attempt of a group of cattlemen in 1887 to control prices by forming a national trust is described in Gene M. Gressley, ''The American Cattle Trust: A Study in Protest,'' *P.H.R.*, XXX (February, 1961).

Invasion of the Indian Territory. An excellent history of the range cattle industry in this area is William W. Savage, Jr., *The Cherokee Strip Live Stock Association: Federal Regulation and the Cattleman's Last Frontier* (Columbia, 1973), which is actually a history of ranching in the area. Carl C. Rister, *No Man's Land* (Norman, 1948), describes the occupation of the Oklahoma Panhandle. Articles by Edward E. Dale canvas the subject thoroughly: ''The Ranchman's Last Frontier,'' *M.V.H.R.*, X (June, 1923) and ''Ranching on the Cheyenne-Arapaho Reservation,'' *C.O.*, VI (March, 1928). The reaction of the Indians to this intrusion is told in William W. Savage, Jr., ''Leasing the Cherokee Outlet: An Analysis of Indian Reaction,'' *C.O.*, XLVI (Autumn, 1968), and Donald J. Berthrong, ''Cattlemen on the Cheyenne-Arapaho Reservation, 1883–1885,'' *A. and W.*, XIII (Spring, 1971).

Ranchers and Cowboys. The literature on the cowboy is voluminous. Any reading on the subject should begin with Joe B. Frantz and Julian E. Choate, Jr., *The American Cowboy: The Myth and the Reality* (Norman, 1955), a penetrating analysis. In Clifford P Westermeier, *Trailing the Cowboy: His Life and Lore as Told by Frontier Journalists* (Caldwell, 1955), are assembled a fine collection of source materials helpful in understanding the true nature of the cowboy; this same author in ''The Cowboy: His Pristine Image,'' *S.D.H.*, VIII (Winter, 1977), traces the evolution of the cowboy's image from the Civil War to the end of the century. The emergence of that myth is also treated in Don Russell, ''The Cowboy: From Black Hat to White,'' *R.R.V.,H.R.*, II (Spring, 1975), and especially in William W. Savage, Jr., *The Cowboy Hero: His Image in American History and Culture* (Norman, 1979). Two collections of essays examine the life and legend of the cowboy more fully: William W. Savage, Jr., ed., *Cowboy Life: Reconstructing an American Myth* (Norman, 1974), and Charles W. Harris and Buck Rainey, eds., *Cowboy: Six-Shooters, Songs, and Sex* (Norman, 1976). That cowboys were sufficiently human to organize for better wages and even to strike on occasion is shown in William H. Hutchinson, "The Cowboy and the Class Struggle, or, Never Put Marx in the Saddle," *A. and W.*, XIV (Winter, 1972), and David E. Lopez, "Cowboy Strikes and Unions," *La.H.*, XVIII (Summer, 1977). Aspects of cowboy life are discussed in Philip D. Jordan, "The Cowboy and the Law," *N.D.H.*, XLVI (Fall, 1979), which shows that most legal infractions were for drunkness or minor misdemeanors, and Don Ricket, *$10 Horse, $40 Saddle* (Ft. Collins, 1976), a description of the equipment used in their work.

Aspects of cowboy history and lore are touched on in such works as Philip Durham and Everett L. Jones, *The Negro Cowboys* (New York, 1965), which maintains that as many as one-fifth of the cowboys were blacks, a figure disputed by some historians. The subject is further explored in Kenneth W. Porter, "Negro Labor in the Western Cattle Industry, 1866–1900," *La.H.*, X (Summer, 1969). More traditional but well worth reading is J. Frank Dobie, *Cow People* (Boston, 1964). The effect of differing environments in producing cowboys is admirably discussed in Stephen Paullada, *Rawhide and Song: A Comparative Study of the Cattle Cultures of the Argentine Pampa and the North American Plains* (New York, 1963).

The best of the several volumes of reminiscences of cowboy life is Andy Adams, *The Log of a Cowboy* (Boston, 1903); an excellent biography of Adams is Wilson M. Hudson, *Andy Adams: His Life and Writings* (Dallas, 1964). Angie Dobie, ed., *The Cowman's Southwest; Being the Reminiscences of Oliver Nelson* (Glendale, 1953), James H. Cook, *Fifty Years on the Old Frontier* (New Haven, 1923), Charles A. Siringo, *A Texas Cowboy, or Fifteen Years on the Hurricane Deck of a Spanish Pony* (New York, 1885), and Willie N. Lewis, *Tapadero: The Making of a Cowboy* (Austin, 1972), are rich in atmosphere and anecdote.

Histories of some of the famous western ranches include: William C. Holden, *The Spur Ranch* (Boston, 1934), Robert H. Burns, "The Newman Ranches: Pioneer Cattle Ranches of the West," *N.H.*, XXXIV (March, 1953),

Lewis Nordyke, *Cattle Empire. The Fabulous History of the 3,000,000 Acre XIT* (New York, 1949), W. M. Pearce, *The Matador Land and Cattle Company* (Norman, 1964), Lester F. Sheffy, *The Francklyn Land and Cattle Company* (Austin, 1963), A. Ray Stephens, *The Taft Ranch: A Texas Principality* (Austin, 1964), Gene M. Gressley, "Teschemacher and deBillier Cattle Company: A Study of Eastern Capital on the Frontier," *B,H.R.*, XXXIII (Summer, 1959), Ellsworth Collins, *The 101 Ranch* (Norman, 1937), Harmon R. Mothershead, *The Swan Land and Cattle Company, Ltd.* (Norman, 1972), Morris F. Taylor, "The Maxwell Cattle Company, 1881–1888," *N.M.H.R.*, XLIX (October, 1974), and Mary W. Clarke, *The Swanson Saga and the SMS Ranches* (Austin, 1976).

Helpful biographies of leading ranchers include Donald E. Green, *Panhandle Pioneer: Henry C. Hitch, His Ranch and His Family* (Norman, 1979). Allen A. Erwin, *The Southwest of John R. Slaughter, 1841–1922* (Glendale, 1965), David B. Gracy II, "George Washington Littlefield: Portrait of a Cattleman," *S.H.Q.*, LXVIII (October, 1964), J. Evetts Haley, *Charles Goodnight; Cowman and Plainsman* (Boston, 1936), A. B. Wood, "The Coad Brothers; Panhandle Cattle Kings," *N.H.*, XIX (January, 1938), and Lincoln Lang, *Ranching with Roosevelt* (Philadelphia, 1926). Memoirs of former ranchers include Frank S. Hastings, *A Ranchman's Recollections* (Chicago, 1921), and John Clay, *My Life on the Range* (Chicago, 1924), while the reminiscences of the meat dealer responsible for helping shape the cattle kingdom are recorded in Joseph G. McCoy, *Historic Sketch of the Cattle Trade of the West and Southwest* (Washington, 1932). Cordia S. Duke and Joe B. Frantz, *6,000 Miles of Fence: Life on the XIT Ranch of Texas* (Austin, 1961), are the reminiscences of the wife of the general manager of the famous ranch between 1885 and 1912.

The Decline of Open-Range Ranching. The cattlemen's financial struggles during the 1880s are described in Louis Pelzer, "Financial Management of the Cattle Ranges," *J.E.B.H.*, II (August, 1930). One of the principal hazards leading to the end of the open range, the grass fire, is the theme of J. A. Rickard, "Hazards of Ranching on the South Plains," *S.H.Q.*, XXXVII (April, 1934), while the disastrous winter that doomed the northern open range industry is pictured in Barbara F. Rackley, "The Hard Winter 1886–1887," *M.*, XXI (Winter, 1971). The transition to 'big pasture' ranching is described in Edward E. Dale, "The Cow Country in Transition," *M.V.H.R.*, XXIV (June, 1937). Henry D.

McCallum and Frances T. McCallum, *The Wire That Fenced the West* (Norman, 1965), is an excellent history of the development and spread of barbed-wire fencing. That this fencing was used by cattlemen to enclose vast areas illegally is demonstrated in William R. White, "Illegal Fencing on the Colorado Range," *C.M.*, LII (Spring, 1975). The effort of Kansas ranchers to protect their economic interests in the 1890s in the theme of Charles L. Wood, "Cattlemen, Railroads, and the Origin of the Kansas Livestock Association— the 1890s," *K.H.Q.*, XLIII (Summer, 1977). A scholarly history of the cattle industry after its transition to the fenced range is John T. Schlebecker, *Cattle Raising on the Plains, 1900–1961* (Lincoln, 1963).

The Spread of the Sheep Range. The standard work is Charles W. Towne and Edward N. Wentworth, *Shepherd's Empire* (Norman, 1945). The coming of herds to the Northwest is discussed in Harold E. Briggs, "The Early Development of Sheep Ranching in the Northwest," *A.H.*, XI (July, 1937), and the rise of the industry in New Mexico in Alvar W. Carlson, "New Mexico's Sheep Industry: 1850–1900: It's Role in the History of the Territory," *N.M.H.R.*, XLIV (January, 1969). Wars between cattlemen and sheepmen on the Idaho-Nevada frontier are described in the biography of a gunman hired by the cattle growers: David H. Grover, *Diamondfield Jack: A Study in Frontier Justice* (Reno, 1968). Trails used by sheep drovers are exhaustively studied in Edward N. Wentworth, *America's Sheep Trails* (Ames, 1948).

32   Opening the Plains

General Works. The concept of the Great Plains country as a region whose hostile environment could be conquered only after the industrial revolution reached maturity is developed in the stimulating book by Walter P. Webb, *The Great Plains* (Boston, 1931). The volume and its point of view are criticized in Fred A. Shannon, "An Appraisal of Walter Prescott Webb's The Great Plains: A Study in Institutions and Environment.," *Critiques of Research in the Social Sciences* (New York, 1940), but Webb's book is nevertheless essential to an understanding of the Plains country. Fred A. Shannon, *The Farmer's Last Frontier* (New York, 1945), and especially Gilbert C. Fite, *The Farmer's Frontier, 1865–1900* (New York, 1966), admirably deal with problems discussed in this chapter, as do Russell McKee, *The Last West: A History of the Great Plains of North America* (New

York, 1974), a journalistic history covering the years from French and Spanish occupation onward, and Thomas Wessel, ed., *Agriculture in the Great Plains, 1876–1936* (Washington, 1977) a series of essays. Fred A. Shannon, *The Centennial Years: A Political and Economic History of America from the Late 1870s to the Early 1890s* (Garden City, 1967) deals more extensively with Far-Western agriculture than the author's earlier writings. A seminal book, comparable in some ways to Webb's study cited above, is James C. Malin, *The Grassland of North America: Prolegomena to Its History, with Addenda and Postscript* (Gloucester, 1967 edn.); an appreciation of this and other works on the grasslands by Malin is Robert G. Bell, "James C. Malin and the Grasslands of North America," *A.H.*, XLVI (July, 1972).

Development of Farm Implements. A series of delightful essays by Earl W. Hayter, *The Troubled Farmer, 1850–1900: Rural Adjustment to Industrialism* (DeKalb, 1968) deal with barbed wire, patent medicines, and farm machinery as they altered the lives of western farmers. The most thorough study of the invention and spread of barbed-wire fencing is in Henry D. McCallum and Frances T. McCallum, *The Wire That Fenced the West* (Norman, 1965). Clarence H. Danhoff, "The Fencing Problem in the Eighteen-Fifties," *A.H.*, XVIII (October, 1944), provides interesting background. Henry D. McCallum, "Barbed Wire in Texas," *S.H.Q.*, LXI (October, 1958), describes the various types of wire employed in fencing.

Shannon, *The Farmer's Last Frontier*, briefly describes improvements in farm machinery, while Leo Rogin, *The Introduction of Farm Machinery in Its Relations to the Productivity of Labor* (Berkeley, 1931), demonstrates the effect of the inventions on frontier expansion. Neil M. Clark, *John Deere: He Gave to the World the Steel Plow* (Moline, 1937), is a laudatory history of a leading plow manufacturer. Alan L. Olmstead, "The Mechanization of Reaping and Mowing In American Agriculture, 1833–1870," *J.E.H.*, XXXV (June, 1975), explains why farmers delayed in accepting new inventions of these implements; similar problems are discussed in Roy Bainer, "Science and Technology in Western Agriculture," *A.H.*, XLIX (January, 1975), an entire issue devoted to western agriculture. The evolution of planting machinery is described in Russell H. Anderson, "Grain Drills Through Thirty-Nine Centuries," *A.H.*, X (October, 1936), and of windmills in T. Lindsay Baker, "Turbine-Type Windmills on the Great Plains and Midwest,"

A.H., LIV (January, 1980). Walker D. Wyman, *Witching for Water, Oil, Pipes and Precious Metals: A Persistent Folk Belief from Frontier Days down to the Present* (Park Falls, 1977), examines methods of dowsing, while a serious study of artificial rain-making efforts is in Clark C. Spence, *The Rainmakers: American "Pluviculture" to World War II* (Lincoln, 1980). Everett Dick, "Water: A Frontier Problem," *N.H.*, XLIX (Autumn, 1968), is a thorough and delightful description of well drilling on the plains. The origins of irrigation in arid regions are discussed in Deryl V. Gease, "William N. Byers and the Case for Federal Aid to Irrigation in the Arid West," *C.M.*, XLV (Fall, 1968), and William Lilley and Lewis L. Gould, "The Western Irrigation Movement, 1878–1902: A Reappraisal," in Gene M. Gressley, ed., *The American West: A Reorientation* (Laramie, 1966). Both stress the fact that private enterprise lacked the resources to develop irrigation projects, and that the frontiersmen readily sought federal aid as a result. A thorough statistical study of the effect of these inventions on farm production is Wayne D. Rasmussen, "The Impact of Technological Change on American Agriculture, 1862–1962," *J.E.H.*, XXII (December, 1962). That dry-farming was generally successful is argued in Mary W. M. Hargreaves, "The Dry-Farming Movement in Retrospect," *A.H.*, LI (January, 1977). An amusing study of the various types of reaper-like machines patented to deal with grasshopper invasions is R. Douglas Hart, "Grasshopper Harvesters on the Great Plains," *G.P.J.*, XVI (Spring, 1977). Reynold M. Wik, *Steam Power on the American Farm* (Philadelphia, 1953), expertly explores that subject.

The Land System. Standard histories are Benjamin H. Hibbard, *A History of the Public Land Policies* (Madison, 1965 edn.), and Roy M. Robbins, *Our Landed Heritage* (Lincoln, 1976 edn.). Harold W. Dunham, *Government Handout: A Study of the Administration of the Public Lands, 1875–1891* (New York, 1970), studies the subject more thoroughly. A number of essays on the formulation and administration of the land system are in Vernon Carstensen, ed., *The Public Lands: Studies in the History of the Public Domain* (Madison, 1963), and Howard W. Ottoson, *Land Use Policy and Problems in the Unites States* (Lincoln, 1963). Ronald R. Brown, "Jonathan Baldwin Turner and the Land-Grant Idea," *J.I.S.H.S.*, LV (Winter, 1962), traces the growth of the idea of land grants for education through the person of an early Illinois advocate of such a plan, while John Y. Simon, "The Politics of the Morrill Act," *A.H.*, XXXVII (April, 1963),

studies the translation of that ideal into legislative form.

The Operation of the Land System. The most essential study is Paul W. Gates and Robert W. Swenson, *History of Public Land Law Development* (Washington, 1968), an important volume. Gates sums up some of his thinking on the disposal of the public domain in "The Homestead Act: Free Land Policy in Operation, 1862–1935," in Howard W. Ottoson, *Land Use Policy and Problems in the United States* (Lincoln, 1963), and "Homesteading on the High Plains," *A.H.*, LI (January, 1977), where he finds the policy sufficiently flexible to accommodate the needs of the area. Everett N. Dick, "Free Homes for Millions," *N.H.*, XLIII (December, 1962), is a popular and informal history of the working of the Homestead Act; he adds to the story in his *The Lure of the Land. A Social History of the Public Lands* (Lincoln, 1970).

The effectiveness of the Homestead Act has continued to intrigue investigators. Using statistical techniques, Homer E. Socolofsky, "Land Disposal in Nebraska, 1854–1906: The Homestead Story," *N.H.*, XLVIII (Autumn, 1967), demonstrates that 57 per cent of the Homestead claims were perfected, a figure only slightly less than those buying land from speculators. Using further samplings in "Success and Failure in Nebraska Homesteading," *A.H.*, XLII (April, 1968), the author came to virtually the same conclusions. On the other hand, Zachariah Boughn, "The Free Land Myth in the Disposal of the Public Domain in South Cedar County, Nebraska," *N.H.*, LVIII (Fall, 1977), finds in an important statistical study that of 212 patents granted for 35,261 acres, only fourteen for 2,176 acres were homesteaded. Robert M. Finley, "A Budgeting Approach to the Question of Homestead Size on the Plains," *A.H.*, XLII (April, 1968), concludes that farmers of the 1870s and 1880s could not have worked a larger plot than 160 acres, as opponents of the Homestead charged. Milton Holtz, "Early Settlement and Public Land Disposal in the Elkhorn River Valley, Cuming County, Nebraska Territory," *N.H.*, LII (Fall, 1971), shows that farmers used various forms of entry to build up farms that they wanted, varying in size and shape as their needs required, regardless of the purpose of the law, while Robert P. Swierenga, "Land Speculation and Frontier Tax Assessments," *A.H.*, XLIV (July, 1970), uses Iowa statistics to prove that absentee landlords paid somewhat higher taxes than residents, thus discouraging speculation. Some of these results are challenged by the most thorough study that has been made to date. Yasuo Okada, *Public*

Lands and Pioneer Farmers: Gage County, Nebraska, 1850–1890 (Tokyo, 1971), demonstrates that in the Nebraska county where the first homestead was granted, only 15 per cent of the land was acquired by Homestead and 40 per cent under the Agricultural College Act. Obviously more case studies over a wider area and timespan are needed to prove or disprove the effectiveness of the Homestead Act. That the imperfections of the measure and other land laws hurried rather than retarded settlement is the theme of Theodore Saloutos, "Land Policy and Its Relation to Agricultural Production and Distribution, 1862 to 1933," *J.E.H.*, XXII (December, 1962). Robert W. Fogel and Jack L. Rutner, "The Efficiency Effects of Federal Land Policy, 1850–1900: A Report on Some Provisional Findings," in William D. Aydelotte, et al., eds., *The Dimensions of Quantitative Research in History* (Princeton, 1972), uses quantitative techniques to prove that the land policy had little effect on farm efficiency; R. Taylor Dennen, "Some Efficiency Effects of Nineteenth-Century Federal Land Policy: A Dynamic Analysis," *A.H.*, LI (October, 1977), uses comparable techniques to prove just the opposite.

The systematic exploitation of the public domain by corporations is treated in William F. Raney, "The Timber Culture Acts," *M.V.H.A., Proceedings,* X (1919–20), and John T. Ganoe, "The Desert Land Act in Operation, 1877–1891," *A.H.,* XI (April, 1937). Two studies on the background of the former measure help explain its nature; Burton J. Williams, "Trees but No Timber: The Nebraska Prelude to the Timber Culture Act," *N.H.,* LIII (Spring, 1972), shows that a Nebraska law of the same nature passed in 1869 had encouraged almost no tree-planting; while David M. Emmons, "Theories of Increased Rainfall and the Timber Culture Act of 1873," *Forest Hist.,* XV (October, 1971), examines rainmaking theories of that day and decides that they were so widely accepted that Congress expected planting to increase rainfall. In a revealing study, Grant K. Anderson, "The Politics of Land in Dakota Territory: Early Skirmishes, 1857–1861," *S.D.H.,* IX (Summer, 1979), demonstrates that the Dakota Land Company and other speculative interests shaped government policy in Dakota Territory.

Railroad Land Grants and Speculation. That railroads received an excessive amount of land in government grants and that their speculative activity hindered the settlement process has been maintained by many historians. That this is not the case is argued in Robert S. Henry, "The Railroad Land Grant Legend in American History Texts," *M.V.H.R.*, XXXII (September, 1945). Leslie E. Decker, "The Railroads and the Land Office: Administrative Policy and the Land Patent Controversy, 1864–1896," *M.V.H.R.,* XLVI (March, 1960), demonstrates that the slowness with which land grants were transferred to railroads was a potent cause of dissatisfaction in the West. An Important aspect of the whole land-grant question is studied in Leslie E. Decker, *Railroads, Lands, and Politics: The Taxation of the Railroad Land Grants, 1864–1897* (Providence, 1964). The economic and social benefits of railroad grants are disputed by investigators. In two pioneering articles, "Land Grants to American Railroads: Social Cost or Social Benefit?" *B.H.R.,* XLIII (Summer, 1969), and "Rates of Return for Land-Grant System Railroads: The Central Pacific System," *J.E.H.,* XXX (September, 1970), Lloyd J. Mercer concludes that the "social" return (the economic growth and higher per-man output in adjacent regions) was as high as 24.1 per cent and the private return (profits to the railroads) only 1.1 per cent. Hence he argues that the land grants were justified. His conclusions are questioned in Stanley L. Engerman, "Some Economic Issues Relating to Railroad Subsidies and the Evaluation of Land Grants," *J.E.H.,* XXXII (June, 1972), largely on the grounds that the returns cannot be measured without comparative studies of areas without land grants. That the controversy is an old one is shown by Edgar I. Stewart, ed., *Penny-an-Acre Empire of the West* (Norman, 1968) which reproduces pamphlets and letters of the 1870s arguing over the benefits achieved by the Northern Pacific Railroad in the form of higher land prices. Further evidence is considered in the studies of profits of the Union Pacific Railroad listed in Chapter XXIX.

Disposal of the Public Domain. Thomas LeDuc, "The Disposal of the Public Domain on the Trans-Mississippi Plains: Some Opportunities for Investigation," *A.H.,* XXIV (October, 1950), stresses the need for further investigation of all aspects of land disposal. The sale of agricultural college land has been investigated in Thomas LeDuc, "State Disposal of the Agricultural College Land Scrip," *A.H.,* XXVIII (July, 1954), and Paul W. Gates, *The Wisconsin Pine Lands of Cornell University: A Study in Land Policy and Absentee Ownership* (Ithaca, 1943).

The operation of the land system in various western states is considered in: Addison E. Sheldon, *Land Systems and Land Policies in Nebraska* (Lincoln, 1936), William J. Stewart, "Speculation and Nebraska's Public Domain, 1863–1872," *N.H.,* XLV (September, 1964), Paul W. Gates, "Land and Credit Problems in Underdeveloped Kansas," *K.H.Q.,* XXXI (Spring, 1965), Paul W. Gates, *Fifty Million Acres: Conflicts over Kansas Land Policy, 1854–1890* (Ithaca, 1954), George L. Anderson, "The Administration of Federal Land Laws in Western Kansas, 1880–1890: A Factor in Adjustment to a New Environment," *K.H.Q.,* XX (November, 1952), which shows that administrative procedures were as ill-suited to the plains environment as the laws themselves, Charles L. Green, *The Administration of the Public Domain in South Dakota* (Pierre, 1940), and Paul W. Gates, "The Homestead Law in Iowa," *A.H.,* XXXVIII (April, 1964), which argues that the measure lessened the debt load and greatly benefited the state. The problems of imposing the American land system in a region where a Spanish system was already operating are explored in Howard R. Lamar, "Land Policy in the Spanish Southwest, 1846–1891," *J.E.H.,* XXII (December, 1962), while Paul W. Gates, "California's Agricultural College Lands," *P.H.R.,* XXX (May, 1961), reveals that California learned nothing from the mistakes of older states. An excellent study, well documented and searching in its implications, is Victor Westphall, *The Public Domain in New Mexico, 1854–1891* (Albuquerque, 1965), which deals with the disposal of the public domain there. R. Hal Williams, "George W. Julian and Land Reform in New Mexico, 1885–1889," *A.H.,* XLI (January, 1967), describes the attempts of the surveyor-general named to that state to secure local reforms and his resulting unpopularity.

33   The Farmers' Frontier, 1870–1890

Forces Encouraging Migration. The best history of the advancing farmers' frontier is Gilbert C. Fite, *The Farmers' Frontier, 1865–1900* (New York, 1966). Useful also is Fred A. Shannon, *The Farmers' Last Frontier* (New York, 1945). A fuller study of population movements is in Carter L. Goodrich, *Migration and Economic Opportunity* (Philadelphia, 1936). Two statistical studies deal with basic forces encouraging migration: C. Knick Harley, "Western Settlement and the Price of Wheat, 1872–1913," *J.E.H.,* XXXVIII (December, 1978), reveals the direct connection between world wheat prices and the rate of westward expansion, while Richard A. Easterlin, "Population Change and Farm Settlement in the Northern United States," *J.E.H.,*

shows that the decline in fertility of the farm population during the period was related to the expectation of multiplying capital. G. Edward White, *The Eastern Establishment and the Western Experience: The West of Frederick Remington, Theodore Roosevelt, and Owen Wister* (New Haven, 1969), is a brilliant exploration of the western image during these years as it served to induce migration. The contrast between these high expectations and the grim reality is the theme of Gilbert C. Fite, "Daydreams and Nightmares: The Late Nineteenth-Century Agricultural Frontiers," *A.H.,* XL (October, 1966).

Social conditions are described in a series of essays in Ray A. Billington, ed., *People of the Plains and Mountains: Essays in the History of the West Dedicated to Everett Dick* (Westport, 1973), while the role of women in the settlement of the Plains country is considered in Mary W. M. Hargreaves, "Women in the Agricultural Settlement of the Northern Plains," *A.H.,* L (January, 1976), and Christine Stansell, "Women on the Great Plains, 1865–1890," *W.S.,* IV (Number 4, 1976). The role of urban communities in the occupation of the Great Plains is described in Oliver Knight, "Toward an Understanding of the Western Town," *We.H.Q.,* IV (January, 1973), which suggests areas in which investigation is needed, and J. Christopher Schnell and Katherine B. Clinton, "The New West: Themes in Nineteenth Century Urban Promotion, 1815–1880," *B.M.H.S.,* XXX (January, 1974), which shows why some towns grew and others failed. Lawrence H. Larsen, *The Urban West at the End of the Frontier* (Lawrence, 1978), compares twenty-four western towns in 1880 on their treatment of municipal problems, finding little difference between West and East.

Migration from Europe to the Great Plains is studied in the histories of immigration, ranging from Carl L. Wittke, *We Who Built America: The Saga of the Immigrant* (New York, 1939), to Philip A. M. Taylor, *The Distant Magnet* (New York, 1971). A useful overall look is in Frederick C. Luebke, "Ethnic Group Settlement on the Great Plains," *We.H.Q.,* VIII (October, 1977), a plea for more research. One important group is studied in Arlow W. Anderson, *The Norwegian-Americans* (Boston, 1975), and Theodore C. Blegen, *Norwegian Migration to the United States,* 2 v. (Northfield, 1931–1940), another in George M. Stephenson, "Background of the Beginnings of Swedish Immigration, 1850–1875, *A.H.R.,* XXXI (July, 1926). Kenneth O. Bjork, *West of the Great Divide: Norwegian Migration to the Pacific Coast,*

1847–1893 (Northfield, 1958), is a detailed history of internal migration. The Mennonite migration from Russia is considered in Charles H. Smith, *The Coming of the Russian Mennonites* (Chicago, 1927). A study of the forces that led the English to migrate to the West in large numbers is Oscar O. Winther, "English Migration to the American West, 1865–1900," *H.L.Q.*, XXVII (February, 1964). A revisionist study showing that one immigrant group at least was usually upraised rather than depressed by migration to the West is Andrew F. Rolle, *The Immigrant Upraised: Italian Adventurers and Colonists in an Expanding America* (Norman, 1968).

The Role of the Railroads. The part played by railroads as colonizing agents in the trans-Mississippi West was first explored in two articles by James B. Hedges, "Promotion of Immigration to the Pacific Northwest by the Railroads," *M.V.H.R.*, XV (September, 1928), and "The Colonizing Work of the Northern Pacific Railroad," *M..V.H.R.*, XIII (December, 1926). Harold Peterson, "Some Colonizing Projects of the Northern Pacific Railroad," *M.H.*, X (June, 1929), deals with the same road, as does Ross R. Cotreneo, "Northern Pacific Officials and the Disposition of the Railroad's Land Grant in North Dakota after 1888," *N.D.H.*, XXXVII (Spring, 1970). An excellent study of the Union Pacific's policy, Barry B. Combs, "The Union Pacific Railroad and the Early Settlement of Nebraska, 1868–1880," *N.H.*, L (Spring, 1969), shows that the company spent more than eight million dollars on promotional activities. John B. Rae, "The Great Northern's Land Grant," *J.E.H.*, XII (Spring, 1952), proves that the line acquired an extensive grant when it assumed control of the St. Paul and Pacific Railroad; the manner in which this was used to promote the agricultural lands along the route is the theme of Ronald Ridgley, "The Railroads and Rural Development in the Dakotas," *N.D.H.*, XXXVI (Spring, 1969). The settlement activities of the Chicago, Burlington, and Quincy Railroad are admirably described in Richard C. Overton, *Burlington West* (Cambridge, 1941), and more briefly in the same author's splendid history of the road, *Burlington Route. A History of the Burlington Lines* (New York, 1965). The policy adopted after 1869 of seeking only settlers from well-to-do backgrounds is described in Ian MacPherson, "Better Britons for the Burlington: A Study of the Selective Approach of the Chicago, Burlington & Quincy in Great Britain," *N.H.*, L (Winter, 1969). An excellent study of the Santa Fe's colonizing policy is in William S. Greever, *Arid Domain. The Santa Fe Railway and Its*

Western Land Grant (Stanford, 1954), and of the Southern Pacific in Edna M. Parker, "The Southern Pacific Railroad and the Settlement of Southern California," *P.H.R.*, VI (June, 1937). Meroe J. Owens, "John Barzynski, Land Agent," *N.H.*, XXXVI (June, 1955), deals with a Polish land agent for the Burlington and Missouri River Railroad. An admirable case study of the manner in which that railroad transported large numbers of Russian Mennonites to the West is in John D. Unruh, Jr., "The Burlington and Missouri River Railroad Brings the Mennonites to Nebraska, 1873–1878," *N.H.*, XLV (March, 1964). Similar studies of other western lines are needed.

The standard work on social conditions in the prairie country is Everett Dick, *The Sod-House Frontier, 1854–1900* (New York, 1937), which describes obstacles as well as living conditions faced by the farmers. A thorough description of the sod house and how it was built is Roger L. Welsch, "The Nebraska Soddy," *N.H.*, XLVIII (Winter, 1967). James C. Malin, "Dust Storms," *K.H.Q.*, XIV (May, 1946) and later issues, and John T. Schlebecker, "Grasshoppers in American Agricultural History," *A.H.*, XXVII (July, 1953), deal with other menaces to settlers. The development of new farming techniques is briefly described in Mary W. M. Hargreaves, *Dry Farming in the Northern Great Plains, 1900–1925* (Cambridge, 1957).

The Kansas-Nebraska Frontier. The problem of adjusting to the Kansas-Nebraska environment is considered in James C. Malin, *Grassland Historical Studies . . . Natural Resources Utilization in a Background of Science and Technology* (Lawrence, 1950). The process is described in histories of the two states, of which the most useful are Robert W. Richmond, *Kansas: A Land of Contrasts* (St. Charles, 1974), and James C. Olson, *History of Nebraska* (Lincoln, 1966 edn.). Dorothy W. Creigh, *Nebraska: A Bicentennial History* (New York, 1977), and Kenneth S. Davis, *Kansas: A Bicentennial History* (New York, 1976), are modest and up to date. The coming of aliens from Europe to Kansas is treated in Charles K. Davis, "A Colony in Kansas—1882," *Am. Jewish Archives*, XVII (November, 1965), describing the migration of a colony of Jews driven from Russia by the persecutions of Alexander III to settle near Cimarron, Emory Lindquist, "The Swedish Immigrant and Life in Kansas," *K.H.Q.*, XXIX (Spring, 1963), George R. Beyer, "Pennsylvania Germans Move to Kansas," *P.H.*, XXXII (January, 1965), and Norman E. Saul, "The Migration of Russian-Germans to Kansas," *K.H.Q.*, XL (Spring, 1974).

Two modern studies describe the "Exodus" of blacks from the lower Mississippi Valley to Kansas in the 1870s: Nell I. Painter, *Exodusters: Black Migration to Kansas after Reconstruction* (New York, 1977), and Robert G. Athearn, *In Search of Canaan: Black Migration to Kansas, 1879–80* (Lawrence, 1978), the latter by a mature scholar. Norman I. Crockett, *The Black Towns* (Lawrence, 1979), deals with the sixty-odd black towns established in Kansas and Oklahoma, while the response of two cities to the influx is the theme of Suzanna M. Grenz, "The Exodusters of 1879: St. Louis and Kansas City Responses," *M.H.R.*, LXXIII (October, 1978). Arvarh E. Strickland, "Toward the Promised Land: The Exodus to Kansas and Afterward," *M.H.R.*, LXIX (July, 1975), places the movement in its proper historical setting. Migration from one area is described in Morgan D. Peoples, " 'Kansas Fever' in North Louisiana," *L.H.*, XI (Spring, 1970). A comparable but more successful colony of Negroes in Oklahoma established in the 1890s is described in Mosell C. Hill, "The All-Negro Communities of Oklahoma: The Natural History of a Social Movement," *J.N.H.*, XXXI (July, 1946).

The promotional writing that helped attract American farmers to Kansas and Nebraska is discussed in David M. Emmons, *Garden in the Grasslands: Boomer Literature of the Central Great Plains* (Lincoln, 1971), while efforts of Nebraska to lure settlers through an "Immigrant Association" are treated in Orville H. Zabel, "To Reclaim the Wilderness: The Immigrant's Image of Territorial Nebraska," *N.H.*, XLVI (December, 1965). William E. Unrau, "The Council Grove Merchants and Kansas Indians, 1855–1870," *K.H.Q.*, XXXIV (Autumn, 1968), demonstrates that merchants banded together to encourage migration, even to bringing pressure for Indian removal from areas near their towns. Other merchants and their efforts to bring railroads to Lawrence, Kansas, are described in I. E. Quastler, *The Railroads of Lawrence, Kansas, 1854–1900: A Case Study in the Causes and Consequences of an Unsuccessful American Urban Railroad Plan* (Lawrence, 1979); the tragic effects of quarrels between promoters is shown in David C. Taylor, "Boom Town Leavenworth: The Failure of the Dream," *K.H.Q.*, XXXVIII (Winter, 1972). That one ethnic group fitted well into the frontier atmosphere and adopted frontier ways is shown in Eleanor L. Turk, "The Germans of Atchison, 1854–1859: Development of an Ethnic Community," *K.H.*, II (Autumn, 1979).

The removal of Indians from Kansas and the beginning of settlement are described in H. Craig Miner and William F. Unrau, *The End of Indian Kansas: A Study of Cultural Revolution, 1854–1871* (Lawrence, 1978), a story comparable to that of the removal of the Five Civilized Tribes from the Southeast. The importation of a brand of wheat that allowed farming in dry Kansas is described in K. S. Quisenberry and L. P. Reitz, "Turkey Wheat: The Cornerstone of an Empire," *A.H.*, XLVIII (January, 1974), while the transition from a pastoral to a farming economy is traced in a statistical analysis in John L. Madden, "An Emerging Agricultural Economy: Kansas 1860–1880," *K.H.Q.*, XXXIX (Spring, 1973). That the army often aided in the settlement process is suggested in one case study: Richard Guentzel, "The Department of the Platte and Western Settlement, 1866–1877," *N.H.*, (Fall, 1975). Studies of the occupation of specific regions include Rita Napier, "Economic Democracy in Kansas: Speculation and Townsite Preemption in Kickapoo," *K.H.Q.*, XL (Autumn, 1974), an excellent account of the early movement into the territory by Missouri speculators, L. Carl Brandhorst, "The North Platte Oasis: Notes on the Geography and History of an Irrigated District," *A.H.*, LI (January, 1977), which describes the beginning of irrigation in the upper Platte country; and James L. Forsythe, "Environmental Considerations in the Settlement of Ellis County, Kansas," *A.H.*, LI (January, 1977), a case study of the hardships that were overcome by a Russian communal settlement. A statistical study showing that British investment in Kansas was double that in Iowa, but still of minor significance, is Larry McFarlane, "British Investment in Midwestern Farm Mortgages and Land, 1875–1900: A Comparison of Iowa and Kansas," *A.H.*, XLVIII (January, 1974).

Everett Dick, *Conquering the Great American Desert: Nebraska* (Lincoln, 1975), is an anecdotal history of the occupation of western Nebraska. That Dick in his earlier studies erred in estimating the nature of the population is shown in David J. Wishart, "Age and Sex Composition of the Population on the Nebraska Frontier, 1860–1880," *N.H.*, LIV (Spring, 1973). The legend of the Great American Desert did not deter settlement so long as the pioneers could be within fifteen miles of timber according to C. Howard Richardson, "The Nebraska Prairies: Dilemma to Early Territorial Farmers," *N.H.*, L (Winter, 1969). One reason for this acceptance was the ability of farmers to adjust their holdings to the environment; Milton E. Holtz, "Early Settlement and Public Land Disposal in the Elkhorn

River Valley, Cuming County, Nebraska,''
N.H., LII (Summer, 1971), tells how such an
adjustment was made. The manner in which
areas rose and fell in popularity during settlement is explored in William H. Breezley,
''Homesteading in Nebraska, 1862–1872,''
N.H., LIII (Spring, 1972), while Thomas R.
Walther, ''Some Aspects of Economic Mobility in Barrett Township of Thomas County,
1885–1905,'' *K.H.Q.*, XXXVII (Autumn, 1971),
traces the migration of sixty-four farm families
as they adjust or fail to adjust to local conditions.

The Northwestern Frontier. A full
version of the occupation of the Dakotas is
Herbert S. Schell, *Dakota Territory During
the Eighteen Sixties* (Vermillion, 1954); briefer
are the same author's *History of South Dakota* (Lincoln, 1975 edn.). The standard history by Elwyn B. Robinson, *History of
North Dakota* (Lincoln, 1966), has not been
displaced by the popularly written D. Jerome
Tweton and Theodore B. Jelliff, *North Dakota: The Heritage of a People* (Fargo,
1976), or Robert P. and Wyona H. Wilkins,
North Dakota: A Bicentennial History (New
York, 1977). An excellent history of the
bonanza farms in the Red River valley is
Hiram M. Drache, *The Day of the Bonanza:
A History of Bonanza Farming in the Red
River Valley of the North* (Fargo, 1964). The
same author explores the economic and social history of the valley, concentrating on
life on the small farms rather than the large
estates, in his *The Challenge of the Prairie:
Life and Times of Red River Pioneers* (Fargo,
1970). Stanley N. Murray, *The Valley Comes
of Age: A History of Agriculture in the Valley
of the Red River of the North, 1812–1920*
(Fargo, 1967), focuses on the Canadian portions of the valley, but contains important
information on American farming there. A
case study of a British firm that invested in
Red River valley lands is Morton Rothstein,
''A British Investment in Bonanza Farming,'' *A.H.*, XXXIII (April, 1959). Additional information may be found in Stanley
N. Murray, ''Railroads and Agricultural Development of the Red River Valley of the
North, 1870–1890,'' *A.H.*, XXXI (October,
1957).

Efforts to induce immigration by a tireless
promoter of Dakota lands are described in
Lewis O. Saum, ''Colonel Donan and the Image of Dakota,'' *N.D.H.*, XXXVII (Fall,
1970), and Kenneth M. Hammer, ''Come to
God's Country: Promotional Efforts in Dakota
Territory, 1861–1889,'' *S.D.H.*, X (Fall, 1980).
The major role of railroads in promoting immigration is admirably described in the standard biography of the builder of the Great

Northern: Albro Martin, *James J. Hill and the
Opening of the Northwest* (New York, 1976).
Kenneth M. Hammer, ''Railroads and Frontier Garrisons of Dakota Territory,'' *N.D.H.*,
XLVI (Summer, 1979), shows that army garrisons played a helpful role in building the
Great Northern, while Bryn Trescatheric,
''Furness Colony in England and Minnesota,
1872–1880,'' *M.H.*, XLI (Spring, 1980), describes the migration of a temperance colony
from England to the Northwest as a project
of another line, the Northern Pacific. That of
the 285 towns planted in Dakota between 1878
and 1887, all but fifty-seven were along railroad routes is demonstrated in James F. Ham-
burg, ''Railroads and the Settlement of South
Dakota during the Great Dakota Boom,
1878–1887,'' *S.D.H.*, V. (Spring, 1975), as
does John Hudson, ''Two Dakota Homestead
Frontiers,'' *A.A.A.G.*, LXIII (December, 1973),
which compares the settlement pattern in two
Dakota counties to show that each was determined by railroad building. Hiram M. Drache,
''The Economic Aspects of the Northern
Pacific Railroad in North Dakota,'' *N.D.H.*,
XXXIV (Fall, 1967), uses statistical evidence
to prove that the railroad was a major factor
in the settlement of North Dakota and its early
economic growth. Information on settlement
is also in Charles L. Green, *The Administra-
tion of the Public Domain in South Dakota*
(Pierre, 1940), and Gerald De Jong, ''The
Coming of the Dutch to the Dakotas,'' *S.D.Q.*,
V (Winter, 1974). John Hudson, ''Frontier
Housing in North Dakota,'' *N.D.H.*, XLIII
(Fall, 1975), argues that cultural tradition no
less than the environment determined the type
of homes erected by the pioneers.

The extension of the farming frontier into
Colorado, Wyoming, and Montana is touched
upon in the histories of the various states listed
in the bibliography to Chapter XXXI. Alvin
T. Steinel, *History of Agriculture in Colorado,
1858–1926* (Denver, 1926), and Merrill G. Burlingame, *The Montana Frontier* (Helena, 1942),
are also useful. Gordon H. Hendrickson, ed.,
*Peopling the High Plains: Wyoming's Euro-
pean Heritage* (Cheyenne, 1977), assembles
six essays dealing with as many ethnic groups,
but pays too little attention to their origins.
A good case study of the influence of one individual in developing a city's early culture is
Dorothea R. Muller, ''Church Building and
Community Making on the Frontier, a Case
Study: Joseph Strong, Home Missionary in
Cheyenne, 1871–1873,'' *We.H.Q.*, X (April,
1979). Interpretative and important is the
study of agricultural adaptation to the arid region in Robert G. Dunbar, ''The Significance
of the Colorado Agricultural Frontier,'' *A.H.*,
XXXIV (July, 1960). An important regional

study is Paul F. Sharp, *Whoop-Up Country. The Canadian-American West, 1865–1885* (rev. edn., Helena, 1960), a scholarly history of the area between Fort Benton on the upper Missouri, and Fort McLeod in Canada.

Governmental Beginnings in the Plains and Rockies. The nature of territorial government has interested scholars. Kenneth N. Owens, "Pattern and Structure in Western Territorial Politics," *We.H.Q.*, I (October, 1970), concludes that one-party rule and resulting factionalism was the normal pattern. The fifty-nine territorial governors who served in the West were drawn from the ranks of lawyers and businessmen with political experience. Hence Jack E. Eblen, "Status, Mobility, and Empire: The Territorial Governors, 1869–90", *P.N.Q.*, LX (July, 1969), concludes that they were far more able than generally supposed. This finding is disputed for Nebraska in Dannis Thavenet, "The Territorial Governorship: Nebraska Territory as Example," *N.H.*, LI (Winter, 1970), who finds that only two of the eight territorial governors were capable. Problems facing Kansas and Nebraska during their territorial periods are examined in Calvin W. Gower, "Kansas Territory and Its Boundary Question: 'Big Kansas' or 'Little Kansas,' " *K.H.Q.*, (Spring, 1967), John L. Madden, "The Financing of a New Territory: the Kansas Territorial Tax Structure, 1854–1861," *K.H.Q.*, XXXV (Summer, 1969), and Gordon J. Blake, "Government and Banking in Territorial Nebraska," *N.H.*, LI (Winter, 1970). Howard R. Lamar, *Dakota Territory, 1861–1889: A Study of Frontier Politics* (New Haven, 1956), is a model study of one state's governmental evolution. Equally valuable is Clark C. Spence, *Territorial Politics and Government in Montana, 1864–89* (Urbana, 1976). T. A. Larson, "Wyoming Statehood," *A. and W.*, XXXVII (April, 1965), is a competent study; the same author's "Dolls, Vassals, and Drudges—Pioneer Women in the West," *We.H.Q.*, III (January, 1972), delightfully describes the triumph of Women's Suffrage in Wyoming. Lewis L. Gould expertly examines the evolution of the state in *Wyoming: A Political History, 1868–1896* (New Haven, 1968). The intolerance of Wyoming's early settlers is shown in Roger D. Hardaway, "Prohibiting Interracial Marriage: Miscegenation Laws in Wyoming," *A. of W.*, LII (Spring, 1980). The statehood process in the Pacific Northwest is described in John D. Hicks, *The Constitutions of the Northwest States* (Lincoln, 1923). A valuable history of the development of one state government is Paul L. Beckett, *From Wilderness to Enabling Act: The Evolution of the State of Washington* (Pullman, 1968).

The Oklahoma Land Rushes. Danney Goble, *Progressive Oklahoma: The Making of a New Kind of State* (Norman, 1979), is an excellent history of the territorial period and statemaking; H. Wayne and Anne H. Morgan, *Oklahoma: A Bicentennial History* (New York, 1977), is brief but well done. An older account still usable is Roy Gittinger, *The Formation of the State of Oklahoma* (Berkeley, 1917). A well-researched account of Boomer activity is in Carl C. Rister, *Land Hunger: David L. Payne and the Oklahoma Boomers* (Norman, 1942); Berlin B. Chapman, "The Legal Sooners of 1889 in Oklahoma," *C.O.*, XXXV (Winter, 1957), deals with teamsters, land agents, and others who were legally in Oklahoma when the rush began. The situation in southern Kansas at the start of the rush is described in Jean C. Lough, "Gateways to the Promised Land: The Role Played by the Southern Kansas Towns in the Opening of the Cherokee Strip to Settlement," *K.H.Q.*, XXV (Spring, 1959). Town planting by the '89ers is described in Gerald Forbes, *Guthrie: Oklahoma's First Capital* (Norman, 1938), John Alley, *City Beginnings in Oklahoma Territory* (Norman, 1939), and Berlin B. Chapman, *The Founding of Stillwater* (Stillwater, 1949). Subsequent rushes are described in Michael H. Reggie, "Troubled Times: Homesteading in Short Grass Country, 1892–1900," *C. of O.*, LVII (Summer, 1979), which deals with the opening of the Cheyenne-Arapaho Reservation in 1892, and Norman L. Crockett, "The Opening of Oklahoma: A Businessman's Frontier," *C. of O.*, LVI (Spring, 1978), a study of five openings and how they were influenced by pressure from merchants. Daniel F. Littlefield, Jr., and Lonnie E. Underhill, "Kildare, Oklahoma Territory; Story of an Agricultural Boom Town," *G.P.J.*, XV (Fall, 1975), is an excellent account of a speculative attempt to create a boom town in the Cherokee Strip.

Aspects of the colonization process are treated in Lonnie E. and Daniel F. Underhill, Jr., "Women Homeseekers in Oklahoma Territory, 1889–1901," *Pac.H.*, XVII (Fall, 1973), a sketchy account of the role of women in the several rushes, and Bobby H. Johnson, "Doctors, Druggists, and Dentists in the Oklahoma Territory, 1889–1907," *A. and W.*, XIX (Summer, 1977), which concludes that anyone who survived their care was fortunate. Two studies of the attempt to establish Negro colonies there under the leadership of Edward P. McCabe are Daniel F. Littlefield, Jr. and Lonnie E. Underhill, "Black Dreams and 'Free' Homes: The Oklahoma Territory, 1891–1894," *Phylon*, XXXIV (December, 1973), and Martin Dann, "From Sodom to the Promised

Land: E. P. McCabe and the Movement for Oklahoma Colonization," *K.H.Q.*, XL (Autumn, 1974).

Two capable works by Glenn Shirley deal with the problems of law enforcement in the territory: *West of Hell's Fringe: Crime, Criminals, and the Federal Peace Officer in Oklahoma Territory, 1889–1907* (Norman, 1978), and *Law West of Fort Smith: A History of Frontier Justice in the Indian Territory* (New York, 1957), while Edward E. Dale and James D. Morrison, *Pioneer Judge: The Life of Robert Lee Williams* (Cedar Rapids, 1958), deals with a principal law-enforcement official. Two able articles by Charles W. Ellinger deal with the statehood process in Oklahoma: "The Drive for Statehood in Oklahoma, 1889–1906," *C.O.*, XVI (Spring 1963), and "Political Obstacles Barring Oklahoma's Admission to Statehood, 1890–1906," *G.P.J.*, III (Spring, 1964). An analysis and description of the 112 delegates elected to prepare the Oklahoma constitution is in Blue Clark, "Delegates to the Constitutional Convention," *C.O.*, XLVIII (Winter, 1970–71). Louise B. James, "The Woman Suffrage Issue in the Oklahoma Constitutional Convention," *C. of O.*, LVI (Winter, 1978–79), describes the efforts of women's rights advocates to insert a clause granting suffrage in the constitution, while James R. Wright, Jr., "The Assiduous Wedge: Woman Suffrage and the Oklahoma Constitutional Convention," *C. of O.*, LI (Winter, 1974), is a careful analysis of the delegates to explain why they failed. LeRoy H. Fischer, "Oklahoma Territory, 1890–1907," *C. of O.*, LIII (Spring, 1975), introduces a series of ten articles dealing with the territorial governors.

The Peopling of New Mexico and Arizona. A masterful study of the effect of the Southwest's environment on institutions is Howard R. Lamar, *The Far Southwest, 1846–1912: A Territorial History* (New Haven, 1966). More recent histories of the two states include Warren A. Beck, *New Mexico: A History of Four Centuries* (Norman, 1962), Marc Simmons, *New Mexico: A Bicentennial History* (New York, 1977), Lawrence C. Powell, *Arizona: A Bicentennial History* (New York, 1976), which is impressionistic, and Jay L. Wagoner, *Early Arizona: Prehistory to Civil War* (Tucson, 1975)., the latter a detailed chronicle of the early period.

Economic developments are the theme of Daniel T. Kelly, *The Buffalo Head* (Santa Fe, 1972), a badly misnamed book that actually deals with the history of a leading mercantile firm, Gross, Kelly Company. A capable sketch of another economic leader active in ranching and mercantile affairs in Arizona is

Elizabeth R. Snoke, "Pete Kitchen: Arizona Pioneer," *A. of W.*, XXI (Autumn, 1979). The problems of reconciling Spanish and American land law in the Southwest are sweepingly surveyed in Iris W. Engstrand, "Land Grant Problems in the Southwest: The Spanish and Mexican Heritage," *N.M.H.R.*, LIII (October, 1978), while two examples of the speculation that was rampant in early Arizona are revealed in Charles A. Cook, "The Hunter Claim: A Colossal Land Scheme in the Papaguerie," *A. of W.*, XV (Autumn, 1973), and Henry P. Walker, "Arizona Land Fraud: Model 1880. The Tombstone Townsite Company," *A. and W.*, XXI (Spring, 1979). Land sales as they affected the occupation of New Mexico are expertly described in Victor Westphall, *The Public Domain In New Mexico, 1854–1891* (Albuquerque, 1965), while the history of a large land grant is considered in Jim B. Pearson, *The Maxwell Land Grant* (Norman, 1961). The Maxwell grant is also expertly studied in Morris F. Taylor, *C. P. McMains and the Maxwell Land Grant* (Tucson, 1979), a thoroughly researched biography of a minister who sought to open the grant to homesteaders, and Norman Cleaveland, *The Morleys: Young Upstarts on the Southwest Frontier* (Albuquerque, 1971), an equally capable biography of the managers of the Maxwell Land Grant Company. The career of an Arizona lawyer and politician which sheds light on life in the territories is Jess G. Hayes, *Boots and Bullets: The Life and Times of John W. Wentworth* (Tucson, 1967).

Two articles on the statehood process in the two territories are John Braeman, "Albert J. Beveridge and Statehood for the Southwest," *A. and W.*, X (Winter, 1968), and Howard R. Lamar, "The Reluctant Admission: The Struggle to Admit Arizona and New Mexico to the Union," in Robert G. Ferris, ed., *The American West: An Appraisal* (Santa Fe., 1963). On Arizona, Jay J. Wagoner, *Arizona Territory, 1863–1912: A Political History* (Tucson, 1970), is a massive chronicle, poorly arranged. Studies dealing with aspects of the Arizona statehood process are Steven A. Frazio, "Marcus Aurelius Smith: Arizona Delegate and Senator," *A. and W.*, XII (Spring, 1970), B. Sacks, "The Creation of the Territory of Arizona," *A. and W.*, V (Spring and Summer, 1963), Bert M. Fireman, "Frémont's Arizona Adventure," *A.W.*, I (Winter, 1964), which describes Frémont's career as territorial governor, and Mary D. Palasson, "The Arizona Constitutional Convention of 1910: The Election of Delegates in Pima County," *A. and W.*, XVI (Summer, 1974), which demonstrates that progressive idealism was less effective in the selection of delegates than practical politics. Competent biographies of two of Arizona's early political leaders are John S. Goff, *George W. P. Hunt and His Arizona* (Pasadena, 1973), dealing with the state's first governor, and Victor Westphall, *Thomas Benton Catron and His Era* (Tucson, 1973), a study of the Republican leader who dominated political affairs for the last four decades of the territorial period.

A fine work on New Mexico's political evolution is Robert W. Larson, *New Mexico's Quest for Statehood, 1846–1912* (Albuquerque, 1968).

34   The Agrarian Revolt, 1873–1896

General Works.   A brief and still usable survey is Solon J. Buck, *The Agrarian Crusade* (New Haven, 1921). This should be supplemented with the stimulating chapters on the causes of unrest in John D. Hicks, *The Populist Revolt* (Minneapolis, 1931). Hicks's conclusions on the importance of the silver issue have been challenged in Lawrence Goodwyn, *Democratic Promise: The Populist Movement in America* (New York, 1976), which argues that the movement originated in Texas and the Southwest, not the Great Plains, and was based on a desire for an alternate culture based on decentralization and democratization of farm life. Political aspects are treated in Russell B. Nye, *Midwestern Progressive Politics; A Historical Study of Its Origins and Development, 1870–1950* (Lansing, 1951), H. Wayne Morgan, *From Hayes to McKinley: National Party Politics, 1877–1896* (Syracuse, 1969), and Nathan Fine, *Labor and Farmer Parties in the United States, 1828–1898* (New York, 1928). Documents on the history of agrarian discontent for the period are assembled in Vernon Carstensen, ed., *Farmer Discontent, 1865–1900* (New York, 1974). Two works dealing with the history of the Democratic Party in two western states also shed light on the unrest: James F. Pedersen and Kenneth D. Wald, *Shall the People Rule? A History of the Democratic Party in Nebraska Politics, 1854–1972* (Lincoln, 1972), and R. Hal Williams, *The Democratic Party and California Politics, 1880—1896* (Stanford, 1973), the latter a particularly competent study.

The southern phase of agrarian discontent has created a large historical literature which is surveyed in Patrick E. McLear, "The Agrarian Revolt in the South: A Historiographical Essay," *L.S.*, XII (Summer, 1973). The standard work on the subject is the schol-

arly study by Theodore Saloutos, *Farmer Movements in the South, 1865–1933* (Berkley, 1960). The story for one southern state is expertly told in William W. Rogers, *The One-Gallused Rebellion: Agrarianism in Alabama, 1865–1896* (Baton Rouge, 1970).

Interpretative investigations into the causes of discontent include such works as Anne Mayhew, "A Reappraisal of the Causes of Farm Protest in the United States, 1870–1900," *J.E.H.*, XXXII (June, 1972), and Jonathan Lurie, "Speculation, Risk, and Profits: The Ambivalent Agrarian in the Late Nineteenth Century," *A.H.*, XLVI (April, 1972). The latter argues that the commercialism of agriculture had converted farmers to a desire for large profits and subjected them to the fluctuations of the market place, thus causing dissatisfaction. This argument was carried a step further in a germinal article by Samuel P. Hays, "The Social Analysis of American Political History, 1880–1920," *P.S.Q.*, LXXX (September, 1965), which uses statistical techniques to prove that most voters remained loyal to the two major parties, and that those who did not were motivated by religious, ethnic, and social purposes. These findings are also stressed in Paul Kleppner, *The Cross of Culture: A Social Analysis of Midwestern Politics, 1850–1900* (New York, 1970), and bolstered in an analysis of 1,216 voters in Indiana's 1870 and 1874 elections: Melvyn Hammarberg, "Indiana Farmers and the Group Basis of the Late Nineteenth-Century Political Parties," *J.A.H.*, LXI (June, 1974). That the Australian ballot was used by Republicans to prevent the fusion of third parties with the Democrats in western states is shown in Peter H. Argersinger, " 'A Place on the Ballot': Fusion Politics and Antifusion Laws," *A.H.R.*, LXXXV (April, 1980), while Cornel J. Reinhart, "Populist Ideology: Mirror or Prism of the Guided Age," *N.D.Q.*, XLIII (Summer, 1975), describes the rhetoric and ideology of leaders of the agrarian reform movement.

The Granger Movement.   The definitive study is D. Sven Nordin, *Rich Harvest: A History of the Grange, 1867–1900* (Jackson, 1974), which holds that the movement was more social than political throughout its history. The assumption in Frank L. Klement, "Middle Western Copperheadism had the Genesis of the Granger Movement," *M.V.H.R.,* XXXVIII (March, 1952), that the Grange received its widest support in areas where Copperheadism was most prevalent is challenged in Ronald P. Formisano and William G. Shade, "The Concept of Agrarian Radicalism," *M.A.*, LII (January, 1970), which uses the elections to the Illinois Constitutional Convention to show that the center of agrarian dissent was in Yankee Republican communities. The early life of the founder of the Grange is studied in Rhoada R. Gilman and Patricia Smith, "Oliver Hudson Kelley: Minnesota Pioneer," *M.H.*, XL (Fall, 1967). That Kelley was no less responsible for founding the organization than William Saunders, and that both conceived of their society as a militant agrarian protest group is demonstrated in William D. Barnes, "Oliver Hudson Kelley and the Genesis of the Grange," *A.H.*, XLI (July, 1967). That wealthy California farmers failed to join the Grange is demonstrated in Gerald L. Prescott, "Farm Gentry vs. the Grangers: Conflict in Rural America," *C.H.S.Q.*, LVI (Winter, 1977–78). An important study of the many cooperative enterprises launched by the Grange is George Cerny, "Cooperation in the Midwest in the Grange Era, 1869–1875," *A.H.*, XXXVII (October, 1963), while Philip N. Backstrom, "The Mississippi Valley Trading Company: A Venture in International Cooperation, 1875–1877," *A.H.*, XLVI (July, 1972), describes a successful cooperative movement to facilitate exchange between the Granges and British cooperatives.

Recent studies have shown that the traditional story of farmers inflicting rate legislation on reluctant railroads requires revision. George E. Miller, *Railroads and the Granger Laws* (Madison, 1971), presents statistical evidence to show that the regulatory measures were adopted with little agrarian support and that the principal advocates of such laws were local businessmen endangered by pricing practices that discriminated against them in favor of large corporations. Gabriel Kolko, *Railroads and Regulation, 1877–1916* (Princeton, 1965), is equally persuasive in showing that the railroads welcomed federal regulation as preferable to ruinous competition or capricious regulation by the states. A case study of California rate control, Ward M. McAfee, "Local Interests and Railroad Regulation in California during the Granger Decade,"*P.H.R.*, XXXVII (February, 1968), demonstrates that railroad regulation was determined by local interests. The same author explains the failure of these attempts in terms of the influence wielded by the Southern Pacific Railroad in "A Constitutional History of Railroad Rate Regulation in California, 1879–1911," *P.H.R.*, XXXVII (August, 1968).

The history of the Grange in certain areas is told in Fred Trump, *The Grange in Michigan: An Agricultural History of Michigan over the Past 90 Years* (Grand Rapids, 1963), a jumble of information, Wayne E. Fuller, "The Grange in Colorado," *C.M.*, XXXVI (October, 1959), Mildred Thorne, "The Grange in Iowa, 1868–1875," *I.J.H.P.*, XLVII (October, 1949), Martin Ridge, "Ignatius Donnelly and the Granger Movement in Minnesota," *M.V.H.R.*, XLII (March, 1956), George H. Miller, "Origins of the Iowa Grange Law," *M.V.H.R.*, XL (March, 1954), Robert A. Calvert, "A. J. Rose and the Granger Concept of Reform," *A.H.*, LI (January, 1977), which explains the successes and failures of the Grange in Texas, and Daniel F. Littlefield and Lonnie E. Underhill, "The Granger Movement in the Cherokee Indians," *R.R.V.H.R.*, IV (Winter, 1979), describing a short-lived movement to establish Granges in Indian Territory.

The Greenback Interlude. An excellent study, which is primarily a political history of money rather than a financial history, is Irwin Unger, *The Greenback Era: A Social and Political History of American Finance, 1865–1879* (Princeton, 1964). Martin Ridge, *Ignatius Donnelly: The Portrait of a Politician* (Chicago, 1962), is an excellent biography of an agrarian leader whose career spans the entire post-Civil War era. The same author's "Ignatius Donnelly and the Greenback Movement," *M.A.*, XXXIX (July, 1957), fits the Greenback movement into the national setting. Edward H. Abrahams, "Ignatius Donnelly and the Apocalyptic Style," *M.H.*, XLVI (Fall, 1978), holds Ridge wrong in saying that Donnelly was driven into his political activities by a sense of failure, and that his convictions were based on his Jacksonian concept of the world. Richard M. Doolen, " 'Brick' Pomeroy and the Greenback Clubs," *J.I.S.H.S.*, LVX (Winter, 1972), deals with a Chicago editor responsible for establishing Greenback Clubs throughout the Midwest, while the movement in key states is studied in John D. Macoll, "Ezra A. Olleman: The Forgotten Man of Greenbackism, 1873–1876," *I.M.H.*, LXV (September, 1969), which deals with Indiana, Judith Berjenbruch, "The Greenback Political Movement: An Arkansas View," *A.H.Q.*, XXXVI (Summer, 1977), and Thomas B. Colbert, "Political Fusion in Iowa: The Election of James B. Weaver to Congress in 1878," *A. and W.*, XX (Spring, 1978). The standard biography of the party's presidential candidate is still Fred S. Haynes, *James Baird Weaver* (Iowa City, 1919).

The Farmers' Alliance. John D. Hicks describes the movement in *The Populist Revolt*, as does Lawrence Goodwyn, *Democratic Promise: The Populist Movement in America*, both listed above. An older work that is still valuable is John D. Hicks and John D. Barnhart, "The Farmers' Alliance," *N.C.H.R.*, VI (July, 1929). The career of a notable leader is described in Roy V. Scott, "Milton George and the Farmers' Alliance Movement," *M.V.H.R.*, XLV (June, 1958). An excellent history of the southern alliances is Robert C. McMath, Jr., *Populist Vanguard: A History of the Southern Farmers' Alliance* (Chapel Hill, 1976), while Michael Schwartz, *Radical Protest and the Social Structure: The Southern Farmers' Alliance and Cotton Tenancy, 1880–1890* (New York, 1976), is a study by a sociologist of the relationship between the alliance and the social structure of the South. The enrollment of more than a million black members is described in Martin Dann, "Black Populism: A Study of the Colored Farmers' Alliance through 1891," *J.Et.S.*, II (Fall, 1974), while the organization's rapid decline under racist attacks is shown in William F. Holmes, "The Demise of the Colored Farmers' Alliance," *J.S.H.*, XLI (May, 1975). That the alliances in the South contained no more than 857,000 members in 21,400 clubs is argued in Michael H. Schwartz, "An Estimate of the Size of the Southern Farmers' Alliance," *A.H.*, LI (October, 1977). The transition from the Alliance movement to Populism is the theme of Donald F. Warner, "Prelude to Populism," *M.H.*, XXXII (Autumn, 1953). A crucial transitional election, marked by remarkable success for the Populists that elevated them to a position as second party is described in Peter H. Argersinger, "Road to a Republican Waterloo: The Farmers' Alliance and the Election of 1890 in Kansas," *K.H.Q.*, XXXIII (Winter, 1967), and Sally S. Zanjani, "The Election of 1890: The Last Hurrah of the Old Regime," *N.H.S.Q.*, XX (Spring, 1977), which deals with the impending demise of the Republicans as a ruling party in Nevada after twenty-six years in power.

The Populist Revolt: Causes and Purpose. The standard works of John D. Hicks, *The Populist Revolt,* and Lawrence Goodwyn, *Democratic Promise: The Populist Movement in America,* cited earlier, are of course essential. Traditionally historians have believed that Populism was supported entirely by disgruntled rural agrarians and wealthy silverites. Their grievances have been linked to the overextension of credit and the depression of the mid-1880s. This subject has been properly studied in Allan G. Bogue, *Money at Interest: The Farm Mortgage on the Middle Border* (Ithaca, 1955). The same author, in "Foreclosure Tenancy on the Northern Plains," *A.H.*, XXXIX (January, 1965), studies the fate

of foreclosed lands after the collapse of the boom, showing that many were purchased by farmers to expand their holdings. In another germinal study, Bogue shows that on the Great Plains and other frontiers adequate credit facilities were available to farmers: "Land Credit for Northern Farmers, 1789–1940," *A.H.*, L (January, 1976). A case study of Whitman County, Washington, Thomas W. Riddle, "Populism in the Palouse: Old Ideals and New Realities," *P.N.Q.*, LXV (July, 1974), shows that well-to-do farmers there had so commercialized their operations that they did not feel the effect of the depression, but favored Populism because of high railroad rates. The ease with which mortgages could be placed, and the reasons for some eastern firms' failure to capitalize on their opportunities, are examined in H. Peers Brewer, "Eastern Money and Western Mortgages in the 1870s," *B.H.R.*, L (Autumn, 1976). Hallie Farmer, "The Railroads and Frontier Populism," *M.V.H.R.*, XIII (December, 1926), links the farm unrest of the late 1880s with dissatisfaction with the railroads. Robert Higgs, "Railroad Rates and the Populist Uprising," *A.H.*, XLIV (July, 1970), argues that there was no trend in rates between 1870 and 1896; this is disputed in Mark Aldrich, "A Note on Railroad Rates and the Populist Uprising," *A.H.*, LIV (July, 1980), which uses statistical techniques to show that rates which had been declining stabilized and began increasing in the late 1880s. In a similar vein, Donald E. Press, "Kansas Conflict: Populist Versus Railroader in the 1890s," *K.H.Q.*, XLIII (Autumn, 1977), shows that a principal thrust of the Kansas Populists was railroad regulation, while this argument is strengthened in H. Roger Grant, "Western Utopians and the Farmers' Railroad Movement, 1890–1900," *N.D.H.*, LXVIII (Winter, 1979), which describes the attempts of utopian groups such as the Colorado Cooperative Company to build their own railroads. Charles Hoffman, *The Depression of the Nineties* (Westport, 1970), is a statistical examination of the cause and impact of the panic.

The best study of the monetary problem as it emerged after the Panic of 1873 is Walter T. K. Nugent, *Money and American Society, 1865–1880* (New York, 1968), a thoughtful and scholarly book. It should, however, be supplemented with the fine volume by Allen Weinstein, *Prelude to Populism: Origins of the Silver Issue, 1867–1878* (New Haven, 1970), which focuses more directly on the problem. In this, the author shows that the wealthy silver-mine owners of Nevada had so diversified their investments by 1880 that they opposed free silver. Allen Weinstein has also demonstrated that a conspiracy of sorts was responsible for the "Crime of 1873," although not so well-organized a one as the free silverites claimed, in "Was There a 'Crime of 1873'?: The Case of the Demonetized Dollar," *J.A.H.*, LIV (September, 1967). That the term "Crime of 1873" was not used until 1889 is proven in Paul Barnett, "The Crime of 1873 Re-examined," *A.H.*, XXXVIII (July, 1964). Jeanette P. Nichols, "The Politics and Personalities of Silver Repeal in the United States Senate," *A.H.R.*, XLI (October, 1935), describes the repeal of the Sherman Silver Purchase Act.

The question of "who were the Populists" has engaged a number of historians. Their queries have led them in two directions. One controversy was launched when Richard Hofstadter explored "The Folklore of Populism" in his *The Age of Reform from Bryan to F.D.R.* (New York, 1955), arguing that Populism was seeking an escape from the industrial age, and that Populists mirrored this cultural lag by their nativistic tendencies. The opposite viewpoint was taken by Norman Pollack, *The Populist Response to Industrial America: Midwest Populist Thought* (Cambridge, 1962), which held that the Populists, rather than seeking a return to a preindustrial social order, were among the most cogent critics of society and truly progressive in their attitudes. The same author in a later essay has repeated these arguments, with additional evidence in, "Fear of Man: Populism, Authoritarianism, and the Historian," *A.H.*, XXXIX (April 1965), stressing that Populists were dedicated to equalitarianism as well as to social change. Three other scholars have studied Populists in different western areas, and all have concluded that they were neither nativistic nor anti-Semitic, but were genuinely progressive and dedicated to social as well as economic reform: Walter T. K. Nugent, *The Tolerant Populists: Kansas Populism and Nativism* (Chicago, 1963), Stanley B. Parsons, "Who Were the Nebraska Populist?" *N.H.*, XLIV (June, 1963), and Donald A. Pickens, "Oklahoma Populism and Historical Interpretation," *C.O.*, XLIII (Autumn, 1965). Theodore Saloutos, "The Professors and the Populists," *A.H.*, XL (October, 1966), surveys this whole controversy and concludes that earlier writers such as John D. Hicks who used archival sources were nearer the truth than the later critics of Populists.

Another group of historians have questioned the traditional belief that Populism attracted only discontented agrarians. The pioneer in this approach was David P. Trask,

"Notes on the Politics of Populism," *N.H.*, XLVI (June, 1965), who argued that the Panic of 1893 drove the small business men of the Midwest into the People's Party where they could combat the giant corporations of the East. This hypothesis has been tested in several states. In an analysis of Populist leaders in Colorado, G. Michael McCarthy, "Colorado's Populist Leadership," *C.M.*, XLVIII (Winter, 1971), finds that the majority were businessmen, lawyers, and professional men, with almost no farmers represented. On the other hand Walter T. K. Nugent, "Some Parameters of Populism," *A.H.*, XL (October, 1966), shows by statistical analysis that the party's members were drawn from rural, not urban, areas, and that they resembled Republicans save for their more precarious financial status. Similarly, Frederick C. Luebke, "Main Street and Countryside: Patterns of Voting in Nebraska During the Populist Era," *N.H.*, (Fall, 1969), using election returns from 186 precincts in the 1892 and 1896 elections, finds that Populism drove small businessmen into the Republican Party while increasing the proportion of farmers who voted Populist or Democratic. A case study of one California county revealed such a diversified membership that no absolute lines could be drawn: Tom G. Hall, "California Populism at the Grass-Roots: The Case of Tulare County, 1892," *S.C.Q.*, XLIX (June, 1967).

More recent scholarship has added new dimensions to the controversy. That Populists were strongly idealistic is suggested in two studies. H. Roger Grant, "Populists and Utopia: A Neglected Connection," *R.R.V.H.R.*, II (Winter, 1975), showing that 81 per cent of the authors of Utopian novels were Populists, and Christine McHugh, "Midwest Populist Leadership and Edward Bellamy: 'Looking Backward' Into the Future," *A.S.*, XIX (Fall, 1978), showing that Populist editors urged their readers to read Utopian novels. That Populism played a pivotal role in the transition of the nation from Jacksonian individualism to neomercantilistic progressivism is the theme of James M. Youngdale, *Populism: A Psychohistorical Perspective* (Port Washington, 1975). Also useful is a study of the basic differences between Populists and earlier Mugwumps, Martin Ridge, "The Populists as Social Critics," *M.H.*, XLIII (Winter, 1973), which pictures the Populists as faithful to the concept that power should be exercised within the limits of the democratic tradition, and not abused by any party or faction.

In a significant book that is far broader than its title indicates, Peter H. Argersinger,

Populism and Politics: William Alfred Peffer and the People's Party (Lexington, 1974), examines Kansas Populists to show that the closer a person lived to an urban area, the less likely he was to be a party member; he holds also that the movement stemmed from the economic grievances of farmers and their alienation from the traditional parties. This view is supported in Karel D. Bicha, *Western Populism: Studies in Ambivalent Capitalism* (Lawrence, 1976), and "The Western Populists: Marginal Reformers of the 1890s," *A.H.*, L (October, 1976), holding that Populism was a rural movement that was basically conservative, and that in the areas that it controlled it was no more reformist than the older parties. Equally suggested is a careful study of Nebraska Populism, Stanley B. Parsons, *The Populist Context: Rural Versus Urban Power on a Great Plains Frontier* (Westport, 1973), which shows that as farmers turned toward railroad and economic reform, the urban reformers who had supported the party broke away fearing laws that would check the flow of capital from the East. The arguments presented in these books are admirably digested in James Turner, "Understanding the Populists," *J.A.H.*, LXVIII (September, 1980), which concludes that isolation from neighbors was the strongest force in creating Populists, following a tradition in which isolation has normally bred a political culture at odds with the mainstream.

The problem of Who Were the Populists has been complicated by the study of voting patterns among ethnic groups. Paul Kleppner, *The Cross of Culture: A Social Analysis of Midwestern Politics, 1850–1900* (New York, 1970), holds that the Wisconsin Populists were largely rural Scandinavian and native pietists, while Frederick C. Luebke, *Immigrants and Politics: The Germans of Nebraska, 1880–1900* (Lincoln, 1969), shows that Republican opposition to liquor drove many Germans into the Populist and Democratic parties. A similar study on a broader scale, Richard Jensen, *The Winning of the Midwest: Social and Political Conflict, 1888–1896* (Chicago, 1971), concludes that party loyalty and religion were responsible for political attitudes and that economic or rural pressures were of minor importance. These findings are substantiated in Roger E. Wyman, "Wisconsin Ethnic Groups and the Election of 1890," *W.M.H.*, LI (Summer, 1968), which demonstrates that opposition to the Bennett Law requiring instruction in the English language in public schools were primarily responsible for driving Germans and Catholics into the Democratic Party. That same author, however, in "Agrarian or Work-ing-Class Radicalism? The Electoral Basis of Populism in Wisconsin," *P.S.Q.*, LXXXIX (Winter, 1974–1975), uses statistical techniques to demonstrate that Populism rose not from agrarian distress, but that its leaders were largely the heads of labor unions who never achieved a coalition with agrarian workers. In an important revisionist study, Gerald H. Gaither, *Blacks and the Populist Revolt: Ballots and Bigotry in the 'New South'* (University, 1977), disputes the traditional view of Populism as encouraging interracial cooperation, holding that on the national level blacks solidly supported Republican candidates. William H. Chafe, "The Negro and Populism: A Kansas Case Study," *J.S.H.*, XXXIV (August, 1968), concludes that Negroes failed to embrace Populism because they felt that their entrance into society would be slowed by such a move.

Rise and Decline of Populism. The Populist Party's role in the election of 1892 is considered in George H. Knoles, *The Presidential Campaign and Election of 1892* (Stanford, 1942). A local study, but with national implications for an understanding of why the Populists did not win in the 1894 elections, is Walter T. K. Nugent, "How the Populists Lost in 1894," *K.H.Q.*, XXXI (Autumn, 1965). Two histories of the 1896 election have been written, both based on extensive research: Stanley L. Jones, *The Presidential Election of 1896* (Madison, 1964), and Robert F. Durden, *The Climax of Populism: The Election of 1896* (Lexington, 1965). Full accounts are also in the many biographies of William Jennings Bryan: Paul W. Glad, *McKinley, Bryan and the People* (New York, 1963), Paolo E. Coletta, *William Jennings Bryan*, 3 v. (Lincoln, 1964–1969), and Louis W. Koenig, *Bryan: A Political Biography of William Jennings Bryan* (New York, 1971). Several scholars have examined the reasons for the Republican victory in 1896. James A. Barnes, "The Myths of the Bryan Campaign," *M.V.H.R.*, XXXIV (December, 1947), shows that prices did not rise spectacularly in 1896, thus encouraging the farmers to vote for McKinley. This interpretation is disputed in Gilbert C. Fite, "Republican Farm Strategy and the Farm Vote in the Presidential Election of 1896," *A.H.R.*, LXV (July, 1960), who shows that a speculative flurry in October, 1896, did create the momentary illusion of an economic recovery. The same author, in an important article on "William Jennings Bryan and the Campaign of 1896: Some Views and Problems," *N.H.*, XLVII (September, 1966), suggests that labor supported Bryan more than has been supposed, that his defeat was due to the lack of support from more prosperous farmers. On the other hand, Robert Higgs, "Railroad Rates and the Populist Uprising," *A.H.*, XLIV (July, 1970), demonstrates that the commonly held belief that freight rates fell steadily during the era is untrue. David S. Trask, in an important article, "A Natural Partnership: Nebraska's Populists and Democrats and the Development of Fusion," *N.H.*, LVI (Fall, 1975), shows that experience with fusion politics in Nebraska allowed the fusion of Populists and Democrats on a national scale to succeed. A detailed history of the election in one state is Richard L. Niswonger, "Arkansas and the Election of 1896," *A.H.Q.*, XXXIV (Spring, 1975).

Many local studies of Populism have been published. Of these the most recent and useful are Roy V. Scott, *The Agrarian Movement in Illinois, 1880–1896* (Urbana, 1962), which carefully studies all phases of post-Civil War agrarian unrest in the state, Kenneth E. Hendrickson, Jr., "Some Political Aspects of the Populist Movement in South Dakota," *N.D.H.*, XXXIV (Winter, 1967), David S. Trask, "Formation and Failure: The Populist Party is Seward County," *N.H.*, LI (Fall, 1970), an excellent analysis of the vote in that Nebraska county, Mary Ellen Glass, *Silver and Politics in Nevada: 1892–1902* (Reno, 1970), which shows that Republicans formed their own "Silver Party" in 1896 and that this helped carry the state for Bryan, Thomas A. Clinch, *Urban Populism and Free Silver in Montana* (Helena, 1970), showing urban workers seeking an eight-hour day as the principal supporters of the party in that state, David B. Griffiths, "Far Western Populism: The Case of Utah, 1893–1900," *U.H.Q.*, XXXVII (Fall, 1969), stressing the liberal support for Populists and their effort in return to democratize governmental structure and enact labor legislation, Terry P. Wilson, "The Demise of Populism in Oklahoma Territory," *C.O.*, XLIII (Autumn, 1965), James E. Wright, *The Politics of Populism: Dissent in Colorado* (New Haven, 1974), a solidly researched study that ranks the silver issue as decisive in that state, G. Michael McCarthy, "The People's Party in Colorado: A Profile of Populist Leadership," *A.H.*, XLVII (April, 1973), which shows that the party was led by lawyers and business men, and Robert W. Larson, *New Mexico Populism: A Study of Radical Protest in a Western Territory* (Boulder, 1974), an excellent analysis proving that the silver issue was only one of many contributing to the rise of Populism.

A number of superior biographies of Populist leaders provide insights not available in more general books. Among the best of these are Martin Ridge, *Ignatius Donnelly. The Portrait of a Politician* (Chicago, 1962), Elmer Ellis, *Henry Moore Teller, Defender of the West* (Caldwell, 1941), Francis B. Simkins, *Pitchfork Ben Tillman, South Carolinian* (Baton Rouge, 1944), Michael J. Brodhead, *Persevering Populist: The Life of Frank Doster* (Reno, 1969), a case study of a small-town lawyer in Nevada who joined the party and remained an uneasy Democrat thereafter, Karel D. Bicha "Jerry Simpson: Populist without Principle," *J.A.H.*, LIV (September, 1967), David B. Griffiths, "Far-Western Populist Thought: A Comparative Study of John R. Rogers and David H. Waite," *P.N.Q.*, LX (October, 1969), contrasting the governors of Colorado and Washington who represented two extremes of Populist thought, Samuel Walker, "George Howard Gibson, Christian Socialist among the Populists," *N.H.*, LV (Winter, 1974), and Harold Piehler, "Henry Vincent: Kansas Populist and Radical Reform Journalist," *K.H.*, II (Spring, 1979). The latter two deal with editors of Populist newspapers and their influence. J. Leonard Bates, "Politics and Ideology: Thomas J. Walsh and the Rise of Populism," *P.N.Q.*, LXV (April, 1974), shows how a long-time Montana senator remained a Democrat but still worked closely with the Populists. That the orator who urged farmers to raise less corn and more hell was active in a number of crusades is demonstrated in Dorothy R. Blumberg, "Mary Elizabeth Lease, Populist Orator: A Profile," *K.H.*, I (Spring, 1978); that she was a detriment rather than an aid to the cause is argued in O. Gene Clanton, "Intolerant Populist? The Disaffection of Many Elizabeth Lease," *K.H.Q.*, XXXIV (Summer, 1968). Despite its title, the same author's *Kansas Populism: Ideas and Men* (Lawrence, 1969), is actually a well-researched study of the eighty-nine leaders of the party.

The economic recovery which spelled doom for the Populists is described in Gerald T. White, "Economic Recovery and the Wheat Crop of 1897," *A.H.*, XIII (June, 1939). The eventual adoption of the Populist program by the United States is the theme of Theodore Saloutos and John D. Hicks, *Agricultural Discontent in the Middle West, 1900–1939* (Madison, 1951). On the other hand Gene Clanton, "Populism, Progressivism, and Equality: The Kansas Paradigm," *A.H.*, LI (July, 1977), concludes that in Kansas at least Progressivism was a small-town, middle class, elitist movement completely at odds with Populist radicalism.

35 The Frontier Heritage

The Frontier and the American Character. That the three centuries of frontiering experience was one of several forces helping shape the character of the people of the United States was the thesis advanced by Frederick Jackson Turner. Substantive arguments for this thesis are contained in the writings of Turner cited in the bibliography to Chapter I, and particularly in Ray A. Billington, *America's Frontier Heritage* (New York, 1966), which attempts to place the whole subject in its modern setting.

That historians have not been unanimous in accepting the frontier hypothesis is amply demonstrated by the controversial writing that it has aroused. Several alternate suggestions have been made. David M. Potter, *People of Plenty: Economic Abundance and the American Character* (Chicago, 1954), ascribes many national traits to the continuing plenty resulting from the sequential exploitation of resources. An alternative interpretation holds that the distinctive traits of Americans are traceable to the habit of mobility; this is vigorously upheld by Everett S. Lee, "The Turner Thesis Re-examined," *A.Q.*, XIII (Spring, 1961), and George W. Pierson, *The Moving American* (New York, 1972). Louis Hartz, *The Liberal Tradition in America* (New York, 1955), holds that the distinctive features of the civilization of the United States stem from the lack of a medieval tradition. Historians will probably never agree on the relative weight of these influences, and others, in forming the national character, but advocates of the frontier theory can point out that had there been no empty continent to be occupied, the abundance stressed by David Potter, the mobility argued by Everett Lee and George Pierson, and the break with the medieval past advanced by Louis Hartz could not have emerged as moulding forces. Hence the frontiering experience is one key to understanding the uniqueness of American civilization.

The Closing of the Frontier. That the dramatic announcement of the closing of the frontier in 1890 was decidedly premature, and was made by a journalist serving as director of the census with little justification, is shown in Gerald D. Nash, "The Census of 1890 and the Closing of the Frontier," *P.N.Q.*, LXXI (July, 1980). Turner's own views on the effect of the closing on American life and character are examined in Ray A. Billington, "Frederick Jackson Turner and the Closing of the Frontier," in Roger Daniels, ed., *Essays in Western History in Honor of T. A. Larson* (Laramie,

1971); this also examines the "Alarmist" belief that the nation would soon face starvation and the exhaustion of its resources with expansion at an end. No single book has attempted to appraise the impact of the frontier's end on the United States; such a book is badly needed. D. W. Brogan, "The Rise and Decline of the American Agricultural Interest," *E.H.R.*, V (April, 1935), deals with agriculture in a nonexpanding land, as does Carl F. Kraenzel, *The Great Plains in Transition* (Norman, 1955). A stimulating article which maintains that awareness of the closing of the frontier stimulated imperialistic sentiments at the close of the century is William A. Williams, "The Frontier Thesis and American Foreign Policy," *P.H.R.*, XXIV (November, 1955). That the ordinary soldier in the Spanish American War was aware of this connection is disproved in Lewis O. Saum, "The Western Volunteer and 'The New Empire,' " *P.N.Q.*, LVII (January, 1966). Professor Williams' translates his belief in the importance of the frontier's closing on foreign policy into the history of that policy in his *The Roots of the Modern American Empire* (New York, 1970). This has been questioned in Lloyd E. Ambrosius, "Turner's Frontier Thesis and the Modern American Empire," *C.W.H.*, XVII (December, 1971).

The effect of the frontier's closing on the western farmer is considered by Louise E. Peffer, *The Closing of the Public Domain* (Stanford, 1951), a legalistic study of land laws and disposal. Agricultural conditions during those years are admirably described in John D. Hicks, "The Western Middle West, 1900–1914," *A.H.*, XX (April, 1946), while the continued expansion into the Far West is the theme of the opening essay in John C. Parish, *The Persistence of the Westward Movement and Other Essays* (Berkeley, 1943). An excellent brief history of the twentieth-century American West is Gerald D. Nash, *The American West in the Twentieth Century: A Short History of an Urban Oasis* (Englewood Cliffs, 1973), while Howard R. Lamar, "Persistent Frontier: The West in the Twentieth Century," *We.H.Q.*, IV (January, 1973), is a stimulating appraisal of the areas needing investigation in the history of the recent West. Carl O. Sauer, *Land and Life* (Berkeley, 1965), contains essays that explore the effects of frontier exploitation on the future.

The movement into the "Last Best West" in Canada's prairie provinces is admirably described in Karel D. Bicha, *The American Farmer and the Canadian West, 1896–1914* (Lawrence, 1968). The efforts of the Canadian governments to encourage this migration are studied in Harold M. Troper, *Only Farmers Need Apply: Official Canadian Government Encouragement of Emigration from the United States* (Toronto, 1972). That this movement northward began as early as the 1870s is shown in James G. Snell, "The Frontier Sweeps Northwest: American Perceptions of the British American Prairie West at the Point of Canadian Expansion (Circa. 1870)," *We.H.Q.*, XI (October, 1980), while the long lag in settlement is explained in K. H. Norrie, "The Rate of Settlement of the Canadian Prairies, 1870–1911," *J.E.H.*, XXXV (June, 1975), as due to inadequate transportation until the completion of the Canadian transcontinental railroads. Governmental policy regulating settlement is discussed in James M. Richtik, "The Policy Framework for Settling the Canadian West, 1870–1880," *A.H.*, XLIX (October, 1975). The failure of this policy to keep peace between farmers and cattlemen is explored in D. H. Breen, "The Canadian Prairie West and the 'Harmonious Settlement' Interpretation," *A.H.*, XLVII (January, 1973).

Two articles by Paul F. Sharp also examine the settlement process: "The American Farmer and the 'Last Best West' " *A.H.*, XXI (April, 1947), and "When Our West Moved North," *A.H.R.*, LV (January, 1950). That the figures used by Sharp are suspect is argued by Karel D. Bicha, "The American Farmer and the Canadian West, 1896–1914: A Revised View," *A.H.*, XXXVIII (January, 1964).

Earl Pomeroy, "What Remains of the West?" *U.H.Q.*, XXV (Winter, 1967), is a searching appraisal of the changes in the nature of the West since the closing of the frontier, while the voluminous literature on conservation that has resulted from that closing is appraised in Gordon B. Dobbs, "Conservation and Reclamation in the Trans-Mississippi West: A Critical Bibliography," *A. and W.*, XIII (Summer, 1971). The need of governmental paternalism to replace the opportunity provided by cheap lands and resources is stressed in Walter P. Webb, *Divided We Stand: The Crisis of a Frontierless Society* (New York, 1937).

Index

859

Hawthorne, William, in Massachusetts fur trade, 79

Haverhill, Massachusetts, Indian attack on, 120

Hazard, Samuel, as land speculator, 146

Header, invention of, 635

Headright System, use of in Virginia, 57, 58

Helena, Montana, settled, 569

Henderson, Richard, buys western lands, 152; interested in Watauga settlements, 166; finances Boone's expeditions, 170; as Kentucky speculator, 175–6; founds Nashville settlements, 190–1

Hennepin, Louis, explores upper Mississippi, 118

Henrico, Virginia, settled, 53

Henry, Andrew, as Rocky Mountain fur trader, 396–7, 400

Henry, James D., in Black Hawk War, 299

Henry, Patrick, as land speculator, 236

Herkimer, New York, settled, 99

Herkimer, Nicholas, in Battle of Oriskany, 186

Herrera, José Maria, considers sale of California, 508–509; as Mexican president, 516–7

Hesse, Emanuel, attacks Illinois Country, 192

Hickok, "Wild Bill," as frontier type, 572

Hidalgo, Francisco, founds Texas missions, 376

Hidalgo, Manuel, as Mexican revolutionist, 436

Hide and Tallow Trade, with California, 493–5

Higgins Land Company, purchases Minnesota lands, 641

Hill, James J., builds Great Northern Railroad, 654–5; on closing of the frontier, 694

Hillsborough, Earl of, formulates western policy, 149–50, 154; opposes Grand Ohio Company grant, 159

Hite, Justus, pioneers in Shenandoah Valley, 103

Holladay, Ben, dominates western transportation, 579–80

Holland Land Company, purchases New York lands, 255; experiments with Hot House method, 256; settles western New York, 256–7; settles western Pennsylvania, 259

Holliday, Cyrus K., builds Santa Fe Railroad, 585–6

Holmes, David, seeks annexation of West Florida, 270

Holston, Stephen, pioneers in eastern Tennessee, 165

Homestake Mining Company, formed, 572

Homestead Act, origins of, 339; promised by Republicans, 548; as sectional issue, 550; to aid freed slaves, 636; failure of on Great Plains, 637; abuses of, 638–40; use of in Dakota Territory, 656; use of in Oklahoma District, 660

Hooker, Thomas, founds Hartford, 74; drafts Fundamental Orders, 74

Hopewell, Treaty of, drafted, 208

Hopi Indians, described, 360

Hopkins, Mark, promotes Pacific railroad, 582

Horse Shoe Bend, Battle of, 283–4; effect of on Indian removal, 311

House of Good Hope, as Dutch trading post, 73

Houston, Sam, migrates to Texas, 437; attends convention, 439; leads Texas Revolution, 442–3; as president of Texas Republic, 445–6; in annexation controversy, 446–7

Hot House Method, used on New York frontier, 255–8

Howard, Benjamin, wins Illinois country in War of 1812, 283

Hudson's Bay Company, founded, 116; in King William's War, 121–2; trade of in Far West, 386; in Oregon Country, 399–400; in Rocky Mountains, 404–405; controls Oregon Country, 453; receives H. J. Kelley, 456; expels Wyeth expedition, 458; welcomes American missionaries, 459–60, 462–3; disliked by Oregon pioneers, 469; aids Oregon provincial government, 471; abandons Oregon Country, 472; in California, 496, 507–508; controls Fraser River rush, 566–7

Hull, William, as governor of Michigan Territory, 272; leads attack on Ft. Malden, 279

Hunt, Wilson Price, leads Overland Astorians, 398

Hunter, John, explores Red River, 392

Hunter, Robert, imports Palatines, 98

Huntington, Collis P., promotes Pacific railroad, 582

Hurdaide, Diego Martínez de, on mission frontier, 372

Huron Indians, described, 25; as allies of French, 46–7; French traders among, 113; in Iroquois wars, 114; in French-English wars, 132–3

Hutchinson, Anne, banished from Massachusetts, 75

I

Ibarra, Francisco de, as governor of Nueva Vizcaya, 369

Iberville, Pierre Le Moyne de, in King William's War, 121–2; founds Louisiana, 123

Idaho, mining frontier in, 567–8, 570; governmental beginnings in, 568; removal of In-

Port Royal, North Carolina, occupied by French, 36; Spanish attacks on, 67

Port Royal, Nova Scotia, founded by French, 44–5; captured by English, 125

Portsmouth, New Hampshire, settled, 75

Portsmouth, Ohio, settled, 363

Portsmouth, Rhode Island, settled, 75

Potawatomi Indians, described, 25; in Iroquois wars, 114; cede lands in Northwest, 272, 296; moved to West, 414; cede Iowa lands, 421; cede Oklahoma lands, 661

Pottawatomie Massacre, in Kansas warfare, 543

Pourée, Eugene, leads St. Joseph expedition in Revolution, 195

Powderly, Terence, in People's Party, 677

Powhatan, tribe of, 24; as friend of English, 54

Pownall, John, formulates British policy, 146

Prairie Cattle Company, profits of, 624–5

Prairie du Chien, in War of 1812, 271, 285; treaty making at, 296; in fur trade, 386

Praying Indians, described, 86; in King Philip's War, 90

Pre-emption Law, adopted, 337; aids settlement of West, 420; used by speculators, 639

Preston, William, as Kentucky speculator, 172

Prevost, George, defeated in Battle of Lake Champlain, 285–6

Printz, Johan, leads Swedish colony, 78

Proclamation of 1763, effect of, 149–50

Proctor, Henry, leads attack on Ohio Country, 281; defeated in Battle of the Thames, 281–2

Prophet, The, rise of to power, 272–4; in Battle of Tippecanoe, 276–7

Prophetstown, founded, 274; destroyed by Harrison, 276

Providence, Rhode Island, settled, 75; in King Philip's War, 86–8, 90

Provo, Utah, settled, 485

Pueblo Indians, described, 360; revolt of, 374

Puget Sound Agricultural Company, established, 453

Pulteney Estates, purchase New York land, 255; settle lands, 255–6

Pulteney, William, heads Pulteney Estates, 255

Putnam, Rufus, forms Ohio Company, 215–6

Pynchon, John, as Connecticut Valley trader, 78; invades Hudson Valley, 79

Pynchon, William, as Connecticut Valley trader, 73–4; founds Springfield, 74; expands trade northward, 78

Q

Quantrill, William C., in Civil War, 554

Quebec, established by France, 45; attack on in Queen Anne's War, 125; captured by English, 140–1; colony of proposed, 147; colony established, 149; mistreatment of settlers in, 149

Quebec Act, adopted, 161

Queen Anne's War, 123–5

Queenstown, Battle of, described, 280

Quivira, visited by Coronado, 367

R

Radisson, Pierre Esprit, as French trader, 115–6; helps found Hudson's Bay Company, 116

Railroads, in Massachusetts, 331; in Maryland, 331; building of between East and West, 340; in Old Northwest, 342–4; effect of on trade, 344–5; influence of on Kansas-Nebraska Act, 537–8; effect of on sectional alignments, 550–2; in Mississippi Valley, 580–1; projected to Pacific, 581–3; built to Pacific, 583–9; as western land holders, 640; lure settlers to Great Plains, 646–7; in Dakota Territory, 653–5; open Oklahoma to settlers, 657, 659, 660; arouse farmer resentment, 664–5; attacked by Patrons of Husbandry, 667–9; regulation of, 681

Raisin River Massacre, described, 281

Raleigh, Walter, attempts to found colony, 48–9

Ramón, Domingo, occupies Texas, 377

Rayneval, Gerard de, in Revolutionary peace negotiations, 197–9

Reaper, invention of, 635

Red Bird, Chief, leads attack, 296–7

Red Cloud, Chief, in Sioux War, 598–600; signs peace treaty, 600

Red River War, described, 603; opens Kansas to settlement, 652

Reeder, Andrew, as Kansas governor, 540–2

Refugee Tract, settlement of, 266

Regulators, uprising of in North Carolina, 111–2; in South Carolina, 112; effect of on migration, 166

Rendezvous System, use of in fur trade, 401–2

Republican Party, formed, 539; growth of, 544; effect of Dred Scott decision on, 545–6; in 1860 election, 548–53; admits Nevada to statehood, 565; admits Omnibus States, 657; relations of with Patrons of Husbandry, 667; passes Sherman Sil-

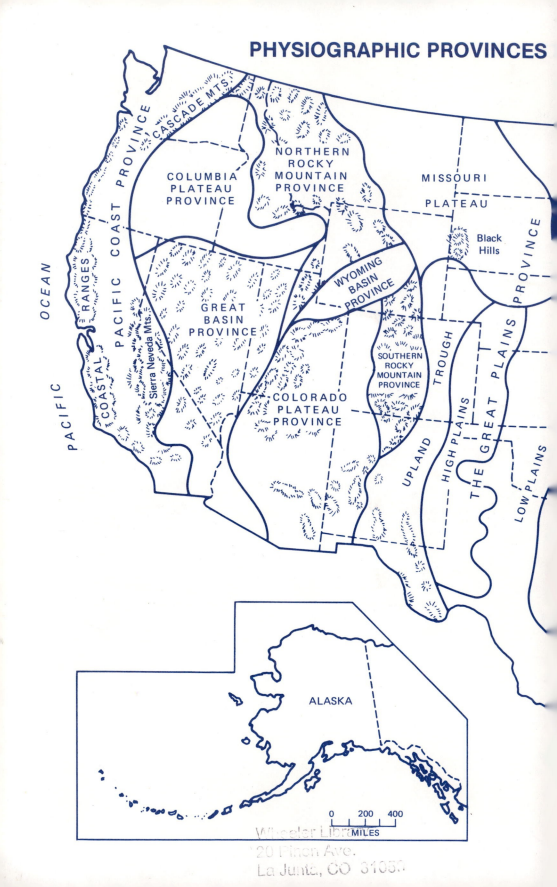

PHYSIOGRAPHIC PROVINCES

OCEAN

PACIFIC

CASCADE MTS.

PACIFIC COAST PROVINCE

COLUMBIA PLATEAU PROVINCE

NORTHERN ROCKY MOUNTAIN PROVINCE

MISSOURI PLATEAU

Black Hills

MISSOURI PLATEAU PROVINCE

COASTAL RANGES

Sierra Neveda Mts.

GREAT BASIN PROVINCE

WYOMING BASIN PROVINCE

SOUTHERN ROCKY MOUNTAIN PROVINCE

COLORADO PLATEAU PROVINCE

UPLAND

TROUGH

HIGH PLAINS

THE GREAT PLAINS

LOW PLAINS

ALASKA

0   200   400
MILES